Current Biography Yearbook 2017

H. W. Wilson

A Division of EBSCO Information Services, Inc.

Ipswich, Massachusetts

GREY HOUSE PUBLISHING

SEVENTY-EIGHTH ANNUAL CUMULATION—2017

International Standard Serial No. 0084-9499

International Standard Book No. 978-1-6192-5848-8

Library of Congress Catalog Card No. 40-27432

Current Biography Yearbook, 2017, published by Grey House Publishing, Inc., Amenia, NY, under exclusive license from EBSCO Information Services, Inc.

CONTENTS

LIST OF BIOGRAPHICAL SKETCHES

List of Biographical Sketches

List of Biographical Sketches

List of Biographical Sketches

LIST OF OBITUARIES

List of Obituaries

List of Obituaries

Current Biography Yearbook 2017

Current Biography Yearbook 2017

David Adjaye

Date of birth: September 22, 1966
Occupation: Architect

"In the last few decades, architecture has become so starstruck that we think it's about glamour and money, but it's not," David Adjaye told Calvin Tomkins for the *New Yorker* (23 Sept. 2013). "For me, architecture is a social act." Indeed, the award-winning British architect's body of work reflects that attitude, featuring numerous highly social and community-oriented spaces—from retail stores and cafés, to an affordable housing development, to the National Museum of African American History and Culture. He has often emphasized social and environmental responsibility through his work: his buildings in areas such as Johannesburg, South Africa, for instance, have been designed for the surrounding climate to lessen reliance on energy-intensive climate control technology.

Despite his protests to the contrary, Adjaye has undoubtedly become one of the architecture field's international stars since the founding of his first firm in the early 1990s, and his high-profile works and slew of celebrity clients could easily be described as glamorous. For Adjaye, though, the focus remains always on the work itself and the constant drive toward improvement. "It takes you 20 years to rehearse before you can actually say that you know what you're talking about, or that people can trust you with vast amounts of money," he told Dodie Kazanjian for *Vogue* (21 June 2016). "I always think I'm just beginning, but I've made it through. I feel like now I'm at the height of my abilities."

EARLY LIFE

David Frank Adjaye was born on September 22, 1966, in Dar es Salaam, Tanzania. He was the first of three sons born to Affram and Cecilia Adjaye, and he also had two older half-brothers from his parents' previous marriages. Adjaye's parents were both from Ghana, and his father, a diplomat, was assigned to Ghana's embassy in Tanzania at the time of his birth. As a child, Adjaye moved frequently due to his father's job. He lived in Uganda, Kenya, Egypt, Lebanon, Ghana, and Saudi Arabia, and attended a series of private international schools.

Jamie McCarthy/Getty Images

In the late 1970s, Adjaye's father transferred to Ghana's London embassy, and the family moved to England. The move was in large part inspired by his parents' desire to obtain better medical care for Adjaye's younger brother Emmanuel, who had become partially paralyzed following an illness. Living in the suburban area of Hampstead, the thirteen-year-old Adjaye had difficulty adjusting to his new surroundings and especially to his new classmates. "The English kids thought their world was so superior," he told Tomkins. "I couldn't understand it, because to me they were more like village kids." After completing secondary school, Adjaye, a talented artist, enrolled in a course in art at Middlesex University.

EDUCATION AND EARLY CAREER

After a year at Middlesex University, Adjaye entered the workforce as an architect, having been commissioned to design a café for some of his former classmates. He was then offered a position with the firm Tchaik Chassay Architects. After working full time in architecture for several years, Adjaye decided to continue his education, enrolling in London South Bank University (LSBU) in 1989.

While studying at LSBU, Adjaye began to solidify his philosophy and approach to architecture, coming to view the field as one that allowed him to combine his longstanding love of art with his familial obligations and desire to accomplish things with his work. "I was interested in what architecture could do, rather than in how beautiful it was," he explained to Tomkins. Speaking of his passion for art and choice of career, he said, "I couldn't see how I could do [art], after the education my parents had given me. They said the best thing we're going to give you is an education, and we were supposed to take that out into the world. It seemed to me that architecture used many of the components of art, but it was a profession, and so I thought, O.K., perfect." At LSBU, he completed an award-winning design for a residential facility for people with physical disabilities like his brother Emmanuel, a project with a socially conscious nature that would become a hallmark of much of Adjaye's most prominent public work. After earning his bachelor's degree, Adjaye traveled to Portugal, where he worked for architect Eduardo Souto de Moura for a year. He then enrolled in graduate school at the Royal College of Art in London, completing his master's degree in architecture and interiors in 1993. While pursuing his degree, he also spent the better part of a year in Japan.

Although Adjaye had previously found work for established architects such as Chassay and de Moura, he next struck out on his own, forming the firm Adjaye and Russell Architecture and Design with classmate William Russell in 1994. Adjaye and Russell later opened an office in London's East End, a formerly industrial neighborhood that was beginning to develop a thriving artistic community. During the firm's early days, Adjaye worked mostly on small-scale projects such as stores and restaurants. In 1997, he began what would become the first of many commissions for Chris Ofili, a critically acclaimed British painter and fellow Royal College of Art alumnus, for whom he renovated a house in the East End. The two became close friends and would later work together on various art installations.

ADJAYE ASSOCIATES

Adjaye and Russell parted ways in 2000, and Adjaye established his solo firm, Adjaye Associates, that June. Adjaye expanded his offerings as an architect while continuing to work on the small residential projects with which he had first made his name. Houses he designed during the first decade of the twenty-first century included the Dirty House, a bitumen-coated converted tavern, and the cubic Sunken House. He also completed a number of large-scale projects in the United Kingdom and beyond, often focusing on

public structures with educational or community purposes. One such building, the Stephen Lawrence Centre in Deptford, South London, is a community center established in honor of a young aspiring architect who was murdered in a 1993 hate crime. Other community-focused buildings designed by Adjaye Associates included two Idea Store locations in London, which combined elements of libraries and community centers, as well as museums such as the Museum of Contemporary Art Denver in Colorado.

Adjaye Associates began to struggle in 2007, as the global economic downturn that began in that year prompted the cancellation of several of the firm's government-funded projects. The firm was in serious financial trouble, but Adjaye was ultimately able to lead the company through some restructuring and further cement its status as an international architectural powerhouse by 2010. In addition to continuing his focus on public and community structures, he explored a growing interest in environmental responsibility, working to design buildings to meet the needs of their specific surroundings rather than to adhere to a preconceived notion of what a building should look like. "It's not a sheer glass building," he told Kazanjian of one of his environmentally conscious designs, an apartment building in Johannesburg, South Africa. "It's all inside-outside space, very layered and lush, with a garden all around it. It has a special membrane roof that protects residents from the harsh sun, but it's virtually carbon-neutral and generates almost all its own energy." Other major projects included the Sugar Hill development in the Harlem neighborhood of New York City, a striking structure that encompassed affordable housing units, a preschool, an art gallery, and a children's museum upon its completion in 2015. Adjaye's designs are not without their detractors, however; some former clients have bemoaned design flaws that led to leaks or other maintenance problems, whereas neighbors of the planned Sugar Hill project objected to the structure's unusual look.

NATIONAL MUSEUM OF AFRICAN AMERICAN HISTORY AND CULTURE

Perhaps one of the most significant design projects that Adjaye has carried out to date is the National Museum of African American History and Culture in Washington, DC. In 2008, the Smithsonian Institution launched a design competition for the creation of a facility for the museum, which had been authorized by Congress in 2003. With Adjaye serving as lead designer, Adjaye Associates collaborated with American firms Freelon Group, Davis Brady Bond, and SmithGroup to create a design that was short-listed and, in April 2009, was selected as the winning plan. Although the design was adjusted significantly over the following years due to structural necessities and budget limitations, construction on the site finally began in February 2012 and the museum officially opened on September 24, 2016.

As lead designer of the project, Adjaye sought to design a building that had cultural significance and reflected African American history. "This is not a project about intuitive whimsy," he told Michael Kimmelman for the *New York Times* (21 Sept. 2016). Speaking of the building's distinctive use of light, he explained, "Most museums on the [National] Mall are closed to the outside in the sense that they take you to another world. They function a bit like cinema. . . . I didn't want that. The experience of being black is not a fiction. There's something important about always coming back to the light of day."

One of the most distinctive physical features of the completed museum is its exterior, which features a tiered structure based on the capitals of columns historically used within the Yoruba culture of West Africa, the region from which many of the Africans enslaved in the Americas were abducted. "I was completely moved by the corona motif," Adjaye told Kimmelman. "It seemed like a way to start to tell a story that moves from one continent, where people were taken, along with their cultures, and used as labor, then contributed towards making another country and new cultures." In addition to its distinctive structure, the museum's exterior is covered with bronze-alloyed aluminum panels. Their intricate decorative patterns were inspired by the metalwork of enslaved and emancipated African American artisans.

OTHER WORK AND RECOGNITION

Although Adjaye focuses primarily on the design of buildings, he has also designed furniture, textile patterns, and fixtures for the companies Knoll and izé, respectively. In 2010, he also designed a line of African print underwear for the sustainable clothing company PACT. In addition to his many architectural and design projects, Adjaye has taught at institutions such as the Harvard University Graduate School of Design.

Adjaye has received numerous architecture and design awards over the course of his career. In 2007, he was named an officer of the Order of the British Empire (OBE) in recognition of his work and, in 2017, was made a knight bachelor, a prestigious honor in the United Kingdom. A retrospective of the work of Adjaye Associates was exhibited at the Haus der Kunst in Munich, Germany, as *David Adjaye: Form, Heft, Material* in 2015 and at the Art Institute of Chicago as *Making Place: The Architecture of David Adjaye* in 2015–16. "I was interested in showing the broad development of our practice, how it has evolved, and its current trajectory," Adjaye told David Ebony for *YaleBooks* (10 Apr. 2015) of the exhibition. "Our office is set up to engage with a range of situations at a variety of scales. This is

the first time that we have shown the full range of our output."

PERSONAL LIFE

Adjaye first met his wife, Ashley Shaw-Scott, when she attended a 2005 lecture he delivered in New York City. They married in January 2014, and have a son named Kwame (b. 2015). Adjaye and his family have homes in London and New York and also own land on Ghana's coast, where they plan to build a house.

SUGGESTED READING

Adjaye, David. "David Adjaye on Designing a Museum That Speaks a Different Language." Interview by Michael Kimmelman. *The New York Times*, 21 Sept. 2016, www.nytimes.com/2016/09/22/arts/design/david-adjaye-museum-of-african-american-history-and-culture.html. Accessed 10 Mar. 2017.

Adjaye, David. "Postcolonial Realism: The Architecture of David Adjaye." Interview by David Ebony. *YaleBooks*, Yale UP, 10 Apr. 2015, yalebooksblog.co.uk/2015/04/10/postcolonial-realism-the-architecture-of-david-adjaye-interview-with-david-adjaye-by-david-ebony. Accessed 10 Apr. 2015.

Kazanjian, Dodie. "With His New Historic Design, Architect David Adjaye Has Hit the Top." *Vogue*, 21 June 2016, www.vogue.com/article/architect-david-adjaye-national-museum-of-african-american-history-and-culture. Accessed 10 Mar. 2017.

Moore, Rowan. "David Adjaye Interview: 'I'm Not Always Looking at the Usual References.'" *The Guardian*, 2 Aug. 2014, www.theguardian.com/artanddesign/2014/aug/02/david-adjaye-interview-not-always-looking-at-usual-references. Accessed 10 Mar. 2017.

Tomkins, Calvin. "A Sense of Place." *The New Yorker*, 23 Sept. 2013, www.newyorker.com/magazine/2013/09/23/a-sense-of-place. Accessed 10 Mar. 2017.

—Joy Crelin

Pamela Adlon

Date of Birth: July 9, 1966
Occupation: Actor, writer, producer

Over the course of more than three decades in film and television, Pamela Adlon has successfully traversed the path from child star to veteran working actor. Although Adlon appeared in films such as *Grease 2* (1982) and television shows such as *The Facts of Life* (1983–84) as a teenager, she struggled to find work for a time before securing a fruitful niche in animation voice acting, which she cemented with her Emmy Award–winning

performance as the young Bobby Hill on the Fox animated series *King of the Hill* (1997–2010). Although she found herself with consistent work, she has frequently emphasized that her career trajectory has not exactly been glamorous. "My actor story is that I'm a punch-the-time-card guy," she explained to Maria Elena Fernandez for *Vulture* (8 Sept. 2016). "I do my jobs when they come. I go into the recording studio and I do my animation. I'm not a star. I'm a periphery person. I always have been."

Since 2006, however, Adlon has moved further and further away from the periphery. That year marked her first collaboration with comedian and television creator Louis C.K., with whom she would appear in the HBO comedy *Lucky Louie* (2006–7) and later the FX series *Louie* (2010–15). With him, Adlon went on to create her own show, *Better Things*, which premiered on FX in the fall of 2016. Despite her frequent collaborator's involvement, however, the show is largely representative of Adlon, who has noted that television rarely reflects the experiences of herself and her friends. "I wanted to tell stories about the friends in my world and things that happen," she told Gwilym Mumford for the Guardian (14 Sept. 2016). "These aren't really big, crazy, extraordinary things. It's just regular life."

EARLY LIFE AND CAREER

Adlon was born Pamela Fionna Segall on July 9, 1966. Her parents, Don and Marina, lived in New York at the time of her birth. Don Segall was a television writer and producer who was nominated for a local Emmy Award for his work on the program *A.M. New York*. He also wrote comic books. Adlon has recalled in interviews that her father worked on a variety of projects and credits him with inspiring her to do the same. "He said you've got to try something new every day," she told Joe Rhodes for the *New York Times* (21 Nov. 2008). "Irons in the fire, that was his thing. You got to have a lot of irons in the fire." Expressing an interest in television from an early age, she made small appearances in the television shows her father wrote and produced as early as the age of nine. Her family split its time between New York and Los Angeles, California, and she began to pursue acting work seriously as a teenager.

In 1982, Adlon made her official television debut with a role in the made-for-television film *Little Darlings*. She followed this role with her first feature film appearance, playing the character of Dolores Rebchuck in 1982's *Grease 2*. The sequel to the 1978 hit musical *Grease*, which starred Olivia Newton-John and John Travolta, *Grease 2* took place at the same high school several years later and starred Michelle Pfeiffer and Maxwell Caulfield. The opportunity to appear in the film was particularly exciting for Adlon, both because it was her first film and because of its connection to its predecessor. "I was *obsessed* with *Grease*," she recalled to Will Harris for the *A.V. Club* (1 Apr. 2014). "So being a part of that was *amazing*." Although she described *Grease 2* to Harris as "a movie that everyone was very ashamed of when it was made," she has noted that her role in the film continued to bring her recognition from its most devoted fans decades after its premiere.

Among Adlon's other notable early roles was that of Kelly Affinado, a recurring character who appeared throughout the fifth season of the sitcom *The Facts of Life* from 1983 to 1984. As she established herself as an actor, she sometimes obtained roles through unusual means. When preparing to audition for a part on the short-lived sitcom *The Redd Foxx Show* in 1986, she and her agent decided that she would pretend to be male for her audition, a ruse that was aided by a short haircut that made her, as she told Harris, "look like Bruce Springsteen at age eleven." The deception continued throughout the audition process and the unusual gambit eventually succeeded in earning her the role of Toni, the teenage foster child of the show's protagonist. She would later go on to make small appearances in numerous television shows, including *Star Trek: The Next Generation* and *21 Jump Street* in 1989.

VOICE WORK

Although Adlon experienced significant success as a teenage actor, opportunities in film and television soon began to dry up. "I went from buying my own condominium and a car for myself when I was seventeen on *The Facts of Life* to not being able to pay my rent," she told Rhodes. "I was at the unemployment office all the time. I had to sell my record collection just to make ends meet." However, the field of voiceover work presented a new career path. Beginning with work in radio, she soon established herself as a voice actor for television and film, particularly animation. In addition to early roles such as a small part in the 1992 animated film *FernGully: The Last Rainforest* and a major role in the animated superhero series *Phantom 2040* (1994–96). she contributed to numerous animated projects, among them *Rugrats* (1992–2002), *Quack Pack* (1996–97), *Recess* (1997–2001), and *Pepper Ann* (1997–2000).

Although Adlon's extensive work as a voice actor brought her success within the field, it was her role in the animated comedy *King of the Hill* that would bring her significant public recognition as well as critical acclaim. In the show, which follows a family and their friends and neighbors in the fictional town of Arlen, Texas, she provided the raspy voice of young Bobby Hill, the son of lead characters Hank and Peggy. The creation of television writer and actor Mike Judge, who had previously created the comedy *Beavis and Butt-Head* (1993–97; 2011) for MTV, and veteran television writer Greg Daniels, *King of the Hill* aired for thirteen seasons following its debut on Fox in 1997.

For Adlon, *King of the Hill* was a dream project. "That was just the greatest show that could ever happen to anybody," she explained to Harris. "The writing was just out-of-the-park incredible. I learned so much, and I just loved it." Fans and critics appreciated Adlon's portrayal of Bobby, and in 2002 she received the Emmy Award for outstanding voice-over performance in recognition of her work. The nomination would be the first of several for her over the next decades, and her 2002 award was one of only two Emmys given to *King of the Hill* during its thirteen years on the air.

RETURN TO LIVE ACTION

Although Adlon specialized in voice work from the early 1990s on, she continued to take on roles in live-action film and television from time to time. She began a far more prominent return to live-action television in 2006, when she joined the cast of the new HBO comedy *Lucky Louie* in the role of Kim, the wife of the titular character. Starring and written by comedian Louis C.K., the show met with mixed critical response and was canceled after a season. Despite that setback, she views her time on *Lucky Louie* as a key moment in the development of her career. "Before *Lucky Louie* nobody would ever cast me to play a mom or a wife, nobody ever saw me in that role, which is weird because [sic] that's who I really am," she recalled to Rhodes. "And

then Louis called and said, 'You have to be my Edith Bunker.'" Between 2007 and 2014, Adlon also costarred in the Showtime series *Californication* along with David Duchovny and appeared in shows such as *Boston Legal* (2007–8).

Adlon's short-lived role in *Lucky Louie* likewise represented the first of multiple collaborations with C.K., a successful stand-up comic and television writer who had previously contributed to *The Dana Carvey Show* and *Late Night with Conan O'Brien*. Their second show together, *Louie*, premiered on FX in 2010. In the recurring role of Pamela, Louie's friend and sometimes love interest, she appeared sporadically throughout the series. She also joined the show as a producer and writer, contributing to several episodes between 2011 and 2015. Unlike *Lucky Louie*, *Louie* found a viewership that appreciated the show's unique brand of comedy and also received significant critical praise, earning Adlon and her colleagues several Emmy nominations. Adlon was nominated for an Emmy for outstanding writing for a comedy series in 2013 and for outstanding guest actress in a comedy series in 2015 for her work on the show.

In addition to her most prominent television roles, Adlon appeared in the 2011 film *Conception* during that period. Along with many other successful voice actors, she was also featured in the 2013 documentary *I Know That Voice*, which highlighted the people behind some of the most iconic voices in twenty-first-century animation.

BETTER THINGS

In September 2016, Adlon moved further into the spotlight with the premiere of her own live-action television comedy, *Better Things*. Largely cowritten and coproduced with C.K., the show airs on FX and follows the life of Sam, an actor and the single mother of three daughters. *Better Things* is semiautobiographical, taking inspiration from Adlon's life in numerous ways. "I was originally trying to think of alternatives to fictionalize myself. I'd say 'maybe I have a daughter adopted from China, or maybe I'm a lesbian, maybe I this, maybe I that,'" she told Mumford of the show's genesis. "But it just seemed better to use my real life as the bones for the show." At the same time, she has confessed in interviews that the process of writing about her own life rather than creating story lines for others proved difficult and somewhat daunting, and she initially had doubts about whether there would be an audience for the more niche premise. "When I started developing the show, I have to admit I got discouraged because so much of what's on TV seems so big and not necessarily real," she confided to Craig Tomashoff for the *Hollywood Reporter* (6 Sept. 2016). "I decided to keep pushing through and it turns out, now is the right time for something like this." Her realistic and relatable depiction of family life resonated with viewers and critics during the airing of the ten-episode first season, and FX announced that the show had been renewed for a second season less than a month after its premiere.

PERSONAL LIFE

Adlon married writer and producer Felix Adlon in 1996. The couple had three daughters before divorcing in 2010. All three of her children have appeared in her projects: her oldest daughter, Gideon, guest starred in *Louie* and *Better Things*, whereas daughters Odessa and Rocky appeared in *Conception*.

SUGGESTED READING

Adlon, Pamela. "Pamela Adlon Can't Believe She Has Her Own Show." Interview by Maria Elena Fernandez. *Vulture*, 9 Sept. 2016, www.vulture.com/2016/09/pamela-adlon-better-things-conversation.html. Accessed 11 Nov. 2016.

Adlon, Pamela. "Pamela Adlon on Snorting Fake Coke, Louie, and the Fate of Her Vulcan Ears." Interview by Will Harris. A.V. Club, Onion, 1 Apr. 2014, www.avclub.com/article/pamela-adlon-snorting-fake-coke-louie-and-fate-her-202837. Accessed 11 Nov. 2016.

Koczwara, Kevin. "The Funniest Emmy Winner You Don't Know Is Ready for Better Things." *Esquire*, 6 Sept. 2016, www.esquire.com/entertainment/tv/a48359/pamela-adlon-profile-better-things. Accessed 11 Nov. 2016.

Mumford, Gwilym. "Pamela Adlon: How Louis CK's Sidekick Became the Star." *The Guardian*, 14 Sept. 2016, www.theguardian.com/tv-and-radio/2016/sep/14/pamela-adlon-better-things-how-louis-cks-sidekick-became-the-star. Accessed 11 Nov. 2016.

Rhodes, Joe. "Her Life as a Mom, an Actress, and a Boy." *The New York Times*, 21 Nov. 2008, www.nytimes.com/2008/11/23/arts/television/23rhod.html. Accessed 11 Nov. 2016.

Tomashoff, Craig. "How Louie (and Girls) Inspired Pamela Adlon's FX Comedy Better Things." *The Hollywood Reporter*, 6 Sept. 2016, www.hollywoodreporter.com/live-feed/fx-better-things-pamela-adlon-924857. Accessed 11 Nov. 2016.

SELECTED WORKS

Grease 2, 1982; *The Facts of Life*, 1983–84; *King of the Hill*, 1997–2010; *Lucky Louie*, 2006–7; *Californication*, 2007–14; *Louie*, 2010–15; *Better Things*, 2016

—Joy Crelin

Riz Ahmed

Date of birth: December 1, 1982
Occupation: Actor, rapper

"I feel kind of lucky, it's been a great couple of years," actor Riz Ahmed told Kyle Buchanan for *Vulture* (20 Dec. 2016). In many ways, that is a colossal understatement. After nearly a decade working primarily in British independent cinema, the London-born actor experienced a career breakthrough beginning in 2014 with a memorable role in the thriller *Nightcrawler*. The year 2016 proved even more significant, bringing with it a major part in the action film *Jason Bourne*, a critically acclaimed performance in the miniseries *The Night Of*, and a crucial role in the international blockbuster *Rogue One: A Star Wars Story*. For Ahmed, however, his dramatic increase in fame comes down to business as usual. "I've just been keeping my head down working hard like I always have," he told Buchanan. "It's just great luck that a couple of the things I've done lately have struck a chord with people, and now they've all come out around the same time. That's the kind of stuff you can't control, so I try not to think too much about it—instead, I think about what I've learned from one job to the next."

In addition to his work as an actor, Ahmed is a rapper who releases music under the name Riz MC. Influenced in large part by 1990s African American rappers such as Tupac Shakur, his music also draws inspiration from a variety of other musical styles, including Qawwali music,

which Ahmed described to Rachel Brodsky for *Spin* (17 Aug. 2016) as "Pakistani gospel-jazz." Indeed, melding musical styles has come naturally to Ahmed, whose experiences growing up in a culturally diverse community would influence both his music and his choices of film roles. "I grew up dancing between different worlds a lot," he explained to Joe Utichi for *Deadline* (15 Dec. 2016), "switching between a working-class household and a middle-class private school that I won a scholarship to and had to take a bus to for an hour-and-a-half each day. In the middle was British Asian street culture, with gangs of kids and its own exciting and really dangerous subculture. I was always pinballing between those different worlds, and so I think a part of me needs that same eclectic range from one project to the next; it just feels normal to me."

EARLY LIFE AND EDUCATION

Rizwan Ahmed was born on December 1, 1982, in London, England. He was the third child born to parents who had immigrated to the United Kingdom from Pakistan in the previous decade. His father worked as a shipping broker. Ahmed and his older brother and sister grew up in Wembley, an ethnically diverse working-class neighborhood in northern London. As a child, he was interested in music, particularly rap. "I decided to focus a lot of my energies as an aspiring MC," he recalled to Brodsky. "It was a very natural way to express yourself as a kid from a certain kind of neighborhood. At the time, we were surrounded by pirate radio stations—before the Internet blew up. I would do sets on pirate radio as an MC."

As a preteen, Ahmed began to attend the Merchant Taylors' School, a prestigious secondary school for boys, after receiving a scholarship. Although he experienced some challenges while in school—he has told journalists that he put a chair through a school window as a child—he soon devoted his attention to acting with the encouragement of his teachers. After completing secondary school, he attended Oxford University, where he studied economics, philosophy, and politics. Continuing to act while at Oxford, he also branched out into directing plays and likewise remained active in music, hosting a club night called Hit & Run. After graduating from Oxford in 2004, Ahmed went on to further his education in acting at the Royal Central School of Speech and Drama in London.

EARLY CAREER

Throughout his early career, Ahmed struggled to find work in a film and television industry that offered limited opportunities for actors of color. "There wasn't a ready-made conveyor belt for someone who looks like me, so I kind of feel like I have to fight my way through the forest," he told Lauren Larson for *GQ* (29 Nov. 2016).

"Maybe it would be different if I were a different person and I held a different shelf space in the culture, but that's not my experience. My experience is, like, out there in the bushes with a machete trying to find a part."

Despite such adversities, Ahmed soon began to obtain challenging roles that earned him significant critical attention. He made his feature film debut in 2006 with the film *The Road to Guantánamo*, a project blending documentary and dramatized elements. Directed by Michael Winterbottom and Mat Whitecross, *The Road to Guantánamo* tells the true story of three British men of Pakistani descent, known as the Tipton Three, who were held in the Guantánamo Bay prison for two years after being mistaken for terrorists in Afghanistan. Ahmed portrayed Shafiq Rasul, one of the three men. The film earned critical recognition from a number of film festivals and awards programs, winning an Independent Spirit Award as well as the award for best director at the Berlin International Film Festival. While returning from the festival in Berlin, Ahmed and several of his colleagues were detained and interrogated by officials at an airport in London, an incident that made a lasting impression on the actor. He has noted in interviews that he has continued to be frequently stopped in airports while traveling for work, even as his film and television projects have gained increasing public recognition.

Ahmed also continued to make music, releasing rap mixtapes and albums as Riz MC. His first song to gain widespread attention in England, "Post 9/11 Blues," was released in 2006. A satire about societal fear and prejudices in the era following the September 11, 2001, terrorist attacks, the song was banned from radio play in England for a time.

A RECOGNIZED TALENT

Having established himself as a talented performer, Ahmed began to find additional roles in British film and television. In 2008, he starred in the independent crime drama *Shifty*, a film that earned him the first of several nominations for a British Independent Film Award. That year, he also appeared in the television miniseries *Dead Set*, about a zombie outbreak that occurs during the filming of a fictional season on the reality show *Big Brother*. Additional prominent roles came during the next several years, including starring roles in 2010's *Four Lions*, a dark comedy about incompetent terrorists, and the 2012 film *The Reluctant Fundamentalist*, based on the best-selling 2007 novel by Mohsin Hamid. Although many of Ahmed's films were released primarily in the United Kingdom, he gained further attention in the United States beginning in 2014, when he played a memorable supporting role in the award-winning thriller *Nightcrawler*.

Ahmed's increasing fame was an interesting adjustment for the actor, who has noted in interviews that meeting well-known actors in the course of his work led to a shift in perspective. "Suddenly, it feels like people who inspire you are within your reach," he explained to Larson. "It kind of boosts your self-belief if you're someone who's given to being very self-critical, or if you can be paralyzed by your own perfectionism at times—I can really nitpick over things. If people you admire are within your reach, it kind of bolsters your aspirations a little bit."

Since 2014, Ahmed has also collaborated with fellow rapper Heems under the name Swet Shop Boys. The group released their first extended-play recording, *Swet Shop EP*, in 2014.

BREAKTHROUGH

The year 2016 marked a turning point for Ahmed, as several high-profile projects premiered in close succession. In the action film *Jason Bourne*, the fifth installment in the series following Matt Damon's rogue intelligence operative, he plays a social media executive who is secretly allowing intelligence agencies to use his technology for mass surveillance. The film was released in the summer of 2016 and was a box office success. Also that summer, he starred in the HBO miniseries *The Night Of*, portraying a New York City college student who is accused of murder. Featuring notable actors such as John Turturro and Michael Kenneth Williams alongside Ahmed, *The Night Of* met with widespread critical acclaim, and Ahmed was nominated for the 2017 Golden Globe Award for best actor in a limited series for his work.

Ahmed's most visible performance yet came near the end of the year, when *Rogue One: A Star Wars Story* opened in theaters worldwide. The first stand-alone film in the blockbuster science-fiction franchise, *Rogue One* tells the story of several individuals who band together to steal the plans for the planet-destroying superweapon known as the Death Star from the evil Empire. Ahmed plays Bodhi Rook, an Imperial pilot who defects to the Rebel Alliance, becomes an integral part of the team that goes after the plans, and even gives the film its name. For Ahmed, the opportunity to costar in a Star Wars film was a mind-blowing one. "You turn up on set and there are hundreds of Stormtroopers standing around. That's . . . you pinch yourself, and you do start fanning out," he recalled to Jacob Hall for *Slashfilm* (6 Dec. 2016). "For a while, I fought that. I was like, 'Come on now, you're Bodhi Rook, you're this guy, you're not a fanboy.' And then I realized that, actually, if being around Stormtroopers and U-Wings and stuff elicits a kind of childlike emotion in you, ride it. Use that." Following *Rogue One*'s theatrical premiere in December

2016, audiences responded enthusiastically to Ahmed's character and to the film itself, which grossed over a billion dollars worldwide.

In addition to his best-known projects, Ahmed starred in several other films and television series that debuted in 2016, including the British film *City of Tiny Lights*, in which he stars as a private detective. He also appeared in several episodes of the Netflix series *The OA*. That year, he also made the mixtape *Englistan*, which he had recorded much earlier, available to the public, and the Swet Shop Boys released their follow-up studio album, *Cashmere*. The group was set to play at a variety of music festivals in 2017, including the California-based festival Coachella and the Primavera Sound Festival in Barcelona, Spain.

PERSONAL LIFE

Ahmed lives in London.

SUGGESTED READING

Ahmed, Riz. "Interview: *Rogue One* Star Riz Ahmed on Playing an Average Guy in the 'Star Wars' Universe." By Jacob Hall. *Slashfilm*, 6 Dec. 2016, www.slashfilm.com/rogue-one-riz-ahmed-interview. Accessed 13 Feb. 2017.

Ahmed, Riz. "*The Night Of* Star Riz Ahmed Leads a Double Life as Riz MC." Interview by Rachel Brodsky. *Spin*, 17 Aug. 2016, www.spin.com/2016/08/riz-ahmed-riz-mc-the-night-of-listening-in-interview. Accessed 13 Feb. 2017.

Ahmed, Riz. "Riz Ahmed on *Rogue One*, Sweeping Reshoots, and His Breakthrough Year." Interview by Kyle Buchanan. *Vulture*, 20 Dec. 2016, www.vulture.com/2016/12/riz-ahmed-on-rogue-one-and-his-breakthrough-year.html. Accessed 13 Feb. 2017.

Ahmed, Riz. "*Rogue One* Star Riz Ahmed Scales 'Star Wars,' Owns *The Night Of*, Celebrates Stratospheric Decade—Q&A." Interview by Joe Utichi. *Deadline*, 15 Dec. 2016, deadline.com/2016/12/rogue-one-star-wars-riz-ahmed-interview-the-night-of-1201868767. Accessed 13 Feb. 2017.

Ahmed, Riz. "Typecast as a Terrorist." *The Guardian*, 15 Sept. 2016, www.theguardian.com/world/2016/sep/15/riz-ahmed-typecast-as-a-terrorist. Accessed 10 Feb. 2017.

Larson, Lauren. *The Night Of*'s Riz Ahmed Goes Rogue (One)." *GQ*, 29 Nov. 2016, www.gq.com/story/riz-ahmed-rogue-one-star-wars. Accessed 13 Feb. 2017.

SELECTED WORKS

The Road to Guantánamo, 2006; *Shifty*, 2008; *Dead Set*, 2008; *Four Lions*, 2010; *The Reluctant Fundamentalist*, 2012; *Nightcrawler*, 2014; *Jason Bourne*, 2016; *The Night Of*, 2016; *Rogue*

One: A Star Wars Story, 2016; *City of Tiny Lights*, 2016; *The OA*, 2016

—Joy Crelin

Kwame Alexander

Date of Birth: August 21, 1968
Occupation: Writer

fourandsixty/CC BY-SA 3.0/Wikimedia Commons

In 2015, Kwame Alexander, already the author of more than twenty books, won both the Coretta Scott King Author Honor Award and the John Newbery Medal for *The Crossover* (2014), his young-adult novel in verse about boys and basketball. In his Newbery acceptance speech, reprinted in *Horn Book Magazine* (July–Aug. 2015), Alexander expressed his sense of awe at earning such recognition and explained how he got there: "I think poetry found me. I think it circled above, for years, until I was ready, and then it swooped down, grabbed me by the arms, lifted me up, and I've been soaring ever since."

Winning both awards led Alexander to further critical acclaim and many guest appearances at libraries, schools, and conferences. In addition, his children's book *Acoustic Rooster and His Backyard Band* (2011), which he initially sold at a local farmers' market, was optioned for a children's television show. Alexander's other awards include the Lee Bennett Hopkins Poetry Award, the Paterson Poetry Prize, and the Charlotte Huck Award for Outstanding Fiction for Children. He was also named the first Dorothy Carter Writer-in-Residence at the Bank Street College of Education Center for Children's Literature.

EARLY LIFE AND EDUCATION

Kwame Alexander was born on August 21, 1968, in New York City, and the family later moved to Chesapeake, Virginia. His mother was an elementary school teacher and administrator, and his father was an academic and publisher; both were authors as well. According to Alexander, his father considered him and his siblings as part of his publishing staff, helping with tasks like stuffing envelopes, causing Alexander to joke that he entered the publishing business at age six. His parents also wanted their children to be aware of social justice issues, and Alexander's father took him at a young age on a march to protest police brutality.

As a child, Alexander liked exploring his home's attic, filled with treasures. There he discovered jazz records that belonged to his father, sparking a lifelong fascination with jazz as well as a deeper appreciation of his father. Alexander also fell in love with words from his mother reading to him. In his daycare days, as he recalled in his Newbery acceptance speech, a teacher told his mother, "Your son intimidates the other children with the things he says. He is a little arrogant." At which point, his mother smiled and said, "Yes, he is. We teach him to use his words, thank you."

Books were everywhere in the Alexander house; Eric Carle, Lee Bennett Hopkins, and Eloise Greenfield were among young Alexander's favorite writers. However, his father later forced Alexander to read the encyclopedia and other books he had no interest in, which led to a dislike of reading. He turned his attention to playing basketball and football. It was only when he discovered the autobiography of boxer Muhammad Ali in middle school that he returned to reading for pleasure. He also developed an interest in poetry in high school in order to write love poems to girls.

Alexander attended Virginia Tech, planning to become a doctor until a course in organic chemistry caused him to rethink the idea. He was involved in student activism pushing for a black studies program on campus. During his sophomore year, he took a poetry class taught by Nikki Giovanni, whose words he had been reading since childhood. Her belief in his ability changed his direction, and Giovanni became his mentor. Writing love poetry to his college sweetheart (who later became his wife) further convinced him to pursue a career in poetry.

BLACKWORDS AND BOOK-IN-A-DAY

Alexander founded BlackWords, Inc. in 1995 to promote the work of black authors, beginning with himself. His father—after telling him there was no money in poetry and to rethink his career—gave him a check for $1,700 to start the imprint. With a thousand copies of his first poetry collection, consisting of love poems, he began a thirty-city book tour. As he told Tracie Currie for *Black Issues Book Review* (Mar.–Apr. 2000), "The idea is that when people think of quality black poetry and literature they will think of BlackWords."

The company became both a bookseller and a publishing house, focusing on—but not limited to—poetry. BlackWords found success in sponsoring author tours, getting black writers opportunities to speak in bookstores, schools, and other venues. Alexander, along with poet Stacey Lyn Evans, began the first tour in 1995 in Los Angeles. The tour led to respectable book sales, and in the first five years of its existence, the Washington, DC–based press sold 10,000 books of poetry.

In 2006 Alexander founded Book-in-a-Day, a workshop program to promote student writing and publishing. It began when a teacher in Detroit asked for his help in getting the poetry of her advanced placement class published. Originally scheduled for two weeks, the session was cut to one day. When Alexander returned home, his wife suggested he use the experience as a model. The program's day-long workshops are held in schools in the United States, the Caribbean, and Canada. Students select a title, create a design, write poems, and can even create a plan for marketing and a book-signing party. As Alexander told Colleen Patrice Clark for *Literacy Today* (Mar.–Apr. 2016), "Through the power of language and literature, young people can learn to open up to a world of possibilities for themselves and say 'yes' to that possibility, whatever it is for them."

In addition to Book-in-a-Day, Alexander cofounded Literacy Empowerment Action Project (LEAP) for Ghana with Tracy Chiles McGhee. After visiting the West African nation, in the fall of 2012 he led a group of five writers and educational professionals to that country to give away books and a library to hold them, as well as to train teachers. The group also planned to expand to other regions. The organization developed a Nikki Giovanni LEAP Scholarship Fund and offered a camp experience to 120 village children.

THE CROSSOVER

Having published two successful picture books and ten books of poetry, including *Crush: Love Poems* (2007), Alexander wanted to try something new. Striving to create literature that would resonate with middle schoolers, who often lose interest in reading as he once did, he worked on the basketball-themed novel *The Crossover* for five years. He told Clark, "I realized I could use sports to get boys in particular and all middle graders engaged with language and literature. . . . It feels authentic." He was inspired by sources ranging from jazz to great basketball players whose games have been considered poetry in motion.

The final work, which took the unusual form of a novel in poems, received twenty rejection letters before being accepted at Houghton Mifflin Harcourt. Yet it quickly proved popular with its target audience, and critics took note. *The Crossover* turned out to be Alexander's major breakthrough, winning him universal accolades and the highly coveted Newbery Medal, among other honors. In his acceptance speech for the Newbery Medal, Alexander described the book as "first and foremost, a novel about fathers and sons. About love. About family."

As an African American author, Alexander acknowledged that *The Crossover* could be viewed in terms of race, especially in the context of widespread concern over discrimination by police in the 2010s. Discussing the book with Jeffrey Brown for *PBS NewsHour* (26 Mar. 2015), he said, "There's a strong race element as it relates to the way they're trying to raise their boys or when the father gets stopped by the police. And I never thought about that when I was writing it." Still, Alexander suggested that his message is universal, and the unspecified race of his characters is unimportant, despite frequent questions from teachers and librarians. Writing for the *New York Times* (26 Aug. 2016), he noted that his young readers, regardless of their race, "believe I am writing about *them*. Why is this so much harder for the grown-ups?" According to Alexander, good literature functions not only as a mirror but also as a window into other worlds.

BOOKED AND OTHER PROJECTS

Following the success of his formula of writing about sports in verse, Alexander penned *Booked* (2016), the tale of Nick, a twelve-year-old soccer player whose academic father forces him to read the dictionary daily. He would note it as his most autobiographical work. Soccer player students whom Alexander met on a school visit had suggested the idea.

Although at the time he had heard the rumor that *The Crossover* was in the running for the Newbery Medal, Alexander decided to focus elsewhere, feeling that he had no chance of winning. He completed *Booked* and sent the finished manuscript to his editor the night before he received the phone call telling him he had won the Newbery. Following this success, Alexander's publisher, Houghton Mifflin Harcourt Books for Young Readers, offered him a four-book deal.

They announced plans for *Rebound*, a prequel focusing on the father in *The Crossover*, as well as a new trilogy aimed at middle schoolers. The historical-fiction trilogy would tell the story of a young boy from Ghana seeking freedom after being taken as a slave, covering subjects including the Middle Passage, the Underground Railroad, and the US Civil War.

Meanwhile, Alexander's educational projects continue. Book-in-a-Day inspired *Kwame Alexander's Page-to-Stage Writing Workshop* (2016), a published manual guiding similar self-publishing programs in any classroom.

ADVOCATING FOR LITERATURE

With his own works, as well as the ongoing efforts of Book-in-a-Day and LEAP for Ghana, Alexander continually strives to empower young people with literature. "Every child has the potential to really excel at reading and writing," he told Clark. "Do we give them that opportunity? Do they recognize they have the potential?" This includes his self-stated mission of bridging the gap between early enjoyment of reading and advanced literature such as the works of William Shakespeare.

Alexander also combines this mission with opportunities to speak to young people in the United States about social issues, including the problem of violence against African Americans. He affirmed his belief in the power of literature, specifically poetry, to help young people grow into tolerance and a better world. As he told Rachel Martin for National Public Radio's *Weekend Edition Sunday* (10 July 2016), "If we don't give them books that are mirrors as well as windows, if they aren't able to see not only themselves, but if they aren't able to see outside of themselves, then how can you expect them to be able to have something in their mind that allows them to connect with this person who looks different, who lives different than they are?"

PERSONAL LIFE

Alexander and his wife, Stephanie, have two children, Nandi and Samayah. Speaking to Clark about the unexpected success of *The Crossover*, Alexander said, "I've always been that confident person who sort of knew his place in this world and that no one could define me for me." He has multiple works going at the same time; if he is blocked on one, he moves to another. Alexander has deep connection to music, using jazz especially as an aid to writing. He also enjoys bossa nova and hip-hop. Basketball and tennis are his favorite sports.

SUGGESTED READING

Alexander, Kwame. "Kwame Alexander on Children's Books and the Color of Characters." *The New York Times*, 26 Aug. 2016, www. nytimes.com/2016/08/28/books/review/ kwame-alexander-on-childrens-books-and-the-color-of-characters.html. Accessed 10 Nov. 2016.

Alexander, Kwame. "Newbery Medal Acceptance." *Horn Book Magazine*, July–Aug. 2015, pp. 67–76. *Academic Search Complete*, search.ebscohost.com/login.aspx?direct=tru e&db=f6h&AN=103656754&site=eds-live. Accessed 10 Nov. 2016.

Alexander, Kwame. "Poet's Novel Turns Young Sports Lovers into Book Lovers." Interview by Jeffrey Brown. *PBS NewsHour*, 26 Mar. 2015, www.pbs.org/newshour/bb/poets-novel-turns-young-sports-lovers-book-lovers. Accessed 10 Nov. 2016.

Clark, Colleen Patrice. "Literature's Empowerment." *Literacy Today*, vol. 33 no. 5, 2016, pp. 22–24. *Academic Search Complete*, search. ebscohost.com/login.aspx?direct=true&db =rch&AN=113496436&site=eds-live. Accessed 10 Nov. 2016.

Currie, Traci. "Poetry in Flight." *Black Issues Book Review*, vol. 2 no. 2, 2000, p. 68. *Academic Search Complete*, http://search.ebscohost.com/login.aspx?direct=true&db=lfh&A N=2930265&site=eds-live. Accessed 10 Nov. 2016.

Sawyer, Jenny. "'Booked' Asks Tweens to Consider the Idea that Being Smart Could Be Cool." Review of *Booked*, by Kwame Alexander. *The Christian Science Monitor*, 6 May 2016, www.csmonitor.com/Books/Book-Reviews/2016/0506/Booked-asks-tweens-to-consider-the-idea-that-being-smart-could-be-cool. Accessed 10 Nov. 2016.

SELECTED WORKS

Crush: Love Poems, 2007; *Acoustic Rooster and His Backyard Band*, 2011; *The Crossover*, 2014; *Booked*, 2016

—*Judy Johnson*

Mahershala Ali

Date of birth: February 16, 1974
Occupation: Actor

For some television audiences, actor Mahershala Ali has been a familiar face for more than a decade and a half. Having taken on his first major recurring role in the crime drama *Crossing Jordan* in 2001, he remained a fixture on television over the next decade, making a variety of guest appearances and joining the casts of series such as *The 4400* (2004–7), *Alphas* (2011–12), and *Treme* (2011–12). He enjoyed increased recognition beginning in 2013, when he landed a role

By Gordon Correll (Mahershala Ali) [CC BY-SA 2.0], via Wikimedia Commons

in the streaming service Netflix's popular political drama *House of Cards*.

It was not until 2016, however, that Ali became a household name. That year, appearances in the Netflix superhero show *Luke Cage* introduced him to wider audiences. Additionally, he costarred in the film *Moonlight*, a critically acclaimed drama that won the Academy Award for best picture, among countless other honors. His performance as the drug dealer Juan, a friend and mentor to the child protagonist of the film's first segment, received critical acclaim, earning him an Academy Award, as well as individual notice from the film's viewers. He was particularly attached to the character and told Steve Rose for the *Guardian* (30 Jan. 2017), "I miss him more than any other character that I've ever played."

By the end of that year, Ali's appearance in other major films such as the critically acclaimed historical drama *Hidden Figures* provided further opportunities for him to experiment with a vast range of genres and characters. At heart, however, he cares most about finding projects and collaborators that truly speak to him. "I'm focused on trying to align myself with people who are like-minded, and trying to build the world I want to live in to the best of my power," he told Rose.

EARLY LIFE

Ali was born Mahershalalhashbaz Gilmore on February 16, 1974, in Oakland, California. As an adult, he later changed his last name to Ali following his conversion to Islam, and he began using the shortened version of his first name

professionally around 2011. He grew up in Hayward, a city southeast of Oakland. His parents, Willicia and Phillip, were high school students at the time of his birth. His mother would go on to work as a hairdresser and later became an ordained minister, while his father was a talented dancer who won a $2,500 prize on the popular dance-oriented television series *Soul Train*. When Ali was still young, his father moved to New York City to pursue his career, later appearing in notable productions such as a 1987 Broadway revival of the musical *Dreamgirls*. Following his parents' separation, Ali lived with his mother but regularly visited his father in New York, where he was exposed to the world of theater and dance. His mother later remarried, and he has younger siblings from that marriage.

As a child, Ali was particularly close to his paternal grandmother, Mamie Gilmore, whom he has credited with helping him develop the self-esteem necessary to pursue his career as an actor. "She would tell me that I was handsome, that I was intelligent, that I could do anything I put my mind to," he recalled in an interview with Stephen Galloway for the *Hollywood Reporter* (15 Feb. 2017). "She said, 'You can be happy or miserable. It's up to you.' She was teaching me to think a certain way, and that has really served me, because at a certain point you believe it enough, where it's not something that you wear as arrogance or armor. There's times when you need to pull that out to encourage yourself."

EDUCATION

Although exposed to acting at a young age, Ali, heavily involved in playing basketball, did not initially consider pursuing a career in the field and was drawn more toward writing. As a teenager, he began composing poems as a means of dealing with stressful aspects of his life. "I wasn't sleeping well at all, and just processing some stuff that was going on," he told Emma Brown for *Interview* magazine (20 Oct. 2016). "So I'd be up all night writing these poems. I eventually started to perform them, especially when I would go visit my dad in New York. And they were essentially monologues."

After graduating from Mt. Eden High School in 1992, Ali enrolled in Saint Mary's College of California on a basketball scholarship. Although initially focused primarily on playing basketball for the school, which competes in the National Collegiate Athletic Association's Division I West Coast Conference, he soon became an avid participant in the school's theatrical productions. Still struggling to determine his path and coping with the loss of his father, he remembers his involvement in the university's production of the play *Spunk* as an especially poignant moment. In an article on Saint Mary's College of California's website (18 Dec. 2012), he was quoted as having said, "I felt a peace during that period of time that seemed to give my life a defining purpose."

After graduating with a bachelor's degree in mass communication in 1996, disenchanted with the competitive nature of sports, he dedicated himself to pursuing a career in acting and took a summer apprenticeship with the California Shakespeare Festival. After a brief period working for a music-industry magazine, he auditioned and became one of eighteen people to enroll in Tisch School of the Arts, part of New York University (NYU), in 1997 to study acting. He earned his master of fine arts degree from the prestigious institution in 2000.

EARLY CAREER

After completing his graduate studies, Ali remained on the East Coast for a short time, obtaining the lead role in a Washington, DC, Arena Stage revival of the Howard Sackler play *The Great White Hope*. Following his tenure with the play as well as a role in an independent film, he returned to California to seek out work in film and television. "I moved to Los Angeles because New York was cold and it was really too quiet for me at that time," he recalled to Brown. "I was out of school; I was hungry." Having already secured an agent during his time at NYU, he quickly found himself cast in the role of Dr. Trey Sanders, a medical examiner, on the crime drama *Crossing Jordan*. He appeared in nineteen episodes of the show's first season, which aired between 2001 and 2002.

Following his season on *Crossing Jordan*, Ali continued to find television work, making single-episode appearances in shows such as *NYPD Blue* and *CSI* in 2002 and 2003. He played a supporting role in several episodes of the short-lived drama *Threat Matrix* from 2003 to 2004, and from 2004 to 2007, he appeared in the science-fiction show *The 4400*. Heavily influenced by hip-hop music, he also performed as a rapper during this early part of his career, releasing the mixtape *Corner Ensemble* (2006) and the album *Curb Side Service* (2007) under the name Prince Ali.

In addition to television work, Ali sought out roles in both short and feature-length films, beginning with independent projects. He made his major film debut in 2008, when he appeared in the award-winning fantasy drama *The Curious Case of Benjamin Button*. Although he continued to work primarily in television following that performance, including appearances in multiple episodes of the shows *Treme* and *Alphas* between 2011 and 2012, he went on to take roles in films such as the 2013 thriller *The Place Beyond the Pines*.

FINDING FAME ON NETFLIX

Having worked in television and film for more than a decade, Ali reached a turning point in his career in 2013, with the debut of the series *House of Cards* on Netflix. One of the service's earliest forays into original content, the show is a political drama that follows the machinations of politician Frank Underwood (played by Kevin Spacey) as he seeks to gain the presidency at all costs. Making his first appearance in the show's fourth episode, Ali portrays Remy Danton, a lobbyist who becomes embroiled in the schemes of Frank and his associates. The show was a critical success throughout its first season and beyond, and viewers particularly noted Ali's strong performance as Remy. Critics agreed with that assessment, and in 2016, he was nominated for an Emmy Award for outstanding guest actor in a drama series for his work.

For Ali, obtaining a role in the show proved crucial to the progression of his career. "There's a part of the business that people just don't see, in the whole auditioning process," he explained to Soraya Nadia McDonald for the *Undefeated* (30 Dec. 2016). "I had many years of that, booking gigs, almost booking jobs and therefore making some real allies in the business, of people who wanted to cast me in things but I just wasn't a big enough name. What *House of Cards* did was gave people permission to cast me." At the same time, he was introduced to fans of science fiction through his role in the final two installments of the dystopian Hunger Games franchise, released in 2014 and 2015.

In 2016, Ali left *House of Cards* after the fourth season; however, in addition to appearing in the historical drama *Free State of Jones* and the independent film *Kicks*, he remained a presence on Netflix upon joining the cast of the new series *Luke Cage*, based on the Marvel Comics superhero of the same name, which debuted in September 2016. As the villainous Cornell "Cottonmouth" Stokes, he made a strong impression on viewers of the series, which was the third of several original Netflix offerings based on Marvel properties.

MOONLIGHT AND BEYOND

Ali's next major project was the film *Moonlight*, written and directed by Barry Jenkins and based on a work written by Tarell Alvin McCraney. Encouraged to read the screenplay by his agency, Ali was instantly drawn to the work. "I thought it was the best thing I had ever read," he told Brown. He quickly signed on to costar in the film.

Moonlight is a coming-of-age story in three parts that focuses on an African American boy, and later man, named Chiron—played by Alex Hibbert, Ashton Sanders, and Trevante Rhodes—who grows up in a rough section of

Miami and struggles with his family life, sexual orientation, and other issues at different stages in his life. Ali appears in the first part of the narrative as Juan, a Miami drug dealer who befriends and mentors young Chiron while at the same time disrupting the boy's life by selling crack cocaine to Chiron's mother. Although Juan appears only in the first segment of the film, Ali was happy with the scope of the role. "I think selfishly, as an actor, we always want to do more," he admitted to Brown. "But in this case—and uniquely in this case—I appreciate Juan disappearing because of what that allows the audience to feel."

After a strong showing at film festivals in the fall of 2016, *Moonlight* proved to be a critical success upon its wide release in the United States in November 2016 and was nominated for numerous awards. Subsequent to Ali's memorable performance in another Academy Award–nominated film, *Hidden Figures, Moonlight* went on to claim the 2017 Academy Awards for best adapted screenplay and best picture. While critics praised many of the film's performances, Ali's was especially lauded, and he ultimately took home the Academy Award for best actor in a supporting role.

Ali was next seen in the film *Roxanne Roxanne*, a biopic based on the life of 1980s rapper Roxanne Shanté, which premiered at the Sundance Film Festival in early 2017. Also in early 2017, it was announced that he would play multiple roles in the upcoming live-action American adaptation of the Japanese comic *Alita: Battle Angel*, which is set to be released in 2018.

PERSONAL LIFE

Ali met his wife, artist and musician Amatus-Sami Karim-Ali, while attending NYU. The couple married in 2013, and their first child, daughter Bari Najma Ali, was born in early 2017. They live in Venice, California.

SUGGESTED READING

Ali, Mahershala. Interview by Emma Brown. *Interview*, 20 Oct. 2016, www.interviewmagazine.com/film/mahershala-ali. Accessed 15 May 2017.

Ali, Mahershala. "*Moonlight* Breakout Mahershala Ali in His Own Words: A Personal Journey from Childhood Upheaval to Spiritual Awakening." Interview by Stephen Galloway. *The Hollywood Reporter*, 15 Feb. 2017, www.hollywoodreporter.com/features/moonlight-breakout-mahershala-ali-his-own-words-a-personal-journey-childhood-upheaval-spiri. Accessed 15 May 2017.

McDonald, Soraya Nadia. "Mahershala Ali Has Been Waiting 16 Years to Become an Overnight Sensation." *The Undefeated*, 30 Dec. 2016, theundefeated.com/features/

mahershala-ali-moonlight-oscar-frontrunner-best-supporting-actor. Accessed 15 May 2017.

Rose, Steve. "From *House of Cards* to *Moonlight*, Why Mahershala Ali Is Having a Moment." *The Guardian*, 30 Jan. 2017, www.theguardian.com/film/2017/jan/30/mahershala-ali-luke-cage-moonlight-hunger-games. Accessed 15 May 2017.

SELECTED WORKS

Crossing Jordan, 2001–2; *The 4400*, 2004–7; *The Curious Case of Benjamin Button*, 2008; *The Place Beyond the Pines*, 2013; *House of Cards*, 2013–16; *Free State of Jones*, 2016; *Luke Cage*, 2016; *Moonlight*, 2016; *Hidden Figures*, 2016

—Joy Crelin

Sam Altman

Date of birth: April 22, 1985
Occupation: Entrepreneur

Sam Altman is one of the most influential figures in the world of start-ups. He is a successful entrepreneur and programmer as well as the president of YC Group and its division Y Combinator—the renowned venture capital company.

Altman first became involved with Y Combinator in 2005, when his start-up Loopt joined the first batch of companies to receive seed money from the newly formed venture capital company. Soon after, Y Combinator turned into a force in its field and became known for providing seed money to prominent companies such as Reddit, Dropbox, and Airbnb. After selling Loopt in 2012, and after running his own venture capital fund, Hydrazine Capital, Altman was recruited to become the next president of Y Combinator by its cofounder Paul Graham. Altman took the position in early 2014, at the age of twenty-eight. In 2016, he became president of the broader YC Group, taking leadership not only of Y Combinator, but also of several other initiatives.

Under Altman's leadership, Y Combinator has continued to fund start-ups seeking to disrupt a variety of industries as well as companies focusing on technologies such as nuclear energy. Likewise, the company has increased its efforts in the areas of education and pure research, launching initiatives such as YC Research, a nonprofit research laboratory.

As groundbreaking as many of the concepts championed by Y Combinator–funded companies are, for Altman, the ideas themselves are less important than the capabilities and dedication of the founders of these companies. "Ideas are cheap and easy and there are a lot of them,"

he explained to Laurie Segall for CNN (9 Apr. 2014). "What we really care about—are the founders that have the strength and determination to go out and build a great company." As an entrepreneur who is himself one of Y Combinator's success stories, Altman brings more than a decade of experience to the table.

EARLY LIFE AND EDUCATION

Samuel H. Altman was born on April 22, 1985. He is the first of four children born to Connie Gibstine, a dermatologist, and Jerry Altman, a real estate developer. Altman has two brothers, Max and Jack, and a sister, Annie. Both of his brothers would later work at technology start-ups funded in part by Y Combinator—Max at Zenefits, an online human resources software, and Jack as cofounder of Lattice, a performance management company.

Altman grew up in Clayton, Missouri, a city just outside of St. Louis. He was an inquisitive child who developed an interest in technology at an early age. When Altman was eight years old, his parents gave him his first computer: a Macintosh. This was a turning point for him because he quickly learned how to disassemble and reassemble the computer as well as how to program. "It was this dividing line in my life: before I had a computer and after," he recalled to Tom Junod for *Esquire* (18 Dec. 2014).

Altman attended the Ralph M. Captain Elementary School in Clayton and the John Burroughs School, a preparatory day school in St. Louis. He graduated from the John Burroughs School in 2003 and went on to attend Stanford

University, where he studied computer science for two years. Together with two other classmates, Altman dropped out, choosing instead to focus on his start-up Loopt.

LOOPT

While at Stanford, Altman and his friends Nick Sivo and Alok Deshpande founded the start-up Loopt in 2005. Sivo became a software developer, and Deshpande, the head of product. Loopt was created with the objective of giving cell phone users the ability to share their locations with friends and family. At the time, smartphones such as the iPhone had not yet been introduced, and the existing forms of cell phones did not make global positioning system (GPS) data available. As such data was necessary for Loopt's product to work, Altman and his team initially developed a work-around; they worked with phone carriers to gain access to location data that was then being used for a 911 service. "Often when you are trying to kind of lead the wave by a little bit in technology, you're willing to put up with some hacks to get something to market a little bit faster," Altman told Andrew Warner for *Mixergy* (24 Oct. 2016) of Loopt's early efforts. "We knew GPS was coming, but it wasn't there yet. We wanted to be first. So we were willing to work around that." The company would later partner with cell phone service providers such as Boost Mobile to make its product available to users, and as mobile technology improved over the following years, the service was introduced to smartphones in the form of an app.

While developing and promoting Loopt, Altman and his colleagues received funding from a variety of venture capital groups including Y Combinator, a newly formed company. Y Combinator was also founded in 2005, by Paul Graham, Jessica Livingston, Trevor Blackwell, and Robert Morris, and it was initially intended to provide seed money as well as guidance to start-ups in exchange for receiving equity in the companies. Loopt became one of eight companies that made up Y Combinator's first batch of start-ups, alongside future successes such as the website Reddit. Although the seed money undoubtedly assisted Altman and his colleagues in developing their product, the connections Altman made in the process would prove even more crucial to his career. These connections would eventually lead him back to Y Combinator.

In 2012, Altman and his cofounders sold Loopt to Green Dot Corporation—a company that specializes in prepaid debit cards—for $43.4 million. He went on to join Green Dot's board of directors, remaining in that role until 2016. Also in 2012, after selling Loopt, Altman cofounded the venture capital fund Hydrazine

Capital with his brother Jack. Jack continued to run the fund after Altman's departure in 2014.

Y COMBINATOR

In February 2014, Paul Graham stepped down as president of Y Combinator and announced Altman as his successor. Graham had begun his attempts to recruit Altman as early as 2012, convinced that the young entrepreneur was the best choice for the position. "Sam is one of the smartest people I know, and understands start-ups better than perhaps anyone I know, including myself," Graham explained in a post on Y Combinator's blog while announcing the leadership change (21 Feb. 2014). "He's the one I go to when I want a second opinion about a hard problem." For Altman, the position represented a welcome challenge and an opportunity to observe innovative start-ups develop from the ground up. "I love working with really early stage start-ups where the outcome is still in doubt," he told Segall. "Maybe they'll go on to greatness or maybe they'll never get off the runway at all."

Uncertainty is one of the defining features of the field of venture capital and of start-ups themselves. In his October 2016 interview with Warner, Altman noted that while Y Combinator had funded 1,500 companies up to that point, it was the top twenty companies that represented the majority of the value. From that perspective, one could consider that the other 1,480 investments have been failures. "It's very humbling to be an investor because you go into each investment with a belief that it's going to be very successful or at least willing to pay for the probability that it will be very successful," Altman explained to Warner. "You are wrong, humiliatingly wrong all the time. At some point, you just stop caring and you realize you'll be wrong most of the time and that is a price of admission for being really right occasionally."

SUPPORTING GREAT IDEAS

As president of Y Combinator, Altman plays a key role in shaping the company's internal and external focus. "A huge part of my job . . . is to say no to good ideas to save firepower for great ones," he told Warner. "And that's a tough thing to learn." At times, start-ups with the most promise might not appear so promising at first. "A couple of years ago, we funded this company called FarmLogs, and everyone was, like, 'This is, like, stupid farming software,'" Altman recalled to Junod. "And now, like, fifteen percent of all crops grown in the United States use this platform, and they're able to hugely increase the efficiency."

In addition to continuing Y Combinator's mission of providing seed money to a variety of start-ups, including companies focusing on mobile applications and disrupting traditional industry practices, Altman has pushed for further investments in hard science, particularly in fields such as nuclear energy. He has also expressed interest in investing in pure research and consequently founded the nonprofit research laboratory YC Research as a division of Y Combinator in 2015. Altman donated $10 million of his personal funds to the laboratory in the hope of funding research that would eventually be released to other researchers and the public for free. Among other areas of research, YC Research plans to study the logistics and effects of universal basic income, a topic of particular interest to Altman.

In 2016, Altman was named president of YC Group. YC Group encompasses Y Combinator and YC Research as well as several other divisions.

PERSONAL LIFE

Altman is openly gay and has talked about how the Internet gave him a sense of hope and community in his youth. "I grew up in the Midwest, sort of struggling with being gay, and I didn't have anyone I could talk to about that," Altman told Junod. "So having the Internet was this unbelievable thing. Just having the human connection, where you can talk about something that no one from your real world would understand, was just unbelievably powerful."

Altman loves classical music. He lives in San Francisco's Mission District.

SUGGESTED READING

Altman, Sam. "How Venture Capitalists Find Opportunities in the Future." Interview by Tom Junod. *Esquire*, 18 Dec. 2014, www.esquire.com/news-politics/interviews/a30763/sam-altman-interview-2014. Accessed 10 Feb. 2017.

Altman, Sam. "Sam Altman on Y Combinator, Loopt & Work Habits." Interview by Andrew Warner. *Mixergy*, 24 Oct. 2016, mixergy.com/interviews/yc-group-with-sam-altman. Accessed 10 Feb. 2017.

Altman, Sam. "YC Changes." *Y Combinator*, 13 Sept. 2016, blog.ycombinator.com/yc-changes. Accessed 10 Feb. 2017.

Chafkin, Max. "Y Combinator President Sam Altman Is Dreaming Big." *Fast Company*, 16 Apr. 2015, www.fastcompany.com/3044282/the-y-combinator-chronicles/california-dreamin. Accessed 14 Feb. 2017.

Friend, Tad. "Sam Altman's Manifest Destiny." *New Yorker*, 10 Oct. 2016, www.newyorker.com/magazine/2016/10/10/sam-altmans-manifest-destiny. Accessed 10 Feb. 2017.

Graham, Paul. "Sam Altman for President." *Y Combinator*, 21 Feb. 2014, blog.ycombinator.com/sam-altman-for-president. Accessed 10 Feb. 2017.

Segall, Laurie. "Meet Silicon Valley's 28-Year-Old Whiz Kid." *CNN*, 9 Apr. 2014, money.cnn.com/2014/04/09/technology/innovation/sam-altman-y-combinator. Accessed 10 Feb. 2017.

—Joy Crelin

Avery Amereau

Date of birth: January 29, 1991
Occupation: Singer

Photo by Hiroyuki Ito/Getty Images

"I don't mean to exaggerate, but this woman made my knees shake," renowned conductor Thomas Crawford told James R. Oestreich for the *New York Times* (21 Sept. 2016). "The voice is just ravishing." He was speaking of Avery Amereau, a young singer who began making waves in the opera world even before she had graduated from New York City's famed Juilliard School. Amereau made her Metropolitan Opera debut in November 2016, performing the small role of a madrigal singer in Giacomo Puccini's *Manon Lescaut*. While critic Corinna da Fonseca-Wollheim devoted much of her review for the *New York Times* (15 Nov. 2016) to lead singer Anna Netrebko, who is considered something of a superstar in that sphere, she was moved enough to write, "The minor role of a musician who recites madrigals written by Manon's rich patron, sung by the captivating Avery Amereau, stood out for the unusually rich, saturated auburn timbre of her voice."

Amereau caused some confusion among fans and critics alike while still in the very earliest days of her career. Although she sings firmly within the alto range, she was often billed as a mezzo-soprano (and continues to be described as such on the website of IMG Artists, which represents her professionally). Amereau has explained in interviews that this was because of the relative lack of good roles for contraltos, the female singers with the lowest vocal range. However, her decision in late 2016 to "rebrand" herself with her true range does not seem to have affected her career. "I'm still singing mezzo-soprano roles," she told James M. Keller for *Pasatiempo* (16 Dec. 2016), the arts-and-entertainment supplement of the *Santa Fe New Mexican*. "In rebranding as a contralto, I didn't change my voice at all."

EARLY LIFE AND EDUCATION

Amereau was born and raised in Jupiter, a town in West Palm Beach, Florida. As a child, she was not fond of her elementary school classmates. In fifth grade, wanting to avoid going on to middle school with the same people, she began searching for alternative schools and discovered the Alexander W. Dreyfoos School of the Arts in West Palm Beach. She auditioned for the school, singing "Colors of the Wind" from the Disney movie *Pocahontas* (1995), and was admitted to the school's voice program, which concentrated on choral singing with some introductory lessons in music theory.

When asked by Zack Singerman for the classical-music podcast *VOICEtalks* (2 Nov. 2016) when she first realized she was a contralto, Amereau recalled a time during her high school years at Dreyfoos when the chorus sang Z. Randall Stroope's "Psalm 23." She loved the song so much that she begged the conductor to put her on soprano so she could sing the melody. "She said, 'Well, no, you're not a soprano,'" Amereau told Singerman. "So that was kind of the first inkling that I had. You know, she said, 'You're a mezzo, that's something special, and you should also look into going to music school.'"

At that point, however, Amereau's musical pursuits were still just "an interest" and "not a passion," she told Oestreich. She was accepted to Florida State University and enrolled, planning to study prelaw. Her parents were thus surprised when she suddenly abandoned those plans, giving up multiple scholarships, in order to enter the Mannes School of Music in New York City.

MANNES AND MEISTERSINGER

An affiliate institution of the well-regarded New School, Mannes has a history of graduating performing-arts professionals who go on to sing with the Metropolitan Opera, accept posts with prestigious orchestras and chamber ensembles, and establish nonprofit arts programs or other philanthropic ventures. At Mannes Amereau studied with Dan H. Marek, a renowned singer, voice teacher, and expert in bel canto, a style of operatic singing that originated in late sixteenth-century Italy. Although she admitted to Singerman that she knew little of his stellar reputation and chose him as a teacher based on his "amazing headshot," Amereau credited Marek with stressing scales and other technical work that allowed her to slowly and methodically build up her skills, with the aim of having a solid and lengthy career.

In summer 2011 she spent six weeks at the Internationale Meistersinger Akademie (IMA) in Neumarkt, Germany, which offers young artists a chance to study languages, opera, and art songs, known as *Lieder* in Germany and *mélodies* in France, with an international array of instructors. Amereau returned to IMA—a popular hunting ground for European agents, promoters, opera directors, and festival managers—each summer through 2014. While there she met Matthew Horner, then vice president and artist manager of IMG Artists' vocal division, who kept in touch and offered her advice and assistance over the years, until Amereau's relationship with the agency became official in 2015. She also became close to the Academy's artistic director, Edith Wiens, who remains an influential coach and mentor. "The first few notes flew up in my head with a rare beauty," Wiens told Oestreich, recalling the first time she ever heard Amereau sing. Of Amereau's voice, she said, "That deep, burnished sound is a gift. It's not a teachable quality." The admiration is mutual: in her interview with Singerman, Amereau described Wiens as "a humongous vessel of inspiration."

JUILLIARD

Upon receiving her bachelor of music degree from Mannes, Amereau enrolled at the Juilliard School, a venerable institution founded in 1905. There she continued to study with Wiens, who was on the faculty, as well as with the well-known instructor Matthew Epstein. Epstein immediately noticed Amereau's unique combination of traits and predicted her success. "Avery is unusual in being a contralto in vocal color and range, combined with a young, physical presence," he said to Oestreich.

In 2015 Amereau earned her master of music degree from Juilliard and was accepted into the school's demanding artist diploma program for opera studies, a two-year advanced course of study that admits no more than ten singers at a time. In addition to intensive training in vocal and acting techniques, the program also focuses on career placement and arranges regular private auditions with top-level managers and opera companies, including the Metropolitan Opera. According to the Juilliard School's website, the goal of the program is to "encourage individuality and humanity in artists" and to produce "collaborative, open, inventive singing actors who can work on any stage, in any style, and with any director."

Throughout her career at Juilliard, from 2014 to 2017, Amereau was the recipient of the school's coveted Kovner Fellowship. She received her artist diploma from Juilliard in 2017, having already made her professional debut years before. When Singerman quipped that she apparently had little need for the artist diploma, she expressed deep appreciation that Juilliard's artist diploma program "is there to invest in you and not to exploit you," as some programs have been known for doing to their young participants.

PROFESSIONAL SINGING CAREER

Amereau's first professional singing engagement came in 2012, when one of her teachers at Mannes, Joshua Greene, hired her to sing alto in the Pro Arte Chorale's performance of Gioachino Rossini's *Petite messe solennelle* (little solemn mass), under Greene's direction. She continued to perform professionally throughout her time at Mannes and then at Juilliard. Her first operatic performance was her role as Olga in Juilliard's 2014 production of Pyotr Tchaikovsky's *Eugene Onegin.*

The following year, her performance in Benjamin Britten's *The Rape of Lucretia*, another Juilliard production, prompted reviewer Anthony Tommasini to write for the *New York Times* (19 Feb. 2015), "With her sensual mezzo-soprano voice, Avery Amereau is achingly perfect as Lucretia, who summons vehement intensity when [villainous prince] Tarquinius attacks her." On the strength of this performance, Amereau was tapped to cover the same role, effectively serving as an understudy, later that year in a production mounted by the Glyndebourne Festival Opera.

Also in 2015 Amereau sang the title role of *Carmen* for the first time, in the New York Opera Exchange's production of Georges Bizet's iconic work. That summer she performed at the Boston Early Music Festival in a Juilliard coproduction with London's Royal Academy of Music, about which critic Jacob Street wrote for the *Boston Musical Intelligencer* (16 June 2015), "Mezzo-soprano Avery Amereau drew the drama from some place deep within herself, the lowest notes a rich, enveloping curtain of clarity and undulating vibrato. Her *sotto voce da capo* (in the voice of the head), achingly mirrored by her orchestral counterparts, was a moment of easy musical magic."

MEZZO-SOPRANO OR CONTRALTO?

Noting that there are few skilled contraltos performing on the opera stage today, Oestreich wondered about Amereau's official designation as a mezzo-soprano, writing, "Why wouldn't a lavishly gifted young contralto shout her arrival from the rooftop?" Amereau explained to him that while contraltos are rare, so are roles suitable for them, and branding herself as such might have limited her possibilities. "I was advised it might put me in a box, that the term was antiquated, that being identified as a contralto might deny me some opportunities," she later said to Keller. She worried that doing so might consign her to singing only Erda—the Earth goddess in Richard Wagner's *Der Ring des Nibelungen*—for much of her career: "Even roles like Olga [in *Eugene Onegin*], Lucretia [in *The Rape of Lucretia*], and Rosina [in *The Barber of Seville*, by Rossini]—these were all written for contraltos, but they got taken over by mezzo-sopranos and sopranos. So people wouldn't automatically consider me for those."

In 2016, however, as exceptionally laudatory reviews began pouring in for her performances, Amereau decided to take the leap. "I just talked to my manager today, and we've decided to rebrand as a contralto," she told Keller. "I've always known that's what I am. The low parts of my voice have always felt the easiest, and I could find the most beauty in them. It's not often that you hear somebody with such ease in the lower part of their voice. I think this color that people are hearing is that I'm an alto." Referring to her previous night's performance of George Handel's *Messiah*, which she sang at the lower, baroque pitch rather than the typical higher, modern pitch, she said, "It said on the program I was a mezzo-soprano, and it just felt like a lie."

SUBSEQUENT SUCCESSES

Since then Amereau has sung in a variety of prestigious settings and groups, including the Spoleto Festival, the Santa Cruz Symphony, the Toledo Symphony, and the New Amsterdam Singers. During the 2016–17 season she sang the title role of *Carmen* again, with Opera Columbus; Wolfgang Amadeus Mozart's *Requiem*, with the Rhode Island Philharmonic; Johann Sebastian Bach's *St. John Passion*, with the Voices of Ascension Chorus and Orchestra; and Handel's *Messiah*, with the St. Paul Chamber Orchestra. Additionally, she returned to the Glyndebourne Festival Opera, this time in a role of her own, as Dryade in Richard Strauss's *Ariadne auf Naxos*.

Amereau considers her 2016 Metropolitan Opera debut, as the madrigal singer in Puccini's *Manon Lescaut*, to be among the highlights of her career thus far. To make her opera-house debut at the Met, so early in her career, was "a huge honor," she told Singerman. "When I

started singing, my dad would always say to me, 'When am I going to see you at the Met? I want to come to the Met,'" she recalled. "And I would tell him, like, 'Listen, it's gonna be in my forties, you have to just wait, you know, that's not the way it works.' And then it did just kind of happen like that."

SUGGESTED READING

Amereau, Avery. "'The Met Will Be My First Opera House'—Avery Amereau." Interview by Zack Singerman. *VOICEtalks*, 2 Nov. 2016, www.voicetalkspodcast.com/2016/11/02/029-avery-amereau. Accessed 5 June 2017.

Fonseca-Wollheim, Corinna da. "*Manon Lescaut* at the Met Opera: A Courtesan in Need of Context." Review of *Manon Lescaut*, produced by Richard Eyre. *The New York Times*, 15 Nov. 2016, www.nytimes.com/2016/11/16/arts/music/puccini-manon-lescaut-metropolitan-opera-anna-netrebko.html. Accessed 5 June 2017.

Keller, James M. "At Home in the Range: Contralto Avery Amereau." *Pasatiempo*, Santa Fe New Mexican, 16 Dec. 2016, www.santafenewmexican.com/pasatiempo/music/in_concert/at-home-in-the-range-contralto-avery-amereau/article_baa5f86d-e891-5a41-b6d8-c9cec04d6798.html. Accessed 5 June 2017.

Oestreich, James R. "Avery Amereau Is a Rarity in Music: A Contralto." *The New York Times*, 21 Sept. 2016, www.nytimes.com/2016/09/22/arts/music/avery-amereau-is-a-rarity-in-music-a-contralto.html. Accessed 5 June 2017.

Street, Jacob. "Technique Abounds, Affect Lacking." *The Boston Musical Intelligencer*, 16 June 2015, www.classical-scene.com/2015/06/16/juilliard415-bemf. Accessed 5 June 2017.

Tommasini, Anthony. "Review: In Britten's *The Rape of Lucretia*, a Savage Act with Resonance Today." Review of *The Rape of Lucretia*, directed by Mary Birnbaum. *The New York Times*, 19 Feb. 2015, www.nytimes.com/2015/02/20/arts/music/review-in-brittens-the-rape-of-lucretia-a-savage-act-with-resonance-today.html. Accessed 5 June 2017.

—Mari Rich

Carol Anderson

Date of birth: June 17, 1959
Occupation: Historian

In the wake of the fatal shooting of a black teenager named Michael Brown by a white police officer in Ferguson, Missouri—and the violent protests and looting that broke out in

Democracy Now Productions, Inc./democracynow.org

response—Emory University professor Carol Anderson was moved to write an op-ed for the *Washington Post*. A specialist in African American studies and history, she was well positioned to comment on the events, which captured national attention in the fall of 2014. "As a historian I understand the power of narratives and how they define and frame reality," she told Elaine Justice for the Emory News Center website (31 May 2016). "In 2014, as I watched the news about Ferguson burning, reporters talked about black rage: Black people burning up where they lived and did they have a right to do so. Because I had lived in Missouri for thirteen years or so, I knew that framing was incorrect. We were so busy looking at the flames that we missed the kindling."

Anderson's op-ed, provocatively headlined "Ferguson Isn't about Black Rage against Cops. It's White Rage against Progress," was published on August 29, 2014, and quickly drew thousands of comments on the *Washington Post* website. The piece became the paper's most widely shared opinion piece of the year, helping to launch Anderson into the public eye. Realizing that as a historian she had a great deal to add to the national conversation on race, Anderson expanded the op-ed into the book *White Rage: The Unspoken Truth of Our Racial Divide*, which was published in 2016 to great acclaim in some quarters and a degree of ire from more conservative or right-leaning sources. Anderson, who was named one of the top fifty "thinkers, doers, and visionaries transforming American politics in 2016" by the editors of *Politico* magazine, took

the varying reactions in stride. "When you say things of consequence, there are consequences," she explained to Justice.

EDUCATION

Carol Elaine Anderson was born on June 17, 1959, but few details of her early life are available. She attended Miami University in Oxford, Ohio, which was chartered in 1809 and is thus one of the oldest public universities in the country. A cum laude graduate and member of the Phi Beta Kappa scholarly honor society, Anderson earned bachelor's degrees in history and political science in 1981, with concentrations in international relations and American and Soviet foreign policy. She remained at the school to earn a master's degree in political science, with the same concentrations, in 1983.

Anderson chose to conduct her doctoral studies at the Ohio State University, in Columbus, Ohio. There she earned her PhD in history in 1995, graduating with particular expertise in the twentieth century, including US international relations, European international history, American history, and the African American experience.

UNIVERSITY OF MISSOURI

Shortly after earning her doctoral degree, in 1996 Anderson accepted a post as an assistant professor of history at the University of Missouri. She taught undergraduate- and graduate-level courses in twentieth-century American history, twentieth-century African American history, twentieth-century US foreign policy, the civil rights movement, human rights policy, and war crimes and genocide. Throughout this period, she also earned numerous fellowships to pursue her research and published various articles. In 2003 Anderson was promoted to an associate professorship.

Also in 2003, Anderson's first book, *Eyes off the Prize: The United Nations and the African American Struggle for Human Rights: 1944–1955*, was published by Cambridge University Press. The book details efforts by black activists to get the United Nations to see de jure and de facto segregation and racism in the United States as human rights issues. It garnered several honors, including the Myrna F. Bernath Book Award from the Society for Historians of American Foreign Relations and the Gustavus Myers Outstanding Book Award from the Gustavus Myers Center for the Study of Bigotry and Human Rights. It was also a finalist for the Harry S. Truman Library Institute's Truman Book Award and the National Conference of Black Political Scientists' W. E. B. Du Bois Book Award. *Eyes off the Prize* was well-received by its audience in academia. In a review, Norman Markowitz wrote for *Political Affairs* (17 Sept. 2004) that

Anderson's work was "a fascinating political narrative" and a "very valuable work for students of African American and general US history."

From 2004 to 2005 Anderson served as the University of Missouri's director of undergraduate studies, in addition to her teaching duties. In 2006 she was named a member of the US State Department's Historical Advisory Committee. Anderson ultimately remained at the University of Missouri until 2008, during which time she sat on numerous theses and dissertation committees and advised several doctoral students in the fields of US foreign policy and African American history.

EMORY UNIVERSITY

Upon leaving the University of Missouri after more than a decade, Anderson joined the faculty of Emory University, an internationally ranked private university in Atlanta, Georgia. There, beginning in 2009, she held an associate professorship in African American studies. At Emory, Anderson found herself as busy and in-demand as she had been in Missouri. In addition to teaching courses on twentieth-century African American history, Cold War–era foreign policy, war crimes and genocide, human rights, and the civil rights movement, she regularly served on dissertation committees—including stints as an outside committee member for history students at the University of Wisconsin–Madison and Arizona State University.

During the 2011–12 academic year, Anderson was appointed interim director of the school's James Weldon Johnson Visiting Fellows Program. Also in 2011, she was made a coordinator of the Mellon Mays Undergraduate Fellowship Program, whose goal is to increase diversity among faculty members at the nation's colleges and universities. In 2013 she was named the Visiting Gladstein Professor of Human Rights at the University of Connecticut.

Anderson's next book was *Bourgeois Radicals: The NAACP and the Struggle for Colonial Liberation, 1941–1960* (2014), published by Cambridge University Press. In a review for the *American Historical Review* (Feb. 2016), Robert Trent Vinton praised Anderson's "characteristic brio and panache" and called the book "essential reading for scholars of African and Asian decolonization, black transnational politics, US foreign policy, and the United Nations."

In 2015, Anderson was promoted from associate professor to an endowed position, becoming the Samuel Candler Dobbs Professor of African American Studies. In this capacity she also took over as chair of Emory's African American Studies department, with a term lasting until 2018. She continued publishing scholarly articles and received further research fellowships over the years.

"WHITE RAGE" AND NATIONAL ATTENTION

Although Anderson's first two books were well received, their audience was generally limited to academic circles. It would take a newspaper opinion piece to bring Anderson into the spotlight in the national conversation on race relations. In 2014, numerous protests and even riots broke out in Ferguson, Missouri, following the shooting of black teenager Michael Brown by a white police officer. The racial tension garnered widespread media attention, with both liberal and conservative commentators seeking to explain why African Americans were rioting. Watching the news at home, Anderson was struck by what she felt was a serious misunderstanding by the press. "As they're talking about what's wrong with Black folk, I'm shaking my head no," Anderson told Tanasia Kenney for the *Atlanta Black Star* (6 July 2016). "We're not looking at Black rage. What we're looking at is white rage. . . . And then I started writing, and it just flowed."

Anderson developed her thoughts into an op-ed that was published by the *Washington Post* in August 2014. The key idea of the piece was captured by the provocative title: "Ferguson Isn't about Black Rage against Cops. It's White Rage against Progress." The article instantly drew controversy, as it upended mainstream thinking from both sides of the political spectrum. It soon became the *Washington Post's* most-shared op-ed of the year, bringing the term "white rage" into the public consciousness and boosting Anderson's profile as a sought-after commentator on race and culture.

Anderson's next book built upon the ideas in her controversial opinion piece, and it too struck a chord with the general reading public. *White Rage: The Unspoken Truth of Our Racial Divide* was published by Bloomsbury in 2016 and was Anderson's first book in the trade press rather than the academic market. She explained the impetus for expanding her op-ed into a book to Sharon Arana for the History News Network website (15 Oct. 2016): "There's only so much you can cover in just over 1,000 words. I, therefore, wrote the book, *White Rage*, to provide a more complete analytical narrative for the ways legislators, presidents, and judges have deployed policy—under the guise of protecting democracy—to actually undermine black aspirations, black achievement, and black access to citizenship rights."

White Rage garnered coverage in several major papers and landed on the best-seller lists of the *New York Times* and online retailer Amazon. Interest in the work only increased as the issue of police shootings of African Americans continued to make headlines. In a review for the *New York Times* (24 June 2016), Jesse McCarthy wrote, "This book is an extraordinarily timely and urgent call to confront the legacy of structural racism bequeathed by white anger and resentment, and to show its continuing threat to the promise of American democracy."

ONGOING SOCIAL COMMENTARY
While *White Rage* brought her a great deal of mainstream attention, Anderson remained dedicated to her primary role as an educator. Her commitment was recognized with numerous teaching awards, including the Crystal Apple Award for Excellence in Undergraduate Education and the Williams Award for Excellence in Teaching, both presented by Emory University in 2016.

Meanwhile, Anderson continued to apply her concept of white rage to explain relevant cultural events as they unfolded. For example, she took the view that a renewed wave of white rage resulted in the 2016 election of Donald Trump as president. In a piece for *Time* (16 Nov. 2016), she dismissed the notion that economic uncertainty facing many white Americans led them to vote for Trump. "The median income of a Trump supporter is more than $70,000 per year, which is well above the national average," Anderson noted. "Clearly, Trump's pathway into the Oval Office is not really about white economic angst. Rather, Barack Obama's election—and its powerful symbolism of black advancement—was the major trigger for the policy backlash that led to Donald Trump." She went on to cite alleged voter suppression tactics targeting minorities enacted by the US Republican Party as proof of her argument.

Despite her perception of deeply entrenched racial bias in the United States, Anderson expressed optimism about the country and its future. "There is a fighting spirit in this nation," she told Arana. "A coalition of African Americans, Latinos, Asian Americans, Native Americans, and whites refuse to accept racism as the operating principle in the United States. . . . There are people who are willing to protest, write, speak, publish, march, demonstrate, knock on doors, and vote. That is the fight . . . that will to ensure that we defuse the power of white rage."

SUGGESTED READING
Anderson, Carol. "Ferguson Isn't about Black Rage against Cops. It's White Rage against Progress." *Washington Post*, 29 Aug. 2014, www.washingtonpost.com/opinions/ferguson-wasnt-black-rage-against-copsit-was-white-rage-against-progress/2014/08/29/3055e3f4-2d75-11e4-bb9b-997ae96fad33_story.html. Accessed 5 Dec. 2016.
Arana, Sharon. "The Book Historian Carol Anderson Had to Write after Ferguson." *History News Network*, 15 Oct. 2016, historynewsnetwork.org/article/163971. Accessed 5 Dec. 2016.
Justice, Elaine. "Anderson Explores Country's Racial Past, Present in *White Rage*." *Emory News Center*, Emory U, 31 May 2016, news.emory.edu/stories/2016/05/upress_white_rage_anderson/campus.html. Accessed 5 Dec. 2016.
Kenney, Tanasia. "Scholar's Controversial New Book Explores 'White Rage' and the Many Ways It Has Worked to 'Undermine Black Advancement' throughout History." Review of *White Rage: The Unspoken Truth of Our Racial Divide*, by Carol Anderson. *Atlanta Black Star*, 6 July 2016, atlantablackstar.com/2016/07/06/scholars-controversial-new-book-explores-white-rage-and-the-many-ways-it-has-worked-to-undermine-black-advancement-throughout-history. Accessed 5 Dec. 2016.
McCarthy, Jesse. "Why Are Whites So Angry?" Review of *White Rage: The Unspoken Truth of Out Racial Divide*, by Carol Anderson. *New York Times*, 24 June 2016, www.nytimes.com/2016/06/26/books/review/white-rage-by-carol-anderson.html. Accessed 5 Dec. 2016.
Poole, Sheila. "Author and Emory Prof Carol Anderson on 'White Rage.'" *AJC.com*, 18 Oct. 2016, www.ajc.com/lifestyles/author-and-emory-prof-carol-anderson-white-rage/wQE85KHAvVLCmADej1eW5J. Accessed 5 Dec. 2016.

SELECTED WORKS
Eyes off the Prize: The United Nations and the African American Struggle for Human Rights: 1944–1955, 2003; *Bourgeois Radicals: The NAACP and the Struggle for Colonial Liberation, 1941–1960*, 2014; *White Rage: The Unspoken Truth of Our Racial Divide*, 2016

—Mari Rich

Piotr Anderszewski
Date of Birth: April 4, 1969
Occupation: Pianist; composer

"I never planned to be professional," pianist Piotr Anderszewski told Jane Cornwell for the *Financial Review* (17 June 2015). "It just happened somehow." Such a statement is perhaps to be expected from the critically acclaimed Polish-born musician, a notorious perfectionist who made headlines in 1990 when, dissatisfied with the quality of his playing, walked off stage midway through his semifinal performance in the prestigious Leeds International Piano Competition. Over the decades that

Photo by Amy T. Zielinski/Redferns for Getty Images

followed, Anderszewski has established himself as a talented and meticulous performer with a particular affinity for works by composers such as Ludwig van Beethoven, Johann Sebastian Bach, Karol Szymanowski, and Robert Schumann. A Grammy Award–nominated recording artist, he has released nearly a dozen albums since his solo CD debut in 1999, including a 2012 album recorded with his sister, the accomplished violinist Dorota Anderszewska. Seemingly surprised by his critical success, Anderszewski remains primarily interested in his relationship to the piano. "As I play it comes alive like an organism. It's really strange," he told Ivan Hewett for the *Telegraph* (20 May 2009). "Sometimes when I'm practicing it feels as if the piano might actually eat me!"

EARLY LIFE AND EDUCATION

Anderszewski was born on April 4, 1969, in Warsaw, Poland, into a Polish and Hungarian family. Music was an important presence in Anderszewski's household. His father was the guitarist in a band, the family enjoyed listening to music and attending concerts, and their home contained an old piano that provided Anderszewski with his first experience with the instrument. As a child, he was likewise influenced by the emphasis placed on music by his extended family and Polish society as a whole. He has said that his biggest memory was of the International Fryderyk Chopin Piano Competition, "which in Poland is bigger than football," he recalled to Hewett. "I remember my aunts and great-aunts arguing about who played the mazurkas better in 1956.

They got so angry they wouldn't speak for days." Beginning his formal studies of piano when he was six years old, Anderszewski quickly demonstrated a talent for music that his parents sought to encourage.

When Anderszewski was seven, his family moved to France, where they spent time in Lyon and Strasbourg. While living in Strasbourg, he studied for several years at the Conservatoire de Strasbourg and learned from the acclaimed pianist Hélène Boschi. Anderszewski returned to Poland at fourteen, attending the Fryderyk Chopin Academy of Music in Warsaw. Although the school enabled him to continue his studies in piano, it also emphasized academics, sometimes to a fault. "What's ridiculous, for a music school, is that an insufficient grade in chemistry would make you have to repeat the whole year, including the year of piano instruction you had just finished," he recalled to Frederic Gaussin for *Piano Mag*. "That terrified me at the end of each year." As an adult, Anderszewski has criticized the Polish form of music education, which he identifies as stifling the potential of young musicians.

After high school, Anderszewski was granted a scholarship to the Thornton School of Music at the University of Southern California in Los Angeles. He enrolled but soon came to realize that the school's teaching style and perceived focus on career success did not appeal to him. "My teachers felt no sense of responsibility for their students," he told Gaussin. "We had to make our way alone, in the middle of the desert, without any guidance or mentoring. This system can bear fruit, and it didn't hurt me, but . . . this is not the proper way to work on this craft." Anderszewski ultimately left the school without completing his degree and returned to Europe. He later took master classes in Italy with such renowned concert pianists as Murray Perahia and Leon Fleisher.

LEEDS COMPETITION

While in his early twenties, Anderszewski began to perform in competitions in Europe, although he typically avoided Polish events such as the Chopin competition, which he remembered vividly from childhood. In 1990, Anderszewski drew significant international attention when he competed in the Leeds International Piano Competition in Leeds, England. Having progressed to the competition's semifinals, he impressed his audience with his rendition of Beethoven's Diabelli Variations, a set of thirty-three piano variations on a waltz originally written by the Austrian composer Anton Diabelli. However, when Anderszewski proceeded to perform a second, much shorter composition—Austrian composer Anton Webern's Variations for Piano, Op. 27—he became unhappy with the quality of his performance and walked off stage after completing two of the piece's three variations.

Anderszewski's abrupt departure from the stage in Leeds was both shocking and highly memorable, and the incident went on to become one of the best-known moments from Anderszewski's early career. For the pianist, however, the incident signaled not only his displeasure with his specific performance of the Webern piece but also his dissatisfaction with music competitions as a whole. "Competitions are a big deal when you're young," he explained to Cornwell. "But why should some random jury decide if you're any good or not? It's not like sport, where you are disqualified for being too slow, or for not jumping high enough." Although Anderszewski did not make a habit of walking off stage later in his career, he would become known for occasionally playing the same piece multiple times in concert when he was dissatisfied with his original performance.

EARLY CAREER

Following the Leeds competition, Anderszewski also gained significant attention for his work as a pianist. He was offered a recording contract shortly after the competition but turned it down, and in 1991, he made his London debut with a performance at Wigmore Hall. He went on to tour internationally with Russian violinist Viktoria Mullova, accompanying her in performances throughout Europe and East Asia.

For Anderszewski, his early years as a professional musician proved to be an intense learning experience. "People hadn't realised that if I couldn't go through with the third round of a competition, how could I support a career?" he told Andrew Clements for a profile in the *Guardian* (14 Mar. 2008). "It was a very tough few years. I was learning what it is to play in public, which engagements you take, which you don't, dealing with conductors. I had very little previous experience of any of that." After touring with Mullova for some time, learning much about the life of a touring performer, Anderszewski began to establish himself as a solo performer. In addition to solo recitals, he went on to make appearances as a soloist with orchestras such as the London Symphony, the Berlin Philharmonic, and the Chicago Symphony, and he at times made appearances as an accompanist for a vocalist.

RECORDINGS

Although he turned down the first recording contract he was offered, Anderszewski later became a prolific recording artist, offering his interpretations of works by famed composers such as Beethoven, Bach, Szymanowski, and Schumann. After beginning his recording career playing on albums by Mullova, he released his first solo

recording, *Bach: Suite Française No. 5; Overture in the French Style*, in 1999. The following year, he became an exclusive artist with the record label Virgin Classics, later known as Erato. His first album with the label, released in 2001, featured his acclaimed performance of the Diabelli Variations. His 2005 album *Szymanowski: Piano Sonata No. 3, Métopes, Masques* was nominated for the Grammy Award for best instrumental soloist performance (without orchestra). Later notable albums included 2009's *Piotr Anderszewski at Carnegie Hall*, a recording of a 2008 concert at the famed New York City venue, and 2012's *Beethoven–Mozart–Schubert*, a collection of violin sonatas recorded with his sister. In February 2017, Anderszewski released the album *Mozart, Schumann: Fantaisies*.

As a musician, Anderszewski is particularly interested in the different forms musical compositions can take when performed live or in a recording studio. "When you record a piece, you want to say everything you know about a piece, and the more you play something, the more difficult that becomes," he told Clements. He noted, "In [concerts] there are other elements that are out of my control and a big mystery. The audience plays its part; you give something, and something comes back to you, and that may make you continue the concert in a different way."

OTHER PROJECTS

In addition to his work as a pianist, Anderszewski has tried his hand at conducting. He enjoys conducting but has no plans to pursue as a second career. "At first I was very enthusiastic, but then I realised that it's a profession, and it's not only about having an exact musical idea of what you want, but about being able to communicate that to the orchestra, of learning the craft of doing that without overdoing it," he explained to Clements. He admitted that he would need to devote a great deal of focus and time to practice that skill and that it is challenging enough for him to play the piano well.

The subject of several documentaries by French filmmaker Bruno Monsaingeon, including *Piotr Anderszewski Plays the Diabelli Variations* (2000), *Piotr Anderszewski, Unquiet Traveller* (2009), and *Anderszewski Plays Schumann* (2010), Anderszewski has likewise begun to experiment with filmmaking. In March 2016, he announced plans to take a sabbatical from performing, one of three such breaks he has taken over the course of his career. During that eight-month period, he returned to Poland to shoot a short documentary film, *Je m'appelle Varsovie* (Warsaw is my name), which he released on DVD alongside *Mozart, Schumann: Fantaisies*. *Je m'appelle Varsovie* is an impressionistic montage of scenes shot around Warsaw, a place that holds both positive childhood associations and painful reminders of the past for Anderszewski, whose paternal grandfather died in a Nazi death camp during World War II.

After his sabbatical ended in November of that year, Anderszewski soon resumed performing at some of the world's most prestigious venues, returning to Carnegie Hall in February 2017.

PERSONAL LIFE
When not touring, Anderszewski lives primarily in Lisbon, Portugal, and Paris, France.

Giannis Antetokounmpo

Date of birth: December 6, 1994
Occupation: Basketball player

Giannis Antetokounmpo quickly became a sensation in the National Basketball Association (NBA) for his star-level talent and his unique path to professional basketball. Hailing from Greece, a country hardly known for basketball, he grew up selling goods on the streets of Athens before discovering his abilities on the court. Standing nearly seven feet tall, he soon came to the attention of NBA scouts and was drafted fifteenth overall by the Milwaukee Bucks in 2013. In just a few seasons he proved his superstar potential at basketball's highest level, becoming affectionately known to fans as the Greek Freak.

Antetokounmpo's greatest strength as a player has been his versatility, blurring traditional differentiations between point guard, center, and small forward. No one label could fully describe his combination of height, athleticism, and ability to read the game. His style of play, Paul Flannery wrote for *SB Nation* (2 Apr. 2017), was like an uninterrupted highlight reel: "You simply can't take your eyes off him at any moment and expect to get the full show. Blink and you'll wish you hadn't." Pundits compared him to all-time NBA greats such as Julius Erving, Magic Johnson, and LeBron James, noting his improvement with each professional season. In 2017, Antetokounmpo dazzled fans in his first All-Star Game, further raising his profile as one of basketball's top rising stars.

EARLY LIFE
Antetokounmpo was born in Greece on December 6, 1994. His parents, Charles and Veronica, had moved to Athens from Lagos, Nigeria, in 1991, leaving their first son to stay with his grandparents. The couple took on menial jobs such as orange picking and selling purses on the street to support themselves in their adopted country, and they soon had four more children. Antetokounmpo grew up with his older brother

By Erik Drost [CC BY 2.0], via Wikimedia Commons

Thanasis and younger brothers Kostas and Alex in Sepolia, a neighborhood in western Athens. The siblings all frequently joined their parents in working to make ends meet, selling items such as sunglasses and watches. Still, the family often struggled to pay rent and were once evicted from their home. Sometimes they made just enough money to cover the cost of a meal or an electricity bill, while other days they went hungry.

For the boys, particularly Antetokounmpo and Thanasis, the neighborhood outdoor basketball court provided a refuge from the struggles of everyday life. Antetokounmpo's mother told Joanna Kakissis for *NPR* (26 Sept. 2013) that playing ball "was a kind of paradise for them"—even when, as they first began playing, they had to share one pair of sneakers between them. The brothers stood out for their impressive height and athletic gifts—their mother had been a high-jumper and their father had briefly played professional soccer. "Outside the court, we didn't have stuff, we didn't have many things in life, but in the court you felt like 'I have everything,'" Thanasis told Kakissis.

A coach named Spiros Velliniatis, who had played professional basketball in Germany, discovered the boys and convinced them to seriously pursue the sport (Antetokounmpo was initially more interested in playing soccer). Making it to practice with the demands of school and work was often a challenge. Velliniatis did what they could to help them succeed because he saw their potential, and neighbors also gave the brothers food and clothes at times. "You're in front of Mozart and he has no food, what do you give him? You have a dilemma," Velliniatis told Ken Maguire for the *New York Times* (25 June 2013). "The answer is not a violin. The answer is a loaf of bread."

EARLY CAREER AND NBA DRAFT

In 2007, when Antetokounmpo was thirteen, Velliniatis invited the brothers to train with a midsize Greek basketball club called Filathlitikos. Velliniatis convinced the club, in a middle-class neighborhood called Zografou, to give the family a monthly stipend so that the brothers would not have to work. Still, money problems continued and Antetokounmpo occasionally went hungry. His coaches sometimes had to convince him and his brother to practice rather than going to work in the street markets. Soon the sport captivated the young player, and he dedicated himself to realizing his full potential. His family eventually moved to live closer to the team's training gym.

Antetokounmpo, who was steadily growing taller, first played point guard for the Filathlitikos youth club. Soon he earned a reputation as one of the best young players in that position in Greece. Later he played small forward for the Filathlitikos men's team, where he averaged 9.5 points and 5 rebounds a game. By the time he was eighteen, Antetokounmpo was six foot nine, playing for the Greek national under-twenty team and garnering international attention. Scouts and NBA executives from the Oklahoma City Thunder, Atlanta Hawks, Boston Celtics, and Houston Rockets, among others, flocked to watch him play. They were impressed not only by his height but also his superior ball-handling skills and his mental game. He signed a contract to play the 2013–14 season for Zaragoza, Spain, in one of Europe's top basketball leagues. However, many sports pundits predicted that his name would be called in the first round of the NBA Draft. They were right.

On June 27, 2013, Antetokounmpo was selected by the Milwaukee Bucks as the fifteenth pick of the first round of the NBA Draft. When his name was announced he hugged his brother Thanasis, who was waving the Greek flag. "It's a wonderful feeling," Antetokounmpo told a reporter that night, as quoted by Kakissis. "I can't describe how I feel. It's a dream come true." His success was all the more remarkable considering the ongoing economic struggles of his home country and his family. Just the month before, Antetokounmpo had finally become an official Greek citizen through a special exception, after years of technically living as an illegal immigrant despite being born and raised in Greece. At the time he was drafted, about two-thirds of young Greeks were unemployed. When Antetokounmpo moved to his new team's home of

Milwaukee, Wisconsin, his whole family came with him.

ROOKIE SEASON

When Antetokounmpo joined the Bucks, the team had a reputation as a perennial middle-of-the-pack finisher, often reaching the playoffs as a low seed only to quickly be eliminated. The team's aging stadium was falling apart, and rumors swirled that the franchise would be moved to Seattle, Washington, or another location. Antetokounmpo struggled to settle in to the new city—one that, jarringly for a man who grew up in the Mediterranean climate, was experiencing its coldest winter in years. He was seen as a curiosity by many basketball fans, unfamiliar and unproven in the sport's home country.

During his rookie season, Antetokounmpo posted relatively modest stats, averaging 6.8 points, 4.4 rebounds, and 1.9 assists per game. However, his dramatic dunks and blocks suggested future greatness. But Milwaukee was in a transitional year, and the Bucks had their worst-ever season record at 15–67. Meanwhile, Antetokounmpo found himself at the center of sometimes unwanted media attention. Treated as a novelty by the American press, he was more obsessively followed by many Greek sports reporters. He also became an object of ire for the Golden Dawn, Greece's racist, anti-immigrant, far-right political party.

For others in Greece, particularly the children of African immigrants, Antetokounmpo was an inspiration. As Greek journalist Nikos Papaioannou told Amos Barshad for the sports website *Grantland* (6 Mar. 2014), "I've heard the teachers in the schools. They say that he is the beacon for all the kids to see where you can go." Antetokounmpo's popularity only increased as his game improved. The young player was a standout in the Rising Stars Challenge during the 2014 All-Star Weekend, and he participated in the Skills Challenge. At the end of the season, he was named to the league's All-Rookie second team. His success came even as many other members of the 2013 Draft class struggled to live up to their billing. Later, many commentators would speculate that were the 2013 Draft to be held again, Antetokounmpo would likely be picked first.

THE GREEK FREAK

Antetokounmpo would look back on his rookie season, during which the press delighted in his innocence regarding American culture, as if it were part of a different life. "I was like a kid in the park, seeing all the cities, seeing LeBron [James] and KD [Kevin Durant], having so much fun," he told Lee Jenkins for *Sports Illustrated* (3 Jan. 2017). "But," he added, "I'm not really that kid anymore." Indeed, his growth as a player was rapid. For his second season, Jason Kidd, one of the best point guards in NBA history, joined the Bucks as head coach. Antetokounmpo had to adjust to Kidd's coaching style, overcoming his initial annoyance at certain decisions after realizing Kidd's illustrious credentials. He also dealt with roster turnover, as many of the teammates he had befriended as a rookie moved on. That year, the Bucks improved drastically, making it to the playoffs before being knocked out of contention by the Chicago Bulls in the first round.

During the 2015–16 season, Kidd and assistant coach Sean Sweeney pushed Antetokounmpo to develop his skills as a point guard, a remarkable decision considering that the position is typically filled by shorter, fast players. Three-time NBA MVP Magic Johnson, who stood about six foot nine, was a notable exception to this rule, and Kidd saw Magic-like potential in Antetokounmpo. Kidd started Antetokounmpo as a guard in a number of games, developing his playmaking skills. The mentorship also imparted other lessons, especially as Antetokounmpo emerged as the Bucks' biggest star: "To make the next step, I've learned you need a little cockiness inside you," he told Jenkins. "I can be a little cocky. . . . I've definitely become more serious. I have a franchise on my shoulders."

STATISTICAL WONDER

In February 2016, in a game against the Los Angeles Lakers, Antetokounmpo recorded his first career triple-double, with 27 points, 12 rebounds, and 10 assists. By the end of the season, he would chalk up several more. However, the team failed to build upon its previous season, finishing 33–49 and missing the playoffs. The Bucks turned to the future, determined to keep their most promising player as a franchise centerpiece. In September 2016, Antetokounmpo signed a four-year, $100 million extension contract with Milwaukee, almost reaching the maximum allowed value.

The signing kicked off a successful 2016–17 season for both the Bucks and Antetokounmpo. In February 2017 he hit a career-high 41 points in a losing game against the Lakers. The same month, he was invited to play in his first All-Star Game, and he was the first Bucks player to do so since 2004. The game marked a rite of passage for the budding superstar, and he did not disappoint, scoring 30 points for the East team. (The West eventually won, 192–182.) To the collective jaw-drop of players and fans, he even dunked on two-time MVP Steph Curry of the Golden State Warriors.

Antetokounmpo was among the league's best players for much of the 2016–17 season. He was named the NBA Eastern Conference Player of the Month for March 2017 and helped the Bucks secure a playoff spot. At the end of the regular season, Antetokounmpo became the first player in NBA history to rank in the top twenty in all of the major stats, finishing fourteenth for total points, fifteenth for rebounds, eighteenth for assists, ninth for steals, and fifth for blocks. Remarkably, he accomplished all of this even before hitting what are typically considered a basketball player's prime years. Already an established star by 2017, he stands poised to build on his success to become a true superstar. Antetokounmpo told Adrian Wojnarowski for *Yahoo! Sports* (18 Mar. 2014) that was indeed his goal: "I don't want to be a good player. I want to be a great one."

PERSONAL LIFE

Antetokounmpo quickly became well liked by teammates, staff, and friends for his good-natured personality. Reporters often noted he was beloved as a charming and sometimes goofy figure, especially when first getting accustomed to the United States. Yet at the same time, he was known to harbor a private and wary side, developed in part through years of being unable to fully trust strangers due to his family's uncertain immigration status.

Devoted to his family, Antetokounmpo helped his relatives adjust to living in the United States. His brothers Thanasis and Kostas also pursued professional basketball.

SUGGESTED READING

Barshad, Amos. "In Giannis We Trust." *Grantland*, 6 Mar. 2014, grantland.com/features/milwaukee-bucks-giannis-antetokounmpo. Accessed 6 Apr. 2017.

Flannery, Paul. "The Giannis Antetokounmpo Dream Becomes Reality." *SB Nation*, 2 Apr. 2017, www.sbnation.com/a/giannis-antetokounmpo-bucks-length-nba-playoffs-sunday-shootaround. Accessed 5 Apr. 2017.

Jenkins, Lee. "Giannis Antetokounmpo: The Most Intriguing Point Guard in NBA History." *Sports Illustrated*, 3 Jan. 2017, www.si.com/nba/2017/01/03/giannis-antetokounmpo-milwaukee-bucks-greek-freak-jason-kidd. Accessed 6 Apr. 2017.

Kakissis, Joanna. "NBA Rookie Wants to Bring Hope to Greece, and to Milwaukee." *NPR*, 26 Sept. 2013, www.npr.org/2013/09/26/226268651/nbas-g-bo-wants-to-bring-hope-to-greece-and-to-milwaukee. Accessed 5 Apr. 2017.

Maguire, Ken. "A Hunger for a Better Life May Lead to the NBA." *The New York Times*, 25 June 2013, www.nytimes.com/2013/06/26/sports/basketball/in-an-athens-suburb-nba-scouts-unearth-a-rare-find.html. Accessed 5 Apr. 2017.

Wojnarowski, Adrian. "From Street Vendor to Surging NBA Player, Greek Freak Living the American Dream." *Yahoo Sports*, 18

Mar. 2014, sports.yahoo.com/news/from-selling-sunglasses-on-street-to-nba-player-on-the-rise--greek-freak-living-the-american-dream-214309752.html. Accessed 6 Apr. 2017.

—*Molly Hagan*

Patrick Awuah

Date of birth: 1965
Occupation: Education entrepreneur

Patrick Awuah is a former Microsoft engineer and the founder and president of Ghana's first private, secular liberal-arts college, Ashesi University.

EARLY LIFE AND EDUCATION

Patrick Awuah was born in Accra, Ghana, in 1965. He is the son of an engineer and a nurse. Although Awuah's parents were members of Ghana's burgeoning middle class, they lived in relative poverty. This was largely due to the decades Ghana spent in political and economic turmoil. In interviews, Awuah has stated that growing up in Ghana during a military dictatorship was challenging (his family could only afford to eat two times a day) and the country's education system was severely deficient. Beyond the overcrowded classrooms, students were taught to memorize information rather than develop their independent critical-thinking skills.

After graduating from high school, Awuah worked for a year as a teacher where he alone was responsible for the welfare of 160 students. His parents, who had both earned their degrees abroad in England, encouraged Awuah to follow suit. With only fifty dollars in his pocket, Awuah left Ghana in 1985 to attend Pennsylvania's Swarthmore College on a full scholarship. Awuah, who as a child had dreamed of becoming an astronaut, spent the next four years studying engineering and economics. In addition to his undergraduate degree, Awuah earned a deep appreciation for liberal-arts education. During his senior year he was hired by Microsoft Corporation after impressing one of their recruiters in an on-campus interview. After graduating in 1989, Awuah moved to Redmond, Washington, to begin working for what was then a little-known company.

LIFE'S WORK

Awuah was employed at Microsoft for eight years as an engineer and program manager. His work there focused on developing Windows components to enable computers to network and share resources. Microsoft proved to be a life-changing experience for Awuah; not only did he meet his wife Rebecca Hulscher, a software-testing engineer, but also his employee stock profits made him a millionaire by the time he was thirty years old.

In 1995, despite all of his success, Awuah felt unfulfilled. His son Nanayaw was born two years earlier, and Awuah began thinking about how he did not want all of Africa's problems to be bequeathed to his children. He and his wife began thinking about how they could make a difference. At first, Awuah considered starting a software company, but he realized that most Africans who had studied coding had only learned how to do it on paper. After researching the pervasive local social and economic challenges of Ghana, Awuah realized that the source of so many of the continent's problems was corrupt and apathetic leadership. In order to improve the lives of its citizens, Africa needed leaders who could fix problems and develop solutions. To that end, Awuah decided to develop a private, nonprofit liberal-arts college with a leadership-based curriculum.

In 1997, Awuah left Microsoft to enroll in University of California, Berkeley's Haas School of Business. The following year he traveled to Ghana with a group of his classmates to complete a feasibility study for opening a private university. The business plan for his Ghanaian liberal-arts school, which he named Ashesi, ultimately became his MBA thesis. (The name Ashesi means "beginnings" in the language of Akan.) After earning his MBA in 1999, Awuah founded the Ashesi University Foundation to help raise money for the school. In addition to donations from his former Microsoft colleagues, he and his wife donated $700,000 of their own money to the foundation.

Ashesi University opened in Accra, Ghana, in 2002. The first class had only thirty students, half of whom were on needs-based scholarships. In the years that followed, the university grew significantly in size. In 2015, it had over 350 enrolled undergraduate students. Ashesi, which once operated out of a rented house, was able to build a one-hundred-acre campus in 2011 after Awuah and board members secured a series of high-profile donors. The university offers four-year degrees in business management, computer science, management information systems, and engineering. Its liberal-arts curriculum, which Awuah based on Swarthmore College's, emphasizes ethical leadership with the "Ashesi Honour Code."

With the help of many experts and advisers, Awuah ultimately succeeded in creating a nonprofit university with a balanced budget. Although tuition covers most operating expenses, Awuah worked hard to secure tens of millions of dollars in philanthropic gifts. In September

2015, Awuah received the so-called genius grant from the MacArthur Foundation, which provides a $625,000 stipend paid over five years. The grant money will help Awuah further his work turning Ashesi into one of Ghana's premier universities. Awuah is also the recipient of the Aspen Institute's John P. McNulty Prize for his outstanding leadership and the Microsoft Alumni Foundation's Integral Fellow Award for his humanitarian efforts. In addition to his work as the acting president of Ashesi University, Awuah is a spokesperson for leadership education and its role in the African renaissance.

IMPACT

Patrick Awuah has created a new generation of leaders who are committed to improving conditions in Africa. Over 95 percent of Ashesi University's graduates work in Ghana and other West African countries, where they continue to espouse Ashesi ethics, leadership, and problem-solving skills. By bringing a nonprofit liberal-arts college to Ghana, Awuah has created an affordable, replicable model to improve the lives of citizens in developing nations.

PERSONAL LIFE

Awuah lives in Ghana with his wife Rebecca, a calculus professor at Ashesi University, and their son Nanayaw and daughter Efia.

SUGGESTED READING

"African Dream: Ghana's Patrick Awuah." *BBC*. BBC, 17 Oct. 2011. Web. 11 Mar. 2016.

Dudley, Brier. "Ghana Native Left Microsoft to Sow Seeds of African Ivy League." *Seattle Times*. Seattle Times, 14 Sept. 2003. Web. 11 Mar. 2016.

Duthiers, Vladimir, and Jessica Ellis. "Patrick Awuah: Millionaire Who Quit Microsoft to Educate Africa's Future Leaders." *CNN*. Cable News Network/Turner Broadcasting System, 1 May 2013. Web. 11 Mar. 2016.

Hallett, Vicky. "Setting Up Ghana's First Liberal Arts College Makes Him a Genius." *NPR*. NPR, 14 Oct. 2015. Web. 11 Mar. 2016.

Lankarani, Nazanin. "Transforming Africa through Higher Education." *New York Times*. New York Times, 16 Jan. 2011. Web. 11 Mar. 2016.

—*Emily Turner*

Chris Bachelder

Date of birth: 1971
Occupation: Writer

In 2016, Chris Bachelder's novel *The Throwback Special* was named as a finalist for the National Book Award. The book examines aspects of the collective modern American male psyche through the experiences of twenty-two middle-aged men, who gather each year to reenact a brutal football play they watched on television during their childhoods. The nomination for the National Book Award has capped a career in which Bachelder has been proclaimed by many fellow writers and literary critics as one of the most incisive voices of his generation by penning novels and stories with considerable humor and grace. In addition to *The Throwback Special*, his major works include *Bear v. Shark* (2001), *U.S.!* (2006), and *Abbott Awaits* (2011).

When asked by Lincoln Michel, in an interview for the National Book Foundation's website, if he wrote with a specific audience in mind, Bachelder responded: "I don't tend to think much about a specific reader or group of readers when I'm writing. Generally speaking, I'm interested in moving deeply and patiently into scene, and in fulfilling the imaginative potential of a premise. When I'm writing, I feel not in the presence of a reader, but rather up against the limits and possibilities of my own premise, which I hope to elaborate with precision, wit, and empathy."

Sylvain Gaboury/Patrick McMullan/Getty Images

EARLY LIFE AND CAREER

Chris Bachelder was born in 1971 in Minneapolis, Minnesota, and raised in Christiansburg, Virginia. He earned his bachelor's degree from Virginia Tech in 1992 and went on to earn his master's degree from the University of Florida at Gainesville in 2002. He has cited Padgett Powell as one of the biggest influences that had pushed him toward pursuing a literary career, especially after he attended a reading by the author and had witnessed his command over language and style. Although Bachelder was able to get his work published frequently early in his career in such literary journals as *Timothy McSweeney's Quarterly Concern* and the *Believer*, he was, like many young authors, unable to support himself by his writing alone.

Eventually, he found work as a virtual tour photographer. In an interview with Daniel Terence Smith for the *New Delta Review*, he recalled, "I was twenty-eight or twenty-nine, living in Houston in this crappy apartment and working as a virtual tour photographer. Driving around in my Plymouth Reliant that squeaked really bad. It was hot. And I was setting up and taking these three-sixty pictures and uploading them to the Russians. Things were not going well. This is not what I thought things were going to be like at that stage." However, he would later make use of his career as a virtual tour photographer by publishing his experiences as McSweeney's first career-development e-book, *Lessons in Virtual Tour Photography*. This digital format for books was still relatively new at the time, but he felt that it was appropriate for a technological manual about being a virtual photographer. By 2004, the free e-book had been downloaded by more than forty-five thousand people.

BEAR V. SHARK

Fortunately for Bachelder, he managed to find a literary agent who was able to sell his first novel, *Bear v. Shark*, to Scribner's; unfortunately, the book was published in 2001, shortly after the terrorist attacks on the World Trade Center towers in New York. The satirical book, which Bachelder has explained was meant to serve as a criticism of America's unhealthy preoccupation with entertainment and the media, is set in a near-future America, in which "reality TV" becomes so pervasive that the entire country becomes obsessed with a computer-generated bear and shark doing battle in a tank of water. (The event of Bear v. Shark has also spun out into everything from breakfast cereals to parental guides on how to talk to children about the experience.) The main characters of the novel, the Norman family, have won tickets to watch these two animals battle it out in Las Vegas. During the road trip, Mr. Norman begins to question not just the

point of the spectacle itself but also the whole trip and, eventually, his whole life.

A critic for *Kirkus Reviews* (1 Sept. 2001) called Bachelder's debut a "quirky first novel, fun especially for wordplay fans," noting that "the author uses his enjoyably silly scenario as a springboard to parody spectacles of the kind our entertainment-engorged culture has become enthralled by—*Survivor*, *Temptation Island*, Monica and Chandra. With its short vignettes, amusing use of language, cartoonish people, science-fiction bent, and its cynicism, the whole is like a slightly less developed preincarnation of Kurt Vonnegut."

U.S.!

U.S.! (2006), Bachelder's second novel, uses the real-life figure of the muckraker Upton Sinclair, who is best known today for his 1906 novel *The Jungle*, about the harsh and unsanitary conditions in the American meatpacking industry, to convey its satirical commentary. In the novel, Sinclair keeps getting assassinated and resurrected and continues to write his particular style of socially conscious novel, long past his one hundredth birthday. The book takes aim at not just the sort of social utopianism that Sinclair espoused but also at the critics of people like Sinclair, who seek to prevent the sort of change represented by the counterculture movement.

In a review of *U.S.!*, a critic for *Kirkus Reviews* (15 Nov. 2005) declared, "Though the novel's depiction of an impotent, intellectually bankrupt leftist movement in America might anger liberal sympathizers, Bachelder ultimately proves an equal-opportunity offender, capable of enraging those on both sides of the cultural divide. Ultimately, his comic vision sparks a comparatively serious inquiry into the nature, power, and possibilities of art, in these times, in this country." In *Publishers Weekly* (21 Nov. 2005), another critic wrote, "Readers require no knowledge of the historical Sinclair to relate to Bachelder's bumbling, endearing idealist grandpa in this entertaining though uneven sophomore outing."

ABBOTT AWAITS

For his next full-length novel, 2011's *Abbott Awaits*, Bachelder, continuing to mature as a writer, decided to turn away from satire. In the years since the publication of his first book, he had communicated in interviews that while he still respected his inexperienced process and intent in writing *Bear v. Shark* and remained proud of the book, he had come to realize that the danger of satire was that the topic of focus may begin to feel too transient after time: "I was troubled by the idea that fiction that responds satirically to superficial and soulless culture runs the risk of being superficial and soulless," he explained to Weston Cutter for the *Brooklyn Rail* (6 Apr. 2016). Focusing on more domestic and emotional issues, *Abbot Awaits* tells the story of an academic named Abbott in the months before the birth of his second child. Abbott, a professor at a university in Massachusetts, is serving as the primary caregiver for his toddler daughter while his wife is enduring a difficult third trimester of pregnancy. During the course of the novel, Abbott, in third-person, diary-like entries, describes the terrors and joys that come with fathering a young child and the worries, concerns, and expectations associated with awaiting another one, as well as the mundane stresses of everyday life.

Because of the similarities between himself and Abbott, Bachelder—who had begun to teach as a more fulfilling way to supplement his income and, at the point of the publication of his third novel, had taught at institutions such as New Mexico State University, the University of Massachusetts Amherst, and the University of Cincinnati, where he has remained since 2011—is frequently asked if the novel is autobiographical. He has stated that while he began to open himself up to inspiration from his own life, especially interactions with his children, his work remains purely fictional: "I discovered that I didn't need to go hunting for big, ambitious American conceits—there were plenty of really interesting things in my head and in my house," he told Cutter.

Abbott Awaits met with considerable praise. Paul Scott Stanfield, writing in *Plowshares* (Spring 2012), said of Bachelder's work, "*Abbott Awaits* is not heavy, but neither is it light. Its structure is simple and elegant—exactly the sort of thing a writer who is a parent of young children could compass. . . . To call *Abbott Awaits* heart-warming would lead you to think of it as exactly the kind of book it is not, so let's borrow Bachelder's own 'heart-expanding'—tart and sweet, painful and funny, all too true."

THE THROWBACK SPECIAL
Bachelder has always remembered watching linebacker Lawrence Taylor of the New York Giants brutally and infamously sack quarterback Joe Theismann of the Washington Redskins on live television in 1985. The sack fractured Theismann's leg and ended his career. In Bachelder's fourth book, *The Throwback Special*, twenty-two middle-aged men meet at a two-and-a-half star hotel, as they have done for the last sixteen years, to reenact that very play and injury, viewed as one of the most horrific in National Football League (NFL) history. It was a collective moment for the country and particularly for the men in Bachelder's novel, who, during their annual recreations of the event, recount the changes in their lives and their wives and children, their jobs and experiences, and their own

sense of impending mortality as they sit fixed in middle age.

Critics have largely praised *The Throwback Special*, which was named as a finalist for the 2016 National Book Award, for its simultaneously comical and poignant portrayal of significant contemporary themes. In a review for the *New York Times* (22 Mar. 2016), John Williams proclaimed, "*The Throwback Special* is about how groups of men interact with one another in a way that nearly subsumes their individuality. What Bachelder is after, and often captures, is akin to the noise he describes at one point emanating from the hotel lobby: 'waves of masculine sound, the toneless song of regret and exclamation.'" A critic for *Kirkus Reviews* (15 Dec. 2015) wrote, "Bachelder's take on manhood is sharply observed and sympathetic and funny enough to win over even those readers who abhor football and its fans."

PERSONAL LIFE
In addition to writing, Bachelder, who resides with his wife and two daughters in Cincinnati, Ohio, teaches in the department of English and comparative literature at the University of Cincinnati.

SUGGESTED READING
Bachelder, Chris. Interview by Daniel Terence Smith. *New Delta Review*, ndrmag.org/interviews/2011/06/an-interview-with-chris-bachelder. Accessed 13 Dec. 2016.

Bachelder, Chris. Interview by Michel Lincoln. *National Book Foundation*, www.nationalbook.org/nba2016finalist_f_bachelder-throwback-special.html#interview. Accessed 13 Dec. 2016.

Bachelder, Chris. Interview by Weston Cutter. *The Brooklyn Rail*, 6 Apr. 2016, www.brooklynrail.org/2016/04/books/chris-bachelder-with-weston-cutter. Accessed 13 Dec. 2016.

Review of *U.S.!*, by Chris Bachelder. *Kirkus Reviews*, 15 Nov. 2005, www.kirkusreviews.com/book-reviews/chris-bachelder/us-2/. Accessed 15 Dec. 2016.

Stanfield, Paul Scott. Review of *Abbott Awaits*, by Chris Bachelder. *Plowshares*, Spring 2012, www.pshares.org/issues/spring-2012/review-abbott-awaits. Accessed 13 Dec. 2016.

Williams, John. Review of *The Throwback Special*, by Chris Bachelder." *New York Times*, 22 Mar. 2016, www.nytimes.com/2016/03/27/books/review/the-throwback-special-by-chris-bachelder.html. Accessed 13 Dec. 2016.

SELECTED WORKS
Bear v. Shark, 2001; *U.S.!*, 2006; *Abbott Awaits*, 2011; *The Throwback Special*, 2016

—Christopher Mari

Kelsea Ballerini

Date of birth: September 12, 1993
Occupation: Singer-songwriter

Grammy-nominated country musician Kelsea Ballerini's debut album *The First Time* went platinum, generating comparisons to Taylor Swift and Carrie Underwood. Though new to the country charts, Ballerini has been perfecting her craft for nearly a decade. As she told Gary Trust for *Billboard* (4 July 2015), "I've been writing songs since I was twelve, and so many times I've wondered if I was good at it. To see it work is so reassuring that this is what I'm supposed to be doing." She saw her first three songs— "Love Me Like You Mean It," "Dibs," and "Peter Pan"—become the top hits on Billboard's Country Airplay chart. Ballerini cites country singers Dolly Parton, the Dixie Chicks, Shania Twain, Kelly Clarkson, Hillary Scott, and Taylor Swift as influences. Part of her success is also due to her admiration for rap, as she told Madison Vain for *Entertainment Weekly* (24 July 2015), "Rap has the most clever phrases, little four-word lines. My favorite thing to do is find tricks like that." *Forbes* named her to its 2017 "30 under 30" list in the category of music.

EARLY LIFE AND CAREER

Ballerini grew up in East Tennessee in the small town of Mascot, near Knoxville; her memories include spending Sunday mornings in church and singing in the choir. That background is evident in her first tattoo, which proclaims, "How sweet the sound," part of the text from the hymn "Amazing Grace." Her father, who is of Italian descent, worked as a sales manager at the radio station WIVK, and Ballerini has memories of the station's frog mascot coming to her birthday parties.

Her parents' divorce when Ballerini was twelve sent her to music for relief and release. As she told Lauren Moraski for the *Huffington Post* (14 Sept. 2016), "I got tall, boys got cute, everything was weird. Then my parents split up on top of that, so it was a big year of change for me. I just randomly started writing songs. It honestly just fell into my lap. It became an obsession." She used the computer program GarageBand to sketch out her songs before discovering Keith Urban, which inspired her love of country music. She attended her first Country Music Fest when she was fourteen, waiting in line for two hours to meet the country musicians she most admired—Hillary Scott of Lady Antebellum and Taylor Swift.

The following year she and her mother, who was then working in religious publishing, moved to Nashville so that Ballerini could live her dream of becoming a country music star.

By Midwest Communications [CC BY-SA 2.0], via Wikimedia Commons

Expressing her gratitude for her mother, Ballerini told Eileen Finan for *People* (9 Nov. 2015), "She's been my champion my whole life. She's the most fiercely independent and compassionate woman, and she instills things in me that I use every day. She texts me every day, 'Kelsea, remember who you are, and remember why you are doing this.' It's what I go back to."

During her years at Centennial High School, where she worked in the counseling office, Ballerini also worked at a bakery and took on babysitting jobs while hustling for opportunities to play and sing. She also competed with a hip-hop dance team. After graduating in 2011, she attended Lipscomb University, where she majored in communications and was a leader in the freshman orientation program.

Ballerini left Lipscomb in 2013 when she signed a deal with Black River Publishing, a new independent label founded just three years earlier. By that time, she had written hundreds of songs. She found success in part through marketing to a very young audience; Radio Disney picked up her first hits. She told Joe Coscarelli for the *New York Times* (8 Feb. 2017) "My album captured me from twelve to twenty-one. That put me down a different path."

SALADGATE AND BRO COUNTRY

During 2015, the so-called "Saladgate" episode brought women in country music into the spotlight. A radio consultant suggested country stations play women artists no more than 15 percent of the time. He likened country music to a salad, saying that men were the lettuce, and women the tomatoes on top. Women country singers were quick to respond, noting that it was a self-perpetuating spiral; with less air time, fewer women would get signed to studios or produce music. Singer Martina McBride developed a line of T-shirts that proclaimed "Tomato Lover." Ironically, the situation brought focus to women artists and the real difficulties they face in a male-dominated music genre.

Commenting on the dominance of men in country music, Ballerini told Moraski, "It was really hard for females at that time. It was just this constant conversation happening in Nashville. . . . I think, like everything, it was a trend. . . . I think that bro country became kind of an era for country music, and I like that there's a new era and it's women."

THE FIRST TIME

Ballerini wrote or cowrote all of the songs on her debut album. She told Bob Doerschuk for *USA Today* (19 Oct. 2016), "I wrote the songs on *The First Time* with my friends. My friends (Glen Whitehead and Jason Massey) coproduced it. To take it from the living room where we were struggling to figure out what we were doing in Nashville to make history with three No. 1 singles, I take a lot of pride in that. But what's really cool is that I get to share that with the people with me."

When her hit single "Love Me Like You Mean It" from her debut album reached number one on the country western charts in 2015, Ballerini was the eleventh woman to have the honor; it had been about nine years since the last time a woman (Carrie Underwood) had done so. Ballerini told Jewly Hight for *Billboard* (17 July 2015), "It wasn't supposed to work—being a new artist, a female artist, an artist on an independent [label]. That's what made it so much sweeter when we hit number one." Ballerini's second hit, "Dibs," was also lighthearted and had one foot firmly in pop music. With the third song, "Peter Pan," she went a bit darker. She told Coscarelli that it was "a songwriter's song."

Ballerini toured with Rascal Flatts on their 2016 Rhythm and Roots tour. Her own thirteen-city First Time tour began in November of that year.

GRAMMY NOMINATION AND 2017 TOURS

Ballerini won Billboard's 2015 Women in Music Rising Star Award and the Academy of Country Music Award for new female vocalist of the year. In December 2016 she was nominated, along with four others, for the Grammy Award for best new artist, from a field of hundreds of new artists. Ballerini and Maren Morris, who was also one of the five nominees, represented the first time that two country singers had been chosen in that category. As she told Coscarelli,

"Whether neither of us wins, or one of us wins, both of us win. There's never been two country singers in that category before. The fact that it's two chicks is just a really cool thing."

The Recording Academy, which sponsors the awards, did away with gender-based categories in 2011. Since that time, women have been nominated as often as or more often than men in the categories of country, rhythm and blues, and pop music. Although she was represented by an independent recording agency, Ballerini was able to gain notice because the Grammy judges are themselves musicians and less likely to be influenced by labels, air time, or album sales. Her record label timed the release of her song "Peter Pan" to give her maximum exposure as a serious songwriter. Her agent wanted the judges to understand that she wrote each of the songs on her first album.

Ballerini was not only nominated, she also performed on the Grammy show on February 12, 2017, along with Lukas Graham, the Danish pop soul group. They sang a mashup of her hit "Peter Pan" and their song "7 Years." Although Chance the Rapper won the award, Ballerini's career received a boost from the nomination. She told Grace Mestad for *Lipscomb Now* (7 Dec. 2016), "To me, every awards show is incredible whether it's industry-voted or fan-voted. All of it's incredible. But the Grammys is the one. It's top-tier. It's the pinnacle. And just to be thought of as one of the five best new artists of this year is so flattering and so incredible and I'm super honored."

Ballerini is a popular opening act for country musicians. She opened for Thomas Rhett's Home Team tour in early 2017. In May 2017 she will begin touring with Lady Antebellum for their You Look Good World tour. Ballerini is close friends with the band's singer, Hillary Scott.

PERSONAL LIFE

As she told Moraski, "I try to be as honest as I can in writing. That's what ends up translating and relating to people. It's so fun to make up stories, but I find that the songs that I'm most proud of came from a real thing in my life."

Australian singer Morgan Evans surprised Ballerini on Christmas Day 2016 with a marriage proposal. As she told the story to *World Entertainment News Network* (26 Dec. 2016), "This morning . . . he got down on one knee in the kitchen while I was burning pancakes and asked me to marry him. Loving him has been the greatest gift of my life. And now I get to do it for life." Ballerina and Evans, who are planning to wed this year, have recorded a duet for her second album.

SUGGESTED READING

Coscarelli, Joe. "Step Aside, Boys, Kelsea Ballerini's in Town." *The New York Times*, 8 Feb. 2017, www.nytimes.com/2017/02/08/arts/music/grammys-kelsea-ballerini.html. Accessed 13 Mar. 2017.

Doerschuk, Bob. "Ballerini Aims for Memorable 'First Time' Tour with Bells, Whistles." *USA Today*, 19 Oct. 2016, www.usatoday.com/story/life/music/2016/10/19/kelsea-ballerini-aims-memorable-first-time-tour-bells-whistles/92356924. Accessed 13 Mar. 2017.

Finan, Eileen. "Kelsea Ballerini I'm Thankful For." *People*, 9 Nov. 2015, pp. C26–28. *MasterFILE Complete*, search.ebscohost.com/login.aspx?direct=true&db=f6h&AN=11061 9712&site=eds-live. Accessed 13 Mar. 2017.

Hight, Jewly. "Country's Next Queen." *Billboard*, 17 July 2015, www.billboard.com/biz/articles/magazine/6634498/kelsea-ballerini-countrys-next-queen. Accessed 13 Mar. 2017.

Moraski, Lauren. "Kelsea Ballerini Believes It's a New Era for Women in Country Music." *The Huffington Post*, 14 Sept. 2016, www.huffingtonpost.com/entry/kelsea-ballerini-its-a-new-era-for-women-in-country-music_us_57d6e679e4b00642712ea77d. Accessed 13 Mar. 2017.

Trust, Gary. "Is Kelsea Ballerini the Next Carrie Underwood?" *Billboard*, 4 July 2015, p.1+.

Vain, Madison. "Breaking Big: Kelsea Ballerini." *Entertainment Weekly*, 21 July 2015, ew.com/article/2015/07/21/breaking-big-kelsea-ballerini. Accessed 13 Mar. 2017.

—*Judy Johnson*

Kelly Barnhill

Date of birth: December 7, 1973
Occupation: Author

Writer Kelly Barnhill won the 2017 John Newbery Medal for her middle-grade novel *The Girl Who Drank the Moon* (2016). The American Library Association (ALA) bestows this annual award, the highest honor in the United States for children's literature. The book was lauded by critics for connecting to young readers while exploring deep, meaningful themes. "I knew I wanted to write a story that grappled with this idea of false narratives," Barnhill told Adam Gidwitz for *School Library Journal* (March 2017). "Stories are powerful. They can transform and amplify and heal—but they can also stagnate and minimize and harm. It just depends on how you tell the story."

A former classroom teacher, Barnhill views her popular books as another way to teach. As she told Barbara Basbanes Richter for *Sewanee Review* (Spring 2015), "Children's-book authors have a bit of the evangelist in them. We are all profound believers in children's literacy and in the power of books for children." The Newbery Medal was only the crowning achievement in a long line of recognition for Barnhill. Among other achievements, she won awards from the Jerome Foundation and the Minnesota State Arts Board and was a finalist for a Minnesota Book Award and a PEN/USA literary prize.

CHILDHOOD AND EDUCATION

As a child, Barnhill was attracted to storytelling even before she could read. Her parents read to her and her four siblings every night; her father often read spooky fairy tales. Barnhill, the eldest, did not especially enjoy reading, and in fact was a delayed reader, but she loved hearing her father read. Informal performances by family members also influenced her, and her family had significant theatrical leanings, though Barnhill had no theater training herself. An aunt and uncle were in the film business and another aunt was an actor, while her cousin also eventually acted in Broadway and Off-Broadway productions; her sister became a playwright and theater artist. The stories and music Barnhill heard at family gatherings would later shape her method of telling stories.

At age nine, Barnhill used money she had saved to buy a cheap plastic record player at a garage sale so she could listen to recordings of adapted radio plays and audiobooks that she found at the public library. Barnhill explained to Gidwitz, "There is an art, I realized then, to the pattern of the voice—tone, diction, pace, inflection—and, by extension, an art to the pattern of language. Internal sounds and subconscious rhythms did as much to make the listener feel the story as the actual story. I didn't know this exactly—of course I didn't; I was only a kid. And yet. I still did understand it in my bones."

Barnhill's interest in folktales and fairy tales deeply influenced her own writing. For example, her childhood desire for a pet dragon later found its way into her novels. Witches were one of her chief obsessions. Her favorite outfit when she was young was a black dress, which she wore with a pair of striped tights, a witch's hat, and shoes that made a satisfying click. Favorite books of her childhood included Roald Dahl's *The Witches* and Anna Elizabeth Bennett's *Little Witch*.

While her imagination flourished, Barnhill struggled socially, and was a victim of bullying in seventh grade. "I was a lonely kid," she told Alice Cary for *BookPage* (Aug. 2016), "I was socially awkward. I just never felt OK in my own body. I was easily targetable." As a result of the bullying, Barnhill's mother transferred her to an all-girl Catholic school. There, Barnhill encountered a principal who had marched with Dr. Martin Luther King, Jr. and nuns dedicated to social justice. She would later credit her own interest in social justice to those teachers. One of her teachers invited the students to write a story a week, and Barnhill discovered she had many stories in her waiting to be written.

Barnhill later attended South High School in St. Paul, Minnesota. After graduation she enrolled at St. Catherine's University, in the same city.

EDUCATING OTHERS

Barnhill held many jobs after college, ranging from janitor to activist to park ranger. Perhaps most important, however, were her time as a school teacher and a job working with homeless young people in a drop-in center in Minneapolis, Minnesota. These experiences provided her with a close-up view of people and relationships that would affect her writing.

In particular, addiction and its effects on families became all too clear to her. She noted how children with parents struggling with addiction faced multilayered challenges, often internalizing their parents' struggles. As she told Richter, "The thing about addiction is that it becomes your first love. People love their addiction and they do love their child. But they love their addiction more, which creates an interesting dynamic." She would later mine this complex dynamic in altered forms in much of her fiction.

Barnhill eventually left her jobs to pursue writing full time. However, she continued to teach through Minnesota's arts education program called COMPAS (Community Programs in the Arts). She also taught workshops at the Loft Literary Center in Minneapolis. She told Amy Goetzman for *MinnPost* (24 Jan. 2017), "Art has ennobled us as human beings, it has enlarged us and made us grew stronger. I know that it matters to kids, teachers and artists. Every time I do work in the schools, I become more of myself and I watch children grow more into themselves."

As a professional writer, Barnhill got her start with nonfiction books for children. Through Capstone Press and Edge Books, she published a series of educational works on sensational topics that might appeal to kids. Examples include *Monsters of the Deep* (2008), *The Wee Book of Pee* (2009), and *The Bloody Book of Blood* (2009).

TURNING TO STORIES

In addition to her nonfiction, Barnhill began publishing short stories in various publications. Much of her work incorporated fantasy, science fiction, and related genres. As she began developing longer works, she chose to focus on writing for a middle grade (MG) audience, generally considered grades five through eight. As she told Julia Smith for *Booklist* (15 Dec. 2016), "What I like about MG literature is its fundamental inclusiveness: they truly are 'big tent stories,' where everyone, whatever their age, is invited to come and participate."

Barnhill's first published novel, released in 2011, was *The Mostly True Story of Jack*. It is a magical tale of a boy sent to live with an aunt and uncle in Iowa who finds himself oddly important in the small town. The novel addresses questions of identity and belonging. She followed that successful debut with the fairy tale *Iron Hearted Violet* (2012). It emphasizes the way we tell stories and the power of words. The book won a Parent's Choice Gold Award.

The Witch's Boy followed in 2014. It is the fantasy tale of Ned, a witch's son whose twin brother is lost in a raft accident in a river, and of motherless Áine, the Bandit King's daughter. The two young people must work together, overcoming their mutual distrust, to prevent war. Barnhill released a novella, *The Unlicensed Magician*, in 2015, winning the 2016 World Fantasy Award. The story concentrates on a magical child who was supposed to have died, but is found alive and raised in secret by a junk seller.

THE GIRL WHO DRANK THE MOON

Despite considerable popular success and critical acclaim for her earlier work, it was Barnhill's 2016 middle-grade novel *The Girl Who Drank the Moon* that took her career to a new phase. The project began when Barnhill suddenly had an image of a swamp monster reciting a poem. She wrote down the poem and then spent two or three years making notes and building a story. Preoccupied by the false news stories circulating in the major media outlets, she wanted to write about false narratives, not only in world news, but also within families and even within a person.

Finding the right setting for the novel took time and travel. She and her husband visited Costa Rica for a long-delayed honeymoon after fifteen years of marriage. The landscape of sinkholes and steam vents that erupted with mud, so different from the landscape of Minnesota, inspired her. The morning following a walk in Rincón de la Vieja National Park, Barnhill began writing. As she told Cary, "Suddenly I realized my characters were on a volcano, and I wasn't expecting them to be there. And once I began, it was like it was always meant to be. I couldn't imagine that story being in any other landscape." The rest of the manuscript then came together relatively quickly.

As with Barnhill's other works, *The Girl Who Drank the Moon* quickly won praise for its take on complex themes in a way accessible to readers of all ages. At its core is the idea of family as a unit bound not necessarily by blood. The book focuses on a witch, an abandoned baby, a dragon, and the swamp monster (named Glerk), who form a family on the literal edge of a volcano. Many of the story's ideas were rooted in Barnhill's years of teaching homeless teenagers in Minneapolis. She told Cary, "When you work in those contexts, you see the different ways in which families organize themselves. This notion of family is much more flexible and fluid than we tend to think."

WINNING THE NEWBERY

The Girl Who Drank the Moon became a *New York Times* Best Seller, with rave reviews from critics and fans alike. Although some friends suggested that Barnhill's fourth novel might have a shot at winning the Newbery Medal, the top award for children's literature, Barnhill did not consider the possibility. The awards committee does not publish a list of nominees or books under consideration for the prestigious medal. So she was startled when her phone rang early in the morning on January 23, 2017. She answered to hear members of the ALA on the line, excitedly telling her *The Girl Who Drank the Moon* was indeed the 2017 winner.

Barnhill was shocked by the news. As she told Goetzman, the book always held a special place in her heart, but "I didn't think anyone else would feel the same way. I thought it was too weird! It breaks too many rules about children's books. It includes the point of view from characters that are adults. It has a lot of complex plot threads." However, she also had a keen understanding of her target audience. "Fourth- and fifth-grade kids, they're very global thinkers," she told Laurie Hertzel for the Minnesota *StarTribune*. "They are literally in the process of writing the universe with every step they take through the world. The world around them is wondrous and strange and complicated and sometimes terrifying. I think that is the type of book that I aspire to write, this book that exists on many levels at the same time."

In the obligatory interviews after winning the medal, Barnhill expressed her hope to use the award as a platform for making a difference in the lives of other writers and artists. Her achievement also resulted in an impromptu celebration that evening at Barnhill's house. Fittingly, the party included children from throughout her neighborhood.

PERSONAL LIFE

Barnhill lives in Minneapolis with her husband, Ted, a designer of sustainable homes, and their three children. She has described herself as noisy and performative, especially while working. As she told Gidwitz, "I'd say a good 75 percent of what I do in my office is out loud. And it is loud. I will read a passage over and over, performing it really only to my dog . . . experimenting with how the story feels in my ear and in my throat and chest and belly and bones." Her hobbies include running, canoeing, hiking, camping, gardening, and baking pies.

SUGGESTED READING

Barnhill, Kelly. "Newbery Magic." Interview by Adam Gidwitz. *School Library Journal*, 1 Mar. 2017, www.slj.com/2017/03/feature-articles/newbery-magic-adam-gidwitz-in-conversation-with-kelly-barnhill. Accessed 2 May 2017.

Barnhill, Kelly. "No Warning: Kelly Barnhill on Winning the Newbery Award." Interview by Amy Goetzman. *MinnPost,* 24 Jan. 2017, www.minnpost.com/books/2017/01/no-warning-kelly-barnhill-winning-newbery-award. Accessed 2 May 2017.

Cary, Alice. "Kelly Barnhill: A Social Crusader with Magic on Her Mind." *BookPage*, Aug. 2016, bookpage.com/interviews/20186-kelly-barnhill. Accessed 2 May 2017.

Hertzel, Laurie. "Minneapolis Author Kelly Barnhill Wins Newbery Award, Children's Literature's Highest Honor." *StarTribune*, 24 Jan. 2017, www.startribune.com/minneapolis-author-barnhill-wins-newbery-award/411521675. Accessed 2 May 2017.

Richter, Barbara Basbanes. "Roald Dahl and Danger in Children's Literature." *Sewanee Review*, vol. 123, no. 2, Spring 2015, pp. 325–34, doi:10.1353/sew.2015.0062. Accessed 2 May 2017.

Smith, Julia. "The State of the Middle-Grade Novel, 2016." *Booklist*, 15 Dec. 2016, www.booklistonline.com/The-State-of-the-Middle-Grade-Novel-2016/pid=8583942. Accessed 2 May 2017.

SELECTED WORKS

The Mostly True Story of Jack, 2011; *Iron Hearted Violet*, 2012; *The Witch's Boy*, 2014; *The Unlicensed Magician*, 2015; *The Girl Who Drank the Moon*, 2016

—*Judy Johnson*

Olivia Bee

Date of birth: April 5, 1994
Occupation: Photographer

Photographer Olivia Bee found early success thanks to a school scheduling mishap and the Internet. As a sixth-grader, she wanted to take a class in video production but ended up in a

Photo by Dominique Charriau/Getty Images for Roger Vivier

photography class instead. Three years later, Bee was still taking pictures, mostly of family and friends, and posting them on the image-hosting website Flickr. Her photographs were spotted by a representative of the Converse shoe company, who contacted her with a job offer, and at age fifteen a professional photographer was born.

Bee's signature style features "dreamy, seventies-inspired photographs of maybe-wasted, increasingly famous young people who just want to have fun, injected with ombre washes of color (often pink)," according to Kurt Soller for the *Cut* (9 Feb. 2013). Her aesthetic influences include the films of Sofia Coppola and the photographs of Ryan McGinley. She considers herself a romantic and her photographs as love letters to the world and to her friends, who are her frequent subjects. She has shown her work in exhibitions in New York, Paris, and Madrid, and her client list includes Fiat Automobiles, Nike, Adidas, and Levi Strauss. In 2016 Bee published her first book of photographs, *Kids in Love*. Yet despite her early fame, Bee is never content with what she has accomplished. "I always want to do more, I'm always striving for the next thing, nothing is ever really good enough, it could always be better," she said in an interview with Lou Noble for the *Photographic Journal* (15 Jan. 2015), "which is a good and a bad thing for your brain, for your work."

CHILDHOOD AND EDUCATION
Olivia Bolles was born in Portland, Oregon, on April 5, 1994, to parents Cara and Houston Bolles. (She adopted a pseudonym for her

photography work at the urging of her parents, who were worried about her safety online.) As a child, Bee displayed an early talent for and interest in art: she made clay sculptures, tried sewing and weaving, drew, painted, and transformed shoe boxes into dollhouses. In this, she took after the rest of her family, who have all been involved in art in some way. Her grandfather was an illustrator; her mother, a hairdresser, also pursues photography, sewing, and knitting; her father, who works in information technology, is also a musician. Bee's younger brother, Max, is a talented musician as well. While growing up, instead of playing sports or studying a musical instrument in her free time, Bee took weekly classes at the Pacific Northwest College of Art.

In 2005, Bee was the last student admitted to da Vinci Arts Middle School, an arts-focused magnet school in Portland that accepts students based on a lottery system. In her first year at the school, Bee intended to sign up for a video production class; she hoped to make movies. Instead, she was placed in a darkroom photography course. "I hated it," she confessed to Sydney Jones and Sophie Hauth for *Grant Magazine* (28 Nov. 2016). "I didn't know how to use the chemicals, and I felt like what I saw in my head was very different than what I was able to make happen in a picture." Still, she persevered, and she soon came to enjoy working in the darkroom to achieve the effects she wanted.

BUDDING PHOTOGRAPHER
Growing up in Portland influenced Bee's work. "I definitely think it affects me a lot, because in Portland it rains all the time," she told fashion blogger Tavi Gevinson in an interview for *Time* magazine (9 Sept. 2011). "So everybody plays an instrument, and is in a band and working on a project. Being in a creative atmosphere 24/7 just encourages me to make something every day. And my friends are my muses." Documenting her life and the lives of her friends gave Bee a way to deal with the difficulties of being a teenager.

She began posting her photographs, mainly of herself and her friends, on the website Flickr, where they caught the eyes of several important contacts. When Bee was fourteen, she was contacted by Converse's advertising agency, VSA Partners. Not having heard of the company, or of advertising agencies in general, Bee ignored what she thought at first were spam e-mails, until finally Converse contacted her directly. The company asked her to attend a photo shoot in Portland and do some work for them. "It was a mentoring thing," Bee explained to Amy Kellner for the *New York Times Magazine* blog the *6th Floor* (23 Nov. 2011). "They wanted to give me a taste of what the business was like. So there weren't any expectations, but they ended up using the stuff, and I got paid for it, so that was my first job."

Until she turned eighteen, Bee was always accompanied by at least one parent on photo shoots, to act as a chaperone on set. "It was a legality thing," she told Kathy Sweeney for the *Guardian* (24 Feb. 2013). "I also had to have a schoolteacher accompany me. It was kind of what actors have to do when they're under eighteen. My parents have been great. They don't help unless I ask for it, they let me do my own thing." Her father has also helped out on set, building bonfires on a beach for one shoot and making snowmen for another.

EARLY CAREER

In 2011, impressed by Bee's photographs of her peers, the *New York Times Magazine* invited her to take photographs that would accompany their upcoming cover article on sex-positive sex education. Bee, then seventeen, chose to work again with friends, all of whom were between the ages of seventeen and nineteen. "All of the shoots that I did were with close friends and their real girlfriend or boyfriend," she said to Kellner later, in a follow-up interview. "I didn't want anything to be faked because I feel like it's really obvious when a photo is fake. It was very low key. . . . There was no hair and makeup or anything like that. I wanted things to be natural and I wanted to capture these people's relationships, so we just did it very simply."

Bee graduated from Grant High School in 2012 with a 3.7 grade point average, despite frequently missing school because she was traveling for her work. She applied to only one college, the Cooper Union for the Advancement of Science and Art in New York City. When she was not admitted, she decided to forgo college and focus full-time on her career. She moved with her boyfriend to Baltimore, where he attended the Maryland Institute College of Art. Later that year she spoke to about three hundred women at a TEDx conference in Amsterdam. "Nothing gets in my way, because I don't accept anything getting in my way," she told the audience there, according to Sweeney.

NEW OPPORTUNITIES

Bee was deeply unhappy in Baltimore. "It was the worst time in my live," she said to Noble. "I was really deep super-depressed, struggling with anorexia a lot, it was the worst five months of my life. Like, rock bottom." So she decided to move to New York: "I just couldn't be in Baltimore anymore, and New York . . . everything in the world happens in New York, you might as well try it out."

Despite early difficulties settling in and meeting new people, Bee found New York to be a much better fit for her. She slowly but steadily built up a stable of commercial clients while adjusting to the changes in her life and how they affected her art photography. "I used to run around with kids all the time and we'd go have a blast and take pictures, but . . . I have less of those magical photo-taking moments in my life because I'm not seventeen anymore," she said to Noble. "So I have to, not stage them, but set those up." By age nineteen she had hired an intern and was regularly working eighty-hour weeks.

In June 2014 Bee debuted a solo exhibition, *Kids in Love*, at the agnès b. Galerie Boutique in New York. Curators initially objected to the title, but Bee defended her choice. "They were like, 'Ah, but I don't know, it's too Patti Smith, it's too Ryan McGinley.' And I was like, 'Those are two people who have definitely influenced me, and I think this is my own thing. I think *Kids in Love* is great,'" she recalled to Lainey R. Sidell for *Paper* magazine (1 Apr. 2016). "And it's not like teenagers—that's stupid. These are kids. I'm still a kid, I feel like a kid. Kid is just a very good word to describe someone who's excited about life and who's just experiencing life with young eyes, which I think you should always do. You should always go through life not with the experience of a child, but with the eyes of a child."

KIDS IN LOVE AND BEYOND

The *Kids in Love* exhibition became the basis of Bee's first published book of photographs, along with another exhibition, *Enveloped in a Dream*, which opened at Bernal Espacio Galería in Madrid, Spain, in September 2014. *Olivia Bee: Kids in Love*, published by the Aperture Foundation in 2016, presents the two collections in separate sections. Initially the book was only meant to include *Kids in Love*, but the publisher suggested adding some of Bee's earlier photographs as well. Bee agreed but insisted the sections not be intermixed, as she sees them as representing two different eras of her work, with distinct styles and themes. The book also features text by Gevinson, Bee's friend and occasional collaborator, including the introduction and an interview conducted by her. After considering asking an older, more established artist to write the introduction, Bee vetoed the idea, preferring somebody of her own generation who, as she said to Sidell, "understands this work and who understands the place it came from and the time it came from."

Bee has also done some directing work, primarily commercials and short films. She hopes to further pursue filmmaking, which, she told Sidell, will require changing the intuitive way in which she works. "I came from just shooting pictures and figuring out the story later; your eye moves faster than your brain when you're a very visual person," she explained. "And so now I'm kind of trying to reverse that, because you can't do that in film. . . . I'm trying to train my brain to think of a story and then shoot it in that way, which I think will really help my films because then I have everything that I need that scene or that image to tell in one frame. And if you can do that in film, you can push every idea to the fullest idea that it can be—that's what makes something really powerful. Less is always more."

SUGGESTED READING

Bee, Olivia. Interview. By Lou Noble. *The Photographic Journal*, 15 Jan. 2015, thephotographicjournal.com/interviews/olivia-bee. Accessed 4 Apr. 2017.

Bee, Olivia. "Our Teenage Photographer of Teenage Lust." Interview by Amy Kellner. *The 6th Floor*, New York Times, 23 Nov. 2011, 6thfloor.blogs.nytimes.com/2011/11/23/our-teenage-photographer-of-teenage-lust. Accessed 4 Apr. 2017.

Bee, Olivia. "Photographer Olivia Bee on Shooting *Kids in Love*." Interview by Lainey R. Sidell. *Paper*, 1 Apr. 2016, www.papermag.com/olivia-bee-kids-in-love-1701957613.html. Accessed 4 Apr. 2017.

Bee, Olivia. "Smells like Teen Spirit: Tavi Gevinson Interviews Olivia Bee." Interview by Tavi Gevinson. *Time*, 9 Sept. 2011, time.com/3780710/smells-like-teen-spirit-tavi-gevinson-interviews-olivia-bee. Accessed 4 Apr. 2017.

Jones, Sydney, and Sophie Hauth. "Capturing the Light." *Grant Magazine*, 28 Nov. 2016, grantmagazine.com/bee. Accessed 4 Apr. 2017.

Soller, Kurt. "The Very Rapid Rise of the Very Precocious Photographer Olivia Bee." *The Cut*, New York Media, 9 Feb. 2013, nymag.com/thecut/2013/02/rapid-rise-of-photographer-olivia-bee.html. Accessed 4 Apr. 2017.

Sweeney, Kathy. "Olivia Bee: 'People Don't Take Me Seriously—Until They See Me Work.'" *The Guardian*, 24 Feb. 2013, www.theguardian.com/artanddesign/2013/feb/24/olivia-bee-interview-photographer-hermes. Accessed 4 Apr. 2017.

—*Judy Johnson*

Jérôme Bel

Date of birth: October 14, 1964
Occupation: Choreographer

Jérôme Bel is an experimental French choreographer who began his career in the 1990s. "I'm more a philosopher of dance," he told Valerie Gladstone for the *Boston Globe* (4 Nov. 2011). Or rather, some have said, "nondance." Bel hates

the term, but it is an appropriate one given that his extensive and provocative body of work explores dance in a very oblique sense. In 2016 his show, *MoMA Dance Company*, was staged at the Museum of Modern Art (MoMA) in New York City, and featured twenty-five nontrained performers culled from the museum's staff. Bel's most famous piece, *The Show Must Go On* (2001), features ten professional dancers and ten amateur dancers bopping around to contemporary pop songs, while the notorious, self-titled *Jérôme Bel* (1995), features four naked performers examining their own bodies and urinating. Using movement and gesture, Bel seeks to strip away the artifice of performance. His work is cerebral but also, as was particularly the case with *The Show Must Go On*, entertaining, even if the performance cannot exactly be labeled as dance. "I love dance," Bel told Roslyn Sulcas for the *New York Times* (24 Feb. 2008). "But I want to know why people go to a theater and sit down in the dark at a particular time. What do you expect, what are you looking for, what does one need to look for? What do you need to dance? For me, those are the fundamental questions."

EARLY LIFE AND SELF-EDUCATION

Bel was born in the south of France on October 14, 1964. His father worked for the United Nations International Children's Emergency Fund (UNICEF), so Bel grew up in Algeria, Iran, Morocco, and South Africa. He knew he wanted to be an artist from a young age, and showed an aptitude for jazz dance. He returned to France as a young man to study at the Centre National de Danse Contemporaine (CND) in Angers in 1984, but dropped out in 1985 because he found the curriculum too traditional. For the next five or six years, Bel danced with companies in France and Italy.

In 1992 he worked as an assistant director to Philippe Decouflé, who was choreographing the opening ceremony for the Winter Olympic Games in Albertville, France. Phil Hersh, writing for the *Chicago Tribune* (9 Feb. 1992), favorably described the ceremony as a "brilliant" and surreal five-ring circus. It was Bel's first turn as a director, and he decided he preferred it to performance. Rather than jump immediately into his new role, however, Bel moved to Paris where he spent two years reading Roland Barthes and Michel Foucault. He lived off of the money he earned working with Decouflé. "I felt the only way to be a choreographer," he told Gladstone, "was to read philosophy and dance history."

Bel also read about an American postmodern choreographer named Trisha Brown, one of the founders of the Judson Dance Theater in New York City. Brown, as the chief dance critic for the *New York Times* (25 Jan. 2013) Alastair Macaulay wrote, is widely considered a "pioneer of pure-dance" movement experimentalism who "changed the way we define dance performance." Brown, who reached the height of her career during the 1960s, often performed in surprising spaces (one famous performance took place across ten SoHo rooftops) and without music. She studied with the late Merce Cunningham, the godfather of American modern dance and romantic partner of avant-garde composer John Cage. Bel also read about Cunningham and Cage, and by absorbing their philosophies, he began to develop his own.

EARLY CAREER

Bel presented his first piece, *Nom donné par l'auteur* (Name given by the author) in 1994. He created the piece with Frédéric Saguette (they performed it together as well) in his Paris apartment. Bel felt that experimentation might be easier outside of the dance studio. The piece was inspired in part by his appreciation for Marcel Duchamp, an early twentieth century conceptual artist. Duchamp is popularly known for a 1917 sculpture called *Fountain*, a porcelain urinal that Duchamp bought and signed with a fake name. With *Nom donné par l'auteur*, Bel set out to investigate the purpose of theater—much like Duchamp, in his cheeky way, set out to investigate the purpose, or at least the bounds, of art objects.

In *Nom donné par l'auteur*, Bel and Saguette move through a black box, variously picking up and holding out various objects like a book or a soccer ball. With these actions, Bel tries to subvert the idea of a theatrical set. The objects

onstage were not specifically chosen for the stage and further, by sitting still and holding them, the "set pieces" become the stars of the show. *Nom donné par l'auteur* set the tone for much of Bel's work in that it is also ironic. As Sanjoy Roy for *The Guardian* (22 Nov. 2011) pointed out, the title of the piece "is the dictionary definition of the word 'title'—hence, a kind of non-title."

"Everyone hated it," Bel told Sulcas of *Nom donné par l'auteur*, "people were snoring." His next piece, *Jérôme Bel* (1995), fared worse with audiences, though it has become an important one in Bel's oeuvre. When it was presented at the International Dance Festival in Ireland in 2002, one audience member sued, claiming that the piece did not include any dance, and that the trauma of viewing the production left him unable to ever attend the theater ever again. (The case was later dismissed.) The piece features four performers, all of them nude. One performer holds a bare light bulb on a string; the bulb serves as the production's only lighting. Another performer hums Bach's "Goldberg Variations," the only music. The other two performers draw on a back wall and on each other's bodies. "As they stretch and squeeze their own skin, not excluding genitalia, or as their bellies expand and deflate in silhouette, they prompt thoughts about bodies as strange things. The experiments, like those of curious children, can strike a viewer as disturbingly gross: fingernails bitten off, hands dipped in someone else's urine," Brian Seibert wrote in his *New York Times* (28 Oct. 2016) review of a revival of the piece. "More often, they crackle with a droll wit. A flow of literal-minded puns, well-paced with little surprises, makes you chuckle and think about identity and language, about bodies (including your own) as absurd."

THE SHOW MUST GO ON

In 1997 Bel choreographed a piece called *Shirtology*, in which a performer removes layer after layer of T-shirts with various slogans or phrases printed on them. In 1998 he staged a piece, called *The Last Performance*, in which he sits at a table and gives a lecture about dance, and in 2000, he worked with Xavier Le Roy to create *Xavier Le Roy*. The piece was actually choreographed by Le Roy, an avant-garde choreographer, but done in the style of Bel and credited to his name.

In 2001 Bel premiered what would become his most famous work, *The Show Must Go On*. The piece begins in total darkness. Familiar songs from the musicals *West Side Story* and *Hair* begin to play, and the performers laugh or clap in recognition. The lights come up on the performers dressed in street clothes and milling around the stage. David Bowie's "Let's Dance" plays and the performers are seized with the inspiration to dance, clumsily and poorly. When

"My Heart Will Go On," the theme song from the movie *Titanic*, plays they throw their arms out in mimicry of the most famous scene from that film. This is the entire show: each performer reacting, alone and together, to each of the eighteen popular songs in the show. Nancy Alfaro, who reviewed a revival of the show for *Dance Magazine* (17 Nov. 2008) called it "brilliant." "Is it dance?" she wrote. "Who cares?"

The show went on tour across the globe, and has since become Bel's most famous work—but early audiences and critics were less enthused. During the premiere, the audience revolted, booing, yelling, and storming the stage. One critic slapped another critic in the face. The piece still sometimes inspires violent reactions. At one performance in Israel in 2004, one spectator got up on the stage and kicked one of the performers. Bel developed the piece over two years during which time he told Kristin Hohenadel for the *New York Times* (20 Mar. 2005), he traveled all over the world collecting inspiration because the songs he chose were so ubiquitous. The piece and the music, he said were "a discourse, a way of thinking about the theater, the community." *The Show Must Go On* won a Bessie Award for its New York premiere in 2005.

RECENT WORK

Bel went on to create a series of biographical pieces about actual dancers including *Véronique Doisneau* (2004), *Pichet Klunchun and Myself* (2005), and *Cédric Andrieux* (2009). In *Cédric Andrieux*, for example, Andrieux, who studied dance with Cunningham, recalls his first dance class with accompanying movements. "He asked me to come up with what I wanted to say about being a dancer," Andrieux recalled to Gladstone. "He's as interested in the ordinary as the virtuosic." Bel's 2012 piece, *Disabled Theater*, he collaborated with Theater HORA, a Swiss performance troupe with mental and physical disabilities. The production, meant to explore empathy and normality, inspired both praise and sharp criticism. Bel's *Ballet (New York)* (2015) and *Gala* (2015), like *The Show Must Go On*, brought together a group of variously trained performers to interpret different genres of music, written on sandwich boards onstage. In 2016, Bel was the first choreographer to be invited to stage a show at MoMA in New York City. Drawing inspiration from the museum itself, Bel selected twenty-five performers from the museum's 750-person staff. In addition to their costumes and choreography, Bel also invited them to choose their own music.

PERSONAL LIFE

Bel lives in Paris with his daughter, Ryo.

SUGGESTED READING

Alfaro, Nancy. "Jérôme Bel Dance Theater Workshop, New York, NY March 24–26." *Dance Magazine*, 17 Nov. 2008, dancemagazine.com/reviews/Jerome_Bel. Accessed 14 Mar. 2017.

Gladstone, Valerie. "Choreographer Jérôme Bel Explains His Philosophy of Dance." *The Boston Globe*, 4 Nov. 2011, www.bostonglobe.com/arts/2011/11/03/choreographer-jerome-bel-explains-his-philosophy-dance/lqzb1mBpg3b75eKS2L9xGL/story.html. Accessed 13 Mar. 2017.

Hersh, Phil. "Albertville Waves in Olympics." *Chicago Tribune*, 9 Feb. 1992, articles.chicagotribune.com/1992-02-09/news/9201120837_1_olympic-cauldron-5-ring-circus-francois-cyrille-grange. Accessed 13 Mar. 2017.

Hohenadel, Kristin. "Nondances That Spur Critics to Brawl and Audiences to Sue." *The New York Times*, 20 Mar. 2005, www.nytimes.com/2005/03/20/arts/dance/nondances-that-spur-critics-to-brawl-and-audiences-to-sue.html. Accessed 14 Mar. 2017.

Macaulay, Alastair. "Pure Dance, Pure Finale." *The New York Times*, 25 Jan. 2013, www.nytimes.com/2015/12/04/arts/dance/a-rousing-end-lifts-a-program-of-jerome-bel-dances-in-paris.html. Accessed 13 Mar. 2017.

Roy, Sanjoy. "Step-by-Step Guide to Dance: Jérôme Bel." *The Guardian*, 22 Nov. 2011, www.theguardian.com/stage/2011/nov/22/step-guide-dance-jerome-bel. Accessed 14 Mar. 2017.

Seibert, Brian. "Jérôme Bel: Naked and Alive, Then Clothed and Dead." *The New York Times*, 28 Oct. 2016, www.nytimes.com/2016/10/29/arts/dance/jerome-bel-naked-and-alive-then-clothed-and-dead.html. Accessed 14 Mar. 2017.

Sulcas, Roslyn. "Unless You Have Another Word, Dance Will Do." *The New York Times*, 24 Feb. 2008, www.nytimes.com/2008/02/24/arts/dance/24sulc.html. Accessed 14 Mar. 2017.

SELECTED WORKS

Nom donné par l'auteur, (1994); *Jérôme Bel*, (1995); *The Show Must Go On*, (2001); *MoMA Dance Company*, (2016)

—*Molly Hagan*

Ali Benjamin

Occupation: Author

Ali Benjamin is an American author best known for her young adult novel *The Thing about Jellyfish*.

EARLY LIFE AND EDUCATION

Ali Benjamin, born Allison Wade, was raised in the greater New York City area. She grew up in a house she described as being filled with books, but was not motivated to write until much later in her life.

As a child, Benjamin loved learning about dinosaurs and the universe and exploring nature. She would only later understand that she was naturally drawn to scientific discovery, and despite becoming known as an author whose work promotes the pursuit of science for young people, Benjamin spent most of her school days pursuing arts, while finding science classes tedious.

Benjamin has said that childhood, and particularly the transition from childhood to teenage years, can be a particularly harrowing experience. She later chose the genre of young adult fiction because she saw it as a path to helping children understand and talk about difficult parts of their lives.

Benjamin graduated from Grinnell College in 1992. She also earned a master of public administration degree from Baruch College, the City University of New York. She lived in West Africa while she served in the United States Peace Corps. She later worked as a health care consultant and as an academic freelance writer.

CAREER

While working for a variety of organizations including corporations and nonprofits, Benjamin published nonfiction writing on lifestyle and healthy living. She cowrote *The Cleaner Plate Club* (2011), a nonfiction guide to healthy food choices for children, with Beth Bader. Benjamin has also contributed to the *Boston Globe Magazine* and *Martha Stewart's Whole Living Online*.

In 2011, Benjamin cowrote two memoirs for American celebrities. The first was *Positive: A Memoir*, detailing the life of Paige Rawl, a teenager with human immunodeficiency virus (HIV) and an antibullying advocate. The same year, Benjamin cowrote the memoir of American soccer player Tim Howard, titled, *The Keeper: The Unguarded Story of Tim Howard*.

Benjamin became fascinated with jellyfish when visiting the New England Aquarium with her children. She began writing a nonfiction piece about jellyfish. Simultaneously, she had been writing a work of fiction about a twelve-year-old girl. Realizing neither work was progressing to her satisfaction, she decided to

Brent N. Clarke/FilmMagic/Getty Images

interweave them into the same story. This work became her debut novel, *The Thing about Jellyfish* (2015).

The novel centers on a girl named Suzy whose best friend mysteriously drowns. Suzy is hit very hard by the death. She later learns about jellyfish, and theorizes that her friend, a good swimmer, must have been stung by a jellyfish. Suzy becomes obsessed with jellyfish and proving that a jellyfish caused her friend's death, with the help of her grade school science teacher.

The Thing about Jellyfish was a best seller and a critical success, earning Benjamin many awards and a nomination as a National Book Award Finalist.

Benjamin has been credited for the manner in which *The Thing about Jellyfish* emphasizes science and the scientific method, which Suzy's teacher helps her to use in investigating her friend's death. Advocates for STEM (science, technology, engineering and mathematics) in primary education have pointed to the novel's potential in attracting young readers to STEM programs.

Benjamin has said that, despite the success of her debut novel, she finds fiction writing difficult. In reflecting on her writing on her website, she observes, "This world of ours is complex, but it's filled with plenty of wonder and sparkle."

IMPACT

Benjamin's *The Thing about Jellyfish* is a *New York Times* Best Seller and was a finalist for the 2015 National Book Award. Pacific Standard Films, a production company owned by actor

Reese Witherspoon, selected the novel for adaptation to a film.

In addition to her writing, Benjamin was the casting director and story researcher for the Emmy Award–winning television special *Sesame Street: Growing Hope against Hunger*.

PERSONAL LIFE

Benjamin lives in Williamstown, Massachusetts, with her husband, Blair Benjamin, and her two daughters, Merrie and Charlotte.

SUGGESTED READING

"About Ali Benjamin." *Ali Benjamin*. N.p., n.d. Web. 23 Jan. 2016.

Benjamin, Ali. "Interview with Ali Benjamin—2015 National Book Award Finalist, Young People's Literature." Interview by Tim Manley. *National Book Foundation*. National Book Foundation, n.d. Web. 4 Apr. 2016.

Benjamin, Ali. "STEAM I: Conversation with Author, Ali Benjamin (National Book Award Finalist)." Interview. *TalkSTEM*. TalkSTEM, 10 Dec. 2015. Web. 23 Jan. 2016.

Burnett, Matia. "Fall 2015 Flying Starts: Ali Benjamin." *PublishersWeekly.com*. PWxyz, 11 Dec. 2015. Web. 23 Jan. 2016.

Young, Robin, and Jeremy Hobson. "Science Plays Lead Role in New Book Aimed at Young Adults." *Here & Now*. Trustees of Boston University, 28 Sept. 2015. Web. 23 Jan. 2016.

SELECTED WORKS

The Cleaner Plate Club (2011); *The Keeper: The Unguarded Story of Tim Howard* (2014); *Positive: A Memoir* (2014); *The Thing about Jellyfish* (2015)

—Richard Means

Melissa Benoist

Date of birth: October 4, 1988
Occupation: Actor

Melissa Marie Benoist became the first female superhero on prime time television in forty years when *Supergirl* debuted in 2015. No woman had helmed a superhero television show since *Wonder Woman*, with Lynda Carter, went off the air in 1979. It is important to Benoist that in a field long dominated by men, *Supergirl* provides a superhero role model for girls and young women. As she told Natalie Abrams for *Entertainment Weekly* (18 Sept. 2015), "I want to do right by women. I want to portray someone they can relate to and look up to. [But] I want her to be complicated *and* flawed." Part of doing so involves a scene with boss Cat Grant (Calista Flockhart) in

By Red Carpet Report on Mingle Media TV from Culver City, USA [CC BY-SA 2.0], via Wikimedia Commons

which Kara complains about the title of Supergirl, pulling for Superwoman, a suggestion Grant does not take. Ultimately, however, Benoist told Bill Keveney for *USA Today* (26 Oct. 2015), *Supergirl* is "all about hope, kindness and doing the right thing."

CHILDHOOD AND EDUCATION

Benoist was born in Houston, Texas, and raised in Littleton, Colorado, near Denver. When she was just two years old, her grandmother put on a video of *Singing in the Rain* to amuse the toddler. Not long after, Benoist was performing in the living room to an audience of her stuffed animals. Two years later, her aunt cast her in a play at church. As Benoist told Laura Jacobs for *Vanity Fair* (8 Dec. 2015), even at that young age, "I just loved the feeling of performing, of using my imagination to take me somewhere else."

As a teenager, she performed in shows at Country Dinner Playhouse, Lakewood Cultural Center, and Littleton Town Hall Arts Center. She played the role of *A Chorus Line*'s Bebe at the Littleton Town Hall Arts Center, a role that was seminal, as she told John Moore for the Denver Performing Arts Center's Newscenter blog (14 Mar. 2016). "That changed my life," Benoist said, "and I think it was totally a precursor to this experience on *Glee* because it required singing and acting and dancing—and having to be honest doing them all at once. We moved at a really fast pace, and I learned really difficult material . . . . It was a really grueling and challenging experience for everyone in that show, and I learned so much."

After graduating from Arapahoe High School, Benoist moved to New York to major in musical theater at Marymount Manhattan College. During her sophomore year, she changed her major to theater arts after falling in love with Shakespeare, George Bernard Shaw, Noel Coward, and the Russian playwrights of the nineteenth century. She starred in shows such as *Thoroughly Modern Millie* and graduated with a bachelor of arts in theater arts in 2011.

GLEE

After appearing in commercials for Clean and Clear and other products, as well as in roles on television series such as *Homeland* and *The Good Wife*, Benoist became part of the ensemble cast of the Fox television show *Glee*. Benoist was part of a new group of actors added to the show around that time. She appeared as the wallflower Marley Rose in seasons four and five, which aired from 2012 through 2014. Her first musical number on the show, *A New York State of Mind*, was performed as a duet with Lea Michele.

Although the show was a musical comedy, it also highlighted some serious issues. One was the bulimia that Benoist's character suffered from, which led to her fainting during a competition. The idea came from the show's writer, Ryan Murphy, as Benoist told Kate Stanhope for *TV Guide* (5 Dec. 2012). When Murphy told her he was considering writing her character as having an eating disorder, Benoist told Stanhope, "It definitely was a daunting thing to hear, but in the best way. As an actor, you can only hope for something with that much depth and something to dig into that much."

To prepare for the role, Benoist read some blogs in which teenage girls who struggled with eating disorders documented their difficulties, even though doing so felt invasive to her. Benoist saw an added benefit from that story arc in the number of people who contacted her about the eating disorder after the episode aired. For her work on *Glee*, she was nominated for the 2013 Teen Choice Award for TV breakout star.

SUPERGIRL

Benoist became the latest superhero to grace television screens in *Supergirl*, one of DC Comics' products. In fall 2015, CBS floated the hourlong pilot, which bears similarities to CW's *The Flash*. She later brought the role to life in other series: *Arrow* (2012–), *The Flash* (2014–), and *Legends of Tomorrow* (2016–).

Executive producer Greg Berlanti, who had already produced two successful superhero series, *The Flash* and *Arrow*, pitched the idea of the show to CBS. Benoist was the first of a thousand actors to audition for the role of Kara Danvers, aka Supergirl, over a three-month period; she prevailed over this stiff competition to land her first major starring role. Berlanti persuaded Calista Flockhart to join the series as Kara's boss.

The pilot was reputed to cost fourteen million dollars; the cast spent a month filming. That hard work paid off; CBS accepted the pilot for a new series. The show was nominated for four 2017 Saturn Awards, given by the Academy of Science Fiction, Fantasy and Horror Films, in the categories of best actress on a television series for Benoist, as well as best supporting actor (Mehcad Brooks), best guest performance (Tyler Hoechlin), and best superhero adaptation television series.

Kara's costume was a plus, as Benoist told Joanna Robinson for *Vanity Fair* (26 Oct. 2015): "I think it's modest in that you can believe someone could fight for their lives in that suit without having a wardrobe malfunction and something popping out. That's what I never understood about Wonder Woman. I'm like, 'How does she fight?'" Benoist also told Keveney for *USA Today* (15 July 2015) that she related to Kara Danvers, saying, "When I put the suit on, I just feel stronger and I feel brave." She went on to comment on the need for a female superhero, saying, "It's high time for it. What I'm more excited about [is that] women have always been superheroes, but now is the time for one to be at the forefront of the story." Benoist used the writer Susan Sontag and political leader Gloria Steinem as inspirations for her role.

CROSSOVER APPEAL

In spring 2016 *Supergirl* featured a guest appearance by *The Flash* star Grant Gustin in the role of Barry Allen, a fellow superhero who poses as Kara's cousin. In contrast to the testosterone-fueled conflicts that often occur when two male superheroes meet onscreen, the meeting between Allen and Danvers was a friendly visit, of benefit to both characters. Allen acts as a mentor to the new superhero, while her enthusiasm gives him a much-needed jolt. Because Greg Berlanti and Andrew Kreisberg produce both series, they wanted to try something that would enhance both shows and the comic book tie-ins. The process was simplified because Warner and CBS also own CW, the channel that broadcasts *The Flash*. Commenting to Laura Prudom for *Variety* (22 Mar. 2016), Benoist said, "I honestly didn't think it was possible between networks. I remember Andrew Kreisberg telling me right before Grant and I presented at the Golden Globes, 'We're gonna just pitch the idea and see how they respond.' . . . There's no way in the world that people wouldn't see how valuable that could be, and how much the fans would love it." Glenn Geller, the head of CBS, saw the potential and was pleased with the organic way in which the narratives blended. His approval left the door open for further collaborations.

Another type of crossover took place on the day of filming, which was a type of family day; several stars, including Fred Savage, brought their children to the set. Kreisberg told Prudom, "As much as we like to say we make this show for ourselves, we really make this show for families and children of all ages, so that was a really special thing."

This was not the first interweaving of superhero worlds. Barry Allen, the alter ego of the Flash, was a character on *Arrow* before being spun off into his own show. The two shows have crossed over several times since. For the second season of *Supergirl*, a broadcast station change occurred, with the show moving to CW, making future melded narrative arcs more likely.

A second crossover took place in 2017, beginning with the March 20 episode of *Supergirl* and continuing on the next night's episode of *The Flash*. The episode reunited Benoist and Gustin with former *Glee* costar Darren Criss in the role of the Music Meister, a supervillain who causes Supergirl and the Flash to hallucinate that they are in a musical. Benoist, who sings "Moon River" during the crossover event, found the experience nostalgic. Although she has focused on acting, she was happy to have a chance to sing again.

THE BIG SCREEN

Benoist has had several roles in films as well. She played the love interest to Miles Teller's jazz drummer in the 2014 Damien Chazelle film *Whiplash*. She was cast in *The Longest Ride*, the 2015 adaptation of a Nicholas Sparks novel. The movie was a best picture Oscar nominee, with Benoist one of five actors participating in that honor. That same year she was in *Danny Collins* with Al Pacino and Annette Benning. Of that experience, she told Amy Spencer for the *New York Post* (1 Dec. 2016), "I [had] such a small role in that movie, yet every single person in that movie went to Al's house to rehearse." She also had a role in the 2016 film about the Boston Marathon bombing, *Patriots Day*, playing the role of Katherine Russell, wife of one of the bombers. She was cast as Lorelei in Eva Longoria's film *Lowriders* (2016) and also netted a leading role in the crime drama *Billy Boy* (2017).

PERSONAL LIFE

Benoist has two sisters, Jessica and Kristina. After a brief marriage, Benoist divorced *Glee* costar Blake Jenner in 2016. Although she lives in Los Angeles, she misses the Colorado landscape, telling Spencer, "I'm not an ocean person. I like being landlocked. I constantly daydream about a ranch in the mountains in Colorado or Montana . . . I think mountains are the most beautiful things in the world." She attended the Women's March on Washington in January 2017, along with other celebrities, to send a message to President Donald Trump about women's rights.

Benoist enjoys cooking, reading, and spending time with her two dogs, and makes pottery as a form of meditation.

SUGGESTED READING

Benoist, Melissa. "Supergirl: Melissa Benoist on Landing the Role of a Lifetime, and Empowering Women." Interview by Natalie Abrams. *Entertainment Weekly*, 2 July 2015, ew.com/article/2015/07/02/supergirl-melissa-benoist-cbs-interview. Accessed 9 Mar. 2017.

Jacobs, Laura. "Why Supergirl Star Melissa Benoist is the 'Annie Hall of Superheroes.'" *Vanity Fair*, 8 Dec. 2015, www.vanityfair.com/hollywood/2015/12/supergirl-star-melissa-benoist. Accessed 15 Mar. 2017.

Keveney, Bill. "For Supergirl, It's 'A Crash Course' in Heroism." *USA Today*, 26 Oct. 2015, www.pressreader.com/usa/usa-today-us-edition/20151026/282248074419087/TextView. Accessed 9 Mar. 2017.

Keveney, Bill. "'Supergirl' Prepares for Iconic Liftoff." *USA Today*, 15 July 2015, www.pressreader.com/usa/usa-today-international-edition/20150715/282368333324639/TextView. Accessed 9 Mar. 2017.

Prudom, Laura. "'Supergirl' Meets 'The Flash': Stars Take Us behind the Scenes on the Crossover (EXCLUSIVE)." *Variety*, 22 Mar. 2016, variety.com/2016/tv/news/supergirl-the-flash-crossover-arrow-legends-of-tomorrow-grant-gustin-melissa-benoist-1201735793. Accessed 10 Apr. 2017.

Robinson, Joanna. "Why Supergirl Star Melissa Benoist Hopes to Talk Less about Gender." *Vanity Fair*, 26 Oct. 2015, www.vanityfair.com/hollywood/2015/10/supergirl-melissa-benoist-gender. Accessed 17 Mar. 2017.

Spencer, Amy. "How 'Supergirl' Melissa Benoist Channeled a Boston Marathon Bomber's Widow." *New York Post*, 1 Dec. 2016, nypost.com/2016/12/01/how-supergirl-melissa-benoist-channeled-a-boston-marathon-bombers-widow. Accessed 18 Mar. 2017.

SELECTED WORKS

Glee, 2012–14; *Whiplash*, 2014; *The Longest Ride*, 2015; *Supergirl*, 2015–; *Patriots Day*, 2016; *Lowriders*, 2017

—*Judy Johnson*

Daniel Berehulak

Date of birth: 1975
Occupation: Photojournalist

Daniel Berehulak earned attention as one of the most prominent and critically acclaimed photographers of his time, winning Pulitzer Prizes in 2015 and 2017, among many other awards. He is known for his dedication to documenting social issues in a way that is both informative and artistic, both sympathetic and objective. Through his publications in the *New York Times* and other outlets, he has opened viewers' eyes to the human experience in historic events worldwide.

The life of an independent freelance photojournalist is not an easy one. In his career, Berehulak must be prepared to leave at a moment's notice to go wherever an assignment requires. He must bear witness to brutal scenes—war, natural disasters, disease, murders—to present to the world pictures that demonstrate unvarnished facts. But the freelance trade also has its benefits: he owns his own photos, makes his own schedules, and can go wherever the story—and his art—leads him, staying for as long as he likes. After taking up photography at the start of the twenty-first century, Berehulak traveled around the globe and captured intimate images the world over. "Daniel is an extraordinary photographer who manages to be artful in dangerous conditions," said Michele McNally, a director of photography at the *New York Times*, as quoted by David Gonzalez and James Estrin for that paper (10 Apr. 2017). "He is brave and courageous and relentless in pursuit of the story."

FORMATIVE YEARS

Daniel Berehulak was born in Sydney, Australia, in 1975, to parents who were Ukrainian immigrants. He grew up on a farm in the nearby town of Camden and received his education at the Homebush Boys High School and the University of New South Wales. Although he had always enjoyed taking photographs, the idea of becoming a professional photographer was simply never one that came into his head—especially not in his practical-minded household. Instead, during his youth, he worked on the family farm and helped at his father's refrigeration business, with the idea of perhaps working in business himself someday.

For a time after graduation Berehulak worked in retail, but after his sister died of lupus when he was twenty-three, he came to realize that it was vitally important to pursue one's dreams. "It kind of put it into perspective that life was short and precious and I quit everything. I had no idea how I wanted to get into photography but I just knew I wanted to do it," he recalled to Melanie Kembrey for the *Sydney Morning Herald* (28 Apr. 2015).

Berehulak started local, taking any assignment he could get but mostly shooting sports matches. Then, in 2002, he began working as a freelancer for Getty Images in Sydney, again mainly shooting sports. He asked his fellow photographers at those events lots of questions, looking for ways to improve his craft. And he continued to take on every assignment that came his way. As he told Kembrey: "I was a young eager kid just wanting to get in, not knowing how. I had a lot of enthusiasm, not much talent at all, and they were really patient and gave a lot of their time."

STAFF PHOTOGRAPHER AT GETTY

As soon as he could, Berehulak shifted away from sports photography and toward news coverage. In 2005 he took a job as a staff photographer at Getty Images, based out of London, England. But that city was only his jumping off point for a highly international range of assignments; his new role meant he was ready to go at a moment's notice anywhere in the world to capture newsworthy images. His first real news assignment came even before he was a full-time staffer. On his way to report to work in London, Getty asked him to cover an earthquake on a small island off the coast of Indonesia. "I flew thirty-six hours," he told Phil Bicker for *Time* (18 June 2014), recalling how unprepared he was. "Had to talk my way on to a military vessel. I had no idea what a fixer was and no translator. I didn't have a satellite phone, no way of transmitting my images."

Berehulak visited more than fifty countries during this period of his life, including time spent in war zones in Afghanistan and Iraq. Between 2006 and 2007 alone, he took images of the twentieth anniversary of the Chernobyl nuclear disaster, recorded the return of politician Benazir Bhutto to Pakistan, and chronicled the trial of former dictator Saddam Hussein in Iraq. He came to realize he preferred field work documenting crisis areas. In 2009 he began operating out of New Delhi, India, and gained more flexibility in shaping his own projects. Among other assignments, he went to Pakistan and was able to cover the massive floods that occurred in that country in 2010. A year later, he returned to Pakistan to document the lives of flood survivors in the aftermath.

As a Getty staff photographer, Berehulak was typically in and out of an area rapidly, moving on to capture the next story as quickly as possible. He recalled the disadvantages of this pace to Jeanette D. Moses for *American Photo* (20 June 2014): "I'd be filing like twenty to forty pictures a day. It sometimes limits the extent to which you can cover a story. You can't stay till midnight or one o'clock, two o'clock—you don't have the luxury of focusing an hour and a half on one person in the crowd and waiting for that moment to get that expression that kind of encapsulates the whole mood."

CRITICAL ACCLAIM

As he gained experience, Berehulak also began to earn attention for the quality of his photography. His photography had been featured in the Getty Images Gallery London Olympic Games Exhibition in 2004 and the Reportage Photojournalism Festival in 2005 and in 2006, but it was in 2007 that he began to receive numerous awards. That year he won third place in World Press Photo's "people in the news" category, an honorable mention in the Serial Portrait Series from the National Press Photographer's Association (NPPA), and foreign news photographer of the year in the UK Picture Editors' Awards. At the 2008 Press Photographer's Year Awards Berehulak won photo of the year and news folio of the year. In 2009 he won first prize in the live news category at the Press Photographer's Year Awards, second prize in sport singles at the Photographers Giving Back Award, and an honorable mention for UNICEF Photo of the Year.

The critical acclaim continued into the next decade. In 2010 Berehulak earned the photograph of the year, three gold prizes, one silver prize, and an award of excellence at the China International Press Photo Contest. He also won further prizes at the Press Photographer's Year Awards and the Photographers Giving Back Award. In 2011 Berehulak was a finalist for the Pulitzer Prize in breaking news photography, while he won the John Faber Award for best photographic reporting from abroad in newspapers and wire services, presented by the Overseas Press Club of America. That year he also earned a first-place World Press Photo award, a third-place prize in the NPPA's Best of Photojournalism contest, and a Special Jury Prize at the Days Japan International Photojournalism Awards.

GOING FREELANCE

Even as he earned significant honors for his staff work with Getty, it was becoming clear to Berehulak that he desired to do more with his photography. "The pros of being a staff photographer [were] a steady salary, having equipment provided and expenses paid [and having my work] disseminated across the globe," he explained to Bicker, but "there was the added frustration that I didn't own the copyright of my own photographs for the duration of my career." In addition, he was bothered by having to take assignments at the expense of major breaking stories, such as when he missed the immediate coverage of the 2011 Japanese tsunami due to being tasked with photographing the Cricket World Cup.

By July 2013, Berehulak decided to leave Getty in favor of a full-time freelance career. He was driven by a desire to spend more time with his subjects, which he saw as essential to progress his art. "I'm trying . . . to take my photography to the next level. Focusing more on storytelling and weaving narratives and doing them with a theme," as he explained to Moses. "Rather than taking the safe route and making sure that I've got [shots] that are going to appease editors and the newspapers I get to step back a little and look at the bigger picture. At the historical value of the imagery, rather than just the daily rush for news."

In addition to working on long-term personal projects, Berehulak quickly found newsworthy assignments from clients such as *Time* and *Der Spiegel*. Most notably, he became a frequent contributor to the *New York Times*, which gave him the flexibility he sought for longer-term photojournalism projects. Berehulak's critical success followed him in his freelance career. He won the Chris Hondros Fund Award in 2014, was named photographer of the year in both 2014 and 2015 by Pictures of the Year International, and received the George Polk Award for Health Reporting in 2015.

PULITZER PRIZE WINNER

In 2014, the *New York Times* asked Berehulak to cover the Ebola virus outbreak in West Africa. Although nervous about the assignment because so little was known about the disease at the time, Berehulak did not hesitate to accept it. He made it his mission to bring attention to a medical crisis that was devastating so many lives. All told, he spent more than four months in West Africa recording the epidemic, at one point working sixty-seven days straight. "For us there is no such thing as failure, you can't miss a deadline, you can't come up short on an assignment," Berehulak told Kembrey. "You have to perform, period." His diligence on the assignment earned him the Pulitzer Prize for feature photography in 2015. As David Furst, international photo editor of the *New York Times*, told Gonzalez and Estrin, "Daniel has this remarkable ability to fuse this strong, forceful, in-your-face, on-the-ground photojournalism with an empathy for his subjects that is second to none."

Berehulak's second Pulitzer Prize (this time in the breaking news category) followed in 2017, for his remarkable coverage of the brutal anti-drug campaign of President Rodrigo Duterte of the Philippines. Over a thirty-five-day period, he captured startling images of some fifty-seven murders and forty-one crime scenes, with drug dealer or user victims killed by vigilantes at the Duterte's urging. In addition to photographing the images for the *New York Times*'s interactive feature "They Are Slaughtering Us like Animals," Berehulak also wrote the accompanying story recounting the atrocities he witnessed. Despite the challenges, his commitment to his work never wavered. "Day in and day out you have to do the story justice," he told Gonzalez and Estrin. "The Pulitzer is a huge honor. But it just reminds us why we do these things. It's the story that's more important than the accolades."

SUGGESTED READING

Berehulak, Daniel. "Interview: Daniel Berehulak on Afghanistan, India and Pakistan." Interview by Jeanette D. Moses. *American Photo*, 20 June 2014, www.americanphotomag.com/interview-daniel-berehulak-afghanistan-india-and-pakistan. Accessed 9 Sept. 2017.

Bicker, Phil. "Daniel Berehulak: The Freelancer's Way." *Time*, 18 June 2014, time.com/3810056/daniel-berehulak-the-freelancers-way/. Accessed 9 Sept. 2017.

"Bio." *Daniel Berehulak*, www.danielberehulak.com/about/1. Accessed 9 Sept. 2017.

Gonzalez, David, and James Estrin. "Photography Pulitzers Recognize Aftermath of Violence Here and Abroad." *The New York Times*, 10 Apr. 2017, lens.blogs.nytimes.com/2017/04/10/photography-pulitzers-recognize-aftermath-of-violence-here-and-abroad. Accessed 9 Sept. 2017.

Kembrey, Melanie. "Pulitzer Prize-Winning Australian Photo-Journalist Daniel Berehulak Eager to 'Get Out There.'" *The Sydney Morning Herald*, 28 Apr. 2015, www.smh.com.au/entertainment/pulitzer-prizewinning-australian-photojournalist-daniel-berehulak-eager-to-get-out-there-20150423-1mrknh.html. Accessed 9 Sept. 2017.

—*Christopher Mari*

David Paul Morris/Bloomberg/Getty Images

Kayvon Beykpour

Date of birth: October 11, 1988
Occupation: Cofounder of Periscope

In 2013, protests were taking place in Taksim Square in Istanbul, Turkey. Although he was able to read about the protests through websites such as Twitter, American entrepreneur Kayvon Beykpour found himself wishing he could see the events that were unfolding for himself. "I wondered why I can't see what's happening right now somewhere in the world," he recalled to Troy McMullen for the *Financial Times* (28 Sept. 2016). "The initial seed of Periscope was born right there and then." Inspired by those ideas, Beykpour partnered with childhood friend Joe Bernstein to develop Periscope, a smartphone app that allowed its users to broadcast live, streaming video from anywhere with an Internet or data connection. With its potential to reshape the way people interact with faraway events, the app drew the attention of Twitter, which acquired the startup before the app was even released.

Although still in his mid-twenties at the time of the sale, Beykpour was already an established entrepreneur, having cofounded the company Terriblyclever Design while in college. Beykpour and his cofounders sold that company, which developed smartphone applications for universities, to the educational technology company Blackboard in 2009. With Periscope, however, Beykpour and his colleagues not only created a successful app but also tapped into an increasing desire to see real life as it was occurring. Since Periscope's launch, the app has been used to broadcast events ranging from a person's everyday life to major protests similar to those that sparked the idea in Beykpour. While often used for entertainment, the app soon took on political significance, allowing citizen journalists to provide on-the-ground views of events such as the Black Lives Matter protests in the United States. For Beykpour, watching Periscope become a success has been a thrilling experience. "It's been a whirlwind, it's been amazing, it's been surreal and we find ourselves continuing to go to bed and wake up every morning really excited to build the thing that we sought to create out of nothing," he told Lance Ulanoff for *Mashable* (9 Apr. 2016).

EARLY LIFE AND EDUCATION

Beykpour was born on October 11, 1988, in California. His parents, who moved to the United States from Iran in the 1970s while they were still in their teens, were both entrepreneurs at various points in Beykpour's life: His father sold rugs with his paternal grandfather, while his mother established a home-based daycare center. Beykpour grew up in Mill Valley, a city north of San Francisco, where he attended local schools. As a teenager, Beykpour attended Tamalpais High School in Mill Valley, where he participated in the school's Academy of Integrated Humanities and New Media program. He graduated from high school in 2006.

Beykpour developed an interest in computer technology when he was as young as five years old, when his father brought home the family's first computer. He soon began experimenting with technology with childhood friends and later colleagues Aaron Wasserman and Joe Bernstein, and the trio created their first website while in sixth grade. Following the advent of smartphones, Beykpour learned to create applications for those devices as well, developing his first apps while in his late teens. In addition to computer technology, Beykpour was an avid photographer and filmmaker, and he won multiple regional Student Emmy Awards for his work.

After high school, Beykpour enrolled at Stanford University to study computer science, specializing in human-computer interaction. As a student, he devoted a portion of his time to completing internships with technology companies such as Autodesk, and he also took on freelance web development and related work for the marketing firm Goodby, Silverstein & Partners. Beykpour earned his bachelor's degree from Stanford in 2010.

TERRIBLYCLEVER DESIGN

While in college, Beykpour and several of his friends, including Bernstein and Wasserman, partnered to launch the company Terriblyclever Design. Officially founded in 2007, the company focused on developing mobile applications, particularly apps that could be used by college students. The company's flagship app, initially known as iStanford, linked into the university's computer system and enabled students to access school systems for class scheduling, check their locations on campus maps, and perform other useful tasks. The app proved successful among Stanford students, and after attracting significant attention off campus, it was named one of the best new inventions of 2008 by *Time* magazine. Having proved that the app functioned as expected through its use at Stanford, Beykpour and his partners next sought to bring their app, which became known as MobileEdu, to other colleges and universities, establishing agreements with a number of institutions.

Although Beykpour and his partners had succeeded in building their company from the ground up, they soon decided to sell it, accepting a $4 million offer from the educational technology company Blackboard in 2009. Following the acquisition, Beykpour joined Blackboard as head of its mobile division, overseeing further efforts to bring education-related technology to mobile devices such as smartphones. He also served as a member of the senior executive team. Over the course of his tenure at Blackboard, Beykpour helped make Blackboard's apps some of the most-downloaded apps in both the iTunes app store and Android devices' Google Play store. He remained with Blackboard for over four years, departing in December 2013.

Although the sale of Terriblyclever was a major financial coup for a group of college students, Beykpour later expressed regrets over the sale. "After we left, that company went through a pretty big transition (after a private equity takeover) and much of what we built (the spirit, product) slowly died, which was very painful to watch," he told Jonathan Chew for *Fortune* (25 Sept. 2015) when asked about the lowest moment in his career.

PERISCOPE

An entrepreneur at heart, Beykpour soon began work on his next project. Inspired by the desire to see live video feeds of events occurring far away, Beykpour and Bernstein began to develop a new app that would allow users to stream live video of whatever subject they chose, from everyday sights to extraordinary events. They began working on the app in early 2014, initially dubbing it Bounty before changing the name to Periscope. Initial funding for the project came from a number of angel investors, individuals who provide funds for startups, typically in exchange for partial ownership of the company in question.

Prior to the app's official launch, Beykpour met with Jessica Verrilli, a Stanford alumna who worked for the social networking site Twitter. Beykpour decided to show Verrilli what he and Bernstein had been working on, a choice that would prove key to Periscope's future success. "She was very complimentary and said, 'What you guys are working on is so important for the world, and you have done a beautiful job, do you mind if I connect you with some people?'" he recalled to Joshi Herrmann for the *Evening Standard* (14 May 2015). "I asked who. And she said 'Jack Dorsey and Dick Costolo' [Twitter's cofounder and CEO]. And I said 'I probably can make time to meet those two people.'"

Founded in 2006, Twitter enabled users to post short messages, known as tweets, from anywhere, thus providing users with an unfiltered glimpse in the lives of people from all over the world. Periscope, with its democratization of live streaming, served a similar purpose, and Twitter's executives identified the app's potential and strong fit with their company's mission. Beykpour agreed with that assessment. "I think about the purpose of Periscope in this world is to show you the world in real-time and, to me, that's what Twitter does," he explained to Ulanoff. "It gives you a pulse of the world through 140 characters. It lets the voiceless have a voice. And Periscope is the same thing, but the medium is live video, rather than tweets with pictures and videos and 140 characters." In early 2015, Twitter acquired Periscope, bringing Beykpour, Bernstein, and their team in to run the company. While neither Twitter nor Periscope publicly announced the terms of the deal, industry journalists estimated that the purchase price may have been between $75 million and $120 million.

The Periscope app launched in March 2015, as Beykpour and his team waited to see how it would be received. "We pressed the release button on the app store at about midnight, and over the course of the next few hours we saw Europe wake up," he told Herrmann. "People in Paris, Germany, and Belgium—you could just see people finding the app for the first time." As users tried out the app for the first time, Periscope's creators, and users viewing others' video streams, were treated to a variety of new and exciting sights. "That morning we saw someone in a hot-air balloon witnessing sunrise in Cappadocia, Turkey, which is just one of the most beautiful things," Beykpour recalled to Herrmann.

LIVE-STREAMING LEADER

Although the core idea behind Periscope was a revolutionary one, the company was far from the first to offer a simple live-streaming solution to its users. Indeed, the app Meerkat, launched slightly prior to Periscope, experienced initial success prior to shutting down in October 2016, and the social network Facebook soon entered the field as well. Beykpour, however, was undaunted by such competition. "One of the nice things about starting a company like Periscope at the time that we did is that we knew from the beginning that we would not be the first," he explained to Ulanoff. "We didn't want to be the first, we weren't the first. There was a graveyard of other companies and active companies that did live video broadcasting even at a time when we started thinking about Periscope."

Perhaps one of the most significant factors in Periscope's success was the cultural era in which it was released. "It's a lot harder to succeed in this space when there isn't cultural appetite for the type of medium that you are building," Beykpour told Ulanoff. "Imagine if we had tried to launch Periscope at a cultural time when people weren't comfortable having phones out in front of them taking pictures or shooting video for that matter." Indeed, in the time since Periscope's launch, a variety of individuals and news outlets have raised privacy concerns about the app, while some mainstream content providers have sought to crack down on illegal broadcasts of copyrighted material that have at times occurred through Periscope. Nevertheless, the app's benefits have far outweighed its drawbacks as it enables anyone, regardless of technological capabilities or social media following, to stream snippets of their lives to anyone who is interested.

PERSONAL LIFE

Beykpour lives in the Telegraph Hill neighborhood of San Francisco, California. In addition to computer science, he remains interested in photography and film and is also a fan of board games, particularly strategy games such as Settlers of Catan and Cyclades. "I bring them out every time I have people over and we can play for hours," he told McMullen.

SUGGESTED READING

Beykpour, Kayvon. "Periscope Interview: Founder Kayvon Beykpour on Helping Create the Livestreaming Phenomenon." Interview by Andrew Griffin. *The Independent*, 22 June 2016, www.independent.co.uk/life-style/gadgets-and-tech/periscope-app-what-is-it-live-streaming-founder-interview-kayvon-beykpour-a7095981.html. Accessed 19 Dec. 2016.

Herrmann, Joshi. "Periscope's Kayvon Beykpour on Scoping Out a Social Media Sensation." *Evening Standard*, 14 May 2015, www.standard.co.uk/lifestyle/london-life/periscopes-kayvon-beykpour-on-scoping-out-a-social-media-sensation-10249651.html. Accessed 19 Dec. 2016.

McMullen, Troy. "Periscope App Chief on San Francisco and Rivalry with Facebook." *Financial Times*, 28 Sept. 2016, www.ft.com/content/1f88edc2-80a3-11e6-8e50-8ec15fb462f4. Accessed 19 Dec. 2016.

Shontell, Alyson. "What It's Like to Sell Your Startup for ~$120 Million before It's Even Launched: Meet Twitter's New Prized Possession, Periscope." *Business Insider*, 26 Mar. 2016, www.businessinsider.com/what-is-periscope-and-why-twitter-bought-it-2015-3. Accessed 19 Dec. 2016.

Ulanoff, Lance. "Up Periscope: Inside Twitter's One-Year-Old Broadcast Startup." *Mashable*, 9 Apr. 2016, mashable.com/2016/04/09/periscope-kayvon-beykpour. Accessed 19 Dec. 2016.

—Joy Crelin

Massimo Bottura

Date of birth: September 30, 1962
Occupation: Chef

In mid-2016, Osteria Francescana in Modena, Italy, was judged to be the very best restaurant in the entire world in an annual competition voted on by some one thousand food critics from around the globe. That distinction, according to a press release by William Reed Business Media, which publishes *Restaurant* magazine and which oversees the contest, is due largely to chef Massimo Bottura's "ongoing creativity, immense skill, undimmed passion and fierce determination to defy the odds."

Diners at Osteria Francescana can expect such signature dishes as the "Five Ages of Parmigiano Reggiano," which features the cheese in various guises, including a creamy sauce, a soufflé, and a crunchy wafer, and "An Eel Swimming up the Po River," which consists of artfully glazed Adriatic eel, served with polenta and apple jelly. As the names imply, Bottura's dishes are meant to evoke specific experiences and emotions. Dana Cowin, a former editor of *Food & Wine* magazine, explained to Stephanie Kirchgaessner for *The Guardian* (17 June 2016), "He is a poet of the land in which he lives and he takes the history of the country and the region and the ingredients and turns that into something that is a dish. Each dish tells a very complete story. . . . His food and thinking are lyrical. It is like the *Odyssey*." In a profile for *T: The New York Times Style Magazine* (17 Oct. 2016), Jeff Gordinier hit upon similar themes, writing, "He cooks food that's about Italy and family and history and memory and art, yes, but ultimately his eclectic platings and flavor combinations reflect the miasmic workings of his own mind."

Bottura has been influenced by such disparate figures as the jazz great Thelonious Monk (who inspired a dish of black cod in squid ink) and the artist Pablo Picasso (whose works led the chef to create a stew of wild hare in custard under a coating of powdered herbs). He does not shy away from placing himself among that continuum. "The chef of the future has a very important sense of responsibility," he asserted to Gordinier. "The contemporary chef is much more than the sum of his recipes."

EARLY YEARS AND EDUCATION

Massimo Bottura was born on September 30, 1962, in the small Italian city of Modena, located in the Po River Valley of Emilia-Romagna. The region is known for its iconic, traditional foods, including what are widely recognized as the world's finest Parmesan cheeses, prosciutto, and balsamic vinegars.

Venturelli/Getty Images for Gucci

Bottura's maternal grandmother had helped found a thriving fuel company, and after his mother, Luisa, married his father, Alfio (who himself hailed from a clan of wealthy landowners), her new husband took over his in-laws' business. Luisa and Alfio had one daughter and four sons; Bottura was the youngest of the boys. Although the family could easily afford household help, Luisa and her mother enjoyed cooking, and Bottura could often be found sitting under the kitchen table watching them roll out pasta dough or perform other kitchen tasks while stealing tastes—a source of endless amusement to his older brothers, who teased him mercilessly about his interest.

In high school, Bottura was part of a social circle known for their raucous parties, fashionable clothing, and love of fast cars and motorcycles. Thanks to the training he had absorbed in the family kitchen, he was acknowledged as the group's designated cook. When he joined the Italian military for a year of service, he enjoyed similar popularity—this time in large part because of his prowess on his unit's sports teams.

Because Alfio wanted to have a lawyer he could trust as part of the family fuel business, Bottura initially agreed to attend law school. Although he found some of his studies interesting, he never really felt he was making the right decision pursuing that profession. His unease intensified one day after he and Alfio fought about a minor business deal. "I started screaming and never went back," Bottura recalled to Jane Kramer for the *New Yorker* (4 Nov. 2013). "I pictured myself waking up, every morning, foggy, fighting with my father over one cent per litre of diesel gas."

LAUNCHING A CULINARY CAREER

Although he had little money, Bottura, who had continued to cook for friends after high school, decided to buy a small, struggling roadside restaurant not far from his childhood home. He was only in his early twenties when he took over Trattoria del Campazzo. "The chipped glasses were as old as the trucks outside, and everything else was brown and muddy yellow except the hideous gold-painted metal food trolley that he wheeled around," Kramer wrote of the establishment. Despite the dismal surroundings, his friends steadfastly came out night after night, and eventually a festive party atmosphere prevailed—particularly after some redecorating by Bottura's then-girlfriend.

Along with the atmosphere, the food improved as well, thanks in no small part to a local woman named Lidia Cristoni, whom Bottura immediately considered almost as important a culinary mentor as his mother and grandmother. Cristoni came to the restaurant each day, using hundreds of eggs at a time to make fresh pasta from scratch. Though he was still learning and building the business was stressful, Bottura remembers those early days fondly: "The way we were working at Campazzo was with a lot of heart, a lot of courage," he told Allan Jenkins for *The Guardian* (14 Sept. 2014). Additionally, he credits the mentorship of a French chef named Georges Cogny, who ran a restaurant, Locanda Cantoniera, in the village of Farini, two hours from Modena. On his days off, Bottura made the trek to cook in Cogny's kitchen and learn from him.

Bottura maintained a small apartment over Campazzo, and each night after dinner service had ended, the party migrated upstairs. It quickly became apparent that these gatherings were too large for the tiny apartment, and in 1989, he purchased a second establishment, this one near Modena's historic center. The Harley Club, as he dubbed it, was soon attracting the region's hottest bands and DJs. Despite the punishing schedule required to keep both businesses running, Bottura has told interviewers that he had never before been that happy.

After making the decision to sell the Harley Club and Campazzo and hoping to elevate his cooking further for a new restaurant, Bottura spent several months working in New York City, where he also met his future wife. Not long after returning to Italy, he was approached by the French chef Alain Ducasse, who was in Modena tasting balsamic vinegars and wandered into Campazzo for lunch. Ducasse invited the younger chef to come to the Hôtel de Paris in Monte Carlo to cook with him. Bottura accepted the invitation and learned a new meticulousness, along with classic techniques.

OSTERIA FRANCESCANA

In the fall of 1994 (a time, Kramer wrote, when "the words 'Italy' and 'new gastronomy' were an oxymoron"), Bottura rented and restored a tiny former inn on one of Modena's picturesque streets. Many of the locals were distrustful of the youthful chef and his avant-garde cuisine. They were, Kramer quipped, "convinced that no one could cook better than the way they had always cooked, meaning exactly the way their mothers and grandmothers, and all the mothers before them, had."

Osteria Francescana opened its doors the following year, and despite severe economic hardship and criticism, Bottura persevered, selling his motorcycle and sports car to pay the rent for the restaurant and enlisting the help of his new in-laws, as he could not approach his own disapproving father. His food continued to attract the attention of established chefs, and he once again had the opportunity to learn more not only about his approach to his food but also the running of a restaurant under the tutelage of Ferran Adrià at his Spanish establishment el-Bulli in the summer of 2000.

GAINING FAME

Then, in 2001, a leading Italian food writer became stuck in bad traffic and happened to stop at Osteria Francescana to eat. He penned an effusive review and other high-profile diners began flocking to Modena. Within a year, Osteria Francescana had earned its first Michelin star. The venerable *Michelin Guide* awards restaurants from zero to three stars, with three stars serving as the ultimate accolade, afforded only to those restaurants that offer "exceptional cuisine" that is "worth a special journey." The stars are highly sought after by chefs because the vast majority of restaurants never receive the honor; Osteria Francescana has held a three-star rating since 2012. Deciding to share his wisdom and experience after comfortably achieving this success, Bottura published *Never Trust a Skinny Italian Chef* (2014), a book containing fifty recipes accompanied by thorough explanations of his inspiration and methods.

Reviews of the restaurant remain almost universally rapturous, with many exploring the deeper meaning of Bottura's cuisine and his commitment to innovation. "Bottura describes his cooking as 'compressing passion into edible bites.' It's much more than that, of course— more like a complicated, and at times contentious, conversation with not just the history of Italian cuisine, but the Italian relationship with food," Gordinier wrote. "Bottura returns again and again to the crumbly cheese and cured meat and pockets of pasta and drizzles of aged vinegar of Modena, where he was born. But he does so by re-engineering the perfected recipes of grandmothers, or nonnas. . . . His cooking is both a love letter to his country and an overthrow of the rigidity that can hold it back."

FOOD MEETS PHILANTHROPY
Bottura has also been widely praised for his dedication to social causes. In 2012, after Emilia-Romagna was devastated by a series of earthquakes, more than three hundred thousand enormous wheels of Parmesan were damaged, and the industry was in danger of collapsing. Bottura quickly devised a risotto recipe calling for large amounts of the aromatic cheese and posted it online. Within months, large amounts of the cheese had been sold to eager cooks, saving the cheese makers from dire consequences and generating proceeds for the benefit of the earthquake victims.

In 2015, during the Milan Expo, Bottura collaborated with a Catholic charity to convert an abandoned theater building into an experimental soup kitchen, using leftovers from the exhibition to raise awareness about food waste. In 2016, during the Summer Olympics in Rio de Janeiro, he replicated that experience, enlisting other high-profile chefs to use food that would otherwise have been wasted to make meals for the poor. "Chefs don't need to rush to have the best caviar, the best truffle," he had told Adam Robb for *T: The New York Times Style Magazine* (26 May 2015) before the Milan Expo. "Emotions can be transferred from a crust of Parmigiano and leftover bread. Foraging for new ingredients is not important. Foraging for ideas, this is important."

PERSONAL LIFE
Bottura married Lara Gilmore, an American he met while working at the same café in the SoHo neighborhood of New York City, not long after opening Osteria Francescana in 1995. Together they have a daughter, Alexa, and a son, Charlie. Both children have inherited their father's love of cooking. Alexa is adept at making passatelli, a pasta dish containing bread crumbs, eggs, and grated Parmesan cheese, while Charlie's specialty is tortellini.

An avid fan of such classic jazz artists as Charlie Parker and Benny Goodman, Bottura has amassed an enormous collection of records. He further explained the importance of music, which also influences his work in the kitchen, as well as contemporary art, in his life to Gordinier, saying, "It's my energy. We cannot live without music, without art."

SUGGESTED READING
Gordinier, Jeff. "Massimo Bottura, the Chef behind the World's Best Restaurant." *T: The New York Times Style Magazine*, 17 Oct. 2016, www.nytimes.com/2016/10/17/t-magazine/massimo-bottura-chef-osteria-francescana.html. Accessed 2 Feb. 2017.

Jenkins, Allan. "Massimo Bottura: The Mercurial Chef Who Reinvented Italian Food." *The Guardian*, 14 Sept. 2014, www.theguardian.com/lifeandstyle/2014/sep/14/massimo-bottura-mercurial-chef-reinvented-italian-food. Accessed 2 Feb. 2017.

Kirchgaessner, Stephanie. "Massimo Bottura, the 'Poet' Chef with the Best Restaurant in the World." *The Guardian*, 17 June 2016, www.theguardian.com/lifeandstyle/2016/jun/17/massimo-bottura-chef-best-restaurant-osteria-francescana. Accessed 2 Feb. 2017.

Kramer, Jane. "Post-Modena." *New Yorker*, 4 Nov. 2013, www.newyorker.com/magazine/2013/11/04/post-modena. Accessed 2 Feb. 2017.

Palling, Bruce. "Massimo Bottura." *Wall Street Journal*, 14 Mar. 2013, www.wsj.com/articles/SB10001424127887323628804578348422312517906. Accessed 2 Feb. 2017.

Robb, Adam. "Massimo Bottura's Pope Francis-Approved Refectory, and Recipe to Turn Stale Bread into Gold." *T: The New York Times Style Magazine*, 26 May 2015, www.nytimes.com/2015/05/26/t-magazine/massimo-bottura-expo-milano-recipe.html. Accessed 2 Feb. 2017.

—*Mari Rich*

Sofia Boutella
Date of birth: April 1982
Occupation: Actor and dancer

For some actors, performing is less of a career option and more of a calling. Such is the case for actor Sofia Boutella, who left a successful career as a backup dancer to pursue work in film. "I knew acting was calling me," she told Kayla Tanenbaum for *Interview* magazine (5 Jan. 2015). "Whether I was good or not it didn't matter. I had to do it." Although risky, Boutella's career change paid off: after obtaining her breakout role as the villainous Gazelle in the spy film *Kingsman: The Secret Service*, abruptly she seemed to be everywhere, costarring in major films such as *Star Trek Beyond* and *The Mummy*.

Born in Algeria, where she began studying ballet as a small child, Boutella evolved significantly as a dancer after moving to France during the Algerian Civil War. Taking up gymnastics as well as hip-hop and street dance, she quickly impressed choreographers and audiences with her dance skills and in 2006 began touring with Madonna. Boutella's talent as a dancer was put

Matthias Nareyek/WireImage for Getty Images

on display at the 2012 Super Bowl, where she performed during Madonna's halftime show, and her command of movement and timing made her performances in action-oriented films such as *Kingsman* and the 2017 spy film *Atomic Blonde* particularly dynamic. For Boutella, her path to stardom has been a rewarding yet surprising one. "I would have been happy just doing smaller movies," she told Kaleem Aftab for the *Independent* (13 Dec. 2016). "I think I got lucky."

EARLY LIFE AND EDUCATION

Boutella was born in April 1982 in Algiers, Algeria. Her father, Safy Boutella, was a well-known jazz musician, while her mother was an architect. Her brother, Seïf, went on to become a visual effects artist. Boutella grew up in the Bab el Oued neighborhood of Algiers, where her family lived in a home with what she described to Emily Baxter for *Harper's Bazaar Arabia* (1 June 2017) as a "big, dishevelled garden."

In 1992, following the start of the Algerian Civil War, Boutella's family moved to France, settling in Paris. Only ten years old at the time, Boutella did not fully understand the significance of the events that were taking place. "It's hard for a ten-year-old to understand the complexity of a civil war and what it means," she told Aftab. "At that age moving to Paris meant that I would get access to more candy and toys. Then in my adolescence, I realised what it meant, especially for my parents to move at their age and how lucky I was." Although she experienced culture shock initially, Boutella soon made friends from a variety of backgrounds.

Growing up in a household that prioritized music and art, Boutella began dancing at an early age and soon developed a passion for it. "As a child I would say that I wanted to become a dancer to honour music," she explained to Aftab. "For me, dancing is the physical translation of the audio recording." At the age of five, Boutella began studying ballet with local dancers who had trained with Russia's prestigious Bolshoi Ballet. Following her family's move to Paris, she began to study jazz and hip-hop styles of dance as well. Boutella likewise began to practice the sport of rhythmic gymnastics and competed on the national level.

DANCE CAREER

Pursuing a career in dance as a young adult, Boutella found herself particularly drawn to hip-hop and street dance styles. "I wanted to be left alone to dance freely, to dance the way that I felt and the way that I wanted," she recalled to Baxter. "So I went and explored and came across some breakdancers and freestylers one day and it just spoke to me. There are no rules to it." Among various other dance gigs during her early career, Boutella starred in the 2002 musical comedy film *Dance Challenge*, released as *Le défi* in France and directed by noted choreographer Blanca Li.

In 2005, Boutella reached a major career milestone when she was chosen to perform in a commercial for the Nike Women line of exercise apparel. The commercial, which featured Boutella breakdancing, was created in partnership with Jamie King, a celebrity choreographer who had a longstanding relationship with pop icon Madonna. Having been brought to King's and Madonna's attention, Boutella was soon hired as a backup dancer for the singer. During the Confessions Tour, an international series of performances publicizing Madonna's 2005 album *Confessions on a Dance Floor*, Boutella and her fellow dancers accompanied the singer throughout North America, Europe, and Japan. She likewise appeared in music videos for several singles from *Confessions on a Dance Floor*, including "Hung Up" and "Sorry."

For Boutella, the process of dancing for Madonna was more than a typical performance. "When you work with her, she has a story behind the steps. We're not just dancers; she always considers her dancers actors," she explained to Tanenbaum. "When I worked with her, she always explained to me why that piece existed, what she wanted to portray. That made me perform the piece on a whole new level than when we were just counting and being musical." After the Confessions Tour, Boutella again performed with Madonna during the Sticky & Sweet Tour in 2008 and 2009. The tour's schedule prevented Boutella from accepting a position as a backup dancer on singer Michael Jackson's This Is It tour, which was ultimately canceled following Jackson's 2009 death. She later went on to star in the 2011 music video for "Hollywood Tonight," a song from Jackson's posthumous album *MICHAEL.* She continued to work with Madonna as well, performing with the singer at the Super Bowl XLVI halftime show in 2012.

TRANSITION TO ACTING

Throughout much of her career as a dancer, Boutella was intrigued by the art of acting. In addition to *Dance Challenge,* she landed a part in the French television movie *Permis d'aimer (Permit Love* 2005) early in her career and went on to study acting at the prestigious Stella Adler Academy of Acting in Los Angeles. In 2012, Boutella played the role of Eva, a salsa dancer who becomes involved in a conflict between rival street dance crews, in the film *StreetDance 2.* Although skilled in various styles of dance, Boutella had no experience with salsa and had the challenging responsibility of mastering the style in only three months. "It was really challenging but really exciting as well as I had to do the work of an actor to really fully explore the character of the film," she told Dean Woodhouse for *MOBO* (*Music of Black Origin*) (30 Aug. 2012). "It made perfect sense for these two dances [salsa and street] to come together as they are so alike."

That year, Boutella decided to stop dancing full time and instead focus on finding work as an actor. The decision was a difficult one, as Boutella was well aware that she could go months or even years without finding work. When an opportunity arose, it came as a surprise. "I woke up one morning at about nine a.m. and I had emails from my agent, saying there's this audition. It [the audition] was the same day at one p.m.," she told Tanenbaum. "The next day they said, 'You're flying this afternoon to audition for [director] Matthew Vaughn. Pack for five months because if you book it, you'll stay, and if not you'll fly back the next day.'" Boutella ultimately claimed the role of Gazelle, a deadly associate of villain Richmond Valentine (Samuel L. Jackson), in the spy film *Kingsman: The Secret Service.* Although Boutella had previously performed for wide audiences at events such as the Super Bowl, *Kingsman* served to introduce her as an actor to moviegoers in the United States and worldwide following its premiere in January 2015 and wide release in February.

In addition to the memorable role of Gazelle, Boutella's early roles included parts in smaller, often independently produced films such as the science-fiction thriller *Monsters: Dark Continent* (2014) and the 2016 crime dramas *Jet Trash* and *Tiger Raid.* For Boutella, independent projects were just as appealing as major films such as *Kingsman*—and potentially even more so. "I

don't necessarily want to be defined as an action star," she told Clarisse Loughrey for the *Independent* (6 June 2017). "I love movies, and my movie culture, luckily because of my parents and my family, is quite obscure and independent."

MAJOR FILMS

Following her breakthrough role in *Kingsman,* Boutella quickly came to be viewed as an up-and-coming actor to watch. Beginning with 2016's *Star Trek Beyond,* she appeared in major roles in a string of films that brought her significant widespread recognition among moviegoers. In *Star Trek Beyond,* the third film in the rebooted Star Trek franchise, Boutella plays an alien scavenger named Jaylah who assists the crew of the USS *Enterprise* in defeating a powerful threat. Although reviews of the film were mixed, critics generally praised Boutella's performance as Jaylah as engaging and humorous.

In 2017, Boutella starred in *The Mummy,* a new take on the often-rebooted monster film and the proposed start of a film franchise dubbed the Dark Universe. Filling the titular role, Boutella plays an ancient Egyptian pharaoh named Ahmanet who sells her soul in an attempt to claim the throne that she believes to be rightfully hers. Millennia after being buried alive for her crimes, she is accidentally released and wreaks havoc in London. In preparing for the role, Boutella sought to identify Ahmanet's character and motivations and drew a great deal of inspiration from actor Boris Karloff, who played the mummy in the original 1932 incarnation of the film. "He had this humanity in the way he acted that made all these characters so fascinating to watch," she told Aftab. "With me playing 'The Mummy' I thought I needed to find that quality because playing a monster is not enough, we need to find why monsters are monsters."

Boutella is also one of the stars of *Atomic Blonde,* a Cold War–era action film based on the acclaimed 2012 graphic novel *The Coldest City* by Antony Johnston. In addition to Boutella, who plays a French spy named Delphine, the film stars Charlize Theron and James McAvoy. The film, which Boutella described to Loughrey as "a fun ride," premiered at the SXSW Film Festival in March 2017 and was released in theaters in July of that year.

PERSONAL LIFE

Boutella lives in Los Angeles with her boyfriend, actor Robert Sheehan, whom she met on location for *Jet Trash.*

SUGGESTED READING

Aftab, Kaleem. "*Jet Trash*'s Sofia Boutella Interview." *The Independent,* 13 Dec. 2016, www.independent.co.uk/arts-entertainment/films/features/

sofia-boutella-jet-trash-charles-henri-bel-leville-the-mummy-tom-cruise-a7472496. html. Accessed 14 July 2017.

Baxter, Emily. "Meet Sofia Boutella: *Bazaar's* June Cover Star." *Harper's Bazaar Arabia*, 1 June 2017, harpersbazaararabia.com/fashion/editorials/sofia-boutella-is-bazaars-june-cover-star. Accessed 14 July 2017.

Boutella, Sofia. "The Comic Book Villain." Interview by Kayla Tanenbaum. *Interview*, 5 Jan. 2015, www.interviewmagazine.com/film/sofia-boutella-15-faces-of-2015#_. Accessed 14 July 2017.

Boutella, Sofia. *"Kingsman: The Secret Service*—Interview with Sofia Boutella." Interview by John T. Chance. *FLUX*, 28 May 2015, www.fluxmagazine.com/interview-with-sofia-boutella. Accessed 14 July 2017.

Boutella, Sofia. "Sofia Boutella Interview." Interview by Dean Woodhouse. *MOBO*, 30 Aug. 2012, www.mobo.com/news-blogs/sofia-boutella-interview. Accessed 14 July 2017.

Loughrey, Clarisse. *"The Mummy* Interview: Sofia Boutella on Breathing New Life into a Classic Monster." *The Independent*, 6 June 2017, www.independent.co.uk/arts-entertainment/films/features/the-mummy-interview-sofia-boutella-ahmanet-backstory-tom-cruise-universal-monsters-universe-sequel-a7775066. html. Accessed 14 July 2017.

Morgan, Philippa. "Algerian Actress Sofia Boutella on Her Meteoric Rise in Hollywood." *Vogue Arabia*, 2 May 2017, en.vogue.me/culture/sofia-boutella-interview-vogue-arabia. Accessed 14 July 2017.

SELECTED WORKS

StreetDance 2, 2012; *Kingsman: The Secret Service*, 2015; *Star Trek Beyond*, 2016; *Tiger Raid*, 2016; *Jet Trash*, 2016; *The Mummy*, 2017; *Atomic Blonde*, 2017

—*Joy Crelin*

Sônia Braga

Date of birth: June 8, 1950
Occupation: Actor

Film critic John Powers, writing for *Vogue* (14 Oct. 2016), called Sônia Braga "the greatest Brazilian film star since banana-hatted Carmen Miranda in the 1930s and 1940s." Braga made a name for herself in such films as *Dona Flor e seus dois maridos* (*Dona Flor and Her Two Husbands*, 1976) and the Oscar-nominated *Kiss of the Spider Woman* (1985). She worked steadily in American film and television throughout the 1980s, 1990s, and 2000s. Her work ran the gamut of genre;

Photo by Carlos Alvarez/Getty Images

she was in an action movie called *The Rookie* (1990), starring Clint Eastwood and Charlie Sheen, and, in 2005, played a KGB assassin in J. J. Abrams's television series *Alias*, starring Jennifer Garner. Braga also made a guest appearance on three episodes of the television show *Sex and the City* in 2001, playing the girlfriend of one of the show's regular characters, Samantha. Despite her impressive oeuvre, Braga has said she is most proud of *Aquarius* (2016), her first Portuguese-language film in over a decade. In it, Braga plays a retired music critic named Clara who, in fighting the developers that have come to buy her old apartment, must reckon with her past. The film is seen as an oblique metaphor for political upheaval in Brazil; this aspect attracted Braga, who was considering her retirement when she received director Kleber Mendonça Filho's script for the film. "I was content doing photography, going for walks, and being happy in life," she told Pam Grady for the *San Francisco Chronicle* (20 Oct. 2016). "I hadn't had a screenplay for the lead in so long and then comes 'Aquarius.' I hadn't done anything in my tongue, in Portuguese. I had so many big issues with Brazil, and there it is, a platform to be able to talk about it." Braga is deeply connected to her country; she famously addressed Brazilians, speaking in Portuguese, when she presented an Academy Award with actor Michael Douglas in 1987.

Braga has earned three Golden Globe nominations and an Emmy nomination; many critics were disappointed when she was not nominated for an Academy Award for *Aquarius*. Braga told Nigel M. Smith for the *Guardian* (9 Mar. 2017) that she was not surprised, saying "The Oscars really only have four spaces for best actress, because one is always reserved for Meryl Streep." She also commented on the dearth of roles for women, particularly older women and women of color. "I'm Latina: I don't see my representation [in Hollywood]," she told Smith. "Not just as a sixty-six-year-old woman, as a person. Where is it?"

EARLY LIFE

Braga was born in Maringá, in the Brazilian state of Paraná, on June 8, 1950. Her father, who was of African and Portuguese descent, was a land broker. Her mother, Maria José, who was of European and indigenous Brazilian descent, was a seamstress. She has six siblings, several of whom have gone on to pursue artistic careers. Sister Ana Braga and brother Julio Braga are also actors; Ana's daughter is actor Alice Braga. Another brother, Helio Braga, is an artist. The family moved to São Paulo, but then, when Braga was eight years old, her father died suddenly of a heart attack or stroke. "I don't have many memories from when I was little, but he loved reading, my father did," Braga told Grady. "There was a bookshelf at home. When my father died, we lost everything. We didn't have money, nothing, but we kept the books." The family divided household chores and one of Braga's tasks was to clean the bookshelf. She would take the books down and read them, imagining that her father was reading to her.

When she was fourteen years old, Braga began playing small roles in television shows, including a role as a princess on the children's show *Jardim encantado* (Enchanted garden), which was presented by her brother Helio. When she was eighteen years old, she joined the original cast of the first Brazilian production of the musical *Hair*.

DONA FLOR AND HER TWO HUSBANDS

Braga appeared in Brazilian soap operas, or telenovelas, throughout the early 1970s, but became an international star after appearing in the 1976 comedy *Dona Flor and Her Two Husbands*. The film, directed by Bruno Barreto, is based on a 1966 novel of the same name by Jorge Amado. Braga plays Dona Flor, a widow who has remarried but is haunted by the ghost of her deadbeat first husband. He was an abusive gambler, but Dona Flor misses making love to him. The central plot of the film revolves around her juggling of her two husbands, one alive and one dead. The film is considered a classic of Brazilian cinema.

Dona Flor and Her Two Husbands cemented Braga's "type" as a sensual siren. In 1981, she starred in the sexy drama *I Love You*, about a woman named Maria who seeks a sexual encounter with a wealthy industrialist (he owns a factory that makes bras) to stave off her loneliness, only to eventually fall in love with him. The film won praise when it premiered at the Cannes Film Festival. In 1983, Braga worked with director Barreto again, starring in the film *Gabriela*, based on Amado's 1958 novel *Gabriela, cravo e canela* (*Gabriela, Clove and Cinnamon*, 1962). Braga first played the character of Gabriela in a Brazilian telenovela in the 1970s. In the film, Gabriela, an impoverished refugee of a drought, takes a job as a cook for a bar owner named Nacib. Their romance is curtailed by the conservative mores of the town. "Braga's performance in 'Gabriela' depends not so much upon her sexuality . . . as upon her winning smile, her tomboy grace, and the cool self-confidence with which she plays a character who is required to seethe [with lust] on demand," Roger Ebert wrote in a review reproduced on his website, *RogerEbert. com* (27 June 1984).

KISS OF THE SPIDER WOMAN

Another of Braga's best-known films is *Kiss of the Spider Woman* (1985), based on the 1976 novel by Argentinian novelist Manuel Puig. The film was written by American screenwriter Leonard Schrader and directed by Brazilian director Hector Babenco. In it, a Brazilian political prisoner named Valentin Arregui, played by Puerto Rican actor Raúl Juliá, shares a jail cell with Luis Molina, a gay movie buff, played by American actor William Hurt. (Hurt won an Oscar for his performance.) Hurt's character describes to his cellmate the plots of his favorite films in great detail to pass the time. Babenco intersperses scenes of these fictional films, which feature Braga as a 1940s movie star. As Janet Maslin wrote for the *New York Times* (26 July 1985), "Several films-within-the-film, illustrating Molina's movie descriptions and starring . . . Braga as a satirically elegant grande dame, serve as refracted images of the main action, couching the larger film's concerns with love and honor in witty, deliberately clichéd terms." *Kiss of the Spider Woman* was a breakthrough independent film, one of the first to achieve mainstream success with both critics and audiences. It premiered at the Cannes Film Festival in 1985 and was nominated for four Academy Awards, including best picture. Braga was nominated for a Golden Globe.

In 1988, Braga appeared in a comedy called *The Milagro Beanfield War*, a fable about the environment and cultural extinction. The film, based on a 1974 John Nichols novel of the same name, was directed by Robert Redford. The same year, Braga appeared in a romantic comedy called *Moon over Parador*, about a failed New York actor turned dictator of a fictional Latin American country. The film stars Richard Dreyfuss, who is thrust into his role as fake dictator when the real dictator dies. Braga earned a Golden Globe nomination for her role as the dead dictator's mistress. In 1990, Braga appeared in a buddy cop action comedy called *The Rookie*. Clint Eastwood starred in and directed the film. Braga plays a villain, and, in one infamous scene, sexually assaults Eastwood's character while he is tied to a chair. The film was poorly received by critics.

THE BURNING SEASON AND OTHER WORKS

In 1994 Braga was nominated for another Golden Globe Award and an Emmy Award for her role in the HBO film *The Burning Season*, about Brazilian environmentalist Chico Mendes. Mendes worked as a rubber tapper and led the fight to unionize workers and preserve the dying rainforest in the 1970s and 1980s. The film chronicles the years before his assassination in 1988. Braga played Regina de Carvalho, an ally of Mendes. The film was praised by American critics, but was less popular with Brazilians. Brazilian filmgoers criticized the film's decision to expunge Mendes's Communist education, as well as its lack of Brazilian actors. Braga is the only Brazilian actor who appears in the film. In 1995 Braga appeared in the miniseries *Streets of Laredo*, an adaptation of Larry McMurtry's 1993 novel of the same name.

In 2001 Braga played Jennifer Lopez's mother in the drama *Angel Eyes*. That same year, Braga made her crowd-pleasing guest appearance as Maria, a Brazilian artist, on three episodes of *Sex and the City*. In 2002 she played a Mexican immigrant named Berta Gonzalez on the PBS television series *American Family*. She then appeared as a former KGB agent on the J. J. Abrams's action drama series *Alias* in 2005. In 2016 she signed on to play the mother of Rosario Dawson's character on Marvel's Netflix series *Luke Cage*.

In *Aquarius*, Braga plays a woman named Clara, based on the director's mother. Clara is a widow with grown children. She is also the last resident of an apartment building in Recife, Brazil, called the Aquarius. Clara fights to stay in her home as developers fight to buy her out of it. Many critics saw the film's story as a metaphor for Brazilian political resistance. The film itself became an emblem of that resistance after Braga and director Mendonça Filho protested the impeachment of Brazilian president Dilma Rousseff at the Cannes Film Festival. In the wake of their political statement, Brazil chose not to enter *Aquarius* into Oscar contention.

Despite the painful snub, the film, and Braga's performance, were widely celebrated. Peter Bradshaw, writing for the *Guardian* (23 Mar. 2017), called Braga's portrayal of the complicated Clara "her finest hour," while Ann Hornaday, for the *Washington Post* (20 Oct. 2016)

wrote, "As a showcase for Braga, 'Aquarius' is nothing less than triumphant, a one-woman show of strength, sensuality and indomitable staying power."

PERSONAL LIFE

Braga lives in the East Village neighborhood of New York City.

SUGGESTED READING

Bradshaw, Peter. "'Aquarius' Review—Sônia Braga Brilliant as a Widow on the Warpath." Review of *Aquarius*, directed by Kleber Mendonça Filho. *The Guardian*, 23 Mar. 2017, www.theguardian.com/film/2017/mar/23/aquarius-review-sonia-braga-filho. Accessed 14 Aug. 2017.

Ebert, Roger. Review of *Gabriela*, directed by Bruno Barreto. *RogerEbert.com*, 27 June 1984, www.rogerebert.com/reviews/gabriela-1984. Accessed 13 Aug. 2017.

Grady, Pam. "Sonia Braga Returns to Starring Roles with 'Aquarius.'" *San Francisco Chronicle*, 20 Oct. 2016, www.sfchronicle.com/movies/article/Sonia-Braga-returns-to-starring-roles-with-9992064.php. Accessed 13 Aug. 2017.

Hornaday, Ann. "Sonia Braga Makes a Triumphant Return to the Screen in 'Aquarius.'" Review of *Aquarius*, directed by Kleber Mendonça Filho. *The Washington Post*, 20 Oct. 2016, www.washingtonpost.com/goingoutguide/movies/sonia-braga-makes-a-triumphant-return-to-the-screen-in-aquarius/2016/10/20/0966195e-948d-11e6-bb29-bf2701dbe0a3_story.html. Accessed 14 Aug. 2017.

Maslin, Janet. Review of *Kiss of the Spider Woman*, directed by Hector Babenco. *The New York Times*, 26 July 1985, www.nytimes.com/movie/review?res=9407E6D81238F935A15754C0A963948260. Accessed 14 Aug. 2017.

Powers, John. "Sonia Braga on Finding the Best Role of her Career in *Aquarius*." *Vogue*, 14 Oct. 2017, www.vogue.com/article/sonia-braga-interview-aquarius-movie. Accessed 13 Aug. 2017.

Smith, Nigel M. "Sônia Braga: 'The Oscars Only Have Four Spaces for Best Actress—One Is Always Reserved for Meryl Streep." *The Guardian*, 9 Mar. 2017, www.theguardian.com/film/2017/mar/09/sonia-braga-aquarius-hollywood-meryl-streep-hsipanic. Accessed 13 Aug. 2017.

SELECTED WORKS

Dona Flor and Her Two Husbands, 1976; *Gabriela*, 1983; *Kiss of the Spider Woman*, 1985; *The Burning Season*, 1994; *Sex and the City*, 2001; *American Family*, 2002; *Alias*, 2005; *Aquarius*, 2016

—*Molly Hagan*

Janicza Bravo

Date of birth: February 25, 1981
Occupation: Writer, director

Janicza Bravo's film *Gregory Go Boom* won the 2014 Sundance Film Festival Short Film Jury Award in the category of US fiction. In May 2013, YouTube hosted Comedy Week, and the film was shown on star Michael Cera's channel. As a woman of color working in the arts, Bravo has experienced difficulty, as she told Melina Gills for the website of the Tribeca Film Festival (23 Mar. 2016) "When I was working on costumes, I would be the only person on the set who was a person of color. I'm talking about a set of anywhere from 50 to 200 people. It starts behind the scenes as well. The question of diversity is a question of who is putting the work together. It's a much larger conversation, and it's about making changes behind as well as in front of the camera."

Photo by Robby Klein/Getty Images Portrait

EDUCATION AND EARLY CAREER

Janicza Michelle Bravo Ford spent her first thirteen years in Panama; her parents are Ana Maria Ford and Rafael Angel Landers. She then moved to the United States during the 1990s. She was prom queen and voted most popular at her high school.

At New York University's (NYU) Playwright's Horizons Theater School, she studied both directing and design for theater. Of the influence of theater on the way she makes films, Bravo told Danielle Massie for Fusion Film Festival (1 Mar. 2014), "I am deeply grateful for my theatre background. It influences all of my choices from framing to blocking to casting. I tend to grain towards wide shots and long takes with very little coverage. I like scenes to play out and breathe, which is definitely a result of my days back at Playwright Horizons."

Bravo received wardrobe or costume credits on more than thirty projects between 2009 and 2011. Taking on so much work was part of freelancing, where the workload is feast or famine, so people end up saying "yes" to every offer of work. As she explained to Conor Riley for *Oak* (15 Nov. 2016), "The sort of inherent problem with not getting to be totally curated about every move of your life when you're a person that doesn't have a ton of money is that you can exhaust yourself on work that is meaningless or work that is heartless, or work that takes you out of it. You kind of forget why you're in the thing in the first place."

One of Bravo's jobs was as wardrobe designer for the film *Notorious* (2009). Yet it was not the career path she envisioned. She explained to Anna Faktorovich for *Pennsylvania Literary Journal* (Spring 2014), "Styling was like waiting tables for me. It was an exhausting, sad making-a-living process and not enough. . . . That work didn't require that much of me. I'm a good shopper, I like clothes and I'm very good at what looks good on people." She was later able to leave that work for directing.

EAT AND *GREGORY GO BOOM*

Christian Sprenger, struck by Bravo's design for a production of *Miss Julie* by August Strindberg, encouraged Bravo to begin a career in film. As Bravo told Faktorovich, "He saw that play and sort of fell in love with how I saw things and pushed me to make a short [film] for him to shoot." He has subsequently shot all of her films.

Bravo's first short film was *Eat*, which she wrote and in which her partner, actor and comedian Brett Gelman, and Katherine Waterston starred. It premiered at the South by Southwest Film Festival (SXSW) in 2011. The film focuses on Gelman's character, a socially awkward man, trying to interact with a young woman who lives in the same building and has been locked out of her apartment. Bravo relies on Gelman and other actors she met while at New York University. As she explained to Faktorovich, "I deeply respect actors and think what they do is incredibly sensitive and raw so for me it's just a matter of finding the right fit."

Bravo's next film, *Gregory Go Boom*, featured Michael Cera, an able-bodied actor in his twenties who convincingly portrayed a paraplegic teenager looking for love. The comedy collective Jash, founded by Michael Cera, Sarah Silverman, Tim Heidecker, Eric Wareheim, and

Reggie Watts, financed the film. Bravo and Gelman created the short after the lead actor for what became their first feature-length film quit and financing dried up. Because of the limited amount of funding for the short film, two of the actors were friends of Bravo's from NYU. In fact, the budget was so tight that they purchased a wheelchair and returned it a week later, after filming had been completed.

When it was screened at the Sundance Film Festival, the film drew criticism. As Bravo explained to Vadim Rizov for *Filmmaker Magazine* (2014), "Some aggressive things were said about me. That I was a bad person and insensitive, and that the film is a bleak picture of being paraplegic. But the film is not about being paraplegic; it's about being dismissed." The idea for the film began when Bravo observed a blind date in progress; clearly, the woman at the restaurant had not expected her date to arrive in a wheelchair. Bravo also drew on her own experiences of being overlooked as the less successful partner in a marriage and as a woman of color. When she visited Salton Sea, California's largest inland lake, she found her setting for the action of the film.

FURTHER WORK

Through connections Bravo made in filming *Gregory Go Boom*, she auditioned for Donald Glover and Hiro Murai, who were also more at home in theater and film. She told Kate Erbland for *IndieWire* (25 Jan. 2017), "Because they had also not done TV, that was a part of why they were attracted to me. They liked my short films. I feel so fortunate that they thought I could do it, because so much of this is about opportunity and unfortunately, women are not given that many opportunities." Bravo was subsequently hired to direct the "Juneteenth" episode of *Atlanta*, a Glover-Murai FX show.

Bravo's 2014 short film *Pauline Alone* featured a woman trying to meet and make connections with strangers in Los Angeles. Of that film, Bravo told Riley, "Most of the protagonists I'm interested in telling stories about are very similar to Pauline. They're people who feel alone. They feel like outcasts, they feel like society has kind of pushed them to the end. And some of them work really hard at trying to be socialized and others don't, but what they all have in common is that they don't have the tools."

EXPLORING VIRTUAL REALITY

In 2016 Bravo created *Hard World for Small Things*, a short fiction work, which premiered at the Tribeca Festival Hub. Seed&Spark, a group that helps indie filmmakers crowdfund their works, approached Bravo because they wanted to promote greater diversity in the world of virtual reality (VR). Set in Los Angeles, the piece focuses on police brutality.

Bravo was initially hesitant about exploring the world of VR film. As she explained to Gills, "I think the selling point for me, as my big entry into it, is that it is rare as an artist to get invited to make the things you want to make. So why would I say no to the possibility of exploring something new and the opportunity to make something that was mine? But I was still kind of hesitant about the medium."

Despite initial misgivings, Bravo came to regard working in VR as akin to directing theater in the round. Part of her inspiration came from a TED talk that Chris Milk gave on empathy. She also researched a cousin who had been shot in Brooklyn by police there in 1999, discovering that the newspaper accounts she found were incorrect. She wanted to portray the full lives of people who were often not granted one in media accounts of their death. The work was the first of hers to deal directly with racism and the world of politics.

LEMON

After making several short films, Bravo directed *Lemon*, a full-length film she cowrote with Gelman, who starred as the deluded protagonist, an actor named Isaac. *Lemon* premiered at the *NEXT* section of the 2017 Sundance Film Festival. It took five years to get the funding and casting in place, which Bravo came to see as the right thing.

When they began writing the script, Bravo and Gelman were thirty and thirty-five, fearful that they would never have their best possible lives—that they would in fact be "lemons," a term used for a car that does not work well. Writing those fears was a way to overcome them, as Bravo explained to Faktorovich, saying the film was "about failure. It's about arriving at an end meant for someone else. It came from a combined anxiety of where it was we thought we might be headed."

Composer Heather Christian used instrumentation to represent moods and characters in the film. On several occasions two of the characters perform a scene from Anton Chekhov's play *The Seagull*; Christian wanted music to reflect that as well.

Lemon opened at the Sundance Film Festival in January 2017. At the screening, as reported by Mark Olsen for the *Los Angeles Times* (23 Jan. 2017), Bravo said, "I cherish this moment, I have wanted to be in a room like this with people like you having this moment and I can't believe it's happening and I get to be a part of it." The film then moved on to the forty-sixth Rotterdam International Film Festival. The film also was shown at SXSW. Magnolia Films acquired *Lemon* for distribution in North America.

COLLABORATING

Bravo has worked consistently with a number of people, including Heather Christian, who composes music for her films. The two have worked together for more than a decade, making it Bravo's longest creative collaboration. As Bravo told Faktorovich, "I trust her deeply. She reads my scripts and tells me what she hears. . . . And then I make the film and send her a very rough cut and she sends me little pieces until we have a full score. . . . I take what she sends and place it where it feels right and then we go from there. We build and we take away."

Perhaps her deepest collaboration is with Gelman. Commenting on the assumption some people made that Bravo's writing was his, Gelman told Zach Gayne for the website ScreenAnarchy (27 Jan. 2017), "If you know things she's written, and you look at the writing of this, it's not very different. So, it's in her voice. I did contribute to the writing, and I'm very proud of our collaboration, but it's got to be known [that she is the writer], you know?" Gelman likened his work to being a dancer, with Bravo as the choreographer, particularly in the film *Lemon*.

PERSONAL LIFE

In 2015 Bravo married Gelman, whom she met when they were both working on a commercial in New York. After living for fifteen years in New York, Bravo moved to Los Angeles, which she appreciates for the amount of physical space and the sunshine. She was one of the women who spoke at the 2017 Sundance Film Festival's Women's March, which drew some five thousand marchers in support of the arts. As Kyle Buchanan reported for *Vulture* (21 Jan. 2017), Bravo told the marchers, "Our greatest power, the thing that I think we have over them, is the power of inclusion."

SUGGESTED READING

Bravo, Janicza. "'Lemon' Director Janicza Bravo on the Art of Rejection and Why Her Film's Not Weird—Sundance 2017." Interview by Kate Erbland. *IndieWire*, 26 Jan. 2017, www.indiewire.com/2017/01/lemon-janicza-bravo-sundance-interview-1201774063. Accessed 25 May 2017.

Bravo, Janicza. "'Hard World for Small Things' Creator Janicza Bravo Tackles Police Brutality through VR." Interview by Melina Gills. *Tribeca*, tribecafilm.com/stories/interview-janicza-bravo-hard-world-small-things-tribeca-film-festival-virtual-arcade. Accessed 27 May 2017.

Bravo, Janicza. "Interview: Janicza Bravo." Interview by Conor Riley. *Oak*, 15 Nov. 2016, oaknyc.com/blog/interview-janicza-bravo. Accessed 25 May 2017.

Bravo, Janicza. "Interview with Janicza Bravo, Director of *Gregory Go Boom*." Interview by Anna Faktorovich. *Pennsylvania Literary Journal*, vol. 6, no. 1, Spring 2014, pp. 27–31.

Bravo, Janicza, and Brett Gelman. "Sundance 2017 Interview: Janicza Bravo and Brett Gelman on Waking Up *Lemon*." Interview by Zach Gayne. *ScreenAnarchy*, 27 Jan. 2017, screenanarchy.com/2017/01/sundance-2017-interview-janciza-bravo-and-brett-gelman-on-waking-up-lemon.html. Accessed 20 May 2017.

Olsen, Mark. "Janicza Bravo's Oddball 'Lemon' Is Tart and Sweet." *Los Angeles Times*, 23 Jan. 2017, www.latimes.com/entertainment/la-et-sundance-updates-janicza-bravo-s-oddball-lemon-is-tart-1485196831-htmlstory.html. Accessed 29 May 2017.

SELECTED WORKS

Eat, 2011; *Gregory Go Boom*, 2013; *Pauline Alone*, 2014; *Hard World for Small Things*, 2016; *Lemon*, 2017

—Judy Johnson

Vera Brosgol

Date of birth: August 1984
Occupation: Cartoonist

"Writing and drawing are pretty connected and kind of come from the same place," cartoonist Vera Brosgol told Rafael Rosado and Jorge Aguirre for *Tor.com* (8 May 2012). "Sort of a magical invisible idea-well." If Brosgol's published works are any indication, her idea-well is magical indeed. The author of the popular graphic novel *Anya's Ghost* and the picture book *Leave Me Alone!*, Brosgol has earned critical acclaim for her work, which blends compelling plots, intriguing explorations of issues such as identity and family, and humor with her signature engaging artwork. In addition to praise from reviewers and readers, her books have won a number of prestigious awards, including the Eisner Award for best publication for young adults.

A visual artist from a young age, Brosgol began her professional career in animation, joining the studio Laika Inc., which is known for its critically acclaimed stop-motion films, including *Coraline* and *Kubo and the Two Strings*. Although employed as a full-time storyboard artist for ten years, she continued to work on original projects as well, establishing herself as a well-regarded comics artist even before the publication of her critically acclaimed graphic novel *Anya's Ghost* in 2011. With the publication of the children's book *Leave Me Alone!* in 2016, Brosgol entered a new field that necessitated a new approach to her work. "In animation and comics, the viewer breezes past the drawings. But with picture books, each page is going to be stared at and touched and read over and over. Maybe even chewed on a little," she explained to Elissa Gershowitz and Katie Bircher for the *Horn Book* (12 Sept. 2016). "Everything needs to be thoughtful and economical, thirty-two little masterpieces." Although the project was challenging, it also proved fruitful: in early 2017, *Leave Me Alone!* was awarded the prestigious Caldecott Honor.

EARLY LIFE AND EDUCATION
Vera Brosgol was born in 1984 in Moscow, Soviet Union (now Russia). In 1989, when she was five years old, her family left the Soviet Union as religious refugees. The family settled in the United States. A budding artist early in life, Brosgol developed a love of drawing at a young age. "I started drawing pretty much as soon as I had my grasping skills figured out," she said in an interview for the website *Media Molecule* (27 Aug. 2009). Although she initially had a difficult time fitting in at school, in part because of her immigrant identity and cultural background, she soon found that her artistic talents appealed to her fellow students, particularly when she drew pictures of popular characters from American television shows. Brosgol's artistic style and skills evolved over the subsequent years, incorporating new influences such as the Japanese comics she enjoyed reading as a teenager. She later began to write and draw a webcomic titled *Return to Sender*, which not only gave her hands-on experience in creating a long-form comic but also gained her valuable connections within the webcomics field and the wider comics industry.

After graduating from high school, Brosgol enrolled in Sheridan College to study classical animation. An arts- and technology-focused college in Oakville, Ontario, Canada, Sheridan College was well known for its animation department, which produced numerous talented graduates in the decades since the program's launch. For Brosgol, the decision to study animation was based on both her longtime interest in art and her desire to find a steady job after completing her education. Learning about numerous different areas of animation, she soon found that she particularly enjoyed working on storyboards, panels of images that create a detailed visual outline of the series of shots that make up an animated work. During her final year of college, Brosgol created a short animated film, *Snow-Bo*, in collaboration with her roommate and fellow animation student Jenn Kluska. *Snow-Bo* was later screened at several film festivals, and the film's creators also made it available online, a decision that ultimately proved beneficial to Brosgol's career. Brosgol earned her diploma

in classical animation from Sheridan College in 2005.

EARLY CAREER
After graduating from college, Brosgol was working as a background painter for a children's DVD when a recruiter from the newly founded animation studio Laika contacted her, having seen and enjoyed *Snow-Bo* online. Brosgol was particularly intrigued by the possibility of working at Laika because she was a fan of the 2002 children's novel *Coraline* by Neil Gaiman, and the studio was then in the process of creating a stop-motion animated adaptation of the novel, its first feature-length project.

After a successful interview process, Brosgol joined Laika as a storyboard artist, moving to Portland, Oregon, in December 2005. She began her tenure at Laika working on *Coraline*, which was ultimately released to critical acclaim in 2009, and went on to contribute to the studio's next stop-motion feature films, *ParaNorman* (2012), *The Boxtrolls* (2014), and *Kubo and the Two Strings* (2016). Brosgol enjoyed the work, not only because of her love of storyboarding but also because she was at heart a fan of Laika's productions. "If I didn't work at Laika I'd probably be stalking the internet for any news of their next movie and seeing them all twelve times," she told Rosado and Aguirre.

In addition to working at Laika, Brosgol pursued independent work in comics. "I don't really have an impulse to make personal animation work, because the part of animation I like best is, oddly enough, storyboarding. I'm a pretty lousy animator and am basically useless in any other part of the process (except cleanup maybe)," she explained to Rosado and Aguirre. "I do have a desire to do personal storytelling, though, and that's where comics step in."

In 2004, prior to Brosgol's graduation from college, her story "I Wish" was included in volume one of *Flight*, a comics anthology series organized by artist Kazu Kibuishi. She went on to have stories featured in the second and fourth volumes in the series, published in 2005 and 2007, respectively. Brosgol likewise contributed art to works such as *Agnes Quill: An Anthology of Mystery* (2006) and *Nursery Rhyme Comics* (2011), and her work would later be featured in publications such as the *Adventure Time* comics series, based on the Cartoon Network show of the same name, and the DC Comics work *Gotham Academy: Endgame* (2015).

ANYA'S GHOST
In 2007, Brosgol began working on what would become *Anya's Ghost*, her debut graphic novel. The young-adult work focuses on a Russian-born American teenager known as Anya who, after falling into a dry well and discovering the

skeleton of a long-dead girl named Emily, finds herself haunted by Emily's ghost. Although the two initially become friends, Emily soon proves to be far more sinister than Anya ever suspected. Hoping to pursue publication, Brosgol contacted Judith Hansen, a literary agent who also represented Kibuishi and the *Flight* anthologies, while in the process of creating the novel. "I came to her with about the first thirty pages and basically told her what was going to happen," Brosgol recalled to Jonathan H. Liu for *Wired* (15 Oct. 2011). "And she took a look at it and said, 'Okay, keep going. Why don't you just finish drawing it, because you don't have a script.'" Working on the project on and off, Brosgol completed the interior artwork for *Anya's Ghost* in 2009, enabling Hansen to approach publishers with a completed work. "Apparently that's easier to sell because then they know there's no surprises," she told Liu. "They know exactly what they're getting."

Anya's Ghost was ultimately published in 2011 by First Second Books, an imprint of Macmillan Publishers that had previously published critically acclaimed graphic novels such as Gene Luen Yang's *American Born Chinese* (2006). Upon its publication, *Anya's Ghost* met with an overwhelmingly positive critical response, with reviewers praising the graphic novel's plot as well as Brosgol's artwork. The novel won a number of prestigious comics industry awards, including the Eisner Award for best publication for young adults and the Harvey Award for best original graphic publication for younger readers. *Anya's Ghost* was similarly popular among readers and became a fixture on school reading lists.

LEAVE ME ALONE!

In 2016, Brosgol left her position at Laika to focus on her original work. Within a matter of months, she signed a deal with Macmillan Children's Books for three books—two picture books and one middle-grade graphic novel. Her first picture book, *Leave Me Alone!*, was published by Macmillan's Roaring Brook Press imprint in September 2016. The book follows an elderly woman's quest to get her knitting done in peace, leaving her crowded home and traveling to the forest, the mountains, and even the moon. In creating the book's illustrations, Brosgol avoided digital artwork and instead used the traditional mediums of ink and watercolor paints. "There's something so nice and tactile about real paint on real paper and I love having all the original paintings in a drawer like a little time capsule," she told Kristian Wilson for *Bustle* (15 June 2016). "I still feel like a fumbly idiot-baby with watercolors but I figure I'll get better if I keep practicing. And if I stop drinking the paint water."

Much like *Anya's Ghost*, *Leave Me Alone!* proved popular among reviewers of children's literature, who called attention to Brosgol's lively artwork, the book's entertaining plotline, and its relatively unusual focus on an adult protagonist. In the spring of 2017, the Association for Library Service to Children (ALSC) awarded the book a Caldecott Honor, one of the most prestigious honors in US children's publishing. "I was, and am, completely shocked," Brosgol wrote in a blog post (21 Mar. 2017) about the award. "I hadn't even considered the possibility of getting a Caldecott, and it's rare in life that you get completely and utterly surprised like that, especially in a GOOD way."

In addition to *Leave Me Alone!* and a second as yet untitled picture book, Brosgol's three-book deal includes the middle-grade graphic novel *Be Prepared*, a memoir about the author's childhood experience at a Russian Orthodox summer camp in upstate New York. "My time at camp was full of loneliness, physical discomfort, and social anxiety," she told Wilson. "This is not a glowing memoir of simpler happier times. Childhood can be pretty dark and unpleasant and I think readers that had a hard time as a kid (at camp or otherwise) will find something to relate to." *Be Prepared* is scheduled for publication in the spring of 2018.

PERSONAL LIFE

Brosgol lives in Portland with her partner, Jeremy Spake, head of the armature department at Laika. In addition to creating comics and illustrations in various mediums, Brosgol enjoys fiber arts and is an avid knitter. "Knitting is repetitive, rewarding, and calms me down like a warm bath," she explained to Gershowitz and Bircher. A lover of animals, Brosgol also regularly fosters dogs rescued from high-kill shelters.

SUGGESTED READING

Brosgol, Vera. "'Anya's Ghost' Author Vera Brosgol Has a New Graphic Novel on the Way!" Interview by Kristian Wilson. *Bustle*, 15 June 2016, www.bustle.com/articles/166864-anyas-ghost-author-vera-brosgol-has-a-new-graphic-novel-on-the-way-exclusive-images. Accessed 9 June 2017.

Brosgol, Vera. "Discovering That You're Russian: Vera Brosgol and 'Anya's Ghost.'" Interview by Rafael Rosado and Jorge Aguirre. *Tor.com*, 8 May 2012, www.tor.com/2012/05/08/discovering-that-youre-russian-vera-brosgol-and-anyas-ghost. Accessed 9 June 2017.

Brosgol, Vera. "Five Questions for Vera Brosgol." Interview by Elissa Gershowitz and Katie Bircher. *The Horn Book*, 12 Sept. 2016, www.hbook.com/2016/09/authors-illustrators/interviews/five-questions-for-vera-brosgol. Accessed 9 June 2017.

Brosgol, Vera. "Frequently Asked Questions." *Verabee*, 31 Dec. 2011, verabee.com/2011/12/

frequently-asked-questions. Accessed 9 June 2017.

Brosgol, Vera. "Mm Interview with Vera Bee." *Media Molecule*, 27 Aug. 2009, www.mediamolecule.com/blog/article/mm_interview_with_vera_bee. Accessed 9 June 2017.

Brosgol, Vera. "Well, I Didn't See THAT Coming." *Verabee*, 21 Mar. 2017, verabee.com/2017/03/well-i-didnt-see-that-coming/. Accessed 9 June 2017.

Brosgol, Vera. "Wordstock Interview: Vera Brosgol." Interview by Jonathan H. Liu. *Wired*, 15 Oct. 2011, www.wired.com/2011/10/wordstock-interview-vera-brosgol. Accessed 9 June 2017.

SELECTED WORKS

Anya's Ghost, 2011; *Leave Me Alone!*, 2016; *Be Prepared*, 2018

—Joy Crelin

Tituss Burgess

Date of birth: February 21, 1979
Occupation: Actor

Although devotees of Broadway musicals have long been familiar with the talents of Tituss Burgess, television audiences were largely unaware of the actor, who for years was best known for originating the role of Sebastian in the Broadway adaptation of Disney's *The Little Mermaid*. A lover of music and theater since childhood, Burgess moved to New York in 2003, after a stint as a performer at Disney World, and soon began to amass credits as a performer in Broadway productions such as *Good Vibrations* (2005), *Jersey Boys* (2005), and the 2009 revival of *Guys and Dolls*.

Burgess's fortunes as a television actor began to change in 2011, when a small role in the critically acclaimed comedy *30 Rock* brought him to the attention of the show's devoted fans. However, it was his costarring role as struggling actor Titus Andromedon in the Netflix-released series *Unbreakable Kimmy Schmidt* that earned him a widespread following as well as critical acclaim after the show's debut in 2015. In the role of Titus, Burgess brings a comedic perspective to the woes of New York City's underemployed actors, a group to which he once belonged. "He's not entirely like myself but certainly I'm able to borrow from personal experiences," he told Jack Smart for *Backstage* (5 Mar. 2015) of Titus. "It's sort of the basis for the character. He's convinced that stardom has skipped over him and he's determined to find it at all costs." Indeed, stardom has certainly not skipped over Burgess; in 2015 and 2016, he was nominated for the Emmy Award for outstanding supporting actor in a comedy series in recognition of his work.

EARLY LIFE AND EDUCATION

Burgess was born on February 21, 1979, in Georgia. As a young child, he lived in the small town of Lexington, Georgia, with his mother, Sandra, and grandparents. After his mother married, the family settled in Athens, Georgia, where Burgess attended Hilsman Middle School. A talented singer who also learned to play piano on his own, Burgess began performing at his church at an early age, and he later became a choir director. He had his first opportunity to act on stage while in middle school, when he appeared in the school production of the 1944 Mary Chase play *Harvey*. Having enjoyed the experience, he continued to participate in performing arts while attending Cedar Shoals High School, from which he graduated in 1997.

After high school, Burgess enrolled in the University of Georgia to study music. Although he initially planned to become a music teacher, he quickly realized that the profession did not suit him and planned to pursue a career in theater instead. He earned his bachelor's degree from the university in 2001. In interviews, he has admitted that because of the social and political climate of his home state, he was eager to leave: "I certainly was not happy in Athens, and I did not feel at home when I was there," he told Kevin Fallon for the *Daily Beast* (12 Apr. 2016).

EARLY CAREER AND BREAKING OUT ON BROADWAY

After graduating from college, Burgess first moved to Florida, where he spent nearly a year as a cast member of *Festival of the Lion King*, a musical performed within the Disney World theme park. Although offered the opportunity to remain with the show after his first contract was up, he chose instead to relocate to New York City and look for work within the city's thriving theater community. It was a "very exciting but very scary time," he told Caryn Robbins for *BroadwayWorld.com* (19 Mar. 2015). During his early years in New York, he supported himself through a variety of odd jobs, including working for a short time as a host at the restaurant Ruby Foo's, a New York City institution that closed in 2015.

During Burgess's early career, he primarily found work in regional theater productions in New York State and elsewhere. In 2004, he joined the workshop of *Good Vibrations*, a jukebox musical based on the music of the Beach Boys. Later that year, he joined another workshop, this one for the musical *Jersey Boys*, about the 1960s group the Four Seasons.

Burgess made his Broadway debut in the production of *Good Vibrations*, which opened in February 2005. He remained with the show until it closed in late April of that year, having unfortunately failed to win over critics or audiences. Within months, however, he had joined the Broadway production of *Jersey Boys* in the role of Hal Miller. The following year, he performed in another regional theater gig as the Lion in a production of *The Wiz* in La Jolla, California. The role proved to be an important one for Burgess, who found inspiration in his character. "I struggled for a very long time to not edit myself," he explained to Smart. "The older I get, the easier it is to be all of me. I no longer take into consideration other people's feelings. That song 'Be a Lion' spoke to me in such a way that . . . I have roared ever since, as cheesy as it sounds."

ESTABLISHING A THEATER REPUTATION

Also a songwriter, Burgess released an album of original songs titled *Here's to You* (2006). He is dedicated to writing music that truly comes from the heart. "People know when something is inspired and when something is not, and I don't want to waste anyone's time," he told Marc Snetiker for *Entertainment Weekly* (27 Mar. 2015). "If I'm telling you you should come and listen to me sing something that I wrote, you can rest assured that I won't waste your time. . . . Why invite you to dinner if I can't cook?"

It was his next Broadway role, however, that would bring Burgess the most fame to date. In January 2008, the stage adaptation of Disney's *The Little Mermaid* opened at New York's Lunt-Fontanne Theatre. Burgess played the role of Sebastian, the crustacean adviser to the titular mermaid and the singer of the iconic *Little Mermaid* song "Under the Sea." Despite his previous experience on Broadway, Burgess did not initially think that he would win the role of Sebastian, in large part thanks to his disastrous audition years before the musical's premiere. "I went in and thought I was off book for the scene, for 'Under the Sea.' And I tanked it," he recalled to Smart. "I remember they said to me, 'Go outside, gather yourself, and come back.' And I went back in and tanked it all over again. I don't think I've ever been so embarrassed. . . . To this day I have no idea why, three years later, they came back and just gave it to me."

In August 2008, Burgess fractured his foot and was forced to go on medical leave from *The Little Mermaid*. Although he planned to return to the musical after recovering, he soon heard from director Des McAnuff, with whom he had worked on *Jersey Boys* and *The Wiz*. McAnuff attempted to recruit him to join the Broadway revival of the 1950s musical *Guys and Dolls* in the role of Nicely-Nicely Johnson, and after considering the role for a while, he agreed. The show opened at the Nederlander Theatre in March 2009.

TELEVISION DEBUT

Having established himself in theater, Burgess next began to explore television, making his on-camera debut in the web series *The Battery's Down* in 2009. His first major television performance came in 2011, however, when he made his first appearance in the comedy *30 Rock*. Helmed by veteran comedian Tina Fey, *30 Rock* follows the antics of the writers and stars of a television sketch comedy show. Burgess's character, a hairdresser named D'Fwan, is a member of the entourage that appears with Angie Jordan, the wife of show-within-a-show star Tracy Jordan, on her reality show, *Queen of Jordan*.

For Burgess, appearing in *30 Rock*, even in a very small role, was a daunting experience. "I'd had no network exposure or experience before, and I definitely didn't have any single camera experience," he told Ryan Butcher for *Gay Times* (13 Apr. 2016). "I was hoping someone else would go first so I could watch what to do when they call 'Action!' But of course, the first scene of the day was me! I don't think I've ever, ever been that horrified. But I just wanted to do a good job. And then, of course, my next scene is with Tina Fey and [Angie Jordan actor] Sherri Shepherd. I made a lot of mistakes that day, but I learned a lot and I walked away with a better understanding of what it takes to be a comedic actor on television." The role of D'Fwan was originally a small one featured in a single episode, but Burgess ultimately returned to *30 Rock* for three more episodes, two of which take the form of episodes of *Queen of Jordan*. Although his time on *30 Rock* was relatively short, he impressed Fey with his performance, and the connections he made on the show would prove crucial to his later television career. In addition to memorable portrayals of D'Fwan on the show as well as the release of a second album, *Comfortable* (2012), he also made single-episode appearances in television shows such as *Blue Bloods* (2012) and *Royal Pains* (2013).

UNBREAKABLE KIMMY SCHMIDT

Following the conclusion of *30 Rock* in early 2013, Fey and fellow writer Robert Carlock began developing their next show, *Unbreakable Kimmy Schmidt*. The off-beat comedy follows the titular woman, who, after being freed from an underground bunker where she had been kept since being abducted as a young teenager, sets out to find a new life in New York City. Burgess won the role of Titus Andromedon, Kimmy's roommate and a struggling actor, which had been written with him in mind. Indeed, actor and character share a number of similarities, although Burgess experienced far more success as an actor than Titus, who supports himself by working as a knock-off superhero in Times Square and as a werewolf in a theme restaurant, among other jobs. At the same time, Burgess worked to distinguish his character from himself with the guidance of the showrunners. "They repeatedly had to tell me to go a lot further, until I finally was like, 'Oh, so this is really not me,'" he explained to Snetiker. "And I don't know that I processed that until I saw the wardrobe . . . and then truly, Titus came out so quickly. I understood exactly who he was."

Although the show was initially developed for NBC, the network ultimately passed on it, and *Unbreakable Kimmy Schmidt* was picked up by the streaming video provider Netflix. The complete first season was made available to Netflix subscribers in March 2015 and was met with largely positive reviews. Viewers and critics particularly enjoyed Burgess's performance as the dramatic Titus, and a clip from the show, in which Titus creates the music video "Peeno Noir," went viral. Inspired by the popularity of the clip, Burgess later launched his own brand of pinot noir wine, Pinot by Tituss. The second season of *Unbreakable Kimmy Schmidt* was released on Netflix in April 2016, several months after Netflix announced that the show would be renewed for a third season. Nominated for the Emmy Award for outstanding supporting actor in a comedy series in both 2015 and 2016 for his work, Burgess often expresses that he has not taken his increased fame and steady gig for granted: "It's a charmed life Tina Fey has given me, and I am so deeply appreciative. The only way I know how to repay her is to show up and be as funny as I possibly can," he told Kristen Yoonsoo Kim for *Complex* (12 Apr. 2016).

PERSONAL LIFE

Burgess lives in the New York City neighborhood of Harlem.

SUGGESTED READING

Burgess, Tituss. "BWW Interview: Tituss Burgess Talks New Netflix Comedy *Unbreakable Kimmy Schmidt*." Interview by Caryn Robbins. *BroadwayWorld.com*, 19 Mar. 2015, www.broadwayworld.com/bwwtv/article/BWW-Interviews-Tituss-Burgess-Talks-New-Netflix-Comedy-UNBREAKABLE-KIMMY-SCHMIDT-20150319. Accessed 6 Jan. 2017.

Burgess, Tituss. "8 Questions with . . . Tituss Burgess." Interview by Jack Smart. *Backstage*, 5 Mar. 2015, www.backstage.com/interview/8-questions-tituss-burgess. Accessed 6 Jan. 2017.

Butcher, Ryan. "Peeno Noirrrr—We Chat with the Unbreakable Tituss Burgess." *Gay Times*, 13 Apr. 2016, www.gaytimes.co.uk/culture/33843/peeno-noirrrr-we-chat-with-the-unbreakable-tituss-burgess. Accessed 6 Jan. 2017.

Kamp, David. "Tituss Burgess on His Vocal Hero, His Bespoke Pinot Noir, and Why He Shaves His Head." *Vanity Fair*, Apr. 2016, www.vanityfair.com/hollywood/2016/04/tituss-burgess-unbreakable-kimmy-schmidt. Accessed 6 Jan. 2017.

Kim, Kristen Yoonsoo. "Tituss Burgess Will Do Whatever the Hell He Wants." *Complex*, 12 Apr. 2016, www.complex.com/pop-culture/2016/04/tituss-burgess-unbreakable-kimmy-schmidt. Accessed 6 Jan. 2016.

Snetiker, Marc. "*Unbreakable Kimmy Schmidt* Breakout Tituss Burgess on His Alter Ego (and 'Pinot Noir')." *Entertainment Weekly*, 27 Mar. 2015, ew.com/article/2015/03/27/tituss-burgess-unbreakable-kimmy-schmidt. Accessed 6 Jan. 2017.

SELECTED WORKS

Good Vibrations, 2005; *Jersey Boys*, 2006; *The Little Mermaid*, 2008; *Guys and Dolls*, 2009; *30 Rock*, 2011–12; *Unbreakable Kimmy Schmidt*, 2015–; *The Angry Birds Movie*, 2016

—*Joy Crelin*

Camila Cabello

Born: March 3, 1997
Occupation: Singer-songwriter

Television audiences were introduced to singer Camila Cabello during the 2012 season of the Fox reality competition series *The X Factor*, after she teamed up with four other solo contestants to form Fifth Harmony, who finished third overall. After signing a joint record deal, the all-girl group quickly made their mark with the debut EP *Better Together* (2013) and the gold single "Miss Movin' On," followed by their first studio album, *Reflection* (2015), which spawned three platinum hits: "BO$$," "Sledgehammer," and "Worth It."

Despite the group's success, Cabello sought a creative outlet and spent her downtime putting her lyrics to paper. "We didn't write our records. We were interpreting somebody else's story," she told Chris Martins for *Billboard* (25 Feb. 2017). Her 2015 collaboration with Shawn Mendes produced her first solo hit and prompted initial speculation regarding Fifth Harmony's future. Cabello also struggled with the group's sexier image, reflected in the lyrics and videos for "Work from Home" and "All in My Head (Flex)," the first two singles from their second studio album, 7/27 (2016). In December 2016—at the height of the group's success and two months after the release of Cabello's second solo hit, "Bad Things"—Cabello split acrimoniously from her Fifth Harmony bandmates, after nearly five years. In May 2017 she released the single and video for "Crying in the Club," the opening track for her upcoming solo album.

EARLY LIFE

Camila Cabello was born Karla Camila Cabello Estrabao on March 3, 1997, in Cojímar, a tiny fishing village east of Havana, Cuba. She spent the early part of her childhood shuttling between Cuba and her father's homeland of Mexico. Cabello's life dramatically changed at age six, when she and her mother, Sinuhe, were seemingly headed on a trip to Walt Disney World in Orlando, Florida. In reality, Cabello's parents were planning to immigrate to the United States.

Armed with a Winnie the Pooh journal and her favorite doll, Cabello hopped on a flight to Mexico with her mother. After visiting her father's family, Cabello and her mother boarded a bus making its way through Mexico, en route to the US border. Upon reaching their destination, the pair, who only had a few hundred dollars and a backpack filled with their belongings, met with an immigration officer who would eventually decide their fate: whether to allow them to enter the United States or to send them back home. "It was me and my mom and two other families

Isaiah Trickey/FilmMagic

in a little room waiting for somebody to come in and let us know," Cabello recalled in a piece she penned for *Popsugar* (8 Apr. 2017). "We were there only a day when we finally got the news. The room [burst] with joy, everybody around me clapping and hugging and screaming and crying! And me yelling out 'Yay! We're all going to Disney!' Little did I know."

Cabello and her mother stayed with a close family friend in Miami, Florida, where Sinuhe, a former architect, found work at a Marshall's department store while also studying English at night. After mastering the AutoCAD Architecture software within a week, Sinuhe found a better-paying job that eventually enabled her to rent an apartment in the village of Pinecrest.

Cabello struggled to adjust to her new life. "A lot of things were suddenly so different—being at a new school without my friends, I didn't speak the language, and I missed my dad," she shared with Erika Hayasaki for *Glamour* (5 Apr. 2017). (The family was eventually reunited a year and a half later.) Music also became a source of comfort for the introverted Cabello, who honed her performance skills by recording YouTube covers and by joining Palmetto Middle School's drama troupe, the Palmetto Thespians. After school, Cabello frequented the local YMCA, where she would borrow a boombox to play some of her favorite CDs.

THE X FACTOR

Growing up, Cabello was a fan of the hugely successful British Irish pop quintet One Direction, who rose to fame after finishing third on the 2010 season of the competitive music series *The X Factor UK*. Inspired by the group's video, which featured audition tips, the fifteen-year-old talked her parents into letting her try out for the American version of the show. "I wasn't going to have quinceañera, so I asked my mom instead if her present could be for her to drive up with me to the audition," she told Noelle Devoe for *Seventeen* (10 Jan. 2017).

In July 2012 Cabello attended *X-Factor* tryouts in Greensboro, North Carolina, and was picked to be an alternate, following a preliminary audition. However, she almost did not perform for the judging panel, which consisted of Simon Cowell, Britney Spears, Demi Lovato, and L. A. Reid. "For two days, I was right about to go audition, and they would tell me, 'Oh no. You can't audition,'" she recalled to Devoe. "I ended up auditioning because they saw how badly I wanted it and how persistent I was—it's a Cuban thing." Cabello's rendition of Aretha Franklin's "Respect" earned her the judges' unanimous approval and qualified her for *X Factor* bootcamp, held in her hometown of Miami.

FIFTH HARMONY

On July 27, 2012, after Cabello failed to advance in the Teens category, the judges grouped her with four other eliminated girls—Normani Kordei Hamilton, Dinah Jane Hansen, Ally Brooke Hernandez, and Lauren Jauregui—to compete in the Groups category. With their version of the Shontelle hit "Impossible," the quintet, who called themselves LYLAS (an acronym for "Love You Like a Sister"), earned a spot among sixteen finalists. When the first live episode aired on October 31, LYLAS had renamed themselves "1432," under the threat of a lawsuit by another all-girl band with the same name. ("1432" means "I love you too" in text slang.) Despite mixed reviews for the group's performance of Taylor Swift's "We Are Never Ever Getting Back Together," Cabello earned praise from Lovato, another of her musical influences. The girls dropped into the bottom two but redeemed themselves with a performance of Lovato's ballad "Skyscraper."

Following Cowell's advice, Cabello and her bandmates scrapped "1432" and let the viewers choose their new moniker, which was unveiled on the episode aired on November 7, 2012. The newly renamed Fifth Harmony was declared safe in week two, after singing Christina Perri's ballad "A Thousand Years." Over the next three weeks, the girls avoided elimination, with their renditions of Mariah Carey's "Hero," The Pretenders' "I'll Stand by You," and Kelly Clarkson's "Stronger," respectively. However, by early December, they found themselves at the bottom again, following performances of Adele's "Set Fire to the Rain" and another Lovato hit: "Give Your Heart a Break." Cabello and the girls reached the semifinals after successfully tackling Carey's "Anytime You Need a Friend" in the week-six sing-off. Their covers of Ellie Goulding's "Anything Could Happen" and Shontelle's "Impossible" earned them a ticket to the two-night finale in late December. After revisiting the Goulding tune and duetting with Lovato on "Give Your Heart a Break," Fifth Harmony performed the Beatles' "Let It Be," eventually finishing third overall and cultivating a loyal fan base known as the "Harmonizers."

BETTER TOGETHER

Cabello, who was then homeschooled, officially launched her music career in January 2013, when Fifth Harmony signed a joint deal with Epic Records and Cowell's Syco label. By late February the girls had started their own YouTube channel, initially posting covers by Frank Ocean, Lana Del Rey, and Ed Sheeran. They spent the next three months (March through May) recording their debut album, for which Cabello cowrote two of the five tracks. "Miss Movin' On," Fifth Harmony's first original tune, debuted in mid-July and featured Cabello belting out the opening verse. The empowering breakup anthem was accompanied by a music video and a month-long Harmonize America mall tour, during which the girls performed songs from their upcoming disc.

The next month Fifth Harmony served as the opener for another former *X Factor* finalist, Cher Lloyd. After releasing the EP *Better Together* in late October, the girls performed a handful of US and Canadian shows before appearing on the American Music Awards (AMAs) preshow, *The X Factor*, and *The Ellen DeGeneres Show* in November—the same month the quintet released acoustic and Spanish-language versions and a remix EP. Then came a December appearance at the iHeart Radio Jingle Ball Tour.

REFLECTION

Cabello and the group started off 2014 by headlining MTV's inaugural Artists to Watch Showcase, supporting Lovato on the first leg of her Neon Lights tour, and working on their full-length debut. In May 2014 the girls embarked on their own tour and performed at KISS 108's annual concert, where they shared a snippet of their upcoming single: the fiercely assertive dance-pop tune "BO$$." Released in early July, "BO$$" sold 75,000 copies in its first week and reached number forty-three on the Billboard Hot 100. Fifth Harmony's sultrier image was also reflected in the accompanying video, which featured the girls sporting leg-baring, body-hugging outfits.

Fifth Harmony, now opening for Austin Mahone (alongside Canadian singer-songwriter

Shawn Mendes), performed the song in August, at the MTV Video Music Awards (VMAs), where Cabello came face-to-face with her idol: pop singer Taylor Swift. "She was one of the artists that inspired me to write songs in the first place," she confided to Ella Ceron for *Teen Vogue* (15 Dec. 2015). However, Cabello's songwriting interests took a backseat to her increasingly successful group, whose next single—the Meghan Trainor–penned synth-pop ballad "Sledgehammer"—was released in late October.

After a series of production delays, *Reflection* finally debuted in early February 2015. The group subsequently embarked on their first major headlining tour and released their third single: the funky, saxophone-driven "Worth It," a collaboration with rapper Kid Ink that featured Cabello singing the second verse. Cabello gained a publicity boost through the Instagram photos of her star-studded, surprise eighteenth birthday celebration, thrown by Swift and attended by Selena Gomez, among others. Swift and Cabello were reunited in August, when Swift invited Fifth Harmony to perform "Worth It" during her 1989 World Tour at Levi's Stadium in Santa Clara, California.

7/27 AND SOLO WORK

While hanging out backstage at one of Swift's concerts, Cabello reconnected with Mendes, Swift's opening act. Their thirty-minute impromptu jam session resulted in "I Know What You Did Last Summer (IKWYDLS)," about a dying relationship, written as a dialogue between an unfaithful girlfriend and her suspicious boyfriend. After releasing the song in late November 2015, Cabello spent the next three months promoting her solo venture and denying Fifth Harmony breakup rumors. "I think that the healthiest thing in a group . . . is to let ourselves explore," Cabello told Brittany Spanos for *Rolling Stone* (24 Nov. 2015). "I don't really believe in music having any sort of rulebook."

On February 26, 2016, Fifth Harmony reunited and released the provocative hip-hop/R & B–flavored track "Work from Home," whose first verse and final chorus are sung by Cabello. For the music video, which takes place at a construction site full of attractive, chiseled men, Cabello dons a long-sleeved bodysuit, overalls, and work boots while her bandmates are wearing more skin-revealing outfits. In its debut week, "Work from Home" reached number twelve on the Billboard Hot 100, making it Fifth Harmony's highest-charting single to date. By early April the song had cracked the top ten. A month later the group's sophomore studio album, 7/27—a nod to the date when Fifth Harmony was created, made its top-five Billboard 200 debut, followed by the release of the second single and only track cowritten by Cabello and her bandmates: the

reggae-tinged "All in My Head (Flex)," which reached the Billboard Hot 100 top forty after just one week and peaked at number twenty-three. During the North American leg of their second headlining tour (late July to early October), Fifth Harmony attended the 2016 VMAs and the AMAs, where they debuted their third single, "That's My Girl," which reached number nineteen on Billboard Pop Songs chart in late November.

GOING SOLO

Despite the group's success, Cabello reignited breakup rumors in 2016, following collaborations with producer Diplo and rapper Machine Gun Kelly (MGK). The latter partnership yielded "Bad Things," a ballad cowritten by Cabello and released in early October. Cabello subsequently performed the song on *The Tonight Show Starring Jimmy Fallon* and *The Late Late Late Show with James Corden*. She also costarred as MGK's love interest in the accompanying video, which debuted in early December. Rumor became a reality on December 18, when Fifth Harmony announced that Cabello's representatives had informed them of her decision to leave. Cabello, whose final group performance was on ABC's *New Year's Rockin' Eve 2017*, denied her bandmates' acrimonious claims, insisting that on multiple previous occasions she had informed her bandmates of her solo plans.

Cabello's first song after leaving Fifth Harmony was the Cashmere Cat collaboration "Love Incredible," released in February 2017. She then appeared alongside Miami rapper Pitbull and reggaeton singer J Balvin on "Hey Ma," the second single from the soundtrack of the film *The Fate of the Furious* (2017). While working on her debut, Cabello cowrote two dance songs, "I Have Questions" and "Crying in the Club," the latter of which she unveiled at the Billboard Music Awards. Cabello's debut album, *The Hurting, The Healing, The Loving*, is scheduled to be released in September 2017.

PERSONAL LIFE

Cabello dated Austin Mahone while they were touring together. Since that relationship ended, she has remained guarded about her love life. Cabello, the new face of Guess Jeans, has also battled anxiety, which caused her to pull out of a Fifth Harmony concert in Missouri in September 2016.

SUGGESTED READING

Cabello, Camila. "Our Dreams Were Bigger Than Our Fears." *Popsugar*, 8 Apr. 2017, www.popsugar.com/latina/Camila-Cabello-Her-Cuban-Background-42239921. Accessed 13 July 2017.

Cabello, Camila, and Sinuhe Cabello. "Camila Cabello Came from Cuba with Only a Doll and a Dream." Interview by Erika Hayasaki. *Glamour*, 5 Apr. 2017, www.glamour.com/story/camila-cabello-came-from-cuba-with-only-a-doll-and-a-dream. Accessed 13 July 2017.

Devoe, Noelle. "Camila Cabello Admits She Was Initially Rejected by X *Factor* Producers." *Seventeen*, 10 Jan. 2017, www.seventeen.com/celebrity/movies-tv/news/a44357/camila-cabello-interview-x-factor-rejection. Accessed 13 July 2017.

Martins, Chris. "Camila Cabello: Gone Girl." *Billboard*, 25 Feb. 2017, features.billboard.com/camila-cabello-talks-solo-music-life-after-fifth-harmony. Accessed 13 July 2017.

Spanos, Brittany. "Camila Cabello, Shawn Mendes Talk 'I Know What You Did Last Summer.'" *Rolling Stone*, 24 Nov. 2015, www.rollingstone.com/music/news/camila-cabello-shawn-mendes-talk-i-know-what-you-did-last-summer-20151124. Accessed 18 July 2017.

SELECTED WORKS

Better Together, 2013 (with Fifth Harmony); *Reflection*, 2015 (with Fifth Harmony); *7/27*, 2016 (with Fifth Harmony); *The Hurting, The Healing, The Loving*, 2017

—*Bertha Muteba*

Andreas Rentz/Getty Images for 100 Lives

Rukmini Callimachi

Date of birth: June 25, 1973
Occupation: Journalist

It is not an exaggeration to say that Rukmini Callimachi is one of the few reporters in the world with a deep understanding of the internal workings of such major terrorist groups as al-Qaeda and ISIS. "From the time ISIS rose to become the most infamous terrorist organization on Earth, no reporter has done more to explain and expose the group than the *New York Times'* Rukmini Callimachi," wrote Isaac Chotiner for *Slate* (12 July 2016). "She has covered everything from ISIS's 'theology of rape' to its alarmingly large presence in Europe." Chotiner is not alone in this assessment. Numerous experts and publications, including *Politico*, the *Atlantic*, and National Public Radio have acknowledged Callimachi's exceptional expertise. Callimachi has been nominated for the Pulitzer Prize twice.

EARLY LIFE AND EDUCATION

Rukmini Callimachi was born in 1973 and grew up in Bucharest, Romania, which at the time was a totalitarian state that proclaimed itself to be communist. Much like the Soviet Union at the time, Romania was not an easy place to leave; the person leaving had to demonstrate that they intended to come back. In 1979, when Callimachi was five years old, she, her mother, and her grandmother left the country, though without any intention of coming back. Even from a very young age, Callimachi clearly had the makings of a reporter. As she later wrote in the *New York Times* (6 Sept. 2015), "The night of our departure, I lined up my stuffed animals and 'interviewed' them to find out which ones wanted to come with me to Paris. I decided they all wanted to come, and so I shoved them into a suitcase . . . only to be scolded by my mother, who said I could take two at most." Callimachi, along with her mother and grandmother, moved first to Switzerland and then to Ojai, California, near Los Angeles. When Callimachi came to the United States, she did not speak any English, only Romanian and French, according to Stuart A. Reid, who profiled Callimachi for the *Dartmouth Alumni Magazine* (July–Aug. 2015).

Callimachi attended Dartmouth College, a private Ivy League university in Hanover, New Hampshire, where she was determined to begin studying to become a doctor. Though she took many science courses relating to what she saw as her future career, she also took various English courses. During her first year, according to Reid, Callimachi applied for a unique study-abroad summer program to study poetry in the Italian Alps. The castle where the studies took place was owned by Mary de Rachewiltz, the daughter of the famous, influential poet Ezra Pound.

Callimachi told Reid that she would later take the lessons she learned in reading Pound's literary theories and apply them to her journalistic writing. "He specifically talks about the use of images—how an image in words becomes the backbone of a poem," she said. "To me, journalism is that. You're taking people through scenes into something that is often very far away from them." She graduated from Dartmouth in 1995.

She then went on to study linguistics and Sanskrit at the University of Oxford in the United Kingdom. While she was in Delhi, India, studying Sanskrit, an ancient and sacred language of Hinduism and Buddhism, the subcontinent was struck by a major earthquake. Callimachi booked a flight to Gujarat, the state that suffered the most damage. For *Time* magazine she performed the function of a stringer, a journalistic term that refers to reporters on the scene who contribute to a story by taking note of the details—in this case deaths, injuries, and destruction—and interviewing survivors and witnesses. From then on she was determined to work in journalism.

EARLY CAREER

Her first job was at the *Daily Herald*, in Arlington Heights, Illinois, where for two years she covered local events. Arlington Heights is a small town, with a population under 100,000, and soon enough Callimachi was eager to move on. In 2003 she a got a job as a night-shift reporter at the Portland, Oregon, bureau of the Associated Press (AP), an international news service. She held this position for two years, but when, in August 2005, Hurricane Katrina hit New Orleans, Louisiana, and the surrounding area, Callimachi wanted to go there and report. Though she was a relatively inexperienced reporter, Callimachi expressed a strong interest, and the AP sent her there to report.

In December 2006 she got the job as AP's West Africa correspondent, in Dakar, Senegal. In less than three years she would earn her first Pulitzer Prize nomination, for a story about child exploitation in the region. Around the time Callimachi arrived in Dakar, an Islamic terrorist group pledged allegiance to al-Qaeda. Effectively, the group became a branch of al-Qaeda operating in North Africa, based in Algeria. Though Callimachi covered the growth of this terrorist group from 2007 to 2012, it was less than thrilling reporting. "To be perfectly frank, I found it quite boring because there were no primary sources to speak to. I would call the same small group of diplomats and analysts who repeated the same specific talking points," she told Chotiner.

REPORTING ON TERRORISM

In 2012, the Islamic terrorist group took over northern Mali, a country in the northwest of Africa, where they brutally imposed Sharia law, a radically fundamentalist interpretation of the Koran: women had to wear veils, and ancient practices such as cutting off hands or stoning were brought back as forms of punishment. The group established its headquarters in Timbuktu, Mali.

In January 2013, French troops went in to fight the Islamists. Three days after the Islamists were beaten by the French troops, Callimachi was in Timbuktu, talking to the residents, as many other reporters were doing. The terrorists were apparently in such a rush to flee that they left thousands upon thousands of pages of documents behind in that city. The documents were in Arabic, and at first, Callimachi told Chotiner, that did not ring any bells for her. However, upon realizing that the language of Mali is French, she went back and filled trash bags full of those documents. With the help of a translator (Callimachi does not speak Arabic), she learned what she had found: letters between leaders and commanders, expense reports, and even debates about whether certain tactics were consistent with Sharia law—such as killing children or civilians—or whether another one, albeit right, was good in terms of public relations—namely the total destruction of mausoleums. It took Callimachi and her translator about a year to go through all those documents. Soon, experts, analysts, and even security agencies, like the Federal Bureau of Investigation (FBI), were contacting Callimachi in search of this information.

In addition to obtaining those documents, Callimachi did something that practically no one covering Islamic terrorism did: she talked to members of al-Qaeda and the Islamic State of Iraq and Syria (ISIS). After the North African branch of al-Qaeda took over Timbuktu, Oumar Ould Hamaha was appointed as the group's spokesman, and he became a frequent contact of Callimachi's. Sometimes they would speak several times a day. At times Callimachi did not report some information because she could not be sure he was telling her the truth—there was no way for her to verify it. But, she told Chotiner, often he would be right; for example, when he told her that during the fall of Libya he was buying surface-to-air weapons, namely the SA-7, she did not initially report it because she was aware that as a member of a terrorist group, one of his goals was to "spread fear." But the documents she later found in Timbuktu confirmed his claims. For her discovery, examination, and reporting of those thousands of pages of documents, Callimachi received her second Pulitzer Prize nomination in 2014. In March of that year, she left the Associated Press for the *New York Times*.

Though she could not come in close physical contact with terrorists because of the risk of being kidnapped or killed, Callimachi fearlessly pushed the boundaries, coming close to the literal border of ISIS-controlled territory, such as northern Iraq. While in northern Iraq, she talked to Yazidi sex slaves who had escaped, asking them what ISIS did about pregnancies. Callimachi was told that such cases were rare, as those women were given birth control. Callimachi broke this news in the *New York Times* in 2015.

Her next major story for the *New York Times* was about the role of al-Qaeda in the terrorist attacks in Paris, France, on the offices of the satirical publication *Charlie Hebdo*. At first counterterrorism experts and journalists could not be sure what role, if any, al-Qaeda played in the attack, but Callimachi soon learned of the terrorist group's involvement from an anonymous source in the organization. That did not sit well with the FBI. The following year Callimachi discussed another terrorist source, a German ISIS operative named Harry Sarfo, with Ailsa Chang on the National Public Radio program *Weekend Edition Sunday* (7 Aug. 2016). "He was very quickly recruited by a secretive branch of ISIS known as the Emni," she said, "which is the branch that is responsible for dispatching fighters abroad to carry out attacks." Callimachi also made the case that Abu Muhammad al-Adnani, the spokesman for ISIS, should be better known, because he was so important to the organization: "He should be as well-known as Osama bin Laden. . . . He's the head of their propaganda. But more importantly, he is the head of the Emni, which is the body that is responsible for exporting terror abroad." In August 2016, the Pentagon announced that al-Adnani was killed in an airstrike. Callimachi took to Twitter to caution those eager to celebrate the death of ISIS: "As important as he is," she wrote, "I would caution [people] not to see this as a blow ISIS can't recover from. Organization is built to survive deaths."

SUGGESTED READING

Callimachi, Rukmini. "A Train Journey from Communism to Freedom, Almost Ended in Hungary." *New York Times*, 6 Sept. 2016, www.nytimes.com/2015/09/07/world/europe/a-train-to-freedom-almost-ended-in-hungary.html. Accessed 16 Dec. 2016.

Callimachi, Rukmini. "How One Journalist Uses Social Media to Get Inside the Minds of ISIS." Interview by Caitlin Roper. *Wired*, 3 Aug. 2016, www.wired.com/2016/08/rukmini-callimachi-new-york-times-isis. Accessed 15 Dec. 2016.

Callimachi, Rukmini. "The ISIS Correspondent." Interview by Isaac Chotiner. *Slate*, 12 July 2016, www.slate.com/articles/news_and_politics/interrogation/2016/07/rukmini_callimachi_the_new_york_times_isis_reporter_discusses_her_beat.html. Accessed 15 Dec. 2016.

Reid, Stuart A. "The Beat of Terror." *Dartmouth Alumni Magazine*, July–Aug. 2015, dartmouthalumnimagazine.com/articles/beat-terror. Accessed 15 Dec. 2016.

—*Dmitry Kiper*

Cam

Date of birth: November 19, 1984
Occupation: Country music singer and songwriter

With its stripped-down sound (acoustic guitars, piano, and strings), singer-songwriter Cam's breakout hit "Burning House" is a clear departure from the genre dominating country music airwaves: the hard-thumping, male-oriented "bro-country" that embraces partying, tailgating, and wooing women. Shortly after Cam's performance on a popular radio show, the ballad quickly climbed the charts to become the fastest-rising country single on iTunes.

Since its official release in June 2015, "Burning House" has achieved several milestones. In addition to selling more than a million downloads in 2015, the ballad reached number two on Billboard's Country Airplay and Hot Country

Photo by Matt Winkelmeyer/Getty Images for SiriusXM

Songs charts while also achieving platinum certification. "Burning House" earned Cam a 2016 Grammy nomination, as well as the distinction of the most-nominated female artist at the 2016 ACM Awards. However, Cam seems less preoccupied with the recognition. "I've never wanted to be famous," she told Jewly Hight for *Billboard* (25 Sept. 2015). "That has never been part of any dream. I do remember being little and thinking I might want to be a singer. But not a famous singer—just . . . a singer."

FALLS IN LOVE WITH MUSIC

Camaron Marvel Ochs (pronounced "oaks") was born to Sharon and Mark Ochs, who worked in construction management, on November 19, 1984, in the surfing capital of the world: Huntington Beach, California. She grew up with her younger sister, Jillian, in Lafayette, a semi-rural community in Northern California. Childhood summers and weekends were spent at their grandparents' horse farm in Oceanside, where Ochs was first exposed to country music. "For our family, the ranch represented our family time when we got to drive down through all that desert farmland and Grandpa would wake us up at 5 a.m. to feed the horses," she shared with Chuck Dauphin for *Billboard* (16 Apr. 2015). "We would listen to Patsy Cline, Bonnie Raitt, and Willie Nelson." She also credits her mother with introducing her to the music of 1960s icons Bob Dylan and Joni Mitchell.

Ochs's love affair with singing began in the fourth grade, when she successfully auditioned for the internationally acclaimed Contra Costa Children's Chorus. Over the next eight years, Ochs became a fixture in the choir, singing in fourteen different languages and performing at various historic churches throughout Europe, including England's Canterbury Cathedral, Notre-Dame in Paris, and the Vatican in Rome. While attending Campolindo High School in Moraga, California, the sixteen-year-old not only cofounded an a cappella group, but also started arranging music.

CHOOSING MUSIC OVER PSYCHOLOGY

Upon completing high school, Ochs majored in psychology at the University of California, Davis. Music remained an important part of her life. In 2004 Ochs honed her vocal arranging skills—first as a member of University of California, Davis's (UC Davis) coed a cappella group the Liquid Hotplates and then as a cofounding member of the Spokes, the university's only all-female a cappella group. She also picked up a guitar for the first time during a study abroad stint in the Netherlands, and occasionally performed on the streets.

After earning her bachelor's degree in 2006, Ochs worked as an assistant in various psychology labs (UC Davis, UC Berkeley, and Stanford University), while also publishing research that focused primarily on human emotions. Her growing appreciation for music was evident in 2007, during a three-month volunteer stint in a rural community in the mountains of Nepal, where she spent her free time playing the guitar. Within two years, Ochs, who eventually became research lab manager at Stanford's Culture and Emotion Lab, had decided to pursue music, after a heart-to-heart conversation with one of her professors. "I was going to go to graduate school," Ochs confided to Hight. "I remember asking [her], 'What should I do?' And she said, 'Picture yourself at eighty. What would you regret not having done more: psychology or music?'"

RELEASES SOLO DISC

Drawing inspiration from her trip to Nepal, Ochs started penning tracks for a record, with the help of cowriter and producer Jason Shafton, also founding chief executive officer of her San Francisco–based independent record label Rubber Room Records. The tunes for the album were all recorded at the homes of family and friends. In January 2010 she released *Heartforward*, a collection of contemporary pop folk songs reminiscent of the Indigo Girls, and then promoted the album with performances at several local venues in the San Francisco Bay area, including the Red Devil Lounge, the Viper Room, Hotel Utah Saloon, Molly Malones, Mama Buzz Café, and Stork Club.

Following several months living in Portland, Oregon, Ochs relocated to Los Angeles. There she met and collaborated with producer-songwriter Tyler Johnson, who eventually introduced her to Lindsay Marias, her manager, as well as Grammy-winning producer and mentor Jeff Bhasker, who provided the pair with honest songwriting critique. "I nitpicked the hell out of them," Bhasker recounted to *Hight*. "All the little details: 'This chord doesn't feel right,' or 'This lyric isn't strong enough.'" The advice paid off. In 2011 one of their demos caught the ear of Tim McGraw's manager Scott Siman; a year later Ochs, living in Nashville at that point, was offered a single-song deal with Siman's RPM Entertainment. The song she cowrote, "Fall Madly in Love with You," eventually appeared on *Cut to Impress* (2013), the debut country album from Maggie Rose, an aspiring artist represented by RPM.

KICKSTARTING HER SINGING CAREER

Next came a surprise collaboration with country singer turned pop star Miley Cyrus. When Bhasker was unable to attend a songwriting session, the duo stepped in and met with album producer Mike WiLL Made-It, who gave them free rein. Still determined to pursue a singing career, Ochs, then an unsigned artist, launched a crowdfunding campaign to finance her first country album. On January 1, 2013, she had successfully raised over $10,000 on the crowdfunding website Kickstarter. Over the next three months, Ochs split her time between studios in Nashville and Los Angeles while collaborating with Johnson.

After she finished recording the album, Ochs continued honing her performance skills by playing live shows, including the 2013 CMA Music Fest in July. Three months later, "Maybe You're Right," the song she penned for Cyrus, was featured on the singer's fourth studio album, *Bangerz*. In December Ochs embarked on a tour of Sweden and Denmark. She also released the iTunes single "Down This Road," which drew the attention of WSIX-FM's program director Michael Bryan, who contacted the unsigned Ochs about adding the song to the station's regular rotation. "He said, 'It means you're going to have more leverage than before. You're going to have a shot without having a label involved,'" Ochs shared with Dana Malone for *Sports & Entertainment Nashville Magazine* (5 Sept. 2014). "It put me in a great spot."

SINGING WITH ARISTA AND RELEASING AN EP

With Bhasker's help, Ochs met with RCA Records executives Peter Edge and Tom Corson, who recommended her to Sony Music Entertainment's chairman and CEO Doug Morris. Accompanied by Lindsay Marias and guitarist Anders Mouridsen, Ochs subsequently auditioned at the label's Manhattan headquarters, where she performed a rough version of a newly written song for Morris, who was instantly hooked. "The three of us are like a rag-tag team sitting in this fancy office and we sing 'Burning House,' just leaning over the arm of [the] sofa kind of singing into Doug's face," she recalled to Nate Rau for the *Tennessean* (25 July 2015). "He's closing his eyes and he starts singing along by the second chorus . . . by the end of it he goes, 'This is the reason why I got into the music business.'" Ochs inked a recording contract with Arista Nashville at the end of 2014, after opening for Dan + Shay on the fall leg of the country music duo's Where It All Began tour.

In early March 2015, *Welcome to Cam Country*, Ochs's four-song debut EP, was released on streaming service Spotify, before it was digitally released weeks later. While promoting the lead single, "My Mistake," her song about a one-night stand, Ochs decided to adopt the stage name of Cam. "I went to my first set of radio remotes, and everybody [would ask] 'What's your last name?' It's not easy to pronounce," she confided to Dauphin. "The first two minutes . . . that's what they wanted to talk about, and sometimes those two minutes is all you get. . . . I decided I couldn't do that." By early April 2015, "My Mistake" had reached number fifty-two on Billboard's Country Airplay chart. Later that month, Cam appeared at Stagecoach, the world's biggest country music festival.

BREAKTHROUGH WITH "BURNING HOUSE"

Cam scored her first breakout hit with the same song that clinched her Sony record deal. The inspiration behind "Burning House" involved a personal dream in which Cam races into a blazing home to rescue an ex-boyfriend before deciding to stay and comfort him in his final moments. She cowrote the tune with key collaborator Johnson, who came up with the two opening lines and the guitar riff, which he modeled after Metallica's "Nothing Else Matters." After listening to a rough demo, Bhasker came up with the chorus and helped produce the haunting ballad at his home studio in Venice, California.

Cam's performance of "Burning House" during her Grand Ole Opry debut on May 29, 2015, led to subsequent appearances on nationally syndicated radio program *The Bobby Bones Show*. "Burning House" was officially released in mid-June, after becoming the fastest-rising country download in iTunes history. By early July the song had entered the top fifty of Billboard's Country Airplay chart and was certified gold in October. That same month, Cam unveiled her accompanying video, in which the singer, clad in a white gown, wanders through a flame-engulfed home to reach her former love. "Burning House" ended the year in the top twenty of two Billboard categories: Hot Country Songs and Country Digital Songs. The singer achieved other December milestones, most notably a Grammy Award nod, as well as the release of her full-length studio debut, *Untamed* (2015).

EARNS MORE ACCOLADES

"Burning House" continued ascending the Billboard charts in 2016, cracking the top thirty of the Hot 100 in January—the same month *Untamed* reached number two on the Billboard's Top Country Albums. In mid-February, while opening for Brad Paisley on the winter leg of his Crushin' It World Tour, she walked the red carpet at the 2016 Grammy Awards before losing out to Chris Stapleton in the best country solo performance category. A month after releasing her third single, "Mayday," Cam performed at April's Academy of Country Music Awards (ACMs), where she was nominated in four categories, including song of the year and single record of the year.

In May 2016 Cam served as the opening act for the first North American leg of Dierks Bentley's Somewhere on a Beach Tour. At the CMT Music Awards in June, she scored a leading three nominations and joined Fifth Harmony for a mash-up performance of "Mayday" and the pop quintet's hit "Work from Home." After concluding her four-month stint with Bentley, Cam embarked on her first headlining tour, which lasted from October to December. During this time, she also racked up two Country Music Award (CMA) nods and another from the American Music Awards (AMAs), where she opened the show, alongside Jennifer Nettles and Martina McBride, with a performance of McBride's "This One's for The Girls."

In January 2017 Cam, who is currently working on her second album, hosted her own TEDx Talk about music's healing power at the University of Nevada in Reno. Two months later she was among the performers at the three-night Country-to-Country festival in the United Kingdom. From April through December, Cam, a 2017 ACM nominee for new female vocalist of the year, will open for George Strait during his Las Vegas residency.

PERSONAL LIFE

Since late September 2016, Cam has been married to Adam Weaver, a business broker and real estate agent. The singer also has a fondness for the color yellow, which has become a staple of her wardrobe and a part of her branding strategy.

SUGGESTED READING

Dauphin, Chuck. "Welcome to Cam Country: Arista Nashville Singer Has a Short Name, Potentially Long Career." *Billboard*, 16 Apr. 2015, www.billboard.com/articles/columns/the-615/6531920/welcome-to-cam-country-arista-nashville-singer-has-a-short-name. Accessed 7 Apr. 2017.

Hight, Jewly. "'Burning House' Singer Cam: 'I Wasn't Sure How Much People Were Going to Take from A New Country Gal." *Billboard*, 22 Nov. 2015, www.billboard.com/articles/news/magazine-feature/6769958/cam-burning-house-untamed-album-interview. Accessed 7 Apr. 2017.

Malone, Dana. "Pathway to a Record Deal: Hard Work, Circumstance and Originality Take Cam Ochs 'Down the Road.'" *Sports & Entertainment Nashville Magazine*, 5 Sept. 2014, sportsandentertainmentnashville.com/pathway-to-a-record-deal-hard-work-circumstance-and-originality-take-camaron-ochs-down-the-road. Accessed 7 Apr. 2017.

Rau, Nate. "Sony Music CEO Doug Morris Touts Nashville Up-And-Comers." *The Tennessean*, 25 July 2015, www.tennessean.com/story/entertainment/music/2015/07/24/sony-music-ceo-doug-morris-touts-nashville-up-and-comers/30641039. Accessed 7 Apr. 2017.

—*Bertha Muteba*

Anne Case

Date of birth: July 27, 1958
Occupation: Economist

Anne Case is a professor of economics and public affairs at Princeton University. The general public might never have known her or her work were it not for a scholarly paper she cowrote in 2015. "Rising Morbidity and Mortality in Midlife among White Non-Hispanic Americans in the 21st Century" was published in September of that year in the *Proceedings of the National Academy of Sciences*, and mainstream media outlets were soon disseminating her findings with eye-catching headlines trumpeting the escalating annual death rates of middle-aged white Americans.

By analyzing data from the Centers for Disease Control and Prevention (CDC) and other such sources, Case and her coauthor concluded that rising death rates among the group were caused not by heart disease or diabetes, as might be expected, but by an epidemic of suicides, accidental overdoses of heroin and prescription painkillers, and the conditions caused by substance abuse, such as cirrhosis of the liver.

Many observers commented on the timeliness of the paper, given the public discussion around that time of the woes being suffered by increasingly disenfranchised blue-collar white Americans—a group whose votes arguably put Donald Trump, with his vows to "Make America Great Again," in the White House. "[We] touched a nerve last fall when we published a

UNU-WIDER from Helsinki, Finland/CC BY 2.0/
Wikimedia Commons

piece in the *Proceedings of the National Academy of Sciences* that documented that, among white non-Hispanics in middle age, mortality, after having fallen for large parts of the last century, actually turned up and started to go the wrong way," Case told Susan B. Glasser and Glenn Thrush for a roundtable interview that appeared in *Politico Magazine* (Sept./Oct. 2016). "The big drivers in that trend are what we call 'deaths of despair' . . . and it appears to be happening all over the country. And that resonated in this political season."

Ronald D. Lee, a professor at the University of California, Berkeley, expressed another reason why Case's findings may have captured people's attention so fully. "Seldom have I felt as affected by a paper," he told Gina Kolata for the *New York Times* (2 Nov. 2015). "It seems so sad."

Politico named Case—who also serves as a member of the World Bank's research committee and the UNAIDS Economic Reference Group—one of the fifty most important thinkers, doers, and visionaries transforming American politics in 2016. Her other laurels include the Kenneth J. Arrow Award for the Best Paper in Health Economics (for a 2002 article on economic status and health in childhood that was published in the *American Economic Review*) and the Princeton University President's Award for Distinguished Teaching. Her citation for the latter award read, in part, "Her students say, 'When I grow up I want to be Anne Case.' . . . She teaches students how to do rigorous scientific research that requires firm theoretical grounding, but that also has the capacity, if done well, to make the world a better place."

EARLY LIFE AND EDUCATION

Anne Catherine Case was born on July 27, 1958. Little other information about her childhood or formative years has been publicly disseminated. In 1980 she earned a BS degree from the State University of New York (SUNY) at Albany, graduating first in her class. (In 2009 the school gave her a Distinguished Alumni Award in recognition of work she was then doing to raise awareness of the effects of AIDS in sub-Saharan Africa.)

After leaving upstate New York, Case made the short trip to New Jersey and a leap to the Ivy League, entering Princeton University's Woodrow Wilson School of Public and International Affairs. There, in 1983, she earned a master's degree in public health, qualifying with distinction. She remained at Princeton for her doctoral studies, and in 1988 she received a PhD in economics.

ACADEMIC POSITIONS AND RESEARCH

Case began her career in academia at another Ivy League institution, Harvard University, where she served as an assistant professor in the department of economics from 1988 to 1991. She had returned to her alma mater, however, as a visiting assistant professor of economics and public affairs during the 1990–91 academic year, and she then made the move permanent, accepting an assistant professorship at the Woodrow Wilson School of Public and International Affairs. Case held that post until 1997, when she became a full professor, and since 2007 she has held an endowed chair as the Alexander Stewart 1886 Professor of Economics and Public Affairs.

In addition to her other teaching and research duties, from 2009 to 2011 she directed Princeton's Center for Health and Wellbeing, whose faculty members seek to understand the role that public policy plays in quality-of-life issues and to educate students who aspire to work in health and health policy. From 2010 to 2012 she was the associate chair of the university's economics department, and she now directs the Research Program in Development Studies, which focuses on such topics as poverty levels, household dynamics, the relationship between health and economic development, the links between income inequality and health status, global well-being, and school quality and educational outcomes.

Among the areas Case has recently researched are the social protection and labor market outcomes of youth in South Africa, the high cost of funerals in that country, and the correlations between suicide and reported well-being. After that last project, Case and her coauthor concluded, "Differences in suicides between men and women, between Hispanics, blacks, and whites, between age groups for men between countries or US states, between calendar years, and between days of the week, do not match differences in life evaluation. By contrast, reports of physical pain are strongly predictive of suicide in many contexts.

ATTENTION-GETTING CONCLUSIONS

In the course of their research, Case and her coauthor found that from 1978 to 1998, the mortality rate for whites between the ages of forty-five and fifty-four fell by 2 percent a year, thanks in large part to advances in medicine. After that, however, they began to rise by a half a percentage point a year. "The rise in death rates among middle-aged white Americans means half a million more people have died in the United States since 1998 than if the previous trend had continued," Ian Sample wrote for *The Guardian* (2 Nov. 2015). "The death toll is comparable to the 650,000 Americans who lost their lives during the [AIDS] epidemic from 1981 to the middle of this year."

The researchers found that deaths from drug and alcohol abuse, along with suicides, had risen dramatically, and that the trend was especially marked for those with no more than a high school diploma. In that group, deaths from drug overdoses and alcohol poisoning quadrupled, suicides rose by more than 80 percent, and deaths from liver disease and cirrhosis by half. Overall, deaths rose more than a fifth during that period for white people without a college degree. "This was absolutely a surprise to us," Case told Sample. "It knocked us off our chairs." (Case has one major point of connection and empathy to some of her statistical subjects; she herself suffered from chronic, debilitating back pain for a dozen years.)

The paper made waves on both the left and the right. In an op-ed for the *New York Times* (9 Nov. 2015) labeled "Despair, American Style" noted economist Paul Krugman wrote, "I'm not the only observer who sees a link between the despair reflected in those mortality numbers and the volatility of right-wing politics. Some people who feel left behind by the American story turn self-destructive; others turn on the elites they feel have betrayed them." He concluded, "At this point you probably expect me to offer a solution. But while universal health care, higher minimum wages, aid to education, and so on would do a lot to help Americans in trouble, I'm not sure whether they're enough to cure existential despair." In a piece for that same paper published two days earlier, noted right-wing commentator Ross Douthat opined that whites were unprepared for the vicissitudes of the recession and the dot-com bust and were thus less resilient than members of minority groups, who had learned, historically, to cope with hardship and disappointment. "If this possibility has policy implications, it suggests that liberals are right to emphasize the economic component to the working class's crisis," he wrote. "But it cautions against the idea that transfer payments can substitute for the sense of meaning and purpose that blue-collar white Americans derived from the nexus of work, faith, and family until very recently."

As often happens in the world of scholarly research, skeptics emerged, asserting that Case's methodology had been flawed or the results skewed. Andrew Gelman, a professor of statistics and political science at Columbia University, for example, wrote for the online magazine *Slate* (11 Nov. 2015), "It was brought to my attention that the observed increase in mortality among a group of Americans aged forty-five to fifty-four could be a statistical artifact resulting from the coarseness of the age category. The culprit is the postwar baby boom, that notorious period from 1946 through 1964 when Americans were producing children like rabbits." When adjusted so that there were equal numbers of people of each age in the group, Gelman found that the death rate had been more or less static since

2005. However, he said, "this is all in no way a 'debunking' of the Case and Deaton paper. Their main result is the comparison to other countries, and that holds up just fine."

PERSONAL LIFE

Case is married to Sir Angus Deaton, a Scottish-born economist who was knighted in 2016. As such, she is entitled to be addressed as Lady Deaton, although few American media outlets do so. Deaton won the Nobel Memorial Prize in Economic Sciences in 2015 "for his analysis of consumption, poverty, and welfare," as the official Nobel site states. A fellow professor at Princeton, he has coauthored many papers with Case, including "Rising Morbidity and Mortality in Midlife among White Non-Hispanic Americans in the 21st Century."

SUGGESTED READING

Case, Anne. "'Deaths of Despair' Are Killing America's White Working Class." *Quartz*, 30 Dec. 2015, qz.com/583595/deaths-of-despair-are-killing-americas-white-working-class. Accessed 3 Jan. 2017.

Gelman, Andrew. "Is the Death Rate Really Increasing for Middle-Aged White Americans?" *Slate*, 11 Nov. 2015, www.slate.com/articles/health_and_science/science/2015/11/death_rates_for_white_middle_aged_americans_are_not_increasing.html. Accessed 3 Jan. 2017.

Glasser, Susan B., and Glenn Thrush. "What's Going On with America's White People?" *Politico Magazine*, Sept./Oct. 2016, www.politico.com/magazine/story/2016/09/problems-white-people-america-society-class-race-214227. Accessed 3 Jan. 2017.

Kolata, Gina. "Death Rates Rising for Middle-Aged White Americans, Study Finds." *New York Times*, 2 Nov. 2015, www.nytimes.com/2015/11/03/health/death-rates-rising-for-middle-aged-white-americans-study-finds.html. Accessed 3 Jan. 2017.

Sample, Ian. "Rising Deaths among White Middle-Aged Americans Could Exceed AIDS Toll in US." *The Guardian*, 2 Nov. 2015, www.theguardian.com/science/2015/nov/02/death-rate-middle-aged-white-americans-aids. Accessed 3 Jan. 2017.

"Tiger of the Week: Anne Case '83 '88." *Princeton Alumni Weekly*, 1 June 2011, paw.princeton.edu/article/tiger-week-anne-case-83-88. Accessed 3 Jan. 2017.

—*Mari Rich*

Chance the Rapper

Date of birth: April 16, 1993
Occupation: Rapper

Chance the Rapper, born Chancelor Bennett, is a Grammy Award–winning hip-hop artist. He released his debut mixtape, *10 Day* (2012), at the age of eighteen and later collaborated with Kanye West on *The Life of Pablo* (2016), most notably on the gospel-inflected track "Ultralight Beam." Chance released his third mixtape, the Grammy Award–winning *Coloring Book*, in 2016. Describing Chance's singular voice, Zach Baron for *GQ* (24 Aug. 2016) wrote, "There's nothing like it in music right now. It's its own jazz instrument, bright and unpredictable as a trumpet, primary colored, a cheerful roar soaked in a meditative sadness. He's an uncommonly dexterous rapper, but it's the voice—the physical quality of it, the way it feels textured by experience and elation—that's truly remarkable." Chance is also notable among his fellow artists for his refusal to sign with a record label. He has released his first three records for free and makes money touring and selling merchandise.

Born and raised in Chicago, Chance has been a prominent advocate for the city's youth. He performs small acts of charity—such as when he took a group of kids to Chicago's Field Museum of Natural History in 2015 or bought out all the showings of the thriller *Get Out* at a Chicago movie theater so people could see the film for free in 2017. He also gives to charity on a much larger scale. In 2015, Chance helped raise $100,000 to purchase technology equipment for six Chicago elementary schools, organized a monthly open-mike night for teens in collaboration with the Chicago Public Library, and helped to organize the first free Teens in the Park Festival, to which he invited Grammy Award–winning rapper Kendrick Lamar. In March 2017, his nonprofit organization, SocialWorks, raised a staggering $2.2 million—including $1 million of his own money—for Chicago public schools. The donation came after Chance met with Illinois governor Bruce Rauner, who had previously vetoed a bill to address the school system's $215 million budget deficit. "While I'm frustrated and disappointed in the governor's inaction, that will not stop me from continuing to do all I can to support Chicago's most valued resources, its children," he said, as quoted by Rodney Carmichael for NPR's *The Record* (6 Mar. 2017).

EARLY LIFE AND MUSICAL INFLUENCES

Chancelor Bennett was born in Chicago, Illinois, on April 16, 1993. He was raised in the West Chatham neighborhood on the city's South

Side, in a home that has been in his family for generations. His mother, Lisa, worked in the office of the Illinois attorney general. His father, Ken, was a community organizer who worked for Barack Obama when Obama was an Illinois state senator and during Obama's first term as president. His father later worked for Chicago mayor Rahm Emanuel; part of his job was to take a call each morning and record a list of the names and ages of people who had been killed in the city the day before. Chance also has a younger brother named Taylor.

Chance came of age during one of the city's most violent eras but also one of its most musically rich. As a teenager, he watched local rappers Chief Keef, King Louie, and Lil Durk rise to stardom, but he was uneasy with the way labels and media outlets chose to portray them. Referring to a 2012 video interview with Chief Keef at a gun range for *Pitchfork*, Chance described the media coverage of Chicago rappers to Baron as "poverty porn that was not something that was afflicting them on a personal level." (*Pitchfork* subsequently retracted the video and removed it from their archives, calling the location selection "insensitive and irresponsible.")

As a child, Chance loved Michael Jackson and he studied Jackson's performance on the *Live in Bucharest: The Dangerous Tour* DVD. "If I hadn't gotten that DVD, I wouldn't be a live performer," he told David Drake for *Complex* (16 Sept. 2013). "That was what I studied, the dancing on stage and incorporation of the crowd and the leg drops and the emotion of the set. Making it a story so that people stay with you the whole time." When he was in fourth or fifth grade, he began listening to Kanye West. Chance and West are less than twenty years apart in age, but their careers are separated by a radical shift in rap music, engineered by West. "I'm a part of the generation that really experienced Kanye as more of an icon and a representative of hip hop, [rather] than [as] a newcomer," Chance told Drake for *Complex* (23 Mar. 2013). West—whose debut album, *The College Dropout*, was released in 2004—paved the way for idiosyncratic rappers like Chance who seek to test the limits of the hip-hop sound.

EARLY RAP CAREER

As a student at the prestigious Jones College Prep High School, Chance began attending a poetry open-mike through the Digital Youth Network (DYN). Chance already considered himself a rapper—he was recording tracks as part of a duo called Instrumentality at the time—but the live performances let him flex his lyric muscles and hone his stage presence. In 2009, with the encouragement of mentor "Brother" Mike Hawkins, he wrote a song called "Beddy Bye" for a citywide contest; the song won second place.

In 2011, when he was a senior in high school, Chance received a ten-day suspension for smoking marijuana. It was an unusually fortuitous turn of events; the young rapper used the two free weeks to start writing his first mixtape, a concept album based on his suspension. Over the course of eight months, he recorded it at the DYN studio space YOUmedia at the Harold Washington Library. The mixtape, titled, appropriately enough, *10 Day*, was released online as a free digital download in April 2012. It confirmed the hype that had been building around Chance's name in Chicago. He described the tape as his "coming out" to Corban Goble for *Pitchfork* (23 Apr. 2013). "This is what it's like to go to a gifted school, to be addicted to drugs, and to be eighteen in Chicago," he said.

However, his success was not immediate. At his own expense, he printed out four thousand physical copies of a mixtape called *5 Day*, which featured different takes of *10 Day* tracks that he handed out for free to people on the streets of Chicago, building a grassroots fan base. *10 Day* landed him a gig at the South by Southwest (SXSW) festival, where Dan Weiner, the publicist for rapper Childish Gambino, saw him perform. Chance went on to contribute lyrics to Childish Gambino's song "They Don't Like Me" and tour with him. While helping to launch his career, *10 Day* also contained certain elements—spaced out vibes, jazzy textures, bittersweet recollections—that would define his next mixtape, *Acid Rap* (2013).

ACID RAP

Working on *Acid Rap*, Chance looked to his influences, including West, Eminem, and the Los Angeles–based jazz rap crew Freestyle Fellowship, to create a sound that would be uniquely his own. "When I found Freestyle Fellowship, I started getting into the construction of rap," he told Drake for *Complex* (16 Sept. 2013). "You get better at it the more you do it, you figure out the science and the math behind it. You can construct [it] like it's a problem instead of listening to the song." The tape's title refers to Chance's incorporation of acid jazz—a genre that traditionally combines elements of soul, funk, and disco—but also to the psychedelic drug; Chance made a good portion of the tape while under the influence. Two songs, "Acid Rain" and "Juice," touch on the 2011 murder of Chance's friend Rodney Kyles Jr., which he witnessed.

Chance released *Acid Rap* as a free digital download in April 2013; the tape was so highly anticipated that fan traffic crashed the hosting site, Audiomack. Critics were equally enthusiastic. "As the album title suggests, the beats, though solidly hooky, have a woozy, psychedelic feel," Jody Rosen wrote for *Rolling Stone* (8 May 2013). "But it's the density of wit, ideas, and verbal invention that makes this one of the year's defining hip-hop releases." *Acid Rap* effectively launched Chance's career; he briefly moved to Los Angeles before returning to Chicago after six months. In 2015, Chance collaborated with his touring band, Donnie Trumpet and the Social Experiment, on their record *Surf*, which includes one of Chance's best-known songs, "Sunday Candy," an expression of Chance's spirituality and his love for his grandmother. That album was also a critical success. David Drake, who reviewed the album for *Pitchfork* (5 June 2015), praised its "wide-ranging, joyfully meandering spirit."

COLORING BOOK

Chance collaborated with West on West's seventh studio album, *The Life of Pablo* (2016). Chance played an integral role in the production of the album, helping to write the songs "Father Stretch My Hands, Pt. 1," "Famous," "Feedback," and "Waves," in addition to the transcendent "Ultralight Beam," on which Chance has a prominently featured verse. On that verse, Chance raps, referencing West, "He said let's do a good ass job with Chance three / I hear you gotta sell it to snatch the Grammy." Chance, who had thus far released all his albums for free online, was referring to the Recording Academy rule that deemed only commercially released albums be eligible for Grammy Award consideration. Despite this rule—and his verse on "Ultralight Beam"—Chance released his third mixtape, *Coloring Book*, as a free digital download in

May 2016. That month, *Coloring Book* became the first streaming-only album to chart on the Billboard 200, where it peaked at number eight. Soon after, with the encouragement of fellow artist Pharrell Williams, Chance started a petition to change this rule. The Recording Academy officially changed its policy regarding streaming albums in June, although it stated that Chance's petition did not influence the decision. In December 2016, Chance was nominated for seven Grammy Awards; he won three, including best new artist, best rap album, and best rap performance for the song "No Problem."

Coloring Book marks an important shift in Chance's personal life. After spending a drug-addled period in Los Angeles, Chance moved back to Chicago, where he and his then girl-friend, Kirsten Corley, gave birth to a daughter, Kinsley Bennett, in September 2015. "Ultralight Beam," released as it was before *Coloring Book*, provides a good aural and thematic introduction to the rapper's third mixtape, which is heavily influenced by gospel music. Songs such as "Same Drugs," which is about two people growing apart ("We don't do the same drugs no more"), and "Blessings," which makes reference to the birth of his daughter and his renewed faith in God, speak to Chance's personal maturation as well as his radical new musical vision. Kris Ex, who reviewed the tape for *Pitchfork* (17 May 2016), described *Coloring Book* as "one of the strongest rap albums released this year" and "an uplifting mix of spiritual and grounded that even an atheist can catch the Spirit to." He went on to praise the mixtape as "personal and panoramic, full of conversations with God, defying hip-hop norms while respecting them, proving that the genre can still dig deeper into its roots."

SUGGESTED READING

Baron, Zach. "How Chance the Rapper's Life Became Perfect." *GQ*, 24 Aug. 2016, www.gq.com/story/how-chance-the-rappers-life-became-perfect. Accessed 7 Sept. 2017.

Carmichael, Rodney. "Chance the Rapper Puts Up $1 Million to Support Chicago Public Schools." *The Record*, NPR, 6 Mar. 2017, http://www.npr.org/sections/therecord/2017/03/06/518864904/chance-the-rapper-puts-up-1-million-to-support-chicago-public-schools. Accessed 7 Sept. 2017.

Drake, David. "Chance the Rapper: Acid Test." *Complex*, 16 Sept. 2013, www.complex.com/music/2013/09/chance-the-rapper-interview-complex-cover-story. Accessed 7 Sept. 2017.

Drake, David. Review of *Surf*, by Donnie Trumpet and the Social Experiment. *Pitchfork*, 5 June 2015, pitchfork.com/reviews/albums/20664-surf. Accessed 7 Sept. 2017.

Drake, David. "Who Is Chance the Rapper?" *Complex*, 23 Mar. 2013, www.complex.com/music/2013/09/chance-the-rapper-interview-complex-cover-story. Accessed 7 Sept. 2017.

Ex, Kris. Review of *Coloring Book*, by Chance the Rapper. *Pitchfork*, 17 May 2016, pitchfork.com/reviews/albums/21909-coloring-book. Accessed 7 Sept. 2017.

Rosen, Jody. Review of *Acid Rap*, by Chance the Rapper. *Rolling Stone*, 8 May 2013, www.rollingstone.com/music/albumreviews/acid-rap-20130508. Accessed 7 Sept. 2017.

SELECTED WORKS

10 Day, 2012; *Acid Rap*, 2013; *Coloring Book*, 2016

—Molly Hagan

Tina Charles

Date of birth: December 5, 1988
Occupation: Professional basketball player

Tina Charles is a forward for the New York Liberty. A two-time National Collegiate Athletic Association (NCAA) Champion with the University of Connecticut (UConn) Huskies, Charles was the first pick of the Women's National Basketball Association (WNBA) draft, going to Connecticut Sun, in 2010. At the end of the season, she was named Rookie of the Year, and in 2012, she was voted the league's most valuable player. Charles, who played on the US Women's Olympic team in 2012 and 2016, is also a two-time gold medalist. The Queens, New York, native joined her hometown Liberty in 2014. Writing for Long Island's *Newsday* (22 Sept. 2016), sportswriter Barbara Barker called the six-feet-four Charles "the most dominant professional athlete in the New York area." In 2016 Charles led the WNBA in scoring and rebounds, and was named Eastern Conference Player of the Month all four months of the regular season. Off the court, Charles has recently become a prominent activist, though the player has always been quietly involved in philanthropy and social justice, particularly through her own Hopey's Heart Foundation, named for her late aunt, Maureen "Hopey" Vaz.

In early July 2016, two unarmed African American men—Philando Castile in St. Anthony, Minnesota and Alton Sterling in Baton Rouge, Louisiana—were killed by police officers. The same week, five police officers were shot and killed in Dallas, Texas. The killings electrified the growing Black Lives Matter civil rights movement, and inspired Charles to take action. Before the Liberty game on July 10, the team wore black t-shirts featuring the hashtags #BlackLivesMatter and #Dallas5. The

By Sphilbrick (Own work) [CC BY-SA 3.0], via
Wikimedia Commons

Liberty was one of a handful of teams to wear such shirts; Christina Cauterucci for *Slate* (25 July 2016) called it "one of the most united, persistent political statements in sports history." The WNBA fined the players for not wearing their official uniform, but Charles doubled down. On July 21, she accepted her Player of the Month Award with her official warm-up uniform turned inside out in protest. (The league later rescinded the fines.) "It shows that there's more to us than putting a ball in a basket," Charles told Seth Berkman for the *New York Times* (30 July 2016) of the protest. "We are women. We have a voice. Oftentimes women are forced to be silent, and that's why I think it's really a beautiful thing what we were able to do, very resilient of us to say, 'No, this time we're not going to be silent.'"

EARLY LIFE AND EDUCATION

Charles was born in New York City on December 5, 1988. Her mother, Angella Holgate, is from Jamaica, and her father, Rawlston Charles, was born in Tobago. In 1972 more than a decade before Charles was born, her father opened up a record shop called Charlie's Calypso City in the Bedford-Stuyvesant neighborhood of Brooklyn. The shop remains the heart of a thriving Caribbean community in the borough. Charles's brother, Rawlston Charles Jr., is a professional basketball player in Europe. Charles grew up in Jamaica, Queens, but from the second to fourth grade, she and her mother lived with Vaz, Charles's aunt and Holgate's sister, in Florida. Charles credits Hopey, as she called Vaz, for introducing her to sports, first baseball and then

basketball. It was only the beginning of her aunt's impact on her life.

Charles attended Christ the King Regional High School in Middle Village, Queens. The small, private school is known for its basketball team—Royals alumni include WNBA stars like Chamique Holdsclaw and Sue Bird, one of the best point guards in WNBA history. Charles played under coach Bob Mackey, who remains at the school. In an interview with Budd Mishkin for New York City's *NY1* (8 Aug. 2016), Charles said that her early success was spurred by a "drive to be consistent." She added, "You know, wanting to be able to finish around the rim. Wanting to set little goals for myself. Wanting to separate myself from others. . . I always had to work for what I have. A lot of individuals believe that, you know, I'm just talented. But no, I had to work on every skill set."

During her junior and senior years, Charles was the lead scorer on the team. She led the Royals to fifty-seven consecutive wins, and finished her high school career ranked number one in the country. She was the Gatorade National Player of the Year and the *USA Today* High School Player of the Year in 2006, the year she graduated and enrolled at the University of Connecticut. Charles majored in psychology and minored in criminology. During her senior year, she interned at Bergin Correctional Institution, a minimum-security prison near the campus. Charles shadowed the correctional officer and the warden, and sat in on counseling sessions in which inmates talked about their hopes for the future. "They are just everyday people, people you would see anywhere you go. They are just people who have made mistakes," Charles told Kristie Ackert for the New York *Daily News* (6 Mar. 2010) of the people she worked with. "Everybody makes mistakes, you have to learn from them and change."

COLLEGE CAREER AT UCONN

Charles played for the UConn Huskies, one of the best women's teams in college basketball, but her tenure there was varied. As freshman in 2006, Charles was named the US Basketball Writers Association (USBWA) Player of the Year as well as the Big East Freshman of the Year, but the player struggled during her sophomore year. After the Huskies lost to Stanford and were knocked out of the 2008 Final Four, Coach Geno Auriemma called Charles out in front of the whole team. "He said we didn't have a post presence, that was why we lost," she recalled to Ackert. "I'm the post, so it was my fault."

Charles's hard work during her junior year paid off; she led the team through an undefeated season to an NCAA Championship title. She registered twenty-five points and nineteen rebounds in the Huskies' winning game over

Louisville, and was named Most Outstanding Player of the 2009 Final Four. In 2010, Charles led the team through another undefeated season to another NCAA Championship, this time over Stanford. Charles ended her college career as UConn's top career scorer and rebounder. The Big East coaches voted her player of the year. She also received the John R. Wooden and the Naismith College Player of the Year Awards.

WNBA CAREER

Less than two days after her NCAA victory, Charles was selected by the Connecticut Sun as the first pick of the WNBA draft. "It's unbelievable, my heart is still pounding out of my chest," Charles told Doug Feinberg for the Associated Press (AP), as it appeared on *Boston.com* (8 Apr. 2010), adding, "I'm more interested what impact I'll have on the team more than just being the No. 1 pick." Charles certainly did have an impact—she set a league record for total rebounds, making 398 during her first year. She was unanimously voted Rookie of the Year in 2010.

In 2011 Charles made 374 rebounds, the second-most single-season rebounds in league history, and set a WNBA record with twenty-three double-doubles (when a player makes a double-digit record in two categories). She was also named a WNBA All-Star for the first time. In 2012 Charles was named the league's most valuable player. She set a Sun record, averaging eighteen points a game, and won her third straight rebounding title, averaging 10.5 rebounds a game. As a member of the US Women's Basketball team, Charles earned her first gold medal at the London Olympic Games. Injuries plagued the end of her 2013 season, and at the end of the 2014 season, Charles put pressure on the Sun to trade her to the New York Liberty. In exchange, the Sun got forward Alyssa Thomas, Kelsey Bone, and the first pick of the 2015 draft. But the Sun were unhappy about the deal, and the franchise and local newspapers took some parting shots at Charles—about her perceived lack of drive or her "diva" desire to choose her own path, according to Berkman for the *New York Times* (11 May 2014)—before she left.

During her first season with the Liberty, Charles averaged 17.1 points and 8.5 rebounds a game. Her 2016 season, her seventh in the league, was one of her best to date. She led the WNBA in scoring, averaging 21.5 points and 9.9 rebounds a game, and became the third player in league history to win both statistical titles in the same season. She became the first WNBA player to sweep the entire regular season player of the month awards, as well as the first to receive four in a row. Charles came in second in MVP voting, and led Team USA to a gold medal, her second, at the 2016 Olympic Games in Rio de Janeiro, Brazil.

HOPEY'S HEART FOUNDATION AND OTHER PHILANTHROPY

Charles has been devoted to charitable causes and social justice since she was young. She began traveling to visit her mother's family in Jamaica when she was a little girl, but was troubled that many of her friends there did not have shoes. Years later, in 2011, Charles bought 5,000 pairs of Nike athletic shoes and donated them to students at St. Jago High School in Spanish Town. In 2012 after reading a story online, she donated $32,000 to build a school in Ganale, a village in Mali. Charles has consistently donated half of her WNBA salary to charity. In 2016, she donated her entire WNBA salary to Hopey's Heart. Her giving is remarkable given that Charles commands the league's maximum salary—about $110,000. Charles, like most WNBA players, plays overseas in the off-season, where women players are paid more.

The idea for Charles's foundation, Hopey's Heart, was born out of her close relationship with her aunt. In 2010, when Charles played in the FIBA World Cup for Women in the Czech Republic, she brought Hopey with her. The two women forged a deep friendship that ended when Hopey passed away of multiple organ failure in 2013. Inspired by Hopey's big and loving heart, Charles founded her own organization to distribute automated external defibrillators (AEDs). She was familiar with the difference AEDs could make, having already donated $14,775 to the New York Department of Education and the Wes Leonard Heart Foundation—named after Wes Leonard, a high school basketball star who collapsed of heart failure during a game in 2011—to put AEDs in schools. She threw herself into the cause as well as the process of building the foundation. "She had really found her passion," Swin Cash, Charles's former teammate, told David Gardner for *Sports Illustrated* (18 Sept. 2015), "and that's important, because your passion keeps you going even when most of your work goes unnoticed. Anybody can write a check, but with Tina you see the passion, and you see the results."

SUGGESTED READING

Ackert, Kristie. "UConn Basketball Star Tina Charles Helping Inmates Make Turns for the Better with Prison Internship." *Daily News*, 6 Mar. 2010, www.nydailynews.com/sports/college/uconn-basketball-star-tina-charles-helping-inmates-turns-better-prison-internship-article-1.171447. Accessed 13 Mar. 2017.

Barker, Barbara. "Nobody Dominates Like Liberty's Tina Charles." *Newsday*, 22 Sept. 2016, www.newsday.com/sports/columnists/barbara-barker/nobody-dominates-like-liberty-s-tina-charles-1.12354679. Accessed 13 Mar. 2017.

Berkman, Seth. "Quiet Protest Helped Tina Charles Find the Voice of Her Conscience." *The New York Times*, 30 July 2016, www.ny-times.com/2016/07/31/sports/basketball/tina-charles-new-york-liberty-wnba-protest.html. Accessed 12 Mar. 2017.

Cauterucci, Christina. "The WNBA's Black Lives Matter Protest Has Set a New Standard for Sports Activism." *Slate*, 25 July 2016. Accessed 13 Mar. 2017.

Feinberg, Doug. "UConn's Charles Taken No. 1 in WNBA Draft." *Boston.com*, 8 Apr. 2010, archive.boston.com/sports/basketball/articles/2010/04/08/uconns_charles_tak-en_no_1_in_wnba_draft/. Accessed 13 Mar. 2017.

Gardner, David. "New York Liberty Star Tina Charles Determined to Help Her Community." *Sports Illustrated*, 18 Sept. 2015, www.si.com/wnba/2015/09/18/tina-charles-wnba-playoffs-new-york-liberty-hopeys-heart-foundation. Accessed 13 Mar. 2017.

Mishkin, Budd. "One on 1 Profile: WNBA Superstar and Queens Native Tina Charles Goes for the Gold Again in Rio." *NY1*, 8 Aug. 2016, www.ny1.com/nyc/all-boroughs/one-on-1/2016/08/8/one-on-1-profile--a-wnba-su-perstar-and-queens-native-tina-charles-goes-for-the-gold-again-in-rio.html. Accessed 12 Mar. 2017.

—*Molly Hagan*

Damien Chazelle

Date of birth: January 19, 1985
Occupation: Film director

At the age of thirty-two, film director and writer Damien Chazelle received the 2017 Academy Award for best director for his musical film *La La Land*, which starred Ryan Gosling and Emma Stone, making him the youngest person ever to receive the Oscar for best director. The film won six Oscars and received fourteen nominations in total. *La La Land* performed exceedingly well at the box office, put the spotlight on the young director, and caused critics to speculate that Chazelle had revived the movie musical.

La La Land is only the third film that Chazelle has directed. The second film he directed, *Whiplash* (2014), tells the story of an ambitious nineteen-year-old jazz drummer and his win-at-all-costs, abusive instructor. That film also received critical acclaim. The film had elements of autobiography, for Chazelle had also played drums in his high school band. *Whiplash* earned him his first Oscar nomination. In addition to writing the screenplays for the three films

By MarinSD [CC BY-SA 2.0], via Wikimedia Commons

he directed, he has also written screenplays for *The Last Exorcism Part II* (2013), *Grand Piano* (2013), and *10 Cloverfield Lane* (2016).

TWO MAJOR PASSIONS

Damien Chazelle was born on January 19, 1985, in Providence, Rhode Island. He and his younger sister, Anna, were raised in Princeton, New Jersey. Anna Chazelle went on to become a professional circus performer and actor, and she has appeared in two of her brother's films, including *La La Land*. Chazelle's father, Bernard Chazelle, who had immigrated to the United States from Paris, France, taught computer science at Princeton University. His mother, Celia Chazelle, taught medieval history at the College of New Jersey. There was some film industry–related work on Chazelle's mother's side of the family—Chazelle's maternal great-grandfather worked in London at Paramount Pictures; his maternal great-grandmother acted in plays in the United Kingdom; and his maternal grandfather, John Martin, appeared in a few films in Los Angeles. Martin, speaking to Eric Volmers for the *Calgary Herald* (3 Feb. 2017), said that he liked to think that Chazelle's interest in filmmaking came from him.

Chazelle did seem to be set on becoming a filmmaker from a very young age. Chazelle had a great interest in music and film from the age of three. He obsessively watched and rewatched movies, such as *Cinderella*. He even told his parents, when he was three years old, that he wanted to make films. The following year, according to a profile by Amy Kuperinsky for *NJ.com* (26

Feb. 2017), four-year-old Chazelle was story-boarding, drawing scene-by-scene outlines of movies he wanted to make. By the time he was thirteen, he was writing movie scripts. He would read them out loud to family members, including Martin. "I would show signs of impatience and he would say, 'Just a minute Grandpa, I'll be finished in forty minutes,'" Martin recalled to Volmers. Chazelle cast his family members in the movies he made with his video camera.

During his adolescence Chazelle attended Princeton High School, where he played in the school band. He played drums and was very passionate about becoming proficient. Both his drive to master the instrument and the harsh treatment he received from his band teacher later served as inspiration for his second feature film, *Whiplash*. Chazelle first learned about jazz from his father, according to Kuperinsky. During high school, Chazelle was fearful and anxious by the pressure to play well with his school band—so much so that he would at times be unable to eat breakfast and lunch. Chazelle was a good drummer, but he wanted to be an excellent filmmaker. By the time he graduated from high school, he knew that his true calling was filmmaking.

HARVARD UNIVERSITY

Chazelle studied filmmaking at Harvard University's Department of Visual and Environmental Studies in Cambridge, Massachusetts. During his freshman year he met fellow Harvard student Justin Hurwitz, who would later score Chazelle's films, most notably *Whiplash* and *La La Land*. Because of their mutual love of music, they became close friends. As freshmen, they formed a band, in which Hurwitz played electric piano and Chazelle played drums. They played around Boston, but the following year they both dropped out of the band yet remained friends.

They often pushed each other creatively, even as their creative pursuits continued to take them in different directions. During their sophomore year they began collaborating on a musical that ultimately became Chazelle's first film, *Guy and Madeline on a Park Bench*. Chazelle took some time off from college to work on the film as his senior thesis. The fact that this musical film was a kind of precursor to *La La Land*—an idea frequently mentioned in profiles of Chazelle—certainly makes sense in retrospect. After graduating from Harvard in 2007, Chazelle moved to Los Angeles, California.

GUY AND MADELINE

Guy and Madeline on a Park Bench began making film festival rounds in 2009 and got a bigger release the following year. It was shot in black and white on 16 mm film. Though it takes place in the present, in Boston and New York City, the feel of the film is somewhat reminiscent of the 1950s and 1960s. In the film, Guy (played by trumpeter Jason Palmer) has a complicated relationship with Madeline (played by Desiree Garcia). The dialogue seems to be less important than the music and unspoken communication of dance moves and facial expressions. There are notable musical numbers that seem improvised, such as when Guy plays his trumpet and his horn call is "answered" by another man tap dancing and banging the floor with a drumstick. Madeline is a waitress, and the film opens as the three month-long relationship between Guy and Madeline begins to dissolve. Much of the film is about how they will (or will not) come back to one another. Guy has a new romantic interest, Elena, so the answer is up in the air.

The musical film was impressive to critics as a first feature. Though plot and character development are not the film's strong points, wrote Jeannette Catsoulis for the *New York Times* (4 Nov. 2010), it had other elements that drove it forward. "The story's dramatic weaknesses," wrote Catsoulis, "are the music's opportunities, and *Guy and Madeline* soars in the cool sizzle of Guy's trumpet solos and the blissed-out atmosphere of his jam sessions. Eruptions of singing and tap-dancing—in a jazz club, a diner, a park—range from joyous to resilient to wistful, their choreographed emotions filling in for the characters' maddening inscrutability." The film was selected as a *New York Times* Critics' Pick. In a review for the *Hollywood Reporter* (15 Oct. 2009), Sura Wood called the film a "distinctive debut feature." Wood went on to add that despite being greatly influenced by the French New Wave directors of the 1960s, Chazelle made something that is unique. "His film suggests," wrote Wood, "that the emotional connection between players and instruments is direct, passionate, and unequivocal and that music, a jazzy, exhilarating soundtrack underscoring daily life, is the lingua franca of human experience."

WHIPLASH

Chazelle's second film, *Whiplash* (2014), continued to explore the relationship between human experience and music—namely jazz. Like his first film, *Whiplash* was first created as a short film that ran just eighteen minutes. Chazelle had to do that to raise the necessary funds, but once the short film got some acclaim at festivals, he proceeded to make a longer version. In some ways, this film was a lot more personal than *Guy and Madeline*. Although Chazelle's first feature incorporated his love of music, particularly jazz, his second feature mined his own experience as a driven drummer of his high school jazz band. Like in the film, he had a particularly strict, tough teacher who drove him to the breaking point. In the film, Andrew (played by Miles Teller) is a promising young drummer who wants to be the best. He is studying at a music conservatory, where his bandleader and instructor, Terence Fletcher (played by J. K. Simmons) is more like a tough, aggressive football coach. Andrew, nineteen years old, pushes himself so hard practicing that his fingers bleed. He trains for drumming as if for a sporting event. Fletcher is abusive and relentless. He does not shy away from making his musicians cry or kicking someone out of the band for seemingly small mistakes, and he thinks nothing of stopping practice to test his musicians, both to see if they know the score and to test their patience and focus by shouting insults at them. He thinks one of the worst things a teacher can say is "good job." Andrew, for his part, is so determined to be the best that he deals with Fletcher by practicing even more and gives up a potentially promising romance with a young lady so he can focus exclusively on drumming. The film received several Academy Award nominations in 2015, including nods for best picture and best adapted screenplay.

The film received a lot of praise, although some critics took issue with Chazelle treating jazz like a physical sport without offering much insight into the genre or the characters' inner lives. Writing for the *Guardian* (18 Jan. 2015), Mark Kermode compared the film to the 1976 boxing movie *Rocky* and the 1987 Vietnam War film *Full Metal Jacket*. Kermode wrote, "Considering the slimness of the plot and the familiar verse-chorus-middle-eight structure of the narrative (boy meets girl, drum meets boy, girl loses boy to drum, etc.) it's dazzling how sprightly and inventive this conspires to be." What Kermode found perhaps most impressive was how Chazelle "manages to turn an impromptu drum solo—that most unforgivably indulgent of musical breaks—into a tense and engrossing dramatic set piece that sets the heart racing."

LA LA LAND

Unlike *Whiplash*, which was a film *about* music, *La La Land* (2016) was a movie musical, featuring characters breaking into song and dance. Although such films enjoyed widespread popularity in the mid-twentieth century, movie musicals are not the most common or most lucrative form of filmmaking today. And unlike Chazelle's first film, this one was full of vivid colors. *La La Land* is about an aspiring actor named Mia (played by Emma Stone) and a talented musician named Sebastian (played by Ryan Gosling). The two meet in a traffic jam. The film, after all, takes place in Los Angeles. But sparks do not fly and no romance ensues after their accidental second meeting either. It is only after their third meeting that they begin their relationship. The story

is their romance, but the driving force of the film is the music and dancing.

La La Land "integrates its numbers, even the most fantastical, as if it were the most natural thing in the world for a guy to tap-dance on a park bench or a woman to dream herself into a waltz," wrote Manohla Dargis for the *New York Times* (23 Nov. 2016). In the review she also suggested that Chazelle may very well have single-handedly made "musicals matter again." Writing for the *New Yorker* (12 Dec. 2016), Anthony Lane, referring to the use of bright colors in the film, confessed that the film "looks so delicious that I genuinely couldn't decide whether to watch it or lick it. The cinematographer, Linus Sandgren, shot it on film, and the colors, rather than merge into the landscape, seem to burst in your face." At the end of his review, Lane encouraged his readers to see the film in theaters on "the largest screen you can find, with a sound system to match." The film received fourteen Oscar nominations and won six of them, including best actress for Emma Stone, best original score and best original song, *City of Stars*, for Justin Hurwitz, and best director for Chazelle. In 2017 the film won a record-breaking seven Golden Globe Awards, including best director, best screenplay, best motion picture musical, best actor, best actress, best original score, and best original song.

PERSONAL LIFE

From 2010 to 2014 Chazelle was married to filmmaker Jasmine McGlade. He currently lives with actor Olivia Hamilton.

SUGGESTED READING

Brody, Richard. "Getting Jazz Right in the Movies." Review of *Whiplash*, directed by Damien Chazelle. *The New Yorker*, 13 Oct. 2014, www.newyorker.com/culture/richard-brody/whiplash-getting-jazz-right-movies. Accessed 3 Apr. 2017.

Catsoulis, Jeannette. "The Blissed-Out Rhythms of the Young and in Love." Review of *Guy and Madeline on a Park Bench*, directed by Damien Chazelle. *The New York Times*, 4 Nov. 2010, www.nytimes.com/2010/11/05/movies/05guy.html. Accessed 3 Apr. 2017.

Dargis, Manohla. "'La La Land' Makes Musicals Matter Again." Review of *La La Land*, directed by Damien Chazelle. *The New York Times*, 23 Nov. 2016, www.nytimes.com/2016/11/23/movies/la-la-land-makes-musicals-matter-again.html. Accessed 3 Apr. 2017.

Kermode, Mark. "'Whiplash' Review—Drumming Up the Tension Nicely." Review of *Whiplash*, directed by Damien Chazelle. *The Guardian*, 18 Jan. 2015, www.theguardian.com/film/2015/jan/18/

whiplash-review-drummer-miles-teller-mark-kermode. Accessed 3 Apr. 2017.

Kuperinsky, Amy. "The Man Who Directed 'La La Land' Is a 32-Year-Old Wunderkind from N.J." *NJ.com*, 26 Feb. 2017, www.nj.com/entertainment/index.ssf/2017/02/damien_chazelle_interview_la_la_land_oscars_best_d.html. Accessed 3 Apr. 2017.

Lane, Anthony. "Fun in La La Land." Review of *La La Land*, directed by Damien Chazelle. *The New Yorker*, 12 Dec. 2016, www.newyorker.com/magazine/2016/12/12/dancing-with-the-stars. Accessed 3 Apr. 2017.

Volmers, Eric. "La La's Local Connection." *Calgary Herald*, 3 Feb. 2017, calgaryherald.com/entertainment/movies/la-las-local-connection-calgary-grandparents-proud-of-oscar-nominated-damien-chazelle. Accessed 3 Apr. 2017.

SELECTED WORKS

Guy and Madeline on a Park Bench, (2009); *Whiplash*, (2014); *La La Land*, (2016)

—*Dmitry Kiper*

Nick Step/Flickr/CC BY 2.0/Wikimedia Commons

Derek Cianfrance

Date of birth: January 23, 1974
Occupation: Filmmaker

Derek Cianfrance is an American film director best known for his 2010 film *Blue Valentine*, about a blue-collar couple falling out of love. Cianfrance's first film, *Brother Tied*, made when he was just twenty-three years old, premiered to some acclaim at the Sundance Film Festival in 1998. Cianfrance eagerly began writing his next feature, *Blue Valentine*, not knowing that it would take him twelve years to secure its production. Ultimately, Cianfrance told Lisa Kennedy for the *Denver Post* (13 Jan. 2011), "I'm thankful that it took so long. I've had life experience. I've been able to sit with the ideas and meditate on them." *Blue Valentine* garnered a best-actress Academy Award nomination for one of its stars, Michelle Williams, and firmly brought Cianfrance, a long-time Brooklynite, into the Hollywood fold. Still, Cianfrance has eschewed directing big-budget films to focus on small, intimate movies like the dark 2012 period drama *The Place beyond the Pines*. His most recent film, *The Light between Oceans* (2016), is based on M. L. Stedman's best-selling 2012 novel of the same name.

Cianfrance is famous for his immersive filmmaking. For *The Light between Oceans*, a film about a lighthouse keeper and his wife in post–World War I Australia, he insisted that actors Michael Fassbender and Alicia Vikander live on an island and tend to a real lighthouse for five weeks. For *Blue Valentine*, he asked actors Michelle Williams and Ryan Gosling, along with the young actor that played their daughter, to live together in the same house for a month, celebrating fake Christmas, fake birthdays, and taking family trips to Sears. By the time Cianfrance was ready to shoot to that section of the film, Gosling told Dave Davies for National Public Radio's (NPR) *Fresh Air* (15 Dec. 2010), "we were drawing on real memories." Cianfrance's dedication to realism has had some real-world consequences. Gosling and Williams were rumored to have begun a romantic relationship during *Blue Valentine*, and Fassbender and Vikander of *The Light between Oceans* met on location and remain a couple. "If the directing ever dries up, Cianfrance could run a dating agency," *New Yorker* critic Anthony Lane wrote (12 Sept. 2016). Cianfrance's films, and filmmaking philosophy, have divided critics. Although *Blue Valentine* was widely praised, Cianfrance's other films, though they deal with similar themes, have largely failed to beguile reviewers in the same way. Currently, Cianfrance is writing an adaptation of S. C. Gwynne's nonfiction epic about the Comanche tribe, *Empire of the Summer Moon*. The film will focus on the story of Quanah Parker, the famous Comanche chief.

EARLY LIFE AND EDUCATION

Cianfrance was born in Lakewood, Colorado, on January 23, 1974. His mother was a teacher and his father worked in retail; he has an older brother named Jason and a younger sister,

Megan. As a young child, Cianfrance recorded movies on HBO and watched them over and over again, studying how they were made. By the time he was in the sixth grade, he had watched George Romero's camp horror film *Creepshow* (1982) dozens of times. Before he began making home movies himself, he took pictures of his family members fighting. In *Interview* magazine (1 Sept. 2016), he told one of his idols, actor Gena Rowlands, "We had all these smiley family pictures all over the walls of my house, but I always found those pictures to be odd because we weren't smiling all the time. I don't want to paint the picture of a total dysfunctional house, but there were a lot of arguments in that house."

Cianfrance graduated from Green Mountain High School with twenty short homemade films under his belt. He hoped to attend the prestigious film school at New York University, but ended up at the University of Colorado in Boulder—a kink in his plans for which he is grateful. At Boulder, Cianfrance studied with avant-garde film masters Stan Brakhage, who made hundreds of short experimental films, including *Dog Star Man* (1964), and Phil Solomon, an award-winning filmmaker who made a lauded short called *Remains to be Seen* in 1989. Cianfrance's aesthetic was deeply influenced by the two men. Brakhage, who died in 2003, first showed nineteen-year-old Cianfrance the John Cassavetes film *Faces* (1968), starring Gena Rowlands. Cianfrance was also deeply influenced by Rowlands's performance in Cassavetes's *A Woman under the Influence* (1974). Cianfrance described Solomon, with whom he remains close, to Rowlands as his "cinematic consciousness." Together, the two professors, he told Kennedy, "taught me how to be a sensitive artist, not just this narrative storyteller."

BROTHER TIED (1998)

In 1998, Cianfrance took an ultimately permanent leave of absence from the University of Colorado to shoot his first film, *Brother Tied*. To raise the necessary $40,000 to make the movie, Cianfrance sold t-shirts and chocolate bunnies; his dentist personally chipped in $5,000. *Brother Tied*, a stylized, black-and-white drama about two brothers and a third male friend who comes between them, premiered at the Sundance Film Festival—a major coup for a first-time filmmaker. The film won a handful of awards on the festival circuit and garnered good reviews, though Emanuel Levy for *Variety* (26 Feb. 1998), wrote that the story of *Brother Tied* was "drowned in style, resulting in a self-conscious work that doesn't engage emotionally."

Cianfrance and his writing partner Joey Curtis, whom he had met at Boulder, were buoyed by their Sundance success, though *Brother Tied* did not receive any distribution offers. They began writing their next film, *Blue Valentine*, inspired in part by Cianfrance's parents' divorce; however, *Brother Tied* languished without a distributor, and Cianfrance's early success seemed quickly forgotten. This was frustrating, but Cianfrance has said it was ultimately necessary for his growth as an artist. There was talk of reviving the film in 2011 after the success of *Blue Valentine*, though Cianfrance has mixed feelings about that. "It's unbearable to watch, because it's trying so hard to be cinematic in a show-offy way," he said of *Brother Tied* to Anthony Kaufman for *Indie Wire* (11 Jan. 2011). "I was a little pretentious and I had a chip on my shoulder and I wanted to prove myself. But it marks a time in my life as a person and a filmmaker. It's like a tattoo or a scar. And as you grow as a filmmaker, your work represents where you are as a person."

BLUE VALENTINE (2010)

After *Brother Tied* was released, Cianfrance supported himself by working on documentaries, some of them about hip-hop legends, such as *Run D.M.C. and Jam Master Jay: The Last Interview* (2002) and *Black and White: A Portrait of Sean Combs* (2006). In 2003, he worked as a cinematographer on friend Curtis's Sundance award-winning drama *Quattro Noza*, about street car racing in Southern California. But it was documentaries, Cianfrance told R. Kurt Osenlund for *Slant* magazine (28 Mar. 2013), that helped him hone his young, self-focused style. "I got into documentaries just to put food on my family's table, and in making them, I went outside myself and was able to tell stories about other people, and fall in love with other people, and kind of humble myself as a filmmaker," he said.

The early 2000s were lean years for Cianfrance and his family. Cianfrance turned down more lucrative projects to keep himself "pure" as an artist, he told Stephen Galloway for the *Hollywood Reporter* (5 Sept. 2012), but the birth of his first son shifted his priorities. "We were buying diapers with change!" he told Galloway. Cianfrance took several jobs directing commercials, and was able to save enough money to shoot *Blue Valentine*, a project that already had its stars. Williams and Gosling had both signed on to the film before receiving the Oscar nominations that made them Hollywood elite—another benefit of the film's long gestation.

Blue Valentine is about a married couple, played by Williams and Gosling, but the film employs an unusual structure to tell their story. Scenes of their early courtship are spliced with their romantic disintegration six years later. Those in-between years, Dennis Lim wrote for the *New York Times* (22 Dec. 2010), are omitted, inviting "the viewer to fill in the blanks."

Gosling told Lim that the movie was like a murder mystery: "You spend the film trying to figure out who the killer [of their love] is. Is it him, is it her, is it the kid, is it money, time, is it their jobs, is it their parents? The answer is up to you." Cianfrance shot the scenes of the end of the relationship—the film's present—in high-definition video, and the past on Super 16-millimeter film with a shaky hand-held camera, adding visual contrast.

Blue Valentine was well received among most critics, who found it to be a powerful and wrenching depiction of love gone sour. Lane, for the *New Yorker* (3 Jan. 2011), called it a "rare creation: a love story that doesn't shy away from sex"—the film was first given an NC-17 rating, changed to R after a challenge—"ignore its consequences, or droop into pointless fantasy." *New York Times* critic A. O. Scott (28 Dec. 2010) was less impressed, and criticized the film as "a muddle of hurt feelings and vague disappointments."

OTHER FILMS

Cianfrance's next film, a crime drama called *The Place beyond the Pines* (2012), was much larger in scope. Starring Gosling, Bradley Cooper, and Eva Mendes, the film—employing another surprising structural twist—sets out to tell a story about fathers and sons. In *Pines*, Gosling plays a carnival performer, travelling from town to town in upstate New York. In Schenectady—which means "place beyond the pines" in the Iroquois language—he encounters a woman with whom he once had an affair. She turns out to have had his son. As the film progresses, the narrative shifts to follow the story of a cop, played by Cooper. Scott, of the *New York Times* (28 Mar. 2013), wrote of the film, "If, in the end, the film can't quite sustain its epic vision, it does, along the way, achieve the density and momentum of a good novel."

A good novel laid the foundation for Cianfrance's next film, *The Light between Oceans*, in 2016. Artistically drained, Cianfrance struggled to find a new project after *Pines* until he read Steadman's 2012 period romance *The Light between Oceans*. Reading the book on the subway for the first time, Cianfrance admits he burst into tears. The film adaptation, which he wrote, is "a companion piece to *Blue Valentine* in a way, because it's about love," he told Kate Erbland for *Indie Wire* (30 Aug. 2016). In it, a World War I veteran (Fassbender) and his wife (Vikander) tend to a lighthouse on a lonely island off the coast of Western Australia. The couple suffers two miscarriages, but then, by a strange twist of fate, they find themselves the guardians of an infant who washes up on their shore. As with Cianfrance's previous film, critics praised the film's visual beauty while regretting its lack of narrative power. *Oceans*, Jon Frosch

wrote for the *Hollywood Reporter* (30 Aug. 2016), is "so busy sweeping us up in a swirl of music, scenery and beautiful, suffering faces that it forgets to do the actual work of earning our emotions."

PERSONAL LIFE

Cianfrance is married to the filmmaker and actor Shannon Plumb. Together they have two sons, Walker and Cody. They live in the Clinton Hill neighborhood of Brooklyn.

SUGGESTED READING

Cianfrance, Derek. "'Blue Valentine' Director Reveals How the Movie Changed his Life (Q&A)." Interview by Stephen Galloway. *The Hollywood Reporter*, 5 Sept. 2012, www.hollywoodreporter.com/news/derek-cianfrance-bradley-cooper-the-place-beyond-the-pines-367893. Accessed 12 Jan. 2017.

Cianfrance, Derek. Interview by R. Kurt Osenlund. *Slant*, 28 Mar. 2013, www.slantmagazine.com/features/article/interview-derek-cianfrance. Accessed 12 Jan. 2017.

Cianfrance, Derek. Interview by Gena Rowlands. *Interview*, 1 Sept. 2016, www.interviewmagazine.com/film/derek-cianfrance-1. Accessed 12 Jan. 2017.

Davies, Dave. "Ryan Gosling: Fully Immersed in 'Blue Valentine.'" *Fresh Air*, National Public Radio, 15 Dec. 2010, www.npr.org/2010/12/15/131963261/ryan-gosling-fully-immersed-in-blue-valentine. Accessed 12 Jan. 2017.

Erbland, Kate. "Why Derek Cianfrance Sees 'The Light between Oceans' as a Companion Piece to His 'Blue Valentine.'" *Indie Wire*, 30 Aug. 2016, www.indiewire.com/2016/08/derek-cianfrance-interview-the-light-between-oceans-michael-fassbender-alicia-vikander-1201721263. Accessed 12 Jan. 2017.

Kaufman, Anthony. "O 'Brother Tied,' Where Art Thou? 'Blue Valentine' Team Seeks to Reclaim Derek Cianfrance's Debut." *Indie Wire*, 11 Jan. 2011, www.indiewire.com/2011/01/o-brother-tied-where-art-thou-blue-valentine-team-seeks-to-reclaim-derek-cianfrances-debut-243927. Accessed 12 Jan. 2017.

Kennedy, Lisa. "Colorado-Reared 'Blue Valentine' Director Is Thankful Film Took Him 12 Years to Make." *Denver Post*, 13 Jan. 2011, www.denverpost.com/2011/01/13/colorado-reared-blue-valentine-director-is-thankful-film-took-12-years-to-make. Accessed 12 Jan. 2017.

SELECTED WORKS

Brother Tied, 1998; *Blue Valentine*, 2010; *The Place beyond the Pines*, 2012; *The Light between Oceans*, 2016

—*Molly Hagan*

Emma Cline

Date of birth: 1989
Occupation: Author

Emma Cline made enormous waves in the literary world even before her highly anticipated debut novel, *The Girls*, hit bookstore shelves in 2016. "Random House took first prize this week in the annual competition for Hypiest Debut Acquisition, sealing a three-book deal . . . with Emma Cline, 25, for a rumored $2 million and change," Boris Kachka wrote for *Vulture* (9 Oct. 2014) when news of the lucrative deal, rare for lesser-known authors, was announced.

The novel, which centers on a group of teenage girls who join a fictional cult modeled in part on the infamous group run by Charles Manson in the late 1960s, received a spate of rapturous reviews, with many critics impressed by Cline's skillful reimagining of her source material. Lexi Pandell noted for *Wired* (14 June 2016), however, that Cline is not morbidly fascinated by her subjects on a prurient level but instead makes a sincere attempt to understand them. "I took it as a challenge to write a book about teenage girls, who are so marginalized and objectified and given no agency and subjectivity," the author explained to Pandell. "How do you write about them in a way that takes them seriously?" Discussing the novel's themes with Caitlin Love for the *Paris Review* (19 July 2016), Cline said, "I'm interested in this moment on the cusp of adulthood—when we encounter how the world treats women and girls—and what it means to be a girl in the world. That age somehow has both a kind of innocence and a burgeoning awareness."

Not yet thirty years old at the time of the deal and the book's publication, Cline received further recognition of her promising talent in early 2017 when she was included in the prestigious British literary magazine *Granta*'s list of best young American novelists, which is released once every decade.

EARLY YEARS

Emma Cline was born in 1989 in California. She grew up in Sonoma, where her parents, Fred and Nancy, own and run a well-regarded winery, Cline Cellars, and an organic farm. The second of seven children, she has two brothers and four sisters. "I'm very sensitive to group dynamics," she told Fan Zhong for *W* magazine (15 June 2016). "The first time I had my own room in my second year in college, I couldn't sleep because I couldn't hear people breathing." In this often chaotic environment, she typically found peace through reading.

Not far from Cline's home in Sonoma was a mansion that had once housed members of a commune called the Chosen Family. The lavish

Photo by David M. Benett/Dave Benett/Getty Images for Shortlist Media

home ultimately burned to the ground, and two youngsters had drowned in the swimming pool on the grounds. "The story has always been in the back of my mind, this great idealistic experiment and its ultimate destruction, side by side," she told Zhong about her lifelong fascination with communes. In interviews, she has explained how stories of Charles Manson and his cult had still been prevalent in her neighborhood and life growing up. Her parents had grown up in California cities that had ties to the cult and the murders, and she can remember being confused as a child, thinking that he was living nearby and feeling that he was a sort of "bogeyman figure," as she told Jane Mulkerrins for the *Telegraph* (3 May 2017). She also read prosecutor Vincent Bugliosi's 1974 book *Helter Skelter: The True Story of the Manson Murders*. But rather than focusing on Manson himself, she became more interested in the girls and women who had followed him.

EDUCATION AND DETERMINING HER CAREER PATH

Cline also harbored dreams of becoming an actor, and as a child, she appeared in the 2001 television movie *When Billie Beat Bobby*, in which she played the young version of the tennis professional and feminist icon Billie Jean King, as well as the little-seen 2003 short film *Flashcards*.

Cline graduated from high school in 2006 and spent a year working on a farm and taking flying lessons before entering Middlebury College, a private college in Vermont. As a freshman, she won a literary award for a short story called "What Is Lost." Interviewed by Sara Black for the school newspaper, the *Middlebury Campus* (17 Oct. 2007), she asserted that she was thinking of dropping out and said, "If I were to return to college, I'd be interested in studying architecture, bioregionalism, landscape and narrative and the West." However, she ultimately chose to remain at Middlebury to focus on writing, and as a junior she won a scholarship to attend the Bread Loaf Writers' Conference, a prestigious event affiliated with the school. She graduated in 2010.

Never having fully given up on her dreams of acting, Cline moved to Los Angeles after leaving Middlebury—but she lasted less than six months there. After going to "a lot of auditions for roles like rape victim," as she wrote in a personal essay titled "See Me" for the *Paris Review* (17 Mar. 2014), she relocated to New York City and enrolled in the master of fine arts (MFA) program at Columbia University. In an interview with Marisa Meltzer for *Vogue* (July 2016), she explained why writing proved more suitable for her than acting: "You control everything. As a woman, it's nice to now write a character who's fourteen and complicated and not the one-note characters I auditioned for."

Cline earned her MFA in 2013, the same year she published the short story "Marion," about a young girl growing up on a marijuana-growing commune, in the *Paris Review*. The following year, the magazine awarded the story its $10,000 Plimpton Prize, named after the legendary editor George Plimpton, who was known for his passion for discovering new writers.

COMPLETING HER FIRST NOVEL AND WINNING A BIDDING WAR

After earning her master's degree, Cline found work at the *New Yorker*, where she was assigned to read the fiction submissions that poured into the venerable publication. Concurrently, she worked on her own novel and found a literary agent, Bill Clegg. She completed *The Girls* over the course of a summer, living in a miniscule shed in a friend's backyard in Brooklyn to save money she would have had to spend on rent and limit distractions. "The best thing about working in such a small room, especially one without Internet access, is the sense of compression, a winnowing down to essential things. . . . There's really not very much to do in here but write," she stated in an interview for the *New York Times Style Magazine* (15 Apr. 2016). She also found, in the process, that she was quite handy, as she ended up doing plumbing, repairing the roof, and building steps.

The Girls had been in the works for several years by then, and Cline incorporated more of the Manson story as she polished it. "I became obsessed with the Manson girls," she wrote in

"See Me." "I was older than they'd been when they killed eight people, when they'd driven home on the Ventura Freeway, stopping at gas stations to clean blood off one another. . . . In the photographs I saw of the girls—pictures striking for their strangely domestic quality— I recognized something of myself at thirteen, the same blip of longing in their eyes." As further inspiration, she consulted her own journals from her years in high school to reengage with the emotional mindset of teenage girls. She continued to make the focus of her book the young female narrator and other female characters who voluntarily become a part of the fictional cult to provide possible perspective into the ambiguities of moral boundaries that had been less explored. "I'm interested in the complex experience, and to me, the women involved in groups like that had never had their story told in a way that I felt fully recognized their humanity," she told Eliza Thompson for *Cosmopolitan* (15 June 2016).

When Clegg, a well-known figure in the publishing world, put *The Girls* up for auction, a frenzied bidding war ensued among a dozen publishers. The victor was ultimately Random House, which paid a reported $2 million for the debut novel, along with a yet-to-be published short-story collection and a sophomore novel. The astonishing figure, especially when viewed in light of Cline's youth, was the subject of numerous headlines and articles—some touting the author's obvious talent and others predicting that no new writer could ever live up to that level of hype.

PUBLICATION AND RECEPTION OF *THE GIRLS*

When the novel was published in June 2016, reviews were divided along the same lines. Even the most hardened critic was forced to admit, however, that hype or not, Cline was a writer of rare skill. "Cline is already a talented stylist, apparently fast-tracked by the Muses," opined James Wood for the *New Yorker* (6 June 2016). "I don't mean this as the critic's dutiful mustering of plaudits before the grim march of negatives. At her frequent best, Cline sees the world exactly and generously. On every other page, it seems, there is something remarkable—an immaculate phrase, a boldly modifying adverb, a metaphor or simile that makes a sudden, electric connection between its poles." Wood also cautioned, however, that "Cline's style may be an obstacle, too. It can be too brilliant—overwritten, flashing rather than lighting. Though it often opens the doors of perception, it also closes a number of windows." In an assessment for the *Washington Post* (31 May 2016), Ron Charles wrote, "The hubbub around *The Girls* threatens to trample what's so deeply affecting about it. . . . With the maturity of a writer twice her age, Cline has written a wise novel that's never showy: a quiet, seething confession of yearning and terror. . . . Debut novels like this are rare, indeed."

Of the hype the novel has attracted, Cline told Pandell, "I've tried to remind myself that this stuff is not real in the way that writing is real to me." Additionally, even after being included in *Granta*'s 2017 list recognizing her as a talented new writer, she remained focused on the writing process itself. "For me, it's of course lovely to get recognition since it's such a private, solitary business. But at the same time I think these external things are not where the real pleasure of writing comes from," she told Kathryn Bromwich for the *Guardian* (21 May 2017).

Readers finding it difficult to wait for Cline's next book were gratified in early April 2017 to see that the *New Yorker* had published her latest short story, "Northeast Regional," about the fallout of an unspecified, but horrific, incident at a boarding school.

PERSONAL LIFE

Although Cline moved out of her writing shed and into her own apartment in Brooklyn in 2016, she continues to use the shed for her work. She has expressed in interviews that there are aspects of her West Coast life that she misses. "I feel much more capable in California, and my life there feels a lot more like life, but I work better in New York," she stated to Jeff Vasishta for *Tin House* (21 June 2016). "I will always be susceptible to a certain kind of mood and late afternoon light that I think of as particular to the West Coast."

SUGGESTED READING

Charles, Ron. "*The Girls*, by Emma Cline: Charles Manson, Reimagined." Review of *The Girls*, by Emma Cline. *The Washington Post*, 31 May 2016, www.washingtonpost.com/entertainment/books/the-girls-by-emma-cline-a-masterly-tale-of-youth-and-the-allure-of-the-mansons/2016/05/31/5afe2e60-2119-11e6-9e7f-57890b612299_story.html. Accessed 6 June 2017.

Cline, Emma. "Beauty, Truth, and *The Girls*: An Interview with Emma Cline." Interview by Caitlin Love. *The Paris Review*, 19 July 2016, www.theparisreview.org/blog/2016/07/19/beauty-truth-and-the-girls-an-interview-with-emma-cline. Accessed 6 June 2017.

Cline, Emma. "See Me." *The Paris Review*, 17 Mar. 2014, www.theparisreview.org/blog/2014/03/17/see-me. Accessed 6 June 2017.

Meltzer, Marisa. "Cult Following: *Vogue* Meets Author Emma Cline." *Vogue*, July 2016, www.vogue.co.uk/article/emma-cline-the-girls-interview. Accessed 6 June 2017.

Pandell, Lexi. "Emma Cline's Turbulent Trip to Literary Superstardom." *Wired*, 14 June 2016, www.wired.com/2016/06/the-girls-emma-cline-anointed-author. Accessed 6 June 2017.

Wood, James. "Making the Cut." *The New Yorker*, 6 June 2016, www.newyorker.com/magazine/2016/06/06/the-girls-by-emma-cline. Accessed 6 June 2017.

Zhong, Fan. "Meet Emma Cline, the Woman behind Summer's Hottest Novel, *The Girls*." *W*, 15 June 2016, www.wmagazine.com/story/emma-cline-the-girls-summer-reading. Accessed 6 June 2017.

—*Mari Rich*

Amal Clooney

Date of birth: February 3, 1978
Occupation: Attorney

Amal Clooney is a British barrister who has represented a number of high-profile clients, including WikiLeaks founder Julian Assange in extradition proceedings and former Ukrainian prime minister Yulia Tymoshenko in a human rights claim regarding her politically motivated detention. Clooney specializes in public international law, international criminal law, and human rights. As many journalists have pointed out, despite her undeniably impressive accomplishments in the field of law, she was largely unknown to the general public until she became romantically involved with—and ultimately married—the award-winning actor George Clooney.

The disparity in their public profiles became media fodder when their relationship was confirmed in early 2014. When the actor received a lifetime achievement award at the Golden Globes in January 2015, host Tina Fey famously joked: "George Clooney married Amal Alamuddin this year. Amal is a human rights lawyer who worked on the Enron case, was an adviser to Kofi Annan regarding Syria, and was selected for a three-person UN commission investigating rules of war violations in the Gaza Strip. So tonight her husband is getting a lifetime achievement award."

Amal Clooney has argued cases in front of the International Criminal Court, the International Court of Justice, and the European Court of Human Rights. Among her most recent cases, she has represented victims of the Yezidi genocide perpetrated by the terrorist group ISIS. The Yezidis are a minority religious group that live predominantly in northern Iraq and Syria. One of Clooney's clients, Nadia Murad, was captured by ISIS militants in 2014 and abused for months before escaping and becoming an activist. ISIS killed some five thousand Yezidi civilians in Murad's community in August 2014 and enslaved

Georges Biard [CC BY-SA 3.0], via Wikimedia Commons

more than six thousand Yezidi women and girls. "We know there's a military campaign going on where ISIS is being taken on on the battlefield," Clooney told Fareed Zakaria for CNN's *Fareed Zakaria GPS* (19 Mar. 2017). "What we want is to see ISIS members also in a courtroom. And at the moment that hasn't happened. So we haven't seen a single prosecution against ISIS in a court anywhere in the world."

EARLY YEARS AND EDUCATION

Amal Clooney (née Alamuddin) was born in 1978 in Beirut, the capital city of Lebanon. Although she and her family fled the war-torn city when she was just two years old, they remain well known and respected among the Druze community there. (The Druze are members of a small religious sect that is an offshoot of Shia Islam and dates back to the eleventh century. They live predominantly in Lebanon, with smaller communities in Jordan, Israel, and Syria.) Clooney's father, Ramzi, who hails from the town of Baakline, became a professor of business studies at the American University of Beirut. Her mother, Baria, was a senior correspondent and editor at the newspaper *Al-Hayat*. Amal Clooney's family also includes a younger sister, Tala, and two half-brothers, Samer and Ziad.

Seeking to escape the violence of the civil war then raging in Lebanon, the Alamuddins settled in London, England, in 1980. Clooney attended Dr. Challoner's High School, an all-girls school in Buckinghamshire, England, where she has been remembered as an exceptional student. She won a scholarship to St. Hugh's College,

University of Oxford, where she studied law and won the Shrigley Award for excellence in law studies. Upon receiving a bachelor's degree and a bachelor of laws in 2000, she entered the New York University (NYU) School of Law, where she received the Jack J. Katz Memorial Award for excellence in entertainment law and earned a master of law degree in 2001. While at NYU, she served as a student law clerk for Sonia Sotomayor, who was then a judge for the US Court of Appeals for the Second Circuit and who later became an associate justice for the US Supreme Court. Clooney won admission to the New York Bar in 2002.

PROFESSIONAL CAREER

Following her graduation from NYU, Clooney joined the prestigious international law firm Sullivan & Cromwell LLP, which is headquartered in Manhattan and advises businesses on international mergers and acquisitions, finance, corporate law, real estate transactions, and taxes and estate planning. She became part of the firm's Criminal Defense and Investigations Group. Early on in her career, she represented clients in a number of complex criminal investigations before state and federal courts, including the criminal probes of the now-infamous energy and commodities firm Enron, which was then embroiled in an accounting scandal and charges of tax fraud, and the accounting firm Arthur Andersen. She later completed a three-year clerkship at the International Court of Justice, commonly known as the World Court or simply The Hague, for the Dutch city in which it is located. During this time, Clooney worked under judges from Russia, Egypt, and the United Kingdom.

In 2010 she was called to the Bar of England and Wales. That year, she returned to London to work as a barrister at Doughty Street Chambers, a well-respected firm known for its work in the arena of human rights and civil liberties. There her clients included WikiLeaks founder Julian Assange; Hamad bin Isa Al-Khalifa, the king of Bahrain; and the former Libyan intelligence chief Abdullah al-Senussi. (Clooney has faced some public backlash because of the infamy of some of her clients, but she has consistently responded by noting that everyone deserves strong representation from a legal expert.)

HIGH-PROFILE CASES

Clooney, who is fluent in Arabic, French, and English, has served in an advisory capacity for numerous organizations and represented clients in a number of high-profile cases. She has served as the legal adviser to the king of Bahrain in connection with the Bahrain Independent Commission of Inquiry, which was established to investigate claims of human rights violations during the 2011 Arab Spring uprisings. She advised Kofi

Annan on human rights violations during the Syrian civil war for the Joint Special Envoy of the United Nations and the Arab League on Syria. She provided legal representation to Yulia Tymoshenko, the former Ukrainian prime minister, in a human rights claim regarding Tymoshenko's politically motivated arrest and detention. She also advised the Greek government on how to negotiate the return of the Elgin Marbles, which were looted from the Parthenon Temple in the early nineteenth century, from the British Museum in London to Greece. She has also represented the Republic of Armenia in the European Court of Human Rights during a case against Turkish politician Doğu Perinçek for denying the Armenian genocide.

She also served as a legal adviser to the head of a United Nations commission that had been established to prosecute those responsible for the 2005 assassination of former Lebanese prime minister Rafik Hariri, who was killed along with twenty-one others when a bomb was detonated near his motorcade. In 2014, five suspected members of the militant group Hezbollah were tried in absentia for Hariri's assassination.

In addition to Murad—the Yezidi woman seeking to bring to justice the ISIS leaders who kidnapped her and killed many members of her family—Clooney's other clients include Mohamed Nasheed, the first democratically elected president of the Maldives who was sentenced to serve thirteen years in prison in what the United Nations has dismissed as a show trial. Clooney has called for targeted sanctions against the Maldivian government in the hopes of securing Nasheed's release. Discussing Nasheed's case in an interview, Cynthia McFadden for *NBC News* (14 Jan. 2016) asked Clooney about the extremely difficult nature of many of her cases. Clooney responded, "If you are a lawyer and you want to take on easier cases, you can prosecute traffic violations or something. You'd have a very high rate of success, and you probably could sleep more easily at night. But that's not what drives me. I want to work on cases that I feel the most passionate about."

PHILANTHROPY

Amal Clooney, who has served as a visiting professor at Columbia Law School's Human Rights Institute, established a scholarship in 2015 that will send one female student from Lebanon to the United World College in Armenia each year to undertake a two-year international baccalaureate program.

In late 2016, Clooney and her husband launched the Clooney Foundation for Justice. Its mission statement reads, according to its official website: "We believe that justice means fighting for the rights of individuals unfairly targeted by oppressive governments through the courts. But justice is more than what is meted out in courts, it is litigated in communities as well. So advancing the cause of justice also means advancing justice for victims of war; justice for vulnerable children deprived of opportunities to learn; and justice for refugees seeking to rebuild their lives abroad." The foundation is funding programs to advance educational opportunities for Syrian refugees and developing its TrialWatch program to monitor the use of courts worldwide as a tool for social and political oppression.

PERSONAL LIFE

Clooney met her husband, Hollywood actor George Clooney, at a charity event in Venice, Italy, in 2013. The pair wed in Venice on September 27, 2014. The couple sold the rights to their wedding photos to *People* and *Hello* magazines, donating the proceeds to various human-rights organizations. In February 2017, the couple announced they were expecting twins in June 2017.

Clooney says that although she does not read the tabloid reports of her attendance and wardrobe at various Hollywood events, she appreciates that such coverage brings increased attention to issues of importance. "There's a lot of my work that takes place behind closed doors that is not ever seen," she told Fiona Bruce for *BBC News at Six* (7 Mar. 2017). "I think if there are more people who now understand what's happening about the Yezidis and ISIS, and if there can be some action that results from that, that can help those clients, then I think it's a really good thing to give that case the extra publicity that it may get."

SUGGESTED READING

Allum, Cynthia. "Amal Clooney to Represent ISIS Survivor Nadia Murad and Victims of Yazidi Genocide." *The New York Times*, 9 June 2016, nytlive.nytimes.com/womenin-theworld/2016/06/09/amal-clooney-to-represent-isis-survivor-nadia-murad-and-victims-of-yazidi-genocide. Accessed 4 May 2017.

"Amal Clooney's Work, Explained by International Human Rights Lawyers." *Vanity Fair*, 29 Mar. 2017, www.vanityfair.com/style/2017/03/amal-clooney-international-human-rights-lawyer-job-explained. Accessed 4 May 2017.

Clooney, Amal. "Amal Clooney Discusses Latest Human Rights Battle in NBC News Interview." Interview by Cynthia McFadden. *NBC News*, 14 Jan. 2016, www.nbcnews.com/nightly-news/video/amal-clooney-discusses-latest-human-rights-battle-in-nbc-news-exclusive-602061379836. Accessed 4 May 2017.

Clooney, Amal. "Nadia Murad and Amal Clooney Demand Justice for Yazidis." Interview by Fareed Zakaria. *Fareed Zakaria GPS*, 19 Mar.

2017, www.cnn.com/videos/tv/2017/03/18/exp-gps-amal-clooney-nadia-murad-isis-yazidi.cnn. Accessed 4 May 2017.

Gonzales, Erica. "Amal Clooney Is Pregnant with Twins." *Harper's Bazaar*, 9 Feb. 2017, www.harpersbazaar.com/celebrity/latest/news/a20578/amal-clooney-pregnant-twins. Accessed 4 May 2017.

Schmidt, Samantha. "A Lawyer Named Amal Clooney Gave a Powerful Speech at the U.N. Some Only Saw Her Baby Bump." *The Washington Post*, 10 Mar. 2017, www.washingtonpost.com/news/morning-mix/wp/2017/03/10/a-lawyer-named-amal-clooney-gave-a-powerful-speech-at-u-n-some-only-saw-her-baby-bump. Accessed 4 May 2017.

—*Mari Rich*

By robbiesaurus [CC BY-SA 2.0], via Wikimedia Commons

Tasha Cobbs

Date of birth: July 7, 1981
Occupation: Singer

Tasha Cobbs Leonard is a Grammy Award–winning gospel singer, best known for her 2013 breakthrough hit "Break Every Chain." The song, which appears on her debut album, *Grace* (2013), earned Cobbs a Grammy Award for best gospel/contemporary Christian music performance in 2014. Over the course of her career, Cobbs has also won three Stellar Gospel Music Awards and three Dove Awards, presented by the Gospel Music Association.

Cobbs, who was born in Georgia and raised by ministers, is a pastor at the dReam Center Church of Atlanta in Decatur and the founder of Tasha Cobbs Ministries (TCM) and iLead Escape, a mentorship program for pastors. Her album *Heart. Passion. Pursuit.* was released in 2017. Its lead single, "I'm Getting Ready," features a verse by rapper Nicki Minaj. In September, the song debuted in the number-one spot on the Billboard Gospel Digital Song Sales chart, Cobbs's fourth single to top the gospel charts. Despite the song's popularity, Cobbs received some blowback for her decision to collaborate with a secular hip-hop artist. Some gospel fans felt Minaj was too racy for Cobbs's wholesome image. Cobbs was quick to defend her fellow artist. "I've seen the Nicki that is off the stage and that Nicki has a great relationship with God," Cobbs told Jessica Littles for *Essence* (29 Aug. 2017). The singer chose to work with Minaj to reach a wider audience, she added. "The testimonies that have come because of this—I would absolutely do it again. I've had thousands of people say to me 'This is the first time I've ever

bought a gospel album. This is first time I've ever felt God. I didn't believe in God until I heard this song."

EARLY LIFE

Cobbs was born in Jesup, Georgia, on July 7, 1981. Her father, the late Bishop Fritz Cobbs, and her mother, Lady Bertha Cobbs, founded a church called Jesup New Life Ministries when Cobbs was ten years old. Her mother is also a singer, and music has been integral to Cobbs's life from an early age. "I've been singing all of my life," she told the Christian Broadcasting Network (CBN) (2014). "On my mother's side of the family we all sing—all my cousins and all my aunts. On Christmas and the holidays, everybody gathers together, and we all sing. It's just part of my life."

Cobbs and her brother grew up in Jesup, and Cobbs sang for the Wayne County Community Choir, but her musical life centered on her family's church. Jesup New Life Ministries began with only seven adults and their children, and Cobbs was involved with the choir from a young age. When she was fourteen, Cobbs was tasked with directing the ministry's choir at a performance at Bennett Union Missionary Baptist Church. At the last minute, the choir's lead singer had to drop out of the event. Cobbs stepped in to sing the song herself. It was a pivotal moment in Cobbs's young life.

MUSIC MINISTRY

Cobbs continued to serve as the musical director at Jesup New Life Ministries into adulthood, but in 2006, she moved to Atlanta to work with Pastor William H. Murphy III at his dReam Center Church in Decatur. Later, she began serving as worship pastor and oversaw four ministry departments, including dance and drama. She also served as worship leader for the young-adult division of the Full Gospel Baptist Church Fellowship, where she trained fellow worship leaders.

Cobbs, who was living with her cousin at the time, happily went to church each Sunday but found herself overwhelmed by feelings of sadness on the other days of the week. Later, in a candid article for *Essence* (21 Feb. 2016), Cobbs recalled being unable to leave her bedroom for days at a time. She knew something was wrong, but she did not know what it was or what to do about it. "It was just a moment where I felt like I couldn't move forward in my career and in my ministry if I kept allowing myself to be in this place," she wrote. Eventually, with the help of her cousin and her pastor, Cobbs found a therapist and was diagnosed with depression. The diagnosis was a major turning point in Cobbs's life. Therapy allowed her to move forward with her life, but it also ignited in her a desire to reach out to others who struggled with mental health issues and perhaps were, as she had been, too ashamed to face those issues head on. "Our culture, and churches in general, should put more focus on depression and people who struggle with mental health," she wrote for *Essence*. "From what I've experienced in sharing my testimony with different people it's something way more prevalent than we acknowledge, and I am willing to stand on the frontline as a leader in our culture and address the mental health issues we have been ignoring."

GRACE

Since joining the dReam Center as a pastor, Cobbs spent some time touring with Murphy, a gospel singer in his own right. "Nobody knew who I was or my name," Cobbs recalled to Angela Wilson for *Vibe* (28 May 2015). In 2010, however, that changed. That year, Cobbs released a self-produced album called *Smile*. One song in particular, "Happy," brought Cobbs wide acclaim. She signed a national recording contract with EMI Gospel in 2012. "Powerful voice, persistent effort, pursuit of worship: these things describe Tasha Cobbs and combined they create a great gospel music sound that we are pleased to record and disseminate to the world," Ken Pennell, the president of EMI Gospel, told Bonnerfide Radio (19 June 2012).

Shortly thereafter, she recorded her second album, *Grace* (2013), at Northview Christian Church in Birmingham, Alabama. The live album contains some songs from *Smile*—such as "Happy" and "Smile"—but also new songs, such as "Break Every Chain," a song written and originally recorded by Will Reagan of the Christian music group United Pursuit. The song has also been recorded by a group called Jesus Culture, and Cobbs told the Christian Broadcasting Network that she was captivated by that version the first time she heard it. "I have ministered it at my church a few times, and it always has the same effect—chains are broken," she said.

"Break Every Chain" was Cobbs's first major hit song. It spent twelve weeks at number one on the gospel music charts in 2013. The album, produced by award-winning gospel singer-songwriter VaShawn Mitchell, was named by Billboard as one of the top ten gospel albums of the year. "At its best it creates raging fires that begin as whispers," Jon Caramanica wrote of *Grace* for the *New York Times* (22 Mar. 2013), specifically highlighting the songs "Break Every Chain" and "For Your Glory," Cobbs's second number-one hit. (That song spent fourteen weeks at number one in 2015.) In early 2014, Cobbs took her parents to the Stellar Gospel Music Awards, where she won new artist of the year, contemporary female vocalist of the year, and contemporary CD of the year. The next day, her father unexpectedly passed away, and a week after that, Cobbs won a Grammy Award for best gospel/contemporary Christian music performance for "Break Every Chain." It was a career-changing accolade, but for Cobbs the moment was bittersweet.

ONE PLACE LIVE

Cobbs released her third album, *One Place Live*, through Motown Gospel in 2015. The album was recorded at Redemption Church in Greenville, South Carolina. Cobbs later said that she wrote the album's lead single, "Jesus Saves," about her struggles with depression. The second single, "Put a Praise on It," featuring gospel artist Kierra Sheard, spent five weeks at number one on the Billboard Hot Gospel Songs chart. Up-and-coming Christian artist Jamie Grace is featured on the song "Solid Rock," which the two women wrote together. Another notable song on the album is the titular "One Place." Cobbs told Timothy Yap for the Christian music website *Hallels* (20 Aug. 2015) of the unusual genesis of the song. "Seventeen years ago, [my mother] woke me and my family up in the middle of the night saying 'God gave me a song. . . .' And she sang just the beginning of 'One Place,'" Cobbs recalled. For years, Cobbs struggled to finish the song. "God finally gave me its completion," she told Yap, in 2015. Her mother appears as a guest artist on the song.

Cobbs's fourth album, *Heart. Passion. Pursuit.*, was released in 2017. "I'm Getting Ready," the album's lead single featuring Minaj, was also a number-one hit for the singer. Cobbs recorded the album over the course of a week in live performances at Doppler Studios in Atlanta. Cobbs invited worship pastors from across the country to accompany her on the recording. "We did it live in the studio. Including the band and worship leaders, there were maybe thirty people in the room," Cobbs told Littles. "We were the singers and we were the audience. It feels very intimate when you listen to it." Featured guest artists include Cobbs's copastor, Murphy, on the song "Forever at Your Feet"; Christian artist Jimi Cravity on "You Know My Name"; and Sheard on "Your Spirit." In a review of the album for the Uniontown, Pennsylvania, *Herald-Standard* (7 Sept. 2017), Clint Rhodes wrote, "In a world that truly needs more examples of heart, passion, and pursuit, [Cobbs] generously delivers the words we need to hear."

PERSONAL LIFE

Cobbs married music producer Kenneth Leonard Jr. on March 3, 2017, in Atlanta, Georgia. The two met at a worship conference nine years prior. Cobbs is stepmother to Leonard's three children.

SUGGESTED READING

Caramanica, Jon. "New Music from Chvrches, Tasha Cobbs and Walter Liars." *The New York Times*, 22 Mar. 2013, www.nytimes.com/2013/03/24/arts/music/new-music-from-chvrches-tasha-cobbs-and-water-liars.html. Accessed 9 Sept. 2017.

Cobbs, Tasha. "Take Me to Church: Tasha Cobbs Talks New Single 'Jesus Saves,' Weight Loss and Fashion." Interview by Angela Wilson. *Vibe*, 28 May 2015, www.vibe.com/2015/05/tasha-cobbs-vixen-interview. Accessed 9 Sept. 2017.

Cobbs, Tasha. "Tasha Cobbs Gives an Exclusive In-Depth Interview about 'One Place Live.'" Interview by Timothy Yap. *Hallels*, 20 Aug. 2015, www.hallels.com/articles/13517/20150820/tasha-cobbs-gives-an-exclusive-in-depth-interview-about-one-place-live.htm. Accessed 9 Sept. 2017.

Cobbs, Tasha. "Gospel Singer Tasha Cobbs Opens Up about Living with Depression." *Essence*, 21 Feb. 2016, www.essence.com/2016/02/22/gospel-singer-tasha-cobbs-opens-about-living-depression. Accessed 9 Sept. 2017.

Littles, Jessica. "Policing Spirituality: Tasha Cobbs Leonard Speaks Out on Backlash from Song with Nicki Minaj." *Essence*, 29 Aug. 2017, www.essence.com/celebrity/policing-spirituality-tasha-cobbs-speaks-out-backlash-song-nicki-minaj. Accessed 9 Sept. 2017.

Rhodes, Clint. Review of *Heart. Passion. Pursuit.*, by Tasha Cobbs. *Herald-Standard*, 7 Sept. 2017, www.heraldstandard.com/entertainment/music/clints_music_review/music-review-tasha-cobbs-leonard---heart-passion-pursuit/article_2949a364-f009-5490-a952-c512017ae311.html. Accessed 9 Sept. 2017.

"Tasha Cobbs: The Music and Ministry of Grace." *Christian Broadcasting Network*, www1.cbn.com/video/tasha-cobbs-the-music-and-ministry-of-grace. Accessed 8 Sept. 2017.

SELECTED WORKS

Grace, 2013; *One Place Live*, 2015; *Heart. Passion. Pursuit.*, 2017

—Molly Hagan

Lily Collins

Date of birth: March 18, 1989
Occupation: Actor

Actor and model Lily Jane Collins may be the daughter of Oscar- and Grammy-winning musician Phil Collins, but she has not relied solely on a famous name to win roles and awards. As she told Matt Diehl for *InStyle* (May 2011), "I always say my name opens doors, but it's up to me to keep them open. If you don't deliver something fresh and new, those doors may close." Collins has kept her doors open: since her first movie role, in 2009's *The Blind Side*, Collins has ascended quickly in Hollywood, landing a lead role by her third film and not slowing down since, playing opposite stars such as Julia Roberts and Warren Beatty.

Collins began her career, however, with an interest in broadcast journalism, and in 2017 she published a book of essays aimed at inspiring young people to pursue their dreams despite pressures of modern life: body-image issues, bullying, and relationships with well-meaning but remote parents.

EARLY LIFE AND EDUCATION

Lily Collins is the daughter of British rock star Phil Collins and American Jill Tavelman, his second wife. Collins was born in England but raised in Los Angeles from age five, after her parents separated. Her father had moved from London to Switzerland after his 1996 divorce from Tavelman; Collins as a young adult realized the harm that relocation did to her when she spent occasional summers with him. As she wrote in her 2017 essay collection, *Unfiltered: No Shame, No Regrets, Just Me*, "Because my dad was often gone, I never wanted to do anything that would make him stay away even longer. I became extra careful about what I said and how I said it, afraid he'd think I was angry or didn't love him. And the truth is, I was angry. I missed him and

By Tony Shek (Lily Collins) [CC BY-SA 2.0], via
Wikimedia Commons

wanted him there. . . . I've realized that many of
my deepest insecurities stem from these issues
with my dad."

Still, as the daughter of Collins, she had an
atypical childhood—she grew up calling Elton
John "Uncle Elton," for example, and her father
wrote the *Tarzan* song "You'll Be in My Heart" as
a lullaby for her. As a child, she played basketball, soccer, and volleyball. She wrote for various publications during her teen years, including
Teen Vogue and the British edition of the now-
defunct *Elle Girl*. At sixteen, she approached
major networks with the idea for a show aimed at
other teens; she had done her research and went
in with graphs and pie charts. It took a few years,
but she landed a job as a teen correspondent for
Nickelodeon, conducting celebrity interviews as
well as covering the 2008 US presidential election. She attended high school at Harvard-West-
lake School in Los Angeles, graduating in 2007.

Collins started college in 2007 as a broadcast journalism and communication major at
the University of Southern California. As her
on-screen career was also starting to blossom, it
made college too difficult; so she left the program. However, she continued to hone her interest in writing, carrying a notebook, taking an
interest in people and characters, and describing herself to Zorianna Kit for *Reuters* (29 Mar.
2012) as "a journalist at heart."

BEGINNING A CAREER
During the summer of 2007, Collins was a presenter on the Nickelodeon road show *Slime
across America*, on which teens could win prizes

or be dunked in slime. The show also featured
celebrity guests, whom Collins interviewed.

Collins wanted a modeling job, which
seemed a natural fit, given her love of fashion,
but at five feet five, she was considered too
short. To compensate, she learned how to walk
in six-inch heels. She began her career as a model after Tommy Hilfiger noticed her on a flight
from New York to Los Angeles. Jobs materialized
at Tommy Hilfiger and British *Vogue*. In 2008
Spain's edition of *Glamour* named her the international model of the year.

Collins lost out at auditions for roles in the
film *Juno* and the television series *Gossip Girl*.
Undeterred, she told Patty Adams Martinez for
Seventeen (March 2012), "I look at auditions as
acting class. I had to learn that each one is its
own experience that you take on to the next."
She had only had a couple of guest spots on the
television show *90210* to her dramatic acting
credit when she was cast as Sandra Bullock's
teenage daughter in the 2009 film *The Blind
Side*. That film brought her wider attention and
further acting jobs.

MIRROR MIRROR AND MORE
After *The Blind Side*, Collins scored a role in
the 2011 movie *Priest*, playing the niece of Paul
Bettany's protagonist in a dystopian saga about a
battle between humans and vampires. It was an
intense role, but Collins tried to do as many of
the stunts herself as possible. She explained to
Diehl, "I want to be a part of whatever is happening in the story. I don't like sitting back when I
know I could be doing something."

Following a leading role opposite Taylor
Lautner in the poorly received thriller *Abduction*
(2011), Collins won her biggest role yet, as Snow
White in the 2012 movie *Mirror Mirror*, with Julia Roberts as the evil Queen. Collins was cast
the day after auditioning, a process she actually
enjoys. Director Tarsem Singh worked with a
script that gave Snow White a more empowered
role and less that of a victim.

For the role, Collins wore a tiara that had belonged to Grace Kelly, the American actor and
later princess of Monaco. It was not all glamour, however—Collins also learned fencing and
sword skills for the role. She told Kit for *Reuters*,
"I too became more open to living life to the fullest and believing that you can put your mind to
doing anything and really accomplish it. I left
a very inspired young woman based on what I
learned as Snow." She was nominated for the
Teen Choice Award for best actress in a sci-fi/
fantasy film.

THE MORTAL INSTRUMENTS: CITY OF BONES
Collins took on the starring role of Clary Fray
in the 2013 movie *The Mortal Instruments: City
of Bones*, based on the first book in Cassandra

Clare's Mortal Instruments young-adult fantasy series. Set in contemporary Brooklyn, the story features Clary battling demons who have kidnapped her mother.

The franchise has been compared to both the Hunger Games and Divergent series. Asked by Piya Sinha-Roy for *Reuters* (21 Aug. 2013) about the difference between her character and that of Katniss in the *Hunger Games* films, played by Jennifer Lawrence, Collins said, "There's a comedic undertone to our stories that is absent in the other ones I think, and Clary is part of that sassiness and part of that comedy. She is on a quest to save her mom and she doesn't let love define her, she's not victimized. She's a fighter, but she's normal too." For her role, Collins was nominated for the 2014 Teen Choice Award for best actress in an action adventure movie.

RULES DON'T APPLY
In 2014, Collins starred in the teen romantic comedy *Love, Rosie* with Sam Claflin. The film did poorly, but Collins was cast next in another romantic comedy, *Rules Don't Apply* (2016), written and directed by Warren Beatty. Collins was nominated for a Golden Globe Award for her performance as a young beauty queen who moves to Hollywood to work for film magnate Howard Hughes (Beatty) and falls in love with the billionaire's driver (Alden Ehrenreich). Collins was more than happy to have Beatty as a mentor on the set. She told Joshua Terry for *Variety* (10 Nov. 2016) that the best advice Beatty gave her was, "Allow yourself to surprise yourself." Although the film itself also did not do well, Collins earned the 2016 New Hollywood Award for her role.

TO THE BONE
Collins's next leading role was in the 2017 drama *To the Bone*, about a young woman suffering from anorexia. Written and directed by Marti Noxon, *To the Bone* was inspired by the director's own early struggles with an eating disorder, but the film resonated on a personal level with Collins too, as she told Annie Martin for United Press International (23 Jan. 2017). Revealing that she herself suffered from anorexia as a teenager, Collins said getting the script "was like the universe kind of putting these things in my sphere to help me face, kind of dead on, a fear that I used to have." She added that the film allowed her "to open up a topic that is considered quite taboo with young people nowadays." The movie had its premiere at the 2017 Sundance Film Festival and was released on Netflix on July 14, 2017.

Collins was subsequently tapped for a television series adaptation of *The Last Tycoon*, the final, unfinished novel by F. Scott Fitzgerald. Set to premiere on Amazon Video in late July 2017,

the series features Collins as Cecelia Brady, daughter of a Hollywood film producer battling rivals in the 1930s. She told Margaret Wappler for *InStyle* (6 Feb. 2017), "I've always been fascinated with old movie stars and the history of the place that I live in. I really love the romanticism and the mystery surrounding the period."

WRITING IT DOWN
Collins's first book, *Unfiltered: No Shame, No Regrets, Just Me*, was published in 2017. In seventeen brief essays, Collins addresses topics of interest to her primary fan base: young women. Chapter dividers that reproduce her handwriting include helpful advice and commentary. For example: "Love will find you again. And you can never, ever change yourself to fix the relationship. So if it isn't healthy, say goodbye." This precedes an essay called "The Great Disappearing Act," about people who are suddenly no longer participating in a relationship. Another chapter discusses in more detail her struggles with disordered eating.

In the chapter about her father, she includes an open letter to him, offering her forgiveness for his absence during her early years and asking to move forward with love and mutual respect. Collins sprinkles the text with black-and-white photographs, mainly of herself and her family. At the end of the book, she includes a list of resources on topics such as eating disorders, dating abuse, and bullying.

PERSONAL LIFE
Collins loves and collects jewelry, and she is a spokesperson for the luxury perfume and cosmetics company Lancôme, as well as the watchmaker Movado. Her grandmother and her mother are both sources of her passion for jewelry. On her eighteenth birthday, her love of jewelry was ignited by her mother's gift, a ring designed by Loree Rodkin. As she told Marion Fasel for *InStyle* (June 2013), "My grandmother, who was a ballerina, schooled me in the classics, like the pearl Chanel necklaces she gave me. She passed away a few years ago, but I'll always remember the lessons she taught me about the value of these traditional designs."

Collins also remains outspoken about the pressures facing young people today. As Collins told Terry for *Variety*, "I'm passionate about speaking out against bullying and speaking up for self-awareness with young people, and body-image issues and self-esteem issues." She has done so since 2014 as a spokesperson for Bystander Revolution, a website that stands against bullying.

SUGGESTED READING
Diehl, Matt. "Blue Belle." *InStyle*, vol. 18, no. 5, May 2011, p. 368+.

Fasel, Marion. "Collins on the Rocks." *InStyle*, vol. 20, no. 6, June 2013, p. 266+.

Kit, Zorianna. "The Fairy Tale Life of 'Mirror Mirror' Star Lily Collins." *Reuters*, 29 Mar. 2012, www.reuters.com/article/entertainment-us-lilycollins-mirrormirro-idUS-BRE82S10720120329. Accessed 9 May 2017.

Martin, Annie. "Lily Collins Says She Struggled with Eating Disorders as a Teen." *UPI*, 23 Jan. 2017, www.upi.com/Entertainment_News/Movies/2017/01/23/Lily-Collins-says-she-struggled-with-eating-disorders-as-a-teen/6501485193614. Accessed 12 June 2017.

Martinez, Patty Adams. "Lily Collins: After Years of Hard Work, This Budding Actress Is Ready for Her Close-Up." *Seventeen*, vol. 71, no. 3, Mar. 2012, p. 104+.

Terry, Joshua. "Lily Collins Reveals the Best Advice She Received from Warren Beatty on 'Rules Don't Apply.'" *Variety*, 10 Nov. 2016, variety.com/2016/film/features/actress-lily-collins-warren-beatty-1201913009. Accessed 12 June 2017.

Wappler, Margaret. "Lily Collins on Being Brave Enough to Share Her Story." *InStyle*, 6 Feb. 2017, www.instyle.com/fashion/lily-collins-new-book-unfiltered. Accessed 12 June 2017.

SELECTED WORKS

The Blind Side, 2009; *Mirror Mirror*, 2012; *The Mortal Instruments: City of Bones*, 2013; *Rules Don't Apply*, 2016; *To the Bone*, 2017

—*Judy Johnson*

Mike Colter

Date of birth: August 26, 1976
Occupation: Actor

After years of finding steady work in supporting roles, veteran actor Mike Colter has finally made his mark as a leading man as the Marvel Comics superhero Luke Cage. Once known as Power Man, Luke Cage is a complex character and a formidable superhero—incredibly strong with bulletproof, nearly impenetrable skin. A man wrongfully convicted of a crime he did not commit, Cage also has a strong moral core and is willing to step in and do the right thing when required. First making memorable appearances as Cage in a supporting role in the Netflix series *Jessica Jones* (2015), Colter went on to star in the streaming platform's show dedicated to the character, *Luke Cage*, beginning in 2016. He heads a majority–African American cast in the crime

Photo by Michael Tullberg/Getty Images

drama, which takes place in New York City's Harlem neighborhood. *The Defenders*, which will follow a cadre of Marvel superheroes that includes Cage, is due out later in 2017.

Despite the media attention that has focused on Colter's depiction of a bulletproof African American hero in an era of controversial confrontations between the police and African American citizens, Colter believes the series transcends race while at the same time touching on some vitally relevant topics. "What makes Luke Cage unique isn't him being black," he said in an interview with Jack Shepherd for the *Independent* (4 Oct. 2016). "Nobody wants to have this agenda being a political show. You're trying to entertain people using a comic book. This is not a Black Lives Matter story, but it kind of still is."

Critics, some of whom dubbed *Luke Cage* Marvel's best television series yet, largely praised Colter's performance as the show's unique hero upon the premier of the first season. In a review for *USA Today* (29 Sept. 2016), Brian Truitt wrote, "The success of the show firmly rests on the burly shoulders of Colter, (*The Good Wife*), who comes into his own as a bona fide star."

EARLY LIFE AND EDUCATION

Mike Colter was born in South Carolina on August 26, 1976, the son of Eddie Lee Colter Sr. and Freddie Colter. From the age of eight, he knew he wanted to be an actor; he was largely inspired to do so after watching *A Soldier's Story* (1984), a film about an African American officer investigating the murder of an African American sergeant at an army base in Louisiana during World War II.

During his time at Calhoun County High School, Colter started his own drama club. The experience convinced him that acting would be his life's work, and he began to look for colleges that would allow him to train for his vocation. "I wanted to be an actor when I was younger, but I didn't know how to get into it," he said to Dionne Gleaton for the *Times and Democrat* (22 July 2012). "I thought school would be the best outlet. I knew there was a way if I could get through school, get some training, and maybe get the chance for someone to see me on a different level and open doors."

Colter spent a year at Benedict College in Columbia, South Carolina, where he studied drama, before transferring to the University of South Carolina upon a professor's recommendation. There, he earned a degree in theater and honed his skills in productions such as *Frankenstein*. Following his graduation in 1998, he went on to study at Rutgers University's Mason Gross School of the Arts, receiving a master of fine arts degree in acting in 2001.

STRUGGLING ACTOR

Upon completing his education, Colter still had to make his bones as an actor. "Like everybody, I decided between Los Angeles and New York," he recalled to Gleaton. "I just took the opportunity to go with an agency in L.A. at the time. I went out there for a year, and it was slow going. It took three months before I got my first acting job. That was a little disconcerting."

After appearing on such shows as *ER* and *The Parkers* in 2002, Colter moved back to New York City, where he landed a role in an independent film titled *Brooklyn Lobster* (2005). Thanks partly to the connection he made with the film's casting director, he managed to secure a good supporting role as a championship boxer in *Million Dollar Baby* (2004), a film directed by and starring film legend Clint Eastwood. Colter said of the experience to Gleaton, "I was young, and I think I was too young to be afraid. Looking back, I wasn't flustered or intimidated. I think I probably should have been because Clint Eastwood's known for doing only one or two takes. When I'm with Clint Eastwood, I've got to have my stuff together." Though he experienced a bit of a dry spell after the film's release as he waited for the right next role, he did have the chance to appear alongside Taye Diggs and Anthony Mackie in a 2005 Off-Broadway production of *A Soldier's Play*, the work on which the 1984 film that had inspired him as a child was based.

Colter continued to find steady work in small roles on television and in films over the next several years, including guest appearances on various *Law & Order* shows. During that time, he began his biggest role up to that point with his powerful recurring performance as Lemond Bishop, a Chicago-based drug kingpin, on *The Good Wife*, a CBS drama that ran from 2010 to 2015. He also secured bigger supporting roles as a Narcotics Anonymous sponsor for a troubled woman in the short-lived Sarah Michelle Gellar series *Ringer* (2011–12); as Will Smith's character's father in *Men in Black 3* (2012); as a Special Operations officer in *Zero Dark Thirty* (2012), a drama depicting the real-life manhunt for Osama bin Laden; and as a Federal Bureau of Investigation agent hunting down a notorious cult serial killer in the popular network show *The Following* (2013–15).

BECOMING LUKE CAGE

It was during this period that Colter won the part of Luke Cage, the Marvel Comics superhero who had been created in 1972 by writer Archie Goodwin and artists John Romita Sr. and George Tuska. Cage had been created in response to the then-burgeoning film genre known as Blaxploitation, which targeted urban African American audiences but soon grew both widely popular and controversial. The character—who later took on the moniker of Power Man—was a street-level superhero who fought criminals and gangsters in New York following an experiment with cell regeneration that exponentially enhanced his body, giving him superhuman strength and durability. When his appeal started to wane, Cage was teamed up with Iron Fist, a martial-arts hero, as the Heroes for Hire—a detective agency for which the two men were paid for their services. Cage would later become a member of two superhero groups: the Defenders and the Avengers.

For the more modern Marvel Netflix series adaptation of the character, Colter would not don a costume, but he would remain true to the character's roots as an urban hero, who had escaped prison and was on the run. "You're not always walking around using superpowers, and you're street level. You don't wear costumes, which is cool. I'm so happy not to wear a costume, I can't tell you," Colter noted to Truitt for *USA Today* (20 Nov. 2015).

The Marvel Netflix plan for their superheroes was similar to what the Marvel films have been doing since the introduction of Iron Man in 2008: premiere each character in their own series, then have them team up. For the Netflix programs, Daredevil was introduced first, followed by Jessica Jones, Luke Cage, and Iron Fist—all of whom will team up as the Defenders in 2017. Colter had an advantage over other heroes, as Cage was first depicted in 2015 as a supporting character in the *Jessica Jones* series, about a super-powered woman who suffers from post-traumatic stress disorder after an encounter with a mind-controlling villain; Cage eventually becomes romantically involved with the titular heroine. Colter's performance was immediately hailed upon the series debut. He credits the appeal of the Cage character with the success of his performance in both that series and Cage's subsequent solo show. "Luke Cage isn't going to throw a pity party for himself," Colter noted to Vinnie Mancuso for the *Observer* (21 Sept. 2016). "He literally says to himself, 'This is the world I'm in. These are the circumstances I have.' He's a self-made man. He's trying to continuously build, and that's what's interesting about him. He's a work in progress."

LOOKING FORWARD
By the end of the first season of *Jessica Jones*, Cage has moved uptown to New York City's Harlem neighborhood, where he tries to maintain a low profile, working and trying to stay out of the eyes of the law. By the beginning of the highly anticipated *Luke Cage*, however, which Netflix premiered in the fall of 2016, his innate morality prevents him from turning a blind eye to the organized crime and political corruption he sees around him, and he comes out of hiding to take it on. Colter's transition to the lead role and his continued portrayal of the character was well received. "Colter brings a great deal of soulfulness and intelligence to Luke, as well as beautifully calibrated shadings of pain and rage," Maureen Ryan wrote for *Variety* (23 Sept. 2016).

Reprising his role as Cage in *The Defenders* series gearing up in 2017, his character will team up with Jessica Jones (Krysten Ritter), Daredevil (Charlie Cox), and Iron Fist (Finn Jones). Colter has said in interviews he is particularly interested in developing the relationship his character has with Iron Fist. "He's a young guy. There's an exuberance that Iron Fist comes with that Luke Cage wants to temper a bit," Colter remarked to Shirley Li for *Entertainment Weekly* (16 Jan. 2017). "It can't help but have a wisdom-versus-youth quality . . . Danny comes out like a bull in a china shop in some ways, and I think Luke has seen the world and knows certain things. It's a cool combination that'll work out."

Colter will likely be playing Cage for some time to come, both in his solo series, which had a second season confirmed in late 2016, and as a part of the Defenders team. And the prospect appeals to him greatly. The actor told Joshua Rivera for *GQ* (29 Sept. 2016), "This is a very unique character, and I just happen to relate to a lot of his struggles—and a lot of his desires. I'm having a great time playing Luke Cage. Hopefully it'll last a little longer." At the same time, he views this role as a springboard for further opportunities. "I think I've just gotten started with my career. It's always very exciting to think about the future in regard to endless possibilities,"

he explained to Emma Brown for *Interview* (30 Sept. 2016).

PERSONAL LIFE
Colter met his wife, Iva, an executive at Netflix, while they were both studying at Rutgers. Together they have a daughter. Colter remains a private person and does not use social media, but he understands that his high-profile acting gig is bringing changes to his life. In an interview with Laura Prudom for *Variety* (28 Sept. 2016), he said, "I try not to think about my life changing. That sort of stuff makes me nervous and self-aware and self-involved, so I try not to focus on that."

SUGGESTED READING
Colter, Mike. "The Making of a Superhero." Interview by Emma Brown. *Interview*, 30 Sept. 2016, www.interviewmagazine.com/culture/mike-colter. Accessed 7 Apr. 2017.

Colter, Mike. "Mike Colter on What Sets Luke Cage Apart from the Rest of the 'Defenders.'" Interview by Laura Prudom. *Variety*, 28 Sept. 2016, variety.com/2016/tv/features/actor-mike-colter-marvels-luke-cage-1201871827. Accessed 7 Apr. 2017.

Colter, Mike. "Luke Cage's Mike Colter on Playing a 'Bulletproof Black Man' in the Time of Black Lives Matter." Interview by Joshua Rivera. *GQ*, 29 Sept. 2016, www.gq.com/story/luke-cage-mike-colter. Accessed 7 Apr. 2017.

Gleaton, Dionne. "Following a Dream: St. Matthews Native Navigating Acting World." *Times and Democrat*, 22 July 2012, thetandd.com/news/topnews/following-a-dream-st-matthews-native-navigating-acting-world/article_d0acca20-d2d7-11e1-a9c1-001a4bc-f887a.html. Accessed 7 Apr. 2017.

Li, Shirley. "*The Defenders*: Mike Colter Talks Luke Cage's Friendship with Iron Fist." *Entertainment Weekly*, 16 Jan. 2017, ew.com/tv/2017/01/15/the-defenders-mike-colter-luke-cage-iron-fist. Accessed 7 Apr. 2017.

Mancuso, Vinnie. "Mike Colter Is Bulletproof." *Observer*, 21 Sept. 2016, observer.com/2016/09/mike-colter-is-bulletproof. Accessed 7 Apr. 2017.

Truitt, Brian. "*Jessica Jones* Star Mike Colter a Powerhouse as Luke Cage." *USA Today*, 20 Nov. 2015, www.usatoday.com/story/life/tv/2015/11/20/jessica-jones-mike-colter-luke-cage/76099760. Accessed 7 Apr. 2017.

SELECTED WORKS
Million Dollar Baby, 2004; *The Good Wife*, 2010–15; *Men in Black* 3, 2012; *Zero Dark Thirty*, 2012; *Jessica Jones*, 2015; *Luke Cage*, 2016–

—*Christopher Mari*

James Corden

Date of birth: August 22, 1978
Occupation: Television host

Before 2015, James Corden was widely known to British television audiences as the creator of the popular sitcom *Gavin & Stacey* and to fans of West End theater for his award-winning turns in *One Man, Two Guvnors* and *History Boys*. He was, however, a mostly unknown entity in the United States. His small American fan base was made up mainly of those who had seen his West End shows when they went up on Broadway. "Indeed, Corden was like one of those UK bands the cool kids in high school told you to listen to," Jason Gay wrote for the *Wall Street Journal* (1 March 2016). "Most people over here had no idea who he was. But those who did bordered on the obsessed."

It was surprising to many industry observers when Corden was given the highly coveted job of hosting the *Late Late Show* on CBS—despite never even having appeared as a guest on an American talk show. His first episode aired on March 23, 2015, and now, thanks to YouTube, even those not awake after midnight, when the show airs, may be familiar with his most popular bit. Many of his clips amass tens of millions of hits, and in 2016 *Time* magazine named him among the most influential people on the Internet.

In that bit, "Carpool Karaoke," Corden and a celebrity guest ride around in a car, chat, and sing along with the tunes playing on the car radio. "We're talking about, genuinely, the biggest stars on the planet, who—not always by choice—are surrounded by people all of the time," Corden told Gay. "Security, makeup, assistant, manager, publicist. Then suddenly they get in a car and are on their own—with me."

Many viewers appreciate how he is changing the often-snarky, acerbic nature of late-night talk shows. "Corden's down-to-earth approach to late-night comedy is refreshing," Jesse Carey wrote for *Relevant* magazine (29 June 2016). "He's funny, but he makes other people funnier. He's sharp, but his humor isn't barbed. . . . [He] isn't angry or cynical." Carey concluded, "James Corden's on-screen persona is giving new life not just to a time slot, but the late-night TV genre itself."

EARLY LIFE AND EDUCATION

James Kimberley Corden was born on August 22, 1978, and was raised in Hazlemere, a village just outside of High Wycombe. A middle child, he has an older sister, Andrea, and a younger sister, Ruth. His father, Malcolm, was a musician in the Royal Air Force who later became a salesman of Christian books, and his mother,

iDominick/CC BY-SA 2.0/Wikimedia Commons

Margaret, was a social worker. Corden's parents were active in the Salvation Army (which functions both as a church and a charity), and he was raised steeped in that culture. As an adult, he has distanced himself from Christianity.

Corden knew from a young age that he wanted to perform in some capacity. In his 2012 autobiography, *Can I Have Your Attention Please?*, he recounts the story of attending Ruth's christening. "There were probably forty or fifty people in the congregation that day, but to my four-year-old self it looked like a sea of millions," he wrote. "I started to pull faces and dance my arms around." Soon, most of the attendees were focused on Corden's antics, rather than on watching his infant sister being welcomed into the church. "Even though I was only four years old, from that moment I knew exactly what I wanted to do," he wrote. "I wanted to entertain people, to act, sing, dance; everything and anything that would mean people would look at me and smile."

When he was young, Corden was forced to contend with bullying in school because of his weight. He used humor to disarm his tormentors. "If you're big at school . . . you're going to be a target," he told Stephen Rodrick for *Rolling Stone* (24 August 2016). "Inside, you're terrified. But if you're a bit funny, if you're quicker than them, they won't circle back on you again."

He found school to be boring and often ignored his studies. "It was just . . . pointless to me—I don't need to know how glaciers separate," Corden recalled to Rodrick. Corden attended secondary school at Holmer Green Senior School. After regular school hours, Corden studied at the Jackie Palmer Stage School and tried fruitlessly to get a boy band off the ground. When he lost his driver's license for riding his scooter recklessly, his father ferried him to auditions in London, most of the time to no avail.

BUILDING A CAREER

In 1996 Corden won his first professional job—speaking one line in a West End production of the musical *Martin Guerre.* "I imagined I would be in the chorus and someone would pick me out and give me a role," he told Esther Zuckerman for *Vulture* (8 January 2016), describing what he characterized as his "out of control" ego at that age. "I was actually at the back of the stage, so far back I could touch the wall. I didn't even have a mic in the second act. I realized then I would have to work in TV."

Although minor, the role opened the door for him somewhat, and he began to get other parts—albeit mainly on the small screen as he had predicted. He appeared in the little-seen 1998 film *Twenty-Four Seven* and garnered a succession of television roles in such British shows as *Boyz Unlimited, Hollyoaks* and *Teachers.*

In 2000 Corden began appearing in the hit series *Fat Friends,* which followed the adventures of a group of people in a British "slimming club," analogous to Weight Watchers in the United States. On the show, which ran for four seasons, he played Jamie Rymer, a heavy-set young man whose story arc includes an attempted suicide, gaining an inheritance, and an Internet romance.

In 2004, near the end of *Fat Friends'* run, Corden returned to the West End, where he won praise for portraying the overweight schoolboy Timms in Alan Bennett's critically acclaimed play *The History Boys.* The play tells the story of two schoolmasters with opposing sensibilities as they prepare their students for university entrance exams. Corden reprised his role as part of the touring company, including during a well-received run on Broadway. In 2006 Corden played Timms in a big screen adaptation that received largely favorable reviews for its wit and humanity.

In addition to the critical praise, *The History Boys* gave Corden the benefit of working with Bennett, a playwright beloved for his sparkling dialogue, warmth, and humor. Recognizing his untapped talent, Bennett advised Corden to write his own works.

GAVIN & STACEY AND SUCCESS

Corden took Alan Bennett's advice. With his *Fat Friends* costar Ruth Jones, he created, wrote, and began costarring in his own BBC Three comedy, *Gavin & Stacey,* in 2007. The show followed the romantic adventures of twenty-somethings

Gavin (Mathew Horne) and Stacey (Joanna Page). Corden played Gavin's best friend, Smithy, while Jones had the part of Stacey's best friend, Nessa. Roderick described the show as "a comedy that celebrated the everyday pleasures of British life—hanging drunk with your mates at the chip shop, a wedding remarkable for its ordinariness, Corden's character singing along to 'Do They Know It's Christmas' on the car radio."

The series garnered a slew of awards, including best male newcomer for Corden and best new British TV comedy at the 2007 British Comedy Awards; a 2008 British Academy of Film and Television Arts (BAFTA) Award for best male comedy performance for Corden and a BAFTA Audience Award for best program of the year; and a 2010 National Television Award for most popular comedy program. The finale, which aired on New Year's Day 2010, attracted 10 million viewers.

The year 2011 saw a change in Corden's fortunes. That year, Corden appeared once more on the West End in the screwball comedy *One Man, Two Guvnors,* portraying a crafty servant trying to keep his two employers (both small-time criminals) apart. The show moved to Broadway in 2012, and Corden, who had hosted various awards shows in his native England, took home a Tony in the category of best actor in a play—despite the fact that he was pitted against James Earl Jones, Frank Langella, John Lithgow, and Philip Seymour Hoffman. He also took home an Olivier Award for his performance in the United Kingdom, the British equivalent of a Tony.

In a review of the Broadway production for the *New York Times* (18 Apr. 2012), Ben Brantley raved, "It's a rich, slow-spreading smile, like butter melting in a skillet over a low flame. And whenever it creeps across James Corden's face in the splendidly silly *One Man, Two Guvnors,* . . . you know two things for sure: You're in for trouble, and you're already hooked."

The following year, Corden and fellow actor Mathew Baynton created and wrote the comedy *The Wrong Mans* for BBC Two. The show centers on two office workers (Corden and Baynton) whose lives are drastically disrupted by a case of mistaken identity. The show received wide critical praise in the United Kingdom. The second season aired in 2014.

A MOVE TO THE UNITED STATES

Les Moonves, the president of CBS, went to see Corden in the Broadway run of *One Man, Two Guvnors.* He walked out of the theater, as he has told interviewers, bowled over by Corden's talent. Moonves initiated talks with Corden, who in 2014 had starred with Meryl Streep and Johnny Depp in a Hollywood adaptation of the Stephen Sondheim musical *Into the Woods.* The two discussed a possible sitcom, and Corden, newly in demand in the United States, also started talks with HBO.

In late 2014 Moonves offered Corden the hosting job on the *Late Late Show*, previously held by Craig Ferguson. He debuted on March 23, 2015, with actor Tom Hanks as a guest. Since then, the show has attracted a solid following, and critics have expressed appreciation that he draws upon the influence of British comedy giants and talk show staples like Graham Norton and Jonathan Ross, making him a quirky rarity in a sea of polished and glib late-night hosts. Of his gentler approach, he told Dave Itzkoff for the *New York Times* (10 May 2015), "Before people fall asleep at night, they want someone to say, 'I know it's tough but it's going to be all right, and we're going to try to make you smile.'"

In 2016 Corden hosted the Seventieth Annual Tony Awards, and that year he also took home an Emmy for his signature "Carpool Karaoke." Stars now consider it an honor to be invited to participate, and Corden's passenger seat has seen the likes of Mariah Carey, Justin Bieber, Elton John, Adele, Stevie Wonder, and First Lady Michelle Obama.

PERSONAL LIFE
Although Corden once had the reputation of being hard-partying and boorish—charges that he does not refute—he is now a family man. He credits his parents for intervening when he was at his lowest, most insufferable point.

Corden recalled to Rodrick. "I met my wife [Julia]; she barely owned a television and worked for Save the Children. We sat down one night and we fell in love and that was it." The couple has two children, Max and Carey.

SUGGESTED READING

Brantley, Ben. "Mistaken Identity May Be Closer Than It Appears." Review of *One Man, Two Guvnors*, dir. Nicholas Hytner. *New York Times,* 18 Apr. 2012, www.nytimes.com/2012/04/19/theater/reviews/james-corden-in-one-man-two-guvnors-at-the-music-box. Accessed 21 Dec. 2016.

Carey, Jesse. "The Prayer That Changed James Corden's Life." *Relevant,* 29 June 2016, www.relevantmagazine.com/culture/prayer-changed-james-cordens-life. Accessed 28 Oct. 2016.

Corden, James. "James Corden on the State of Late Night." Interview by Dave Itzkoff. *New York Times,* 10 May 2015, www.nytimes.com/2015/05/11/arts/television/james-corden-on-the-state-of-late-night.html. Accessed 28 Oct. 2016.

Gay, Jason. "Late Night Redefined: James Corden." *Wall Street Journal Magazine,* 1 Mar. 2016, www.wsj.com/articles/late-night-redefined-james-corden-1456851745. Accessed 28 Oct. 2016.

Rodrick, Stephen. "How James Corden Conquered Late Night One 'Carpool Karaoke' at a Time." *Rolling Stone,* 24 Aug. 2016. www.rollingstone.com/tv/features/carpool-karaoke-king-how-james-corden-won-late-night-tv-w435702. Accessed 28 Oct. 2016.

Zuckerman, Esther. "Tonys Host James Corden Is No Stranger to the Broadway Stage." *Vulture,* 10 June 2016, www.vulture.com/2016/06/looking-back-at-james-cordens-broadway-past.html. Accessed 28 Oct. 2016.

SELECTED WORKS
Fat Friends, 2000–5; *Gavin & Stacey*, 2007–10; *The Wrong Mans*, 2013–14; *Into the Woods*, 2014; *Late Late Show with James Corden*, 2015–

—Mari Rich

Marion Coutts

Date of birth: ca. 1965
Occupation: Artist and author

Marion Coutts is an award-winning British artist, writer, and former musician. Coutts, who is also a senior lecturer at Goldsmiths, an arts college at the University of London, began her career as a musician, playing trumpet and singing in a Scottish anarcho-punk band called the Dog Faced Hermans from the late 1980s until 1995. She went on to become a renowned artist, creating films and sculptures beginning in the late 1990s. Some of her best-known works include *Fresh Air* (1998–2000), *Everglade* (2003), *Twenty Six Things* (2008), and *Aiming or Hitting* (2017).

Her first book, *The Iceberg* (2014), a memoir about the illness and death of her husband, the art critic Tom Lubbock, won the Wellcome Book Prize in 2015. *The Iceberg*, she has said in numerous interviews, began as a series of short texts written during her husband's illness. After Lubbock died, she realized the writings could be strung together to form a book. Even as a writer, she thinks like an artist. "I have a very sculptural way of thinking about things," she told Claire Meadows for the British magazine *After Nyne* (2017). "I used to make videos and sculpture works and now I make photographs and sculpture works. I am interested in how experience can be configured materially. I don't see my writing as particularly connected to my artworks but the way I think about writing is similar to how I think around objects."

EARLY LIFE AND MUSIC CAREER

Coutts was born in Nigeria, where her parents were working as Salvation Army ministers. She grew up there and in London, but she spent most of her adolescence in Edinburgh, Scotland. In 1982, she enrolled as a student at the Edinburgh College of Art. While in school, she began spending time with an improvisational music group that eventually named itself Volunteer Slavery and whose first concert was a benefit for a local miners' strike. She graduated with a bachelor's degree in fine art in 1986, the same year that she and others from the experimental group formed a punk band called the Dog Faced Hermans, which included Andy Moor, Colin McLean, and Wilf Plum. Coutts played the trumpet, an instrument she had essentially learned to play with a church group when she was ten years old, and sang. She has described the band's beginnings as a social group, and in an interview with Vanessa Thorpe for the *Guardian* (30 Dec. 2001), she explained the band's more unique style: "We were very performance-oriented, fitting in somewhere between the improvised new music and the alt-rock, weirdo leftie music scene." In 1989, Coutts won a British Council Scholarship to study at the State School for the Arts in Wroclaw, Poland. The scholarship ended in 1990; she spent the next five years living and working with her band in the Netherlands.

Largely resisting aligning themselves with one genre over another, the Dog Faced Hermans were ultimately part of a larger movement of British anarcho-punk bands such as the Ex, with whom they toured and sometimes played, and Chumbawamba, best remembered in the United States as one-hit wonders for their mainstream 1997 single "Tubthumping." Dog Faced Hermans released a number of albums—including *Humans Fly* (1988), *Everyday Timebomb* (1989), *Mental Blocks for All Ages* (1991), *Hum of Life* (1993), *Those Deep Buds* (1994), and *Bump and Swing* (1995)—but always considered themselves, first and foremost, a live band. For almost a decade, they toured extensively, particularly throughout Europe and the United States. Following a final world tour, feeling that they had managed to fully express themselves as a musical group, the Dog Faced Hermans disbanded in 1995.

CAREER AS A VISUAL ARTIST

Returning to settle in London, Coutts focused on finding her voice as a visual artist. Meanwhile, she met Tom Lubbock, a writer and art critic for the *Independent*, through mutual friends in 1996. They married in 2001.

Coutts's work is varied in medium and tone. Between 1998 and 2000, she created a trio of tennis tables in the shape of different London parks for a piece called *Fresh Air*. The theme of this work and others of the same period, James Hall wrote for *Artforum* magazine (Jan. 2003), is "mythologiz[ing] the mundane." He added, "With the insouciance and economy of a professional magician, [Coutts] makes the one-dimensional multidimensional and transforms stale habit into compelling ritual." In addition to ensuring that her artistic style could not be pigeonholed through making each piece unique in its form and representative ideas, she remained committed from the beginning to concentrating her work on what she described to Thorpe as "the sort of objects which are invested with collective emotion, things that gather people to them, entertainments, utilities—social objects."

In 1998, Coutts created a sculpture called *Eclipse*, in which a small garden greenhouse periodically fills with smoke. She shot her first films on a Super 8 camera as a Rome Scholar at the British School at Rome in 1999, and she incorporated superimposed film footage of migrating starlings in her piece *Assembly* (2000). She won the Momart Fellowship, a nine-month residency, at Tate Liverpool in 2000. Two years later, she exhibited a new work called *Cult*, an exploration of group psychology, at London's Chisenhale Gallery. The installation, as Hall put it, "wryly transfigured the domestic cat." In the center of the low-lit gallery, nine video monitors were mounted at eye level on pedestals. The videos played on a loop and featured the motionless, life-sized face of a cat. Hall praised the piece, but Elisabeth Mahoney, writing for the *Guardian* (5 Sept. 2002), was less impressed. "Coutts neatly subverts the twee sweetness of cats as they are conventionally represented, but only for a fleeting moment," she wrote.

In 2003, Coutts held a Kettle's Yard Artist Fellowship at St. John's College, Cambridge. That same year, she presented her piece *Everglade*, a video projection that captures individual scenes of a suburban park, some of which include distant figures walking, talking, and sitting. Her next piece, *Mountain* (2004), focused on the elaborate dining rituals at St. John's. In an eighteen-minute sequence shot in black and white that ran on a loop, Coutts's video captured two staff members laying a long table, their figures becoming smaller as they move away from the camera. Coutts, working with composer Adrian Johnston, recorded a soundtrack for the piece featuring two pianos.

TEACHING, CREATING, AND WRITING

In addition to crafting her own work, Coutts has lent her talents to teaching others, including stints as a senior visiting lecturer at the Norwich School of Art and Design from 2004 to 2005 and associate lecturer at the University of the Arts from 2005 to 2010. She began her longest lecturer tenure to date at the University of London's

Goldsmiths in 2007; holding the position of senior lecturer in fine art, she had begun working there as a visiting tutor in 2001.

In 2008, Coutts completed a commission from the Wellcome Collection in London, a short film called *Twenty Six Things*. Henry Wellcome, who died in 1936, made a fortune as a pharmacist in the late nineteenth century, and he became a well-known philanthropist and collector. In *Twenty Six Things*, Coutts filmed objects from his collection, creating a memory game for the viewer.

In September 2008, Lubbock was diagnosed with a late-stage tumor located in the part of his brain that controls language and speech. For the next two years, Coutts cared for him—in addition to the couple's nearly two-year-old son, Eugene—as he lost his ability to read, write, and speak. He wrote a book about his own deterioration, titled *Until Further Notice, I Am Alive* (2012), for which Coutts wrote the introduction. Lubbock died on January 9, 2011, at the age of fifty-three. During Lubbock's illness, Coutts had written fragments of text in a number of Microsoft Word documents on her computer. She eventually rearranged the fragments in chronological order and published them as the memoir *The Iceberg*, which was published in the United Kingdom in 2014. In an interview with Katie Law for the *Evening Standard* (30 June 2014), Coutts explained her motivation for turning to writing at such a tragic time: "I started to write in the summer of 2009, and really it was writing against annihilation. We were going to go under. . . . It was somehow a way of externalizing the things I was given to see and the things that were given to us to do. I felt like it was something I could orchestrate."

IMPACT OF *THE ICEBERG*

As Law wrote, *The Iceberg* is not "like any other bereavement memoir—it is written in the first-person, present tense—it reads like a huge juggernaut, its inevitable awful ending hurtling towards you at full speed from the first page." The book was unique in another way, too; as Dwight Garner, a book critic for the *New York Times*, pointed out, Coutts observes her husband lose his faculties while Eugene gains his. "Tragedy set beside joy throws both into topographical relief," Garner wrote (26 Jan. 2016). *The Iceberg* was short-listed for the 2014 Pol Roger Duff Cooper Prize, the 2014 Costa Biography Award, and the 2014 Samuel Johnson Prize for nonfiction. After winning the Wellcome Book Prize in 2015 and being published in the United States in 2016, the memoir was also a finalist for a National Book Critics Circle Award in 2017.

In 2017, Coutts created an installation of sculpture, photographs, drawing, and text called *Aiming or Hitting*, a title taken from a line in her memoir. The centerpiece of the exhibit, her first in around eight years, and the impetus for the project as a whole, was *Library*, a photograph of the remains of Lubbock's extensive book collection. (Coutts sold most of the collection to raise money for the hospice where Lubbock died.) The show, like Coutts's book, was born out of grief, but it drew inspiration from the work of the late Felix Gonzalez-Torres. "I worked on . . . his first major exhibition in the UK and I have strong memories of it," Coutts told Susie Pentelow for *Traction* (Apr. 2017). "The work was formal, sculptural, and intimate. I'm interested in what happens in the encounter with an artwork that moves you and I made some work based on one of his posters." Another part of the exhibit, a photograph titled *Boy Looks at Rock on Top of Another Rock*, is about the experience of viewing art as well. The photo is cropped in such a way that the boy's looking (at a work by Peter Fischli and David Weiss) becomes the focus of the piece, rather than the object itself.

PERSONAL LIFE

Coutts lives in London, where she is raising her son, Eugene, who was born in 2007. In addition to writing her memoir, Coutts has promoted increasing awareness and resources regarding brain tumor research since the death of Lubbock in 2011. In 2015, she supported the opening of a new research center dedicated to studying brain tumors funded by the British charity Brain Tumour Research by reading an excerpt from *The Iceberg* at the launch.

SUGGESTED READING

Coutts, Marion. "Aiming or Hitting: Nine Minutes with Marion Coutts." Interview by Claire Meadows. *After Nyne*, 2017, www.afternynemagazine.com/aiming-hitting-nine-minutes-marion-coutts. Accessed 12 June 2017.

Coutts, Marion. "Marion Coutts." Interview by Susie Pentelow. *Traction*, Apr. 2017, traction-magazine.co.uk/post/158924514301/145-marion-coutts. Accessed 12 June 2017.

Garner, Dwight. "Review: A Widow Documents Her Loss in *The Iceberg*." Review of *The Iceberg*, by Marion Coutts. *The New York Times*, 26 Jan. 2016, www.nytimes.com/2016/01/27/books/review-a-widow-documents-her-loss-in-the-iceberg.html. Accessed 12 June 2017.

Hall, James. "Marion Coutts." Review of *Cult*, by Marion Coutts. *Artforum*, MutualArt, Jan. 2003, www.mutualart.com/Article/Marion-Coutts/4062FADD802EED0C. Accessed 12 June 2017.

Law, Katie. "It Was My Duty to Stop Tom Being Destroyed before His Death—and Eugene by It." *Evening Standard*, 30 June 2014, www.standard.co.uk/lifestyle/london-life/it-was-my-duty-to-stop-tom-being-destroyed-before-his-death-and-eugene-by-it-9572592.html. Accessed 12 June 2017.

Thorpe, Vanessa. "Welcome to My World." *The Guardian*, 30 Dec. 2001, www.theguardian.com/theobserver/2001/dec/30/features.review27. Accessed 12 June 2017.

SELECTED WORKS

Fresh Air, 1998–2000; *Cult*, 2002; *Everglade*, 2003; *Twenty Six Things*, 2008; *Aiming or Hitting*, 2017

—*Molly Hagan*

Kelly Fremon Craig

Born: ca. 1980
Occupation: Director; writer

Kelly Fremon Craig's 2016 film *The Edge of Seventeen* garnered several awards, including her nomination for outstanding achievement of a first-time filmmaker by the Directors Guild of America, as well as the New York Film Critics Circle Award for best first film. Fremon Craig explained to Jordan Raup for the website The Film Stage (14 Feb. 2017), "The message of the film is really that nobody gets out of this unscathed. Nobody gets out of life without some real bumps and bruises, even if they look like they are faring a lot better. I think the truth is that just some of us hide it better. Some of us just pretend better, but the truth is that everybody goes through stuff that is really difficult." The film's success opened new opportunities, including participating in a panel at Chapman University's Women in Focus: In the Director's Chair in April 2017. Offering her advice to directors, Fremon Craig told Laura Berger for the blog *Women and Hollywood* (15 Sept. 2016), "There are no small things. Everything matters. I find that filmmaking requires brutal precision, little details matter hugely, and a wrong costume or prop or music cue can sink a scene."

EARLY LIFE AND EDUCATION

Kelly Fremon Craig was born in Whittier, California, where she grew up watching films by Christopher Guest and reading David Sedaris and Nick Hornby. She attended the University of California, Irvine, graduating with a bachelor's degree in English literature. During her college days, she performed both spoken-word poetry and comedy routines at coffeehouses.

An internship changed the direction of her life, as she explained to Matthew Ross for *Variety* (21 June 2007): "When I was still in college, I got an internship in the film division at Immortal Entertainment. I read one script and

By Gordon Correll [CC BY-SA 2.0], via Wikimedia Commons

immediately knew this was what I wanted to do." Level 1 hired Fremon Craig after college to write a contemporary version of *Cyrano de Bergerac* set in a high school.

For a brief period, Fremon Craig worked in children's group homes as a social worker. She left the job, as she explained to Dylan Callaghan for the Writers Guild of America website (18 Nov. 2016), because "it was so painfully sad, and I felt like I couldn't really fix it. I also couldn't not take it home with me, like some people could."

EARLY CAREER

Fremon Craig worked with Allan Loeb to write the screen story for *Streak*, a sixteen-minute film released in 2008. The short film portrays a female college student agonizing over whether to join others in running across campus in the nude. Demi Moore directed the film.

Fremon Craig next embarked on *Post Grad*, a full-length PG-13 film focusing on the dilemmas of a young woman having difficulty with real-world life after college. The cast included Alexis Bledel of *Gilmore Girls* fame in the role of the protagonist, a recent English major graduate without a job forced to move back home with her bizarre family. Other actors included veterans Carol Burnett, Jane Lynch, and Michael Keaton.

Ivan Reitman, who worked with Fremon Craig on the script, produced the film. He told Ross, "Over the past year, Kelly has written at least fifteen drafts of the script. Although she completely was open to doing the work that was necessary to improve it, she also worked very hard to maintain her own language and the integrity of her characters. She really has her own voice, which is her greatest strength."

Critics were not kind to the movie, comparing it unfavorably to the 2006 comedy *Little Miss Sunshine*. They took the film to task for its clichéd portrayal of a young woman who is nothing without a man, despite a college education and ambition.

THE EDGE OF SEVENTEEN

Fremon Craig wrote and directed the 2016 film *The Edge of Seventeen*, which she originally titled *Besties*. When it debuted at the Toronto International Film Festival, it drew comparisons to *Mean Girls* (2004), *Juno* (2007), and the teen films by John Hughes. It was Fremon Craig's directorial debut.

James L. Brooks, who directed hits such as *Terms of Endearment* and *Broadcast News* and television shows such as *The Simpsons*, mentored her. He decided to do so after a meeting about that possibility; as she was leaving, Fremon Craig told him no one would work harder than she would. That sold Brooks, who heads the production company Gracie Films, which is distributed by Sony Pictures. With a small company, Brooks ensures that most writers get to direct or produce their scripts.

Brooks encouraged Fremon Craig to do some research to get the right tone for the interactions of contemporary teenagers. To do so, Fremon Craig told Brent Lang for *Variety* (12 Sept. 2016), "I did six months of interviewing high school kids. . . . And those interviews would turn into little therapy sessions. I hung out at high schools. Went to a high school dance. I tried to be a fly on the wall." Her research gave her a greater respect for the difficulties of the teen years, which are easily dismissed by many adults. The research she did led Fremon Craig to rewrite the script to honor the messiness of teenagers' lives, rather than simply set up jokes. Nothing remained of her first effort, but the second draft became the basis for the film.

Asked by Raup about her portrayal of high school students, Fremon Craig said she had, for the first time since graduating, visited her college, explaining, "There was this sense of gnawing loneliness that I remember having there and that I remember having in high school. I think it's just a part of that age, at least it was for me. This feeling of being all alone in the world. Does anybody understand? At some point feeling like nobody, *nobody* could possibl[y] get what you are feeling. I guess that was so central to my experience through high school and college that I didn't know how to write a movie without that. It was just so in the bones of it."

Hayden Szeto and Hailee Steinfeld play the film's protagonists. Fremon Craig's choice to make the male lead Korean American was a reflection of the friends she had during college, as well as a response to the "whitewashing" of films and the underrepresentation of Asians. Szeto drew on his own experiences as a high school student in Vancouver, where some of the film was shot. Finding the female lead, Nadine, required more than a year and a thousand auditions. Brooks was convinced getting that character right was the lynchpin of the entire film. Steinfeld, famed for her role in the 2010 remake of *True Grit*, nailed the audition.

Fremon Craig's first meeting with Brooks, who has three Oscars and produced the first films of both Wes Anderson and Cameron Crowe, changed not only her script but also how she writes. As she began discussing issues such as structure and plot, Brooks stopped her. As she explained to Scott Myers for his website Go into the Story (27 Nov. 2016), "He stopped and said, 'The first and biggest question you have to answer is, what are you saying about life?' That just changed everything for me. It changed everything because I had felt that in myself always, as I was writing and trying to find something, but I had never really articulated it until he said that and I will never write anything the same ever again because of that." Fremon Craig spent the next weeks writing in a journal to answer that question, revising her script to focus not on the jokes, but on honest emotion. Her internal seeking led her to focus on the loneliness of adolescence and the fear of not being good enough.

Over the four years that Brooks worked with Fremon Craig to develop the script and film it, he also encouraged her to film each scene in several different ways to enhance her directing, as she explained to Berger. "When you're shooting a scene, get choices. Get variations beyond whatever you had in your head. You make your film in the edit and you will be so glad to have the option to push the energy one direction or another when you're staring at it all in context."

A WRITER FIRST

Asked by Peter Hall for *Movie.com* (18 Nov. 2016) whether the words on the page or on the set made the script come alive for her, Fremon Craig responded, "Because I'm a writer first, and I always write, write, write, it was important to have it on the page before we ever got to the set. That these felt like real people saying real things and going through real emotions. I think I would have been terrified to jump into anything [with] actors without feeling like everything is there. And the great thing is when you work with really talented people, they then further expand from that."

She works a regular nine-to-seven writing day, treating the writing as if she were going to an office to work and then coming home. She first hears a character's voice and begins to write, trying to determine what the voice is saying. At times she will use music in the background to get the right feel for the characters.

Fremon Craig told Lang, "I am definitely one of those people that as soon as I put my hands on the keys something clicks in. Some ideas strike you in the shower, but mostly it's just showing up to the laptop, not knowing how I'm going to get where." This was true of the script for *The Edge of Seventeen*; she first came up with the opening scene between Nadine and her teacher (played by Woody Harrelson), without knowing anything else about the plot or the characters. Fremon Craig has tried to use voice dictation to write, but finds it impossible, although her mentor, Brooks, can do so, a feat she considers magical.

PERSONAL LIFE

Fremon Craig looks forward to further adventures in writing film scripts; as she told Ross, "Character-based comedy is what I love to do; those are the types of movies that move me, so I'll be happy writing them for a while." She cites Sofia Coppola's film *Lost in Translation* (2003) as her favorite film directed by a woman. Fremon Craig believes that social media is a leading contemporary cause of the feelings of loneliness and isolation that her first film depicts. As she told Myers, "All you have to do is get online for two seconds and you'll be hit with a barrage of perfectly filtered pictures of people having more fun then you are. On some level . . . that makes everyone feel a little bit lonelier everyday." Fremon Craig is married; the couple have a young son, who was born while Fremon Craig was working on the script for *The Edge of Seventeen*.

SUGGESTED READING

Berger, Laura. "TIFF 2016 Meet the Women Directors: Kelly Fremon Craig—'The Edge of Seventeen.'" *Women and Hollywood*, 15 Sept. 2016, blog.womenandhollywood.com/tiff-2016-women-directors-meet-kelly-fremon-craig-the-edge-of-seventeen-9f6524c350a3. Accessed 22 June 2017.

Fremon Craig, Kelly. "Heartbreak High." Interview by Dylan Callaghan. *Writers Guild of America West*, 18 Nov. 2016, www.wga.org/writers-room/features-columns/the-craft/2016/the-edge-of-seventeen-kelly-fremon-craig. Accessed 28 June 2017.

Fremon Craig, Kelly. Interview by Scott Myers. *Go into the Story*, 27 Nov. 2016, gointothestory.blcklst.com/interview-kelly-fremon-craig-bea8502e86c. Accessed 22 June 2017.

Fremon Craig, Kelly. "'The Edge of Seventeen' Director Kelly Fremon Craig on Loneliness, Reception, and 'Moonlight.'" Interview by Jordan Raup. *The Film Stage*, 14 Feb. 2017, thefilmstage.com/features/the-edge-of-seventeen-director-kelly-fremon-craig-on-loneliness-reception-and-moonlight/. Accessed 20 June 2017.

Fremon Craig, Kelly, and James L. Brooks. "Interview: James L. Brooks and Kelly Fremon Craig Talk Their Fantastic Teen Comedy 'The Edge of Seventeen.'" Interview by Peter Hall. *Movies.com*, 18 Nov. 2016, www.movies.com/movie-news/edge-of-seventeen-interview-kelly-fremon-craig-james-l-brooks/21688. Accessed 27 June 2017.

Lang, Brent. "Brooks, Craig on 'The Edge' Together in Toronto." *Variety*, 12 Sept. 2016, pp. 1+.

Ross, Matthew. "10 Screenwriters to Watch." *Variety*, 21 June 2007, variety.com/2007/film/features/kelly-fremon-1117967389. Accessed 22 June 2017.

SELECTED WORKS

Streak, 2008; *Post Grad*, 2009; *The Edge of Seventeen*, 2016

—Judy Johnson

Adam Curtis

Date of birth: May 26, 1955
Occupation: Documentary filmmaker

Adam Curtis's documentaries are distinct and instantly recognizable: a declarative sentence fills the screen followed by juxtaposed images, as well-chosen music provides ambient sound. His hypnotic, kaleidoscopic films are edited in such a way to prompt viewers to make intuitive leaps and identify patterns amid the chaos of modern life. A longtime BBC employee, Curtis makes use of the BBC's extensive film archives, which date back to the early twentieth century. His central theme: that everyone has been listening to the wrong story, which has been created by politicians and cultural influencers to maintain control.

He is, to his many supporters, the contrarian journalistic voice of the modern world; to his critics, he is an arrogant intellectual seeking to oversimplify complex issues and situations to fit a single worldview: his own. Curtis explained his work in an interview with Paul MacInnes for *The Guardian* (24 Jan. 2015): "All reality is incredibly complex and chaotic. To make sense of it we have to tell stories about it—which inevitably simplifies. And that is what politicians—and journalists—do. What *I* try to do is to find new facts and data, things you haven't thought about, and turn them into new stories. My aim is to use those stories to try and make the complexity and chaos intelligible."

Vivien Killilea/Getty Images

EARLY LIFE AND EDUCATION

Kevin Adam Curtis was born in Dartford, Kent, England, on May 26, 1955. His grandfather ran for parliament as a socialist, while his father, Martin Curtis, was a cinematographer who worked with the British documentary filmmaker Humphrey Jennings, as well as other notable directors such as Michael Winner of *Death Wish* (1974). Curtis earned a scholarship to Sevenoaks independent school. He then went to Mansfield College at the University of Oxford, where he studied human sciences. For a brief time he taught and did postgraduate work at Oxford, with the idea of earning his PhD, but left before completing it. "I very quickly realized I hated academia," Curtis recalled to Andrew Anthony for *The Guardian* (3 Jan. 2015).

Curtis subsequently joined the BBC training course. By the early 1980s he was at work as a segment producer on a television program called *That's Life!*, which was a hybrid program that mixed serious investigative reporting with light-hearted entertainment pieces. While working on the show, he had something of an epiphany about what he wanted to do with his life. He had been sent to Edinburgh, to film a dog that sang while his owner played the bagpipes. Yet, no matter what they did, neither the owner nor the film crew could get the dog to sing on film. Curtis called his producer to ask what he should do. She told him to keep on filming the man playing the bagpipes and the dog doing nothing at all.

He recalled the lessons of the experience to Jonathan Lethem for the *New York Times Magazine* (27 Oct. 2016): "That time with a dog

taught me the fundamental basics of journalism. That what really happens is the key thing; you mustn't try and force the reality in front of you into a predictable story. What you should do is notice what is happening in front of your eyes, and what instinctively your reaction is. And my reaction was that I hated the dog as it looked at me silently. So I made a short film about that."

DEVELOPING HIS STYLE

Although he had found his calling, it took Curtis some time to develop his signature style. His first two documentary films for the BBC as producer include *The Italians* (1984) and *The Great British Housing Disaster* (1984). He then directed two episodes of the BBC documentary series *Forty Minutes: Bombay Hotel* (1987) and *The Kingdom of Fun* (1989). The work he believes was the first that was distinctly his was *Inside Story: The Road to Terror* (1989). On that documentary he was supposed to detail how Ayatollah Khomeini's followers tortured and executed left-wing opponents in Iran. Finding that story uninteresting, he added a discussion of the French Revolution into the film. Although his superiors at the BBC threatened to can the project, Alan Yentob, who was the controller of BBC 2 at the time, saw the documentary and loved it, saving not only the film but likely Curtis's job. Since that time Curtis has worked practically unopposed at the BBC, able to make whatever films he wanted using the BBC's vast treasure trove of archival footage. "He's been quite overt in his hatred of the BBC," a BBC insider told Anthony for *The Guardian*, "and yet no one seems to mind. Instead he enjoys a creative freedom at the BBC that exists for a minority of one."

British television audiences came to know Curtis through his work on a series of documentaries he directed in the 1990s. The first was Pandora's Box (1992), a six-part series about exploiting technological and political ideas without regard for the outcome of those decisions. Pandora's Box earned Curtis a British Academy of Film and Television Arts (BAFTA) Award for best factual series. His next major work was *The Mayfair Set* (1999), a four-part series about a group of British entrepreneurs who, in the 1960s, weakened British regulated industries and introduced free-market principles into politics. He then followed this with *The Century of the Self* (2002), a four-part documentary series that looks at the way Sigmund Freud's psychological theories were used to influence public relations, consumerism, and politics. Each of these films used the vast archival footage of the BBC to pose a simple argument: that ideas were manipulated by those in power or those seeking to acquire power. Brandon Harris wrote of Curtis's films for the *New Yorker* (3 Nov. 2016), explaining, "His films posit that the official history of the twentieth century—told to us by states-men and newsreaders, amplified by the main-stream media in all its technologically enhanced forms—is the work of 'managers of perception,' people who avoid telling the public the uncom-fortable and complicated truths about the world in order to retain power within a status quo that isn't ever quite what it seems to be."

Curtis's subsequent films helped to raise his profile in the United States, particularly *The Power of Nightmares: The Rise of the Politics of Fear* (2004), a three-part series that theorizes that the radical Islamist and neoconservative movements run on parallel tracks, with each looking to instill fear in the general population of a changing world. In the film he also made the argument—a year prior to the London bomb-ings of July 7, 2005, and just a few years after the terror attacks of September 11, 2001, on the United States—that there was no organized global network of radicalized jihadists looking to overthrow Western liberalism but rather a frac-tured set of individual operatives. He followed this film with *The Trap: What Happened to Our Dream of Freedom* (2007), which looked at how modern concepts of freedom are actually restric-tive and paranoid; and *All Watched Over by Ma-chines of Loving Grace* (2011), which presents an argument that the computers and machines people have built to bring ease to their lives have in fact colonized them and control their way of thinking.

BITTER LAKE

Curtis's 2015 documentary, *Bitter Lake*, took its name from a meeting between President Frank-lin D. Roosevelt and King Ibn Saud of Saudi Arabia aboard a yacht on the Great Bitter Lake of the Suez Canal in February 1945. During the meeting the American president and the Saudi monarch made a deal that Curtis believes con-tinues to have ramifications for modern times: the United States agreed to protect the newly formed Saudi kingdom in exchange for a con-tinuing supply of oil to Western nations. As Curtis sees it, the meeting had the unintended consequences leading down to the Western involvement in wars in Iraq and Afghanistan, as well as the spread of radical Islamic funda-mentalism. Curtis released the film directly to BBC iPlayer. "I'd always known about the Bitter Lake meeting," Curtis explained to MacInnes for *The Guardian*. "I'd seen the footage, this re-ally gloomy, almost Edward Hopper–style shot of President Roosevelt—who is about to die—sit-ting on a warship meeting the king of Saudi Ara-bia, who'd ruthlessly created this new kingdom twenty years before. I'd always thought this was rather an epic moment and it has stuck in the back of my brain."

The film, like many of Curtis's other docu-mentaries, met with considerable critical ac-claim. However, it exposed him to a growing criticism that he was an arrogant intellectual seeking to provide an overly simplified alternate history of modern society that was more in keep-ing with his worldview—that little-known and underreported forces are really at work in shap-ing the world—than with reality. As MacInnes observed: "He's been praised as an auteur and one of the most original thinkers on TV. He's also been denounced as a dangerous contrarian and a teller of tales that simplify the complex realities of the modern world."

HYPERNORMALISATION

Curtis's latest film, *HyperNormalisation*, released in 2016, did little to squelch the criticism or the praise surrounding his work. This documentary, which again made liberal use of the BBC's ar-chives, argues that the modern world is suffer-ing from a mass delusion deliberately created and cultivated by powerful politicians and busi-ness interests to create a simplistic black-and-white narrative of good and evil because these same leaders have been unwilling to make hard choices about complex issues. He further ar-gues that this fake world has existed since the 1970s, when financial institutions realized they could run society better than elected leaders. In a review of the film for *The Guardian* (9 Oct. 2016), Tim Adams wrote, "Curtis suggests that the trending opposites of our times—the chat-ter of social media and the stricture of Islamic fundamentalism—represent a retreat from com-plexity into an existence that constantly reflects our desires and anxieties back to us."

Like its predecessors, *HyperNormalisation* met with a great deal of critical praise. In the *New Yorker*, Brandon Harris proclaimed: "*Hy-perNormalisation* is a searching and essential document of our times, a movie that leaves us, as in its opening shot, groping through a pitch-black forest with only a flashlight, wondering what lies in all that terrifying darkness that no one has found a way through." Jonathan Lethem declared in an article for the *New York Times Magazine* that "*HyperNormalisation* is a summa-tion of one of Curtis's major themes: that liberal-ism—since the collapse of certainty about how its values would transform politics, finance, and journalism—has in fact become genuinely con-servative. In a world of unpredictability, it has retreated from genuine frontiers, instead opting for holding actions that can make it feel stable and safe."

SUGGESTED READING

Anthony, Andrew. "Adam Curtis: Cult Film-Maker with an Eye for the Unsettling." *The Guardian*, 3 Jan. 2015, www.theguardian.

com/theobserver/2015/jan/04/adam-curtis-bitter-lake-documentary-iplayer. Accessed 5 Jan. 2017.

Curtis, Adam. "Adam Curtis: Why *South Park* Is the Best Documentary of Them All." *The Guardian*, 14 Nov. 2016, www.theguardian.com/film/2016/nov/14/adam-curtis-documentary-south-park-american-honey. Accessed 10 Jan. 2017.

Harris, Brandon. "Adam Curtis's Essential Counterhistories." *New Yorker*, 3 Nov. 2016, www.newyorker.com/culture/culture-desk/adam-curtiss-essential-counterhistories. Accessed 5 Jan. 2017.

Lethem, Adam. "Adam Curtis and the Secret History of Everything." *New York Times Magazine*, 27 Oct. 2016, www.nytimes.com/interactive/2016/10/30/magazine/adam-curtis-documentaries.html. Accessed 10 Jan. 2017.

MacInnes, Paul. "Adam Curtis: 'I Try to Make the Complexity and Chaos Intelligible.'" *The Guardian*, 24 Jan. 2015, www.theguardian.com/tv-and-radio/2015/jan/24/adam-curtis-bitter-lake. Accessed 5 Jan. 2017.

SELECTED WORKS

Pandora's Box, 1992; *The Mayfair Set*, 1999; *The Century of the Self*, 2002; *The Power of Nightmares: The Rise of the Politics of Fear*, 2004; *The Trap: What Happened to Our Dream of Freedom*, 2007; *All Watched Over by Machines of Loving Grace*, 2011; *Bitter Lake*, 2015; *HyperNormalisation*, 2016

—*Christopher Mari*

Dennis Daugaard

Date of birth: June 11, 1953
Occupation: Governor of South Dakota

As the thirty-second governor of South Dakota, Dennis Daugaard has helped the state to overcome many economic challenges and achieve a sound fiscal standing and economic growth.

EARLY LIFE AND EDUCATION

Dennis Daugaard was born on June 11, 1953, in Garretson, South Dakota. Both of his parents were deaf, and he grew up on his family's dairy and cattle farm near Dells Rapids. He attended a one-room country school until seventh grade and then moved to a larger school when two local school districts merged. He graduated from Dells Rapids High School in 1971 and enrolled in the University of South Dakota.

Daugaard worked his way through college doing a variety of jobs, including working as a welder, dish washer, and waiter. He majored in

government with minors in mathematics and psychology, and he graduated with a bachelor's degree in 1975 before entering Northwestern University School of Law in Chicago, Illinois. He worked as a bus driver, law clerk, and security guard. He also became certified as a sign language interpreter. After earning his law degree in 1978 and passing the Illinois bar exam, he stayed in Chicago for three years and worked as a lawyer.

In 1981 he returned to South Dakota and married Linda Schmidt, his high school girlfriend. During this time, Daugaard worked as an executive at what is now US Bank, where he was responsible for trust administration and business development. In the early 1980s, Daugaard and his wife purchased the Daugaard family homestead and built a house on it.

In 1990, Daugaard left US Bank and became the development director for the Children's Home Foundation, a nonprofit organization founded in 1982 to provide funding for the Children's Home Society of South Dakota (CHS). CHS had operated an orphanage until the mid-1960s, when the organization transitioned to a residential treatment center that provided services to children with emotional or behavioral problems. Daugaard led the group through a major building and expansion period and helped secure gifts totaling several million dollars for new construction and an endowment fund.

In 2002 Daugaard moved from the Children's Home Foundation to CHS and became its executive director. He resigned in 2009 to campaign for governor of South Dakota.

POLITICAL CAREER

Daugaard is a member of the Republican Party. He entered politics in 1996, when he was elected to the South Dakota state senate. He was reelected in 1998 and 2000. As a state senator, he served on multiple committees, including the state affairs, education, taxation, commerce, judiciary, and government operations committees. In 2002, he was elected lieutenant governor on the ticket with Governor Michael Rounds. They were reelected in 2006. Daugaard served as the president of the state senate from 2003 to 2011.

In 2011 he successfully ran for governor, with Matt Michels as his running mate for lieutenant governor. His campaign issues focused on financial stewardship, including balancing the state budget, improving economic conditions and job creation, and his opposition to raising taxes. He also reiterated his support for the right of citizens to bear arms, which he had demonstrated by voting against gun control legislation while a senator. His stance on other issues included opposition to the federal health-care reform law, the Patient Protection and Affordable Care Act, and support for a 2006 amendment to the South

Dakota Constitution that defined marriage as between one man and one woman and prohibited civil unions and same-sex marriages.

Daugaard was sworn in as governor on January 8, 2011. During his first term as governor, he kept his promise not to raise taxes, made cuts in government spending (including his own salary), and worked to improve the state's economy. In his first year as governor, he joined a group of thirty-two governors who signed a letter to President Barack Obama expressing opposition to some mandates required by the Patient Protection and Affordable Care Act. That same year, he signed the nation's most restrictive antiabortion law. It requires a three-day waiting period as well as antiabortion counseling before a woman seeking an abortion can terminate her pregnancy in South Dakota.

In 2013 Daugaard signed legislation granting school employees the right to carry a gun on school property. The law does not allow all school employees the right to carry guns; rather, it enables school boards to designate particular individuals, called sentinels, to carry guns in school after they complete special training.

In 2013 Daugaard also signed the Public Safety Improvement Act to reform the adult judicial system in order to reduce the prison population, particularly of nonviolent offenders. The law eliminated the need for South Dakota to construct two new prisons, which would have cost the state more than $220 million. Judicial reform encompassed drug courts that seek to reduce the incarceration rate of individuals convicted of minor drug offenses.

Other accomplishments during Daugaard's first term included reducing government regulations by repealing several hundred sections of codes and policies that were unnecessary or redundant and exploring oil development within the state.

In 2015 Daugaard and Michels were reelected by a wide margin, and Daugaard was sworn in to his second term as governor on January 6, 2015. During his second term, he signed legislation to raise taxes, such as the gasoline tax and other vehicle taxes, in order to fund infrastructure projects, and announced his intent to reform the juvenile justice system along similar lines as those of the adult system. He also prepared his fourth consecutive state budget with a surplus.

IMPACT

Daugaard has helped establish a balanced budget in South Dakota during a postrecession period when many other states are struggling with high debt and a sluggish economic recovery. His initiatives and reforms have drawn the attention of other states looking for solutions to similar economic, social, and government issues.

PERSONAL LIFE

Daugaard married Linda Schmidt in 1981. They have three children—Laura, Sara, and Chrisas as well as several grandchildren. Daugaard's hobbies include hunting, fishing, carpentry, and canoeing.

SUGGESTED READING

Colias, Meredith. "Five Questions with Gov. Dennis Daugaard." *Rapid City Journal*. Rapid City Journal, 20 Jan. 2015. Web. 13 Sept. 2015.

Daugaard, Dennis. "2015 State of the State Address." South Dakota State Capitol, Pierre, South Dakota. 13 Jan. 2015. Address.

"Dennis Daugaard on the Issues." *On the Issues*. OntheIssues.org, 18 June 2015. Web. 13 Sept. 2015.

Nord, James. "Daugaard: South Dakota Ends 2015 Budget Year with Surplus." *Washington Times*. Washington Times, 13 July 2015. Web. 13 Sept. 2015.

Paulson, Amanda. "South Dakota Anti-Abortion Law Breaks New Ground." *Christian Science Monitor*. Christian Science Monitor, 22 Mar. 2011. Web. 13 Sept. 2015.

South Dakota Governor Dennis Daugaard Site. State of South Dakota, 2015. Web. 13 Sept. 2015.

Swisher, Kaija. "Straight from the Governor: Dennis Daugaard Candidly Discusses SD's Future." *Black Hills Pioneer*. Black Hills Pioneer, 26 Jan. 2011. Web. 13 Sept. 2015.

—*Barb Lightner*

Jason Day

Date of birth: November 12, 1987
Occupation: Golfer

A fan and player of golf since early childhood, professional golfer and PGA Tour fixture Jason Day could be said to have grown up with the sport. From the day his father brought home Day's first gold club, to his debut on the professional circuit in 2006, to his 2015 PGA Championship win and beyond, Day's growth and development as a person has gone hand in hand with his achievements as an athlete. Day has overcome a variety of childhood challenges to become one of the rising stars of international golf. His journey was in many ways a collaborative one, strongly influenced by the guidance of coach and mentor Colin Swatton as well as the crucial choices of Day's mother and the inspiring influence of successful athletes such as American golf legend Tiger Woods. Yet despite such crucial connections, Day is fully at home

Keith Allison (Flickr: Jason Day)/CC BY-SA 2.0/
Wikimedia Commons

on the golf course, as a lone player immersed in the solitude inherent to the sport. "I definitely like the solitude of golf," he explained to David Von Drehle and Julia Lull for *Time* magazine (14 July 2016). "I have always practiced by myself. It's just because that is when I can do the most work, the most efficient work, is when I am by myself, and I think I just find a little bit of peace when it comes to being able to be out here on the golf course, and you are just you and yourself and your thoughts."

EARLY LIFE

Jason Day was born on November 12, 1987, in Beaudesert, a town south of Brisbane in eastern Queensland, Australia. The youngest of three children born to Dening and Alvin Day, he has two older sisters, Kim and Yanna, as well as four half siblings from his father's previous two marriages. When Day was a child, the family lived on a farm, where his father raised cattle. His mother worked various jobs during Day's childhood, and both parents later found work at a slaughterhouse. After spending Day's early childhood in Beaudesert, the family moved to the city of Rockhampton when he was six.

Golf became a fixture in Day's life early on, beginning the day his father brought a beat-up golf club home from the local junkyard. Day, then three years old, amused himself by playing with the club, and his parents soon recognized his apparent talent as a fledgling golfer. He began training seriously at the age of six, accompanied by his father. Although Day excelled at the sport from an early age, the pressure associated

with the sport proved detrimental at times. His father struggled with alcoholism and was physically abusive, and Day has recalled in interviews that his father would beat him if he did not perform well enough on the golf course. Such experiences, as well as his father's death when Day was almost twelve, led Day to drink and act out at home and at school.

EDUCATION

Hoping to prevent him from going down the wrong path, Day's mother eventually decided to send him to the Kooralbyn International School, a boarding school in southern Queensland. This decision proved beneficial for Day, who credits his mother with helping him through the difficult times in his life. "With everything that went on, for me and my sisters to come out pretty normal on the other side, I think a lot of that has to do with our mom," he told Karen Crouse for the *New York Times* (5 Apr. 2016).

At the heavily sports-focused Kooralbyn International School, Day continued his golf training under the guidance of coach Colin Swatton. Swatton soon became a mentor to Day, who has noted the important role the coach played in both his training and his personal development. "Col had open arms to me. I really needed him. He shaped who I am," he told Cameron Morfit for *Golf* magazine (9 Oct. 2015). "I never had that type of family growing up. It's a safe place." When Swatton took a position at Hills College in Jimboomba, Queensland, Day transferred to that school, from which he graduated in 2004. Swatton later served as Day's caddy, accompanying the golfer to many high-profile tournaments.

EARLY CAREER

While still in school, Day competed on the amateur golf circuit in Australia, appearing in a variety of youth tournaments. Following his graduation, he began to pursue a career in golf in earnest and soon demonstrated his skill at the sport in events such as the 2005 Victorian Junior Masters, in which he placed first. Other events in which Day competed during his amateur years included the 2004 Wilson Australian Junior Amateur Championship, the 2005 Queensland PGA Championship in his native Australia, and the 2005 Porter Cup in the United States.

Day's years of training paid off in 2006, when he made his debut on the professional golf circuit and qualified for his first PGA Tour. First established by the Professional Golfers Association of America, from which it separated in the late 1960s, the PGA Tour consists of more than forty events, held primarily in the United States, in which qualifying professional players compete. In addition to smaller competitions such as the Barbasol Championship and the Puerto Rico Open, the PGA tour includes four major golf championships, known collectively as the majors: the Masters Tournament (held at Augusta National), the US Open, the Open Championship (or British Open), and the PGA Championship.

Over the course of his debut season in the PGA Tour, Day competed in seven events, including the Reno-Tahoe Open and the John Deere Classic. His best performance came at Reno-Tahoe, where he placed eleventh. Day did not qualify to compete in the PGA Tour the following year. However, he competed instead in the 2007 Nationwide Tour (known since 2012 as the *Web.com* Tour), a series of events overseen by the PGA Tour organization and geared toward professional golfers who did not qualify for the main tour. Day competed in nineteen events over the course of the tour and took first place at the Legend Financial Group Classic, held in Highland Heights, Ohio. In recognition of his performance on the Nationwide Tour, Day took home winnings of more than $330,000.

MAJOR COMPETITIONS

Day returned to the PGA Tour in 2008 and would continue to compete on that circuit over the following eight years. He proved to be a strong competitor, earning numerous top-twenty-five and top-ten finishes and winning more than a million dollars in prize money each year beginning in 2009. In May of 2010, Day achieved his first first-place finish in a PGA Tour event, overcoming the competition at the HP Byron Nelson Championship in Texas.

Despite Day's success in the sport during his first years as a professional golfer, he seriously considered quitting golf in 2011. "I wasn't having a good time on the golf course," he explained to an incredulous David Feherty for the Golf Channel program *Feherty* (28 Mar. 2016). However, those close to Day managed to convince him to keep playing, Day said. Only days after his brush with quitting, he competed in the 2011 Masters, taking second place in the prestigious championship.

As Day entered the latter half of his first decade as a professional golfer, he began to rack up an array of impressive wins on the PGA Tour as well as in international tournaments. In addition to his second-place finish in the 2011 Masters, he brought strong performances to the PGA Tour's other majors, placing second in the US Open in both 2011 and 2013 and taking fourth place at the 2015 British Open. Perhaps the greatest milestone in his career to date, however, came in August 2015. At the PGA Championship, held that year in Wisconsin, Day took first place by a margin of three strokes, defeating American golfer Jordan Spieth to claim his first championship in the majors. His performance in the 2015 PGA Tour, which included first-place finishes in

the PGA Championship and four other events as well as eleven top-ten and fifteen top-twenty-five finishes, earned him more than $9.4 million in prize money, his highest winnings yet. A decade after his first PGA Tour, Day returned to the tour in 2016, competing in twenty events and placing first in three of them. He played in all four of the majors, claiming second place at the PGA Championship. Day ended the 2016 season as number-one in the world, according to the PGA Tour's official world golf ranking.

In October 2016, Day announced that he would be withdrawing from professional play for several months to focus on recovering from a back injury. However, he remained intent on competing in the 2017 season and particularly hoped to participate in competitions held in his native Australia. He resumed playing in early January 2017 at the Tournament of Champions in Hawaii.

THE EVOLUTION OF GOLF

For a lifelong golfer such as Day, the chance to play in the sport's major competitions is both a dream come true and an opportunity to see firsthand just how much competitive golf has evolved since his early days watching the sport on television. "When I was growing up, sitting there watching Augusta National, the Masters, we just watched golf," he explained to Von Drehle and Lull. "Now the stats pop up telling where the guys hit it, the technology has changed a lot and we have to advance with that technology just to keep the game going forward and make it more exciting for everyone to try and pick up."

Although Day has embraced the use of such technology in golf and also hopes to make golf accessible to both young athletes and potential spectators, he has been resistant to changing the speed of the notoriously slow game. While some in the golf media have called for golfers to speed up play, identifying the game's slow pace as off-putting to casual spectators, Day argues that such a change would prove detrimental to players on the professional level. "I don't care so much about speeding up my game. I've got to get back to what makes me good. If that means I have to back off five times, then I'm going to back off five times before I have to actually hit the shot," he told Ewan Murray for the *Irish Times* (4 Jan. 2017). He continued, "For golfers that are trying to win and that one shot that could take you out of a play-off, that's important, and you need to make sure that you get everything correct. Because we're driven by results; we want to be the best and we want to do everything but the average Joe just doesn't get it."

PERSONAL LIFE

Day met his wife, Ellie, while visiting Ohio with Swatton. The two married in 2009. They have a son and a daughter and live in Westerville, Ohio.

The Days are the cofounders of the Brighter Days Foundation, a charitable organization that contributes to a variety of causes in Ohio and elsewhere. Day has likewise expressed an interest in working to give back to the Australian golf community and promote the sport in his native country. "Australian golf did so much for me and that is why I am here today," he explained to Von Drehle and Lull. "Golf is not huge back in Australia. . . . I would like to see a lot more boys and girls being able to pick up the game back home so that we can make the game healthy back there."

SUGGESTED READING

Crouse, Karen. "Jason Day's Long Rise to No. 1 Began with a Mother's Save." *New York Times*, 5 Apr. 2016, www.nytimes.com/2016/04/06/sports/golf/jason-day-masters.html. Accessed 6 Jan. 2017.

Day, Jason. Interview by David Feherty. *Feherty*, season 6, episode 4, Golf Channel, 28 Mar. 2016.

Day, Jason, Jack Niklaus, and Jordan Spieth. "Jack Niklaus, Jason Day, Jordan Spieth Talk Success." Interview by David Von Drehle and Julia Lull. *Time*, 14 July 2016, time.com/4405031/nicklaus-day-spieth-interview. Accessed 6 Jan. 2017.

Morfit, Cameron. "Jason Day's Greatest Save." *Golf*, 9 Oct. 2015, www.golf.com/tour-and-news/jason-days-greatest-save-golf-magazine-interview. Accessed 6 Jan. 2017.

Murray, Ewan. "Jason Day Indignant about Pressure to Speed Up Play." *Irish Times*, 4 Jan. 2017, www.irishtimes.com/sport/golf/jason-day-indignant-about-pressure-to-speed-up-play-1.2925806. Accessed 6 Jan. 2017.

—*Joy Crelin*

Matt de la Peña

Occupation: Writer

The critically acclaimed author of young-adult literature and picture books, Matt de la Peña is best known for writing compelling stories about the lives of working-class urban teenagers. De la Peña has received numerous accolades for his work and has been the darling of critics, frequently earning starred or praiseworthy reviews from such publications as *Booklist*, *School Library Journal*, and *Kirkus Reviews*. Moreover, his essays and short fiction have been published in

acclaimed periodicals, including the *New York Times*, the *Vincent Brothers Review*, *Chiricú Journal*, the *George Mason Review*, and the *Allegheny Review*.

In 2016, de la Peña became the first Hispanic author to earn the John Newbery Medal, for his picture book *Last Stop on Market Street* (2015), which was illustrated by Christian Robinson. The Newbery Medal, given by the American Library Association (ALA), is a prestigious literary award presented to authors of children's literature. "As a writer, you work in such solitude," de la Peña said to Shannon Maughan for *Publishers Weekly* (12 Jan. 2016) shortly after winning the Newbery Medal. "You aspire to do great work and when someone validates what you're doing it's more emotional than I could have imagined. That they thought this book was worthy of an award chips away at the imposter syndrome that I think all writers secretly have."

EARLY LIFE AND EDUCATION

Matt de la Peña was born in National City, California, into a working-class family. His father was Mexican American and his mother was white. His parents, who had him when they were teenagers, were both hardworking people. Their work ethic would make an impact on de la Peña and his future writing career. "I saw my dad get up every single day—never took a sick day," he told Scott Simon for NPR's *Weekend Edition* (23 Nov. 2013). "So, that experience of seeing my dad work so hard and my mom work so hard, it translates for me into the writing process in this way. I have to clock in every day, just like my dad did going to work at the zoo. Just that I'm sitting at a desk writing a book."

De la Peña was not much of a student in high school. He was, however, a good athlete. He was particularly good at playing basketball, which would allow him to attend college on a scholarship. Although de la Peña was not studious, he did have a creative streak. "I wrote all through high school and never showed anyone," he confessed to Jessie Grearson for *Kirkus* (18 Nov. 2013). "The weird thing was I was not a reader and hadn't yet fallen in love with books— that didn't happen until college—but I was writing a lot of spoken-word, hip-hop-y poetry. Very shallow, very on the surface, but I loved the rhythm of language."

After graduating from high school, de la Peña attended the University of the Pacific in Stockton, California, on a full basketball scholarship. There, he studied English. During his undergraduate years, he was exposed to a wide variety of authors. "It really just changed everything," he recalled to Lilliam Rivera for the *Rumpus* (6 Nov. 2013). "I was introduced to authors like Sandra Cisneros, Gabriel García Márquez, Junot Díaz, and a lot of African American literature, as well."

Thinking that it was unlikely that he would become a professional basketball player, de la Peña began to consider becoming a writer. After earning his bachelor's degree in 1996, he earned his MFA in creative writing from San Diego State University in 2000. Graduating from both institutions made him the first member of his family to not only go to college but also earn an advanced degree.

YOUNG-ADULT NOVELS

De la Peña's debut novel, *Ball Don't Lie* (2005), about a high school basketball prodigy with a tragic past, was named a best book for young adults by the ALA Young Adult Library Services Association (ALA-YALSA). It was also named an ALA-YALSA quick pick for reluctant readers. The book's recognition in these categories was surprising to the author, as he had not thought of it as a young-adult novel. De la Peña did not even know what young-adult literature was. "As a matter of fact, when my agent told me my book was sold and it was going to come out as young adult, I had to Google it," he confessed to Simon. In 2008, *Ball Don't Lie* was adapted for the screen starring Rosanna Arquette, Grayson Boucher, Ludacris, and Nick Cannon.

For his second novel, *Mexican WhiteBoy* (2008), de la Peña drew on his own youth and made liberal use of Spanglish, a mix of the Spanish and English languages, to explore the adolescence of a biracial boy. Like its predecessor, the novel garnered considerable critical acclaim, with many reviewers praising its dialogue and characterization. *Mexican WhiteBoy*

was also named an ALA-YALSA best book for young adults, a 2009 Notable Book for a Global Society, and a Junior Library Guild Selection. Furthermore, the novel made the 2008 Bulletin for the Center of Children's Literature Blue Ribbon List.

In 2009, de la Peña published his third young-adult novel, *We Were Here*. As with his earlier novels, de la Peña explored the experiences of a working-class urban teenager, in this case, Miguel. After being convicted of a crime, Miguel is sentenced to a year in a group home. There, following the judge's instructions, he writes a journal. Told through first-person journal entries, *We Were Here* also earned favorable reviews and was named an ALA-YALSA best book for young adults, an ALA-YALSA quick pick for reluctant readers, and a Junior Library Guild Selection.

In 2010, de la Peña published his fourth young-adult novel, *I Will Save You*. Like the rest of his novels, this one also found considerable praise. *I Will Save You* unfolds the story of seventeen-year-old Kidd Ellison, an orphan who finds himself in a group home for young adults who have experienced traumatic events. When Kidd flees the group home and finds a job at a beach, he meets and falls in love with a girl named Olivia. Unfortunately for him, Devon, a friend from the group home who is a danger to himself and others, finds Kidd and begins to pursue Olivia. The novel was named an ALA-YALSA quick pick for reluctant readers and a Junior Library Guild Selection. Furthermore, *I Will Save You* was a finalist for the 2011 Amelia Elizabeth Walden Award.

EXPLORING THE APOCALYPSE

For his fifth young-adult novel, *The Living* (2013), de la Peña went in a different direction. Although he continued to explore the lives of minority teens, he did it in a new setting. In the novel, a teenager named Shy and his friend Carmen take summer jobs on a cruise ship. Unfortunately for them, a massive earthquake hits California, causing a giant tidal wave that cripples the ship. This unfavorable event leads to a desperate fight for survival among those who are still left alive. Despite the page-turning quality of the novel, de la Peña sought to continue exploring the way race and class influence relationships—even in a postapocalyptic setting. "My one fear of writing a more 'commercial' novel is that people would not see it as literary," the author admitted to Grearson. "For me, the literary value of a novel is *the* absolute most important part of a book I'm reading or writing—I just love the stuff that resonates long after you finish the story."

In 2015, de la Peña published *The Hunted*, the sequel to *The Living*. In this book, Shy and a group of cruise ship survivors make landfall on the California coast. There, they learn that the massive earthquake has flattened whole cities, leaving precious few survivors. While Shy is still on the life raft, he learns a terrible secret that could change everything—and because of that knowledge he finds himself being hunted.

Both *The Living* and *The Hunted* received considerable acclaim when they were published, including glowing reviews from *Booklist*, the *New York Times*, *Kirkus Reviews*, and *VOYA*.

WINNING THE NEWBERY MEDAL

In addition to penning young-adult books, de la Peña is also the author of picture books. Although *Last Stop on Market Street* (2015) is the author's most notable work in this genre, it is not his first. In 2011, he published *A Nation's Hope*. Illustrated by Kadir Nelson, the book explores the life of Joe Louis, one of the greatest boxers of all time.

Illustrated by Christian Robinson, *Last Stop on Market Street* describes the experiences of CJ, a young African American boy, as he rides the crosstown bus after church with his grandma one Sunday. During the trip, CJ asks his Nana many questions as she teaches him gratitude and shows him all of the beauty of the everyday world. The book earned renowned accolades, including the 2016 John Newbery Medal. It was only the second time the Newbery Medal had been given to a picture book, and de la Peña was the first Hispanic author to win the prestigious award. "I just literally could not comprehend it," de la Peña said to Maughan. "To tell you the truth, I still can't believe it. I threatened to kiss him and everyone on the committee when I see them. It was a huge, huge shock."

Shortly after winning the Newbery, de la Peña noted that he had completed work on two new books: a young-adult novel and a picture book. The novel, tentatively titled *One of Those Lights That Used to Love Me*, is about a young man who is the first in his family to go to college. In the picture book, *Carmela Full of Wishes*, the protagonist is a Mexican American girl.

PERSONAL LIFE

De la Peña is married to Caroline Sun, the senior publicity director at HarperCollins Children's Books. They live in Brooklyn, New York, with their daughter, Luna. When not at home writing, de la Peña can be found teaching creative writing or speaking at high schools and colleges—where he encourages students to live up to their full potential.

SUGGESTED READING

De la Peña, Matt. "Matt de la Peña." Interview by Jessie Grearson. *Kirkus*, 18 Nov. 2013, www.kirkusreviews.com/features/making-leap. Accessed 1 Apr. 2017.

De la Peña, Matt. "Wouldn't You Like to Know . . . Matt de la Peña." Interview by Stacey Hayman. *VOYA*, 28 Sept. 2014, voyamagazine.com/2014/09/28/wouldnt-you-like-to-know-matt-de-la-pena. Accessed 1 Apr. 2017.

De la Peña, Matt. "'A Huge, Huge Shock': Matt de la Peña on His 2016 Newbery Medal." Interview by Shannon Maughan. *Publishers Weekly*, 12 Jan. 2016, www.publishersweekly.com/pw/by-topic/childrens/childrens-authors/article/69124-a-huge-huge-shock-matt-de-la-pe-a-on-his-2016-newbery-medal.html. Accessed 3 Apr. 2017.

De la Peña, Matt. "The Rumpus Interview with Matt de la Peña." Interview by Lilliam Rivera. *The Rumpus*, 6 Nov. 2013, therumpus.net/2013/11/the-rumpus-interview-with-matt-de-la-pena. Accessed 1 Apr. 2017.

De la Peña, Matt. "Even on the Water, Class Remains in Session." Interview by Scott Simon. *Weekend Edition*, 23 Nov. 2013, www.npr.org/2013/11/23/246380621/even-on-the-water-class-remains-in-session. Accessed 1 Apr. 2017.

SELECTED WORKS

Ball Don't Lie, 2005; *Mexican WhiteBoy*, 2008; *We Were Here*, 2009; *I Will Save You*, 2010; *A Nation's Hope*, 2011; *The Living*, 2013; *The Hunted*, 2015; *Last Stop on Market Street*, 2015

—*Christopher Mari*

Michaela DePrince

Date of birth: January 6, 1995
Occupation: Ballet dancer

Michaela DePrince is a soloist with the Dutch National Ballet. Born in Sierra Leone during the country's brutal civil war, DePrince was left by an uncle at an orphanage after both of her parents died. There she saw a picture of a ballet dancer in a magazine and vowed to become one herself. At the age of four, she was adopted by an American couple and began taking dance classes in Philadelphia. DePrince's harrowing and inspirational tale was included in the 2011 documentary *First Position*, which chronicles the experiences of six young people competing in the 2010 Youth America Grand Prix, where DePrince ultimately won a scholarship to the Jacqueline Kennedy Onassis School at the American Ballet Theatre in New York.

With her mother, Elaine DePrince, she also wrote a book about her early life called *Taking Flight: From War Orphan to Star Ballerina* in 2014. In 2015 MGM secured the film rights to the book. In 2016 she appeared in Beyoncé's

Jason Kempin/Stringer for Getty Images

best-selling visual album *Lemonade*, and in 2017 she was promoted to the rank of soloist at the Dutch National Ballet. "When I look back at all the things I've been through and everything I've accomplished," DePrince told Erika Hayasaki for *Glamour* (16 July 2015), "I realize, Wow, I am very blessed."

EARLY LIFE AND ADOPTION

DePrince was born Mabinty Bangura in 1995. In her birth country, Sierra Leone, a bloody civil war had already been raging since 1991 and would not end until 2002. The war took some fifty thousand lives. DePrince's father was killed in a massacre while working in the diamond mines when DePrince was three years old. A week later, her mother starved to death. An uncle left DePrince, who was just four years old, at a local orphanage. DePrince suffers from a skin disease called vitiligo; her skin is speckled with white patches across her neck and chest. Because of the vitiligo, adults at the orphanage called her "devil child" and told her she was too ugly to be adopted. They ranked the children according to favor, doling out less food and clothing to those ranked lowest. They placed DePrince last; she was known as Number 27. At the orphanage, DePrince witnessed horrific events, including the gruesome murder of her favorite teacher, who was dismembered and left to die.

DePrince was miserable, but she found solace in a secret talisman: a magazine photograph of an American ballerina en pointe. "All I remember is she looked really, really happy," DePrince recalled to Carley Petesch for the Associated Press (7 July 2012). "I ripped the page out and I stuck it in my underwear because I didn't have any place to put it." DePrince did not know what ballet was, but whatever the woman in the picture was doing, she wanted to do it too. Soon after DePrince discovered the magazine photograph, word came that the orphanage was going to be bombed. DePrince and the other children walked for miles without shoes to reach a refugee camp in Ghana in 1999.

At the refugee camp, DePrince met an American couple, Elaine and Charles DePrince. (Elaine DePrince is the author of the 1997 memoir *Cry Bloody Murder: A Tale of Tainted Blood*, about the deaths of two of her sons from a product used to treat hemophilia.) The DePrinces were there to adopt DePrince's friend, a young girl named Mia, but when they heard about the "devil child" DePrince, they decided to adopt her as well. (Mia became a musician and singer-songwriter.) In total, the DePrinces have adopted nine children. DePrince was raised in Cherry Hill, New Jersey, but memories of the orphanage and the war plagued her for years. Her mother helped her write down those memories; the notes helped DePrince write *Taking Flight*, published internationally under the title *Hope in a Ballet Shoe*.

EARLY DANCE CAREER

Elaine DePrince recalls her young daughter sifting through her suitcase in the hotel room in Ghana—the little girl, assuming that all Americans wore pointe shoes, was looking for her mother's pair. DePrince showed her mother the magazine photograph, and when they returned to the states, the five-year-old was enrolled at the Rock School of Dance, forty-five minutes away in Philadelphia. DePrince thrived in her classes, but she was painfully shy about her vitiligo. She also had to contend with the prejudice of classical ballet, a predominantly white art form. Her mother spent hours dyeing DePrince's beige, "nude" leotards and pointe shoes to match her brown skin, and DePrince was unceremoniously pulled from a production of *The Nutcracker* when she was eight by a teacher who told her that she could not dance because, as DePrince recalled to Petesch, "America's not ready for a black girl ballerina." When she was nine, another teacher told her mother that the school did not bother investing in black ballerinas because they soon grew hips and breasts. The young DePrince was crushed by the comments, but she told Petesch that they also made her more determined to succeed.

When DePrince was fourteen, she appeared as one of the stars of the former dancer Bess Kargman's documentary *First Position* (2011), about a group of young people competing in the 2010 Youth America Grand Prix, an annual, international student dance competition. Thousands of young dancers compete, but only a couple hundred get to perform at the finals in New York City. Winners of the competition receive scholarships to dance schools around the world. The pressure of the event alone is too much to bear for some dancers, but DePrince consented to let Kargman's documentary crew follow her around for a year while she prepared to compete. In the end, DePrince won a scholarship to the prestigious Jacqueline Kennedy Onassis School at the American Ballet Theatre in New York.

DUTCH NATIONAL BALLET

Appearing in *First Position* made DePrince a minor celebrity. As a student at the School at the American Ballet Theatre, she made a guest performance in the Netherlands and took a class with the Dutch National Ballet. "I just loved the way everyone danced," she told a reporter for *Dance Spirit* magazine (13 Mar. 2012). "They express themselves in a unique, exciting way. I want to be part of something like that." DePrince graduated in 2012 and briefly joined the Dance Theater of Harlem, also in New York. But Dutch National Ballet artistic director Ted Brandsen remembered DePrince and asked her to join the Dutch National Ballet junior company in 2013. "It was immediately clear that she was really strong technically and had an amazing jump," Brandsen told a reporter for *Dance Spirit* (17 Sept. 2015). "I offered her a position straightaway." She was promoted to the main company in August 2014 and was able to dance a soloist role in *Swan Lake* a few weeks later.

The Dutch National Ballet, a diverse company that performs both classical and contemporary pieces, was a comfortable fit for DePrince, even though, as of mid-2017, she has yet to learn Dutch. Thanks to her dogged work ethic, DePrince has excellent technique, but dancing with the Dutch National Ballet has allowed her to focus on developing her voice, she told *Dance Spirit*. To help her during her first months in the main company, Brandsen placed a moratorium on media requests for DePrince who, thanks to her inspiring story, was constantly in demand. (DePrince did, however, give a popular TEDx talk in late 2014.) In 2016 DePrince was promoted to grand sujet (or demi-soloist), and in January 2017, she was promoted to soloist. With this success came a flurry of media attention, but much of it focused on DePrince's difficult childhood rather than her art, which disappointed DePrince. "I'm here not because of my story," she told *Dance Spirit* (17 Sept. 2015), "but because of who I am as an artist."

LEMONADE AND OUTREACH

In 2015, DePrince's mother received an email from Beyoncé's publicist. DePrince said later that she thought the email was a joke, but after following up, she realized that she really had been sought out by one of the most famous pop stars in the world. Beyoncé was working on *Lemonade* (2016), her secret, feature film–length visual album celebrating black women, and wanted DePrince to be a part of it. DePrince appears in the portion of the video devoted to the song "Freedom." Shooting on an old Southern plantation, DePrince danced a short piece she choreographed herself. Blue Ivy, Beyoncé's young daughter, was taken with DePrince, as the dancer recalled to Desiree Murphy for *Entertainment Tonight* (6 May 2016). "She showed me that she had learned the five ballet positions," DePrince told Murphy.

As a young girl, DePrince has said that she was inspired by other black ballerinas, such as Heidi Cruz, who danced for the Pennsylvania Ballet. As an adult, DePrince takes time to work with young black ballerinas herself. "I've always wanted to be a role model, especially to young black girls," DePrince told Jordan Levin of the *Miami Herald* (17 July 2015) after teaching a workshop in Miami. "I think I can inspire them to . . . just push and believe in yourself and become whatever you want. I've been through so much, but I was able to go forward to what I've always believed in." One day, DePrince hopes to open a school for dance and the arts in Sierra Leone; she works as an ambassador for a nongovernmental organization (NGO) called War Child Netherlands and sponsors a child from Sierra Leone through the American nonprofit ChildFund International.

SUGGESTED READING

Friscia, Suzannah. "Michaela DePrince Gets Promoted at Dutch National." *Pointe Magazine*, 5 Jan. 2017, pointemagazine.com/news/michaela-deprince-gets-promoted. Accessed 27 Apr. 2017.

Hayasaki, Erika. "I Was Orphan Number 27: Ballerina Michaela DePrince's Inspiring Story." *Glamour*, 16 July 2015, www.glamour.com/story/world-class-ballerina-michaela-deprince. Accessed 24 Apr. 2017.

Levin, Jordan. "Michaela DePrince's Journey from War to Ballet Stardom Inspires Miami Gardens Dancers." *Miami Herald*, 17 July 2015, www.miamiherald.com/entertainment/ent-columns-blogs/jordan-levin/article27496714.html. Accessed 27 Apr. 2017.

"Michaela DePrince." *Dance Spirit*, 13 Mar. 2012, www.dancespirit.com/michaela-deprince-2326094798.html. Accessed 27 Apr. 2017.

Murphy, Desiree. "Exclusive: Ballerina Michaela DePrince on Her Personal Journey to 'Freedom' in Beyoncé's 'Lemonade.'" *Entertainment Tonight*, 6 May 2016, www.etonline.com/features/188266_beyonce_lemonade_ballerina_michaela_deprince_set_secrets_personal_freedom_journey. Accessed 27 Apr. 2017.

"The Next Chapter." *Dance Spirit*, 17 Sept. 2015, www.dancespirit.com/the-next-chapter-2326646281.html. Accessed 27 Apr. 2017.

Petesch, Carley. "Star Dancer Born into War Grows Up to Inspire." *Associated Press*, 7 July 2012, www.usnews.com/news/world/articles/2012/07/11/star-dancer-born-into-war-grows-up-to-inspire. Accessed 26 Apr. 2017.

—Molly Hagan

Loretta Devine

Date of birth: August 21, 1949
Occupation: Actor

Loretta Devine is an award-winning actor best known for her roles on the television series *Boston Public* and *Grey's Anatomy* and for her performance in the 1995 film *Waiting to Exhale*.

BACKGROUND

Loretta Devine was born on August 21, 1949, in Houston, Texas, to James Devine, a laborer, and Eunice (O'Neal) Devine, a beautician. After Devine's parents divorced, she and her five siblings were raised by their mother and grandmother in the Acres Home neighborhood of northwest Houston, where Devine attended George Washington Carver High School for Applied Technology, Engineering and the Arts. There she was active in the pep squad and performed in the school's talent shows.

Devine continued her education at the University of Houston and graduated in 1971 with a bachelor's degree in speech and drama. She was a member of the Epsilon Lambda Chapter of the Alpha Kappa Alpha sorority, the first sorority established by African American women. Devine went on to receive her master's degree in 1976 from Brandeis University in Waltham, Massachusetts.

Following her graduation from Brandeis, Devine moved to New York where she took acting and dancing classes and began working in Off-Broadway theater productions. She made her theater debut in a 1977 production of *Hair*. From there Devine was part of the original Broadway cast of the musical *Dreamgirls*, which opened on December 20, 1981, and closed on August 11, 1985. The production won several Tony Awards, Drama Desk Awards, and a 1983 Grammy Award for best cast show album.

LIFE'S WORK

After the successful run of *Dreamgirls* on Broadway, Devine moved to Los Angeles to pursue an acting career in film and television. One of her first film roles was small but was alongside renowned actor Sidney Poitier in the thriller *Little Nikita* (1988). She appeared in other small roles in several more films and got her first big television role on the sitcom *A Different World*, which aired from 1987 to 1993 and was a spinoff of the hit sitcom *The Cosby Show* (1984–92). Devine played a dormitory director at the fictional Hillman College, and as with *The Cosby Show*, the series *A Different World* was notable at the time for having a primarily African American cast.

Devine landed her first major film role in the romantic drama *Waiting to Exhale* (1995) as Gloria Matthews, a beauty salon owner and single mother who falls in love with her neighbor. The film was a financial success, and Devine won an Image Award for outstanding supporting actress in a motion picture for her performance. The following year, Devine won a second Image Award in the same category for her role as Beverly in *The Preacher's Wife* (1996), a romantic comedy starring Denzel Washington and Whitney Houston.

In the late 1990s, Devine appeared in films such as the period thriller *Hoodlum* (1997), the horror thriller *Urban Legend* (1998), and the comedy *The Breaks* (1999). She returned to television as a voice actor on the Claymation animated series *The PJs* (1999–2001), and during this time, Devine landed a regular role on the high school drama *Boston Public* (2000–5) where she played history teacher Marla Hendricks.

Devine appeared on eighty-one episodes of *Boston Public* and won a third Image Award, this time for outstanding actress in a drama series. She was also nominated for a Satellite Award for best supporting actress. In 2004 she costarred in the drama *Crash* (2004), which won the Academy Award for best picture. Devine was nominated for a Black Reel Award for best supporting actress for her role as a case worker.

Her next recurring television roles were on the long-running medical drama series *Grey's Anatomy* from 2005 to 2013 and on the drama series *Eli Stone* from 2008 to 2009. She won the 2011 Primetime Emmy Award for outstanding guest actress in a drama series for her role as Adele Webber on *Grey's* as well as an Image Award for outstanding supporting actress in a drama series. She was also nominated for the same Image Award in 2009 for her role as Patti Dellacroix on *Eli Stone*.

In 2010 Devine returned to theater with *Pieces of Me*, a one-woman show that she wrote and starred in. The show featured Devine's original songs and poetry that addressed both social and personal issues and contained childhood stories told by Devine as well as pieces of visual art. *Pieces of Me* earned her NAACP Theatre Award nominations for best one-woman show and best musical director. She returned to television in 2015 with a regular role on the sitcom *The Carmichael Show*.

IMPACT

Since her first theater role in the 1970s to her film and television career that began in the 1980s, Devine has consistently been celebrated for her performances. She is a five-time Image Award winner and has won and been nominated for several other major acting awards.

PERSONAL LIFE

Devine married Lamar Tyler in 1973, and they have a one son, James Lawrence Tyler. Devine and Tyler separated in 1980 and divorced in January 2008. In April 2001, she became engaged to financial expert Glenn Marshall, whom she married after her divorce from Tyler was finalized.

SUGGESTED READING

Holden, Stephen. "Four Divas Have Lots of Fun Telling Off Mr. Wrong." *New York Times*. New York Times, 22 Dec. 1995. Web. 9 May 2016.

Jay, Adam. "Original 'Dreamgirls' Sheryl Lee Ralph, Loretta Devine, and Jennifer Holliday Reunite for Broadway under the Stars Concert in LA, 7/10." *Broadway World*. Wisdom Digital Media, 27 Apr. 2016. Web. 9 May 2016.

Loewenstein, Melinda. "Emmy Nominee Loretta Devine Reflects on a Divine Career." *Backstage*. Backstage, 19 Aug. 2011. Web. 7 May 2016.

Mays, Raqiyah. "Loretta Devine Tackles Topical Comedy on 'The Carmichael Show.'" *Ebony*. Ebony Magazine, 26 Aug. 2015. Web. 8 May 2016.

Weaver, Neal. Rev. of *Pieces of Me*, dir. Loretta Devine. *Backstage*. Backstage, 22 Sept. 2010. Web. 9 May 2016.

SELECTED WORKS

A Different World, 1987–88; *The PJs*, 1999–2001; *Boston Public*, 2000–5; *Grey's Anatomy*, 2005–15; *Waiting to Exhale*, 1995; *The Preacher's Wife*, 1996; *Crash*, 2004; *Dreamgirls*, 1981–85; *Pieces of Me*, 2010

—*Patrick G. Cooper*

Elio Di Rupo

Date of birth: July 18, 1951
Occupation: Former Prime Minister of Belgium

Elio Di Rupo was the fiftieth prime minister of Belgium and is a Francophone Socialist Party politician.

EARLY LIFE AND EDUCATION

Elio Di Rupo was born on July 18, 1951, in Morlanwelz, Belgium, a small town located in the French-speaking region of Wallonia. Di Rupo's parents were Italian immigrants who moved to the migrant town of Morlanwelz in search of work. His father, a coal miner, died in a car crash when Di Rupo was one year old. Unable to raise all seven of her children on her own, his mother was forced to send three of his brothers to a nearby orphanage while she raised Di Rupo and his sisters on six pounds a month. In interviews, Di Rupo has attributed his ability to stay positive during difficult times to his mother, who had nothing to offer her children but happiness.

At the age of twelve, Di Rupo was sent to a nearby boarding school. Due to chronic migraines induced ·by sinusitis, he had to repeat his first year of high school twice. A gifted student, Di Rupo became dedicated to the subject of chemistry after receiving encouragement from his science teacher. He went on to earn a master's degree and PhD in chemistry from the University of Mons-Hainaut. From 1977 to 1978, while working on his doctorate, Di Rupo guest lectured at the University of Leeds in Yorkshire, England.

EARLY CAREER

Elio Di Rupo first became involved with the Francophone socialist party Parti Socialiste as a student of the University of Mons-Hainaut. In 1982, after deciding to pursue a career in politics rather than chemistry, Di Rupo became a municipal councillor to the city of Mons. He soon moved up to the national political stage in 1987 when he was elected to represent the French-speaking constituency of Mons-Borinage in the Belgian Federal Parliament's Chamber of Representatives.

Di Rupo served as the representative of Mons-Borinage until 1989, when he left to become a member of the European Parliament. In 1991 Di Rupo returned to the Belgian Federal Parliament to serve in the Senate, where he was appointed the minister for education of the French community. In 1994 Di Rupo became the deputy prime minister and minister for communications and publicly owned companies. Upon the formation of the next federal government in 1995, he was appointed deputy prime minister and minister of the economy and telecommunications.

In 1999 Di Rupo was made the minister-president of the Walloon region. In this position, Di Rupo became the executive power of Wallonia, one of Belgium's three regions. He stepped down several months later, however, when he was elected the president of Parti Socialiste, because he felt he needed to focus his energy on reforming the party. In October 2000 Di Rupo was elected the mayor of the city of Mons. He resigned as mayor in 2005 when he was reappointed as the minister-president of Wallonia. As minister-president, Di Rupo developed the Wallonia "Marshall Plan" to help get the region out of an economic depression.

In July 2007 Di Rupo was reelected as the president of Parti Socialiste. Secure in his position as party president, Di Rupo resigned as minister-president so that he could become the mayor of Mons once again.

PRIME MINISTER

Following the country's general election on June 13, 2010, a political crisis emerged in Belgium. As none of the eleven political parties running had secured more than 20 percent of the seats in the Parliament, forming a cabinet was impossible. The New Nationalist Party won the most seats with twenty-seven total, whereas Elio Di Rupo's Parti Socialiste came in second with twenty-six seats. On May 16, 2011, after months of fruitless negotiations, Albert II, king of the Belgians, tapped Di Rupo to lead the formation of a coalition government.

Di Rupo succeeded in getting six of the eleven parties to forge a government coalition. On December 6, 2011, after 589 days without a government, Di Rupo was sworn in as prime minister of Belgium. During his term, Di Rupo was credited with getting Belgium's debt costs under control and subsequently preventing an economic crisis. After losing the elections on May 25, 2014, Di Rupo gave his resignation to King Philippe (who had ascended to the throne in 2013). He stepped down officially on October 11, 2014, when Charles Michel of the Mouvement Réformateur Party assumed office.

IMPACT

Throughout his political career, Di Rupo has made strides in reducing the tensions between the French and Flemish regions of Belgium. His appointment as prime minister in 2013 marked the first time since the 1970s that Belgium was led by a Francophone. During the 2010–11 Belgian political crisis, Di Rupo was successful in facilitating the collaboration of opposing political parties to create the sixth Belgian state reform.

PERSONAL LIFE

Di Rupo's sexuality was made public in 1996 during a media scandal where he was wrongly accused of having sex with an underage man. At one point, a group of journalists followed Di Rupo down the street demanding to know if he was gay. Di Rupo famously replied, "Yes. So what?"

SUGGESTED READING

"An End to Waffle?" *Economist*. Economist Newspaper, 3 Dec. 2011. Web. 25 Jan. 2016.

Castle, Stephen. "18 Months after Vote, Belgium Has Government." *New York Times*. New York Times, 1 Dec. 2011. Web. 25 Jan. 2016.

Fontanella-Khan, James. "Elio Di Rupo: Belgium's Unlikely Prime Minister." *Financial Times*. Financial Times, 12 Nov. 2012. Web. 25 Jan. 2016.

Jackson, Patrick. "Profile: Belgium's Elio Di Rupo." *BBC News*. BBC, 5 Dec. 2011. Web. 25 Jan. 2016.

Lichfield, John. "Gay, Socialist, and Born in a Squatters' Camp—Meet the New PM of Belgium." *Independent*. Independent.co.uk, 7 Dec. 2011. Web. 25 Jan. 2016.

—*Emily E. Turner*

Daveed Diggs

Date of birth: January 24, 1982
Occupation: Actor, rapper

Daveed Diggs won the 2016 Tony Award for best featured actor in a musical for his dual role as Thomas Jefferson and the Marquis de Lafayette in the Broadway musical *Hamilton*. Diggs was also among the six male and six female actors who received the 2015 Theatre World Award for outstanding performances by new actors in Broadway or Off-Broadway productions. The cast recording for *Hamilton* also won a Grammy Award for best musical theater album. President Barack Obama and First Lady Michelle Obama saw the show twice.

The success is welcome but feels strange to Diggs, who worked a variety of jobs, including teaching, before working on *Hamilton*. As he told a writer for the *New York Post* (21 Oct. 2016), "It's a radical change for me to eat and drink what I want and not worry about it too much at the end of the night. I'm not used to it yet. I still get nervous when I take cabs too much!" His newfound financial success is partly due to the actors getting a share of the revenues from the show, which is not commonly done in theater.

D Dipasupil/Getty Images

EARLY LIFE AND EDUCATION

Daveed Daniele Diggs grew up in Oakland, California. His name is a phonetic spelling of the Hebrew pronunciation of David, a name meaning "beloved." His father, an African American, drove a bus; during the late 1970s and early 1980s, Diggs's Jewish mother, Barbara, was a disc jockey. The two met at a club where his mother was the DJ. Diggs now prizes all the vinyl albums he inherited from that time of her life. Although Diggs attended Hebrew school, he decided not to have a bar mitzvah, a Jewish coming-of-age ceremony and celebration. He has said, however, that he identifies with both parents' cultures. He has one brother.

Diggs felt awkward as a child, but that sense of alienation ended in fourth grade, when the teacher challenged the class to memorize and recite poems. The organization Youth Speaks, which creates opportunities for teenagers to write and perform poetry, was just beginning during his years attending Berkeley High School. Participating in the poetry slams organized by Youth Speaks further cemented his love of writing and performing. As he told Shayla Love for the *Washington Post* (18 July 2016), "It was a part of what you did growing up. It was woven in the fabric of the community. I don't think I realized how special that was until I left. I didn't know that it wasn't part of what everyone did when they were teenagers, which was to go watch your friends spit poems." Although he considered himself a good speaker, he told Love, he was not a good writer until Youth Speaks showed him how to be. Youth Speaks helped him organize his

thoughts and consider his choice of word and structure. Diggs began excelling at freestyle rap, a fast-paced, improvisational form.

Brown University recruited him to run track, focusing on hurdles; during his sophomore year, Diggs broke the university's record in the 110-meter hurdles. During his freshman year, along with recent Brown graduate Judy Green, he developed a program for Central Falls High School Arts Literacy Program, encouraging students to deconstruct and then rewrite plays and perform them in modern language. Their success led to working with students in the English as a Second Language program as well, rewriting *Romeo and Juliet* in hip-hop language. He earned a degree in theater in 2004.

EARLY CAREER

After earning his degree, Diggs began auditioning for theater roles in New York City; unable to afford the city's high rents, he stayed with friends or rode the subway all night. When nothing came of these efforts, Diggs returned to Oakland to teach middle school classes in poetry and acting. Teaching rap brought immediate results. As he explained to Danielle Henderson for *Esquire* (26 May 2016), "The awesome and equally tragic thing is that all of those kids are old enough to form complicated opinions about things, and nobody cares what they have to say. It was nice to give them a place to read something they had written and the audience—the rest of the class—wasn't allowed to leave." The job lasted until 2012, when he began getting more acting jobs.

One of those jobs was a role in *Word Becomes Flesh*, a show performed in spring 2013 at Intermedia in Minneapolis, Minnesota. The text is based on a series of letters from a new single father to his unborn son. Written and directed by Marc Bamuthi Jacobs, it looks at the roles of fathers and sons, as well as the place of the male body in culture.

Being in the San Francisco Bay area was good for Diggs artistically, as he told Danielle Henderson, saying, "I think it's important that your work is in conversation with artists in your community. It's nice to come from a place where I actually had and have a community of artists who call each other on the phone and make something new." Diggs joined several hip-hop groups, including Lin-Manuel Miranda's group Freestyle Love Supreme, while back in the Bay Area.

HAMILTON

Miranda read a biography of Alexander Hamilton by Ron Chernow while on a vacation in Mexico; doing so changed his life and the lives of many others. Diggs, who had met Miranda through a friend while teaching in the Bay Area, first learned about the script Miranda was developing during the 2013 Super Bowl in New Orleans, where Freestyle Love Supreme was performing for the ESPN show *SportsNation*. He flew to New York to work with Miranda on some of the show's early readings. The producers sometimes paid his fare, but often he flew at his own expense, using his mother's frequent flier miles.

Even the early readings of Miranda's script were significant for Diggs. As he told Branden Janese for the *Wall Street Journal* (17 July 2015), "Watching Chris Jackson play George Washington for a week, I left thinking that the dollar bill looked wrong. I walked out of the show with a sense of ownership over American history. Part of it is seeing brown bodies play these people."

Diggs was cast in dual roles in the resulting musical, *Hamilton*, and the play's score had rap, hip-hop, and R & B influences. The musical opened Off-Broadway at the Public Theater in February 2015 and moved to Broadway in August of that year, winning eleven Tony Awards. In a show with about twice the number of songs that Broadway musicals commonly have, Diggs played the Marquis de Lafayette in Act I and Thomas Jefferson in Act II. The pace of the work required a rapper, clocking 144 words a minute. In one three-second speech, Diggs rapped nineteen words; his overall rate for that number, "Guns and Ships," was 6.3 words per second. The opening number, four minutes long, condenses the first forty pages of the Chernow biography.

Diggs extended his research beyond Chernow's book. As he told Jack Smart for *Back Stage* (2016), "I needed to get a sense of who they were. I looked for personal letters. Lafayette . . . had these aspirations of being known, of being remembered. Also, there's a kind of sweetness about him. There's not that sweetness to Jefferson! It's been so crazy to come in contact with history in this way. It always deepens things."

The musical's authenticity is also clear in Miranda's writing, as Diggs told Kathy Henderson for *Broadway.com* (30 July 2015), "If another writer tried to put rapping into characters for whom rap music didn't exist, it would feel forced, but that's how Lin speaks. He quotes rap, R & B, and Broadway musicals in conversation! It feels natural to perform because it's real." To embody the charm needed for Jefferson, who is not easy to like in the production, Diggs based his performance on his grandfather, who, Diggs told Barbara Hoffman for the *New York Post* (18 July 2015), "ran some . . . illegal businesses and he's a great storyteller."

A unique feature of the show is the lottery for ten-dollar tickets, with cast members providing free entertainment for those waiting. The performances are called "Ham4Ham." Making *Hamilton* available to people who may not be able to afford the average ticket price of $150 is part of the show's commitment to diversity; as Diggs told Jennifer Ashley Tepper for *Playbill* (4 Jan. 2016), "it opens the doors and gives people access."

MOVING ON

In July 2016 Diggs became the fifth principal actor to leave *Hamilton*. He left the party held in his honor, quickly packed, and headed for Brave New Voices, a teen poetry slam founded in 1996 by Youth Speaks and held at the Kennedy Center in Washington, DC. He was the emcee for the finals, and, as Love reported, he told the crowd, "It's not hyperbole when I say, I need this so bad right now. . . . It's been a while since I was just in a room where kids were being brilliant and honest. I need this for myself. I really wanted to make sure I had the space to come here, and be inspired, and remember what this is like."

In fall 2016 Diggs joined the ABC comedy *Black-ish* during its third season in an extended arc of at least six episodes as Johan, brother of Rainbow, played by Tracee Ellis Ross. Both characters are biracial, as are Diggs and Ross.

A musician as well as an actor, Diggs is the lyricist for the hip-hop trio clipping, with Jonathan Snipes and William Hutson. The three, who do not use musical instruments, have worked together since 2009, though not consistently, and released their first full-length album, *CLPPNG*, in 2014. The group's second album, *Splendor and Misery* (2016), dealt with more overtly political topics, including a slave rebellion in space. The album was in part inspired by science fiction from African American writers such as Samuel Delany, Octavia Butler, and N. K. Jemisin. As Diggs explained to Jon Caramanica for the *New York Times* (11 Sept. 2016), "The world we live in right now makes it pretty difficult not to be political."

Diggs contributed a song to the soundtrack of the movie *Zootopia* and appeared in several episodes of the Netflix original series *The Get Down*, a fictionalized account of the birth of hip-hop in the 1970s. He plays an English teacher opposite actor Julia Roberts in the 2017 film *Wonder*, based on the novel of the same name. He is also featured in Andy Samberg's mockumentary on doping in sports, *Tour de Pharmacy* (2017).

PERSONAL LIFE

Diggs encourages young people to be involved in art, regardless of their level of success. As he told Smart, "Oftentimes it feels like we spend so much of our life waiting to make art, waiting for somebody to let us do something. You don't really have to do that. You can make it all the time and make it with your friends."

Diggs lives in Washington Heights in Upper Manhattan with his girlfriend, actor Jalene Goodwin, and their dog, Soccer. He flies to the West Coast for his television work. Diggs founded a hip-hop theater workshop, called #BARS, with his friend Rafael Casal. The two are collaborating on a play about masculinity, and Diggs clearly values the role of friends in creativity; as he told Danielle Henderson, "When people who know and believe in each other get together to make a thing they feel powerfully about, those are the best things. We end up loving those things. Those are the things that last."

SUGGESTED READING

Caramanica, Jon. "Jetting from 'Hamilton' into the Future." New York Times, 8 Sept. 2016, www.nytimes.com/2016/09/30/arts/music/daveed-diggs-hamilton-clipping-blackish.html. Accessed 6 Dec. 2016.

Diggs, Daveed. "Spotlight On . . . Daveed Diggs." Interview by Jack Smart. Back Stage, vol. 57, no. 19, 2016, p. 10.

Diggs, Daveed. "Daveed Diggs on His Hebrew School Roots, Meeting Crazy Celebrities & Getting His Shot on Broadway in Hamilton." Interview by Kathy Henderson. Broadway.com, 30 July 2015, www.broadway.com/buzz/181630/daveed-diggs-on-his-hebrew-school-roots-meeting-crazy-celebrities-getting-his-shot-on-broadway-in-hamilton. Accessed 6 Dec. 2016.

Diggs, Daveed. "'Hamilton' Roles Are This Rapper's Delight." Interview by Brandon Janese. Wall Street Journal, 15 July 2015, www.wsj.com/articles/hamilton-roles-are-this-rappers-delight-1436303922. Accessed 6 Dec. 2016.

Henderson, Danielle. "Hamilton's Daveed Diggs Is the Most Charismatic Person in the Room." Esquire, 26 May 2016, www.esquire.com/entertainment/music/a45240/daveed-diggs-profile-hamilton. Accessed 6 Dec. 2016.

Love, Shayla. "'Hamilton' Star Daveed Diggs: Slam Poetry Saved My Life." Washington Post, 18 July 2016, www.washingtonpost.com/lifestyle/style/daveed-diggss-first-stop-after-leaving-hamilton-a-teen-poetry-slam/2016/07/18/56ac2d6a-4c45-11e6-aa14-e0c1087f7583_story.html. Accessed 6 Dec. 2016.

—*Judy Johnson*

Mike Duncan

Occupation: Podcast host

Mike Duncan found an unlikely path to fame by turning his amateur interest in history into a wildly successful podcasting career. While working as a fishmonger, he began his first podcast, *The History of Rome*, in 2007 as nothing more than a hobby on the weekends. The series went on to run for almost two hundred episodes and was downloaded more than 56 million times, becoming one of the most popular history podcasts of all time and winning a People's Choice Podcast Award for best educational podcast in 2010. After *The History of Rome* concluded in 2012, Duncan launched his next series, *Revolutions*, in 2013. Also a hit, *Revolutions* covered significant revolts throughout world history, including the English Civil War, the American War of Independence, the French Revolution, the Haitian Revolution, and the European Revolutions of 1848.

Duncan's success as a podcaster also launched his career as an author and popular historian. His first published book, *The History of Rome: The Republic* (2016), is an edited transcript of part of Duncan's original series. His second book, *The Storm before the Storm: The Beginning of the End of the Roman Republic* (2017), chronicles the turbulent period between approximately 133 BCE and 80 BCE in ancient Rome. Duncan has also collaborated with cartoonist Jason Novak, and their work has appeared in the *New Yorker* and the *Paris Review*, among other publications.

EARLY LIFE AND EDUCATION

Duncan was born in Redmond, Washington, in the Seattle area. From a young age, he developed an interest in history, being drawn to entries on ancient civilizations in his family's encyclopedia. However, he did not pursue this interest in his formal education. Instead, Duncan studied political science at Western Washington University, specializing in political theory. His political studies hardly touched on ancient Rome, the civilization that had always stood out to him as the largest, most complex, and most important in history.

After college, Duncan worked as a fishmonger, cutting and selling fish for high-end grocery stores. Still, in his spare time he indulged his love of history through extensive reading. By 2007 he was eagerly consuming the works of ancient historians such as Tacitus, Livy, Suetonius, and Polybius "just for fun," as he said in an interview for the *Age of Revolutions* blog (5 Oct. 2016). He was motivated by a desire to learn about details of Roman history that fall outside the range of popular knowledge, and he enjoyed what he found. "There were all of these stories that were buried inside this really, really dry text," he told Matthew Yglesias for *Vox* (9 Nov. 2015).

Around the same time, Duncan discovered podcasts, which were then still a new and developing medium. Naturally drawn to series focusing on history, he tuned in to programs such as

Lars Brownworth's *12 Byzantine Rulers: The History of the Byzantine Empire*, which had begun in 2005. Duncan was hooked, but he had his doubts that podcasting had a sustainable future. "I thought I was late to the party because there was already a pretty rich history podcasting community out there," he told *Age of Revolutions*. "I figured podcasting was going to be a fad that came and went, but instead it just kept getting more and more popular with each passing year. Now looking back it turns out I was actually super early to the party—like setting out chairs and running to the store for ice early."

THE HISTORY OF ROME

As Duncan listened to every history podcast he could find, he searched in vain for a series about the history of ancient Rome. Finally, he determined he would make one himself: "I decided to take what I was reading and translate it into a podcast: 'I'll narrate the entire Roman Empire from beginning to end. Easy.' I have no idea why I thought I could pull it off," he told *Age of Revolutions*. To begin, he had nothing more than an iMac computer with a built-in microphone and the GarageBand recording software.

The project was a labor of love. After ten episodes, Duncan ditched his built-in microphone for a slightly better piece of equipment, but for two years the podcast was little more than an after-work hobby—albeit a time-consuming one. Duncan wrote and edited each episode before recording it. Research, editing, and revising at first took days, but as the episodes grew longer the process began to take weeks. There was no revenue stream in the early days, as the podcast was downloadable for free and included no ads. Duncan did not even include a mechanism on his website allowing listeners to donate money until he had already been broadcasting for two years.

With his attention devoted to producing *The History of Rome*, Duncan did virtually nothing to promote it. He posted episodes on iTunes, Apple's popular digital media hub, and other podcast sites, but he had neither the budget nor the experience to market his work. However, thanks to the popularity of his subject, listeners quickly found the show, and Duncan grew an enthusiastic following. "Mostly, I think, what got me an audience to begin with was there was a persistent audience for Roman history," he told Yglesias. "People went looking for a podcast about Roman history the same way I did, but instead of finding nothing they found my show." Listeners responded favorably to Duncan's presentation style and tone, which was widely seen as engaging and accessible. The show's clear progression, beginning with the myths and facts of the founding of Rome and moving forward chronologically, also helped its popularity.

COMMERCIAL SUCCESS AND NEXT STEPS

Mainly through word of mouth, *The History of Rome* earned thousands of downloads, numbers that attracted attention even beyond the podcast community, which remained somewhat outside the mainstream. In the spring of 2009, a representative from Duncan's hosting site, Libsyn, reached out to him. Libsyn had seen that *The History of Rome* had a steady listenership, and the representative asked if Duncan would be willing to sell advertising space. Though hesitant at first, fearing that ads would detract from the program, Duncan agreed after understanding that he could choose which advertisers he would host. He accepted ads from Audible, an audio book company, including some he read himself on the air. The company sponsored two episodes a month for the rest of the show's run.

The advertising revenue, along with a new donations button on his website, allowed Duncan to cut down his hours at work and devote more time to his podcast. Listeners and critical acclaim continued to pour in. *The History of Rome* won a People's Choice Podcast Award for best educational podcast in 2010. The show continued for two more years, collecting more fans as it chronicled the turbulent late years of the Roman Empire. When Duncan began the podcast, he speculated that covering the full breadth of Roman history would take about seventy-five episodes. It was a daunting prospect, he recalled on the show's one hundredth episode, but as he continued to record, the material only grew. He finally ended the show after 179 episodes (189 counting supplemental episodes) in May 2012.

Even after its run had ended, *The History of Rome* remained popular. By 2017 it had been downloaded more than 56 million times, making it one of the most popular history podcasts of all time. But with the conclusion of his labor of love in 2012, Duncan was asked by many fans what his next project would be. He initially planned to take time off before earning a graduate degree in history and developing that into a career. To that end he enrolled at Texas State University to study public history.

REVOLUTIONS

Duncan's graduate school experience did not last long. He was only at Texas State for about a year before his wife took a job in Madison, Wisconsin, and he dropped out to make the move with her. With free time once again, he began his second podcast series in September 2013 with the aim of making it a full-time job.

Duncan's new show, *Revolutions*, focused on examining various political revolutions in world history. In his introduction he defined the term "revolution" (in part) as "a sudden radical change" displacing one regime for another, radically different, one. Like his earlier work, *Revolutions* balances the complexity of history and political theory with good storytelling. He aimed to approach his subjects in such a way that someone with no prior knowledge of a particular revolution will come away with a general understanding of it. "History as a discipline has also really abandoned narrative history as a genre, which I think makes it difficult for people to approach topics for the first time," Duncan explained in his interview for the *Age of Revolutions*. "The bookshelves tend to be filled with stuff that focuses narrowly on some particular topic or aspect of a historical era: there are narrow books about fashion, art, and the role of paper currency in the French Revolution, but there are surprisingly few options for people who want to find out simply *what happened during the French Revolution*. So my show is for people looking for an in-depth narrative of events."

For *Revolutions*, Duncan devotes a season, with a variable number of episodes, to each revolution he covers. As with *The History of Rome*, the progression is chronological, naturally drawing listeners along to the next installment. Among the first events he covered were the English Civil War, the American Revolution, the French Revolution, and the Haitian Revolution. As Duncan put it in his interview for *Age of Revolutions*, "The eternal question that hangs over my show is: 'What happened next?'"

Revolutions proved to be another hit for Duncan, with more than 12 million downloads by 2017. Once again, the popularity of the podcast was driven by word of mouth, with Duncan's reputation providing a boost. Duncan was also able to capitalize on his established success by partnering with tour companies to provide guided tours of historic sites based on both his podcasts.

PUBLISHING AS A POPULAR HISTORIAN
In addition to his podcast work, Duncan branched out as a historian by focusing on his original passion: ancient Rome. His first book, *The History of Rome: The Republic* (2016), was an outgrowth of his first podcast, presenting the story of the early Roman Republic. His second book, *The Storm before the Storm*, homed in on the beginning of the end of that era of Roman history. It explores the period between 133 BCE to 80 BCE, when Roman expansion into Spain, Gaul, Africa, and Asia threatened to tear the empire apart.

The Storm before the Storm was met with largely positive reviews. "Duncan writes with evident enthusiasm, and his style is accessible and colloquial," a reviewer for *Kirkus* wrote (21 Aug. 2017). Critics also noted that Duncan adeptly draws disturbing parallels between this period of upheaval preceding the end of the Roman

Republic and American current events of the early twenty-first century. Duncan admitted that these similarities, such as polarized politics and rising inequality, pushed him to write about the period.

PERSONAL LIFE
Duncan and his wife, Brandi, were married in 2009. The birth of their first child coincided with the conclusion of *The History of Rome* podcast, and Duncan spent time as a stay-at-home parent after Brandi accepted the job that brought the family to Madison, Wisconsin. The couple later had a second child.

SUGGESTED READING
Duncan, Mike. "Podcasting Revolution: An Interview with Mike Duncan." *Age of Revolutions*, 5 Oct. 2016, ageofrevolutions. com/2016/10/05/podcasting-revolution-an-interview-with-mike-duncan. Accessed 7 Sept. 2017.

Review of *The Storm before the Storm: The Beginning of the End of the Roman Republic*, by Mike Duncan. *Kirkus*, 21 Aug. 2017, www. kirkusreviews.com/book-reviews/mike-duncan/the-storm-before-the-storm. Accessed 7 Sept. 2017.

Yglesias, Matthew. "How Mike Duncan Turned a Passion for History into a Podcasting Career." *Vox*, 9 Nov. 2015, www.vox. com/2015/11/9/9694154/mike-duncan-interview. Accessed 29 Aug. 2017.

—*Molly Hagan*

Mark Duplass
Date of birth: December 7, 1976
Occupation: Director and actor

Mark Duplass and his brother, Jay, have been credited with being pioneers of mumblecore, a genre of independent film characterized by low production values, naturalistic acting, and a focus on dialogue-heavy scenes rather than on action. They first made a name for themselves with the release of their 2005 picture, *The Puffy Chair*, which centers on a young man who has purchased the titular chair as a birthday gift for his father. (Mark Duplass took on the role of the protagonist as well as cowriting the screenplay and codirecting.) The film won the Audience Choice Award at the Sundance Film Festival that year, and, as Gwynedd Stuart wrote for *LA Weekly* (21 Mar. 2016), made "their mutual inclusion in conversations about young filmmakers-to-watch almost instantaneous." Stuart explained that the brothers seemingly tapped

By Greg Hernandez [CC BY-SA 2.0] via Wikimedia Commons

into the era's zeitgeist, asserting, "Major record labels were fixating on all things indie rock, and major film studios were fixating on quiet, quirky dramas being made for $15,000 rather than $15 million."

In an interview with Mickey Rapkin for *GQ* (18 Jan. 2012), Duplass said of his prolific early years: "Most people have one independent film in them, because it's so hard. . . . The thing is, I am willing to hang lights and suffer and keep doing it over and over again because I kind of like it. It's the same thing that makes you want to go camping. You get into it."

More recently, the brothers have moved on to somewhat higher-budget productions, including *Cyrus* (2010), which featured such big-names as John C. Reilly and Jonah Hill, and *Jeff, Who Lives at Home* (2011), starring the popular comic actor Jason Segel. The pair have also inked production deals with HBO (for the comedic series *Togetherness* and *Room 104*) and Netflix (in a four-film agreement that includes the 2016 romantic drama *Blue Jay*).

Despite possessing impressive indie credentials, Duplass has also been embraced by a mainstream general audience, which knows him for his star turn in the long-running FX Network comedy *The League* (2009–15), in which he portrayed avid football fan Pete Eckhart. Commenting on the Duplass oeuvre as a whole, Gavin Edwards wrote for the *New York Times Magazine* (18 May 2012), "Taken together, their body of work forms a vivid portrait of twenty-first-century masculinity in all its stunted absurdity."

EARLY YEARS

Mark Duplass was born on December 7, 1976, in New Orleans, Louisiana, and raised in the suburb of Old Metairie. (Many sources mention the family's Cajun roots.) His mother, Cynthia (née Ernst), was a homemaker who hailed from a dairy-farming family, and his father, Lawrence, was a lawyer. Duplass and his brother, Jay, who was born in 1973, were raised as Roman Catholics and sent to parochial schools.

The two enjoyed an especially close sibling relationship. "I was extremely dependent on Jay," Duplass recalled during an interview for the National Public Radio (NPR) show *Fresh Air* (10 Feb. 2016). "He was my spiritual leader. He was my god. He was just—he was everything to me. And he was sweet enough to let me play with him 'cause, you know, what brother who has a four-years-his-younger little brother wants to hang out with him?" Because Duplass was afraid of the dark as a child, the two often spent the night huddled in a single bed.

The brothers were big fans of television growing up, although their taste differed from that of their friends. Jay Duplass said on *Fresh Air*, "We were in a very specific situation where cable came to our neighborhood in like 1982. And so at that time HBO was uncurated, so all these movies were coming down the pipeline. . . . Our friends were really into *Star Wars* and *Empire Strikes Back*, but we were just watching whatever showed up on HBO. And at that time you'd come home from school and, like, *Ordinary People* would be on or *Kramer vs. Kramer* or *Sophie's Choice*."

EDUCATION

They began making rudimentary films together—with Jay manning their father's clunky VHS camera and Duplass appearing on screen. When not engaged in that pursuit, they played Ping-Pong for hours. (Years later, after Jay had left home to attend the University of Texas at Austin, the game provided a valuable outlet for Duplass; he and his conservative-minded father often played as a way of connecting when they avoided conversation because of their opposing views and attitudes.)

While in his teens, Duplass regularly flew to Austin to visit Jay, and the brothers often visited a local art-house cinema, where they would sometimes see filmmakers doing question and answer sessions after the showings; he once heard cult-favorite auteur Richard Linklater discuss his work. "And I was like, 'Wait a minute, he's not like smoking a cigarette and wearing a beret. This dude's a filmmaker? He looks and feels like me,'" Duplass marveled to Laura Rice during an interview for Austin's NPR station, WKUT (5 Sept. 2014). "And he gave me the hope and the courage to feel like I could make a movie too."

When it came time to choose a college, Duplass joined his brother at the University of Texas. Although he studied film there and credits the town of Austin with shaping his artistic sensibilities, he was also a serious singer-songwriter, and he later made the move to the East Coast to study composition at City College, part of the City University of New York (CUNY) system.

A START IN THE MUSIC INDUSTRY

"In some alternate universe, Mark Duplass would not be a name most people associate with low-budget indie films about coming to terms with adulthood," Dan Ozzi wrote for *Vice* (1 Feb. 2016). "In this parallel dimension, Mark Duplass would instead be a name listed among the indie rock acts on Coachella's lineup and written about on cool music blogs." Ozzi was referring to Duplass's time in a band with an improbable name: Volcano, I'm Still Excited!!

Duplass had made a few solo records and self-released them as a teen, but when tendonitis prevented him from playing the acoustic guitar—leaving him to accompany himself only on a Casio keyboard he was still able to play—he decided to form a band, joining forces with two close friends. The trio released a debut album on the Polyvinyl label in 2004. "The self-titled album was very of its time, capturing the lo-fi, Casio keyboard–heavy style popular among the band's peers," Ozzi explained. "Polyvinyl founder Matt Lunsford cites it as the most underrated album the label ever put out."

Duplass and his brother had, however, never stopped making short films, and not long after the release of *Volcano, I'm Still Excited!!*, the films began attracting some buzz at Sundance. (One of them, *This Is John*, was shot on their parents' old camera for three dollars—the price of the VHS tape they used.) Traveling to promote the album, Duplass felt torn. As he drove the band's van to various tour venues, he dictated his next script into a cassette recorder, and by the end of the label-sponsored run, he was still conflicted. He and Jay assembled a crew and began shooting the film that would cement their reputation as darlings of the indie film scene—*The Puffy Chair*—yet concurrently he was making plans to fly to Europe for a seven-week tour with his bandmates. It gradually dawned on him that he would not be able to do both while maintaining his health and sanity, so when *The Puffy Chair* was accepted at Sundance, he made his choice and, as he told Ozzi, "I haven't really looked back since. But I'd be lying if I said I didn't miss it. . . . My experience in the music industry 100 percent shaped, not only my creative process, but it shaped the [low-budget] producing models that I've built inside the film industry."

FILM CAREER

The brothers made *The Puffy Chair* with $15,000 they borrowed from their parents, paying each actor $100 a day and marketing the film by surreptitiously plastering stickers on the sides of public buses and bathroom stalls. The movie received wildly varying reviews, with some critics charmed by its quirkiness and others annoyed by it, but it is almost universally credited with launching the Duplass brothers' career.

They followed it in quick succession with such low-budget projects as *Baghead* (2008) before their growing fame attracted financing for higher-budget fare like *Cyrus* (2010), about a troubled man-child who interferes with his mother's budding romance, and *Jeff, Who Lives at Home* (2011), about a slacker who helps his married brother track his adulterous wife. Industry observers have pointed out that although those latter movies had relatively modest budgets by Hollywood standards, the $6.5 million that *Cyrus* cost could have financed *The Puffy Chair* four hundred times.

The success of their studio-backed efforts has led in recent years to attention from HBO, and the brothers created the HBO series *Togetherness* (2015–16). The show, which follows two couples attempting to navigate life, relationships, and careers, stars Duplass, who took on the role in addition to his directing and writing duties. He can also be seen on screen in multiple episodes of the sitcom *The Mindy Project*, which originally aired from 2012 to 2016 on Fox and Hulu, and in big-screen pictures such as *Safety Not Guaranteed* (2012), *Zero Dark Thirty* (2012), *The One I Love* (2014), and *Blue Jay* (2016). (The last-named film, about two former high-school sweethearts who meet again as adults, is part of a major production deal with Netflix.)

As an actor, Duplass is perhaps best known for his portrayal of a cubicle dweller who runs a fantasy football league in the FX show *The League*, which aired for seven seasons and won him plaudits for his relatability and humor. Recently the brothers tried their hands at producing an animated series: *Animals.*, which airs on HBO and depicts a group of anthropomorphic creatures whose neuroses and foibles mirror the human condition.

PERSONAL LIFE

Since 2006 Duplass has been married to actor Katie Aselton, who has costarred with him in several projects, including *The Puffy Chair* and *The League*. They have two daughters, Molly and Ora.

SUGGESTED READING

D'Addario, Daniel. "Mark and Jay, Who Live in L.A.: The Post-Mumblecore Duplass Brothers

Grow Up." *Observer*, 14 Mar. 2012, observer.com/2012/03/mark-and-jay-who-live-in-l-a-the-post-mumblecore-duplass-brothers-grow-up. Accessed 28 June 2017.

Duplass, Mark. "Mark Duplass Looks Back at the Time He Almost Had a Career as an Indie Rock Star." Interview by Dan Ozzi. *Vice*, 1 Feb. 2016, noisey.vice.com/en_us/article/rn-w5eq/mark-duplass-volcano-im-still-excited-interview. Accessed 28 June 2017.

Duplass, Mark. "Live from Sundance: A GQA with Mark Duplass." Interview by Mickey Rapkin. *GQ*, 18 Jan. 2012, www.gq.com/story/mark-duplass-interview-sundance-film-festival. Accessed 28 June 2017.

Duplass, Mark, and Jay Duplass. "Duplass Brothers on Filmmaking, Siblings and Parenting's 'Fugue State.'" Interview by Terry Gross. *Fresh Air*, NPR, 10 Feb. 2016, www.npr.org/2016/02/10/466079805/duplass-brothers-on-filmmaking-siblings-and-parentings-fugue-state. Accessed 1 Aug. 2017.

Edwards, Gavin. "The Duplass Brothers Have Kidnapped Hollywood!" *The New York Times Magazine*, 18 May 2012, www.nytimes.com/2012/05/20/magazine/the-duplass-brothers-have-kidnapped-hollywood.html. Accessed 1 Aug. 2017.

Stuart, Gwynedd. "How the Duplass Brothers Changed Hollywood by Refusing to Change at All." *LA Weekly*, 21 Mar. 2016, www.laweekly.com/arts/how-the-duplass-brothers-changed-hollywood-by-refusing-to-change-at-all-6730298. Accessed 28 June 2017.

—*Mari Rich*

Carson Ellis

Date of birth: October 5, 1975
Occupation: Artist

Artist Carson Ellis received a Caldecott Honor in 2017 for *Du Iz Tak?*, a book she wrote and illustrated for young children, with dialogue in an invented language. Of her experience being both author and illustrator, she told Jeff Baker for the *Oregonian* (9 June 2015), "Now that I'm finding my own narrative voice, I can see how with each successive book it will become more fine-tuned and I'll be able to hear it better in all the clutter of my creative consciousness." She first gained notice as the designer of album covers for the Portland, Oregon, indie rock band the Decemberists. She has also created some of the backdrops for the band's tours. Among her other illustrated works is Lemony Snicket's *The Composer Is Dead* (2009). She described her distinctive "folksy, old-world" artistic style to Allison Gibson

By Dennis Bratland (Own work) [CC BY-SA 3.0], via Wikimedia Commons

for the *Huffington Post* (25 May 2011), saying, "I do feel like I always want to draw times gone by, but it's not really turn of the century England that's intriguing; it's really more like the countryside of Siberia or something."

CHILDHOOD AND EARLY CAREER

Carson Friedman Ellis loved to draw even as a child. She also enjoyed nursing wounded animals back to health and exploring nature in Westchester County, New York, north of the city, where she and her sister were raised. She was also a reader, and told Aaron Scott for Oregon Public Radio (19 Feb. 2015), "As [a] kid, I loved to use my own imagination and apply it to an illustration to fill in blanks and answer the questions that the picture suggested." She credits Pauline Baynes, the original illustrator for *The Chronicles of Narnia* series by C. S. Lewis, as an early inspiration and influence. As a teenager, she also became interested in the art of Maurice Sendak, Aubrey Beardsley, and Arthur Rackham.

Although she knew she was interested in illustration, Ellis was also attracted to wild spaces and loved to snowboard, so she attended the University of Montana in Missoula, which had no courses in illustration. She graduated in 1998 with a degree in painting but no knowledge of the illustration field. After graduating, Ellis worked as a bartender and cocktail waitress in four states. For a time she lived in San Francisco, where she painted as a fine artist in oil rather than an illustrator. As she explained to Baker, "I think if I had stayed down there I eventually would have found some recognition, in a different sphere. I had my first solo paint-ing show in a gallery in San Jose and I feel like I was on some sort of path there, though it didn't make as much sense to me as my illustration path does."

She settled in Portland and reconnected with her college friend Colin Meloy, who later became the frontman for the Decemberists. She designed posters for his first band, Tarkio, and for other bands and art events in the city un-til she was able to get a few editorial jobs. She learned to use Photoshop; the art editor who hired her to do a color cover for the Portland weekly *Willamette Week* walked her through the process over the telephone. Her work attracted the attention of literary agent Steve Malk, who contacted her to ask if she might be interested in illustrating children's books.

COVER ART

Ellis does all the illustration for the Decem-berists, including the band's album covers and tour posters. She prefers to hand-letter all the words on the band's work rather than use or create a standardized font. As she told Douglas Wolk for *Print* magazine (Spring 2015), "I'm not a calligrapher, or a very precise person in gen-eral. Handlettering, for me, has to be a wonky, imperfect affair. I never try to get it right; I leave it loose and let it be expressive."

In 2016, Ellis was nominated for a Grammy Award for the cover she created for the band's release *What a Terrible World, What a Beautiful World*. For that illustration, Ellis expanded her usual palette, which until then had consisted of white, burnt umber, cadmium scarlet, paynes gray, Prussian blue, and raw sienna. She ex-plained to Wolk, "I came home from the art sup-ply store and I told my family, 'I bought magenta! . . . You don't understand—this is huge! . . . It's a huge departure!'" Using the same basic palette for nearly two decades gives her work a feeling of cohesion for her.

ILLUSTRATOR

Ellis's first credits as a book illustrator came with the 2007 launch of the Mysterious Benedict Society series, written by Trenton Lee Stewart. Published in four volumes starting with *The Mysterious Benedict Society*, the series is filled with riddles and puzzles for readers to solve, and features four gifted children working on behalf of other orphans at L.I.V.E.—the Learning In-stitute for the Very Enlightened. The series be-came a *New York Times* Best Seller, and National Public Radio (NPR) selected it for its Backseat Book Club, which highlights recommended books for young readers, in March 2012.

Ellis won her first award as an illustrator for *Dillweed's Revenge: A Deadly Dose of Magic*, a 2010 children's book by Florence Parry Heide.

Originally written in the 1970s with the intent that Edward Gorey, of Addams Family fame, was to illustrate it, the manuscript was shelved for four decades before being dusted off and Ellis chosen to illustrate it. For her work on it, the Society of Illustrators gave Ellis the 2010 Sil-ver Medal. Ellis was working in gouache, a new medium for her at the time, adding to her usual pen-and-ink drawings.

Asked by Julie Danielson for the blog *Sev-en Impossible Things before Breakfast* (17 May 2011) about the differences between illustrat-ing a picture book and a chapter book, Ellis re-sponded, "I think picture books are *harder*. They need to have a visual arc that matches their story arc. The text and the images are interdependent. Any given page has a relationship to the page that came before and the one that comes after. There's a craft to it that I think the casual reader might take for granted."

WILDWOOD

For her next project, Ellis teamed up with Colin Meloy, to whom she was now married. In 2010, publisher HarperCollins announced it had signed a three-book deal for a middle-grade se-ries eventually called the Wildwood Chronicles, written by Meloy and illustrated by Ellis. The series, set in Portland, Oregon, resembles classic children's fantasy series such as the Chronicles of Narnia. In the HarperCollins press release, Meloy said, "The germ of this series goes back a long way. For me, this is the culmination of a long-term collaboration with Carson, matching words and art. I grew up on a steady diet of Lloyd Alexander, Roald Dahl, and Tolkien; this is our humble paean to that grand tradition of epic ad-venture stories."

The book began with Ellis drawing a map of Forest Park, a 5,000-acre urban forest reserve in western Portland. The two then added details of the imaginary landscape. Although the first chapter book in the series, *Wildwood* (2011), has eighty-five illustrations, designing the jacket art turned out to be most challenging; the pair went through more than twenty drafts. Ellis told Dan-ielson for *Seven Impossible Things before Break-fast*, "Colin and I have been hoping to collabo-rate on something like this for the past ten years but, between touring and illustrating and parent-ing and everything else, we could never seem to make time for it. Last year, at long last, we had a window in our schedules and sat down to work on it." Ellis would suggest narrative ideas, but her experience of the books only confirmed to her that she was an illustrator rather than a writer. All three books in the series—*Wild-wood, Under Wildwood* (2012), and *Wildwood Imperium* (2014)—all became *New York Times* Best Sellers.

She and Meloy also collaborated on *The Whiz Mob and the Grenadine Kid*, a middle-grade novel set in 1961 France, set for release in October 2017.

AUTHOR AND ILLUSTRATOR

The first picture book that Ellis both wrote and illustrated was *Home*, published in 2015 by Candlewick Press, exploring all the different kinds of dwellings that people and animals around the world call home. Although she said the words came to her in half an hour, it took several years to complete the book. As she told Julie Danielson, this time for *Kirkus Reviews* (5 Feb. 2015), "I must've written it three or four years ago. I illustrated at least one other book and had a baby in the meantime, so it took me a bit to get working on it in earnest." The book touches on architectural ideas that Ellis has explored in other books. Once she let go of the need to write a narrative, she could explore different living environments, ranging from a wigwam to an igloo to a snail's shell. As Ellis told Danielson, "It's about homes. . . . It's also, because I'm in the book myself, about being an artist and celebrating the things that artists are attracted to and inspired by—all the worlds that we can't stop thinking about, reading about, conjuring up, visiting, and inhabiting."

The original manuscript required little change, though at the request of her editor, Ellis dropped the spread on soldiers in a trench. She replaced it with a tour bus, a home she knows well from traveling with the Decemberists. She also seeded the book with illustrations, such as Odin at Valhalla and a person from the mythical city of Atlantis, that she knew would interest her older son, who considered himself too old for picture books.

After *Home*, Ellis felt she could embark on a picture book that incorporated more narrative, and in 2016 published *Du Iz Tak?* In it, two damselflies discover an unfamiliar green thing sprouting from the ground. They puzzle over what it might be, asking, "Du iz tak?" Comments from other insects follow in a language Ellis invented, but which can be deciphered because of syntax, much like Lewis Carroll's poem "Jabberwocky." The book is delightfully absurd, with one insect providing a ladder from his home in a log so that others may build a tree fort in the growing plant. When the flower finally unfurls, the insects joyfully exclaim, "Unk gladdenboot!" The seasons progress; insects leave and the plant dies, but drops seeds. When it is again spring, another insect appears to wonder, "Du iz tak?" The book's 2017 Caldecott Honor (one of a number of runner-up awards to the Caldecott Medal) was Ellis's most prominent recognition yet.

PERSONAL LIFE

Ellis has said she is intrigued by her Russian and Polish heritage, and her drawing style at times evinces an Old-World sensibility. Ellis and Meloy have two young sons, Hank and Milo. The family lives on a five-acre farm south of Portland, complete with llamas, goats, chickens, and a sheep; Ellis's studio there is a converted shed once used to dry nuts. Ellis, who also sells embroidery patterns and wallpaper prints, knits to relax after everyone else has gone to bed, and has enjoyed teaching drawing workshops for teenagers at Portland Art Museum.

SUGGESTED READING

Baker, Jeff. "Carson Ellis Finds 'Home' with New Children's Book, Art for the Decemberists." *The Oregonian*, 9 June 2015, www.oregonlive.com/books/index.ssf/2015/06/carson_ellis_finds_home_with_n.html. Accessed 11 May 2016.

Danielson, Julie. "Home Sweet Home with Carson Ellis." *Kirkus Reviews*, 5 Feb. 2015, www.kirkusreviews.com/features/home-sweet-home-carson-ellis. Accessed 11 May 2017.

Ellis, Carson. "Seven Questions over Breakfast with Carson Ellis." Interview by Julie Danielson. *Seven Impossible Things before Breakfast*, 17 May 2011, blaine.org/sevenimpossiblethings/?p=2136. Accessed 11 May 2017.

"HarperCollins Signs Colin Meloy and Carson Ellis for 'Wildwood' Series." *HarperCollins*, 29 Apr. 2010, corporate.harpercollins.com/us/press-releases/163/HARPERCOLLINS%20SIGNS%20COLIN%20MELOY%20AND%20CARSON%20ELLIS%20FOR%20%22WILDWOOD%22%20SERIES. Accessed 11 May 2017.

Heyman, Stephen. "A Dark Lyricist Turns to Tales for Children." *The New York Times*, 12 Oct. 2011, www.nytimes.com/2011/10/12/books/wildwood-a-book-by-the-decemberists-colin-meloy.html. Accessed 11 May 2017.

Wolk, Douglas. "An Imperfect Affair." *Print*, vol. 69, no. 2, Spring 2015, p. 23.

SELECTED WORKS

The Mysterious Benedict Society (Trenton Lee Stewart), 2007; *The Composer Is Dead* (Lemony Snicket), 2009; *Dillweed's Revenge* (Florence Parry Heide), 2010; *Wildwood* (Colin Meloy), 2011; *Under Wildwood* (Colin Meloy), 2012; *Wildwood Imperium* (with Colin Meloy), 2014; *Home*, 2015; *Du Iz Tak?*, 2016

—*Judy Johnson*

Luke Evans

Date of birth: April 15, 1979
Occupation: Actor

Throughout most of his twenties, Luke Evans was just one of many struggling actors seeking work in London's competitive theater scene. Although he played major roles in local productions of stage musicals such as *Taboo* (2002) and *Rent* (2007), he received little recognition for his work from the theater media despite his own confidence in his abilities. "I knew I could act," he told Jonathan Heaf for *GQ* magazine (14 Mar. 2017). "I was angry and frustrated; I just couldn't catch a break." Evans's fortunes improved, however, in 2008, when he won a lead role in a revival of the play *Small Change* at London's prestigious Donmar Warehouse. Although he had been working in London for nearly a decade, his performance in the play brought him his first true taste of widespread critical recognition. "Literally overnight my life changed," Evans recalled to Heaf. "I'll never forget what I had to do to get to that moment." Following his breakthrough performance in Small Change, he began to attract the attention of film casting directors. He made his first feature-film appearance in the 2010 fantasy film *Clash of the Titans*.

After Evans's break into film, his career accelerated quickly as he moved from small parts to major roles, such as the lead in 2014's *Dracula Untold*. Appearances in multiple installments in the Fast and the Furious franchise as well as the trilogy of Hobbit films further solidified his status as a talented and entertaining performer in addition to introducing him to broad audiences. An even greater boost in international fame came in 2017, when he starred as the narcissistic villain Gaston in Disney's live-action musical *Beauty and the Beast*. For Evans, starring in such a film—which grossed more than $1.2 billion worldwide—was an unbelievable and unexpected opportunity. "I'm having experiences and moments I never thought would be my experiences. I thought they would be somebody else's or something I'd see on TV," he told Robin Swithinbank for the Jackal (2017). "It's a lovely thing."

EARLY LIFE AND EDUCATION

Luke George Evans was born on April 15, 1979, in Pontypool, Wales. His mother, Yvonne, worked as a cleaner, while his father, David, worked in construction. Evans grew up in Aberbargoed, a small town in southeastern Wales, where he attended Bedwellty Comprehensive School.

As a child and teenager, Evans faced bullying from his peers, which he has noted was in part religiously motivated. His parents were Jehovah's Witnesses, and Evans was required to

By Gage Skidmore [CC BY-SA 2.0], via Wikimedia Commons

accompany them as they spread the word about their faith, going door to door in town. "Imagine," he explained to Ryan Gilbey for the *Guardian* (22 Sept. 2016). "You're knocking while they're watching *He-Man* on a Saturday morning. Who wants to be interrupted when they're watching *He-Man*?" Although he found ways to avoid his bullies during much of the week, his family's weekend routine made that hard to do. "There were streets I wouldn't walk down in case the bullies were there. I wouldn't play out in the evening with my friends," he told Gilbey. "Then I'd have to stand on a bully's doorstep in a suit with my parents behind me on a Saturday morning." The experience proved to be a formative one for Evans, who would later discuss it often in interviews in the hope of raising awareness and helping others who are bullied.

Evans demonstrated talent as a singer throughout his childhood, and after leaving Bedwellty Comprehensive at the age of sixteen, he sought to save up money to pursue training in singing and acting. After a stint working in a local store, he received a scholarship to the London Studio Centre, a well-regarded dance and musical theater school. He moved to London at seventeen to study musical theater, a decision that he told Emma Brown for *Interview* magazine (5 Oct. 2016) left his parents "a little freaked out." Nevertheless, they remained supportive of their son's career path. "They saw that I was good at it; I was winning singing and performance competitions and stuff," he told Brown. "They could see that I was doing something that really made me happy." He graduated from the London Studio Centre in 2000.

STAGE CAREER

After training as an actor for several years, Evans began his professional acting career with a small role in the London production of the musical *La Cava*, which opened in June 2000. Following his professional stage debut, in 2002, Evans became the first actor to play the lead role of Billy in the new musical *Taboo*, based in part on the life of singer Boy George and on the New Romantic movement of the 1980s. The production opened at the Venue Theatre in London's West End in early 2002. A recording of the West End production was released on DVD in 2003. He then went on to obtain parts in a variety of musicals, including London productions of well-known shows such as *Avenue Q* in 2006 and *Rent* in 2007.

Amid Evans's stage performances, he worked a variety of jobs to support himself, including a stint working public relations for "Z-list celebrities" whom he described to Swithinbank as "awful people." Although he had found some success on stage, he received relatively little recognition for his work and had difficulty breaking out of musical theater and into straight plays or film. However, a turning point in his career came in 2008, when he claimed a lead role in a revival of the 1976 play *Small Change* at London's Donmar Warehouse. Written by playwright Peter Gill, *Small Change* explores two young Welsh men's relationships with their respective mothers and with each other. For Evans, the opportunity to act in the play was tantalizing. "I thought, 'This is my role, this has to be mine,'" he told Brown. After his agent was unable to get him an audition, he wrote a letter to the casting director expressing his interest in the role and identifying himself as a Welsh actor. The letter led to an audition, and Evans ultimately won the role. His performance in *Small Change* received widespread critical acclaim, and he was even nominated for the Milton Shulman Award for outstanding newcomer by the *Evening Standard* newspaper, despite having been acting on London stages for the better part of a decade. In his interview with Brown, he emphasized the importance of the role in illustrating his versatility as an actor: "It allowed people to see me in a different light to this musical theater actor."

BIG SCREEN BEGINNINGS AND BECOMING A FRANCHISE FIXTURE

Evans began a concerted effort to break into film in 2009, auditioning for a variety of projects. He made his feature film debut in 2010, playing the small role of the Greek god Apollo in the fantasy film *Clash of the Titans*. That year also saw the release of several additional films featuring performances by Evans, including the music biopic *Sex & Drugs & Rock & Roll* and the film *Tamara Drewe*, an adaptation of a comic strip of the same name.

Although Evans's roles in his early films were typically small ones, they not only demonstrated his potential as a bookable actor but also provided him with the ability to learn more about the craft of acting for film. As Evans had never studied screen acting formally, he sought to learn as much as possible from the actors around him. "If you work with amazing actors, you've got a master class happening in front of you," he explained to Brown. Evans continued to develop as an actor as he took on more significant roles in films such as 2011's *The Three Musketeers*, an adaptation of the classic 1844 work by French writer Alexandre Dumas, and *Immortals*, an action film inspired by Greek mythology.

Having established himself as a performer through his early films, Evans also went on to gain significant fame for his roles in popular film franchises. In 2013, he played the role of Owen Shaw, the antagonist of the action film *Fast and Furious 6*. A former British operative turned weapons thief, Shaw leads a gang of criminals that faces off against the long-running film franchise's heroes, who ultimately defeat him. Unlike many of the villains of the Fast and the Furious series, who to that point typically did not recur in additional films, Shaw remains important following the end of the film.

Evans likewise gained international recognition as a member of the large ensemble cast of the Hobbit trilogy. Based on the 1937 novel by J. R. R. Tolkien and serving as prequels to the Lord of the Rings film franchise (2001–3), the three Hobbit films tell the story of the titular hobbit, Bilbo Baggins (Martin Freeman), who embarks on a dangerous journey to help a group of dwarves reclaim their ancestral homeland from the dragon Smaug. Making his first appearance in the second film in the series, *The Hobbit: The Desolation of Smaug* (2013), Evans plays Bard, an archer of Laketown and a descendant of Girion, the last ruler of the long-destroyed city of Dale. He additionally portrays his character's ancestor in a flashback scene in the film. In the series' final installment, *The Hobbit: The Battle of the Five Armies* (2014), Bard manages to defeat Smaug and ultimately becomes the leader of the people of Laketown. In addition to bringing Evans greater name recognition among moviegoers, the films were a major commercial success. Also in 2014, Evans played the lead role in *Dracula Untold*, a historical horror film that details the origins of Vlad the Impaler, better known as Dracula. Returning to his role as Shaw, his character's brother seeks revenge against the franchise's heroes in 2015's *Furious 7*.

EXPANDING REPERTOIRE

Over the course of his film career, Evans became particularly known for his work in action films and period pieces. However, he rejected the title of action hero and instead sought out a more diverse array of opportunities. "I want to be a chameleon," he explained to Swithinbank. In light of that goal, he took on roles in a wide range of films, including the 2015 drama *High-Rise*, the 2016 thriller *Message from the King*, and the 2016 mystery *The Girl on the Train*. He also filmed a new television series, *The Alienist*, which is set to air on TNT in the United States.

In addition to Evans appearing once more as Shaw for the 2017 installment *The Fate of the Furious*, in which Shaw and brother Deckard (Jason Statham) team up with the Fast and the Furious franchise's heroes to take down a greater threat, the year 2017 saw the release of one of Evans's most popular films yet, the musical *Beauty and the Beast*. A live-action adaptation of the 1991 animated Disney film, the film gave him the opportunity to return to his musical theater roots and surprise fans unfamiliar with his theatrical background with his singing abilities. He filled the role of Gaston, a narcissistic antagonist who attempts to woo the film's protagonist, Belle (Emma Watson), and subsequently seeks to kill the titular Beast (Dan Stevens). For Evans, playing the role of Gaston, one of many iconic animated Disney characters, presented an interesting opportunity. "It's a role you want to take on and own. You want it to be yours and you want people to remember your version of it," he told Julie Kosin for *Harper's Bazaar* (13 Mar. 2017). "I find it a challenge and I find it quite an honor to bring something to life that's already been imagined in so many people's minds." One of the most popular films of 2017, *Beauty and the Beast* became an international success, introducing Evans to the widest audience to date.

PERSONAL LIFE

When not working elsewhere, Evans lives in London. He enjoys visiting family in Wales, where he still feels most comfortable. "In the pub with my cousin or in the garden drinking cheap booze by the bonfire—that's where I'm at home," he told Gilbey.

SUGGESTED READING

Evans, Luke. "Luke Evans." Interview by Emma Brown. *Interview*, 5 Oct. 2016, www.interviewmagazine.com/film/luke-evans. Accessed 18 July 2017.

Evans, Luke. "Luke Evans on Becoming Gaston for *Beauty and the Beast*." Interview by Julie Kosin. *Harper's Bazaar*, 13 Mar. 2017, www.harpersbazaar.com/culture/film-tv/news/a21381/luke-evans-gaston-beauty-and-the-beast-interview. Accessed 18 July 2017.

Gilbey, Ryan. "*The Girl on the Train* Star Luke Evans: 'I Wasn't Looking for Fights. . . .'" *The Guardian*, 22 Sept. 2016, www.theguardian.com/film/2016/sep/22/luke-evans-interview-the-girl-on-the-train. Accessed 18 July 2017.

Heaf, Jonathan. "*Beauty and the Beast* Star Luke Evans on His Big Break, Olive Oil, and Being Bullied at School." *British GQ*, 14 Mar. 2017, www.gq-magazine.co.uk/article/luke-evans-beauty-and-the-beast. Accessed 18 July 2017.

Swithinbank, Robin. "Roll the Tape: Luke Evans." *The Jackal*, 2017, thejackalmagazine.com/roll-the-tape-luke-evans/. Accessed 18 July 2017.

SELECTED WORKS

Clash of the Titans, 2010; *Fast and Furious 6*, 2013; *The Hobbit: The Desolation of Smaug*, 2013; *Dracula Untold*, 2014; *The Hobbit: The Battle of the Five Armies*, 2014; *Furious 7*, 2015; *The Girl on the Train*, 2016; *Beauty and the Beast*, 2017; *The Fate of the Furious*, 2017

—*Joy Crelin*

David Fahrenthold

Date of birth: 1978
Occupation: Journalist

David Fahrenthold is a George Polk Award–winning investigative political reporter for the *Washington Post* who became recognized as "the guy with the legal pad" during the 2016 US presidential campaign. He joined the cable and satellite television news channel CNN in January 2017 as a contributor, which was approximately one year after he wrote an article for the *Washington Post* that developed into a major political story about Republican presidential candidate Donald Trump's charitable giving.

While on the campaign trail in February 2016, Trump attended a rally in Waterloo, Iowa, where he gave a $100,000 check to a local veterans group. The money came from Trump's personal charity, the Donald J. Trump Foundation, which had also held a fundraiser for veterans the previous month. The fundraiser was reported to have raised $6 million, which included a $1 million personal donation from Trump. Fahrenthold, who was covering the event in Waterloo, suspected that the candidate may have broken the law by mixing his charity and his presidential campaign, but he also wondered where the rest of the money from the fundraiser had gone.

Trump had publicly and frequently discussed his charitable contributions for decades. Fahrenthold, whose suspicions were raised following the rally in Waterloo, embarked on a nine-month quest to corroborate those claims, and his very public inquiry into Trump, aided by an army of Twitter tipsters, helped Fahrenthold break a second explosive story: an audio tape on which Trump is heard bragging about what many perceived as sexual assault against women. That story became the most-read story of all time on the *Washington Post*'s website.

These stories, combined with the unusually public way in which Fahrenthold was able to crowdsource leads about the Trump Foundation, contributed to Fahrenthold becoming a widely known and recognized figure during the 2016 US presidential election. He was one of few reporters at the time who thoroughly investigated and reported on Trump's myriad business and financial claims. Fahrenthold's reports brought unanticipated publicity and praise and invited criticism and death threats. According to Fahrenthold for the *Washington Post* (29 Dec. 2016) in an overview of his experience, one person even referred to the reporter as "a time traveler from the future trying to carefully fix the darkest timeline."

Fahrenthold's work yielded important information about candidate Trump as well as important ways in which contemporary journalists collect information. Dan Gillmor, director of the Knight Center for Digital Media Entrepreneurship at Arizona State University, wrote for the *Atlantic* (21 Dec. 2016) that Fahrenthold is not "the first to have used what some call crowdsourcing to deepen his sources and knowledge. But . . . he's taken it into new areas, notably by using social media in a particularly smart way. And his methods offer a lesson to others in journalism."

EARLY LIFE AND EDUCATION

Fahrenthold was born in 1978 and raised in Houston, Texas. His mother, Jeane, worked as an elementary school teacher, and his father, Peter, worked for Continental Airlines. Fahrenthold attended Memorial High School in Hedwig Village and wrote "Musings of the Omnipotent Leroy," a humor column that appeared in the school newspaper, the *Anvil*. He also covered school football games, which, as he explained to Blake Paterson for the *Houston Chronicle* (8 Nov. 2016), gave him his first exposure to difficult interview subjects. The football coaches and players, he recalled, acted like they "were talking about state secrets. You had to really work to get information out of them." He graduated from high school in 1996.

Fahrenthold attended Harvard University, where he studied history and later became the associate managing editor of the Harvard *Crimson*. In 1998, he interned at the city desk for the *Seattle Times*, and in 1999, he was a reporting

intern in the city and suburban bureau at the New Orleans *Times-Picayune*. Fahrenthold graduated from Harvard in 2000 and joined the *Washington Post* as an intern. His first assignment as a full-time reporter was covering news related to the Washington, DC, police department.

Fahrenthold went on to cover environmental issues, and in 2010 he became the newspaper's political reporter. In 2013 and 2014, and during the increasing nationwide influence of the Tea Party, a US political party interested in limited government, he did a series of stories about government waste. He wrote several articles about the so-called National Raisin Reserve, which is the now-defunct reserve that functioned in accordance with a World War II–era law by which the government seized a portion of raisin-growers' grapes each year. The guiding question of these stories, Fahrenthold told Canadian journalist Jonah Keri for the *Jonah Keri Podcast* (12 Dec. 2016), was, why do some government programs get cut, while others—like the raisin reserve—stick around well beyond their era of usefulness? Fahrenthold told Keri that his favorite article during this period was "Sinkhole of Bureaucracy," which appeared in the March 22, 2014, issue of the *Washington Post* and reported on a Pennsylvania limestone mine that had been converted into a federal agency assigned to process truckloads of paper personnel records of government employees. The "paper cave," as Fahrenthold came to call it, was a prime example of government inefficiency, housing over 20,000 filing cabinets.

2016 US PRESIDENTIAL ELECTION

Fahrenthold began covering the 2016 presidential election at the end of 2014 and followed several Republican campaigns along the way. In January 2016, candidate Donald Trump decided to skip a televised debate, moderated by Megyn Kelly of Fox News, between the remaining Republican candidates and instead, he held a televised fundraiser for veterans.

Trump gave away $100,000 from that fundraiser a few days later in Waterloo, Iowa, comingling his charity, the Donald J. Trump Foundation (which signed the check), and his presidential campaign (the slogan of which, "Make America Great Again," was printed on the check). Fahrenthold suspected that this highly unusual move was also illegal, and the experts he contacted tentatively agreed but added that such a violation would take years to investigate and prove. Undaunted, Fahrenthold wondered what had happened to the rest of the $6 million (including, as Trump had publicly stated, $1 million of his own money).

Fahrenthold called Corey Lewandowski, Trump's then-campaign manager, who reported that the money had been given away, but he refused to divulge when or to what groups it was given. Fahrenthold then combed through Trump's Twitter account for mention of any veterans' groups the candidate had supported in the past. He then asked those groups if they had received any money from Trump, tagging Trump's Twitter handle in his inquiries so the candidate would be aware that his claims were being investigated.

When Trump later contacted Fahrenthold, he contradicted Lewandowski and explained to Fahrenthold that the money had been given to a friend's charity. Trump then held a press conference to officially comment on the money raised and where it had gone. The story was so big that Fahrenthold began appearing on news shows like MSNBC's *Morning Joe*. It was the beginning of Fahrenthold's career as a pundit, but he and his editor at the *Washington Post* had another facet of the story they wanted to investigate.

DONALD J. TRUMP FOUNDATION

As Fahrenthold recalled in his overview, his editor, Marty Baron, was generally curious about Trump's foundation. "The logic was that Trump had just tried to wiggle out of a charitable promise he'd made on national TV," Fahrenthold wrote. "What, Marty wondered, had he been doing before the campaign, when nobody was looking?" Working with a researcher, Fahrenthold scoured old newspaper clippings going back to the 1980s where Trump talked about donating to charities. He also looked at the Donald J. Trump Foundation's tax filings and later recalled that he was surprised to find "two very different stories."

Trump claimed that over the years, through his foundation he had given away at least $12 million. The tax filings, however, revealed that Trump had only provided his foundation with $5.5 million since 1987. When asked, Trump's team explained that they had intentionally kept the other donations a secret, but Fahrenthold was not willing to take their word for it. Instead, he took out a legal pad, which would become his signature journalistic tool after appearing with it in several tweeted photographs as his handwritten list grew, and began writing down the names of charities Trump might have ever given money to. After calling over three hundred charities from his list (none of which claimed to have received money from Trump), Fahrenthold said that his quest began to remind him of another investigative story he wrote for the *Washington Post*. In "Sinkhole of Bureaucracy," Fahrenthold resorted to interviewing former US government employees because government officials refused to discuss the existence and inefficiency of an underground mine used to house and store federal paperwork. Fahrenthold explained in his overview article that "in reporting jargon, I'd tried the front door: I asked to tour the mine.

[The Office of Personnel Management] said no. So then I went looking for windows. I sought out ex-employees, who had firsthand knowledge of the place but weren't beholden to OPM's desire for secrecy. I found them. By piecing together their recollections, I got the story that the government didn't want me to find."

Fahrenthold employed a similar strategy with the Trump Foundation. He ultimately found his "window" on the three-hundred twenty-fifth charity that he contacted. HomeSafe, a Florida children's charity, had received $20,000 from the Trump Foundation in exchange for a painted portrait of Trump that was created at a charity event. This was important because it suggested something called self-dealing, whereby charity leaders use charity funds to buy things for themselves. If the portrait was hanging in one of Trump's resorts, for example, it would prove the self-dealing claim. Fahrenthold and an army of Twitter users scoured the Internet for the portrait. They did not find it, but remarkably, they found another portrait of Trump that the foundation had purchased from another children's charity. That portrait was hanging at Trump's golf resort in Doral, Florida.

Fahrenthold's very public investigation of Trump was likely the impetus for an anonymous tipster sending him a short video one month before the presidential election. The now-infamous video contained audio of Trump and entertainment reporter Billy Bush snickering about an attractive woman and Trump bragging about grabbing women inappropriately and without their consent. Fahrenthold verified and published that video, which became an explosive story in the final days of the campaign.

For his work throughout the campaign, Fahrenthold received the George Polk Award and the inaugural Ben Bradlee Prize, named after the late *Washington Post* editor. He joined CNN as a contributor in 2017.

PERSONAL LIFE

Fahrenthold married Elizabeth Lewis, a fellow Harvard graduate who works for the World Resources Institute, in 2005. They have two children and live in Washington, DC.

SUGGESTED READING

Fahrenthold, David A. "David Fahrenthold Tells the Behind-the-Scenes Story of His Year Covering Trump." *The Washington Post*, 29 Dec. 2016, www.washingtonpost.com/lifestyle/magazine/david-fahrenthold-tells-the-behind-the-scenes-story-of-his-year-covering-trump/2016/12/27/299047c4-b510-11e6-b8df-600bd9d38a02_story.html. Accessed 15 Mar. 2017.

Fahrenthold, David. "Sinkhole of Bureaucracy." *The Washington Post*, 22 Mar. 2014, www.

washingtonpost.com/sf/national/2014/03/22/sinkhole-of-bureaucracy. Accessed 16 Mar. 2017.

Gillmor, Dan. "How One Reporter Turned to His Readers to Investigate Donald Trump." *The Atlantic*, 21 Dec. 2016, www.theatlantic.com/politics/archive/2016/12/what-journalists-can-learn-from-david-fahrentholds-trump-coverage/511277. Accessed 9 Mar. 2017.

Keri, Jonah. "The Jonah Keri Podcast #76: David Fahrenthold." *Nerdist*, 12 Dec. 2016, nerdist.com/the-jonah-keri-podcast-76-david-fahren-thold. Accessed 10 Mar. 2017.

Paterson, Blake. "Before His Trump Scoops, the Memorial High Anvil." *Houston Chronicle*, 8 Nov. 2016, www.houstonchronicle.com/local/gray-matters/article/Before-his-Trump-scoops-the-Memorial-High-Anvil-10599567.php. Accessed 9 Mar. 2017.

—*Molly Hagan*

Georges Biard [CC BY-SA 3.0], via Wikimedia Commons

Elle Fanning

Date of birth: April 9, 1998
Occupation: Actor

For actor Elle Fanning, entering the world of film and television was in some ways an inevitability. The younger sister of fellow actor Dakota Fanning, who became well known as a child actor and continues to work into early adulthood, Fanning first found work on-screen playing younger versions of her sister in such films as the 2001 drama *I Am Sam*. Over the following years, however, Fanning established her own identity as an actor separate from her sister with roles in films such as *Babel* (2006) and *The Curious Case of Benjamin Button* (2008). A turning point of sorts came in 2011, when she appeared in a major role in the J. J. Abrams–directed science-fiction film *Super 8*. Later roles, such as that of Aurora in the 2014 live-action Disney film *Maleficent*, solidified Fanning's reputation as a talented performer in her own right.

As a young adult, Fanning continued to branch out, taking on more mature roles in projects such as director Nicolas Winding Refn's 2016 horror film *The Neon Demon* and the 2017 drama *The Beguiled*. Despite having spent nearly her entire life in the film industry, she remains enthusiastic about her work and intrigued by the possibility of exploring new opportunities as a performer. "If you're not having a great time and loving it still, then you should do something else," she told Gill Pringle for the *Independent* (3 Jan. 2017). "Everything still feels fresh for me—every new character, new script, new environment, and I still get very excited by it."

EARLY LIFE AND FOLLOWING HER SISTER INTO ACTING

Mary Elle Fanning was born in Georgia on April 9, 1998. She was the younger of two daughters born to Steven and Heather Fanning, athletes who had played minor-league baseball and professional tennis, respectively. Her father went on to pursue work in electronics sales. Fanning spent the first years of her life in Conyers, a small city east of Atlanta, Georgia. In 2000, her older sister, Dakota, began finding regular work as a child actor, and the family eventually decided to move to Los Angeles, California, for the elder Fanning's career.

Fanning's initial steps into the world of acting came while she was still a toddler. "When my sister started acting I knew I wanted to try it too," she told Amelia Abraham for *Refinery29* (5 July 2016). As Dakota found work in television and film, those in the industry who met both Fanning sisters noted that they shared a resemblance, which in turn provided Fanning with her first opportunities in the industry. In the 2001 drama *I Am Sam*, she played a two-year-old version of her sister's character, Lucy. The following year, she had a small role in the television miniseries *Taken*, again playing a younger incarnation of Dakota's role.

Although homeschooled by her grandmother as a young child, Fanning later began attending schools in Los Angeles, balancing her time in the classroom with her acting work. She and her sister both attended Campbell Hall, a day school located in the Studio City neighborhood of Los Angeles, where the family lived. In addition to acting from a young age—though neither she nor her sister ever received any formal acting training—she began studying ballet as a child, first in school and later with a private teacher. Although not interested in pursuing a career in dance, she enjoyed the physical and mental aspects of the demanding dance style. "You have to be aware of every single muscle," she explained in a conversation with fellow actor Scarlett Johansson for *Interview* magazine (5 May 2014). "It's cool to be able to have the ability and the posture. I also like the discipline of it. You can't be goofing around. You have to be very serious."

A CHILD ACTOR IN HER OWN RIGHT

Having established herself as a child actor with those first small parts, Fanning next began to appear in film and television projects that did not feature her sister, gaining experience with films such as *Daddy Day Care* (2003), *The Door in the Floor* (2004), and *Because of Winn-Dixie* (2005). "I was four when I did *The Door in the Floor*," she recalled to Johansson. "I don't remember every single thing about it, but I liked the costumes, and they always put my hair in pigtails. In one scene I got to eat grilled cheese and I was so excited." Aside from her sister, one of her biggest role models had become Marilyn Monroe, particularly after seeing *The Seven Year Itch* (1955) at age seven. "I watched that all the time when I was little. I liked the dress. I was her for Halloween when I was seven. I did the makeup and the mole and I did all the poses with blowing kisses and all that," she told Lauren Tabach-Bank for *Interview* (9 Dec. 2010).

In the latter half of that decade, Fanning's projects came to include critically acclaimed films such as the 2006 drama *Babel* and the 2008 film *The Curious Case of Benjamin Button*, both of which went on to be nominated for several Academy Awards, including the award for best picture. Although Fanning often filled relatively small roles, playing the child or younger version of a film's protagonist on numerous occasions, that was not always the case. In the 2008 independent drama *Phoebe in Wonderland*, she played the role of the title protagonist, a young girl struggling with Tourette syndrome.

BREAKTHROUGH

As a teenager, Fanning took on major roles in a series of culturally significant films that earned her both wider recognition among audiences and praise from critics, directors, and others in the film industry. In 2011, she appeared in several high-profile films, including the science-fiction film *Super 8*. She enjoyed her role and particularly appreciated how the film, which was written and directed by filmmaker J. J. Abrams, respected the points of view of its child protagonists. "This movie is not condescending at all

to the kids," she told Geoff Boucher for the *Los Angeles Times* blog *Hero Complex* (7 June 2011). The year 2011 also saw the release of the horror film *Twixt* by legendary director Francis Ford Coppola, whose guesthouse Fanning stayed at during the filming process. "We would eat dinner every night with him, and he showed me how to make pasta sauce," she recalled to Johansson. In addition to such projects, she went on to appear in films such as *We Bought a Zoo* (2011); *Ginger & Rosa* (2012), a coming-of-age drama in which she played a lead role as a character meant to be sixteen years old, despite only having been thirteen at the time of filming; and *Young Ones* (2014).

The year 2014 saw the premiere of Fanning's largest film to date, the live-action Disney film *Maleficent*. A twist on the classic animated Disney film *Sleeping Beauty* (1959), the film starred Angelina Jolie as the titular fairy and Fanning as Aurora, better known as Sleeping Beauty. Popular both in the United States and internationally, *Maleficent* introduced Fanning to audiences all over the world. Fanning herself was thrilled to have worked with Jolie and also appreciated having the opportunity to be in a film that made extensive use of special effects. "I felt like a newbie," she told Johansson. "I had never done something with so much visual effects before. Every time I had a hair change or a makeup change, they would put me on the turntable, turn me, and do the scanning while I made all these facial expressions." Following *Maleficent*, Fanning appeared in the biopic *Trumbo* (2015) and the drama 3 *Generations* (2015), in which she played a transgender teen preparing to transition. In addition to her film work, Fanning began to model for clothing designers during her teen years, working for fashion brands such as Marc by Marc Jacobs and Miu Miu.

ADULT ROLES

Having begun her career as a toddler and gained much of her acclaim as a child actor, Fanning has relished the opportunity to take on more mature roles and increasingly challenging, diverse projects since reaching her late teens. "I love a risk. If something seems impossible, then that's what I want to try," she explained to Pringle. She strongly signaled her turn toward such projects in 2016 with the release of *The Neon Demon*, a horror film by critically acclaimed filmmaker Nicolas Winding Refn. An exploration of the fashion industry, the film sparked controversy with its graphic violence and depictions of practices such as cannibalism, and it received a mixed critical response upon its premiere at the Cannes Film Festival. For Fanning, however, the film's distasteful elements are crucial to its overall message, tone, and stylistic approach. "I knew *Neon Demon* would be violent and that my character does go to a very dark place," she told Abraham. "I guess I am a little squeamish but it was fine. I think the blood in this film is very glamorous and beautiful. It's stylized in a pretty way. . . . It's not icky."

In addition to *The Neon Demon*, Fanning played major roles in a variety of films in 2016, including the Academy Award–nominated drama *20th Century Women* and the historical crime film *Live by Night*. That same year, she graduated from Campbell Hall. Although pursuing an education as well as an acting career was challenging at times, she has no regrets about her choice to attend a traditional school. "I'm glad I had the experience of going to a totally normal high school," she told Pringle. "Some of my friends have gone to college, others aren't, but we are in this limbo where we talk about 'Oh, we're not in high school anymore, it's such a strange thing.'"

Fanning costarred in a number of films released in 2017 as well, including *Sidney Hall* and *How to Talk to Girls at Parties*. Her film *The Beguiled*, directed by filmmaker Sofia Coppola and costarring Nicole Kidman, Kirsten Dunst, and Colin Farrell, met with a largely positive reception at Cannes, earning a nomination for the prestigious Palme d'Or and winning Coppola the award for best director. *The Beguiled* was released in the United States in June 2017.

Like many actors, Fanning has also expressed an interest in directing and has noted in interviews that she hopes to begin pursing opportunities in that field in the near future. "As an actor you're exploring someone else's vision. I'd like to be able to create that vision instead," she told Nathan Heller for *Vogue* (10 May 2017). "It's a *huge* challenge. But I want that."

PERSONAL LIFE
When not filming on location elsewhere, Fanning has spent much of her life living in her family's home in the Studio City neighborhood of Los Angeles. "Because I travel a lot, going back home and being with my family is always special," she told Pringle. "I live in the house that I grew up in since I was seven years old, so, being in my own room, with my family right there, is a very comforting feeling."

SUGGESTED READING

Abraham, Amelia. "Elle Fanning on *Neon Demon*, Her Prom Night and #CareerGoals." *Refinery29*, 5 July 2016, www.refinery29.uk/2016/07/115655/elle-fanning-interview-neon-demon. Accessed 13 June 2017.

Berrington, Katie. "Experimental Elle." *Vogue UK*, 1 July 2016, www.vogue.co.uk/article/elle-fanning-interview-the-neon-demon. Accessed 13 June 2017.

Fanning, Elle. "Elle Fanning." Interview by Scarlett Johansson. *Interview*, 5 May 2014, www.interviewmagazine.com/film/elle-fanning-1. Accessed 13 June 2017.

Fanning, Elle. "Elle Fanning Opens Up about Being Cast as the World's Most Beautiful Woman." Interview by Julie Kosin. *Harper's Bazaar*, 27 June 2016, www.harpersbazaar.com/culture/film-tv/a16322/elle-fanning-neon-demon-interview. Accessed 13 June 2017.

Heller, Nathan. "Elle Fanning Is an Old Soul Who Has Visions of the Future—and Directing." *Vogue*, 10 May 2017, www.vogue.com/article/elle-fanning-interview-marilyn-monroe-technology-june-vogue-cover. Accessed 13 June 2017.

Pringle, Gill. "*Live by Night*'s Elle Fanning Interview: Now That I'm 18, the Role Matched Up to the Place That I'm at Now." *Independent*, 3 Jan. 2017, www.independent.co.uk/arts-entertainment/films/features/live-by-night-elle-fanning-ben-affleck-sienna-miller-zoe-saldana-loretta-figgis-warner-bros-a7507711.html. Accessed 13 June 2017.

SELECTED WORKS
I Am Sam, 2001; *Babel*, 2006; *The Curious Case of Benjamin Button*, 2008; *Super 8*, 2011; *Twixt*, 2011; *Ginger & Rosa*, 2012; *Maleficent*, 2014; *The Neon Demon*, 2016; *20th Century Women*, 2016; *The Beguiled*, 2017

—*Joy Crelin*

Elena Ferrante

Date of birth: 1943
Occupation: Author

Elena Ferrante is the pen name of an unknown Italian author best known for her Neapolitan Novels series.

EARLY LIFE AND EDUCATION
Elena Ferrante is a pseudonymous fiction writer living in Italy. She has been publishing novels since 1992. She earned global popularity for the English translations of her Neapolitan Novels series, the first of which was published in English translation in 2012.

Ferrante was born in Naples, Italy, where she lived into her early adulthood. She is presumed to have grown up in the 1950s and is known to have lived outside of Italy for some periods of her life.

Ferrante's youth was spent reading and aspiring to write, but she felt discouraged by an early anxiety about the validity of fiction centered on female protagonists. She worried as a young reader that only a man could be the hero of a great work of fiction. Her greatest influences in her youth were writers such as Gustave Flaubert, Victor Hugo, and Leo Tolstoy, as she found many women writers' stories were not bold enough for her tastes. She resolved to write about young women with the same dazzling characteristics she saw attributed to male literary protagonists. Eventually she also found female authors who inspired her, such as the mid-twentieth-century Italian writer Elsa Morante.

When she was thirteen years old, Ferrante began writing fiction. She earned a degree in classics at university. Ferrante began writing in earnest in her twenties, but at first had no plans to publish her writing, or even allow it to be read by others.

LITERARY CAREER

Ferrante has published seven novels under her pen name. Her first novel, *Troubling Love*, was published in Italian in 1992. At the time of its writing, she told her publisher she wished to remain pseudonymous, saying that working with her would be inexpensive, as the publisher would not need to invest in promoting her as an individual. *Troubling Love* was adapted into an award-winning 1995 movie by director Mario Martone.

Her second novel, *The Days of Abandonment*, was not published until 2002; in the intervening time, she had written constantly, but had not produced anything she felt worth publishing. *The Days of Abandonment* was made into a film in 2005.

The four so-called Neapolitan Novels are a series centered on a friendship between two women named Lena and Lila living in Italy between the 1950s and the 2010s. The series, which comprises *My Brilliant Friend* (2012), *The Story of a New Name* (2013), *Those Who Leave and Those Who Stay* (2014), and *The Story of the Lost Child* (2015), details the tumultuous political climate of Italy and the equally tumultuous personal lives of the two women it follows. Ferrante has suggested that Lena and Lila's friendship is inspired by a relationship in her own life.

The Neapolitan Novels were translated into English by Ann Goldstein from 2012 to 2015. While *Troubling Love* and *The Days of Abandonment* had been successful in Italy, the English translations of the Neapolitan Novels earned Ferrante great success and global acclaim. The *New York Times* named *The Story of the Lost Child* one of the ten best books of 2015.

Ferrante says her pseudonymity is not intended to protect her private life, but to protect her writing from the pressure to publish.

IMPACT

Ferrante's work has risen to popularity worldwide after many years of publishing to little acclaim. In 2014, she was shortlisted for the Best Translated Book Award for *The Story of a New Name*, as translated to English by Ann Goldstein.

PERSONAL LIFE

The enigmatic Ferrante has not revealed any significant details about her personal life, nor her true identity. She is known to have children and is believed to have been previously married. She has been uninterested in public attention and has consistently rejected invitations for in-person media events. Ferrante conducts interviews only by email, with few exceptions; in 2015 she granted the *Paris Review* her first known in-person interview. Her city of residence is not known, but she occasionally visits family in Naples. She has said that she studies, translates, and teaches in addition to writing.

SUGGESTED READING

Ferrante, Elena. "'Writing Has Always Been a Great Struggle for Me.'" Interview by Rachel Donadio. *New York Times*. New York Times, 9 Dec. 2014. Web. 24 Jan. 2016.

Ferrante, Elena. "Elena Ferrante, Art of Fiction No. 228." Interview by Sandro and Sandra Ferri. *Paris Review*. Paris Review, Spring 2015. Web. 24 Jan. 2016.

Ferrante, Elena. "Women of 2015: Elena Ferrante, Writer." Interview by Liz Jobey. *Financial Times*. Financial Times, 11 Dec. 2015. Web. 24 Jan. 2016.

Lewis-Kraus, Gideon, Meghan O'Rourke, and Emily Gould. "Who Is Elena Ferrante?" *New York Times*. New York Times, 21 Aug. 2014. Web. 24 Jan. 2016.

O'Rourke, Meghan. "Elena Ferrante: The Global Literary Sensation Nobody Knows." *Guardian*. Guardian News and Media, 31 Oct. 2014. Web. 24 Jan. 2016.

Simpson, Mona. "Elena Ferrante Writes Fiction That Feels Autobiographical. But Who Is She?" *New Republic*. New Republic, 10 Oct. 2014. Web. 24 Jan. 2016.

Wood, James. "Women on the Verge." *New Yorker*. Condé Nast, 21 Jan. 2013. Web. 24 Jan. 2016.

SELECTED WORKS

L'amore molesto, 1992 (*Troubling Love*, 2006); *I giorni dell'abbandono*, 2002; (*The Days of Abandonment*, 2005); *La frantumaglia*, 2003 (*Fragments*, 2013); *La figlia oscura*, 2006 (*The Lost Daughter*, 2008); *L'amica geniale*, 2011 (*My Brilliant Friend*, 2012); *Storia del nuovo cognome*, 2012 (*The Story of a New Name*, 2013); *Storia di chi fugge e di chi resta*, 2013 (*Those Who Leave and Those Who Stay, 2014); Storia della bambina perduta, 2014 (The Story of the Lost Child, 2015)*

—*Richard Means*

Angela Flournoy

Date of birth: ca. 1985
Occupation: Author

Angela Flournoy's novel *The Turner House* (2015)—about an African American family grappling with what to do with their now-vacant family home in a blighted section of Detroit—was the kind of literary debut young authors dream of: both critically acclaimed and commercially successful, topping numerous "best of" lists, and being recognized as a *New York Times* notable book of the year. It also became a finalist for several awards, including the National Book Award, the Center for Fiction First Novel Prize, the PEN/Robert W. Bingham Prize for Debut Fiction, and an NAACP Image Award. Flournoy herself was honored by being named to the National Book Foundation's "5 under 35" list for 2015. Her writing has also appeared in the *Paris Review*, the *New York Times*, the *New Republic* and the *Los Angeles Times*.

EARLY LIFE AND CAREER

Angela Flournoy was born around 1985 and grew up in Southern California. Her mother hailed from Los Angeles, while her father had grown up in a large family in Detroit, Michigan. She spent a lot of time in Detroit as a child, visiting extended family who still lived there. She vividly recalls an early visit there with her father and sister, as they drove around her father's old East Detroit neighborhood, with him pointing out sites of significance to him that had, in the years since his own childhood, changed irrevocably. Once-vibrant Detroit was now blighted and abandoned, with whole neighborhoods emptied as the flight to the suburbs began to speed up in the 1960s. The memories formed by those visits with her father would help to shape the way young Angela saw how cities evolved and changed.

In an interview with Deesha Philyaw for the *Rumpus* (13 Feb. 2016), Flournoy recalled how her mother's work ethic helped spur on her own ambitions: "My mom used to wake us up at four to drive us to my aunt's house, who would take us to school so she could continue driving downtown to work at the phone company. And she wouldn't get back until eight o'clock at night. And I'm not doing that. So, I'm working hard, not necessarily to be a credit to the race, but because that's just the background I come from."

Janette Pellegrini/Getty Images for Girls Write Now

In a number of interviews Flournoy has stated that she has always known she wanted to be a writer. She recalled writing poetry in high school—what she would later consider "bad poetry"—but turned to writing prose as an undergraduate. Her English professors were always encouraging of her work, something that helped to motivate her during her undergraduate years and afterward. Flournoy earned her bachelor's degree in English with a creative writing emphasis from the University of Southern California Dornsife in 2007. She also earned a communications degree from the Annenberg School for Communication and Journalism, which is also part of USC. She subsequently studied at the Iowa Writers' Workshop, where, beginning in 2010, she started to research and write *The Turner House*.

Since earning her degrees she has taught at a number of institutions, including the University of Iowa, the New School, and Columbia University. In 2016 she was named the Rona Jaffe Foundation Fellow at the New York Public Library and Lewis B. Cullman Center for Scholars and Writers. The fellowship lasts one year.

DOING THE RESEARCH

Initially, Flournoy had nothing but the vague kernels of an idea for her novel: a story that took place in Detroit, with a woman named Lelah, who was squatting in her family's vacant house. She had assumed that all of the book would take place in 2008, the year of the subprime mortgage crisis that led to the sharp economic downturn that would become known as the Great Recession. But her research into Detroit's rich history took her into other, unexpected directions. "I started with that house, a house that was similar in condition and geography to the house that my father grew up in on the east side of Detroit," Flournoy recalled in an interview with Jeffery Gleaves for the *Paris Review* (4 June 2015). "I remember thinking, What is the future of this house? But then, obviously, a house is only as important as the people and the relationships within it. Coming from several large families, I thought that showing the various opinions about what should be done with the house would highlight how difficult the situation really is. I wanted to show how so much can change in one generation. The more I researched homeownership in Detroit, the more I realized that there are a lot of obstacles involved with that idea. And once I started researching the family I'd decided to create, I realized that they needed to be tied into the political history of the city."

Flournoy's research brought her into places both anticipated and familiar: the city's complicated history of race relations, the outsized influence of the auto industry, the flight of mostly white Detroiters to the suburbs, and the 1967 riots, which led to the deaths of 43 people, over 7,200 arrests, and the destruction of more than 2,000 buildings. Another 1,189 people were injured. The riot was one of the most destructive in the history of the United States, just behind the 1863 Draft Riots in New York City during the Civil War (1861–65) and the 1992 Los Angeles riots that followed the acquittal of the police officers who were caught on videotape beating African American motorist Rodney King.

The Detroit riot would forever change the face of the city. In an interview for the National Book Award's website, Flournoy remarked: "When I first learned about Black Bottom and Paradise Valley, neighborhoods that no longer exist in Detroit that were home to black migrants from the south, I was unsure about addressing this history in my novel. I feared it was a diversion, that I'd spend months researching and it wouldn't make sense to include this information anywhere in the novel. Ultimately, I couldn't resist jumping down that research rabbit hole, and all the others that came after it."

THE TURNER HOUSE

Although Flournoy's debut novel, *The Turner House*, is set in 2008, it provides space for a series of flashbacks to flesh out the history of the Turner family, as well as the history of the city of Detroit. A significant portion of the flashbacks take place during the 1967 riot, and another significant set of flashbacks return to the years 1944 and 1945, when the family patriarch, Francis, works to establish himself in Detroit as his wife, Viola, waits for him to summon her north from their home in Arkansas.

The Turners ultimately raise thirteen children in their house on Yarrow Street. They watch as children grow up and move away, as grandchildren are born, as the neighborhood declines and various addictions take hold of different family members. After Francis dies and Viola is eventually forced to leave the family home in her old age, the children all come back to decide what to do with the house—now worth just a tenth of its mortgage value. But as the family comes together, they also find themselves confronting their own history—as well as a "haint," or ghost, that has settled into the house.

Upon its publication, Flournoy's debut met with nearly universal praise. Writing for the *Washington Post* (23 Apr. 2015), Stacia L. Brown declared: "'The Turner House' is an elegant and assured debut that takes a refreshing approach to discussing mental health issues within a black family that's resistant to direct conversation about them. In the end, it doesn't matter if the haint that drew us into the narrative is "real" to anyone but [eldest son] Cha-Cha. His belief in it is enough for readers to invest in his exorcism of it and of all the other hounds of history that haunt him." Matthew Thomas, for the *New York Times Sunday Book Review* (29 Apr. 2015), called the novel "an engrossing and remarkably mature first novel" and went on to note, "That Flournoy's main characters are black is central to this book, and yet her treatment of that essential fact is never essentializing. Flournoy gets at the universal through the patient observation of one family's particulars. In this assured and memorable novel, she provides the feeling of knowing a family from the inside out, as we would wish to know our own."

On the subject of how her novel deals with race, Flournoy told Andrew Purcell for the *Sydney Morning Herald* (22 July 2016), "It's a novel about reality. It's a novel about black people living in a world that's very similar to ours, and that's a world in which racism does exist."

Flournoy is often asked what she believes her success means to black writing in America in general. Although she is involved in seminars about African American literature, such as her participation in a summer retreat established by the Kimbilio Center for African American Fiction in 2015, she remains ambivalent about the relation of her individual efforts to the collective whole.

She noted to Philyaw: "My ambition is personal. I don't think I need to succeed so that the race can succeed. We've seen that. We've been succeeding since we were sneaking to learn how to read. We've been showing ourselves to be exceptional. . . . For me, it's much more on a craft level, and the level of writing things that may not be lower-case-t true, but capital-T True, to some aspect of black experience. And the biggest thing that I can contribute to any sort of understanding of black lives is to not explain it. I don't want to write books that explain black people to non-black people. I want to write books that pick apart aspects of black life and talk about it. And that's it."

SUGGESTED READING

Brown, Stacia L. "'The Turner House' Takes on Mental Health in Black Families." Review of *The Turner House*, by Angela Flournoy. *Washington Post*, 23 Apr. 2015, www.washingtonpost.com/news/act-four/wp/2015/04/23/the-turner-house-takes-on-mental-health-in-black-families/. Accessed 18 Jan. 2017.

Flournoy, Angela. "Haunting Houses: An Interview with Angela Flournoy." By Jeffery Gleaves. *The Paris Review*, 4 June 2015, www.theparisreview.org/blog/2015/06/04/haunting-houses-an-interview-with-angela-flournoy. Accessed 17 Jan. 2017.

Flournoy, Angela. "The Saturday Rumpus Interview: Angela Flournoy." By Deesha Philyaw. *The Rumpus*, 13 Feb. 2016, therumpus.net/2016/02/the-saturday-rumpus-interview-angela-flournoy-2. Accessed 18 Jan. 2017.

Purcell, Andrew. "Angela Flournoy Interview: Almost Every Novel in the US Is Bound to Be about Race." *The Sydney Morning Herald*, 22 July 2016, www.smh.com.au/entertainment/books/angela-flournoy-interview-almost-every-novel-in-the-us-is-bound-to-be-about-race-20160715-gq6bqw.html. Accessed 18 Jan. 2017.

Thomas, Matthew. Review of *The Turner House*, by Angela Flournoy. *New York Times*, 29 Apr. 2015, www.nytimes.com/2015/05/03/books/review/the-turner-house-by-angela-flournoy.html. Accessed 18 Jan. 2017.

"'The Turner House', by Angela Flournoy, 2015 National Book Award Finalist, Fiction." *National Book Foundation*, www.nationalbook.org/nba2015_f_aflournoy.html. Accessed 18 Jan. 2017.

—*Christopher Mari*

Claire Foy

Date of birth: April 16, 1984
Occupation: Actor

Claire Foy is one of the most successful actors working in British film and television today. She first came to prominence in 2008 when she portrayed the title character in the BBC miniseries *Little Dorrit*, an adaptation of Charles Dickens's 1857 novel of the same name. Since that time

Steve Granitz/WireImage/Getty Images

she has gone on to give a number of critically acclaimed performances, most notably in her roles as Anne Boleyn in the television series *Wolf Hall* (2015), an adaptation of Hilary Mantel's 2009 novel of the same name, and as Elizabeth II in the popular Netflix series *The Crown*, which debuted in 2016. Her performances in each of these roles have earned her nominations for a number of notable awards, including a British Academy of Film and Television Arts (BAFTA) Award, a Critics' Choice Television Award for best supporting actress in a movie or miniseries, a Golden Globe Award for best performance by an actress in a television drama series, and a Screen Actors Guild (SAG) Award for outstanding performance by a female actor in a drama series. In 2017 Foy went on to win the Golden Globe and SAG Awards for best actress.

Despite her growing success, Foy maintains she has no interest in pursuing a career in Hollywood but would rather continue to find roles in the United Kingdom. "The American mentality is lost on me," she admitted in an interview with Gabriel Tate for the *Independent* (10 Jan. 2015). "You've got to want to do anything to make it. [People say] don't you want to go to Hollywood? Well, no—if you knew what it was like, you wouldn't either. I'd rather just work."

EARLY LIFE AND EDUCATION

The youngest of three siblings, Claire Elizabeth Foy was born on April 16, 1984 in Stockport, Greater Manchester, England, and raised in Buckinghamshire. Her father was a salesman; her mother worked for a pharmaceutical company. Foy has claimed that she always sought to dominate the spotlight as a child, much to the annoyance of her brother and sister. Despite her desire to perform, she has confessed that she never saw herself pursuing a career in acting. She developed an early and abiding love of film and initially thought of becoming a cinematographer.

The first major change in her life came at age eight, when her parents divorced. Although it was more difficult for her older siblings to cope with, it was a relatively painless experience for her. "As divorces go, on a scale of one to ten? I don't remember a thing—so, ten, amazing," Foy recalled in an interview with Gerard Gilbert for the *Independent* (17 Feb. 2012) "I didn't really know what was going on. Or maybe I just chose not to remember, but mum and dad didn't shout at each other or anything. . . . And we moved to another house in the same village so we didn't have to change school or anything."

At the age of seventeen, Foy suffered a more traumatic episode, when she developed a benign tumor in one eye. "I was like a Cyclops and it was all a bit scary," she said of the experience to Gilbert in the *Independent*. "I was on steroids for about a year-and-a-half afterwards that makes you put on a lot of weight and have really bad skin."

Foy was admittedly the least academically inclined of her siblings, but she managed to do well enough in her entrance exams to get a spot at Liverpool John Moores University, where she studied drama and screen studies. After earning her degree, she decided to study acting. She enrolled in a yearlong course at the Oxford School of Drama. There, she soon realized, she had found her place and her purpose. "If you wanted to say what was outstanding in her, it would be her inventiveness; she was always very bold," George Peck, the principal of the school, told Emine Saner for *The Guardian* (21 Aug. 2015). "It was partly her sense of humour and the way she approached the course meant that it was very accessible to her. Often when you go to drama school, the ideas are quite new and she was able to receive those and run with them in a very creative way."

RISING STAR

After a casting director saw Foy perform in one her school's drama showcases, she landed her first role on British television with a small part in the pilot episode of the television series *Being Human* in 2008. But her breakout performance occurred when she was cast in the title role of *Little Dorrit*, the BBC miniseries adaptation of the Charles Dickens novel of the same name. Foy has admitted that she did not feel that she would win the part during her auditions, but she believed she was cast in the role for two reasons:

first, she sensed that casting director Rachel Frett was advocating for her, and second, that screenwriter Andrew Davies enjoyed placing relatively unknown actors in major parts. "Davies likes doing that because then people think you are that character," she explained to Gilbert. Others, however, have credited Foy's unique ability to communicate a variety of emotions in still moments. "What stood out was her fragility, and her extraordinary eyes—big saucer eyes that were like a window into her soul," Dearbhla Walsh, who directed several episodes of *Little Dorrit*, told Saner. "It was very clear [from casting meetings] that there was something exciting about her."

The success of that miniseries raised Foy's profile considerably. She quickly snagged parts in the two-part television miniseries *Going Postal* (2010), the television movie *Pulse* (2010), and a big Hollywood production called *Season of the Witch* (2011) starring Nicholas Cage. While she admired Cage's attention to his craft, she found the Hollywood experience to be too much for her and sought to return to British television work, where she felt she could secure higher quality roles.

She found such a part in a four-part television miniseries, *The Promise* (2011), in which Foy portrayed a young woman named Erin Matthews, who travels to Israel and Palestine to better understand her grandfather's experiences in Palestine during the time it was under British control. The series was written and directed by the noted filmmaker Peter Kosminsky, who found in Foy an actor with considerable versatility. "Casting is probably the most important part of the way I go about making films," Kosminsky said to Saner. "I was casting for the best part of six months and I think Claire has said she had about seven interviews. The role she played in *Little Dorrit* couldn't have been more different from the role she was to play in *The Promise*. I was looking to see whether she had that range and of course it turns out she absolutely did have."

Foy followed this successful turn with starring roles in the television movie *The Night Watch* (2011) and in a low-budget film *Wreckers* (2011) with Benedict Cumberbatch. She earned plaudits for her role as a budding feminist in 1960s London on the television series *White Heat* (2012) and as a Nazi sympathizer named Lady Persephone Towyn in the remake of the famed British television series *Upstairs Downstairs* (2010–12).

BECOMING ANNE BOLEYN

Foy's next highly acclaimed role came when she teamed up with Kosminsky again as he and Peter Straughan sought to adapt Hilary Mantel's 2009 historical novel, *Wolf Hall*, about the life of Thomas Cromwell in the court of Henry VIII. The production, which aired in 2015, was highly anticipated prior to its release, as Mantel's book had won several notable awards, including the Man Booker Prize. Foy earned acclaim for her role as Henry VIII's second wife, Anne Boleyn, who was ultimately beheaded on trumped-up charges of high treason. Anne's daughter, Elizabeth, subsequently became the British monarch.

Several critics credited Foy for holding her own against far more established actors, including Damian Lewis, who portrayed Henry, and Mark Rylance, who played Cromwell. Cromwell, during the course of the six-part miniseries, goes from being Anne's ally to her enemy. "I just didn't imagine her as Anne," Kosminsky told Tate. "It was a failing in me. Anne can be really quite unpleasant, but in the end she has to break your heart and Cromwell's heart. Claire both pushes the audience away and seduces us."

THE CROWN
Foy then took on the role of another British queen in the leading role for *The Crown*, a Netflix series that debuted in 2016. In it, she portrays Queen Elizabeth II, who took the throne in 1952 at the age of twenty-five, following the death of her father, George VI, who had led Britain through much of the Great Depression of the 1930s and World War II. The first season depicts the life of Britain's now-longest reigning monarch from her marriage to Philip, Duke of Edinburgh (played by Matt Smith), in 1947 to the mid-1950s, a time when the nation was undergoing a period of great change, including the loss of its colonial holdings abroad.

Foy found the role to be particularly challenging, in part because the woman she portrays continues to be such a major part of British daily life. She remarked in an interview with Gabriel Tate for the *Telegraph* (1 Nov. 2016): "When you're a British citizen, you just accept that they're there and take them for granted. And then you stop and realise, hang on, this was a young couple with two young children who didn't think this [their accession to the throne] would happen for another twenty years. Their lives change in an instant, while they're still grieving and going through something terrible personally. I don't know how anyone can't sympathise with that."

The show's creators have suggested they plan on producing up to six seasons of the series, possibly following Queen Elizabeth II and her family into modern times. The queen's popularity flagged somewhat in the 1990s, as the divorce of her son Prince Charles and scandal overwhelmed the royal family, but she continues to remain popular, both at home and abroad. As to the future of the British monarchy, Foy told Tate for the *Telegraph*: "It's in interesting hands. I think everyone thinks there'll be a revolutionary change, but the one thing I'd say after doing this is that history and the heritage are what sustain it. You're being propelled forward by all the kings and queens before you, which is huge."

However, Peter Morgan, who has written for and coproduced *The Crown*, suggested that Foy's role in the show will end after the second season, despite plans for six seasons. "I feel that when we reach 1963–64 we've gone as far as we can go with Claire Foy without having to do silly things in terms of makeup to make her look older," he said in an interview with Orlando Parfitt for *ScreenDaily* (8 Feb. 2017). "She can't help the fact she's as young as she is, and if we were to go further forward we'd probably need to think about the issue of recasting everybody." Nevertheless, her performance in the show's first season earned her widespread critical acclaim, including the Golden Globe and Screen Actors Guild (SAG) Awards for best actress in a television drama.

PERSONAL LIFE
Foy lives in the United Kingdom with her husband and fellow actor, Stephen Campbell Moore, and their young daughter.

SUGGESTED READING
Gilbert, Gerard. "A Class Act: Claire Foy on Criticism, Tumours and Embarrassing Sex Scenes." *The Independent*, 17 Feb. 2012, www.independent.co.uk/news/people/profiles/a-class-act-claire-foy-on-criticism-tumours-and-embarrassing-sex-scenes-6940774.html. Accessed 27 Jan. 2017.

Saner, Emine. "Claire Foy: An Actor Bringing a Subtle Talent to Majestic Roles." *The Guardian*, 21 Aug. 2015, www.theguardian.com/tv-and-radio/2015/aug/21/claire-foy-actor-subtle-talent-majestic-roles-crown-wolf-hall. Accessed 27 Jan. 2017.

Tate, Gabriel. "Claire Foy Interview: The 'Wolf Hall' Star on Politics in the Tudor Court and Hollywood." *Independent*, 10 Jan. 2015, www.independent.co.uk/arts-entertainment/tv/features/claire-foy-interview-the-wolf-hall-star-on-politics-in-the-tudor-court-and-hollywood-9968549.html. Accessed 27 Jan. 2017.

Tate Gabriel. "'You See Them as Real Human Beings': Matt Smith and Claire Foy on Netflix's Royal Drama *The Crown*." *The Telegraph*, 1 Nov. 2016, www.telegraph.co.uk/on-demand/2016/11/01/you-see-them-as-real-human-beings-matt-smith-and-claire-foy-on-n. Accessed 27 Jan. 2017.

SELECTED WORKS
Little Dorrit, 2008; *Season of the Witch*, 2011; *The Promise*, 2011; *Upstairs Downstairs*, 2010–12; *Wolf Hall*, 2015; *The Crown*, 2016–

—*Christopher Mari*

Michael Fulmer

Date of birth: March 15, 1993
Occupation: Baseball player

Michael Fulmer, a right-handed pitcher for the Detroit Tigers, was named American League Rookie of the Year in 2016. Fulmer, who was drafted by the New York Mets out of high school in 2012 and traded to the Tigers in 2015, shocked baseball fans after pitching 33.3 straight innings without allowing a single run during his rookie season. Fulmer's is the second-longest stretch of scoreless innings by a rookie pitcher in the last forty-five years. Fulmer's secret weapon, his changeup, is a relatively new pitch in his arsenal, which also includes one of the hardest fastballs, at 96 mph, in the league. Just after he was called up, Fulmer worked with Tigers pitching coach, Rich Dubee, to perfect the pitch. He had thrown changeups before, but this time something about the loose grip of the pitch clicked.

Dubee told Dave Brown for *Vice* (21 Sept. 2016) that Fulmer "understood that he needed" a third pitch in addition to his deadly fastball and slider, which Blue Jays manager John Gibbons once compared to a "razor blade," as quoted by Brown. Fulmer's "baseball IQ allowed him to commit himself to doing what he had to do," Dubee told Brown. "He picked [the changeup] up pretty quickly and he started throwing a bunch of them when he got good results." According to teammates and coaches, Fulmer, who was also a serious contender for the Cy Young Award in 2016, is an intelligent player who asks smart questions and works hard to improve his game. He approaches baseball with the same technical, methodical mind that made him a strong math student and, in his unusual second career, makes him a good plumber. "Baseball is very humbling and it can humble you quickly," Veteran Tigers' second baseman Ian Kinsler told Brown. "You see Rookies of the Year and they're out of the game in the next four years. You've always got to try to improve yourself. This game's difficult. I think Michael's got the makeup to do that. He's going to be a lot of fun to watch."

EARLY LIFE AND HIGH SCHOOL CAREER

Fulmer was born in Lafayette, Louisiana, on March 15, 1993. His family moved to Tulsa, Oklahoma, when he was in the sixth grade, and then to Edmond, north of Oklahoma City, in 2005, when Fulmer was in the eighth grade. His father, J.P., works as a petroleum engineer and his mother, Lisa, is a legal secretary. He has a younger brother named Austin. Fulmer attended Deer Creek High School and played for the school's baseball team, the Antlers. In coach Ron Moore's eyes, at least at first, Fulmer was

By Keith Allison on Flickr (Original version) UCinternational (Crop) [CC BY-SA 2.0], via Wikimedia Commons

not a natural player. He was "chunky," Moore told Stephanie Apstein for *Sports Illustrated* (2 Feb. 2017); he had a strong arm, but then again, he had been cut from his Little League baseball team. In other words, he was a good player, but his talent did not appear to be anything special. But then, between freshman and sophomore year, Fulmer transformed. The pitcher grew five inches and his baby fat was replaced by muscle.

Fulmer joined the varsity team his sophomore year. He was one of the best players during his junior year, but it was during his senior year that he really established himself as a player to watch with his 95 mph fastball. Under Moore's guidance, he began playing third base and developed his hitting. That season, he hit .436 with 6 home runs and 43 RBIs, and was named the Oklahoman's Big All-City Baseball Player of the Year. His stats garnered him attention from Division I teams like the University of Texas, Wichita State, and Arkansas University. Fulmer graduated in 2011, and committed to play for the Arkansas Razorbacks, but as the June major league draft approached, insiders suggested the young pitcher might be drafted. "Mentally he's mature enough to do whatever he wants to do," Moore told Robert Przybylo for the *Oklahoman* (4 June 2011). "If he wants to go professional, he can hang with the 24-26-year-old guys out there." Later, Moore would recall the night Fulmer was drafted.

Family and friends gathered at the local Hooters chain restaurant when Fulmer got the call from New York Mets manager, David Wright. The franchise had selected him with the forty-fourth pick of the 2011 draft. The restaurant erupted in cheers and celebration. Moore told Anthony Fenech of the *Detroit Free Press* (13 Nov. 2016) that there was a feeling of collective pride. "Kind of like it's what we did," Moore said. "It wasn't really what Michael did. . . look what we did. It was a pretty neat atmosphere." The next morning, at 7:45 a.m., Moore recalled, Fulmer showed up to help Moore run a Little League baseball camp. Moore was flabbergasted; Fulmer just shrugged. "But that's just typical Michael," Moore explained to Fenech. Fulmer signed with the Mets, pocketing a $900,000 signing bonus, in July.

MINOR LEAGUE CAREER

Fulmer joined the Gulf Coast Mets, a rookie-level team in the Gulf Coast League, in Port St. Lucie, Florida, to finish out the 2011 season. In 2012, he joined the Savannah Sand Gnats, a Class-A minor league team. Fulmer thrived with the team, with a 2.74 ERA in 21 starts, but injuries sidelined Fulmer's early career. He underwent surgery after he tore his meniscus at spring training in 2013. Fulmer pitched only 46 innings that season, mostly with the Class-A Advanced St. Lucie Mets, but still managed to be named a top prospect within the Mets franchise. The next season, 2014, was another difficult one for the young player. Fulmer underwent another surgery for bone spurs and bone chips in his elbow, and his stats suffered. In 2015, Fulmer played one game with the St. Lucie Mets before transferring to Double-A Binghamton Rumble Ponies in New York. Fulmer took the league by storm, posting 1.88 ERA in 86 innings. At midseason, he was ranked the number eight prospect in the Mets franchise.

In July 2015, fifteen minutes before the trade deadline, Fulmer was traded, along with pitcher Luis Cessa, to the Detroit Tigers for outfielder Yoenis Cespedes. "It kind of was out of nowhere," Fulmer recalled to Howie Kussoy for the *New York Post* (11 June 2016). "I didn't have any idea. I walk inside and all my teammates start clapping, saying there's the new Tiger. They're watching MLB Network, my name and face are up there with Cespedes. That moment was kind of surreal [but] it was nice to be wanted." The Tigers assigned Fulmer to their Double-A affiliate, the Erie SeaWolves in Erie, Pennsylvania, keeping the pitcher in the Eastern League. Fulmer pitched 27.2 innings with the SeaWolves, posting a 2.60 ERA and striking out 29 batters. At the end of the season, he was named the Double-A Eastern League Pitcher of the Year.

ROOKIE OF THE YEAR

Fulmer, the number-one ranked prospect in the Tigers franchise, began the 2016 season with the Mud Hens, a Triple-A minor league team in Toledo, Ohio. He was called up on April 29, 2016, in a game against the Minnesota Twins after right-handed pitcher Shane Greene got a blister and was put on the disabled list. "I've been dreaming about this since I was four years old playing T-ball," he told George Sipple of the *Detroit Free Press* (28 Apr. 2016), adding that after he got the call he "put my face in my hands and took a moment." He started four games, but as pitching coach Dubee told him in mid-May: his signature fastball and slider were not enough to keep him in the major leagues. The two perfected Fulmer's changeup, and worked to change his pitching philosophy as well. Taken altogether, the changes radically altered his game. By the end of the season, insiders speculated that his changeup was the sixth-hardest pitch to hit in baseball. In June, he recorded a 33.3 inning scoreless streak—the second-longest scoreless streak by a rookie pitcher in forty-five years, and the longest streak by any Tigers pitcher since 1961. The feat, Tigers manager Brad Ausmus told Katie Strang for *ESPN* (18 June 2016), is "impressive for anyone" but "much more impressive for a rookie."

Still, Fulmer never took his position for granted. He fully expected to be shunted back to the minors, and lived in the same Detroit hotel room from April to October. He suffered a mid-season slump—relative to his attention-grabbing major league debut—and finished out the season with a 3.06 ERA. Yankees slugger Gary Sanchez made a strong bid for the Rookie of the Year prize after his major league debut later in the season, but Fulmer won the accolade handily, with twenty-six first place votes to Sanchez's four. In 2017 Fulmer has settled into his role as a starting pitcher, and sought out superstar pitcher Justin Verlander as a mentor. At the Tigers season opener on April 7, Fulmer threw six shut-out innings.

PERSONAL LIFE

Fulmer has worked as a plumber for a local Oklahoma company called Cyrus Wright Plumbing since the fall of 2014. From October to January, Fulmer joins the two-man operation three or four days a week, installing sinks, digging ditches for sewage lines, and fixing leaks. Fulmer enjoys the challenge of the work, but remarkably, has yet to be recognized by a client. Fulmer married his high school sweetheart, Kelsey Miles, in January 2016. The couple met during their first year of college, when Miles (now Fulmer) was working as the student manager of the baseball team. They live in Guthrie, Oklahoma.

SUGGESTED READING

Apstein, Stephanie. "No Pipe Dream: Tigers Pitcher Michael Fulmer Is the AL Rookie of the Year—And a Plumber." *Sports Illustrated*, 2 Feb. 2017, www.si.com/mlb/2017/02/02/michael-fulmer-tigers-rookie-year-plumber. Accessed 9 Apr. 2017.

Brown, Dave. "How Rookie Michael Fulmer Established Himself as the Tiger's New Ace." *Vice Sports*, 21 Sept. 2016, sports.vice.com/en_us/article/how-rookie-michael-fulmer-established-himself-as-the-tigers-new-ace. Accessed 9 Apr. 2017.

Fenech, Anthony. "Detroit Tigers' Michael Fulmer Shifts from Pitching to Plumbing." *Detroit Free Press*, 13 Nov. 2016, www.freep.com/story/sports/mlb/tigers/2016/11/13/detroit-tigers-michael-fulmer/93729076. Accessed 9 Apr. 2017.

Kussoy, Howie. "How Michael Fulmer Learned of Cespedes Trade: 'Kind of Surreal.'" *New York Post*, 11 June 2016, nypost.com/2016/06/11/how-michael-fulmer-learned-of-cespedes-trade-kind-of-surreal. Accessed 9 Apr. 2017.

Przybylo, Robert. "Big All-City Baseball Player of the Year: Deer Creek's Michael Fulmer Becomes Complete Player." *The Oklahoman*, 4 June 2011, newsok.com/article/3574391. Accessed 9 Apr. 2017.

Sipple, George. "Michael Fulmer Shocked to Hear He Was Called Up to Detroit Tigers." *Detroit Free Press*, 28 Apr. 2016, www.freep.com/story/sports/mlb/tigers/2016/04/28/detroit-tigers-michael-fulmer/83671752. Accessed 9 Apr. 2017.

Strang, Katie. "Michael Fulmer Sets Tigers Record but Sees Scoreless Streak End." *ESPN*, 18 June 2016, www.espn.com/blog/detroit-tigers/post/_/id/2120/tigers-michael-fulmer-sets-tigers-record-but-sees-scoreless-streak-come-to-an-end. Accessed 9 Apr. 2017.

—*Molly Hagan*

Julia Garner

Date of birth: February 1, 1994
Occupation: Actor

Julia Garner is gaining increasing recognition for her on-screen roles, becoming the "coil-haired poster girl of indie cinema," according to Brooke McCord for *Wonderland Magazine* (1 Oct. 2015). Similarly, in a profile for *Filler Magazine* (6 Aug. 2014), Jennifer Lee deemed Garner "an acclaimed staple on the film festival circuit" and praised her performances in such pictures as *Martha Marcy May Marlene* (2011), *Electrick Children* (2012), and *The Perks of Being a Wallflower* (2012). "Petit with a halo of blond curls and a voice that drips syrup, the actress's touch of the celestial lends itself to roles where

By Vera Mulyani [CC BY 2.0], via Wikimedia Commons

innocence and naivety are paramount character features," Lee wrote, noting Garner's portrayals of quirky but sympathetic characters, such as her role in *Electrick Children*. In this film, Garner plays Rachel, a sheltered Mormon teen who believes she has been impregnated by the sound of a man's voice singing a 1980s-era pop tune on a cassette tape.

Garner's reputation as an indie darling, however, may soon be in danger. In 2015, she appeared on the popular FX drama series *The Americans*, which follows the adventures of two Cold War–era Soviet spies posing as a married couple in a suburb of Washington, DC. In 2016, Garner joined such stars as Jaden Smith and Jimmy Smits in *The Get Down*, a Netflix drama directed by Baz Luhrmann. This series follows a group of teens coming of age in the Bronx, New York, in the 1970s. "I like anything with a good story," Garner asserted to McCord, "I mean, if you have a studio film with better writing and an indie film with poor writing, I would pick the studio film. But I only do things with stories that interest me. If it's bad writing, I'm just not going to go for it."

EARLY YEARS AND EDUCATION

Garner was born in Riverdale, New York, on February 1, 1994. Her father, Thomas, is an art teacher, and her mother, Tami, is a therapist and former actor. Her older sister, Anna, is an artist and writer who often uses social media to cheer her accomplishments. Garner grew up in a loving and open family atmosphere. "There were no secrets in my house," Garner recalled to Sean

T. Collins for *Vulture* (1 Apr. 2015), discussing the Soviet spy intrigue at the center of *The Americans.* "I always knew what was going on. When a child knows there's a secret, they don't know what it is, but they know it's there, and they know they're being lied to. When you know something's up, it's a very uneasy feeling."

The family often curled up on the sofa to watch Turner Classic Movies together. Garner's favorites included *Annie Hall*, *Rosemary's Baby*, and the 1928 film *The Student Prince in Old Heidelberg.* Upon seeing Bette Davis star in the cult classic *What Ever Happened to Baby Jane?* and the perennial classic *All About Eve*, Garner became fascinated by the actor. "I was like: 'Who's this woman? She's amazing,'" she told Kathryn Shattuck for the *New York Times* (1 Mar. 2013). "The first thing I noticed is that I forgot she was acting. [Davis] just lights up the screen," Garner marveled to Scott Macaulay for *Filmmaker* (19 July 2012), echoing sentiments critics would later express about her performances.

Seeking to overcome her shyness, Garner began taking acting lessons when she was fifteen years old. She studied with Pamela Scott at the acclaimed T. Schreiber Studio for Film and Theatre in Manhattan, New York. During one class, Garner had an epiphany. "I all of a sudden got lost in the moment," she recalled to Lee. "And when I snapped back into reality, I just really liked that feeling. I was like, What just happened? That was amazing! So I kind of just became addicted to it, and thought, this acting thing is unbelievable." When she announced her intention to pursue acting seriously, her mother, who knew the vicissitudes of the industry from firsthand experience, was supportive but cautious. "She was like, 'Are you sure? It's a really hard profession, you know,'" Garner told McCord.

ACTING BEGINNINGS

Garner started her acting career doing student films. While working with a film student at Columbia University, she heard about an audition for an American version of the British teen drama *Skins* and decided to audition. Although Garner made it to the final rounds, she was ultimately not cast. Fortunately for her, Susan Shopmaker, the casting director of the series, was also casting for the film *Martha Marcy May Marlene.*

Garner's first film was *Martha Marcy May Marlene*—she was sixteen at the time. The movie, which premiered at the 2011 Sundance Film Festival, unfolds the story of a young woman, played by Elizabeth Olsen, who escapes an abusive cult only to find her ability to heal emotionally hampered by painful memories. "From the actors to the [production assistants], it seemed like most of the people were just starting; it was a lot of people's first big thing, really," Garner recalled to Colleen Kelsey for *Interview* magazine

(14 June 2016). "It was really special. For me, I learned how to be on a movie set. I didn't know what it would be like. Basically, everything that I learned, it's from that movie."

In 2012, Garner appeared in *Electrick Children.* She self-taped her audition on a Monday, was hired the following Wednesday, and flew to Utah to start filming less than a week later. In Utah, Garner, raised in the Jewish faith in a relatively cosmopolitan region, was taken aback to see fundamentalist Mormon girls like her character strolling the streets sporting braids and long prairie dresses. In *Electrick Children*, directed by Rebecca Thomas, Garner stars as Rachel, a teenager growing up in a Mormon household. Rachel stumbles across a forbidden cassette tape and listens to a rendition of the Blondie classic "Hanging on the Telephone." When she discovers to her bewilderment that she is pregnant, she convinces herself that the man on the tape is involved. After her horrified parents attempt to arrange a hasty marriage to a local boy, she runs away to Las Vegas—hoping to find the man on the tape.

Electrick Children made something of a splash on the festival circuit and brought Garner a measure of critical acclaim. Calling it "a whimsical coming-of-ager lightened with a few fanciful elements," Justin Lowe wrote for the *Hollywood Reporter* (11 Nov. 2012) that "Garner is a revelation in Thomas's film, playing the divinely inspired teenager with rare conviction and authenticity."

MAINSTREAM SUCCESS AND *GRANDMA*

Also in 2012, Garner appeared in the film *The Perks of Being a Wallflower*, starring Logan Lerman, Emma Watson, and Ezra Miller. The film, released more widely than her previous films, marked her first involvement in a mainstream box-office success—albeit a modest one. *The Perks of Being a Wallflower* grossed almost $34 million worldwide.

In 2013 Garner starred as a young cannibal in *We Are What We Are*—the American remake of the Mexican horror film *Somos lo que hay.* The movie received a rapturous response when it screened at the 2013 Cannes Film Festival. "[The movie] is mostly about how [the sisters] relate to their mother's death," she explained to Macaulay. "It's weird—they don't exactly know what they are, and they don't know much harm they do." Macaulay, in turn, opined: "With her ethereal look . . . it's not surprising that Garner has played otherworldly characters. But what's striking about Garner is not just her presence, but also the utter naturalness of her performances."

In 2014, Garner reached a growing audience when she appeared alongside Joseph

Gordon-Levitt in the hard-boiled crime drama *Sin City: A Dame to Kill For*.

In 2015, Garner held her own on screen with veteran actor Lily Tomlin in *Grandma*, a road-trip movie with a twist. In the film, she plays Sage, a teenager forced to ask her gay grandmother for the money to pay for an abortion. The two embark on a quest to try to scrape together the cash, visiting various acquaintances and selling their possessions. "They usually just have the kid in the movie," Garner told Esther Zuckerman for *Refinery29* (19 Aug. 2015). "It's like, realistically, you're not going to have the kid. You're going to have an abortion." Although *Grandma* deals with the theme of abortion, she cautioned that it also contains broader themes. "The movie, at the end of the day, is not about abortion," Garner asserted. "It's about generations of women learning about one another and finding their shared history."

In addition to her work on the big screen, Garner has had recurring roles in the television dramas *The Americans* (2015–16) and *The Get Down* (2016–17). She is slated to appear in the upcoming Netflix series *Ozark* opposite Jason Bateman and Laura Linney. The series will revolve around a man in debt to a Mexican drug lord. Garner currently has multiple other projects in various stages of completion, including the sci-fi drama *Everything Beautiful Is Far Away* and the film *One Percent More Humid* alongside Juno Temple.

PERSONAL LIFE

Having grown up in New York, Garner never learned to drive. She does hope, however, to learn soon. "A lot of the movies that I'm in, I'm always in a car. I'm like, this is a sign," she quipped to Zuckerman.

In 2016, Garner modeled in a campaign for the design house Miu Miu; she also appeared on the cover of *Vogue Italia*. Journalists often comment on her classic sense of style. "Because my hair is really crazy, I don't like wearing things that are too, too crazy. I like things that are simple, but at the same time make a statement," Garner told Lee.

SUGGESTED READING

Garner, Julia. "Already a Cinema Veteran at 19." Interview by Kathryn Shattuck. *The New York Times*, 1 Mar. 2013, www.nytimes.com/2013/03/03/movies/julia-garner-in-electrick-children.html. Accessed 12 Feb. 2017.

Garner, Julia. "Here's What *Grandma* Star Julia Garner Learned from Working with Lily Tomlin." Interview by Kate Erbland. *IndieWire*, 20 Aug. 2015, www.indiewire.com/2015/08/heres-what-grandma-star-julia-garner-learned-from-working-with-lily-tomlin-59101. Accessed 12 Feb. 2017.

Garner, Julia. "Julia Garner." Interview by Colleen Kelsey. *Interview Magazine*, 14 June 2016, www.interviewmagazine.com/film/julia-garner. Accessed 12 Feb. 2017.

Garner, Julia. "Julia Garner on Her Difficult Role on *The Americans*, and Kimmy's 'Daddy Issues.'" Interview by Sean T. Collins. *Vulture*, 1 Apr. 2015, www.vulture.com/2015/04/americans-julia-garner-kimmys-daddy-issues.html. Accessed 12 Feb. 2017.

Garner, Julia. "Julia Garner on *Grandma*: 'You're Going to Have the Abortion.'" Interview by Esther Zuckerman. *Refinery29*, 19 Aug. 2015. www.refinery29.com/2015/08/92597/julia-garner-grandma-interview. Accessed 12 Feb. 2017.

Garner, Julia. "Simply Divine." Interview by Jennifer Lee. *Filler*, 6 Aug. 2014, fillermagazine.com/culture/film/celebrity-news-interviews-actress-julia-garner-of-sin-city-a-dame-to-kill-for. Accessed 12 Feb. 2017.

McCord, Brooke. "Best of the Next: Julia Garner." *Wonderland Magazine*, 1 Oct. 2015, www.wonderlandmagazine.com/2015/10/01/julia-garner. Accessed 12 Feb. 2017.

SELECTED WORKS

Martha Marcy May Marlene, 2011; *Electrick Children*, 2012; *The Perks of Being a Wallflower*, 2012; *We Are What We Are*, 2013; *Sin City: A Dame to Kill For*, 2014; *Grandma*, 2015; *The Americans*, 2015–16; *The Get Down*, 2016–17

—*Mari Rich*

Joachim Gauck

Date of birth: January 24, 1940
Occupation: Former President of Germany

Joachim Gauck became the eleventh president of the Federal Republic of Germany in March 2012, making it the first time that both the head of state and the head of government of Germany were from East Germany.

EARLY LIFE AND EDUCATION

Joachim Gauck was born on January 24, 1940, in Rostock, Germany, a large industrial city near the Baltic Sea. His father, for whom Gauck was named, was a ship captain and inspector in a shipbuilding company. His mother, Olga Gauck, was an office clerk.

After World War II ended, the Soviets occupied the region of Germany that included Rostock, and in 1949 it became the German Democratic Republic (GDR). Two years later Gauck's father was arrested for crimes against the state. Convicted of espionage and antidemagogy for possessing materials written in the West, he was sent to a forced labor camp in Siberia. He was released after four years, having suffered abuse that left him physically disabled.

His father's experiences in the Gulag and the Soviet occupation made a deep impression on the young Gauck and helped to shape his personal and political beliefs. He became a vehement opponent of communism and a firm supporter of human rights. Because he refused to join the Communist Youth Organization, he was not allowed to study journalism or most other subjects. Instead he studied theology at the University of Rostock from 1959 to 1965.

Upon the completion of his studies, he became a pastor of the Lutheran Church in East Germany. He became active in anticommunism groups and used his pulpit to preach support for human rights and freedom. He increasingly used the pulpit as a springboard for a growing anticommunism movement, leading people in prayers before they participated in mass demonstrations. He served as a pastor until 1982.

In 1989 Gauck helped found the prodemocracy movement New Forum and became one of its leaders. He was involved in protests that led to the end of one-party rule by the Soviet-backed Socialist Unity Party of Germany in late 1989.

POLITICAL CAREER

On March 18, 1990, the GDR held its first free elections, and Gauck was elected to the only democratic parliament of the GDR. He served as a member of the East Germany parliament until East Germany was reunited with West Germany in October 1990.

Following the reunification of Germany, Gauck became the federal commissioner of a new government agency that archived the records of the Stasi, the secret police of the former GDR. As commissioner, he gained national prominence for his work for civil rights, democracy, and anticommunism. He has been called Germany's "Nelson Mandela" for his human rights activism and dedication to individual freedom.

Gauck left the agency in 2000, then worked as a host for the TV show *Joachim Gauck*. From 2001 to 2004 he served as an honorary member for European Monitoring Centre on Racism and Xenophobia. From 2003 to 2012 he was the leader of the prodemocracy organization Gegen Vergessen–Für Demokratie (Against Forgetting–For Democracy).

In 2010 Gauck was nominated for the presidency of Germany, but he lost to Christian Wulff. In February 2012 Wulff resigned due to corruption allegations. Gauck, who has never belonged to a political party, ran for the presidency. He was hugely popular—in fact, many people had wanted him to win the 2010

election, but Chancellor Angela Merkel had backed Wulff at the time, which helped him to win. In 2012 Merkel initially failed to support Gauck, but she capitulated as his overwhelming support grew. Gauck had the support not only of the liberal Free Democrats, but of most major parties and the majority of the Federal Assembly. On March 18, Gauck won the election with 991 of the 1,228 valid votes cast. He was sworn into office on March 23.

Although the presidential position is ceremonial, it is highly influential because it represents Germany's moral authority. Shortly after becoming president, Gauck announced his intention to continue to advocate for human rights and freedom. He especially planned to focus on migrant-related issues and increasing Germany's role in international politics.

Gauck demonstrated his commitment to human rights in 2014 when he boycotted the Winter Olympics in Sochi, Russia, due to Russia's history of human rights abuses, which included a new law criminalizing gay propaganda.

Gauck has authored or coauthored several books, including *Freedom: A Plea* (2012). He also has received numerous honors, including the 1997 Hannah Arendt Prize.

IMPACT

In mid-2015 Gauck sought to become the moral compass not only of Germany, but of the international community when he called on world leaders to do more to help the millions of refugees fleeing Africa for Europe. He not only called for compassion and an increased willingness to accept refugees, but stressed the need for countries to work together to address humanitarian crises.

PERSONAL LIFE

Gauck has four children with Gerhild "Hansi" Radtke, whom he married in 1959. They separated in 1991. Gauck's partner since 2000 has been journalist Daniela Schadt, who served as the First Lady of Germany.

SUGGESTED READING

Der Bundespräsident [English]. Bundespräsidialamt, 2015. Web. 9 Oct. 2015.

Evans, Stephen. "Profile: Germany's Joachim Gauck." *BBC*. BBC, 18 Mar. 2012. Web. 9 Oct. 2015.

Marsh, Sarah. "Former Rights Activist Gauck to Become German President." *Reuters*. Thomson Reuters, 19 Feb. 2012. Web. 9 Oct. 2015.

"'Moral Duty' to Save Mediterranean Migrants, Says Gauck." *DW*. Deutsche Welle, 20 June 2015. Web. 9 Oct. 2015.

Oltermann, Philip. "German President Boycotts Sochi Winter Olympics." *Guardian*. Guardian

News and Media, 8 Dec. 2013. Web. 9 Oct. 2015.

Strategic Information and Developments. Vol. 1 of *Germany: Country Study Guide.* Washington: International Business Publications, 2013. Print.

Tronson, Mark. "Germany's New President a Protestant Minister Whose Key Word Is 'Freedom.'" *Christian Today.* Christian Media Corporation, 27 Mar. 2012. Web. 9 Oct. 2015.

—*Barb Lightner*

Tyrese Gibson

Date of birth: December 30, 1978
Occupation: Actor, singer

Tyrese Gibson is an award-winning actor, model, television personality, and R&B singer known for his Grammy-nominated music as well as his roles in film series *Fast and Furious* and *Transformers.*

EARLY LIFE AND EDUCATION

Tyrese Darnell Gibson was born on December 30, 1978, the youngest of four children, in the Watts neighborhood of Los Angeles, California. His father left the family in 1983, leaving Gibson's mother Priscilla Murray Gibson to raise the children alone. Gibson's early life was challenging growing up in Watts, which was a tough neighborhood with increased violence and gang activity. Also, because of his family's financial situation, he often went without eating during the day, which led him to join an after-school program that provided meals and where he met music teacher Reggie Andrews. Andrews encouraged Gibson to pursue his singing talent and audition in local competitions. As a teenager, he would compete in talent shows around Watts, and his obvious talent for singing landed him a part in a 1994 Coca-Cola commercial in which Gibson sings a soulful version of the "Always Coca-Cola" jingle.

Gibson's performance in the commercial caught the attention of members of the fashion industry, and in 1995, he began modeling for the fashion lines Guess and Tommy Hilfiger. During his modeling work, Gibson continued to pursue a singing career. After three years he was given a recording contract by RCA Records, who released his debut album *Tyrese* on September 29, 1998.

LIFE'S WORK

Tyrese went on to sell over a million copies in the United States and earn Gibson the 2000 favorite

soul/R&B new artist award from the American Music Awards. The album's single "Sweet Lady" received a 2000 Grammy nomination for best R&B vocal performance, male. At the same time his singing career was taking off, Gibson also pursued a career in acting. After working as an MTV VJ on the popular music cable television network in the late 1990s, Gibson appeared in the television drama *Love Song* (2000).

Gibson's role in *Love Song* was small, but his next role was as the lead in the 2001 urban drama *Baby Boy* (2001). The movie, which director John Singleton explained is not a follow-up to his 1991 hit *Boyz 'n the Hood* but rather a complement to it, follows Gibson's character, Joseph "Jody" Summers, an unemployed African American father in Los Angeles who still lives with his mother. The film was well received by critics, but it was Gibson's performance that stood out among critics and audiences alike. His performance earned him a nomination for outstanding actor in a motion picture at the 2002 Image Awards. The song "Just a Baby Boy," which is from *2000 Watts* (2001), Gibson's second studio album, was featured on the *Baby Boy* soundtrack.

Gibson was nominated for a 2002 Image Award for outstanding hip-hop artist for *2000 Watts,* and his third album, *I Wanna Go There* (2002) sold 500,000 copies in the United States and earned him a second Grammy nomination. His fourth album, *Alter Ego* (2006), was not as popular.

Gibson worked with Singleton again in the action drama *2 Fast 2 Furious* (2003), a sequel to the hugely popular *The Fast and the Furious* (2001), in the role of Roman Pearce, a wisecracking convict who joins a crew of car thieves. He reprised the role in the sequels *Fast Five* (2011), *Fast & Furious 6* (2013), and *Furious 7* (2015). He is scheduled to appear in two subsequent sequels in the franchise, *Fast 8,* which is scheduled to be released in 2017, and *Fast and Furious 9,* which is scheduled to be released in 2019. Gibson also collaborated with Singleton in the film *Four Brothers* (2005), about a group of brothers avenging the death of their mother.

Gibson has had roles in other notable films, including the military drama *Annapolis* (2006) and the crime drama *Waist Deep* (2006). The latter film earned him a Black Movie Award nomination for outstanding performance by an actor in a leading role. In 2007, he played a sergeant in the big-budget science fiction action film *Transformers* (2007), which earned over $700 million at the box office. He reprised this role in the sequels *Transformers: Revenge of the Fallen* (2009) and *Transformers: Dark of the Moon* (2011).

Gibson earned a Grammy nomination for best R&B album for his fifth album, *Open Invitation* (2011). In 2013, Gibson teamed up with friends and fellow artists Ginuwine and Tank to release their first studio album as the group TGT. *Three Kings* debuted at number three on the Billboard 200. Gibson's sixth studio album, *Black Rose*, was released in 2015 and debuted at number one on the Billboard 200. The single "Shame" was nominated for two Grammy awards: best traditional R&B performance and best R&B song.

In 2012, the Trumpet Awards honored Gibson with their Pinnacle Award, which recognizes African Americans who succeeded against poverty and racism.

IMPACT

Gibson grew up in poverty, in a neighborhood plagued by gang violence, and went on to become a renowned singing and acting talent. He has used his fame to help support several charities, particularly ones that focus on at-risk and disadvantaged youths in the inner cities.

PERSONAL LIFE

Gibson married Norma Mitchell in 2007 and they divorced in 2009. They have a daughter, Shayla Somer. Gibson lives in Los Angeles.

SUGGESTED READING

Caito, Angela. "Tyrese Gibson Shares His Life with the World in Exclusive Interview." *News Hub*. News Hub, 30 Mar. 2015. Web. 13 May 2016.

Douglas, Edward. "Tyrese Gibson on His Fourth Turn as Roman in 'Furious 7.'" *Coming Soon*. Crave Online Media, 30 Mar. 2015. Web. 13 May 2016.

Flanigan, Sarah. "Tyrese Talks Real-Life Connection to First Acting Role in 'Baby Boy.'" *Entertainment Tonight*. CBS Studios, 23 Mar. 2015. Web. 12 May 2016.

Larson, Jeremy D. "A Long Conversation with Tyrese about Race, 'Empire,' and 'Black Rose.'" *Radio*. CBS Local Media, 18 Aug. 2015. Web. 12 May 2016.

Valentini, Valentina I. "Tyrese Builds His Own Empire." *Ebony*. Ebony Magazine, 14 Oct. 2015. Web. 13 May 2016.

SELECTED WORKS

Tyrese, 1998; *2000 Watts*, 2001; *Baby Boy*, 2001; *2 Fast 2 Furious*, 2003; *Transformers*, 2007; *Black Rose*, 2015

—*Patrick G. Cooper*

Adam Gidwitz

Date of birth: February 14, 1982
Occupation: Author

Children's author Adam Gidwitz was a teacher before he discovered his talent for capturing the attention and imagination of young people as a storyteller. His first three books reimagined Grimm brothers' tales through the point of view of a modern narrator: *A Tale Dark and Grimm* (2010), *In a Glass Grimmly* (2012), and *The Grimm Conclusion* (2013). He is also the author of *Star Wars—The Empire Strikes Back: So You Want to Be a Jedi?* (2015), the second volume in a series for young readers that retells the three original Star Wars films; and *The Inquisitor's Tale: Or, The Three Magical Children and Their Holy Dog* (2016). Inspired by Geoffrey Chaucer's *The Canterbury Tales*, *The Inquisitor's Tale* presents the story of three unique children with superpowers in thirteenth century France. The book was designated one of three Newbery Honor Books for 2017 by the Association of Library Service to Children, a division of the American Library Association (ALA).

EARLY LIFE AND EDUCATION

Adam Gidwitz was born in 1982 in San Francisco, California. When he was just a few years old, he and his family moved to Baltimore, where he lived until it was time to leave for college. In the mini-autobiography that appears on his official website, Gidwitz said he often got in trouble at school when he was a kid. He

Larry D. Moore [CC BY-SA 4.0], via Wikimedia Commons

was at the principal's office, he wrote, throughout "my entire middle school career." He got his act together in high school, however, and after graduating from the Park School of Baltimore in 2000, he moved to New York City to attend Columbia University.

At Columbia, Gidwitz considered several majors, namely religion and philosophy, before choosing English literature. He finally decided upon English literature because, he wrote on his site, "I think that the deepest truths about life tend to be written in works of fiction." Also, he wrote, he was thrilled to have a reading list of several books as his homework. During his freshman year, he volunteered working with elementary school students as part of the East Harlem Tutorial Program. The following year he became more involved with the program and would continue to stay in touch with some of the pupils.

LEARNING TALES

Another significant time during his college years was his junior year abroad in England as part of the Oxford/Cambridge Scholars Program. He had a lot of free time, much of which he spent walking around, reading the poetry of John Keats, and writing. Despite having a lot of time, or perhaps because of it, he began to schedule and manage his time better so he could write on a regular basis. In fact, Gidwitz wrote on his site, he would later realize that it had been during his year abroad in England that he had "discovered I could be a writer."

Even though he enjoyed the well-known Grimm brothers' stories when he was a kid, he did not delve into them as serious works of literature until he was a university student. According to a profile by Grace Laidlaw for *Columbia College Today* (Mar./Apr. 2011), a major turning point in Gidwitz's thinking about the Grimm brothers' tales occurred during a seminar he took on children's books, which was taught by Karl Kroeber. "Kroeber taught Gidwitz to look at Grimm—and other children's literature, including *Winnie the Pooh* and the Harry Potter series—from an academic standpoint," wrote Laidlaw. Speaking to Laidlaw, Gidwitz said, "I learned to take the stories for what they were rather than imposing my own structure on the text."

TEACHING TALES

After graduating from Columbia, in 2004, Gidwitz taught at St. Ann's School, a private K–12 academy in the New York City borough of Brooklyn. He simultaneously studied in the evenings at the Bank Street College of Education. After he received a master's degree in general education and special education from Bank Street College, Gidwitz continued teaching at St. Ann's, where, according to Laidlaw, he has taught elementary,

middle, and high school students "everything from basic math to advanced literary theory."

It was at St. Ann's that the idea of creating new versions of Grimm stories occurred to Gidwitz. Substituting for a school librarian, he read *Grimms' Tales for Young and Old* to grade-school students, but with his own flair. He would use dramatic pauses, foreshadowing (hinting at plot twists), and just kidding around to further engage his young listeners. And it worked. He says that even though he is a teacher, his fairy tales are not intended to have a specific lesson or moral. "The Grimm brothers don't moralize," Gidwitz told Laidlaw. "Instead, they use symbol, magic, and laughter to help children discover and navigate their own interior lives. My goal is the same."

THE GRIMM BOOKS

The first volume in Gidwitz's Grimm Books trilogy is *A Tale Dark and Grimm* (2010), in which the main characters, Hansel and Gretel, exit their own story to experience new adventures in an alternative version of old fairy tales. The reviews were somewhat mixed, but were positive overall. "The narrator contributes unnecessary platitudes," according to the *Kirkus Review* (24 Sept. 2010), "but on the plus side, savvily warns when little kids should leave the room, effectively cautioning big kids that upcoming content is sad or gory—and it really is. . . . Old Grimm tales and Gidwitz's original additions weave together into one arc, with fiercely loyal siblings Hansel and Gretel at the heart." A reviewer for *Publishers Weekly* (18 Oct. 2010) also expressed a slight reservation about the narrator, but generally praised Gidwitz for humor and originality: "The rhythms and rhetoric of the prose are heavily influenced by verbal storytelling, which can on occasion strike a false note, but mostly add the intended wry wink to an audacious debut that's wicked smart and wicked funny."

His second book of stories, *In a Glass Grimmly* (2012), featured Jack, Jill, and a frog, all in search of a magic mirror. A reviewer for *Publishers Weekly* (6 Aug. 2012) called it "more enjoyable" than his first book, because it was funnier and grislier. It was also more original than his first book, less reliant on retelling old fairy tales. "Parental cruelties," wrote the reviewer, "are more ordinary this time—mockery, neglect, and recrimination—but what the children find in their quest for the Seeing Glass is horrifying enough to compensate for any perceived softness at the outset."

The third and final book of the series, titled *The Grimm Conclusion* (2013), followed brother and sister Joringel and Jorinda through a series of Grimm-inspired tales. Although the characters' names are new, the stories offer much of what the previous two books offered: grotesque and humorous tales of murder, misadventure, neglect, and violence. A writer for *Kirkus Review* (31 Aug. 2013) pointed out that the narrator seems to have an even larger presence in this final book: "So intrusive a narrator that even his characters hear him, Gidwitz offers commentary and (necessarily frequent) warnings about upcoming shocks. He then later steps in to shepherd his protagonists to modern Brooklyn for some metafictional foolery before closing with notes on his sources."

SO YOU WANT TO BE A JEDI?

In 2015 Disney/Lucasfilm Press released a trilogy of Star Wars–based books for readers in grades three to six, with each volume in the trilogy retelling one of the three original Star Wars films. Gidwitz wrote the second volume, titled *Star Wars—The Empire Strikes Back: So You Want to Be a Jedi?* In the author's note at the beginning of the book, Gidwitz anticipates that some of his readers might be surprised that he has chosen to write about a Star Wars episode. In response, he explains that George Lucas, creator of the original Star Wars franchise, had always thought of the saga as a modern fairy tale, saying (as quoted by Gidwitz) that the films are a "tool that can be used to make old stories be new, and relate to younger people"—which, Gidwitz writes, is exactly what he was trying to do with the Grimm tales. Gidwitz goes on to write that Luke, as a character, may seem "a little bland. A little empty," but that this quality makes him, like other archetypal heroes, an avatar for the reader, who may then "inhabit" the avatar character within the narrative. Gidwitz then invites readers to become Luke, saying that they will need to do so in order to become Jedis. Accordingly, the narrator addresses the reader as "you" and tells the story as if the reader was Luke in some chapters, while chapters that follow Leia, Han, and other characters are narrated from the more conventional third person perspective. Interspersed between chapters are Jedi lessons, training exercises, and tests, which the narrator provides for the reader.

THE INQUISITOR'S TALE

After *So You Want to Be a Jedi?*, Gidwitz published—with illustrator Hatem Aly—*The Inquisitor's Tale: Or, The Three Magical Children and Their Holy Dog* (2016). This time the structure of the story is based not on tales of the Brothers Grimm but on Chaucer's *The Canterbury Tales*. Set in France in the year 1242, the book tells the tale of three children: William, an incredibly strong, biracial monk who is on a mission from his monastery; Jacob, a Jewish boy who has fled his burning village and has the ability to heal the sick; and Jeanne, a peasant girl who has prophetic visions yet hides them. They are on the move to escape persecution and prejudice.

"What Gidwitz . . . accomplishes here is staggering," wrote Soman Chainani for the *New York Times* (7 Oct. 2016). "'The Inquisitor's Tale' is equal parts swashbuckling epic, medieval morality play, religious polemic and bawdy burlesque, propelling us toward a white-knuckle climax where three children must leap into a fire to save . . . a Talmud. And yet, the rescue of this single book feels like higher stakes than any world-incinerating superhero battle." One of the reasons the book works so well, wrote Chainani, is because Gidwitz has managed to make these three characters feel human, like real children, despite their superhuman abilities.

PERSONAL LIFE

Gidwitz lives in the New York City borough of Brooklyn with his wife, Lauren Mancia. According to Gidwitz, the couple met in a college class on Chaucer. Mancia teaches medieval history at Brooklyn College.

SUGGESTED READING

Chainani, Soman. "Are the Children in This Novel Saints, or Heretics?" Review of *The Inquisitor's Tale: Or, Three Magical Children and Their Holy Dog*, by Adam Gidwitz. *The New York Times*, 7 Oct. 2016, www.nytimes.com/2016/10/09/books/review/inquisitors-tale-adam-gidwitz-hatem-aly.html. Accessed 15 May 2017.

Gidwitz, Adam. "Q & A with Adam Gidwitz." Interview by Sue Corbett. *Publishers Weekly*, 27 Sept. 2016, www.publishersweekly.com/pw/by-topic/childrens/childrens-authors/article/71596-q-a-with-adam-gidwitz.html. Accessed 15 May 2017.

Gidwitz, Adam. "What Makes a Children's Book Good?" *The New Yorker*, 3 Oct. 2016, www.newyorker.com/culture/cultural-comment/the-goosebumps-conundrum-what-makes-a-childrens-book-good. Accessed 15 May 2017.

Gidwitz, Adam. "The Writer's Block: An Interview with Adam Gidwitz." Interview by Kevin Springer. *Middle Grade Mafia*, 30 Apr. 2015, middlegrademafia.com/2015/04/30/the-writers-block-an-interview-with-adam-gidwitz. Accessed 15 May 2017.

Laidlaw, Grace. "Adam Gidwitz '04 Reinvents the Brothers Grimm." *Columbia College Today*, Mar./Apr. 2011, www.college.columbia.edu/cct/archive/mar_apr11/bookshelf1. Accessed 15 May 2017.

Review of *Star Wars—The Empire Strikes Back: So You Want to Be a Jedi?*, by Adam Gidwitz. *Kirkus*, 5 Sept. 2015, www.kirkusreviews.com/book-reviews/adam-gidwitz/so-you-want-to-be-jedi. Accessed 15 May 2017.

Review of *The Grimm Conclusion*, by Adam Gidwitz. *Kirkus*, 31 Aug. 2013, www.

kirkusreviews.com/book-reviews/adam-gid-witz/the-grimm-conclusion/. Accessed 15 May 2017.

SELECTED WORKS
A Tale Dark and Grimm, 2010; *In a Glass Grimmly*, 2012; *The Grimm Conclusion*, 2013; *Star Wars—The Empire Strikes Back: So You Want to Be a Jedi?*, 2015; *The Inquisitor's Tale: Or, The Three Magical Children and Their Holy Dog*, 2016

—Dmitry Kiper

Brendan Smialowski / Stringer for Getty Images News

Jeffrey Goldberg

Date of birth: September 22, 1965
Occupation: Editor in chief of the *Atlantic*

In October 2016 Jeffrey Goldberg, a highly respected journalist who had written for a host of notable periodicals, was tapped to become the next editor in chief of the *Atlantic*, one of the oldest and most venerated magazines published in the United States. Goldberg, who had been serving as a national correspondent for the *Atlantic* since 2007, succeeded James Bennet. As the magazine's fourteenth editor in chief since its founding in 1857, Goldberg looks to continue the *Atlantic's* adherence to high-quality long-form journalism, while at the same time hoping to continue its expansion into new formats in the digital age. He also brings to it a passionate commitment to a better understanding of international affairs, particularly issues pertaining to the Middle East, where he served as both a foreign correspondent and as a member of the Israel Defense Forces when he was a young man. A central theme of his reporting throughout his career has been the relationship of the Jewish people to the wider world and how that relationship plays out both in the United States and abroad.

The *Atlantic's* president, Bob Cohn, and its parent company's owner, David G. Bradley, explained that they had searched for months and considered hundreds of top-tier journalists for the position. They ultimately chose Goldberg, in large part because he "exemplifies *Atlantic* editorial values: he's smart, creative, resourceful, and iconoclastic—and has a sense of humor to go with his core commitment to fairness and integrity," Cohn stated, as quoted by Krishnadev Calamur in the *Atlantic* (11 Oct. 2016).

FORMATIVE YEARS

Being Jewish has been central to Jeffrey Goldberg's identity since childhood. Born in 1965 in the Brooklyn borough of New York City, New York, to Daniel and Ellen H. Goldberg, he and his family moved to Malverne on the south shore of Long Island during his childhood. There, he discovered how his Judaism made him stand out uncomfortably in a community of mostly Irish American, Catholic neighbors. In interviews he has recalled being jumped by Irish kids in middle school because he was Jewish and how he learned to fight back from African American children who were similarly mistreated. "I knew well that Jews were disliked—I knew this in an uncomfortably personal way," he wrote of his childhood in his 2006 book *Prisoners: A Muslim and a Jew across the Middle East Divide*. "I didn't like the dog's life of the Diaspora. We were a whipped and boneless people."

His experiences quickly made him a fledgling Zionist—a supporter of the maintenance of a Jewish homeland in the Middle East, specifically the state of Israel. He read numerous books by a range of Zionist leaders and was deeply impacted by accounts of the Holocaust. He summered in the Catskills at a socialist Zionist camp and, after a bar mitzvah trip to Israel, dreamed of living in Israel and joining the Israel Defense Forces.

SPENDING TIME IN ISRAEL

Goldberg studied for a short time in the mid-1980s at the University of Pennsylvania but left without completing a degree. In interviews, he has explained that while attending the university, he became more invested in his editorial role with the institution's newspaper, *The Daily Pennsylvanian*, than his studies or classes. "I knew what I wanted to do. It was a fantastic adventure, where you got to go anywhere and do anything. It taught me that journalism could be the shortcut to interesting things—and it certainly made academic work at the time pale in comparison," he told Jordana Horn for the *Pennsylvania Gazette* (May/June 2011) regarding his experience writing for the paper. Still intent on going to Israel, he took a leave of absence from school to accomplish his goal.

Expecting to shed his American identity in favor of an Israeli one, he spent his first weeks and months in Israel on a kibbutz as an agricultural worker before joining the Israeli army. During his training, he was thrilled by his experience. However, his initial enthusiasm dissipated after he was assigned to serve as a police officer at a large prison in the Negev desert called Ketziot. Most of his interactions were with Palestinian prisoners, which led him to question his reason for being in the army. After completing his service, he worked for a brief period as a humor columnist for the *Jerusalem Post*. Then, realizing he was too tied to his American upbringing and sensibility, he left Israel. In an interview with *New York* (16 Oct. 2006), he told Boris Kachka why he left Israel: "I grew up venerating the Freedom Riders, not Bull Connor, and I didn't want to carry a nightstick. But you can't hold a country to the standard of perfection that I held Israel to. It's a real place with real people."

EARLY CAREER

After returning to the United States, Goldberg sought work as a journalist. Having already worked as a police reporter for the *Washington Post*, he became the New York bureau chief for the *Forward* before going on to cover the Mafia and other organized crime for *New York* and write about the Middle East and Africa for the *New York Times Magazine*. In 2000 he joined the staff of the *New Yorker*, where he served as the magazine's Middle East correspondent and Washington, DC, correspondent. It was during this period that he came to be recognized as one of the leading reporters on the Middle East, writing from such varied countries as Iraq, Afghanistan, Pakistan, Egypt, Syria, and Lebanon, as well as in such places as the Gaza Strip and the West Bank. In addition to interviewing leaders of such radical organizations as Hezbollah, al-Qaeda, and the Taliban, among others, he also got to know all of the major political leaders in Washington and internationally.

In the run-up to the war in Iraq (2003–11), during which the George W. Bush administration argued that the Iraqi dictator Saddam Hussein should be overthrown because of his unwillingness to give up his weapons of mass destruction, as required by United Nations' resolutions, Goldberg found himself favoring Hussein's overthrow. This was due in part to the

dictator's brutal tactics against his own people, as well as a feeling in the world after the terrorist attacks on September 11, 2001, that threats to US security should be neutralized before they come to bear on US citizens. "Saddam Hussein is uniquely evil, the only ruler in power today—and the first one since Hitler—to commit chemical genocide," against the Kurds, Goldberg wrote for *Slate* (3 Oct. 2002). "Is that enough of a reason to remove him from power? I would say yes, if 'never again' is in fact actually to mean 'never again.'"

Goldberg's growing expertise and thoroughness in covering radical Middle Eastern politics earned him and the *New Yorker* a National Magazine Award from the American Society of Magazine Editors in 2003. The award was given to recognize his reporting skills in writing the piece "In the Party of God," about the militant Lebanese organization Hezbollah.

PRISONERS

In 2006, Goldberg published his memoir, *Prisoners*, about his experiences growing up and his time in the Israeli army. Largely well received, the book describes his relationship with Rafiq Hijazi, a prisoner he met while serving as a guard at Ketziot in 1991. He goes on to describe how their on-again, off-again friendship developed through the years, including their time in Washington, while Goldberg was a reporter and Rafiq, who was becoming more and more fundamentalist in his beliefs, was earning his doctorate in statistics.

The book earned considerable praise upon its publication. Writing for the *New York Times* (12 Nov. 2006), Elena Lappin called *Prisoners* "a lucid, richly layered memoir." In a review for the *Washington Post* (29 Oct. 2006), Haim Watzman called the book a "sensitive, forthright and perceptive account," and remarked, "*Prisoners* offers a modicum of hope but also a healthy dose of despair. These days, the work of bringing peace to Israel and Palestine often looks like an impossible mission. Still, as the Jewish sages taught, even if we cannot hope to complete the task, we are not allowed to shirk it."

THE *ATLANTIC*

Goldberg would remain at the *New Yorker* until 2007, when he left the magazine to become a national correspondent for the *Atlantic*. Between 2007 and 2016, he wrote eleven cover stories for the *Atlantic*, as well as numerous pieces for the magazine's website. In addition to conducting interviews with major politicians such as former president Barack Obama, former secretary of state Hillary Clinton, and former British prime minister David Cameron, his work has looked at such issues as whether or not Jews should leave Europe, if Israel should attack Iranian nuclear facilities, and the pros and cons of Obama's foreign policy during his presidency. In 2011, Andrea Mitchell, chief foreign affairs correspondent for NBC News, told Horn that Goldberg "is not your average reporter, who goes to briefings and spews out the info that's handed to him. He digs and travels and has great sources overseas, and he's original. He has a rising reputation as one of the most thoughtful people about Middle East policy."

In October 2016, Cohn announced that Goldberg had been promoted to serve as the magazine's editor in chief. He would take over stewardship of the magazine at a critical time, as the *Atlantic* was continuing its transformation into a multimedia news organization but was still characterized by a commitment to serious, long-form, quality journalism. Print sales continued to be strong, and the *New York Times* reported that, within the United States, the magazine's website drew nineteen million unique online visitors in August 2016 alone, which was an increase of about 50 percent from the previous year. Despite being familiar with the *Atlantic*'s values and teams, Goldberg intimated that he would be conducting a thorough amount of research to determine the best way to fulfill his new role and the task of bringing the publication forward, just as he would for writing a story. "The challenge is to maintain somewhere between dramatic and explosive growth on all platforms while adhering to *Atlantic* standards and being true to the *Atlantic*'s history and purpose," he explained to Jake Sherman for *Politico* (14 Oct. 2016). He also expressed confidence in the magazine's place within the publishing industry. "The miracle of the *Atlantic* is this is literally a nineteenth-century brand that is firing on all pistons in a really ruthless twenty-first-century media environment," he said to Sydney Ember for the *New York Times* (11 Oct. 2016).

Not long after his promotion, it was announced that Goldberg was also being honored with Georgetown University's Institute for the Study of Diplomacy prestigious 2016 Edward Weintal Prize for Diplomatic Reporting. Recognizing his entire journalism career, the institute also specifically noted the significance of his early 2016 *Atlantic* article "The Obama Doctrine," which details the former president's foreign policies discussed over several interviews.

PERSONAL LIFE

Goldberg has been married to Pamela Ress Reeves since 1993. They have three children. He has received numerous awards for his journalism, including, among others, the Overseas Press Club Joe & Laurie Dine Award, the Abraham Cahan Prize in Journalism, and the 2005 Anti-Defamation League's Daniel Pearl Award.

SUGGESTED READING

Calamur, Krishnadev. "*The Atlantic*'s New Editor in Chief." *The Atlantic*, 11 Oct. 2016, www.theatlantic.com/news/archive/2016/10/jeffrey-goldberg-atlantic-editor-in-chief/503573/. Accessed 10 May 2017.

Ember, Sydney. "*Atlantic* Names Jeffrey Goldberg Its Editor in Chief." *The New York Times*, 11 Oct. 2016, www.nytimes.com/2016/10/12/business/atlantic-is-expected-to-name-jeffrey-goldberg-its-editor-in-chief.html. Accessed 10 May 2017.

Goldberg, Jeffrey. "Brave Heart: Jeffrey Goldberg." Interview by Boris Kachka. *New York*, 16 Oct. 2006, nymag.com/arts/books/profiles/22294/. Accessed 10 May 2017.

Goldberg, Jeffrey. "The Playbook Interview: Jeffrey Goldberg." Interview by Jake Sherman. *Politico*, 14 Oct. 2016, www.politico.com/story/2016/10/the-playbook-interview-jeffrey-goldberg-229783. Accessed 10 May 2017.

Horn, Jordana. "Journalism, Jews, and Jeffrey Goldberg." *The Pennsylvania Gazette*, May/June 2011, www.upenn.edu/gazette/0511/PennGaz0511_feature4.pdf. Accessed 10 May 2017.

Starobin, Paul. "Jeffrey Goldberg, Washington's Most Pugnacious Journalist." *Washingtonian*, 29 Jan. 2013, www.washingtonian.com/2013/01/29/jeffrey-goldberg-washingtons-most-pugnacious-journalist/. Accessed 10 May 2017.

SELECTED WORKS

"The Great Terror," *New Yorker*, 25 Mar. 2002; "In the Party of God," *New Yorker*, Oct. 2002; *Prisoners: A Muslim and a Jew across the Middle East Divide*, 2006; "The Obama Doctrine," *Atlantic*, Apr. 2016

—*Christopher Mari*

Sara Goldrick-Rab

Date of Birth: ca. 1977
Occupation: Professor

According to Sara Goldrick-Rab, the affordability and accessibility of higher education is one of the most significant issues facing the United States in the early twenty-first century. "Affordability is a much bigger deal [to undergraduates] than policy people currently think," she explained to Karen Herzog for the Milwaukee *Journal Sentinel* (21 Jan. 2016). "The amount of money in financial aid is insufficient, the delivery system is too complex, too few people are helped, and the current situation is driving

Sara Goldrick-Rab/Wikimedia Commons

students to drop out of college. The approach is not cost effective."

A professor of higher education and sociology at Temple University who previously spent more than a decade at the University of Wisconsin–Madison, Goldrick-Rab has devoted her career to exploring policies that are already in place and ways in which such efforts can be improved. In addition to authoring numerous influential studies as well as several books, including the 2016 book *Paying the Price: College Costs, Financial Aid, and the Betrayal of the American Dream*, she has sought to influence higher-education policy on multiple levels, from national to local. Goldrick-Rab has not shied away from controversy on that quest, sparking public debate over her outspoken opposition to politicians such as Wisconsin governor Scott Walker as well as to members of the University of Wisconsin leadership. Above all, however, she hopes to raise awareness of the issues surrounding higher education. "There are so many people who have their eyes closed so tightly to what is going on in the world," she told Emily Scott for the *Temple News* (6 Sept. 2016). "I need to go open those eyes."

EARLY LIFE AND EDUCATION

Sara Goldrick-Rab was born Sara Youcha Rab, one of two daughters born to Sydney Rab and Victoria Youcha. Her father was a lawyer who eventually came to work for the Virginia attorney general's office, while her mother was an academic specializing in early childhood education. Goldrick-Rab and her sister, Lisa, grew up in Fairfax, Virginia, not far from Washington, DC.

As a child and teenager, Goldrick-Rab was acutely aware of the importance of attending college. "I've always kind of understood the privileges I have and that were given to me because my grandparents went to college," she told Scott. "There was a legacy in my family of college-going that I always understood to be a big deal." However, despite that legacy and her mother's own career in academia, Goldrick-Rab was not yet drawn to studying higher education as a career, nor was she yet devoted to a particular discipline.

After graduating from high school, Goldrick-Rab initially enrolled at the College of William and Mary in Williamsburg, Virginia. She later transferred to George Washington University in Washington, DC, where she pursued a degree in sociology, which proved to be her area of interest. "I was immediately attracted to sociology because it was about real people's lives," she recalled to Scott. While at George Washington University, she also became a member of the Phi Beta Kappa honor society. She earned her bachelor's degree from the university in 1998. Following her time at George Washington University, Goldrick-Rab left the Washington, DC, area to pursue graduate studies at the University of Pennsylvania in Philadelphia. She earned her master's degree in sociology in 2001 and completed her doctorate three years later.

UNIVERSITY OF WISCONSIN–MADISON

After completing her doctorate, Goldrick-Rab began her job search still unsure whether she wanted to be a professor. "I spent most of graduate school saying I was not going to be a professor, I was going to be an applied researcher at a research shop in New York or Washington," she told Todd Finkelmeyer for the Madison, Wisconsin, *Capital Times* (2 May 2011). She continued, "I didn't want to be in an ivory tower. I really wanted to make a difference and I really wanted to engage with policy, with students."

Goldrick-Rab remained opposed to the idea of becoming a professor even after seeing a posting for a position at the University of Washington–Madison that seemed closely aligned with her academic background and professional interests. She reconsidered, however, after multiple friends sent her the same job posting. After applying and making her way through the interview process, Goldrick-Rab was offered the position of assistant professor at the University of Wisconsin–Madison in 2004.

Having at last decided to pursue a career in academia, Goldrick-Rab nevertheless found it difficult to adjust to her newfound career path at times. "My students knew more than I did," Goldrick-Rab told Scott of her early days at the university. "That is so humbling. I went home after teaching the first couple times and just cried because of how insecure I felt, but what it did was push me to be a much better faculty member." Over the course of more than a decade, Goldrick-Rab advanced from assistant professor to associate professor, and in 2014 she was promoted to full professor. She was likewise granted tenure, achieving that milestone in 2011.

While at the University of Wisconsin–Madison, Goldrick-Rab developed an interest in blogging and social media, which were beginning to become widely popular. Her blog, *The Education Optimists*, which focuses on a variety of education issues, laid the foundation of Goldrick-Rab's educational consultancy group, the EduOptimists, which she launched in 2013. In addition to long-form blogging, she joined the social network Twitter in April 2009, using the site to engage in discussions about higher education as well as to educate her readers about the issues at hand.

AN OUTSPOKEN ACTIVIST

Throughout her years at the University of Wisconsin–Madison, Goldrick-Rab developed a reputation as a committed and outspoken activist who did not hesitate to challenge those in power. In 2011, she strongly opposed a proposed plan to separate the University of Wisconsin–Madison from the rest of the University of Wisconsin system, coming into conflict with Chancellor Biddy Martin. Goldrick-Rab argued that such a move could have detrimental effects on the affordability of the university. She similarly spoke out against statewide education budget cuts on various occasions, and in one notable instance she referred to Wisconsin governor Scott Walker as a fascist on Twitter.

In light of such conflicts, Goldrick-Rab was no stranger to controversy during her time at the University of Wisconsin–Madison, and indeed, her use of platforms such as Twitter made her statements all the more public. In 2015, following news of budget cuts and changes to the tenure process that she believed would negatively affect the quality of the university's education, she contacted incoming students on Twitter to warn them of those changes at the school. Some of the students complained, and the university issued a public statement criticizing Goldrick-Rab's actions, which were characterized by some as overstepping boundaries and damaging the university's reputation. Although Goldrick-Rab issued an apology for the incident, she continued to oppose the issues that had sparked it as well as defend her right to dissent. "I don't want to be in a place where the unpopular people can't have a voice," she told Herzog. "I don't want to be in an environment where I'm told that to do my job, I am to 'sift and winnow,' but I am told in very covert, quiet, yet clear ways that I am to be quiet. I can't do that. It's untenable."

JOINING TEMPLE UNIVERSITY

In 2016, Goldrick-Rab left the University of Wisconsin–Madison to return to Pennsylvania, where she had accepted the position of professor of higher education and sociology at Temple University. She was pleased by the idea of once again living in Philadelphia, a place she has loved since she earned her graduate degrees there.

Prior to joining the institution, Goldrick-Rab expressed concerns about whether those in charge of hiring for the position were familiar with her sometimes controversial viewpoints and means of expressing them. However, it soon became clear that for those at Temple, her outspoken nature and devotion to higher education affordability were significant points in her favor. "Looking objectively at her record, it's really a no-brainer for any serious college or university to want to have faculty like her, based on her funding productivity, her scholarly and research activity, and her impact on public policy and the postsecondary arena," Temple University dean of education Greg Anderson explained to Susan Snyder for *Philly.com* (9 Mar. 2016). Assuming her position at Temple in the summer of 2016, Goldrick-Rab quickly began to establish a new academic home for herself at the university.

COLLEGE AFFORDABILITY

Over the course of her career at both the University of Wisconsin–Madison and Temple University, Goldrick-Rab has conducted extensive research into a variety of issues related to higher education affordability and accessibility. Much of her work considers the ways that factors such as education, economics, and opportunity intersect. "The things I noticed as a kid—the homes and neighborhoods we live in, our differing levels of wealth and education—these things play out over our lives," she told Herzog. "I'm concerned about the extent to which people who have less are increasingly locked out and kept in economically fragile circumstances. I am intent on doing something about that."

To further her research goals, Goldrick-Rab founded the Wisconsin HOPE Lab, the first research laboratory dedicated to studying college affordability, in 2013. She is the author of numerous papers on such topics as student loans, federal grants, and food insecurity among college students and has contributed to books such as *Putting Poor People to Work: How the Work-First Idea Eroded College Access for the Poor* (2006), coauthored with Kathleen Shaw, Christopher Mazzeo, and Jerry A. Jacobs. Goldrick-Rab's book *Paying the Price* was published in 2016.

In addition to examining the educational and financial policies in place and their effects on students and would-be students, Goldrick-Rab seeks to influence the development of future policy by advising organizations and individual lawmakers on local, state, and national levels. Although the issue of higher education is undoubtedly a complex one, Goldrick-Rab is quick to provide potential solutions. "We need accountability for pricing, improved political support for how we finance higher ed, and a much more substantial discount that also helps address living costs," she told Herzog. "I support experimentation with universal public higher education including via state and local promise programs."

PERSONAL LIFE

Goldrick-Rab has two children with her former husband, Liam Goldrick, who works in education policy. The couple collaborated on *The Education Optimists* blog prior to their divorce. Goldrick-Rab lives in Philadelphia.

SUGGESTED READING

Finkelmeyer, Todd. "Outspoken Professor Gives Biddy Martin's Plan a Failing Grade." *Madison.com*, 2 May 2011, host.madison.com/news/local/education/campus_connection/outspoken-professor-gives-biddy-martin-s-plan-a-failing-grade/article_81452a4e-7456-11e0-9e9d-001cc4c03286.html. Accessed 10 Nov. 2016.

Goldrick-Rab, Sara. "Interview with Social Class Scholar Dr. Sara Goldrick-Rab." Interview by Tori Svoboda. *NASPA*, 17 Mar. 2015, www.naspa.org/constituent-groups/posts/interview-with-social-class-scholar-dr.-sara-goldrick-rab. Accessed 10 Nov. 2016.

Gunn, Dwyer. "Talking Student Loans with Sara Goldrick-Rab." *Pacific Standard*, 10 Oct. 2016, psmag.com/talking-student-loans-with-sara-goldrick-rab-b7a1b143211#.68kp2o55o. Accessed 10 Nov. 2016.

Herzog, Karen. "Reviled by Some, Revered by Others, Madison Professor Pushes On." *Journal Sentinel*, 21 Jan. 2016, archive.jsonline.com/news/education/reviled-by-some-revered-by-others-madison-professor-pushes-on-b99649971z1-366093081.html. Accessed 10 Nov. 2016.

Scott, Emily. "Focusing on Inequities at Universities." *The Temple News*, 6 Sept. 2016, temple-news.com/lifestyle/focusing-inequities-universities. Accessed 10 Nov. 2016.

Snyder, Susan. "Temple Gets Outspoken Education Prof with National Profile." *Philly.com*, 9 Mar. 2016, www.philly.com/philly/education/20160310_Temple_gets_outspoken_education_prof_with_national_profile.html. Accessed 10 Nov. 2016.

SUGGESTED WORKS

Putting Poor People to Work: How the Work-First Idea Eroded College Access for the Poor (2006), coauthored with Kathleen Shaw, Christopher Mazzeo, and Jerry A. Jacobs, *Paying the Price: College Costs, Financial Aid, and the Betrayal of the American Dream*, 2016.

—*Joy Crelin*

Neil Gorsuch

Date of birth: August 29, 1967
Occupation: Supreme Court Justice

After the death of conservative Supreme Court Justice Antonin Scalia on February 13, 2016, the battle over his replacement became heated. Although President Barack Obama tried filling the seat with the well-respected appeals court judge Merrick Garland, Senate Republicans refused to grant Garland a hearing in order to keep the seat vacant until after the presidential election later that year. The tactic worked for them, and following his January 2017 inauguration, President Donald Trump nominated Neil Gorsuch, who was serving as a judge on the US Court of Appeals for the Tenth Circuit. Gorsuch, like Scalia, was known as an "originalist"—one who believes that any reading of the US Constitution must be based on the ordinary and accepted meaning of the text at the time it was drafted by the Founding Fathers, with no room for modern reinterpretation.

Although Democrats threw as many procedural roadblocks in the way as possible, Gorsuch was ultimately confirmed as the 113th Justice

By United States Court of Appeals for the Tenth Circuit, via Wikimedia Commons

of the Supreme Court on April 7, 2017. While Trump congratulated himself on his successful pick, and most conservatives agreed that Gorsuch was a solid choice, liberals mourned what the confirmation might mean for the country for decades to come.

"Given the lengthy tenure of most modern justices, Gorsuch could still be pulling the Supreme Court to the right in 2045," Mark Joseph Stern wrote for *Slate* (17 May 2017). "Depending on the longevity of his colleagues, he may have the opportunity to cast the deciding vote in 5–4 decisions that overturn *Roe v. Wade*, roll back marriage equality, eradicate campaign finance restrictions, hobble unions, weaken environmental regulations, permit more executions, and sanction voter suppression." Although it is early in Gorsuch's tenure, some of his opinions and actions have lent credence to attitudes such as Stern's, particularly Gorsuch's vote in late April to deny a stay of execution for Ledell Lee, an Arkansas man sentenced to death in 1995 for murder, despite evidence of ineffective counsel, a conflict of interest on the part of the presiding judge, and the state's refusal to conduct DNA testing. "It's not entirely fair to judge a Supreme Court justice based on his first vote. Urgent matters arise unexpectedly, and the court must sometimes act quickly," the editorial board of the *New York Times* wrote on the paper's opinion page on April 21, 2017. "Still, it's worth paying special attention to Justice Neil Gorsuch's vote. . . . [He] held the power of life and death in his hands Thursday night. His choice led to Ledell Lee's execution, and gave the nation an early, and troubling, look into the mind-set of the high court's newest member."

EARLY YEARS AND EDUCATION

Neil McGill Gorsuch was born on August 29, 1967, in Denver, Colorado. He has a younger brother, J.J., and a younger sister, Stephanie. Their parents, David Gorsuch and Anne Gorsuch Burford, were attorneys who had met as students at the University of Colorado's School of Law and married in the mid-1960s. (They got divorced in 1982, and Anne subsequently married Robert Burford, a rancher and mining engineer who served for a time as director of the US Bureau of Land Management.)

In 1981, Gorsuch Burford was appointed by President Ronald Reagan to head the Environmental Protection Agency (EPA). The first woman ever to hold that post, she found her tenure marked by controversy numerous times; she tried cutting the agency's budget severely, rolled back regulations, reduced the number of lawsuits mounted against polluters, and approved the use of certain restricted pesticides, for example, and in 1982 she was held in contempt of Congress after refusing to release EPA documents relating to the agency's possible mishandling of a $1.6 billion toxic waste fund.

Gorsuch, who developed an early love of hiking, skiing, and fishing as a child, had attended Christ the King Catholic School, in Denver, but when his mother assumed her EPA position, he moved to the DC area and entered Georgetown Preparatory School, a Jesuit-run all-boys institution in Maryland. By all accounts, he was a serious and studious pupil who loved sparring over politics and law with his more liberal teachers. Liked by peers, he was elected president of his senior class.

Gorsuch took only three years to earn his undergraduate degree from Columbia University, graduating in 1988 having been elected to Phi Beta Kappa. At Columbia, he wrote for the student newspaper and cofounded his own, more conservative publication, which he dubbed the *Federalist Paper*. In 1991 he earned his law degree from Harvard, counting Barack Obama as a classmate. Later, in 2004, he earned a doctoral degree in legal philosophy from Oxford University.

LEGAL CAREER

Gorsuch launched his legal career in 1991 as a clerk for Judge David B. Sentelle of the US Court of Appeals for the District of Columbia Circuit. In 1993 he began clerking for Supreme Court justices Anthony M. Kennedy and Byron R. White.

With several high-level jobs offered to him as a result of those prestigious clerkships, in 1995 Gorsuch joined the Washington-based firm Kellogg, Huber, Hansen, Todd, Evans & Figel, where he specialized in complex litigation cases, including contracts, antitrust, and securities fraud. He was named a partner in 1998.

In 2005, the year after he earned his Oxford degree, Gorsuch left private practice to join the US Justice Department, tasked with defending the George W. Bush administration's controversial policies regarding the detainees at Guantanamo Bay and other such issues. His official title was principal deputy to the associate attorney general.

Bush nominated Gorsuch, then still under forty, to the US Court of Appeals for the Tenth Circuit, in Denver, and he was unanimously confirmed for the lifetime post. During his tenure there he established himself as a favorite with conservatives, asserting that making a campaign finance contribution, even on the part of a large corporate entity, is a form of free speech, and siding with Hobby Lobby during the craft store's 2013 battle to disregard Obamacare's mandated coverage of contraception, among other such views.

SUPREME COURT

On January 31, 2017, Donald Trump nominated Gorsuch to fill the Supreme Court seat left vacant by Scalia's death. Partisan bickering immediately ensued. For three days in March, he sat before the Senate Judiciary Committee to answer questions about his views and qualifications. He worked hard to reassure members that he would remain independent from Trump and was discreet about the controversy surrounding the failed nomination of Merrick Garland, who had many supporters on the committee. Despite what most observers characterized as a solid, unobjectionable performance, minority leader Chuck Schumer announced a plan on the part of Democrats to filibuster Gorsuch's nomination. "There was no filibuster for Clarence Thomas, whose Supreme Court confirmation hearings provoked a national uproar over sex, race and the behavior of powerful men," Matt Flegenheimer wrote for the *New York Times* (31 Mar. 2017). "Antonin Scalia, for a generation the court's irrepressible conservative id, earned 98 votes in the Senate. Ruth Bader Ginsburg, now the patron saint of liberal jurisprudence, got 96. But with the Senate careering toward a chamber-rattling showdown over President Trump's nominee, Judge Neil M. Gorsuch, the body's long history of relative collaboration on Supreme Court matters has come to this: Next week, the last bastion of comity is expected to fall over a plainly qualified, mild-mannered nominee who had no major stumbles in his hearings."

On April 6, Senate Democrats followed through with the plan, denying Gorsuch the 60-vote supermajority needed for his confirmation to proceed, but Republicans responded by launching what is known as the "nuclear option," a parliamentary procedure that allows the Senate to override a rule or precedent with a simple majority of 51 votes. The following day, Gorsuch was confirmed by a vote of 54 to 45, and he was sworn in on April 10 at the White House. Opinion of him remains sharply divided along partisan lines, although some observers are advocating for a "wait-and-see" attitude. Accurately characterizing Gorsuch's philosophy is difficult this early in his tenure, Supreme Court analyst and law professor Carl Tobias told Joseph P. Williams for *US News & World Report* (10 May 2017). "I find that so speculative it's unhelpful. You have to give new justices some slack to see how they come out in a number of cases."

By the time the Supreme Court's 2016 term ended at the end of June 2017, however, Gorsuch was on record as having voted 100 percent of the time with the court's most conservative justice, Clarence Thomas, and almost as often with its other strong conservative, Samuel Alito. All three, for example, voted to allow the Trump travel ban on visitors from six majority-Muslim nations to go into full effect while waiting to give Trump's executive order a full review in October; however, they were overruled by the other six justices, who allowed people with a pre-existing relationship in the United States to travel here while the case is pending.

In June, Gorsuch received a spate of media attention when he spoke at a Harvard event and made a statement that some observers took as a veiled criticism of Trump, who had just the previous day excoriated the majority ruling on the travel ban. During Gorsuch's widely quoted remarks, he said that "judges can safely decide the law according to their conscience, without fear of reprisal" and deemed it admirable "that government can lose, in its own courts, and accept the judgment of those courts without an army to back up the judgments. Just nine old people in polyester black robes that we have to buy at the uniform supply store. . . . . That is a heritage that is very special." He added, "I know there is a lot of cynicism about government and the rule of law today, but I don't share it."

PERSONAL LIFE

Gorsuch met his wife, Louise, while they were both students at Oxford. They have two daughters: Emma and Belinda. He has told interviewers that his preferred birthday gift is a family promise to watch a Western movie with him. He has retained his boyhood love for skiing, fishing, and hiking, and he has raised chickens, horses, and goats at the family home in Boulder, Colorado.

He has served as a visiting professor at the University of Colorado Law School, where he taught ethics and antitrust law, and in 2006 he published the book *The Future of Assisted Suicide and Euthanasia*, arguing against the practice.

Even those who disagree with his rulings and conservative bent consider Gorsuch to be a warm and engaging person. "He's someone who knows the names of the security guards at the courthouse and gets to know who their families are," his former law clerk Theresa Wardon explained to Nancy Benac and Mark Sherman for the *Associated Press* (18 Mar. 2017).

SUGGESTED READING

Benac, Nancy, and Mark Sherman. "Disarmingly Warm Gorsuch Loves 'Cold Neutrality' of Law." *Associated Press*, 18 Mar. 2017, apnews.com/d2253f289339431490ffa32d2c613627/disarmingly-warm-gorsuch-loves-cold-neutrality-law. Accessed 5 June 2017.

Bravin, Jess. "Gorsuch Decries Public Cynicism over 'Rule of Law.'" *Wall Street Journal*, 4 June 2017, www.wsj.com/articles/

gorsuch-decries-public-cynicism-over-rule-of-law-1496574000. Accessed 5 June 2017.

De Vogue, Ariane. "Gorsuch Shows an Independent Streak to Begin Life at Supreme Court." *CNN*, 2 May 2017, www.cnn.com/2017/05/02/politics/gorsuch-cert-pool/index.html. Accessed 1 June 2017.

Flegenheimer, Matt. "The Roots of the Battle over Neil Gorsuch: 'They Started It.'" *The New York Times*, 31 Mar. 2017, www.nytimes.com/2017/03/31/us/politics/supreme-court-neil-gorsuch-senate.html. Accessed 1 June 2017.

Liptak, Adam. "Gorsuch Rejects Doubts over 'Rule of Law Today.'" *The New York Times*, 3 June 2017, www.nytimes.com/2017/06/03/us/politics/gorsuch-rejects-doubts-over-rule-of-law-today.html. Accessed 5 June 2017.

"Neil Gorsuch and the State's Power to Kill." *The New York Times*, 21 Apr. 2017, www.nytimes.com/2017/04/21/opinion/neil-gorsuch-and-the-states-power-to-kill.html. Accessed 1 June 2017.

Stern, Mark Joseph. "Trump's Justice." *Slate*, Slate Group, 17 May 2017, www.slate.com/articles/news_and_politics/jurisprudence/2017/05/neil_gorsuch_will_be_the_enduring_symbol_of_a_disastrous_presidency.html. Accessed 5 June 2017.

—*Mari Rich*

Clio Gould

Date of birth: 1968
Occupation: Violinist

"I didn't want a career that went down one route," violinist Clio Gould told Colin Anderson for the website *Classical Source* (11 Aug. 2017). Indeed, Gould's career has gone down a multitude of different routes in the decades since she first began studying violin at the age of three. A talented soloist, she has performed in that capacity with numerous ensembles in her native England and beyond, and in the 1990s she established herself as the long-serving principal first violinist for the London Sinfonietta. She likewise made a name for herself as a musical leader, beginning with her appointment as artistic director of the twelve-player Scottish Ensemble in 1993, then drew further attention in 2002 when she was named leader of the Royal Philharmonic Orchestra, a post she would hold for more than a decade. Gould is also a passionate educator who has led ensembles of student musicians at London's Royal Academy of Music and taught violin to young musicians worldwide. "What I find really stimulating is that I haven't

been forced to channel my energies into one area," she said to Anderson. "I've been able to do so many things that have fed off and stimulated each other."

EARLY LIFE AND EDUCATION

Clio Cassia Gould was born in London, England, in 1968. Her parents, Frank and Lesley, both worked in education, and her father would later serve as vice-chancellor of the University of East London. One of three children, Gould grew up in north London.

Music was a priority in the Gould household, and Gould began taking violin lessons at the age of three. From early childhood, she studied with Sheila Nelson, a well-known violinist, teacher, and writer based in London. Nelson emphasized the importance of group lessons, and after several years of individual lessons, Gould began to learn to play alongside other musicians as well. "We used to basically take over her house," she recalled to Eva Radich for the Radio New Zealand program *Upbeat* (14 Apr. 2016). "She used to send one quartet off to the bedroom, and somebody was in the kitchen with a trio. We were sort of swarming all over the house, doing our little bits of quartet playing."

Nelson's approach to musical education made an enduring impression on Gould. "I really think it's kind of made me the player with the interests that I have," she said to Radich. Gould's early musical endeavors also had a lasting effect on her brother, Thomas, who was fifteen years her junior. "Clio was always bringing these really lively, interesting people home to rehearse," he said to Ivan Hewett for the *Telegraph* (21 Apr. 2011). "It seemed an exciting life she was leading." Thomas Gould would go on to study violin himself and would later lead the Aurora Orchestra and the Britten Sinfonia.

In addition to training extensively as a child and teenager, Gould participated in public performances on various occasions. Among her notable performances were two appearances in *Fanfare for Young Musicians*, a televised competition that showcased talented ensembles made up of players under the age of thirteen. Launched in 1978, the program aired annually on the channel ITV until 1982. Gould led her ensemble on both occasions, demonstrating an early affinity for musical leadership. After completing her primary and secondary schooling, Gould studied violin at London's Guildhall School of Music and Drama, from which she graduated in 1990.

EARLY CAREER

Having established herself as both a talented violinist and a capable leader before reaching adulthood, Gould continued to prove herself after completing her studies, finding work with some of the United Kingdom's many orchestral groups. In 1993, she was appointed artistic director of the Scottish Ensemble, a group founded in 1969 as the Scottish Baroque Ensemble and later known as the BT Scottish Ensemble. With the ensemble, which consisted of twelve core players as well as occasional guest performers, Gould spent the winters performing in Scotland and the summers touring throughout the United Kingdom. "We have a bus and have done thousands of miles," she said to Anderson in 2002. "We just pound around in our little bus, which is like another member of the ensemble." As artistic director of the group, Gould was tasked with ensuring that the ensemble functioned harmoniously both on and off the stage. "It's a group thing but I keep an overview, someone has to keep things moving," she explained to Anderson. "I'm keeping an eye on the whole process. The players make suggestions for repertoire that I shape into a season."

Gould remained with the Scottish Ensemble until 2005. Throughout her twelve years with the group, she continued to work with other musical ensembles and explore her interests in varying forms of classical music. "In London, there's a very broad freelance scene, and you can be in an orchestra but also in other orchestras," she recalled to Radich. "At one crazy point in my life I had three jobs running concurrently." One such job was that of principal violinist with the London Sinfonietta, a small ensemble devoted to performing, and often premiering, works of contemporary classical music. In 1997, while performing with the London Sinfonietta, Gould was first lent the Ruston Stradivarius, a prized violin that belongs to the Royal Academy of Music. The instrument was crafted in 1694 by the acclaimed Italian violin maker Antonio Stradivari, whose instruments are widely considered to be among the best in the world. In addition to performing with the Sinfonietta, Gould served as leader of the group for a time. She stepped down from the position of principal violinist in 2012.

ROYAL PHILHARMONIC ORCHESTRA

Gould gained additional notice in the world of classical music in 2002, when she was appointed leader of the prestigious Royal Philharmonic Orchestra. Founded in 1946, the orchestra consists of more than fifty individual musicians and plays at major venues such as London's Cadogan Hall and Royal Albert Hall. Gould was the first woman to serve as leader of the orchestra, in which she also played as a first violinist.

Over the course of more than a decade with the Royal Philharmonic, Gould performed with the group in London as well as throughout the United Kingdom. Although many of the orchestra's concerts went as planned, Gould's tenure with the orchestra also featured its fair share of surprises. In one notable 2012 concert, the Royal Philharmonic was set to perform composer Ralph Vaughan Williams's orchestral piece *The Lark Ascending* (1920), which prominently features the violin. Not long before the concert, the scheduled soloist, violinist Nicola Benedetti, became sick and was unable to perform. Gould, as one of the orchestra's first violinists, was tasked with performing the piece on very short notice. As she later noted to Hannah Nepil for the orchestra's newsletter, *Ovation* (Aug. 2012), the task was particularly challenging because she did not have her copy of the sheet music with her. "My husband photographed it with his iPhone and sent it over," she recalled to Nepil. "It was like trying to read off an old pirate map— totally brown and crumpled at the edges. But still better than using somebody else's music." Gould's last-minute scramble paid off, as she won praise from critics for her performance of the composition.

Gould remained with the Royal Philharmonic until early 2016, when she announced that she was stepping down as leader and leaving the violin section's ranks to focus on her teaching work. "It has been an immense privilege to be here and work with you all. However, I feel it's now time to hand the privilege over," she said to the members of the orchestra, as quoted in the *Strad* (18 Mar. 2016). "I've had an absolutely amazing time here. This orchestra has such heart, soul, spirit, and courage." She led her final rehearsal in March of that year.

EDUCATION AND OUTREACH

Gould holds a teaching position at the Royal Academy of Music in London, one of the United Kingdom's most prestigious music conservatories, and serves as director of the Sainsbury Royal Academy Soloists, the institution's highest-level string ensemble. In addition to her work with adult students, she has participated in numerous efforts to educate young violinists and has run master classes and group educational programs at institutions such as New Zealand's Pettman National Junior Academy of Music. For Gould, the opportunity to work with young musicians is a compelling one. "It is always . . . a really exciting time to get together with young people, maybe take them through a piece," she said to Radich.

Shaped greatly by her early studies with Nelson, Gould frequently asserts the importance of group study for violinists and emphasizes such practices in her work as a music educator. "For really fine string players, there's an enormously long sort of gestation period where they're . . . putting in a lot of hours alone in a room, learning how to master these difficult instruments," she explained to Radich. "One thing that doesn't always get the same amount of attention is actually playing with other people, and so you come out of the end of that process and you're sort of brilliant playing on your own, but not necessarily the rounded musician that this sort of work can encourage you to become." Through her educational efforts, Gould hopes to encourage young musicians to develop a well-rounded array of skills that will benefit them in the future.

NOTEWORTHY PROJECTS

In addition to her work with her primary ensembles, Gould has performed with numerous additional large and small groups, including the BBC Symphony Orchestra, the Royal Scottish National Orchestra, and Ireland's RTÉ National Symphony Orchestra. In 1999, the BBC Scottish Symphony Orchestra accompanied Gould and viola player Philip Dukes for a performance at the BBC Proms, a prestigious series of classical concerts held each summer in London.

Though perhaps best known for her live performances, Gould has played violin on numerous albums, both as a soloist and as a member of groups such as the Scottish Ensemble and the London Sinfonietta. Albums featuring Gould's playing include the BT Scottish Ensemble's *The Celtic* (1997), the 2006 concert recording *Warp Works and Twentieth Century Masters*, and the 2014 album *Ypakoë*, a compilation of works by twentieth-century British composer John Tavener. She has also contributed to the scores for numerous works, including the films *Elizabeth: The Golden Age* (2007), *The Great Gatsby* (2013), and *Fantastic Beasts and Where to Find Them* (2016), as well as the 2015 video game *Everybody's Gone to the Rapture*.

PERSONAL LIFE

Gould met her husband, fellow violinist Jonathan Morton, when he first auditioned for the Scottish Ensemble. The couple married in 2002. In addition to their work with the Scottish Ensemble, Gould and Morton have performed together on numerous occasions and have also collaborated on educational programs. Following the end of Gould's tenures as artistic director of the Scottish Ensemble and principal violinist for the London Sinfonietta, Morton succeeded her in both posts. They have two children and live in Woodbridge, Suffolk, in southeastern England.

SUGGESTED READING

Anderson, Colin. "Carry On Clio." *Classical Source*, Aug. 2002, classicalsource.com/db_control/db_features.php?id=866. Accessed 11 Aug. 2017.
Campbell, Curtis. "The Royal Philharmonic Orchestra Is Here and Excited." *The Gleaner*, 12 Sept. 2012, jamaica-gleaner.com/gleaner/20120912/ent/ent1.html. Accessed 11 Aug. 2017.
"Clio Gould." *Royal Academy of Music*, Uwww.ram.ac.uk/about-us/staff/clio-gould. Accessed 11 Aug. 2017.
"Clio Gould Steps Down as Royal Philharmonic Orchestra Concertmaster." *The Strad*, 18 Mar. 2016, www.thestrad.com/clio-gould-steps-down-as-royal-philharmonic-orchestra-concertmaster/1604.article. Accessed 11 Aug. 2017.
Gould, Clio, and Jonathan Morton. Interview. By Eva Radich. *Upbeat*, Radio New Zealand, 14 Apr. 2016, www.radionz.co.nz/concert/programmes/upbeat/audio/201797066/clio-gould-and-jonathan-morton. Accessed 11 Aug. 2017.
Nepil, Hannah. "Clio Gould on Life as a Professional Musician." *Ovation*, Aug. 2012, www.rpoonline.co.uk/newsletter/aug12/ovation.html. Accessed 11 Aug. 2017.

—*Joy Crelin*

Adam Grant

Date of birth: August 13, 1981
Occupation: Professor

Adam Grant, the youngest professor ever to earn tenure at the University of Pennsylvania's prestigious Wharton School, has a long list of accomplishments to his credit. As a psychologist, he emerged as one of the most popular thinkers in the field, earning mentions in various publications as a top influencer in academia, for business management, and among the general public. He has been highly sought after as a consultant for a diverse range of major organizations, including Amazon, Disney, Google, Goldman Sachs, and the National Football League (NFL). As Richard Rys wrote for *Wharton Magazine* (Spring 2016), "Across the vast galaxy of gifted professors, at the University of Pennsylvania and beyond, Grant's star is bright and easily seen with the naked eye."

Besides his teaching duties and consultant work, Grant is also a best-selling author. His book *Give and Take: Why Helping Others Drives Our Success* (2013) examines how acts of professional generosity can enhance one's own life and career, and it was deemed one of the best books of 2013 by several outlets. *Originals: How Non-Conformists Move the World* (2016) was also highly lauded, and Grant was Sheryl Sandberg's coauthor on *Option B: Facing Adversity, Building Resilience, and Finding Joy*, the highly praised 2017 volume she penned after the untimely death of her husband. Grant also maintains his own blog and writes regularly for such publications as the *New York Times*.

By אדם גרנט (אדם גרנט) [CC BY-SA 3.0], via Wikimedia Commons

Despite the heights his career has reached, Grant remains exceptionally accessible to his students, down-to-earth, and willing to offer help to anyone who needs it. As his mentor, psychology professor Brian Little, told Rys, "With all of his brilliance and enthusiasm, he's also just a hell of a nice guy. Somebody that driven can often have a negative side. They're a bit abrasive, inconsistent in their allegiances. Adam is just a really good man."

EARLY YEARS
Adam Grant was born on August 13, 1981, and was raised in the suburbs of Detroit by his father, Mark, an attorney, and mother, Susan, a teacher. Although he was, by all accounts, a relatively happy child and served for a time on the student council of his elementary school, he was somewhat socially awkward. He would later tell interviewers that he was a rule-following introvert who would cry if he got called to the principal's office for any reason—even if he knew he had done nothing wrong. Additionally, he was plagued by a variety of food allergies and prone to unreasonable aversions to such seemingly innocuous things as denim jeans and haircuts. As a youngster he was so addicted to video games that he was featured in a local newspaper article headlined "The Dark Side of Nintendo." Still, he had numerous other interests, including swimming, soccer, and basketball.

Grant grew to be deeply appreciative of his parents and the upbringing he received from them. "My mother was always the person who looked for ways to recognize and appreciate other people," he told Robert Strauss for *Philadelphia Style* (24 Sept. 2013). "My dad coached every youth sports team. He would volunteer to do the civil air patrol as a pilot and taught swimming to children with disabilities. Their lives were replete with success."

At age twelve Grant began performing as a magician at birthday parties and other local events. He would continue to moonlight as a professional magician up until he entered academia. Meanwhile, he also took up springboard diving, despite a fear of heights. In high school he trained for hours a day, ultimately becoming an All-American and qualifying for the Junior Olympics twice. Grant was accepted to Harvard University, where he continued competing for a year before taking up coaching instead.

The summer before entering college, Grant launched an e-mail chain to connect with other incoming Harvard freshmen. The list quickly grew to more than two hundred members, and Grant would later note to interviewers that in a way it served as a precursor to the social media site Facebook.

EDUCATION
Although Grant was initially undecided between studying psychology and physics, he ultimately chose the former, inspired in large part by a course he took with Brian Little, a popular Harvard professor and a pioneer in the field of personality and motivational psychology. "It was a completely transformative experience," Grant recalled to Rys. "I gained a tremendous amount of self-awareness in that class. I thought if I could have even a fraction of the impact on students that Brian has had on me, then this would be the most meaningful career I could imagine."

In addition to excelling at his studies, Grant earned money by selling advertising at a company called Let's Go Publications. Although initially bad at the job, he realized how the company was providing jobs for students and resolved to improve. He then set numerous sales records, and at the age of just nineteen he was promoted to a director's position that found him overseeing an annual budget of more than $1 million. The experience sparked a deep interest in the field of organizational psychology, and upon graduating magna cum laude and Phi Beta Kappa from Harvard in 2003, he embarked upon the University of Michigan's organizational psychology graduate program. (Little had wanted to nominate him as a Rhodes Scholar, but so intent was Grant on participating in Michigan's top-ranked and highly competitive program that he declined the offer.)

While at Michigan, Grant conducted a research project that greatly informed his later work. Seeking to motivate workers at a university call center whose aim was to drum up donations for scholarships, he mounted a simple and low-cost experiment: Grant invited in one of the scholarship recipients to give a short talk to the center's operators, explaining how he had benefited from their efforts. Within a month, the workers were spending 142 percent more time talking with potential donors and bringing in 171 percent more revenue. The experiment was successfully replicated multiple times, and the hard data supporting the results won much attention in the fields of motivational and organizational psychology. As organizational behavior researcher Stuart Bunderson told Susan Dominus for the *New York Times Magazine* (27 Mar. 2016), "I don't know the last time there was a study in our field that had such striking results. In terms of an intervention that has practical significance and moves the needle on employee behavior—you don't see them that often."

Grant earned his MS and PhD in organizational psychology in 2005 and 2006, respectively, completing the graduate program in just three years. Among the academic honors he garnered as a student were a National Science Foundation (NSF) Graduate Research Fellowship and an American Psychological Association (APA) Early Graduate Student Researcher Award.

AWARD-WINNING PROFESSOR

After earning his doctoral degree, Grant became a visiting scholar at the University of Sheffield's Institute of Work Psychology in 2007. Later that year he accepted a post as an assistant professor of organizational behavior at the University of North Carolina's Kenan-Flagler Business School. Despite initially being very nervous about speaking in front of a class, he was quickly recognized for excellence in undergraduate teaching, winning the institution's Weatherspoon Award and the university-wide Tanner Award. Among his most popular activities was a challenge wherein he divided MBA students and undergraduates into teams to raise as much money as possible for the Make-A-Wish Foundation.

In 2009, Grant joined the faculty at the Wharton School of Business at the University of Pennsylvania, where he continued to develop his reputation as a respected and popular teacher. In 2011, at age twenty-nine, he became the youngest tenured professor in Wharton history, and he earned the school's Excellence in Teaching Award for several consecutive years. His success also continued to raise his national profile, and he was on several occasions listed by various publications as a top professor in the country.

Part of Grant's popularity stemmed from his personal attention to his many students. He became known for challenging himself to learn the name of each of his three hundred or so students in a semester within two weeks. He also made time for every single person who showed up during his office hours, even when the line stretched far down the hallway, and answered hundreds of e-mails each day. He encouraged students to use the networking contacts listed on his personal social media pages, confident that contacts he helped in the past would be happy to help his current students in turn. Grant told Rys that despite the demands his altruism places on him, he can envision no other way of working and living. "If anything, I want to put more pressure on myself," he said. "The higher my expectations of myself are, the more I'm able to contribute."

RESEARCHER AND BEST-SELLING AUTHOR

At Wharton, Grant continued his research into motivation and organizational behavior. He led a team focused on research that would have meaningful practical applications, earning the group the nickname the Impact Lab. "Grant's research on job design, work motivation, and proactive behavior addresses fundamental questions about the forces that drive employees to invest high levels of time and energy in their work, achieve effective performance, and take the initiative to change how work is done," the editors of *American Psychologist* (Nov. 2011) wrote, explaining why they were awarding Grant their Award for Distinguished Scientific Early Career Contributions to Psychology. "Grant's guiding purpose is to practice what he preaches: Do research that makes a difference for scholars, students, employees, and managers." He conducted several well-known studies supporting his central idea that people can be motivated by altruism, not just selfishness. For example, one experiment placed different signs at different sinks in a hospital. Doctors and nurses reading a message emphasizing how hand hygiene prevents patients from catching diseases were found to use significantly more soap than those reading a message emphasizing their own health.

Grants's students helped push him to turn his research into a book for general audiences. After a first attempt was abandoned for being too academic, in 2013 he published *Give and Take: Why Helping Others Drives Our Success*, which captured the public imagination and shot to the top of the New York Times Best Sellers list. As Andrew Hill opined for the *Financial Times* (10 Apr. 2013), "What makes the book more bracing than the many soppy manuals for better living is that Grant provides convincing evidence in support of dubious-sounding popular theories, such as 'what goes around, comes around' and 'karma.'" The work was cited by many publications as one of the best books of the year and top business books, helping to popularize the concept of prosocial behavior.

Building on that success, Grant released his second book, *Originals: How Non-Conformists*

Move the World, in 2016. Another immediate best seller, it is built around examples of inspiring figures whose success was reached despite conventions suggesting otherwise, and suggests everyone has such potential. "*Originals* succeeds by marrying sound research and insightful anecdotes to a breezy narrative style that belies Grant's academic roots," Iain Morris wrote for the *Guardian* (16 Feb. 2016). Grant also cowrote with Sheryl Sandberg *Option B: Facing Adversity, Building Resilience, and Finding Joy* (2017), a compassionate and clear-headed look at grief and resiliency and another best seller. Meanwhile, his articles on raising creative and moral children for the *New York Times* were shared hundreds of thousands of times on social media, and his TED talks on various topics have been viewed more than 8 million times.

PERSONAL LIFE
Grant and his wife, Allison, a psychiatric nurse practitioner, met while both were in graduate school. They have three children together. He has noted that he was mostly able to overcome his social awkwardness and fear of public speaking through practice and building on his strengths, but that he remained an introvert at heart. Those close to him confirm that he personally lives up to his research on being a "giver" who is happy to help others.

SUGGESTED READING
"Adam Grant: Award for Distinguished Scientific Early Career Contributions to Psychology." *American Psychologist*, vol. 66, no. 8, Nov. 2011, doi:10.1037/a0025016. Accessed 8 June 2017.

Dominus, Susan. "Is Giving the Secret to Getting Ahead?" *The New York Times Magazine*, 27 Mar. 2013, www.nytimes.com/2013/03/31/magazine/is-giving-the-secret-to-getting-ahead.html. Accessed 8 June 2017.

Grant, Adam. "Adam Grant, a Workplace Magician, Reveals His Secrets." Interview by David Gelles. *The New York Times*, 6 Feb. 2016, www.nytimes.com/2016/02/07/business/adam-grant-a-workplace-magician-reveals-his-secrets.html. Accessed 8 June 2017.

Hill, Andrew. "Nice Guys Don't Always Finish Last." Review of Give and Take: A Revolutionary Approach to Success, by Adam Grant. *Financial Times*, 10 Apr. 2013, www.ft.com/content/c292d86c-9d48-11e2-88e9-00144feabdc0?mhq5j=e2. Accessed 8 June 2017.

Morris, Iain. Review of *Originals*, by Adam Grant. *The Guardian*, 16 Feb. 2016, www.theguardian.com/books/2016/feb/16/originals-adam-grant-end-of-average-todd-rose-review. Accessed 8 June 2017.

Rys, Richard. "Adam Grant, Original." *Wharton Magazine*, Spring 2016, whartonmagazine.com/issues/spring-2016/adam-grant-original/#sthash.gP5yKVLL.dpbs. Accessed 8 June 2017.

Strauss, Robert. "Adam Grant Gives Back to Wharton." *Philadelphia Style*, 24 Sept. 2013, phillystylemag.com/author-professor-adam-grant-gives-back-to-wharton. Accessed 8 June 2017.

SELECTED WORKS
Give and Take: Why Helping Others Drives Our Success, 2013; *Originals: How Non-Conformists Move the World*, 2016; *Option B: Facing Adversity, Building Resilience, and Finding Joy* (with Sheryl Sandberg), 2017

—Mari Rich

Mirga Gražinytė-Tyla
Date of birth: August 29, 1986
Occupation: Conductor

To those unfamiliar with the process of orchestral conducting, the role of conductor might seem to be an isolated and perhaps even lonely one, as the conductor is surrounded by orchestra and audience yet is set apart from both. For conductors such as Mirga Gražinytė-Tyla, however, that perception could not be less accurate. The child of a choir conductor and a pianist, the Lithuanian-born conductor was immersed in the world of music at a young age and quickly discovered the intensely collaborative and highly social nature of the field. "Music was the only profession I could imagine," she recalled to Rick Fulker for *DW* (5 Sept. 2016). "And as a conductor, you're simultaneously with music and with people. Both are very important to me."

After coming to the attention of the international conducting community through a number of major performances as well as strong showings in international conducting competitions, Gražinytė-Tyla embarked on a steady trajectory toward international fame, conducting orchestras throughout Europe and the United States. After completing a fellowship with the Los Angeles Philharmonic, she joined the orchestra as an assistant conductor and later associate conductor. In early 2016, she was named music director of the renowned City of Birmingham Symphony Orchestra in Birmingham, England. Yet despite her international success as a conductor, Gražinytė-Tyla remains committed to developing a deeper understanding of her profession and her own personal approach to conducting. "I'm still developing my style," she explained to David Ng

Jay L. Clendenin/Los Angeles Times via Getty Images

for the *Los Angeles Times* (26 Dec. 2014). "I'm just interested in continuing to explore how clear a conductor should be—how much organizing does an orchestra need, how much inspiration should a conductor give? It's a very interesting subject, and you're never done researching."

EARLY LIFE AND EDUCATION

Mirga Gražinytė-Tyla was born in Vilnius, Lithuania, on August 29, 1986, the first of three children. Born into a highly musical family, she was surrounded by music and musicians from birth. Her extended family included organists, violinists, and composers, and her parents, Romualdas Gražinis and Sigutė Gražinytė, worked as a choral conductor and a pianist, respectively. As a child, Gražinytė-Tyla frequently attended her parents' practices and performances, and she would later tour Europe as a member of the choir led by her father. Although Gražinis's work as a choral conductor significantly influenced Gražinytė-Tyla's later career aspirations, she has noted in interviews that she found her father's style of conducting to be too commanding and has consciously avoided emulating his style when conducting orchestras.

In addition to her family's influence, Gražinytė-Tyla has often credited her Lithuanian culture and heritage with shaping her relationship with music. "We have a special culture and tradition of singing, and that is what helped us regain our human rights," she explained to Fulker, noting that Lithuania and its people were long oppressed by Russian czars and then by the Soviet Union. "Song and singing paved the way

to freedom for the Baltic countries. . . . They helped form our cultural identity." This close historical relationship between nationalism and music led to the formation of many choirs in Lithuania beginning in the late nineteenth century, which in turn influenced the development of a strong system of musical education that has lasted into the twenty-first century. "There are more than five schools in the country where you can start to learn choral conducting at age thirteen," Gražinytė-Tyla noted to Fulker. "They joke that every second citizen of Lithuania is a choral conductor."

Yet despite her family background and the available musical education opportunities, Gražinytė-Tyla was sent to school in Vilnius to study the visual arts. Although she was interested in music, her parents did not allow her to pursue musical studies at first, as they worried about her future career prospects. "They wanted me to have a real profession, unlike them," she explained to Ivan Hewett for the *Telegraph* (16 Aug. 2016). "So they encouraged me to study painting at the arts college I attended." In keeping with her parents' wishes, Gražinytė-Tyla initially studied painting and French. However, they were unable to distract her from her love of music. "I told them when I was eleven that music was all I wanted," she recalled to Hewett. At the time, few of the musical programs at her school had openings for new students, so she decided to follow in her father's footsteps and enroll in the school's choral conducting program. She conducted a choir for the first time at the age of thirteen.

TRAINING AND EARLY CAREER

Gražinytė-Tyla continued to study conducting in university, enrolling in the University of Music and Performing Arts in Graz, Austria, so that she could study under Professor Johannes Prinz, whom she considered the best choral conducting professor in the world. She was surprised to discover that students at Austrian universities were allowed a great deal of academic freedom, particularly in regard to course selection, as the Lithuanian educational system was far more structured. "This was such a liberation for me!" she told Hewett.

Although Gražinytė-Tyla initially focused on choral conducting, as she had for much of her early life, she later began to explore the realm of orchestral conducting and eventually decided to focus on orchestras. She earned her bachelor's degree from the University of Music and Performing Arts in 2007. After completing her university studies, Gražinytė-Tyla expanded her knowledge further at music conservatories in Germany, Italy, and Switzerland.

Throughout her early career, Gražinytė-Tyla had the opportunity to conduct a variety of orchestras and other groups of musicians in European cities such as Salzburg, Austria, as well as to appear in international competitions. In the spring of 2007, she traveled to Budapest, Hungary, to compete in the fourth International Competition of Young Choral Conductors, where she won first place. She gained significant attention in 2009, when the German Dirigentenforum, or Conducting Forum, recognized her talents and she subsequently appeared in a seminar on conducting the works of the composer Ludwig von Beethoven. Gražinytė-Tyla joined the German Theater Heidelberg as second Kapellmeister, or conductor, in 2011 and conducted a variety of musical performances and operas for the theater. In 2012, she received the Nestlé and Salzburg Festival Young Conductors Award, a prestigious honor in the world of conducting.

As Gražinytė-Tyla became well known within the international music community, journalists frequently asked her about her experiences as a woman working in a profession that remains male-dominated in the United States and many other countries. Gražinytė-Tyla, however, generally does not think of her career in such terms. "The only thing that counts is to feel authentic and be what you are," she told Fulker. "I feel very free and have rarely experienced discrimination. I feel very fortunate and have trailblazing women colleagues to thank for that."

LOS ANGELES PHILHARMONIC
The next milestone in Gražinytė-Tyla's international conducting career came in 2012, when she was selected to complete a Dudamel Fellowship with the Los Angeles Philharmonic. Established in 2009 by conductor and Los Angeles Philharmonic music director Gustavo Dudamel, the Dudamel Fellowship Program enables its participants to develop their skills as conductors through various educational and mentorship programs. In addition to those benefits, the fellowship program presented Gražinytė-Tyla with an unexpected challenge: a week into her fellowship, conductor Ludovic Morlot fell ill during a performance, and Gražinytė-Tyla was tasked with filling in for him. "I had two hours to prepare, maybe less," she recalled to Ng. "In your stomach, you have storms going on, without having done any rehearsals. It's really an adventure." Her surprise appearance with the Los Angeles Philharmonic met with positive reviews, signaling her later success with the orchestra.

Although Gražinytė-Tyla's Dudamel Fellowship ended in 2013, she did not leave the Los Angeles Philharmonic for long. She returned to the orchestra in 2014 as an assistant conductor, making her Hollywood Bowl debut with the group in August of that year. In 2016, she was promoted to associate conductor and was set to conduct performances of works by composers

such as Wolfgang Amadeus Mozart and Joseph Haydn during the orchestra's 2016–17 season.

For Gražinytė-Tyla, conducting orchestras in cities such as Los Angeles provided her with ample opportunities not only to learn from a vast array of musicians and fellow conductors but also to take note of the differences between the cities and their musical communities. "It's incredibly exciting to observe these differences," she told Fulker. "Even a city has its own personality. For a while, I worked mainly in Salzburg and Los Angeles. I love both, yet can hardly imagine two more different cities."

MUSIC DIRECTOR AND MORE
In addition to her work with the Los Angeles Philharmonic, Gražinytė-Tyla has served as a guest conductor for numerous other orchestras in the United States and Europe, including the Seattle Symphony, the San Diego Symphony, the Lithuanian National Symphony Orchestra, the Danish National Symphony Orchestra, and the Camerata Salzburg. She made her New York City debut with the Juilliard Orchestra in September of 2016. Beginning in 2015, Gražinytė-Tyla made several appearances with the prestigious City of Birmingham Symphony Orchestra in Birmingham, England, and in the winter of the following year, it was announced that she would be taking on the role of music director for that orchestra. She likewise served as music director of the Salzburg Landestheater from 2015 to 2017.

As a conductor, Gražinytė-Tyla works to tap into the spirit of each orchestra she leads and assist the musicians in sharing great music with their audiences. At times, the process can be challenging, particularly when she is conducting an orchestra that is new to her. "There are many psychological challenges when you are faced with a big group, which are very different from the challenges that face each individual," she explained to Hewett. "If you see somebody who is not happy, or under pressure, you tend to take it personally, but of course you can't. You have to help that person, while standing apart from them." Ultimately, Gražinytė-Tyla considers the process of making music to be akin to a collaborative partnership, and she works to foster that relationship when conducting each orchestra. She explained to Hewett, "In the end, it's the music that saves us, because it is the music we are all there to serve."

PERSONAL LIFE
When not conducting orchestras in Los Angeles, Birmingham, and other cities, Gražinytė-Tyla makes her home in Heidelberg, Germany.

SUGGESTED READING

Chute, James. "Mirga Gražinytė-Tyla on the Art of Collaboration." *The San Diego Union-Tribune*, 28 Nov. 2015, www.sandiegouniontribune.com/entertainment/classical-music/sdut-san-diego-symphony-mirga-profile-2015nov28-story.html. Accessed 10 Feb. 2017.

Gražinytė-Tyla, Mirga. "Mirga Gražinytė-Tyla: 'Music Can Build Cultural Identity.'" Interview with Rick Fulker. *DW*, 5 Sept. 2016, www.dw.com/en/mirga-gra%C5%BEinyt%C4%97-tyla-music-can-build-cultural-identity/a-19240471. Accessed 10 Feb. 2017.

Hewett, Ivan. "Meet Conducting's Next Superstar: Mirga Gražinytė-Tyla." *The Telegraph*, 16 Aug. 2016, www.telegraph.co.uk/music/classical-music/meet-conductings-next-superstar-mirga-grainyt-tyla/. Accessed 10 Feb. 2017.

Ng, David. "LA Phil's Mirga Gražinytė-Tyla Conducts Herself with Aplomb." *Los Angeles Times*, 26 Dec. 2014, www.latimes.com/entertainment/arts/classical/la-et-cm-ca-music-person-20141228-story.html. Accessed 10 Feb. 2017.

Oestreich, James R. "Review: A Rising Conductor Makes Her New York Debut." *New York Times*, 27 Sept. 2016, www.nytimes.com/2016/09/28/arts/music/review-a-rising-conductor-makes-her-new-york-debut-mirga-grazinyte-tyla-juilliard-orchestra.html. Accessed 10 Feb. 2017.

Platt, Russell. "The Rise of a Young Lithuanian Maestro." *New Yorker*, 26 Sept. 2016, www.newyorker.com/magazine/2016/09/26/the-rise-of-a-young-lithuanian-maestro. Accessed 10 Feb. 2017.

Swed, Mark. "The LA Phil's Mesmerizing Mirga Gražinytė-Tyla Leaps to the Birmingham Orchestra." *Los Angeles Times*, 5 Feb. 2016, www.latimes.com/entertainment/la-et-cm-mirga-grazinyte-tyla-20160205-column.html. Accessed 10 Feb. 2017.

—*Joy Crelin*

A. J. Green

Date of birth: July 31, 1988
Occupation: Football player

"From Day One I always wanted to be a role model," professional football player A. J. Green told Paul Dehner Jr. for *Cincinnati.com* (16 June 2017). Indeed, for many football fans and commentators, Green has already succeeded in meeting that goal. Since being drafted by the

By Navin75 [CC BY-SA 2.0], via Wikimedia Commons

Cincinnati Bengals as the fourth overall pick of the 2011 National Football League (NFL) Draft, the wide receiver has worked to establish himself as a valuable contributor to the team as well as a true team player. "For me, that's who I am. I didn't have to be somebody I wasn't coming into the league," Green told Dehner. "I had a great foundation from my family. This is who I am as a person. I really didn't have to change who I am."

A talented football player since his early days growing up in South Carolina, Green enjoyed a successful high school career before playing three seasons at the University of Georgia, where he received recognition as one of the best players in the Southeastern Conference. Following his junior season, Green joined the Bengals on a four-year contract, which would go on to be extended for an additional five years. In addition to contributing to the team's regular-season victories and becoming a fixture in the annual NFL Pro Bowl games, Green has focused closely on one particularly meaningful goal: winning a Super Bowl. Although the Bengals have yet to win a Super Bowl in the team's fifty-year history, Green considers that goal achievable thanks to the talent of his teammates and the dedication of the franchise's fans. "They see the talent that we have and they see the potential that we have to go all the way, and why not?" he told Jordan Schultz for the *Huffington Post* (16 Dec. 2015). "And it's 'why not' for us. 'Why not' for the Cincinnati Bengals winning the Super Bowl."

EARLY LIFE AND EDUCATION

Adriel Jeremiah Green was born on July 31, 1988, in Ridgeville, South Carolina. He grew up in Summerville, a town north of the city of Charleston. Green's father, Woodrow, worked for a steel mill and later a cement company, and his mother, Dora, worked for Walmart. He had an older brother named Avionce who died in a car accident when Green was four. Green's household was highly family oriented, and he grew up close to his extended family and particularly enjoyed building treehouses with his cousins. His childhood experiences proved influential, setting the stage for his later approach to adult life. "All I know is family," he told Dehner. "That's what I want for myself."

From a young age, Green demonstrated a talent for a variety of sports. His family encouraged his talents, and he has recalled in interviews that both his parents and members of his extended family were convinced that he would go on to do great things. "My granddaddy, when I was six years old, he was telling me, 'You'll be something. I don't know what, but you've got talent I've never seen,'" he recalled to Geoff Hobson for *Bengals.com* (24 July 2014). "When I was ten years old I was playing basketball with fifteen-year-olds. I'd run everywhere, jumping over fences with no hands. Just clearing them."

Green particularly excelled at football and concentrated on that sport while attending Summerville High School, where he played under the guidance of legendary coach John McKissick. He was likewise influenced by his middle school football and basketball coach, Louis Mulkey, whose death in 2007 affected Green greatly. Having gained the attention of multiple colleges and universities during his early high school years, as a junior Green committed himself to attending the University of Georgia, a member of the National Collegiate Athletic Associate (NCAA)'s Division I.

COLLEGE CAREER

After graduating from Summerville High School, Green honored his earlier commitment and enrolled in the University of Georgia (UGA), where he joined the Georgia Bulldogs football team. Green immediately proved himself to be a valuable member of the team during his debut season, setting freshman records in a variety of areas, including touchdowns. Over the course of three seasons, Green tallied 166 receptions for 2,619 yards and led the Southeastern Conference in touchdowns on multiple occasions. During his college career, he suffered some minor setbacks: as a junior, Green was suspended for the first 4 games of the season for selling his jersey from the previous year's Independence Bowl to a buyer who was considered an agent, an act prohibited under NCAA regulations.

Nevertheless, Green's teammates and Bulldogs leadership stood by him during that incident, and upon his return to the team, he began a successful season that featured a team-leading 57 catches and 9 touchdowns.

In January 2011, Green announced that he planned to enter the NFL Draft, in which the league's professional football teams choose eligible new players to join their rosters. His decision meant that he would leave UGA a year early, missing what would have been his senior season with the Bulldogs. Despite his early exit from the university, Green remained strongly connected to his alma mater, which he has credited with preparing him to enter the NFL and the world of adulthood. In 2015, he announced that he was endowing two scholarship programs at the university, the A. J. Green Family Football Scholarship, which would benefit football players, and the A. J. Green Family Scholarships, a need-based program that would benefit two students each year, preferably students from Green's home state of South Carolina. "I'm very excited and very thankful that we were in the position to give back to the University of Georgia," he said in a press release, as quoted by Robby Kalland for *CBS Sports* (2 Nov. 2015). "My time at UGA is still close to my heart. It was definitely important for me to give back while I'm still playing professionally and I'm fortunate that we are able to do that." In recognition of his achievements, Green received the Young Alumni Award from the university's alumni association in 2017.

CINCINNATI BENGALS

On April 28, 2011, Green was selected by the Cincinnati Bengals as the fourth pick in the first round of the 2011 NFL Draft. He signed a four-year, $19.6 million deal with the team and made his regular season debut with the Bengals on September 11, 2011, in a game against the Cleveland Browns. The Bengals won the game 27–17, and Green distinguished himself by catching a 41-yard pass from teammate Bruce Gradkowski for a touchdown. Over the course of his debut season with the Bengals, Green played in a total of 15 games, achieved 65 receptions for 1,057 yards, and scored 7 receiving touchdowns. Following the end of the season, the Bengals claimed a Wild Card spot in the NFL playoffs and faced off against the Houston Texans in a January 2012 game. Although the team ultimately lost 10–31, the game represented the first of many playoff appearances for Green, who also went on to participate in the Pro Bowl later that month.

Over the following seasons, Green continued to make substantial contributions to his team, achieving eleven receiving touchdowns in both the 2012 and 2013 seasons. The Bengals made it to the playoffs in both seasons and were

American Football Conference (AFC) North division champions in 2013 but ultimately lost their Wild Card games against the Houston Texans and the San Diego Chargers, respectively. In the 2014 season, Green suffered multiple injuries that led him to play in only 13 of the team's 16 regular season games. During the season's final contest, a December 2014 game against the Pittsburgh Steelers, Green sustained a concussion that prevented him from participating in what would have been his fourth consecutive playoff game. The Bengals were eventually defeated by the Indianapolis Colts, 10–26.

Green's performance during his first four seasons in Cincinnati pleased Bengals leadership, who sought to keep him on the team beyond the end of his original contract. In 2014, the team exercised a fifth-year option, signing Green to another year with the Bengals for more than $10 million. Although generally positive about his work during his first several seasons, Green remained convinced that he could continue to improve and take the team to new heights. "I still feel like I haven't hit my peak," he told Hobson in 2014. "I want to be much better."

EYES ON THE FUTURE
Having recovered from his concussion, Green returned to regular play with the Bengals at the start of the 2015 season, in September of that year. That same month, he extended his commitment to the Bengals for an additional four years, signing a $60 million contract. The Bengals performed well during the 2015 season, finishing with a season record of 12 wins and 4 losses and claiming first place in the AFC North division. Green appeared in all 16 regular-season games, achieving 86 receptions for 1,297 yards and 10 receiving touchdowns. In the postseason, the Bengals again entered the Wild Card playoffs, playing the Steelers on January 9, 2016. Although the Bengals lost the painfully close game by only two points, Green hit a new milestone when he caught a pass from teammate A. J. McCarron and scored a receiving touchdown, his first in a postseason game.

Green played in only 10 regular-season games in 2016, having torn a hamstring during the latter half of the season. During the postseason, the Bengals missed the opportunity to enter the playoffs for the first time during Green's tenure with the team. Despite such setbacks, he remained focused on his goal of helping the Bengals win a Super Bowl one day, which would be a first in the team's fifty-year history. "I think we have a team to do it," he told Schultz. "I think this is the most talented team I've been a part of, the most of these last couple years I've been here. I think anything less than that is a disappointment. I think that is the standard we hold to each other." With the start of the 2017 season

in September of that year, Green set out to strive toward his goal once again.

PERSONAL LIFE
Green and his wife, Miranda, met on Facebook while Green was still attending the University of Georgia. They married in 2015, and their first child, a son named Easton, was born the following year. In interviews, Green has noted that he looks forward to taking his son to football games when he is old enough. In addition to his work with the Bengals and family commitments, Green has starred in commercials for a variety of brands, including Champs Sports and Beats by Dre.

SUGGESTED READING
Dehner, Paul, Jr. "Fatherhood Enhances All Sides of A.J. Green." *Cincinnati.com*, 16 June 2017, www.cincinnati.com/story/sports/nfl/bengals/2017/06/16/fatherhood-enhances-all-sides-a-j-green/403872001/. Accessed 8 Sept. 2017.

"Georgia Star Receiver A.J. Green Suspended 4 Games for Selling Bowl Jersey for $1,000." *Fox News*, 8 Sept. 2010, www.foxnews.com/sports/2010/09/08/georgia-star-receiver-aj-green-suspended-games-selling-bowl-jersey.html. Accessed 8 Sept. 2017.

Green, A. J. "A.J. Green: It's Super Bowl or Bust for the Bengals." Interview by Jordan Schultz. *Huffington Post*, 16 Dec. 2015, www.huffingtonpost.com/entry/aj-green-cincinnati-bengals_us_56687e23e4b080eddf569a0e. Accessed 8 Sept. 2017.

Harvey, Coley. "Who Is A.J. Green? Bengals Dish on (Mostly) Silent Superstar." *ESPN*, 11 Nov. 2015, www.espn.com/blog/cincinnati-bengals/post/_/id/20000/bengals-aj-green-silent-superstar-who-is-he-dish. Accessed 8 Sept. 2017.

Hobson, Geoff. "A Modest Proposal: Green Rules as Downhome Superstar." *Cincinnati Bengals*, 24 July 2014, www.bengals.com/news/article-1/A-modest-proposal-Green-rules-as-downhome-superstar/56b6b201-530a-472f-90c5-f53c04623e53. Accessed 8 Sept. 2017.

Kalland, Robby. "Former UGA Star WR A.J. Green Endowing Scholarships to School." *CBS Sports*, 2 Nov. 2015, www.cbssports.com/college-football/news/former-uga-star-wr-aj-green-endowing-scholarships-to-school/. Accessed 8 Sept. 2017.

Shipgel, Ben. "A Fierce Playmaker Who Shrugs Off Praise." *The New York Times*, 28 Dec. 2012, www.nytimes.com/2012/12/29/sports/football/bengals-aj-green-is-fierce-playmaker-with-quiet-approach.html. Accessed 8 Sept. 2017.

—*Joy Crelin*

John Green

Date of birth: August 24, 1977
Occupation: Author

John Green is an American author of young adult fiction best known for his 2012 novel, *The Fault in Our Stars*. Green also operates several web-based entertainment and educational video channels aimed at his primarily teenage audience.

EARLY LIFE AND EDUCATION
John Michael Green was born in Indianapolis, Indiana, on August 24, 1977, to Mike and Sydney Green. Green's younger brother, Hank, was born in 1980. The family moved to Orlando, Florida, where Green spent most of his youth, before moving to Birmingham, Alabama. Green graduated from the Indian Springs School in 1995.

Green has noted that although he was fortunate to have a stable upbringing, he often felt isolated and was the target of bullying in school. These struggles in school helped form his personality and his interest in reading and writing. His fiction would later draw upon his experiences with bullies and teenage social dynamics.

Green attended Kenyon College, where he studied English and religion. Upon graduating in 2000, Green planned to enroll at the University of Chicago Divinity School, but first began his career as a student chaplain at a children's hospital in Columbus, Ohio. Working closely with the families of sick and dying children greatly affected Green. Though he had an interest in writing, he had not considered it a career option until he decided to leave the children's hospital and not pursue divinity school. He moved to Chicago, Illinois, seeking a new career in literature.

YA NOVELIST
For the next five years, Green worked at *Booklist*, a Chicago-based magazine published by the American Library Association (ALA). He decided to write for teenage audiences, and began reading young adult novels in preparation for writing what would become his first book, *Looking for Alaska*.

Looking for Alaska, published in 2005, was partially based on Green's experience at the Indian Springs School in Alabama. The novel's themes, which include teenage romance, bullying, and death, would characterize much of Green's later work. Having succeeded in publishing his first young adult novel, Green left his job at *Booklist* to write full time.

Following his debut, Green published a second novel, *An Abundance of Katherines* (2006),

and several short stories. His third novel, *Paper Towns* (2008), debuted at number five on the *New York Times* Best Sellers list.

ONLINE CREATIVE WORK
While his career as a best-selling young adult author was on the rise, Green began using the video-sharing website YouTube to create video diaries, or vlogs, as a way to communicate with his brother, Hank. In 2007 the Greens launched *Brotherhood 2.0* (later renamed *VlogBrothers*), a YouTube-based video blog that expanded into a platform for the brothers to discuss their varied interests and social concerns. The channel grew in popularity and launched Green into his second career as an online video host and presenter, primarily of educational and entertainment content. The *VlogBrothers* audience developed into "Nerdfighteria," a subculture among Green's fans that promotes humanitarian causes and charity events. Members of the community, known as "Nerdfighters," collaboratively raise awareness and funds for various charities in an annual online event dubbed the Project for Awesome. In 2012 Green also launched *Crash Course*, an online educational channel hosted by the Green brothers, aimed at helping students learn essential information about a topic in under fifteen minutes.

Green's web-based creative work is characterized by fast-paced talking, dry humor, personal anecdotes, and sincere encouragement of his viewers. Green often reminds his audience, "Don't forget to be awesome," a slogan his Nerdfighteria following abbreviate as DFTBA. This slogan and its abbreviation are used in social media posts, clothing, and artwork within the Nerdfighteria subculture.

THE FAULT IN OUR STARS
Green published *The Fault in Our Stars* in 2012. Centered on a terminally ill heroine, the novel was inspired by Green's previous interactions with children's hospital patients. *The Fault in Our Stars* debuted at the top of the *New York Times* Best Seller list and remained on the young adult chart for seventy-eight consecutive weeks; by the summer of 2014 it had sold over 10.7 million copies. Critics praised the work for its compelling depictions of romance and sickness, as well as the storytelling's insightful combination of humor and melancholy. The popularity of the novel led to its adaptation as a film, which premiered in 2014 and starred Shailene Woodley and Ansel Elgort. The film—a critical and commercial success—increased Green's fan base and solidified his status as a leading figure in young adult fiction.

In the summer of 2015 the film adaptation of *Paper Towns* premiered and was a box office success. Shortly after, Green was offered a first-look producing deal with Fox 2000 Pictures to begin work as a film producer.

IMPACT

The popularity of Green's fiction gave rise to a literary movement within young adult fiction that A. J. Jacobs of the *New York Times* described as "GreenLit." Authors included in this group, such as Andrew Smith, are noted for their use of witty teenage narrators and unsentimental representations of trying emotional circumstances.

Looking for Alaska earned Green the 2006 Michael L. Printz Award. *The Fault in Our Stars* reached the top of both the *New York Times* and *Wall Street Journal* best seller lists. His books are taught at secondary schools throughout the United States, and in 2015 Rutgers University announced that it was offering a course that would examine Green's works as compared to classic fiction.

PERSONAL LIFE

In 2006 Green married art curator Sarah Urist Green, with whom he cocreated the PBS Digital Studios program, *The Art Assignment*. Their son, Henry, was born in 2010, and their daughter, Alice, was born in 2013. Green lives in Indianapolis, Indiana. Green identifies as an Episcopalian Christian and as a feminist.

SUGGESTED READING

Barkdoll, Jayme K., and Lisa Scherff. "'Literature Is Not a Cold Dead Place': An Interview with John Green." *English Journal* 97. 3 (2008): 67–71. Print.

Grose, Jessica. "The Green Movement." *Mental Floss*. Mental Floss, 15 Jan. 2014. Web. 15 Sept. 2015.

"John Green's Biography." *JohnGreenBooks.com*, n.d. Web. 15 Sept. 2015.

McEvoy, Marc. "Interview: John Green." *Sydney Morning Herald*. Fairfax Media, 21 Jan. 2012. Web. 15 Sept. 2015.

Rosen, Rebecca J. "How John Green Wrote a Cancer Book but Not a 'Bullshit Cancer Book.'" *Atlantic*. Atlantic Monthly Group, 25 Feb. 2013. Web. 15 Sept. 2015.

Talbot, Margaret. "The Teen Whisperer." *New Yorker*. Condé Nast, 9 June 2014. Web. 15 Sept. 2015.

SELECTED WORKS

Looking for Alaska, 2005; *An Abundance of Katherines*, 2006; *Paper Towns*, 2008; *Will Grayson, Will Grayson* (with David Levithan), 2010; *The Fault in Our Stars*, 2012

—*Richard Means*

Garth Greenwell

Date of birth: 1978
Occupation: Poet and novelist

Garth Greenwell's debut novel *What Belongs to You* was a finalist for the National Book Award in 2016. A poet who studied singing, Greenwell began the novel while working as a high school English teacher in Sofia, Bulgaria. *What Belongs to You* was praised by longtime *New Yorker* critic James Wood and hailed by Gabe Habash of *Publishers Weekly* (4 Dec. 2015) as "the first great novel of 2016." Novelist Aaron Hamburger, who reviewed the book for the *New York Times* (29 Jan. 2016), called it "a rich, important debut, an instant classic to be savored by all lovers of serious fiction."

Set in Sofia, the novel follows an unnamed protagonist who, like Greenwell, is an American expat poet teaching in the Eastern European city. He meets a young male prostitute named Mitko—Hamburger called Mitko a "twenty-first-century answer to Christopher Isherwood's shabbily charming Sally Bowles," who was brought to life in the musical *Cabaret*—in a public restroom under the National Palace of Culture. Told in three parts, *What Belongs to You* describes the fraught relationship between the two men, the protagonist's traumatic childhood in Kentucky, and a reunion with Mitko years after the relationship had ended.

Max Freeman

EARLY LIFE AND EDUCATION

Greenwell was born in Louisville, Kentucky, in 1978. Growing up as a gay young man in his rural hometown in the 1980s and early 1990s fostered in Greenwell a profound sense of alienation and loneliness that he succored through his first experiences "cruising," a term used to describe anonymous sexual encounters in public spaces. In an essay for *BuzzFeed*, Greenwell wrote about attending a camp at Western Kentucky University in Bowling Green as an adolescent and finding an empty men's bathroom covered in messages and graffiti depicting gay sex. The bathroom, he reasoned, appeared to be a place where men like him met. All Greenwell had ever heard about being gay was filtered through the horror of the AIDS virus, shame, and punishment. "Those [bathroom] notes," Greenwell writes, "were the first real evidence I had that the world might offer some answer to the desire I felt." Greenwell is careful to point out that cruising can be dangerous—men are routinely assaulted or robbed in such places—but later, when Greenwell began meeting men in cruising zones himself, the encounters were a crucial step to understanding the "joys of being a queer person, not just the trauma of being a queer person," he told Jason Howard for *Salon* (24 Feb. 2016).

Greenwell studied voice at Louisville's Youth Performing Arts School at duPont Manual High School. His early teenage years were extremely difficult. When he was fourteen, his father threw him out of the house when he discovered that Greenwell was gay; Greenwell's mother took him in. Flunking most of his classes, including English, he found a kind mentor in a voice teacher who encouraged him to apply to and helped him gain admittance to the Interlochen Arts Academy in Michigan. By his own account, the move saved his life. "To be a gay kid in Kentucky in the early '90s was to be told again and again, in ways overt and implicit, that your life had no value," Greenwell told Jayne Moore Waldrop for the Louisville *Courier-Journal* (12 Feb. 2016).

EDUCATION AND TEACHING IN BULGARIA

Greenwell moved to Michigan in 1994 at the age of sixteen. He thrived at Interlochen, graduated in 1996 and went on to study at the Eastman School of Music at the University of Rochester in Rochester, New York. As a junior, he rethought his life path, and decided to study poetry. He transferred to SUNY Purchase in New York, where he earned a bachelor's degree. He studied with the award-winning poet Carl Phillips at Washington University in St. Louis, Missouri, where he earned his MFA degree, and began (but did not finish) a doctorate in English and American literature at Harvard. In Cambridge, Massachusetts, Greenwell decided that he did not want to lead the life of a cloistered academic. He quit his degree to teach high school English in Ann Arbor, Michigan. "Teaching high school was my real training as a novelist: it got me out of my head, and (at least a little) out of books, and invested me in the lives of others and the world around me," he told Alden Jones for the *Rumpus* (1 Feb. 2016). In 2009 he moved to Bulgaria and began teaching high school at the American College of Sofia.

Greenwell learned Bulgarian and made Bulgarian friends. For many of his students, he was also the first openly gay man they had ever met; he soon became a mentor for queer and questioning students. Their struggles reminded him of his own. "The stories they told, and also the stories that gay men I met who were my own age told, were exactly the stories I heard in Kentucky when I was fourteen, fifteen, and sixteen," he told Tara Anderson for WFPL News in Louisville (11 Feb. 2016). "I kept thinking, the horizon of possibility that gay people have for their lives here is the same as it was in Kentucky in the early '90s."

Greenwell also began writing prose. In 2010 he published a novella called *Mitko*, about a young Bulgarian prostitute. It won the Miami University Press Novella Prize in 2011. After the unexpected success of his first prose publication, Greenwell planned to return to poetry, but was seized by an inspiration to continue Mitko's story. (A revised version of the novella became the first section of Greenwell's novel.) He continued to write, waking early in the morning to work before class. He left Sofia in 2013 to attend the prestigious University of Iowa Writers' Workshop, where he revised a draft that would become *What Belongs to You* (2016). He graduated from the program in 2015, but remained at the university as the Richard E. Guthrie Memorial Fellow.

WHAT BELONGS TO YOU

What Belongs to You was published in early 2016 to critical acclaim. In it, an unnamed protagonist meets a young Bulgarian prostitute named Mitko. The two men embark on an unequal relationship; the narrator needs Mitko, but sours on him when he asks for money. They converse only in Bulgarian, a language that the narrator speaks imperfectly. The shifting dynamics of their relationship evoke the poet Audre Lorde, who wrote, as cited by Greenwell in a number of interviews, that sex can bridge racial and socioeconomic divides. Love is not merely "a matter of looking at someone . . . but also of looking with them, of facing what they face," Greenwell writes in the book.

In the second section of the book, the narrator reflects on his traumatic upbringing in Kentucky. The prolonged recollection is brought on by an e-mail that announces his father's illness and imminent death. Walking around Sofia, the narrator carries a printed-out copy of the e-mail and remembers his first erotic encounter with a boy and his father's violent reaction to his homosexuality. He crumples the letter in a ball and throws it in a stream, deciding not to see his father. Wood praised this section of the novel, writing that Greenwell's "long swerve from and around" a conventional plot point speaks to the "originality and power" of his writing.

In the third section of the book, the narrator is in a relationship with a man from Portugal known only as R. His life is interrupted by the reappearance of Mitko, who tells the narrator that he has syphilis. The revelation reminds the narrator of the AIDS era, during which being gay seemed, as the narrator described it, like living in a "morality tale." "Disease was the only story anyone ever told about men like me where I was from, and it flattened my life to a morality tale, in which I could be either chaste or condemned," Greenwell writes in the book.

Wood compared Greenwell's style to the kinetic ease of Virginia Woolf or the German writer W. G. Sebald. Hamburger described him as working in an "all over" prose style—like novelists Ben Lerner and Karl Ove Knausgaard—"in which all compositional details seem to be given equal weight." Like those writers, Greenwell has used autobiographical details in his fiction, though he denies that the story is entirely true. "The lines between genres seem in large part arbitrary to me, or at least I don't really care about them," Greenwell said in a lecture, as quoted by Jeffrey Zuckerman of the *New Republic* (19 Jan. 2016).

OTHER WRITING

Greenwell began to publish literary criticism as a student at Iowa. In his critical writing, Greenwell is interested in centering queer narratives, or more specifically, creating and fostering writing that speaks directly to queer readers. In 2015, in an essay for the *Atlantic* (31 May 2015), Greenwell argued that Hanya Yanagihara's best-selling novel *A Little Life* (2015) was the long-sought "great gay novel," describing it as "the most ambitious chronicle of the social and emotional lives of gay men to have emerged for many years." On August 25, 2015, Greenwell published an essay for the *New Yorker* blog called "The Wild, Remarkable Sex Scenes of Lidia Yuknavitch." Yuknavitch's explicit works, Greenwell argues, draw "on a specifically queer and feminist tradition of thought." He compares her "assaultive presentation of sexuality" to the French thinker Michel Foucault and the experimental poet and performance artist Kathy Acker.

SUGGESTED READING

Anderson, Tara. "Garth Greenwell Returns to Louisville amid Glowing Praise for First Novel." *WFPL News*, 11 Feb. 2016, wfpl.org/louisville-garth-greenwell-novel-garners-praise. Accessed 3 Jan. 2017.

Greenwell, Garth. "'Queer Sexual Bodies Are Despised:' Garth Greenwell on Writing His Debut Novel and Why Everything Comes Back to Kentucky for Him, 'For Better and for Worse.'" Interview by Jason Howard. *Salon*, 24 Feb. 2016, www.salon.com/2016/02/24/queer_sexual_bodies_are_despised_garth_greenwell_on_writing_his_debut_novel_and_why_everything_comes_back_to_kentucky_for_him_for_better_and_for_worse. Accessed 3 Jan. 2017.

Greenwell, Garth. "The Rumpus Interview with Garth Greenwell." Interview by Alden Jones. *Rumpus*, 1 Feb. 2016, therumpus.net/2016/02/the-rumpus-interview-with-garth-greenwell. Accessed 3 Jan. 2017.

Greenwell, Garth. "From Flunking English to Celebrated Author." Interview by Jayne Moore Waldrop. *Courier-Journal*, 12 Feb. 2016, www.courier-journal.com/story/entertainment/books/2016/02/12/flunking-english-celebrated-author/80239000. Accessed 3 Jan. 2017.

Habash, Gabe. "Staff Pick: 'What Belongs to You' by Garth Greenwell." *Publishers Weekly*, 4 Dec. 2015, www.publishersweekly.com/pw/by-topic/industry-news/tip-sheet/article/68856-staff-pick-what-belongs-to-you-by-garth-greenwell.html. Accessed 3 Jan. 2017.

Hamburger, Aaron. Review of *What Belongs to You*, by Garth Greenwell. *New York Times*, 29 Jan. 2016, www.nytimes.com/2016/01/31/books/review/what-belongs-to-you-by-garth-greenwell.html. Accessed 3 Jan. 2017.

Wood, James. "Unsuitable Boys." Review of *What Belongs to You*, by Garth Greenwell, and *Black Deutschland*, by Darryl Pinckney. *New Yorker*, 8 Feb. 2016, www.newyorker.com/magazine/2016/02/08/unsuitable-boys. Accessed 4 Jan. 2017.

—*Molly Hagan*

Luca Guadagnino

Date of birth: 1971
Occupation: Director

The Italian-born film director Luca Guadagnino has directed such notable films as the coming-of-age story *Call Me by Your Name* (2017), the quietly seductive *A Bigger Splash* (2015), and

Elena Ringo [CC BY 4.0], via Wikimedia Commons

the beautiful, sensuous *I Am Love* (2009), the latter two of which star actor and critical darling Tilda Swinton. The combination of Guadagnino's abilities as a visual filmmaker—his use of rich color and exquisite attention to detail—and Swinton's ability to express the subtlest of emotions without saying a word has proven to be unique. While in college, Guadagnino, on the advice of a film director he admired, did not attend film school; he simply decided he was a film director and set out to make films.

LOOKING THROUGH A CAMERA LENS

Luca Guadagnino was born in Palermo, Italy, in 1971, to a Sicilian-born father and an Algerian-born mother. Only a month after his birth, his family moved to Ethiopia, where his father taught history and Italian. The family returned to Palermo when Guadagnino was six years old, and Guadagnino remained there until he was in university.

From early on, films made quite an impression on Guadagnino. "I think cinema has always been with me. In a way, there was no other path for me to follow, since I knew that this idea of a big screen giving you image after image was something that made me as a person, ever since I saw *Lawrence of Arabia [1962]* when I was a little kid with my mother," he recalled in an interview with Armelle Leturcq for the French magazine *Crash* (7 Apr. 2016). "Of course, I didn't understand anything about the film at the time, but the actual power of those images and the strangeness of the screening—showing a big version of reality—was really appealing to

me. So I always believed I wanted to become a film director." He began making his own Super 8 films around the age of eight. He told Leturcq that he would shoot scenes around his native Palermo, making "little documentaries about what was around [him]," learning how to use a camera and what a camera can do.

From an early age, Guadagnino had a keen eye for detail. In response to Leturcq's question about his films' "strong connection to fashion"—specifically, his exquisite use of fashion in the visual medium—Guadagnino recalled how even at a young age he would pay attention to the smallest details. "I remember looking at my mother's bags, or the silhouettes of a character played by Bette Davis, or the way things changed between the '70s and the '80s in people's silhouettes," he said. "I developed an interest in fashion's capacity to speak the language of the future."

A DIFFERENT KIND OF FILM SCHOOL

Guadagnino studied literature at the University of Palermo. During his time in college he met Patrizia Allegra, whom Dana Thomas described for the *New York Times* (1 Aug. 2016) as "a fixture of Sicily's cultural scene." The young director, already a devotee of the prolific Swedish director Ingmar Bergman, would go to dinner parties with Allegra, who would in turn introduce him to such filmmakers as Danièle Huillet and Jean-Marie Straub. Guadagnino told Thomas about a life-changing exchange he had with Straub when he was nineteen and still studying literature at the University of Palermo. "Patrizia said: 'Oh, Monsieur Straub, Luca wants to be a director. What is your advice? Should he go to film school?'" he recalled. "Straub looked at me and said, 'If you want to be a director then you are a film director. You don't need to go to school. Don't.'"

Following this advice, Guadagnino moved to Rome and finished his studies at Sapienza University, graduating with a degree in literature and cinema history, then began to pursue filmmaking full time. His education in film began when he met the actor Laura Betti. "I approached her in complete naïveté, and she said, 'Come visit me,' and we became friends—this big, nasty lady and this very skinny young man," he recalled. "I could cook very well, so she used me a lot—'You have to come now because I have guests!' Everybody from [director] Bernardo Bertolucci to Valerio Adami, the painter—these big personalities, together. That was my film school." Years later Guadagnino made a documentary about the famous director, titled *Bertolucci on Bertolucci* (2013).

MEETING HIS MUSE

Around this time, when Guadagnino was in his early twenties, he began to notice—and become increasingly impressed with—the acting of a young Tilda Swinton, starting with her first role, as Lena in *Caravaggio* (1986), and her performance in other early films, such as *War Requiem* (1989) and *The Garden* (1990). By the time she played the title character in *Orlando* (1992), based on Virginia Woolf's 1928 novel of the same name, Guadagnino told Thomas, "I was obsessed." He wrote a short script, titled "The Penny Arcade Peepshow" inspired by the work of author William S. Burroughs, and sent it to her agent along with a personal letter for Swinton, but received no response. Several months later, upon learning that Swinton would be in Rome, he sought her out and eventually caught her attention. "[I] was staring at her like a stalker. Staring!" he told Thomas. "After one hour, she said, 'What can I do for you?'"

Despite being completely unknown at the time, Guadagnino managed to convince Swinton to star in the film, which would have been his first. Though the Burroughs-based film was never completed, the director and actor developed a unique bond. Swinton went on to star in his first feature film, *The Protagonists* (1999), playing an actor who is part of an Italian film crew that is filming a documentary about a murder case in London. She later appeared in Guadagnino's short documentary film *Tilda Swinton: The Love Factory* (2002), in which the director interviews her about acting and how love relates to loneliness.

I AM LOVE

Guadagnino's first feature film to achieve significant international success was *I Am Love* (2009), titled *Io sono l'amore* in Italian. The film, which was generally well received, features much of what the director loves: good food, exquisite attention to detail, a subtle examination of romantic love as well as lust, and Tilda Swinton in the lead role. In the opening scene, the patriarch of the Recchi family, Edoardo Recchi, makes a surprising announcement: he is leaving his textile business not only to his son, Tancredi, as everyone in the family expected, but also to his grandson, Edoardo Jr. Swinton plays Emma, a Russian woman who is married to Tancredi and is the mother of Edoardo Jr. Viewers first meet Emma at the opening-scene gathering, in which her face noticeably transforms through exhaustion. In a review of the film for the *New York Times* (17 June 2010), Manohla Dargis observed, "Amid all the luxuries on display in the Italian film *I Am Love*—the chandeliers, tapestries, and paneled walls, the paintings, statuary, and white-gloved servants—nothing holds your gaze as forcefully as Tilda Swinton's alabaster face." The film was selected by Dargis as a New York Times Critics' Pick.

A BIGGER SPLASH

In Guadagnino's next feature film, which takes place on an island not far from Sicily, Swinton plays a rock star named Marianne Lane who, viewers are certain to notice, somewhat resembles the famously androgynous real-life rock star David Bowie, particularly his look from the early 1970s. Swinton agreed to do the film on the condition that she would have no lines and would not speak at all. Guadagnino agreed. In the film Swinton's character, the rock star, comes to the island to rest her vocal cords—for which it is best that she does not utter a word—with her filmmaker boyfriend Paul (Matthias Schoenaerts), a recovering alcoholic. This seemingly paradise-like setup is disturbed by the presence of two other tourists, Harry (Ralph Fiennes) and his daughter Penelope (Dakota Johnson). Harry, a music producer, is in fact an old lover of Marianne's. With the help of heat and alcohol, the erotic tension rises.

Dargis, in another review for the *New York Times* (3 May 2016), commended the director's attention to detail, observing that Guadagnino "knows how to decorate a movie, from Marianne's manicured head to Penelope's perfectly photographed bellybutton. Every fetishized element—the glorious house, the tiled pool, Marianne's Dior outfits, and the scrubbiest of vistas—looks ravishing, ready for a close-up, too." Dargis, who again selected Guadagnino's film as a New York Times Critics' Pick, added that "the world that . . . Guadagnino creates is at once seductive and aspirational." Christy Lemire, in a review for the website RogerEbert.com (5 May 2016), praised Guadagnino as "a master craftsman" and the film as "simultaneously lush and lurid, sumptuous and startling."

CALL ME BY YOUR NAME

The year 2017 saw the release of Guadagnino's next film, *Call Me by Your Name*, an adaptation of essayist and writer André Aciman's acclaimed 2007 novel of the same name. In the film, which is set in 1983, Professor Perlman, an archaeologist, art historian, and scholar of Greco-Roman sculpture, is staying in a villa with his French wife and his son, Elio. The trio is joined by Oliver, a smart, handsome research assistant. Eventually Elio, who is seventeen years old, becomes smitten with Oliver, who is twenty-four. Eventually the two kiss, and slowly but surely, a romance blooms. As for how much of this relationship the parents are privy to, that unfolds in parts.

In a review for *Variety* (23 Jan. 2017), Peter Debruge pointed out that the film is "not necessarily a gay movie at all—at least, not in the sense of being limited to LGBT festivals and audiences." Instead, he wrote, it is "above all a story of first love—one that transcends the same-sex dynamic of its central couple." The book on which the film is based was a big success and was enthusiastically embraced in the gay and lesbian communities, winning the 2008 Lambda Literary Award for general gay fiction. For Guadagnino, who is gay, this film was "a very personal project, and making it was a moving journey," he said in advance of its debut at the Sundance Film Festival, as reported by the *Hollywood Reporter* (6 Jan. 2017). In an interview with Nick Vivarelli for *Variety* (13 Feb. 2017), he mused, "I would say the reason this film is striking deep chords is probably due to the way I approached it. It was a way of absolute simplicity. . . . I chose to make the movie in the most lighthearted and simple way. I think it's probably the movie I made with the most calmness, applying in a very specific and literal way my motto, that we should live with a sense of *joie de vivre.*"

And he brought the story to life with exceptional skill. "Guadagnino recreates Elio's life-changing summer with such intensity that we might as well be experiencing it first-hand," Debruge wrote. "It's a rare gift that earns him a place in the pantheon alongside such masters of sensuality as Pedro A[l]modóvar and François Ozon." There is a touching scene at the end of the film, an exchange between father and son, Professor Perlman and Elio, to which many critics have given special praise. In his review for the *Guardian* (23 Jan. 2017), Jordan Hoffman called it "one of the best exchanges between father and son in the history of cinema."

In 2015 Guadagnino announced that he would be directing a remake of the classic 1977 Italian horror film *Suspiria*, with a projected release in 2017, and that the cast would include Swinton and Dakota Johnson—one-half of the main cast of *A Bigger Splash*. Filming began in 2016 and completed in March 2017.

SUGGESTED READING

Dargis, Manohla. "*A Bigger Splash*, with a Speechless Tilda Swinton, Is Ready for Its Close-Up." Review of *A Bigger Splash*, directed by Luca Guadagnino. *The New York Times*, 3 May 2016, www.nytimes.com/2016/05/04/movies/a-bigger-splash-review-tilda-swinton.html. Accessed 18 May 2017.

Dargis, Manohla. "From Tapestried Villa to Sylvan Glade, Aristocratic Women in Love." Review of *I Am Love*, directed by Luca Guadagnino. *The New York Times*, 17 June 2010, www.nytimes.com/2010/06/18/movies/18iamlove.html. Accessed 18 May 2017.

Debruge, Peter. "Sundance Film Review: *Call Me by Your Name*." Review of *Call Me by Your Name*, directed by Luca Guadagnino. *Variety*, 23 Jan. 2017, variety.com/2017/film/reviews/call-me-by-your-name-review-1201966646/. Accessed 18 May 2017.

Guadagnino, Luca. "Berlinale: Luca Guadagnino on Why *Call Me by Your Name* Strikes Such Deep Chords." Interview by Nick Vivarelli. *Variety*, 13 Feb. 2017, variety.com/2017/film/global/berlinale-luca-guadagnino-call-me-by-your-name-1201986720/. Accessed 18 May 2017.

Guadagnino, Luca. "Luca Guadagnino on Inspiration." Interview by Armelle Leturcq. *Crash*, 7 Apr. 2016, www.crash.fr/luca-guadagnino-interview-on-inspiration/. Accessed 18 May 2017.

Hoffman, Jordan. "*A Bigger Splash* Director Makes Waves with Superb Gay Romance." Review of *Call Me by Your Name*, directed by Luca Guadagnino. *The Guardian*, 23 Jan. 2017, www.theguardian.com/film/2017/jan/23/call-me-by-your-name-review-italian-romance. Accessed 18 May 2017.

Thomas, Dana. "One Italian Filmmaker's Ultimate Set—His Own Home." *The New York Times*, 1 Aug. 2016, www.nytimes.com/2016/08/01/t-magazine/luca-guadagnino-home-italy-interior-design.html. Accessed 18 May 2017.

SELECTED WORKS

The Protagonists, 1999; *Melissa P.*, 2005; *I Am Love*, 2009; *Bertolucci on Bertolucci*, 2013; *A Bigger Splash*, 2015; *Call Me by Your Name*, 2017

—*Dmitry Kiper*

David Guetta

Date of Birth: November 7, 1967
Occupation: DJ

David Guetta is a Grammy Award–winning French DJ and producer whose decades-long career played a major role in the mainstreaming of dance culture and the rise of electronic dance music (EDM) in the United States. Guetta has collaborated with some of the world's biggest pop stars and hip-hop artists, including Rihanna, Usher, Nicki Minaj, and Sia. After spending years as a DJ and nightclub entrepreneur in Paris and Ibiza, Guetta began making his own music. His early records capture the euphoria of the 1980s club scene, but his later breakthrough singles—"When Love Takes Over," featuring Kelly Rowland; the Black Eyed Peas hit "I Gotta Feeling"; and "Titanium," featuring Sia—meld pop, hip-hop, and R & B with percussive, heart-thumping EDM. For Guetta, the allure of EDM—the making of it and the performance of it at clubs, festivals, and raves—is how it brings people together. "My studio is a laptop," Guetta

Alain Zirah from Paris, France/CC BY 2.0/Wikimedia Commons

told Luke Bainbridge for the *Guardian* (22 Apr. 2012). "Everybody I work with is the same. We make computer music, we're the laptop generation. . . . It's a different way to make music, but for me, I love it, because it's more connected to the world."

EARLY LIFE AND CAREER

Pierre David Guetta was born in Paris, France, on November 7, 1967, to Pierre Guetta, a Sephardic Jewish sociologist from Morocco, and Monique, a psychoanalyst from Belgium. He has an older half-brother, political journalist Bernard Guetta, and an older sister, actor Nathalie Guetta. In his interview with Bainbridge, Guetta described his family as politically "extreme left" and recalled his nontraditional upbringing, which included walking barefoot around Paris when he was eight. He started experimenting with mixing vinyl records when he was thirteen, but when he began deejaying at age seventeen, his parents were skeptical at first. "For them, nightclubs, and all of this life, was terrible and fake," he told Bainbridge. "But when I stopped doing only this, and became an artist, my mother was like, 'OK, now I'm proud of you.' Which is crazy."

In the mid-1980s, house music was just starting to take hold in the United States. It first emerged in Chicago, where young, black club DJs would sample and remix songs from various genres, including disco and funk, to create new sounds. DJ Frankie Knuckles presided over one such club, the Warehouse in Chicago, and allegedly the term "house music" was born from

its name. Clubs such as the Warehouse were havens for African Americans and the gay community, and the latter was true in Paris as well; Guetta was working at the Broad, a gay nightclub, when he heard house music for the first time. Inspired by the sound, and by American DJs such as Knuckles and Farley "Jackmaster" Funk, Guetta and his friend and fellow DJ Kien began mixing their own music to play during their sets, first at the Broad and then at other, larger venues.

Guetta met Cathy Lobé, then a waiter and nightclub host, in 1989. He was moving from seedy club to seedy club, but after Guetta and Lobé started dating, they decided to throw their own parties and, later, open their own clubs. Together they organized and promoted events at, and later took over management of, nightclubs such as Queen, Le Palace, and Les Bains Douches. While Guetta was running Queen, he began inviting guest DJs to play, "which is completely basic today, but at the time it was a total revolution," he recalled to Nick Murray for *Rolling Stone* (11 Nov. 2014). Through this initiative, he met DJs such as Danny Tenaglia, Louie Vega, David Morales, DJ Pierre, and Thomas Bangalter of Daft Punk. In 1996, Guetta and Lobé launched a hugely successful party called F—— Me, I'm Famous (FMIF) in Ibiza, Spain. "Then I started to make music by making beats that are missing in my sets," he told Craig McLean for the *Independent* (27 Aug. 2011).

FROM DJ TO MUSICIAN

Guetta released his first single, "Nation Rap" (a collaboration with French rapper Sidney Duteil), in 1990, but he would not gain serious traction as a musician for another decade. In 2001, he met gospel singer Chris Willis. Guetta wanted to work with Willis, but as he explained in his documentary *Nothing but the Beat*, released in 2011 to accompany the album of the same name, Willis was hesitant to make the leap from gospel to house music because he was afraid the latter was sinful. Guetta encouraged him to look at house music as a church unto itself, saying that he would just be "preaching to a different kind of people." Guetta and Willis first collaborated on the single "Just a Little More Love," released in 2001; however, it was their second single together, "Love Don't Let Me Go," that proved to be Guetta's first real breakthrough. Both songs appeared on his debut album, *Just a Little More Love* (2002), and Guetta and Willis would go on to collaborate on Guetta's next three albums. Guetta played *Just a Little More Love* for Bangalter, who immediately called the president of his record label in France. "It was like God was calling the president of the company," Guetta told Murray. He signed a contract with Virgin Records the same day.

Guetta released his second album, *Guetta Blaster*, in 2004. Jack Smith, who reviewed the album for the BBC (2005), wrote that it was "weighted more towards the mainstream than underground," successfully modeling itself on pop bands from the 1980s such as Depeche Mode, Yazoo, Dead or Alive, and New World Order. "Guetta certainly seems to have grown up from the pop-dance that made his name," Smith wrote, adding that Guetta "should be wary not to alienate the audience that feeds him." By the time Guetta released his third album, *Pop Life* (2007), he was a huge celebrity in Europe who had appeared in ads for the French car manufacturer Citroën and for cosmetics company L'Oreal. "David Guetta is probably the first DJ and club promoter to turn himself into a bona fide brand," London nightclub owner Nick House told Simon Mills for the *Sunday Times* (31 July 2005). Although *Pop Life* garnered a top-ten hit with "Love Is Gone," the record as a whole failed to impress critics. In a review for the *Guardian* (18 Aug. 2007), Betty Clarke described it as "sound[ing] tired," writing, "In trying to unite his trance roots with his love of pop, Guetta ends up betraying both."

ONE LOVE

Guetta was working on his fourth record—what would become *One Love* (2009)—when R & B singer Kelly Rowland, formerly of Destiny's Child, approached him while he was deejaying at a club in Ibiza. She asked him what he was playing, and when he told her that the music was his own, she asked if she could sing on it. "I felt so much emotion from the track; something happened the first time I heard it, and it was just beautiful," Rowland told Jason Lipshutz for *Reuters* (22 May 2009). The result of their collaboration was the song "When Love Takes Over," Guetta's first major hit in the United States. The song signaled the ascension of EDM as an international, mainstream phenomenon; in an article for *Billboard* (1 Oct. 2013), Kerri Mason and Zel McCarthy called it "an indelible part of dance music history," highlighting Rowland's vocals in particular, and listed it as the number-one dance-pop collaboration of all time. In 2010, "When Love Takes Over" earned Guetta a Grammy Award for best nonclassical remixed recording.

The same week Guetta met Rowland, he received a text message from the rapper and producer Will.i.am asking to collaborate. Guetta teamed up with Will.i.am's band, the Black Eyed Peas, to write and compose the song "I Gotta Feeling," which he also produced. The song skyrocketed to number one on the Billboard charts and broke digital sales records. In 2014, *Billboard* named it one of the best songs of the decade, and it won the 2010 Grammy Award for best pop performance by a duo or group with vocals. While working on the song, Guetta and Will.i.am found an instant rapport and decided to continue collaborating. "We were creating this bridge between European electronic culture and American urban culture," Guetta told Cortney Harding for *Billboard* (12 Mar. 2010). "We were having so much fun in the studio, dancing like two little kids. We kept making songs, even though our albums were finished, just for the fun of it."

Later the same month, Guetta met the singer and rapper Akon, and the two collaborated on the song "Sexy Bitch," another big hit for Guetta. Collectively, the three songs served as a turning point in Guetta's career, but also, he believes, in American pop music. EDM, he told Murray, "became accepted by radio, which was not the case before, and opened lots of doors for many DJs." *One Love*, which also featured performances by Ne-Yo, Kid Cudi, and Will.i.am, was well received as Guetta's official crossover offering. (A reissue of the album the following year included the popular song "Who's That Chick?," featuring Rihanna.) "For the most part . . . Guetta knows what he's doing here," Mikael Wood wrote in a review for the *Los Angeles Times* blog *Pop & Hiss* (24 Aug. 2009). "Bring America to the club? Nah. He'll bring the club to America."

NOTHING BUT THE BEAT AND LISTEN

In 2011, Guetta won his second Grammy Award for his remix of Madonna's 2009 single "Revolver," and *Nothing but the Beat* (2011), his follow-up to *One Love*, was nominated for a Grammy for best dance/electronic album in 2012. *Nothing but the Beat* featured an impressive array of guest artists, including Flo Rida, Nicki Minaj, Taio Cruz, Ludacris, Snoop Dogg, Usher, Chris Brown, Lil Wayne, Jennifer Hudson, and Sia. The album's first single, "Where Them Girls At" (featuring Minaj and Flo Rida), reached number one on the iTunes dance chart less than a week after it was quietly released, and "Titanium," a powerhouse pop single featuring Sia, set a Billboard record as the longest-running title (over twenty-eight weeks on the chart) since Michael Jackson's "Thriller." Other hits included "Without You," featuring Usher, and "Turn Me On," featuring Minaj, both of which peaked at number four on the Billboard charts.

If *Nothing but the Beat* was one big party, Guetta's next album, *Listen* (2014), was the exhausted and reflective morning after—or at least Guetta saw it that way. He characterized the album as his most personal, with a focus on songwriting and classic pop melodies. The album's hit singles "Dangerous" and "Lovers on the Sun" both featured singer-songwriter Sam Martin. Other songs on the album featured Sia, Minaj, and John Legend. In particular, the piano-driven pop song "What I Did for Love," featuring Emeli Sandé, was a departure from Guetta's usual party-centric fare. "I still love to party and have fun, and I'm full of happiness," he told Matt Medved for *Billboard* (26 Nov. 2014). "But I've been through some hard stuff lately. I think you can feel it in the songs."

PERSONAL LIFE

Guetta married Cathy Lobé in 1992. They had two children, Tim Elvis Eric and Angie, before divorcing in 2014. The split influenced the more mellow tone of *Listen*.

SUGGESTED READING

Bainbridge, Luke. "David Guetta: Lord of Dance." *The Guardian*, 22 Apr. 2012, www.theguardian.com/music/2012/apr/22/david-guetta-dance-music-dj. Accessed 16 Nov. 2016.

Guetta, David. "The Reinvention of David Guetta: EDM Giant on His Surprising New Sound." Interview by Nick Murray. *Rolling Stone*, 11 Nov. 2014, www.rollingstone.com/music/features/reinvention-of-david-guetta-listen-20141111. Accessed 16 Nov. 2016.

Harding, Cortney. "David Guetta: The Billboard Cover Story." *Billboard*, 12 Mar. 2010, www.billboard.com/articles/news/958972/david-guetta-the-billboard-cover-story. Accessed 16 Nov. 2016.

Mason, Kerri, and Zel McCarthy. "The Top 10 Dance-Pop Collaborations of All Time." *Billboard*, 1 Oct. 2013, www.billboard.com/articles/list/5740702/the-top-10-dance-pop-collaborations-of-all-time. Accessed 17 Nov. 2016.

McLean, Craig. "The Dance Messiah: How David Guetta Became the World's Biggest DJ." *The Independent*, 27 Aug. 2011, www.independent.co.uk/arts-entertainment/music/features/the-dance-messiah-how-david-guetta-became-the-worldrsquos-biggest-dj-2343097.html. Accessed 17 Nov. 2016.

Medved, Matt. "Tired at the Top: David Guetta Talks Love, Loss & New Album *Listen*." *Billboard*, 26 Nov. 2014, www.billboard.com/articles/news/6327812/david-guetta-listen-new-album-interview. Accessed 16 Nov. 2016.

Mills, Simon. "Guetta Fabulous." *The Sunday Times*, 31 July 2005, Style sec., p. 34. *Newspaper Source Plus*, search.ebscohost.com/login.aspx?direct=true&db=n5h&AN=7EH3464704938. Accessed 17 Nov. 2016.

SELECTED WORKS

Just a Little More Love, 2002; *Guetta Blaster*, 2004; *Pop Life*, 2007; *One Love*, 2009; *Nothing but the Beat*, 2011; *Listen*, 2014

—Molly Hagan

Vanita Gupta

Date of Birth: November 15, 1974
Occupation: Department of Justice, Civil Rights Division

Vanita Gupta serves as the interim head of the Civil Rights Division of the US Department of Justice (DOJ) where she oversees areas such as fair housing, voting rights, and employment violations. At age thirty-nine, she became the youngest, first woman, and first South Asian to hold the position. Gupta has been praised for her ability to work with conservatives and liberals and, as Grover Norquist, president of Americans for Tax Reform, explained to Sari Horwitz for the *Washington Post* (15 Oct. 2014), she is "good to work with and a serious person" who has "played a strong role in the left–right cooperation in criminal justice issues." Among her many awards and recognitions is being named a Minority 40 Under 40 in 2011 by the *National Law Journal*. The publication profiles the country's most influential minority lawyers under the age of forty who have utilized the practice of law to implement change at the national level.

EARLY LIFE AND EDUCATION

Gupta's father, Raj, worked as the business manager for an international company, and although Gupta was born in the Philadelphia area, she spent several of her early years living in England and France. She recalls being in a McDonald's in London as a four-year-old with her mother,

Dimitrios Kambouris/WireImage/Getty Images

sister, and grandmother. People threw french fries at the women and insulted them because of their dark skin. Her paternal grandmother was murdered in India when Gupta was a teenager; the unsolved case fueled her desire to work for justice.

Gupta graduated with high honors in 1998 from the Ezra Stiles College at Yale University. Majoring in history and women's studies, she is remembered as often speaking out against discrimination and for organizing campus protests in defense of immigration. She earned her law degree from New York University School of Law in 2001 where she received the Vanderbilt Medal and the Anne Petluck Poses Prize. For several years beginning in 2008, she was an adjunct instructor at the university and taught classes on civil rights litigation and advocacy clinics. She was asked to deliver the 2016 commencement address, which was reprinted by the Department of Justice (19 Aug. 2016), and she advised graduates that "history does not reward timidity. And even when other people in implicit, quiet ways tell you to know your place, do not stay silent."

NAACP
Following graduation from law school and passing the bar exam in 2001, Gupta was hired as assistant counsel for the NAACP Legal Defense Fund. Her first major case took place in Tulia, Texas, where the testimony of one white undercover police officer had put approximately ten percent of the town's African Americans in prison following a 1999 drug sweep. As the convening and lead lawyer on the case, Gupta brought in powerful and respected attorneys from firms in Washington, DC; New York; and California to coordinate the defense strategy, which involved presenting evidence of the officer's misconduct, misrepresentation, and perjury.

In March 2003 a judge recommended reversing all original guilty verdicts, and a special bill was passed by the Texas legislature to allow the defendants to be released on bail while the courts, the state's attorney general, and the US Department of Justice reviewed and investigated the case. The following month, Gupta spoke with Lynda Richardson for the *New York Times* (16 Apr. 2003) and admitted that she was "still trying to process what happened" and that the judge's recommendation and the national attention the case received was "completely overwhelming." She went on to clarify that she saw the Tulia case as important "not just in terms of prominence, but with the power to affect systemic reform." In August, Texas Governor Rick Perry pardoned the defendants, freeing them four years after being arrested. Following the pardon, Gupta and her team negotiated a $6 million settlement for the defendants. As a result of her work on this case she was awarded the first India Abroad Publisher's Special Award for Outstanding Achievement.

AMERICAN CIVIL LIBERTIES UNION (ACLU)
Between 2006 and 2010, Gupta worked as a staff lawyer within the Racial Justice Program at the American Civil Liberties Union (ACLU). The program worked on immigration detention and education cases, and Gupta's first notable achievement occurred in 2007 when a settlement was reached for immigrant children who were held with their families at the T. Don Hutto detention center in Texas. Her work also marked the end of the detention of families at that facility.

As early as 2009, Gupta began voicing her opposition to the reliance of the United States on mass incarceration of its citizens rather than on widespread social reform, and ACLU executive director Anthony Romero credits Gupta with initiating the development of the organization's National Campaign to End Mass Incarceration, which was launched in 2014 with Gupta as its head. He described Gupta, as quoted by *NYU Law* magazine (7 Sept. 2015), as someone who "knows where true north is, how to navigate choppy water, and keeps her hands firmly on the tiller."

In 2010, Gupta was promoted to deputy legal director and named director of the ACLU's newly formed Center for Justice, which focused its work on capital punishment, prisoners' rights, and criminal justice reform.

THE JUSTICE DEPARTMENT
In 2013, Thomas E. Perez, assistant attorney general for civil rights at the US Department of Justice, was confirmed as secretary of the Department of Labor. President Obama then nominated NAACP special counsel Debo Adegbile as Perez's official replacement. After the US Senate blocked the nomination, Adegbile later removed himself from consideration for the position. In October 2014, Vanita Gupta was appointed acting assistant attorney general for the Civil Rights Division, with the expectation that she would be officially nominated to the position and confirmed by the Senate.

In his announcement of Gupta's interim appointment, reprinted as a press release by the DOJ (15 Oct. 2014), Attorney General Eric Holder stated that "Vanita has spent her entire career working to ensure that our nation lives up to its promise of equal justice for all." Her appointment put Gupta into the center of several high-profile civil-rights cases that then thrust her and the Division into the national spotlight. According to Ryan J. Reilly for the *Huffington Post* (6 May 2015), former ACLU colleague Steve Shapiro described Gupta's first six months with the Department of Justice as "a baptism by fire." Since joining the DOJ and heading up the Civil Rights Division, Gupta has been instrumental in investigating potential civil rights violations across the county and in working to enforce the laws of civil rights legislation.

Within weeks of her 2014 appointment, Gupta represented the DOJ in the formal announcement of a settlement with and an agreement to reform the Albuquerque, New Mexico, police department following a federal investigation that revealed Albuquerque police officers engaged in excessive use of force. The DOJ and the city of Albuquerque agreed to work together to reform the city's police department and police practices. This was the first of several investigations that Gupta led into police department practices across the United States and potential civil-rights violations by department officers in such cities as Ferguson, Missouri; Cleveland, Ohio; and Baltimore, Maryland.

INVESTIGATING POLICE DEPARTMENTS

In November 2014, a St. Louis, Missouri, grand jury found insufficient cause to charge white Ferguson, Missouri, police officer Darren Wilson with the August 2014 shooting death of Michael Brown, an unarmed black teenager. The decision ignited protests, which escalated into riots, and the Justice Department began an investigation. In its March 4, 2015, press release, the DOJ announced that although Officer Wilson had not violated any civil rights laws, the Ferguson Police Department had "routinely violated the Fourth Amendment in stopping people without reasonable suspicion, arresting them without probable cause, and using unreasonable force against them." Gupta is quoted in the press release as looking forward to working with Ferguson officials "to develop and institute reforms."

In November 2014, twelve-year-old Tamir Rice was shot and killed after police mistook his toy gun for an actual firearm. When a grand jury then failed to indict the officer, lawyers for the Rice family requested the Justice Department investigate the case. On May 26, 2015, the DOJ released a press statement noting that the Cleveland police department had violated the Fourth Amendment in its use of excessive force and that "a court enforceable agreement" had been reached in which significant changes in most every facet of the department would be implemented, beginning with the recruitment and training of officers. As reported in USA Today (27 May 2015), Gupta stated about the case that "constitutional policing is key to building trust between police departments and the communities they serve."

Several weeks after the April 2015 death of Freddie Gray, an African American man, while in Baltimore, Maryland, police custody, the six officers involved were indicted on homicide and assault charges. In May 2015, the DOJ began an investigation of the Baltimore Police Department (BPD) for potential constitutional violations and announced its findings in an August 10, 2016, press release, stating that the DOJ had "found reasonable cause to believe that the BPD . . . [had violated] the First and Fourth Amendments . . . as well as federal anti-discrimination laws" for many years, which "exacerbated community distrust of the police." John Bacon and Melanie Eversley for USA Today (11 Aug. 2016) quoted Gupta explaining that "policing that violates the Constitution or federal law severely undermines community trust, and blanket assumptions about certain neighborhoods can lead to resentment against police." The Civil Rights Division and the city of Baltimore began negotiations for reform of department policy and officer training, with Gupta stating in the press release that she felt "optimistic" because she has witnessed "transformative reform rebuild relationships and advance public safety."

Although not formally nominated by the president or confirmed by the Senate as of November 2016, Gupta is listed by the DOJ as principal deputy assistant attorney general and head of the Civil Rights Division. Many feel that the absence of an official nomination has been due in part to the controversial nature of the Civil Rights Division, which handles high-profile civil rights cases that are often entwined with Constitutional protections. Following the 2016 US presidential elections and the administrative and party shift that will occur when Republican president-elect Donald Trump takes office in January 2017, many analysts anticipate that Gupta will be replaced.

PERSONAL LIFE

In 2003, Gupta married Chinh Q. Le, legal director of the Legal Aid Society of the District of Columbia. They have two sons, Rohan and Chetan.

SUGGESTED READING

"Attorney General Holder Announces Vanita Gupta to Serve as Acting Assistant Attorney General for the Civil Rights Division." Department of Justice, 15 Oct. 2014, www.justice.gov/opa/pr/attorney-general-holder-announces-vanita-gupta-serve-acting-assistant-attorney-general-civil. Accessed 15 Nov. 2016.

"Head of the Civil Rights Division Vanita Gupta Delivers Remarks at New York University School of Law's Convocation." United States Dept. of Justice, 19 Aug. 2016, www.justice.gov/opa/speech/head-civil-rights-division-vanita-gupta-delivers-remarks-new-york-university-school-law-s. Accessed 10 Nov. 2016.

Horwitz, Sari. "Obama to Nominate ACLU Lawyer to Lead Justice Department's Civil Rights Division." *Washington Post*, 15 Oct. 2014, www.washingtonpost.com/world/national-security/obama-to-nominate-aclu-lawyer-to-lead-justice-departments-civil-rights-division/2014/10/15/3630985e-5472-11e4-892e-602188e70e9c_story.html. Accessed 15 Oct. 2016.

Johnson, Kevin, and Yamiche Alcindor. "Cleveland to be Monitored as it Implements Changes." *USA Today*, 27 May 2015, www.pressreader.com/usa/usa-today-us-edition/20150527/281599534096354. Accessed 6 Oct. 2016.

Reilly, Ryan J. "Vanita Gupta Is Setting the Tone for Obama's Civil Rights Division." *The Huffington Post*, 6 May 2015, www.huffingtonpost.com/2015/05/06/vanita-gupta-doj-civil-rights-division_n_7190982.html. Accessed 15 Nov. 2016.

Rhodan, Maya. "Obama Nominates Vanita Gupta to be Civil Rights Chief." *Time*, 15 Oct. 2014, time.com/3511429/obama-nominates-vanita-gupta-to-be-civil-rights-chief/. Accessed 6 Oct. 2016.

Richardson, Lynda. "Public Lives; Young Lawyer, Old Issue: Seeking Social Justice." *The New York Times*, 16 Apr. 2003, www.nytimes.com/2003/04/16/nyregion/public-lives-young-lawyer-old-issue-seeking-social-justice.html. Accessed 19 Oct. 2016.

—*Judy Johnson*

Ameenah Gurib

Date of birth: October 17, 1959
Occupation: President of Mauritius

As an internationally known scientist and the sixth president of Mauritius, Ameenah Gurib has championed science and technology as the key to capitalizing on Africa's natural resources and promoting its economic development.

EARLY LIFE AND EDUCATION

Ameenah Gurib was born on October 17, 1959, in Surinam, Mauritius, to Hassenjee Gurib, a primary school teacher, and Firdaus Durgauhee, a housewife. Her parents believed education was as important for her as it was for her brother, and even though education was not free before 1979, they paid for her to attend school.

Gurib developed a strong interest in science while in secondary school, realizing that science held the answers to questions that could change people's lives. The birth of the first test-tube baby in 1978 had a profound impact on her, and she chose to study chemistry at the University of Surrey in the United Kingdom. After graduating with a bachelor of science degree in 1983, she studied at Exeter University, receiving a PhD in organic chemistry in 1987.

SCIENTIFIC CAREER

After completing her doctoral studies, Gurib considered going to the United States for postdoctoral research. Instead, she returned to Mauritius and became a lecturer in organic chemistry at the University of Mauritius. She also pursued her interest in research, immersing herself in the new field of phytochemistry, which deals with plants and plant products. Recognizing that she lived on a continent with immense biodiversity, she hoped to find ways to use plants and their compounds for new product development in the areas of medicine, health, and cosmetics. From 1990 to 1995 she led the Regional Research Project of the Indian Ocean Commission, which inventoried and studied medicinal and aromatic plants in Mauritius and the Rodrigues Islands.

In 1995, she became an associate professor in the faculty of science at the University of Mauritius and a research manager with the Mauritius Research Council. She continued pursuing her interest in plant diversity and was the national coordinator for a project that identified and monitored biodiversity in small island developing states (1997–98) and for the Indian Ocean University (1998–2000). She also served as the project leader for a multicountry distance-education program, the CAERENAD Project (1998–2000).

Gurib's career at the University of Mauritius continued to progress, and she was named a professor in 2001 and given an endowed chair in organic chemistry. She served as the dean of the faculty of science from 2004 to 2006, then served as the pro-vice chancellor for teaching and learning from 2006 to 2010. In 2011, she became the managing director for research and innovation at the Centre for Phytotherapy Research, a newly founded plant-based research and development firm.

Gurib has written numerous scientific articles and more than twenty-eight books, including coauthoring a scholarly tome on botanicals, *African Herbal Pharmacopoeia* (2010). She is highly regarded in the international science community and has received numerous awards for her contributions to biodiversity and sustainable development, including being elected a fellow of the Linnean Society and the African Academy of Sciences. In 2007, she won the L'Oreal–UNESCO Women in Science Award for Africa. The next year, the government of Mauritius named her a Commander of the Order of the Star and Key of the Indian Ocean.

POLITICAL CAREER

For most of her life, Gurib's main interest was science, and she was relatively uninvolved in politics. However, when she was asked to be the presidential candidate for the Alliance Lepep (Alliance of the People) party, she agreed because she saw it as a way to serve her country. In May 2015, then-president Kailash Purryag, who had been appointed by the Labour Party prior to the party's defeat in the December 2014 elections, resigned. The new prime minister, Sir Anerood Jugnauth, nominated Gurib, and she was unanimously elected president by the National Assembly. On June 5, 2015, she was sworn in as the country's first nonpolitician president. On the same day, she received Mauritius's highest distinction, Grand Commander of the Order of the Star and Key of the Indian Ocean.

Gurib's duties are primarily ceremonial. She is responsible for upholding the constitution and heading the country's paramilitary units. After her inauguration, Gurib announced her intent to be more than a figurehead. She promised to remain apolitical, but to expand her presidential role to promote initiatives that foster science, technology, and sustainability. She also planned to promote education and gender equality.

IMPACT

Since taking office, Gurib has met with many world leaders and attended regional and global forums, such as the African Ministerial Conference in 2015 and the Global Women's Forum Dubai in 2016, to share her knowledge and vision of transforming Africa through science, technology, education, and empowerment of women. In 2015, *Foreign Policy* magazine named her one of the world's one hundred leading global thinkers, citing her advocacy for science and technology investment throughout Africa and desire to narrow the science gap between northern and southern Africa.

PERSONAL LIFE

Gurib married Anwar Fakim, a surgeon, in 1988. They have two children, Adam and Iman. She speaks Urdu, English, and French.

SUGGESTED READING

"Ameenah Gurib-Fakim." *University Pierre and Marie Curie*. UPMC, 12 Dec. 2013. Web. 19 Apr. 2016.

Carey, Sean. "Mauritius Gets Its First Female President." *New African*. IC Publications, 4 June 2015. Web. 19 Apr. 2016.

Indramalar, S. "Mauritius' First Woman President Shatters the Glass Ceiling." *Star2.com*. Star Media Group, 15 Jan. 2016. Web. 19 Apr. 2016.

"The Leading Global Thinkers of 2015." *Foreign Policy*. Foreign Policy, Dec. 2015. Web. 19 Apr. 2016.

Muraya, Joy Wanja. "President Gurib-Fakim Is at Home among Scientists." *Standard Digital*. Standard Group, 20 Sept. 2015. Web. 19 Apr. 2016.

Perdani, Yuliasri. "Ameenah Gurib-Fakim: Mauritius President on Biodiversity, Science & Women." *Jakarta Post*. Jakarta Post, 30 Nov. 2015. Web. 19 Apr. 2016.

"The President of the Republic." *Republic of Mauritius Portal*. Republic of Mauritius, 2016. Web. 27 Feb. 2016.

—*Barb Lightner*

Yaa Gyasi

Date of birth: 1989
Occupation: Author

A seven-figure advance for a first-time novelist is extremely rare; rarer still is the novel that lives up to such a payday. Yet such was the case with *Homegoing*, the award-winning 2016 novel by Ghanaian American writer Yaa Gyasi, who wowed critics and readers alike with her spellbinding debut. The novel has landed at or near the top of multiple best-of lists and has received acclaim from many notable media outlets, including NPR, the *New York Times*, and the *Washington Post*.

Homegoing impresses in large part because of its humanity, in addition to its unusual structure and its sweeping ambition. The novel tells of historical black experiences in Ghana and the United States by following the descendants of two half sisters in both countries over more than two centuries. It has been cheered as a tour de force by well-respected critics and as a harbinger of great things to come from an author who, at the time of the book's publication, had not yet reached her thirtieth birthday. As for Gyasi herself, she seeks to keep herself apart from the hype, wanting her work to speak for itself, and perhaps to contribute to discussions of institutional racism and how it became embedded in Western, especially American, society. "I hope that we can start to have a longer view of our history and how that informs the way that we treat people in the present," Gyasi said to Sarah Begley for *Time* (5 June 2016). "Every moment has a precedent and comes from this other moment, that comes from this other moment, that comes from this other moment."

Photo by Paul Marotta/Getty Images

FORMATIVE YEARS

Yaa Gyasi was born in Mampong, Ghana, in 1989. Her mother, Sophia, is a nurse, and her father, Kwaku Gyasi, is a professor of French language and francophone literature. When Gyasi was about two years old, her parents brought her and her two brothers to the United States so that her father could complete his graduate studies. After he earned his doctorate in French from Ohio State University, the family moved to Illinois and then to Tennessee before ultimately settling in Huntsville, Alabama. "Whenever we moved to a new place, my dad would get out the phone book and look up Ghanaian-sounding last names and just call people," Gyasi said to Eli Wolfe for *SFGate* (28 June 2016). "And in Alabama there were really very few."

Gyasi has said that she had difficulty making friends during her youth. "I was a really shy kid, and for long periods of my life the only people I felt really close to or understood by, I guess, were my brothers, who had the same experience not just of moving around but also being a Ghanaian in Alabama, which is a very unique position to be in," she said to Begley. "We share a lot of trauma and a lot of joy and all the things that all families feel for each other."

She also felt like she never quite fit in—not Ghanaian, apart from birth, and not exactly African American. "One thing I ran up against a lot as a child was that saying 'black' or 'Afro-American' implies a certain cultural identity that was different from mine as an immigrant," she said to Kate Kellaway for the *Guardian* (8 Jan. 2017). "I found it difficult to feel I was being black in

the right way. The older I got, the more I realized there's no right way, that everything I do and am is also allowed to be black."

EDUCATION AND BOOK DEAL

In order to cope with her feelings of isolation, Gyasi disappeared into books. Before long, her love of reading inspired her to begin writing stories of her own. She even submitted a story to the Reading Rainbow Young Writers and Illustrators Contest, which earned her a certificate of achievement signed by actor and *Reading Rainbow* host LeVar Burton. "It was my most prized possession, and I was just hooked from there," she recalled to Begley. "But I don't think I really understood that you could choose writing as a profession for many years later." That revelation came at age seventeen, when she read Toni Morrison's novel *Song of Solomon* (1977) for the first time. "It was kind of like the tipping point for me in terms of understanding that I could be a writer—that black women do this work and do it well," she said to Maddie Oatman for *Mother Jones* (7 June 2016).

When she told her pragmatic parents that she wanted to become a writer, they were less than pleased. Nevertheless, she forged on and, in 2011, earned her bachelor's degree in English from Stanford University. Then, after a brief period working at a technology startup company in San Francisco—a job her parents loved and she hated—she entered the Iowa Writers' Workshop in 2012, aided by a Dean's Graduate Research Fellowship from the University of Iowa. She completed the program and earned her MFA in creative writing in 2014.

All this time, both during college and afterward, she was at work on *Homegoing*, the novel that would establish her as a young writer to watch. Her work on the book was methodical and sometimes painfully slow, but upon completing it in 2015, she found almost instantaneous success. The first agent to whom she sent the draft loved it and signed her as a client; that agent in turn sold it to Alfred A. Knopf, following a bidding war that drove the price above $1 million. Selling the novel was an almost painless process, and every writer's dream. Gyasi has admitted to having mixed feelings about the hefty advance. "It's great that it brings the work attention . . . [but] it also makes me nervous that people are going to have kind of harsher expectations for my work than they might have otherwise," she said to Begley.

HOMEGOING

Homegoing was inspired by Gyasi's visit to Ghana in the summer of 2009, funded by a research grant for novel writing that she received from Stanford in advance of her junior year. During the trip to her homeland, which she had not seen since leaving at the age of two, she reconnected with extended family but found herself feeling uninspired and unable to work on her novel. That changed when she visited Cape Coast Castle, a former outpost for the European slave trade. In the upper floors of the castle, British soldiers lived in luxury with the local woman they took as wives, while in the dungeons below, those who had been sold into slavery endured brutal and horrific conditions before being shipped overseas to colonies in the Americas.

The experience both haunted and inspired Gyasi. She began to imagine writing a novel about two half-sisters who lived in the castle, one as a soldier's wife and one as a slave, without knowing each other. Initially she imagined that the novel would take place in the present day, with flashbacks to the 1700s, but that began to change as Gyasi came to realize she wanted to tell a generational story, one that would depict the black experience in both Ghana and America. The half-sisters are Effia, who marries an English commander at the castle, and Esi, who is captured from her village and sent to toil as a slave in Alabama. The novel then follows these women and their descendants on two continents; as Effia and her children benefit from their familial relationship with the British, Esi and her children and grandchildren struggle to survive. Their stories progress through the brutal conflict between the Fante and Asante people, the full British colonization of Ghana, the American Civil War, the Great Migration, and varied civil rights milestones, up until the modern day.

Despite the numerous characters, locations, and events involved, Gyasi claims it was not as difficult to structure as one might think. "I didn't outline," she said to Wolfe. "I made a family tree that I put up on my wall, and I just had the sisters on either side of the page and their descendants, then the years in which the bulk of their chapter would take place." She added, "The research really wasn't crazy extensive. I say that my research was wide but shallow."

Upon its publication, *Homegoing* received stellar reviews. In a review for the *New York Times* (13 June 2016), Michiko Kakutani wrote, "It's impossible not to admire the ambition and scope of *Homegoing*, and thanks to Ms. Gyasi's instinctive storytelling gifts, the book leaves the reader with a visceral understanding of both the savage realities of slavery and the emotional damage that is handed down, over the centuries, from mothers to daughters, fathers to sons." Ron Charles wrote for the *Washington Post* (13 June 2016) that "the speed with which Gyasi sweeps across the decades isn't confusing so much as dazzling, creating a kind of time-elapsed photo of black lives in America and in the motherland."

Homegoing won the 2017 PEN/Hemingway Award for best debut novel or short-story collection and the National Book Critics Circle's John Leonard Award for best debut novel of 2016. Writer and 2015 MacArthur Fellow Ta-Nehisi Coates, an early promoter of the book, selected Gyasi as one of the National Book Foundation's "5 under 35" honorees for 2016.

SUGGESTED READING

Begley, Sarah. "A 26-Year-Old Looks to the Past for Her Literary Debut." *Time*, 5 June 2016, time.com/4357214/homegoing-yaa-gyasi-profile. Accessed 6 June 2017.

Charles, Ron. "*Homegoing*, by Yaa Gyasi: A Bold Tale of Slavery for a New *Roots* Generation." Review of *Homegoing*, by Yaa Gyasi. *The Washington Post*, 13 June 2016, www.washingtonpost.com/entertainment/books/homegoing-by-yaa-gyasi-a-bold-tale-of-slavery-for-a-new-roots-generation/2016/06/13/f5802cee-2e85-11e6-9de3-6e6e7a14000c_story.html. Accessed 6 June 2017.

Gyasi, Yaa. "Yaa Gyasi: 'Slavery Is on People's Minds. It Affects Us Still.'" Interview by Kate Kellaway. *The Guardian*, 8 Jan. 2017, www.theguardian.com/books/2017/jan/08/yaa-gyasi-slavery-is-on-peoples-minds-it-affects-us-still-interview-homegoing-observer-new-review. Accessed 6 June 2017.

Kakutani, Michiko. "Review: In *Homegoing*, What Slavery Costs One Family." Review of *Homegoing*, by Yaa Gyasi. *The New York Times*, 13 June 2016, www.nytimes.com/2016/06/14/books/review-homegoing-by-yaa-gyasi.html. Accessed 6 June 2017.

Oatman, Maddie. "The Slavery Story You Haven't Heard Yet." *Mother Jones*, 7 June 2016, www.motherjones.com/media/2016/06/yaa-gyasi-debut-novel-homegoing-slavery. Accessed 6 June 2017.

Wolfe, Eli. "How Yaa Gyasi Found Her Story in Slavers' Outpost." *SFGate*, Hearst Communications, 28 June 2016, www.sfgate.com/books/article/How-Yaa-Gyasi-found-her-story-in-slavers-8329849.php. Accessed 6 June 2017.

—*Christopher Mari*

Rebecca Hall

Date of birth: May 3, 1982
Occupation: Actor

Rebecca Hall is an award-winning actor for her work both in film and on stage. Yet she has faced some criticism she feels is unwarranted. As she explained to Cara Buckley for the *New*

Siebbi derivative work: César/CC BY 3.0/ Wikimedia Commons

York Times (4 Oct. 2016), "There was a lot of, 'Well, you really came out in the movie world, and you've blown it because you've gone off and done theater.' But I want a career in movies forever and a career in theater forever. They both have a very important place in my heart." Hall seeks to balance these two worlds and, because of this, she has created a rule for herself where she must appear in at least one stage production for every three films. As the child of artistic parents, Hall knew from a young age that she wanted a career in theater. Discussing her approach to acting, she told Josh Ralske for *MovieMaker* (10 Oct. 2016), "For me—I don't know if this is the same with all actors—but for me the voice comes first. The sound and the intonations, and the way someone speaks, and how they express themselves, comes first, and then the physical life is almost sort of instinctive after that." Hall has established herself as a versatile actor who regardless of the character she portrays—in film or theater—never fails to deliver in an impeccable manner.

EARLY LIFE AND EDUCATION
Rebecca Hall was born in London, England, on May 3, 1982. Hall's mother, Maria Ewing, is an acclaimed American opera singer. Ewing told Leah Rozen for the *New York Times* (8 Sept. 2010), "The only thing that matters—I know this sounds clichéd—is the art itself. The fame stuff, that's something you should never aim for, never. Rebecca doesn't have that sort of ego. She's never needed that." Hall's father, Peter Hall, a celebrated British theater director, founded the

Royal Shakespeare Company and was also the director of the National Theatre. Their marriage ended when their daughter was five. Of her parents, Hall told Naomi West for the *Telegraph* (29 Oct. 2011), "My mother is incredibly instinctual and emotional, so I've got all of those tools from her and all the analytical tools from my dad. I'm very grateful to both of them for that." Hall has several half siblings, all in the entertainment industry. Hall spent part of her childhood with her mother in Los Angeles and New York. She also lived in England where she attended Roedean School.

Hall made her acting debut in 1992, at the young age of ten, playing Sophy in *The Camomile Lawn*. This miniseries, based on the 1984 British novel by Mary Wesley, was directed by Hall's father. After her debut, offers for additional roles followed, but when her father asked her if she wanted to be an actor or if she wanted to be a child actor, Hall responded that she wished to become an actor one day. After hearing this, her father advised her to have a rich childhood and become an actor afterward. Hall attended the University of Cambridge, where she focused on English literature but dropped out in 2002 after two years.

THEATRICAL BEGINNINGS
In 2002, Hall's father cast her in George Bernard Shaw's play *Mrs. Warren's Profession*. This was Hall's first West End stage production. On opening night, Hall could see that her father was nervous for her. She told Buckley, "He knew the reviews were coming out. And the media being what it is, and people's views, rightly so, about nepotism being what they are, if I wasn't good enough, I would have got completely and utterly slayed. My career would absolutely be over in that minute." Fortunately for Hall and her father, she had no need to worry. Her performance as Vivie Warren in the play won Hall first prize at the Ian Charleson Awards that year.

Hall also performed several William Shakespeare productions at the Brooklyn Academy of Music (BAM). In 2003, casting director Juliet Taylor saw Hall in a performance of *As You Like It*. This was significant for Hall's future film career because it was Taylor who later encouraged Woody Allen to cast Hall in the movie *Vicky Cristina Barcelona*.

Hall again called on his daughter in 2004 for a production of *Galileo's Daughter*, a play by Timberlake Wertenbaker based on the book of the same name by Dava Sobel. The play was presented by the Theatre Royal in Bath, England. Matt Wolf commented for *Variety* (2004) on the significance of Hall directing his daughter in a play about the close relationship of the astronomer and his illegitimate daughter Maria Celeste, "[W]hat one mostly senses is the versatility yet again of Rebecca Hall in the title role, this time in a play about a daughter's love for her father, starring a daughter who has been directed by her real-life father." Hall also performed that season in George Bernard Shaw's 1903 play *Man and Superman*, in which she played a character named Ann.

In 2009, Hall was cast in productions of Shakespeare's *The Winter's Tale* and Anton Chekhov's *The Cherry Orchard* during the first year of BAM's Bridge Project. The Bridge Project was a transatlantic collaboration of companies in New York and London in which actors united to perform under director Sam Mendes.

For her father's eightieth birthday celebration in 2011, Hall played Viola in a National Theatre production of Shakespeare's *Twelfth Night*. Although she had spent time at that venue as a child, it was Hall's first theatrical performance there.

A MOVIE CAREER

In 2006, Hall appeared in her first film, *Starter for 10*. In this romantic comedy, Hall plays Rebecca, a student at Bristol University who falls in love with Brian Jackson, played by James McAvoy. Brian, however, is in love with Alice—another student, portrayed by Alice Eve.

That same year, Hall appeared in *The Prestige*, a film directed by Christopher Nolan. In this movie, Hall plays Sarah Borden, the wife of Alfred Borden, a competitive magician played by Christian Bale. This movie included well-known actors such as Hugh Jackman and Scarlett Johansson. It was here where Hall first shared the big screen with Johansson. The two actors would later reunite for another project.

Hall's breakout role was in the 2008 Woody Allen film *Vicky Cristina Barcelona*. When Hall met Allen, she had no idea there was a script nor that she was being considered for a role. Then she was cast to play Vicky alongside Johansson, who played Cristina. In the film, the two are friends and rivals, both in love with a local painter played by Javier Bardem. She found Allen's process, which included improvising, as she told Jon Weisman for *Variety* (24 Oct. 2008), "Initially terrifying, but I loved it. I found it enormously liberating." For her role in the film, Hall was nominated for a 2009 Golden Globe Award for best performance by an actress in a motion picture. The film won a 2008 Gotham Independent Film Award for best ensemble performance as well as a 2009 Golden Globe Award for best motion picture.

Following the success of *Vicky Cristina Barcelona*, Hall appeared that same year in *Frost/Nixon* directed by Ron Howard. This historical drama presents a version of the conversations that Richard Nixon had with British television interviewer David Frost after the Watergate political scandal. In the movie, Hall plays Frost's girlfriend, Caroline Cushing—a promising journalist. *Frost/Nixon* was critically acclaimed and nominated for a 2009 Golden Globe Award for best motion picture. The film was also nominated for a 2009 Oscar for best motion picture of the year.

In 2010, Hall appeared in *The Town*, a crime thriller directed by Ben Affleck. In the film, Hall plays Claire Keesey, a bank manager who falls for a professional bank thief played by Affleck. Speaking of the experience, Affleck told Rozen, "Rebecca is beautiful, engaging, smart—I mean really, really smart—and a joy to work with."

In 2013, Hall played botanist Maya Hansen opposite Robert Downey Jr. in *Iron Man 3*, the third installment of the *Iron Man* superhero franchise. According to director Shane Black, Hall's Hansen was originally supposed to have been the main villain, and would have been the first female antagonist in the Marvel Cinematic Universe. Her role was changed, however, because of corporate concerns that a female action figure depicting her character would not sell as well as a male one.

ON TELEVISION AND BROADWAY

Also in 2013, Hall starred alongside Benedict Cumberbatch—with whom Hall had worked in *Starter for 10*—in the BBC-HBO production of *Parade's End*. The five-episode miniseries was Tom Stoppard's adaptation of four World War I–era novels by Ford Madox Ford. Hall and Cumberbatch play a married couple in the miniseries. Of her character, Hall told Adrienne Gaffney for the *Wall Street Journal* (17 Jan. 2013), "I don't think it's very often that you come across characters that are intensely unlikable, borderline sadistic, complicated and yet redeeming at the same time. She was fascinating to me and very out of my realm of experience. She's a force."

In 2014, Hall made her debut on Broadway in a revival of the play *Machinal*. Written by Sophie Treadwell in 1928, the original production featured a young Clark Gable and had not been done since. Hall first learned of the play—which was directed by Lyndsey Turner—through a friend who suggested she to read the play, feeling there was a role for Hall in it.

Hall found in Turner a director with ideas about the production similar to those of her own: no overpowering technical design elements to overwhelm the text and no grotesque scenes. When David Gordon asked Hall for *WhatsOnStage* (4 Feb. 2014) if the show would work on London's West End, Hall replied in the affirmative, saying, "I think it has a strong effect on people. I don't think people instantly come out and say 'I love it' because I think people feel a bit shaken for a while. It will always have a tendency to shake people up and polarize people."

CHRISTINE

Hall continued solidifying her career as an actor by steadily appearing in different types of films. Playing the lead role in the film *Christine* in 2016 was certainly different as well as a challenge for Hall. The film is based on the story of news reporter Christine Chubbuck. In 1974, Chubbuck fatally shot herself while on air in Sarasota, Florida. Years later, Craig Shilowich wrote a screenplay about the event, trying to understand what had motivated Chubbuck to commit such a tragic act.

When Hall first received the script for the film, she felt uncomfortable. Hall hid the script under coffee-table books and magazines. As she told Buckley, "I think my reaction was like a lot of people's reactions. It seems very morbid and feels exploitative, and why's there a film about this?" Because of the subject matter, getting funding for the movie was difficult. The film was shot in only twenty-two days as a result.

Hall prepared for the role by watching the only twenty minutes of footage of Chubbuck still alive; the on-air violence has not been saved. At both the Toronto and Sundance film festivals, Hall was praised for her work on the film—especially for her ability to make Chubbuck a sympathetic character. Hall appreciated the opportunity to play an antihero, which is a rare role for women. "It's about time women started being the heroes of things. They can also be the antiheroes of things and that's what I feel I'm getting to do with Christine," she said, as quoted by Mark Daniell for Postmedia Network (*Toronto Sun*, 13 Sept. 2016). Hall won the 2016 Courage in Acting Award, granted by the Women Film Critics Circle, for her portrayal of Chubbuck. At the Chicago Film Festival that year, she also received the Silver Hugo for best actress.

PERSONAL LIFE

Hall does not read reviews of her performances. After false accusations were made about her in a British tabloid, Hall has refused to discuss her personal life. As she told Rozen, "If I don't have that, I have nothing." She is married to the actor Morgan Spector and the couple lives in Brooklyn, New York.

SUGGESTED READING

Daniell, Mark, Postmedia Network. "Rebecca Hall Says Marvel Reduced Her Part in 'Iron Man 3.'" *Toronto Sun*, 13 Sept. 2016, www.torontosun.com/2016/09/13/tiff-16-rebecca-hall-says-marvel-reduced-her-part-in-iron-man-3. Accessed 13 Feb. 2017.
Hall, Rebecca. "When She First Got This Script, She Hid It." Interview by Cara Buckley. *New York Times*, 4 Oct. 2016, www.nytimes.com/2016/10/09/movies/rebecca-hall-interview-christine.html. Accessed 4 Jan. 2017.
Hall, Rebecca. "Ready for Her Close-Up." Interview by Adrienne Gaffney. *Wall Street Journal*, 17 Jan. 2013, www.wsj.com/articles/SB10001424127887324407504578187312387487542. Accessed 30 Jan. 2017.
Hall, Rebecca. "Rebecca Hall Takes the Lead." Interview by Naomi West. *The Telegraph*, 29 Oct. 2011, www.telegraph.co.uk/culture/film/starsandstories/8852878/Rebecca-Hall-takes-the-lead.html. Accessed 27 Jan. 2017.
Hall, Rebecca. "Rebecca Hall." Interview by Jon Weisman. *Variety*, 24 Oct. 2008, www.variety.com/2008/film/awards/rebecca-hall-1117994647/. Accessed 3 Jan. 2017.
Rozen, Leah. "Off and Running around the World." *New York Times*, 8 Sept. 2010, www.nytimes.com/2010/09/12/movies/12rozen.html. Accessed 4 Jan. 2017.
Wolf, Matt. "Hall Takes Another Dip in Bath." *Variety*, 15 Aug. 2004, www.variety.com/2004/legit/news/hall-takes-another-dip-in-bath-1117909081/. Accessed 3 Jan. 2017.

SELECTED WORKS

Vicky Cristina Barcelona, 2008; *Frost/Nixon*, 2008; *The Town*, 2010; *Parade's End*, 2013; *Iron Man 3*, 2013; *Machinal*, 2014; *Christine*, 2016

—*Judy Johnson*

Halsey

Date of birth: September 29, 1994
Occupation: Singer

Halsey was barely out of her teens when she became a pop star. An in-demand singer and performer with a troubled past, she has openly discussed in interviews and songs her experiences with heartbreak and addiction, as well as her struggle with bipolar disorder. Halsey's first song, "Ghost," was an overnight success in 2014, leading to several offers from major record companies. When her first album, *Badlands*, came out in 2015, Halsey was only twenty years old. Two years later, she released her second album, *Hopeless Fountain Kingdom* (2017). Featuring the singles "Now or Never" and "Eyes Closed," the album tells the tale, inspired by Romeo and Juliet, of a dystopian romance suited to young millennials. Writing for *Rolling Stone* (1 June 2017), reviewer Rob Sheffield described Halsey as "bisexual, biracial, bipolar, but definitely not buying your next drink."

EARLY LIFE AND EDUCATION

Halsey was born Ashley Nicolette Frangipane on September 29, 1994, the oldest of three children in suburban northern New Jersey. In interviews she has likened the small town she grew up in to the football-obsessed town that is the setting of *Friday Night Lights*, the 2006 NBC television sports drama. Because football was such a big part of high school life, Halsey had a hard time in school. She felt different and looked different. The side of her head was shaved, she had tattoos, and emotionally she was very sensitive. Adding to her sense of marginal identity was the fact that, although she looks white, she is biracial, with a black father and a white mother. Before high school Halsey played various string instruments, such as cello, viola, and violin, but then around age fourteen she switched to acoustic guitar. She grew up with her parents listening to bands like Nirvana, the Cranberries, Coldplay, and the Gin Blossoms, and she has cited poetic singer-songwriters such as Bob Dylan and Leonard Cohen among her strongest influences.

The Frangipane family moved a lot. They lived in cramped quarters, and her mother and father—both dropped out of college after they became pregnant with Halsey—often worked long hours. At the age of seventeen Halsey took a combination of over-the-counter pills, trying to commit suicide by overdose; but as soon as she swallowed the pills, she realized she did not want to die—and told her parents. As a result, she ended up being hospitalized at a children's psychiatric hospital for two-and-a-half weeks. She was diagnosed with bipolar disorder, a psychiatric condition also known as manic depression, in which a person can experience drastic shifts in mood, from high-energy mania to periods of deep depression. Halsey later found out that her mother is also bipolar. "The thing about having bipolar disorder, for me, is that I'm really empathetic," Halsey told Justine Harman for *Elle* magazine (27 May 2015), in the first interview in which she publicly disclosed her mental illness. "I feel everything around me so much," she said. "I *feel* when I walk past a homeless person, and I feel when my friend breaks up with someone, or I feel when my mom and my dad get into a fight and my mom's f—— crying over dishes in the sink." But she said her mother always considered her sensitivity a gift, asking, "'Would you rather be blissfully ignorant or would you rather be pained and aware?' . . . She's encouraging of what I'm doing because she knows that even if sometimes I might be in pain, I'm aware."

EARLY MUSIC CAREER

At the end of high school Halsey was accepted into the Rhode Island School of Design but could not afford to go; she tried community college for a while but eventually dropped out and left home. She did a lot of traveling in the northeastern United States, playing her acoustic guitar and singing songs, performing in various small venues where she could get a gig. At times she would stay the night in crowded, unsafe surroundings. Other times she would stay with her then-boyfriend in Brooklyn, New York. She also developed a large following on the website *Tumblr*, where she posted her songs. The time she spent at various lofts on Halsey Street, in Brooklyn, where she met various creative young people, made a strong impression—so much so that she decided to perform under the name Halsey, which is also an anagram of her first name.

One night she was hanging out at a hotel party, and she happened to meet Anthony Li, a member of the band Action Item. Li had heard the entertaining satirical songs she posted online on topics such as the celebrity relationship between pop singers Taylor Swift and Harry Styles, and he was impressed enough to suggest that she record a serious song. Li sent her to the home studio of a friend of his in New Jersey, and Halsey wrote and recorded the first version of her song "Ghost." It took her about an hour. Then they put the song online. The reaction was immediate and overwhelming, and the very next day several major record labels expressed interest: Atlantic, Republic, RCA, and Island wanted to talk to Halsey. She went with Astralwerks, a subsidiary of Capitol Records, which she felt offered her the most creative freedom.

BADLANDS

After the release of her five-song EP *Room 93* (2014), which featured the song "Ghost," Halsey began touring intensively, opening for such acts as Imagine Dragons and the Weeknd. She also gave a memorable performance at the 2015 South by Southwest music festival in Austin, Texas. Her debut album, *Badlands*, was released by Astralwerks in August 2015. The album was a combination of the sound and feel of such young female pop sensations as Lorde, Miley Cyrus, and Lana Del Rey, but it was still very much Halsey's album. She was only twenty years old at the time. Some reviewers, such as Joe Levy in a review for *Rolling Stone* (28 Aug. 2015), emphasized that what makes the album stand out in the world of young female pop singers is what Halsey has to say: "The music recalls Lorde or Rihanna heard from across a suburban football field, and it wears out faster than the lyrics—which vibrate with the twists and turns of a young woman taking command of her body, mind, and then the world."

The album again featured the song "Ghost," a synth-heavy love song about her then-boyfriend, a heroin addict who came and went. In a mixed review of the album for the music website *Pitchfork* (2 Sept. 2015), Nathan Reese wrote of the single "New Americana" that it "reconstitutes Lana Del Rey's Hollywood Babylon-isms and Lorde's tongue-in-cheekiness as a millennial call-to-arms." The chorus of the song goes: "We are the new Americana / High on legal marijuana / Raised on Biggie and Nirvana." Reese cited this lyric as just one example of how Halsey's songs are "calculated, defiant, and, ultimately, hollow." The more personal songs, however, such as "Ghost" and "Hurricane," wrote Reese, succeed because they are specific, because they paint a picture. Critical reservations aside, however, Halsey struck a major chord with her fans. *Badlands* debuted at number two on the Billboard 200 chart, and the song "New Americana" peaked at number 60 on the Billboard Hot 100.

HOPELESS FOUNTAIN KINGDOM

Halsey's fame was further cemented in 2015 when she was featured on the Justin Bieber song "The Feeling," and the next year on the Chainsmokers song "Closer"; the latter was a huge hit, and Halsey's social media following continued to grow. Her second album, *Hopeless Fountain Kingdom*, was released in June 2017 and hit number one on the Billboard 200 charts. This time around expectations were high, and her fame even higher. The album opens with Halsey reciting the prologue from Shakespeare's *Romeo and Juliet*, a line that is tattooed on her arm: "These violent delights have violent ends." After the intro, the first song on the album, "100

Letters," succeeds in the same way "Ghost" and "Hurricane" did on Halsey's first album: by being specific. "I said, 'I'm not something to butter up and taste when you get bored,'" sings Halsey. "Cuz I have spent too many nights on dirty bathroom floors / To find some peace and quiet right behind a wooden door." The song has a 1990s feel to it, as does the song "Alone," which includes brass and cellos. Other songs on the album are more standard-issue pop.

In a review for *Pitchfork* (7 June 2017), Katherine St. Asaph wrote, "On an album full of radio experiments, some succeed—'100 Letters,' 'Walls Could Talk,' and 'Alone' demonstrate the perennially fertile sound of alt-pop—and some inevitably fail. The two R & B tracks are a swagger void. . . . More damningly, style never quite matches substance." Whereas St. Asaph generally heard the album as something for young millennials, others heard a growing maturity in Halsey's sophomore effort. In a review for *Rolling Stone* (1 June 2017), Rob Sheffield called *Hopeless Fountain Kingdom* a "bold second album that consolidates all the strengths of her 2015 debut." Sheffield observed that aside from being influenced by fellow female pop vocalists, Halsey is as much influenced by darker, more adult fare: Trent Reznor and Depeche Mode. "Most daringly of all," Sheffield concluded, "Halsey strips down musically to lean on her voice in the vulnerable piano ballad 'Sorry,' where she worries whether she'll ever like herself enough to let anyone get close to her. She's hardly the first twenty-something pop upstart to face this dilemma. But judging from *Hopeless Fountain Kingdom*, Halsey could go anywhere from here."

SUGGESTED READING

Harman, Justine. "Halsey Opens Up about Being a Reluctant Role Model." *Elle*, 27 May 2015, www.elle.com/culture/celebrities/q-and-a/a28577/halsey-music-bipolar. Accessed 10 Aug. 2017.

Morris, Alex. "Inside Halsey's Troubled Past, Chaotic Present." *Rolling Stone*, 28 July 2016, www.rollingstone.com/music/features/inside-halseys-troubled-past-chaotic-present-w431261. Accessed 10 Aug. 2017.

Ringen, Jonathan. "Billboard Cover: How Halsey Became the Voice of Her Generation through Tweets, Tumblr and Truth-Telling." *Billboard*, 10 Mar. 2016, www.billboard.com/articles/news/cover-story/6971430/billboard-cover-halsey-on-fans-fame-music-success. Accessed 10 Aug. 2017.

SELECTED WORKS

Room 93, 2014; *Badlands*, 2015; *Hopeless Fountain Kingdom*, 2017

—*Michael Tillman*

Corey Hawkins

Date of birth: October 22, 1988
Occupation: Actor

Corey Hawkins is an actor best known for his breakout role as legendary rapper Dr. Dre in the Academy Award–nominated N.W.A. biopic *Straight Outta Compton* in 2015. That same year, he also began appearing as Heath on the long-running AMC television series *The Walking Dead*. Hawkins, who trained at the Juilliard School in New York and cut his acting chops performing on stage, also briefly starred as former Army Ranger Eric Carter in the show *24: Legacy*, a spin-off of the popular television series *24*. The show premiered on Fox in February 2017 but was canceled a few months later in June. In 2017, in addition to a role in the film *Kong: Skull Island*, Hawkins appeared alongside Emmy Award–winning actor Allison Janney and Tony Award–winning actor John Benjamin Hickey in the Broadway revival of John Guare's *Six Degrees of Separation*. He was nominated for a Tony Award for best performance by an actor in a leading role in a play for his portrayal of Paul, a scam artist masquerading as the son of legendary actor Sidney Poitier. Ben Brantley, in a review for the *New York Times* (25 Apr. 2017), praised the revival and wrote of Hawkins's performance, "Equal parts radiance and shadow, Mr. Hawkins transforms a fatally mixed-up character into something close to a tragic hero."

Hawkins has expressed that he does not simply take any role that comes his way. Remaining selective of the projects he chooses to work on, he told Briana Rodriguez for *Backstage* (8 Feb. 2017), "I just have no interest in doing anything that's easy or anything that people expect."

EARLY LIFE

Corey Antonio Hawkins was born on October 22, 1988, and raised by his single mother, Monicamarie Hawkins, in Washington, DC. She has been a police officer with the DC Metropolitan Police Department for almost three decades. His grandmother was heavily involved in her church and often brought her grandson with her; the spirit, energy, and faith characteristic of the church atmosphere would continue to affect him throughout his career.

When Hawkins was nine years old, he auditioned for a 1998 Kennedy Center production of a children's musical titled *The Brothers of the Knight*, a contemporary retelling of the classic Brothers Grimm fairy tale "The Twelve Dancing Princesses." He wanted the role of a character named Teeny Tiny Tappin' Theo and did not let the fact that he did not know how to tap dance deter him. "I just bought these brand new tap shoes—like, the stickers were still on [them]. . . .

By Gage Skidmore [CC BY-SA 2.0], via Wikimedia Commons

And I just remember, like, just tapping my feet," he recalled to Elizabeth Blair for National Public Radio (21 Apr. 2017) of his audition. Debbie Allen, the show's director, loved his tenacity. "He was just so alive. He had confidence," she told Blair. She cast him in the show, which proved a critical hit. "Only a sensory-overloaded curmudgeon could remain unmoved—both literally and figuratively—by *Brothers of the Knight*," Pamela Sommers wrote for the *Washington Post* (20 Apr. 1998). Allen became a mentor to the young actor and continued to cast him in shows. She pushed Hawkins's mother to see the star path she saw for the young actor. When his mother balked at letting Hawkins star in a show because of his grades, Allen told her, as she recalled to Blair, "You better listen to me: This child is gonna go the distance."

Hawkins attended the Duke Ellington High School of the Arts in DC. He had thrown himself into acting but worried about the dearth of roles for African American actors outside of the academic setting. In an article about race and casting, a fifteen-year-old Hawkins told S. Mitra Kalita for the *Washington Post* (13 June 2004), "I know that people get cast based on how they look in Hollywood. We work so hard on our craft, and once we get out of Duke Ellington, there are not going to be people looking for technique. I worry about that a lot."

EDUCATION AND EARLY THEATER AND FILM CAREER

Hawkins spent a brief amount of time in California following his graduation from high school before deciding to audition for the prestigious Juilliard School in New York City to provide structured support for further acting training. For his audition, he prepared to perform a monologue he had worked on for years, an excerpt from James Baldwin's 1954 play *The Amen Corner*, which he had performed in as part of his high school's production. However, he was so focused on acting his "behind off," as he put it to Stephen Colbert on *The Late Show with Stephen Colbert* and Ruthie Fierberg quoted for *Playbill* (19 May 2017), that he completely forgot the words to the monologue. Nevertheless, he was accepted to the school on a scholarship.

At first, Hawkins feared that the conservatory would turn him into "this classically trained robot," he told Elisabeth Vincentelli for the *New York Times* (19 Apr. 2017). But after reading *The Artist as Citizen*, a book by Juilliard's long-serving president Joseph Polisi, he realized that the work at the school was rooted in humanity and not cold, impersonal technique. As a student, he won the John Houseman Prize for excellence in classical acting in 2010. Hitting the ground running both before and after graduating from Juilliard, he appeared in the regional theater production *Piece of My Heart* before serving as a member of the cast of the Off-Broadway show *Suicide, Incorporated* in 2011 while simultaneously getting his first real taste of acting work outside of theater with a small role in an episode of the television series *Royal Pains*.

In 2012, after acting in another Off-Broadway production, *Hurt Village*, Hawkins appeared on the big screen for the first time in the independent military drama *Allegiance*. He subsequently made his Broadway debut as Tybalt in a 2013 production of William Shakespeare's *Romeo and Juliet*, starring Orlando Bloom and Condola Rashad.

STRAIGHT OUTTA COMPTON

Hawkins made his major motion picture debut playing a bit role in *Iron Man 3* (2013), starring Robert Downey Jr. and Gwyneth Paltrow. In 2014, he appeared in the Liam Neeson thriller *Non-Stop*. His breakout role, however, came when he played iconic rapper and record producer Dr. Dre in the highly anticipated biopic *Straight Outta Compton* in 2015. He won the role after taking a risk and sending the film's director, F. Gary Gray, who explained in interviews that he had been deliberately searching for fresh faces to fill the lead roles, an audition tape. Gray liked the tape, and crucially, so did Dre, who was a producer on the film. *Straight Outta Compton* tells the origin story of the pioneering hip-hop group N.W.A., with original members Dre, MC Ren, Eazy-E, DJ Yella, and Ice Cube. Growing up, Hawkins was a fan of the group—whose debut album *Straight Outta Compton*

was released in 1988—and wanted to do his idols justice.

An added pressure, Dre and other surviving members of the group were fixtures on the film set. One day, Hawkins was shooting a difficult scene in which Dre breaks down after learning that his brother has died. Dre abruptly walked out; Hawkins was worried that he had done something wrong but later found that his performance had moved the mogul. "Corey's performance took him back," Gray told Angela Dawson for the entertainment news website *Front Row Features* (11 Aug. 2015). "This big guy who you don't associate with vulnerability was overcome because of Corey's performance. He just couldn't stay. He had to leave the set."

The film was well received by audiences and critics, though there was some controversy about what (and who) was included in the film and what was not. The film received an Academy Award nomination for best screenplay. Richard Brody, writing for the *New Yorker* (15 Aug. 2015), noted that the personal relationships between each of the men and their families "emerge with a remarkable vividness, thanks to the actors' extraordinarily relaxed and conversational performances."

TELEVISION CAREER AND ACCLAIMED RETURN TO BROADWAY

Hawkins also joined the cast of the popular AMC drama *The Walking Dead* in its sixth season in 2015. Based on a graphic novel series about a zombie apocalypse, the show follows a band of humans as they struggle to survive. On the show, Hawkins played a character named Heath, a supply runner at an outpost in Alexandria, Virginia. Heath mysteriously vanishes during an episode in the seventh season, leaving many commentators to speculate that Heath's abrupt departure had something to do with Hawkins being cast as the star of the new Fox drama *24: Legacy*, a spin-off of the popular drama starring Kiefer Sutherland that ran from 2001 to 2010. His memorable performance as Dr. Dre earned him the significant television role.

The much-hyped show was given a splashy opening, premiering directly after the Super Bowl in February 2017. Hawkins played Eric Carter, a former Army Ranger who must stop a terrorist attack. Like its predecessor, the show takes place over the course of twenty-four hours, with each episode representing an hour of real time. Hawkins told Natalie Stone for *People* magazine (7 Feb. 2017) that he took the role over several film offers. "Eric Carter is not a perfect guy. He has flaws. He can be an anti-hero, which is even more interesting. That's why I chose this instead of a film—it was like, 'this might be our only chance.' You know how trends go with television. Next year, the networks might not be open to taking risks," he said.

The premiere of the show, however, was diminished by the world that surrounded it, landing a week after President Donald Trump engendered mass protests for his attempt to institute a ban on Muslim immigrants entering the United States. The plot of *24: Legacy* revolves around a radical terrorist group plotting an attack against the United States and killing members of the armed forces. For many commentators, the story line, as it presented in the show's early episodes, sat uneasily alongside the administration's vitriolic and racist rhetoric. *24: Legacy* was canceled after twelve episodes in June 2017.

At the same time, in addition to playing a geologist in the star-studded King Kong film *Kong: Skull Island*, Hawkins made a triumphant return to his theater roots when he joined the 2017 production of the Broadway revival of John Guare's *Six Degrees of Separation*, which originally premiered in 1990. Aside from the talent associated with the play, he was especially drawn to his character, Paul, telling Jeremy Gerard for *Deadline Hollywood* (1 June 2017), "I remember reading this play and seeing a bit of myself in this young man, in his imagination and will to keep going, to dream, to envision himself and create this reality." He was formally recognized for his performance with his first Tony Award nomination that year.

PERSONAL LIFE
A largely private person who does not often use social media, Hawkins resides in New York.

SUGGESTED READING
Blair, Elizabeth. "From D.C. Theater to *24*: The Rise of Actor Corey Hawkins." *NPR*, 21 Apr. 2017, www.npr.org/2017/04/21/524749803/from-d-c-theater-to-24-the-rise-of-actor-corey-hawkins. Accessed 19 July 2017.

Brantley, Ben. "Review: A Scam Artist's Masterwork in *Six Degrees of Separation*." Review of *Six Degrees of Separation*, directed by Trip Cullman. *The New York Times*, 25 Apr. 2017, www.nytimes.com/2017/04/25/theater/six-degrees-of-separation-review.html. Accessed 19 July 2017.

Dawson, Angela. "Straight Outta D.C.: Corey Hawkins Plays Dre in Rap Biopic." *Front Row Features*, 11 Aug. 2015, frontrowfeatures.com/features/film-features/straight-outta-d-c-corey-hawkins-plays-dre-in-rap-biopic-12838.html. Accessed 19 July 2017.

Rodriguez, Briana. "How Risk-Taking Made Corey Hawkins' Career." *Backstage*, 8 Feb. 2017, www.backstage.com/interview/how-risk-taking-made-corey-hawkins-career/. Accessed 19 July 2017.

Vincentelli, Elisabeth. "Rapper. Hero. Swindler. Corey Hawkins Changes It Up." *The New York Times*, 19 Apr. 2017, www.nytimes.com/2017/04/19/theater/corey-hawkins-six-degrees-of-separation-broadway.html. Accessed 19 July 2017.

SELECTED WORKS
Iron Man 3, 2013; *Romeo and Juliet*, 2013; *Straight Outta Compton*, 2015; *The Walking Dead*, 2015–16; *24: Legacy*, 2017; *Six Degrees of Separation*, 2017

—Molly Hagan

Carla Hayden
Date of birth: August 10, 1952
Occupation: Librarian of Congress

Carla Diane Hayden was sworn in as the fourteenth librarian of Congress on September 14, 2016. Her appointment was widely viewed as historically significant because, as Daniel A. Gross explained for the *New Yorker* (20 Sept. 2016), "American public libraries, though founded to expand access to information, also inherit a history of exclusion—something that Hayden has seen firsthand. More than eighty per cent of American librarians are women, but for two hundred years the role of Librarian of Congress was filled exclusively by white men. Hayden is the first woman, and the first African American, to hold the position." She is also the first librarian of Congress to have actually trained and practiced as a librarian since Lawrence Quincy Mumford, who retired in 1974; her immediate predecessor was a scholar of Russian studies, and the one before him was a historian. President Barack Obama made the appointment, acknowledging having known her since he had lived and worked in Chicago, where she began her career. Of her appointment, Hayden told Nicholas Fandos for the *New York Times* (14 Sept. 2016), "To be the head of an institution that's associated with knowledge and reading and scholarship when slaves were forbidden to learn how to read on punishment of losing limbs, that's kind of something."

EARLY LIFE AND EDUCATION
Hayden was born in Tallahassee, Florida, on August 10, 1952. She grew up first in the Queens borough of New York City and then in Chicago, Illinois, where her family moved when she was ten years old. In an interview with Sarah Begley for *Time* magazine (15 Sept. 2016), Hayden said that her favorite book as a child was *Bright April* (1946), by Marguerite de Angeli, which features

Sarah L. Voisin/The Washington Post/Getty Images

a young African American girl as the protagonist. "What's so important about kids' books—they can be windows to introduce them to the world, but [kids] also need to see a reflection," she said. "They should be a window and a mirror."

In high school Hayden became interested in British history, particularly Anne Boleyn, an interest that began her love of all things English. She graduated from Chicago's Roosevelt University with a bachelor's degree in political science in 1973. The same year she graduated, Hayden began working as a children's librarian and library associate at Chicago Public Library (CPL), a post she held until 1979. Only after beginning to work there did Hayden consider librarianship as a career. She earned her master's degree in library science from the University of Chicago Graduate Library School in 1977. Her doctorate, from the same institution, was granted in 1987.

From 1979 to 1982 Hayden was CPL's young adult services coordinator. She became library services coordinator at Chicago's Museum of Science and Industry in 1982 and remained there until 1987, when she left for a position as assistant professor for library and information science at the University of Pittsburgh. In 1991 she returned to Chicago, where she served as CPL's chief librarian and deputy commissioner. Two years later she left Chicago to take a position as chief executive of the Enoch Pratt Free Library in Baltimore, a job she would hold for the next twenty-two years.

ENOCH PRATT FREE LIBRARY

The library board of the Enoch Pratt Free Library chose Hayden from a field of nearly one hundred applicants. Upon learning that Hayden was planning to accept the job, CPL offered her the job of commissioner, its top position. However, Hayden was determined to go to Baltimore, accepting the challenges of running a troubled and underfunded library system. Within two years, the library had gained nearly ten million dollars in grants and donations, on top of more than a million additional dollars from the city.

Under Hayden's guidance as chief executive officer, the library became the largest provider of free computer access in all of Maryland. In addition, the infrastructure was upgraded and expanded; Hayden pushed through the opening of the library's first new branch in thirty-five years, oversaw a major renovation of the central library (still in progress when she left), and led numerous other improvement efforts, including the digitization of special collections and the creation of college and career counseling programs. By the time she left, Enoch Pratt had twenty-two locations, more than five hundred staff members, and an annual budget of forty million dollars. According to Peggy McGlone for the *Washington Post* (24 Feb. 2016), Winston Tabb, the dean of university libraries and museums at Johns Hopkins University, said of Hayden, "She is loved by the people of Baltimore for building new buildings, renovating old ones, making them the center of life in Baltimore."

In 2015, when civil unrest followed the death of Freddie Gray, a young African American man, in police custody, Hayden decided Baltimore needed safe spaces. She determined that all of the library branches would remain open, including one across the street from a CVS store that had been looted and set on fire. "The library was still that safe place, that place for opportunity," Hayden said, as reported by Brenna Williams and Sophie Tatum for CNN (13 Oct. 2016). "My decision to make sure it was open and available, right in the middle of all of the unrest, the next day, in fact, was really based on what I knew what the community needed and what they expected. And there they were, lined up, the next day to get into that library."

AMERICAN LIBRARY ASSOCIATION PRESIDENT

In spring 2002 Hayden, then still the head of Enoch Pratt, was elected president of the American Library Association (ALA) for a one-year term starting in July 2003. Pamela A. Goodes reported for *American Libraries* (Aug. 2002) that she had said in an interview that she "plan[ned] to develop a model for 21st-century library practices encompassing all formats, all people, all means of delivery, and all types and sizes of libraries."

One aspect of that vision included better recruiting for an aging profession. Hayden believes that children need to be exposed to what librarians do early in life, perhaps through career-day involvement at schools. "We have to do more, even beginning in preschool, to let our children know that this profession has a lot to offer. You have to start early, not just exposing them to what libraries can do, but also to what the people who work in libraries do," she told Goodes. She also believes that librarianship could be an attractive option for adults seeking a career change.

By 2003 Hayden was already concerned about the possible impacts of the USA PATRIOT Act on libraries. She suggested that a fund for legal cases and challenges be established. In this, she was prescient.

PATRIOT ACT

In the wake of the terrorist attacks on September 11, 2001, Congress passed the USA PATRIOT Act, one aspect of which allowed for members of the Federal Bureau of Investigation (FBI) to collect patron data from libraries. Most librarians opposed this provision on the grounds that it violated the First Amendment.

In a speech before the National Restaurant Association in 2003, John Ashcroft, then the attorney general, mocked fears of privacy invasion. As president of the ALA at the time, Hayden responded to his making light of the FBI's requests for patron information, as reported by Norman Oder in *Library Journal* (15 Oct. 2003), by saying, "Librarians have a history with law enforcement dating back to the McCarthy era that gives us pause." Her remark was an allusion to Senator Joe McCarthy and the House Un-American Activities Committee that promulgated a climate of fear of Communism during the late 1940s and 1950s. Accusations of harboring Communist sympathizers were made at that time against the Library of Congress. She also mentioned the FBI's Library Awareness Program of the 1980s, in which agents of the organization visited several libraries in New York City to investigate patrons' reading habits, particularly foreign patrons. The story made the front page of the *New York Times* in 1987, prompting an eventual congressional hearing and a curbing of the FBI's activities, deemed to be in conflict with intellectual freedom.

Librarians opposed to the relevant portions of the PATRIOT Act found a friend in a then-independent congressional representative, Bernie Sanders, who led an effort to repeal section 215 of the act, which had granted these powers. According to Ashcroft, the powers granted by section 215 had never been used in libraries or bookstore. Nonetheless, the ALA reported that several libraries were seeking legal counsel. It also began accepting donations for a program to protect the privacy rights of library patrons, which it called Keep Big Brother Out of Your Library.

For her efforts in opposing the act on behalf of the ALA, Hayden was named one of *Ms.* magazine's ten women of the year for 2003.

NOMINATION AND APPOINTMENT

President Barack Obama nominated Hayden to the office of librarian of Congress in 2016. There were concerns that her appointment, which needed Senate confirmation, would be delayed, as was the case with Merrick Garland, whom Obama had nominated the same year to succeed the late Supreme Court justice Antonin Scalia but who was never confirmed because of the Senate's refusal to hold a hearing. However, despite concerns raised by some conservative legislators over Hayden's previous stance with respect to the PATRIOT Act, the Senate Rules Committee unanimously voted to recommend her, and in July 2016 Hayden's nomination was confirmed by the Senate with a 74–18 vote.

Prior to her confirmation hearing, Hayden's nomination was met with enthusiastic support from countless library and educational institutions. In addition to her proven track record as an accomplished library director, part of the reason for her widespread support among librarians in particular was that Hayden is herself a trained librarian—the first one appointed to the position since the eleventh librarian of Congress, Lawrence Quincy Mumford, who had a bachelor's degree in library science and who served from 1954 to 1974. She also has experience working at almost all levels of a library system. In an effort led by the ALA, more than 140 schools, libraries, and nonprofit groups nationwide signed a letter to the Senate in support of her confirmation. Among those recommending Hayden for the position was White Plains Public Library director Brian Kenney, who wrote in a column for *Publishers Weekly* (16 May 2016), "Hayden is well equipped to naturally reposition LC as not just a research library, but a library in service to the American people, extending our complex cultural heritage beyond the walls of the Jefferson Building." In March 2016, while she was still a nominee, *Fortune* magazine named Hayden to its annual list of the world's fifty greatest leaders.

LIBRARIAN OF CONGRESS

At the time of Hayden's appointment, as Robert Gebelhoff wrote for the *Washington Post* (25 Mar. 2016), the Library of Congress was "in the midst of a massive crisis of mission, and undoubtedly, its next leader faces a daunting challenge to preserve—and possibly revitalize—a symbol of our country's democracy and culture." With more than 162 million items occupying 863 miles of shelving, the Library of Congress is the nation's largest library. It is also its oldest cultural institution, having been founded in 1800 when Thomas Jefferson donated his library as the core of the collection. Hayden's predecessor, James Billington, had resigned in 2015 following the release of a Government Accountability Office (GAO) report rebuking him for failing to meet the challenges of the digital age or to provide a strategic plan for new technologies. At the time of his resignation, the Copyright Office, which is overseen by the library, was making plans to leave and reestablish itself as an independent agency.

Hayden took the oath of office with her hand on the Bible that had belonged to Abraham Lincoln, a treasure of the Library of Congress. Hers is a ten-year term with an option for reappointment, due to an act of Congress passed in 2015; before that, the position of the librarian of Congress had no term limits.

One of Hayden's first steps was celebrating Constitution Day, September 16, using Twitter to chat with students across the nation.

PERSONAL LIFE

Hayden told Begley that her favorite piece in the Library of Congress was Abraham Lincoln's life mask. "My family's from Illinois, and in fact most of my relatives are buried in the same cemetery as Abraham Lincoln," she said. "It's just part of our legacy. As a child I spent every summer in Springfield, Ill. So to actually see the life mask of Abraham Lincoln, it resonated." Hayden decorates her home with practical items, such as bowls and baskets, that are meant for everyday use as well as for beauty. Many of them were purchased while visiting Africa in 2003 as part of her duties as ALA president.

SUGGESTED READING

Fandos, Nicholas. "New Librarian of Congress Offers a History Lesson in Her Own Right." *New York Times*, 14 Sept. 2016, www.nytimes.com/2016/09/15/us/librarian-of-congress-carla-hayden.html. Accessed 11 Jan. 2017.

Gebelhoff, Robert. "The Most Important Obama Nominee No One's Talking About." *Washington Post*, 25 Mar. 2016, www.washingtonpost.com/news/act-four/wp/2016/03/25/the-most-important-obama-nominee-no-ones-talking-about. Accessed 4 Jan. 2017.

Goodes, Pamela A. "Hayden Presidency to Center on Diversity and Equity of Access." *American Libraries*, Aug. 2002, p. 11.

Gross, Daniel A. "Carla Hayden Takes Charge of the World's Largest Library." *New Yorker*, 20 Sept. 2016, www.newyorker.com/books/pageturner/carla-hayden-takes-charge-of-the-worlds-largest-library. Accessed 13 Jan. 2016.

Hayden, Carla. "10 Questions with Librarian of Congress Carla Hayden." Interview by Sarah Begley. *Time*, 15 Sept. 2016, time.com/4494775/carla-hayden. Accessed 11 Jan. 2017.

McGlone, Peggy. "Obama Nominates African American Woman to Be Librarian of Congress." *Washington Post*, 24 Feb. 2016, www.washingtonpost.com/lifestyle/style/obama-nominates-african-american-woman-to-be-librarian-of-congress/2016/02/24/0dff9f14-db18-11e5-925f-1d10062cc82d_story.html. Accessed 4 Jan. 2017.

Williams, Brenna, and Sophie Tatum. "Former History Major Makes History as Librarian of Congress." *CNNPolitics*, CNN, 13 Oct. 2016, www.cnn.com/2016/10/13/politics/librarian-of-congress-carla-hayden. Accessed 4 Jan. 2017.

—*Judy Johnson*

Simon Helberg

Date of birth: December 9, 1980
Occupation: Actor

Simon Helberg is best known for portraying Howard Wolowitz, a Jewish aerospace engineer, on the CBS comedy series *The Big Bang Theory*. Created by Chuck Lorre and Bill Prady, this sitcom, which first aired in 2007, has continued to gain popularity and, for the last several seasons, has averaged an astonishing twenty million viewers per episode. This successful show has made Helberg and his costars some of the most recognizable actors on television.

Throughout the series, Helberg's character has evolved from a wannabe womanizer who lives at home with his mother to a specialist on the International Space Station to a married man and father. And just as his character has developed, Helberg himself has been branching out into film. In 2014, Helberg wrote, directed, and starred in *We'll Never Have Paris*, a comedy based on his real-life relationship with his wife. Furthermore, in 2016, the actor costarred with Meryl Streep and Hugh Grant in the film *Florence Foster Jenkins*, a comedy about a woman who sold out concert halls in the first half of the twentieth century—despite being an awful singer.

Despite his growing success, however, Helberg remains uncertain as to whether he is any good as a comedic actor. Helberg admitted to Catherine Shoard for *The Guardian* (5 May 2016), "I'm deeply insecure. I ask my wife all the time: 'Was that OK? Are people lying?' I'm not as happily oblivious as I'd like."

EARLY LIFE AND EDUCATION

Simon Maxwell Helberg was born in Los Angeles, California, on December 9, 1980, to Sandy and Harriet B. Helberg. Although his father was an actor and his mother a casting director, Helberg was not interested in acting or the entertainment industry during his childhood. Helberg's central passion at the time was karate, for which he earned a black belt at the young age of ten. He also learned to play the piano when he was ten years old and aspired to become a musician. During his teen years, Helberg played in rock and jazz bands. "I played the Sunset Strip at the Roxy, had braces, and had my dad drop me off for gigs in hotel lobbies, and I was not super cool," Helberg told Kathryn Shattuck for the *New York Times* (12 Aug. 2016). "But I kept thinking, if I can get good enough, I can probably get girls."

In his late teens, Helberg began to develop an interest in acting. After graduating from Crossroads School in Santa Monica, California, Helberg attended the Tisch School of the Arts at New York University and completed acting training at the Atlantic Theater Company.

STRUGGLING ACTOR

Starting off in the entertainment industry was not easy for Helberg. As he recalled in an interview with Amy Kaufman for the *Los Angeles Times* (4 Aug. 2016), "When you're starting out, there's no incentive to tell you anything but the truth. You'll get feedback that's like, 'You're not handsome enough.' They will dress up those things a little bit too by saying, 'You're too

character-y,' which means too ugly or too Jewish or too short. 'They thought you were pushing it too big,' or 'They don't know if you're funny enough.' Those are hard things to hear."

For years, Helberg divided his career between sketch comedy and small acting roles in film and television. From 2002 to 2004, Helberg appeared on the sketch comedy series *MADtv*, which ran on FOX for fourteen seasons. In 2007, Helberg appeared as the comedy partner of Derek Waters on the web series *Derek & Simon*.

Furthermore, Helberg had small roles in film comedies such as *Van Wilder: Party Liaison* (2002), where he played a character named Vernon. He also appeared in the movie *Old School* (2003), a comedy that included actors such as Ellen Pompeo, Will Ferrell, and Vince Vaughn. Helberg's first significant television run was on *Studio 60 on the Sunset Strip*. The show, which ran from 2006 to 2007, was critically acclaimed but received poor ratings. While working on this show, Helberg heard about an opportunity to audition for a new comedy on CBS called *The Big Bang Theory*.

SITCOM SUPERSTAR

The successful television series *The Big Bang Theory* first aired in 2007. This sitcom follows the misadventures of four brilliant but socially awkward men: Leonard Hofstadter and Sheldon Cooper, both physicists at Caltech; Howard Wolowitz, an aerospace engineer; and Raj Koothrappali, an astrophysicist. These characters are played by Johnny Galecki, Jim Parsons, Helberg, and Kunal Nayyar, respectively. As the series progresses, it is evident that they are all fascinated with various aspects of geek culture—including comic books, science fiction, and fantasy. The early part of the series involves their awkward interactions with Penny, portrayed by Kaley Cuoco. Penny is Leonard and Sheldon's neighbor and an aspiring actor who has considerably better social skills and more common sense than all of them. Throughout its many seasons, additional characters have joined the show, including Bernadette, a microbiologist who eventually marries Helberg's character. Bernadette is played by Melissa Rauch.

Despite the show's success, Helberg has been critical of those who do not see the work they do in the series as having artistic significance. "I don't think Hollywood respects multicamera television. Well, I don't think they disrespect it, but I don't think it gets respect for its artistry," Helberg told Kaufman. "We shoot for nine months. We make twenty-four episodes. We shoot one every five days, and we shoot for three hours live in front of an audience. . . . We are one of the few multi-cams that year after year keeps ending up at the Emmys and the Globes and the SAG Awards."

Furthermore, Helberg admits that he continues to be amazed by the show's lengthy success, which may likely extend into future seasons. Helberg remarked to Alison Rowat for the *Herald* (3 Oct. 2015), "Just the longevity of it, the quality, all things that make it not feel like a job at all. That's incredible." For his role as Howard Wolowitz on *The Big Bang Theory*, Helberg won the 2013 Critics' Choice TV Award for best supporting actor in a comedy series. Also, Helberg and his castmates have been nominated for several awards, including the 2017 Screen Actors Guild (SAG) Award for outstanding performance by an ensemble in a comedy.

BEYOND *THE BIG BANG THEORY*

In recent years, Helberg has sought to branch out from his role on *The Big Bang Theory* by working in film. One of his more notable efforts is *We'll Never Have Paris* (2014). Helberg and Jocelyn Towne, his wife, directed this semiautobiographical comedy, which was inspired by their fractured courtship. Helberg, who is also the protagonist of the movie, plays a socially awkward character named Quinn who abandons his plans to propose marriage to his girlfriend when he learns that a beautiful coworker has a crush on him. When his attempt to date his coworker turns out to be a disaster, he realizes that leaving his ex-girlfriend was a mistake and decides to follow her to Paris—hoping to win her back.

The film received mixed reviews upon its release, but many critics highlighted Helberg's comedic skills. In a review for the *Los Angeles Times* (22 Jan. 2015), Gary Goldstein wrote, "Helberg . . . undeniably channels Woody Allen in his character's persona and verbal delivery as well as the script's anxiously droll observations and asides. Although Quinn may strike some viewers as more annoying narcissist than self-deprecating charmer, he's a vivid creation."

In 2016, Helberg had another major role in the film *Florence Foster Jenkins*. This comedy follows the story of a real-life opera singer, portrayed by Meryl Streep, who sold out concert halls from the 1920s to 1940s despite being a terrible singer. In the film, Helberg portrays Jenkins's long-suffering pianist, who is haughty but also sympathetic. Throughout the movie, Helberg's character and Jenkins's husband, played by Hugh Grant, conspire to keep critics paid off and concert halls packed.

Although Helberg knew how to play the piano, he understood the importance of the role and worked to hone his musical skills further. Helberg told Kaufman, "I rented an apartment to practice the piano and to work, because that's how scared I was to make this movie. It was in Koreatown. I Airbnb-ed it. It had a piano, and I had to practice for, like, three or four months. Aside from learning the pieces, it was more about the technique—having a crash course in classical technique. Watching a lot of Vladimir Horowitz and [Arthur] Rubinstein videos—seeing how they sat and held themselves."

Helberg found the experience of working alongside well-known actors such as Streep and Grant inspiring. He admits, however, that he was intimidated by the prospect. Although he received critical praise for his performance in the film—with some reviewers going so far as to suggest the role could be a breakout performance—it was clear to everyone on the set that Helberg was nervous. "I didn't think it was humanly possible to be more neurotic as an actor than me," Grant said to Shoard. "Simon proved me wrong. I introduced him to my panic bag—pills, inhalers, unguents."

PERSONAL LIFE

Helberg married actor Jocelyn Towne in 2007. The couple has two children: a daughter named Adeline, born in 2012, and a son, Wilder, born in 2014. Due to the success of *The Big Bang Theory*, the series has been renewed through the 2018-19 season.

SUGGESTED READING

Engel, Allison. "Simon Helberg of *The Big Bang Theory* Makes a Strong Impression at USC." *USC News*, 12 Sept. 2016, news.usc.edu/107236/simon-helberg-of-the-big-bang-theory-makes-a-strong-impression-at-usc. Accessed 10 Mar. 2017.

Goldstein, Gary. Review of *We'll Never Have Paris*, dir. Simon Helberg. *Los Angeles Times*, 22 Jan. 2015, www.latimes.com/entertainment/movies/la-et-mn-well-never-have-paris-review-20150123-story.html. Accessed 10 Mar. 2017.

Helberg, Simon. "*The Big Bang Theory* Star Simon Helberg Freshens Up His Piano Skills to Work with Meryl Streep." Interview by Amy Kaufman. *Los Angeles Times*, 4 Aug. 2016, www.latimes.com/entertainment/movies/la-ca-mn-conversation-simon-helberg-20160726-snap-story.html. Accessed 10 Mar. 2017.

Helberg, Simon. "Simon Helberg Interview: *The Big Bang Theory* Star on His Directorial Debut, *We'll Never Have Paris*." Interview by Alison Rowat. *The Herald*, 3 Oct. 2015, www.heraldscotland.com/arts_ents/13802108.Simon_Helberg_interview__The_Big_Bang_Theory_star_on_his_directorial_debut__We_ll_Never_Have_Paris. Accessed 10 Mar. 2017.

Helberg, Simon. "Simon Helberg Trades His 'Big Bang' Geek for Meryl Streep." Interview by Kathryn Shattuck. *The New York Times*, 12 Aug. 2016, www.nytimes.com/2016/08/14/movies/simon-helberg-trades-his-big-bang-geek-for-meryl-streep.html. Accessed 10 Mar. 2017.

Helberg, Simon. "Simon Helberg: From Big Bang Nerd to Meryl Streep's Cartoonish Pianist." Interview by Catherine Shoard. *The Guardian*, 5 May 2016, www.theguardian.com/film/2016/may/05/simom-helberg-big-bang-theory-cartoonish-pianist-florence-foster-jenkins. Accessed 10 Mar. 2017.

SELECTED WORKS

The Big Bang Theory, 2007–; *We'll Never Have Paris*, 2014; *Florence Foster Jenkins*, 2016

—*Christopher Mari*

Brooke Henderson

Date of birth: September 10, 1997
Occupation: Golfer

Mary Beth Lacy (Sunice Golf)/CC0/Wikimedia Commons

Professional golfer Brooke Henderson was already a dominant force in the sport by the age of nineteen. After earning her tour card halfway through the 2015 season with a win at the Cambia Portland Classic, Henderson won her first Ladies Professional Golf Associaiong (LPGA) major, the KPMG Women's PGA Championship, in 2016, becoming the youngest winner in the event's history and the first Canadian to win an LPGA major in forty-eight years. Her historic win made her, according to the Rolex rankings, the number two female golfer in the world; she finished the season ranked eighth, but ranked third on the LPGA Official Money List. The Canadian Press gave her the Bobbie Rosenfeld Award, naming her the female athlete of the year in 2015. She is the first golfer to receive the honor since 2000.

Henderson, a former hockey player, is a hard hitter with an unusually flexible backswing. She is known as a friendly person, but she is also a fierce competitor who attacks the green. She is not as concerned with technique as other golfers (such as her sister Brittany), preferring to golf by feel. "I do a lot of things you don't normally see," she told Ron Kaspriske for *Golf Digest* (13 Feb. 2017). "I hover the club at address. I grip down a lot. My backswing is long. But it works for me. I think standing in goal all that time made my legs stronger, too, and that helps me hit the ball farther." Going into the 2017 season, Henderson boasts three tour wins, including a major, and stands poised to collect many more.

EARLY LIFE AND EDUCATION

Henderson was born in Smiths Falls, a small town in Ontario, Canada, on September 10, 1997. Her mother, Darlene, is retired but worked as a social worker for Lanark County Support Services. Her father, Dave, a former teacher, is also retired. He played hockey in college and once appeared in a 7Up commercial with Canadian great Wayne Gretzky. Henderson's older sister Brittany is a professional golfer herself, and in 2017 took over as Henderson's full-time caddie. (Henderson's former caddie was her father, who is also her coach.) Henderson inherited her first set of clubs from her great-grandmother, and began golfing with her father and sister when she was four. At that age, she thought the first person to hit the ball in the hole won the game. The family owned a cottage near Rideau Lakes Golf Club in Westport, where the girls learned the basics of the sport. At home in Smiths Falls, Henderson began working for the semiprivate Smiths Falls Golf and Country Club, cleaning clubs, picking up golf balls, and selling raffle tickets. "Brooke had an amazing work ethic," the general manager at the club, Dan McNeely, recalled to Tim Baines for the *Ottawa Sun* (4 Aug. 2016). "I was always amazed at how she had the energy level to go out on her own and hammer out three-foot putts for two hours."

Henderson attended Chimo Elementary School and then Smiths Falls District Collegiate Institute, taking online courses after her career took off. She graduated in 2015. Like many Canadian children, Henderson also learned to play hockey. She even played goalie on the Canadian national girls' junior hockey team when she was fourteen. She told Kaspriske that her experiences as a goalie prepared her for her career as a professional golfer. "They say you have to be a little bit crazy [to be a goalie]. You're either the hero or no one wants to talk to you after a game. It was a great way to learn to deal with pressure."

AMATEUR CAREER

Henderson began playing in junior tournaments when she was nine years old, and played in her first big tournament, the Ladies Club Championship at her hometown Smiths Falls Golf and Country Club, when she was ten. She came in second. Though she was playing with women many times her own age, her success was not surprising. Henderson was already well known as a junior champion. She was the youngest member ever on the Ontario provincial junior team. By the time she was eleven, Canadian pros like Alena Sharp had heard her name. "I heard someone say, 'She's the real deal,'" Sharp, who is now friends with Henderson on tour, recalled to Kristina Rutherford for *Sportsnet Magazine* (1 May 2016). "You don't hear that about a player that age unless they're really great, because golf is a fickle game. But Brooke is amongst that class." In 2010, at twelve years old, Henderson recorded her first ever hole-in-one at the Royal Canadian Golf Association (RCGA) Royale Cup Canadian Junior Girls Championship, which she also won.

In 2012 Henderson won both the Canadian and Ontario junior titles. As the youngest member of Team Canada's Development Squad, she also won a CN Canadian Women's Tour event in Beloeil, Quebec. Henderson beat Lisa Ferrero, an LPGA Tour member, by two strokes, becoming the youngest golfer ever to win a professional tournament. She was fourteen years old. Henderson now points to that victory as the moment she knew she wanted to pursue becoming a professional golfer. "I had really good scores on a very long and tough golf course, and against a very strong field of world-class players," Henderson recalled to Andrea Karr for *Canadian Living* (2016). "I knew at that time that I was on the right track." That win earned her an exemption to qualify for the Canadian Women's Open, the youngest golfer ever to do so. It was also her first LPGA event. In 2013, Henderson qualified for, and made the cut at, the US Women's Open, where she was proud to birdie the seventy-second hole.

Henderson went into 2014 as the sixth-ranked amateur female golfer in the world. Early that year she won both the Junior Orange Bowl and the South Atlantic Ladies Amateur. In the summer she won the Scott Robertson Memorial, the Women's Porter Cup, and the Ontario Women's Amateur Championship. She also won

the PGA Women's Championship of Canada, the youngest golfer ever to do so, and finished thirteen under par, setting a new championship scoring record. In June, she was the lowest-scoring amateur at the US Women's Open, where she led the pack at three under par for ten holes, and ended the tournament tied for tenth place. By September, she was officially the number one female amateur in the world, and the first Canadian to ever hold the title.

TURNING PRO IN 2015

Henderson had publicly considered accepting an athletic scholarship at the University of Florida, but after her stunning 2014 season, she decided to turn pro in early 2015. Henderson was not a full-time member of the LPGA Tour because she was not yet eighteen; her family petitioned the organization to make an exception and let her qualify through the tour's ultra-competitive Q-School, but their request was denied. This made Henderson's road to membership tricky at the outset, but was ultimately immaterial. In June, she tied for fifth at the KPMG Women's PGA Championship and won the Four Winds Invitational on the Symetra Tour. In July, she tied for fifth at the US Women's Open, and in August, Henderson earned her tour card by winning her first LPGA event, the Cambia Portland Classic, by eight strokes, the largest margin of victory on the tour that year. Membership changed her life in an instant, earning her over $700,000 and catapulting her world ranking to eighteenth. She also became the first Canadian woman to win an LPGA event in fourteen years, and she joins Lydia Ko and Lexi Thompson as the third player ever to win an LPGA event before her eighteenth birthday.

Henderson completed the 2015 season as an LPGA rookie. "I'm hoping this is just the start of a pretty long career, and one where I can chase after some bigger dreams and goals that I've set for myself," Henderson told Gregory Strong for the Toronto *Globe and Mail* (28 Dec. 2015). "Really I think that there are no limits and I think anything is possible. My 2015 year proves that it's true—that anything is possible."

Henderson made the most of her first full season on the LPGA tour. She played a tour-high thirty-one events, ranked second on the tour in birdies (with 455), racked up fifteen top-ten finishes, and peaked at number two in the world before finishing at eighth. In June, Henderson got off to the right start at the KPMG Women's PGA Championship when she sank a hole-in-one on the fourth hole. She ended up tying with Ko, the top-ranked player in the world, and forcing a play-off. Henderson birdied the eighteenth hole for the win—her first major championship victory.

Two weeks later, in July, Henderson successfully defended her title at the Cambia Portland Classic, beating Stacy Lewis by four strokes to take her third LPGA victory. In August, Henderson competed for Canada in the Olympic Games in Rio de Janeiro, Brazil. It was the first time golf was included in the summer games since 1904. Henderson was excited to compete in the games and determined to bring home a medal for Canada, but, unusual for the young athlete, the pressure of the event rattled her. Henderson appeared to be within swiping distance of a medal through the first two-and-a-half rounds, but fell apart in the third, after she double-bogeyed the sixteenth hole. Had she even made par, she might have been in contention for a bronze medal. She learned a lot from her uncharacteristically scattershot performance, she said later, but she allowed herself a moment to think about what could have been. As she put it at a golf clinic in Alberta a week later, as quoted by Eric Francis for the *Calgary Sun* (23 Aug. 2016), "I was right there."

PERSONAL LIFE

Henderson continues to live in Smiths Falls. When not on the golf course, she enjoys watching movies and listening to country music. In 2017, she participated in the Morgan Pressel Foundation's annual Morgan & Friends Fight Cancer Tournament to raise money for cancer research.

SUGGESTED READING

Baines, Tim. "Smiths Falls Golfer Brooke Henderson Set to Carry Small Town's Hopes into Rio Olympics." *Ottawa Sun*, 4 Aug. 2016, www.ottawasun.com/2016/08/04/smiths-falls-golfer-brooke-henderson-set-to-carry-small-towns-hopes-into-rio-olympics. Accessed 19 Feb. 2017.

Francis, Eric. "Canada's Brooke Henderson Gained Insight into Herself from Her Olympics Experience." *Calgary Sun*, 23 Aug. 2016, www.calgarysun.com/2016/08/23/canadas-brooke-henderson-gained-insight-into-herself-from-her-olympics-experience. Accessed 20 Feb. 2017.

Henderson, Brooke. "Brooke Henderson: A Q&A with Canada's Next Golf Superstar." Interview by Andrea Karr. *Canadian Living*, 2016, www.canadianliving.com/life-and-relationships/community-and-current-events/article/brooke-henderson-a-q-a-with-canada-s-next-golf-superstar. Accessed 19 Feb. 2017.

Henderson, Brooke. "Could Brooke Henderson Be Canada's Best Golfer Ever?" Interview by Ron Kaspriske. *Golf Digest*, 13 Feb. 2017, www.golfdigest.com/story/could-brooke-henderson-be-canadas-best-golfer-ever. Accessed 19 Feb. 2017.

Rutherford, Kristina. "The Young and the Limitless." *Sportsnet Magazine*, 1 May 2016, www.sportsnet.ca/golf/brooke-henderson-young-limitless. Accessed 19 Feb. 2017.

Strong, Gregory. "Golfer Brooke Henderson Named Canadian Press Female Athlete of Year." *The Globe and Mail*, 28 Dec. 2015, www.theglobeandmail.com/sports/golf/golfer-brooke-henderson-named-canadian-press-female-athlete-of-year/article27943147. Accessed 19 Feb. 2017.

—Molly Hagan

Laurie Hernandez

Date of birth: June 9, 2000
Occupation: Gymnast

Little known outside the gymnastics community prior to the summer of 2016, Laurie Hernandez became one of the most famous gymnasts in the world in August of that year, when she was one of five athletes to compete for the United States in the artistic gymnastic events at the 2016 Olympic Games. Referred to by the media as the Final Five, Hernandez and her fellow athletes brought an impressive skill set to the games, held in Rio de Janeiro, Brazil. Hernandez performed particularly well, winning a silver medal for her balance-beam routine and contributing to the team's gold-medal win in the team all-around event. In addition to earning her Olympic medals, Hernandez's performance in the competition made her an overnight star in the United States, earning her widespread acclaim as well as role-model status for many girls. For many, this would be a daunting responsibility, but Hernandez handled her newfound fame with aplomb. "Gosh, I want to be a role model," she told Steve Helling for *People* (21 Aug. 2016). "I want to be able to know that I inspired girls to work hard and go for their dreams, and to never give up. I hope that is the message that people get when they see me."

Although best known for her Olympic performance, Hernandez has been a competitive gymnast since childhood. "My whole life revolved around gymnastics because I loved it so much," she said of her early life in an interview for *Time* (8 Nov. 2016). Prior to making her debut on the senior circuit in 2016, she competed in numerous national and international youth tournaments, honing the skills that would ultimately take her to the Olympics. All the while, she cultivated the positive attitude and demeanor that, along with her skill on the balance beam and in other events, would come to characterize Hernandez through both her Olympic performance and her subsequent stint on the reality

Agência Brasil Fotografias/Flickr/CC BY 2.0/Wikimedia Commons

show *Dancing with the Stars.* "I want to make sure I always show off my smile and have a positive attitude the whole time, whether it's during a performance, practice, or doing an interview," she explained to Luis Miguel Echegaray for *The Guardian* (8 July 2016). "I never really stop. I would say I'm like this 23/7."

EARLY LIFE AND EDUCATION

Lauren Hernandez was born in New Brunswick, New Jersey, on June 9, 2000. The youngest child born to Anthony and Wanda Hernandez, she has two siblings, a sister and a brother. Hernandez's father works as a clerk for the New York City Supreme Court, and her mother, a former US Army reservist, is a social worker.

Hernandez's interest in gymnastics developed early in life. When she was five years old, her parents enrolled her in ballet classes, which the young Hernandez found boring. She soon transitioned to studying gymnastics, in large part inspired by gymnastic competitions she saw broadcast on television. "My earliest memory was watching gymnastics on live TV, and wanting to do what the 'big girls' did," she recalled to Julia Fincher for the NBC Olympics website (29 July 2016). Hernandez quickly demonstrated her gymnastic talent, performing cartwheels and splits after studying under instructor Carly Haney for less than two months. Noticing Hernandez's potential, the instructor put the Hernandez family in touch with her sister, gymnastics coach and former gymnast Maggie Haney, who would become Hernandez's primary instructor. Over the years, Hernandez developed

a productive working relationship with Haney, who in turn considered Hernandez to be like a daughter to her. "I can't see myself with anybody else," Hernandez told Echegaray of her work with Haney. "I don't think I would have come even close to this far with anybody else."

As Hernandez became increasingly serious about gymnastics, questions arose regarding whether she would be able to balance her training with a traditional school schedule. Her family ultimately decided to homeschool her beginning in third grade, allowing her to continue her education while also participating in extensive training sessions—as many as six per week as a teen—to hone her skills. "I've learned how to fit my schooling in—weekends, evenings," Hernandez told Helling. "I'm good with the time management. I'm keeping up with my studies."

While they have worked to nurture their daughter's talents, Hernandez's parents have at the same time sought to prevent her success from overshadowing their lessons about positivity and strong values. "Our goal as parents is to keep her grounded at all times," Wanda Hernandez told Echegaray. "Regardless of the outcome in any meet or championship, we are truly proud and amazed of who she is as a person."

GYMNASTICS CAREER

At the age of nine, Hernandez gained admittance to development camps hosted by USA Gymnastics, the United States' national governing body for the sport. The camps instruct talented young gymnasts who, like Hernandez, have demonstrated significant skill through an assessment known as the Talent Opportunity Program (TOP). Learning a variety of new skills through such programs and from Haney, Hernandez soon began to compete in major youth gymnastics events, making her first appearance in the USA Gymnastics National Championships in 2012. Over the following years, she competed within the United States and also accompanied other young US gymnasts to international competitions, winning gold medals in competitions such as the US Classic. Although such major competitions could easily have been intimidating, Hernandez's focus on the tasks at hand helped her tune out any potential distractions. "When I perform and the crowd is cheering, there's a ringing noise in my head," she said to Echegaray. "I'm just zoned in and even though I know there are people watching me all I hear is this ringing inside of me."

After several years of competing on the junior circuit, Hernandez made her senior debut in 2016. In July of that year, she competed in the US Olympic Trials, a series of competitions that determine which athletes will represent the United States at the next Olympic Games. The 2016 Olympics, held in Rio de Janeiro, Brazil, represented a new and exciting opportunity for Hernandez, who was in her first year of eligibility, as official policy mandated that all Olympic gymnasts be at least sixteen years old at the time of competition. In the trials, Hernandez placed first in the balance-beam event and second in the all-around event, in which gymnasts compete on several different apparatuses, including the balance beam, vault, and uneven bars. Her performance qualified her for a spot on the US women's gymnastics team, along with team captain Aly Raisman and fellow competitors Simone Biles, Gabby Douglas, and Madison Kocian. At sixteen, Hernandez was the youngest member of the team.

OLYMPIC GYMNAST

In August 2016, Hernandez and the other members of the US women's gymnastics team, who came to be known in the media as the Final Five, traveled to Brazil to compete in the Olympics. The women's gymnastics events began on August 7, two days after the opening ceremonies, starting off with a series of qualification competitions. Along with her teammates, Hernandez competed in the team all-around finals on August 9, delivering a strong performance that helped push the US team to a nearly ten-point victory over China. She likewise performed well in the individual balance-beam competition, finishing behind Dutch gymnast Sanne Wevers to win the silver medal in the event.

In addition to competing, Hernandez enjoyed having the opportunity to experience her first Olympic Games and meet athletes whom she had previously seen only on television. "My favorite part was seeing all the other countries and what sports they do," she told *Time*. "The Olympic Village was awesome because [my teammates and I] were able to see all these amazing athletes, like [swimmer] Michael Phelps and [sprinter] Usain Bolt. I mean, we would say to each other, 'Oh, hey, look, it's Michael Phelps just casually roaming around.' We met Usain Bolt in the cafeteria." Most of all, however, the Olympics represented an opportunity to compete as part of a team alongside older, more experienced gymnasts. "It was great to really experience it with these other girls," she told Helling. "We were all from different backgrounds, but we came together for a reason. I loved that about it."

DANCING WITH THE STARS

As the media response to previous teams of US gymnasts might have suggested, Hernandez and her teammates were met with significant attention upon their return to the United States, appearing on numerous talk shows and embarking on a tour of the country. Hernandez herself received an especially significant reception, as many Americans, particularly

young girls, identified with her positive attitude and expressive demeanor in competition. The media likewise highlighted Hernandez's status as the first Latina US gymnast to compete in the Olympics since 1984, when gymnast Tracee Talavera was part of the silver-medal-winning team.

Although the media attention surrounding the Final Five was to be expected, Hernandez's next move was perhaps less so. In the fall of 2016, Hernandez joined the cast of the twenty-third season of the competitive reality show *Dancing with the Stars*. In the show, celebrities are paired with trained dancers and compete by learning and performing dance routines. Hernandez was paired with dancer Valentin Chmerkovskiy, with whom she performed a variety of dances, including the samba, the foxtrot, and the Argentine tango. Hernandez and Chmerkovskiy earned consistently high scores, proceeding through the competition while celebrities such as Olympic swimmer Ryan Lochte and Republican politician Rick Perry were eliminated. In the season's final episode, Hernandez defeated race-car driver James Hinchcliffe to win the competition. Following the conclusion of the season, she announced that she would join a national *Dancing with the Stars* tour, which would enable her to perform routines outside of a competition. "It's nice to be able to go and just be yourself without having to compete at the same time," she told Zach Seemayer for *Entertainment Tonight* (5 Dec. 2016) about the tour.

PERSONAL LIFE

When not competing, Hernandez lives in Old Bridge Township, New Jersey. She initially planned to attend the University of Florida after completing her high school education, hoping to compete for the college as a National Collegiate Athletic Association (NCAA) athlete. However, in August 2016 she announced that she would give up the scholarship she had been offered and instead pursue a career as a professional gymnast.

SUGGESTED READING

Echegaray, Luis Miguel. "Laurie Hernandez: The US Latina Gymnast with Dreams of Olympic Glory." *The Guardian*, 8 July 2016, www.theguardian.com/sport/2016/jul/08/laurie-hernandez-usa-olympic-gymnastics-trials. Accessed 15 Dec. 2016.

Fincher, Julia. "Who Is . . . Laurie Hernandez." *NBC Olympics*, NBCUniversal, 29 July 2016, www.nbcolympics.com/news/who-laurie-hernandez. Accessed 15 Dec. 2016.

Hernandez, Laurie. "Laurie Hernandez Talks Homeschooling, Being a Hispanic Athlete and Her Legion of Tween Fans." Interview by Steve Helling. *People*, 21 Aug. 2016, people.

com/sports/laurie-hernandez-i-want-to-be-a-role-model/. Accessed 15 Dec. 2016.

Hernandez, Laurie. "This 16-Year-Old Gymnast Is Doing Hispanics Proud." *Time*, 8 Nov. 2016, time.com/4555468/laurie-hernandez-american-voices/. Accessed 15 Dec. 2016.

Seemayer, Zach. "Exclusive: Laurie Hernandez on Life after Winning *DWTS* and Upcoming Tour: 'This Should Be a Lot of Fun!'" *Entertainment Tonight*, CBS Interactive, 5 Dec. 2016, www.etonline.com/news/204305_laurie_hernandez_on_life_after_winning_dwts_and_upcoming_tour_this_should_be_a_lot_of_fun/. Accessed 15 Dec. 2016.

—*Joy Crelin*

Marcel Hirscher

Date of birth: March 2, 1989
Occupation: Skier

Erich Spiess/CC0/Wikimedia Commons

Austrian Marcel Hirscher is one of the best technical skiers in the world. An Olympic silver medalist and consecutive five-time World Cup overall champion, Hirscher, who is twenty-seven, is at the peak of his career and poised to make a strong showing at the 2018 Winter Olympic Games in PyeongChang, South Korea.

Hirscher began the 2016–17 season by registering his fortieth career win in the slalom event in Levi, Finland. The win made him the fifth winningest alpine skier in history. In addition to his dominance on the slopes, Kelley McMillan for the *New York Times* (11 Feb. 2015) dubbed Hirscher a "new kind of Austrian ski star" for his unorthodox training methods, which include CrossFit and motocross, and his cult-like social media following. In ski-crazy Austria, Hirscher is a huge celebrity; he cannot walk through Salzburg without being mobbed by fans.

Hirscher competes in slalom and giant slalom, two of the fastest and most challenging events in alpine skiing. In the slalom, skiers find the fastest possible line as they weave down a course designated by flexible gates. Giant slalom functions on the same principle, but the gates are posted farther apart. These are known as ski racing's technical events. Slalom and giant slalom require speed, technique, and daring. Hirscher, an extreme sports enthusiast, seems drawn to the third qualification. He explained to Matt Majendie for CNN (16 Mar. 2016) that "fear helps you to feel alive."

EARLY LIFE

Marcel Hirscher was born on March 2, 1989, and raised in the ski village of Annaberg, Austria, which is two hours from Salzburg. His father,

Ferdinand, is Austrian, and his mother, Sylvia, is Dutch. Both parents worked as ski instructors, and Hirscher first learned to ski when he was two years old. A 1992 home video that Hirscher posted on YouTube shows the young skier cruising down a hill with a pacifier in his mouth. He entered his first competition when he was six, and as Hirscher got older, Ferdinand Hirscher instilled in his son an appreciation for technique. "He told me, 'Listen, if you want to win races, it doesn't matter what level, you have to ski technically brilliant,'" Hirscher recalled to McMillan for the *New York Times* (15 Nov. 2013). "It was the most important thing of my career, to have this technique." The elder Hirscher remains one of Hirscher's coaches.

EARLY CAREER

As a young teenager, Hirscher seemed destined for greatness. He won five Junior World Ski Championship medals, three of them gold, in the slalom, giant slalom, and super G events. He made his World Cup debut before turning eighteen in 2007. He made his Olympic debut when he was twenty years old at the Vancouver Games in 2010, where he finished fourth in the giant slalom and fifth in the slalom. In 2011, Hirscher faced the first major setback of his young career. A week before the Alpine World Championships in February, he fell during a giant slalom race in Hinterstoder. He fractured a bone in his left foot and was forced to sit out the rest of the season. Hirscher had yet to win a single World Cup race, and the injury threatened to end his career for good. Hirscher, who has never been known as an ambitious sportsman, used the time off to reflect on whether he wanted to continue down the path of professional skiing. After seven weeks of rest, however, Hirscher decided that he did. "After my injury," he told McMillan (15 Nov. 2013), "I was certain that being a professional skier was the biggest, most important thing in my life."

Hirscher hired a new fitness coach and doubled down on his training. His hard work paid off: First was his win in December 2011 in Colorado at the second giant slalom race of the season. Next was all of 2012, which became what many analysts dubbed as Hirscher's breakthrough year. The skier dominated in the slalom and giant slalom races all year, posting nine World Cup victories and landing on the podium fourteen times. He also won the World Cup overall title—the most prestigious title in alpine racing—and the giant slalom title. He placed third in the slalom and was given the Skieur d'Or Award by the International Association of Ski Journalists (AIJS) in October 2012. (He won the award again in 2015 and 2016.)

DISQUALIFICATIONS AND LESSONS LEARNED

Hirscher's "sterling season," as McMillan called it, was marred, however, by accusations of cheating. He was disqualified from two separate races for a violation known as straddling, which occurs when a skier does not clear a gate with both skis. As McMillan explained in a January 24, 2012, article for the *New York Times*, straddling is difficult to spot with the naked eye because the racers are achieving such high rates of speed. The infraction is obvious to the skiers themselves, however, and competitors are supposed to voluntarily ski out of a race if they violate. Judges can spot straddling on high-resolution video, and the penalty for skiers who do not self-check is disqualification, a fine, and the enmity of one's peers. In 2012, Hirscher was accused of skiing through two slalom races—one in Switzerland and one in Austria—after straddling, a fairly serious allegation.

Croatian skier Ivica Kostelić was furious. "It is just one race," he said as quoted by McMillan for the *New York Times* (24 Jan. 2012), "but the shame lasts forever." Kostelić's denunciation sparked anger among fans—officials called for extra police protection at one race, fearing violence between Croatian and Austrian fans—and prompted the International Ski Federation (FIS), the sport's governing body, to review Hirscher's most recent victories. Hirscher later told McMillan (15 Nov. 2013) that he was shaken by the episode. "I learned a big lesson from this situation," he said. "That I can go from hero on one day to zero the next day."

2014 OLYMPIC GAMES IN SOCHI, RUSSIA

Hirscher's 2012–13 season was mercifully free of scandal. He was awarded the World Cup overall title for a second time with six victories and eighteen podium finishes. Aksel Lund Svindal of Norway congratulated Hirscher on a "fantastic season, worthy of great skiers of the past," comparing him to Sweden's Ingemar Stenmark, considered one of the great slalom specialists of all time, and Alberto Tomba, the Italian ski star of the 1980s and 1990s. Hirscher also won the FIS World Alpine Ski Championship title in the slalom and team events in front of more than 40,000 screaming fans in Schladming, Austria.

In 2014, Hirscher competed in his second Olympic Games and remembers his first Olympics as a youthful blur, describing his twenty-year-old Olympic self to the *Ski Resort Advisor* blog (2014) as "young, thirsty, and not the questioning type of guy at that age." An older and wiser Hirscher entered the Sochi games as the heavy favorite in both the slalom and giant slalom events. Despite a stellar season, Hirscher finished a disappointing fourth in the giant slalom. After it, Hirscher posted on Twitter, "For me it's going to be difficult today." But Hirscher dug deep and turned out a beautiful second run, enough to win him a silver medal behind Austrian teammate Mario Matt's gold.

MAKING WORLD CUP HISTORY

As if to make up for his Sochi performance in that event, Hirscher dominated the World Cup giant slalom in 2015, winning five times. He achieved his fifth win in March at a competition in Garmisch-Partenkirchen, Germany, making history by winning with an unheard of 3.28 second lead, the largest victory margin in thirty-six years. At the end of the season, he won the giant slalom title for the second time in his career. He made history again in the slalom in January, when he achieved his fifteenth win in a World Cup slalom race, beating Austrian Benjamin Raich's record of fourteen wins. (Hirscher also won the last race of the season, pushing the record to sixteen wins.) Hirscher ended the season, for the third year in a row, with the slalom title, and for the fourth year in a row, the World Cup overall title as well. At the 2015 World Championships in Vail, Colorado, Hirscher won two gold medals—in the super combined and team events—and a silver medal in giant slalom.

In December in Madonna di Campiglio, Italy, Hirscher was nearly hit by a falling drone during the second run of his slalom race. The drone was carrying a mounted camera for an aerial view of the race and crashed down on the course, inches from Hirscher, who was horrified at the thought of the drone hitting him and causing serious injury. He also saw the absurdity of the situation. Taking to social media, he posted a photograph of the incident on Instagram with the caption: "Heavy air traffic in Italy." A few days later, the FIS announced a ban on camera drones during World Cup races.

In 2016, Hirscher won eight races and appeared on the podium nineteen times. He kept his World Cup giant slalom title, but more importantly, he matched Austrian Marc Girardelli's record for winning five overall World Cup titles. Unlike Girardelli, who accomplished that feat over the course of nine years, Hirscher is the first skier in World Cup history to win the title five years in a row. The distinction is mind-boggling to him still. "If you have a dream and you have already reached it, it's not so easy to find motivation for it. My biggest dream was to be once the overall World Cup champion. I reached it," he told McMillan for the *Times* (29 Oct. 2015). "What is more motivating: to reach your biggest goal or that you have already reached it?"

SUGGESTED READING

Graham, Pat. "Austria's Mario Matt Wins Men's Olympic Slalom." *NBC San Diego*, 22 Feb. 2014, www.nbcsandiego.com/news/sports/Alpine-Skiing-mens-slalom-Sochi-Winter-Games-246678551.html. Accessed 22 Dec. 2016.

Majendie, Matt. "Marcel Hirscher: Alpine Skiing's Reluctant Superstar." *CNN*, 16 Mar. 2016, edition.cnn.com/2016/03/15/sport/marcel-hirscher-world-cup-skiing. Accessed 22 Dec. 2016.

McMillan, Kelley. "Austria's Marcel Hirscher Hopes to Continue Alpine Dominance." *New York Times*, 29 Oct. 2015, www.nytimes.com/2015/10/30/sports/austrian-skier-marcel-hirscher-alpine-world-cup-overall-dominance.html. Accessed 22 Dec. 2016.

McMillan, Kelley. "For Hirscher, Injury Lifted Career." *New York Times*, 15 Nov. 2013, www.nytimes.com/2013/11/16/sports/for-hirscher-injury-lifted-career.html. Accessed 22 Dec. 2016.

McMillan, Kelley. "For Young Austrian, Victory amid Accusations of Cheating." *New York Times*, 24 Jan. 2012, www.nytimes.com/2012/01/25/sports/skiing/austrias-hirscher-wins-slalom-amid-allegations-of-cheating.html. Accessed 22 Dec. 2016.

McMillan, Kelley. "Marcel Hirscher, a New Kind of Austrian Ski Star, Is Set to Add to His Title Collection." *New York Times*, 11 Feb. 2015, www.nytimes.com/2015/02/12/sports/skiing/having-met-expectations-marcel-hirscher-is-poised-for-more.html. Accessed 22 Dec. 2016.

—*Molly Hagan*

Tom Holland

Date of birth: June 1, 1996
Occupation: Actor

In June 2015, British actor Tom Holland was checking the photo-sharing app Instagram when he learned the news that would change his life forever: he had been chosen to play Marvel Comics character Peter Parker—better known as the superhero Spider-Man—in a widely anticipated addition to the Marvel Cinematic Universe. A fan of Spider-Man since childhood, he was stunned by the news that he would be playing the iconic character and would soon become part of one of the most recognizable and profitable cinematic franchises in the world. "I could see my future changing," he recalled to costar Zendaya for *Interview* magazine (5 June 2017). After making a small but well-received appearance in the Marvel film *Captain America: Civil War* in 2016, he reprised his role in the solo film *Spider-Man: Homecoming*, which prompted an overwhelmingly positive response upon its theatrical release in July 2017.

Although best known for his work in *Spider-Man: Homecoming*, Holland in fact began his career nearly a decade earlier, when he made his debut on the London stage in *Billy Elliot the Musical* in 2008. After two years of first playing the titular Billy's best friend and then playing Billy himself, he made the transition into film with a lead role in the 2012 drama *The Impossible*. Roles in projects such as the 2015 television miniseries *Wolf Hall* and historical film

In the Heart of the Sea followed, bringing him further attention as a young actor worth watching. Although he has worked steadily since his final bow as Billy Elliot, he values quality over quantity where projects are concerned. "I don't mind sitting at home playing the guitar for a year as long as I'm making good films," he told Jeff Labrecque for *Entertainment Weekly* (23 Apr. 2013).

EARLY LIFE AND EDUCATION

Thomas Stanley Holland was born on June 1, 1996, in England's Kingston upon Thames region of Greater London. His mother, Nicola, was a photographer, while his father, Dominic, was a published writer as well as a stand-up comic. Holland would later credit his father with helping him navigate the entertainment industry. "He knows all the dos and don'ts and the ins and outs and stuff," he told Zendaya. The oldest of his parents' children, he has three younger brothers who have likewise found some work in media; his brother Harry, for instance, played the United Kingdom's Prince Harry in the 2013 biopic *Diana*.

According to Holland's parents, their oldest son demonstrated a talent for dance from a very young age. "My mom thought I could dance because I used to dance to this Janet Jackson song she'd play when I was a baby," he told Zendaya. Although he did not pursue intensive training, he began to participate in hip-hop dance classes, which he soon found that he enjoyed.

Holland completed his primary schooling at Donhead Preparatory School before moving on to Wimbledon College. In addition to dancing and acting, he enjoyed playing rugby.

BILLY ELLIOT

Holland's first experience in the entertainment industry began following a regional dance showcase, where he performed with the other members of his dance class. He drew the attention of an individual connected to the West End production *Billy Elliot the Musical*, who encouraged him to audition for the show. An adaptation of the 2000 film *Billy Elliot*, *Billy Elliot the Musical* tells the story of a boy who secretly pursues ballet lessons, set against the backdrop of the miners' strike that took place in the United Kingdom during the 1980s. The show was written by Lee Hall and directed by Stephen Daldry, both of whom had worked on the original film, and featured musical compositions by popular performer Elton John. Following its premiere at the Victoria Palace Theatre in London's West End in 2005, the musical continued to run for more than a decade.

Although Holland's initial audition for *Billy Elliot the Musical* was unsuccessful due to his lack of ballet training, Daldry believed that he would be a good fit for the production after being trained further in dance. Following the audition, Holland trained for two years and continued to audition on a regular basis. Although he trained for the purpose of securing a part in one specific musical, he has since noted that his resulting dance and gymnastics experiences have been important overall career skills. "I'm very happy I had that training," he told Zendaya. "It's been so valuable to my career, and I've used it on almost everything I've done since."

By mid-2008, Holland's training had finally paid off. He made his stage debut in June of that year, playing the role of the titular Billy's best friend, Michael. After several months, he moved to the lead role, first playing Billy in early September. His performance was received well by audiences, whom he impressed with his particularly acrobatic dance moves that often featured flips. He remained with the production until 2010, when he stepped down from the role with the intention of returning to school full time.

FILM DEBUT

Although Holland had intended to resume his education without any further interruptions, he remained in school for only a short time before leaving to film his first screen project, the drama *The Impossible*. Based on real events, *The Impossible* follows a British family in Thailand as they fight to survive the tsunami that devastated the region in 2004. Holland plays the key role of Lucas, the oldest son of parents Maria and Henry, portrayed by actors Naomi Watts and Ewan McGregor. Despite his years of experience singing, dancing, and acting on stage, he viewed the filming of *The Impossible* as a particularly educational experience. "I was taught how to act," he told Tom Teodorczuk for the *Independent* (11 Dec. 2015). "Naomi Watts was there every day constantly teaching me. That was where I discovered I wanted to be an actor." Following the film's premiere in 2012, he was widely praised for his performance and was nominated for a variety of awards highlighting youth actors.

After establishing himself as a talented young performer in *The Impossible*, and enrolling at the prestigious BRIT School for Performing Arts and Technology, Holland went on to find additional film roles, including a voiceover-based role in the 2013 drama *Locke* and a supporting part in the 2013 apocalyptic drama *How I Live Now*. He made his first television appearance in 2015, playing sixteenth-century English nobleman Gregory Cromwell in the historical miniseries *Wolf Hall*. Perhaps his most physically grueling film work to that point came during the shooting of the 2015 film *In the Heart of the Sea*, directed by critically acclaimed filmmaker Ron Howard. The film is based on a historical nonfiction book of the same name, which chronicles the 1820 sinking of a whaling ship by a whale and the crew's subsequent desperate efforts to survive. Holland plays cabin boy Thomas Nickerson, one of the few survivors of the event. Working alongside well-known actors such as Chris Hemsworth and Cillian Murphy, he had to learn to play the part of a sailor convincingly, which required significant physical training. "We were in the gym every day with a trainer and spent days on the boat learning how to row and assemble the sail once we were marooned," he explained to Teodorczuk. "But the physical training was fun as we were working out together."

BECOMING SPIDER-MAN

The films in which Holland would play his most recognizable role yet were a long time in the making. Although Marvel Studios had achieved significant critical and commercial success since the advent of their so-called Marvel Cinematic Universe with 2008's *Iron Man*, the company had been unable to include one of Marvel Comics' most iconic costumed heroes—Spider-Man, known in his civilian guise as Peter Parker—in that universe due to a long-standing film rights agreement with Sony Pictures. However, in 2015, the two companies reached an agreement that would allow the character to appear in films created by Marvel Studios. In light of that new agreement, film executives from both companies sought to find an actor to play the character—the third, after Tobey Maguire and Andrew Garfield, to play Spider-Man in less than two decades.

A fan of Spider-Man since childhood, Holland was excited to audition for the role and spent five months completing eight separate auditions, which included self-taped line readings and in-person auditions alongside actors Chris Evans and Robert Downey Jr., who play superheroes Captain America and Iron Man, respectively. In addition to demonstrating his acting talents, Holland impressed film executives with the results of his many years of dance and acrobatic training. "I was like, 'Shall I do a backflip?'" he told Zendaya. "And all the Sony guys were like, 'Can you *do* a backflip?' 'F——, yeah. I've been sending you videos for the last five months of me doing a backflip. How do you not know this?'"

After completing the lengthy audition process, Holland waited anxiously to hear whether he had secured the role. When the news came, it was unexpected. "One day I was sitting on my bed with my dog just scrolling through Instagram, and there it was. It said, 'Go to our website and check out who the new Spider-Man is.' And I did. It said my name," he recalled to Zendaya. "I went crazy. My poor dog had a fit." He debuted his take on the character in 2016's *Captain America: Civil War*, capturing the interest of filmgoers despite his character's limited screen time. At the same time, he continued to appear in films outside of the Marvel universe such as 2016's *The Lost City of Z* and *Edge of Winter*.

SPIDER-MAN: HOMECOMING

Following his appearance in *Captain America: Civil War*, Holland prepared to star in *Spider-Man: Homecoming*, a film that would pick up some time after the character's first appearance. He spent two days shadowing a student at the prestigious Bronx High School of Science under an assumed name, with the goal of gaining a better understanding of Peter's life beyond his crime-fighting activities. "A lot of the students were very confused about why I was there, and I think a lot of the teachers were too," he told Brent Lang for *Variety* (27 Mar. 2017). "So the teachers kept testing me and asking me questions, and believe me, I am by no means a scientist."

Premiering in July 2017, *Spider-Man: Homecoming* proved popular among viewers and critics, many of whom appreciated the film's differences in approach from the previous Marvel superhero films. "You've seen the billionaire, the scientist, the soldier. Now it's time to see the kid," Holland told Tatiana Siegel for the *Hollywood Reporter* (9 Nov. 2016). "Every decision we make on set is based off how would a kid react in this situation, so every fight scene we have is designed in a way that's almost child-friendly, so he never actually punches anyone. It's all done kind of by accident. I think the biggest difference is his youth and innocence."

Following *Spider-Man: Homecoming*, Holland costarred in the 2017 historical adventure film *Pilgrimage*. He is set to reprise his role as Peter Parker in 2018's *Avengers: Infinity War* as well as in further solo Spider-Man projects. In addition to acting, he hopes one day to try his hand at directing a feature film, having previously directed the 2015 short film *Tweet*.

PERSONAL LIFE

Holland owns an apartment in London, not far from his family's home. Despite often working elsewhere, he prefers life in his home city. "There's not many judgmental people, which I love," he told Siegel. Along with his younger brothers, Holland launched a charity, the Brothers Trust, in 2017.

SUGGESTED READING

Hawkes, Rebecca. "From Rihanna Lip-Syncing to His Embarrassing Dad: Why Tom Holland Is Hollywood's Most Lovable New Star." *The Telegraph*, 9 May 2017, www.telegraph.co.uk/films/0/spider-man-actor-tom-holland-hollywoods-lovable-new-star/. Accessed 15 Aug. 2017.

Holland, Tom. "*The Impossible* Blu-Ray." Interview by Jeff Labrecque. *Entertainment Weekly*, 23 Apr. 2013, ew.com/article/2013/04/23/the-impossible-blu-ray-tom-holland/. Accessed 15 Aug. 2017.

Holland, Tom. "Tom Holland." Interview by Zendaya. *Interview*, 5 June 2017, www.interviewmagazine.com/film/tom-holland. Accessed 15 Aug. 2017.

Holland, Tom. "Tom Holland Learned He Got His *Spider-Man: Homecoming* Role from a Marvel Instagram Post." Interview by Tatiana Siegel. *The Hollywood Reporter*, 9 Nov. 2016, www.hollywoodreporter.com/amp/news/tom-holland-his-spider-man-incarnation-time-see-kid-945320. Accessed 15 Aug. 2017.

Holland, Tom. "Tom Holland on *Spider-Man: Homecoming*, Spinoffs and Planning for Bathroom Breaks." Interview by Brent Lang. *Variety*, 27 Mar. 2017, variety.com/2017/film/news/tom-holland-spiderman-homecoming-2-1202017512/. Accessed 15 Aug. 2017.

Teodorczuk, Tom. "Tom Holland: From the Stage of *Billy Elliot* to a Star-Studded Hollywood Blockbuster *In the Heart of the Sea*." *Independent*, 11 Dec. 2015, www.independent.co.uk/arts-entertainment/films/features/tom-holland-from-the-stage-of-billy-elliot-to-a-star-studded-hollywood-blockbuster-in-the-heart-of-a6768851.html. Accessed 15 Aug. 2017.

SELECTED WORKS

The Impossible, 2012; *How I Live Now*, 2013; *Wolf Hall*, 2015; *In the Heart of the Sea*, 2015; *Captain America: Civil War*, 2016; *Edge of Winter*, 2016; *The Lost City of Z*, 2016; *Pilgrimage*, 2017; *Spider-Man: Homecoming*, 2017

—Joy Crelin

Braden Holtby

Date of Birth: September 16, 1989
Occupation: Hockey player

Goaltender Braden Holtby was selected in the fourth round of the 2008 National Hockey League (NHL) Draft by the Washington Capitals, often referred to as the Caps, and made his NHL debut on November 5, 2010, in a game against the Boston Bruins. Holtby replaced Caps goalie Michal Neuvirth with the game tied 3–3 and with ten minutes remaining on the clock. He stopped four shots on goal, and the Caps scored two goals for the win.

Since then, Holtby has accumulated some of the best statistics in the NHL, including 149 career wins, 23 shutouts, 248 games played, a

Sanford Myers/Getty Images

2.37 goals-against average, and a .921 save percentage. He won the 2016 NHL Vezina Trophy, presented to the best goaltender in the league, in recognition of his 48 wins, which was a Caps record for wins in a season, and his 22-game streak of regulation wins, which was the second-longest streak by a Caps goaltender. Holtby was also the second NHL goalie in twenty years to achieve twenty-two or more consecutive regulation wins.

Holtby renewed his contract with the Caps in 2015, obtaining an impressive five-year $30.5 million deal. "Since day one I've wanted to be the guy in the Washington Capitals net," he told Katie Brown for NHL.com (24 July 2015). "As a goalie, you're only as good as your last game. My job is to just keep pushing forward, keep challenging myself, keep challenging our team, and see what we can accomplish."

EARLY LIFE AND EDUCATION

Braden Holtby was born on September 16, 1989, in the Canadian city of Lloydminster, which overlaps the line between the Alberta and Saskatchewan provinces. He was raised in the nearby Saskatchewan town of Marshall. "Marshall is about five hundred people," he told Joe Heim for the *Washington Post* (26 Nov. 2014). "We have one paved road, one stop sign. No lights. We have a school, a post office, and one convenience store."

Holtby's talent on the ice had been apparent since he was four years old. Taryn, his older sister and only sibling, also showed talent from an early age. Now a veterinarian, she is also a member of Saskatchewan's curling team, a popular sport in Canada and one that Holtby and his sister played throughout junior high school. The game uses stones that have handles and are large, flat, and round. Players slide the stone on the ice and release it while teammates use brooms to sweep the ice ahead of the stone to control its direction and speed. "Unfortunately, he was probably better than me," Taryn joked to Sean Fitz-Gerald for the *National Post* (17 Feb. 2013). "Thank goodness he wanted to play hockey."

Holtby's parents, Greg and Tami, own a six-thousand-acre farm, where they grow grain and raise beef cattle; they also run a small country store. From 1983 to 1985, Holtby's father was a goaltender with the Saskatoon Blades, a junior league team in the Western Canadian Hockey League (WHL), which may be why his son's aspirations to play professional hockey were always supported. As Holtby explained to Scott Burnside for *ESPN.com* (19 Feb. 2015), his father cared more that he and his sister were "passionate" and "worked hard" than he cared about them going into farming, because "that's basically how you make yourself happy is doing what you want to do," Holtby clarified. For years, Holtby's father shuttled him to and from practices and games, with Holtby often changing into his uniform in the car on the way to the rink.

Holtby's mother was in a rock band during her teen years. After marrying Holtby's father and moving to Saskatchewan, she switched her focus to country music, which was more popular in that area and thus more lucrative. Using her maiden name, she formed the band Tami Hunter and Walkin' after Midnight, which played cover tunes and original songs in bars, lounges, and rodeos throughout western Canada during the 1980s and 1990s. She received several awards and nominations for her music and released two albums in Canada.

Holtby and his sister were always included in their mother's band life, often tagging along when she toured. Holtby took guitar lessons for a time, but his main focus remained on hockey.

EARLY CAREER AND PROFESSIONAL DEBUT

Holtby began his assent to professional goaltending in 2005 with the major junior league Saskatoon Blades, the same team on which his father had played. Holtby was with the Blades until 2009, and his first three seasons were unremarkable with just 42 wins out of 116 games. His final season with the team, however, was the most notable, with 40 wins out of 61 games.

In 2007, Holtby was recruited to represent Canada at the International Ice Hockey Federation (IIHF) World U18 Championship in Finland, where he served as backup goalie for future Colorado Avalanche draft pick Trevor Cann. Later that year, he was passed over for Canada's

World Junior Championship team and would not represent his country again on the international stage until 2016, when he played at the World Cup of Hockey.

Despite his relatively lackluster performance in the junior league, Holtby was picked by the Washington Capitals in the fourth round of the 2008 NHL Entry Draft. For the next several years, he played primarily for the South Carolina Stingrays, a Capitals' affiliate minor-league team, and the Hershey Bears, a professional team in the American Hockey League (AHL) and the main training environment for the Capitals. Between 2009 and 2013, Holtby posted 74 wins in 132 games with the Bears and 7 wins in 12 games with the Stingrays.

Holtby made his NHL debut on November 5, 2010, when the Capitals faced the Boston Bruins at the Verizon Center in Washington, DC. Replacing veteran goalie Michal Neuvirth with only ten minutes remaining and the game tied, Holtby stopped four Bruins shots while the Caps scored two goals as the clock ran down, giving a win for the Caps.

He played his first NHL game as a starter two days later against the Philadelphia Flyers and in the third period won a standing ovation from the crowd after blocking two back-to-back point-blank shots. The Capitals ultimately won 3–2 in overtime and prevented the Flyers from reaching their first seven-game streak since January 2002. With a total of twenty-three saves during the game, Holtby was matter-of-fact when talking to reporters: "I knew they'd be crashing the net hard, and I like it when guys do that," Jeff Klein reported for the *New York Times* (7 Nov. 2010). "It gets me into the game."

RISING NHL STAR

Holtby's first shutout game as a professional came on March 9, 2011, against the Edmonton Oilers when he stopped twenty-two shots on goal, allowing the Capitals to take the game in a 5–0 victory. The Caps recorded four wins and no losses that week, and Holtby was named the NHL's first star of the week.

Because regular goaltenders Tomáš Vokoun and Michal Neuvirth were sidelined with injuries at the start of the 2012 Stanley Cup quarter-finals against the Boston Bruins, the winners of the 2011 Stanley Cup, Holtby started in the first game and saved 29 of 30 shots for a 1–0 overtime loss. In the next game, he stopped 43 of 44 shots in a 2–1 double-overtime win to tie the series at 1–1. Although Neuvirth and Vokoun were then fit to play, head coach Dale Hunter chose to start Holtby in subsequent games, including the series-winning seventh game.

Despite losing to the top-seeded New York Rangers in the semifinals, Holtby's playoff performance earned him the distinction of becoming only the third NHL rookie goaltender, twenty-years-old or younger, to achieve a .920 save percentage or better and a 2.0 goals-against average in the playoffs. He was also named the starting Caps goaltender for the following season.

The next two seasons were disappointing for the Caps and for Holtby. Despite advancing to the 2013 quarterfinal playoffs, they lost the series to the New York Rangers. In 2014 the team did not even make it to the postseason playoffs, which broke a seven-year streak for the Caps. Compounding these disappointments, Holtby had, as Katie Carrera remarked for the *Washington Post* (11 Apr. 2014), "his worst season in the NHL" during 2013–14. Burnside wrote (13 Mar. 2015) that Holtby's performance that season "suffered as a result of defensive deficiencies around him."

At the start of the 2014–15 season, Holtby remarked to journalists that he felt encouraged, especially after the hiring of respected goaltending coach Mitch Korn by the Caps' new head coach Barry Trotz. Holtby explained that he "was just looking forward to a new start [as a] team" and to focus on his own skills "with the help of a lot of guys involved, especially Mitch [Korn]."

AWARD-WINNING GOALTENDER

By all accounts, Holtby did move forward, and Korn is credited with helping him gain control of his play and boost his confidence. The 2014–15 season found Holtby becoming the first Caps goaltender in almost ten years to achieve three or more shutout games against the Boston Bruins in one season. Additionally, his forty-one wins tied him with Caps goalie Olaf Kölzig for most wins in a single season.

During the 2015–16 season, a newly confident and mature Holtby started in all sixty-six games. When the Capitals defeated the St. Louis Blues, 5–1, on April 9, 2016, he earned his forty-eighth win of the season, tying him with New Jersey Devils goalie Martin Brodeur for the record of most wins in a single season.

Despite Holtby's historic season, the Caps were not able to advance past the semifinals in the 2016 Stanley Cup playoffs, losing the series to the Pittsburgh Penguins, 2–4. However, Holtby's talent and contributions were recognized by the League when he was selected to play in the 2016 NHL All-Star Game, was chosen as goalie for Team Canada for the World Cup of Hockey, was nominated for the Hart Memorial Trophy (awarded to the NHL player who has contributed the most to his team), and won the 2016 Vezina Trophy, which is presented to a NHL goaltender voted by NHL general managers to be the best at his position. Holtby's memorable 2015–16 season was also formally recognized by

the Caps franchise on October 18, 2016, in a pregame ceremony.

Holtby has several rituals and routines, known as Holtbyisms, that he performs prior to and during games. The best-known Holtbyism is perhaps what many fans refer to as the "Holtby Shuffle," a series of movements he performs before the start of every game during national anthems. He explained that he began doing this as a way to keep his body loose and that growing up it was something he always noticed goalies doing. "I don't know why mine became so noticeable," he confessed to Heim.

PERSONAL LIFE

Holtby and his wife, Brandi, have a son, Benjamin, who was born in 2012, and a daughter, Belle, who was born in 2014. They live in Alexandria, Virginia. Holtby has said that having a family has, in some respects, made him a better player. "You know in order to be successful [as a goalie] you have to be able to block things out," he explained to Burnside (13 Mar. 2015). "Obviously, having a family makes it a lot easier. You go home and you have responsibilities that don't let you think about or dwell on the game. That definitely helps. [But] I think anyone would say that at the same time, it does present challenges. It's harder to be on the road and be away from them."

Holtby and his wife support several causes, including civil rights for lesbian, gay, bisexual, and transgender (LGBT) individuals. In 2016 they marched in Washington's Capital Pride Parade, which the Caps franchise also supported in conjunction with You Can Play, a group that works to ensure equality in sports without regard to sexual orientation or gender identity. Holtby is an avid reader, guitar player, and crossword puzzle fan.

SUGGESTED READING

Brown, Katie. "Capitals Sign Goaltender Holtby to Five-Year Contract." *NHL*, 24 July 2015, www.nhl.com/ice/m_news.htm?id=775599. Accessed 22 Oct. 2016.

Burnside, Scott. "Even in the NHL, They're Just Hockey Dads." *ESPN*, 19 Feb. 2015, www.espn.com/nhl/story/_/id/12345679/nhl-even-nhl-washington-capitals-fathers-just-hockey-dads. Accessed 22 Oct. 2016.

Burnside, Scott. "Braden Holtby Getting the Job Done." *ESPN*, 13 Mar. 2015, www.espn.com/nhl/story/_/id/12474963/nhl-washington-capitals-goalie-braden-holtby-thriving-spotlight. Accessed 22 Oct. 2016.

Fitz-Gerald, Sean. "Curler Taryn Holtby, Like Brother Braden of Capitals, Keeps Mother on the Edge of Her Seat." *National Post*, 17 Feb. 2013, news.nationalpost.com/curling/curler-taryn-holtby-like-brother-braden-of-capitals-keeps-mother-on-the-edge-of-her-seat. Accessed 22 Oct. 2016.

Heim, Joe. "Just Asking: The Capitals' Braden Holtby." *The Washington Post*, 26 Nov. 2014, www.washingtonpost.com/sports/capitals/just-asking-the-capitals-braden-holtby/2014/11/12/bad359e2-6116-11e4-8b9e-2ccdac31a031_story.html. Accessed 22 Oct. 2016.

Prewitt, Alex. "Braden Holtby Has His Game in Tune." *Sports Illustrated*, 11 Apr. 2016, www.si.com/nhl/2016/04/11/braden-holtby-washington-capitals-pregame-routine-music-guitar. Accessed 22 Oct. 2016.

Steinberg, Dan. "Braden Holtby's LGBT Support Goes beyond a Parade." *Washington Post*, 8 June 2016, www.washingtonpost.com/news/dc-sports-bog/wp/2016/06/08/braden-holtbys-lgbt-support-goes-beyond-a-parade. Accessed 22 Oct. 2016.

—*Mari Rich*

By SciBiograph (Own work) [CC BY-SA 4.0], via Wikimedia Commons

Jacob Hooker

Date of birth: 1980
Occupation: Scientist

When chemist and molecular imaging researcher Jacob Hooker was in the final year of his doctoral studies in chemistry at the University of California, Berkeley, he attended a presentation that changed the course of his career forever. At that presentation, delivered by Brookhaven Research Laboratory scientist Joanna Fowler, he learned about a particular technique for studying processes in the human brain through the use of positron emission tomography (PET) technology and synthesized radioactive molecules called radiotracers. "It was incredibly exciting that a chemist could label a small molecule and observe something fundamental about the brain using that molecule they made," he explained to Bob Grant for the *Scientist* (1 Oct. 2015). After completing his studies, Hooker joined Fowler's team at Brookhaven for several years, gaining expertise in the research that so intrigued him, before joining the faculty of Harvard Medical School in 2009.

In addition to his work at Harvard, Hooker serves as director of radiochemistry at the Athinoula A. Martinos Center for Biomedical Imaging at Massachusetts General Hospital, where he also heads the Hooker Research Group. Along with the other researchers in his laboratory, Hooker has been responsible for developing numerous radiotracers that enable scientists to locate and study specific compounds within the human body. The team is perhaps best known for developing and patenting [11C]Martinostat, a radiotracer used to study enzymes that control gene deactivation processes in the brain. As such processes may be linked to brain disorders such as Alzheimer's disease, the research group's work could play a key role in the understanding and treatment of Alzheimer's and similar disorders. Even as Hooker acknowledges the important implications of his team's research, however, he likewise remains excited about the nature of the work itself. "How many other people get to make new molecules and see them moving in and interacting with the human brain?" he asked Gary Boas for the Martinos Center (25 Mar. 2015).

EARLY LIFE AND EDUCATION

Jacob Matthew Hooker was born in 1980 to Timothy and Donna Hooker. He grew up in Candler, North Carolina, an unincorporated community west of the city of Asheville, where he attended Enka High School. A strong student, he was a regular competitor in the Western Carolina University Annual High School Mathematics Contest and placed first in the competition's Algebra I division while in middle school. Hooker graduated from Enka High School in 1998.

After completing high school, Hooker attended North Carolina State University. Inspired by a college representative who had visited his high school to speak about the university's textile chemistry program, he double majored in both that discipline and the broader field of chemistry. During his time at North Carolina State, Hooker began to hone the research and teaching skills that would prove crucial to his later career, working as a research assistant for some of the institution's professors and also serving as a teaching assistant for laboratory courses in organic chemistry. A strong academic performer, he was inducted into Phi Beta Kappa honor society, and was ultimately valedictorian of his graduating class. Hooker earned his bachelor's degrees in chemistry and textile chemistry from North Carolina State University in 2002.

Later that year, Hooker moved to California to pursue graduate studies in chemistry at the University of California (UC), Berkeley, on a National Science Foundation Graduate Research Fellowship. In addition to expanding his knowledge of chemistry in the classroom, he carried out research in the chemistry laboratory headed by Professor Matt Francis, focusing primarily on the modification of organic compounds. Papers Hooker coauthored during that period would be published in prestigious venues such as the *Journal of the American Chemical Society*. Hooker earned his PhD from UC Berkeley in 2007.

FOWLER LAB

A turning point in Hooker's career trajectory came in 2006, when he first became aware of research being carried out by Joanna Fowler, an organic chemist working at the Brookhaven National Laboratory on Long Island. Combining elements of chemistry and neurobiology, Fowler was using positron emission tomography (PET) techniques to study the brain through the targeted introduction of carefully designed radioactive molecules. "I had some familiarity with imaging from my PhD work," he recalled to Boas, "but Joanna's lecture opened my eyes to new possibilities for applying physical organic chemistry concepts to neuroscience."

After completing his studies at UC Berkeley, Hooker returned to the East Coast to take a research position in Fowler's laboratory at Brookhaven. Founded in 1947 and operated by the US Department of Energy (DoE), the Brookhaven National Laboratory is home to researchers in numerous fields, including chemistry, biology, and physics. Hooker joined the facility's body of researchers as a member of the Gertrude and Maurice Goldhaber Distinguished Fellowships Program, a three-year program designed to fund exceptional researchers who are recent doctoral graduates, and he was also a recipient of the Ruth L. Kirschstein grant, sponsored by the National Institutes of Health (NIH).

During his tenure at Brookhaven, Hooker proved to be a valuable contributor to Fowler's research efforts. "He's the best I've ever seen," she told Grant of Hooker. "He's going to ask questions we haven't thought of before." In recognition of his work, Hooker was named Brookhaven's inventor of the year by the Battelle

Memorial Institute, a nonprofit company that comanages the laboratory, in 2009. After relocating to Massachusetts later that year, Hooker remained affiliated with the Brookhaven National Laboratory for some time, taking on the titles of assistant scientist and associate scientist.

INDEPENDENT CAREER

In the fall of 2009, Hooker joined the faculty of Harvard Medical School as an assistant professor. He would serve in that role until late 2014, when he was promoted to associate professor of radiology. In addition to his prestigious teaching position, Hooker's 2009 move to the greater Boston area likewise enabled him to join the Athinoula A. Martinos Center for Biomedical Imaging, a research center affiliated with Massachusetts General Hospital (MGH). Taking on the position of director of radiochemistry at the Martinos Center, Hooker also established his own research group at the institution, the Hooker Research Group. Building upon the areas of science that Hooker first learned about in Fowler's lab at Brookhaven, the Hooker Research Group focuses primarily on developing new techniques and applications for molecular imaging, particularly in relation to the human brain. Although the nature of Hooker's research necessitates contributions from scientists from vastly different disciplines, the researchers are brought together by a common goal as well as a common manner of thinking about the topics at hand. "What unifies us is the fact that I'm a chemist and think about things from a molecular basis," Hooker told Bethany Halford for *Chemical & Engineering News* (14 July 2014).

In addition to his work at Harvard Medical School and the Martinos Center, Hooker served as associate director of the PET Core Laboratory at MGH from 2009 to 2013. He became an associate editor of the journal *ACS Chemical Neuroscience* in 2013 and has likewise been a part of the Madrid–MIT M+Visión Consortium and its successor, MIT linQ, an organization dedicated to promoting and facilitating biomedical research. Hooker has received significant recognition for his work since beginning his career as an independent researcher, including a number of prestigious awards and grants. In 2010, he was one of eighty-five scientists to be granted the Presidential Early Career Award for Scientists and Engineers by President Barack Obama, an award accompanied by funding from the US Department of Energy. In light of Hooker's ongoing research into the use of molecular imaging to understand brain disorders, the Brain and Behavior Research Foundation awarded Hooker a NARSAD (National Alliance for Research in Schizophrenia and Affective Disorders) Independent Investigator grant in 2015. The following year, he was named the Phyllis and Jerome

Lyle Rappaport MGH Research Scholar, a title that comes with a grant of $500,000, distributed over five years.

INNOVATIONS IN IMAGING

Since the foundation of the Hooker Research Group at the Martinos Center, Hooker's research has focused primarily on studying the human body, especially the brain and nervous system, through the use of molecular imaging technology, and particularly PET technology. In PET research, radioactive particles with specific properties are introduced into the body, where they bond with molecules already in the body to form compounds known as radioactive tracers. By using specialized technology that can detect and create an image of the locations of the radioactive tracers, researchers are able to determine where the original molecules are located in the body. This not only enables researchers to create a map of sorts but also to observe and analyze the chemical processes taking place. In light of such capabilities, PET is widely considered "an extremely valuable tool for understanding human physiology," as Hooker noted in a press release published by the Brookhaven National Laboratory (24 Apr. 2009).

Despite the valuable research implications of PET technology, however, research in that area is limited by the existing understanding of radiotracers. "Many, if not most, molecules people are interested in studying with PET cannot be radiolabeled right now, so there is a huge need for basic science to develop new strategies for making radiotracers," Hooker explained in the Brookhaven press release. In light of that need, Hooker and his colleagues have worked to develop and synthesize new radiotracers that allow researchers to observe different substances within the body. Among other imaging tools, scientists in the Hooker Research Group have developed the radiotracer [11C]Martinostat, which binds to enzymes known as histone deacetylases (HDACs) and therefore enables researchers to study those particular enzymes and their role in gene expression. Named for the Martinos Center, Martinostat is the name of the molecule that inhibits HDACs, and 11C refers to the radioactive isotope carbon-11, which when tagged to Martinostat makes it visible with PET scanning. The team began to test [11C]Martinostat in human research subjects in late 2014.

Although the Hooker Research Group initially worked in the area of developing new radiotracers, by 2015 the group's focus had shifted primarily to developing "applications aimed at relating a particular class of enzyme to brain function in disease," Hooker told Boas. In particular, the team used [11C]Martinostat to conduct research on the action in the brain of HDACs, which are capable of deactivating genes—essentially, switching genes off. Prior to the development of such techniques, gene activation and deactivation could not be studied in living brains, rendering research efforts inadequate. "We simply can't study it outside of its natural context," Hooker explained to Sharon Begley for *Stat* (10 Aug. 2016). "[Dead] brains and living brains will look very different." The technique developed by Hooker and his colleagues, however, enables researchers to observe gene deactivation in living brains. Hooker hopes that by observing the areas of the brain where such deactivation occurs, scientists will be able to determine the causes of brain disorders such as Alzheimer's disease, which scientists theorize may be related to gene deactivation.

PERSONAL LIFE

Hooker met his wife, Rebekah (Miller) Hooker, a fellow doctor of chemistry and alumnus of the lab of Matt Francis, while attending UC Berkeley. They married in 2012. The couple lives with their children outside of Boston.

SUGGESTED READING

"Battelle Honors Jacob Hooker as Brookhaven Lab's 'Inventor of the Year.'" *Brookhaven National Laboratory*, 24 Apr. 2009, www.bnl.gov/newsroom/news.php?a=110942. Accessed 9 June 2017.

Begley, Sharon. "In Living Color: New Technique Sees Gene Activity in Human Brains." *Stat*, 10 Aug. 2016, www.statnews.com/2016/08/10/living-brain-gene-activity/. Accessed 9 June 2017.

Boas, Gary. "PET Project: Imaging Modality Offers New Insights into Neurodegenerative Disease." *Athinoula A. Martinos Center for Biomedical Imaging*, 25 Mar 2015, www.nmr.mgh.harvard.edu/news/20150325/pet-project-imaging-modality-offers-new-insights-neurodegenerative-disease. Accessed 9 June 2017.

Grant, Bob. "Jacob Hooker: Weaver of Brain Science." *The Scientist*, 1 Oct. 2015, www.the-scientist.com/?articles.view/articleNo/44064/title/Jacob-Hooker--Weaver-of-Brain-Science. Accessed 9 June 2017.

Halford, Bethany. "PET Project." *Chemical & Engineering News*, 14 July 2014, cen.acs.org/articles/92/i28/PET-Project.html. Accessed 9 June 2017.

"Jacob Hooker: The Mind Mapper." *C&EN's Talented 12*, 2015, talented12.cenmag.org/jacob-hooker/. Accessed 9 June 2017.

—*Joy Crelin*

Al Horford

Date of birth: June 3, 1986
Occupation: Basketball player

For professional basketball player Al Horford, the sport has been a fixture of his life since birth. The son of retired athlete Tito Horford, who in 1988 became the first player born in the Dominican Republic to be drafted onto a National Basketball Association (NBA) team, Horford grew up learning about the sport from his father. As a teenager, Horford distinguished himself as a player on his high school team in Grand Ledge, Michigan. After three successful seasons at the University of Florida, Horford was drafted by the Atlanta Hawks in 2007 and went on to play nine seasons and appear in eight playoff tournaments with the team. In addition to cementing his status as a valuable contributor to the Hawks, Horford—who has played as a center and as a forward at various points in his career—has also represented the Dominican Republic in international competition and seeks to help the country of his birth "reach new heights," as he told Damon Salvadore for the *Latin Post* (22 Aug. 2015).

The summer of 2016 presented Horford with a dilemma, as his contract with the Hawks ended and he became an unrestricted free agent. Although he considered remaining in Atlanta, where he had spent his entire NBA career to that point, he evaluated competing offers and ultimately signed a deal with the Boston Celtics. The choice was difficult for Horford, but he viewed the change as an opportunity. "I was put in a tough position and situation that I had to make a choice," he told Chris Vivlamore for the *Atlanta Journal-Constitution* (11 July 2016). "But it's a new challenge for me. I'm excited and looking forward to it." His decision proved to be a fruitful one, bringing him both a four-year, $113 million contract as well as a successful debut season that saw the Celtics claim the top spot in the NBA's Eastern Conference.

EARLY LIFE AND EDUCATION

Al Horford was born on June 3, 1986, in Puerto Plata, Dominican Republic. His parents, Arelis Reynoso and Alfredo "Tito" Horford, later separated, and Horford spent his early years living in Santo Domingo, the capital city of the Dominican Republic, with his mother. When Horford was in his early teens, he moved to Michigan to live with his father, stepmother, and four younger siblings.

The sport of basketball was a fixture in Horford's life from infancy. At the time of Horford's birth, his father was a member of the University of Miami Hurricanes basketball team. Tito Horford went on to be drafted into the NBA in 1988, joining the Milwaukee Bucks. Although

By Keith Allison [CC BY-SA 2.0], via Wikimedia Commons

Horford's father left the NBA after several seasons, he continued to play internationally during Horford's childhood and passed his love of the sport down to his children. "Watching him is what motivated me to start playing basketball and become interested in it," Horford recalled to Salvadore. "He always gave me good advice." In addition to Horford himself, his brothers and sisters played basketball growing up, and his brother Jon went on to play for the Canton Charge, a development team affiliated with the Cleveland Cavaliers.

After moving to the United States, Horford enrolled at Grand Ledge High School in Grand Ledge, Michigan. He became a valuable addition to the school's basketball team, scoring the most points of any player in the team's history over the course of his high school career. He graduated from Grand Ledge High School in 2004.

FLORIDA GATORS

As Horford prepared for life after high school, he decided to begin his career in basketball by playing for a college team. He ultimately chose to enroll in the University of Florida, which appealed to him on multiple levels. "I was really sold as soon as I came in—the nice campus and the buildings and the palm trees and everything. I fell in love with that," he told Adam Silverstein for *Only Gators* (8 Feb. 2010). "I never told Coach [Billy Donovan] that. I tried to act tough on my visit, but I knew that I wanted to go there as soon as I saw all of that."

Horford made a strong first impression during his freshman year with the university's Florida Gators basketball team, playing in thirty-two games over the course of the season and averaging 5.6 points and 6.6 rebounds per game. The following year proved to be even better, with Horford averaging 11.3 points and a team-high 7.7 rebounds per game. At the end of the season, he accompanied the team to the 2006 National Collegiate Athletic Association (NCAA) Division I championship. The Gators defeated George Mason University in the semifinals before beating the University of California, Los Angeles (UCLA), to claim the NCAA title, the team's first.

Although successful as a college basketball player, Horford looked forward to playing professionally and considered leaving school after his sophomore year to do so. His father encouraged him to remain in school for a while longer and devote more time to developing his skills. Horford followed his father's advice and remained at the University of Florida for a third year, which proved fortuitous for the Gators. In his third and final season with the team, he averaged 13.2 points and 9.5 rebounds per game over 38 games, and near the end of the season he reached the milestone of 1,000 points scored with the team. To the surprise of the team and their fans, the Gators again fared well in the postseason, defeating UCLA in the semifinals before beating Ohio State University (OSU) to claim their second consecutive championship win.

ATLANTA HAWKS

On June 28, 2007, Horford was selected by the Atlanta Hawks as the third pick in the first round of that year's NBA Draft. He made his debut with the team, a member of the NBA's Eastern Conference, on November 2 of that year, playing for nearly twenty-three minutes in a game against the Dallas Mavericks. The Hawks won Horford's debut game by 7 points, and Horford personally contributed 9 points to the team's score. He went on to play in a total of eighty-one games over the course of the season. Although the Hawks struggled at times during the season, which ended with more losses than wins, the team nevertheless performed well enough to advance to the playoffs for the first time in nearly a decade. The team was ultimately eliminated in the first round after losing to the Boston Celtics in seven games.

Following his strong debut season with the Hawks, Horford played an additional eight seasons for the team, during which he continually worked to improve his skills and contribute to the team's success. "I think the key with the NBA is I'm still staying hungry, I feel like I can get a lot better still. I'm still working on my game," he told Silverstein. "I have not reached my full potential yet. I think that's why I'm able to improve every year."

The next three years saw Horford become a major contributor to the Hawks during both the regular season and the postseason. He was a member of the starting lineup for each game he played in during those three seasons, and in the 2010–11 season he hit a new personal record for points scored per game, with an average of 15.3. Horford played an important role in Atlanta's postseason efforts, which included a victory in the first round of the 2009 NBA Playoffs. In 2010, the team again progressed past the first round and into the Eastern Conference Semifinals, where they lost to the Orlando Magic. Horford was a key contributor to the team, scoring a total of 161 points in the postseason. The team again went to the playoffs in 2011 but fell to the Chicago Bulls in the Conference Semifinals. In light of his strong performance during his early seasons with the Hawks, Horford was selected to play in the NBA All-Star Game in both 2010 and 2011.

INJURIES AND TRIUMPHS

Following a late start due to an NBA labor dispute, the 2011–12 season brought trouble for Horford. Although he started the season off strong, averaging 12.4 points per game in the first eleven games, he tore a muscle while on the court and was forced to miss the majority of the season while recovering from surgery. He returned to the team in the postseason and played in three of the Hawks' six games against the Celtics, a choice that he later noted was not ideal. "I hadn't even practiced with the team when I decided to come back," he told Charles Bethea for *Grantland* (28 Nov. 2012). "I was in good shape, but it was two and a half months after the surgery. My doctors, they didn't really recommend that. But it's the playoffs, you see your team hurting, they really want you to be out there."

Horford returned to regular play in the 2012–13 season, starting in all seventy-four regular-season games he played. He achieved several personal bests, including a career-high average of 17.4 points per game, and he led the team in points and rebounds during several games in the postseason. He finished the regular season having scored the sixth-most double-doubles of any NBA player. Injured again in December 2013, Horford played only twenty-nine games in the 2013–14 season, although he recorded a career-high average of 18.6 points per game in that time. For the first time in his NBA career, he did not accompany the Hawks to the playoffs, instead devoting himself to making a full recovery. The subsequent seasons were successful for Horford and the Hawks, as the team advanced into the postseason in 2015 and achieved the team's best result in some time, advancing to the Eastern Conference Finals, where they fell to the Cavaliers. In addition to his performance with the Hawks, Horford was again selected to play in the NBA All-Star Game in 2015 and 2016.

MOVE TO BOSTON

Following the 2016 postseason, in which the Hawks were eliminated in the Conference Semifinals, Horford became an unrestricted free agent. Although Horford considered remaining in Atlanta, he came to acknowledge that after nine seasons the time had come for him to move on. "After the season, my agent and I sat down and looked at the possibilities of other teams if it didn't work out in Atlanta," he explained to Vivlamore. "There were three or four teams that emerged in case things didn't work out that I would look at." After evaluating his offers, which included offers from the Hawks and the Washington Wizards, Horford decided to join the Boston Celtics and in July 2016 signed a four-year, $113 million contract with the team.

Horford made his first appearance with the Celtics on October 26, 2016, in a winning game against the Brooklyn Nets. Over the course of the season, which resulted in a 53–29 record for his new team, Horford played in sixty-eight games and averaged 14.0 points per game. The team claimed the number-one spot in the Eastern Conference and defeated the Chicago Bulls and the Washington Wizards in the first two rounds of the tournament. Horford was a major contributor to the Celtics' success, scoring 271 points during the playoffs and becoming the third-highest-scoring player on the team and first in rebounds per game. The Celtics ultimately lost to the Cleveland Cavaliers in the Conference Finals.

PERSONAL LIFE

Horford met his wife, entertainer and 2003 Miss Universe winner Amelia Vega, while attending the Latin Pride Awards. They later met again while they were both working on the same charity campaign, and the couple soon began dating. They married in December 2011. Horford and Vega have a son, Ean, and a daughter, Alía.

SUGGESTED READING

"Al Horford, Celtics Agree on Deal; Agent Says 4 Years, $113 Million." *ESPN*, 3 July 2016, www.espn.com/nba/story/_/id/16712043/al-horford-boston-celtics-agree-terms-four-year-113-million-deal-according-league-sources. Accessed 14 July 2017.

Coyne, Josh. "CelticsLife Exclusive: An Interview with the Horfords." *CelticsLife*, 1 Mar. 2017, www.celticslife.com/2017/03/basketball-horford-family-business.html. Accessed 14 July 2017.

Horford, Al. "Al Horford Opens Up about His Decision to Leave Atlanta." Interview by Chris Vivlamore. *The Atlanta Journal-Constitution*, 11 July 2016, www.myajc.com/sports/basketball/horford-opens-about-his-decision-leave-atlanta/wLF0O26kyzG1GG6WGRZ9hP. Accessed 14 July 2017.

Horford, Al. "Atlanta Hawks' Al Horford: 'I Tried to Act Tough.'" Interview by Adam Silverstein. *Only Gators*, 8 Feb. 2010, www.onlygators.com/02/08/2010/atlanta-hawks-al-horford-i-tried-to-act-tough. Accessed 14 July 2017.

Horford, Al. "Q&A: Al Horford on Reading Gabriel Garcia Marquez, Doing Yoga with Ivan Johnson, and James Harden's Beard." Interview by Charles Bethea. *Grantland*, 28 Nov. 2012, grantland.com/the-triangle/qa-al-horford-on-reading-gabriel-garcia-marquez-doing-yoga-with-ivan-johnson-and-james-hardens-beard. Accessed 14 July 2017.

Horford, Al. "Ten Questions with Al Horford: Dominican NBA Star Reflects on Career, Looks Ahead to Upcoming Season." Interview by Damon Salvadore. *The Latin Post*, 22 Aug. 2015, www.latinpost.com/articles/73025/20150822/atlanta-hawks-exclusive-interview-nba-star-al-horford-talks-basketball-family-free-agency.htm. Accessed 14 July 2017.

King, Jay. "Al Horford Extols Boston Celtics' Family Values after Missing Game to Celebrate Daughter's Birth." *MassLive*, 29 Nov. 2016, www.masslive.com/celtics/index.ssf/2016/11/al_horford_rejoins_boston_celt.html. Accessed 14 July 2017.

—*Joy Crelin*

Eric Hosmer

Date of birth: October 24, 1989
Occupation: Baseball player

Eric Hosmer is a left-handed hitter and first baseman for the Kansas City Royals. Hosmer's star turn came during the Royals' miraculous 2014 postseason run, but he clinched his place in baseball history in a dash for home plate in Game 5 of the 2015 World Series. Hosmer's "calculated bit of baseball brilliance," as Gabe Lacques put it for *USA Today* (2 Nov. 2015), tied the game, and ultimately won the Royals their first World Series title since 1985. Hosmer, the third pick of the Major League Baseball Draft out of high school in 2008, made his major-league debut in May 2011. The date—May 6— is considered a turning point in Royals history,

By Keith Allison [CC BY-SA 2.0] via Wikimedia Commons

and the beginning of their miraculous transformation from one of the worst teams in baseball to World Series champion. The three-time Gold Glove winner was named All-Star MVP in 2016, a season during which he hit twenty-five home runs. Hosmer is also one of the most beloved Royals players; young fans of the team emulate his faux-hawk haircut, calling it the "Hoz." After the Royals swept the Los Angeles Angels in the American League Division Series (ALDS) in 2014, Hosmer famously sent out an open invitation to Royals fans to come to a downtown bar, and helped pay for an open bar for an hour. As of 2017, Hosmer is in his prime, but his contract is set to expire at the end of the season and his future with the Royals is uncertain.

EARLY LIFE AND EDUCATION

Hosmer was born on October 24, 1989, and raised in South Florida. His father, Mike, was a Miami firefighter (now retired) and his mother, a Cuban refugee named Ileana, is a nurse. Growing up, Hosmer and his older brother, Mike Jr., fell in love with baseball. Their parents bought them a Tony Gwynn Solohitter, a backyard training system with a net. The two boys hit balls for hours. "Our neighbors probably hated us," Hosmer's mother told Kent Babb for the *Kansas City Star* (2 July 2011). When the boys began to play for travel teams, like the state and national-champion Diamond Kings, their father rearranged his work schedule so that he could go to see their games, sometimes traveling as far as upstate New York. Ileana began filming the boys' games when Hosmer was eight. Both boys

studied the tapes and compared their swings to those of their favorite players. When the family went to Marlins games, Hosmer dreamed of playing for the major leagues himself. "We'd just watch the games and hope that one day, we might get here," Hosmer told Babb years later.

Both Hosmer and his brother attended the American Heritage School in Plantation, Florida. The high school has one of the top baseball teams in the nation; his mother had to take a second job in the science lab of the local high school to help pay their tuition. Hosmer quickly emerged as one of the team's star players. (Former American Heritage teammate and close family friend Deven Marrero plays for the Boston Red Sox.) Hosmer was a great hitter as a child, but an eight-inch growth spurt between eighth and tenth grade—putting him at six feet four inches and 200-plus pounds—made him a powerhouse. The first baseman could also throw a 94-mph pitch. "We all knew he was going to be good," former head coach Todd Fitzgerald told Stephen Spiewak for the high school sports website *MaxPreps* (2008). "We just didn't know he was going to be that tall or that good." His sophomore season, Hosmer batted .500, and his junior year, he hit .380 with nine home runs. One of the most powerful sports agents in the business, Scott Boras, first approached Hosmer when he was just sixteen years old.

During his high school career, Hosmer was a two-time *Miami Herald* state player of the year, the Connie Mack and World Wood Bat Association MVP, and a Rawlings High School Gold Glove winner. During his senior year, 2008, he batted .470 with eleven home runs. He also led the American Heritage team, the Patriots, to a state championship. The team was named Baseball America's 2008 Team of the Year. When the season ended, Hosmer was widely considered the country's best high school player and the best position player overall. He signed a letter of intent to attend Arizona State University, but was chosen by the Kansas City Royals as the number three overall pick of the draft in June 2008. That summer he played for the Midland Redskins in Cincinnati, finishing second in the Connie Mack World Series, as Boras hammered out a deal with the Royals. Hosmer signed with the team, earning a $6 million bonus, a franchise record, just before the August 15 deadline.

MINOR LEAGUE CAREER

Hosmer's professional career got off to a rough start. He hit .241 with six home runs during his first full professional season with the Burlington Royals in North Carolina and then the Class A Wilmington Blue Rocks in Delaware in 2009. He noticed that he had trouble seeing the ball during night games, and underwent corrective surgery for a vision problem called astigmatism.

He returned to his team a week later and hit a triple on his first at-bat. In 2010, Hosmer moved from Wilmington to Arkansas to play for the Class AA Northwest Arkansas Naturals. He hit .338 and twenty home runs. Hosmer hoped to be sent directly to the majors in 2011, but instead began the season with the Class AAA Omaha Storm Chasers. In his first twenty-six games with the team, Hosmer was hitting .439, the highest average of any minor league regular in the country. In May, Hosmer was at batting practice in Albuquerque before a game when he got a call from the Royals. The team was giving him his "call up." They wanted him to play for the team the next night in Kansas City. Hosmer called his parents, he told Babb. "I told them we made it—not just I made it," he said. "They've been there every step of the way for me."

KANSAS CITY ROYALS

Hosmer made his major-league debut on May 6, 2011, in a game against the Oakland Athletics. The Royals were suffering through yet another losing season when Hosmer arrived. That summer, the team called up a handful of new players, including third baseman Mike Moustakas. But Hosmer was the first. The players' collective effect on the team was so significant that in 2016, Rustin Dodd, writing for the *Kansas City Star* (5 May 2016), called May 6, 2011, "a pivot point in the franchise's history." Royals general manager Dayton Moore has the jersey Hosmer wore that day framed in his house. Hosmer hit his first major league home run a few days after his debut in a game at Yankee Stadium. He ended the 2011 season with a .293 average—the highest among the league's rookies—with 19 home runs in 128 games. He finished third in the voting for American League Rookie of the Year.

In 2012, Hosmer's stats slumped. He told Zach Schonbrun for the *New York Times* (23 May 2012), "You want to rush out of [the slump] and break out of it as soon as possible, but at the time it's not going to happen with one swing. You've got to be patient and take your walks. You can't go out of the zone." He finished the season with a .232 batting average and fourteen home runs. Hosmer fared better in 2013. He finished the season with a .302 average and seventeen home runs, and won his first Rawlings Gold Glove Award. (He was a finalist for the award in 2012.) Hosmer suffered a wrist injury in July, just as the Royals started heating up in the summer of 2014. In late August, Hosmer played two games with the Storm Chasers to rehabilitate, but he returned to the majors in time to participate in the Royals history-making postseason run. In September, the team secured their first ever wild card slot.

The Royals won the game against the Oakland Athletics 9–8 in a harrowing, twelve-inning walk-off. Hosmer hit a triple and scored the tying run in the twelfth inning. "This will go down as the craziest game I ever played," he told Bob Nightengale for USA Today (1 Oct. 2014). The Royals, so recently one of the worst teams in baseball, then went on to sweep the Los Angeles Angels in the Amerian Leage Division Series (ALDS). Hosmer hit a two-run home run to win Game 2 in extra innings. Improbably, the Royals' luck held. They swept the Baltimore Orioles in the American League Championship Series, becoming the first major league team to win their first eight postseason games. The Royals ultimately lost to San Francisco Giants in Game 7 of the World Series.

The 2015 season proved to be another banner year for the franchise. Yet again, they made a dramatic postseason showing, setting a major-league record: eight of their eleven playoff wins were comebacks. In October, the Royals faced the New York Mets in the World Series. In Game 5, Hosmer made an inspired and risky dash for home plate to tie the game in the ninth inning. The Royals went on to win the game and the series, snatching their first World Series victory in thirty years. Tim Kurkjian for *ESPN* (25 Mar. 2016) wrote an entire article about the play, calling it "the most important and most provocative play of the 2015 World Series." Hosmer told Kurkjian that he was driven by the prospect of a potential Game 6 and a Game 7. "We didn't want that," he said. "I thought this was the time to take a chance."

Hosmer made an impressive debut in his first All-Star Game in 2016. He hit a home run and was named the game's MVP. That season, he aimed to hit twenty home runs and hit twenty-five.

SUGGESTED READING

Babb, Kent. "Eric Hosmer Takes His Family's Legacy to the Major Leagues." *The Kansas City Star*, 2 July 2011. *archive.is*, archive.is/fqrnq. Accessed 13 Aug. 2017.

Dodd, Rustin. "Five Years Ago Today, Eric Hosmer's Debut Sent a Jolt through Kansas City." *The Kansas City Star*, 5 May 2016, www.kansascity.com/sports/mlb/kansas-city-royals/article76004442.html. Accessed 13 Aug. 2017.

Kurkjian, Tim. "Hosmer's Mad Dash." *ESPN*, 25 Mar. 2016, www.espn.com/espn/feature/story/_/id/15007298/hosmer-mad-dash. Accessed 13 Aug. 2017.

Lacques, Gabe. "Eric Hosmer Paves Way to Royals' World Series Win with Bold, Brilliant Move." *USA Today*, 2 Nov. 2015, www.usatoday.com/story/sports/mlb/royals/2015/11/02/eric-hosmer-kansas-city-royals-world-series-new-york-mets-david-wright-lucas-duda-salvador-perez/75028018/. Accessed 13 Aug. 2017.

Nightengale, Bob. "Amazing! Royals Advance to ALDS on 12-Inning Walk-Off." *USA Today*, 1 Oct. 2014, www.usatoday.com/story/sports/mlb/2014/10/01/al-wild-card-athletics-royals-walk-off/16516853/. Accessed 13 Aug. 2017.

Schonbrun, Zach. "Royals' Hosmer Is Grappling with a Sophomore Slump." *The New York Times*, 23 May 2012, bats.blogs.nytimes.com/2012/05/23/royals-hosmer-is-grappling-with-a-sophomore-slump/. Accessed 13 Aug. 2017.

Spiewak, Stephen. "American Heritage Has Hardball Stars, Too." *MaxPreps*, CBS Interactive, 2008, www.maxpreps.com/news/6ZNrirTbv0u8V-AB0-im4Q/american-heritage-has-hardball-stars,-too.htm. Accessed 13 Aug. 2017.

—*Molly Hagan*

Photo by Paul Archuleta/FilmMagic

Vivian Howard

Date of birth: March 8, 1978
Occupation: Chef

Chef Vivian Howard has "a problem with food TV," she told Andy Dehnart for his website *Reality Blurred* (3 Sept. 2015), because "they exalt the role of chef to something that it's not. They make these people seem like gods, and they make the industry seem glamorous." Although such an assertion may seem strange coming from the winner of the 2016 James Beard Award for best food television personality, it is entirely consistent with Howard's culinary ethos. The star of the award-winning PBS documentary-style reality program *A Chef's Life*, which premiered in 2013, Howard focuses not on glamorizing her career or promoting her personal brand but on the realistic day-to-day aspects of running a restaurant and the people, ingredients, and techniques central to the creation of authentic regional southern food.

Born and raised in rural North Carolina, Howard trained in cooking in New York City during her twenties and planned never to return to her childhood home. Plans changed, however, and in 2006 Howard and her business partners opened a restaurant, Chef and the Farmer, in the city of Kinston, North Carolina. Since its opening, Chef and the Farmer has received widespread acclaim for its farm-to-table approach and inventive take on traditional food, and Howard herself has been credited with helping revitalize Kinston and the surrounding communities. Indeed, the restaurant, with its heavy focus on local ingredients, has become a significant source of income for local farmers, while *A Chef's Life* has drawn tourists who had never before heard of Kinston to the small city. Howard has expressed discomfort, however, with the media's perception of her as a local savior of sorts. "Saving a town was not what I was trying to do," she told Kim Severson for the *New York Times* (17 Jan. 2017). "I'm just a storyteller. A storyteller who cooks."

EARLY LIFE AND EDUCATION

Howard was born in North Carolina in 1978, the youngest of four daughters of John and Scarlett Howard. She grew up in the small rural community of Deep Run in eastern North Carolina, where her parents farmed and raised hogs. Although she was not interested in cooking as a child, she did develop a love of eating at an early age and would later cite the meals her parents prepared as key influences from her childhood

During her early years, Howard became acutely aware of the differences between urban and rural life as she compared her own experiences, in rural areas heavily shaped by tobacco farming, with life in the nearby small city of Kinston. "Even in this very small place, there was the country and there was the town," she said to Jane Black for the *Washington Post* (7 Oct. 2014). "I felt as if the kids who went to the city schools looked down on the kids that went to the country school. We were river rats and rednecks."

Hoping to explore the world beyond Deep Run, Howard attended boarding school as a teenager, following the example of one of her older sisters. She initially attended Salem Academy in Winston-Salem, North Carolina, before moving to attend Virginia Episcopal School in Lynchburg, Virginia, for her last two years of high school. After graduating in 1996, Howard enrolled in North Carolina State University, where she majored in English. She earned her bachelor's degree from the university in 2000. Later lauded as one of North Carolina State's famous alumni, she would eventually return to the university to speak at its winter 2014 commencement ceremony.

EARLY CAREER

Howard did not initially pursue work in the culinary world, instead exploring fields such as journalism and advertising. She completed an internship at the newsmagazine television program *CBS Sunday Morning* and later found a job at the Grey Worldwide advertising agency in New York City, where she remained for a year and a half. Advertising work made her miserable, however, and Howard eventually quit her position. She then took on a string of unrelated jobs before being hired as a server at Voyage, a restaurant in New York's West Village neighborhood, then headed by executive chef Scott Barton. Intrigued by the behind-the-scenes operations of the restaurant, Howard began to consider pursuing work as a food writer but ultimately found that cooking appealed to her more than writing. With guidance from Barton, she began to learn more about cooking and soon found herself pursuing a career as a cook.

To expand her knowledge of culinary techniques, Howard enrolled in the Institute of Culinary Education (ICE), where she studied until 2003. She went on to work in the critically acclaimed Manhattan establishment wd~50, which specialized in modernist culinary techniques such as molecular gastronomy, and the Asian-inspired Spice Market. Although she gained valuable experience from these jobs, Howard hoped to pursue more entrepreneurial ventures, and in 2004 she opened a soup company, Viv's Kitchen, which she and future husband Ben Knight operated out of their Harlem apartment. The company proved successful, and not long after its launch, a satisfied customer offered Howard and Knight financial assistance to open a store in New York. They ultimately turned the offer down, choosing instead to move to North Carolina and open a restaurant in Kinston with the assistance of Howard's family.

CHEF AND THE FARMER

Howard's first restaurant, Chef and the Farmer, opened in Kinston in June 2006. At first the restaurant was not particularly successful, in part because of Howard's attempts to serve New York–style food at New York prices. "I was cooking down to people," she admitted to Severson. "I didn't feel like these people had anything to teach me." However, her outlook—and, subsequently, the success of the restaurant—changed when she began to delve into the traditional cuisine of the region, presenting fresh interpretations of much-loved dishes while retaining their authenticity. At times, that mission prompted Howard to mine the memories of local residents to uncover nearly forgotten recipes, as in the case of the long-neglected traditional sausage known as the tom thumb. "Tom thumb is a relic from the era when folks came together and had hog killings in the early winter," she explained to Antoinette Bruno for *StarChefs* (Nov. 2013). "They salted hams, made sausage and pickled pork. Out of the need to waste nothing, people would stuff their sausage mix into the pig's appendix and hang it in the smokehouse till Christmas or New Year's. So tom thumb is a semicured, celebration sausage. . . . It's delicious and no one even knows how to make it anymore. We developed our recipe from one country butcher and my dad's memory." The re-creation process was successful, and the result is often featured in the restaurant's menu.

In addition to its focus on eastern North Carolina cuisine, Chef and the Farmer is known for its heavy use of local ingredients, particularly produce, dairy products, and meats. The restaurant's menu reflects ingredients that are available locally and in season, and Howard has noted that the use of local ingredients both gives her food its unique character and supports the local rural economy. "Our region is ideal for small farms that do great things," she said to Bruno. "Being where we are we've been able to nurture relationships with farmers and guide them to grow the things we want, to make our cuisine unique."

Although Chef and the Farmer experienced some notable setbacks, including a fire in early 2012 that caused severe smoke damage and forced the restaurant to close for nearly four months, the establishment became a popular dining option in Kinston. Diners began to travel from out of town—or even out of state—to taste Howard's recipes. Building on the success of Chef and the Farmer, Howard and her business partners opened a second restaurant in Kinston, the Boiler Room Oyster Bar, in 2013. Inspired by the tradition of eastern North Carolina oyster bars, the restaurant also serves such items such as hamburgers, fish and chips, and ribs. In late 2016, Howard announced plans to open a new restaurant called Benny's Big Time Pizzeria in Wilmington, a coastal city about ninety miles south of Kinston. That year also saw the publication of Howard's first cookbook, *Deep Run Roots: Stories and Recipes from My Corner of the South*.

A CHEF'S LIFE

Several years after returning to North Carolina, Howard began to think about creating a documentary that would chronicle her experiences at Chef and the Farmer and highlight some of her local suppliers and the ingredients featured in her restaurant. She eventually reached out to Cynthia Hill, a filmmaker who had grown up in the region and whom Howard had known as a child. The pair began filming what would become the pilot episode of Howard's television series, *A Chef's Life*, documenting the process of preserving corn for winter as well as the events surrounding the fire at Chef and the Farmer.

Although Howard was enthusiastic about documenting the culinary traditions of the region, she did not originally plan to become a nationally known television personality. "We still thought we were making a little documentary," she told Marian Bull for *Food52* (16 Dec. 2014). "We wouldn't have had the confidence to make a series had it not been for a producer out of New York, who told us to call it a pilot and make a series out of it."

After sending the pilot to a PBS affiliate in South Carolina, Howard and Hill were tasked with filming a full season of the show, which would then air on PBS stations throughout the United States. The debut season of *A Chef's Life* premiered in September 2013 and quickly received critical acclaim, winning a prestigious Peabody Award in 2014 and earning a nomination for the 2014 James Beard Award for best on-location television program. Three additional seasons aired between 2014 and 2016 and received further recognition, including the 2015 Daytime Emmy Award for outstanding direction in a lifestyle, culinary, or travel program. In 2016 Howard was nominated again for a James Beard Award, for outstanding personality or host, and this time she won.

Perhaps more notable than the show's critical acclaim has been the recognition that it has received for its role in revitalizing Kinston and the surrounding communities, which had suffered economically in the decades since Howard's childhood. Along with Chef and the Farmer, *A Chef's Life* has been credited with bringing visitors to Kinston and introducing the local way of life to people throughout the United States. "Until recently, everyone who lives in Lenoir County apologized for it," Howard told Black. "'I live in Kinston, but I only moved back here because I need to take care of my mom.' Or, 'I'm here because I run my parents' business.' Or, 'Doesn't this place suck?' Now that other people are interested in this place, they say, 'I live in Kinston—you know? *A Chef's Life*.' That's the first step in really making a difference."

PERSONAL LIFE

Howard met her husband, painter Ben Knight, while they were both working at Voyage. They have two children, twins Florence and Theodore. The family lives in a farmhouse in Deep Run.

SUGGESTED READING

Black, Jane. "Vivian Howard Lives *A Chef's Life*, Her Attempt to Show the Real North Carolina." *The Washington Post*, 7 Oct. 2014, www.washingtonpost.com/lifestyle/food/vivian-howard-lives-a-chefs-life-her-attempt-to-show-the-real-north-carolina/2014/10/06/b8e1d0b8-4a51-11e4-891d-713f052086a0_story.html. Accessed 12 June 2017.

Dehnart, Andy. "How Chef Vivian Howard, Who Offended Food Network, Is Trying to Change Food TV." *Reality Blurred*, 3 Sept. 2015, www.realityblurred.com/realitytv/2015/09/a-chefs-life-vivian-howard-interview/. Accessed 12 June 2017.

Howard, Vivian. *Deep Run Roots: Stories and Recipes from My Corner of the South*. Little, Brown, 2016.

Howard, Vivian. "Interview with Chef Vivian Howard of Chef & the Farmer—Kinston, NC." Interview by Antoinette Bruno. *StarChefs*, Nov. 2013, www.starchefs.com/cook/interview/interview-chef-vivian-howard-chef-farmer-kinston-nc. Accessed 12 June 2017.

Howard, Vivian. "An Interview with Vivian Howard of *A Chef's Life*." Interview by Marian Bull. *Food52*, 16 Dec. 2014, food52.com/blog/11950-an-interview-with-vivian-howard-of-a-chef-s-life. Accessed 12 June 2017.

Howard, Vivian, and Scarlett Howard. "Carolina Conversations with PBS' *A Chef's Life* Vivian Howard & Mom, Scarlett." *OutreachNC*, 31 July 2015, www.outreachnc.com/carolina-conversations-with-pbs-a-chefs-life-vivian-howard-mom-scarlett/. Accessed 12 June 2017.

Severson, Kim. "Vivian Howard, a TV Chef, Offers Hope for Her Rural Hometown." *The New York Times*, 17 Jan. 2017, www.nytimes.com/2017/01/17/dining/vivian-howard-north-carolina-chef-and-the-farmer.html. Accessed 12 June 2017.

—*Joy Crelin*

Ollanta Humala

Date of birth: ca. June 27, 1962
Occupation: President of Peru

Former left-wing radical and army official Ollanta Humala became the president of Peru in 2011. During his presidency, he attempted to balance center-right economic policies with leftist social policies.

BACKGROUND AND EDUCATION

The second eldest of seven children, Ollanta Humala was born on either June 26 or 27, 1962, in Ayacucho, Peru. His father, Isaac Humala, was a left-wing radical who espoused *etnocacerismo*, a political ideology based on ethnic nationalism and the restoration of the Inca heritage. He encouraged his children to become revolutionaries. He founded the Ethnocacerist Movement, and some of his children, including Ollanta, became involved in it. Other family members were not active in the movement but held strong leftist views.

Humala attended high school in Lima then briefly studied at the National Agrarian University. In 1980, he enrolled in the Chorrillos Military School. Two years later he graduated with the rank of junior officer. He later did graduate work at several universities, studying political science at Pontifical Catholic University of Peru, national defense at the Center of Higher Military Studies, and international law at the University of Paris.

LIFE'S WORK

Following his 1982 graduation from the Chorrillos Military School, Humala joined the national army. He received additional training at the School of the Americas, a US Army training facility for Latin American military personnel. By 1992 he had earned the rank of army captain and led a group to fight the Shining Path guerrilla rebels in Tingo Maria. His actions there later led to allegations of human rights abuses, which he denied. In 1995, Humala fought in the Cenepa War, a brief skirmish between military forces over the border between Ecuador and Peru.

In October 2000, Humala and his brother, Antauro Humala, led a rebellion against then-president Alberto Fujimori, claiming he was corrupt. The rebellion was immediately suppressed and both brothers were subsequently imprisoned. Humala was discharged from the army, and plans to court martial him were initiated. Soon, however, Fujimori's corruption became known, and Humala was reinstated in the army and given a congressional pardon.

In 2004, Humala was sent to France as an assistant military attaché and then to South Korea as a military attaché. While in South Korea, army leadership shifted, and Humala was forced out. He resigned in 2005 with the rank of lieutenant colonel.

Returning to Peru in 2005, Humala founded the Partido Nacionalista Peruano (the Peruvian Nationalist Party). Previously unable to garner sufficient signatures to register as a candidate for the 2006 presidential election, he ran as the candidate for the Peruvian Nationalist Party. Although he won the first round, he failed to gain the necessary 50 percent majority plus one to claim victory. In the runoff election, he lost to Alan Garcia.

Humala ran again for president in the 2011 election. Although he had modeled himself in 2006 after Hugo Chávez, the socialist president of Venezuela, he took a more moderate approach in 2011, modeling himself after Luiz Inácio Lula da Silva, the president of Brazil. Humala pledged to continue his predecessors' free-market policies but also to address social and environmental problems, to make Peru more inclusive, and to give local communities more say in regional mining activities. He also promised to raise taxes on mining companies and to use the increased revenues to reduce poverty, to create a pension system for people sixty-five years and older, and to raise the minimum wage. Humala narrowly defeated his chief opponent, Keiko Fujimori, the daughter of the former president, in the runoff election and was sworn in as president on July 28, 2011.

As president, Humala kept many of his campaign promises. He continued the free-trade economic policies of his predecessors while implementing leftist social policies. He raised the taxes on mining companies and passed a law giving communities a voice in mining developments. Despite his efforts to balance the needs of foreign investors with those of the largely poor population, he was unable to quell social conflicts and protests. Many Peruvians opposed mining developments for environmental reasons, and violent protests were commonplace—so, too, was crime, which increased during Humala's term.

Humala also struggled politically. He lost the support of many on the far-left who felt that he had abandoned their interests. He shuffled around members of his cabinet several times. A number of members of his administration were accused of corruption, with Humala implicated in a bribery scandal in early 2016.

IMPACT

Despite his ability to maintain high foreign investments and implement some social reforms, Ollanta Humala was unable to make significant headway in reducing poverty and inequality in Peru. By the last year of his term, his administration was mired in allegations of corruption, several large mining projects were on hold, and Humala's approval rating among voters had significantly declined.

PERSONAL LIFE

Humala is married to Nadine Heredia. They have two daughters and a son.

SUGGESTED READING

"A Jarring Defeat: The Loneliness of Ollanta Humala." *Economist*. Economist, 4 Apr. 2015. Web. 24 Feb. 2016.

Chauvin, Lucien. "Peru Swears in New President. Who Is Ollanta Humala?" *Christian Science Monitor*. Christian Science Monitor, 28 July 2011. Web. 24 Feb. 2016.

Chauvin, Lucien. "Peru's President: Why Does His Family Hate Him?" *Time*. Time, 29 June 2012. Web. 24 Feb. 2016.

Collyns, Dan. "Peru Election: Is Ollanta Humala the Great Transformer?" *BBC*. BBC, 7 June 2011. Web. 24 Feb. 2016.

Kozak, Robert. "Peru's President Humala Shuffles Cabinet as Popularity Weakens." *Wall Street Journal*. Wall Street Journal, 17 Feb. 2015. Web. 24 Feb. 2016.

"Ollanta Humala." *Peru Reports*. Peru Reports, n.d. Web. 24 Feb. 2016.

St. John, Ronald Bruce. "Peru's Humala Is Washington's Next 'Worst Nightmare.'" *Foreign Policy in Focus*. Institute for Policy Studies, 24 Apr. 2006. Web. 24 Feb. 2016.

—*Barb Lightner*

By Activités culturelles UdeM [CC0], via Wikimedia Commons

Justin Hurwitz

Date of birth: ca. 1985
Occupation: Composer, writer

The composer Justin Hurwitz has created some of the most well-known and memorable contemporary film music, namely for the films *Whiplash* (2014) and *La La Land* (2016). The former won him notice and critical attention. *La La Land*, a musical film about the love of two people and the love of jazz, received fourteen Oscar nominations. It ultimately won six Oscars, including best actress for its lead actor Emma Stone and best original score for Hurwitz, who was only thirty-two years old at the time. Aside from his musical career, he has ventured into the comedy realm, writing one episode of *The Simpsons* and a few episodes of *The League*, and writing and producing for the highly anticipated ninth season of the cult HBO comedy *Curb Your Enthusiasm*.

EARLY YEARS

Justin Hurwitz was born circa 1985 and spent his early childhood years in California. When he was in eighth grade his family moved to Fox Point, Wisconsin, where he would go on to attend Nicolet High School. Hurwitz was a precocious child, playing piano from the age of six and composing music at the age of ten. He studied music at the Wisconsin Conservatory of Music, where one of his teachers was Stefanie Jacob. In

an interview with National Public Radio (NPR) host Scott Simon (18 Feb. 2017), Jacob recalled how diligent and hardworking Hurwitz was as a student. During his senior year of high school, he performed (with a community orchestra) Beethoven's entire first piano concerto, and he "played it really well," she added. As talented as Hurwitz was when it came to his piano playing, however, he did not like practice very much. In an interview with Colleen Walsh for his alma mater's newspaper, the *Harvard Gazette* (20 Jan. 2017), Hurwitz said that when he was in high school, piano practice was "like pulling teeth." But composing music—putting together all the elements of music, such as melody, harmony, tempo, and rhythm, and inserting complex elements such as counterpoint—came naturally to him, even at a young age. When he was composing, he told Walsh, "the hours would just disappear."

STUDYING MUSIC AT HARVARD

After graduating from Nicolet High School in 2003, Hurwitz studied music at Harvard University, in Cambridge, Massachusetts. As rich and valuable as many of his experiences at Harvard were, Hurwitz told Walsh that taking the class Music 51 was "the most life-changing thing I did at Harvard." Thanks to his teacher, John Stewart, Hurwitz learned a great deal about music by delving deeply into the works of composer Johann Sebastian Bach. Specifically, he studied Bach's chorales, works that incorporate four voices interacting simultaneously in strange and fascinating ways. In that class, wrote Walsh,

Hurwitz learned the quintessential ingredients of musical composition: rhythm, timbre, harmony, form, and counterpoint. Hurwitz would later go on, in such films as *La La Land*, to use counterpoint—two or more contrasting melodies being played or sung simultaneously—as a storytelling device.

During his freshman year Hurwitz met fellow Harvard student Damien Chazelle, who was studying at the university's Department of Visual and Environmental Studies. Because of their mutual love of music, they became close friends. As freshmen they played in a band, with Hurwitz on electric piano and Chazelle on drums, but in the middle of their sophomore year—by which point they were roommates and good friends—they dropped the band to focus more on their studies. Hurwitz and Chazelle often pushed each other creatively, even as their creative pursuits continued to take them in different directions. From sophomore year onward, they would talk about their aspirations, wrote Walsh. One of the things that brought Hurwitz and Chazelle closer, Hurwitz told Walsh, was how much they both valued "working really hard and sacrificing." It was also during their sophomore year that they began collaborating on a musical film that would become Chazelle's directorial debut, *Guy and Madeline on a Park Bench*, a sort of precursor to *La La Land*.

GUY AND MADELINE ON A PARK BENCH

Guy and Madeline on a Park Bench, for which Hurwitz wrote the music, began making film festival rounds in 2009 and got a wider release the following year. It was shot in black and white on 16mm film. Though it takes place in the present, in Boston and New York City, the feel of the film is somewhat reminiscent of the 1950s and '60s. Guy, played by trumpeter Jason Palmer, has a difficult relationship with Madeline, played by Desiree Garcia. Madeline is a waitress, and the film opens with the three-month-long relationship between Guy and Madeline dissolving. What is most important in this film is not the plot or the question of whether the leads will get back together, but the music and the unspoken communication of dance moves and facial expressions. There are some musical numbers that seem improvised, such as when Guy plays his trumpet, and his call is "answered" by another man tap dancing and banging the floor with drumsticks.

This level of improvisation, a common feature of jazz but generally nonexistent in classical music, was something new for Hurwitz. At Harvard he primarily composed classical music, namely piano fugues and string quartets. "I remember the very first recording sessions we had for *Guy and Madeline*, we brought jazz musicians from Berklee [College of Music, in Boston] into the studio, gave them lead sheets, and then let them do what jazz musicians do," Hurwitz told Kevin Slane for *Boston.com* (24 Feb. 2017). "Hearing them come up with things that I never would have written on the page, it was so exciting."

Though plot and character development are not the film's strong points, wrote Jeannette Catsoulis for the *New York Times* (4 Nov. 2010), it had other elements that drove it forward. "The story's dramatic weaknesses," wrote Catsoulis, "are the music's opportunities, and *Guy and Madeline* soars in the cool sizzle of Guy's trumpet solos and the blissed-out atmosphere of his jam sessions. Eruptions of singing and tap-dancing—in a jazz club, a diner, a park—range from joyous to resilient to wistful, their choreographed emotions filling in for the characters' maddening inscrutability." The film was selected as a *New York Times* Critic's Pick. In a review for the Associated Press (15 Oct. 2009), Sura Wood called the film a "distinctive debut feature." Wood went on to add that despite being greatly influenced by the French New Wave directors of the 1960s, the film was unique.

WHIPLASH

The film *Whiplash* (2014), also directed by Chazelle and scored by Hurwitz, continued to explore the relationship between human experience and music, specifically jazz. Although Chazelle's first feature incorporated his love of music, his second feature mined his own experience as a drummer of his high school jazz band. Like the protagonist of the film, he had a particularly strict, tough teacher who drove him to the breaking point. In the film, Andrew (Miles Teller) is a young drummer who wants to be the best. He is studying at a music conservatory, where his bandleader and instructor, Fletcher (J. K. Simmons) is more like a ridiculously tough football coach. Fletcher is abusive and relentless: he does not shy away from making his musicians cry or kicking someone out of the band for seemingly small mistakes, and he thinks nothing of stopping practice to test or mock his musicians. He thinks one of the worst things a teacher can say is "good job." Andrew, age nineteen, pushes himself so hard practicing drums that his fingers bleed. He trains for drumming as if for a sporting event. He is so determined to be the best that he deals with Fletcher by practicing even more and gives up a potentially promising romance with a young lady so he can focus exclusively on drumming. There seems to be no limit to what he will sacrifice.

The film received several Academy Award nominations in 2015, including best picture and best adapted screenplay. It also received praise and positive reviews. Robbie Collin, for the *Telegraph* (16 June 2015), compared the structure of the film to the rhythms of jazz, and concluded, "However genius may flourish, you know it when you see it, and *Whiplash* is it." Writing for the *Guardian* (18 Jan. 2015), Mark Kermode compared the film to the boxing movie *Rocky* and the Vietnam War film *Full Metal Jacket*. Kermode wrote, "Considering the slimness of the plot and the familiar verse-chorus-middle-eight structure of the narrative (boy meets girl, drum meets boy, girl loses boy to drum, etc.) it's dazzling how sprightly and inventive this conspires to be." Some critics, however, took issue with the film's portrayal of jazz. The movie's "very idea of jazz is a grotesque and ludicrous caricature," wrote Richard Brody for the *New Yorker* (13 Oct. 2014). Brody took issue with the fact that Andrew, the film's young hero, does not actually do what a jazz musician should do to improve: jam with fellow students. Instead he plays drums—by himself. The film, Brody concludes, is not about jazz; it is about "abuse of power."

LA LA LAND

Around 2010, about a year after *Guy and Madeline*, Hurwitz and Chazelle began their collaboration on *La La Land*. The film seemed grand in budget and ambition, and the two creative partners could find no studio that would back them. *La La Land* was a movie musical, with music composed by Hurwitz, featuring characters breaking into song and dance—not the most common or most lucrative form of filmmaking in the twenty-first century. After the success of *Whiplash*, however, Summit Entertainment picked up the project.

La La Land is about an aspiring actor named Mia (Emma Stone) and a talented musician named Sebastian (Ryan Gosling). The two meet in a traffic jam in Los Angeles, but despite the classic boy-meets-girl setup, sparks do not fly. No romance ensues after their accidental second meeting either. It is only after their third meeting that they begin their relationship. The story is about their romance, but the driving force of the film is the dancing and music—jazz in particular.

The film received fourteen Oscar nominations, and won six of them, including best actress for Stone, best original score for Hurwitz, and best director for Chazelle. Writing for the *New Yorker* (12 Dec. 2016), Anthony Lane, referring to the use of bright colors in how the film was shot, confessed that the film "looks so delicious that I genuinely couldn't decide whether to watch it or lick it." As impressive as the film was visually, a musical film succeeds or fails based on the music. *La La Land* "integrates its numbers, even the most fantastical, as if it were the most natural thing in the world for a guy to tap-dance on a park bench or a woman to dream herself into a waltz," wrote Manohla Dargis for the *New York Times* (23 Nov. 2016). In the review she also suggested that the film may very well have made "musicals matter again."

SUGGESTED READING

"Behind 'La La Land,' a Long Relationship between a Director and a Composer." *WBGO. org*, 18 Feb. 2017, wbgo.org/post/long-relationship-director-and-composer-la-la-land. Accessed 8 June 2017.

Dargis, Manohla. "*La La Land* Makes Musicals Matter Again." Review of *La La Land*, directed by Damien Chazelle. *The New York Times*, 23 Nov. 2016, www.nytimes.com/2016/11/23/movies/la-la-land-makes-musicals-matter-again.html. Accessed 8 June 2017.

Hurwitz, Justin. "How 'La La Land' Composer Justin Hurwitz Used 'Sleight of Hand and Deception' to Create His Dynamic Score." Interview by Matt Grobar. *Deadline*, 15 Feb. 2017, deadline.com/2017/02/la-la-land-justin-hurwitz-oscars-best-original-score-bafta-interview-news-1201910726. Accessed 8 June 2017.

Lane, Anthony. "Fun in *La La Land*." Review of *La La Land*, directed by Damien Chazelle. *The New Yorker*, 12 Dec. 2016, www.newyorker.com/magazine/2016/12/12/dancing-with-the-stars. Accessed 8 June 2017.

Levy, Piet. "Oscar-Nominated 'La La Land' Composer Justin Hurwitz Got His Start in Milwaukee." *Milwaukee Wisconsin Journal Sentinel*, 17 Feb. 2017, www.jsonline.com/story/entertainment/music/2017/02/17/la-la-lands-justin-hurwitz-composing-music-life-long-obsession/98029448. Accessed 8 June 2017.

Walsh, Colleen. "From Harvard to 'La La Land.'" *Harvard Gazette*, 20 Jan. 2017, news.harvard.edu/gazette/story/2017/01/harvard-and-its-la-la-land-connection. Accessed 8 June 2017.

SELECTED WORKS

Guy and Madeline on a Park Bench, 2009; *Whiplash*, 2014; *La La Land*, 2016

—*Dmitry Kiper*

Roksanda Ilinčić

Date of birth: May 1970
Occupation: Fashion designer

Since the start of the twenty-first century, fashion designer Roksanda Ilinčić has striven to design clothing that both is aesthetically pleasing to her customers and fits within their busy, multifaceted lives. The Serbian-born British founder of the fashion label Roksanda, Ilinčić developed

Ricky Vigil / Stringer for GC Images

an interest in fashion early in life and launched her company after completing graduate studies at the prestigious Central Saint Martins school in London. In the years since the debut of her first collection of eveningwear at London Fashion Week, her designs have become fixtures on red carpets and at important events of all kinds, worn by celebrities and major figures such as Kate Middleton and Michelle Obama. While Ilinčić's success as a designer has become clearly apparent, she insists that she cares far more about the fashion itself. "I'm not doing this for the money," she told Ian Wright for *Drapers* (22 June 2013). "I do it for the love."

Although Ilinčić's company's focus has expanded over the years, encompassing more casual pieces in addition to the eveningwear with which she first made her name and introducing new lines of handbags, jewelry, and children's clothing, she remains focused on designing for a very specific sort of customer. "It's a woman who likes to dress not to please others but to please herself," Ilinčić explained to Meadhbh McGrath for the Irish *Independent* (29 June 2016). "She's somebody who is very inquisitive and interested in many different things, she's very independent and very modern. Somebody who likes and enjoys fashion for her own sake."

EARLY LIFE AND EDUCATION

Ilinčić was born in May 1970 in Belgrade, Serbia, then part of Yugoslavia. As a child Ilinčić was introduced to the world of fashion by her pharmacist mother, Ranka, who was a devoted fan of designers such as Yves Saint Laurent as well as the owner of numerous bespoke pieces of clothing. "She had her own seamstresses who made clothes for her, and she'd make dresses for me out of the leftover pieces of fabric," Ilinčić recalled to Sophie de Rosee for the *Telegraph* (9 June 2011). "I was like a mini-me. She loved dressing me, which I wasn't very happy about because I wanted to dress myself."

Although as a child Ilinčić aspired to be a ballerina, she was likewise drawn to the field of clothing design, inspired in part by the costumes featured in ballet and theatrical performances. She soon began creating her own designs but ultimately studied architecture and applied arts upon her enrollment in the Faculty of Applied Arts at the University of Arts in Belgrade. Although she lived in the city during the Yugoslavian Civil War of the 1990s and endured privations such as lack of heat at school, Ilinčić has said that one of the most memorable hardships she faced during that period was an inability to obtain foreign fashion magazines.

In 1999, Ilinčić moved to London, England. There, she enrolled in the prestigious art school Central Saint Martins, one of six schools that make up the University of the Arts London. The alma mater of many notable creatives, Central Saint Martins has educated numerous well-known clothing designers, including Alexander McQueen and Stella McCartney. Ilinčić, however, was primarily interested in having the opportunity to study under Professor Louise Wilson, who served as course director of the college's graduate-level fashion program. Ilinčić earned her master's degree in fashion with a concentration in womenswear in 2000. During that time, she also gained fashion industry experience working as a model signed to the Storm agency.

LAUNCHING A LABEL

In 2005, Ilinčić launched her own clothing line, Roksanda Ilinčić (later renamed simply Roksanda in 2014). Ilinčić's early design efforts focused on eveningwear, and her first official collection consisted of only about a dozen dresses. She debuted the collection officially her spring/summer 2006 offering during London Fashion Week (LFW) in September 2005. As a devotee of fashion who had lived in London for several years at that point, Ilinčić was highly aware of the importance of LFW to new designers and was pleased to be part of it—an attitude that she has maintained years after finding fame as a designer. Speaking of the event in an interview with Jo Glynn-Smith for *Harper's Bazaar* (16 Feb. 2016), she said, "London is such a creative melting pot. Designers here are much more experimental and free than in other fashion capitals. It's always exciting to see what type of new aesthetic will emerge during Fashion Week."

The response to Ilinčić's debut collection was largely positive, and she soon established herself as one of the United Kingdom's major up-and-coming designers. Over the following year, her label found its niche creating fashionable clothing for women who are both practical and well dressed. "I'm always designing for a modern woman with a varied day," Ilinčić explained to Glynn-Smith. "I want to make clothes for women taking their child to school, running around during a busy day at work, and going out for dinner in the evening." At the same time, she sought to distinguish her pieces from the countless other clothing items available for purchase by adding various distinctive touches—such as bold blocks of color or exaggerated bell sleeves—that would surprise and intrigue her customer base. "It's good to challenge yourself, but also to challenge your customer, because it's good to offer something that the customer doesn't necessarily know or feel that they needed," she told McGrath.

AN APPEALING AESTHETIC
Although the many seasonal collections Ilinčić has created since the launch of her label have featured a vast range of design elements and materials, much of her work is characterized by an assertive use of color rather than the monochromatic tones favored by many other designers. "Color brings happiness," she told Emma Sells for the fashion magazine the *Edit* (5 Nov. 2015), produced by Net-a-Porter, one of the prominent online retailers that sells her label. "It's a point of difference, a way of making a statement with something that is not shape or fabric, but something that just makes you feel comfortable and positive. I think that positive energy is very important."

Over the course of her career, Ilinčić has drawn inspiration from a variety of cultural and day-to-day influences, including such quotidian objects as LEGO blocks and Australian recycling bins. In addition to the more obvious hallmarks of her designs, such as her frequent use of bright colors and recurring shapes, her design strategy is characterized by a level of attention to detail that comes across in her runway shows as well. For a 2016 runway show, Ilinčić and stylist Mark Hampton paid close attention not only to the clothing the models were wearing but also the specific colors of ponytail holders used in their hair. Although audiences likely would not have noticed such details, Ilinčić believes that such small touches can have a significant impact on the overall aesthetic appeal of a collection. "At the end of the day that's the point, you just get the feel of something, something you can't quite grasp," she explained to McGrath. "That connection with a person at a show is very important, because the emotions that they take out

are what makes you relevant and what makes you desirable." Ilinčić's design aesthetic proved popular among many in the United Kingdom and beyond, and her designs have been notably worn by actors such as Cate Blanchett, Sandra Bullock, and Kerry Washington as well as political figures such as Kate Middleton, Samantha Cameron, Michelle Obama, and Melania Trump.

BRAND EXPANSION
In the Roksanda brand's first decade of existence, Ilinčić and her business partners sought to expand the label's scope and reach. Although Ilinčić's earliest pieces were primarily eveningwear intended for fancy occasions, she quickly came to realize that the brand could reach a broader base of customers by offering more separates and more practical, casual pieces. Her resort collection, which encompasses a wider range of ready-to-wear clothing, proved particularly popular following its introduction, and Ilinčić does not shy away from the commercial appeal of such designs. "Resort is definitely the main collection. I'm always expanding all the collections but resort is certainly the bestseller," she told Wright. "Commercial is seen as this ugly word. I call [the pieces] 'must-haves.' Perfectly priced garments are very important—resort and pre-collections have become so vital to everyone's business."

In addition to her collections of clothing for everyday wear, Ilinčić introduced a collection of children's clothing, BLOSSOM, in 2012. The Roksanda brand also encompasses collections of jewelry and handbags. While focusing on expanding the company's offerings, the label has likewise sought to reach its customers through additional retail avenues. In 2014, Roksanda opened its first retail store in the Mayfair neighborhood of London. Designed by award-winning British architect Sir David Adjaye, the boutique's design featured bold colors and eye-catching shapes reminiscent of Ilinčić's designs. Seeking to boost growth further, in 2015 the company brought in its first CEO, Carmela Acampora, a former executive at Burberry and Aspinal of London.

PERSONAL LIFE
Ilinčić met her future husband and business partner, Philip Bueno de Mesquita, not long after moving to London. De Mesquita is himself an entrepreneur who cofounded the shoe brand Acupuncture in 1993. Their daughter, Efimia, was born in August 2010. In interviews, Ilinčić has noted that raising a young child has given her a greater understanding of the intersections between work and family life that many of her designs' buyers encounter. "Before I had a child I couldn't even understand how women can have several children and still run successful

businesses," she explained to Wright. "But once you get your own child you realise things are possible and you can create things just as good as before but with a slightly different approach. Things aren't a matter of life or death as they used to be."

Although Ilinčić primarily wears her own label's clothing, she is an avid collector of clothing, including designer pieces and vintage items. "I love collecting clothes but they don't have to be labels, they can just be beautiful pieces," she told Imogen Fox for the *Guardian* (14 Sept. 2008). Like her mother before her, Ilinčić particularly enjoys collecting Yves Saint Laurent clothing and claims to have amassed more than five hundred individual pieces.

SUGGESTED READING

Ilinčić, Roksanda. "The Close-Up." Interview by Imogen Fox. *The Guardian*, 14 Sept. 2008, www.theguardian.com/lifeandstyle/2008/sep/15/fashion1. Accessed 12 May 2017.

Ilinčić, Roksanda. "Five Minutes with Roksanda Ilinčić." Interview by Dolly Jones. *Vogue*, 10 June 2014, www.vogue.co.uk/article/five-minutes-with-roksanda-Ilinčić-interview. Accessed 12 May 2017.

Ilinčić, Roksanda. "Work It Out: Roksanda Ilinčić." Interview by Jo Glynn-Smith. *Harper's Bazaar*, 16 Feb. 2016, www.harpersbazaar.co.uk/people-parties/bazaar-at-work/news/a36544/work-it-out-fashion-special-london. Accessed 12 May 2017.

Ilinčić, Roksanda. "World of Designer Roksanda Ilinčić." Interview by Sophie de Rosee. *Telegraph*, 9 June 2011, fashion.telegraph.co.uk/columns/sophie-derosée/TMG8555379/World-of-designer-Roksanda-Ilinčić.html. Accessed 12 May 2017.

McGrath, Meadhbh. "The Interview: Roksanda Ilinčić Talks Designer Burnout, A-List Fans, and Embracing Her Dark Side." *Independent*, 29 June 2016, www.independent.ie/style/fashion/style-talk/the-interview-roksanda-Ilinčić-talks-designer-burnout-alist-fans-and-embracing-her-dark-side-34813321.html. Accessed 12 May 2017.

Sells, Emma. "The Interview: Roksanda Ilinčić." *The Edit*, Net-a-Porter, 5 Nov. 2015, www.net-a-porter.com/magazine/324/18. Accessed 12 May 2017.

Wright, Ian. "Close Up: Roksanda Ilinčić, Designer." *Drapers*, 22 June 2013, www.drapersonline.com/people/the-drapers-interview/close-up-roksanda-Ilinčić-designer/5050119.article. Accessed 12 May 2017.

—*Joy Crelin*

Imagine Dragons
Occupation: Band

DAN REYNOLDS
Date of birth: July 14, 1987
Occupation: Lead vocalist

DANIEL PLATZMAN
Date of birth: September 28, 1986
Occupation: Drummer, film composer

BEN MCKEE
Date of birth: April 7, 1985
Occupation: Bass guitarist

WAYNE SERMON
Date of birth: June 15, 1984
Occupation: Lead guitarist

The popular Grammy Award–winning band Imagine Dragons likes to mix it up style-wise. They have been called pop rock or arena rock, though they also incorporate dance and electronic elements into their music. When they released their first album in 2012, listeners compared them to Coldplay, the Killers, and Mumford & Sons. Their songs stayed on the Billboard Hot 100 chart for extensive periods of time, getting much airplay around the country as well as abroad. Hits like "It's Time," "Radioactive," "I Bet My Life," and "Believer" have been heard tens of millions of times across the globe. Though the group has its critics, who say that Imagine Dragons is safe or overproduced, the band has set chart records. Between 2012 and 2014, "Radioactive" had the longest Billboard Hot 100 run in the chart's history.

ECLECTIC ELECTRICS AND INFLUENCES

Imagine Dragons consists of four main members: lead singer Dan Reynolds, from Las Vegas, Nevada; drummer Daniel Platzman, from Atlanta, Georgia; bass player Ben McKee, from Forestville, California; and lead guitar player Wayne Sermon, from American Fork, Utah. Three of the band's members—McKee, Sermon, and Platzman—all went to the Berklee College of Music in Boston, Massachusetts. In an interview with Alyssa McCord for the *Berklee Groove* (4 Aug. 2013), the college's student publication, Ben McKee recalled how he, Sermon, and Platzman played together for three years in an all-guitar group called Eclectic Electrics for a performance ensemble class. The group played mostly fusion—a blending of rock, jazz, and various kinds of music from across the world. In the

By Alexandra Sermon [CC BY-SA 3.0], via Wikimedia Commons

interview with McCord, McKee also said that aside from the ensemble class, two other classes were instrumental to his growth as a musician. The first was atonal solfege, which examined very challenging music that does not rely on the major-minor scale system. McKee said that the class proved to be "some of the best ear training that you could ever do." The second class was a jingle writing class, "one of the most practical and usable classes I ever took," he said, in which he learned about the connection between jingles and pop songs.

In an interview with the *Columbian* (14 Mar. 2013), Sermon, reflecting on Imagine Dragons' first album and musical identity, pointed to the band members' early years as a major influence on the band's later sound: "I think the sound arose out of just a collection of everything we've listened to, everything that has influenced us individually," he said. "There's definitely a lot of classic rock influence in everything we do because we've all listened to that growing up." Specifically, he cited Led Zeppelin, the Beatles, the Rolling Stones, Simon & Garfunkel, and the little-known but influential singer-songwriter Harry Nilsson. At Berklee, however, McKee, Sermon, and Platzman also learned about jazz, avant-garde, and experimental music. They have drawn on these influences and added in modern elements, especially regarding rhythm, effects, and production.

UTAH TO LAS VEGAS

After graduating from the Berklee College of Music, Sermon returned to his hometown of Provo, Utah. "I had come back just to kind of figure out what I wanted to do," Sermon said in his interview with the *Columbian*. "I knew I wanted to do music. I knew I wanted to be very serious about it. So I just kind of began exploring the scene a little bit, and a friend told me about this guy that sang and played guitar. So I went to a show he was doing in Provo and just kind of liked what he was doing." The guy was Dan Reynolds, and the year was 2008. The two musicians got to know one another, and eventually Reynolds decided to return to his hometown of Las Vegas, Nevada, where he was going to form a band. He wanted to know if Sermon was interested. And it turned out he was.

The band officially formed in 2009 (some sources say 2008). The group's name, which has been the subject of much speculation and mystery, was agreed upon by all members. The name Imagine Dragons, McKee told McCord, is an anagram: the letters are rearranged from another word or phrase. What that word or phrase is has never been revealed because the band members swore themselves to secrecy. The only thing McKee did say was that the original word or phrase from which the band name derives has "some meaning to the band." In 2009 the band got a lucky break at the Bite of Las Vegas music festival, where they played an early afternoon slot. When the singer of the band Train, who was supposed to headline a later show, fell ill, Imagine Dragons performed in his stead, playing to a crowd that topped 26,000 people. After that performance, word about the band began to spread locally.

In 2010 the group recorded EPs (records consisting of only a few songs), including *Hell and Silence*, at Battle Born Studios, the recording studio of the popular Las Vegas rock band the Killers. Imagine Dragons' third EP, *It's Time*, came out in 2012, and based on its strength, the band landed a deal with Interscope Records. Prior to the signing of that deal, the group's original drummer, Andrew Tolman, left the group, and that is when Platzman joined Imagine Dragons on drums. The foursome—Reynolds, Platzman, Sermon, and McKee—went on to release a full album and dominate the music charts.

NIGHT VISIONS

Imagine Dragons' first full-length album, *Night Visions* (2012), debuted at number two on the Billboard 200, Top Rock, and Alternative Albums charts. Although the album was not much of a critical success—many critics viewed it as safe and middle-of-the-road—the music struck a chord with fans. The album sold 3.9 million copies worldwide. There were instant comparisons to the arena rock group Coldplay, the folk-pop group Mumford & Sons, and the electro-rock group the Killers. The sound of the songs was larger than life, catchy, and unselfconsciously earnest. The hit "It's Time" was somewhat reminiscent of the post–Mumford & Sons sound that was popular at the time, featuring big drums, strummed guitars, and emotive vocals. Another hit off the album, "Demons," was somewhat reminiscent of Coldplay, and musically somewhere between their first and second hit songs off this album. "Demons" peaked at number six on the Billboard Hot 100 chart in 2013. The most successful song of the album, "Radioactive," combined elements of dubstep, pop, and alternative rock, and became a major hit in the summer of 2013, when it peaked on the Billboard Hot 100 chart at number three. "Radioactive" stayed on the chart for eighty-seven weeks from September 29, 2012 until May 10, 2014—the longest Billboard Hot 100 chart run in the chart's fifty-five-year history. The hit also went on to win a Grammy Award for best rock performance in 2014.

In a review for AllMusic, Gregory Heaney wrote, "Dramatic and sweeping, the Las Vegas band works in the same vein as pop giants Coldplay, offering up track after track of hooky and emotional midtempo jams. While a move like this might seem overly ambitious for a freshman band, Imagine Dragons are able to pull the sound off." Heaney's review was a mixed one, for he later added: "The problem is, while the band's electronically reinforced sound is definitely big, it sometimes feels as though it lacks depth." Still, he admitted that the band does do in part what a pop band should do, adding that the songs on the album "at least for a few minutes at a time, will make everyday life seem just a little bit bigger."

SMOKE + MIRRORS

Following the success of their first album and subsequent world tour—130 dates and 50 festivals—the band received more attention as well as more pressure to succeed. The band's second album, *Smoke + Mirrors* (2015), was clearly a follow-up to *Night Visions*. The album debuted at number one on the Billboard Top Rock and Alternative charts. *Smoke + Mirrors*, wrote Stephen Thomas Erlewine for AllMusic, "captures a band so intoxicated with their sudden surprise success that they've decided to indulge in every excess." This album, wrote Erlewine, is even "bigger and bolder" than their first. However, the first single off the album, "I Bet My Life," was clearly an Imagine Dragons song, in its stomp, sincerity, and grandiosity. "I Bet My Life" peaked at number fifty-four on the Billboard Hot 100 chart, and the other single off the album, "Shots," which had dance music elements, peaked at number seventy-five.

Erlewine offered a qualified review of the album: "Despite the bloozy bluster of 'I'm So Sorry'—a Black Keys number stripped of any sense of R & B groove—the group usually favors the sky-scraping sentiment of Coldplay, but where Chris Martin's crew often seems pious, there's a genial bros-next-door quality to Imagine Dragons that deflates their grandiosity." Erlewine then added that Imagine Dragons' "straight-faced commitment to the patently ridiculous has its charm, particularly because they possess no sense of pretension." In other words, there might be excessive reverb and effects, and it might be overproduced and the lead singer might overemote, but they are sincere. In a review for *Rolling Stone* (17 Feb. 2015), however, Jon Dolan was not buying it. On Imagine Dragons' first album, he wrote, the band "found a way to reheat old-fashioned arena-rock catharsis for the segmented pop world of the 2010s." Their new album, wrote Dolan, "builds on its predecessor's multifaceted bombast . . . . Throughout the album, the genre mash-ups come fast and furious—from the New Wave–tinged dance-rock of 'Shots' to 'Friction,' a whirl of Eastern strings, art-metal yammering, R & B Auto-Tune and electronic knock-hockey." Other critics offered similar observations, noting that taking elements of various kinds of music is not enough to be original or make an impact. Or as Dolan put it, "being mildly inventive isn't the same as being good."

TOURING

Imagine Dragons' first tour, to support *Night Visions*, was put together rather quickly in 2014 after "Radioactive" became a big hit worldwide.

For their second tour, the group was better prepared and put a lot more effort into its stage show. They used the production team of the band Nine Inch Nails. As the name of their second album indicates, the band intended to play with people's perceptions, use illusions and visual trickery. In an interview with Patrick Doyle for *Rolling Stone* (3 June 2015), Reynolds said that the band would offer a "full-scale arena production." He said the group's second album is "introspective," in that he was trying to see "what's real and what's not real," so he wanted their stage shows to follow that theme. Another well-known aspect of Imagine Dragons live shows is their unpredictable covers, covering quite a variety of genres. In the interview with Doyle, Reynolds expressed his deep admiration for Paul Simon and said he would like to cover his hit song "You Can Call Me Al."

EVOLVE

Prior to recording their third album, all four members of Imagine Dragons took a break from touring and performing. In an interview with Nicole Sands for *People* (11 May 2017), Reynolds said the break was "significant" because time off allowed him to "connect with real life again—to go home, be with friends and family . . . mentally, I needed it." Reconnecting with friends, family and life in general, and being able to appreciate the wonderful aspects of life made Reynolds approach the third album differently. Whereas in writing the second album he was "looking in"—inside himself—for the third album he was "looking out and seeing the color and beauty of the world."

The group's third album, *Evolve*, came out in June 2017 and debuted at the top of the Billboard Top Rock Albums and Alternative Albums charts. The singles off the album, however, began coming out in early 2017. Even before the album came out, the singles made it to the Billboard Hot 100 chart: "Thunder" peaked at number fifty-four, "Whatever It Takes" at number ninety-two, and "Believer" was at number six as of July 15, 2017. The latter, starting with its grand, pounding drums and tight, rap-like singing, is an optimistic anthem. Reynolds elaborated on the song's meaning, telling Sands that the song is about "specific things in my life that were painful, whether it was anxiety and dealing with crowds, feeling overwhelmed by that or the success of the band, disease, going through depression—anything that was a source of pain in my life." But the underlying message, he said, is "rising above that," using that pain as inspiration.

SUGGESTED READING

Dolan, Jon. Review of *Smoke + Mirrors*, by Imagine Dragons. *Rolling Stone*, 17 Feb. 2015, www.rollingstone.com/music/albumreviews/ imagine-dragons-smoke-mirrors-20150217. Accessed 12 July 2017.

Erlewine, Stephen Thomas. Review of *Smoke + Mirrors*, by Imagine Dragons. *AllMusic*, www.allmusic.com/album/smoke-mirrors-mw0002803699. Accessed 12 July 2017.

Heaney, Gregory. Review of *Night Visions*, by Imagine Dragons. *AllMusic*, www.allmusic. com/album/night-visions-mw0002409529. Accessed 12 July 2017.

McKee, Ben. "Imagine Dragons Interview." By Alyssa McCord. *The Berklee Groove*, 4 Aug. 2013, www.berkleegroove.com/2013/08/04/ staff-pick-of-august-imagine-dragons-interview/. Accessed 12 July 2017.

Reynolds, Dan. "Imagine Dragons Frontman Dan Reynolds Says He Was in a 'Really Healthy Space' While Writing New Album *Evolve*." Interview by Nicole Sands. *People*, 11 May 2017, people.com/music/imagine-dragons-dan-reynolds-healthy-headspace-evolve/. Accessed 12 July 2017.

Reynolds, Dan. "Imagine Dragons on Trippy New Arena Show, Paul Simon Obsession." Interview by Patrick Doyle. *Rolling Stone*, 3 June 2015, www.rollingstone.com/music/features/imagine-dragons-on-trippy-new-arena-show-paul-simon-obsession-20150603. Accessed 12 July 2017.

Trust, Gary. "Imagine Dragons' 'Radioactive' Ends Record Billboard Hot 100 Run." *Billboard*, 9 May 2014, www.billboard.com/ articles/columns/chart-beat/6084584/imagine-dragons-radioactive-ends-record-billboard-hot-100-run. Accessed 12 July 2017.

SELECTED WORKS

Night Vision, 2012; *Smoke + Mirrors*, 2015; *Evolve*, 2017

—*Michael Tillman*

Klaus Iohannis

Date of birth: June 13, 1959
Occupation: President of Romania

Klaus Iohannis became the fifth president of Romania in 2014. Prior to becoming president, he served as the mayor of Sibiu from 2000 to 2014.

EARLY LIFE AND EDUCATION

Klaus Iohannis was born in Sibiu, Romania, on June 13, 1959. The oldest of two children born to Gustav Heinz Johannis and Susanne Johannis, he grew up in a community of ethnic Germans in Transylvania. (Johannis is the German spelling of the family's surname.) After graduating from Babeş-Bolyai University of Cluj-Napoca in 1983, he taught physics in secondary schools from 1983 to 1997. He then worked as a school inspector for Sibiu County from 1997 to 2000.

After the fall of communism in 1989, many ethnic Germans in the region, including Iohannis's parents, left Romania, but Iohannis stayed. He joined the newly founded centrist Democratic Forum of Germans in Romania (FDGR) in 1990. In 1997, he became a member of the party's education committee. The following year, he was made head of that committee and elected to the leadership committee. In 2002, he was elected president of the FDGR; he was re-elected twice and served through 2013.

POLITICAL CAREER

Iohannis entered politics in 2000 when he was elected mayor of Sibiu. He won reelection in 2004, 2008, and 2012. Iohannis considered his responsibility as a mayor to be a public manager, and he was actively involved in the hands-on management of the city. He quickly gained public approval for building roads and resolving problems such as a lack of heat in schools. Iohannis's popularity increased after he transformed Sibiu into a leading tourist attraction and increased jobs by attracting foreign investors. In 2007, Sibiu was named a European Capital of Culture, partly because of Iohannis's efforts to revitalize the city.

In October 2009, several political groups in opposition in parliament proposed Iohannis as a candidate for prime minister. Despite parliament adopting a near-unanimous declaration in favor of Iohannis, President Traian Băsescu denied their requests and chose someone else. Around that time, Iohannis voiced an interest in running for president sometime in the future.

Iohannis joined the National Liberal Party (PNL) in 2013. He became the party's first vice president in 2013 and its president in 2014. In August 2014, the ACL chose Iohannis as its candidate for the upcoming presidential elections.

Many voters considered Iohannis an outsider because of his German ethnicity and relative political independence, but, for Romanians fed up with government corruption, that worked to his advantage. With a proven track record as mayor of Sibiu, Iohannis had gained a reputation as an honest and hardworking steward of government.

Iohannis campaigned on promises to combat corruption, reform the judicial system, and improve relations with the European Union. In the first round of the elections, he lost to Prime Minister Victor Ponta. In the second round, he captured a large share of the votes cast by Romanians living abroad, winning the round with nearly 54.5 percent of the votes to Ponta's 45.5 percent. He was declared the winner on November 16, 2014, and was sworn in as prime minister on December 21, 2014.

In his inaugural speech, Iohannis repeated his pledge to rid the country of corruption. The country had experienced multiple corruption scandals during the prior decade, with several politicians and elected officials convicted of crimes such as electoral fraud, embezzlement, bribery, and forgery.

Iohannis's first year as president was characterized by difficulties with the ruling government and conflicts with Prime Minister Ponta, his opponent in the presidential election. Parliament thwarted many of Iohannis's efforts to effect reform, such as refusing to lift criminal immunity for government officials. Despite these challenges, Iohannis was able to implement several reforms to the electoral process. He also made strides in foreign-policy matters, meeting with the leaders of several countries, strengthening Romania's role in the European Union (EU), and developing stronger partnerships with other countries, especially members of NATO and the EU and neighboring countries. He also called for a greater NATO presence along the Baltic and the Black Seas. For several months, Iohannis spearheaded talks with Moldova after it experienced a financial and political crisis in 2015. In early 2016, he negotiated an assistance package that required Moldova to take specific actions to combat corruption and work with international bodies to restore its financial stability.

Iohannis's conflicts with the prime minister intensified after Ponta was charged with numerous crimes, including conflict of interest, tax evasion, money laundering, and forgery, in June 2015. Despite Iohannis's repeated requests for him to resign, Ponta refused until November 4, 2015, after tens of thousands of protesters demanded his resignation following a nightclub fire in which more than forty-five people lost their lives. Iohannis then appointed Dacian Cioloş, an independent, the prime minister.

IMPACT

At the onset of Klaus Iohannis's presidency, many political analysts predicted divisions between Iohannis and the ruling Social Democratic Party (PSD) coalition would lead to political stalemates and crises. Instead, opinion polls in 2015 showed public support for the PSD had declined and support for the PNL had increased. With a new prime minister and the formation of a technocrat government, Iohannis is better positioned to work with the government in a smooth manner and to make significant reforms to combat corruption and create a more independent judicial system.

PERSONAL LIFE

Iohannis is married to Carmen Iohannis, an English teacher. He speaks German, Romanian, and English.

SUGGESTED READING

Kulish, Nicholas. "Grim Romanians Brighten over a German Connection." *New York Times*. New York Times, 5 Dec. 2009. Web. 19 Feb. 2016.

Lupu, Victor. "President Klaus Iohannis' Balance Sheet after One Year in Office." *Romania Journal*. Romania Journal, 16 Nov. 2015. Web. 14 Apr. 2016.

"Romania Presidential Election: Profile of Klaus Iohannis." *BBC*. BBC, 17 Nov. 2014. Web. 14 Apr. 2016.

"Who Is Klaus Iohannis, Romania's New President?" *Romania-Insider.com*. Business Insider, 17 Nov. 2014. Web. 14 Apr. 2016.

—*Barb Lightner*

Marin Ireland

Date of birth: August 30, 1979
Occupation: Actor

By Peabody Awards [CC BY 2.0], via Wikimedia Commons

Marin Ireland has become a fixture not only of Broadway and Off-Broadway stage productions but also in film and television. Although the wide-ranging nature of her work might be challenging for some actors, for Ireland, the seemingly disparate worlds of stage and screen are anything but. "I always feel like they are so complementary," she explained to Benjamin Lindsay for *Backstage* (2 Mar. 2017). "The theater I continue to do helps remind me to stay in the moment exactly where I am on the day when doing TV and film. The most important thing is to be present in the moment on the day."

Since first catching the attention of theatergoers with her work in Adam Rapp's *Nocturne*, Ireland has appeared in numerous stage productions, perhaps most notably the 2009 Broadway comedy *reasons to be pretty*, for which she was nominated for a Tony Award. Her screen work has included mainstays of the New York television scene such as *Law & Order*, independent films such as the 2012 drama *28 Hotel Rooms*, and various higher-profile television series, among them *Homeland*, *The Divide*, *The Slap*, and *Sneaky Pete*. In 2016, she played a supporting role in the crime drama *Hell or High Water*, which went on to be nominated for four Academy Awards.

Despite her increasing fame, Ireland continues to be more interested in taking on roles in projects that challenge both actor and audience, including the 2017 debut of the solo play *On the Exhale*, about gun violence. "To be able to use my voice as an interpreter for something that is not only beautiful, but relevant to a broader political conversation—to feel useful in some way while also having the privilege to deliver these exquisite words—is a great honor," she told Ted Sod for the blog of the Roundabout Theatre Company (8 Mar. 2017). "I feel enormously grateful."

EARLY LIFE AND EDUCATION

Marin Ireland was born in Camarillo, California, a small city northwest of Los Angeles. Although she was shy as a child, Ireland's elementary school required her to participate in two plays each year, which introduced her to public performance early in life. "When I started playing bigger parts in those, it was completely transformative for me," she recalled to Sod. Ireland was drawn to acting, and dreams of a performing arts career soon overtook her earlier thoughts of becoming a writer.

Ireland participated in local community theater as a young teen and was formally trained in acting at Idyllwild Arts Academy, an arts-focused preparatory school where she completed her final two years of secondary education. After graduating, she enrolled in the newly established undergraduate theater program at the Hartt School, the performing arts conservatory at the University of Hartford in Connecticut. She graduated from the institution in 2000.

EARLY CAREER

By the time Ireland entered into professional theater, she could already act in union productions, having earned her Actors' Equity membership through summer stock theater productions. Seeking work, she pursued opportunities in an unorthodox—yet sometimes successful—manner. "I threw all my belongings in my little Honda Accord and drove around to all the theaters in the northeast," she told Sod. "I'd call a theater up, like a maniac, ask to speak to their casting person or associate artistic director and just say, 'Hi, I'm an Equity actor! When can I audition for you?' And sometimes it worked."

Ireland's first major opportunity came when she was cast in Adam Rapp's play *Nocturne*, set to be performed at the American Repertory Theatre in Cambridge, Massachusetts, from October to November 2000. Although she had no lines—she stood nude and silent on stage during one scene—Ireland impressed reviewers with the emotion she brought to her performance. She reprised her role when the play moved to the New York Theatre Workshop in 2001. After her move to New York, Ireland also worked as a school office manager for a time, having inherited the job from a friend who left the city.

ON STAGE

Over the next sixteen years, Ireland made a name for herself as a versatile and dedicated actor who took on wide-ranging roles in theatrical productions. Working primarily Off-Broadway—that is, in theaters with between one hundred and five hundred seats—she appeared in more than a dozen different plays between 2002 and 2012. Her projects included Off-Broadway productions of *Far Away* (2002), *Where We're Born* (2003), *Sabina* (2005), *Cyclone* (2006), *Beebo Brinker Chronicles* (2008), and *In the Wake* (2010). Ireland won the 2006 Obie Award—the highest Off-Broadway honor—for her performance in *Cyclone*. She also received attention for her performance as the exploited lover Cate in the 2008 New York production of *Blasted*, by the late British playwright Sarah Kane—a work critics often described as brutal and disturbing. In interviews, Ireland has recognized the disturbing nature of some plays and the characters she has embodied, but she notes that above all, she finds herself drawn to works that present new stories and perspectives. "It's such a luxury as an actor to think of your career as something you're choosing for yourself, because so much of the time as an actor you're just hoping that exciting projects come your way," she told Maggie Lange for *Interview* magazine (16 Nov. 2012). "The thing I respond to the most is just great writing, interesting characters."

Ireland made her Broadway debut in 2009, starring in *reasons to be pretty* at the Lyceum Theatre. The romantic dramedy by Neil LaBute began previews in March 2009 and officially opened on April 2 of that year. The cast and playwright earned critical praise for their work, with the play ultimately earning a nomination for the Tony Award for best play and Ireland herself being nominated for best featured actress

in a play. After *reasons to be pretty*, Ireland returned to Broadway in the fall 2009 production of *After Miss Julie* and again in the spring 2013 revival of *The Big Knife*, both at the American Airlines Theatre.

Perhaps Ireland's most challenging and powerful stage role came in 2017, when she performed as the sole actor in the Off-Broadway premiere of *On the Exhale*. Written by Martín Zimmerman and helmed by Tony-nominated director Leigh Silverman, *On the Exhale* centers on a mother's complex response to a school shooting. "It's never been just me onstage, so I really was looking for a director who I already trusted," Ireland explained to Sod about working with Silverman, who had previously directed her in *Beebo Brinker Chronicles* and *In the Wake*. *On the Exhale* ran from February to April 2017, and Ireland was nominated for that year's Drama Desk and Outer Critics Circle Awards for outstanding solo performance.

FILM STAR

Ireland has also been a prolific screen actor since early in her career, when she first landed bit parts in films such as *The Manchurian Candidate* (2004) and *I Am Legend* (2007). She went on to claim lead roles in several independent films, including *The Understudy*, which was shot in 2008 and had a limited release in the United States in 2012.

In the 2012 film *28 Hotel Rooms*, Ireland costarred with Chris Messina, a former colleague from the New York Theatre Workshop, as unnamed lovers in an extended affair. Ireland enjoyed working on the film and particularly appreciated how filmmaker Matt Ross and Messina, who collaborated on the film's development, approached her character. "Something they were interested in was finding the flip-side to the female character that shows up in a lot of indie movies, where she's really quirky and emotionally available and charming and cute," she told Lange. "They felt like they were allergic to that at this point, so they were like, 'Okay let's do the opposite of that.'"

Another major point in Ireland's film career came in 2015, when she played a supporting role in the crime drama *Hell or High Water*. Directed by David Mackenzie and written by Taylor Sheridan, the film follows two brothers who rob banks to save their family's ranch. After *Hell or High Water* premiered at the Cannes Film Festival in 2016, *Hell or High Water* received significant praise from critics and was ultimately nominated for an Academy Award for best picture and a Golden Globe for best motion picture, among other honors.

TELEVISION

Ireland began her career in television with small roles in series such as *Law & Order* and its spin-offs. In 2011, she appeared as a maid in the HBO period miniseries *Mildred Pierce* and began a character arc on the Showtime thriller series *Homeland* as terrorist Aileen Morgan. Over the following years, Ireland appeared as a recurring character in the series *A Gifted Man*, *Boss*, *Masters of Sex*, and *Girls*, among others. She also played major roles in the short-lived 2014 legal drama *The Divide* and the 2015 miniseries *The Slap*.

Ireland gained further notice upon joining the main cast of *Sneaky Pete*, an Amazon Studios original crime series. The show's 2015 pilot and 2017 first season were a hit, and it was renewed for a second season days after the first was released on Amazon Prime. For Ireland, the success of *Sneaky Pete* was to be expected: "It's a caper, it's got heart, it's thrilling, it's moving, and it's funny," she told the trend webzine the *New Potato* (27 Jan. 2017). "I think maybe some of our viewers are enjoying a serious show that's not heavy, and that's not so light it becomes insignificant. It's fun, but it's not junk food."

AGITATING FOR CHANGE

In 2012, Ireland's then boyfriend, a fellow actor, struck her so forcefully during a dispute that she got a black eye. Since then, she has sought to raise awareness of issues such as sexual harassment and violence within the acting community, which she asserts are rarely dealt with in appropriate and productive ways. "Many actors don't know what to do when behavior—physical, sexual, harassment, bullying—crosses a line," she explained to Patrick Healy for the *New York Times* (15 Mar. 2015). To that end, she has urged theater unions such as the Actors' Equity to establish clear procedures for making complaints and receiving confidential mediation and to explain such policies thoroughly before work begins on any professional show.

PERSONAL LIFE

Ireland lives in New York's East Village.

SUGGESTED READING

Healy, Patrick. "Sex and Violence, Beyond the Script." *The New York Times*, 15 Mar. 2015, nytimes.com/2015/03/15/theater/sex-and-violence-beyond-the-script.html. Accessed 8 Sept. 2017.

Ireland, Marin. "Actress Marin Ireland: On *Sneaky Pete*, Personal Mantras & Halloumi." Interview. *The New Potato*, 27 Jan. 2017, www.thenewpotato.com/2017/01/27/marin-ireland-2017. Accessed 8 Sept. 2017.

Ireland, Marin. "Checking in with Marin Ireland." Interview by Maggie Lange. *Interview*, 16 Nov. 2012, www.interviewmagazine.com/film/marin-ireland-28-hotel-rooms. Accessed 8 Sept. 2017.

Ireland, Marin. "Five Minutes with Marin Ireland." Interview by Vanessa Lawrence. *W*, 22 Apr. 2013, www.wmagazine.com/story/marin-ireland-actress-interview-the-big-knife-play. Accessed 8 Sept. 2017.

Ireland, Marin. "How Marin Ireland Has 'Survived' 15 Years Working in NYC." Interview by Benjamin Lindsay. *Backstage*, 2 Mar. 2017, www.backstage.com/interview/how-marin-ireland-has-survived-15-years-working-nyc. Accessed 8 Sept. 2017.

Ireland, Marin. "*On the Exhale*: Interview with Actor Marin Ireland." Interview by Ted Sod. *Roundabout Theatre Company*, 8 Mar. 2017, blog.roundabouttheatre.org/2017/03/08/on-the-exhale-interview-with-actor-marin-ireland. Accessed 8 Sept. 2017.

Milzoff, Rebecca. "Marin Ireland, Theater's Best-Kept Secret, May Not Be a Secret Much Longer." *Vulture*, 7 Feb. 2017, www.vulture.com/2017/02/marin-ireland-may-not-be-a-secret-much-longer.html. Accessed 8 Sept. 2017.

SELECTED WORKS

Nocturne, 2000–2001; *The Understudy*, 2008; *Blasted*, 2008; *reasons to be pretty*, 2009; *Mildred Pierce*, 2011; *Homeland*, 2011–12; *28 Hotel Rooms*, 2012; *Sneaky Pete*, 2015– ; *Hell or High Water*, 2016; *On the Exhale*, 2017

—Joy Crelin

Nicky Jam

Date of birth: March 17, 1981
Occupation: Singer, songwriter

Reggaeton artist Nicky Jam started rapping at the young age of ten. When he was thirteen years old, he released his first album called *Distinto a Los Demás* (*Unlike Any Other*). Although the album did not receive the attention that he had hoped for, by the age of twenty, Nicky Jam was collaborating with well-known reggaeton artists, including Daddy Yankee. During this time, however, he also started to battle with alcohol and drug abuse. In 2004, he released the album *Vida Escante*, but his addictions continued and eventually damaged his career and reputation. In 2010, Nicky Jam left his home in Cataño, Puerto Rico, for Medellín, Colombia—where he envisioned a more promising life for himself. With this, he intended to rebuild his reputation and focus on his music career—and he succeeded. In 2015, Nicky Jam released

Siednji Leon/CC BY 2.0/Wikimedia Commons

the hit song "El Perdón" ("The Forgiveness"), featuring international Latin star Enrique Iglesias. The song earned him a 2015 Latin Grammy Award for best urban/fusion performance. His new album, *Fenix*, was released in January 2017.

EARLY LIFE
Nicky Jam was born Nick Rivera Caminero in Boston, Massachusetts, on March 17, 1981. His mother is from the Dominican Republic, and his father is from Puerto Rico. He started to develop his musical talent at an early age and showcase his skills at local talent shows. When he was ten years old, Nicky Jam and his family moved to Puerto Rico. Growing up in Puerto Rico, Nicky Jam was exposed to a variety of music styles, but he took a special liking to reggaeton. This music genre—which originated in Latin America in the 1990s—is characterized by its fusion of hip-hop, reggae, and Latin music, and usually rapped in Spanish.

It did not take Nicky Jam long to get discovered after coming to Puerto Rico. In fact, it took about a year. One day, while he was bagging groceries at a local store, a woman overheard Nicky Jam rapping and, impressed, took him to her husband. "I went with her. She took me to her husband . . . a CEO of a record company in Puerto Rico and she was like, 'OK, rap for him.' So I started rapping. I started freestyling for him and he was like, 'Wow, this guy is money!'" Nicky Jam told Shoboy for *AMP Radio* (4 Sept. 2015). This man eventually signed Nicky Jam, whose first album, *Distinto a Los Demás*, came out in 1994, when he was only thirteen years old.

The album did not do well on the charts, but it did catch the attention of some important reggaeton performers.

MANAGING FAME AT A YOUNG AGE
Nicky Jam started making a name for himself by rapping on various mixtapes, compilation albums featuring different rappers and singers. His appearances on DJ Playero's mixtapes got him noticed and earned him respect in the music industry. He appeared with such artists as Don Chezina, Big Boy, RKM & Ken-Y, and, perhaps most important to his future career, Daddy Yankee. Daddy Yankee was more established than Nicky Jam when he asked him to perform as a backup singer in the Dominican Republic. After that, Nicky Jam and Daddy Yankee became close. They collaborated on hits such as "Guayando," and "En La Cama." *Haciendo Escante* (2001), Nicky Jam's second album, came out when he was twenty years old, and featured Daddy Yankee on a few songs. Though the album received more notice than *Distinto a Los Demás*, it did not make Nicky Jam a household name.

Also around 2001, after Daddy Yankee became his mentor, Nicky Jam was becoming overwhelmed by attention, pressure, and money. He started drinking and doing drugs. "I was making too much money. I was too young," he told Nick Murray for *Billboard* (29 Oct. 2015). "I didn't know how to deal." Nicky Jam's struggles with fame and substance abuse led to conflicts with Daddy Yankee, who was somewhat like a father figure—or at least like an older brother—in addition to a professional collaborator. Daddy Yankee told his protégé to clean up his act and sometimes mentioned him in his songs, though not explicitly. Upset by this, Nicky Jam recorded a "diss track"—a song written to disparage another artist—in retaliation. This led Daddy Yankee to write the song "Gasolina" in 2004, which proved to be a major hit and made reggaeton more popular than ever before.

BREAKTHROUGH
In 2004, the same year Daddy Yankee released the hit song "Gasolina," Nicky Jam released the album *Vida Escante* on Pina Records, which proved to be a turning point in his career. He also had a major breakthrough the following year with the rerelease of *Vida Escante* with bonus tracks—titled *Vida Escante: Special Edition*. The album featured guest appearances by the likes of RKM & Ken-Y, Don Chezina, and Taina. Although Nicky Jam gained new fans with this album and gave those who were already fans a solid, consistent reggaeton record, the album did not receive any significant press coverage outside Puerto Rico. As Evan C. Gutierrez wrote in an album review for *AllMusic*, "The upside of using all the usual suspects is that Pina Records

releases are consistent in theme and quality. The downside is that they tend to lack variety. Fans of the Pina reggaeton sound will love *Vida Escante*. For listeners looking for something different, look elsewhere."

Nicky Jam's next album, *The Black Carpet*, was released in 2007; this was his first album to have an English title, which was perhaps indicative of greater ambitions to appeal to mainstream American audiences. The album included such songs as "Gas Pela," featuring RKM, and "Ton Ton Ton," featuring RKM & Ken-Y. Notably missing from the album, however, was Nicky Jam's mentor and early musical partner, Daddy Yankee. The reason for this was that a few years prior, the two went their separate ways.

By this time Daddy Yankee was a star in the reggaeton world. Nicky Jam, however—still battling with his addictions—decided to quit recording. He was depressed, wrote Murray, and singing cover songs in a hotel lounge, trying not to be recognized, and using that hotel gig to support his drug habit. Although the hotel gig did help him improve at singing, wrote Murray, Nicky Jam knew he could not keep doing it forever.

Around 2010, Nicky Jam decided to start a new life in Medellín, Colombia—where, unlike Puerto Rico, he was still a respected reggaeton artist. This decision would turn out to be a good one—both for getting clean and starting a new chapter in his musical career.

TOPPING THE HOT LATIN SONGS CHART

Nicky Jam became part of the reggaeton scene in Colombia, particularly Medellín, along with such performers as J Balvin and Maluma. But it was slow going. In a sense, he had to start over. He played occasional shows, but what started to rebuild his fame and reputation were the freestyle rap videos he posted online. In 2014, he had a hit with "Voy a Beber," which peaked at number twenty-nine on the Billboard Latin Digital Songs chart. His next hit was "Travesuras," which reached number four on the Billboard Hot Latin Songs chart. The success of "Travesuras" not only led to a record deal with Sony but a call from—and eventually a collaboration with—international Latin star Enrique Iglesias.

"Enrique fell in love with 'Travesuras,'" Nicky Jam told Leila Cobo for *Billboard* (10 Oct. 2016). "He was into my story, because normally when a reggaeton artist leaves, he doesn't come back. I was an embarrassment. And when he read about me, he was obsessed about doing something with me." This was not mere boasting. Iglesias really did become fascinated with Nicky Jam's life story and reached out to him personally. As Nicky Jam told Murray, when Iglesias called him and said, "Hey, I'm Enrique Iglesias," Nicky Jam did not believe him and hung up. But then Iglesias called again, and the two ended up talking for hours.

"I've been a fan of Nicky Jam's for a while," Iglesias told Cobo. "His career is as long as mine, and what's interesting is how he started with Daddy Yankee, they split, and he moved to Colombia and how that shook his musical style and his lyrics. I usually write or cowrite most of my songs. But when he sent me the song, I called him up and I said, 'I love it. I don't care that I didn't write it.'" Iglesias ended up singing on Nicky Jam's big hit "El Perdón," which climbed Billboard charts, including reaching number one on *Billboard*'s Greatest of All Time Hot Latin Songs chart, number thirty on the Pop Songs chart, and number fifty-six on the Hot 100 chart. The song's success also led to a reunion of sorts with Daddy Yankee, with whom he went on tour. Nicky Jam also went on to receive a Latin Grammy Award for best urban/fusion for "El Perdón" in 2015. He also had two other Latin Grammy Award nominations that year.

In January 2017, Nicky Jam released the album *Fenix*, proving, once more, that he is here to stay.

SUGGESTED READING

Cobo, Leila. "The Amazing Story behind Nicky Jam and Enrique Iglesias' 'El Perdon.'" *Billboard*, 10 Oct. 2016, www.billboard.com/articles/columns/latin/7534429/nicky-jam-enrique-iglesias-el-Perdon-story-hot-latin-songs. Accessed 11 Jan. 2017.

Gutierrez, Evan C. Review of *Vida Escante*, by Nicky Jam. *AllMusic*, www.allmusic.com/album/vida-escante-mw0000633936. Accessed 10 Jan. 2017.

Murray, Nick. "How Nicky Jam Triumphed over Drugs, Weight Gain and Beef with Daddy Yankee: 'I Was Too Young.'" *Billboard*, 29 Oct. 2015, www.billboard.com/articles/news/6745299/nicky-jam-beef-daddy-yankee-drug-abuse-comeback. Accessed 10 Jan. 2017.

Nicky Jam. "Nicky Jam Opens Up about His Rocky Past, Family Life and Brand New Outlook." Interview by Shoboy. *The New 923 AMP Radio*, 4 Sept. 2015, 923amp.cbslocal.com/2015/09/04/nicky-jam-shoboy-interview. Accessed 10 Jan. 2017.

SELECTED WORKS

Vida Escante, 2004; *Vida Escante: Special Edition*, 2005; *The Black Carpet*, 2007; *Fenix*, 2017

—*Dmitry Kiper*

Azéde Jean-Pierre

Date of birth: 1988
Occupation: Fashion designer

For fashion designer Azéde Jean-Pierre, clothing is both an art form and a conversation, decorating the people it wears while creating a tangible link between wearer and designer. "I think it's interesting to be able to live in what you create," she said to Lauren David Peden for *Elle* (22 Nov. 2013). "Your customer has such a strong and personal connection with you and your work since they can own it, wear it, and live in it." Indeed, many notable figures, including former First Lady Michelle Obama and singer Solange Knowles, have formed such connections with Jean-Pierre, wearing her designs in magazines and at high-profile events while the young designer was still only in her twenties. Jean-Pierre began exhibiting collections of her clothing while still a student at the Savannah College of Art and Design (SCAD) and later earned critical acclaim for her self-titled clothing line following showings at the New York and Paris fashion weeks.

As a refugee from Haiti whose family settled in Georgia when she was a young child, Jean-Pierre has often credited her cultural background with inspiring her approach to fashion. "I'm not quite American yet. I am a Haitian citizen still, but I am, in many ways, first-generation or could identify with being first-generation," she said to Amber Alexander for the *Fader* (30 Mar. 2017). "It brings on an interesting perspective because I understand clothing and culture from multiple points of views, even how you wear things or what is considered classy or good or what is traditionally acceptable for a woman or a man. It influences it, but I also like to turn things on their head and do things that are polarizing." Although some of Jean-Pierre's pieces could certainly be described as polarizing, with their inventive uses of color and shape and their unexpected motifs, her body of work has received widespread critical acclaim, and she has been named one of the top young designers to watch by publications such as *Forbes*.

EARLY LIFE AND EDUCATION

Jean-Pierre was born in Pestel, Haiti, the fourth of eight children. When she was five years old, her family left Haiti and spent several months in a refugee camp at Guantánamo Bay, Cuba, before traveling on to the United States. The family went on to settle in Atlanta, Georgia, where Jean-Pierre spent the remainder of her childhood. She has noted in interviews that immigrating to the United States at such a young age made it easy for her to learn English and become acclimated to life in Atlanta, although she still retained close ties to Haitian culture. "I pretty

Photo by Monica Schipper/FilmMagic

much grew up in America, but I had multiple cultural pulls," she told Alexander. "I think my childhood was a cool one because I had all those different influences."

An artist from an early age, Jean-Pierre enjoyed drawing but soon found herself particularly interested in sketching clothing designs. "I used to draw little characters growing up and the clothing [I drew for them] just became much more interesting so I was like, 'Oh okay, I'll keep doing this,'" she recalled to Alexander. By the time Jean-Pierre was in her early teens, she had begun transforming her sketches into handmade clothing. Wanting to continue her education in fashion while remaining close to home, she enrolled in the Savannah College of Art and Design (SCAD) after graduating from high school, pursuing a bachelor of fine arts in fashion at the college's Atlanta campus.

EARLY CAREER

Already a talented designer, Jean-Pierre continued to design and manufacture clothing while at SCAD, creating capsule collections that she exhibited at both SCAD-sponsored and independent fashion shows. Her designs drew attention from a variety of fashion websites as well as major publications such as *Vogue Italia*, and one of the pieces from her Spring/Summer 2011 collection was displayed in the window of the department store Neiman Marcus's Atlanta location. She obtained her first major client when she designed a dress for Shirley Franklin, then the mayor of Atlanta, to wear to a mayoral ball.

Although Jean-Pierre had established herself as an up-and-coming designer while still in college, she still considered it important to learn from established designers and fashion brands. "I want to intern and learn the business," she said to Claire Sulmers for *Vogue Italia* (4 July 2011). "I have to prove I am worthy. When the right opportunity knocks, I'll answer." That year, Jean-Pierre completed an internship with the independent fashion label Ohne Titel, which was founded in 2007 by designers Flora Gill and Alexa Adams. "I learned 'cool' at Ohne Titel," Jean-Pierre told Peden. "They have a strong belief and confidence in their uniquely cool aesthetic. Their signature cut is a fit that women can live in. I cherish a pair of pants that Flora gave me at the end of my time there. They are so special yet livable that they are now a part of my daily uniform—they almost define my personal style."

Jean-Pierre went on to complete an additional internship, at Ralph Rucci, in 2012. Although her time spent working for other designers took some of her attention away from her own projects, Jean-Pierre has noted that gaining experience as an intern was something she considered essential rather than an impediment to her own progress. "I'm so dedicated to hard work. I definitely know how important it is," she told Sulmers. "For me, it's just a matter of time."

FASHION LABEL

After moving to New York, Jean-Pierre officially launched her self-titled ready-to-wear design label, Azéde Jean-Pierre, in February 2012. The label's first official offering, its Fall/Winter 2013 collection, was well received and drew further critical and commercial attention to Jean-Pierre's creations. Jean-Pierre made her New York Fashion Week (NYFW) debut in September 2013, presenting her Spring/Summer 2014 collection at MADE Fashion Week, an event run by New York–based Milk Studios. "It was very exciting showing during NYFW and we were elated to have the opportunity to show with Milk MADE," she said to Peden. "They have a very supportive program and we are grateful to have been a part of it. It was also rewarding to see our vision finally realized. We had been working on it for such a long time that the show allowed us to exhale a bit." Visually inspired in part by beetle shells, the designs featured in the collection received positive responses from fashion critics, and several pieces were later worn by a number of celebrities, including singers Solange Knowles and Lady Gaga. Another major milestone came in the summer of 2014, when then First Lady Michelle Obama wore a custom Azéde Jean-Pierre dress in a photo shoot for *Essence* magazine.

Over the years following her label's debut, Jean-Pierre has designed a variety of collections, drawing from a vast range of influences and styles. Her Spring/Summer 2015 collection, for instance, was inspired by nature and featured fabrics with leaf prints, as well as items more subtly evoking leaves and flowers. Her Fall/Winter 2016 collection featured asymmetrical wrap dresses and shirts and the prominent use of color blocking. When speaking about her work, Jean-Pierre has often noted that her own background has shaped her approach to fashion. "Being native of Haiti, living in suburban America, and working in fashion, I've seen the world from many different perspectives," she said to Amelia Diamond for *Man Repeller* (27 Jan. 2016). "I can relate to the marginalized groups in developing countries as well as the world traveler and fashion connoisseur. My brand is the bridge between those cultures." With their mingled cultural influences, Jean-Pierre's creations appeal to fashion lovers of many different backgrounds, and her distinctive pieces have made frequent appearances on red carpets.

PARIS AND BEYOND

Having held multiple successful shows at New York Fashion Week, Jean-Pierre took her designs to an even more prestigious venue when she presented her Spring/Summer 2017 collection at Paris Fashion Week in September 2016. She received significant critical attention for her newest pieces, many of which featured insect or bird imagery. Other pieces in the collection, such as a tiered white dress with colorful details, were inspired by styles of clothing worn in the West Indies. Following her debut showing in Paris, Jean-Pierre has focused on expanding the reach of her brand, partnering with a financial backer and working on creating clothing items that are both practical and distinctive in design.

In addition to her work for her Azéde Jean-Pierre brand, Jean-Pierre has been involved in a number of philanthropic efforts, many of them related to improving the lives and livelihoods of the people of Haiti. In early 2017, it was announced that she was partnering with the organizations Artists for Peace and Justice, Prodev, and the Pestel-based Centre de Facilitation et de Développement Communautaire (CEFADEC) to design new school uniforms for underprivileged students in Haiti. "I am excited about the project," Jean-Pierre said to Lindsay Peoples for the *Cut* (15 Mar. 2017). "All education in Haiti is private, and I know firsthand how difficult it is for families to afford the tuition, let alone the additional necessities like books, transportation, and the uniforms. This project gives parents much-needed support, and it's my hope that it will increase the efficiency of the traditional attire, as well as boost student self-esteem." Jean-Pierre has likewise partnered with a number of veterinary and animal-welfare groups to vaccinate Haiti's dogs against rabies in order to prevent the spread of the disease among the human population. She has also sought to do good through her own company's work, employing artisans in Haiti and other developing nations to complete embroidery work and other fiber arts essential to the construction of her pieces.

PERSONAL LIFE

After leaving Atlanta, Jean-Pierre settled in New York City, where she lives in an apartment at the edges of the Clinton Hill and Bedford-Stuyvesant neighborhoods of Brooklyn. "It's wonderfully scenic," she told Diamond for *Man Repeller* (26 Sept. 2016). "I like the beautiful brownstones and the cinematic tree-canopied streets, the organic gardens, the bodega and coffee shops on alternating corners, the young, cool residents, and that it's a cultural melting pot."

SUGGESTED READING

Diamond, Amelia. "Know Your Labels: Azede Jean-Pierre." *Man Repeller*, 27 Jan. 2016, www.manrepeller.com/2016/01/know-your-labels-azede-jean-pierre.html. Accessed 7 Apr. 2017.

Jean-Pierre, Azéde. "Meet Azede Jean-Pierre, the Haitian Designer Dressing Today's World Travelers." Interview by Amber Alexander. *The Fader*, 20 Mar. 2017, www.thefader.com/2017/03/20/azede-jean-pierre-interview. Accessed 7 Apr. 2017.

Jean-Pierre, Azéde. "Real Cool People, Real Cool Apartments: Azede Jean-Pierre." Interview by Amelia Diamond. *Man Repeller*, 26 Sept. 2016, www.manrepeller.com/2016/09/cool-nyc-apartments.html. Accessed 7 Apr. 2017.

Jean-Pierre, Azéde. "Why Designer Azede Jean-Pierre Is the Next Big Thing (Just Ask Solange)." Interview by Lauren David Peden. *Elle*, 22 Nov. 2013, www.elle.com/fashion/news/a18781/azede-jean-pierre-interview. Accessed 7 Apr. 2017.

Nnadi, Chioma. "Azede Jean-Pierre and Shala Monroque Bring French Caribbean Flair to Paris." *Vogue*, 29 Sept. 2016, www.vogue.com/article/inside-azede-jean-pierres-first-show-in-paris. Accessed 7 Apr. 2017.

Peoples, Lindsay. "Designer Azede Jean-Pierre Is Creating School Uniforms for Haitian Schoolchildren." *The Cut*, New York Media, 15 Mar. 2017, nymag.com/thecut/2017/03/azede-jean-pierre-designs-uniforms-for-students-in-haiti.html. Accessed 7 Apr. 2017.

Sulmers, Claire. "Azede Jean-Pierre." *Vogue Italia*, 4 July 2011, www.vogue.it/en/vogue-black/the-black-blog/2011/07/azede-jean-pierre-. Accessed 7 Apr. 2017.

—*Joy Crelin*

Barry Jenkins

Date of birth: November 19, 1979
Occupation: Filmmaker

Writing for the *New York Times* (6 Sept. 2016), A. O. Scott described director Barry Jenkins's Academy Award–winning film *Moonlight* (2016) as "a reality check about the state of black America and an intensely personal, almost dreamy, meditation on desire, identity, and friendship." Other critics waxed similarly rhapsodic about the film, which focuses on a gay African American man growing up in a rough section of Miami. Hilton Als, in an essay for the *New Yorker* (24 Oct. 2016), wrote of what the movie meant to him personally: "Did I ever imagine, during my anxious, closeted childhood, that I'd live long enough to see a movie like *Moonlight*, Barry Jenkins's brilliant, achingly alive new work about black queerness?" Als added, "Did any gay man who came of age, as I did, in the era of Ronald Reagan, Margaret Thatcher, and AIDS, think he'd survive to see a version of his life told onscreen with such knowledge, unpredictability, and grace?"

Others viewed the film as a crucial and necessary response to the lack of minority representation in Hollywood. During an interview in which they discussed what writer Greg Tate referred to as the "ravenous Black spectatorship hungering for a cinema resonant with this #BlackLivesMatter millennium," Jenkins told Tate for the *Village Voice* (21 Dec. 2016), "I think this is an amazing time to be a Black artist, not

By Jared eberhardt [CC BY-SA 2.0], via Wikimedia Commons

just for the reception of the work, but because I didn't have to look far to find other Black artists to take inspiration from, or to take counsel from . . . . We're all adding to the complexity of what it means to be a Black person in America, a Black person in the world. It just feels right to be a part of it."

Before the success of *Moonlight*, which is Jenkins's second feature film, he had written and directed the critically acclaimed independent film *Medicine for Melancholy* (2008). Although it did not receive as much mainstream attention and recognition upon its release, it did herald Jenkins's promising talent.

EARLY LIFE

Barry Jenkins was born on November 19, 1979, in Miami, Florida. He was raised in Liberty City, a predominately African American neighborhood in northern Miami. Liberty City had not always been as desolate as it became in the 1980s, when Jenkins was growing up. It was the site of Liberty Square, one of the first federal public housing projects in the nation for African Americans, and with its indoor plumbing and electricity, it attracted solid, working-class residents. It was, however, walled off from the white neighborhoods surrounding it, and the area's economic and social conditions began to deteriorate after the construction of a nearby interstate highway. Protesters staged occasional riots and businesses left, allowing crime and poverty to flourish. "Very, very slowly certain areas of the neighborhood began to be off limits," Jenkins recalled to Nikole Hannah-Jones for the *New York Times* (4 Jan. 2017). "I just remember this moment where it went from being this thing where you could wander anywhere, almost like Huck Finn, to places you had to avoid."

When the area fell prey to the epidemic of crack cocaine sweeping the nation, Jenkins's family was not immune. His mother had already had a difficult life by the time the highly addictive drug made its initial appearances in Miami in the 1980s. Likely a victim of sexual abuse, she had become pregnant with the first of Jenkins's three older siblings when she was still a teenager. She and Jenkins's father ultimately separated. Jenkins does not hold animosity toward his mother, who eventually contracted HIV. "She beat all these things, and she couldn't beat this," he recalled to Hannah-Jones. "And I think she had held on for so long and eventually you break, and I think crack cocaine filled that break. I don't judge her."

Jenkins, still a preschooler when his mother began abusing crack cocaine, was raised largely by an older family friend. Money was generally tight, and her two-bedroom apartment was crammed with about eight people. He has told interviewers of utilities being shut off because of missed bills and going without needed toiletries. Still, life was not all bleak. He has also recalled playing football on Thanksgiving with other Liberty City boys, frequenting the corner store, and going to the playground.

EDUCATION AND INTEREST IN FILMMAKING

Jenkins attended Miami Northwestern Senior High School, where he played for the varsity football team and thought about becoming an English teacher. He entered Florida State University (FSU) with that goal in mind, but he happened to see a poster touting a filmmaking class. Knowing that he would have to essentially start over, he switched majors, only to find that he felt out of place. He had heard whispers from some of his fellow students that he had been accepted into the program only because he was a member of an underrepresented minority, and he told Michael Cieply for *Deadline Hollywood* (5 Dec. 2016) that he thought, "What am I doing here? I'm a kid from the projects. It was a rude awakening."

Jenkins dropped out of FSU for a year but felt a sense of guilt for wasting what he knew was a valuable opportunity. He returned with new resolve and determination to make something that would stand out, watching every foreign film he could get at his neighborhood video store and voraciously reading global film magazines. He remains profoundly grateful to the school. In addition to living and working with classmates in a house near campus, an experience he described to Dave Heller for the *Florida State University News* (20 Feb. 2017) as "otherworldly," he explained to Heller that professors were nurturing and encouraging. "They gave us the freedom to create whatever box we thought was most appropriate for our voice," he told Heller. "FSU changed me."

While in school he also got his first taste of the annual Telluride Film Festival, held in Colorado. In 2002, he participated in the Student Symposium program there, watching movies and then returning to a classroom to discuss them. Required to complete a short film before graduating, Jenkins made *My Josephine* in 2003. Written shortly after the terrorist attacks of September 11, 2001, the main characters are Middle Eastern owners of a laundromat, and the eight-minute short is narrated almost entirely in Arabic. He remains proud of that work, which set him apart from his classmates.

Even after graduating in 2003, Jenkins continued to return to Telluride as a staffer, progressing from making popcorn and ushering to moderating panels and hosting presentations—making industry connections along the way.

STRUGGLING TO ESTABLISH A PROFESSIONAL FILM CAREER

As Jenkins moved to California and worked to get his filmmaking career off the ground, he took on other jobs, including one as a retail clerk. "Working around non-film people every morning on this job, getting the muscles going, having a dialogue with real people and not about 'projects' was a great way to start the day, open up the brain, and get some positive energy going," he told Scott Macaulay for *Filmmaker* magazine (4 Aug. 2009). It was during that period, partly inspired into action by a tough breakup, that he made his first full-length feature on his own, a romantic drama titled *Medicine for Melancholy* (2008), which follows twenty-four hours in the lives of a young black couple in a gentrifying neighborhood of San Francisco. The picture, shot with a small crew and a budget of thirteen thousand dollars, won awards at festivals in Sarasota, Woodstock, and San Francisco before being picked for art-house distribution by IFC Films. In a review for the *New York Times* (29 Jan. 2009), A. O. Scott wrote, "It is an exciting debut, and a film that, without exaggeration or false modesty, finds interest and feeling in the world just as it is."

Over the following years, Jenkins embarked on a variety of projects but battled with a lack of confidence, especially as more time passed without production of a major work. He began to fear that the momentum he had gained from his first feature was disappearing. Regardless, he started a production house that created branded content for Bloomingdale's and other companies, worked on an ill-fated screenplay that involved the iconic musician Stevie Wonder and time travel, adapted Bill Clegg's 2010 memoir *Portrait of an Addict as a Young Man* for the screen, made an occasional short film, and accepted a short-lived job as a staff writer on the HBO series *The Leftovers*.

BREAKING OUT WITH *MOONLIGHT*

In 2011, while working on the short film *Chlorophyl* for the Miami film collective Borscht Corporation, Jenkins read a compelling, semiautobiographical work titled "In Moonlight Black Boys Look Blue," which had been written by young playwright Tarell Alvin McCraney. McCraney had also grown up in Liberty City and been the son of a mother addicted to crack cocaine; he was also friends with one of the founders of the collective. The piece needed some changes and revisions, and after about two years and encouragement from his longtime friend and former FSU classmate Adele Romanski to make another feature film, Jenkins decided that this project was worth taking on, seeing commonalities in his and McCraney's backgrounds.

McCraney gave him the green light to work on the screenplay.

Plan B Entertainment, the production company cofounded by Brad Pitt (who became a producer for the film), became interested in Jenkins's script and brought on the independent entertainment company A24 to provide financing. Filmed in Liberty City, *Moonlight* stars the well-known entertainers Mahershala Ali and Janelle Monáe, but Jenkins found much of his supporting cast by combing Liberty City's schools and community centers. "I had to re-prove my bona fides," Jenkins told Rebecca Keegan for the *Los Angeles Times* (21 Oct. 2016). He explained that during filming, current residents of the neighborhood gave him advice about how best to represent the area. "It was about them taking possession of the piece."

Pleased with the finished product, Jenkins had come to terms with his initial hesitations to make such a personal film. "The beautiful thing about *Moonlight* is that it's like, This is who I am. This is where I'm from. This is my DNA," he said to Carl Swanson for *Vulture* (1 Dec. 2016). *Moonlight* went into limited release in October 2016 and, within just weeks of its debut, it had grossed more than three million dollars. The film subsequently won a number of prizes, including a Golden Globe Award for best dramatic motion picture and Academy Awards for both best picture and best adapted screenplay (along with an Oscar nod for Jenkins as best director). Of the rapturous reception *Moonlight* received, Jenkins told Keegan, "Having grown people cry in my arms at screenings is a surreal experience." His mother, he assures journalists, has been in recovery for several years but has not watched *Moonlight*. "I understand it because there are things in the film that are hard for me to watch, so they could be doubly hard for her," he said to Gregg Kilday for the *Hollywood Reporter* (11 Nov. 2016).

Following the success of *Moonlight*, Jenkins inked a deal to adapt Colson Whitehead's acclaimed 2016 novel *The Underground Railroad* for television, and he is reportedly considering a variety of other future projects as well.

PERSONAL LIFE

Jenkins lives in Los Angeles.

SUGGESTED READING

Als, Hilton. "*Moonlight* Undoes Our Expectations." Review of *Moonlight*, directed by Barry Jenkins. *The New Yorker*, 24 Oct. 2016, www. newyorker.com/magazine/2016/10/24/moonlight-undoes-our-expectations. Accessed 1 Mar. 2017.

Hannah-Jones, Nikole. "From Bittersweet Childhoods to *Moonlight*." *The New York Times*, 4 Jan. 2017, www.nytimes.com/2017/01/04/

movies/moonlight-barry-jenkins-tarell-alvin-mccraney-interview.html. Accessed 1 Mar. 2017.

Jenkins, Barry. "Barry Jenkins on *Moonlight*, a Tale of Black America and Personal Adversity." Interview by A. O. Scott. *The New York Times*, 6 Sept. 2016, www.nytimes.com/2016/09/07/movies/barry-jenkins-interview-moonlight.html. Accessed 1 Mar. 2017.

Keegan, Rebecca. "To Give Birth to *Moonlight*, Writer-Director Barry Jenkins Dug Deep into His Past." *Los Angeles Times*, 21 Oct. 2016, www.latimes.com/entertainment/movies/la-et-mn-moonlight-barry-jenkins-feature-20161006-snap-story.html. Accessed 1 Mar. 2017.

Swanson, Carl. "*Moonlight* Director Barry Jenkins Thought He'd Fled His Past, Then He Accidentally Made a Movie about It." *Vulture*, 1 Dec. 2016, www.vulture.com/2016/11/barry-jenkins-moonlight.html. Accessed 1 Mar. 2017.

Tate, Greg. "How Barry Jenkins Turned the Misery and Beauty of the Queer Black Experience into the Year's Best Movie." *The Village Voice*, 21 Dec. 2016, www.villagevoice.com/film/how-barry-jenkins-turned-the-misery-and-beauty-of-the-queer-black-experience-into-the-years-best-movie-9478791. Accessed 1 Mar. 2017.

—*Mari Rich*

Tyehimba Jess

Date of birth: ca. 1966
Occupation: Poet

Tyehimba Jess has received near-universal critical praise for his two books of poetry, *Leadbelly* (2005) and *Olio* (2016). *Olio*, which won the Pulitzer Prize for poetry in 2017, is a multifaceted examination of minstrelsy and the people who took part in this musically and theatrically significant—yet racist and racially charged—form of performance and entertainment. As a young African American poet fresh out of college, Jess aimed his poems directly at black people. In the early 2000s, however, he not only gained a new maturity and subtlety in his verse, but also decided to write for everyone. Jess's poetry takes inspiration from many sources, such as songs, letters, dances, jazz, blues, theater, and American history.

BIRTH OF A YOUNG POET
Tyehimba Jess was born Jesse S. Goodwin around 1966. Jess and his older brother and sister were raised in Detroit, Michigan. His father,

Jesse F. Goodwin, was the first vice president of the local National Association for the Advancement of Colored People (NAACP) chapter. He also worked for the Detroit Department of Public Health. Jess's mother, Della McGraw Goodwin, established the nursing school at Wayne County Community College District. Jess's father grew up in South Carolina, though he did not like to talk about it, and moved north to a measure of reprieve from the racism of the South. His mother grew up in Oklahoma and completed high school in Little Rock, Arkansas—a hotbed of both racism and civil rights activism. She left Oklahoma, where she was barred from nursing school because of her race.

Jess's childhood home was a very literary one. His parents insisted that their children read—a lot. His father subscribed to dozens of magazines, and there were books everywhere. In an interview with Jessica Kinnison for the *Fourth River* literary journal (12 July 2013), Jess said, "I think that my parents' support and insistence upon college and that exposure to the necessity of reading at a very young age affected me." He began writing poems in high school, at the age of sixteen. At about eighteen, he placed second at an NAACP poetry competition.

Jess graduated from high school in 1984. He then matriculated at the University of Chicago in part to be different from his brother, who was enrolled at the much closer Michigan State University and with whom he had attended lower-levels schools.

EDUCATION
Jess entered the University of Chicago as an English major, fully intending to study poetry, but he changed his major to public policy after getting a C+ on a paper after several rewrites. At the time, Jess told Michael Marsh in an interview for *Chicago Reader* (6 June 2002), he could not bring himself to work with a white instructor on creative writing, though he added that that later changed. The socially and politically aware Jess found other students, even many of the black students, were less aware of and outraged by social issues of the day such as apartheid in South Africa. He dropped out of the University of Chicago in 1987.

Jess went on to work odd jobs here and there, interning at a bank and substitute teaching for Chicago Public Schools. Two years later Jess returned to the University of Chicago, resuming his education in public policy. In addition, Jess sought informal education elsewhere—for example, with the All-African People's Revolutionary Party, with the New African People's Organization, and at Freedom Found Books in Hyde Park. He also studied many literary figures of the Harlem Renaissance and the Black Arts movement of the 1960s and 1970s at the University of

Illinois at Chicago. All of these activities led Jess to again focus on poetry. He graduated in 1991.

CALL ME TYEHIMBA JESS

Though he did not legally change his name until 1999, he began to go by Tyehimba Jess soon after graduation. The name change not only points to his African heritage—*Tyehimba* in the Tiv language of Nigeria means "We stand as a nation"—but also rejects his last name Goodwin, which Jess has stated comes from the slaveholders who owned his ancestors. He also became a regular at poetry slams and continued to work on his performance for years. He went on to compete in the National Poetry Slam in 2000 and 2001. Eventually his talent and hard work were recognized: in 2000 he won the Illinois Arts Council Fellowship and the following year placed first in the *Chicago Sun-Times* poetry competition.

In 1993 Jess self-published seven hundred copies of a chapbook of his poetry, *When n——s love Revolution like they love the bulls*. The title poem, written in 1992, reflects the speaker's disappointment with the discrepancy between how well young black men know obscure basketball statistics and how many do not know facts that are much more relevant to their lives: "fbi stats, / infant mortality stats, / police brutality stats." The poem was anthologized in *Soulfires: Young Black Men on Love and Violence* (1996). His works are also found in a handful of other poetry anthologies. Notably, "retired, ronald reagan sits in his dayroom and wonders," about President Ronald Reagan's policies in Latin America, was included in the 2002 collection *Role Call: A Generational Anthology of Social and Political Black Literature and Art*.

In the late 1990s and early 2000s, Jess participated in several Cave Canem Foundation writing retreats for poets of color. By 2002, he had changed his focus, sharpening his poems while making them more nuanced. His poems, he told Marsh, became "more concerned with the human struggle that we have to deal with on a day-to-day basis, like how we relate to our children, the question of whether or not we will have children, the romantic relationships we have as a people." He later elaborated on his transformation in his interview with Kinnison: "I used to write for political purposes strictly. I was interested in writing poems that would inspire [black] people to take political action." He continued, "After a while, I came to accept the idea that I was writing for everybody. . . . It is difficult to say that you are writing for one particular group of people. It can limit your imagination. After a while, I was like, 'OK, I am writing for the entire world.'"

LEADBELLY

In 2004, Jess earned his master's degree in creative writing from New York University (NYU). By then important others were gaining confidence in his work. The National Endowment for the Arts gave him a grant that helped him publish his debut collection of prose poems, *Leadbelly* (2005). The title refers to Huddie William Ledbetter, a Louisianan folk and blues singer-songwriter and guitarist. He served time in Angola Prison, where he was first recorded by the American musicologists and folklorists John and Alan Lomax. Leadbelly, as he was known, became famous in the 1930s and 1940s for such songs as "Goodnight Irene," "Rock Island Line," and "Where Did You Sleep Last Night?" Those songs, or Leadbelly's versions of them, were performed by many artists throughout the twentieth century, including the Weavers, Johnny Cash, and Nirvana, respectively. In his collection, Jess tells the story of Leadbelly through various voices, including Ledbetter's wife Martha and John Lomax.

A review in *Publishers Weekly* called the book an "addictive amalgamation of approaches," acknowledging that its "strength lies in its contradictory forms; from biography to lyric to hard-driving prose poem, boast to song, all are soaked in the rhythm and dialect of Southern blues and the demands of honoring one's talent." The reviewer further noted how Jess's poems are crafted for reading aloud, rather than remaining silently on the page. The esteemed, award-winning poet Cornelius Eady wrote the following blurb: "I suspect this book, about one man's journey through the blues, is as close as a book of poetry may get to describing what it means and what it costs to have this music in your veins." The book was a National Poetry Series selection and a *Black Issues Book Review* top book of the year.

Leadbelly opened up new possibilities for Jess. The following year, he joined the faculty of the University of Illinois at Urbana-Champaign and then received the prestigious Whiting Award. In the spring of 2007, he served as a Lannan Foundation resident.

OLIO

It took Jess more than a decade to put out his next collection of poems, but judging by the awards and praise, the wait was worth it. The poetic forms, structure, and subject matter of his second book, *Olio* (2016), constitute a collage of art objects, poems, songs, and prose histories and fictions imbued with a vast amount of subtle historical detail and meaning. The book was also clearly meant to be read in a multitude of ways, given Jess's syncopation and counterpoint—the simultaneous use of various rhythms and themes—as well as its physical construction with foldouts and perforated cutouts. The subject matter and the characters were all taken from the complex American musical and theatrical performance type known as the minstrel show, which featured music, comedy, skits, and dancing. It was a very popular form of entertainment in the nineteenth century and the early twentieth century. The performers, both white and black, performed in "blackface," their faces painted black in a form of caricature. What Jess sought to explore in his book were the characters behind the caricature, the people behind the show—though he also delved into the multiple racial and historical implications of the performances themselves.

The book received almost unanimous praise. "Many of the poems are written from the direct perspective of the artists, all of them acting as the speaker," Hanif Willis-Abdurraqib wrote for the *Rumpus* (6 Apr. 2016). "For Jess to pull this off so effectively, in artists spanning different backgrounds, eras, and genders, is indicative as his skill as a writer, and I imagine his skill as a listener. Someone with an ear towards conversation, tone, and urgency." In another very positive review for the *Kenyon Review*, Jacob Sunderlin lauded Jess's "technical wizardry," noting some of the many forms in which he works, including "most spectacularly, the double-jointed sonnet, which can be read a total of three, or possibly infinite ways, both down and across the caesura, or diagonally." Sunderlin concludes, "In these poems, two voices emerge from the poem, distinct, and two voices combine into a single song." *Olio* was a National Books Critics Circle Award finalist for 2016. In 2017 it received the Pulitzer Prize and the Anisfield-Wolf Book Award, which recognizes important works of literature that celebrate racial diversity or further interracial dialogue.

PERSONAL LIFE

Jess teaches in the College of Staten Island's English Department and edits poetry and fiction for the *African American Review*. He lives in Brooklyn.

SUGGESTED READING

Fitzgerald, Adam. "Tyehimba Jess on Excavating Popular Music through Poetry: Exploring the Sustenance of Song and Historical Clapbacks." *Literary Hub*, 5 May 2016, lithub.com/tyehimba-jess-on-excavating-popular-music-through-poetry. Accessed 15 Aug. 2017.

Jess, Tyehimba. "Telling Two Stories in One Breath." Interview by Jessica Kinnison. *The Fourth River*, 12 July 2013, www.thefourthriver.com/index.php/2013/07/telling-two-stories-in-one-breath-an-interview-with-tyehimba-jess. Accessed 15 Aug. 2017.

Marsh, Michael. "Local Lit: Can Tyehimba Jess Wake Up the World?" *Chicago Reader*, 6 June 2002, www.chicagoreader.com/chicago/local-lit-can-tyehimba-jess-wake-up-the-world/Content?oid=908783. Accessed 15 Aug. 2017.

Sunderlin, Jacob. "'The Gut Meaning of Grace': Tyehimba Jess's *Olio*." Review of *Olio*, by Tyehimba Jess. *Kenyon Review*, www.kenyonreview.org/reviews/olio-by-tyehimba-jess-738439. Accessed 15 Aug. 2017.

Wanschura, Dan. "The Unconventional Poetry of Tyehimba Jess." *Weekend Edition Saturday*, National Public Radio, 15 July 2017, www.npr.org/2017/07/15/537381252/the-unconventional-poetry-of-tyehimba-jess. Accessed 15 Aug. 2017.

—*Michael Tillman*

Dustin Johnson

Date of birth: June 22, 1984
Occupation: Golfer

Since bursting onto the PGA Tour in 2007, Dustin Johnson has developed into one of golf's most naturally gifted players. With his unusually powerful swing and soft hands, he has managed to win at least one PGA title in his first ten seasons, becoming only the third player behind Jack Nicklaus and Tiger Woods to accomplish such a feat. Johnson, however, struggled to capture that elusive major championship, amassing a number of near misses at the 2010 US Open and PGA Championships, and most recently, the 2015 US Open. He finally claimed his first major championship at the 2016 US Open, and secured the world's number-one ranking in 2017.

"I think we all knew the talent was there. I think the last couple of years you've seen him grow on and off the golf course and see him become the player we all knew he could be," fellow golfer Brandt Snedeker told Joseph Person for the *Charlotte Observer* (5 Apr. 2017). "It's been fun to see him reach his potential."

DISPLAYS RAW POTENTIAL

Dustin Johnson was born on June 22, 1984, in Columbia, South Carolina, into a family of athletes. Art Whisnant, Johnson's maternal grandfather, is a former University of South Carolina basketball standout. His father, Scott Johnson, played basketball, baseball, and football at Chapin High School. When he was young, Johnson was a frequent presence at Mid Carolina Club, where his father was the head golf professional, and the Weed Hill Driving Range, where he drew the attention of range owner Jimmy

By Keith Allison [CC BY-SA 2.0], via Wikimedia Commons

Koosa. "Little DJ had a swing with rhythm and tempo, and he could hit the fool out of the ball," Koosa recalled to Jaime Diaz for *Golf Digest* (29 Apr. 2015).

Johnson played several other sports, including basketball and Little League baseball, before focusing exclusively on golf. From 1999 to 2002, he competed in six tournaments on the American Junior Golf Association (AJGA) circuit, recording his best finish at the 2001 Greater Greensboro Chrysler Junior, where he tied for tenth.

EARLY TROUBLE AND TURN AROUND

Although Johnson was an up and coming high school athlete, he went through a troubled period during his sophomore and junior years after his parents divorced and his father lost his job. In addition to skipping classes, Johnson was suspended from the golf team, fell in with the wrong crowd, and, in 2001, became involved in a home burglary. The sixteen-year-old Johnson was arrested after a stolen item—a handgun—was linked to a murder investigation involving Steve Gillian, the older brother of Johnson's close friend. After alleging that Gillian had pressured him into purchasing ammunition with a fake ID, as well as pawning several watches and a coin collection, Johnson pled guilty to second degree burglary, paid restitution, and testified against Gillian, who received life without parole. Johnson was granted a full pardon in 2009.

Johnson was able to turn his life around during his senior year at Dutch Fork High School. "Getting in trouble actually kind of helped me

realize that I needed to get my [act] together," he said to Jim Moriarty for *Golf Digest* (26 Jan. 2009). "That was when I started playing golf all over again." His friends talked him into rejoining the Silver Foxes boys' varsity golf team, which went on to score a record-breaking 882 points against the Hillcrest Rams to capture the South Carolina High School League (SCHSL) 2002 Class AAAA State Golf Championship. Johnson's 218 points earned him a fourth-place tie for the individual title.

After graduating from Dutch Fork that spring, Johnson did not have enough credits to attend college, so he enrolled at Midlands Technical College in Columbia, South Carolina. "I was smart in school, it just wasn't my thing," he admitted to Alan Blondin for *Myrtle Beach Online* (21 Sept. 2016). "I wanted to go to college to play sports, not necessarily to get an education."

Johnson's wish came true when Allen Terrell, the golf coach at Coastal Carolina University (CCU), in Conway, South Carolina, recruited him. Initially, Johnson struggled during his freshman season (2003–4). "All of a sudden, he's got a guy telling him he needs to get up and work out in the morning and be at practice at a certain time and he's got to study. He fought it like hell," Terrell recalled to Moriarty.

Johnson eventually thrived, helping lead the Chanticleers to four consecutive Big South Conference Championships and their first three NCAA Championship appearances (2005–7). Furthermore, he was a three-time All-American, three-time Big South Golfer of the Year (2005–7), and four-time All-Big South honoree.

TURNS PRO AND CLINCHES FIRST TITLE

In 2007, a few credits shy of graduation, Johnson left CCU to pursue golf full time. He had a strong start to his career, helping the United States defeat Europe at the Arnold Palmer Cup in June, before capping off the month with prestigious victories at the Monroe Invitational and the Northeast Amateur. Following a fiftieth-place finish at the Nationwide Children's Hospital Invitational in July, Johnson represented the winning US team at the Walker Cup in September. Despite missing the cut at the Valero Texas Open in October, his fourteenth-place tie at December's PGA Qualifying Tournament earned him a PGA Tour card for the 2008 season.

In 2008, after two impressive top-ten finishes in his first four starts—the Sony Open in Hawaii and the AT&T Pebble Beach National Pro-Am—Johnson struggled over the next four months to make cuts and to crack the top thirty. Despite a nineteenth-place finish at the Greater Milwaukee Open in July, his woes continued. In addition to withdrawing from the RBC Canadian Open and the Wyndham Championship, as well as missing the cut at the Barclays, Johnson barely reached the top forty at the Viking Classic in September. To regain his early-season form, he rededicated himself, focusing on his putting game. The hard work paid off at the Turning Stone Resort Championship in October, when Johnson birdied the final two holes to clinch a one-shot victory over veteran Robert Allenby and pocket the $1.08 million prize.

WINS BACK-TO-BACK AT PEBBLE BEACH

Johnson's win qualified him for the 2009 Mercedes-Benz Championship, where he finished eleventh. Following another top-twenty finish at the Buick Invitational, Johnson held a four-stroke lead after three rounds at the AT&T Pebble Beach Pro-Am, eventually claiming his second PGA title when a washout cancelled the final round. The victory made him the youngest winner since Woods in 2000. Johnson followed that up with a top-ten finish at the Northern Trust Open in February 2009. A month later, however, Johnson was arrested for driving under the influence of alcohol (DUI). Despite the incident, he continued to play well during the rest of the 2009 season, finishing no lower than fortieth in every tournament, except the Players Championship, where he tied for seventy-ninth. Johnson's top-ten finishes came at the HP Byron Nelson Championship, the Deutsche Bank Championship, and the PGA Championship—golf's final major of the year.

Johnson had a strong start to 2010, recording consecutive sixteenth-place finishes at the Hyundai Tournament of Champions and the Sony Open, as well as a third-place tie at the Northern Trust Open. In February, he successfully defended his title at the AT&T Pebble Beach Pro-Am with a one-stroke victory over David Duval and J. B. Holmes. With the win, Johnson became the first player in two decades to claim back-to-back titles at the event, and the first player since Woods to win in each of his first three years on the PGA Tour. In June, Johnson, fresh off a seventh-place finish at the HP Byron Nelson Championship, returned to Pebble Beach for the US Open—with different results. He held a three-stroke lead into the final round until consecutive bogeys on the second and third holes dropped him into an eighth-place tie. Johnson also fell short at the PGA Championship, tying for fifth after being assessed a two-stroke penalty for grounding his club in a bunker. He rebounded nicely with a ninth-place finish at the Barclays, and victories at the BMW Championship—his fourth PGA title—as well as the Ryder Cup to reach the top five in world ranking.

MAKING HEADLINES ON AND OFF THE COURSE

Johnson picked up where he left off in 2011, with top-ten showings at the Hyundai Tournament of Champions and the Farmers Insurance Open. He, however, also generated controversy—on and off the court. Despite missing the cut at the Northern Trust Open, he was penalized two shots for being late for his tee time. Shortly after this incident, the highway patrol released the video of his DUI arrest. He ultimately pleaded guilty to reckless driving and was fined.

Johnson, however, maintained his solid play, finishing second at the WGC-Cadillac Championship in March and fourth at the Memorial Tournament in June. His best result that year was at the Open Championship, where he pulled within two shots of the lead but finished second, following a double bogey on the fourteenth hole. After winning the Barclays in August, Johnson helped the United States claim the Presidents Cup in October.

Johnson's 2012 season started off promising. After flirting with his third AT&T Pebble Beach National Pro-Am title, he placed among the top ten at the Northern Trust Open and WGC-Accenture Match Play Championship. In early April, a back injury forced him to withdraw from the Masters. Johnson, however, was successful in his return, finishing nineteenth at the Memorial Tournament and clinching his sixth title at the FedEx St. Jude Classic. He ended the year ranked eighth in the world, following a strong second half that included top-ten finishes at the Open Championship and the Barclays.

Johnson opened the 2013 season with his seventh PGA win at the Hyundai Tournament. After placing thirteenth in his Masters return, the FedEx St. Jude Classic's defending champion finished tenth and eighth at the PGA Championship. Furthermore, Johnson won the WGC-HSBC Champions, his eighth title, and finished third at the RBC Canadian Open and fifth at the TOUR Championship.

Johnson remained competitive in the first half of 2014, claiming runner-up honors at the AT&T Pebble Beach National Pro-Am and Northern Trust Open. Furthermore, he finished sixth at the Hyundai Tournament of Champions, fourth at the WGC-Cadillac Championship, and seventh at the HP Byron Nelson Championships. In late July, after finishing fourth at the US Open and twelfth at the Open Golf Championship, Johnson took an indefinite hiatus—citing personal reasons. In early August 2014 Michael Bamberger for *Golf* reported that Johnson had been placed on a six-month suspension from the PGA Tour after testing positive for cocaine, and that he had previously failed two other drug tests in 2009 and 2012. As a result of the suspension, Johnson missed competing in the PGA Championship, the FedEx Cup playoff series, and the Ryder Cup in Scotland that year.

RETURNS TO GOLF

Upon returning to the golf course in February 2015, Johnson finished fourth at the AT&T Pebble Beach National Pro-Am and second at the Northern Trust Open. In March, he captured his ninth title at the WGC-Cadillac Championship. He then placed sixth in his next two events: the Valero Texas Open and the Masters. Furthermore, Johnson finished second at the US Open, where he lost by one stroke to Jordan Spieth, and finished seventh at the PGA Championship. He ended the 2015 season with a Presidents Cup victory, and three more top-ten results—the Barclays, BMW Championship, and TOUR Championship.

Johnson had a breakthrough season in 2016. In April, he finished fourth at the Masters. After finishing third at the Memorial Tournament and fifth at the FedEx St. Jude Classic, Johnson was part of the final group at the US Open, where he secured a three-shot victory to claim his tenth title—and first major championship. Although Johnson's ball moved while he was lining up a putt on the fifth hole, the United States Golf Association waited until two hours before reversing its initial judgment not to assess a one-shot penalty, drawing heavy criticism from fellow golfers, including Spieth and Rory McIlroy. Johnson added two more individual titles—the World Golf Championships-Bridgestone Invitational and the BMW Championship—and a Ryder Cup win to his collection.

BECOMES NUMBER ONE

Johnson continued his dominance in 2017, with a sixth-place showing at the SBS Tournament of Championship, and a third-place result at AT&T Pebble Beach Pro-Am. In February, Johnson's Genesis Open victory earned him the world's number-one ranking. In March, he extended his winning streak at the World Golf Championships-Mexico Championship, and the World Golf Championships-Dell Technologies Match Play. In April, however, Johnson injured his back falling down the stairs, which forced him to withdraw from the Masters. In May, he returned to action at the Wells Fargo Championship.

PERSONAL LIFE

Since 2013, Johnson has been engaged to Paulina Gretzky, with whom he has a son, Tatum. In February 2017, it was reported that they were expecting their second child.

SUGGESTED READING

Bamberger, Michael. "Dustin Johnson Suspended from PGA Tour after Positive Drug Test." *Golf*, 2 Aug. 2014, www.golf.com/tour-and-news/dustin-johnson-suspended-pga-tour-after-positive-test-cocaine. Accessed 17 May 2017.

Blondin, Alan. "Dustin Johnson Has Persevered to Reach the Summit of Professional Golf." *Myrtle Beach Online*, 21 Sept. 2016, www.myrtlebeachonline.com/sports/golf/article103334822.html. Accessed 5 May 2017.

Diaz, Jaime. "The New DJ." *Golf Digest*, 29 Apr. 2015,www.golfdigest.com/story/the-new-dustin-johnson. Accessed 5 May 2017.

Moriarty, Jim. "Recovery Act." *Golf Digest*, 26 Jan. 2009, www.golfdigest.com/story/gw-20090202moriarty. Accessed 16 May 2017.

Person, Joseph. "Fall at Rental House Puts World-No. 1 Dustin Johnson's Masters in Jeopardy." *The Charlotte Observer*, 5 Apr. 2017, www.charlotteobserver.com/sports/other-sports/article142926119.html. Accessed 5 May 2017.

—*Bertha Muteba*

Kellie Jones

Date of birth: May 16, 1959
Occupation: Art historian and curator

In 2016, art historian and curator Kellie Jones was honored with a MacArthur Fellowship from the John D. and Catherine T. MacArthur Foundation. According to the terms of the fellowship, Jones, an associate professor and the director of undergraduate studies in Columbia University's Department of Art History and Archaeology and a research fellow at the university's Institute for Research in African-American Studies, will receive $625,000 paid in quarterly installments over five years. "This is major recognition for the arena that I have dedicated so much time and energy to," Jones said in response to the award, as reported in an article for *Columbia News* (22 Sept. 2016), the website of Columbia's Office of Communications and Public Affairs. "The efforts I have put towards making art history and museum culture more reflective of the world we inhabit by recognizing global and gendered creators has paid off."

EARLY LIFE AND EDUCATION

Jones is the eldest of two daughters of Amiri Baraka, a celebrated writer and activist and the founder of the Black Arts Movement, and Hettie Jones, an author of more than twenty books who is best known for her memoir of her life during the Beat movement. According to Jones's younger sister, writer and journalist Lisa Jones, Kellie Jones was ahead of her time even as a child. "[She] had us do paper dolls that were multi-culti superstars before there were multi-culti superstars. She was so attuned to organizing the world in our own image, even when we were children,"

John D. & Catherine T. MacArthur Foundation

Lisa recalled at a Columbia University event in which the sisters discussed Jones's then recently released book *EyeMinded: Living and Writing Contemporary Art* (2011), as reported by John Uhl for the *Record* (22 Dec. 2011). Growing up in lower Manhattan at a time when the area was home to a vibrant multicultural arts and music scene, the sisters were surrounded by such cultural and artistic diversity from a young age; as Jones noted in response to her sister's comment, again according to Uhl, "People talk about globalization, but if you grew up on the Lower East Side, you experienced that on every block."

During her years at Manhattan's High School of Music & Art (now Fiorello H. LaGuardia High School of Music & Art and Performing Arts), Jones began to wonder why her art history textbooks devoted so little space to artists of color outside the context of ancient civilizations. As she recalled to Dayna Evans for the *Cut* (24 Oct. 2016), "They were Egyptians, they were Aztecs, they were Ancient Chinese people. There were no contemporary people. I thought hmm, this is not right. I was going to school with all these people. This was just a mistake from the beginning."

Jones graduated magna cum laude from Amherst College in 1981 with an interdisciplinary degree in black studies, Latin American studies, and fine arts. She engaged in self-directed study at Amherst and also attended classes in South America and California, where she was able to learn more about Latin American art and artists.

EARLY CAREER

Although Jones grew up surrounded by artists, she knew she did not want to be an artist herself. Her earliest ambition was to become a diplomat for the United Nations (UN), and she studied Spanish and French in pursuit of this goal, but ultimately abandoned the idea to return to the world she was most familiar with. "I realized that there are a lot of artists but not a lot of people who write about them and help them—the curator, the writer, the critic. I said, 'Wow, I could actually do this,'" she said to Uhl. "You're kind of the go-between between the artist and the institution. It was the same kind of life that I imagined the diplomatic life to be." Rather than pursue a master's degree in business administration with the goal of becoming a museum director, Jones set her sights on a PhD in art history, which she earned from Yale University in 1999. "My interest in art was really in the ideas, not so much in the selling," she explained to Uhl. "At the end of the dissertation process, I realized that I had grown to really like teaching and the life of the mind."

After graduating from Amherst in 1981, Jones began working at the Studio Museum in Harlem, where she had held an internship the summer before. For her first nine months, she was an intern under a program of the National Endowment for the Arts (NEA), which allowed her to work in each department for a few weeks before deciding on an area of interest. She chose to remain with curatorial work and was promoted to assistant curator, with the main task of overseeing the art collection at the Adam Clayton Powell Jr. State Office Building.

JAMAICA ARTS CENTER

Jones later continued her career at the Jamaica Arts Center in Queens, holding the position of visual arts director from 1986 until 1990. In her first year there, she collaborated with the center's executive director, William P. Miller, to produce an exhibition titled *Masters and Pupils: The Education of the Black Artist in New York, 1900–1980*. The goal of the exhibition, which featured more than fifty works by forty artists, was to show the professional and artistic development of African American artists during this period. "In the beginning, there were no black teachers to study with," Miller told C. Gerald Fraser for the *New York Times* (7 Dec. 1986). "But suddenly we had in the black community black artists who were becoming teachers. In the 1940s there were black art teachers in major universities. Now there are black art teachers all over; many are chairmen of art departments." The exhibition focused on how the artists were influenced by their white teachers, and how they may have influenced those teachers in turn. "We'll hang a work of an instructor or master next to the work of a pupil at that time," Jones explained to Fraser. "This will illustrate the intertwining of the white and black artists." The exhibition also featured video interviews with some of the artists as well as written documents.

Another of Jones's activities while at Jamaica Arts Center was to serve as moderator of a 1987 panel discussion at the Metropolitan Museum of Art entitled "The Education of an Artist." The topic, which dovetailed nicely with the exhibit at Jamaica Arts Center, was part of the larger discussion series Contemporary Issues: The Artist in the Museum. In 1989 Jones proposed and subsequently curated the official US entry to the São Paulo Bienal, an exhibition featuring the work of sculptor Martin Puryear, which won the grand prize for best individual exhibition.

In 1991 Jones moved to the Walker Art Center, where she remained until 1998. While there, she followed her earlier success at the São Paulo Bienal by curating an exhibition for the 1997 Johannesburg Biennale.

ACADEMIC LIFE

Jones taught as an assistant professor at Yale University from 1999 until 2006 before accepting a position at Columbia. While at Yale, she curated an exhibit of black abstract expressionist artists, *Energy/Experimentation: Black Artists and Abstraction, 1964–1980*, at the Studio Museum. Limited by the constraints of space, the show featured only fifteen artists. Most of the works were from the 1960s and 1970s, though the artists included painters from different generations.

Jones shares her passions with the students she teaches, including them in her research, which gives them something significant to add to a résumé as they seek jobs. "Kellie Jones is a path-breaking scholar, an influential critic, and an inspiring teacher," said Michael Cole, the chair of the Department of Art History and Archaeology, as quoted by *Columbia News*. "From an academic post, moreover, she has become one of the most visionary curators of modern and contemporary art working anywhere in America. Few of us can aspire to follow her example, writing with the learnedness, originality, and insight that made her a leader of her field while also establishing an important public voice."

Jones also has written several works about art, including *EyeMinded*. Published in 2011, it is both a memoir of growing up in New York's Lower East Side and a consideration of African American and multicultural art movements. The anthology, which contains essays spanning twenty years of her writing as well as essays written by family members and friends, ponders the question of how artists form various connections and communities.

NOW DIG THIS! AND OTHER WORK

In 2011, Jones curated *Now Dig This! Art and Black Los Angeles, 1960–1980*, an exhibition at Los Angeles's Hammer Museum. It was part of a larger project by the Getty Foundation titled Pacific Standard Time, a series of exhibitions in cultural institutions throughout Southern California that showcased the multicultural history of art and architecture in the region. *Now Dig This!* featured 140 works by more than thirty artists, most of them African Americans, as well as information about political activities and attempts to end segregation. Jones wanted to explore the effects of the civil rights movement and Black Power on the African American sense of identity as well as on their art. After closing in Los Angeles, the exhibit traveled to MoMA PS1 in Queens, New York City, and to Williams College Museum of Art in Williamstown, Massachusetts. In 2016 the Hammer Museum, with support from the Andrew W. Mellon Foundation, created a digital archive of the exhibit. The digitized content includes the eight essays that Jones wrote for the catalog, which was published in 2011 and is now out of print, as well as interviews with the artists.

In addition, to mark the fiftieth anniversary of the passage of the Civil Rights Act of 1964, Jones cocurated the exhibition *Witness: Art and Civil Rights in the Sixties*, which opened at the Brooklyn Museum in March 2014, with Teresa A. Carbone. The two also cowrote the catalog for the exhibit.

In 2016, Jones was among twenty-three people in various fields awarded a MacArthur Fellowship, an unrestricted grant given annually to "talented individuals who have shown extraordinary originality and dedication in their creative pursuits and a marked capacity for self-direction." Jones told Jessica Gelt for the *Los Angeles Times* (21 Sept. 2016) that the first thing she planned to do with the money was buy a new desk, as she had owned the same desk since college, bringing it with her from Amherst to Yale to Columbia. She also spoke with Evans about the importance of intergenerational work, saying, "With this MacArthur grant, I want to collaborate more with younger scholars, younger curators, younger people. What the award signaled to me is to take more risks. Think bigger. What could we come up with that would make things look different? How can we really look to the future? Collaborating with younger people is my way of focusing on things in the future, by working with people who the future is their now."

Jones's second noncatalog book, *South of Pico: African American Artists in Los Angeles in the 1960s and 1970s*, was published by Duke University Press in 2017, with extra funding provided by the Institute for Research in

African-American Studies, the Columbia University Department of Art History and Archaeology, and a grant from the College Art Association's Wyeth Foundation for American Art. According to Jones's website, the book "explores how the artists in Los Angeles's black communities during the 1960s and 1970s created a vibrant, productive, and engaged activist arts scene in the face of structural racism."

PERSONAL LIFE

Jones is married to Guthrie P. Ramsey Jr., a professor of music at the University of Pennsylvania. She remains committed to art as an agent of change. Speaking to Evans of her college years and her desire at the time to work for the UN, she said, "I wanted to change the world. I'm not so naive to think that art is the only thing that can change the world, but art allows us to dream, to think, to imagine something different."

SUGGESTED READING

"Columbia's Kellie Jones, Sarah Stillman, and Alum Claudia Rankine Receive MacArthur 'Genius Grants.'" *Columbia News*, Columbia U, 22 Sept. 2016, news.columbia.edu/macarthur2016. Accessed 16 Mar. 2017.
Cooper, Rand Richards. "Breaking the Frame." *Amherst Magazine*, 13 Feb. 2017, www.amherst.edu/amherst-story/magazine/issues/2017-winter/breaking-the-frame. Accessed 16 Mar. 2017.
Evans, Dayna. "How to Work in the Art World without Selling Out Your Politics." *The Cut*, New York Magazine, 24 Oct. 2016, nymag.com/thecut/2016/10/career-advice-from-curator-and-art-historian-kellie-jones.html. Accessed 16 Mar. 2017.
Fraser, C. Gerald. "America's Black Artists Are Seen in New Light." *The New York Times*, 7 Dec. 1986, www.nytimes.com/1986/12/07/arts/america-s-black-artists-are-seen-in-new-light.html. Accessed 16 Mar. 2017.
Gelt, Jessica. "What This MacArthur Winner, an Expert in African American Art History, Plans to Do with Her Grant." *Los Angeles Times*, 21 Sept. 2016, www.latimes.com/entertainment/arts/la-et-cm-kellie-jones-macarthur-grant-20160921-snap-story.html. Accessed 16 Mar. 2017.
Jones, Kellie. "Now Dig This: Seeing through the Artistic Eye of Prof. Kellie Jones." Interview by John Uhl. *The Record*, 22 Dec. 2011, pp. 1+. *Columbia News*, archive.news.columbia.edu/files_columbianews/imce_shared/vol3705.pdf. Accessed 16 Mar. 2017.

SELECTED WORKS

Now Dig This! Art and Black Los Angeles, 1960–1980, 2011; *EyeMinded: Living and Writing Contemporary Art*, 2011; *Witness: Art and Civil Rights in the Sixties* (with Teresa A. Carbone), 2014; *South of Pico: African American Artists in Los Angeles in the 1960s and 1970s*, 2017

—*Judy Johnson*

Ariya Jutanugarn

Date of birth: November 23, 1995
Occupation: Golfer

Thai golfer Ariya Jutanugarn is, as of April 2017, the number-three-ranked woman golfer in the world, according to the officially sanctioned Rolex Rankings. Jutanugarn joined the Ladies Professional Golf Association (LPGA) Tour in 2015 and enjoyed a breakout year in 2016. That year, she won five tournaments, including the Ricoh Women's British Open; earned a number of honors, including the Heather Farr Player Award and the LPGA Award for Rolex Player of the Year; and won the Race to the CME Globe title, sponsored by the CME (Chicago Mercantile Exchange and Chicago Board of Trade) Group, which came with a $1 million bonus.

A relative newcomer to professional golf, Jutanugarn has already established herself as a powerful hitter, a precise putter, and a carefree tour mate with a naturally sunny disposition. Following a turbulent, stress-plagued rookie season in 2015 and a disappointing showing at the ANA (All Nippon Airways) Inspiration championship in March 2016, her improved

By Keith Allison from Hanover, MD, USA [CC BY-SA 2.0], via Wikimedia Commons

mental game—including her coaches' suggestion that she smile before each hit and putt to relax herself—carried her to the top of the rankings. "She's a player who has everything to win a tournament, and she seems like she is having lots of fun while she's playing," fellow golfer Lydia Ko told Lisa D. Mickey for the *New York Times* (14 Sept. 2016) after Jutanugarn's impressive winning streak in spring 2016. "It's always hard to beat someone with great skills who is having fun."

EARLY LIFE AND AMATEUR CAREER

Jutanugarn was born in Bangkok, Thailand, on November 23, 1995, to mother Narumon Tiwattanasuk and father Somboon Jutanugarn. She has an older sister, Moriya Jutanugarn, who is also a professional golfer on the LPGA Tour. The two also have four older half siblings through their father.

The Jutanugarn sisters joke that they began golfing in the womb because their mother played while she was pregnant with each of them. After Moriya was born in 1994, Narumon hired a caddie to babysit while she hit the course. Jutanugarn's parents owned four golf pro shops, including the pro shop at the Rose Garden Golf Course near Bangkok, which they still manage. The sisters first learned to golf on the driving range at the Rose Garden, when Moriya was seven and Ariya was five. "We didn't have toys growing up. We had golf clubs," Jutanugarn told Randall Mell for the Golf Channel website (7 June 2016). Their first coaches were range regulars.

Early on, Jutanugarn showed a natural gift for the sport. In 2007, when she was eleven, she qualified for the Honda LPGA Thailand tournament, becoming the youngest player to ever qualify for an LPGA event. Three years later, in 2010, she won medalist honors at the US Women's Amateur Public Links Championship and placed first in the Junior Orange Bowl International Golf Championship. In 2011 she won the Junior PGA Championship, the United States Girls' Junior Golf Championship, and the American Junior Golf Association (AJGA) Rolex Girls Junior Championship. Ranked number one among juniors, she also won the Rolex Junior Player of the Year in the girls division, a feat she repeated the following year.

Jutanugarn earned low amateur honors at the 2011 and 2012 Kraft Nabisco Championship (now the ANA Inspiration), an LPGA major to which she gained entry through a sponsor exemption. Also in 2012, although Jutanugarn struggled to maintain control over her swing, she won a slew of tournaments thanks to her focused putting skills: the Women's Western Amateur, the Junior PGA Championship (again), the Canadian Women's Amateur, the Rolex Girls Junior Championship (again), and the AJGA Polo Golf Junior Classic. She also won the Ladies European Tour (LET) final qualifying stage, earning status on the LET for 2013. Jutanugarn finished the season as the top-ranked junior player and the number-two-ranked amateur woman golfer in the world.

EARLY PROFESSIONAL CAREER AND INJURY

In 2012 Jutanugarn petitioned the LPGA for an age waiver (members must be eighteen to qualify, and Jutanugarn was only seventeen) but was denied. In early 2013, Jutanugarn finally got to play the first professional tournament she had ever qualified for—the Honda LPGA Thailand—as a member of the LET. She narrowly missed the title, finishing second to Inbee Park, a Korean golfer who continues to challenge Jutanugarn on the LPGA. Jutanugarn earned her first professional title in March 2013 at the Lalla Meryem Cup in Morocco, her fourth start on the LET. She established an advantage early, birdying the first three holes. That advantage dwindled on the second nine holes, but the seventeen-year-old was able to pull out a victory in the end.

Sponsorships allowed her to play a handful of LPGA tournaments in 2013, including the Kingsmill Championship (tying for third), the HSBC Women's Champions (finishing fourth), and the Mobile Bay LPGA Classic (tying for fourth). In June 2013, however Jutanugarn was preparing to play the Wegmans LPGA Championship, thanks to another sponsor exemption, when she tripped over a tee box while chasing her older sister with a water bottle during a practice round. The fall resulted in a tear in the labrum in her right shoulder. Jutanugarn returned to Bangkok for surgery, but her injury forced her to put her professional career on hold for the next eight months.

Jutanugarn was ranked fifteenth in the world before her injury, and clawing her way back to the top proved difficult. She returned to the green in 2014, but she struggled to adjust her swing so that she could play without pain. "I felt OK after the surgery, and I thought I would be OK after a few months, but I wasn't getting better," she recalled to Mell for another article for the Golf Channel website (7 June 2016). "I couldn't hit the ball the same way, and then I really started worrying." Still, Jutanugarn, finally eighteen, managed to win her LPGA Tour card through the league's qualifying school with a third-place finish in December. In 2015, she played in twenty-nine tournaments and enjoyed four top-ten finishes, including a tie for runner-up at the Pure Silk–Bahamas LPGA Classic, but, as Jutanugarn told Mell, she was "playing scared." "I kept thinking about all the bad things that could happen, and things just got worse," she said.

BREAKOUT SEASON

The turning point for Jutanugarn came in March 2016 at the ANA Inspiration, an LPGA major championship. Jutanugarn was on track to win her first LPGA tournament and her first major, but she squandered her chances on the final holes. She was devastated. Knowing that her mental game was holding back her physical one, Jutanugarn began working with performance coaches Pia Nilsson and Lynn Marriott, cofounders of Vision54, whose previous clients include World Golf Hall of Famer Annika Sörenstam. "All players change in some way under pressure," Nilsson said to Mell. "Some get too tight, some get too fast. Some overread putts, and they get too slow. Everyone reacts to stress." According to Marriott, Jutanugarn "was speeding up. She looked tighter, around her mouth and shoulders. Her smiles were becoming forced. She wasn't taking as deep breaths." Among other recommendations, Marriott and Nilsson told her to smile before taking a swing. Their advice has helped center Jutanugarn.

In addition to improving her mental game, Jutanugarn and her caddie decided to shelve her driver in favor of the rarer two-iron club to help her control her swing. The unusual decision has improved her game dramatically. In May 2016, Jutanugarn won her first LPGA Tour event, the Yokohama Tire LPGA Classic in Prattville, Alabama. John Zenor noted for the Associated Press (8 May 2016) that she "gave cheering fans a wave and smile as she approached the final green." Jutanugarn faced close competition from Amy Yang, Morgan Pressel, and Stacy Lewis, but she managed to take the win by a stroke. "Right now, I'm really happy," she told Cheryl Wray for the website *AL.com* (8 May 2016). "Like proud of myself, but, you know, after the back nine, I didn't feel anything. I was just like, I'm out. Right now I'm still a little bit excited, but [in the] last three hole my hands shake, yeah."

FIRST MAJOR TITLE

After her victory at Yokohama, Jutanugarn won the next two LPGA tournaments: the Kingsmill Championship and the LPGA Volvik Championship. She is the first player in LPGA history to make her first three title wins consecutively. In July, she won her first major at the Ricoh Women's British Open in Milton Keynes, England. Jutanugarn was leading by six strokes when she saw her lead narrow after double-bogeying the thirteenth hole. She got mad, she later said, but then caught herself and refocused to win by three strokes over Mo Martin and Miriam Lee. The victory made her the first Thai golfer to win a major title in the sport's history. "I think it's really important for me and for Thai golf, also," Jutanugarn said, as reported by the Associated Press (31 July 2016). "After

my first tournament on tour, my goal is I really want to win a major. I did, so I'm very proud of myself."

Jutanugarn won her fifth title in August 2016 at the Canadian Pacific Women's Open. After that, she was slated to play in the first-ever golf event in the modern Olympic Games at the summer games in Rio de Janeiro, Brazil, but she withdrew due to a sore knee. When the season ended, Jutanugarn led the tour with five title wins and eleven additional top-ten finishes. She also led the tour with 469 birdies, breaking a two-year-old record, and topped the tour's money list, making about $2.5 million. She earned an additional $1 million when she won the Race to the CME Globe title. She won the title of Rolex Player of the Year, an accolade determined by a point system, by twenty points. As of April 2017, Jutanugarn was ranked third in the world. In March, she finished second behind Inbee Park at the HSBC Women's Champions and tied with Amy Yang for eighth place at the ANA Inspiration.

PERSONAL LIFE

In 2016 Jutanugarn purchased a house at Lake Nona in Orlando, Florida. She and her sister, Moriya, who go by the nicknames May and Mo, respectively, share the house with their mother, who also accompanies them on tour.

SUGGESTED READING

Mell, Randall. "A. Jutanugarn Turns Fear of Failure into Winning Focus." *Golf Channel*, NBCUniversal, 7 June 2016, www.golfchannel.com/news/randall-mell/jutanugarn-turns-fear-failure-winning-focus. Accessed 10 Apr. 2017.

Mell, Randall. "Sister Act: Jutanugarns Fueled by Family Bond." *Golf Channel*, NBCUniversal, 7 June 2016, www.golfchannel.com/news/randall-mell/sister-act-jutanugarns-fueled-family-bond. Accessed 10 Apr. 2017.

Mickey, Lisa D. "Winning Smile Is Ariya Jutanugarn's Secret Weapon." *The New York Times*, 14 Sept. 2016, www.nytimes.com/2016/09/15/sports/golf/ariya-jutanugarns-evian-championship.html. Accessed 10 Apr. 2017.

"Thailand's Ariya Jutanugarn Wins Women's British Open." *The Big Story*, Associated Press, 31 July 2016, bigstory.ap.org/article/6db8569aab174df0aeb0423045025a12/thailands-ariya-jutanugarn-wins-womens-british-open. Accessed 10 Apr. 2017.

Wray, Cheryl. "Ariya Jutanugarn Wins Yokohama Tire LPGA Classic in Prattville." *AL.com*, Alabama Media Group, 8 May 2016, www.al.com/sports/index.ssf/2016/05/ariya_jutanugarn_wins_yokohama.html. Accessed 10 Apr. 2017.

Zenor, John. "Ariya Jutanugarn Becomes LPGA Tour's First Thai Winner." *The Big Story*, Associated Press, 8 May 2016, bigstory.ap.org/article/f3335fa212534432828b5b4b4947e863/ariya-jutanugarn-holds-alabama-first-lpga-tour-win. Accessed 10 Apr. 2017.

—*Molly Hagan*

Andrew Kaczynski

Date of birth: November 30, 1989
Occupation: Journalist

Andrew Kaczynski joined CNN as a political reporter in October 2016. Kaczynski began working for *BuzzFeed* in 2012 while he was still a college student at St. John's University in New York City. A former intern at the Republican National Committee (RNC), Kaczynski, by his own account, was drawn to political journalism after discovering a talent for rooting out old videos of politicians on the Internet. Kaczynski cut his teeth during the 2012 election, uncovering damning footage of Republican presidential candidate Mitt Romney contradicting himself on health care reform. But the reporter became a fixture of the field in the run-up to the 2016 presidential election, researching and fact-checking claims by front-runners Hillary Clinton and Donald Trump. As a reporter with CNN, Kaczynski broke several stories about Andrew Puzder, a fast-food executive who was President Trump's pick for the position of US secretary of labor in early 2017. The stories created such a cloud over Puzder that he withdrew his nomination in February.

EARLY LIFE AND CAREER

Kaczynski was raised in a suburb of Cleveland, Ohio. His father, Stephen J. Kaczynski, is a partner with the international law firm Jones Day, where he served as a senior litigator on the national coordinating counsel team for the R. J. Reynolds Tobacco Company. His mother, Theresa Kaczynski, was a teacher's aide and later a stay-at-home mother. At the age of nineteen, Kaczynski was diagnosed with pancreatitis; after his bout with the illness, he neither smokes nor drinks alcohol. At the private Cleveland Benedictine High School, Kaczynski wrote for the school newspaper, the *Bennet*. He graduated in 2008 and enrolled as a student at Ohio University in Athens, Ohio. He studied at Ohio University for two years before he transferred to St. John's University in the Queens borough of New York City, where he studied early American history. While he was a student there, he interned

By Some Brooklynguy [CC BY 2.0], via Wikimedia Commons

for the RNC and the offices of Dana Rohrabacher, a Republican US representative for California, and Bob Turner, a former US representative for New York who took over the seat vacated after Anthony Weiner was ousted in 2011.

Kaczynski also developed an interesting hobby. In 2011, Kaczynski unearthed an embarrassing video clip of New York Assemblyman David Weprin, Turner's Democratic opponent in the special election, dancing at a Brooklyn festival in 2009. He posted the video on his Twitter page, and it quickly went viral. The video was posted by national news outlets, including the *New York Times*, and was featured on a segment of the late-night comedy show *Jimmy Kimmel Live*. "I realized there's this space to fill for people who want to see politically related videos, whether archival or recent," he told a reporter for the St. John's University website. "They're so polished and put forth an image they want people to accept, but these videos really show how they've evolved until their current political self appears." Living in a Russian family's basement in Queens, Kaczynski spent hours searching for old video footage of politicians on the Internet between classes at St. John's, combing over a variety of sources, including Google Videos, YouTube, AOL Video, the C-SPAN archives, and local news sites. One of his first targets was Texas politician Rick Perry, who had recently entered the Republican primary race for president. Kaczynski found and posted some of Perry's earliest political advertisements. When Kaczynski found something interesting, he sent it to Ben Smith, then an editor at the political news website

Politico. When Smith left the site to become the editor in chief at *BuzzFeed* in late 2011, he hired Kaczynski as a part-time contributor. Kaczynski was one of the first reporters in the site's news division. He officially began the job in January 2012, and he ultimately left university to work full time without completing his degree.

2012 PRESIDENTIAL ELECTION

During the 2012 election, Kaczynski found a number of compromising videos of Republican presidential candidate Mitt Romney. "I hate to pick on Mitt Romney," he told Jason Zengerle for *New York Magazine* (11 Dec. 2011). "I think he's the most electable Republican other than [former Utah governor Jon] Huntsman." Kaczynski's interest in the candidate was twofold; people seemed to enjoy videos that reinforced Romney's socially awkward persona—in one video unearthed by Kaczynski, Romney tells a teenager at a local festival that he likes "music of almost any kind, including this"—but Kaczynski was also trying to parse Romney's hazy ideology after the candidate had been leveled with charges of flip-flopping on key positions.

Romney, a former Republican governor of Massachusetts, a strongly liberal state, gained traction during the Republican primaries by touting his conservative bona fides. He was particularly critical of President Barack Obama's health care plan, the Patient Protection and Affordable Care Act, popularly known as Obamacare. Romney made repealing Obamacare the centerpiece of his campaign, but his aversion to the legislation was odd considering that he had signed into law a similar health care policy in Massachusetts in 2006. Romney repeatedly insisted that the two plans were totally different and that he had never intended for his model to be implemented at the national level, but it did not take long for Kaczynski to challenge his claim. In March 2012, several months before Romney won the Republican nomination, Kaczynski unearthed a 2009 op-ed that Romney had written for *USA Today*, as well as three different interview clips from the same year, in which Romney urged President Obama to use the Massachusetts health care plan as a template for Obamacare. "You can find the history of everybody," Kaczynski told Jeff Sonderman for *Poynter* (20 Mar. 2012). "The Internet is an archive in itself now, and when something gets put on YouTube, it's there forever. You can really find anything that you need on these people."

FEUD WITH RAND PAUL

In many ways, the campaign preparation for the 2016 presidential election began shortly after President Obama was inaugurated to his second term in 2013, and Kaczynski, and his small band of political researchers at *BuzzFeed*, known as the K-File, began digging for dirt on presidential hopefuls early on. In October 2013, MSNBC talk show host Rachel Maddow aired a segment about Rand Paul, a US senator for Kentucky, plagiarizing a *Wikipedia* entry in a speech. Shortly thereafter, Kaczynski published other examples of the senator doing the same thing. In the article "Rand Paul Has Given Speeches Plagiarized from Wikipedia Before" (29 Oct. 2013), Kaczynski noted that in a June 2013 speech, Paul had used passages from the *Wikipedia* page on the 1988 film *Stand and Deliver*. A few days later, Kaczynski found that an entire passage of Paul's 2012 book *Government Bullies* was plagiarized from a 2003 case study from the conservative think tank the Heritage Foundation. Another passage came from a report by a senior fellow at the conservative Cato Institute. Paul dismissed Kaczynski's reporting, taking umbrage at being called "dishonest," he said in a speech as reported by Annalisa Quinn for NPR's *The Two-Way* (4 Nov. 2013). "If dueling were legal in Kentucky, if they keep it up, it'd be a duel challenge," he said.

In June 2015, Kaczynski and fellow *BuzzFeed* reporter Megan Apper found that many of the quotes attributed to Founding Fathers in Paul's books *Government Bullies* and *The Tea Party Goes to Washington* (2011) were "either fake, misquoted, or taken entirely out of context." Fake Founding Fathers quotes are favorite niche beat for Kaczynski—he has outed a handful of politicians, including former Arkansas governor Mike Huckabee, for fabricating such quotes—but Paul's missteps in that regard became an ongoing story. Kaczynski found Paul using fake historical quotes in speeches to constituents and in Congress on a number of occasions. Kaczynski and Apper published an article in the cheeky spirit of *BuzzFeed* (27 Oct. 2015) that was composed as a letter to the senator citing similar objections to a slew of false quotations in Paul's 2015 book, *Our Presidents & Their Prayers: Proclamations of Faith by America's Leaders*. Many of the purported quotations, the reporters wrote, were revealed to be fake after a quick Internet search.

2016 PRESIDENTIAL ELECTION

Keeping politicians honest in the manner Kaczynski had practiced since 2012 became an increasingly Sisyphean task as the election wore on. Still, Kaczynski and his team managed to break a few stories that shaped election coverage. In November 2015, Kaczynski and his colleague Nathan McDermott published a 1998 video clip of Republican candidate Ben Carson giving a commencement address in which he asserts that the Egyptian pyramids were built by the biblical figure Joseph for the purpose of storing grain. (When CBS News reached out to Carson for comment in response to Kaczynski's reporting, Carson confirmed that he still held this view.) The same year, Kaczynski challenged former secretary of state and Democratic candidate Hillary Clinton's assertion that all four of her grandparents were immigrants; only one was foreign-born. They also found a 1996 video clip of Clinton referring to children in gangs as "superpredators."

Kaczynski and McDermott broke the K-File's biggest story in the campaign in February 2016. On the campaign trail, Republican candidate Donald Trump repeatedly insisted that he had opposed the American invasion of Iraq. Kaczynski found a September 2002 clip from *The Howard Stern Show* radio program in which Trump says that he supported the invasion. Kaczynski went on to cite other sources, including Trump's 2000 book, *The American We Deserve*, and a 2003 interview with Neil Cavuto that reinforce Trump's supportive stance. Kaczynski broke other major news regarding Trump when he found evidence that former Ku Klux Klan leader David Duke had urged followers to support the candidate. In the fall, Kaczynski unearthed a clip of Trump's cameo in a 2000 soft-core porn video for Playboy.

JOINING CNN

In early October 2016, one month before the election, Kaczynski and his investigative team accepted positions with the news network CNN. Andrew Morse, the executive vice president of the network and the head of CNN Digital, said that Kaczynski first caught his attention after the story about Trump's stance on the Iraq War months earlier. Smith was reportedly unhappy about losing Kaczynski and the K-File team, but he wished Kaczynski the best, telling Sridhar Pappu for the *New York Times* (16 Oct. 2016), "He's a great person, a brilliant researcher, and the ultimate one-man show—I'm sure he'll do great wherever he goes." Kaczynski was positive about the transition. "To be at the biggest name in news for the last month of what has been the craziest election in modern history is just a great opportunity for me and everybody on our team," he told Michael Calderone for the *Huffington Post* (3 Oct. 2016). Kaczynski explained his decision to join CNN to Pappu, stating, "When I worked at *BuzzFeed*, it was always validation for me when my stories were getting talked about on MSNBC or CNN or Fox News."

As a reporter for CNN, Kaczynski broke several stories about Trump's labor secretary nominee Puzder, the former chief executive of CKE Restaurants, which owns the fast food chains Hardee's and Carl's Jr. On January 23, 2017, Kaczynski published the transcripts of two separate 2011 speeches in which Puzder disparaged his own employees as "the best of the worst," a characterization at odds with his public statements. About two weeks later, Kaczynski, with K-File teammate Chris Massie, published a story revealing that Puzder had previously described about 40 percent of his employees as undocumented immigrants. (Puzder had made several comments to that effect over a number of years.) This detail in particular sat uneasily with Republicans in Congress. Puzder subsequently withdrew his nomination.

PERSONAL LIFE

Kaczynski is engaged to Rachel Louise Ensign, a banking reporter for the *Wall Street Journal.* They live in Brooklyn.

SUGGESTED READING

Ember, Sydney. "Four from BuzzFeed Politics Defect to CNN." *The New York Times*, 3 Oct. 2016, www.nytimes.com/2016/10/04/business/media/four-from-buzzfeed-politics-defect-to-cnn.html. Accessed 9 June 2017.

Pappu, Sridhar. "A Onetime BuzzFeed Wunderkind, Now at CNN." *The New York Times*, 15 Oct. 2016, www.nytimes.com/2016/10/16/style/andrew-kaczynski-buzzfeed-politics-cnn.html. Accessed 9 June 2017.

Quinn, Annalisa. "Book News: Rand Paul to Plagiarism Accusers: 'If Dueling Were Legal in Kentucky . . .'" *The Two-Way*, NPR, 4 Nov. 2013, www.npr.org/sections/thetwoway/2013/11/04/242935941/book-news-rand-paul-to-plagiarism-accusers-if-dueling-were-legal-in-kentucky. Accessed 9 June 2017.

"St. John's Student Goes Viral." *St. John's University*, www.stjohns.edu/academics/schools-and-colleges/st-johns-college-liberal-arts-and-sciences/success-stories/andrew-kaczynski. Accessed 9 June 2017.

Sonderman, Jeff. "How BuzzFeed's Andrew Kaczynski Mines the Internet for Video Gold." *Poynter*, 20 Mar. 2012, www.poynter.org/2012/how-buzzfeeds-andrew-kaczynski-mines-the-internet-for-video-gold/166797. Accessed 9 June 2017.

—*Molly Hagan*

Daniel Kaluuya

Date of birth: May 8, 1989
Occupation: Actor

Daniel Kaluuya is an English actor best known for his starring role in the 2017 American horror movie *Get Out*. In the film, written and directed by actor Jordan Peele of the comedy television show *Key & Peele*, Kaluuya plays an African

Rodin Eckenroth/Getty Images for Universal Home Entertainment

American photographer named Chris who accompanies his white girlfriend, played by Allison Williams, on a trip to meet her parents. Though his girlfriend tries to reassure him, Kaluuya's character is uneasy about the trip and her parents' disconcertingly enthusiastic welcome. Bad omens accumulate, and soon Chris finds himself living in a nightmare. *Get Out* is a sharp satire indicting liberal racism; it is also, as critics attest, genuinely frightening, illustrating the ways in which white people inadvertently terrorize the black people who enter their lives. Peele marries classic horror tropes with images that evoke slavery and instances of police brutality—depicting an "evil," as critic Manohla Dargis wrote in her glowing review for the *New York Times* (23 Feb. 2017), "that isn't obscured by a hockey mask."

It was precisely this visceral, real-life dimension of *Get Out*—which Kaluuya has described as "groundedness" in various interviews—that attracted the actor to the script in the first place. "I remember sending an email to my agent which said, 'This is *12 Years a Slave: The Horror Movie*,'" he told Ashley Clark for the *Guardian* (18 Mar. 2017), referencing the hyperrealistic, Academy Award–winning 2013 film about American slavery. *Get Out* was Kaluuya's first starring role in an American film, though he appeared in the 2015 film *Sicario* with actors Emily Blunt and Benicio del Toro. Kaluuya, who is also a writer, got his start writing and acting for the British television series *Skins* in 2007. He will appear in the highly anticipated superhero film *Black Panther*, slated for release in 2018.

EARLY LIFE AND EDUCATION

Kaluuya was born on May 8, 1989. His mother is Ugandan but moved to London to give birth to Kaluuya. The actor and his mother lived in hostels across the city, but when Kaluuya was two years old, they moved to Camden in North London. Camden, the birthplace of British punk music, is a working-class neighborhood and is also, as Kaluuya wrote in an article for *Vice* (24 Feb. 2017), "the biggest drug market in Europe."

Kaluuya showed his artistic stripes early. When he was nine years old, he wrote a play inspired by the popular 1990s teen sketch comedy show *Kenan & Kel*. "I was obsessed by their dynamic," Kaluuya recalled to Emma Brown for *Interview Magazine* (24 Feb. 2017), adding that his own play "was just two guys that worked at McDonald's or something." The play won a competition at his school and was later performed at Hampstead Theatre. On his mother's suggestion, he soon began acting, taking an improv class at the Anna Scher Theatre in nearby Islington. Still, throughout Kaluuya's teenage years, writing appeared to be his primary passion. He wrote more plays for the Hampstead Theatre's youth theater and London's National Youth Theatre.

SKINS

Kaluuya attended an all-boys Catholic high school in North London called St. Aloysius, but by his own admission, he was a poor student. His mother pushed him to get better grades, but he was bored by the material. "I knew from an early age that school was a test of your memory, rather than a test of your intellectualism," he wrote in the *Vice* article. At sixteen, he got a job as a runner for a shopping channel, but he soon booked his first acting gig, a role in a TV movie called *Shoot the Messenger* (2006), starring David Oyelowo. "It was quite surreal being on set and going back at school," he wrote for *Vice*.

In 2007, when Kaluuya was seventeen years old, he landed a job as a writer on a new television show called *Skins*. The show was about a group of friends attending school in Bristol, but its inclusion of young writers and performers made it unique among shows depicting teenage life. Kaluuya, who later played a character named Posh Kenneth on the show, recalls writing down quips he heard from his friends at school and bringing them into the writers' room. "What's great about *Skins* is that the characters are exactly like people around you," Kaluuya told Chris Green for the *Independent* (11 Feb. 2008). *Skins* aired on the British channel E4 from 2007 to 2013 and launched the careers of a number of writers and actors, including Nicholas Hoult, Hannah Murray, Joe Dempsie, and Dev Patel. The show was popular with audiences and critics alike; ten years after it premiered, Rebecca Nicholson, in an article for the *Guardian* (25

Jan. 2017), wrote that "watching it again makes it clear that it's still great. It's a brilliant, original drama, full of warmth and wit and fun, still entertaining, still outrageous, and still far more grown-up than it ever let on."

EARLY CAREER

After working on *Skins*, Kaluuya landed an agent and appeared in a handful of plays, television shows, and movies. In 2009 he appeared in an episode of the long-running television series *Doctor Who* called "Planet of the Dead," and in 2010 he starred in a play called *Sucker Punch* by award-winning playwright Roy Williams at London's Royal Court Theatre. Set in the 1980s, the play follows the story of two black boxers from South London. In 2011, Kaluuya appeared in an episode of *Black Mirror*, a British television anthology series in the mold of the 1960s science-fiction series *The Twilight Zone*. Kaluuya's episode, called "Fifteen Million Merits," remains one of the show's best known. In it, Kaluuya's character, Bing, lives in a dystopian world wherein people pedal stationary bikes to power the city in which they live. Based on how much they pedal, they earn points for food or the chance to appear on a competitive reality television show.

In 2013, Kaluuya appeared in the British premiere of Aimé Césaire's 1966 play *A Season in the Congo* at the Young Vic in London. (The production starred Chiwetel Ejiofor, most famous for his starring role in *12 Years a Slave*.) The play follows the story of Congolese leader Patrice Lumumba and, through that story, explores decolonization in the Congo in the 1950s and early 1960s. Kaluuya won praise in the role of Mobutu Sese Seko, who, after Lumumba's death, serves as the country's military dictator for more than thirty years. Also in 2013, Kaluuya had a small role in the American movie *Kick-Ass 2*, an action comedy starring Chloe Grace Moretz, and in 2015 he played a larger role in the American drama *Sicario*, a thriller about Mexican drug cartels. Kaluuya played an FBI agent alongside actor Emily Blunt. The film premiered at the Cannes Film Festival in 2015 and was nominated for three Academy Awards.

Although Kaluuya was beginning to dip his toes into the Hollywood pool, he never left British theater entirely. In 2016, he appeared in a revival of Joe Penhall's Olivier Award–winning play *Blue/Orange* at the Young Vic. Kaluuya was praised for his performance as Christopher, a young man suffering from mental illness who desperately wants to leave the psychiatric hospital where he has spent the last twenty-eight days. The play explores issues of mental health, race, and power.

GET OUT

Kaluuya read an early draft of Peele's script for *Get Out* and immediately wanted to be a part of it. In March 2015 he interviewed with Peele over Skype, and several months later, after *Sicario*'s premiere, the actor formally auditioned for the lead role in Los Angeles. Peele was impressed by Kaluuya's role in *Black Mirror*, which places the actor in a similarly nightmarish world. Kaluuya told Clark for the *Guardian* that Peele sent him a list of horror films to watch in preparation for the role, but Kaluuya did not do so: "I'd be too aware of it being a film, a fiction," he told Clark. "I just like playing guys, normal dudes. That's the stuff I really enjoy watching, when it feels grounded." In a number of interviews, Kaluuya said he drew on his own experiences as a dark-skinned black man to prepare for his role. In one harrowing episode in 2010, Kaluuya was pulled off of a bus in Camden, thrown to the ground by four police officers, and strip-searched at the local police station. Wrongly identified as a suspected drug dealer, Kaluuya contends that he was stopped because of his race, and he sued the police department in 2014. *Get Out*, which was also directed by Peele, was shot in a whirlwind twenty-three days and premiered to critical and popular acclaim in February 2017. Despite the film's paltry $4.5 million budget, it went on to make nearly $200 million, making it the highest-grossing original debut in Hollywood history.

Peele described the film as a "social thriller" to Brandon Harris for the *New Yorker* (4 Mar. 2017). "In a social thriller, the monster at hand is society," he said. Elaborating on this point, Harris wrote, "The movie's sharp scares, gallows humor, and insidious intelligence are informed by the sensibility, and insistent paranoia, that lurks within the hearts of blacks who must navigate white spaces." Amid celebration of the film and Kaluuya's performance, the actor found himself on the receiving end of a critical comment from legendary African American actor Samuel L. Jackson. Jackson criticized Hollywood for casting British actors as African American characters in movies and television shows—a surprisingly common practice—but he also questioned Kaluuya's ability, as a Brit, to relate to the racism that the film portrays. Kaluuya expressed admiration for Jackson, but frustration with the actor's comments. "I really respect African American people. I just want to tell black stories," he told Shakeil Greely for *GQ Magazine* (13 Mar. 2017). "This is the frustrating thing, bro—in order to prove that I can play this role, I have to open up about the trauma that I've experienced as a black person. I have to show off my struggle so that people accept that I'm black. No matter that every single room I go to I'm usually the darkest person there. You know what I'm saying? I kind of resent that mentality. I'm just an individual."

SUGGESTED READING

Clark, Ashley. "Get Out Star Daniel Kaluuya: 'This Is 12 Years a Slave: The Horror Movie.'" *The Guardian*, 18 Mar. 2017, www.theguardian.com/film/2017/mar/18/get-out-daniel-kaluuya-horror-movie-jordan-peele. Accessed 2 May 2017.

Dargis, Manohla. "Review: In 'Get Out,' Guess Who's Coming to Dinner? (Bad Idea!)." Review of *Get Out*, directed by Jordan Peele. *The New York Times*, 23 Feb. 2017, www.nytimes.com/2017/02/23/movies/get-out-review-jordan-peele.html. Accessed 2 May 2017.

Green, Chris. "Teen Writers Show Their 'Skins.'" *The Independent*, 11 Feb. 2008, www.independent.co.uk/news/media/teen-writers-show-their-skins-780666.html. Accessed 2 May 2017.

Harris, Brandon. "The Giant Leap Forward of Jordan Peele's 'Get Out.'" Review of *Get Out*, directed by Jordan Peele. *The New Yorker*, 4 Mar. 2017, www.newyorker.com/culture/culture-desk/review-the-giant-leap-forward-of-jordan-peeles-get-out. Accessed 2 May 2017.

Kaluuya, Daniel. "Daniel Kaluuya's Journey from the Streets of London to Hollywood." *Vice*, 24 Feb. 2017, www.vice.com/en_us/article/daniel-kaluuya-early-works-interview. Accessed 2 May 2017.

Kaluuya, Daniel. "Daniel Kaluuya's Next Move." Interview by Emma Brown. *Interview Magazine*, 24 Feb. 2017, www.interviewmagazine.com/film/daniel-kaluuya-1. Accessed 2 May 2017.

Kaluuya, Daniel. "Get Out Star Daniel Kaluuya: 'I Resent That I Have to Prove I'm Black.'" Interview by Shakeil Greeley. *GQ Magazine*, 13 Mar. 2017, www.gq.com/story/daniel-kaluuya-get-out-interview. Accessed 2 May 2017.

Nicholson, Rebecca. "10 Years of Skins: The Show That Revealed the Explicit Truth about Teenage Life." *The Guardian*, 25 Jan. 2017, www.theguardian.com/tv-and-radio/2017/jan/25/skins-tv-teenage-life-truth-10-years-on. Accessed 2 May 2017.

SELECTED WORKS

Skins, 2007–13; *Sicario*, 2015; *Get Out*, 2017

—*Molly Hagan*

Mary Jepkosgei Keitany

Date of birth: January 18, 1982
Occupation: Runner

Mary Jepkosgei Keitany is a Kenyan long-distance runner and the second-fastest woman marathoner ever. In 2017, Keitany won her third London Marathon with a time of 2:17:01, setting a world record for women-only marathons and coming in second for the all-time record behind Paula Radcliffe, who posted a time of 2:15:25 in a mixed-gender setting at the 2005 London Marathon. (The International Association of Athletics Federations, or IAAF, recognizes two records for female athletes: "mixed gender," for races that include both men and women, and "women only.") The previous year, Keitany had won her third consecutive New York City Marathon, becoming the first person to win the women's race three years in a row since 1986 (the sixth consecutive win of late Norwegian Olympian Grete Waitz), and did so by the largest margin of victory—about three and a half minutes—since 1980.

Keitany, who grew up in a small village in Kenya's Rift Valley Province, always knew she wanted to be a runner. After winning a local race, she was afforded an opportunity to pursue her dream, and finish school, at the National Hidden Talents Academy in Nairobi. She graduated in 2005, and focused on half marathons, shattering records around the world, before making her highly-anticipated marathon debut in New York in 2010. Unlike most contemporary elite

By Acrb [GFDL CC BY-SA 3.0], via Wikimedia Commons

runners, Keitany trains by instinct. This attitude could be attributed to a faulty watch that threw off her split times in the 2011 New York marathon or merely experience; whatever the reason, she told Nick Pachelli for the *New Yorker* (5 Nov. 2016) that she rarely thinks about her splits, particularly while she is running. "I just follow my fatigue," she said. "With this, I can push my pace or go a bit easier or go and make a move."

EARLY LIFE AND EDUCATION

Keitany was born on January 18, 1982, in Kisok, a village in the Baringo District (now Baringo County) of Kenya's former Rift Valley Province. She was the fourth of six children, and her parents, both of Kalenjin descent, worked as subsistence farmers. It was a difficult life, Keitany recalled to Joe Battaglia for the website FloTrack (26 Oct. 2015). "My parents . . . have cattle to raise and they have a farm to dig and do the plantation," she said. "They grow maize, beans, and other vegetables. It was not easy growing up because my parents work hard but basically have nothing."

Keitany began running while she was a student at Kanjulul Primary School. Her family did not have enough money to send her to secondary school, so she worked on the family farm in Koibatek for a year. Keitany had big dreams, though: she dreamed of one day riding in an airplane, and of becoming a professional athlete like her heroes, Paul Tergat, who held the marathon world record from 2003 to 2007, and Tegla Loroupe, the first African woman to win the New York City Marathon. She continued running, and after she won a race in the nearby town of Kabarnet, her brother-in-law saw her name in the newspaper and suggested that she move to Nairobi to attend a school for gifted runners, for which her family would not have to pay.

Keitany enrolled at the school, called the National Hidden Talents Academy, in 2002. Enos Oumo, a Ugandan refugee turned pastor, had founded the Dagoretti Corner Rehabilitation Centre for children in need in the early 1990s; the National Hidden Talents Academy was established as a program within the center to support academically and athletically gifted, but economically disadvantaged, children and teenagers. It was difficult for Keitany to leave her parents, she told Battaglia. Still, she said, "I knew if I stayed at home, there would be no secondary school for me for sure. So I said, 'Let me just go and do well in everything there.' I was going to work hard to become successful." Keitany lived and studied at the National Hidden Talents Academy for three years, training twice or three times a day and competing four or five times a semester. She ran both track and cross-country, but by the time she graduated in 2005, she knew she wanted to focus on road racing.

EARLY CAREER

Following the path of her idols Tergat and Loroupe, Keitany moved to Iten, Kenya, a small town overlooking the Great Rift Valley, about eight thousand feet above sea level. The modest training facilities in Iten generate the lion's share of the world's elite long-distance runners. Keitany ran her first major race, the Shoe4Africa ten-kilometer race (10K) in Iten, in the fall of 2006. She placed twenty-first in the race, in which only the first twenty finishers won prizes, but her performance impressed her then-coach, Philip Singoei, a champion marathon runner. Singoei encouraged Keitany, who had been competing primarily in 10K and 15K races, to try running longer distances. In December 2006, she boarded a plane for the first time to run the Medio Maratón de Sevilla (Seville Half Marathon) in Spain. She won that race, as well as the Corrida de São Silvestre dos Olivais (São Silvestre dos Olivais Race) 10K in Lisbon, Portugal, two weeks later. In early 2007, Keitany won two more half marathons, the Meia Maratona Manuela Machado (Manuela Machado Half Marathon) in Viana do Castelo, Portugal, and the Medio Maratón Ciudad de Almería (Almería Half Marathon) in Spain.

Also in 2007, Keitany began training with coach Gabriele Nicola and an elite group of runners, including Olympian Peninah Arusei and marathon specialist Helena Kirop, in Iten. In the spring, Keitany broke a personal record when she ran the Humarathon, a half marathon between Ivry-sur-Seine and Vitry-sur-Seine in France, in 1:08:36; in October, she broke her own record again, the 2007 IAAF World Road Running Championships (formerly and subsequently the World Half Marathon Championships) in Udine, Italy, in 1:06:48. She came in second behind Kenyan Dutch runner Lornah Kiplagat, who won the race in 1:06:25, a world record. Recalling the race, Keitany told Battaglia, "That was the first time I showed the world that I was capable of running very fast."

CHASING RECORDS

After marrying in 2007 and having her first child in 2008, Keitany marked her return to the sport in May 2009 with a new personal best time in the 10K, 32:09, placing second to Aselefech Mergia of Ethiopia at the World 10K Bengaluru in Bangalore, India. That September, she won the Semi-Marathon de Lille Métropole (Lille Métropole Half Marathon) in France with a time of 1:07:00, the fastest so far that year, making her a favorite in the 2009 IAAF World Half Marathon Championships in Birmingham, England, the following month.

Keitany won in Birmingham with a time of 1:06:36, the world's second-fastest women-only time after Kiplagat's world record at the same race in 2007 (and officially the World Half Marathon Championships women's record, since the 2007 race was technically the World Road Running Championships). The win and record came despite less than desirable conditions: the day was windy, the road was slick, and Keitany was understandably a bit strained, having been trapped in a full elevator for nearly an hour the day before. Mary Wittenberg, a former New York City Marathon race director, told David Powell for the IAAF website (11 Oct. 2009) that Keitany's natural talent and assured race demeanor that day would make her a great marathon runner, saying, "Mary clearly has what it takes. . . . She has the speed, the strength, and it looks like mental tenacity to be one of the best we have ever seen."

In January 2010 Keitany won the Zayed International Half Marathon in Abu Dhabi, a goal she had set for her post-pregnancy return. After following this victory with a world-record-breaking win (1:19:53) at the BIG 25 Berlin (25K) in Germany and then winning the London 10,000 (10K) with a personal best time of 31:06, Keitany decided to make her marathon debut in New York the same year.

RECORD BREAKER

Marathons, which cover just over 26.2 miles, require an entirely different set of skills, even for professional distance runners such as Keitany. At the New York City Marathon in November 2010, Keitany placed an impressive third in the women's race, with a time of 2:29:01. "After I finished, I was saying that maybe I will not run another marathon," she recalled to Battaglia. "My whole body was paralyzed. Both legs, my back, everywhere was feeling bad. I told [training partner] Helena [Kirop] and all of my training men that would be the last marathon for me."

In February 2011, Keitany shattered Kiplagat's half-marathon world record at the Ras Al Khaimah (RAK) Half Marathon in the United Arab Emirates, posting a time of 1:05:50. She was the first woman to break the sixty-six-minute mark. Couched in that record were four others: 20K (1:02:36), ten miles (50:05), 15K (46:40), and 8K (24:30).

A few months later, in April, Keitany found herself where she had said she would never be: at the starting line of her second marathon. Keitany's performance in the 2011 London Marathon established her as a fierce competitor at that distance. She won the race in 2:19:19, besting her previous time by nearly ten full minutes. Keitany returned to the New York City Marathon later that year, but a faulty watch confused her about her pace, prompting her to run too fast too soon, and she came in third again with a time of 2:23:38. The following year, in April 2012, Keitany took her second crack at the London Marathon and set a Kenyan national record, winning with a time of 2:18:37—the third-fastest time in women's marathon history.

OLYMPICS AND MORE MARATHONS

Keitany's career-defining moment at the 2012 London Marathon set high expectations for her Olympic debut at the 2012 Olympic Games later that year, also in London. Due in large part to the humidity, however, she finished in fourth place, with a time of 2:23:56. "What I can say is maybe I was not used to running in a rainy place," Keitany explained to Battaglia. "In Kenya when it is raining, we stay in, and then if the rain stops, we can go for the training. When it rained in London, it was harder for me to move on faster. The Olympics was just not my day."

After her Olympic disappointment, Keitany took another break from the sport. She returned again in 2014, setting course records at the Ottawa Race Weekend 10K (31:22) and the Great North Run half-marathon in North East England (1:05:39). In November, Keitany ran for the third time in the New York City Marathon and earned her first victory in the race, besting fellow Kenyan Jemima Sumgong in one of the closest races in the event's history. Far ahead of the pack, the two women battled one another for the last four miles of the race. Keitany won with a time of 2:25:07, three seconds faster than Sumgong.

In 2015 Keitany, who had recently struggled with bouts of pneumonia and malaria during training, made a second-place showing at the London Marathon in April. In November, however, she returned to the New York City Marathon to successfully defend her title, leaving Ethiopian Tigist Tufa, who had beaten her in London, in the dust. Keitany finished the marathon with a time of 2:24:25, shaving more than forty seconds off her previous year's time.

In 2016, Keitany finished ninth in the London Marathon. Her uncharacteristically poor showing was likely to blame for Kenya's decision to leave her off of its official Olympic team that year. (She did travel to the games in Rio de Janeiro, Brazil, as a reserve runner; her teammate Sumgong took home the gold.) But Keitany bounced back from her second Olympic disappointment to win her third consecutive New York City Marathon in November. Keitany pulled away from the pack in the tenth mile and finished out of sight of her competition in 2:24:26. Lindsay Crouse, writing for the *New York Times* (6 Nov. 2016), called it "an extraordinary race of one." Keitany's momentum carried her into 2017, and she returned to the London Marathon in April to win for the third time. She finished in 2:17:01, a world record for a women-only marathon event and the second-fastest time in women's marathon history.

PERSONAL LIFE

Keitany married Charles Koech, a fellow runner, in 2007. The couple's first child, Jared Kipchumba, was born in June 2008; their second, Samantha Cherop, was born in April 2013. Keitany and her family live in Iten.

SUGGESTED READING

Battaglia, Joe. "Kenya's Mary Keitany Looks to Continue Ascent at TCS New York City Marathon." *FloTrack*, FloSports, 26 Oct. 2015, www.flotrack.org/article/36254-kenyas-mary-keitany-looks-to-continue-ascent-at-tcs-new-york-city-marathon. Accessed 17 July 2017.

Crouse, Lindsay. "New York Marathon: Keitany Wins Third Title and Ghebreslassie Wins First." *The New York Times*, 6 Nov. 2016, www.nytimes.com/2016/11/06/sports/nyc-marathon-2016.html. Accessed 17 July 2017.

Pachelli, Nick. "Mary Keitany and the Power of Not Knowing." *The New Yorker*, 5 Nov. 2016, www.newyorker.com/news/sporting-scene/mary-keitany-power-not-knowing-marathon. Accessed 17 July 2017.

Powell, David. "Marathon Beckons for Keitany—World Half Marathon, Birmingham." *IAAF—International Association of Athletics Federation*, 11 Oct. 2009, www.iaaf.org/news/news/marathon-beckons-for-keitany-world-half-mar. Accessed 17 July 2017.

Rotich, Benard. "Victorious Mary Keitany Shifts Focus to World Championship." *Daily Nation*, 9 Nov. 2016, www.nation.co.ke/sports/athletics/Victorious-Mary-Keitany-shifts-focus-to-World-Championship/1100-3446726-t2j6d-dz/index.html. Accessed 17 July 2017.

—*Molly Hagan*

Angelique Kerber

Date of birth: January 18, 1988
Occupation: Tennis player

In September 2016, Angelique Kerber became the first professional tennis player from Germany to be ranked number one since Steffi Graf, who dominated the sport in the late 1980s and 1990s. Kerber turned pro almost fifteen years before reaching the number-one position, but only hit her stride in the five years leading up to it. After respectably grinding away for years on tour, Kerber unexpectedly won her way to the semifinals of the US Open in 2011. After a breakthrough 2012 season, a brief lull gave way

Julian Finney/Getty Images

to a sensational 2016 in which Kerber won two Grand Slam titles and became the best female tennis player in the world.

Kerber is a right-hander who plays with her left hand, and her style of play could be described as indefatigable. She is not necessarily the most graceful or naturally gifted player, but she is one of the most creative; Kerber finds a way to get it done. Previously known for her defensive play, Kerber has doubled down on her offense, a decision that has helped her rise. Louisa Thomas, for the *New Yorker* (2 Sept. 2016), described her transformation this way: "[Kerber] is a brawler whose game matches up well with big hitters, but also a smart, crafty, improvisational player with unusual strokes and a thrilling style. Her game is reactive but imaginative, using her opponent's pace but also using her strength, especially in her legs, to redirect the power and make it her own. With her consistency, she baits her opponents into trying too much, while her shotmaking punishes them for their safe retorts."

EARLY LIFE AND EDUCATION

Kerber was born on January 18, 1988, in Bremen, Germany. Her father, Slawek, is Polish, and her mother, Beata, is German. Kerber also has a sister named Jessica. Kerber's family moved to Kiel, Germany, when she was one; she began playing tennis with her father when she was three. Later, the family lived in an apartment at a tennis academy where Kerber trained and her parents worked. Her maternal grandparents own a training facility in Puszczykowo, Poland, named Centrum Tenisowe Angie after Kerber.

Kerber turned pro at fifteen in 2003, after she finished school, and played her first major tournament in Hasselt, Belgium, in 2006; she lost to Ana Ivanovic of Serbia in the second round.

EARLY CAREER

In May 2007, at the age of nineteen, Kerber broke the top one hundred in player rankings for the first time after winning four titles on the International Tennis Federation tour. She played Wimbledon and the French Open for the first time, but was unable to progress in either. The same was true at the US Open, where Kerber played superstar Serena Williams for the first time. Williams bested Kerber, 6–3, 7–5. At the 2008 Australian Open, Kerber beat Estonian Maret Ani in the first round. It was the first time in her career that she had advanced in a Grand Slam tournament. (The four Grand Slam tournaments are the Australian Open, the French Open, Wimbledon, and the US Open.) She lost to Francesca Schiavone of Italy in the second round. In 2009, she beat fellow German Andrea Petkovic to make it to the second round of the US Open, and in 2010, she lost to Russian star Svetlana Kuznetsova in the third round of the Australian Open. Kerber also made it to the third round of Wimbledon, where she lost to the Slovakia-born Australian Jarmila Wolfe. If Kerber's career seemed to be moving on a slow upward trajectory, the beginning of the 2011 season was a blow to that assumption. Kerber reached the second round of just three tournaments out of thirteen; she considered retiring.

At the US Open that year, Kerber, who was ranked ninety-second in the world, went on an unexpected run, winning five matches and reaching the semifinals of the Grand Slam tournament. She lost to the number nine seed, Samantha Stosur of Australia, who went on to beat Serena Williams for the title. It was Kerber's first taste of real professional success; by the time she had reached the quarterfinals, she had more than doubled her earnings for the year and halved her ranking. Fans were charmed by Kerber's "Cinderella run," as Mike Vorkunov for *NJ.com* (10 Sept. 2011) described it. Kerber, however, recognized her success not as an end, but as a beginning. When the tournament began, she recalled to the Associated Press (AP) (11 Sept. 2016), "I was just telling myself, 'OK, just win a few rounds, and then you can get main draw in Australia.'" By the time it was over, she saw the 2011 US Open as "the turnaround" of her career.

PROFESSIONAL RISE

In 2012, Kerber made it to the quarterfinals of the French open, and the semifinals at Wimbledon. She won her first two Women's Tennis Association (WTA) titles in Copenhagen and Paris,

and beat Venus Williams to make it to the quarterfinals of the Olympic Games in London. In August, Kerber broke Wimbledon champion and Olympic gold medalist Serena Williams's nineteen-match winning streak, beating her 6–4, 6–4 at the Western & Southern Open in Cincinnati. After the match, Ben Rothenberg for the *New York Times* (17 Aug. 2012) marveled that Kerber had "redefined her career over the last twelve months." Ranked fifth in the world, Kerber also made it to the WTA Tour Championships, in which the top eight players of the season face off against one another, for the first time.

Kerber's breakout season was followed by a less sensational 2013. That year, she won a title in Linz, Austria, but failed to make it past the second round at Wimbledon, falling to Estonia's Kaia Kanepi after three sets. She made it to the fourth round at both the French Open and US Open, and made her second appearance at the WTA Championships. Kerber ended the season ranked ninth in the world, and in December, decided to separate from her longtime coach, Torben Beltz, and begin working with Benjamin Ebrahimzadeh. In 2014, Kerber made it to the quarterfinals at Wimbledon, but lost to twenty-year-old Eugenie Bouchard of Canada, 6–3, 6–4. She maintained her number-nine ranking at season's end, but at beginning of 2015, after a tough series of losses, she saw herself slipping out of the top ten.

In February 2015, Kerber dropped Ebrahimzadeh and rehired Beltz. Together, Kerber and Beltz agreed that she needed to make a change. Kerber vowed to be more aggressive offensively, and developed a new focus on her fitness and endurance. Throughout the 2015 season and in the postseason, she told Bryan Armen Graham for *The Guardian* (11 Sept. 2016), "I really tried to play more intensely in practice and not play like maybe two, three hours just like that. I just go to court and spend a lot of hours as well on gym, or just make a lot of sprints and movement." With Beltz's help—as well as the help of Kerber's idol and friend Steffi Graf—Kerber was able to turn her 2015 season around, winning four WTA titles. She did not make it to the late rounds in any Grand Slam tournament, though she did turn in one of the best match performances of her career. Kerber lost to Belarusian Victória Azárenka in the third round of the US Open in a riveting, nearly three-hour confrontation. Her satisfaction in her performance, Kerber told Thomas later, made up for the loss. "It was not the feeling like I lost a match," she said. "It was more the feeling that I played good and she won it at the end, and this is what gives me a lot of confidence when I come to the new tournaments."

GRAND SLAM CHAMPION AND NUMBER ONE

In January 2016, after nearly losing in the first round, Kerber reached the finals of the Australian Open, where she faced off against Serena Williams. Both women were vying for an accolade once held by Graf: Williams was hoping to tie Graf's record as a twenty-two-time Grand Slam champion, while Kerber was hoping to become the first German to win a major tournament since Graf won the French Open in 1999. Williams, who is likely the greatest player the sport has ever seen, was the odds-on favorite to win the match, but after two hours, Kerber had upset the champion with a final score of 6–4, 3–6, 6–4. Williams was gracious in her defeat, seeming to even take some small pleasure in watching Kerber's decade-plus grind pay off. Kerber, meanwhile, was euphoric. In a rambling post-game speech, she said, as quoted by Nick McCarvel for *USA Today* (30 Jan. 2016), "My dream come true tonight, on this night. My whole life I was working so hard and now I can say that I'm a Grand Slam champion . . . . It sounds so crazy." Kerber, who had gone into the match ranked sixth, emerged as the number two women's player in the world.

Kerber won a tournament in Stuttgart in the spring, but lost in the first round of the French Open, complaining of a sore shoulder. After a period of rest, she appeared at Wimbledon as a fourth seed. Kerber admitted that she had succumbed to the pressure of being a newly minted Grand Slam champion in Paris, but at Wimbledon, she was able to tap into the focus she had found in Australia. Kerber faced off against Venus Williams in the semifinals, and beat the veteran 6–4, 6–4. She did not lose a single set at Wimbledon until she reached the final, a rematch with Serena Williams, who was still seeking her historic twenty-second victory. Williams scorched Kerber, 7–5, 6–3.

In August, Kerber competed for Germany in the 2016 Olympic Games in Rio de Janeiro, Brazil. Kerber made it to the final, but was defeated in a stunning upset by the number thirty-four seed, Monica Puig of Puerto Rico. Kerber went home with the silver medal. At the US Open in September, Kerber was all but guaranteed to become the number one female tennis player in the world after Karolína Plíšková of the Czech Republic knocked Serena Williams out of contention in the semifinals. Kerber faced off against Plíšková—who had beaten her in a final a month earlier in Cincinnati, Ohio—and came out on top, beating her in three sets, 6–3, 4–6, 6–4, to earn the second Grand Slam title of the season and also of her career.

Kerber's 2017 season got off to a rocky start with early losses on tour. She was knocked out of contention at the Australian Open in January in the fourth round and lost her number-one ranking to Williams, who won the title as well as her record twenty-third Grand Slam.

PERSONAL LIFE

Kerber moved to Poland in 2012 to be close to her grandparents, and owns a house there, though she continues to compete for Germany. In her free time, she enjoys swimming, soccer, Formula 1 (F1), figure skating, handball, shopping, sleeping, swimming, dancing, and hanging out with friends.

SUGGESTED READING

Associated Press "New No. 1, U.S. Open Champion Angelique Kerber: 'It Still Sounds a Little Bit Crazy.'" *Tennis*, 11 Sept. 2016, www.tennis.com/pro-game/2016/09/us-open-champ-kerber-starting-to-like-sound-of-no-1-ranking/60985. Accessed 18 Feb. 2017.

Graham, Bryan Armen. "Angelique Kerber Says Patience and Hard Graft Turned Her into No. 1." *The Guardian*, 11 Sept. 2016, www.theguardian.com/sport/2016/sep/11/angelique-kerber-world-no1-karolina-pliskova-us-open-womens-final-serena-williams. Accessed 19 Feb. 2017.

McCarvel, Nick. "Angelique Kerber Stuns Serena Williams in Australian Open Final." *USA Today*, 30 Jan. 2016, www.usatoday.com/story/sports/tennis/aus/2016/01/30/angelique-kerber-stuns-serena-williams-australian-open-final/79560674. Accessed 19 Feb. 2017.

Rothenberg, Ben. "For Williams Sisters, a Split in Cincinnati." *New York Times*, 17 Aug. 2012, www.nytimes.com/2012/08/18/sports/tennis/serena-williams-is-upset-at-western-southern-open.html. Accessed 18 Feb. 2017.

Thomas, Louisa. "The Mysterious Transformation of Angelique Kerber." *New Yorker*, 2 Sept. 2016, www.newyorker.com/news/sporting-scene/the-mysterious-transformation-of-angelique-kerber. Accessed 18 Feb. 2017.

Vorkunov, Mike. "U.S. Open: Samantha Stosur downs Angelique Kerber in semifinals." *NJ.com*, 10 Sept. 2011, www.nj.com/tennis/index.ssf/2011/09/us_open_sam_stosur_downs_angel.html. Accessed 18 Feb. 2017.

—*Molly Hagan*

Chloe Kim

Date of Birth: April 23, 2000
Occupation: Snowboarder

If Chloe Kim's success in competitions such as the Winter X Games and Youth Olympic Games (YOG) are any indication, she may be one of the best elite snowboarders in the world—and one

Tom Pennington/Getty Images

of the youngest. At sixteen, she has amassed an impressive array of medals earned in national and international competitions. Her skill in snowboarding events such as the halfpipe has enabled her to break the records set by many of the elite female snowboarders who came before and set new milestones of her own. At the 2016 US Grand Prix, held in Park City, Utah, Kim completed two consecutive 1080 maneuvers while competing in the halfpipe event. The first woman ever to achieve that feat, she went on to receive a perfect score for her run.

Kim began snowboarding at an early age, and it was not always apparent that she would become a major force in the sport. "I definitely didn't like it at the beginning," Kim recalled to Nelson Rice for *Sports Illustrated* (27 Jan. 2016). "Probably because I was four and it was cold out." She soon became devoted to the sport, which has brought her opportunities most teens would never dream of. "Every time I'm on the mountain, I'm just so thankful to be there," she told Rachel Axon for *USA Today* (21 Jan. 2015). "And I'm always texting my friends, 'Haha, how's school going?'"

EARLY LIFE AND EDUCATION
Chloe Kim was born on April 23, 2000, in Long Beach, California. She was the third of three daughters born to Jong Jin Kim and Boran Yun Kim. Her father worked in engineering, while her mother worked for Korean Air. Her parents were born in South Korea but met in Switzerland prior to immigrating to the United States. Growing up in La Palma, California, Kim

attended elementary and middle school at La Palma Christian School. She later enrolled in the Independent Learning Center at Mammoth High School, which allowed her to continue her education by scheduling her schoolwork around her training sessions and competitions.

When Kim was four years old, her father took her to Mountain High Resort, a winter resort located in Southern California's San Gabriel Mountains. There, he established the foundation for Kim's later mastery of snowboarding as his daughter learned the basics of the sport. "My dad pretty much dragged me into it," she recalled to Audrey Cleo Yap for *NBC News* (23 May 2016). However, Kim quickly demonstrated her skill in the sport and did not remain a reluctant snowboarder for long. "My dad was like, 'All right, she's really good so we're going to start doing this for real,'" she told Axon. She began participating in snowboarding competitions as the age of six and soon began to compete on the national level.

TRAINING
Although Kim primarily lived in California, she spent third and fourth grades in Geneva, Switzerland, where she lived with her aunt. When her father visited, the two would travel across the border into France, where Kim would practice her sport at a local mountain resort. While in Switzerland, Kim learned to speak fluent French, adding the language to her repertoire alongside English and Korean. After returning to the United States, Kim began to train at California's Mammoth Mountain. Initially, Kim and her parents traveled to the mountain on weekends and rented a home nearby when necessary, but they later purchased a property closer to Kim's training grounds.

For a time, Kim supplemented her snowboarding training with skateboarding, with the hope that it would improve her ability to compete in halfpipe events. The strategy gave her a competitive edge and provided her with a strong foundation for her later efforts. Indeed, US Olympic snowboarding coach Mike Jankowski cited Kim's training background as having been critical to her success, telling Rice, "You can really tell when someone has that touch on the snow with the way they approach the mountain and attack the mountain. Chloe has that."

COMPETITIVE SUCCESS
Kim has made appearances in numerous competitions both within the United States and internationally. She joined the US snowboarding team in 2013. That year, Kim competed in several international events, including the Burton European Junior Open, in which she placed first in both halfpipe and slopestyle events. In halfpipe events, snowboarders ride down a snow-covered

curved ditch and are often propelled into the air, performing tricks such as spins all the while. In slopestyle events, the athletes ride down a declined course that features a variety of obstacles used to perform a variety of maneuvers.

In 2014 Kim made her first appearance in the Winter X Games, an extreme sports competition operated by the broadcaster ESPN. Entering the superpipe competition, Kim demonstrated her ability to compete on the signature extra-large halfpipe, placing second in the women's division. She returned to the X Games the following two years and competed in the 2016 X Games Oslo, held in Norway, earning first place in the women's superpipe event in each. In the World Snowboard Tour, in which Kim competed beginning in 2013, she earned consecutive honors for the halfpipe in 2015 and 2016 and also placed first in her division overall in 2014.

Perhaps Kim's most significant accomplishment came at the 2016 US Grand Prix. Although Kim performed well at previous Grand Prix competitions, she made history in 2016 when, during her halfpipe run, she completed two back-to-back 1080 maneuvers. In a 1080, an airborne snowboarder spins 1,080 degrees in the air and lands successfully—a difficult feat when performed once, let alone twice in a row. Kim became the first woman to achieve that milestone in a competition, also scoring a perfect score of 100 for her run. Even more surprising was the fact that Kim did not plan to complete the difficult maneuver. "It was definitely pretty spontaneous," she told Yap. "I think I did it once at the X Games during practice. I didn't think I would get it at the Grand Prix. It was pretty crazy actually."

THE FUTURE OF SNOWBOARDING

In light of both her age and her success in the sport, Kim has frequently been called the future of snowboarding. Among other successful female snowboarders, Kim is often compared to Kelly Clark, a veteran snowboarder who won a gold medal in the sport at the 2002 Olympics and has continued to compete in the X Games and other major competitions. Although some sports commentators tend to pit the two against each other in a rivalry, Kim considers Clark to be a mentor, and Clark herself has expressed her hope that younger snowboarders such as Kim will build upon her successes and achieve new feats in the sport.

Although snowboarding, like many of the sports included in the X Games, tends to be dominated by male athletes, Kim has never viewed her status as a female snowboarder as a challenge, or even something worth notice. "I've never really thought about it in that way," she told Hannah May for *Popmania* (10 May 2016). "I mean, it's always a good time. I feel like, the

women are slowly catching up to the men, so it's nice to see."

OLYMPIC HOPES

As Kim's success in national and international competitions has demonstrated, her skill level would certainly qualify her to compete with the US snowboarding team in the Winter Olympic Games. "She rides with a tremendous amount of amplitude and carries a lot more speed than any other female in the halfpipe," US Snowboarding halfpipe coach Ricky Bower told Yap. "She's in a whole different league. There's really no one that can ride like that." However, despite her skill and dedication to the sport, Kim was unable to compete in the 2014 Winter Olympics in Sochi, Russia, as she was only thirteen years old at the time. Although she would have appreciated having the opportunity to compete, she acknowledged in interviews that the pressure would have been difficult to manage. Her parents concurred, with her father commenting in interviews that the age regulations in place prevent overly competitive parents from pushing their children to compete too early. Although unable to compete in the 2014 games, Kim later traveled to Lillehammer, Norway, in 2016 to participate in the Youth Olympic Games. Continuing her string of successes, she placed first in her division in the halfpipe and slopestyle events.

In addition to the many US and international events in which she regularly competes, Kim has set her sights on the 2018 Winter Olympics, scheduled to take place in Pyeongchang, South Korea. The opportunity to compete in Pyeongchang would be a particularly meaningful one for Kim, as her parents were born in South Korea, and some of Kim's family members still live there. Based on her performance in competitions such as the X Games and the Grand Prix, Kim's coaches predict that she will not only make the Olympic team but also excel in the competitions themselves. "She's just riding that good," Bower told Yap. "Going forward, she's got Olympic gold medals in halfpipe and maybe even slopestyle."

PERSONAL LIFE

Although Kim has devoted much of her life to snowboarding, she is likewise well aware of the need to plan for her future and has told interviewers that she hopes one day to go to college. "Snowboarding is a huge part of my life, but I also feel like it's important to have a plan B or a back-up plan for after my career because I can't snowboard for my whole life competitively," she told Yap.

In many ways a typical teenager, Kim has an active social media presence and is a lover of music. "I always listen to music when I ride," she told May. "I just listen to my favorite song and it helps calm me down or put me in a good mood."

SUGGESTED READING

Axon, Rachel. "At 14, Snowboarder Chloe Kim Has Big Dreams, Big Potential." *USA Today*, 21 Jan. 2015, www.usatoday.com/story/sports/olympics/2015/01/21/chloe-kim-x-games-halfpipe-star/22121475/. Accessed 10 Nov. 2016.

"Chloe Kim, 13, Might Be the Best Snowboarder in US, but Is Too Young for Olympic Team." *Boise Weekly* [Boise, ID], 18 Jan. 2014, boiseweekly.com/boise/chloe-kim-13-might-be-the-best-snowboarder-in-us-but-is-too-young-for-olympic-team/Content?oid=3041708. Accessed 10 Nov. 2016.

Kim Ji-Han, and Choi Hyung-Jo. "Chloe Kim Can't Wait for 2018." *Korea JoongAng Daily*, 18 Feb. 2016, mengnews.joins.com/view.aspx?aid=3015194. Accessed 10 Nov. 2016.

May, Hannah. "Exclusive: Meet Your Girl Crush, Snowboarder Chloe Kim!" *Popmania*, 10 May 2016, popmania.com/exclusive-chloe-kim-interview-snowboarder-2016. Accessed 10 Nov. 2016.

Rice, Nelson. "Queen of the Snow: Chloe Kim Looks to Rule Snowboarding for Years to Come." *Sports Illustrated*, 27 Jan. 2016, www.si.com/edge/2016/01/27/chloe-kim-snowboarding-queen-of-the-snow-x-games-aspen. Accessed 10 Nov. 2016.

Yap, Audrey Cleo. "16-Year-Old Snowboarding Champion Chloe Kim Is Just a Regular Teenager." *NBC News*, 23 May 2016, www.nbcnews.com/news/asian-america/16-year-old-snowboarding-champion-chloe-kim-just-normal-teenager-n575411. Accessed 10 Nov. 2016.

—*Joy Crelin*

Si Woo Kim

Date of birth: June 28, 1995
Occupation: Golfer

In May 2017, golfer Si Woo Kim stunned golf fans and his fellow players when he completed an error-free final round to secure first place at the Players Tournament, a prestigious Professional Golf Association (PGA) Tour event considered by some to be golf's unofficial fifth major event. Kim's win, which earned him nearly two million dollars in prize money as well as five-year PGA Tour eligibility, was particularly meaningful because of the athlete's age—he was only twenty-one at the time—and relatively recent

Photo by Gregory Shamus/Getty Images North America

entry into the ranks of professional golf and the PGA Tour.

An avid golfer since his childhood in South Korea, Kim first gained PGA Tour eligibility in 2012, when he completed the PGA Tour Qualifying Tournament at the age of seventeen. Following a disappointing PGA Tour debut and several seasons on the developmental Web.com Tour, Kim returned to the PGA Tour in 2016, claiming first place in that year's Wyndham Championship. His win at the Players Championship the following season cemented Kim's status as a player to watch and likewise marked him as one of only four players to win two PGA Tour events while under the age of twenty-two. For Kim, however, records, statistics, and scores are best left off the golf course. "I just focused on myself, and I didn't try to think about others' scores," he told Karen Crouse for the *New York Times* (14 May 2017) of his strategy at the Players Championship. "I think that really helped me to be stable."

EARLY LIFE AND EDUCATION

Si Woo Kim, also known as Kim Si-woo, was born on June 28, 1995, in Seoul, South Korea. He attended Sinsung High School in Seoul before moving to California with his family to pursue his career in professional golf. As a child and teenager, Kim enjoyed watching major golf competitions and was inspired by the talented golfers he observed, including the American player Tiger Woods. He was particularly inspired by South Korean golfer K. J. Choi, who would later assist Kim in preparing for some of his professional competitions. "He's been a great golfer representing Korea, and I always wanted to be like him," Kim said of Choi, as quoted by Brian Wacker for *GolfDigest* (14 May 2017).

Kim learned to play golf himself at an early age, having first developed an interest in the sport while watching his father, a golf teacher, play. When Kim demonstrated a talent for the sport, his father stopped teaching other children and focused on his son, serving as Kim's sole coach until Kim was in his twenties.

Q-SCHOOL

Like many aspiring professional golfers, Kim focused on gaining eligibility to play on the PGA Tour, the high-level professional golf tour. In 2012, he competed in the PGA Tour Qualifying Tournament, also known as Q-School, in an attempt to earn his tour card, or right to play on the PGA Tour. The following year would bring significant changes to the qualification process: players who successfully complete Q-School could earn the right to compete on the developmental Web.com Tour, where they could then earn their PGA Tour eligibility. In 2012, however, placing within the top twenty-five players automatically gained a golfer PGA Tour eligibility.

Performing well in the tournament, which took place over several stages in the fall and winter of 2012, Kim tied for twentieth place in Q-School. He was surprised to find, however, that he could not yet make use of his hard-earned automatic tour eligibility, as he was still only seventeen years old. PGA Tour regulations stipulated that players must be eighteen or older to become automatically eligible for the tour, and younger players such as Kim could enter tour events only if they performed adequately in a qualifier or received an exemption from an event's sponsor. Despite this setback, Kim nevertheless considered Q-School to have been a valuable experience. "I probably would have tried it even if I found out there was an age issue," he told Kevin Dunleavy for the *Washington Examiner* (30 May 2013). "I don't think it's unfair. I was just a little disappointed to find it out later." Considering his limited ability to participate in PGA Tour events, Kim instead played in a number of events on the Web.com Tour over the course of 2013. His best performance came at the Mid-Atlantic Championship in Maryland in late spring 2013, when he tied for eleventh place and earned a prize of more than thirteen thousand dollars.

PGA DEBUT

Although unable to exercise his automatic eligibility to play in PGA Tour events, Kim managed to secure a spot in eight events on the tour during the 2013 season, including the Wyndham Championship, the RBC Canadian Open, and the John Deere Classic. Although he played in the initial rounds of the tournaments, his scores failed to qualify him to participate in the later rounds, and he was cut from the competitions.

Following his largely unsuccessful PGA Tour debut, Kim returned to the Web.com Tour for the 2014 and 2015 seasons, during which time he continued to develop his skills as a professional golfer. In the 2014 season, he played in nineteen events on the tour, in addition to the qualifier tournament, and ultimately made the cut in four of them. His best performance came in June 2014, when he competed in the Cleveland Open, later known as the Rust-Oleum Championship, at Lakewood Country Club in Westlake, Ohio. He finished in third place with a score of 271, which is 13 under par, and claimed not only his highest placement on the Web.com Tour to that point but also more than forty thousand dollars in prize money.

Kim had a more eventful 2015 season, participating in twenty-five events on the Web.com Tour and making the cut in eighteen of them. He claimed seventh place in the Rust-Oleum Championship in June and tied for second at the News Sentinel Open Presented by Pilot in Knoxville, Tennessee, in August. The most pivotal moment of his career to that point came in mid-July of that year, when Kim played in the Stonebrae Classic. A four-round tournament held at the Stonebrae Country Club in Hayward, California, the event—later renamed the Ellie Mae Classic—proved to be Kim's best professional performance yet. Kim performed well through the initial rounds, tying for first place by the end of the third, and in the final round of the tournament he claimed a victory with a total score of 268, which is 12 under par. His first tour win, Kim's victory at the Stonebrae Classic made him the second-youngest player to win an event on the Web.com Tour. Kim's performance during the 2015 season ultimately won him a total of $225,268, nearly half of which was due to his win at Stonebrae. His impressive earnings placed him among the top ten earners on the Web.com Tour, which earned Kim the right to play on the PGA Tour during the following season.

GOLF CHAMPION

In 2016, Kim returned to the PGA Tour for a far more successful season than his first on the tour. He competed in thirty-four tour events over the course of the season, making the cut in twenty-three of them. Kim achieved top-ten finishes in five different events, including the TOUR Championship, in which he tied for tenth place, and the Barbasol Championship, in which he placed second. Kim also made his first appearance in one of the competitions known as the majors, the four most important tournaments in professional golf, with an appearance in the

2016 PGA Championship. However, he was cut from the tournament after two rounds.

In August 2016, Kim traveled to Greensboro, North Carolina, to compete in the Wyndham Championship. Performing well during the early stages, he took an aggressive approach to play that paid off when he finished the tournament in first place, with a score of 259 and 21 under par, five strokes ahead of English golfer Luke Donald. His first PGA Tour victory, the win earned him more than one million dollars in prize money and made Kim both the youngest player on the PGA Tour to win a competition in 2016 and the second-youngest player ever to win the Wyndham Championship. Thanks in large part to his win at Wyndham, Kim ended the 2016 season with more than three million dollars in winnings and a rank of seventeenth in the overall PGA Tour standings.

PLAYERS CHAMPIONSHIP

In comparison to the success of his first full season on the PGA Tour, Kim started the 2017 season off slowly, failing to make the cut at a number of events and withdrawing from play on several occasions. The tide turned, however, in May, when Kim entered the 2017 Players Championship at the Tournament Players Club at Sawgrass—commonly known as TPC Sawgrass—in Ponte Vedra Beach, Florida. Although not one of golf's four majors—which include the Masters Tournament, the US Open, the Open Championship, and the PGA Championship—the event is considered by some in the golf world to be an unofficial fifth major of sorts, and a win would be a significant victory for any golfer.

To the surprise of many observers, Kim excelled at the event, claiming first place with a total score of 278 and 10 under par. His finish was three strokes better than that of his closest competitors, South African player Louis Oosthuizen and English player Ian Poulter, who tied for second place. Although they were undoubtedly disappointed by the missed opportunity, Kim's competitors recognized the strength of his performance. "You have to respect some good golf, and that's exactly what he's done," Poulter said following the championship, as quoted by Wacker. One of only four players to win two PGA Tour events while under the age of twenty-two, Kim was awarded $1.89 million for his win, which also granted him five-year eligibility for the PGA Tour.

2017 AND BEYOND

Over the remainder of the 2017 season, Kim's performance on the golf course was mixed. Although he was cut from two of the four majors, the Masters Tournament and the Open Championship, he tied for thirteenth place in the US Open, achieving his first majors finish. He participated in the 2017 PGA Championship as well but withdrew after the first round due to a back injury.

Although now eligible to participate in PGA Tour events for five years, Kim announced that he may put his golf career on hold in the near future to complete two years of military service, which is mandatory for most South Korean men between the ages of eighteen and thirty. Although the South Korean government grants exemptions to the winners of certain athletic competitions, neither of Kim's PGA Tour victories meet the official criteria. "I really wish we could have that benefit," Kim said after the Players Championship, as quoted by Joel Beall for *GolfDigest* (15 May 2017). "However, regardless of me winning this tournament, I really have to go to the military service, and I've already decided I'm going to go, too, so I'm ready for that."

PERSONAL LIFE

When not competing in tournaments elsewhere, Kim lives in Fullerton, California. His local course is the Los Coyotes Country Club in Buena Park, California. In addition to golf, Kim enjoys soccer and is a fan of the British soccer team Manchester United.

SUGGESTED READING

Beall, Joel. "Despite Winning Players, Si Woo Kim Still Has to Fulfill South Korean Military Service." *GolfDigest*, 15 May 2017, www.golfdigest.com/story/despite-winning-players-si-woo-kim-still-has-to-fulfill-south-korean-military-service. Accessed 8 Sept. 2017.

Crouse, Karen. "Si Woo Kim, 21, Claims the Players Championship." *The New York Times*, 14 May 2017, nytimes.com/2017/05/14/sports/golf/players-championship-si-woo-kim.html. Accessed 8 Sept. 2017.

Dunleavy, Kevin. "17-Year-Old Si Woo Kim Makes the Grade at Mid-Atlantic Championship." *The Washington Examiner*, 30 May 2013, www.washingtonexaminer.com/17-year-old-si-woo-kim-makes-the-grade-at-mid-atlantic-championship/article/2530887. Accessed 8 Sept. 2017.

Myers, Alex. "Si Woo Kim Was So Young When He First Earned His PGA Tour Card That He Wasn't Allowed to Play." *Loop*, 14 May 2017, www.golfdigest.com/story/si-woo-kim-was-so-young-when-he-first-earned-his-pga-tour-card-that-he-wasnt-allowed-to-play. Accessed 8 Sept. 2017.

Romine, Brentley. "Andrew 'Beef' Johnston, Si Woo Kim Withdraw from PGA Championship." *Golfweek*, 10 Aug. 2017, golfweek.com/2017/08/10/andrew-beef-johnston-withdraws-from-pga-championship. Accessed 8 Sept. 2017.

"Si Woo Kim." *PGA Tour*, 2017, www.pgatour.com/players/player.37455.si-woo-kim.html. Accessed 8 Sept. 2017.

Wacker, Brian. "Si Woo Kim's Introduction to Golf World: Players Champion." *GolfDigest*, 14 May 2017, www.golfdigest.com/story/si-woo-kims-introduction-to-golf-world-players-champion. Accessed 8 Sept. 2017.

—*Joy Crelin*

Christopher Kimball

Date of birth: June 5, 1951
Occupation: Chef

For more than two decades, avid home cooks recognized Christopher Kimball from his many culinary media efforts, which included the popular magazines *Cook's Illustrated* and *Cook's Country* as well as the public-television shows *America's Test Kitchen* and *Cook's Country*. Although he left those enterprises in late 2015, he is still a force to be reckoned with in the culinary world, with a new magazine, *Milk Street*; a kitchen and cooking school located on Milk Street in downtown Boston, Massachusetts; and new radio and television shows.

Regardless what media outlet he employs, Kimball is a steady and reliable presence, widely lauded for his extensive recipe testing and belief that anyone can become a competent cook, given the right instruction. Discussing *Cook's Illustrated*, the magazine with which Kimball remains most closely associated in the public mind, Alex Halberstadt wrote for the *New York Times Magazine* (11 Oct. 2012), "In simplest terms, *Cook's Illustrated* focuses on preparing middlebrow American dishes at home with supermarket ingredients and omits everything glossy cooking magazines have come to be known for. If you are interested in recreating a Tuscan-style Passover feast or wonder what David Chang, the Momofuku Ko chef, thinks about contemporary art, *Cook's Illustrated* may not be for you." Kimball, known for his rural pragmatism and sartorial stodginess (he favors button-down shirts worn with bow ties), told Halberstadt, "I hate the idea that cooking should be a celebration or a party. Cooking is about putting food on the table night after night, and there isn't anything glamorous about it."

EARLY YEARS

Christopher Kimball was born on June 5, 1951, in a wealthy area of Westchester County, north of New York City. His father, Edward Norris Kimball, was a successful business consultant, and his mother, Mary Alice White, was a professor of psychology at Columbia University.

The Kimballs owned a farm in southwest Vermont, where they spent summers and weekends. Kimball's mother raised Angus cattle and Yorkshire pigs, paying a local man to butcher them when the time came and selling the meat to area restaurants. She loved to hunt and fish and gave Kimball a rifle of his own before he entered his teens. He became so steeped in Vermont culture, greatly admiring residents' simple family cooking, that many fans assume he was born and raised there. "At the heart of it, Kimball makes his money by sticking to two lessons he learned from the old-timers in southwest Vermont," Kris Frieswick wrote for the *Boston Globe Magazine* (2 Aug. 2009). "The first: There is a right way and a wrong way to do everything. . . . The second lesson: Pay attention, or else." Kimball explained to Frieswick, "[Vermonters'] method of teaching was they never tell you something explicitly. They always demonstrate."

Although meals at home in New York were prepared by the family's cook, he got his first experience in the kitchen when he learned to bake from a local woman in Vermont named Marie Briggs. Reminiscing about this inspirational time in an interview with Claire Lui for the Columbia University alumni magazine *Columbia College Today* (July/Aug. 2010), he explained, "Food was the center of that community and she was the center of that community because she was the cook. The food was simple, but it was really good. I really liked that, and that's how I got started."

EDUCATION AND FIRST FORAYS INTO PUBLISHING

Kimball attended Phillips Exeter Academy, a preparatory school in Exeter, New Hampshire, before entering Columbia University in 1969. Despite later adopting a staid appearance, he was an active participant in the campus's counterculture. Columbia was then a hotbed of anti-war activities and protest marches, and he has recalled missing many tests because of frequent student strikes. He earned pocket money by driving a cab on the weekends and spent much of it going to Grateful Dead concerts, which often ended in the early hours of the morning.

Kimball graduated in 1973 with a bachelor's degree in primitive art and was accepted into a graduate art-history program at Cornell University. Unsure of the career path he wanted to follow, he declined admission, later taking a job at the Center for Direct Marketing in Connecticut. He moved to the suburbs, cut off his 1970s-era long hair, and married for the first time.

While living in Connecticut, Kimball began taking cooking courses but found himself frustrated by the imprecision of the instruction. "I used to get really irritated, because I would ask all these questions and be incredibly annoying in these classes, but nobody knew [the answers]," he recalled to Frieswick. "They were just repeating what someone told them. Nobody actually tested anything."

Kimball got the idea of launching a cooking magazine for those like him who would appreciate rigorous recipe testing and the absence of glitz. "The other food magazines weren't really about food," he told Lui. In 1980, with approximately $100,000 raised from family and friends, he began publishing *Cook's Magazine*. Some of his early staff, including Mark Bittman and Melanie Barnard, went on to some success in the culinary world. He soon discovered that keeping a new niche publication afloat, combined with his inexperience, was a difficult proposition, however, and after just three years, he sold partial ownership to the *New Yorker*. That company, in turn, sold their interest to S. I. Newhouse's publishing conglomerate in 1985. Ultimately, in 1989, he sold off *Cook's Magazine* in its entirety to Bonnier, a Swedish publishing house; shortly afterward, the publication was shut down.

Kimball spent the next few years bouncing around the publishing world, working on a men's magazine that was defunct even before the first issue came out and turning around a troubled special-interest publication on alternative health. By 1993, however, he was more than ready to try his hand at another culinary venture.

AMERICA'S TEST KITCHEN

That year, Kimball rehired many of the employees who had worked on *Cook's Magazine* and launched the similarly named *Cook's Illustrated*. Totally free of advertising and supported solely by subscribers, the largely black-and-white magazine had what many critics have characterized as a Victorian feel, filled with scrupulously tested recipes (with scientific explanations where needed), meticulous line drawings, and a chatty letter from Kimball himself in the front of every issue. Kimball, dividing his time between a farmhouse in Vermont and a townhouse in Boston, typically wrote about southwest Vermont, and the letters often unsentimentally detailed the joys and tribulations of living in the area among eccentric locals, survivalists, aging hippies, and newly arrived New Yorkers seeking more peaceful environs.

For each cover Kimball chose a Flemish-style still-life oil painting of food, believing that it gave the publication a timeless look. It was the recipes themselves, however, that won the magazine legions of avid readers. Each recipe was assigned to a test-kitchen cook who prepared several versions, attempting to isolate which factors contributed to or detracted from success. Only after as many as one hundred variations were created and judged was it decided which version of the recipe, if any, warranted inclusion in a bimonthly issue. "I am not against people playing around with recipes, but they should get to the point where they really understand the recipe first," Kimball told Jessica Gross in an interview for the blog *Longreads* (June 2015). Expounding his decisions regarding the layout of the publication, he said, "Black and white tells you right at the beginning this is a serious magazine about cooking, not a lifestyle magazine. We're not trying to sell you on something; we are there to explain something."

After also publishing the well-received cookbooks *The Cook's Bible: The Best of American Home Cooking* (1996), *The Yellow Farmhouse Cookbook* (1998), and *The Dessert Bible* (2000), a second magazine, *Cook's Country*, was launched in 2004, featuring rustic comfort food and dishes from various parts of the nation. Each magazine spawned a television show: Kimball hosted *America's Test Kitchen* (also the name of his umbrella media company), the instructional cooking program with the highest number of viewers on public television, from 2001 to 2016 and *Cook's Country* from 2008 to 2016 on PBS. While the former is filmed at a kitchen in Massachusetts, the latter is filmed at a farmhouse in Rupert, Vermont, purchased specifically to highlight the approachable, rural focus of the show's companion magazine. Kimball became well known for his steady presence in the test kitchen, asking questions and prompting his cooks to explain their process and ingredients. A team of America's Test Kitchen's editors eventually put together *The America's Test Kitchen Cooking School Cookbook* (2013), which includes favorite recipes from *America's Test Kitchen* as well as summaries of cooking basics.

Discussing Kimball's overall ethos, Frieswick wrote, "What readers and viewers get are recipes that use ingredients available at any major supermarket in America and that yield consistent, predictable, excellent results. . . . His recipes are nearly bulletproof."

MILK STREET KITCHEN

In late 2015, shortly after parent company Boston Common Press had installed someone in the newly created position of chief executive officer, it was announced that Kimball was severing his connection to *America's Test Kitchen*. The following year marked the launch of his new venture: a magazine, cookbook, television, radio, and cooking-school empire named after the Boston street where it is headquartered.

Milk Street Kitchen focuses on techniques and recipes from around the world, rather than the comfortingly traditional fare that had long been Kimball's trademark. "Instead of using Eurocentric techniques that rely on concentrating flavors through long applications of heat, Mr. Kimball is exploring ways to build dishes that rely on texture, spice and freshness," Kim Severson wrote for the *New York Times* (31 May 2016). Kimball defended his decision to Alexandra Hall for *Boston* magazine (Dec. 2016), saying, "I finally realized that the world offers almost infinite possibilities in how to think about food and how to prepare it. I still think apple pie is one of the greatest culinary ideas of all time, but I want to introduce home cooks to all the other options."

Details soon emerged that made plain the acrimonious nature of his split with *America's Test Kitchen*, which filed a major lawsuit against him in the fall of 2016. Among the allegations was that he had built what is now a direct competitor while still on *America's Test Kitchen*'s payroll, essentially stealing company resources.

Despite being painted as something of a villain in the press, Kimball maintains that he is uniquely suited to his new mission. "We're not translating the ethnic soul of a community," he told Severson. "We're just saying this is a good idea. You need someone who knows a fair amount about cooking to do this, who has the thoughtfulness and testing to translate Thai cooking to our kitchens."

PERSONAL LIFE

Kimball has been married three times. He has a son and three daughters with his second wife,

Adrienne, whom he divorced in 2012. The following year he married Melissa Lee Baldino, whom he met when she interviewed for a job as his assistant at *America's Test Kitchen*; they continued to work together as Baldino went on to become an executive producer of the company's radio and television shows. In addition to cooking, he enjoys playing guitar, and he continues to live in both Massachusetts and Vermont.

SUGGESTED READING

Frieswick, Kris. "Perfection, Inc." *The Boston Globe Magazine*, 2 Aug. 2009, archive. boston.com/bostonglobe/magazine/articles/2009/08/02/perfection_inc. Accessed 5 Apr. 2017.

Halberstadt, Alex. "Cooking Isn't Creative, and It Isn't Easy." *The New York Times Magazine*, 11 Oct. 2012, www.nytimes.com/2012/10/14/magazine/cooks-illustrateds-christopher-kimball.html. Accessed 5 Apr. 2017.

Hall, Alexandra. "Christopher Kimball: Bow Ties, Recipes, and Lawsuits." *Boston*, Dec. 2016, www.bostonmagazine.com/restaurants/article/2016/11/20/christopher-kimball-atk-milk-street-lawsuit. Accessed 5 Apr. 2017.

Hall, Alexandra. "Country Style." *Boston*, June 2004, www.bostonmagazine.com/2006/05/country-style. Accessed 5 Apr. 2017.

Krystal, Becky. "Home Cooking's Headed for a Mash-Up 'Watershed Moment.'" *The Washington Post*, 17 Oct. 2016, www.washingtonpost.com/lifestyle/food/christopher-kimball-starts-afresh-with-milk-street-magazine/2016/10/17/210af11a-9186-11e6-a6a3-d50061aa9fae_story.html. Accessed 5 Apr. 2017.

Lui, Claire. "Cooking 101." *Columbia College Today*, July/Aug. 2010, www.college.columbia.edu/cct/archive/jul_aug10/features0. Accessed 5 Apr. 2017.

Severson, Kim. "Why Christopher Kimball Is Moving On from 'America's Test Kitchen.'" *The New York Times*, 31 May 2016, www.nytimes.com/2016/06/01/dining/americas-test-kitchen-christopher-kimball.html. Accessed 5 Apr. 2017.

—Mari Rich

Pom Klementieff

Date of birth: May 3, 1986
Occupation: Actor

In May 2017, the cosmic superhero film *Guardians of the Galaxy Vol. 2* introduced a new character into the rapidly expanding Marvel Cinematic Universe: the empathic alien Mantis.

By Florida Supercon [CC BY 2.0], via Wikimedia Commons

For the actor who portrays the character, Pom Klementieff, the introduction of the character not only fulfilled her longtime dreams of appearing in a Marvel film and playing an alien, but also granted her the opportunity to add a new type of character to the cinematic universe's selection of superheroes, secret agents, and associated allies. "Female characters in Marvel films are usually cool and badass and strong, and I love that!" Klementieff explained to Seth Plattner for *Elle* (1 May 2017). "But Mantis is something different. She's childlike. She listens rather than fights. She's also weird! I get to be the total weirdo!"

Although the "weird" role of Mantis is unlike any Klementieff had previously played, it is in many ways consistent with her overall approach to her craft. A Canadian-born French actor who gained notice for her early roles in films such as 2007's *Après lui*, she gained international attention for her part in director Spike Lee's 2013 remake of the 2003 South Korean film *Oldboy*—a part she wanted so badly that she began taking boxing lessons in preparation for the role prior to even auditioning. Indeed, Klementieff delights not simply in playing so-called total weirdoes but in pushing herself in new, exciting, and challenging directions. "It makes it more interesting to do work," she told Jerome Maida for the *Inquirer* (3 May 2017), "and I'm a very passionate person who enjoys challenging myself."

EARLY LIFE AND EDUCATION

Pom A. Klementieff was born on May 3, 1986, in Quebec City, Quebec, Canada. Her Russian French father was a diplomat who was stationed at a consulate in Quebec at the time of her birth. Klementieff's family left Canada when she was one and went on to live in Japan, Cote d'Ivoire, and France.

When Klementieff was five years old, her father died. As her mother was struggling with mental illness and was unable to take care of her children, Klementieff and her older brother, Namou, moved in with their aunt and uncle, who resided in the Vallée de Chevreuse region of the French countryside. Klementieff's uncle later died on her eighteenth birthday, and her brother committed suicide seven years later, also on her birthday. Although Klementieff has noted that the painful events of her childhood and young adulthood still affect her, acting has played a key role in helping her process her grief. "It's cathartic in a way," she told Maida. "You relive it and become accepting of it and you touch other people's hearts with your experience and performance. It's beautiful!"

As a child, Klementieff was not allowed to watch much television and instead primarily watched older black-and-white films, which she enjoyed. She later became a fan of late twentieth- and early twenty-first-century films featuring strong female lead characters. Although long interested in acting, Klementieff did not consider it to be a viable career path and, as a young adult, set out to study law at the urging of her aunt. She soon found that the legal field did not appeal to her and began to reconsider her options. "It felt like a pretentious fantasy to say, 'I want to be an actress,'" she recalled to Angela Ledgerwood for *Interview* (3 May 2017). "But when I didn't connect with law, I saw my chance." At the age of nineteen, Klementieff enrolled in Cours Florent, a drama school in Paris, to study acting. Shortly after beginning her studies, she won two years of free classes, and she gained representation by a talent agent not long afterward.

EARLY CAREER

Klementieff made her film debut in the 2007 drama *Après lui* (After Him), which starred critically acclaimed actor Catherine Deneuve. Although her role was a small one, Klementieff's debut proved successful, and she went on to appear in numerous additional French films over the next several years. For the 2009 film *Loup* (Wolf), which focused on a group of Siberian reindeer breeders, she traveled to Siberia and lived in a remote camp while filming. The experience was particularly memorable for Klementieff in part because of the cold environment. "When you breathed in the air, you could feel ice crystals in your nose," she told Kee Chang for *Anthem* (7 May 2017). She also learned to work with reindeer and how to cook reindeer meat.

In addition to her film work, Klementieff played a supporting role in the television series *Pigalle, la nuit* (Pigalle, night), which aired on television in France in 2009. She primarily found work in film, however, with roles in films such as *Sleepless Night* (2012; originally released in 2011 as *Nuit blanche*) and *Paris à tout prix* (2013; *Paris or Perish*). Yet despite her growing résumé, Klementieff soon became tired of the limited types of roles available to her in French cinema and began to consider moving to the United States to pursue new opportunities in Hollywood. "I want to play independent strong female characters, not the heart-broken girls I was playing in Paris," she told Jennifer Lee for *Filler*. Klementieff ultimately made the move overseas, settling in California.

BREAKTHROUGH ROLES

Primarily known in France, Klementieff began to receive significant international attention in 2013, when she played the supporting role of Haeng-Bok in *Oldboy*, American director Spike Lee's remake of South Korean director Chan-wook Park's 2003 film of the same name. Klementieff first saw the original film as a teenager and became an instant fan. "I wanted to be inside the film and part of the creative process that made it come to life," she told Ledgerwood. When she heard that Lee was remaking the film and was seeking a female actor of Asian descent for the role of the villain's bodyguard, Klementieff, whose mother is Korean, began to take boxing lessons with the goal of preparing herself to win the part.

After claiming the role, Klementieff was tasked with helping to choose an appropriate name for the character, who had been played by a man in the original film. Klementieff and the filmmakers settled on the name Haeng-Bok, which is based on the Korean word for happiness. She likewise continued to train extensively to prepare for her role in the film, which chronicles a man's quest for revenge and search for the truth after being imprisoned for decades by a mysterious enemy. "I had to train three hours a day for two months," she recalled to Lee. "You are sore every day, and you're working on your soreness!" Klementieff's hard work paid off: although *Oldboy* itself received mixed reviews, her performance as Haeng-Bok brought her to the attention of international audiences.

BECOMING A GUARDIAN OF THE GALAXY

The most significant opportunity to date came in 2017, when Klementieff costarred in the highly anticipated *Guardians of the Galaxy Vol. 2*. The first sequel to 2014's well-received *Guardians of the Galaxy* follows the further adventures of the first film's main cast, with the several new additions. Following a series of auditions with casting directors and film director James Gunn, Klementieff claimed the role of one of the new characters: Mantis, a sheltered young alien with empathic powers. A longtime fan of the films in the Marvel Cinematic Universe—which encompasses numerous superhero films set on Earth in addition to the space-focused Guardians franchise—Klementieff found the role appealing because of Mantis's alien perspective and unusual abilities. Although initially apprehensive about her status as a newcomer, Klementieff soon found herself at home among the main cast, which included actors Chris Pratt and Zoe Saldana. "I didn't know how the other actors would react," Klementieff told Julie Kosin for *Harper's Bazaar* (5 May 2017) of her experience joining an established cast. "It could have been a bad experience, but it was the total opposite. They were really welcoming and adorable. I felt adopted, in a way."

Unlike the majority of Klementieff's previous films, *Guardians of the Galaxy Vol. 2* featured extensive use of special effects, particularly computer-generated ones. Klementieff's own appearance was modified significantly via makeup and prosthetics, but computer effects were used to give her character a set of long, mobile antennae. Although interacting with digitally created backgrounds and characters was a new experience for her, doing so proved to be less of a challenge than she expected. "Sometimes instead of an actor, you have to talk to something that is next to the camera, because it gives a better angle for the shot. When you're an actor, you have to imagine," Klementieff explained to Rob Keyes for *ScreenRant* (20 Apr. 2017). "You have to imagine things, like, 'Oh there is something coming here!' Or, 'You're in a beautiful countryside. It's beautiful. There is a tree there. There are birds.' And then you imagine stuff, so it's kind of the same." Upon its release in May 2017, *Guardians of the Galaxy Vol. 2* performed well with critics and audiences, introducing both Klementieff and Mantis to new audiences worldwide. She was confirmed to reprise the role of Mantis in *Avengers: Infinity War*, which is scheduled for release in 2018.

In addition to the role of Mantis, Klementieff gained attention in 2017 for her supporting role in *Ingrid Goes West*, a dark comedy about a troubled young woman who becomes obsessed with a popular user of the photo-sharing app Instagram. Klementieff plays Harley Chung, one of the other Instagram influencers in the two women's social circle, a role that she has noted in interviews is at odds with her real-life preference for privacy. The film premiered at the Sundance Film Festival and later debuted in theaters in the summer of 2017.

PERSONAL LIFE

Klementieff lives in Los Angeles, California, a city that she has said she prefers over her former home of Paris. "I feel free here," she explained to Lee. "There was always personal drama in Paris, I felt like I had to build something somewhere else." Los Angeles has been more professionally fulfilling for Klementieff as well. "All my auditions here are so interesting," she told Lee. "In Paris it was all about girls mad because their boyfriends cheated on them."

In addition to acting, Klementieff enjoys boxing and has also trained in Tae Kwon Do. She is an avid lover of fashion and enjoys both watching fashion shows at events such as Paris Fashion Week and experimenting with fashion herself. "I just love things that bring more happiness, fun, and light into my life and clothes are a big part of that," she told Chang. "It's just great to have the possibility to look like a babydoll or a badass, depending on your mood."

SUGGESTED READING

Chang, Kee. "The Archives: Pom Klementieff." *Anthem*, 7 May 2017. anthemmagazine.com/qa-with-pom-klementieff/. Accessed 8 Sept. 2017.

Keyes, Rob. "What Pom Klementieff Told Us on *Guardians of the Galaxy* 2 Set." *ScreenRant*, 20 Apr. 2017. screenrant.com/guardians-of-the-galaxy-2-pom-klementieff-interview/. Accessed 8 Sept. 2017.

Klementieff, Pom. Interview by Angela Ledgerwood. *Interview*, 3 May 2017. www.interviewmagazine.com/film/pom-klementieff. Accessed 8 Sept. 2017.

Kosin, Julie. "Pom Klementieff Is the Real Star of *Guardians of the Galaxy Vol. 2*." *Harper's Bazaar*, 5 May 2017. www.harpersbazaar.com/culture/film-tv/amp9611006/pom-klementieff-guardians-of-the-galaxy-interview/. Accessed 8 Sept. 2017.

Lee, Jennifer. "Little Trouble Girl." *Filler*, 2015, fillermagazine.com/culture/film/celebrity-news-and-interviews-actress-pom-klementieff-from-spike-lees-oldboy/. Accessed 8 Sept. 2017.

Maida, Jerome. "In Playing Mantis, Pom Klementieff Keeps Laughing through the Pain." *The Inquirer*, 3 May 2017. www.philly.com/philly/entertainment/geek/Pom-Klementieff-Mantis-Guardians-of-the-galaxy-vol-2.html. Accessed 8 Sept. 2017.

Plattner, Seth. "Pom Klementieff on Being the 'Total Weirdo' of the Marvel Universe." *Elle*, 1 May 2017. www.elle.com/culture/celebrities/amp44332/pom-klementieff-profile/. Accessed 8 Sept. 2017.

SELECTED WORKS

Après lui, 2007; *Loup*, 2009; *Pigalle, la nuit*, 2009; *Oldboy*, 2013; *Hacker's Game*, 2015; *Guardians of the Galaxy Vol. 2*, 2017; *Ingrid Goes West*, 2017

—*Joy Crelin*

Solange Knowles

Date of birth: June 24, 1986
Occupation: Singer-songwriter, actor

Through a long and varied career, as well as an unfailing conviction in her own voice, Solange Knowles has successfully distinguished herself as an accomplished singer-songwriter apart from her famous family. This is more evident than ever with the release of her third studio album, *A Seat at the Table* (2016). "It feels like a breakout moment for the star. Perhaps, for the first time in her career, her release has generated a level of excitement among critics and fans on par with that [of] her older sister," Chris Riotta wrote for *Mic* (30 Sept. 2016). "Solange is very much her own identity. She's long worked to cultivate a diverse career rooted in New Orleans with jazz, modern rhythm and blues, and old school influences into a sound that's separate from [Beyoncé's] commercially accessible brand."

A Seat at the Table is also Knowles's highest-charting album to date, topping Billboard's 200

CLAIRE/CC BY-SA 4.0/Wikimedia Commons

chart. With this feat, Knowles and Beyoncé achieved another milestone, becoming the first pair of sisters in *Billboard*'s history to each have a number-one record in the same calendar year. (Beyoncé's *Lemonade* debuted at number one earlier that year.)

EARLY LIFE

Solange Piaget Knowles was born on June 24, 1986, to Tina and Matthew Knowles in Houston, Texas. She and Beyoncé were raised in Houston's Third Ward. Knowles credits her parents—a beauty salon owner of Louisiana Creole descent and an African American corporate salesman—with her early exposure to music. "I grew up watching a lot of videos from the 60s R & B movement. My mother played The Supremes, The Veltones, The Marvelettes," she shared with Ali Shaheed Muhammad and Frannie Kelley for *NPR* (12 Feb. 2014). "My father would play the Jackson 5 and . . . New Edition."

Knowles was also raised in a household that embraced creativity. She became fascinated with dance, taking her first ballet class at age three. When Knowles was five, she sang in front of an audience for the first time at an amusement park. She penned her first song for a United Way songwriting competition while in the third grade.

ON THE ROAD WITH DESTINY'S CHILD

Knowles had aspirations of becoming a contemporary ballet dancer, however, and visited the Juilliard School, the renowned conservatory in New York City, at age twelve. At the time her sister's music career was taking off; Destiny's Child released their self-titled debut album in 1998, a year after signing with Columbia Records. The group was already a family enterprise. Not only was their father managing the group, but their mother was also serving as the group's stylist and choreographer.

It was not long before Knowles became a part of the operation. At age thirteen she stepped in as a backup dancer during the group's international tour. "It was really nice, 'cause in a weird way, we were able to have a lot more of a consistent family life," she shared with Amber Bravo for *Fader* (12 Feb. 2013). Knowles recalled being heavily influenced by a tour stop in Jamaica. "When I [came] home, I was constantly writing, whether it was songs or melody or poetry or essays. I wanted to be a writer," she recalled to Tavi Gevinson for *Rookie* magazine (30 Sept. 2016). Knowles also adopted Rastafarian fashion and culture, including becoming a vegetarian.

BECOMING A SOLO ARTIST

In 2000 when Destiny's Child opened for pop diva Christina Aguilera, Knowles subbed for group member Kelly Rowland, who was sidelined with two broken toes. She sang backup on a rendition of "Little Drummer Boy," from the group's holiday disc 8 *Days of Christmas* (2000). She followed that up with a cameo in rapper Lil' Bow Wow's music video for "Puppy Love," which premiered in June 2001. That September, Knowles assumed lead vocal duties on the theme song for the animated Disney Channel series *The Proud Family*, with Destiny's Child providing backup vocals. In the summer of 2002, Knowles reunited with her big sister for "Hey Goldmember," a single featured on the soundtrack of the spy parody *Austin Powers in Goldmember* (2002), which also costarred Beyoncé. The sisters also appeared on the soundtrack for another summer comedy that year, *The Master of Disguise* (2002).

Determined to launch a solo career, the sixteen-year-old signed with Music World Entertainment, the management firm owned by her father, who subsequently helped her land a recording contract with Columbia Records. She next participated in another Destiny's Child collaboration, with cowriting credits on three songs on Kelly Rowland's 2002 solo album, including the title track "Simply Deep." Knowles's year ended with the release of her debut single "Feelin' You."

For her first studio album, *Solo Star*, Knowles cowrote a majority of the sixteen tracks—a mixture of up-tempo R & B, pop, rock, and reggaeton—and enlisted the help of several notable producers, including Timbaland, the Neptunes, Linda Perry, and Jermaine Dupri. In February 2003, nearly two weeks after its release, *Solo Star* cracked Billboard 200's top fifty before falling off the chart three weeks later. She was able to go on tour opening for Justin Timberlake, but after contracting strep throat and losing her voice, she went home for a much-needed break.

Instead of returning immediately to music, however, Knowles married her high-school sweetheart, Texas Southern University football player Daniel Smith, in February 2004 and subsequently moved to Idaho. After making her big-screen debut opposite Bow Wow in the comedy *Johnson Family Values* (2004), a pregnant Knowles appeared in the music video for Destiny's Child's "Soldier."

TRYING OUT A NEW SOUND

In 2006 Knowles starred in the straight-to-DVD cheerleading movie *Bring It On: All or Nothing*. She also cowrote two tracks for Beyoncé's second solo record, *B'day*: "Upgrade U" and "Get Me Bodied." Despite success with these songs for her sister, Knowles had a hard time getting traction with her songwriting otherwise. As she told Amber Bravo from *Fader* (12 Feb. 2013), "I was writing these '60s soul and pop records and no one was picking them up. That's kind of what transitioned me into doing [the Sol-Angel] record, because I just kept writing them and nothing was happening, and I was like, 'Well, I guess I can give it another go.'"

In 2007 she moved to Los Angeles and inked a recording contract with Interscope/Geffen Records. Knowles collaborated with legendary Motown songwriter Lamont Dozier, retro-soul producer Mark Ronson, and hip-hop artists Pharrell Williams and Cee-lo Green, among others on the new record. In April 2008 "I Decided," Knowles's collaboration with Williams and the lead track from her upcoming album, was released and the single eventually topped several Billboard chart categories.

When *Sol-Angel and the Hadley St. Dreams* hit shelves in August, it became Knowles's first album to crack both the top ten of Billboard's 200 and the top five of another chart, Top R & B/Hip-Hop Albums. Knowles embarked on a six-week summer tour, followed by a United Kingdom leg in November, to promote the album.

BREAKING FREE AND HONING HER VOICE
In March 2009 Knowles released "T.O.N.Y.," the album's third single and her third chart-topping single on *Billboard*'s Dance Club Songs. That fall she began moonlighting as a deejay, and in November 2009, made the decision to shake up her career and leave her record label to pursue an independent route. Knowles expressed her displeasure with the music business in the track "F—k the Industry (Signed Sincerely)," which was digitally released in May 2010.

That year Knowles began working with singer-songwriter-producer Dev Hynes on a new EP, which incorporated elements of funk, soul, and New Wave. She also honed her deejay skills at various New York City hotspots and high-profile events including the Coachella Music Festival. In 2011 Knowles's unique, trend-setting style, which often incorporated bold colors and funky patterns, landed her major beauty contracts with Carol's Daughter and Rimmel London.

By the year's end she had relocated to Brooklyn, and became involved in the indie music scene there. She also started to work on her next record, taking the time to grow into the sound she wanted. As she remarked to Bravo, "[In] four years, there's been so much artistic growth, so much growth just as a woman in [my] twenties, but especially as an artist. You're exposed to so much more from age twenty-one to twenty-six, and you sure as hell care a lot less."

In October 2012 Knowles debuted "Losing You," the lead track from her new EP. Following the November release of her critically acclaimed seven-track EP *True*—under the indie label Terrible Records—Knowles kicked off 2013 with a mini-tour of New York City and several major European cities. In late January *True* peaked at number seventeen on Billboard's Top R & B/Hip-Hop Albums chart. Knowles spent the next

few months performing at several major events, such as Bonnaroo, South by Southwest (SXSW), Glastonbury, as well as the Essence and Pitchfork Music festivals.

In May 2013 Knowles founded her own label, Saint Records, with Sony Music serving as distributor. The first release under the new imprint, *Saint Heron*, a twelve-song collection from Knowles's favorite up-and-coming R & B artists, performed admirably. That accomplishment was overshadowed by a falling-out with Hynes, after he implied that he had penned most of Knowles's EP himself. (The two have since mended their rift.)

GETTING *A SEAT AT THE TABLE*
As Knowles has continued to develop as an artist, she has also continually turned her attention towards the issue of race relations in America. At a May 2015 event, she unveiled "Rise," a song she penned about police killings of unarmed black men in Baltimore and Ferguson, as well as the lead track for her upcoming album. Knowles recalled her own experience with race at a Kraftwerk concert in early September 2016, when a group of four white women yelled for her and her son to sit down and pelted her with a lime after she kept dancing. She described the incident in a second-person essay she posted on the *Saint Heron* website.

Knowles capped off September with the release of *A Seat at The Table* (2016), a black girl's manifesto which she cowrote, arranged, and coproduced. Knowles wanted the album to be a conversation about the life of the modern black woman, and an exploration of her personal and cultural history, as well as that of black music. In the album's twenty-one songs, Knowles alludes to many artists across the spectrum of black musical history in the construction of her songs. As she explained to her sister for *Interview Magazine* (10 Jan. 2017), "the album really feels like storytelling for us all and our family and our lineage. And having mom and dad speak on the album, it felt right that, as a family, this closed the chapter of our stories. And my friends' stories—every day, we're texting about some of the micro-aggressions we experience, and that voice can be heard on the record, too. The inspiration for this record came from all of our voices as a collective, and wanting to look at it and explore it."

Audiences responded well to Knowles's third full-length disc, which debuted at the top of the Billboard 200—her first record to do so. In October she released videos for the singles "Don't Touch My Hair" and "Cranes in The Sky," which she directed with her husband, music video director Alan Ferguson. Her year ended with another milestone: a first-ever Grammy nod for "Cranes in The Sky," which earned her the prize for best R & B performance at the 2017 Grammy Awards.

On the small screen, Knowles serves as music consultant for comedian Issa Rae's HBO comedy series *Insecure*.

PERSONAL LIFE

Solange Knowles married Daniel Smith in 2004, when she was seventeen and he was nineteen. She gave birth to their son, Daniel Julez Smith, Jr. (known as Julez) on October 18, 2004. In 2007, Knowles and Smith divorced and she moved with her son to Los Angeles. Knowles became engaged to Alan Ferguson after they had been together for five years. The two married in November 2014 at New Orleans's Marigny Opera House. Since 2013, the self-proclaimed Southerner has split her time between Los Angeles and New Orleans.

SUGGESTED READING

Bravo, Amber. "Solange: Rise and Shine." *Fader*, 12 Feb. 2013, www.thefader.com/2013/02/12/solange-rise-and-shine. Accessed 9 Feb. 2017.

Gevinson, Tavi. "First Drafts: Solange Knowles," *Rookie*, 30 Sept. 2016, www.rookiemag.com/2016/09/first-drafts-solange-knowles. Accessed 9 Feb. 2017.

Knowles, Solange. "Solange." Interview by Beyoncé Knowles. *Interview Magazine*, 10 Jan. 2017, www.interviewmagazine.com/music/solange. Accessed 9 Feb. 2017.

Muhammad, Ali Shaheed, and Fannie Kelley. "Solange Knowles on Nas, Juvenile, and Dance Moves," *NPR*, 12 Feb. 2014, www.npr.org/sections/microphone-check/2014/02/12/272432827/solange-knowles-on-nas-juvenile-and-dance-moves. Accessed 9 Feb. 2017.

Riotta, Chris. "How Solange Knowles Has Evolved from Beyoncé's Sister to R & B Queen in Her Own Right," *Mic*, 30 Sept. 2016, mic.com/articles/155544/how-solange-knowles-has-evolved-from-beyonc-s-sister-to-r-b-queen-in-her-own-right. Accessed 9 Feb. 2017.

SELECTED WORKS

Solo Star, 2003; *Sol-Angel and the Hadley St. Dreams*, 2008; *True*, 2012; *A Seat at the Table*, 2016

—*Bertha Muteba*

Sasha Lane

Date of birth: September 29, 1995
Occupation: Actor

Sasha Lane did not intend to become an actor. One day, however, while she was on the beach in Panama City, Florida, British filmmaker Andrea Arnold discovered Lane and quickly cast her in a leading role in her film *American Honey* (2016). In the movie, Lane portrays a troubled teen who escapes an abusive foster home and joins a gang of misfits on a road trip. *American Honey* impressed audiences at the Cannes Film Festival—where it won the prestigious Jury Prize.

Lane's electrifying debut dazzled critics. Although she had no acting experience before the film, she was able to hold her own against more seasoned actors, such as Shia LaBeouf and Riley Keough. Lane, who describes herself as an anxious person, presents a poised and experienced demeanor on film, which has allowed her to find other acting opportunities since her debut. Her upcoming films include *The Miseducation of Cameron Post*, *Shoplifters of the World*, *Hunting Lila*, and *Shotgun*.

"I'm a really anxious person and a really uncomfortable person and a people-pleaser. Putting all those together with this type of industry, it's pretty much everything that makes me uncomfortable and that I dislike. People literally have told me like, 'Sasha, you're doing everything that you hate,'" Lane confessed to Colleen Kelsey for *Interview Magazine* (30 Sept. 2016). "But to make a film like that and those connections you

By Gordon Correll (Sasha Lane) [CC BY-SA 2.0], via Wikimedia Commons

make and then to meet people who felt inspired or connected to you through film, and you could put your energy across, you're like, 'Wow, this is worth it.' That's the beautiful part, so I want to do more stuff to where I feel good about it, or else I would not be in this."

FORMATIVE YEARS

Sasha Lane was born on September 29, 1995, in Houston, Texas. Her parents divorced when she was young, and her brother went to live with her father. Lane and her mother eventually settled in Dallas, Texas. Lane's unique looks come from her blended heritage—her father is African American, and her mother is of New Zealand Maori descent. Growing up, Lane had no interest in pursuing an acting career. "I always thought it'd be cool to portray these certain things, make people feel a certain way. I was kind of fascinated with that, but I wasn't the type to do acting school or theater," she told Kelsey. "I didn't have the best views of Hollywood, so it wasn't something that I was going to try and pursue. But I always said, if someone randomly found me, I would do it."

After graduating from high school, Lane left her hometown to attend Texas State University in San Marcos, Texas, where she intended to major in social work and psychology. Many of her classes, however, left her feeling isolated and depressed. "It made me feel very alone because I didn't learn a certain way," she recalled to Noah Jackson for *Nylon* (15 Nov. 2016). "I had to take classes that I didn't feel connected to, so I didn't want to be in them."

Feeling directionless and lost, she headed to Panama City, Florida, for spring break. "I was in a very hopeless place," Lane told Jackson. "I had this feeling that something was going to happen, but by that point I was very exhausted." It was her mother who convinced Lane to go to Florida. What her mother did not realize, however, was how fateful that trip would be. While partying with friends on the beach, Lane was approached by someone who would change her life.

FILMING *AMERICAN HONEY*

The person who approached Lane was Andrea Arnold, a British director best known for films such as *Red Road* (2006), *Fish Tank* (2009), and *Wuthering Heights* (2011). At the time, Lane did not know Arnold was looking to cast the role of Star in her film *American Honey*. The director, however, believed Lane was perfect for the part. "She asked to come to my hotel room that night, and I said 'sure,'" Lane recalled to Jackson. "I didn't think she'd come, but she did, and she videotaped me and my friend talking, and then asked me to breakfast the next morning."

Shortly after meeting with Lane, Arnold offered her the role. Lane's family, particularly her father, was concerned about her running off with someone she did not know. They found it difficult to believe a British director had asked Lane to make a road trip movie. Her mother, however, was more encouraging and believed Arnold was who she said she was. After thinking it over, Lane agreed to take the role.

To provide realism to the story, Lane and the other first-time actors Arnold had chosen for the film lived just as their characters did, in and out of motels, in a chaotic world, partying. Without a script and with little direction from Arnold, the young actors discovered that many scenes would be improvised. In the film, all the main characters are part of a traveling magazine sales crew, or "mag crew"—young scam artists who sell magazine subscriptions door to door. Arnold had been inspired to write and direct a film about magazine crews after reading an investigative piece in the *New York Times*. *American Honey* is Arnold's look at the grubby outskirts of towns across the United States, where marginalized individuals, like the characters in the film, do their best to survive in places with very limited opportunities.

In the film, the crew's leading salesman, a character played by Shia LaBeouf, approaches Lane's character, asking her to join the group. She agrees to leave with him, believing the possibility of making up to three hundred dollars a day would be far better than the scavenging life she has at home. As the two characters become involved, they come into conflict with the crew's boss, played by Riley Keough.

Shot like a documentary over three months in small towns across states such as Oklahoma and North Dakota, *American Honey* depicts the brutal existence of these magazine crews, who often suffer from drug and alcohol abuse as well as exploitation. Upon its release in 2016, the nearly three-hour film was met with considerable praise. Critics enjoyed the chemistry between the actors—particularly the chemistry between Lane and LaBeouf. Furthermore, critics almost universally praised Lane's performance, with Mark Kermode for the *Guardian* (16 Oct. 2016) calling it "revelatory" and Michael O'Sullivan for the *Washington Post* (6 Oct. 2016) praising Lane as "mesmerizing newcomer."

FAME

After filming was complete, Lane found herself adrift again, bouncing between friends' couches in Texas and Los Angeles, California. In May 2016, she was reunited with her cast mates for the film's premiere at the Cannes Film Festival. There, *American Honey* earned the prestigious Jury Prize. "Nothing will top that. It was so intense and so emotional and so unreal. To walk away and be proud of something that you created, and something that is going to be out there, I think that's amazing. That was the first time we were all back together again. That was the first time I saw the movie," Lane told Kelsey, describing her experience at the Cannes Film Festival. "It was very beautiful, and lively, and there was a lot of love, and plus, with *American Honey*, we make everything fun. So we ditched all of the high-end stuff and just had a great time."

Since winning such accolades for her performance in *American Honey*, Lane is quickly becoming an in-demand actor—and her schedule reflects it. "I never know if I'll be free on what day," Lane said of her new life to Jackson. "Everything is planned out for you, but things just pop up as you go. It's been free living. Sometimes I try to escape to Texas, but life is very 'whatever happens next.' It's crazy."

FUTURE ENDEAVORS

Despite her success, Lane has been trying to take things slow and adjust to the opportunities her role has given her. "I've been reading books and looking at articles, trying to find things that I enjoy in the midst of my auditions and everything," Lane told Kelsey. "I'm going with the flow of it. I don't really know what I want exactly, but I know as far as the energy I'm trying to put out into the world in hopes to get it back and get those things that I want to be a part of, without me being like, 'This is a plan. This is a goal.' So, we'll see."

Since *American Honey* premiered, she has completed work on a video short called *Great Performers: LA Noir* (2016). Lane's upcoming films include *The Miseducation of Cameron Post*, an adaptation of the 2012 young-adult novel of the same name by Emily M. Danforth; *Shoplifters of the World*, directed by Stephen Kijak and starring Joe Manganiello; *Hunting Lila*, a film adaptation of the young-adult series by Sarah Alderson; and *Shotgun*, a romantic comedy starring Maika Monroe and Jeremy Allen White. Release dates for these films have not yet been set.

SUGGESTED READING

Cohen, Finn. "*American Honey*: Open Highways, Free Spirits." *The New York Times*, 28 Sept. 2016, www.nytimes.com/2016/10/02/movies/american-honey-open-highways-free-spirits.html. Accessed 22 Apr. 2017.

Ford, Rebecca. "*American Honey* Breakout Sasha Lane Joins Indie Drama *Shotgun* (Exclusive)." *The Hollywood Reporter*, 5 Apr. 2017, www.hollywoodreporter.com/news/american-honey-breakout-sasha-lane-joins-indie-drama-shotgun-991143. Accessed 10 May 2017.

Kermode, Mark. "*American Honey* Review—A Magical Mystery Tour of the US." Review of *American Honey*, directed by Andrea Arnold. *The Guardian*, 16 Oct. 2016, www.theguardian.com/film/2016/oct/16/american-honey-review-mark-kermode. Accessed 22 Apr. 2017.

Lane, Sasha. "Sasha Lane on How Her Role in *American Honey* Changed Everything." Interview by Noah Jackson. *Nylon*, 15 Nov. 2016, www.nylon.com/articles/sasha-lane-american-honey-interview. Accessed 22 Apr. 2017.

Lane, Sasha. "Sasha Lane: Star Rising." Interview by Colleen Kelsey. *Interview Magazine*, 30 Sept. 2016, www.interviewmagazine.com/film/sasha-lane. Accessed 22 Apr. 2017.

O'Sullivan, Michael. "*American Honey*: Travels with a Youthful Subculture, Fleeing Crushed Dreams." *The Washington Post*, 6 Oct. 2016, www.washingtonpost.com/goingoutguide/movies/american-honey-travels-with-a-youthful-subculture-fleeing-crushed-dreams/2016/10/06/f81b465e-8723-11e6-92c2-14b64f3d453f_story.html. Accessed 22 Apr. 2017.

—*Christopher Mari*

Zara Larsson

Date of birth: December 16, 1997
Occupation: Singer

Swedish pop music stars have long had crossover appeal in the United States, beginning in the 1970s with ABBA and including such diverse artists as Europe, Ace of Base, Robyn, Icona Pop, and Avicii. By 2016, the singer-songwriter Zara Larsson joined that list, as she skyrocketed from fame in her native country to international success with a musical style that drew comparisons to superstars Rihanna and Lorde. Her breakthrough came while still just a teenager—she amassed a string of hit singles in Europe and reached top of the American dance music charts before turning nineteen years old. Her hits include such songs as "Never Forget You," a collaboration with British artist MNEK, which became a number-one dance song in the United States, and "Lush Life," which also topped the charts across Europe.

Larsson's rise to pop stardom was fast but foreshadowed from a young age, as she won a major Swedish talent competition television program at age ten. After a few of her recordings gained attention, her first full-length solo album, *1*, debuted in 2014 to critical and commercial acclaim. By the end of 2016, her music videos had amassed millions of views—"Lush Life" surpassed 421 million views on YouTube alone—and she had built a social media following in the millions, including major popularity on the music-streaming service Spotify. Admittedly ambitious, Larsson approached music

Frankie Fouganthin/CC BY-SA 3.0/Wikimedia Commons

from the beginning with the goal of becoming a worldwide pop phenomenon. "I'm proudly mainstream," she noted in an interview with Maggie Lange for *GQ* (20 Apr. 2016). "I want to make music that I just love. A good song is a good song. I want my songs to be played on the radio. I want people to like it. I don't over-think stuff. Not what I do, not what I wear, not what I say. I'm just like, *Yeah, I like that, let's do it!*"

EARLY LIFE AND CAREER

Zara Larsson was born on December 16, 1997, in Stockholm, Sweden, to Agnetha and Anders Larsson. She grew up with her younger sister, Hanna, who eventually went on to pursue a mu-sical career herself. Larsson's parents were both very supportive of having an open atmosphere in their household, so both sisters were allowed to question everything and frequently spent hours at the dinner table having debates over a wide variety of issues. Such free expression enabled young Zara to frequently argue for her causes—including her future plans for her professional life. From a young age she wanted to be a singer, and a famous one at that, often telling her moth-er during her childhood that she wanted to be the next Elvis Presley.

That drive led Larsson to begin performing, which in turn reinforced her ambition. She told Arielle Castillo for *Rolling Stone* (8 Apr. 2016): "When I was about nine or ten, I was on a few random talent shows in shopping malls. And I just thought that was so fun, and then I heard about the TV show thing and then I was like,

'Wow, that's what I want to do! I want millions of people to see me.'"

The "TV show thing" was what enabled Larsson to make good on her childhood hope. At age ten, she competed on the 2008 season of *Talang Sverige*, the Swedish version of the Got Talent television series. Despite her youth and inexperience, she won the contest. The song that secured her win, "My Heart Will Go On," was first made famous by Celine Dion, and Lars-son recorded it as her first single. "It went really fast," she recalled of her experience on the tal-ent show to Rob LeDonne for *Teen Vogue* (29 Mar. 2016). "I auditioned and all of the sudden I was the winner. When I look back at it, I'm like, 'How did I do that?' I think that I was so small I was just like, 'Yeah!'"

EXPLODING ONTO THE EUROPEAN MUSIC SCENE

Despite her early and overwhelming success on television, Larsson did not sign with a record la-bel right away because she was still just a child. "I met with a lot of labels and record companies after I won and they were all like, 'You're way too young for this,'" she told LeDonne. "I was devastated and thought my career was over. Now when I look back on it, I realize why. No one wants to sign a ten-year-old unless it was Disney or Nickelodeon and I wasn't interested in that."

Larsson waited just four years—until 2012, when she was a teenager—to sign with TEN Music Group, an independent music company in Sweden. Over the next year, she worked with various songwriters and producers on a five-song EP, which was released in January 2013 under the title *Introducing*. She had low expectations for this early effort. "I thought that so many good artists were releasing music, why would anyone buy mine? I was really doubting myself," she told LeDonne. However, the listening public soon put her fears to rest. The first single off the re-cord, "Uncover," topped the charts in her native Sweden, as well as in Norway, and reached num-ber three in Denmark. The song was eventually certified triple platinum in Sweden.

Larsson's follow-up EP, *Allow Me to Rein-troduce Myself*, debuted in June 2013, produc-ing the double-single, "She's Not Me (Pt. 1)" and "She's Not Me (Pt. 2)." As her social media following grew, eventually reaching millions of followers on Facebook, Twitter, and Instagram, Larsson was recognized as one of the brightest up-and-coming pop stars throughout Europe. With fame in Sweden achieved and European success rapidly growing, she turned her atten-tion to America, signing a three-year contract with Epic Records in the United States in April 2013.

MAKING IT IN AMERICA

Larsson's debut full-length album, *1*, was released in October 2014. It was another smash success in Sweden, spawning top-ten hits with the singles "Rooftop," "She's Not Me," and "Carry You Home." However, it was not released globally and so could not attract wide popularity in the United States. That breakthrough came in 2015, thanks to the release of new singles and Larsson's social media presence.

In January 2015 Larsson had her first experience with the power of the American media when a post she made on the social media site Instagram went viral. The post showed a photo of her pulling a condom over her foot and lower leg, with a caption indicating that no man could claim his penis was too big for a condom. Larsson expressed surprise at the attention and controversy the post generated across social media. "I posted it because I thought it was funny and it wound up exploding," she told LeDonne. "People have done that joke since fourth grade, so I don't know why everyone was like, 'Oh, my God!' I guess it was the caption. It was obviously a joke, but let's be honest: It's got some truth."

Even as she drew attention on social media, Larsson worked on extending her musical success. Her international debut EP, *Uncover*, containing versions of some of her previous hits, was released by Epic in early 2015. Meanwhile, she was busy crafting a follow-up full-length album, and provided previews through a series of singles. The first of these, "Lush Life," was released in June 2015. It not only became a multiplatinum hit in Sweden, topping the charts there, but also reached the upper ends of the charts in such countries as Great Britain, Australia, Denmark, Ireland, and Germany, among others.

Larsson followed this success with a collaboration with British artist MNEK, "Never Forget You," a dance track that topped charts in numerous countries, including the United States. She was particularly proud of that song's success, as it represented her progression as an artist. "'Never Forget You' was the first song I cowrote," she told Joey Nolfi for *Entertainment Weekly* (13 Apr. 2016). "Before that, I wasn't really writing, I was just singing. . . . But I wanted to be an even bigger part of the whole thing." However, she noted that she had no plans to record only her own material and would not turn down the chance to record a song she enjoyed written by someone else. "I'm not proud like that. . . . If it's a good song, it's a good song. I'll take it," she told Nolfi. Larsson went on to perform "Never Forget You" live on *The Tonight Show Starring Jimmy Fallon* in April 2016. That performance was met with such acclaim that she was asked to return, which she did in September, to perform "Lush Life."

FURTHER SUCCESS

By the end of 2016 Larsson had indeed achieved breakthrough success in the United States and other markets around the world. Many critics noted that a large part of Larsson's international allure comes from her considerable vocal dexterity. "Much of Larsson's appeal lies in her ability to fit into a song. Her vocalizations are chameleon-like," Lange wrote, noting that the singer effortlessly shifts styles from song to song, invoking established superstars such as Rihanna and Mariah Carey. Demonstrating this versatility, Larsson was featured in an advertising campaign by cosmetics maker Clinique that tied different lipstick colors and fashion looks to different musical styles. The campaign used an interactive music video of "Lush Life" that saw Larsson performing acoustic, country, pop, and dance versions of the track.

In October 2016, *Time* magazine named Larsson as one of the thirty most influential teenagers of the year. The honor recognized not only her status as one of the biggest young pop stars of the time but her reception as something of a feminist spokesperson. For example, her 2016 single "Ain't My Fault" was interpreted as a song about empowered women, while her outspoken social media comments frequently channeled women's rights messages.

Larsson's next full-length record was planned for release in January 2017. Like her previous effort, she collaborated with a number of songwriters and producers and had a hand in cowriting roughly half the tracks. In an interview for *Harper's Bazaar* (29 Nov. 2016), Erica Gonzales asked the singer if her new record was different from *1*, to which Larsson replied: "I feel like it's not too different, it's just better. The melodies are better, the production is better, the lyrics are better. I just feel like you just take it up a few notches. It's still kind of the same vibe but a little bit more grown."

PERSONAL LIFE

Larsson openly cites fellow pop star Beyoncé as her greatest idol, both in terms of music and in being a feminist and social activist. As she told Nolfi, "I met her once and I just cried so much." Larsson has described taking advantage of her social media celebrity in her dating life. She is also noted for being very forthright and has freely described her personality as attention-seeking. "I want people to look at me all the time. I was the clown in class," she told Lange. "Everybody wants attention, more or less. I just want a lot."

SUGGESTED READING

Larsson, Zara. "Swedish Pop Sensation Zara Larsson Previews Her Anticipated Second Album." Interview by Joey Nolfi. *Entertainment Weekly*, 13 Apr. 2016, www.ew.com/

article/2016/04/13/zara-larsson-interview. Accessed 13 Dec. 2016.

Larsson, Zara. "Zara Larsson: From Swedish Reality TV Star to EDM-Pop Sensation." Interview by Arielle Castillo. *Rolling Stone*, 8 Apr. 2016, www.rollingstone.com/music/news/zara-larsson-from-swedish-reality-tv-star-to-edm-pop-sensation-20160408. Accessed 13 Dec. 2016.

Larsson, Zara. "Zara Larsson Is Gunning for Your Attention." Interview by Maggie Lange. *GQ*, 20 Apr. 2016, www.gq.com/story/zara-larsson-wcw. Accessed 13 Dec. 2016.

LeDonne, Rob. "Meet Zara Larsson, the 18-Year-Old Swedish Export Taking Over the Pop World." *Teen Vogue*, 29 Mar. 2016, www.teenvogue.com/story/zara-larsson-interview. Accessed 13 Dec. 2016.

SELECTED WORKS

Introducing, 2013; *Allow Me to Reintroduce Myself*, 2013, *1*, 2014

—*Christopher Mari*

Credit: Simon Prosser

Deborah Levy

Date of birth: 1959
Occupation: Writer

Deborah Levy is the acclaimed playwright, poet, and author of such novels as *Swimming Home* (2012) and *Hot Milk* (2016), both of which were shortlisted for the prestigious Man Booker Prize. "While the settings in Levy's novels shift and slide, her subjects have stayed markedly the same," Sarah Crown wrote for *The Guardian* (19 Mar. 2016). "Questions of identity, exile, and dislocation thread their way through her fiction," she continued. When Levy was asked by Crown whether she would agree that her published work consisted of "variations on a single theme," Levy, who is a native of South Africa but moved as a young child to Great Britain, rejected the notion and explained to Crown that any child who has "left one country and arrived in another" experiences a "sort of rupture." Therefore, it is unsurprising and perhaps even expected that "those sorts of questions [of identity, exile, and dislocation] will come up."

Another hallmark of Levy's work is her ability to conjure convincing and unforgettable female protagonists. "I want to walk my female characters into the center of my work," she explained to Kate Kellaway for *The Guardian* (20 Sept. 2012). "They don't have to be likable, but they have to be compelling and complicated."

EARLY LIFE AND EDUCATION

Levy was born in 1959 in Johannesburg, South Africa, during the era of racial segregation and political oppression known as apartheid. She and her younger brother, Sam, lived with their parents on the city of Johannesburg. Her father was of Lithuanian Jewish descent, and his own parents had been shopkeepers. While they owned a fish store when they first came to South Africa, they later began selling lingerie, because Levy's grandmother had grown tired of the smell of fish. "I've always loved that mix of fish and lingerie," Levy quipped to Jacques Testard for the *White Review* (Aug. 2013). Levy's mother hailed from a patrician British family, and her parents were shocked when Levy chose to marry the penniless Jewish son of a merchant.

Levy's father worked as a professor of history, and he was a staunch member of the African National Congress (ANC), which fought to end apartheid and grant voting rights to blacks. Because the ANC was officially banned by the ruling whites, he was arrested in 1964 and held for four years as a political prisoner. During those formative years, Levy and her brother knew him only from a photo their mother kept out on display and from the occasional letters he was allowed to send.

Levy's mother was a voracious reader who helped the children cope with their father's absence by spinning complex bedtime tales. She raised them with the aid of a tall Zulu housekeeper the family called Maria (although her real name was Zama). Despite their best efforts, Levy was considered something of a troublemaker at her all-white school. After the headmaster beat Levy with a ruler for not following her teacher's instructions, Levy's mother sent her to the town of Durban to live with a family friend and attend a Catholic school.

This marked only a short-lived exile; one day, unable to bear the thought of the family's beloved budgie locked in a cage like her father, she released the bird. Although it was retrieved only a few hours later by one of the family's servants, Levy had angered the matriarch so greatly that she was sent back to Johannesburg to live with her family.

Levy's father was finally released when Levy was nine years old. "He came out of prison looking quite different from that photo [we had on display]," Levy recalled to Danny Danziger for the *Independent* (2 Oct. 1994). "He was much thinner, and he was wearing a suit that was years out of date. It was shocking." He remained under house arrest, making it impossible to find work, so, like many former political prisoners, he was forced to move with his family out of the country.

The family sailed on an ocean liner called the *Edinburgh Castle* and arrived on the south coast of England in July 1968. In her memoir, *Things I Don't Want to Know* (2014), Levy writes that although she cherishes her memories of Maria, "I don't want to know about my other memories of South Africa. When I arrived in the UK, what I wanted were new memories."

The family settled in the nondescript London suburb of Wembley Park and lived in a small apartment above a menswear shop where her parents had both secured employment. The couple, who were still enduring the task of getting to know each other again after so many years apart and who still suffered financial difficulties, began to fight frequently and finally divorced when Levy was fifteen years old. "I suppose I realized . . . that in many ways the real world was very disappointing," Levy recalled to Danziger. "And I remember deciding at the end of that first year in England, when I was ten, that that was enough snot and tears for a lifetime."

Remembering advice she had gotten from a nun while attending Catholic school in Durban, Levy began to put her thoughts down on paper. "Writing made me feel wiser than I actually was," she recalls in her memoir. "Wise and sad. That was what I thought writers should be."

Levy intended to study English literature after secondary school, but before embarking on that pursuit she took a year off from schooling and spent that time working as an usher at an art house cinema in the then bohemian neighborhood of Notting Hill. While working there one day, she met the filmmaker Derek Jarman, who recognized her love of drama and suggested she attend Dartington College of Arts to study

playwriting, which she then attended. "I wound up having an avant-garde theatre and contemporary arts training," she explained to Testard. Throughout her time at Dartington, Levy continued to write short stories and plays, some of which she submitted to *London Magazine*. After many rejections, the editor finally agreed to publish one, which then drew the attention of an agent.

WRITING CAREER

Levy's debut novel, *Beautiful Mutants*, was published in 1989, as was her short-story collection *Ophelia and the Great Idea*. Those volumes brought her a small measure of acclaim in London's literary circles; anthologists began including her short stories and poetry in their collections, and the Royal Shakespeare Company staged some of her plays.

Levy did not aspire to write bestselling commercial fiction but was nonetheless distressed when she had difficulty finding a publisher for *Swimming Home*, a novel that had taken her five years to write. The online bookstore and e-commerce site Amazon had already begun to change the publishing landscape, and in a generally tight economy, publishers were reluctant to take on a work as complex and cerebral as Levy's. Finally, a small nonprofit press whose founder was a fan took a chance on *Swimming Home*. The novel garnered glowing reviews, won a National Book Award, and was shortlisted for the 2012 Man Booker Prize, bringing it to the attention of readers far outside Levy's usual small audience.

In a November 12, 2012, review published in the *New York Times*, Francine Prose called *Swimming Home* a "wry, accomplished novel" and elaborated that the book makes readers wonder whether they have "seen something like this in an early Chabrol thriller or in that Ozon film with Charlotte Rampling? Don't the tone and the milieu suggest an improbable hybrid of Virginia Woolf, Edward St. Aubyn, *Absolutely Fabulous* and Patricia Highsmith?" Despite the feeling of familiarity or even of repetition, Prose concludes that the reader will decide "that *Swimming Home* is unlike anything but itself."

Due in large part to the success garnered from *Swimming Home*, it was easy for Levy to find a publisher for her next novel, *Hot Milk*, which hit shelves in 2016 and was also shortlisted for the Man Booker. The novel traces the adventures of Sofia Papastergiadis, a waitress and former PhD candidate, and her mother, Rose, as they travel by car across southern Spain in order to visit a clinic they hope will provide a cure for Rose's unexplained paralysis. "*Hot Milk* is a powerful novel of the interior life, which Levy creates with a vividness that recalls Virginia Woolf," Erica Wagner wrote in a review for *The*

Guardian (27 Mar. 2016). She continued that "the sense of Sofia's life with her mother (or against her mother) is built through an accumulation of detail, a constellation of symbols and narrative bursts."

PERSONAL LIFE
Levy has two daughters, Sadie and Leila, with the playwright David Gale. In her memoir, she writes of the experience of motherhood, "We were all shadows of our former selves, chased by the women we used to be before we had children. . . . We had metamorphosed . . . in to someone we did not entirely understand."

Levy lives in London and writes each day in a backyard garden shed where the late poet Andrew Mitchell once wrote. Mitchell's widow is a family friend and rents the space to Levy. The two women usually end the day by having a drink together.

Levy swims daily for exercise, either at a local gym or, when the weather is nice, at one of the ponds within Hampstead Heath, a large public park in London. Levy is an avid amateur chef.

SUGGESTED READING
Crown, Sarah. "A Life in. . . Deborah Levy." *The Guardian*, 19 Mar. 2016, www.theguardian.com/books/2016/mar/19/books-interview-deborah-levy-hot-milk. Accessed 29 Jan. 2017.
Danziger, Danny. "The Worst of Times: Life after Apartheid: Snot and Tears." *Independent*, 2 Oct. 1994, www.independent.co.uk/life-style/the-worst-of-times-life-after-apartheid-snot-and-tears-deborah-levy-talks-to-danny-danziger-1440660.html. Accessed 29 Jan. 2017.
Kellaway, Kate. "It's a Page-Turner about Sorrow." *The Guardian*, 20 Sept. 2012, www.theguardian.com/books/2012/sep/20/deborah-levy-swimming-home-interview. Accessed 29 Jan. 2017.
Levy, Deborah. "Interview with Deborah Levy." Interview by Jacques Testard. *The White Review*, Aug. 2013, www.thewhitereview.org/interviews/interview-deborah-levy/. Accessed 29 Jan. 2017.
Miller, E. CE. "Who Is Deborah Levy?" *Bustle*, 20 Oct. 2016, www.bustle.com/articles/188013-who-is-deborah-levy-the-hot-milk-author-is-one-of-the-best-of-our-time. Accessed 29 Jan. 2017.
Prose, Francine. "Naked Came the Stranger." Review of *Swimming Home*, by Deborah Levy. *The New York Times*, 21 Nov. 2012, www.nytimes.com/2012/11/25/books/review/swimming-home-by-deborah-levy.html. Accessed 29 Jan. 2017.
Wagner, Erica. "Powerful Novel of Interior Life." Review of *Hot Milk*, by Deborah Levy. *The Guardian*, 27 Mar. 2016, www.theguardian.com/books/2016/mar/27/hot-milk-deborah-levy-review. Accessed 29 Jan. 2017.

SELECTED WORKS
Beautiful Mutants, 1989; *Ophelia and the Great Idea*, 1989; *Swallowing Geography*, 1993; *Swimming Home*, 2011; *Black Vodka: Ten Stories*, 2013; *Things I Don't Want to Know*, 2014; *Hot Milk*, 2016

—*Mari Rich*

Tomas Lindahl
Date of birth: January 28, 1938
Occupation: Biochemist

Tomas Lindahl is a Nobel Prize–winning biochemist who demonstrated that the DNA molecule is unstable and requires a molecular maintenance system. In particular, he described a repair mechanism known base excision repair.

EARLY LIFE AND EDUCATION
Tomas Lindahl was born on January 28, 1938, in Kungsholmen, Stockholm, Sweden, to Folke and Ethel Lindahl. He studied at the Karolinska Institutet in Stockholm, completing his PhD in 1967. He spent two years in the United States pursuing postdoctoral work at Princeton University in New Jersey and Rockefeller University in New York City, and he then returned to Karolinska as a faculty member and to complete his medical degree, which he was awarded in 1970.

During Lindahl's doctoral research, the reigning biological understanding of DNA was that it was a stable molecule. Lindahl disagreed, and he suspected that DNA was much less stable than was generally assumed and that it was much more prone to random mutations, copying errors, damage from external chemicals and energy sources, and other injuries to its integrity. He chose the stability of DNA as the topic of his doctoral thesis, which was titled "On the Structure and Stability of Nucleic Acids in Solution."

DNA: AN UNSTABLE MOLECULE
Lindahl's doctoral research demonstrated that DNA was indeed inherently unstable and that it needed a system of repair to maintain itself. He set about investigating those mechanisms of repair. DNA is made up of four nitrogen bases—adenine, thymine, cytosine, and guanine—which are attached to a sugar-phosphate backbone. In his previous work, Lindahl had noted a common mutation: cytosine can lose one of its chemical components and spontaneously become uracil, which is normally only found in

RNA, and which then negatively affects the encoded message of the molecule.

In the early 1970s, Lindahl determined the ways in which DNA repairs this particular type of error, a mechanism that was named base excision repair. To execute a base excision repair, a specialized enzyme first detects the error and snips out the mutated base. Another two enzymes then deliver a fresh, error-free cytosine molecule and attach it to the DNA's backbone. Lindahl was the first to describe this mechanism, and once he felt he had described the base excision repair mechanism in bacteria well enough, he moved on to describing its function in human cells.

The failure of DNA repair mechanisms in human cells, Lindahl discovered, is a root cause of many cancers. In particular, Lindahl was one of the first researchers to show how the Epstein-Barr virus can cause cancer by changing the DNA of its host.

In 1978 Lindahl left his long-time home at Karolinska to take a position as a professor of medical and physiological chemistry at the University of Gothenburg in Gothenburg, Sweden. By the early 1980s, he had moved to London to join the Imperial Cancer Research Fund (later renamed Cancer Research UK) Mill Hill Laboratories in London, in large part due to the cancer-oriented implications of his research on DNA repair. He left the Mill Hill Laboratories in 1984 to direct Clare Hall Laboratories (later absorbed into the Francis Crick Institute), where he remained until the early 2000s. He was elected as a Fellow of the prestigious Royal Society in 1988.

Lindahl retired in 2009 but maintained emeritus positions with Cancer Research UK and honorary appointments at institutions around the world. His retirement has included roles as a scientific adviser for the Beijing Institute of Genomics, Chinese Academy of Sciences; the International Foundations of Medicine in Milan; and the Cancer and Ageing Centre at the University of Nice, France.

IMPACT

Lindahl was one of three biochemists awarded the 2015 Nobel Prize in Chemistry. He shared the award with the Turkish-American Aziz Sancar and American Paul L. Modrich. The Royal Swedish Academy of Sciences, which awards the Nobel Prize, described the separate but related work of Lindahl, Sancar, and Modrich as "a decisive contribution to the understanding of how the living cell functions, as well as providing knowledge about the molecular causes of several hereditary diseases and about mechanisms behind both cancer development and aging."

Lindahl, in particular, upended the biological orthodoxy presuming that DNA must be a stable molecule. He instead showed that DNA requires complex and efficient machinery to account for the massive amount of errors it incurs because of the wear and tear of everyday life. In addition to his own achievements, his research laid the groundwork for other researchers to map the various mechanisms of DNA repair. In doing so, he had a revolutionary impact on how doctors and scientists approach the causes and treatments of various genetic diseases, particularly cancers with a genetic origin.

PERSONAL LIFE

Lindahl was married to Alice Adams from 1967 until their divorce in 1980. They have a son and a daughter. Lindahl enjoys advising fellow scientists and tracking the accomplishments of his students and is proud of the acclaim he has brought both to Cancer Research UK and his alma mater the Karolinska Institutet.

SUGGESTED READING

Anderson, Malin. "Tomas Lindahl: A Laureate with Absolute Pitch for DNA Repair." *Nordic Life Science*. Media Value, 30 Mar. 2016. Web. 28 June 2016.

Broad, William J. "Nobel Prize in Chemistry Awarded to Tomas Lindahl, Paul Modrich, and Aziz Sancar for DNA Studies." *New York Times*. New York Times, 7 Oct. 2015. Web. 31 May 2016.

Cressey, Daniel. "DNA Repair Sleuths Win Chemistry Nobel." *Nature*. Macmillan Publishers, 7 Oct. 2015. Web. 1 June 2016.

Fernholm, Ann. "DNA Repair—Providing Chemical Stability for Life." *Nobel Prize*. Royal Swedish Academy of Sciences, 2015. Web. 28 June 2016.

Huss, Madeline Svärd. "The 2015 Nobel Prize in Chemistry—Tomas Lindahl Conducted Crucial Research at Karolinska Institutet." *KI News*. Karolinska Institutet, 14 Dec. 2015. Web. 1 June 2016.

Lindahl, Tomas. "My Journey to DNA Repair." *Genomics, Proteomics, & Bioinformatics* 11.1 (2013): 2–7. Print.

—*Kenrick Vezina, MS*

Little Big Town

Occupation: Country music group

KAREN FAIRCHILD
Date of birth: September 28, 1969
Occupation: Vocalist

KIMBERLY SCHLAPMAN
Date of birth: October 15, 1969
Occupation: Vocalist

PHILLIP SWEET
Date of birth: March 18, 1974
Occupation: Vocalist, guitarist

JIMI WESTBROOK
Date of birth: October 20, 1971
Occupation: Vocalist, guitarist

Photo by Terry Wyatt/Getty Images for ACM

Since 1998, the vocal quartet of Karen Fairchild, Kimberly Schlapman, Jimi Westbrook, and Phillip Sweet, also known as Little Big Town (LBT), has captivated country music listeners with their signature four-part harmonies and multiple lead vocals. After a commercially disappointing debut album, the group has established themselves as one of country music's elite, with three number-one country albums and eight top-10 country singles under their belt. They have also tested the bounds of country music sensibilities, with their controversial number-one hit "Girl Crush" (2014), a provocative ballad about a jilted woman who is envious of her ex-boyfriend's latest love. Lyrics implying same-sex attraction resulted in radio listener complaints that led the song to be taken off the air by some country radio stations, but it also earned the group their first crossover hit—and mainstream recognition.

LBT has also not shied away from joining forces with fellow country musicians such as Vince Gill and Miranda Lambert, as well as artists from other genres, including rock singer John Mellencamp and, most recently, rapper Pharrell Williams. Williams produced their 2016 album *Wanderlust*, which also featured an appearance from pop singer Justin Timberlake. Their latest album, 2017's *The Breaker*, includes the Taylor Swift–penned tune "Better Man," the group's third number-one song.

FAIRCHILD AND SCHLAPMAN

Karen Fairchild was born to Brenda and Butch Fairchild in Gary, Indiana, on September 28, 1969. She grew up with her two siblings in Marietta, Georgia, where her father was a sales executive. Fairchild's parents exposed their middle child to gospel and traditional country, including Dolly Parton and Kenny Rogers. She first heard pop and rock music while listening to her older sister's car radio. At Lassiter High School in Marietta, Fairchild was involved in the school's music program, where she developed her singing voice and gave her first-ever solo performance on stage. "I was terrified," she admitted to Steve Helling for *People* (21 Jan. 2017). "But it changed my life. It gave me self-confidence."

After graduating from high school, Fairchild studied early childhood education at Alabama's Samford University. She also successfully auditioned for the Samford Singers, the school's a cappella choir—a major turning point. "I never stopped singing after that," she told Sarah Mausolf for *Vail Daily* (16 July 2009). "It kind of took off from there." So did Fairchild's friendship with choirmate and fellow Georgia native Kimberly Schlapman, whom she first met while traveling by bus to choir camp.

Born on October 15, 1969, in the rural, blue-collar town of Cornelia, Schlapman grew up surrounded by music. Schlapman's earliest memories were of singing in the church alongside her father and her younger sister, as well as singing harmony with her family. Her turning point came around age eleven or twelve, when a friend gave her a copy of Emmylou Harris's bluegrass-flavored album *Roses in the Snow* (1980). "I remember staying in my room and listening to those songs and standing in front of my mirror and hoping that one day I [would be] singing in front of other people," she recounted to Wayne Bledsoe for the *Knoxville News Sentinel*

(14 Nov. 2014). Schlapman spent her teens honing her vocal skills in local talent competitions, community theater, and several choral groups. Schlapman's stint as a Samford Singer was also instrumental in introducing her to another choir member: Steven Roads, who became her spouse as well as the band's lawyer.

MOVING TO NASHVILLE

By 1990, Fairchild had graduated and was working as a substitute teacher in Georgia. Schlapman had transferred to the University of Tennessee in Knoxville, where Roads was an attorney for the university. Despite earning a degree in family and human development in 1992, Schlapman still hoped to pursue music. "I did a lot of singing in Knoxville and kind of developed a deep desire to make it in the business," she told Bledsoe. Fairchild also spent the early 1990s performing, with a couple of different Christian contemporary vocal groups.

The two college friends reunited in 1996 after moving to Nashville, where they were trying for solo careers. One day, they came up with a unique idea. "One thing that hadn't been done was a guy-and-girl group singing harmonies," Fairchild told Mary Colurso for *AL.com* (17 Sept. 2010). However, she added, "Chemistry is everything. Kimberly and I had this deep bond, and we had to find boys who would share it." The first guy Fairchild contacted was Jimi Westbrook.

Westbrook was born on October 20, 1971, in Jacksonville, Arkansas, and raised with his older sister in Sumiton, Alabama, where he grew up playing sports and singing in the choir. Westbrook fell in love with music as a twelve-year-old, after performing his first-ever choir solo. He was a member of vocal ensembles in high school and college, eventually graduating from Lee University in Tennessee.

BECOMING A QUARTET

Fairchild's phone call led Westbrook, who had recently resigned from a sales position, to relocate from Birmingham, Alabama, to Nashville. The newly formed trio subsequently honed their soulful harmonies while searching for their fourth group member. They found the missing piece of the puzzle in aspiring singer-songwriter Phillip Sweet. Like Westbrook, Sweet is an Arkansas native. Born on March 18, 1974, he was raised in a musical family in Cherokee Village, a resort community in the Ozark Mountains. By age ten, Sweet, whose mother is a guitarist, was not only playing guitar and keyboards but was also singing in church. Music became Sweet's main focus in high school and at Arkansas State University, in Jonesboro.

In 1998, a year after moving to Nashville, Sweet auditioned with his future bandmates in Schlapman's living room. "We knew when we heard the blend of our voices, that it was the blend we were looking for," Fairchild recalled to Brian Dagger for the *Toledo Blade* (29 Jan. 2006). "It's almost a sibling harmony." The quartet named themselves Little Big Town, and auditioned for several labels, including Mercury Nashville Records, who signed them to a recording contract in early 1999.

FINDING A LABEL

Following their performing debut at the Grand Ole Opry in May 1999, LBT started work on their debut album, recording four songs within eight months. However, the deal with Mercury fell through due to creative differences. Despite failing to produce a single or an album, Little Big Town managed to make inroads in country music, providing backing vocals on Collin Raye's album *Can't Back Down* (2001). Thanks to a publishing deal with Warner-Chappell Music, Sweet and Schlapman (as Kimberly Roads) also earned songwriting credit for "Back Where I Belong," a track from Sherrie Austin's 2001 album *Followin' a Feelin'*.

By January 2002, LBT had joined Sony Music Nashville's Monument Records. In May, they released their self-titled debut album, cowriting six of the ten tracks, including "Everything Changes" and "Don't Waste My Time," which reached the Billboard Hot Country Songs chart. "I think we were still trying to figure out who we are," Fairchild admitted to Chuck Dauphin for *Billboard* (9 October 2012). "We really hadn't been together that long."

While promoting the pop-leaning album, which only sold 31,000 copies, the group experienced more than its share of setbacks that year: the death of Westbrook's father; the end of Fairchild and Sweet's marriages; and the 2004 Sony-BMG merger and dissolution of Monument Records' Nashville division, which left LBT without a label—again.

EQUITY MUSIC

Undeterred, the quartet stayed together while working part-time to support themselves. Westbrook parked cars at a Nashville restaurant, Fairchild worked as a Music Row booking agent, while Sweet accepted a telemarketing gig. They returned to the studio to write and record material for their follow-up. Songwriter-producer Wayne Kirkpatrick, who cowrote the song "Pontiac" on the group's debut, financed the second album and provided them with free studio time and session musicians. Little Big Town continued to perform, driving themselves to low-paying gigs in a rented minivan. In 2005 LBT successfully shopped their demo to the independent Equity Music Group. The sudden passing of Roads to a heart attack in April 2005 overshadowed that joy.

Determined to keep going, LBT released "Boondocks" a month later. The small-town anthem—and lead single from their sophomore album, *The Road to Here*—resonated with country audiences, cracking the Billboard Hot Country Songs top ten in January 2006. It was outperformed by the top-five country hit "Bring It on Home." Two more top-twenty singles followed—"Good as Gone" and "A Little More You"—and the group took home the 2006 Academy of Country Music Award for top new vocal group or duo, along with nominations from the Grammy Awards and the Country Music Association Awards (CMA), among others. To promote *The Road to Here*, which achieved platinum status in February 2007, Little Big Town opened for Keith Urban and John Mellencamp.

CAPITOL RECORDS

LBT went on to release another album for Equity: *A Place to Land* (2007), which spawned two top-forty hits on the Hot Country Songs chart: "I'm with the Band" and "Fine Line." In May 2008, the band abandoned Equity for a multirecord deal with Capitol Records Nashville. Capitol also acquired the rights to their second album, which they rereleased with bonus tracks, including their Grammy- and CMA-nominated live rendition of The Dream Academy's "Life in a Northern Town," a collaboration with Sugarland and Jake Owen. Fairchild lent her voice to several tracks on Mellencamp's 2008 album *Life, Death, Love and Freedom*, including "A Ride Back Home." LBT closed out the year opening for Carrie Underwood and earning another CMA nod before headlining their 2009 tour.

The following March, the band released "Little White Church," their third top-ten hit—and third Grammy-nominated tune—from their fourth studio disc, *The Reason Why* (2010), also their first number-one record on the Billboard Country Albums chart. Over the next year, the group headlined another tour, opened for Sugarland, and performed at several Miranda Lambert concert dates.

The group's fifth album, *Tornado*, was released in 2012, and its first single, "Pontoon," became LBT's first number-one song and first platinum single, while the album's title track made the top ten. "Pontoon" went on to earn the group its first Grammy Award, for best country duo/group performance in 2012; yet another single from the album, "Your Side of the Bed," was nominated for a Grammy in 2013.

FURTHER COLLABORATIONS

The band's sixth album, *Pain Killer* (2014), delivered a summer hit with "Day Drinking," which reached number four on the Billboard Hot Country Songs chart. The band achieved another milestone on October 3, 2014, when Reba McEntire personally invited them to join the Grand Ole Opry, where they were officially inducted two weeks later. LBT entered uncharted territory in December 2014, however, with the release of "Girl Crush," the second single off *Pain Killer*. An ode to the charms of an ex-boyfriend's latest love, Fairchild sings, "I want to taste her lips / Yeah, 'cause they taste like you." Many listeners regarded the song as affirming same-sex attraction, and several country music radio stations bowed to pressure from listeners to take the song off the air, prompting a wider conversation about homophobia in country radio. "We were secretly hoping people would use their brain power a little better and listen to the whole song," Sweet told Jewly Hight for *Billboard* (6 Apr. 2017). Despite the controversy, "Girl Crush" managed thirteen weeks atop the Hot Country Songs chart; it also crossed over to the mainstream, reaching into the top thirty of the Billboard Adult Contemporary and Adult Pop Songs charts. The single earned LBT several accolades, including single of the year honors at the 2015 CMAs, as well as the 2015 Grammy for best country group performance.

For the first two months of 2016, LBT performed at the C2C: Country to Country music festival in the United Kingdom and provided backing vocals on "Take Me Down," a track on Vince Gill's *Down to My Last Bad Habit*. "They don't sound like anybody else," Gill told Hight. "In the history of country music, there's nobody like them." The crossover success of "Girl Crush" spurred the band to explore music outside their usual genre, resulting in *Wanderlust* (2016), their collaboration with hip-hop producer Pharrell Williams. Craig Jenkins's review for *Vulture* (13 June 2016) described the album as "the most eclectic offering in the group's catalogue," pushing the band "out of country and into funk, dance, and Caribbean music." *Wanderlust*, however, was not embraced by country music audiences and failed to chart. The quartet returned to their country music roots on their eighth studio album, *The Breaker* (2017), whose lead single, "Better Man," was written by Taylor Swift, a pop superstar with country roots; it became the band's third chart-topper on the Hot Country Songs chart.

In February 2017, LBT embarked on a yearlong, six-date inaugural residency at Nashville's Ryman Auditorium, former home of the Grand Ole Opry.

PERSONAL LIVES

The band made headlines in 2007 following Fairchild and Westbrook's secret wedding, as well as Schlapman's marriage to Stephen Schlapman. Fairchild and Westbrook are parents to Elijah Dylan Westbrook, born in March 2010. The Schlapmans have two daughters: Daisy

Pearl, born on July 27, 2007, and Dolly Grace, who was adopted in January 2017. Since March 2007, Sweet has been married to Rebecca Arthur, with whom he has daughter, Penelopi Jane, born on December 27, 2007.

Fairchild and Schlapman have pursued enterprises outside of music. In addition to hosting the Great American Country cooking series *Kimberly's Simply Southern* from 2012 to 2015, Schlapman has launched Oh Gussie!, a home and kitchenware collection, and penned a cookbook by the same name. In 2016 Fairchild unveiled her own clothing line.

SUGGESTED READING

Bledsoe, Wayne. "'Pain Killer': Life, Love and Tragedy Brought Little Big Town to Just the Right Mix." *Knoxville News Sentinel*, 14 Nov. 2014, archive.knoxnews.com/entertainment/music/pain-killer-life-love-and-tragedy-brought-little-big-town-to-just-the-right-mix-ep-748351348-353986191.html. Accessed 10 Aug. 2017.

Colurso, Mary. "Karen Fairchild: Little Big Town's on the Map, but There's Still Room to Grow." *AL.com*, 17 Sept. 2010, blog.al.com/mcolurso/2010/09/little_big_towns_on_the_map_bu.html. Accessed 10 Aug. 2017.

Dauphin, Chuck. "Little Big Town on No Lead Singer: 'It Worked for the Beatles.'" *Billboard*, 9 Oct. 2012, www.billboard.com/articles/columns/the-615/474736/little-big-town-on-no-lead-singer-it-worked-for-the-beatles. Accessed 10 Aug. 2017.

Dugger, Brian. "Nashville Dreaming: Little Big Town Reaches for the Top in Music City." *The Blade*, 29 Jan. 2006, www.toledoblade.com/Music-Theater-Dance/2006/01/29/Nashville-dreamin-Little-Big-Town-reaches-for-the-top-in-Music-City.html. Accessed 10 Aug. 2017.

Helling, Steve. "Little Big Town Surprises a High School Choir to Promote Music Education." *People*, 21 Jan. 2017, people.com/country/little-big-town-surprises-a-high-school-choir-to-promote-music-education/. Accessed 10 Aug. 2017.

Hight, Jewly. "Little Big Town, Nashville Royalty with an Outlaw Streak, Wants to Heal America." *Billboard*, 6 Apr. 2017, www.billboard.com/articles/news/magazine-feature/7751676/little-big-town-interview-cover-story. Accessed 10 Aug. 2017.

Jenkins, Craig. "Little Big Town and Pharrell Made a Country Album (Barely)." Review of *Wanderlust*, by Little Big Town. *Vulture*, 13 June 2016, www.vulture.com/2016/06/album-review-little-big-towns-wanderlust.html. Accessed 10 Aug. 2017.

SELECTED WORKS
The Road to Here, 2005; *The Reason Why*, 2010; *Pain Killer*, 2014; *The Breaker*, 2017

—*Bertha Muteba*

Carli Lloyd

Date of birth: July 16, 1982
Occupation: Soccer player

Midfielder Carli Lloyd is perhaps one of the most successful female soccer players in the United States, but her journey to the professional soccer field was not exactly a straight shot. In fact, as the title of her memoir, When Nobody Was Watching (2016), suggests, much of her development as a player occurred largely out of the spotlight, and Lloyd was for many years far less known than some of her teammates. After more than a decade in the sport, however, Lloyd has begun to receive far more recognition, in large part thanks to her performances at events such as the 2015 Fédération Internationale de Football Association (FIFA) World Cup, in which her three goals in quick succession helped push the US team to victory in their gold-medal game against Japan.

While those unfamiliar with soccer might be tempted to chalk many of Lloyd's accomplishments on the field up to good luck, Lloyd makes it clear that her World Cup goals, and others, have been nothing but the result of years of hard

Jamie Sabau/Getty Images

work. A talented soccer player from an early age, Lloyd nearly quit the game after being cut from the national youth team while in college. Turning her attitude and career around with the help of trainer James Galanis, Lloyd rededicated herself to the sport to great success, going on to play for teams such as the Houston Dash and traveling to three Olympics as part of the US national team. Even with such success, however, Lloyd is not content to stop working, particularly when goals such as pay equality for female soccer players have yet to be reached. "I know how hard I've had to work to get to this point. I know that it hasn't been an easy journey for me," she told Jonathan Tannenwald for *Philly.com* (29 July 2016). "I know that I want to continue to work hard for the rest of my career, and I have a lot of other things that I want to accomplish."

EARLY LIFE AND EDUCATION

Carli Lloyd was born on July 16, 1982, in Marlton, New Jersey. Her father, Steve, operated a machine shop, while her mother, Pam, worked as a paralegal. Lloyd, her brother, Stephen, and her sister, Ashley, grew up in Delran, a township in western New Jersey, where she attended Millbridge Elementary School.

Lloyd began playing soccer informally when she was five, practicing constantly at home and in a nearby park. "I used to kick the ball up against the curb for hours upon hours," she recalled in an interview with David Greene for National Public Radio's *Morning Edition* (29 Sept. 2016). She soon started to play on local teams, among them the Delran Dynamite, for which her father served as assistant coach, and the under-thirteen team the Medford Strikers. Lloyd continued to play while attending Delran High School, scoring twenty-six goals during her senior season with the Delran Bears. She graduated from high school in 2001.

After high school, Lloyd enrolled in New Jersey's Rutgers University, where she studied exercise science and sport studies. As a member of the Rutgers Scarlet Knights soccer team, she scored more goals than any other player by the time of her graduation and was thrice named an All-American player by the National Soccer Coaches Association of America. Lloyd graduated from Rutgers in 2006.

OVERCOMING CHALLENGES

While in college, Lloyd also served as a member of the US national under-twenty-one team. Although she had honed her soccer skills since childhood, she did not demonstrate the teamwork and physical fitness necessary to be a successful team member and was ultimately cut from the roster prior to her senior year of college. "I think for so many years I relied on my talent," Lloyd explained to Greene. "I didn't

have someone who really spoke the truth—told me that I wasn't fit, told me that I'm not a good teammate, I don't have good character: all of those things that are necessary at the top . . . . I made a lot of excuses, it was everybody else's fault."

After being cut from the team, Lloyd seriously considered quitting soccer for good. "I didn't know how to face adversity and be able to get through it," she told Greene of that period in her life. Her parents, however, convinced her to begin training with James Galanis, an Australian-born soccer trainer who forced Lloyd to confront her limitations as a player and work to overcome them. Working with Galanis not only enabled Lloyd to improve her physical fitness and soccer skills but also brought about a shift in Lloyd's understanding of teamwork and her role on the soccer field.

PROFESSIONAL SOCCER

After the Women's Professional Soccer (WPS) league was founded in 2010, Lloyd began playing for professional soccer teams that belonged to the league. She joined the Chicago Red Stars in 2009 and went on to play for the Sky Blue Football Club (FC) and the Atlanta Beat. The WPS shut down in 2012 but was soon replaced by the National Women's Soccer League (NWSL), and Lloyd began playing with the Western New York Flash for the 2013 season. Lloyd and the Flash placed second in the 2013 NWSL championship, ultimately losing to the Portland Thorns FC. After two seasons with the Flash, Lloyd was traded to the Houston Dash for the 2015 season. She remained with the team in 2016, although her work with the US national team and other professional commitments meant that she made only seven appearances with the Dash in 2016.

NATIONAL TEAM

Although Lloyd's experience on the youth national team had been challenging at times, she was nevertheless admitted onto the adult national team in 2005, making her first appearance in a game against Ukraine in July of that year. She proved herself to be a capable part of the team and in 2007 accompanied her teammates to her first FIFA Women's World Cup. At the World Cup, held in China in September 2007, the US team proceeded through the group phase and into the knockout stage, defeating England to move onward into the semifinals. In the semifinals, the team lost to the eventual second-place team, Brazil, before moving on to claim third place after beating Norway 4–1.

Although the United States did not manage to win the first World Cup in which she played, Lloyd remained determined to help achieve a US victory. The team got closer to that goal in 2011, placing second at the World Cup in Germany when a tied game against Japan ended in penalty kicks. Finally, at the 2015 Women's World Cup in Canada, the United States proceeded to the finals after eliminating the Colombian, Chinese, and German teams during the knockout stage. Facing Japan in the final match for the second time in a row, the team started off strong in large part thanks to Lloyd, who scored three goals in the game's first sixteen minutes. The third goal proved particularly impressive, as Lloyd managed to get the ball past Japanese goalkeeper Ayumi Kaihori from halfway across the field. "When I got the ball at midfield, I took a touch. I looked up and saw the keeper off her line," she recalled to Hallie Grossman for *ESPN* (23 May 2016). "I took another touch to prep. I just hit it. As perfect as could be. When it came off my foot, I knew it was perfect." That goal, the fourth achieved by that point in the game, gave the US team a commanding lead, and they ultimately won the final 5–2.

Following the team's World Cup victory, only the third by the US women's team, Lloyd was widely praised for her three-goal streak, which many commentators referred to as a lucky or miraculous event. Lloyd, however, characterized her performance differently. She explained to Grossman, "The thing is those 16 minutes were 13 years of hard, hard work." Lloyd's hard work was recognized in January 2016, when she was named the FIFA Women's World Player of the Year for 2015.

In addition to her World Cup appearances, Lloyd accompanied the US national team to the Olympic Games on several occasions. She played a key role in the 2008 and 2012 Games, scoring the winning goal in the gold-medal matches in both years. In 2016, Lloyd accompanied the United States women's soccer team to her third Olympics, this time in Rio de Janeiro, Brazil. Although the team succeeded in progressing through the group phase, the players were unable to proceed beyond the quarterfinals, during which the team tied with Sweden and ultimately lost during penalty kicks.

WAGE EQUALITY
In addition to her efforts on the soccer field, Lloyd has been engaged in an ongoing campaign to secure equal pay for members of the US women's soccer team. In March 2016, Lloyd and fellow players Alex Morgan, Becky Sauerbrunn, Hope Solo, and Megan Rapinoe filed a federal complaint in which they asserted that the women's team was subject to wage discrimination. Lloyd and the other players argued that despite their victories in major tournaments such as the FIFA Women's World Cup and the Olympics, they were receiving less than half the pay received by their male counterparts. Sports commentators have noted that the issue was

a complex one that was based not only on US Soccer's pay decisions but also on the collective bargaining agreements of both teams and the financial decisions made by FIFA. While the players seeking wage equality acknowledge the complexity of the situation, they argue that the time to act has come. "We have been quite patient over the years with the belief that the federation would do the right thing and compensate us fairly," Lloyd noted to Andrew Das for the *New York Times* (31 Mar. 2016).

PERSONAL LIFE
Lloyd married golf professional Brian Hollins in November 2016. The two began dating in high school. When not training or traveling to games, Lloyd lives in Mount Laurel, New Jersey.

In 2016, Lloyd published her first book, the memoir *When Nobody Was Watching: My Hard-Fought Journey to the Top of the Soccer World*. The book, cowritten with Wayne Coffey, chronicles both the evolution of her career and challenges in her personal life. Perhaps most striking is Lloyd's discussion of her relationship with her parents, which suffered as Lloyd sought to come into her own as an athlete. Although she was initially reluctant to discuss such personal challenges in her memoir, she ultimately decided that they played an important role in her development as a person and a player. "It's part of my journey," she told Greene, "and I think that I'd be lying to readers if this wasn't in there." A young readers' version titled *All Heart: My Dedication and Determination to Become One of Soccer's Best* came out later that same year.

SUGGESTED READING
Das, Andrew. "Top Female Players Accuse U.S. Soccer of Wage Discrimination." *New York Times*, 31 Mar. 2016, nytimes.com/2016/04/01/sports/soccer/uswnt-us-women-carli-lloyd-alex-morgan-hope-solo-complain.html. Accessed 15 Dec. 2016.

Grossman, Hallie. "16 Minutes of Fame." *ESPN*, 23 May 2016, www.espn.com/espn/feature/story/_/page/espnw-lloyd160523/carli-lloyd-ready-prove-2016-rio-olympics. Accessed 15 Dec. 2016.

Lloyd, Carli. "Carli Lloyd: U.S. Women's Soccer Team Is 'More Sophisticated.'" Interview by Jonathan Tannenwald. *Philly.com*, 29 July 2016, www.philly.com/philly/blogs/thegoalkeeper/Carli-Lloyd-US-womens-national-soccer-team-is-more-sophisticated.html. Accessed 15 Dec. 2016.

Lloyd, Carli. "How Carli Lloyd Became a Soccer Star 'When Nobody Was Watching.'" Interview by David Greene. *Morning Edition*. NPR, 29 Sept. 2016, www.npr.org/2016/09/29/495497578/

how-carli-lloyd-became-a-soccer-star-when-nobody-was-watching. Accessed 15 Dec. 2016.

Lloyd, Carli, and Wayne Coffey. *When Nobody Was Watching: My Hard-Fought Journey to the Top of the Soccer World.* Houghton, 2016.

Politi, Steve. "Carli Lloyd: Relationship with Rutgers Is 'Not Really Existent.'" *NJ.com,* 3 Oct. 2016, www.nj.com/rutgersfootball/index.ssf/2016/10/carli_lloyd_new_book_rutgers_story.html. Accessed 15 Dec. 2016.

—Joy Crelin

Lisa Lucas

Date of birth: January 1, 1980
Occupation: Executive director of the National Book Foundation

For as long as Lisa Lucas can remember, reading has been a fundamental part of her life. "There were books everywhere in my house," she told Hope Wabuke for the *Root* (27 Feb. 2016). "Books were very present. I just loved books. I never understood reading as anything but a pleasurable activity from a very young age." Despite her own lifelong love of reading, however, Lucas is well aware that the hobby, though a passion for some, is perceived by others as boring, tedious, or homework-like. As executive director of the National Book Foundation (NBF), a nonprofit organization responsible for the prestigious National Book Award, among other initiatives, Lucas seeks to combat the latter perception and promote reading and literature as diverse, inclusive, and accessible to anyone in the United States, regardless of location or demographic.

A professional with a background in nonprofits who began her career with theater- and film-focused organizations such as the Steppenwolf Theatre Company and the Tribeca Film Institute, Lucas gained notice within the publishing and literary fields for her work at the literary magazine *Guernica,* for which she first served as volunteer publisher and later joined full time in that role. After the NBF embarked on a search for a new executive director, Lucas was offered the job in early 2016 and took on the role in March of that year. She was in many ways an ideal candidate for the position, thanks to her nonprofit and publishing experience as well as her passion for books. Still, Lucas acknowledges that the role of executive director will present a difficult—yet rewarding—ongoing challenge due to the broad scope of the foundation's work. "Our mission is to enhance the cultural value of good writing in America," she explained to Ana

Sylvain Gaboury/Patrick McMullan via Getty Images

Marie Cox for the *New York Times Magazine* (7 Sept. 2016). "That's a big job!"

EARLY LIFE AND EDUCATION

Lisa Lucas was born on January 1, 1980, in New York City. Her father, Reggie, was a guitarist, music producer, and songwriter who worked with notable musicians such as Miles Davis and Madonna, while her mother, Kay, worked in advertising. The couple operated their own recording studio in New Jersey when Lucas was very young. An only child until she was a teenager, Lucas grew up in suburban Teaneck and Montclair, New Jersey. Following her parents' divorce, she lived primarily with her mother but regularly spent time at her father's home.

Lucas was an avid reader from an early age, having grown up in a family of readers and educators. "I was always a reader," she recalled to Wabuke. "My grandfather would come and pick me up every Tuesday night for our date night, which was the sweetest thing in the entire world. And if we got to go to the bookstore, that was the best." As a child growing up in the 1980s and 1990s, Lucas enjoyed many of the youth-oriented series of the era, such as the Sweet Valley High series, and she has also cited Madeleine L'Engle's classic science-fiction novel *A Wrinkle in Time* as a particular childhood favorite.

After graduating from high school, Lucas enrolled in the University of Chicago to study English. She earned her bachelor's degree from the university in 2001.

EARLY CAREER

Lucas made her first foray into the literary world at the age of fifteen, when she served as an intern at *Vibe* magazine. After graduating from college, she initially found a job with the Steppenwolf Theatre Company, a regional theater group operating out of Chicago. Lucas's work in regional theater would greatly influence her later perspective on the geographic diversity of great art, as the efforts of such theater organizations demonstrated that high-quality work was not limited to cultural centers such as New York City. "Regional has been fighting the good fight in the shadows of Broadway and Off-Broadway for years despite the fact that some of the most exciting, diverse, boundary-pushing work comes out of regional theater," she explained to Claire Kirch for *Publishers Weekly* (9 Mar. 2016). "Coming from that background, it's hard to discount the incredible work that's coming out of so many different parts of the country."

Over the next several years, Lucas continued to work in theater, joining TADA! Youth Theater as development and special events manager in 2003. In 2005 she shifted her focus to film, joining the staff of the Tribeca Film Institute. A nonprofit organization founded by actor Robert De Niro, producer Jane Rosenthal, and philanthropist Craig Hatkoff, the Tribeca Film Institute provides a variety of professional development opportunities for filmmakers and seeks to foster an interest in film among youth. As the organization's director of education, Lucas hoped to take advantage of new technology and implement inclusive and accessible programs to educate the next generation of filmmakers. "When I started working at Tribeca, things in film were changing dramatically," she recalled to Kirch. "As the medium became more digital, and more driven by social media, it became more accessible and affordable. We were able to think about how film education programming could reach students more broadly." Lucas remained with the Tribeca Film Institute into 2011.

Over the following years, Lucas worked as a consultant for a number of organizations and events related to the arts and literature, including the Scholastic Arts and Writing Awards, the Sundance Institute, and Scenarios USA. She developed curriculum for the San Francisco Film Society and in 2012 began to serve as cochair of the Brooklyn Book Festival's nonfiction committee. She continued to cochair the committee until 2016 and also became a member of the festival's literary council.

GUERNICA

Although much of Lucas's early work focused on the fields of theater and film, she remained an avid reader throughout and continued to be aware of the power of literature. In 2012 she took a further step into the literary world, volunteering as publisher of the literary magazine *Guernica*. Founded in 2004, *Guernica* is an online magazine that publishes fiction and poetry as well as a variety of nonfiction pieces. The magazine is operated as a nonprofit, and at the time of Lucas's first involvement, it was operated solely by volunteers. In 2014 *Guernica* announced that Lucas would be joining the magazine as a full-time, paid publisher, becoming the magazine's first such employee.

For Lucas, taking on *Guernica's* first full-time position represented an opportunity to take the magazine to a new level. "Coming on full-time means I'm not distracted and can take some of the burden off the staff. Everyone has a paying job [outside of the magazine], and on top of that they're spending hours and hours sneaking *Guernica* in before breakfast, sneaking it in at lunch, because everybody loves it so much," she told Cat Richardson for *Poets & Writers* (15 Oct. 2014). "There's nothing that I'm more passionate about or believe in more. Now more of our ideas can be made real more quickly, whereas sometimes we took a year to do something because there just wasn't the manpower." Lucas remained publisher of *Guernica* until early 2016, when she joined the NBF as executive director.

NATIONAL BOOK FOUNDATION

Founded in the 1980s, the National Book Foundation is a nonprofit organization devoted to promoting books and reading in the United States. Among its many initiatives, the foundation is responsible for overseeing the prestigious National Book Awards, which had been initially established in the 1950s but were reimagined under the NBF's leadership. The National Book Awards recognize excellence in four literary categories: fiction, nonfiction, poetry, and young people's literature.

When seeking and evaluating potential executive directors, the NBF's search committee pinpointed Lucas as an ideal candidate to take over the position and replace departing executive director Harold Augenbraum, only the second person to head the foundation. "We were looking for someone who could engage people of all kinds about books," David Steinberger, the chair of the organization's board of directors and a member of the search committee, told Calvin Reid for *Publishers Weekly* (16 Dec. 2016) about Lucas. "What's striking is her contagious energy and drive, inside and outside the book community. She has that ability to relate to everybody."

Delighted by the opportunity, Lucas joined the NBF in March of 2016 and immediately set out to further the foundation's mission of celebrating the importance of reading. For Lucas, and many of her colleagues, literature plays a significant role in enabling people to understand the world and people around them. "There are moments where we don't understand the world we live in—where we don't understand our own lives, our sadness or our joy," she told Wabuke. "I have always felt that books help me feel less alone in the world. They make our lives bigger—they help us to feel feelings we wouldn't otherwise feel and to understand feelings that we don't have a framework for. And learning from books is so empowering—whether it be from history, a novel or a poem. When you come away from reading having learned something, you yourself are bigger." As executive director, Lucas seeks to spread the transformative power of reading nationwide.

SHARING LITERATURE

Since taking the position of executive director, Lucas has worked to continue the NBF's ongoing initiatives as well as expand the organization's focus. She is particularly concerned with promoting diversity and inclusivity in the literary and publishing communities, which are often perceived as exclusionary or limited only to individuals from specific racial, geographical, socioeconomic, and educational backgrounds. "There are so many preconceived notions of who reads books," she explained to Kirch. "Our job at NBF is to celebrate great work, but also to make sure that that great work gets into the hands of more people. We'll keep building—keep thinking nationally, keep thinking digitally, and keep thinking about those who aren't being recognized as a strong, supportive community of readers." In an interview with NBC News (12 Sept. 2016), she noted that her first months in the position were about learning and adjusting before exploring ways to implement her goals. Interviewer Lesley-Ann Brown asked how Lucas would begin to expand readership and focus on diversity, and Lucas responded that "I think the answer is taking a step back now that I am in place, knowing what I believe in, knowing what the staff and the board believe in and trying to harness all that energy into something that can be more accessible."

For the 2016 National Book Awards, Lucas teamed up with the *New Yorker* to announce the finalists on Facebook Live. The livestream had 60,000 viewers. For the November 16 awards, Lucas selected comedian and television show host Larry Wilmore to host the ceremony that presented awards to Colson Whitehead, Ibram X. Kendi, Daniel Borzutzky, and graphic novel collaborators Congressman John Lewis, Andrew Aydin, and Nate Powell. Lucas has also expressed a desire to broadcast the awards to a wider audience, as she considers them the Oscars of the book industry.

PERSONAL LIFE

Lucas lives in Brooklyn, New York.

SUGGESTED READING

Brown, Lesley-Ann. "National Book Foundation's Lisa Lucas: Get to Know 'the Other NBA.'" *NBC News*, 12 Sept. 2016, www.nbcnews.com/news/nbcblk/national-book-foundation-s-lisa-lucas-get-know-other-nba-n602706. Accessed 10 Jan. 2017.

Gregg, Helen. "A More Literary Union." *University of Chicago Magazine*, 2016, mag.uchicago.edu/arts-humanities/more-literary-union. Accessed 6 Jan. 2017.

Lucas, Lisa. "Four Questions for . . . New National Book Foundation Head, Lisa Lucas." Interview by Claire Kirch. *Publishers Weekly*, 9 Mar. 2016, www.publishersweekly.com/pw/by-topic/industry-news/people/article/69604-four-questions-for-new-nbf-head-lisa-lucas.html. Accessed 6 Jan. 2017.

Lucas, Lisa. "A Lifelong Lover of Books Breaks Ground atop the Literary World." Interview by Hope Wabuke. *The Root*, 27 Feb. 2016, www.theroot.com/articles/culture/2016/02/q_a_with_lisa_lucas_the_1st_woman_and_1st_african_american_to_head_the_national/2. Accessed 6 Jan. 2017.

Lucas, Lisa. "Lisa Lucas Looks to Guernica's Future." Interview by Cat Richardson. *Poets & Writers*, 15 Oct. 2014, www.pw.org/content/lisa_lucas_looks_to_guernica_s_future. Accessed 6 Jan. 2016.

Lucas, Lisa. "Lisa Lucas Wants to Make Reading Fun Again." Interview by Ana Marie Cox. *New York Times Magazine*, 7 Sept. 2016, www.nytimes.com/2016/09/11/magazine/lisa-lucas-wants-to-make-reading-fun-again.html. Accessed 6 Jan. 2016.

Reid, Calvin. "PW Notables of the Year: Lisa Lucas." *Publishers Weekly*, 16 Dec. 2016, www.publishersweekly.com/pw/by-topic/industry-news/people/article/72334-pw-notables-of-the-year-lisa-lucas.html. Accessed 6 Jan. 2017.

—*Joy Crelin*

Tyronn Lue

Date of birth: May 3, 1977
Occupation: Basketball coach

Tyronn Lue had never served as a head coach at any level when, in January 2016, he was hired to replace David Blatt as head coach of the National Basketball Association (NBA)'s Cleveland Cavaliers. Despite his inexperience at the helm, Lue, a former NBA journeyman point guard,

Christian Petersen/Getty Images

led the Cavaliers to the top record in the Eastern Conference and a 12–2 postseason record, and the team advanced to the NBA Finals for the second straight season. In the championship series, Lue helped the Cavaliers overcome a 3–1 deficit against the reigning NBA champion Golden State Warriors to win the franchise's first-ever title.

Prior to joining the Cavaliers organization as Blatt's assistant coach in 2014, Lue served as an assistant coach under his mentor, Doc Rivers, for five seasons with both the Boston Celtics and Los Angeles Clippers. Known as a "player's coach," Lue has won the respect of fellow coaches and players around the league for his no-nonsense style, defensive acumen, and low-key, humble nature. He explained to Joe Vardon for Cleveland.com (23 Sept. 2016), "I'm not the type of guy who wants the credit. . . . I love the game of basketball, I love coaching. The attention, being on TV, all that stuff, that's not what it's about for me."

EARLY LIFE

Tyronn Jamar Lue was born on May 3, 1977, in the small town of Mexico, Missouri. Along with his brother and sister, Lue was raised by his mother, Kim Miller. Growing up, he saw little of his biological father, Ronald Kemp, who was in and out of prison on various drug-related offenses. Lue's mother, too, battled drug addiction and often resorted to stealing to provide for the family.

Lue's grandparents, Tyrone and Olivia George, helped raise him and his siblings, as his mother struggled to find steady work. His grandfather stepped in as a father figure and steered him into sports. Like his father, who was "a local basketball legend," according to Kurt Streeter for *ESPN The Magazine* (21 Dec. 2016), Lue learned how to play basketball at Mexico's Garfield Park. Despite being undersized compared to his peers, he used grit and determination to overcome his physical shortcomings.

Lue attended Mexico High School, but after his freshman year, his mother, who became a minister, sent him to live with her brother and his wife in Kansas City. The move offered Lue better basketball opportunities and distanced him from his friends, many of whom were already going to jail for petty crimes. Lue would nonetheless later credit Mexico with molding his personality and perspective. "I carry that place with me everywhere I go," he told Streeter. "It is who I am and where I am from. It taught me everything I know about life."

HIGH SCHOOL AND COLLEGE CAREER

Lue enrolled at Raytown High School, in the Kansas City suburb of Raytown, where he played on the varsity basketball team under coach Mark Scanlon. Not long after arriving at the school, Lue boldly predicted to Scanlon that he would eventually play in the NBA. Living up to his prediction, he emerged as one of Raytown's top playmakers, averaging twenty-three points per game as a senior. "He's a natural leader. He's got great people skills. Those two things always stood out," Scanlon said, as quoted by Steve Aschburner for *NBA.com* (10 Feb. 2016).

Upon graduating from Raytown High School, Lue earned a scholarship to the University of Nebraska. He spent three seasons as the Cornhuskers' starting point guard, during which he racked up 1,577 points, 432 assists, and 145 three-pointers, good for seventh, third, and fourth on the school's all-time list. One of the most decorated players in Nebraska basketball history, Lue, who earned first-team All–Big 12 honors as a junior, decided to forgo his senior season and entered the 1998 NBA Draft.

The Denver Nuggets selected Lue as the twenty-third overall pick in the draft's first round. Then, on draft night, Lue was traded to the Los Angeles Lakers, along with forward Tony Battie, in exchange for guard Nick Van Excel. Making it to the NBA was always "a goal I had," Lue said early in his career, as quoted by Aschburner. "It was a far-fetched goal, but it was something I was able to accomplish. People doubted me and I used it as motivation."

NBA PLAYING CAREER

Standing at only six feet tall and weighing 175 pounds, Lue saw little playing time in his first three seasons with the Lakers, serving as a backup guard on a team that featured superstars Kobe Bryant and Shaquille O'Neal. During the 1999–2000 season, he played in just eight games due to various injuries.

Lue was relatively unknown to the NBA world until the 2001 playoffs, when he emerged as one of the Lakers' most valuable reserves. Named to the Lakers' postseason roster by coach Phil Jackson for his defensive abilities, Lue helped contain that year's most valuable player (MVP), the Philadelphia 76ers guard Allen Iverson, during the 2001 NBA Finals. In game one of the series, the Lakers lost to the 76ers in overtime on a last-minute jumper by Iverson, who upon making the shot memorably stepped over Lue, who had fallen while defending him. However, Lue held Iverson to subpar shooting percentages the rest of the series, and the Lakers swept the next four games to win their second of three consecutive NBA titles.

During the 2001–2 offseason, Lue signed with the Washington Wizards, where he became a teammate of the then recently unretired superstar Michael Jordan, widely considered to be the greatest basketball player of all time. Lue received significantly more playing time as a backup guard for the Wizards, with whom he spent two seasons. He then played for the Orlando Magic during the 2003–4 season, in which he notched career-highs in games (76) and starts (69). The Magic, however, finished with the worst record in the NBA, compiling a dismal 21–61 record. At the end of the season, Lue was traded to the Houston Rockets in a multiplayer deal.

Serving almost exclusively as a role player, Lue would play in the NBA for five more seasons, bouncing around with the Rockets, the Atlanta Hawks, the Dallas Mavericks, and the Milwaukee Bucks, before ending his career with the Magic in 2009. He retired with modest career averages of 8.5 points and 3.1 assists per game, but was described by Streeter as "the beating heart of every team he'd ever been part of."

TRANSITION INTO COACHING

Following the conclusion of his playing career, Lue decided to go into coaching. Prior to the 2009–10 season, he landed a job with the Boston Celtics as director of basketball development. The position was created specifically for Lue by the Celtics' then head coach Doc Rivers, who had first become acquainted with him while coaching the Magic during the 2003–4 season. Though Rivers was fired only eleven games into that season after leading the Magic to a 1–10 start, he immediately became impressed with Lue's cerebral and detail-oriented approach to the game and tagged him as a future coach.

Lue spent two seasons as the Celtics' director of basketball development before being promoted to an assistant coach on the team's staff during the 2011–12 season. He held this role for another two seasons. During this time, Lue became a protégé of Rivers, as he dedicated himself to learning the intricacies of coaching. "I like his brain," Rivers told Jake Fischer for *Sports Illustrated* (7 June 2016). "Every time I drew up an ATO [after timeout] or anything, he would write it down. If it was something in practice we were experimenting, he loved coming in and wanted to know why."

Rivers's confidence in Lue prompted him to bring him along as a member of his staff when he left the Celtics to become head coach of the Los Angeles Clippers in 2013. Lue was an assistant coach with the Clippers for one season. Serving as Rivers's "de facto defensive coordinator," as Fischer put it, he helped the Clippers win a franchise-best fifty-seven games during the 2013–14 season, which saw the team advance to the Western Conference semifinals.

CLEVELAND CAVALIERS

After a season with the Clippers, Lue emerged as a top candidate for the Cavaliers' head-coaching vacancy. He lost the job, however, to David Blatt, one of the most decorated coaches in European basketball history. The Cavaliers were nonetheless impressed enough to hire Lue as an associate coach. The team signed Lue to a four-year, $6.5 million contract, making him the highest-paid assistant coach in NBA history.

During the 2014–15 season, Lue served as the Cavaliers' main defensive coach under Blatt. The Cavaliers, led by homegrown superstar forward LeBron James, who rejoined the team in free agency after spending the previous four seasons with the Miami Heat, finished with a 53–29 record, enjoying a twenty-game improvement from the previous season. The Cavaliers won the Central Division and advanced to the 2015 NBA Finals, where they were defeated by the Golden State Warriors in six games.

The Cavaliers picked up where they left off in 2015–16, entering the season's midpoint with the best record in the Eastern Conference at 30–11. Despite their record, however, Blatt was fired by the team's general manager, David Griffin, for failing to establish a collective rapport with players, particularly with James. The move came as a shock to many observers around the league and drew harsh criticism from several NBA coaches, among them Rivers.

MOLDING AN NBA CHAMPION

On January 22, 2016, immediately after Blatt's firing, Lue was persuaded by Griffin to become the Cavaliers' head coach. He held off on signing the three-year, $9.5 million contract extension offered to him, however, because he "wanted to make sure it was the 'right fit,'" as he put it to Vardon.

Upon taking over, Lue overhauled the Cavaliers' style of play, quickening their tempo while emphasizing more passing, stronger defense, and better conditioning. Unlike Blatt, he also began holding players accountable for their actions on and off the court. This included confronting James and the team's other two superstars, forward Kevin Love and guard Kyrie Irving, when necessary.

Lue's changes paid dividends as the Cavaliers went 27–14 the rest of the regular season, finishing first in the Eastern Conference with a 57–25 overall record. The Cavaliers carried their momentum into the playoffs, winning their first ten games en route to a second straight NBA Finals appearance. Lue became the first coach in NBA history to win their first ten postseason games.

In a rematch of the previous year's NBA championship series, the Cavaliers again faced the Warriors, who had won a league-record seventy-three games during the regular season. Despite falling down three games to one in the series, the Cavaliers ultimately defeated the Warriors in seven games to win the franchise's first-ever championship. The Cavaliers became the first team in league history to overcome a 3–1 deficit in the finals and their victory marked the first championship title by a Cleveland sports franchise in fifty-two years. Lue became the fifth rookie head coach to win an NBA title. He also became the fourteenth person to win a title as both a player and coach.

During the summer of 2016, Lue signed a five-year, $35 million contract extension with the Cavaliers. Living up to his new contract, he guided the Cavaliers to a 20–6 record to open the 2016–17 season. Commenting on Lue's team-first coaching philosophy, James explained to Streeter, "He is not coming from an 'I'm doing this for me' standpoint. He's doing it from an 'I'm doing this for us. I'm going to tell you the truth no matter what.' I respect that."

PERSONAL LIFE

In addition to his coaching career, Lue has done extensive charitable work in his hometown of Mexico, where he frequently visits family and friends.

SUGGESTED READING

Aschburner, Steve. "Cleveland's Tyronn Lue, Accidental Coach No More." *NBA.com*, 20 June 2016, www.nba.com/2016/news/features/steve_aschburner/06/20/tyronn-lue-accidental-coach-no-more-cleveland-cavaliers. Accessed 4 Jan. 2017.

Aschburner, Steve. "Tuning Out Dissenters Nothing New for Tough-Minded Lue." *NBA.com*, 10 Feb. 2016, www.nba.com/2016/news/features/steve_aschburner/02/10/tyronn-lue-eastern-conference-all-star-coach-still-getting-his-feet-wet-with-cleveland-cavaliers. Accessed 4 Jan. 2017.

Fischer, Jake. "Napkin Plays, Film Sessions and a Call: How Doc Rivers Groomed Tyronn Lue." *Sports Illustrated*, 7 June 2016, www.si.com/nba/2016/06/07/nba-finals-cleveland-cavaliers-tyronn-lue-doc-rivers-lebron-james. Accessed 4 Jan. 2017.

Gregorian, Vahe. "Cavaliers Coach Tyronn Lue Stays True to His Hometown of Mexico, Mo." *The Kansas City Star*, 20 June 2016, www.kansascity.com/sports/spt-columns-blogs/vahe-gregorian/article84975122.html. Accessed 4 Jan. 2017.

Streeter, Kurt. "Tyronn Lue and the Art of Igniting Lebron." *ESPN The Magazine*, 21 Dec. 2016, www.espn.com/espn/feature/story/_/id/18318471/the-unique-dynamic-lebron-james-cavs-coach-tyronn-lue. Accessed 4 Jan. 2017.

Vardon, Joe. "Tyronn Lue Wondered If He Was 'Right Fit' to Coach the Cavaliers." *Cleveland.com*, 23 Sept. 2016, www.cleveland.com/cavs/index.ssf/2016/09/tyronn_lue_lebron_james_kevin_1.html. Accessed 4 Jan. 2017.

—*Chris Cullen*

Emmanuel Macron

Date of birth: December 21, 1977
Occupation: President of France

In May 2017, Emmanuel Macron—at the age of thirty-nine—became the youngest president in the history of modern France, younger even than Louis-Napoléon Bonaparte (Napoleon III), who assumed that office at the age of forty in 1848. Macron's election is particularly remarkable when one considers that he ascended to the presidency of France without ever having held elective office. Apart from stints as deputy secretary general for President François Hollande from 2012 to 2014 and economic minister from 2014 to 2016, he has not served extensively in public office. Moreover, he won the presidency without the support of either the Socialists or the Republicans, the two major political parties in France.

Macron's victory came in part because he appealed to French citizens to renounce fixed ideas of right- and left-wing politics and to embrace a concept of France as a significant force on the world stage. His policies aim both to be

Kremlin.ru [CC BY 4.0] via Wikimedia Commons

business-friendly and to maintain social welfare, drawing from both the right and left, respectively. "This is a man who, certainly, began his career in the Socialist Party, and he says that he is not a centrist," Pascal Perrineau, a political science professor at Sciences Po in Paris, explained to Alissa J. Rubin for the *New York Times* (19 Apr. 2017). "He is, as he says, from the right and from the left and this is an invention that our political family has not seen before." Macron has also been particularly critical of what he sees as the weakening of the French presidency—one of the most powerful executive offices in the Western world—and seeks to make it vibrant again, as it had been under French president Charles de Gaulle. Since taking office, however, his centralized approach to authority has drawn unfavorable comparisons to another French leader: Napoléon Bonaparte.

EARLY LIFE AND EDUCATION

The eldest of three children, Emmanuel Macron was born on December 21, 1977, in Amiens, France, a city located about seventy miles north of Paris. Both of Macron's parents were doctors, but arguably the most influential person in his young life was his maternal grandmother, Manette, whom he has credited with cultivating many of his political and intellectual leanings. Manette was a schoolteacher and reformist socialist who stressed upon her grandson the need for a good education and a well-honed intellect. It was also through her that he developed a love of the French countryside. Macron recalled, as quoted by Rubin: "It was she and my grandfather

who for years and years led me to live in Bagnères-de-Bigorre, to walk there, to run there, to learn how to bicycle, to ski, to be rooted in our country."

Macron studied at a private Jesuit school in Amiens. There, he excelled as a student and was well regarded as an actor and pianist. It was there that he met Brigitte Trogneux, the woman he would later marry. A Latin and French teacher who ran the school's theater group and who was more than twenty years his senior, Trogneux and Macron formed an almost instantaneous bond. Macron ultimately fell in love with his teacher and, because of it, was sent away by his parents to complete his schooling in Paris at the prestigious Lycée Henri IV. Despite the distance and the age difference, the relationship eventually flourished. "He called me all the time," she recalled, as quoted by Rubin. "We spent hours on the telephone. Little by little he conquered all my resistance in a manner that was incredible—with patience."

Between 1999 and 2001, Macron attended the Université Paris Ouest Nanterre La Défense, where he earned a master's degree in philosophy and wrote a dissertation on Niccolò Machiavelli, the Italian Renaissance author and philosopher who is often credited as being the father of political science. During this time, he also served as an editorial assistant to philosopher and historian Paul Ricœur, who was then writing his book *La mémoire, l'histoire, l'oubli* (2000). Macron then earned a master's degree in public policy at Sciences Po in 2001 and graduated from the prestigious École Nationale d'Administration in 2004.

EARLY CAREER

Upon leaving school, Macron served as an inspector of finances in the French Ministry for the Economy and Finance from 2004 to 2008. In 2006, he became a member of the Socialist Party for a brief time, but he had been uncomfortable with the two major political parties in France—the conservative Republicans and the liberal Socialists—since at least 2002, when Jean-Marie Le Pen, the leader of the far-right National Front Party, made it to the final round of the presidential elections. Macron feared that if the two major parties did not reform, the far right would eventually come into power in France.

Macron left his inspector position in 2008 to work for the investment bank Rothschild. Although he took on the job knowing little about investment banking, he moved up from director to managing director and earned more than three million dollars during the four years he worked there. His main task at the bank was to broker deals, and he advised Nestlé during its acquisition of Pfizer's infant nutrition unit in

2012. "You're sort of a prostitute," Macron told Stacy Meichtry and William Horobin for the *Wall Street Journal* (8 Mar. 2015). "Seduction is the job."

In 2012, President François Hollande appointed Macron as his deputy chief of staff, but Macron quit in 2014 after becoming frustrated with Hollande's reluctance to implement business-friendly reforms. However, shortly after he stepped down from his position as deputy chief of staff, Hollande asked Macron to serve as minister of economy. Macron served about two years in the post, from 2014 to 2016, during which time he orchestrated the implementation of what has become known as the "Macron law," deregulation measures designed to cut red tape for businesses and increase market flexibility. The pro-business policies were derided by the Socialists in Hollande's own government but won favor in the business community.

THE 2017 PRESIDENTIAL ELECTION

Macron stepped down from his position of economy minister in 2016, with an eye toward running for the French presidency in the 2017 election. He was disenchanted with the way Hollande had rammed the Macron law through a controversial form of presidential decree instead of through a parliamentary vote, which Macron felt could have been successful. He was also unhappy with President Hollande's promise to strip French citizens convicted of terrorism of their dual citizenship after a terrorist attack in Paris in November 2015 left 130 people dead.

Initially it seemed that Macron was a long shot for the presidency. With little government experience and without a political party behind him, apart from En Marche! (meaning "Forward!" or "Onward!"), the independent party Macron founded in April 2016, it seemed unlikely that he could win. But luck favored him: Hollande decided not to run for another term; Alain Juppé, a moderate and former prime minister of France, lost the Republican primary race; François Fillon, a right-leaning politician, fell behind in the polls due to scandal; and left-wing Benoît Hamon defeated centrist candidate Manuel Valls in the Socialist Party primaries— all of which left the center open for a candidate like Macron.

Before launching his campaign, Macron asked his supporters to go door-to-door to ask French citizens what was wrong with France and how to fix it. Many of his policy positions during the campaign could be generally described as pro-business, favoring deregulation, as well as pro–social welfare, aiming to maintain the strong social safety net the French Republic has long enjoyed. His message, though somewhat vague on specifics, found favor with young, urban, and educated voters.

His favorability in the race earned him enough votes in the first round of the election, held on April 23, 2017, to allow him to compete in a runoff against Marine Le Pen, the current leader of the National Front, the far-right party that advocates France's withdrawal from the European Union (EU) and stricter control of France's borders. Although many Western leaders feared that a Le Pen victory would further degrade the cohesion of Europe after the British vote to withdraw from the EU in June 2016, these fears proved to be unfounded: Macron won more than 66 percent of the vote in his runoff against Le Pen, held on May 7. Macron wooed French voters by appealing to moderation.

Hollande, the outgoing French president, said that Macron's victory "confirms that a very large majority of our fellow citizens wanted to gather around the values of the Republic and mark their attachment to the European Union as a gateway for France to the world," as quoted by Yasmeen Serhan for the *Atlantic* (7 May 2017). Shortly after Macron's victory, his party, renamed "La République En Marche!," secured a comfortable majority in the National Assembly, the lower house of the French legislature, winning 308 out of 577 seats in the parliamentary elections held in June 2017.

IN OFFICE

Since taking office on May 14, 2017, Macron has seen his popularity decline. Unlike his predecessors, he has made few public appearances and infrequently speaks to the press. He has used his majority in the legislature to push through favored pieces of legislation: Parliament, controlled by members of Macron's party, voted to allow the president to pass reforms to the country's labor code by ordinance, drawing the ire of labor unions and left-wing politicians.

Macron has also faced criticism from the right. During his campaign, he pledged to increase military spending, a promise he ultimately decided to abandon when faced with a budget shortfall left by the Hollande government. In order to meet the European Union's requirement that national budget deficits should not surpass 3 percent of a member country's gross domestic product, Macron proposed a cut of $980 million to defense spending. When General Pierre de Villiers, the head of the French armed forces since 2014, criticized the proposal, Macron publicly criticized him, prompting the general's resignation in July. "In the current circumstances I see myself as no longer able to guarantee the robust defense force I believe is necessary to guarantee the protection of France," de Villiers said in a statement announcing his resignation, as quoted by Simon Carraud and Michel Rose in an article for *Reuters* (19 July 2017). Macron's public comments about de Villiers prompted some media outlets to question his judgment and temperament.

Macron has drawn comparisons to the current US president, Donald Trump, who also came to the highest office in the land by running as a political outsider, by eschewing traditional political leanings, and without ever holding elected office. "They both want a monopoly on public attention and are attracted by constant media coverage. And there is a similar kind of narcissism in their attraction to power," said Patrick Weil, a French constitutional scholar, as quoted by Jenna Johnson and James McAuley for the *Washington Post* (14 July 2017). "Both show a will to govern without the Parliament and against the press—without any separation or balance of power."

Critics have been wary of what they consider to be Macron's Napoleonic, authoritarian style, whereas others believe he is demonstrating the key political instincts of a bold leader. "He wants to be both lion and fox," Jean-Yves Boriaud, a Machiavelli specialist at the University of Nantes, explained to Adam Nossiter for the *New York Times* (30 June 2017). "Machiavelli said the two must coexist. This is enlightening. Authority and ruse."

PERSONAL LIFE
Macron married Trogneux in 2007. Through his marriage, Macron is the stepfather of three adult children. His stepdaughter Tiphaine Auzière worked for Macron's presidential campaign.

SUGGESTED READING
Chrisafis, Angelique. "Emmanuel Macron: The French Outsider Who Would Be President." *The Guardian*, 17 Feb. 2017, www.theguardian.com/world/2017/feb/17/emmanuel-macron-the-french-outsider-president. Accessed 22 July 2017.

Gopnik, Adam. "Why Is Emmanuel Macron Being So Nice to Donald Trump?" *The New Yorker*, 14 July 2017, www.newyorker.com/news/daily-comment/why-is-emmanuel-macron-being-so-nice-to-donald-trump. Accessed 17 July 2017.

Johnson, Jenna, and James McAuley. "Trump and Macron, Once Cast as Adversaries, Show They Have Much in Common." *The Washington Post*, 14 July 2017, www.washingtonpost.com/politics/trump-and-macron-once-cast-as-adversaries-show-they-have-much-in-common/2017/07/13/0ed71dda-67ea-11e7-8eb5-cbccc2e7bfbf_story.html. Accessed 17 July 2017.

Nossiter, Adam. "French Puzzle over Macron as Their New President Gathers Up Power." *The New York Times*, 30 June 2017, www.nytimes.com/2017/06/30/world/europe/emmanuel-macron-france-president-power.html. Accessed 17 July 2017.

Rubin, Alissa J. "Macron Wants to Change France. But Will Voters Elect an Unknown?" *The New York Times*, 19 Apr. 2017, www.nytimes.com/2017/04/19/world/europe/france-election-emmanuel-macron.html. Accessed 17 July 2017.

Serhan, Yasmeen. "Macron's Win: The Center Holds Firm in France." *The Atlantic*, 7 May 2017, www.theatlantic.com/international/archive/2017/05/macron-wins-french-election-2017/525390. Accessed 17 July 2017.

—*Christopher Mari*

Karan Mahajan
Date of Birth: April 24, 1984
Occupation: Novelist

Karan Mahajan is an award-winning American-born Indian writer. His second novel, *The Association of Small Bombs*, was a finalist for the National Book Award in 2016. *Bombs* describes a terrorist attack in New Delhi in 1996 from the perspectives of the survivors, the families of the victims, and the terrorists themselves. Fiona Maazel, who reviewed the book for the *New York Times* (15 Mar. 2016), called it "smart, devastating, unpredictable, and enviably adept in its handling of tragedy and its fallout."

Mahajan was born in Connecticut, grew up in New Delhi, and attended college in California; his first novel, a social satire called *Family Planning*, was published in 2008, when he was just twenty-four years old. *Family Planning* won the Joseph Henry Jackson Award and was a finalist for the International Dylan Thomas Prize. As a writer, Mahajan explores contemporary life in New Delhi with curiosity, empathy, and humor and has explored the cultural divide between his home in India and his home in the United States. In addition to his novels, he has also contributed essays and book reviews to a variety of publications, including the *Daily Beast*, the *New Yorker*, the *New York Times*, the *Los Angeles Review of Books*, the *Wall Street Journal*, *Newsweek*, *Granta*, and the *Believer*.

EARLY LIFE AND EDUCATION
Mahajan was born in Stamford, Connecticut, on April 24, 1984. His parents had lived in the United States for fourteen years but moved back to India when Mahajan was two years old. The family settled in Friends Colony, an affluent neighborhood in South Delhi. In May 1996, when Mahajan was twelve, terrorists set off a

Sylvain Gaboury/Patrick McMullan/Getty Images

bomb in the nearby Lajpat Nagar market, where Mahajan bought his uniforms for his school. Thirteen people were killed. "My grandmother had visited the market a day before the blasts—to buy yarn, I think—and perhaps the possibility that a family member might have perished in the attack stuck with me," he told Antonio Ruiz-Camacho for the *Millions* (22 Mar. 2016). The event would later become the subject of his second novel, *The Association of Small Bombs*.

Mahajan moved to Stanford, California, to attend Stanford University in 2001. He graduated with degrees in English and economics in 2005, but he only began writing during his senior year. Mahajan and his family had envisioned that he would return to India and snag a high-paying job in finance; a career in writing had never been in the cards. After deciding to pursue a career as a novelist, Mahajan's family was supportive but, as he conceded to Ruiz-Camacho, the distance helped. "If I hadn't moved to the United States, I wouldn't have become a writer," he said. "I was too meek to break with the weight of cultural expectations."

FAMILY PLANNING

After college, Mahajan worked as an editor for MacAdam Cage Publishing, an indie book publisher in San Francisco. In 2007 he briefly returned to Delhi before moving to Brooklyn in 2008. Mahajan kept a hectic schedule, writing in the mornings before going to his job at New York City's strategic planning department. In November 2008, a series of deadly terrorist attacks in Mumbai inspired him to sit down and

write the opening of his second novel, *The Association of Small Bombs*, in a single sitting. By this time, Mahajan had already secured an agent and was about to publish his first novel, *Family Planning*.

That novel satirizes contemporary life in India through the story of a government official in New Delhi named Rakesh Ahuja. Rakesh designs "flyovers," or overpasses, although the story's primary plot involves his thirteen children. When the novel begins, his exhausted wife is pregnant again. Rakesh's teenage son Arjun is frustrated with his father's insistence on having so many children. (Rakesh is too embarrassed to tell him the answer: He is simply more attracted to his wife when she is pregnant.) Against the backdrop of bustling life in New Delhi, Rakesh and Arjun try to win each other's approval. Joan Frank, who reviewed the novel for the *San Francisco Chronicle* (7 Dec. 2008), described *Family Planning* as "a fearless cultural and domestic tour, and a kind of sorrowing valentine to a bedeviled city."

THE ASSOCIATION OF SMALL BOMBS

Mahajan spent years researching his second novel, *The Association of Small Bombs*. Although the focus of the story is on the Lajpat Nagar market bombing he remembered from his childhood, the book also drew inspiration from Mahajan's extensive travels through India from 2010 to 2012, an assignment in which he was compiling a history of entrepreneurship in India for a tech billionaire in Bangalore. He used this experience to create the world of the novel. "This job took me to small towns; it was my mandate to interview people and hear their life-stories," he told Jeff Vasishta for *Interview* magazine (21 Mar. 2016). "Along the way I picked up a lot of odd, incidental details." In 2012, Mahajan accepted a writing fellowship at the Michener Center for Writers at the University of Texas at Austin while continuing to flesh out what would become *The Association of Small Bombs*. He graduated from the program in 2015, although he continues to live in Austin.

Like his debut novel, *The Association of Small Bombs* is also set in Delhi. It opens on the day of the bombing in 1996. Two young boys are among the people killed, but their friend, a boy named Mansoor, survives. The novel follows Mansoor's story and explores his wounds both physical—the shrapnel wound on his wrist refuses to heal—and emotional, as well as the stories of Shaukat, a terrorist, and Deepa and Vikas Khurana, the parents of the two killed boys. "I didn't feel that modern literature—fiction or nonfiction—had done an honest job describing so-called 'radicalization,'" he told Ruiz-Camacho. Shaukat, or Shockie, and his collaborators are not religious extremists, but political activists. Mahajan explained to Ruiz-Camacho that he was more interested in "the torn people, who try to make meaning out of their alienation," than those who were raised to hold certain beliefs. Shockie, of course, is no angel; according to Mahajan's description, he is a murderer who dreams of making a statement on the scale of Ramzi Yousef, one of the men behind the 1993 World Trade Center bombing.

Compared to the scale of many terrorist attacks, the Lajpat Nagar bombing was relatively small—it killed thirteen people and injured thirty. But Mahajan questions the "smallness" of an event that disrupts the lives of the people it touches. He told Nandini Nair for *Open* (20 May 2016), an English-language Indian weekly, that he wanted to write about the victims and perpetrators of a so-called small bombing because "they are linked to a large international phenomenon, but their suffering is relatively—and I say this with a degree of irony—meaningless. Victims of these blasts are forced to make their own meaning out of what has happened to them. This makes them worthy subjects of inquiry for fiction." *The Association of Small Bombs* won the 2017 Bard Fiction Prize and was included on the short list for the 2016 National Book Award.

OTHER WRITINGS

Mahajan's other writings, for newspapers and magazines such as the *Wall Street Journal* and the *New Yorker*, explore contemporary India through a cultural, historic lens. In 2007, he reviewed Yasmin Khan's *The Great Partition: The Making of India and Pakistan* (2007), about the creation of the two nations after India's independence in 1947, for the New York *Sun* (10 Oct. 2007). The book chronicles the hubris of the British politicians who engineered the partition, and Mahajan was careful to point out its modern-day relevance; at the time, American politicians were considering a similar sectarian partition of Iraq. In 2010 Mahajan wrote about a memoir called *Curfewed Night: One Kashmiri Journalist's Frontline Account of Life, Love and War in His Homeland* (2010) by Basharat Peer for the *Daily Beast* (27 Mar. 2010). Kashmir is a northern territory divided between India and Pakistan. Mired in conflict since 1947, Indian Kashmiris revolted in 1989 and have lived in a state of armed suppression ever since. (Shockie, of Mahajan's novel, is a Kashmiri separatist who believes in an independent Kashmir.)

In 2015, Mahajan wrote about *This Is Not That Dawn* by Yashpal, a Hindi novel he called "India's forgotten feminist epic," for the *New Yorker* (27 Mar. 2015). Published in two installments in 1958 and 1960—and first published in English in 2010—the novel follows two siblings who are coming of age during the partition. Mahajan wrote about the novel in light of India's ongoing crisis of sexual violence and the release of the documentary *India's Daughter* (2015), about the brutal gang rape and murder of a Delhi medical student named Jyoti Singh. (The movie was banned in India.) Mahajan also wrote a review of Sunil Khilnani's 2016 book *Incarnations: India in Fifty Lives* for the *New Yorker* (1 Nov. 2016). In it, he coopted the slogan of Donald Trump's divisive American presidential campaign to describe an India gripped by Hindu nationalism: "Make India Great Again." He elaborated, "In India, right now, the past is violently alive, and it is being bandied about like a blunt instrument, striking down those who try to speak sense to the present or who try to point out that this past is itself a fiction" and described *Incarnations* as an anecdote to the madness.

Caught between two countries, Mahajan has cast a sharp eye on both, but he also writes humorously of the cultural divide. In July 2016, he wrote a personal essay for the *New Yorker*, in honor of American Independence Day, about his struggle to master the American art of small talk. Ordering coffee distressed him because he knew the barista was likely to ask him, "How's it going?" Indians do not like meaningless chatter, he insisted, and he questioned the American desire to exchange money with a smile. The two-pronged analysis led him to an interesting observation, characteristic of his outlook. He wrote: "In the East, I've heard it said, there's intimacy without friendship; in the West, there's friendship without intimacy."

SUGGESTED READING

Frank, Joan. Review of *Family Planning*, by Karan Mahajan. *The San Francisco Chronicle*, 7 Dec. 2008, www.sfgate.com/books/article/Family-Planning-by-Karan-Mahajan-3182224.php. Accessed 5 Nov. 2016.

Maazel, Fiona. Review of *The Association of Small Bombs*, by Karan Mahajan. *The New York Times*, 15 Mar. 2016, www.nytimes.com/2016/03/20/books/review/the-association-of-small-bombs-by-karan-mahajan.html. Accessed 4 Nov. 2016.

Mahajan, Karan. "I Want Complete Freedom When I Write." Interview by Antonio Ruiz-Camacho. *The Millions*, 22 Mar. 2016, www.themillions.com/2016/03/i-want-complete-freedom-when-i-write.html. Accessed 4 Nov. 2016.

Mahajan, Karan. "Karan Mahajan Reinterprets Home." Interview by Jeff Vasishta. *Interview*, 21 Mar. 2016, www.interviewmagazine.com/culture/karan-mahajan. Accessed 4 Nov. 2016.

Nair, Nandini. "Karan Mahajan: A Case of Exploding Metaphors." *Open*, 20 May 2016, www.openthemagazine.com/article/books/

karan-mahajan-a-case-of-exploding-meta-phors. Accessed 7 Nov. 2016.

SELECTED WORKS
Family Planning, 2008 and *The Association of Small Bombs*, 2016.

—*Molly Hagan*

Susanna Mälkki

Date of birth: March 13, 1969
Occupation: Conductor

By MITO SettembreMusica derivative work: MagentaGreen [CC BY 2.0], via Wikimedia Commons

"Every conductor is different," Finnish conductor Susanna Mälkki explained to Antti J. Peltonen for *FMQ: Finish Music Quarterly* (Dec. 2010). "How you use the space. How you communicate with musicians. How you adjust your energy levels depending on the size of the orchestra. See, conducting is both psychological and physical." If Mälkki's critically acclaimed career as a conductor is any indication, she has mastered both aspects of her craft. In the decades following her studies at the prestigious Sibelius Academy, Mälkki has distinguished herself as a talented conductor of orchestras, small ensembles, and opera companies. She has not only obtained a series of high-profile positions with European orchestras but also become a fixture on the guest-conducting circuit in Europe and the United States.

Having earned widespread praise for her work with Norway's Stavanger Symphony Orchestra and France's Ensemble Intercontemporain, Mälkki joined the Helsinki Philharmonic Orchestra in her native Finland as chief conductor in 2016. That year also marked her debut appearance at the Metropolitan Opera in New York City and her appointment as principal guest conductor with the Los Angeles Philharmonic. One of the keys to Mälkki's success has been the insight she gained during her first career as a cellist, playing with youth orchestras and later Sweden's Gothenburg Symphony Orchestra. "I've learnt probably half of what I know as a conductor through being a player in orchestras, watching," she told Charlotte Higgins for *The Guardian* (21 Mar. 2001). Still, watching a conductor work is nothing compared to the experience of leading a room full of musicians. "I am fascinated by being in charge of the whole picture, and putting all the pieces together," she explained. "There are so many details to find and colours to produce."

EARLY LIFE AND EDUCATION
Susanna Ulla Marjukka Mälkki was born on March 13, 1969, to an art teacher and an oceanographer. She and her two older brothers grew up in Vuosaari, outside Helsinki. Music was an important part of Mälkki's life from an early age. Her family often listened to classical music at home, and her father sang in a choir. All three Mälkki children took music lessons, with Mälkki herself beginning her studies in violin at the age of five. After four years, she switched to cello, which she found better suited her personality.

Although Mälkki enjoyed playing music in youth orchestras, she did not realize that she wanted to pursue a career in the field until she was a teenager. "I was attending a music camp in Kuhmo [in eastern Finland] . . . I was deeply touched by some of the concerts, performances, teachers, and the overall atmosphere," she recalled to Peltonen. "When I returned home my relationship with music had transformed. I became 100 percent certain that I wanted to make a living out of music." With her career goal in mind, Mälkki began studying the cello seriously, working toward becoming a professional musician. She graduated from the Conducting Department at the Royal Academy of Music, University of London, in 1994.

EARLY CAREER
Mälkki's years of study paid off in the mid-1990s, when she established herself as a talented professional cellist. In 1995, she joined the Gothenburg Symphony in Gothenburg, Sweden, as a musician. Although Mälkki had achieved her goal of becoming a concert cellist, she began

to dream of transitioning to conducting. "I had always been interested in conducting," she explained to Higgins. "As an orchestral player I'd always analysed what worked and what didn't. Even after my cello studies the idea was still in my head." Unsure of which direction to pursue, she applied to both the cellist position in Gothenburg as well as the conducting course at the prestigious Sibelius Academy, located in her native Finland. To her surprise, she was accepted. "I didn't have any experience," she recalled to Higgins. "It's difficult to say why they chose me. Maybe they saw I had something in my eye—even though my hands were not quite working."

Over the next years, Mälkki worked to balance her studies under notable conductors such as Jorma Panula and Leif Segerstam with her professional commitments to the Gothenburg Symphony. At one point, she took a yearlong leave of absence from Sibelius to focus on her work in Gothenburg. "It was wonderful," she told Zachary Woolfe for the *New York Times* (15 May 2015). "But I knew it was not where I was supposed to be. And then things went very well relatively quickly after that." Having found her true calling in conducting, Mälkki devoted herself to refining her skills in that arena, leaving the Gothenburg Symphony in 1998 to return to Finland.

UP-AND-COMING CONDUCTOR

While completing her studies at the Sibelius Academy, Mälkki began to establish herself as a noteworthy up-and-coming conductor. During the March 1999 Musica Nova Helsinki festival, she demonstrated her skills by conducting a performance of British composer and conductor Thomas Adès's opera *Powder Her Face*. Adès was in the audience and enjoyed the performance. He later recruited Mälkki to assist him on a short UK tour with the Birmingham Contemporary Music Group, for which she conducted a handful of performances. She would later conduct the group in its home city of Birmingham, England.

In 2002, Mälkki joined the Norwegian-based Stavanger Symphony Orchestra as music director. She remained with the orchestra through 2005. The following year, she took the position of music director of L'Ensemble Intercontemporain (EIC), a chamber orchestra based in Paris, France, which she had previously conducted at the 2004 Lucerne Festival in Switzerland. Founded in 1976 by French conductor Pierre Boulez, the ensemble specializes in twentieth- and twenty-first-century chamber music. The EIC presents a unique challenge to its conductors, as the thirty-one-member ensemble consists entirely of soloists. "Bigger symphony orchestras too are full of personalities, but some sort of hierarchy is still recognised and accepted.

In EIC all the musicians carry similar top status," Mälkki explained to Peltonen. "In theory, equality is a good thing but in practice it can create problems. In the end it is all about music. Personal opinions must be put aside. Someone must make the final decision. And that, of course, is my job." Mälkki remained music director of the EIC until September 2013, when she was succeeded by German conductor Matthias Pintscher.

INTERNATIONAL APPEARANCES

As Mälkki's work with ensembles such as the Stavanger Symphony Orchestra and the EIC gained widespread critical notice, she became a sought-after guest conductor of ensembles and large orchestras throughout Europe and the United States. Over the course of her career, she has made guest appearances with orchestras such as the Helsinki Philharmonic Orchestra, the Chicago Symphony Orchestra, the Oslo Philharmonic, the Swedish Radio Symphony Orchestra, and the London Philharmonic Orchestra, as well as the National Opera of Paris and the Finnish National Theatre. In 2013, she was named principal guest conductor of the Gulbenkian Orchestra in Lisbon, Portugal, a role she held into 2016.

In April 2011, Mälkki conducted a performance at the prestigious Teatro alla Scala in Milan, Italy, leading the premiere performance of composer Luca Francesconi's opera *Quartett*. In December 2016, Mälkki made her debut with New York City's Metropolitan Opera, conducting *L'Amour de Loin* (Love from Afar) by Finnish composer Kaija Saariaho. For Mälkki, conducting such a wide variety of music groups from different countries proved to be an exciting challenge, which she has noted was shaped in part by regional and cultural differences in conducting style. "Nationality and the cultural background matters too," she explained to Peltonen. "In some countries musicians simply do not respect the conductor if he or she is being too friendly. On the other hand, the last time I conducted in Finland, the musicians seemed to be amused by my un-Finnish politeness. That was funny." Mälkki earned critical acclaim for her work as a guest conductor, and her numerous appearances with major ensembles led critics to speculate about her candidacy for a number of positions with high-profile symphonies.

HELSINKI PHILHARMONIC

In September 2014, the Helsinki Philharmonic Orchestra announced that Mälkki was to be appointed the orchestra's next chief conductor, beginning in the fall of 2016. Although initially hired for a three-year term, Mälkki has noted that she does not see the orchestra as a temporary assignment. "I would really like to build something on the long term," she told Woolfe. "There are different kinds of careers and there are conductors who are doing positions a couple of years here and a couple of years there, and I'm not that kind."

In addition to marking the beginning of her term with the Helsinki Philharmonic, 2016 saw the announcement that Mälkki had been selected as the third conductor to fill the role of principal guest conductor with the Los Angeles Philharmonic, starting the 2017–18 season. Mälkki was particularly pleased with the assignment due to the Los Angeles Philharmonic's commitment to reaching younger audiences and promotion of contemporary composers. "Contemporary music is the music of our time," she explained to Jessica Gelt for the Los Angeles Times (6 Apr. 2016.) "If we don't take care of the time we live in, how can we secure the future?" At the same time, Mälkki remains committed to showcasing classic works of orchestral music. "We want to make sure the masterpieces of the past are also being heard in the best possible way," she told Gelt.

In addition to conducting, Mälkki has resumed playing the cello, both for her own enjoyment and with small ensembles. "As a conductor you have your territory," she explained to Woolfe. "But then there's this area that belongs to the musicians that is about the exact sound and articulation. I respect that, and if I play also, I can do it myself. I enjoy the physical act of producing sound."

The recipient of numerous industry honors, she has also received national honors from the governments of Finland and France for her services to the arts. In addition to listening to classical music and opera, Mälkki enjoys musical theater and the work of bands such as Led Zeppelin.

SUGGESTED READING

Gelt, Jessica. "L.A. Phil Appoints Susanna Malkki as Principal Guest Conductor." The Los Angeles Times, 6 Apr. 2016, www.latimes.com/entertainment/arts/la-et-cm-susanna-malkki-phil-20160404-story.html. Accessed 10 Mar. 2017.

Higgins, Charlotte. "In a Class of Her Own." The Guardian, 21 Mar. 2001, www.theguardian.com/culture/2001/mar/22/artsfeatures. Accessed 10 Mar. 2017.

Mälkki, Susanna. "Facing the Music: Susanna Mälkki." Interview. The Guardian, 27 July 2015, www.theguardian.com/music/2015/jul/27/facing-the-music-conductor-susanna-malkki. Accessed 10 Mar. 2017.

Mälkki, Susanna. "10 Questions: Susanna Mälkki." Interview. Good News from Finland, 1 Dec. 2016, www.goodnewsfinland.com/questions/10-questions-susanna-malkki. Accessed 10 Mar. 2017.

Peltonen, Antti J. "An Interview with a Conductor—Susanna Mälkki." FMQ: Finnish Music Quarterly, Dec. 2010, www.fmq.fi/2010/12/an-interview-with-a-conductor-susanna-malkki. Accessed 10 Mar. 2017.

Wolfe, Alexandra. "Susanna Mälkki, Center Stage." The Wall Street Journal, 21 Oct. 2016. www.wsj.com/articles/susanna-malkki-center-stage-1477067425. Accessed 10 Mar. 2017.

Woolfe, Zachary. "Susanna Malkki's Wide Appeal on Both Sides of the Atlantic." The New York Times, 15 May 2015, www.nytimes.com/2015/05/17/arts/music/susanna-malkkis-wide-appeal-on-both-sides-of-the-atlantic.html. Accessed 10 Mar. 2017.

—Joy Crelin

Chen Man

Date of birth: 1980
Occupation: Visual artist

Visual artist Chen Man has long defied categorization. Initially known for art pieces that blended traditional photography techniques with extensive digital manipulation to create a distinctive new aesthetic, Chen won widespread recognition for her early work while also drawing criticism from photography traditionalists who objected to her use of post-processing. She went on to establish herself as an in-demand fashion photographer and to further blur the lines between art forms, experimenting with more minimalist approaches as well as media such as film and calligraphy. Her development as an artist has been met with an overwhelmingly positive response from critics, some of whom have compared her to more established artists, such as American photographer Annie Leibovitz, whereas others put her in a category unto herself. For Chen, her inability to be categorized is part of her appeal. "I treat every picture like art pieces," she said to Alexa Tietjen for WWD (8 May 2017). "The people in the fashion industry or art industry cannot define me."

A graduate of the Central Academy of Fine Arts in Beijing, Chen was artistic from an early age and trained as a painter before moving into graphic design. After developing a passion for photography in college, she began contributing work to magazines, which would later come to feature Chen's portraits, editorial photographs, and advertising work. In addition to her work with popular celebrities such as actor and singer Fan Bingbing, Chen has made a point of spotlighting models who represent Chinese cultural and ethnic groups that have little representation in the country's media and dominant culture. Through her work, Chen has sought to provide a greater vision of the country's history, society, and people. "I want to show what contemporary China is and what contemporary Chinese beauty is," she told Valeriya Safronova for the *New York Times* (10 May 2017).

EARLY LIFE AND EDUCATION

Chen Man was born in Beijing, China, in 1980. Her parents, a doctor and a graphic designer, had met while living in the Inner Mongolia region of northern China, having been forced to settle there during the Cultural Revolution. The couple later moved to the Dashilar neighborhood of Beijing, where Chen spent her childhood.

Taking after her artist father, Chen demonstrated artistic talent from an early age and impressed her parents with her drawing skills while she was still a toddler. She began taking painting classes at the age of three and continued to paint throughout her childhood. "While other children went on holiday, I was always painting," she recalled to Safronova. "I always stared at people. People were actually uncomfortable about that." Although her success in local art competitions underscored her talent, Chen initially hoped to pursue a career far from the world of exhibitions and celebrity photo shoots that she would later inhabit. "I used to want to draw court portraits, like for the wanted posters," she told Safronova.

Chen attended a high school affiliated with the prestigious Central Academy of Fine Arts (CAFA) in Beijing, where she studied a variety of traditional art forms, including painting and sculpting. After graduating from high school, she enrolled in the Central Academy of Drama and studied there for a time before enrolling in CAFA's design program. During her time at the institution, Chen had the opportunity to study photography for the first time. Immediately drawn to the medium, she soon developed a passion for it and made photography the primary focus of her studies. She also studied graphic design, which she came to consider an important complement to photography. Chen earned her bachelor's degree from CAFA in 2005.

EARLY CAREER

Chen first gained widespread notice as a photographer during her junior year of college, when she began to contribute cover images to the Chinese fashion and lifestyle magazine *Vision*. Her covers blended photography and graphic design, featuring photographs of models that she had extensively retouched and embellished to create otherworldly final products. The vibrant and modern aesthetic displayed in her work for *Vision* would come to define the first stage of Chen's career, as she became strongly associated with the practice of retouching photographs for artistic purposes, as opposed to the

purpose of correcting flaws in a photograph or altering its subject's features to conform to prevailing standards of beauty. Although some critics found Chen's use of digital retouching to be unappealing and argued that her work should be classified as graphic design rather than photography, her *Vision* covers attracted significant positive attention and set Chen on the path to global recognition.

From the early days of her career, Chen's aesthetic and thematic interests were shaped in part in response to the existing trends in Chinese photography during her early life. "At that time, Chinese photographers often imitated foreigners," she explained in an interview for *K Magazine* (4 Feb. 2016). "They'd find a Western-looking space and shoot a foreign-looking picture. Or you'd have nostalgic photos, imitating old Shanghai or ancient China. No one was capturing what was happening right now." Chen's early work for publications such as *Vision* made it instantly clear that she was not attempting to create Western-looking or nostalgic art, instead presenting images that were both distinctly modern or futuristic and unabashedly Chinese.

MAJOR PROJECTS

In the years following Chen's graduation from CAFA, her profile as a photographer steadily grew as she produced memorable photographs that went on to be featured in magazines and gallery exhibitions. Among Chen's most noteworthy projects have been her photographs dedicated to highlighting the diversity of China's population. "People think Chinese look the same, but we are kind of like the Americans. We have fifty-six different races," she told Safronova. For the pre-spring 2012 issue of the fashion magazine *i-D*, known as the "Whatever the Weather" issue, Chen photographed not only established models but also a group of Tibetan teenagers who were attending a high school for students of Tibetan descent. Four of Chen's portraits were featured on the print magazine's covers, while the other eight photographs she took for the series were made available online. For Chen, such projects present an opportunity to feature women who are underrepresented in Chinese culture and to challenge prevailing notions of beauty. "I wanted this shoot to represent the breadth of beauty in China today," she told Sarah Raphael for *i-D* (30 Jan. 2014) of her work for the issue.

In addition to challenging the norms of the fashion industry and society as a whole, Chen seeks to showcase modern China in her work while remaining mindful of the country's history. Her work often reflects the cultural juxtapositions that are part of everyday Chinese life yet often surprise foreigners visiting the country. "Europeans watch [the 1993 film] *Farewell My Concubine* and come to China with all these romantic expectations, but when they arrive they're met with skateboarders, break-dancers, fashion photographers, and a hip hop scene," she said to Raphael. "I want to package this together and not only show it to China but show it to the world." To that end, Chen's *Funky Great Wall* series (2007) features a model dressed in a modern, funky style atop the centuries-old Great Wall of China. Another series, *Long Live the Motherland* (2010), combines elements of modern Chinese life with historically resonant imagery through a series of photographs that place models against backdrops such as the Shanghai skyline and Beijing's Tiananmen Square. Later works include *Four Seasons* (2011) and *Five Elements* (2011), two series of photographs inspired by the four seasons and the five elements of traditional Chinese philosophy, respectively. Photographs from Chen's major series have met with significant critical acclaim and have been exhibited in China as well as in galleries and exhibitions in Paris, Tokyo, and New York. Her work has also been displayed in major museums such the Museum of Contemporary Art Shanghai and the Victoria and Albert Museum in London.

CELEBRITY PHOTOGRAPHER

Over the course of her career, Chen has become best known for her fashion and celebrity photography, which has been widely featured in such international magazines as *Vogue*, *Harper's Bazaar*, and *Elle* and in advertisements for such fashion brands as Guess and Dior. Although demonstrably capable of taking traditionally glamorous celebrity portraits, Chen tends to bring her own creative twist to the proceedings, creating eye-catching and memorable images of popular public figures. In a 2010 series of photographs published in the Chinese edition of *Esquire* magazine, for instance, Chen presents Fan Bingbing, one of China's most popular film stars, in a new and surprising light. "They wanted to shoot a woman as a man but left the details to me," Chen told *K Magazine* about the shoot. The cover image used for the issue featured Fan dressed as Che Guevara, with her hair and clothing styled to resemble that of the Marxist revolutionary, and images within the magazine depicted Fan as Bruce Lee, Superman, and Elvis Presley, among others. However, instead of dressing Fan in different clothes for each shot, she simply painted the outfits on Fan's body. "[*Esquire*] never imagined that Fan Bingbing would get naked. So it was up to me to bring that up," she recalled for *K Magazine*. "So I did and she got naked and let me draw clothes on her and we shot it like that." Following that shoot, Chen became a favorite photographer of Fan, and the two went on to collaborate on numerous photo shoots. Chen has also photographed a number of other celebrities from China and elsewhere,

including Zhang Ziyi, Li Bingbing, Rihanna, and Nicole Kidman.

Due to her artistic success as well as her association with major celebrities such as Fan, Chen has become a celebrity herself, and photographs of the artist—often self-portraits—have been featured in magazines and advertisements. A frequent collaborator with international fashion and beauty brands, she has partnered with companies such as MAC Cosmetics, which in 2012 released a line of makeup inspired in part by Chen's use of color. Chen herself serves as a brand ambassador for the jewelry company Qeelin and the watchmaker Hublot. A special edition Hublot watch inspired by Chen was introduced in early 2017.

PERSONAL LIFE

Chen is married to Raphael Ming Cooper, an American-born entrepreneur who cofounded the skateboard company Society Skateboards. They have two children. Chen divides her time between Beijing, where she maintains a studio, and San Marino, California, where she and Cooper own a home. "I really fell in love with California because of the sunshine, the beach, the mountains. Here people have everything, here lies the real heaven on earth," she told Frances Anderton for KCRW's design and architecture blog *DNA* (7 Jan. 2015). "But actually I bounce back and forth; I am from China but I do not belong only there. Each of us can now say we are all one universe."

In addition to her work as a photographer, Chen continues to paint and draw and has created works of art inspired by traditional Chinese calligraphy. She is also interested in film and has directed a number of short videos for brands such as Cadillac, Sharp, and Beats. In 2016 Chen signed with the Creative Artists Agency, a talent agency with offices in both California and Beijing, among other places, with the goal of pursuing directorial work.

SUGGESTED READING

Anderton, Frances. "Chen Man: Fashion Photographer, Artist, and Poster Child for the Post-1980 Chinese." *DNA Design and Architecture*, KCRW, 7 Jan. 2015, blogs.kcrw.com/dna/chen-man-high-flying-fashion-photographer-and-poster-child-for-the-post-1980s-chinese. Accessed 14 July 2017.

Chen Man. "Meet Chen Man, the 'Chinese Annie Leibovitz.'" Interview by Valeriya Safronova. *The New York Times*, 10 May 2017, www.nytimes.com/2017/05/10/fashion/meet-chen-man-the-chinese-annie-leibovitz.html. Accessed 14 July 2017.

"Man on Top: Chinese Photographer Chen Man Exposed." *K Magazine*, 4 Feb. 2016, www.

kering.com/en/magazine/man-top. Accessed 14 July 2017.

Newell-Hanson, Alice. "Chen Man Is Not the Annie Leibovitz of China, She's Chen Man." *i-D*, 10 May 2017, i-d.vice.com/en_us/article/chen-man-is-not-the-annie-leibovitz-of-china-shes-chen-man. Accessed 14 July 2017.

Raphael, Sarah. "Chen Man, the Chinese Princess of Fashion Photography." *i-D*, 30 Jan. 2014, i-d.vice.com/en_gb/article/chen-man. Accessed 14 July 2017.

Rosenfeld, Cynthia. "Insider: Chen Man's Guide to Beijing." *Surface*, 9 Mar. 2017, www.surfacemag.com/articles/travel-guide-beijing-chen-man-fashion-photographer/. Accessed 14 July 2017.

Tietjen, Alexa. "Chen Man on Perfection, Michael Jackson and Chinese Philosophy." *WWD*, 8 May 2017, wwd.com/eye/people/chen-man-talks-michael-jackson-chinese-philosophy-10883120/. Accessed 14 July 2017.

SELECTED WORKS
The Astronaut, 2003; *Funky Great Wall*, 2007; *Long Live the Motherland*, 2010; *Four Seasons*, 2011; *Five Elements*, 2011

—Joy Crelin

Joe Manganiello

Date of birth: December 28, 1976
Occupation: Actor

Joe Manganiello rocketed to fame while starring as a werewolf with a heart of gold on HBO's paranormal Southern gothic series *True Blood*, about the adventures of a psychic waitress and her associations with supernatural beings. Although sometimes dismissed as nothing more than a lightweight actor with an impressively chiseled body, Manganiello has attempted to move beyond his typecasting by writing a book, producing and directing a documentary, and taking on varied film roles—everything from comedic turns to action-adventure to a villainous turn in Ben Affleck's upcoming *Batman* feature film. When asked by Delphine Chui of *GQ* (4 July 2014) to name some of the public misconceptions about him, Manganiello answered: "I think a lot of people don't realize I've been acting for [more than twenty] years. They think that I just started a few years ago [when *True Blood* was on]. There are probably a lot of people out there that also don't think I can walk and chew gum at the same time because they are focused on the exterior, which you know is fine. When you're underestimated, you spend an entire lifetime

Srakirei derivative work: RanZag/CC BY-SA 2.0/Wikimedia Commons

sneaking up on people and it's easy to get ahead that way, so it's all good."

EARLY LIFE AND CAREER
Joe Manganiello was born on December 28, 1976, to Susan and Charles Manganiello, who also have a younger son, Nick. Joe and his brother were raised in Pittsburgh, Pennsylvania. As a child, Joe was a self-described "nerd," obsessed with comic books and super heroes, as well as fantasy and science fiction. When Mickey Rapkin asked in *Elle* (23 Sept. 2013) who his first crush was, Manganiello answered: "Princess Leia from *Star Wars*. I actually met Carrie Fisher a couple of years ago. When I told her that she was my first crush, she insisted that we get married and have a reality show about it. I'm lucky to have made it out of that weekend without getting married."

Despite being a scrawny teenager, Manganiello trained his body and went out for high school sports, including football. He had other interests, however, besides sports. At Mount Lebanon High School, he worked in the school's television studios, sometimes borrowing cameras and making short films on the weekends with friends. When he was sixteen, he dressed up in a promotional Captain Morgan pirate costume and worked local bars for twenty-five dollars an hour. After a football injury sidelined him, he decided to pursue acting in school productions, which made him few friends among his old teammates. "The linebacker coach would stop me in the hall and say really snide comments to me because I wasn't playing football anymore, and the volleyball coach told me I was making a huge mistake with my life," Manganiello recalled in an interview with Rob Owen for the *Pittsburgh Post-Gazette* (25 June 2010). Then he got a part in the high school production of *Oklahoma*. "After that the linebacker coach stopped me in the hall again and said, 'I was wrong. You were really good.' It was a victory."

The vindication helped encourage him to try out for Carnegie Mellon University's acting program in his senior year of high school. When he failed to make the cut, he studied at the University of Pittsburgh for a year, then reapplied to the acting program. This time he got in. He graduated from Carnegie Mellon in 2000.

A *TRUE BLOOD* WEREWOLF

Manganiello had an early success in the film industry when he was cast to play Flash Thompson, the high school rival of Spider-Man's alter ego Peter Parker, in *Spider-Man* (2002), directed by Sam Raimi. (He would reprise the role several years later in *Spider-Man 3*, which premiered in 2007.) When his career, however, did not begin to take off as he hoped it would, Manganiello found himself spiraling deeper into self-destructive behavior, smoking two packs of cigarettes a day and drinking heavily. He worked construction for a few years instead of acting. Then he quit drinking and smoking and returned to performing, building his résumé through television appearances on such shows as *CSI* (2006), *Las Vegas* (2006), *American Heiress* (2007), and *ER* (2007). He found steadier work as Owen Morello on *One Tree Hill* (2008–10) and in a series of appearances on *How I Met Your Mother* (2006–12). But his breakthrough role came through *True Blood*, HBO's adaptation of Charlaine Harris's *Sookie Stackhouse* novel series.

True Blood, which premiered in 2008, follows the adventures of Sookie Stackhouse, a telepathic waitress (played by Anna Paquin in the series), who finds herself getting involved with an odd assortment of supernatural creatures, including most notably vampires and werewolves. Manganiello played a werewolf named Alcide Herveaux in the critically acclaimed series from 2010 to 2014.

"'True Blood' as a whole delves a lot deeper than other supernatural shows or movies," Manganiello remarked to Rob Owen for the *Pittsburgh Post-Gazette*. "It's a lot richer, more character-driven. What's interesting about this character to me is it really gets into the backstory. It gets into what it must have been like to grow up with this. He was a kid who was born with this thing that manifests itself around puberty, and you get an idea that he had to live as a recluse and hide and not let people know what he really is."

Playing Alcide brought Manganiello a legion of fans—particularly female fans who admired his character's salt-of-the-earth decency as well as his chiseled good looks. His only regret while being contracted for the series was being unable to try out for the various super hero films that were being cast at the time, particularly Superman in the *Man of Steel* film of 2013. That part eventually went to British actor Henry Cavill, who would reprise the role in *Batman v. Superman: Dawn of Justice* (2016).

MAGIC MIKE AND OTHER PROJECTS

One film Manganiello was able to make during his time on *True Blood* was *Magic Mike* (2012), a comedy about male strippers. It was directed by acclaimed director Steven Soderbergh and costarred Channing Tatum as Magic Mike, Matthew McConaughey as Dallas, and Matt Bomer as Ken. Manganiello would reprise his role as Richie in the sequel, *Magic Mike XXL* (2015). Manganiello's costar Matt Bomer, whom he first met at drama school at Carnegie Mellon, told Jessica Shaw for *Men's Fitness* (Jan./Feb. 2015): "[Joe] has an enviable amount of courage and self-confidence, but not in an egotistical way. Watching him on set has made the job easier for me. I just have to do what he does, which is not be scared to throw myself into it." Manganiello's experience in the world of male strippers would later prompt him to direct his first film, *La Bare*, a 2014 documentary about Le Bare Dallas, one of the most popular male strip clubs in the world. He and his brother, Nick, would also serve as producers for the film.

In 2013, Manganiello published his first book, *Evolution*, a book that describes his fitness training regimen and how he transformed himself from a skinny teenager into one of the fittest men working in Hollywood. Actor Arnold Schwarzenegger, a former Mr. Universe and former governor of California, wrote the introduction to the book. Schwarzenegger met Manganiello while the pair worked together on the action film *Sabotage* (2014). Schwarzenegger recalled of his costar for Shaw: "I really got to know him when we rehearsed. We all trained very carefully for a month before the movie, and when you do that you get to know the people very well, very quickly. You see who's the lazy bastard and who goes all out. Joe goes all out."

Manganiello has also appeared in such films as *Knight of Cups* (2015), *Tumbledown* (2015), and *Pee-wee's Big Holiday* (2016), in which he costars alongside one of his childhood comedic heroes, Pee-wee Herman, the alter ego of Paul Reubens. The film, which was produced by Reubens and Judd Apatow, is a sort of buddy movie, in which Manganiello is playing himself and inspires Pee-wee to take his first vacation outside of his idyllic hometown. Manganiello had been friends with Reuben since 2011, when the pair met at an Emmy Awards party. "What I love about Joe so much is that he's this amazing-looking guy, 6'5", and he's on the cover of *Men's Fitness*," Reubens told Jason Adams for *Men's Fitness* (April 2016). "But when you peel all that away, he's like a dorky nerd."

UPCOMING PROJECTS
When asked if he would still like to be in a su-perhero movie, Manganiello told Adams: "I missed that whole boom because I was on *True Blood*. All of the primary superheroes were be-ing cast when I was contracted on a series. So I wasn't even allowed to screen-test, you know? They got mad when I set up meetings with di-rectors about those projects. They're all cast now—at least all the ones I loved as a kid. There might be an obscure character left for me some-where out there." In September 2016 the *Wall Street Journal* reported that Manganiello would finally get his chance to work in a superhero film when he costars as the main villain in the upcoming Batman film, provisionally titled *The Batman*, in which Ben Affleck will reprise his role as the caped crusader. (Affleck first played Batman in 2016's *Batman v. Superman: Dawn of Justice*.) In the film Manganiello is expected to play Slade Wilson, also known as Deathstroke, a longtime DC Comics villain known for his skills as an assassin and for his genetically augmented abilities. Deathstroke most notably has only one eye, the other having been shot out, but the loss of the eye does not make him any less lethal an opponent.

PERSONAL LIFE
Since November 2015, Manganiello has been married to Sofía Vergara, the Colombian Ameri-can actor best known for her comedic turn as Gloria Delgado-Pritchett on the long-running hit television series *Modern Family*, which began airing in 2009.

SUGGESTED READING
Adams, Jason. "Joe: The Man Behind the Mus-cle." *Men's Fitness*, Apr. 2016, pp. 68–175. *MasterFILE Complete*, search.ebscohost.com/login.aspx?direct=true&db=f6h&AN=113375479&site=eds-live. Accessed 15 Dec. 2016.

Chui, Delphine. "Joe Manganiello Would Prefer to Keep His Shirt On, If You Wouldn't Mind." *GQ*, 4 July 2014, www.gq-magazine.co.uk/ar-ticle/joe-manganiello-true-blood-magic-mike-la-bare-interview. Accessed 13 Dec. 2016.

Holub, Christian. "Joe Manganiello Cast as Deathstroke in Ben Affleck's Batman Movie." *Entertainment Weekly*, 8 Sept. 2016, www.ew.com/article/2016/09/08/

joe-manganiello-deathstroke-ben-affleck-bat-man. Accessed 13 Dec. 2016.

Owen, Rob. "CMU Grad, Joe Manganiello's, 'True Blood' Role May Be a Starmaker." *Pittsburgh Post-Gazette*, 25 June 2010, www.post-gazette.com/tv-radio/2010/06/25/CMU-grad-Joe-Manganiello-s-True-Blood-role-may-be-a-starmaker/stories/201006250206. Ac-cessed 15 Dec. 2016.

Rapkin, Mickey. "Joe Manganiello Knows What Women Want." *Elle*, 24 Sept. 2013, www.elle.com/culture/celebrities/a13846/joe-mangani-ello-interview. Accessed 13 Dec. 2016.

Shaw, Jessica. "Super Manganiello." *Men's Fit-ness*, Jan./Feb. 2015, p. 66. *MasterFILE Com-plete*, search.ebscohost.com/login.aspx?direc t=true&db=f6h&AN=100323597&site=eds-live. Accessed 4 Jan. 2017.

SELECTED WORKS
Spider-Man, 2002; *One Tree Hill*, 2008–10; *True Blood*, 2010–14; *Magic Mike*, 2012; *Sabotage*, 2014; *Magic Mike XXL*, 2015; *Pee-wee's Big Hol-iday*, 2016

—Christopher Mari

Simone Manuel

Date of birth: August 2, 1996
Occupation: Swimmer

Although elite American gymnast Simone Biles was considered an odds-on favorite to win a gold medal at the 2016 Summer Olympic Games, it was another female athlete with the same first name who made headlines in Rio de Ja-neiro that summer. Simone Manuel emerged from relative obscurity to take center stage in the women's 100-meter freestyle. Despite trail-ing in third place after the first 50 meters, she managed to keep pace with the world record-holder, Australia's Cate Campbell, eventually overtaking her and finishing first in a dead heat with sixteen-year-old Canadian Penny Oleksiak. Manuel's gold medal was the first since 1984 for the United States in the women's 100-meter freestyle event.

Manuel's accomplishment was also notable for another reason. With this victory, the twen-ty-year-old became the first African American woman to win an individual gold in swimming. Manuel, who also added another gold and two silvers to her medal collection, recognizes the importance of her achievement, especially in a sport with so few people of color. "This medal is not just for me," Manuel shared with Dahleen Glanton for the *Chicago Tribune* (12 Aug. 2016). "It's for some of the African Americans that . . .

Wesley Hitt/Getty Images

came before me and have been inspirations and mentors to me. I hope that I can be an inspiration for others."

EARLY LIFE

Simone Ashley Manuel was born in Sugar Land, Texas, to Sharron and Marc Manuel on August 2, 1996. She hails from an athletic family. Her mother was a member of her high school basketball and volleyball teams, while her father played basketball for Xavier University, a historically black institution in New Orleans, Louisiana. Manuel, whose two older brothers played college basketball, developed a fascination with water at a very early age. "I remember taking her to Water World when she wasn't even a year old," Manuel's mother recalled to Taryn Burnett for *Sugar Land Magazine* (Spring 2014). "The second we put her in the water, she splashed and splashed and splashed. It was like a transformation." Even Manuel's older brother Ryan noticed his sister's passion from the time she was just eighteen months old. "I had the water running and was sitting in the tub," he shared with Paul Newberry for the *Associated Press* (6 Mar. 2015). "Out of nowhere, my little sister comes around the corner and jumps in the tub with all her clothes on. I think that's when my parents knew she wanted to be a swimmer."

By age four, Manuel was enrolled in swim classes where she displayed a natural ability and was able to swim across the pool on her second day of class. She joined a summer recreational swim league at age six, and within three years

was swimming competitively year-round. By eleven years old she joined the First Colony Swim Team (FCST), a USA Swimming–affiliated club in Sugar Land.

MAKING A SPLASH ON THE COMPETITIVE CIRCUIT

A turning point for Manuel came in May 2010, when she attended the USA Swimming's Diversity Select Camp at the Olympic Training Center on the recommendation of FCST coach Allison Beebe. "I met people in the sport who were a minority like me, who'd also had feelings of being excluded. I saw that it wasn't just me and they were such amazing people with different stories," she shared with Rhonda Marable for *USASwimming* (6 Oct. 2014).

Manuel notched her first major victory in early August 2011, posting a time of 55.22 to capture the gold medal in the women's 100-meter freestyle at the Speedo Junior National Championships, a biannual competition for the nation's best female swimmers aged eighteen and under. Her performance earned her a chance to join USA Swimming's National Team at the 2011 FINA World Junior Championships in Lima, Peru, where the fifteen-year-old won another gold (in the 4×100-meter freestyle relay) and barely missed the podium with a fourth-place finish in the 100-meter freestyle. Manuel closed out the year ranked fifteenth nationally and sixty-first in the world in the 100-meter freestyle.

RISING UP IN THE JUNIOR RANKS

In June 2012, Manuel qualified to compete at the US Olympic Trials for the London Summer Olympics. After failing to make the Olympic team, Manuel headed to Hawaii in late August to compete for Team USA in the Junior Pan Pacific Championships, where she claimed the 100-meter freestyle gold. Two months later at the Gulf Swimming Senior Meet, Manuel won the girls' 50- and 100-yard freestyles in the fifteen-and-over category. Her time in the latter event (49.82) qualified her for the 2012 AT&T Winter National Championships in Austin, Texas, where she finished fourth in the 100-yard freestyle and fifth in the 200-yard freestyle.

In early March 2013, Manuel triumphed in the 50-yard freestyle and 200-yard butterfly at another thirteen-and-over meet—the Gulf 2013 Short Course Champs II. By mid-March she had racked up three more individual titles (the 50-, 100-, and 200-yard freestyles) from the 2013 National Club Swimming Association's (NCSA) Junior Nationals, while also setting records in the 15–16 National Age Group (NAG) records in the 50-yard freestyle (22.04) and the 100-yard freestyle (47.73). At the FCST Gulf April Open, she competed in the fifteen-and-over category and claimed wins in three freestyle events (the 50-, 100-, and 400-meter), along with the 200-meter backstroke and 100-meter breaststroke.

COMPETING AGAINST THE BEST

That summer Manuel held her own against many of the country's top swimmers at the 2013 Phillips 66 USA Swimming National Championships, capturing two freestyle medals—a silver in the 50-meter and bronze in the 100-meter—and qualifying for the World Championships in Barcelona, Spain, where she won gold in the 400-meter relay preliminary and placed seventh in the 50-meter freestyle, with a personal-best time of 24.80. Manuel's winning time (23.09) in the girls fifteen-and-over 50-yard freestyle at an October 2013 Gulf Swimming Senior meet qualified her for the 2014 Winter National Championships. She followed that up with victories in the 50-, 100-, and 200-yard freestyle, as well as the 100-yard backstroke and the 200-yard individual medley (IM) at the AGS Gulf Senior Championships, held at Texas A&M University. Manuel closed out the year in Glasgow, Scotland, competing at the Duel in the Pool, which is swimming's version of the Ryder Cup. Along with her 100-meter freestyle gold and her 50-meter freestyle bronze, Manuel helped lead Team USA's relay squad to a gold in the 200-meter mixed medley and silver in the 400-meter freestyle.

Following first-place finishes in the 50- and 100-yard freestyle at the Gulf 2014 SC Champs II Meet, as well as three individual freestyle golds (in the 50-, 100-, and 200-yard) at the 2014 NCSA Spring Championships, Manuel claimed the 100-yard freestyle, backstroke, and IM crowns, along with the 50-yard butterfly, at the NASA Junior National Championship Cup in late March. She continued her medal-winning run at the 2014 Phillips 66 Nationals, with a gold in the 50-meter freestyle and a silver in the 100-meter freestyle. Manuel's performance earned her a berth at the Pan Pacific Championships, where she placed second in two relay events (the 4×200-meter freestyle and 4×100-meter medley) and third in the 100-meter freestyle.

MAKING HER MARK AT THE COLLEGE LEVEL

In September 2014, the heavily recruited Manuel began attending Stanford University in Palo Alto, California, and kicked off her freshman season by winning the 50-meter freestyle and 100-meter butterfly to help propel Stanford over fellow Pac-12 school the University of Utah. Her victories in the 200- and 500-meter freestyle, as well as the 200-meter IM propelled the Stanford Cardinals over the Oregon State Beavers. In late November 2014 Manuel

turned in a record-setting performance at the Art Adamson Invitational by becoming the first female swimmer in history to clock the fastest relay split (45.81) during the 400-yard medley and by notching personal bests in her three individual wins: the 50-meter freestyle (21.59); the 100-meter freestyle (46.62 and a 17–18 NAG record); and the 200-meter freestyle (1:42.03). She was also a member of the gold medal-winning 200-meter free relay squad and helped the Cardinals finish second overall to tournament host Texas A&M University.

On January 23, 2015, Manuel put on another dominant performance against the University of Arizona (UA) Wildcats, sweeping the 50-, 100-, and 200-yard freestyle en route to winning the Saturday tournament. She capped off the weekend road trip with her first-place finish in the 200-yard IM during a successful meet against UA's rival, Arizona State University. (Her time of 2:01.72 set a school swimming record.) Over the next month, the Cardinal squad posted convincing home wins over two more Pac-12 schools, University of California, Los Angeles (UCLA) and University of Southern California (USC).

BECOMING A PAC-12 AND NCAA CHAMPION

In late February, the third-ranked Stanford Cardinals competed at the 2015 Pac-12 Championships. The first day, Manuel anchored Stanford's 800-yard freestyle relay team that came in second. On day two, Manuel clocked a personal best (1:41.15) in the 200-yard freestyle but came in second and also came in second in the 50 freestyle. Manuel wrapped up the Pac-12 championship on a high note, anchoring Stanford's winning 400-yard freestyle relay team and capturing the 100-yard freestyle in a time of 46.70—a Pac-12 record.

Manuel's overall Pac-12 performance qualified her for the 2015 National Collegiate Athletic Association (NCAA) Division I Women's Championships. She was impressive in her debut, claiming gold and setting NCAA records in the 50-yard freestyle (21.32) and the 400-yard medley relay (3:36.41) while also finishing second in the 200-yard freestyle relay. On day two, Manuel earned runner-up honors in an individual event (the 200-yard freestyle) and relay (the 800-yard free) before finishing first in the 400-yard medley relay (3:26.41) and the 100 free (46.09)—both NCAA and American records. For the latter event, she shared the podium with two other African American swimmers: Lia Neal and University of Florida's Natalie Hinds—an unprecedented occurrence. In April 2015, Manuel was named Pac-12 Swimming Freshman/Newcomer of the Year.

THE 2016 SUMMER OLYMPICS

During the summer of 2015, Manuel swam in the 2015 FINA World Championships and helped the US national team clinch a bronze medal in the finals of the 400-meter freestyle relay. Manuel made headlines again in October 2015 when she sat out the 2015–16 season to train for the 2016 Olympics. She closed out the year by competing at the 2015 AT&T Winter Nationals. Her first-place finishes in the 50- and 100-meter freestyle helped her qualify for the 2016 US Olympic Trials in Omaha, Nebraska, where she fulfilled her lifelong Olympic dream by finishing in second place in both events, earning her a berth to the Summer Olympics in Rio de Janeiro, Brazil. Manuel was one of only two African American women to make the US Olympic swim team.

Manuel's Olympic debut on August 6 was impressive, swimming leadoff for a US women's 4×100-meter freestyle relay team and achieving a silver medal-winning performance (3:31.89), which set an American record. However she had a more impressive finish five days later with a come-from-behind effort to tie Canada's Penny Oleksiak for the 100-meter freestyle gold. With her win, Manuel set an Olympic record (52.70) and became the first African American swimmer in Olympic history to win an individual gold medal. On the final night of the swimming competition, she added two more medals to her collection—another silver, in the 50-meter freestyle, and another gold, as anchor of the women's 4×100-meter medley relay team.

Since her Olympic glory, Manuel has returned to the Stanford women's swim team for the 2016–17 season.

PERSONAL LIFE

In her spare time, Manuel, whose nickname is Swimone, loves to cook and visit art museums. She cites Beyoncé as her favorite singer and the romantic drama *Beyond the Lights* (2014) as her favorite film.

SUGGESTED READING

Barnett, Taryn. "Finding Her Place in the Water." *Sugar Land Magazine*, Spring 2014, www.sugarlandmagazine.com/wp-content/uploads/2014/04/Simone-Manuel.pdf. Accessed 6 Jan. 2017.

Glanton, Dahleen. "Reflecting on Black Women, Hair, and Swimming after Simone Manuel Wins Gold." *Chicago Tribune*, 12 Aug. 2016, www.chicagotribune.com/news/columnists/ct-simone-manuel-glanton-20160812-column.html. Accessed 11 Jan. 2017.

Marable, Rhonda. "Multicultural Heroes: Simone Manuel." *USASwimming*, 6 Oct. 2014, www.usaswimming.org/viewnewsarticle. aspx?db_oem_id=30600&tabid=0&itemid=6397&mid=14491. Accessed 6 Jan. 2017.

Newberry, Paul. "Manuel Siblings Thriving on Court, in Pool." *The Augusta Chronicle*, 7 Mar. 2015, chronicle.augusta.com/sports/college/2015-03-06/manuel-siblings-thriving-court-pool. Accessed 6 Jan. 2017.

—*Bertha Muteba*

Helen Marten

Date of birth: 1985
Occupation: Artist

The British multimedia artist Helen Marten has earned international acclaim for her unique installation pieces, which often make use of ordinary objects to form abstract, thought-provoking creations. Critics have struggled to definitively describe her work, which is often called whimsical, but most have agreed that it is among the most interesting contemporary art. "Marten makes you want to look very closely at the things she makes and the traces she leaves," Adrian Searle wrote for *The Guardian* (25 Nov. 2012) in a review of one of the artist's earliest major solo shows. "Her way of thinking, with its word salads and trap-door metaphors, is dangerously infectious." Marten rose to prominence in the art world rapidly, achieving recognition as an important figure while still in her twenties. She cemented her role as one of the brightest stars of contemporary art in 2016 when she won both the inaugural Hepworth Prize for Sculpture and the exceptionally prestigious Turner Prize.

Marten's work focuses on assemblage and sculpture, but she never hesitates to think outside the box. She has used media ranging from found objects to video installations to develop her artistic vision. She provided some insight into that vision to Christopher Bollen for *Interview Magazine* (6 Dec. 2012): "I suppose I'm trying to upset the expected rhythms of daily circumstance, exploring what it means to be a tribal human preoccupied with the status of toothpaste, the floppiness of pasta, eroticism of rubbish, or tedium of hair."

EARLY YEARS AND EDUCATION

Marten was born in 1985 in Macclesfield, a historic town in Cheshire, England. Her father was a chemist who worked for a pharmaceutical company; she has described him as somewhat pedantic, with a love of labeling and scheduling every element of his life. Her mother was a biologist who later earned advanced degrees in psychology and semiotics. Marten has told interviewers that she takes after her mother, who was

Michael Stewart/Getty Images

often deeply engrossed in works of literature. She grew up with a twin sister, who would later become an accountant. "We're different brain hemispheres," the artist quipped to Skye Sherwin for *W* magazine (27 Aug. 2014).

Although Marten's parents would later encourage her artistic career, she had little idea as a youngster that art might be a realistic path for her to take. "The fact that this would ever be a viable profession never seemed like an option for me," she recalled to Sherwin, remarking on the conventionality of her childhood. "I didn't think, I'm going to be an artist when I grow up." Still, she both wrote and made art from a young age.

Even once her interest had been sparked and she had received validation of her artistic talent from family and teachers, Marten wavered between pursuing a literary career or one in the visual arts. In 2004 she hit upon the idea of doing an introductory foundation year at the Byam Shaw School of Art, part of Central Saint Martins, itself a constituent college of the University of the Arts London. Following that, she enrolled at the Ruskin School of Art at the University of Oxford. She decided to study in the tradition-bound halls of Oxford, rather than in London, as she told Sherwin, because in the city "all the art schools seemed to be about the posture of being an artist."

As a student Marten discovered the work of husband-and wife architects Robert Venturi and Denise Scott Brown. She was so taken with their 1972 treatise, *Learning from Las Vegas*, cowritten by Steven Izenour, that she embarked on a trip to the locations mentioned in the book, including

the massive sign company responsible for much of Las Vegas's iconic neon. Upon earning her degree in 2008 and realizing that she needed to find a job that would pay a steady wage, Marten worked for an essay-writing company, an experience she detested.

BEGINNING AN ART CAREER

Marten soon returned to her hometown and, thanks to the abundance of cheap raw materials that could be found there, began making art in her parents' garage. She began experimenting with industrial metalworking techniques such as powder coating and laser cutting. Soon her work started attracting attention. In 2009, not long after she began working on her sculptures in earnest, one of her former professors, Richard Wentworth, included one of her pieces in an exhibition at the Lisson Gallery in London. The next year, Wentworth described her in a feature article for *The Guardian*'s Observer column headlined "Meet the Best New Artists in Britain" (16 Oct. 2010). "She is like a fantastic tourist: intelligently acquisitive, yet editorially selective. . . . She knows how to look," Wentworth said. "She is making codes—her work is like a contemporary Rosetta stone. It is part of a broad conversation. She is enormously respected. She has a hidden grandeur but no grandiosity."

Following those high-profile accolades, Marten's career took off rapidly. She earned a mention by well-known curator Hans Ulrich Obrist, and her video installation *Dust and Piranhas* (2011) was shown as part of a series by the Serpentine Galleries of London. Her show *Take a stick and make it sharp* appeared the same year at the Johann König gallery in Berlin, Germany. Another show at that gallery won Marten the Prix Lafayette, awarded by France's FIAC (International Contemporary Art Fair) to artists exhibiting at emerging galleries. Also in 2011, she was shortlisted for the LUMA Award for contemporary art, before winning it in 2012.

CRITICAL BREAKTHROUGH

One of the selectors for the LUMA Award was the esteemed curator Beatrix Ruf, who would become one of Marten's biggest promoters. Under her guidance, the artist would progress from promising newcomer to in-demand star. Ruf was then the head of the gallery Kunsthalle Zürich, in Zürich, Switzerland, which became the site of Marten's first major solo show. Aoife Rosenmeyer reviewed that show, originally titled *Almost the exact shape of Florida*, for *Art in America* (27 Dec. 2012): "Marten belongs to the first generation for which the choreography of clicking and exploring on the computer is as natural as walking and opening doors. Her fluency with form is impressive, and here she used it to create an environment redolent of the digital realm."

Marten's breakthrough show eventually became known as *Plank Salad*, and was exhibited 2012–13 at the Chisenhale Gallery, London—her first major solo show in her native country—before traveling to the United States. The works in the exhibition were mostly multimedia sculptures, with images and objects combined in ways that invited contemplation as well as a sense of humor. The assemblages and the textual descriptions in the show's accompanying literature bordered on the surreal, avoiding concrete representation or description.

Many art critics have admitted that it can be difficult to accurately convey a sense of Marten's work, but they have been virtually united in their acclaim for it and its complex, ambiguous messages. Writing for the *Atlantic* (5 Dec. 2016), Sophie Gilbert suggested, "Her sculptures create swooping, almost rhythmic structures out of seemingly disconnected objects—suitcases, cotton buds, eggshells, coffee cups—that encapsulate the ephemera of modern life. At first glance it seems haphazard, but Marten's intention is to create order from disorder: to piece together disconnected fragments into a more intelligible narrative." Others have been similarly confused and impressed. As Charlotte Higgins wrote for *The Guardian* (22 Dec. 2016), "If you submit yourself to this art—approaching the sculptures like free verse whose meaning you might rather absorb than decode—you realize you are in a place unlike any you've entered before, where a distinctive mind has messed with the world of objects and meaning, creating her own strange, compressed archaeology, which you are invited to expand into imaginary life."

Marten would follow her breakthrough success as a solo exhibitor with several other well-received group and solo shows in various venues. Her solo exhibitions included *No borders in a wok that can't be crossed* (2013) at CCS Bard in New York City, *Parrot Problems* (2014) at the Fridericianum in Kassel, Germany, and *Drunk Brown House* (2016) at the Serpentine Sackler Gallery in London. Major group shows included displays at the prestigious Venice Biennial in 2013 and 2015.

HEPWORTH AND TURNER PRIZES
Marten came to widespread attention even well outside of the art world in 2016, when international news outlets reported that she had won not one, but two, major prizes. In November of that year she received the inaugural £30,000 (approximately US$38,000) Hepworth Prize for Sculpture. Aimed at recognizing and supporting important contributors to sculpture from or based in Great Britain, the biennial prize is named after Barbara Hepworth (1903–75), one of Britain's most acclaimed practitioners of the art. Marten surprised some members of the art

world when she announced she would share the prize money with the other artists shortlisted for the award. "I'm lucky enough to be here and to be given a visible and audible platform to be doing what I'm doing and the fact that I'm supported by an enormously generous infrastructure of other artists, critics, curators, galleries is enough for me," she said, as quoted by Clarisse Loughrey for the *Independent* (18 Nov. 2016).

Then, in December 2016, it was announced that Marten was the recipient of the Turner Prize, administered by the Tate Gallery and widely considered among the United Kingdom's most prestigious awards for young visual artists. Alex Farquharson, the director of Tate Britain, compared Marten to a poet in explaining the judges' decision to Sophie Gilbert for the *Atlantic* (5 Dec. 2016). He specifically cited "the complexity of the work, its amazing formal qualities, its disparate materials and techniques, and also how it relates to the world." The reference to poetry was apt, as Marten often mentioned the ongoing influence of written words on her art. "Before I touch anything in the studio, before I do anything tangible or physical, I spend three or four months reading and researching, but not with a specific end goal in mind," she explained to Higgins. "It could be fiction, theory, news, philosophy. I read a lot of poetry. The primary impulse more often than not is linguistic."

Upon receiving the prize, Marten again said she would share the money with her fellow shortlisted artists. The Turner Prize, as many art critics pointed out, has often been a lightning rod for controversy. Past winners such as Damien Hirst have scandalized some gallery-goers with unconventional works that often pushed the boundaries of art. Marten's pieces shown at the 2016 Turner exhibition—including an assemblage of oddly curated objects such as fish skin and blocks of pool-hall chalk—did not incite fury, but many observers nonetheless admitted to some confusion. "It's really a kind of humbling lesson doing public exhibitions, because sometimes people have no idea," Marten told Higgins, "and curators often don't get it."

SUGGESTED READING
Bollen, Christopher. "Art: Helen Marten." *Interview*, 6 Dec. 2012, www.interviewmagazine.com/art/london-helen-marten/. Accessed 9 Jan. 2017.

Gilbert, Sophie. "Helen Marten's Intricate Sculptures Win the Turner Prize." *The Atlantic*, 5 Dec. 2016, www.theatlantic.com/entertainment/archive/2016/12/helen-marten-wins-the-2016-turner-prize/509669/. Accessed 9 Jan. 2017.

Higgins, Charlotte. "Helen Marten: From a Macclesfield Garage to Artist of the Year." *The Guardian*, 22 Dec. 2016, www.theguardian.

com/artanddesign/2016/nov/22/helen-mar-ten-from-a-macclesfield-garage-to-artist-of-the-year. Accessed 9 Jan. 2017.

Rosenmeyer, Aoife. Review of *Almost the exact shape of Florida*, by Helen Marten, at Kunsthalle Zürich, Zürich, Switzerland. *Art in America*, 27 Dec. 2012, www.artinamerica-magazine.com/reviews/helen-marten/. Accessed 9 Jan. 2017.

Searle, Adrian. "Monkeying with Mozart: The Striking Art of Helen Marten." Review of *Plank Salad*, by Helen Marten at the Chisenhale Gallery, London, England. *The Guardian*, 25 Nov. 2012, www.theguardian.com/artanddesign/2012/nov/25/monkeys-mozart-helen-marten-artist. Accessed 9 Jan. 2017.

Shea, Christopher D. "Multimedia Artist Helen Marten Wins Turner Prize." *New York Times*, 5 Dec. 2016, www.nytimes.com/2016/12/05/arts/design/multimedia-artist-helen-marten-wins-turner-prize.html. Accessed 9 Jan. 2017.

Sherwin, Skye. "Object Lessons." *W*, 27 Aug. 2014, www.wmagazine.com/story/helen-marten-artist. Accessed 9 Jan. 2017.

SELECTED WORKS
Take a stick and make it sharp, 2011; *Almost the exact shape of Florida*, 2012; *Plank Salad*, 2012–13; *No borders in a wok that can't be crossed*, 2013; *Parrot Problems*, 2014; *Drunk Brown House*, 2016

—Mari Rich

Hisham Matar

Date of birth: 1970
Occupation: Author

Libyan novelist Hisham Matar won the 2017 Pulitzer Prize in biography or autobiography for his memoir *The Return: Fathers, Sons and the Lands in Between* (2016). The book is about Matar's father, an exile and strong critic of Libyan dictator Muammar al-Qaddafi who was kidnapped by the regime in 1990. Libya, a country in northern Africa, gained its independence from France and Britain in 1951. Qaddafi, then a young army officer, seized power in a bloodless coup in 1969. Throughout the 1970s, the years that comprise Matar's early childhood, Qaddafi helped Libya cash in on its plentiful oil reserves, but his regime grew more and more oppressive. Matar grew up in Tripoli, Libya's capital, but he moved with his family to neighboring Cairo, Egypt, in 1979, after his father was forced into exile. Matar did not return to Libya again until 2012, after Qaddafi was overthrown in a popular uprising. Most of *The Return* takes place during this

period—after Qaddafi but before the country slid into civil war. Matar is also the author of two novels, *Anatomy of a Disappearance* (2011) and *In the Country of Men* (2006), the latter of which was short-listed for the Man Booker Prize.

EARLY LIFE AND EXILE
Matar was born in New York City in 1970, but he spent his early years in Tripoli. His paternal grandfather, Jaddi Hamed, was a poet who fought in the resistance against the Italian occupation in the 1930s and 1940s. Later, members of that family stood up to Qaddafi in similar fashion and were similarly persecuted. Growing up in Tripoli, Matar has recalled his talent for Arabic, and another distinction that could only be described as a superior recklessness: he could swim farther out into the Mediterranean Sea than any of his friends—far enough to lose sight of the shore. "Even though my heart would be pounding by now and there was no one to see me, I would dare myself even further: I would close my eyes and spin around myself until I lost direction," he wrote for the *Guardian* (25 June 2016). "I would make a guess and begin swimming back where I thought the shore might be. Somehow, I never got it wrong."

Matar loved language and grammar, but he hated school, where teachers beat students on the hands with olive branches when they made mistakes. Outside of school, Matar and his brother, Ziad, felt the oppressive regime weighing on them with the threat of a more sinister disciplinary hand. From a young age they knew that they must be careful about what they said about the regime in public. In 1979, ten years after Qaddafi seized power, Matar's father, Jaballa Matar, a former officer in the Libyan Royal Army and member of the Libyan mission to the United Nations, was accused of being a reactionary. At the time, the elder Matar was in Cairo, and the family left Libya to join him there.

EDUCATION IN EGYPT AND ENGLAND

Matar continued to struggle in school in Egypt, though he suggests that the corrupt public school system was to blame. Teachers gave him failing grades, forcing Matar's parents to pay for extra tutoring. Once the payment was secured, the same teachers gave him high marks, no matter what he wrote down on exams. The only alternative was private school, but all the private schools in Egypt were European or American, and all their languages were foreign to Matar. When his parents offered to pay for private schooling, Matar arbitrarily chose an English one. He began attending the Cairo American College, where he read novels by Jane Austen, Herman Melville, and Charles Dickens. He became familiar with American cultural figures such as Bob Dylan and Billie Holiday, on whom he developed a serious crush. Though his English progressed, he had trouble relating to his American classmates, who only made fun of his taste and his clothes. The harassment intensified, and Matar began drinking and smoking at the age of thirteen.

Matar moved to a boarding school in England in 1986. Like his brother before him, he attended school under a false identity, as Qaddafi's agents were known for targeting dissidents and their families abroad. His new name was Bob. Surrounded by English speakers, he eventually took to the language in the way he had taken to Arabic as a child. Matar frequently sent letters home to his family in Cairo; he wrote several to his father in English but received a package back, containing the letters with a note telling him to write in Arabic. Matar has said that being a writer born into Arabic but having adopted English as his primary language is complicated. "It never feels completely okay that I'm not writing in Arabic," he told the British novelist Hari Kunzru in an interview for *Guernica* magazine (15 Oct. 2011). "On some level it's sort of a betrayal. But at the same time, English gives me that distance. . . . It makes me braver, but it also makes me more restrained."

Despite his love of language, Matar eventually enrolled at Goldsmiths College, University of London, and elected to study architecture. In March 1990, while Matar was still living in London, his father was abducted by the Egyptian secret service and returned to Libya, where he was taken to Tripoli's notorious Abu Selim prison, known for inmate torture. Matar's mother received a smuggled letter from his father in 1992 and another in 1995. Piecing together bits of information received over the course of many years, Matar discovered that his father was moved to another prison in April 1996, a few months before Libyan authorities massacred some 1,200 prisoners at Abu Selim. Matar's father was last seen in 2002—though Matar acknowledges in his book *The Return* that some or all of this information, gleaned after the elder Matar's last letter, could be false.

IN THE COUNTRY OF MEN

After receiving his master's degree from Goldsmiths College, Matar worked briefly as an architect. In 2002, he moved to Paris, determined to write a novel. After a period of anguish, he began what would become his first novel, *In the Country of Men* (2006). The book, based partly on Matar's own life experience, takes place in Tripoli in 1979. The book's protagonist is a young boy named Suleiman. Suleiman's father, Faraj, is a dissident. Matar's narrative grapples with Faraj's heroism, but also, through the lens of Suleiman's mother, Najwa, the heartbreak and fear of his family. Matar uses the muddled understanding of Suleiman, who is nine, as a literary device to humanize the complicated politics of the Libyan regime. Matar, who was deeply in debt by the time he finished the book, sold the novel for a huge sum. *In the Country of Men* was published to wide acclaim in 2006.

Lorrain Adams, who reviewed the book for the *New York Times* (4 Mar. 2007) after it was released in the United States in 2007, was particularly drawn to the way that Suleiman's point of view rendered the mechanisms of the regime grotesquely absurd. *In the Country of Men* is a realistic novel, but she compared it to science fiction classics about totalitarianism such as George Orwell's *Nineteen Eighty-Four* and Ray Bradbury's *Fahrenheit 451* "in the way [that] it posits a cruelly simplified and nonsensical universe." *In the Country of Men* was short-listed for Britain's prestigious Man Booker Prize and the *Guardian*'s First Book Award in 2006, and it won the Royal Society of Literature's Ondaatje Prize in 2007.

Matar published his second novel, *Anatomy of a Disappearance*, in 2011. This novel also draws from Matar's life experience, again featuring the young child of a Libyan dissident as its protagonist. Nuri el-Alfi is fourteen when the book begins in 1972. Nuri falls in love with his father's new wife, Mona, but then his father, like Matar's, disappears. Throughout the rest of the book, Nuri searches for his father. When it was published, *Anatomy of a Disappearance* suffered in comparison to its predecessor. "For all its elegance, *Anatomy of a Disappearance* is a little disappointing," Robert F. Worth wrote for the

New York Times (9 Sept. 2011), voicing a common complaint among critics. "The narrative voice has a coldness, a pained fragility, utterly at odds with the vividness and spontaneity of *In the Country of Men.*"

THE RETURN

Anatomy of a Disappearance was published several months after the Arab Spring, a series of popular uprisings across the Middle East that saw the fall of, among others, Libyan dictator Qaddafi. Matar wrote a slew of articles about Libya during this period and made a vow. "As soon as the revolution is complete," Matar told Cressida Leyshon for the *New Yorker* (7 Mar. 2011), "I will return to search for my father." Matar's 2016 memoir, *The Return: Fathers, Sons and the Lands in Between*, describes the author's return to Libya in 2012. It also contains meditations on art, exile, and authoritarianism and chronicles the abuses of Qaddafi's brutal regime through interviews with extended family members who were held as political prisoners. *The Return* was embraced by critics. In a review for the *New York Times* (5 July 2016), Robyn Creswell wrote that *The Return* is "a more mature and ultimately more satisfying book" than Matar's previous novels. "Like many elegies," she wrote, "*The Return* is a text of carefully controlled rage." It won the inaugural PEN/Jean Stein Book Award, and the *New York Times* named it one of the ten best books of 2016. In the spring of 2017, Matar was awarded the Pulitzer Prize in biography or autobiography.

PERSONAL LIFE

Matar is married to American photographer Diana Matar. She published a book of photographs depicting her 2012 journey to Libya with Matar called *Evidence* in 2015.

SUGGESTED READING

Adams, Lorraine. "The Dissident's Son." Review of *In the Country of Men*, by Hisham Matar. *The New York Times*, 4 Mar. 2007, www.nytimes.com/2007/03/04/books/review/Adams.t.html. Accessed 24 Apr. 2017.

Cresswell, Robyn. "Libya's Prisons Were Emptying. But Hisham Matar's Father Was Nowhere to Be Found." Review of *The Return: Fathers, Sons and the Land in Between*, by Hisham Matar. *The New York Times*, 5 July 2016, www.nytimes.com/2016/07/10/books/review/hisham-matar-the-return.html. Accessed 24 Apr. 2017.

Kunzru, Hari. "Libya's Reluctant Spokesman." *Guernica*, 15 Oct. 2011, www.guernicamag.com/matar_kunzru_10_15_11. Accessed 24 Apr. 2017.

Leyshon, Cressida. "Hisham Matar on Libya." *The New Yorker*, 7 Mar. 2011, www.

newyorker.com/books/page-turner/hisham-matar-on-libya. Accessed 23 Apr. 2017.

Matar, Hisham. "Hisham Matar: 'I Don't Remember a Time When Words Were Not Dangerous.'" *The Guardian*, 25 June 2016, www.theguardian.com/books/2016/jun/25/hisham-matar-i-dont-remember-a-time-when-words-were-not-dangerous. Accessed 23 Apr. 2017.

Worth, Robert F. "A Libyan Author Writes of Exile and a Vanished Father." Review of *Anatomy of a Disappearance*, by Hisham Matar. *The New York Times*, 9 Sept. 2011, www.nytimes.com/2011/09/11/books/review/anatomy-of-a-disappearance-by-hisham-matar-book-review.html. Accessed 24 Apr. 2017.

SELECTED WORKS

In the Country of Men, 2006; *Anatomy of a Disappearance*, 2011; *The Return: Fathers, Sons and the Land in Between*, 2016

—Molly Hagan

Melina Matsoukas

Date of birth: January 14, 1981
Occupation: Director

Director Melina Matsoukas has, as she once explained in an interview for the *Alice Initiative* (Jan. 2017), "an undying need to diversify the stories and imagery we've seen on screen historically." Indeed, her expansive body of work has made that need quite clear. Primarily a director of music videos, Matsoukas has worked with a diverse array of artists—from Rihanna to Lady Gaga to Snoop Dogg—to create short-form works that incorporate powerful imagery and thematic content. Since 2007, she has been a frequent collaborator of Beyoncé, directing numerous music videos for the artist and forming a close working relationship that in 2016 led to the creation of the music video for the artist's song "Formation," the first single from the cultural phenomenon that was Beyoncé's visual album *Lemonade*.

As a work dealing with the southern African American experience and touching on the relationship between the African American community and law enforcement, the "Formation" video drew criticism from some viewers and organizations while receiving critical acclaim from others. The music video earned Matsoukas her second Grammy Award, however, the conversations the video began were the ultimate reward, in her opinion. "I feel like there's been a lot of racial injustice in our community, and we're hungry for somebody to say something and for somebody as strong as Beyoncé to say something and show

Photo by Rodin Eckenroth/FilmMagic

value to people of color," she explained to Wesley Morris for the *New York Times* (28 Dec. 2016). In addition to her work in music videos, Matsoukas had directed advertisements for brands such as Nike, Absolut, and Lexus. In 2016 she made her television directorial debut as an executive producer and director for the critically acclaimed HBO series *Insecure*.

EARLY LIFE AND EDUCATION

Melina Matsoukas was born on January 14, 1981 in New York. Her mother, Diana-Elena, was a high school math teacher, while her father, David, was a carpenter. Matsoukas spent her early years in the New York City borough of the Bronx, where her family lived in the Co-Op City cooperative housing development. The family later moved to Hackensack, New Jersey, where Matsoukas spent her late childhood and adolescence.

Although Matsoukas grew up in an era in which music videos were becoming a major force in popular culture, she did not grow up dreaming of directing them. "I definitely was an MTV baby," she explained to Brenna Egan for *Refinery29* (27 Feb. 2013), "but it wasn't until college when I figured out I wanted to be in film and videos." Instead, the young Matsoukas found a creative outlet in photography, which proved a fruitful starting point for her later work. "When I got to NYU I just thought it was a natural progression and a way for me to speak to the world," she told Egan of her later switch to directing. "With music videos, I felt like I could be

extremely experimental with my art and have fun at the same time. I just love them."

After graduating from high school, Matsoukas returned to New York City to enroll at New York University's Tisch School of the Arts, a well-regarded training ground for creatives in a multitude of fields. Her early experiments with filmmaking at the school awakened a newfound passion for the field, although she has admitted in interviews that some of her earliest class projects were far from noteworthy. Matsoukas graduated from New York University in 2003, earning a bachelor of fine arts. She went on to pursue graduate studies at the American Film Institute, from which she earned her master of fine arts in cinematography in 2005.

EARLY CAREER

Matsoukas began making music videos early in her career, starting with her NYU thesis, a video for a singer with whom she was friends. Although she sometimes found herself spending money out of pocket for her earliest videos, she soon moved on to paid work, earning $250 for a video she created for her cousin Red Handed, a rapper based in Houston, Texas. Matsoukas also served as an assistant director for more established professionals during her early career, working under director Rachel Watanabe-Batton on the video for Lil Jon and the Eastside Boyz' song "Play No Games" in early 2003. After completing her studies at the American Film Institute in 2005, Matsoukas settled permanently in Los Angeles, where she began to make a name for herself as a director. Over the following year, she gained notice for videos she directed for artists such as the Ying Yang Twins and Ali & Gipp. Perhaps her most prominent video of 2006, however, was for the song "Money Maker," which was performed by rapper Ludacris and featured artist Pharrell Williams. The video proved popular among hip-hop fans, and the popularity of the artists involved drew further attention to Matsoukas's talents.

In addition to videos by artists such as Eve and Snoop Dogg, the year 2007 brought one of the most important steps in Matsoukas's career to date: her first collaboration with singer Beyoncé. The previous year, the singer had released her second solo album, *B'Day*, which proved popular among listeners and produced several hit singles and accompanying music videos. In 2007 Beyoncé released the *B'Day Anthology Video Album*, a collection of music videos for nearly all of the songs on the original album as well as additional songs from the album's 2007 deluxe edition. Matsoukas directed four of the videos featured on the video album: "Green Light," "Upgrade U," "Kitty Kat," and "Suga Mama." In an email to Alexis Okeowo for the *New Yorker* (6 Mar. 2017), Beyoncé remarked, "I feel safe working with her and expressing or revealing things about myself that I wouldn't with any other director." The opportunity to work with Beyoncé, who was already among the most popular solo acts in the United States, alone would likely have had a transformative effect on Matsoukas's career. For Matsoukas, however, her early collaborations with Beyoncé were the start of an ongoing professional relationship that shaped her overall outlook on the process of creating music videos. "I've almost killed Beyoncé a few times—she's either taken a fall, which I was responsible for, or tried some daring stunt," she told Egan. "She really set the tone for me in terms of an artist who will try and do anything for the art." Having become a popular choice of directors among solo pop and R & B performers, Matsoukas went on to direct videos for Solange—Beyoncé's sister—as well as artists such as Katy Perry, Ne-Yo, and Lily Allen. In 2008, she directed the video for "Just Dance," singer Lady Gaga's debut single.

SPARKING CULTURAL CONVERSATIONS

Within a decade of entering the industry, Matsoukas was well established as a director of eye-catching, entertaining, and often thought-provoking music videos. In addition to her work with Beyoncé, with whom she collaborated on videos such as "Diva" in 2008 and "Pretty Hurts" in 2013, Matsoukas established an ongoing working relationship with the singer Rihanna beginning in 2009, with her video for the singer's song "Hard." After directing two videos for Rihanna in 2010, "Rude Boy" and "Rockstar 101," she went on to collaborate with the artist on three videos the following year. The video for the song "S&M," released in February 2011, sparked controversy due to its sexual imagery and was banned in several countries. Later that year, Matsoukas's video for Rihanna's single "We Found Love," featuring Scottish DJ Calvin Harris, likewise met with criticism from some organizations due to its depictions of drug use, violence, and sexual content. Despite such criticism, the video was popular among viewers and industry professionals and in 2013 was awarded the Grammy Award for best short-form music video, making Matsoukas the first female solo director to win the award.

In 2016, Matsoukas directed her most culturally significant music video to date. That year, Beyoncé prepared to release her groundbreaking visual album *Lemonade*, which not only sheds light on painful aspects of the singer's personal life but also highlights the discussion of African American life in the United States. Matsoukas was selected to direct the video for the album's lead single, "Formation," which premiered online in February of that year. A striking work set in Louisiana and featuring imagery related to Hurricane Katrina and police brutality, among other elements, the video became the subject of extensive public discussion, with some viewers protesting what they identified as antipolice content in the video and others praising the work's depiction of southern African American culture. For Matsoukas, the reception of the video and the conversations it prompted came as a surprise. "That wasn't anything expected," she told Morris. "I had no idea that it would have that reaction and initiate those kinds of conversations. That was very satisfying as an artist to be a part of that." In recognition of their work, Matsoukas, Beyoncé, and the other key figures involved in the making of "Formation" were honored with the award for best short-form music video at the 2017 Grammys.

TELEVISION AND FILM

In addition to her work in music videos, Matsoukas has branched out into other forms of media throughout her career, putting her training in cinematography to use for several short films during and after her time at the American Film Institute. She has also directed commercials for several prominent brands, including Adidas, Lexus, and Nike. The next step in her directorial career came in 2016, when she made her television debut as the director and executive producer of the comedy series *Insecure*. Premiering on HBO in October of that year, the show was created by and stars writer Issa Rae, who had previously created the popular web series *The Misadventures of Awkward Black Girl*, and deals with topics such as friendship, dating, and identity. For Matsoukas, the opportunity to helm a television series for the first time was an incredible one. "Directing and executive producing an entire season of *Insecure* is probably my greatest achievement thus far, professionally," she told Stacy-Ann Ellis for *Vibe* (13 Mar. 2017). A hit with critics and audiences, *Insecure* was nominated for a variety of awards, including an Image Award nomination for Matsoukas for outstanding directing in a comedy series. Building upon her experience directing for television, Matsoukas went on to direct two episodes of the series *Master of None*, released on Netflix in 2017 and starring comedian and series cocreator Aziz Ansari.

Although Matsoukas enjoys directing music videos and television episodes, she has long sought to direct a feature film but has struggled to find the perfect project. "I've been searching for my first film for over a year now," she told Egan in 2013. "It's a tedious process that involves a lot of reading and developing, but hopefully it will start to manifest itself. I would love to do a film that has a strong character-based story and is intimate, artful, and provocative in some way." Despite her long search, Matsoukas remains optimistic. "I haven't found the exact story that speaks to me yet," she told Egan, "but I'm definitely on the hunt."

SUGGESTED READING

Ellis, Stacy-Ann. "Melina Matsoukas Trusts the Vision, the Voyage, and the Victories Sure to Come." *Vibe*, 13 Mar. 2017, www.vibe.com/2017/03/melina-matsoukas-director-interview. Accessed 12 May 2017.

Matsoukas, Melina. "The Lenny Interview: Melina Matsoukas." Interview by Laia Garcia. *Lenny*, 15 Apr. 2016, www.lennyletter.com/culture/news/a339/the-lenny-interview-melina-matsoukas. Accessed 12 May 2017.

Matsoukas, Melina. Interview. *The Alice Initiative*, www.thealiceinitiative.com/melina-matsoukas-interview. Accessed 12 May 2017.

Matsoukas, Melina. "Melina Matsoukas Touched Nerves from behind the Camera." Interview by Wesley Morris. *The New York Times*, 28 Dec. 2016, www.nytimes.com/2016/12/28/arts/music/melina-matsoukas-beyonce-formation-interview.html. Accessed 12 May 2017.

Matsoukas, Melina. "My Style: Director Melina Matsoukas Shows Off Her Sensational Style!" Interview by Brenna Egan. *Refinery29*, 27 Feb. 2013, www.refinery29.com/melina-matsoukas. Accessed 12 May 2017.

Matsoukas, Melina. "The Squeeze: Q&A with Video Director Melina Matsoukas." Interview by Mariel Concepcion. *Billboard*, 3 Feb. 2011, www.billboard.com/articles/columns/the-juice/473242/the-squeeze-qa-with-video-director-melina-matsoukas. Accessed 12 May 2017.

Okeowo, Alexis. "The Provocateur behind Beyoncé, Rihanna, and Issa Rae." *The New Yorker*, 6 Mar. 2017, www.newyorker.com/magazine/2017/03/06/the-provocateur-behind-beyonce-rihanna-and-issa-rae. Accessed 12 May 2017.

SELECTED WORKS
"Money Maker," 2006; "Sensual Seduction," 2007; "Green Light," 2007; "Upgrade U," 2007; "Kitty Kat," 2007; "Suga Mama," 2007; "Just Dance," 2008; "Rude Boy," 2010; "Why Don't You Love Me?," 2010; "S&M," 2011; "We Found Love," 2011; "Pretty Hurts," 2013; "Formation," 2016; *Insecure*, 2016–

—*Joy Crelin*

Gugu Mbatha-Raw

Date of birth: April 21, 1983
Occupation: Actor

From her early performances with youth theater companies in her native England to her breakthrough in both British and American film and television, actor Gugu Mbatha-Raw has remained intently focused on channeling her passion for acting into a productive career. "This is what I've always wanted to do ever since I was a little girl," she told Lindsay Peoples for the *Cut* (20 June 2016). "The idea of making my hobby into my job was the ultimate quest." Indeed, her quest has been a successful one by all measures. She established herself as a working actor in England shortly after completing her studies at the prestigious Royal Academy of Dramatic Art, soon appearing on well-known television shows such as *Spooks* (2006) and *Doctor Who* (2007) before breaking into the US market with a short-lived but attention-grabbing role in the spy series *Undercovers* (2010). A series of well-regarded performances in films such as 2014's *Belle* and *Beyond the Lights* followed, and by 2016, she was a known entity in Hollywood, making prominent appearances in major films such as *Free State of Jones* and *Miss Sloane*, as well as in the critically acclaimed anthology series *Black Mirror*. With such work, Mbatha-Raw has cemented her status as a fixture in international film and television.

By GabboT (Flickr: Belle 20) [CC BY-SA 2.0], via Wikimedia Commons

EARLY LIFE AND EDUCATION

Mbatha-Raw was born Gugulethu Sophia Mbatha on April 21, 1983, in Oxford, England. Her mother, Anne Raw, was a nurse, and her father, Patrick Mbatha, was a doctor. Her parents separated a year after she was born, and she went on to live primarily with her mother, who settled in the town of Witney, outside of Oxford.

Growing up in Witney, Mbatha-Raw went to primary school at Our Lady of Lourdes and later attended the Henry Box School. She was drawn to the arts at an early age, starting ballet lessons at the age of four and performing on stage by six. Soon developing an interest in theater, she began acting with groups such as Dramascope and institutions such as the Oxford Playhouse and the Oxford Youth Music Theatre. It was her experience with the National Youth Music Theatre as a teenager, however, that further fueled her desire to pursue acting as a career. "During the school summer holidays we rehearsed and then toured, including performing at the Oxford Playhouse. Everything was done to a really high professional standard, and it was definitely a turning point for me," she recalled to Gill Oliver for the *Witney Gazette* (23 Aug. 2007). "I think I already knew that I wanted to be an actor, but the whole experience made me more confident and allowed me to believe I really could do it."

When Mbatha-Raw was seventeen, she auditioned for the Royal Academy of Dramatic Art (RADA), a prestigious institution in London. She was accepted, and after completing her education at the Henry Box School in 2001, she moved to London to enroll in a three-year program at RADA.

EARLY CAREER

Mbatha-Raw initially became known for her stage work, performing at a variety of prestigious venues in the United Kingdom. In addition to earning critical praise, her experiences in theater as both an audience member and an actor helped further her education in the field as well as deepening her appreciation for the works of playwrights such as William Shakespeare. She has noted that she was particularly inspired by watching actor Josette Bushell-Mingo play the role of Cleopatra in a Royal Exchange Theatre production of Shakespeare's *Antony and Cleopatra* in 2005, an experience that took on even greater significance when Mbatha-Raw went on to star in the Royal Exchange production of *Romeo and Juliet* later that year. "To return to the same stage six months later playing a lead role, was incredible," she told Peoples. "I fell in love with the poetry and the breadth of the language so much that I didn't want it to end."

In addition to her theater roles, Mbatha-Raw began to find television and film work soon after leaving RADA. Early projects included the 2005 made-for-television films *Legless* and *Walk Away and I Stumble*, and she went on to obtain roles in television series such as *Spooks* (2006), known in the United States as *MI-5*. In 2007, she was introduced to a wider international audience when she appeared in several episodes of the long-running science-fiction series *Doctor Who*, playing the sister of the time-traveling Doctor's companion Martha. Continuing to work in theater as her career developed, she traveled to New York in 2009 to play the role of Ophelia alongside Jude Law as Hamlet in a Broadway production of *Hamlet*.

STARRING ROLES

Mbatha-Raw's first major starring role came in 2010, when she costarred alongside German-born actor Boris Kodjoe in the US television show *Undercovers*. Created by television veterans J. J. Abrams and Josh Reims, *Undercovers* follows a married pair of former secret agents, played by Mbatha-Raw and Kodjoe, who are reactivated as agents and sent on a series of missions. The project excited Mbatha-Raw from the very beginning. "I was really thrilled to read the script because it was just so fast-paced and so action-packed, and so exciting and just had such kind of charismatic characters, you know, to play with," she told the website *Fellowship of Fools* in a 2010 interview. *Undercovers* premiered on NBC in September of that year and aired eleven of its thirteen produced episodes prior to its cancellation. After making her Hollywood film debut with a small part in the 2011 Tom Hanks film *Larry Crowne*, she went on to play a major supporting role in the first season of the series *Touch*, which aired in 2012 on Fox and starred Kiefer Sutherland.

In 2014, Mbatha-Raw made her first starring appearance in a feature film with the historical drama *Belle*. Set in eighteenth-century England, the film focuses on the historical figure Dido Elizabeth Belle, the daughter of a British naval officer and an enslaved African woman who was brought to England as a child and raised by her aristocratic great-uncle. A longtime fan of British historical dramas, particularly the 1995 television adaptation of Jane Austen's novel *Pride and Prejudice* (1813), Mbatha-Raw was thrilled to have the opportunity to star in such a film. "Speaking as a mixed-race woman, there aren't many historical stories about people like me," she explained to Olivia Cole for the *Spectator* (21 June 2014). "When people think of 'dual heritage' they think it's a modern concept, but really it's not." Screened at numerous film festivals prior to its international release, *Belle* was received well by critics, and Mbatha-Raw won the British Independent Film Award (BIFA) for best actress for her work.

BRANCHING OUT

Mbatha-Raw had the opportunity to show off her other performing abilities in 2014, starring as R&B singer Noni in the romantic drama *Beyond the Lights*. Written and directed by Gina Prince-Bythewood, who is best known for films such as *Love & Basketball* and *The Secret Life of Bees*, the film took a long time to be made, in part due to studio reluctance to make a film about a pop star that features an actor rather than an established singer. For Mbatha-Raw, however, the wait provided a valuable opportunity to work closely with Prince-Bythewood while developing the character of Noni. "I met Gina for the project almost two years before we actually got to shoot it, so there was a long journey in developing the character. And even though the film wasn't fully greenlit at the time, she was very determined and we just began working on the character before the reality of it sort of started," she recalled to Jai Tiggett for *IndieWire* (23 Oct. 2014). "That was very empowering, because then it felt like we were almost manifesting this thing into being by just starting rehearsals and research." To prepare for the role, Mbatha-Raw also trained extensively with a vocal coach and choreographer Laurieann Gibson, who had previously worked with many of the world's most famous pop singers. The film, which costars Minnie Driver as Noni's overbearing mother and Nate Parker as her police officer love interest, received critical acclaim upon its US release in late 2014, with much of the praise focusing on Mbatha-Raw's performance.

As Mbatha-Raw's career continued to develop, she was dismayed by the one-dimensional nature of many of the roles offered to female actors. "I don't really want to just play the girlfriend or the love interest," she told Cole. "I get so many scripts like that and, not to moan because I'm really fortunate, but I just look at those scripts and my heart sinks a little bit because I think there's so much more to us than that." Actively resisting taking on such roles, she instead sought out a wide range of projects that offered her opportunities to explore new types of characters, among them a deer-woman in 2015's *Jupiter Ascending*, a runaway slave in 2016's *Free State of Jones*, and a gun-control lobbyist in 2016's *Miss Sloane*.

OTHER PROJECTS

Mbatha-Raw returned to television in late 2016, in the third season of the British science-fiction anthology series *Black Mirror*. "I got sent the script by my agent, and I was like, 'Ohhh, *Black Mirror*. I've heard that's cool,'" she told Emma Dibdin for *Cosmopolitan* (28 Oct. 2016). "So I started reading it instantly on my phone and I was actually at Oxford Circus [in London] about to get a bus to Brixton. I read the whole script between Oxford Circus and Brixton because it was such a page-turner." She ultimately costarred with actor Mackenzie Davis in "San Junipero," the fourth episode of *Black Mirror*'s third season. The episode, which features the series' signature style of science-fiction twists yet is far more optimistic in tone than its predecessors, was named by many critics as one of *Black Mirror*'s best.

In 2017, Mbatha-Raw appeared as Plumette, a woman who has been transformed into an anthropomorphic feather duster, in the much-anticipated live-action adaptation of Disney's classic *Beauty and the Beast*; in interviews, she explained that the more lighthearted role was a welcome change of pace compared to the more serious parts she had taken on up to that point in her career. She was also scheduled to appear in a film that year initially known as *God Particle*, about a group of astronauts who face a mysterious threat aboard a space station, which industry publications speculated may in fact be the third installment in J. J. Abrams's Cloverfield franchise. In addition, she was set to play a supporting role in director Ava DuVernay's adaptation of Madeleine L'Engle's 1962 novel *A Wrinkle in Time*, which was scheduled for release in 2018. She has expressed her excitement about being part of the film, in which she plays the protagonist's mother, Dr. Kate Murry. "I didn't grow up with the book as a little girl in the UK, but I'm reading it now," she told Lakshmi Singh for National Public Radio (26 Nov. 2016). "And, you know, Ava is just so dynamic, and it's just such a phenomenal cast in that film. So I'm really thrilled to be able to get to work on that."

PERSONAL LIFE

In between projects, Mbatha-Raw has expressed an affinity for yoga and travel, including visiting her family. After finishing filming scenes for *Beyond the Lights*, she took a trip to her father's home country of South Africa for the first time. "After spending so much time trying to be another person, I always think it's good to go somewhere to regain perspective," she told Danielle Stein Chizzik for *Town & Country* (10 Feb. 2015).

SUGGESTED READING

Cole, Olivia. "Belle Fleur." *The Spectator*, 21 June 2014, life.spectator.co.uk/2014/06/belle-fleur. Accessed 13 Mar. 2017.

Mbatha-Raw, Gugu. "'Belle' of the Big Screen: Gugu Mbatha-Raw Stays Busy in Film." Interview by Lakshmi Singh. *NPR*, 26 Nov. 2016, www.npr.org/2016/11/26/503446703/belle-of-the-big-screen-gugu-mbatha-raw-stays-busy-in-film. Accessed 13 Mar. 2017.

Mbatha-Raw, Gugu. "*Black Mirror*'s Gugu Mbatha-Raw on the Heartbreaking and Hopeful 'San Junipero.'" Interview by Emma Dibdin. *Cosmopolitan*, 28 Oct. 2016, www.cosmopolitan.com/entertainment/tv/a7700702/black-mirror-gugu-mbathaw-raw-san-junipero. Accessed 13 Mar. 2017.

Mbatha-Raw, Gugu. "Interview: Gugu Mbatha-Raw Tells S&A about Becoming a Pop Star in *Beyond the Lights*." Interview by Jai Tiggett. *IndieWire*, 23 Oct. 2014, www.indiewire.com/2014/10/interview-gugu-mbatha-raw-tells-sa-about-becoming-a-pop-star-in-beyond-the-lights-157515. Accessed 13 Mar. 2017.

Oliver, Gill. "Henry Box Girl on the World Stage." *Witney Gazette*, 23 Aug. 2007, www.witneygazette.co.uk/news/wgheadlines/features/1638929.Henry_Box_girl_on_the_world_stage. Accessed 13 Mar. 2017.

Peoples, Lindsay. "Gugu Mbatha-Raw Isn't Trying to Be Like Anyone Else." *The Cut*, New York Media, 20 June 2016, nymag.com/the-cut/2016/06/gugu-mbatha-raw-interview.html. Accessed 13 Mar. 2017.

SELECTED WORKS

Doctor Who, 2007; *Larry Crowne*, 2011; *Undercovers*, 2010; *Belle*, 2014; *Beyond the Lights*, 2014; *Jupiter Ascending*, 2015; *Concussion*, 2015; *Free State of Jones*, 2016; *Miss Sloane*, 2016; *Beauty and the Beast*, 2017

—*Joy Crelin*

By Danny Karwoski [CC BY-SA 4.0-3.0-2.5-2.0-1.0], via Wikimedia Commons

Angel McCoughtry

Date of birth: September 10, 1986
Occupation: Basketball player

A small forward with the Atlanta Dream WNBA team since 2009, basketball player Angel McCoughtry has been a valuable addition to the franchise, winning Rookie of the Year following her debut season and helping lead the Dream to the WNBA Finals in 2010, 2011, and 2013. Yet despite the hard work inherent to a career in professional basketball, McCoughtry views the game as less a job than a calling. "I get paid to do what I love," she told Mark Pollard for *Kontrol* (17 Feb. 2016). "It's like I don't have a real job and that's what makes it enjoyable."

A talented player from an early age, McCoughtry first displayed her skills on youth teams before moving on to newsworthy careers at Baltimore's St. Frances Academy and the Patterson School in Lenoir, North Carolina. Recruited to join the University of Louisville Cardinals, she led the team to its first NCAA final and left such an impression on the school that her jersey was subsequently retired. Her performance with the Dream has been similarly successful, and she has been a member of two consecutive gold

medal–winning Olympic basketball teams. "I've basically accomplished everything," she told Ryne Nelson for *Slam* (2 Mar. 2017). "All that's left is a WNBA championship. I definitely want to fulfill that goal, but if not, I'm satisfied with how my career has went." Although McCoughtry announced in early 2017 that she would be taking time off from the Dream during the 2017 season, she remained dedicated to living out an entirely different dream: opening her own ice cream shop, McCoughtry's Ice Cream.

EARLY LIFE AND EDUCATION

McCoughtry was born on September 10, 1986, in Baltimore, Maryland. She was the first of three daughters born to Roi and Sharon McCoughtry. During McCoughtry's early years, her father served as the pastor of the Holy Nation Tabernacle in Baltimore, while her mother worked as an administrative assistant. Family was very important to McCoughtry, who has noted in interviews that her desire for her parents' approval has remained with her into adulthood. "I always wanted to be perfect for my family and parents and always wanted to make them proud," she told Mechelle Voepel for *ESPN* (28 May 2015).

Displaying an aptitude for basketball at an early age, McCoughtry soon began to focus heavily on the sport. Her father had played basketball while attending Coppin State University, and he encouraged McCoughtry and helped improve her athletic performance over the years. She played on a number of youth teams, including the Baltimore Cougars under-seventeen team, and after enrolling in Baltimore's St. Frances

Academy, she distinguished herself as a member of the high school's girls' basketball team. As a key member of the St. Frances Panthers, she helped lead the team to several conference titles and in 2003 was named All-Metro Player of the Year by the *Baltimore Sun*. McCoughtry graduated from St. Frances Academy in 2004.

Following her graduation, McCoughtry initially planned to attend St. John's University in New York City, where she hoped to play for the St. John's Red Storm basketball team. However, National Collegiate Athletic Association (NCAA) regulations mandate that student athletes meet minimum grade-point average and SAT score requirements to play for a Division I team, and McCoughtry did not qualify to join the team as a freshman. Although she considered enrolling in a junior college, she ultimately spent a year at the Patterson School, a private preparatory school in Lenoir, North Carolina. Over the course of that school year, McCoughtry focused on academic improvement and also played basketball, helping the school's team obtain its first National Association of Christian Athletes (NACA) national title. Although McCoughtry told Dave Caldwell for the *New York Times* (21 Mar. 2009) that "nothing is worse" than spending a year in prep school, she later credited her time at the Patterson School with helping to prepare her for college.

UNIVERSITY OF LOUISVILLE

McCoughtry drew the attention of college scouts during her year at the Patterson School, and she was soon recruited by the University of Louisville, a Division I school that she had not previously considered. "When the coach first called, I was like: Where is Louisville? Where is this place on the map?" McCoughtry said, as quoted by Caldwell. In the fall of 2005, she moved to Kentucky to join the university as a communications student and one of the newest members of the Louisville Cardinals.

As a member of the Cardinals, McCoughtry quickly gained widespread recognition as a talented player, playing in twenty-nine games during her first season. She scored a total of 754 points during the following season, setting a team record, and in 2007 was named Big East Player of the Year. She continued her strong performance during her junior season, earning All-American honors from a variety of sports publications and scoring 858 points during the season, beating her own record.

In 2009, McCoughtry's senior season, she yet again broke her scoring record with 901 points. She also led the Cardinals to the team's first NCAA Division I women's championship appearance, defeating the Oklahoma Sooners in the semifinals to face the University of Connecticut Huskies in the championship. Although the Cardinals ultimately lost to the Huskies 54–76, the game was a major milestone for both the team and McCoughtry, who scored 23 points over the course of the game. McCoughtry graduated from the University of Louisville in the spring of 2009, having earned a bachelor's degree in communications. In recognition of her strong performance during her time with the Cardinals, the team retired McCoughtry's jersey, number 35, in November 2010.

ATLANTA DREAM

On April 9, 2009, the teams of the Women's National Basketball Association (WNBA) held their annual college draft. The number-one draft pick, McCoughtry was selected by the Atlanta Dream, a new WNBA team that had only begun playing the previous season. After making one preseason appearance with the Dream, in a game against the Connecticut Sun, McCoughtry made her regular-season debut with the team on June 6, 2009, contributing fifteen points to the Dream's victory over the Indiana Fever. She played in all thirty-four games of the first season and accompanied the dream to the playoffs in the postseason; however, the Dream was eliminated after losing to the Detroit Shock in the Eastern Conference semifinals. In light of her strong performance in her debut season, McCoughtry was named Rookie of the Month on multiple occasions and in October 2009 was named WNBA Rookie of the Year.

Over the next several years, McCoughtry remained a valuable member of the Dream, frequently leading the team in metrics such as scoring, steals, and minutes played. In 2010, McCoughtry led the team in points scored as the Dream defeated the New York Liberty in the Eastern Conference Finals, moving on to the team's first WNBA Finals. The Dream ultimately lost to the Seattle Storm in the three-game matchup, despite strong showings by McCoughtry and her teammates. The Dream returned to the WNBA Finals in 2011 and 2013 but ultimately lost to the Minnesota Lynx in both championships.

Having seen the Dream nearly win the championship on three separate occasions, McCoughtry was disappointed that they had been unable to claim the title for Atlanta. "It used to weigh on me a lot," she recalled to Voepel. "I would be so hard on myself. I felt I let down the fans and the city of Atlanta. They wanted a championship so bad, but it wasn't our time." Nevertheless, she remained optimistic about the team's chances. "I feel like when our time will be, it will be," she told Voepel. "We want to play hard and do what we can to win it. I feel like we have paid our dues, so hopefully it will come soon." McCoughtry continued to devote herself to the Dream over the next few years, taking the team to the playoffs in 2014 and 2016. In January 2017, she announced that she would be taking time off during the 2017 season to rest, having spent the better part of a decade playing basketball year-round.

INTERNATIONAL BASKETBALL AND ICE CREAM

Like many WNBA players, McCoughtry plays basketball internationally during the off-seasons, playing on teams in countries such as Slovakia and Hungary. Beginning in 2011, she joined Istanbul's Turkish Women's Basketball League team Fenerbahçe, with which she remained for several years. Having gained exposure to both American and international attitudes about basketball, McCoughtry found that playing internationally was at times more rewarding. "People appreciate women's basketball more overseas," she explained to Nelson. "In the States, all I hear is the comparison: You can't jump as high; you're not as fast. Well, of course, I'm a woman. Over here, they just appreciate the art of the game."

In 2015, McCoughtry abruptly ended her association with Fenerbahçe, a parting initially attributed to a contract dispute. However, she later revealed that she had faced discrimination after the news that she was in a same-sex relationship with fiancée Brande Elise became public and that the team had instructed her to write a letter stating that she was not in a relationship with Elise. Although McCoughtry initially complied, she later decided to leave the team anyway. "I [wrote the letter] because I wanted to continue to play for that team," she told Voepel. "But I shouldn't have to write a fake letter lying about who I love. Actually, most of the fans were really supportive; they were like, 'We don't care; we love you.' The team was too involved in my personal life, and it was good for me to move on." After her departure from Fenerbahçe, McCoughtry went on to play with another Turkish team before joining the Russian team Dynamo Kursk in 2016.

In addition to her off-season work with international teams, McCoughtry has represented the United States in a number of international basketball competitions. She made her first international appearance in the 2007 Pan-American Games while still in college, and in 2009, she joined the US National Team to compete in the Ekaterinburg International Invitational in Russia. She was likewise a member of the gold medal–winning teams at the 2010 and 2014 International Basketball Federation (FIBA) Women's Basketball World Cups. In 2012, McCoughtry accompanied the US women's team to London for the Olympic Games, where the team took the gold. She traveled to Rio de Janeiro, Brazil, with the US team in 2016, helping the United States claim another Olympic gold medal.

In 2016 McCoughtry, a lover of ice cream, announced plans to open her own ice cream shop in Atlanta. The store, known as McCoughtry's Ice Cream, remained in development into early 2017 and is set to begin operations in Atlanta's Castleberry Hill neighborhood later in the year.

PERSONAL LIFE

McCoughtry met her fiancée, blogger Brande Elise, through a mutual friend and became close after Elise interviewed McCoughtry for her Atlanta-focused blog. They celebrated their engagement in 2014, and in January 2016, the couple was featured in an episode of the reality series *Say Yes to the Dress*. Although McCoughtry has noted that she faced discrimination after taking her relationship with Elise public, she has likewise made clear that the relationship has had an overwhelmingly positive influence on her life. "I was never comfortable with myself, and I think that was a big part of my frustrations in life," she told Voepel. "But when I met Brande, she really helped me to just be who I am and love myself."

SUGGESTED READING

Caldwell, Dave. "Louisville's Angel McCoughtry Credits Prep School for Transformation." *The New York Times*, 21 Mar. 2009, www.nytimes.com/2009/03/22/sports/ncaabasketball/22louisville.html. Accessed 7 Apr. 2017.

"Dream's Angel McCoughtry Plans to Rest during 2017 Season." *WNBA*, 4 Jan. 2017, www.wnba.com/news/atlanta-dream-angel-mccoughtry-rest-2017-season. Accessed 7 Apr. 2017.

Nelson, Ryne. "Grindin' for the Longest." *Slam*, 2 Mar. 2017, www.slamonline.com/wnba/angel-mccoughtry-atlanta-dream-interview-wnba. Accessed 7 Apr. 2017.

Pollard, Mark. "Olympic Gold Medalist Angel McCoughtry Talks Life, Love, and Basketball." *Kontrol*, 17 Feb. 2016, www.kontrolmag.com/life-love-basketball-with-olympic-gold-medalist-angel-mccoughtry. Accessed 7 Apr. 2017.

Shaffer, Jonas. "Baltimore's Angel McCoughtry Puts Her Own Twist on Olympic Basketball Experience." *The Baltimore Sun*, 17 Aug. 2016, www.baltimoresun.com/sports/olympics/bs-sp-olympics-angel-mccoughtry-0818-20160817-story.html. Accessed 7 Apr. 2017.

Voepel, Mechelle. "McCoughtry Now 'Living My Own Life.'" *ESPN*, 28 May 2015, www.espn.com/wnba/story/_/id/12971110/atlanta-dream-star-angel-mccoughtry-now-living-my-own-life. Accessed 7 Apr. 2017.

—Joy Crelin

Tarell Alvin McCraney

Date of birth: October 17, 1980
Occupation: Playwright

Tarell Alvin McCraney is a playwright and Academy Award–winning screenwriter. In 2017 the film *Moonlight* (2016), an adaptation of his semiautobiographical play *In Moonlight Black Boys Look Blue*, won the Academy Awards for best picture and best adapted screenplay. Before the flurry of critical acclaim that enveloped *Moonlight*, McCraney was best known as the playwright behind the Brother/Sister Plays, a cycle of three plays set in Louisiana that draw on Yoruba cultural and religious influences.

McCraney was born and raised in Miami, Florida. After studying acting in Chicago and playwriting at the Yale School of Drama, he soon found success in the theater world, winning a slew of awards—among them a 2007 Whiting Award, a 2009 Steinberg Playwright Award, and a prestigious MacArthur Fellowship, worth $625,000, in 2013—and becoming the RSC/Warwick international playwright in residence at the Royal Shakespeare Company (RSC) in 2008. He has also received the 2008 Paula Vogel Playwriting Award, the 2008 Evening Standard Theatre Awards' Charles Wintour Award for Most Promising Playwright, the 2009 New York Times Outstanding Playwright Award, a 2013 Windham-Campbell Literature Prize for drama, and the 2017 PEN/Laura Pels International Foundation for Theater Award for an American playwright in mid-career. In December 2016, McCraney was named the next head of the playwriting program at the Yale School of Drama.

EARLY LIFE

Tarell Alvin McCraney was born on October 17, 1980, in Miami, Florida, the oldest of four children. His mother was a teenager when she gave birth to him; his father left the family when he was a child. He was raised in Liberty City, a Miami neighborhood that began as a federal housing project for African Americans during the Great Depression. Though the neighborhood originally housed middle-income families, the construction of Interstate 95 through the nearby low-income neighborhood of Overtown in the 1960s caused the displaced residents to migrate into Liberty City, prompting businesses and middle-class families to flee. The poverty of the area made it particularly vulnerable to the crack cocaine epidemic of the 1980s.

While McCraney was growing up, he and his friends would make up stories and games as a refuge from the realities of their lives. "We sort of found a narrative that allowed us to still have an imagination and grow within that atmosphere, which I found and still find incredibly

inspiring," he said to Nikole Hannah-Jones for the *New York Times* (4 Jan. 2017). McCraney was thirteen before he realized his mother was addicted to crack, as a result of which she contracted HIV, which then developed into AIDS. He said to Maddy Costa for the *Guardian* (28 Oct. 2008) that he understands how her addiction began: "I saw her trying to take care of four kids on her own, with an abusive boyfriend. Her mother and father passed away at the ages of fifty and forty-nine, so she lost her support system. Then Hurricane Andrew came, in 1992, and we lost everything. . . . I'm not excusing any of her behavior, but I feel those things were the catalysts." And there were good moments; it was McCraney's mother who exposed him to books, reading him the entirety of Stephen King's lengthy novel *It* (1986), from which he developed his love of literature.

When McCraney was fourteen years old, his mother entered rehabilitation for her addiction, and he and his younger brother moved in with their father. The trauma of the change and his mother's illness took a toll; he told a school counselor that he thought he might be depressed. The counselor suggested that McCraney pursue an activity that would allow him to feel as though he were helping others. On his counselor's advice, McCraney joined Village South Improv, a local community theater troupe that "work[ed] in drug and alcohol rehabilitation," according to Costa. McCraney had been interested in theater from an early age, and he had participated in a magnet program for drama in middle school. But it was his experience with Village South Improv, run by a man named Teo Castellanos, that encouraged him to pursue theater as a career.

THEATER EDUCATION

Castellanos became McCraney's first artistic mentor. "I thought, here is a young man who is into the arts, but he has nowhere to go" to practice it, Castellanos told Bill Hirschman for *Florida Theater on Stage* (30 Aug. 2011). "When he auditioned for me . . . he didn't do too well, but I took him anyway. But pretty quickly, I think within six months to a year, you could see it . . . . I said, 'Wow, he's really good.'" McCraney wrote his first play—a monologue about a man doing battle with his body after contracting HIV, inspired by his mother's experiences—when he was fourteen or fifteen years old, and he performed the piece himself. The performance was a success, in that it evoked the intended emotions from the audience, but McCraney learned an important lesson, he told Costa: "You can't bury people in the depths of your emotional chasm and expect them to want to come back."

McCraney was accepted to the New World School of the Arts, a magnet high school in Miami, when he was in tenth grade. There, he found another mentor in the school guidance counselor, Sylvan Seidenman, who helped him get accepted to the Theatre School at DePaul University in Chicago; years later, McCraney would refer to Seidenman and his wife as his godparents.

While studying acting at DePaul, McCraney drew the attention of famed English director Peter Brook, who worked with him for two years. Though a talented actor, McCraney soon realized he was not suited to the profession. "I can be extremely self-deprecating—and on stage, you can't be judging yourself that much all the time," he explained to Costa.

When he graduated from DePaul in 2003. McCraney had already applied to and been accepted by the competitive Yale School of Drama, to pursue a master's degree in playwriting, and was scheduled to take a year off first to perform in a play for Brook. That summer, his mother died of AIDS-related illness, and McCraney's life was upended; then the play with Brook fell through, and he was left to grapple with his mother's death on his own. "Since thirteen, I've kind of been wading through that water and finally, to get to the arrival of her death, was sort of surprisingly calm," he said to Hannah-Jones. "But then, I started to continuously have these memories, thoughts of growing up in Miami and my mother in that time. I had bad guilt for not being at her bedside when she died, terrible guilt about not asking her the questions you always regret not asking your parents when they pass away." He explored these unanswered questions

in a play he wrote during that summer, which he called *In Moonlight Black Boys Look Blue*.

THE BROTHER/SISTER PLAYS

During McCraney's time at Yale, he served briefly as an assistant to legendary playwright August Wilson, before Wilson's death in 2005. McCraney graduated from Yale in 2007; the same year, while he was still a student, his play *The Brothers Size* premiered Off-Broadway at the Public Theater. The play, the second part of a three-play cycle called the Brother/Sister Plays, follows the story of three brothers living in the bayou country of Louisiana. Their tale is loosely based on Yoruba myth. *New York Times* critic Jason Zinoman was captivated by the play and deemed the young playwright an important new theatrical voice. McCraney's play *Wig Out!*, about drag queens living in Harlem, was first staged Off-Broadway at the Vineyard Theatre in 2008. That play also combines real life and mythology; it is narrated by a Greek chorus that resembles the Supremes. Ben Brantley, another critic for the *New York Times*, praised the richness of McCraney's language and the originality of *Wig Out!*'s world.

In 2009, the Brother/Sister Plays premiered in their entirety at the Public Theater. The cycle (McCraney dislikes the term trilogy) consists of the plays *In the Red and Brown Water*, *The Brothers Size*, and *Marcus; or, The Secret of Sweet*. Set in a housing project in Louisiana with interlocking stories and character arcs, the plays hover somewhere between realism and ritual. According to McCraney they are drawn from real life but also not, set in a time he calls the "distant present," as reported by Brantley in his review for the *New York Times* (17 Nov. 2009). *In the Red and Brown Water* follows a young track star named Oya, named for the Yoruban goddess of the wind; *The Brothers Size* follows two brothers after one of them has just been released from prison; and *Marcus* concerns the queer awakening of a young boy in the days before Hurricane Katrina. Brantley did not hold back his praise for the plays, writing, "Watching them, you experience the excited wonder that comes from witnessing something rare in the theater: a new, authentically original vision. It's what people must have felt during productions of the early works of Eugene O'Neill in the 1920s or of Sam Shepard in the 1960s."

McCraney's other plays include *The Breach* (2006), written with Catherine Filloux and Joe Sutton, about Hurricane Katrina; and *Choir Boy* (2012), a coming-of-age story about a group of high school boys who sing in a choir. His play *Head of Passes* (2013), a parable about a matriarch living at the mouth of the Mississippi River that is based on the book of Job, premiered Off-Broadway at the Public Theater in 2016.

While serving as the RSC/Warwick international playwright in residence with the RSC from 2008 to 2010, he wrote a one-act play called *American Trade* (2011), which was marketed as "a contemporary restoration comedy." In 2013 he wrote and directed an adaptation of William Shakespeare's *Antony and Cleopatra*; the play, which McCraney set in eighteenth-century Haiti on the eve of the revolution, was a coproduction of the RSC, the Public Theater, and GableStage in Miami.

MOONLIGHT

In 2011, a mutual friend of McCraney's and director Barry Jenkins, who also grew up in Liberty City, e-mailed McCraney's script *In Moonlight Black Boys Look Blue* to Jenkins. Although the two men had grown up in the same neighborhood and attended the same middle school, they had never met before. Jenkins was captivated by the script; coming off the success of his first film, *Medicine for Melancholy* (2008), he had wanted to tell a personal story, but attempts to write about his own mother's struggles with addiction felt too raw. McCraney's story, about a young boy grappling with his sexuality—based on his own experiences—was similar to Jenkins's, yet the differences provided necessary distance.

Jenkins approached McCraney about adapting the script, but McCraney, who had recently won a MacArthur Fellowship, was too busy. A few years went by before Jenkins decided to take a crack at adapting the script himself. The experience, he told Hannah-Jones, shattered any illusions he had about the safety of McCraney's story versus his own. "I thought I could hide behind Tarell in this piece, thinking, 'This is personal for this cat; it's not personal for me,'" Jenkins said. "I was wrong."

The result was the film *Moonlight*, which, like the play it is based on, draws elements directly from McCraney's life. The main character, Chiron, is mercilessly bullied as a child, in part for his sexuality, as McCraney was; the character Juan (played by actor Mahershala Ali, who won the Academy Award for best supporting actor for his performance) is based on a man named Blue, the father of one of McCraney's younger brothers. Blue sold drugs to McCraney's mother, but he also took the young boy under his wing. In the film, Juan teaches Chiron how to swim; in real life, Blue taught McCraney many things, including how to make salmon croquettes. Blue was murdered when McCraney was six, and his death rocked the boy's young life.

Moonlight premiered at the Telluride and Toronto International Film Festivals in 2016, where it received glowing reviews from critics and standing ovations from early audiences. "There's insight to *Moonlight* that should pierce viewers to their core, even if Chiron's life is very different from their own," David Sims wrote in his review for the Atlantic (26 Oct. 2016). "This is not an 'issue' film that's mainly 'about' race or sexuality; this is a humane movie, one that's looking to prompt empathy and introspection most of all. On those terms alone, *Moonlight* is one of the year's most gripping viewing experiences." The film was nominated for eight Academy Awards and won three, for best picture, best adapted screenplay, and best supporting actor.

In December 2016, McCraney was appointed chair of the playwriting department at the Yale School of Drama. His three-year term began in July 2017.

SUGGESTED READING

Brantley, Ben. "Lives in the Bayou Tap All the Realism of Dreams." Review of the Brother/Sister Plays, by Tarell Alvin McCraney. *The New York Times*, 17 Nov. 2009, www.nytimes.com/2009/11/18/theater/reviews/18brother.html. Accessed 11 Aug. 2017.

Costa, Maddy. "Miami Voice." *The Guardian*, 28 Oct. 2008, www.theguardian.com/stage/2008/oct/29/theatre. Accessed 11 Aug. 2017.

Hannah-Jones, Nikole. "From Bittersweet Childhoods to *Moonlight*." *The New York Times*, 4 Jan. 2017, www.nytimes.com/2017/01/04/movies/moonlight-barry-jenkins-tarell-alvin-mccraney-interview.html. Accessed 11 Aug. 2017.

Hirschman, Bill. "Tarell Alvin McCraney Comes Home—for a While." *Florida Theater on Stage*, 30 Aug. 2011, www.floridatheateronstage.com/news/tarell-alvin-mccraney-comes-home-for-a-while/. Accessed 11 Aug. 2017.

McCraney, Tarell Alvin. "Tarell Alvin McCraney on *Moonlight*'s Message: 'I Think People Were Hungry for That.'" Interview by Amanda N'Duka. *Deadline Hollywood*, 17 Feb. 2017, deadline.com/2017/02/tarell-alvin-mccraney-moonlight-barry-jenkins-a24-oscars-interview-1201915105/. Accessed 11 Aug. 2017.

Sims, David. "*Moonlight* is a Film of Uncommon Grace." Review of *Moonlight*, by Tarell Alvin McCraney, adapted and directed by Barry Jenkins. *The Atlantic*, 26 Oct. 2016, www.theatlantic.com/entertainment/archive/2016/10/moonlight-barry-jenkins-review/505409/. Accessed 11 Aug. 2017.

SELECTED WORKS

The Breach, 2006; *Wig Out!*, 2008; The Brother/Sister Plays, 2009; *Choir Boy*, 2012; *Head of Passes*, 2013; *Moonlight*, 2016

—Molly Hagan

Connor McDavid

Date of birth: January 13, 1997
Occupation: Hockey player

Awarded the 2017 Hart Memorial Trophy for most valuable player by the National Hockey League (NHL), the Ontario-born Connor Mc-David is one of hockey's brightest stars. During his second season with the Edmonton Oilers (a fractured collarbone had kept him on the bench for thirty-seven games during his rookie season), he scored thirty goals, seventy assists, and one hundred points to win the Art Ross Trophy for leading scorer in the league. He also won the Ted Lindsay Award, voted by fellow players, for most outstanding player.

Like many young Canadians, McDavid, who was born and raised in Ontario, grew up playing hockey. But from an early age, McDavid revealed himself as a prodigy, capturing the attention of hockey legend Bobby Orr—who now serves as his agent—when he was just thirteen years old. When he was fifteen, McDavid was awarded "exceptional player status," allowing him to be drafted into the Ontario Hockey League (OHL) a year early. He was the first pick of the OHL Draft and began playing for the Erie Otters in 2012. He was the first pick of the NHL Draft in 2015, and the Oilers made him the youngest team captain in NHL history in 2016. When he won the Hart Memorial Trophy in 2017, he joined Pittsburgh Penguins captain Sidney Crosby and legend Wayne Gretzky as one of the only players to claim the prize before his twenty-first birthday. "He's had the touch from Day 1, you could just tell," Don Cherry, the Hall of Fame coach and player, told the Rochester *Democrat and Chronicle* (1 Mar. 2014) of McDavid when McDavid was just seventeen years old. "Good skater, good shot, hockey sense. I'm the expert and I guarantee he'll be a star. . . . He's one of those that come along every five to ten years. You hear the term 'can't-miss guy.' Well, he's a can't-miss guy. He's special."

EARLY LIFE

McDavid was born on January 13, 1997. His father, Brian, is a consultant for the Hudson's Bay Company; his mother, Kelly, is human resources director for the German appliance manufacturer Miele. McDavid and his older brother, Cameron, were raised in Newmarket, Ontario, north of Toronto. McDavid tried on his first pair of ice skates when he was three years old. When he was four, his parents lied about his age so that he could join a hockey team. McDavid took the sport seriously: at five, he was wearing a shirt and tie to his brother's hockey games, following and explaining every play and sitting in on locker room pep talks.

By Connor Mah (Own work) [CC BY-SA 3.0], via Wikimedia Commons

He begged his mother and grandmother to play games with him in the family's basement for an audience of stuffed animal fans. Later, he played with his older brother and trained for hours with in-line skates in the driveway, timing himself on an obstacle course he built with paint cans and bricks. McDavid's father, a youth hockey coach, saw something special in the young player. His mother dismissed the idea—"Every kid thinks they are going to play in the NHL," she recalled to Marty Klinkenberg for the *Globe and Mail* (18 Sept. 2015)—but by the time Mc-David was a preteen, she started to see it too.

EARLY CAREER

Between the ages of eight and twelve, McDavid led the York Simcoe Express to five Ontario Minor Hockey Association championships. Coaches remember him as singularly focused, even then. At nine years old, trainer Alex Nanos recalled to Sean Fitz-Gerald for the *Toronto Star* (7 Oct. 2015), "He'd come back and kick the boards and get mad at himself because he should have passed when he shot, or he should have shot when he passed." He was discovered by Orr at a skills camp in Toronto when he was thirteen and played for the Express until he was fifteen. He then played, briefly, for the minor-league Toronto Marlboros, where he was the Greater Toronto Hockey League's player of the year in 2012. (McDavid attended school at the Premier Elite Athletes' Collegiate in Toronto for three years; after that he attended a public high school part time and then worked with a tutor to finish school).

The same year, McDavid was granted exceptional player status, making him eligible for the major junior OHL Draft a year early, at the age of fifteen instead of sixteen. With Orr as his agent, McDavid, the league's first pick, went to the Erie Otters in Erie, Pennsylvania. McDavid lived with a host family who shuttled him to and from practice, as he was too young to drive. The Otters were struggling when McDavid joined their ranks. They missed the playoffs his rookie season, and the loss stirred in McDavid a deep desire to win. "He hates losing more than he likes winning," Bob Catalde, McDavid's host father, observed to Tim Rohan for the *New York Times* (18 Feb. 2013). Still, McDavid was named the OHL rookie of the year. The Otters scored 106 points during McDavid's next season—as opposed to 47 points the year before—and McDavid led them to two playoff series. During his third season, McDavid got in a fight during a game with Bryson Cianfrone of the Mississauga Steelheads in 2014. He fractured his hand in the brawl and was forced to sit for twenty games.

McDavid's hand healed in time for him to play for Canada in the World Junior Championship in early 2015. He led the team to a gold medal against Canada's historic rival, Russia. McDavid later told Kevin McGran for the *Star* (28 Dec. 2015) that the tournament helped prepare him for the NHL. "You definitely learn some skills in dealing with the media, dealing with the pressure that comes from that tournament," he said. Returning to the Otters, McDavid led the team to the championship finals and won the trophy for OHL Playoff MVP. In the 47 games he played that season, McDavid scored 44 goals, 76 assists, and 120 points. In three seasons with the Otters, McDavid scored 285 points and became the most-decorated player in OHL history, winning, among other individual honors, the Red Tilson Trophy for most outstanding player in 2015.

NHL DRAFT AND EDMONTON OILERS

McDavid turned eighteen in 2015, and excitement for his entry into the NHL built to a fever pitch. In June, he was drafted, number one overall, by the Edmonton Oilers. Fans were ecstatic for McDavid's major-league debut but also his return to Canada. The young phenom starred in commercials for Adidas and Reebok before playing in a single NHL game. The Oilers had last gone to the Stanley Cup Playoffs in 2006, and McDavid joined the team as it struggled to rebuild itself. Fans even took to calling their new player "McJesus." But McDavid and general manager Peter Chiarelli were more pragmatic in considering McDavid's first season with the team. McDavid was, after all, still a teenager and underwent serious strength training to prepare to play against the burly, adult men of the NHL.

"There's going to be battles he loses and there's going to be mistakes he makes," Chiarelli told Adam Kimelman for *NHL.com* (26 June 2015). "I've been asked if he's going to be an impact player next season and I would say no."

Chiarelli turned out to be right, but for a different reason. In November 2015, McDavid fractured his left collarbone in a game against the Philadelphia Flyers. The injury sidelined him for several months. In the 45 games he did play that year, he scored 16 goals, 32 assists, and 48 points. (Despite his injury, McDavid finished third in the voting for NHL Rookie of the Year.) His second season with the Oilers, in 2016, was far more successful. In anticipation of future glory, the team overhauled its arena and made a series of strategic staffing changes. It was clear that Edmonton saw McDavid as the second coming of its first truly great player, the inimitable Wayne Gretzky, who led the Oilers to four Stanley Cup victories in the 1980s. McDavid, who was named team captain—the youngest in NHL history—in October, was remarkably calm in the face of such pressure. "You can definitely sense they're expecting a lot out of us this year, and that's good," he told Ben Shpigel for the *New York Times* (27 Oct. 2016). "Because we're expecting even more out of ourselves."

By November 2016, McDavid was tied for lead scorer in the league. In a game against the Dallas Stars, he scored 3 goals to win the game and end a five-game drought. In January 2017, McDavid scored his career one hundredth point. He accomplished the feat in 92 NHL games, one of the fastest in league history. (Gretzky did it in 61 games.) In the spring, McDavid led the team to the playoffs for the first time in a decade, though their bid ended in Game 7 of the Western Conference semifinals against the Anaheim Ducks. A newly media-savvy McDavid told Dan Greenspan for the Canadian Press (11 May 2017), "Obviously it's going to take some time to get over [the loss]. But I think there are a lot of positives we can take from this year." Individually, McDavid enjoyed a stellar season; he led the league in scoring to win the Art Ross Trophy, the third-youngest player to ever claim the prize. The two younger players were Gretzky and McDavid's idol Crosby. McDavid joined their ranks again when he was voted league MVP; only he, Gretzky, and Crosby won the honor before turning twenty-one. McDavid also won the Ted Lindsay Award, an MVP award voted by NHL players.

SUGGESTED READING

"Connor McDavid: Hockey's 'Next Great One.'" *Democrat and Chronicle*, 1 Mar. 2014, www.democratandchronicle.com/story/sports/columnist/roth/2014/03/01/

connor-mcdavid-hockeys-next-great-one/5933211. Accessed 5 Sept. 2017.

Fitz-Gerald, Sean. "Connor McDavid's Hockey Greatness Was Evident from Day 1." *The Toronto Star*, 7 Oct. 2015, www.thestar.com/sports/hockey/2015/10/07/connor-mcdavids-hockey-greatness-was-evident-from-day-1.html. Accessed 5 Sept. 2017.

Greenspan, Dan. "Edmonton Oilers' 2017 Playoff Bid Ends with 2–1 Loss to Ducks in Game 7 of Western Conference Semifinal." *Canadian Press*, 11 May 2017, globalnews.ca/news/3443176/edmonton-oilers-2017-play-off-run-ends-with-2-1-loss-to-ducks-in-game-7-of-western-conference-semifinal. Accessed 6 Sept. 2017.

Kimelman, Adam. "Connor McDavid Drafted No. 1 by Edmonton Oilers." *NHL.com*, 26 June 2015, www.nhl.com/news/connor-mcdavid-drafted-no-1-by-edmonton-oilers/c-772405. Accessed 5 Sept. 2017.

Klinkenberg, Marty. "Family Ties: While His Father Helped Develop Connor McDavid's Hockey Skills, It Was His Mother Who Nurtured His Heart." *The Globe and Mail*, 18 Sept. 2015, beta.theglobeandmail.com/sports/hockey/family-ties-while-his-father-helped-develop-connor-mcdavids-hockey-skills-it-was-his-mother-who-nurtured-his-heart/article26423586. Accessed 3 Sept. 2017.

McGran, Kevin. "Connor McDavid Shares His Thoughts on World Juniors and Being a Pro." *The Toronto Star*, 28 Dec. 2015, www.thestar.com/sports/breakaway_blog/2015/12/connor-mcdavid-shares-his-thoughts-on-world-juniors-and-being-a-pro.html. Accessed 5 Sept. 2017.

Rohan, Tim. "A Prodigy on the Way to Stardom." *The New York Times*, 18 Feb. 2013, www.nytimes.com/2013/02/18/sports/hockey/connor-mcdavid-excels-in-ontario-hockey-league-and-is-on-way-to-stardom.html. Accessed 5 Sept. 2017.

—*Molly Hagan*

Arthur B. McDonald

Date of birth: August 29, 1943
Occupation: Physicist

Arthur B. McDonald is a Nobel Prize–winning Canadian astrophysicist and particle physicist credited with the joint discovery that neutrinos possess mass and can change identity.

EARLY LIFE AND EDUCATION

Arthur B. McDonald was born on Cape Breton in Sydney, Nova Scotia, in 1943. As a child, he loved fishing and science. His mother, Valerie McDonald, told the Canadian Broadcasting Corp. (CBC) in 2016 that McDonald was always a curious child who, even as a toddler, tried to understand how their family clock worked.

In 1964, McDonald graduated with a bachelor's degree from Dalhousie University in Halifax, Nova Scotia, and went on to earn a master's degree in physics at the university in 1965. He then attended the California Institute of Technology (Caltech) in Pasadena, California, where he earned a PhD in nuclear physics in 1969.

Having completed his university studies, McDonald worked for the Chalk River Nuclear Laboratories of Atomic Energy of Canada from 1969 until 1982. He became a professor in Princeton University's physics department in 1982, where he worked with the Palmer Cyclotron, a noteworthy tool for studying particle physics, which was built in the 1930s and decommissioned in 1998.

As a particle physicist and astrophysicist, McDonald has studied neutrinos for the majority of his career. Neutrinos are a type of lepton, one of the basic particles that make up all matter. In the 1980s, he helped to develop a neutrino observatory center 6,800 feet (2,070 meters) underground in Sudbury, Ontario. In 1989, he became the Sudbury Neutrino Observatory's first director and also began teaching as a professor at Queens University in Kingston, Ontario.

The Sudbury Neutrino Observatory (SNO) was built underground to allow neutrinos to pass through layers of rock and reach a large water tank that made up the observatory's detector. The underground position of the detector also allowed the scientists to observe neutrinos in isolation from cosmic rays. It was at SNO that McDonald began to develop his research into the question of whether solar neutrinos possess mass.

NOBEL PRIZE WINNER

Despite being the second-most abundant particle in the universe after photons, little was understood about neutrinos and their properties as matter prior to research McDonald directed at SNO. Theoretical physicist Wolfgang Pauli theorized the existence of neutrinos in 1930, but he believed that they were undetectable and did not collide with matter.

McDonald's SNO team studied a group of electron neutrinos originating at the sun. The tests had shown two-thirds of these neutrinos disappearing when they reached the Earth, raising the question of whether the particles were dissipating.

McDonald's findings proved that the neutrinos were changing identity from electron neutrinos to other neutrino types, tau and muon neutrinos. This ensured that the neutrinos were not disappearing on their way to the Earth from the sun, and consequently proved that neutrinos have mass. In fact, McDonald's team's findings suggest that neutrinos, which are created by cosmic rays, may collectively have as much mass as the collective weight of stars.

Having successfully proven that neutrinos do have mass and can change identities, McDonald won the 2015 Nobel Prize in Physics. He shared the award with Takaaki Kajita, whose research team at Japan's Super-Kamiokande neutrino detector developed the same findings about neutrinos. In 2016, McDonald's SNO team was one of five teams to split the Breakthrough Prize in Fundamental Physics, worth $3 million. Japan had three winning teams, one of which was Kajita's Super-Kamiokande team.

IMPACT

McDonald has authored more than 120 scientific papers and is a decorated scientist, having won many awards. In 2006, he earned one of Canada's highest national honors when he was made an Officer of the Order of Canada. In addition to the Nobel Prize and the Fundamental Physics Prize, his other honors include a Herzberg Medal (2003) and a Benjamin Franklin Medal in Physics (2007). McDonald was elected as a Fellow of the Royal Society of London in 2009, and was promoted to Companion of the Order of Canada in 2015.

The neutrino mass question had been investigated for more than fifty years prior to McDonald's breakthrough findings. The *Wall Street Journal* noted that the outcome of McDonald's research "opened the door to a new world of physics." The finding that neutrinos have mass has forced particle physicists to revise their understanding of how the universe works.

PERSONAL LIFE

McDonald lives in Canada with his wife. He serves as professor emeritus at Queens University, where he has taught since 1989.

SUGGESTED READING

"Arthur McDonald, Nobel Winner, Snags 2nd Major Science Honour." *CBCnews*. CBC/Radio Canada, 9 Nov. 2015. Web. 28 Mar. 2016.

"Arthur McDonald's Mother Proud of Nobel Prize–winning Son." *CBCnews*. CBC/Radio Canada, 7 Oct. 2015. Web. 28 Mar. 2016.

Gregersen, Erik. "Arthur B. McDonald." *Encyclopedia Britannica Online*. Encyclopedia Britannica, 12 Feb. 2016. Web. 28 Mar. 2016.

Grodin, Claire. "Meet the Newest Nobel Laureates in Physics." *Fortune*. Time, 6 Oct. 2015. Web. 27 Mar. 2016.

Naik, Gautam, and Anna Molin. "Nobel Prize in Physics Won by Takaaki Kajita and Arthur B. McDonald for Work on Neutrinos." *Wall Street Journal*. Dow Jones, 6 Oct. 2015. Web. 27 Mar. 2016.

Overbye, Dennis. "Takaaki Kajita and Arthur McDonald Share Nobel in Physics for Work on Neutrinos." *New York Times*. New York Times, 6 Oct. 2015. Web. 27 Mar. 2016.

"Past Winner 2003 NSERC Award of Excellence: Arthur McDonald." *Natural Sciences and Engineering Research Council of Canada*. NSERC, 13 Aug. 2010. Web. 27 Mar. 2016.

—*Richard Means*

Tatyana McFadden

Date of birth: April 21, 1989
Occupation: Paralympic athlete

Tatyana McFadden is a seventeen-time Paralympic medalist with a remarkable backstory. McFadden, who was born in Russia with a condition that left her paralyzed below the waist, spent her first years in an orphanage. She was adopted by two American women at the age of six, but doctors predicted that she would not survive into adulthood. McFadden, however, thrived in her new home. She took up a number of sports and ultimately, wheelchair racing. She won two medals in her first Paralympic Games in Athens, Greece in 2004 when she was just fifteen years old. The same year, McFadden began high school and, after not being allowed to compete in track meets alongside her able-bodied teammates, successfully sued the school district for equal inclusion. The case paved the way for a state law and a national mandate requiring public schools to offer equal access to all students.

In 2016 McFadden, with author Tom Walker, published a book for young adults called *Ya Sama! Moments from My Life. Ya sama* is a Russian phrase that means "I can do it myself." After winning three gold medals at the 2012 Summer Paralympic Games in London, she tried skiing for the first time. Two years later, at the Winter Paralympic Games in Sochi she won a silver medal in the sport. To date, McFadden ranks as one of the best athletes in the world; she has been the world-record holder in five major racing events—the 100, 400, 800, 1,500 and 5,000 meters—and in 2013 she became the first person to ever win the four major marathons—New York, Boston, London, and Chicago—in one year. She repeated the feat in 2014 and 2015. In 2016

Katie Chan/CC BY-SA 4.0/Wikimedia Commons

she won the Excellence in Sports Performance (ESPY) Award for best female athlete with a disability, the sixth time she was nominated for the award.

EARLY LIFE
Tatyana McFadden was born in St. Petersburg, Russia, on April 21, 1989, with spina bifida, or a hole in her spine that left her paralyzed below the waist. Doctors expected that she would live only a few days, and her parents gave her to a local orphanage called Orphanage 13. There was no access to medical care in the orphanage; nor could she use a wheelchair because the orphanage did not have one. Instead, as McFadden told Johnny Dodd for *People* magazine (24 Nov. 2016), she learned to "walk on my hands or scoot myself across the floor." She added, "I just wanted to be like the other kids, to go wherever they were going and never saw myself as any different than they were."

When McFadden was six years old, she met Deborah McFadden, the commissioner for disabilities in the US Department of Health and Human Services under the George H. W. Bush administration, who was touring the orphanage. Deborah McFadden could not stop thinking about the little girl and McFadden recalled telling the other children of the American visitor, "That's my mom. She's going to be my mom," she told Dodd. Indeed, Deborah McFadden adopted her, though she was told, as McFadden's birth parents were told six years earlier, that the little girl would not survive to adulthood.

Deborah McFadden brought Tatyana home to live with her and Deborah's partner, Bridget O'Shaughnessy. The two women, who have been partners for over thirty years, met while Deborah McFadden was still recovering from a rare autoimmune disease called Guillain-Barré syndrome that left her paralyzed from the neck down. She used an electric wheelchair for four years and crutches for eight. Her experience during that time inspired her to become an advocate for disabled people. In 1990 she helped write the historic Americans with Disabilities Act.

The transition to life in America was difficult for Tatyana, and her health worsened after her arrival. But again, McFadden beat the odds. Her new parents took her to the Kennedy Krieger Institute in Baltimore, Maryland, for treatment. After examining McFadden, her doctors were astounded at her resilience and that she had survived as long as she had under the negligent care of the orphanage. At their home in Clarksville, Maryland, Deborah McFadden and O'Shaughnessy, who works in information technology for the United States Department of Health and Human Services, nursed Tatyana back to health and bought her a wheelchair. They later adopted two more daughters, Hannah and Ruthi, from Albania. Hannah, who is seven years younger than McFadden, was born without a femur in her left leg and is an above-the-knee amputee. She walks with a prosthesis, but like her older sister, races in a wheelchair. In 2016 she too competed in the Paralympic Games in Rio de Janeiro, Brazil.

EARLY RACING CAREER
Concerned about McFadden's weakened state after an early life of neglect, her parents signed her up for basketball, sled hockey, swimming, gymnastics, and track. "I was very anemic and weak," McFadden told Joseph Shapiro for *Weekend Edition Sunday* on National Public Radio (NPR) (31 Aug. 2012). "And so the only point that saved my life was sports." She immediately took to racing, and began competing for the Bennett Blazers in the Kennedy Krieger Institute's Physically Challenged Sports Program. "Fairly early on, you recognized she was a special athlete," Gerry Herman, who coached McFadden for ten years, told Kevin Cowherd for the *Baltimore Sun* (25 Aug. 2012). "Some of it is her will. And she's just genetically blessed with fast-twitch muscles."

When McFadden was twelve, Herman recalled, she broke the world record in the women's 100-meters in an unsanctioned meet. With the encouragement of her mothers, McFadden continued to play other sports as well; she particularly excelled as a basketball player. When McFadden was fifteen, she was the youngest member of the US Paralympic team. In the

2004 Athens Games, she won a silver medal in the 100-meters and a bronze medal in the 200-meters. The same year, McFadden began her freshman year at Atholton High School in Columbia, Maryland.

LANDMARK DISABILITY CASE

At Atholton, McFadden was told that she would not be allowed to compete against other athletes on the school's track-and-field team. McFadden's results were already scored separately, but under the dictate of the school, which cited safety concerns, McFadden was made to race after her teammates on an empty track. McFadden felt alienated from her peers and her mother made an appeal to the school. As Deborah McFadden recalled to Cowherd, "I went back to the school, and said 'Look, guys, I have 400 attorneys that work for me. I helped write the [Americans with Disabilities Act.] If I sue you, it'll be nuclear war. I'm begging: just give her a uniform." Still the school said no.

When the family sued Howard County Board of Education in 2005, filing no damages, the fallout was indeed substantial. The case garnered national media attention, but McFadden was booed by her teammates and ostracized at school. A fellow teammate, the coach's daughter, wrote an angry letter to the local newspaper in which she said, as quoted by Kelly Whiteside for the *New York Times* (1 Sept. 2016), "I will no longer sit back and watch runners be treated unfairly because they are NOT disabled."

It was a difficult time for McFadden. She told Whiteside that O'Shaughnessy's mother, Jo, who moved in with the family while Deborah McFadden ran the International Children's Alliance, an orphan advocacy group, helped her through her darkest days. McFadden's case went to federal court, where a judge ruled in her favor in 2006. The decision paved the way for Maryland's Fitness and Athletic Equity for Students with Disabilities Act, which passed in 2008. As a result of these laws, the United States Department of Education Office of Civil Rights issued a federal mandate in 2013 solidifying schools' obligation to ensure equity in access to extracurricular activities.

PARALYMPIC CAREER

In high school, McFadden began to focus more seriously on her racing career. In 2008 she competed in the Beijing Paralympic Games, winning silver medals in the 200-meters, 400-meters and 800-meters, and a bronze medal in the 4-by-100-meter relay. After the Paralympics, McFadden began her freshman year at the University of Illinois where she majored in human studies and family development. She continued to race and joined the school's wheelchair basketball team. Though McFadden was a sprinter, she decided

on a whim to enter the Chicago Marathon in 2009. "I thought it would be a good workout," she recalled to Cowherd; more than a good workout, she won the race.

McFadden would go on to win the New York Marathon in 2010, and the Chicago and London marathons in 2011. When asked how a sprinter could perform so well in such a long and grueling race, McFadden said, as quoted by Cowherd, that she loved the 400-meters and simply told herself that she was "just doing it 100 times." In 2012 McFadden competed in the London Paralympic Games, winning gold medals in the 400-meters, 800-meters and 1500-meters, and a bronze medal in the 100-meters. That same year, she presented her 2010 New York Marathon medal to the orphanage director at Orphanage 13.

In 2013 McFadden completed her first historic Grand Slam of the four major marathons, beginning in Boston in April. That year, she also tried cross-country skiing for the first time. McFadden graduated from Illinois in December 2013 and gave the graduation speech to her class two months before competing in her first Winter Paralympic Games as a Nordic skier. In Sochi, Russia, McFadden won a silver medal in the 1 kilometer sprint, her eleventh career Paralympic medal. Among those watching her cross the finish line was her biological mother, Nina Polevikova, whom she met for the first time briefly in 2012. In 2015, McFadden won the New York Marathon in one hour and forty-three minutes, smashing the previous record for the course by over seven minutes. She also completed her Grand Slam for an unprecedented third year in a row.

At the 2016 Paralympic Games in Rio de Janeiro, McFadden sought to become the first athlete to sweep all seven distances in wheelchair racing. She fell short of that goal, but took home four gold medals—in the 400-meter, 800-meter, 1500-meter, and 5000-meter race—and silver medals in the 100-meters (in which she was narrowly edged out by Liu Wenjun of China) and the marathon.

McFadden, who has garnered lucrative sponsorships from BMW, BP, Coke, Nike and Samsung, is perhaps the most visible wheelchair athlete in the United States. David Elbert, whose daughter, Ruby, races for McFadden's old team, the Bennett Blazers, told Whiteside, "Tatyana brings pride and recognition. She makes these kids stand up taller sometimes.'"

PERSONAL LIFE

McFadden shares a house with her sister Hannah in Champaign, Illinois, where both study at the University of Illinois. McFadden is working toward a postgraduate degree with the aim of working with critically ill children as a child-life specialist.

SUGGESTED READING

Cowherd, Kevin. "Tatyana McFadden Looking to Go Far and Fast at Paralympics." *The Baltimore Sun*, 25 Aug. 2012, articles.baltimoresun.com/2012-08-25/sports/bs-sp-paralympics-mcfadden-0826-20120825_1_paralympics-wheelchair-racing-green-gables. Accessed 4 Jan. 2017.

Dodd, Johnny. "Meet My Two Moms: Wheelchair Racing Sensation Tatyana McFadden Reveals How She Was Saved from a Bleak Russian Orphanage." *People*, 24 Nov. 2016, people.com/sports/tatyana-mcfadden-parents-and-upbringing-in-orphanage. Accessed 4 Jan. 2017.

Shapiro, Joseph. "Paralympian's Pursuit Enables Aspiring Athletes." *Weekend Edition Sunday*, 31 Aug. 2012 www.npr.org/2012/09/02/160382788/paralympians-pursuit-enables-aspiring-athletes. Accessed 4 Jan. 2017.

Whiteside, Kelly. "A Paralympian Races to Remove Obstacles for the Next Generation." *New York Times*, 1 Sept. 2016, www.nytimes.com/2016/09/04/sports/olympics/paralympics-tatyana-mcfadden-wheelchair.html. Accessed 4 Jan. 2017.

—*Molly Hagan*

Conor McGregor

Date of birth: July 14, 1988
Occupation: Mixed martial artist

Conor "The Notorious" McGregor, a former plumber-in-training from Dublin, Ireland, is the reigning Ultimate Fighting Championship (UFC) lightweight champion, former UFC featherweight champion, and one of the most exciting-to-watch mixed martial artists in the world. Dana White, the president of the UFC, signed McGregor, then a local unknown, to a five-fight deal in 2013 without even having watched him fight. White was deeply impressed by their first meeting, recalling to Chris Jones for *Esquire* (15 Apr. 2015), "He's one in a million. He has that thing that you can't teach people, whatever it is that makes people gravitate toward you. He has that more than any fighter I've ever met. He makes you believe everything he believes."

A flamboyant character both inside the octagon—the chain-linked cage within which mixed martial arts (MMA) bouts are fought—and out, McGregor enjoyed a dramatic rise in 2013

Andrius Petrucenia/Flickr/UCinternational (Crop)/CC BY-SA 2.0/Wikimedia Commons

before eventually enduring a humbling fall, after tapping out in the second round of his fight with welterweight Nate Diaz in 2016. He won a rematch with Diaz and a few months later claimed the UFC lightweight title in an historic bout with Eddie Alvarez. McGregor believes a lot about his own ability and his potential for greatness. He also seems to genuinely believe in his own infallibility, which makes it all the more remarkable when he loses. Following an unorthodox training regimen, he has often studied footage of animals hunting prey, Jones wrote, adding cryptically that in doing so, McGregor "became closer to one of them than one of us."

EARLY LIFE

McGregor was born on July 14, 1988, and raised along with his two siblings in the working-class Crumlin neighborhood of Dublin. His father, Tony, a taxi driver, said of his son in an interview with Andrea Smith for the *Independent* (19 June 2016), "His fists were clenched coming out of the womb so he was ready to fight." Growing up, McGregor got into fights with other boys, and though initially he had been involved in soccer, he eventually became interested in and took up boxing, largely to learn to defend himself. He began training at the Crumlin Boxing Club at a young age.

Around 2006 his family moved to the Dublin suburb of Lucan, but McGregor's heart remained in Crumlin. For a while, he would commute back to his Crumlin gym, but at the same time, a new schoolmate introduced him to MMA, which quickly became his new passion.

Because it is traditional in Ireland either to continue with schooling or to enter a trade, and he did not have any real desire to pursue a university education, at the behest of his mother, he became a plumber's apprentice. At first he attempted to both train and work, but the grueling schedule led him to quit his job after several months of twelve-hour workdays to train in MMA full time. "I know there are passionate, skilled plumbers," he told Donald McRae for *The Guardian* (10 Aug. 2015). "But I had no love for plumbing."

EARLY PROFESSIONAL CAREER

McGregor still barely knew what the sport of MMA was, but he was determined to blaze his own trail. "I just felt I was going to be the person I wanted to be, regardless of what anyone said," he told McRae. His parents were nervous but supportive. He fought his first professional MMA bout in March 2008 in Dublin—and won. Though he did suffer his first, rather devastating, loss that year, he also achieved victory in three of his fights. He loved not only the fighting but also the glitz and the braggadocio of the fighters, and after witnessing a UFC fight in Dublin in 2009, he saw opportunity for himself. "I saw all the fans and fighters and I didn't see me. I was different. I knew people would love that," he told McRae.

McGregor spent all of 2009 and most of 2010 on hiatus from competition. He continued training at Straight Blast Gym in Dublin with Coach John Kavanagh, honing his technique before making his successful return, fighting in the Chaos Fighting Championships in October 2010. In early 2011 he embarked on an impressive winning streak and quickly became known for his devastatingly powerful left-hand punch. "Most punches blemish," Jones wrote. "When McGregor lands a punch, his fists behave more like chisels, like awls. His punches cut. They don't bruise the skin; they break it." In March 2011 it took McGregor only sixteen seconds to knock out English fighter Mike Wood using his left hand; a month later he knocked out Irishman Paddy Doherty in four seconds.

By 2013 McGregor, who had been fighting under the Cage Warriors promotion banner, was famous enough in the United Kingdom to catch the attention of White and the UFC. White was in Dublin to receive an award from Trinity College, but as he told Jones, everywhere he went he heard whispers about McGregor. He invited the young fighter to Las Vegas for an interview and was so beguiled by their meeting that he signed him to a five-fight contract without ever seeing him fight.

EARLY UFC CAREER

McGregor came to the UFC at a unique and very lucrative time in MMA's history. The UFC, the sport's dominant promotion company, held its first event—UFC 1—in 1993; its earliest iteration was closer to a street brawl, with an emphasis on bloodletting over technique. In 1996 Senator John McCain famously called MMA "human cockfighting" and successfully lobbied to have the sport banned from cable television in thirty-six states. The ban speeded the evolution of the sport; the UFC introduced a more cohesive set of rules, and fans tired of boxing flocked to MMA, making it one of the most popular sports in the country.

At 145 pounds, McGregor began his UFC career as a featherweight. His first fight, against Marcus "The Bama Beast" Brimage, took place on April 6, 2013. His debut lived up to the hype, and he won the fight on a technical knockout (TKO). His second fight came in August, by which time he was already becoming one of the most popular figures in the UFC. He beat Max Holloway in a decision victory but tore his Anterior Cruciate Ligament (ACL) in the process. After knee surgery, he was advised to rest up and recover; he was out of the octagon for almost a year, during which time he changed his training regimen, doing away with conventional weights and workouts and adopting a more fluid and perhaps even spiritual program aimed at exhausting his seemingly limitless energy and his desire to gain more control over his body. Sometimes he hit the gym in the middle of the night, just to move around. "Movement is medicine to me," he told Jones.

Luckily for McGregor, his injury came at the beginning of his UFC career, not just before it. If had he injured himself at a local show, he told Damon Martin for the *Bleacher Report* (23 Sept. 2013), it would have been a "career-ender." Instead, he made a triumphant return to the sport on July 19, 2014, with a fight against Brazilian jujitsu black belt Diego Brendão in Dublin. The city showed up in droves to support their homegrown fighter, and McGregor did not disappoint his fans, winning in a TKO in the first round. The fight solidified his ascent as an international star.

UFC FEATHERWEIGHT CHAMPION

In September 2014 McGregor faced his first world-class UFC fighter, Dustin "The Diamond" Poirier. With the fight considered a crucial moment for his career, he disposed of his opponent quickly, beating Poirier in a TKO in less than two minutes. Displaying characteristic bravado, he used his victory to put other fighters on notice. "What the other featherweights don't understand, is that it's a whole 'nother game when they get hit by me," he said, as quoted by Dave Doyle for the website MMA Fighting (27 Sept. 2014). "The world title is next."

Although the UFC has never garnered the press attention of sports organizations such as the National Football League (NFL), it maintains a booming, multibillion-dollar industry—in large part due to McGregor's contributions to making MMA more mainstream. For McGregor, who was living off welfare checks when he began his fighting career, this became one of the UFC's most enticing aspects. His career, he told McRae, "started with a love for the sport and it's been strengthened by a love for the money it brings."

McGregor was slated to fight José Aldo, the reigning featherweight champion, for his title in July 2015, but Aldo bowed out ten days before the match due to a rib injury. He fought Chad Mendes instead, knocking him out in the second round to claim the interim featherweight title. In December he finally faced Aldo; for all of the buildup, however, the fight set a surprising record as the swiftest title bout in UFC history, with McGregor knocking Aldo out in just thirteen seconds to become the official UFC featherweight champion.

UFC LIGHTWEIGHT CHAMPION
In the spring of 2016 McGregor's UFC record was 7–0. Seeking to be the UFC's first dual-weight champion, he challenged Rafael dos Anjos, the reigning lightweight champion, for his belt. The fight, UFC 196, was slated for March, but Anjos broke his foot in training two weeks before the event. Nate Diaz, a popular welterweight, replaced him. Now, instead of moving up just one weight class (from 145 pounds to 155 pounds), McGregor found himself moving up two weight classes (to welterweight at 170 pounds) to face Diaz. As usual, McGregor was smug about the match. However, Diaz proved too large to be fazed by McGregor's punches. He delivered a stunning loss to McGregor, forcing him to tap out after applying the brutal rear naked choke in the second round. Following the defeat, Mike Bohn, writing for Rolling Stone (6 Mar. 2016), quoted McGregor as saying, "It's a tough pill to swallow, but we can either run from adversity or we can face our adversity head-on and conquer it. That's what I plan to do." The two men fought a rematch in August 2016 at UFC 202 that lasted all five rounds, ending in a decision victory—based on judges' scores—for McGregor.

In November McGregor fought Eddie Alvarez for the lightweight title at UFC 205 at Madison Square Garden, the first UFC event in New York after a twenty-year ban. He became the first UFC fighter to hold dual-weight titles after knocking Alvarez out in the second round. Two weeks later the UFC stripped him of his featherweight title because he had yet to defend it.

This created, White said in a press conference, as quoted by Marissa Payne for the *Washington Post* (3 Dec. 2016), a "logjam" of disgruntled fighters. Though White claimed to have made the decision with McGregor, McGregor himself said he would not relinquish the title in December 2016. It was not the first time McGregor and White resorted to public negotiation tactics; earlier that year McGregor announced his retirement in an effort to prod White. White called his bluff, briefly dropping McGregor's name from the UFC roster. As of early 2017, in anticipation of the birth of his first child, McGregor was reportedly on paternity leave from competition for several months.

PERSONAL LIFE
McGregor and his longtime girlfriend, Dee Devlin, began dating in 2008. They are expecting their first child in 2017. He has emphasized in interviews that his success would not have been possible without the support of Devlin, who has admitted that she still gets nervous before watching every one of his fights.

SUGGESTED READING
Doyle, Dave. "UFC 178 Results: Conor McGregor Finishes Dustin Poirier in Less Than Two Minutes." *MMA Fighting*, 27 Sept. 2014, www.mmafighting.com/2014/9/27/6855887/ufc-178-results-conor-mcgregor-finishes-dustin-poirier-in-less-than. Accessed 11 Jan. 2017.

Jones, Chris. "Conor McGregor Doesn't Believe in Death." *Esquire*, 15 Apr. 2015, www.esquire.com/sports/interviews/a34377/conor-mcgregor-interview-0515. Accessed 11 Jan. 2017.

McRae, Donald. "UFC's Conor McGregor: 'I Pinch Myself Because I Am Surrounded by Luxury but It Is Built on Sacrifice.'" *The Guardian*, 10 Aug. 2015, www.theguardian.com/sport/2015/aug/10/ufc-conor-mcgregor-floyd-mayweather-fight. Accessed 11 Jan. 2017.

Parker, James. "The Rise and Fall of Ultimate Fighter Conor McGregor." *The Atlantic*, June 2016, www.theatlantic.com/magazine/archive/2016/06/the-penultimate-fighter/480732/. Accessed 11 Jan. 2017.

—*Molly Hagan*

Sara Mearns

Born: January 19, 1986
Occupation: Dancer

Writing for the *New York Times* (18 Jan. 2015), Roslyn Sulcas named Sara Mearns one of five

Photo by Hiroyuki Ito/Getty Images

from Russia's famed Bolshoi Ballet Company. Indeed, Mearns looks for her inspiration not to earlier American dancers, but to Russian ballerinas. As she told Laura Jacobs for *New Criterion* (Apr. 2011), "[Natalia] Makarova was and still is my all-time inspiration." Mearns uses videos of other dancers to inspire and inform her own choices in dance roles. She admits to watching her recording of Makarova's 1976 *Swan Lake*, performed in New York, repeatedly.

At age fourteen, Mearns spent a year at the South Carolina Governor's School for the Arts and Humanities, studying with Stanislav Issaev. She spent four summers taking intensive courses at the School of American Ballet, the official school of the New York City Ballet, and enrolled full time in the fall of 2001, following her year at the Governor's School. She was insecure in her first year, fearing she would not be asked to return. The second year, however, she gained a great deal of notice. In 2003, she became an apprentice at the NYCB; that year she received the Mae L. Wien Award for Outstanding Promise.

NEW YORK CITY BALLET

Mearns was invited to join the New York City Ballet in 2004 as a dancer in the corps de ballet. In 2007 she danced in *The Sleeping Beauty* as Lilac Fairy, earning praise for the way she used her atypical ballerina body. As Jacobs wrote, "She used the broad set of her shoulders and ribs to find amplitude, a serene space around torso, head, and neck. This wreath of space—a feeling of sovereignty—is necessary to ballerina roles and to Lilac Fairy in particular."

During the spring 2008 season, Mearns danced a number of leads, including Diamonds in George Balanchine's *Jewels*, the Sugar Plum Fairy in *The Nutcracker*, and in Jerome Robbins's *The Goldberg Variations*. As a result of her stellar performances, she was promoted to principal dancer later that year.

Mearns felt the pressure of her elevated status, as she explained to Leda Meredith for *Pointe* (30 Nov. 2001): "You feel like you have to go out there and deliver. But if you dance like you did before you were promoted, well, they know what you're going to be like onstage because that's why they promoted you. I don't think about the expectations. I want to keep the fun." She also avoids the temptation to over-rehearse, believing that could create boredom.

Much of the NYCB's repertoire is the choreography of its late cofounder, George Balanchine, who died a few years before Mearns was born. Speaking to Tom Phillips for *DanceView* (Summer 2010) about Balanchine's work, Mearns said, "I just feel like when you see the choreography and hear the music, it goes together. You see what he was trying to do. You don't have to read too much into it, there's no story. You just know exactly what he wanted to

principal ballerinas at the New York City Ballet (NYCB) who satisfy the public longing for "absolute technical mastery . . . musicality, dramatic power, charm, assertiveness and radiance . . . [and] who are at the peak of their powers and among the greatest exemplars of the art form." Mearns has been featured in some eighty roles since joining the NYCB in 2004. Of her style, choreographer Christopher Wheeldon told Astrida Woods for *Dance Magazine* (9 Mar. 2012), "Sara has a very distinct personality. Her movement quality is voracious. If you don't pull her back a little, her fiendish abandon can get the better of her. But when it is fully realized it is unlike anything I have seen onstage. Sara is one of the most important dancers of her generation."

CHILDHOOD AND DANCE EDUCATION

Mearns grew up in Columbia, South Carolina. She began dancing and acting when she was three; she competed in jazz and tap. From ages three to twelve, Mearns's teacher was Ann Brodie of the Calvert-Brodie School of Dance. Before Brodie died, she told Mearns's mother, Sharon, that Sara needed to go to the School of American Ballet in New York. Mearns's mother encouraged her daughter's interest in dance, driving her to rehearsals and competitions more than an hour away and making her costumes. Mearns's older brother, Keith, also danced.

All of the late rehearsals and the performing allowed Mearns to become very comfortable on stage. She also trained at the Carolina Ballet Academy with Shamil Yagudin, a ballet master see, what he was going for. And it feels so nice to dance his ballets, because you feel beautiful, it's good on the body. It's exhausting, but it feels good."

One of Balanchine's characteristic devices was to have dancers make their move a brief second before the beat of the music. Audience members saw the leap or pirouette, then heard the music. This aspect of Balanchine's style had been lost during the early years of the twenty-first century; Mearns has brought it back into fashion.

SWAN LAKE

Swan Lake, her favorite ballet, was Mearns's first role as a soloist, performing the dual roles of Odette (the White Swan) and Odile (the Black Swan) when she was nineteen, in 2006. She was chosen to replace an injured dancer, with a three-week rehearsal. Choreographer Peter Martins condensed Tchaikovsky's four-act work into two acts, requiring a quick change in the second act from the black swan to the white. Mearns found that haste helpful, as she explained to Phillips: "I was so drained and so emotional, I was just so down after black swan that it actually helps you, because you become that devastated character." Mearns had a bout of stomach flu the day prior to the performance, but went on as scheduled.

Mearns continued to dance the role. She had a breakthrough on Valentine's Day 2011 with Jared Angle as her partner, Siegfried. It had been a taxing week of performances; Mearns was too exhausted to do any thinking about her dancing, but relied on passion and muscle memory, which made for a better performance.

Mearns tries to bring the same intensity to dance that Tchaikovsky put into the music. As she told Joseph Carman for *Dance Magazine* (Jan. 2017), "With Tchaikovsky it's very emotional and dramatic. It's not small in any way, even in a quiet moment. Every moment means something. Tchaikovsky has a way of tapping into those really deep parts that enable you to let yourself go and let it all out." She continues to watch the video of Natalia Makarova before every performance she gives of *Swan Lake*.

IDENTIFYING GENDER BIAS

During 2016, Mearns was one of the dancers who began to question the lack of women choreographers at New York City Ballet and other major ballet companies. The ballet master in chief of NYCB, Peter Martins, rejected the idea of sexism in hiring choreographers. Rather, he attributed the imbalance to the predominance of women's roles in ballet, leaving women dancers less time to develop skills in choreography, whereas male dancers tend to have more free time. As he told Gia Kourlas for *New York Times* (26 June 2016), "It's hard work. In Balanchine's

choreography, you don't stand idly by—you dance. And it's less so for the men."

Women choreographers are more prevalent in modern dance, where men and women have greater equality. In ballet, the women are often showcased as muses or beauty incarnate, leading to passivity. Also, ballerinas are trained to be obedient. They are nearly always referred to as "girls," a term they never grow out of.

Mearns pointed out that little girls dream of being ballerinas and tend to stick to that dream as long as possible. About the lack of women choreographers, she told Kourlas, "I don't think it really concerned me until recently, when it came to my attention that we had five choreographers coming [to City Ballet], and none of them were female. I was like, wait a minute. There can't be at least *one* woman in this whole group?"

MOVING A NEW WAY

Taking matters into her own hands, Mearns worked with Jodi Melnick, the contemporary dancer and choreographer, during a residency at Jacob's Pillow Dance in western Massachusetts during the fall of 2015. The two had met as part of a Danspace Project that matched contemporary and ballet dancers from New York City Ballet. Jared Angle, with whom Mearns frequently is paired onstage, and Gretchen Smith, a member of the corps, joined Mearns for the residency. Melnick did not initially warm to the idea of choreographing a ballet, until Mearns suggested the work was about the process rather than the final project. The resulting collaboration was *Working in Process/New Bodies*, performed at the Guggenheim Museum.

Melnick began with improvisational exercises, so common for modern dance and so foreign to ballet. She told Gia Kourlas for *New York Times* (6 Nov. 2016), "It was so much new information [for Mearns]. I was like: 'I've been where you are: You don't get it, it seems meaningless. This is what process is, Sara. I'm asking you to think and manipulate and be on the spot and be vulnerable and not worry about how you look.'"

The work changed Mearns's approach to ballet, particularly Balanchine's *Diamonds*. As she told Kourlas, "This [residency] wasn't for an external reason. It was about me. Can I be a deeper artist in some way? It was an opportunity to see what else my body could do."

Mearns continues to try new approaches to dance, working with Lori Belilove, who specializes in the work of Isadora Duncan, the famed twentieth-century modern dancer. Mearns performed a solo in Belilove's production of Chopin's *Narcissus* in New York in June 2017. Mearns is also working with a hip-hop group for a performance at Jacob's Pillow in New York.

PERSONAL LIFE

In 2009 Mearns sustained a lower back injury, which at first caused her to doubt her career. However, she returned to NYCB to dance *Swan Lake* again the following year. She told Phillips, "Being injured was horrible at first because I had nothing, but it was good because I learned how to live on my own and start from the ground up, and get the confidence back that I needed to be independent and my own person." Mearns was injured on stage again in 2012 and was sidelined for eight months; since then she has become an outspoken advocate for injury prevention in dance.

She has learned to enjoy watching television with her dogs, Rocky and Ozzie. She shares a twenty-seventh floor Lincoln Center apartment in New York City with her boyfriend, Emmy Award–winning choreographer Joshua Bergasse. In 2015 he added a small cameo for her to the Broadway production of Leonard Bernstein's *On the Town*.

SUGGESTED READING

Carman, Joseph. "Three Principal Ballerinas Who Are One with Their Role." *Dance Magazine*, 29 Dec. 2016, www.dancemagazine.com/the-arc-of-artistry-2307053132.html. Accessed 13 July 2017.

Jacobs, Laura. "The Birds: Odette-Odile at NYCB." *New Criterion*, vol. 29, no. 8, Apr. 2011, p. 36.

Kourlas, Gia. "When These Dancers Collaborated, 2 Learning Curves Met as One." *The New York Times*, 4 Nov. 2016, www.nytimes.com/2016/11/06/arts/dance/when-these-dancers-sara-mearns-jodi-melnick-collaborated-2-learning-curves-met-as-one.html. Accessed 13 July 2017.

Kourlas, Gia. "Dance Luminaries Weigh In on the Conspicuous Absence of Female Choreographers." *The New York Times*, 26 June 2016, www.nytimes.com/2016/06/26/arts/dance/ballet-luminaries-weigh-in-on-a-conspicuous-absence.html. Accessed 13 July 2017.

Meredith, Leda. "A New Breed of Ballerina." *Pointe*, 30 Nov. 2001, www.pointemagazine.com/a-new-breed-of-ballerina-2412798993.html. Accessed 13 July 2017.

Phillips, Tom. "Romance in Repertory." *Danceview*, vol. 27, no. 3, Summer 2010, pp. 3–8.

Woods, Astrida. "No Holds Barred." *Dance Magazine*, 9 Mar. 2012, www.dancemagazine.com/no_holds_barred-2306893826.html. Accessed 13 July 2017.

—*Judy Johnson*

Ben Mendelsohn

Date of birth: April 3, 1969
Occupation: Actor

"Scenes where you've either got to hurt or physically love another person," actor Ben Mendelsohn told Killian Fox for *The Guardian* (6 Dec. 2014), are "the hardest to do." Indeed, in the decades since launching his career in the late 1980s, Mendelsohn has had ample opportunities to do both. The Australian actor entered the world of film and television at an early age, appearing as a teenager in television shows such as *The Henderson Kids* (1985) and the soap opera *Neighbours* (1986–87) as well as the film *The Year My Voice Broke* (1987). As he grew older, he continued to work steadily in Australia and beyond, making inroads into Hollywood and establishing himself as a talented character actor especially known for playing dangerous men.

Mendelsohn's true breakthrough, however, came in 2010, when his critically acclaimed performance in the Australian crime drama *Animal Kingdom* earned him both widespread praise and the attention of Hollywood filmmakers. The following years would be productive ones, bringing roles in films such as *The Place beyond the Pines* (2012) as well as the Netflix series *Bloodline* (2015–17), for which he would win the Emmy Award for best supporting actor in a drama series in 2016. That same year, his career took yet another turn with the premiere of *Rogue One: A Star Wars Story*, a stand-alone film in the blockbuster Star Wars franchise that introduced

Eva Rinaldi/Flickr/CC BY-SA 2.0/Wikimedia Commons

Mendelsohn to the series' legion of devoted fans. Although well aware of the dramatic changes that projects such as *Bloodline* and *Rogue One* have brought about in his professional life, he remains open about the long journey he has taken and his many roles, both the critically acclaimed ones and those far less glamorous. "I am fortunate enough to have been uptown and downtown in terms of the type of work I've done," he told Emma Brown for *Interview* (20 Mar. 2015).

EARLY LIFE AND EDUCATION

Paul Benjamin Mendelsohn was born on April 3, 1969, in Melbourne, Australia. He was the first of three sons born to Frederick and Carole Ann Mendelsohn. His parents both worked in the medical field, with his mother working as a nurse and his father as a medical researcher who served for a time as head of the Florey Institute of Neuroscience and Mental Health in Melbourne. His parents divorced when he was still a child, and he has two half-brothers from his father's later relationship.

Following his parents' separation, Mendelsohn lived in a number of different places, moving frequently due to his father's career. He spent time in Germany and England and lived for a year in the United States, where he attended a boarding school in Pennsylvania while his father worked for the National Institutes of Health (NIH). He returned to Australia as a young teen, settling in the Melbourne area with his grandmother. During his time in Australia, he attended Eltham High School, a secondary school in the Melbourne suburb of Eltham, among other schools.

While in high school, Mendelsohn enrolled in a drama course in the hope that it would be an easy class. However, he soon developed an interest in acting, and when a group of his friends planned to audition for an acting job, he decided to join them. "We were all going to go answer this ad in the paper," he recalled to Brown. "None of [the others] actually did, but I did." The decision would prove to be a crucial one. He booked the part, beginning what would be a decades-long career in Australian and international film and television. "Had I not got that job, I don't think I would have pursued acting," he told Brown. "But, I did." He soon left home and school to pursue further acting gigs, leaning on his work even at such a young age to fill the void created by his rather dysfunctional family life and supporting himself during lean times with jobs in restaurants, bars, and even a slaughterhouse.

EARLY CAREER

Mendelsohn made his television debut in a 1984 episode of the television show *Special Squad*. He went on to establish himself as a teen actor, appearing in series such as *The Henderson Kids* in 1985 and *Neighbours* between 1986 and 1987, a soap opera known for featuring early appearances by Australian actors who would go on to become international stars. Notable actors who appeared on *Neighbours* at the same time as Mendelsohn included actor Guy Pearce and actor and pop star Kylie Minogue, the latter of whom had also appeared alongside Mendelsohn in *The Henderson Kids*.

After appearing in his first film, *The Still Point*, in 1986, Mendelsohn began to win further big-screen roles. He gained notice in 1987 for his performance in the period drama *The Year My Voice Broke*, winning the award for best performance by an actor in a supporting role from the Australian Film Institute (AFI), as well as for his starring role in 1990's *The Big Steal*, in which a teenager's attempt to impress a girl by purchasing a used Jaguar automobile results in a series of unexpected antics. *The Big Steal* was nominated for nine AFI Awards, and Mendelsohn himself was nominated for the award for best actor for his performance. As inspiration during these first years of acting, a time when, he explained to Ryan Gilbey for *The Guardian* (11 Mar. 2014), he shunned praise for his achievements as he still did not feel "ready or good enough," he claims to have watched and studied Robert De Niro's legendary performance as mentally unstable Vietnam War veteran Travis Bickle in the classic *Taxi Driver* (1976) at least seventy times.

Over the following two decades, Mendelsohn continued to work steadily in Australia as well as the United States and other countries. His work was not always glamorous. "There was a subset of work that you used to be able to get that was known as a corporate video," he recalled to Brown. "I can remember doing one about how to get fuel correctly from a tanker into the fuel dump. I did a bunch of that stuff." In addition to such informational videos, Mendelsohn frequently found work in film and television, appearing in high-profile films such as Terrence Malick's *The New World* (2005) and Baz Luhrmann's *Australia* (2008).

BREAKTHROUGH

Although Mendelsohn had been successful as an actor over the decades, he found that it was difficult to gain wide notice while living and working in Australia. "I think one of the dilemmas for any English speaking place that isn't America is that that sort of hovers around the vibe of things," he explained to Brown. "And it's bull——, but it carries a lot of currency in the wider community and therefore in the work communities themselves."

In 2010, however, Mendelsohn experienced a breakthrough that would prove crucial to the further development of his career. That year, he starred in the film *Animal Kingdom*, a drama about a family of Australian criminals.

The film received critical acclaim and numerous awards, and Mendelsohn won the Australian Film Institute Award for best actor for his work. In addition to bringing him critical praise from the Australian film community, the film gained significant notice outside of Australia, and both Mendelsohn and numerous interviewers have credited it with bringing him a wave of opportunities during the second decade of the twenty-first century.

After appearing in the films *Killer Elite* and *Trespass* in 2011, Mendelsohn had a particularly productive 2012, playing major supporting roles in the superhero film *The Dark Knight Rises* and the crime films *Killing Them Softly* and *The Place beyond the Pines*. The latter film represented a new experience for him, as his character was reshaped significantly after rehearsals and filming had already begun. "It's very rare. It had never happened to me," he told Sam Fragoso for *A.V. Club* (26 Sept. 2015) of such rewriting. "There are things that might change, but not something as substantial." Although the experience was an unfamiliar one for him, he ultimately appreciated director and cowriter Derek Cianfrance's commitment to the character's development. "It's very admirable, it's very brave," he told Fragoso. "And it's very alive, I think, to what's actually going on." Following a role in Ridley Scott's epic film *Exodus: Gods and Kings* (2014), he went on to play major roles in films such as 2015's *Slow West* and *Mississippi Grind*.

BLOODLINE

Mendelsohn returned to television in 2015, joining the new Netflix original drama *Bloodline*. Released in full to subscribers of the streaming-video service, the first season of the show follows a family that is thrown into conflict when the oldest brother, played by Mendelsohn, returns to town. For Mendelsohn, the experience of acting in a show released directly on Netflix rather than in accordance with a weekly television schedule was in many ways a liberating one. "There was always a feeling that there was nothing you had to get right," he told Brown. "There was never that imperative to get to some sort of destination. I think that changed the dynamic a lot. And that's very unusual in my experience—it's never been that naked between creators-slash-writers and their cast."

Bloodline's first season was generally well received by viewers and was nominated for a variety of awards, with critics focusing particularly on Mendelsohn's performance as Danny Rayburn and that of costar Kyle Chandler. Mendelsohn was nominated for the Emmy Award for outstanding supporting actor in a drama series in both 2015 and 2016 for his work, and he took home the award in the latter year. Although he was recognized for his work in the show's second season, the season was somewhat less well received than its predecessor, and in September 2016, Netflix announced that *Bloodline* would be canceled after the 2017 release of a third season.

ROGUE ONE

Mendelsohn was introduced to an even broader international audience in December 2016 with the premiere of *Rogue One: A Star Wars Story*. A stand-alone film set within the world of the Star Wars franchise, *Rogue One* follows the adventures of a group of rebels trying to steal the plans for the Death Star, a superweapon developed by the villainous Empire. Mendelsohn's character, Orson Krennic, is an Imperial officer tasked with overseeing the construction of the Death Star. A fan of the Star Wars films since childhood, Mendelsohn was thrilled to have secured a role in the influential franchise, having been unsuccessful in doing so when the prequel trilogy had filmed in Australia more than a decade before. "If that's not the dream, then please don't wake me," he told Emily Zemler for *Esquire* (15 May 2015). "I was in the real sweet spot when the first [Star Wars film] came out. There are very few film experiences that have been that magical. That was like an explosion going off. It was revelatory. I drank the whole bottle of Kool-Aid."

By the point that he had earned the role in *Rogue One*, Mendelsohn had finally begun to feel secure in his talent and career: "The thing about acting is you have to wait to be asked to the dance. I'm fairly confident now they'll keep asking," he told Gilbey.

PERSONAL LIFE

Mendelsohn met his future wife, English writer Emma Forrest, at an event highlighting Australians in film, at which they were introduced by *Animal Kingdom* director David Michôd. The couple married in 2012. Mendelsohn and Forrest have one child together, and the actor also has a child from a previous relationship.

SUGGESTED READING

Gilbey, Ryan. "Ben Mendelsohn: 'I Don't Do Talky-Talky Chummy-Chummy.'" *The Guardian*, 11 Mar. 2014, www.theguardian.com/film/2014/mar/11/ben-mendelsohn-starred-up-neighbours-interview. Accessed 16 Dec. 2016.

Kamp, David. "*Bloodline*'s Ben Mendelsohn on American Accents and Australian Mongrels." *Vanity Fair*, Oct. 2015, www.vanityfair.com/hollywood/2015/09/ben-mendelsohn-bloodline-mississippi-grind. Accessed 16 Dec. 2016.

Mendelsohn, Ben. "Ben Mendelsohn Interview: 'Scenes Where You've Got to Hurt Another Person Are the Hardest to Do.'" Interview by Killian Fox. *The Guardian*, 6 Dec. 2014, www.theguardian.com/film/2014/dec/07/

ben-mendelsohn-interview-black-sea-exodus-god-and-kings. Accessed 16 Dec. 2016.

Mendelsohn, Ben. "Our Interview with *Mississippi Grind*'s Ben Mendelsohn Gets Personal." Interview by Sam Fragoso. *A.V. Club*, 26 Sept. 2015, www.avclub.com/article/our-interview-mississippi-grinds-ben-mendelsohn-ge-225859. Accessed 16 Dec. 2016.

Mendelsohn, Ben. "There Will Be Blood." Interview by Emma Brown. *Interview*, 20 Mar. 2015, www.interviewmagazine.com/culture/ben-mendelsohn/#_. Accessed 16 Dec. 2016.

Zemler, Emily. "Ben Mendelsohn Makes the Case for His Rumored *Star Wars* Role." *Esquire*, 15 May 2015, www.esquire.com/entertainment/interviews/a35035/ben-mendelsohn-interview/. Accessed 16 Dec. 2016.

SELECTED WORKS

The Year My Voice Broke, 1987; *The Big Steal*, 1990; *Australia*, 2008; *Animal Kingdom*, 2010; *The Dark Knight Rises*, 2012; *The Place Beyond the Pines*, 2012; *Mississippi Grind*, 2015; *Slow West*, 2015; *Bloodline*, 2015–17; *Rogue One: A Star Wars Story*, 2016

—*Joy Crelin*

Shawn Mendes

Date of birth: August 8, 1998
Occupation: Singer-songwriter

By the time the guitar-strumming singer Shawn Mendes was fifteen years old, he had become a major sensation on the video-sharing application Vine, posting six-second-long covers of popular songs by the likes of Justin Bieber, Sam Smith, and Ed Sheeran. He had 200,000 followers, and soon found himself signed to a major label, Island Records. He would go on to gain millions of followers on Twitter and, more impressively, have two number-one albums by the age of eighteen: *Handwritten* (2015) and *Illuminate* (2016). After his first hit song, "Life of the Party," he continued to release hit after hit, such as "Something Big," "Stitches," and many others. His major inspirations include John Mayer and Ed Sheeran, and he has embraced them as musical mentors. His second album was a major improvement over his first, say critics, and his career appears to be just warming up.

EARLY LIFE AND EDUCATION

Shawn Peter Raul Mendes was born in 1998 and raised in Pickering, Ontario. He has a younger sister, Aaliyah. His mother, Karen, a real estate agent, is originally from England, and his father, Manuel, who owns a bar and restaurant supply company, is the son of Portuguese immigrants. Neither of his parents sing or play any musical instrument. As a boy, Mendes played ice hockey and soccer and loved skateboarding with his

Adam Bettcher/Getty Images

school pals. While he was attending Pine Ridge Secondary School in Pickering, he could not have imagined what was to come: the social media following, the musical success, and the fame.

VINE SENSATION

In August 2012, Mendes uploaded a video to Vine, a now-defunct platform for sharing videos of no longer than six seconds. The video was a very, very short cover version of the song "As Long as You Love Me" by pop sensation and fellow Canadian Justin Bieber. Mendes sang and played guitar, an instrument he had been playing for only about a year. Although he had music lessons in school, Mendes primarily learned to play guitar by watching how-to videos on YouTube. One of the first songs he learned was "Soul Sister" by the band Train. He would practice playing for hours, and kept at it. He practiced singing too, later claiming that at the beginning his voice was not very good. In an interview with Siân Ranscombe for the *Telegraph* (16 Jan. 2015), Mendes said, "I was terrible actually. I promise you, if you look at YouTube and see some of my first covers you will hear that I don't sound good. But I was so obsessed with it and wanted so much to be good at it that I forced myself to figure out what sounds right and what sounds wrong. I'm not the best singer in the world; I'm just good at picking up what I want to sound like." Mendes, through trial and error, honed his singing voice, and his guitar playing improved as well.

Only one day after posing his cover of Bieber's "As Long as You Love Me" on Vine, Mendes already had 10,000 likes. For an unknown fourteen-year-old kid, this was incredible. He kept uploading videos, and soon gained millions of followers on Vine and Twitter. His six-second cover versions became his trademark in those early days. Mendes told Ranscombe that when he started uploading his minivideos to Vine, he had no ambitions. "I was just doing it for fun," he said.

However, it didn't take long for Mendes to figure out that he was doing something that resonated with young music fans. He had teen-idol looks, charisma, a soulful singing voice, and he was doing something original: no one had taken advantage of Vine in quite the way Mendes did. He did minicovers of dozens of hit songs, mostly pop and R & B, including Sam Smith's "Stay with Me"; Ed Sheeran's "Don't," "Sing," and "Give Me Love"; One Direction's "Little Things"; Bill Withers' "Ain't No Sunshine"; Beyonce's "Drunk in Love"; John Legend's "All of Me"; and many more.

MAJOR-LABEL DEAL

Late in 2013, a little over a year after Mendes began posting his Vine videos, music manager Andrew Gertler saw Mendes's cover—a full cover version, not a short Vine video—of A Great Big World's "Say Something," and he wasted no time reaching out to a major label. He contacted Ziggy Chareton, the head of artists and repertoire (A&R) at Island Records. Chareton was immediately impressed and jumped to sign Mendes. In May 2014, the fifteen-year-old flew to New York City with his father and signed a recording contract with Island Records' president and chief executive, David Massey.

At the time of his signing, Mendes had 200,000 followers on Vine. But for someone to get a major-label deal from putting out Vine videos was unheard of. "There had never been anyone that emerged from Vine as a recording artist," Massey told Joe Coscarelli for the *New York Times* (20 Sept. 2016), adding, "I'm naturally wary of those things because they haven't really translated, apart from Justin [Bieber] and YouTube." Though Mendes's having a strong social-media following certainly didn't hurt his prospects, it was not the main reason he was signed. Clearly Massey saw something in Mendes. In 2014, the very year Mendes was signed by Island Records, the label released Mendes's first single, "Life of the Party." Without any real radio play, the single reached number one on iTunes in about half an hour; and it sold nearly 150,000 copies after only one week. What soon followed was the four-song *Shawn Mendes EP*, which was a preface of sorts for Mendes's first full-length album.

HANDWRITTEN

Shawn Mendes's first album, *Handwritten* (2015), came out when he was sixteen years old and still in high school. The album had twelve songs, including "Life of the Party," and some of them became major hits. "Something Big" was released as a single before the album came out, and was followed by the single "Stitches." Other noteworthy songs included "Air" and "I Don't Even Know Your Name." The album debuted at number one in both the United States and Canada. "The thrill for smitten admirers is that Mendes seems to be singing straight to their ears," wrote Carl Wilson in a review for *Billboard* (11 Apr. 2015), "either snuggling up for pillow talk or falling pleadingly to his knees, as generously cheek-boned crooners have done since the days of Rudy Vallee and Paul Anka (two other teen idols with Canadian backgrounds). The drawback for other listeners, particularly grown-up ones, is that there's not much else to hear." Wilson wrote that the album is somewhat hit-and-miss, though it does have "confident hooks" on singles such as "Life of the Party" and "Stitches," on which "big dynamics make the syrup go down smoothly." Writing for *AllMusic*, Thomas Erlewine offered a harsher assessment. He called the album "pretty thin gruel," adding that the songs often "feel like a laboratory-generated fusion of Jason Mraz's singsong loverman schtick and Ryan Tedder's icy adult contemporary." The main issue, in Erlewine's view, was that Mendes was still stuck in his Vine phase, not able to hold a listener's attention for more than a few seconds. But mixed reviews did not keep the album from soaring in the charts.

ILLUMINATE

Mendes's second album, *Illuminate* (2016), would go on to win over even some critics who had dismissed him earlier as little more than a Vine sensation. For one, by the time his first album was released, Mendes had mostly stopped posting on Vine, and he also decided to expand his reach, aiming not just for teens, primarily teenage girls, but also adults. When the album came out, in the fall of 2016, he was eighteen years old. He was getting older and wanted to be taken more seriously. Coscarelli observed that Mendes had taken a page from the playbook of both Ed Sheeran and John Mayer. Whereas some artists try to avoid explicitly citing their inspirations, wrote Coscarelli, Mendes openly admitted that Sheeran and Mayer are both strong influences, and both, "serve as his big-brother figures in the industry."

The songs on the second album were more mature. One track, "Bad Reputation," is about a girl who is made to feel ashamed of her sexuality; but Mendes, still the good-hearted guy, sings that others don't know what she has been through, but "I could be the one to treat you like a lady." The second single from the album, "Ruin," a bluesy bedroom number, sounded more adult than anything on Mendes's first album. The song "Lights On" is a song about sex, in which Mendes promises to keep the lights on and "keep you up all night long." For Mendes, this transition and maturity was logical. "I'm releasing a song about sex at 18, which is appropriate," he told Coscarelli. "I wouldn't have done it if I were 16 or 17. I'll release a song about drinking at 21, you know what I mean?"

Writing for *Rolling Stone* (23 Sept. 2016), Joe Levy wrote that the songs on the album are "at once as disarmingly intimate as a singer-songwriter confession and as layered with melodic and rhythmic bait as a Major Lazer single." Levy added that the album "mixes professions of romantic agony like 'Mercy' (where a quietly hummed hook explodes into crashing drums), with nice-boy valentines like 'Treat You Better' and bedroom come ons like 'Lights On.'" Even Thomas Erlewine of *AllMusic*, who had essentially dismissed Mendes's first album, observed that *Illuminate* was better both musically and lyrically. He pointed out that the singer's "wide-eyed puppy dog routine is the key to Mendes's appeal. He's not forceful, and whenever he slides into a loverman routine, there's never a sense that he's a player: his voice is so small and sweet, it feels as if he's whispering sweet nothings to his high school sweetheart." The album, wrote Erlewine, is a coherent collection of songs, because Mendes has "gelled into his pop persona; he's charming because he embraces his ordinariness." In other words, Mendes is a regular nice guy, and he embraces it fully. And like his first album, *Illuminate* hit number one on the Billboard 200 Chart.

SUGGESTED READING

Coscarelli, Joe. "Shawn Mendes, Pop Idol, Is Not Banking on a Gimmick." *New York Times*, 20 Sept. 2016, www.nytimes.com/2016/09/21/arts/music/shawn-mendes-illuminate-interview.html. Accessed 16 Feb. 2017.

Haithcoat, Rebecca. "Shawn Mendes Brings Back Hunky, Guitar-Strumming Sensitivity." *Billboard*, 25 Aug. 2016, www.billboard.com/articles/news/7486993/shawn-mendes-illuminate-billboard-cover-story. Accessed 16 Feb. 2017.

Ranscombe, Siân. "Shawn Mendes: How a Six-Second Video Launched the Next Justin Bieber." *The Telegraph*, 16 Jan. 2015, www.telegraph.co.uk/culture/music/11340960/Shawn-Mendes-How-a-six-second-video-launched-the-next-Justin-Bieber.html. Accessed 16 Feb. 2017.

SELECTED WORKS

The Shawn Mendes EP, 2014; *Handwritten*, 2015; *Illuminate*, 2016

—*Dmitry Kiper*

Chrissy Metz

Date of birth: September 29, 1980
Occupation: Actor

Chrissy Metz has become well known to television audiences for her role in the hit NBC drama *This Is Us*, which follows the members of a family as they negotiate sibling relationships, romantic attachments, career woes, parental problems, and more. Metz portrays Kate, a woman who meets her love interest at a support group for overeaters. "*This Is Us* belongs to a genre that used to be more common on big-network TV: cry-time dramas, those heart-on-sleeve series about ordinary people with ordinary problems," James Poniewozik wrote about the show for the *New York Times* (19 Sept. 2016). Commenting on Metz's role within the series, which is helmed by Dan Fogelman, Poniewozik continued, "It's refreshing to see a broadcast series spotlight an overweight character who's not a sitcom dad with a hot wife, but Kate is characterized almost wholly in terms of her weight." Metz, who struggled for years to find suitable roles, told Maria Cavassuto for *Variety* (14 Sept. 2016), "So many people are defined by a number. If there was going to be a pioneer of the plus-size girl of my shape on TV, why not me? We're not defined by our weight or what we wear but this is a very poignant story that needs to be told."

Now instantly recognizable thanks to the immense popularity of the show and the press attention that came with her nomination for a 2017 Golden Globe Award, Metz is often

Photo by Alberto E. Rodriguez/Getty Images

approached on the street by women grateful for her relatable portrayal of the character. "I hope they take away that no matter what we're all contending with—whether it's a weight issue, a self-esteem issue—it's never too late to do what it is that you know in your heart what you should be doing," she asserted to Jessica Radloff for *Glamour* (20 Sept. 2016). "At the end of the day we all want to be loved."

EARLY LIFE AND EDUCATION

Metz was born on September 29, 1980, in Homestead, Florida. She spent her earliest years in Japan, where her father, a Navy officer, was stationed. Her parents divorced when she was eight years old, and her mother, Denise, raised Metz and her older brother, Phil, and older sister, Monica, on her own back in Florida. Money was often in short supply, and her mother's electricity was cut off for nonpayment on occasion. Metz, who was heavy even as a young child, has recalled that her mother sometimes gave up her own dinner to ensure that the children had enough to eat. "In retrospect I think that's why food equals love in my family," she told Alex Morris for *Glamour* (1 Feb. 2017). "It's the way we showed love—my grandmother would make me a grilled cheese sandwich every time she'd pick me up from school. I really valued that attention."

Metz's mother ultimately remarried—she has two half-sisters—but money remained tight even then. Once, Metz has said, a friend offered her a small Keds label to glue onto her off-brand sneakers to fool their status-conscious classmates. In addition to her lack of trendy clothes, her weight made her the target of class bullies. "I remember being at Weight Watchers at, like, eleven years old and my mom just trying to figure it out for me," she told Lanford Beard for *People* (26 Oct. 2016). "It's one of those things where it's heartbreaking because, as a parent, you want your child to have the best life possible and you want them to be protected and in this little bubble where everybody finds them to be beautiful and perfect and their lives to be amazing. But that's not always the case."

Growing up, Metz enjoyed roller-skating and biking, and she found great solace in comedy, gradually gaining a reputation as a class clown. She toyed with the idea of acting after high school but had no idea how to go about breaking into the field. One day, she accompanied her sister to a casting call, held at a small Holiday Inn in Gainesville. There, a woman encouraged her to audition herself. Metz, who had sung in the school's chamber choir, performed Christina Aguilera's "Beautiful" and was contacted the next day by her soon-to-be manager, who encouraged her to pursue a career in the arts. (Her sister was offered a modeling contract.)

EARLY CAREER

Metz, at that point attending community college and teaching preschool, drove cross-country with a group of other girls to California. "Some young women and I caravanned all the way from Florida, then lived in a two-bedroom apartment, three of us to each room, in Burbank," she recalled to Morris. "We were all on a budget—we spent nights playing Uno in our living room—but most of the other kids' parents were footing their bills." Metz's stepfather chipped in for car insurance, but she felt she could not ask him for more, given his own financial constraints, so she supported herself by working as a nanny or doing other odd jobs. That first year, she had few auditions and, by her own admission, spent much of her time in tears.

While Metz eventually found work at a Hollywood talent agency, scheduling auditions for other actors "was like watching your boyfriend take out another woman every single day," as she told Margaret Wappler for *Harper's Bazaar* (13 Mar. 2017). She began engaging in stress-eating, binging on the baked goods brought in by actors seeking to curry favor with the agents.

Occasionally, Metz found an acting job, but most were small bit parts. In 2005, for example, she appeared in an episode of *Entourage*, whose credits listed her as simply "Counter Girl," and three years later she won a role in an episode of *My Name Is Earl*, playing a character called Chunk. Her first major recurring role came in 2014, when she was cast to portray Ima "Barbara" Wiggles, the fat woman in a carnival freak show, on the FX anthology series *American Horror Story*. Although she thought the part would provide an effective launch pad for her career, once the season had wrapped, she received few other calls. Dispirited, she prepared to move back to Florida. Her mother encouraged her to tough it out, however. "[She] said, 'You can either be miserable here and not pursue your dreams, or you can be miserable in L.A. and at least pursue what you want,'" Metz recalled to Morris.

Deciding to follow that maternal advice, Metz lived on ramen noodles and racked up credit card debt in order to stay in Los Angeles. Though she had the support of friends, at one point, she had just eighty-one cents in her bank account.

THIS IS US

It was at that low point that Metz read the script for *This Is Us*. "I remember reading the breakdown and thinking, 'I want this. This is me,'" she told Radloff. With the same small group of plus-size actors who were at every audition she attended, she steeled herself for rejection despite her conviction that she was perfect for the role of Kate.

The casting directors agreed with Metz's assessment, however, and she got the part. In 2016,

This Is Us premiered on NBC with an ensemble cast that included Milo Ventimiglia (as Kate's father), Mandy Moore (as her mother), Sterling K. Brown (as her adopted brother), Justin Hartley (as her twin brother), Susan Kelechi Watson (as her sister-in-law), Chris Sullivan (as her love interest), and Ron Cephas Jones (as her adopted brother's long-lost biological father).

The show struck an immediate chord with audiences, and although some reviewers carped at the saccharine nature of portions of the plotlines—the headline of Poniewozik's review is "*This Is Us* Is Skillful, Shameless Tear-Jerking"—all recognized the appeal to viewers who missed the heartwarming family dramas of years past. In a review echoed by many, Molly Eichel wrote for the *AV Club* (15 Mar. 2017), "I tuned in because I wanted to feel, and I didn't want ambiguity of those feelings. I wanted a simple emotional outlet, and *This Is Us* provided that fabulously. This first season wasn't great TV, but I don't think I want *This Is Us* to be great TV. Here are my heartstrings. Tug away."

Metz used her first paychecks to clear up her debts, and while she has told interviewers that she very much wanted to purchase a washer and dryer for her grandmother, the elderly woman passed away before she could do so. "I've had women—average women, older women, teenagers—who say to me, 'Your role and this show has changed my life,'" she told Morris. "That makes all the struggle, all the ramen noodles, all the times when I couldn't pay my bills, all the times where I was like, 'I can't do this,' worth it." Among the most buzzed-about scenes of the series is one in which Kate, clad only in underwear, steps onto a scale. "It was super liberating and very scary initially, but then I thought, 'It's not a secret that I'm a plus-size woman,'" Metz recalled to Radloff. "'How much more real could we get from exposing her mentally, emotionally, and now physically?'"

Despite suffering a knee injury, Metz attended the Golden Globes ceremony in January 2017 as she had been nominated for best performance by an actress in a supporting role in a series, limited series, or motion picture made for television, a moment that she expressed in interviews that she had always dreamed of. Her next high-profile project, the feature film *Sierra Burgess Is a Loser*, was in postproduction as of the summer of 2017 and is scheduled for release in 2018.

PERSONAL LIFE

Metz was married for several years to screenwriter Martyn Eaden; their marriage ended in divorce. She met her boyfriend, Josh Stancil, a cameraman, on the set of *This Is Us*. An avid reader and music lover, she hopes one day to make both an autobiographical film and an album. She also looks forward to the day when her weight does not dominate every conversation.

"I'm just happy to be doing what I do, and if I inspire people and bring hope it's only more reason to do this," she told Barbara J. King for NPR (10 Nov. 2016). "It will be exciting to talk about things other than my weight. I'm an actress and a human being."

SUGGESTED READING

Beard, Lanford. "*This Is Us* Star Chrissy Metz: I Was in Weight Watchers When I Was 11." *People*, 26 Oct. 2016, people.com/bodies/this-is-us-chrissy-metz-weight-watchers-age-11/. Accessed 15 Aug. 2017.

Cavassuto, Maria. "*This Is Us* Actress Chrissy Metz on Her Plus-Sized Role: This Is a 'Story That Needs to Be Told.'" *Variety*, 14 Sept. 2016, variety.com/2016/tv/news/this-is-us-chrissy-metz-sterling-k-brown-mandy-moore-1201860347/. Accessed 15 Aug. 2017.

Eichel, Molly. "*This Is Us* Ends Its Solid First Season with an Episode That Disappoints." *AV Club*, 15 Mar. 2017, www.avclub.com/tvclub/us-ends-its-solid-first-season-episode-disappoints-252098. Accessed 15 Aug. 2017.

King, Barbara J. "Authenticity, Weight and Character Portrayals in TV's *This Is Us*." *NPR*, 10 Nov. 2016, www.npr.org/sections/13.7/2016/11/10/501541437/authenticity-weight-and-character-portrayals-in-tvs-this-is-us. Accessed 15 Aug. 2017.

Metz, Chrissy. "Chrissy Metz: 'When I Booked *This Is Us*, I Had 81 Cents in My Bank Account.'" Interview by Alex Morris. *Glamour*, 1 Feb. 2017, www.glamour.com/story/this-is-us-chrissy-metz-always-be-grateful. Accessed 15 Aug. 2017.

Metz, Chrissy. "*This Is Us* Star Chrissy Metz Talks Plus-Size Labels: 'I'm So Much More Than the Weight I Carry on My Body.'" Interview by Jessica Radloff. *Glamour*, 20 Sept. 2016, www.glamour.com/story/this-is-us-star-chrissy-metz-talks-plus-size-labels. Accessed 15 Aug. 2017.

Poniewozik, James. "*This Is Us* Is Skillful, Shameless Tear-Jerking." Review of *This Is Us*, created by Dan Fogelman. *The New York Times*, 19 Sept. 2016, www.nytimes.com/2016/09/20/arts/television/review-this-is-us-is-skillful-shameless-tear-jerking.html. Accessed 15 Aug. 2017.

SELECTED WORKS

My Name Is Earl, 2008; *American Horror Story*, 2014–15; *This Is Us*, 2016–

—*Mari Rich*

Von Miller

Date of birth: March 26, 1989
Occupation: Football player

On July 15, 2016, when linebacker Von Miller signed a $114.5 million contract with the Denver Broncos that included $70 million in guaranteed money, he became the highest-paid defensive player in National Football League (NFL) history. The signing received particular attention in the sports press as previously only star quarterbacks had received such lucrative NFL contracts. Miller began attracting attention during his college days at Texas A&M, where he earned the Butkus Award as the best college linebacker in the country. That attention continued after he was tapped by the Broncos as the second overall draft pick in 2011, and it reached a fever pitch when his Broncos defeated the Carolina Panthers in Super Bowl 50 in 2016.

Miller was named Super Bowl MVP at the close of the season and subsequently enjoyed a "whirlwind off-season, the six months that vaulted him from elite football star to the mainstream," as Greg Bishop wrote for *Yahoo Sports* (16 Aug. 2016). He furthered his position in the public eye with appearances on national television programs, including as a contestant on the popular competition *Dancing with the Stars*. Not all of the attention on Miller has been positive, however. Personal problems, a failed drug test, and an arrest for missing a court appearance over traffic charges combined with injuries to derail his career and caused him to miss the Broncos' Super Bowl push in 2013. Recalling those dark days and the process of redeeming himself, Miller told Jenny Vrentas for the *MMQB*, a *Sports Illustrated*-affiliated blog (8 Feb. 2016), "I didn't want to be injured. I didn't want to be a guy who was getting in trouble. I just wanted to be great. I wanted to be the player this organization brought me in to be."

EARLY YEARS

Von B'Vsean Miller was born on March 26, 1989, in Dallas, Texas. He and his younger brother were raised in the Dallas suburb of DeSoto by their parents, Von and Gloria, who operated a variety of business ventures to support the family. Both his parents were former college athletes, and physical ability and competitive drive were passed down to Miller.

Miller's father forbade him from playing football until he had fully matured physically, but Gloria gave in to her son's entreaties and signed him up for a pee-wee team when he was in fifth grade. The two hid that fact from Von Sr., stashing the needed equipment in the back of Gloria's SUV and laundering soiled jerseys only when he was out of the house. One day, however, Miller's father decided to clean the car, and

Wesley Hitt/Getty Images

when he opened the rear door, knee pads, helmets, and other equipment tumbled out, making it clear that his son had defied his edict. "By then, quite honestly, he was entrenched," Von Sr. told Andrew Lawrence for *Sports Illustrated* (18 Apr. 2011). "I wasn't gonna take football away from him."

As a teen, Miller, who was known for his love of practical jokes in addition to his athletic prowess, participated in track-and-field activities and played football for the DeSoto High School Eagles. By his junior year he had emerged as a star, and as a senior he only improved, helping his team into the notoriously competitive state playoffs. When it came time to choose a college, Miller fielded offers from such schools as the University of Oklahoma (whose team is known as the Sooners), the University of Florida (the Gators), and the University of Mississippi, affectionately known as Ole Miss (the Rebels). The most attractive offer, however, came from Texas A&M University and its much-lauded football team, the Aggies.

COLLEGE CAREER

Miller entered Texas A&M in 2007 and found immediate success. The editors of the *Sporting News* named him to the Freshman All-Big 12 team after he recorded 22 tackles—10 on his own—and 2 sacks. His performance on the field was far better than his work in the classroom, however. His dismal academic record and poor attitude caused head coach Mike Sherman, newly hired for Miller's sophomore season, to suspend him indefinitely in the spring of 2008. Miller considered transferring to a different school, but his father encouraged him to remain at Texas A&M and listen to his coach's advice. Finally, Sherman's message got through to the talented player. "He kept telling me, 'You can't live double lives,'" Miller recalled to Lawrence. "Once I cleaned up off the field, football became a lot easier."

Reinstated to the team, Miller was assigned to be weakside linebacker (the member of a standard, three-person defensive crew who serves as a pass defender when needed). That season he posted 44 tackles, 25 of which were solo stops, and led the team with 3.5 sacks. As a junior he was given another positional shift, acting as both a defensive end and linebacker. That season his 17 sacks led the nation in sacks, and his 21 tackles for loss were the fifth-most in college football. Following that performance, he was named a first-team All-American by *Sporting News* and *Sports Illustrated*, becoming the first Aggie to have that honor since 1999.

Miller toyed with the idea of turning pro before his senior year but found that he was beginning to enjoy school, thanks in large part to a class he had signed up for only because it had seemed like an easy A. The class—in poultry farming—was more engaging than Miller had imagined, and poultry science became a real passion for him. He was especially fascinated by the field trips to farms and hatcheries, and he soon purchased his own chickens and launched a small-scale egg-producing venture. During his senior year Miller made first-team All-Big 12 and All-American honors and received the coveted Butkus Award, given to the nation's top college linebacker. He was invited to play in the Senior Bowl, a postseason all-star game that features the best NFL Draft prospects, and was named the game's MVP.

Following his college success, Miller was predicted to be a top-five draft choice. Before the draft, however, in March 2011, he was tapped by the NFL Players Association to participate in a lawsuit against the NFL. The group of plaintiffs, which included superstars like Tom Brady and Peyton Manning, sought a high-profile rookie like Miller to join their antitrust claims against the league. Out of respect for his fellow players, he accepted a place in the lawsuit. Miller was thus "in the unusual position of suing his potential employers, something NFL teams might hold against him if he weren't the best pass rusher coming out of college this year," as Lawrence wrote. When team owners and the Players Association could not come to a consensus on a new collective bargaining agreement, a lockout ensued, ending just prior to the start of the 2011 regular season.

JOINING THE BRONCOS

Despite his active role in the lawsuit, Miller's talents were too apparent for NFL teams to ignore.

He was picked second overall in the 2011 draft, taken by the Denver Broncos. He became the Aggies' highest draft pick since 1992 and the highest selected linebacker since 2000.

During his first season with the Broncos, Miller was named an AFC Defensive Player of the Week. Selected to the 2012 Pro Bowl and named AP Defensive Rookie of the Year, he posted 11.5 sacks, 19 quarterback hits, and 29 quarterback hurries. His aggressive play also led to numerous fines for dangerous hits and other offenses, however. That pattern continued during his sophomore pro season, as his statistics continued to improve. He was fined $21,000 for one hit on quarterback Cam Newton of the Carolina Panthers, for example, but was nonetheless named first team All-Pro and finished in second place for defensive player of the year honors.

The 2013 season, however, proved to be challenging for Miller on many levels. He was suspended for six games for allegedly trying to cheat on a drug test (charges he denied). Then, after being reinstated, he tore his anterior cruciate ligament (ACL) in a December game, prematurely ending his season. He could only watch from the sidelines as the Broncos lost Super Bowl XLVIII to the Seattle Seahawks. There was also trouble for Miller outside of football: in August 2013 he was arrested on a failure-to-appear warrant for driving-related charges, and the following month he was cited for speeding and driving with a suspended license.

As he had done back at Texas A&M, Miller vowed to turn things around. "Every guy that's up here has had to deal with adversity and had second thoughts," Miller said to Benjamin Hoffman for the *New York Times* (7 Feb. 2016). He succeeded once again, deleting all his social media accounts so he could focus on the game, having long talks with his father about his professional goals, and putting in maximum effort on the field. "Those were my finest hours getting back right and grinding and getting back with my teammates and becoming the Von I am today," Miller told Hoffman.

SUPER BOWL MVP

Miller recovered from his injury to play all sixteen regular-season games in 2014, posting strong numbers with 14 sacks, 48 tackles, and 18 assists. Denver went 12–4 to win the AFC West division, but lost to the Indianapolis Colts in the first round of the playoffs.

While Miller had already proven himself as a game-changing player, 2015 proved to be his true breakout season. On September 17 of that year he became one of the fastest players in NFL history to hit 50 sacks. Miller's personal statistics for the regular season were solid but not outstanding, but it was his postseason performance that stood out. The Broncos again finished 12–4, but this time beat the Pittsburgh Steelers in the first playoff round and faced the New England Patriots in the AFC Championship. In that game, Miller's 2.5 sacks of New England quarterback Tom Brady set a new Broncos playoff record and helped Denver win 20–18.

Advancing to Super Bowl 50, the Broncos relied on Miller's strong defense against the heavily favored Carolina Panthers, who behind Newton had the NFL's top offense. Thanks in large part to Miller's 6 tackles, 2.5 sacks, 2 forced fumbles, and 2 quarterback hurries, Denver contained the Panthers' attack and won 24–10. Named Super Bowl MVP, Miller set out on an offseason that broadened his profile beyond the world of football. His story of perseverance—and his flair for style—brought him attention including national television appearances and a visit to the White House. Perhaps most notably, he appeared as a contestant on the reality show *Dancing with the Stars* in 2016, finishing in eighth place.

With Miller's demonstrated talent, relative youth, and approaching free agency, much speculation surrounded his contract negotiations. Tensions rose between player and organization as Miller rejected what he felt were low offers on an extension with the Broncos. As many pundits noted, his playoff and Super Bowl success drove his value up greatly, and signings by other players shaped the market as the Broncos sought to retain their star. Finally, in February 2016 Denver placed an exclusive franchise tag on Miller, and in mid-July he signed a six-year deal with the team worth $114.5 million, with $70 million guaranteed. He thus became the highest paid defensive player in NFL history, with the highest amount of guaranteed salary of any non-quarterback player.

PERSONAL LIFE

In 2013, Miller, who is known for sporting stylish eyeglasses, created the nonprofit Von's Vision to provide Denver-area youngsters with free eye exams and glasses. Miller's sense of style also extends to his footwear, and he became known for wearing a wide variety of unconventional cleats and sneakers, including pairs decorated with rooster feathers (in homage to his chicken farming) or optometrists' eye charts (to draw attention to his charity). Miller has also signed endorsement deals with numerous companies, including Microsoft, Beats by Dre, Adidas, and Old Spice.

SUGGESTED READING

Bishop, Greg. "Von Miller's Whirlwind Summer as the NFL's Busiest, Most Interesting Man." *Yahoo Sports*, 16 Aug. 2016, sports.yahoo.com/news/von-millers-whirlwind-summer-nfls-132943493.html. Accessed 4 Jan. 2017.

Hoffman, Benjamin. "Von Miller Recounts Adversity." *New York Times*, 7 Feb. 2016, www.nytimes.com/live/super-bowl-50/von-miller-recounts-adversity-that-could-have-derailed-his-career. Accessed 4 Jan. 2017.

Lawrence, Andrew. "Locked Out And Loaded." *Sports Illustrated*, 18 Apr. 2011, www.si.com/vault/2011/04/18/106057671/locked-out-and-loaded. Accessed 4 Jan. 2017.

Stephens, Mitch. "Von Miller Cherishes Dallas Roots Heading into NFL Draft." *MaxPreps*, 28 Apr. 2011, www.maxpreps.com/news/vJsL-gnF7EeCkhgAcxJSkrA/von-miller-cherishes-dallas-roots-heading-into-nfl-draft.htm. Accessed 4 Jan. 2017.

Su, Caleb. "Von Miller on the One NFL Rule He Wants to See Changed and His Affinity for Custom Cleats." *Complex*, 15 Dec. 2016, www.complex.com/sports/2016/12/von-miller-nfl-rule-custom-cleats. Accessed 4 Jan. 2017.

Vrentas, Jenny. "From the Depths, Von Miller Reaches the Top." *MMQB*, Time, 8 Feb. 2016, mmqb.si.com/mmqb/2016/02/08/nfl-super-bowl-50-von-miller-mvp. Accessed 4 Jan. 2017.

—*Mari Rich*

MØ

Date of birth: August 13, 1988
Occupation: Singer

The Danish singer MØ (pronounced "mu") has had major worldwide success by combining the attitude of punk and grunge with the feel of contemporary soul and R & B and the manic energy of electronic music. She first hit it big with the singles "Pilgrim" and "XXX 88" in 2013 and "Don't Wanna Dance" and "Walk This Way" in 2014. She would later go on to have hits with Major Lazer's songs "Lean On" (2015)—which, for a time, was Spotify's most streamed song of all time—and "Cold Water" (2016), as well as with her own single "Final Song" (2016). "There's something a little different about Mø, compared to most artists featured on songs with a billion views," Owen Myers wrote in a profile of her for the *Fader* (13 May 2016), referring to the record-breaking view count of "Lean On." "You can feel it when she dances, the way she throws her limbs around and finds power in the fists, not the hips. . . . Behind the sheen and sparkle of her songs, there's a young woman who once lived in an anarchist commune and started her career screaming songs with titles like 'P—— in Your Face.'"

FROM SPICE GIRLS TO SONIC YOUTH

MØ was born Karen Marie Aagaard Ørsted on August 13, 1988, to parents Mette Ørsted, a

Photo by Noam Galai/WireImage

teacher, and Frans Ørsted, a psychologist. She was raised in the small town of Ejlstrup, on the Danish island of Funen. When she was young she liked sugary, cheerful pop music, particularly that of the Spice Girls, whom she has said in interviews inspired her to want to be a pop star and to try writing songs. Once, after taking some piano lessons, she convinced her friends to form a band, under her direction, and to stay after school with her and practice. "It was mainly me writing a song, and then we would make a dance for it," she recalled to Myers. "We each had our own part to sing, like All Saints and Spice Girls. I was very ambitious in my dream of being a pop star."

When Ørsted was thirteen, her older brother, Kaspar, introduced her to the punk band Black Flag and noise-rock group Sonic Youth. She was particularly enthralled by Sonic Youth bassist Kim Gordon, who found musical success without playing up to conventional standards of beauty. "It spoke to me so much, because I was not a pretty girl at all," Ørsted said to Myers. "No boys would look at me. So I was like, 'You can be f—— successful and badass and be yourself, no matter who you are.' To me, secretly wanting to be a pop star, that was really nice for me to know: that there are other ways. You don't have to be Mariah Carey." She began listening to other rock groups, such as Nirvana, the Smashing Pumpkins, the Yeah Yeah Yeahs, Mudhoney, and Guns N' Roses, and became involved with the scene at a punk café in Odense, a city just outside of Ejlstrup. Her musical world widened, and with it her political awareness; she began attending activist meetings at the café, including a feminist

group for which she designed T-shirts with body-positive slogans. "I really felt like I started getting my identity," she said to Myers. At age of seventeen, she and her friend Josefine Struckmann Pedersen formed an electronic punk duo called MOR, which is Danish for "mother."

MOR TO MØ

For five years, Ørsted and Pedersen toured as MOR, playing political songs at small venues throughout Europe. They recorded two singles on the computer music program GarageBand, and released those singles in 2009 via Mastermind Records, a Danish record label. It was also in 2009 that Ørsted, then attending art school, began to develop her "alter ego" MØ, originally by experimenting with rapping. "Everybody thought I was crazy," she recalled to Sander Amendt for *Electronic Beats* magazine (24 June 2014). "But the fact that I could think and act conceptually liberated me. It has an ironic edge to it so that I called it MØ, which means 'virgin' in Danish. I liked the idea that my alter ego had a bizarre name and was constantly agitating. It wasn't about letting off emotional steam anymore. Everything had changed."

In 2012 Ørsted and Pedersen got internships with former Le Tigre member J. D. Samson in New York, working for Samson's art-and-music collective MEN, mainly in promotion and marketing. In addition to gaining valuable experience, they took advantage of the opportunity to play at house parties and underground venues in Brooklyn.

After completing her internship, Ørsted returned to Denmark, where she moved into an anarchist communal house in Copenhagen. She decided to pursue a solo music career, inspired by female electronic musicians such as Peaches (whose music incorporates aspects of performance art) and Uffie (whose pop music melds electronic and rap), and began writing new songs and recording them on her laptop computer. Many of the songs had provocative, sexually themed titles, such as "Grease Me Up with Gravy Baby" and "A Piece of Music to F—— To." She began performing under the name MØ (which, in addition to meaning "virgin" or "maiden," was chosen to represent Ørsted's middle and last names), for the first time, bringing her art-school persona into the punk clubs of Copenhagen. "I tried to provoke as much as possible," she recalled to Myers. "For me it was a super political thing about youth culture gone wild, so I was putting on this alter ego as a crazy, insane, young bitch girl. I think people were like, 'Are you being for real? Do you smoke crack?' It also sounded like crap. But it was a time."

Still, Ørsted drew the attention of award-winning music producer Ronni Vindahl—not for her deliberately provocative, rap-inflected songs, but rather for a stripped-down composition titled

"Maiden" that offered a glimpse of the vulnerability behind her punk persona. "[Vindahl] always liked me, but he never liked my sick raps," she said to Amendt. "When he noticed that I had started singing he immediately asked me if I could record some vocals for him. He then produced some music around it, and we called the track 'Maiden.'" Of the song, Ørsted said to Jim Easterhouse for the *Los Angeles Times* (6 June 2014), "'Maiden' . . . was the first time in a long time that I was very personal and vulnerable, but still having the aggression without crunk rapping, or hiding behind a filter." It would later be released as a B-side to "Pilgrim," the second single from MØ's debut studio album.

NO MYTHOLOGIES TO FOLLOW

The year 2013 was a good one for Ørsted. She signed a record deal with the record label RCA, which led to the release of her extended-play album (EP) *Bikini Daze* in October 2013. The EP consisted of four songs, including "Never Wanna Know" and "XXX 88," both of which would later appear on her debut full-length album. Also in 2013, Ørsted released two singles from her upcoming debut, "Glass" and "Pilgrim," and appeared in the electro-pop song "Dear Boy" by Avicii, which did a lot to boost her popularity. Finally, in the spring of the following year, she released her debut album, *No Mythologies to Follow* (2014).

The album was both critically and commercially successful, receiving overall positive reviews and peaking at number two on the Hitlisten (Danish record chart), number eleven on the Australian Recording Industry Association (ARIA) Hitseekers albums chart, and number fifty-eight on the UK Albums Chart, among others. Music critic Renato Pagnani wrote for *Pitchfork* (7 Mar. 2014) that the album "finds MØ . . . ditching shock-rap for more mature but no less immediate electro-pop that explores the swirling confusion of young adulthood. Its sound is one that's equally as indebted to the forward-thinking Scandinavian pop scene she comes from as it is to the sounds of Southern rap and modern bass music." He concluded, "Although it makes no apologies for the bits and pieces it takes from her contemporaries, *No Mythologies to Follow* doesn't work because it assembles the right ingredients in the right amount—it works because a likable persona is something you just can't teach."

COLLABORATIONS

Later in 2014, while on tour in North America, Ørsted received an offer that had the potential to greatly increase her popularity: she was asked to sing on Iggy Azalea's song "Beg for It," from her forthcoming album *Reclassified* (2014). She later told Myers that she was uncertain about taking part in a song she "wasn't a part of emotionally,

artistically, or creatively," but that it seemed to be a logical career move. When the two debuted the single on an October episode of *Saturday Night Live*, however, Ørsted looked lost and uncomfortable, and her vocal timing was off. She explained the next day on Twitter that technical difficulties with her equipment had caused "latency" (delay) on her vocals, which confused her and threw her off. "I looked lost, and I sang like I was lost, and that was it. . . . I was like, 'This is the end of my career,'" she recalled to Myers. "But . . . you just gotta get on that damn horse." And she did.

Ørsted had collaborated with electronic music trio Major Lazer, of which Diplo was a founding member, on writing the latter's song "All My Love." Released in November 2014 and featuring vocalist Ariana Grande, the song was a commercial success, peaking at number fifteen on the Billboard Dance/Electronic Songs chart and appearing on the *Hunger Games: Mockingjay—Part 1* (2014) soundtrack. But it was Ørsted's next collaboration with the group that would rocket her to mainstream success.

"LEAN ON"

In March 2015, Major Lazer released their single "Lean On," cowritten by Ørsted, Diplo, and French producer DJ Snake and featuring Ørsted's vocals. Diplo (real name Thomas Pentz) had originally offered a slower, reggae version of the song to musicians Rihanna and Nicki Minaj, but when both declined, the song was rewritten and recorded with Ørsted instead. Diplo later said to Nolan Feeney for *Time* (19 Aug. 2015) that the rejections from Rihanna and Minaj were "a blessing in disguise" and that Ørsted "sounds better than anybody was going to sound on that record."

Audiences agreed: "Lean On" peaked at number four on the Billboard Hot 100 chart, reached number two on the UK Singles Chart, and hit number one in multiple countries, including Australia, Ireland, Mexico, and New Zealand. In November 2015, the music-streaming service Spotify named "Lean On" as its most streamed song ever, with 526 million plays worldwide; by June 2017, that number had increased to over one billion. "Lean On" eventually lost the title of "most streamed song" to Drake's "One Dance" (2016), but this did not diminish the achievement, or the boost it gave to Ørsted's career. "I couldn't really analyze it until some time had passed. But now I've digested the whole thing, I can see it changed things for me, on many levels," Ørsted said to Nick Levine for New Music Express (*NME*) (12 May 2017). "Of course the media started to be more aware of me. But also, a lot of doors opened: people you want to work with are suddenly open to working with you. I mean, I've always dreamed about having a song that became a hit. But also, very importantly, it was a song I really loved and didn't compromise how I see myself as an artist."

Ørsted collaborated again with Major Lazer on their 2015 cover of Frank Ocean's song "Lost," and then again on 2016's "Cold Water," which also featured Justin Bieber. She was also featured on Cashmere Cat's song "9 (After Coachella)" (2017), a nod to the major music festival, along with Los Angeles–based DJ Sophie.

SECOND ALBUM

Ørsted capped off 2015 by performing at the Nobel Peace Prize Concert, held in December in Oslo, Norway. She had released "Kamikaze," the first single from her as-yet-unnamed second studio album, just two months earlier, and the completed album was expected to arrive sometime in 2016. Yet although Ørsted kept writing new songs, the projected release date kept being pushed back, with no official date announced. This was due partly to her busy touring schedule, which interfered with the work, and partly to Ørsted's determination to get the album right.

The issue was not a lack of material, but rather an uncertainty as to how she wanted her songwriting to evolve. "At the beginning of [2016], I wrote a lot of songs that I thought were great, but weren't so much 'me,'" Ørsted said to Will Richards for *DIY* magazine (4 Feb. 2016). She added, "To begin with I wanted to try out some very new things, and work in ways I never had before, but I realized that above anything else I had to be myself through it all. I had to be naked and honest and say what I wanted to say instead of trying to sound like something I thought was awesome but couldn't relate to." She discarded between five and ten of the songs she had written in the past year, which still left her with "thirty or forty songs" to choose from, she told Richards. "One of my problems as a songwriter sometimes is that I overcomplicate things," she admitted. "I'm going for simplicity. It's the hardest thing to make something simple though; it's got to be f—— brilliant if it's gonna last."

Still, as she continued to work, Ørsted continued to release singles for the upcoming album. After "Kamikaze" came "Final Song," in May 2016; "Drum," in October 2016; and "Nights with You," in April 2017. Of these, all were praised, but "Final Song" was the most successful, earning platinum certification in four countries (two of them double platinum) and gold certification in another four.

As of summer 2017, Ørsted's second album was expected to be released before the end of the year. "I needed it to be right, in the sound and the concept and everything," she said to Alexandra Pollard for *Nylon* (4 July 2017) of the repeated delays. "I'm such a f—— perfectionist when it comes to those things."

PERSONAL LIFE

Ørsted began dating Mads Damsgaard Kristiansen, cofounder and frontman of the music-duo-turned-collective Reptile Youth, in 2014. It was Kristiansen who encouraged Ørsted to try stage diving (jumping from the stage into the audience), something Reptile Youth was known for, when she expressed an interest. "Before [Kristiansen] was my boyfriend he was the one who was encouraging me and said, 'Hey, you have to do it!'" she recalled to Sarah Rowland for *Nylon* (27 May 2015). "I was telling him that I really wanted to stage dive like he did, because it's just so cool. It's the ultimate way of letting go when you're performing, to just throw yourself out there and not really know what's going to happen."

SUGGESTED READING

Easterhouse, Jim. "Danish Songstress MO Ready to Break Out in America." *Los Angeles Times*, 6 June 2014, www.latimes.com/entertainment/music/posts/la-et-ms-danish-singer-mo-20140606-story.html. Accessed 15 Sept. 2017.

Levine, Nick. "MØ: Where the Danish Popstar Went after Co-Writing the Biggest Song of All Time." *NME*, 12 May 2017, www.nme.com/blogs/nme-blogs/mo-interview-major-lazer-lean-on-2017-2069251. Accessed 15 Sept. 2017.

MØ. "Band Crush: MØ." Interview by Sarah Rowland. *Nylon*, 27 May 2015, nylon.com/articles/band-crush-mo. Accessed 15 Sept. 2017.

MØ. "'Society Waits for Nobody': Pop's Newest Outsider MØ Interviewed." Interview by Sander Amendt. *Electronic Beats*, 24 June 2014, /www.electronicbeats.net/society-waits-for-nobody-sander-amendt-talks-to-mo/. Accessed 15 Sept. 2017.

Myers, Owen. "How Mø Finessed Anarchist Punk Life into Global Pop Stardom." *The Fader*, 13 May 2016, www.thefader.com/2016/05/13/mo-interview-final-song-new-album. Accessed 15 Sept. 2017.

Pollard, Alexandra. "After One Track Launched Her into Music's Mainstream, MØ Is Ready for the Next Level." *Nylon*, 4 July 2017, nylon.com/articles/nylon-mo-june-july-2017. Accessed 15 Sept. 2017.

Richards, Will. "MØ: 'It's Gotta Be F—— Brilliant If It's Gonna Last." *DIY*, 4 Feb. 2016, diymag.com/2016/02/04/mø-interview-new-album. Accessed 15 Sept. 2017.

—*Michael Tillman*

Ottessa Moshfegh

Date of birth: May 1981
Occupation: Author

Ottessa Moshfegh has garnered several awards for her first two books and her many short stories. These honors include the Plimpton Prize for Fiction, a grant from the National Endowment for the Arts (NEA), and the Wallace Stegner Fellowship at Stanford University. In addition, her first book, the novella *McGlue*, received the Fence Modern Prize in Prose. Her first novel, *Eileen*, received a Hemingway/PEN Award for debut fiction, which carries a $25,000 prize and a residency from the Distinguished Visiting Writers Series of the University of Idaho's MFA creative writing program. *Eileen* was also named to the short lists for the National Book Critics Circle Award and the Man Booker Prize.

All of the attention does not faze her. "I don't care about being a literary personality—that doesn't appeal to me, especially because the literary world doesn't appeal to me. I actually don't feel like I even belong in it," she told Meredith Turits for *Vanity Fair* (17 Aug. 2015). "If this was high school, I would be sitting with the goths, looking at everyone, being like, *Whatever*." Moshfegh's works carry the sense of alienation that she herself experiences. As she told Sarah Gerard for *Hazlitt* magazine (2 July 2015), "I'm like an alien in a human body. I come from a different place, a different plane of existence. . . . I'm not comfortable with life on Earth. This life here feels really harsh and painful. It has felt like torture here a lot of the time."

CHILDHOOD AND EDUCATION

Moshfegh's father is from Iran. He met her mother, who is from Croatia, while they both attended a music program in Belgium. Her father is a violinist with large family land holdings in Iran; her mother is a viola player whose parents joined partisan armies to fight the Nazis during World War II.

Her parents settled in Iran, but left the country during the revolution that deposed the shah. Her mother left Tehran on the last airplane out of the country before the borders closed. She smuggled a small dog out as well, hiding her in her coat. After traveling to a few different countries, the family settled in Massachusetts, where Moshfegh was born and raised. Moshfegh has a sister and a brother.

By the age of seven, Moshfegh could play four musical instruments. For more than a decade she took piano lessons from a Russian woman named Valentina Lass until she graduated from high school. Of that time, she told Sasha Frere-Jones for *Los Angeles Times* (2 Nov. 2015), "My piano teacher growing up was probably the most important teacher I've ever had. . .

Tristan Fewings/Stringer/Getty Images

. In an indirect way, she taught me that art could be a container for my relationship with myself." In an interview with Nathan Martin for *Antenna* (2 Apr. 2013), she described Lass's influence on her writing: "The way she talked about the compositions I was learning, the characters, the innuendos, the ecstasy, all of that, influenced me profoundly. Seeing the divine order of a piece was heartbreaking and magical. That's what I want to do in my stories."

EARLY WRITINGS

Moshfegh's early writing, produced when she was a teenager, was influenced by her love of music and was more atmospheric and mood-expressive than narrative. She eventually stopped playing piano, realizing she would never be good enough to be a professional musician. At the same time, she grew to love writing more. "I learned that I enjoyed telling stories. And once I started to do that, the piano became very limiting," she told Frere-Jones.

As a child, she read whatever she pleased of the many books she found in her home. Her favorite writers then were James Baldwin and Richard Wright. In sixth grade she read writers such as Ray Bradbury, Herman Hesse, and Alice Walker. By the time she was twelve, she knew she wanted to be a writer.

Her parents separated when Moshfegh was in her late teens, but her family relationships remained positive. As Moshfegh told James Yu for *Iowa Review* (10 Aug. 2015), "I can't hide it [her work] from my family. They read it. They love me. They are all artists. They are amazing.

Sometimes I worry that something might hurt them, but they never let on if it does."

During her early twenties, Moshfegh lived for two years in China. She co-owned a bar in the city of Wuhan. As an English speaker, she was tapped to record English-language learning tapes, which she did for three months. Back in the United States, living and working in New York City, Moshfegh contracted cat scratch fever, a bacterial infection that kept her bedridden for more than a month. She had to quit her job and return to her mother's home. Migraines, seizures, and numbness in her hands prevented her from writing much. After recovering from her illness, she determined not to waste her life on jobs other than writing just to be able to afford to live in New York City.

While she was ill, she applied to Brown University and was accepted into the school's master of fine arts graduate writing program. As she told Carl Sekaras for *Gawker* (19 Aug. 2015), "I'd heard Brown had a reputation for being weird, and that sounded good. I went and it was like the universe gave me this ticket: 'Get busy writing.'"

MCGLUE

Moshfegh's first book, which won the 2013 Believer Book Award, is experimental in its structure. Moshfegh was inspired to write the novella after reading an article in a New England periodical from 1851 that detailed the story of a sailor imprisoned in a ship's hold for the murder of his best friend, an act he does not remember committing. She explained her process of writing to Lorin Stein for *BOMB* magazine (28 Oct. 2014), "I'd grown up in New England and could relate to McGlue's self-destructive rebellion in the face of all that Puritanical cold. Once I started working on the book, I could hear him rambling around in my brain, impatient and wild. I spent my writing-energy trying to squeeze that chaos down into prose."

One of Moshfegh's techniques during the writing process was to research what life was like in the United States during the mid-nineteenth century. Doing so provided the distraction she needed to get the story down correctly. She listens for the voices of her characters as she writes; as she told Stein, "Finding the voice has less to do with the imagination, and more to do with designation, like casting an actor in a movie. I ventriloquize the voices at first, but then they pretty much take over. That was particularly true in *McGlue*."

McGlue drinks to excess, as Moshfegh once did for five years, beginning when she was seventeen or eighteen. Ultimately she stopped because the physical pain of drinking grew too great; she attended Alcoholics Anonymous meetings for eight years.

FUNDING A CAREER

Moshfegh's writing has been made possible in large measure by the awards she has received. She considered this ironic, as she told Sekaras: "Being a writer, an artist, that's a calling. People don't seem to get that—there are industries built up for people for whom writing isn't a calling, so they can learn how to fake it. I'm not a fake, so being in institutions has always been unpleasant, although I couldn't have afforded to write without funding from a few schools." Moshfegh's stories were published in several literary magazines, including the prestigious literary journal *Paris Review*. One of those, "Bettering Myself," received the 2013 Plimpton Prize for Fiction.

In 2014 she was awarded a grant from the NEA, for her short stories. In her artist's statement for the NEA website, Moshfegh wrote, "Beyond just relieving me of a number of financial burdens, this grant has inspired me with courage and optimism. I had figured my values and interests as a writer were too peculiar to draw any sort of substantial readership. . . . Knowing that my fiction can find a place in this world brings a wonderful audaciousness to how I choose to live and write."

EILEEN

Despite her early success, Moshfegh was unsatisfied. As Paul Laity wrote in an article for *The Guardian* (16 Sept. 2016), "She is candid about *Eileen* being a deliberate exercise in playing with the format of commercial fiction to get the attention of a big publisher. *McGlue* and her early short stories might have won awards, but they didn't pay much." Moshfegh admitted to Laity that she "wanted to write a novel to start a career where I could live off publishing books. That was my prime motivation for writing *Eileen*."

Writing her first novel was also a challenge to herself. As she told Frere-Jones, "I discovered that I enjoyed the challenge of the long game—the psychic taunts and misshapen emotional crescendos involved in fooling myself and the world that something I pulled out of thin air could exist as an imaginary reality, complete and meaningful in some way."

She wrote the first draft in only two months and then put it away for six months before revising it, producing three subsequent drafts. The genesis of the novel was not the main character, Eileen, but the character of Lee Polk, who was based on a real person who had killed his abusive father and was serving a life sentence without the possibility of parole. That setting moved Moshfegh to write a novel that has been described as noir, mystery, thriller, and coming-of-age. It is told through dual perspectives—Eileen at twenty-four and as an older woman.

Eileen, whose story is told in flashbacks, is not an entirely likeable or trustworthy narrator. Moshfegh explained to Laity, "Eileen is a character that makes people uncomfortable. She is not going to, you know, cheer you up. But might it not be liberating to hear the thoughts of someone who is completely ignored by society?"

Scott Rudin, the producer behind such films as *The Social Network* (2010) and *The Grand Budapest Hotel* (2014), has optioned the book. Comparisons have been drawn to the work of Shirley Jackson and Flannery O'Connor, as well as to contemporary novels such as Gillian Flynn's *Gone Girl* (2012) and Paula Hawkins's *The Girl on the Train* (2015).

SHORT FICTION

Moshfegh returned to short stories after *Eileen*, writing new ones and supplementing them with previously published stories to form the 2017 collection *Homesick for Another World*. As she explained to Stein, after *McGlue* was published, "I began to write honestly from my own experiences for the first time and fell in love with the short story form, its elegance, power, divine beauty, all over again." She recalled reading "The Necklace," Guy de Maupassant's short story, in sixth grade and the impact it had on her.

For Moshfegh, novels touch her mind, but short stories touch her heart. They seem to her to be less contrived. "My novels aim to entertain and provoke and engross. My short stories don't have aims. Because of their brevity, I can allow them to bubble up organically, one cell splits into two, the story emerges. I have little to do with it. A novel requires way more forethought," she explained to Stein. "Novels require so much human tinkering. The author's fingerprints are all over the place. When I read a short story, a good one, the author disappears for me."

PERSONAL LIFE

Moshfegh has refused to allow an author photograph in her books. As she explained to Yu, "Our capitalistic structure would fall apart if women actually started loving the way they looked. Women are judged by appearance first." She has problems with her sight and cannot read more than twenty or thirty pages at a time. She favors black-and-white speckled composition books; she once wrote her stories in them, but no longer does. The more than twenty-five books she has filled are lists, notes, and feelings.

SUGGESTED READING

Frere-Jones, Sasha. "Ottessa Moshfegh on Becoming a Writer and Her Buzzed-About Novel, 'Eileen.'" *Los Angeles Times*, 2 Nov. 2015, www.latimes.com/books/jacketcopy/la-et-jc-ottessa-moshfegh-interview-20151102-story.html. Accessed 19 Dec. 2016.

Laity, Paul. "Ottessa Moshfegh Interview: Eileen Started Out as a Joke—Also I'm Broke, Also I Want to Be Famous." *The Guardian*, 16 Sept.

2016, www.theguardian.com/books/2016/sep/16/ottessa-moshfegh-interview-book-started-as-joke-man-booker-prize-shortlist. Accessed 19 Dec. 2016.

Moshfegh, Ottessa. "A Necessary Trauma." Interview by Carl Sekaras. *Gawker Review of Books*, 19 Aug. 2015, review.gawker.com/a-necessary-trauma-ottessa-moshfegh-on-eileen-and-risi-1724791494. Accessed 19 Dec. 2016.

Moshfegh, Ottessa. Interview by James Yu. *The Iowa Review*, 10 Aug. 2015, iowareview.org/blog/interview-ottessa-moshfegh. Accessed 19 Dec. 2016.

Moshfegh, Ottessa. "Voice, Vulnerability, and Putting the Intellect to Bed." Interview by Lorin Stein. *BOMB*, 28 Oct. 2014, bombmagazine.org/article/1000261/ottessa-moshfegh. Accessed 19 Dec. 2016.

Turits, Meredith. "Don't Google Ottessa Moshfegh." *Vanity Fair*, 17 Aug. 2015, www.vanityfair.com/culture/2015/08/ottessa-moshfegh-eileen-interview. Accessed 19 Dec. 2016.

SELECTED WORKS

McGlue, 2014; *Eileen*, 2015; *Homesick for Another World*, 2017

—*Judy Johnson*

Jessie Mueller

Date of Birth: February 20, 1983
Occupation: Actor

Jessie Mueller, who polished her acting and singing chops in Chicago, made her Broadway debut in New York City in her late twenties and has gone on to appear in five Broadway productions to date. After her Broadway debut, in 2011, in a revival of the musical comedy *On a Clear Day You Can See Forever*, Mueller became the musical actor to cast. She then went on to perform in *Nice Work If You Can Get It*, *The Mystery of Edwin Drood*, *Beautiful: The Carole King Musical*, and *Waitress*. In his review of *Waitress* for the *New York Times* (24 Apr. 2016), Charles Isherwood complimented Mueller's "rich, soulful, and emotionally translucent voice, and an ability to bring heaping cupfuls of subtext to her acting." Isherwood called her performance of the show-stopping song "She Used to Be Mine" not only the "high point of the show" but also "a high point of the Broadway season."

FAMILY OF ACTORS

Jessica Ruth Mueller was born on February 20, 1983, in Evanston, Illinois, where she lived until she went to college. Mueller comes from a theatrical family: her parents, Roger Mueller and

Slaven Vlasic/Getty Images

Jill Shellabarger, and siblings Abby, Matt, and Andrew are all actors, too. From a young age Mueller got to see that acting is a real profession, full of struggle, hard work, and disappointment but also joy. She got a rare peak at actors' lives that most theatergoers never get: what goes on behind the scenes and at home. "I was taken with theater from the beginning," Mueller told Tim Teeman for the *Daily Beast* (16 May 2016). She added, "It was the coolest thing for me. I was entranced, and it was the most natural thing because it was what my parents did." According to Teeman's profile, at around the age of four to five, Mueller saw Sherman Edwards's *1776* and Stephen Sondheim's *Gypsy*, which made an impression on her. Mueller told Teeman that she especially loved the strippers in *Gypsy* because "they had the best songs and outfits." So from a young age, the fascination was there. She saw some of the greatest plays and musicals. What drew her to theater most, she told Teeman, was "the magic of becoming someone else, the music, and I was fascinated with the actresses coming out of the stage door with their lashes still on—it seemed otherworldly to me."

While attending Evanston Township High School, Mueller began to act and sing in such musicals as *The Wiz* and *Working*, which are frequently performed by high school and college theater troupes. She had never acted before, so this was new. And it was then that she decided that she wanted to go into theater. She did not dream of Broadway, however. She did not quite fully understand what Broadway was, Mueller told Teeman, but she knew she wanted to be part of a theater community, much like her parents.

In addition to acting, Mueller loved to paint with acrylics and even took some art classes. But her ambitions lay with acting.

ACTING AGAINST TYPE

After she graduated in 2001, Mueller studied theater at Syracuse University in upstate New York. In an interview with Victoria Myers for the *Interval* (11 Oct. 2016), she admitted that she was in a sense "really lucky in that people didn't know what to do with me," meaning they did not know how to typecast her. Mueller said that became an advantage, but it was also a personal, even philosophical, principle: "Because I didn't feel like I had one thing that I was good at or one thing I was supposed to develop because I didn't really have anybody saying that to me," she told Myers. Mueller credited her teachers "who let me explore things and let me do this belty song here, and do this soprano song here." She particularly admired her "amazing" voice teacher Tish Oney, who was classically trained but also sang jazz. What Mueller said she learned from Oney was that she did not have to limit herself to singing or performing in one style. Mueller graduated in 2005, after which she returned to Chicago.

SETTING CHICAGO ON FIRE

In Chicago—and the nearby area—Mueller began her work as a professional musical actor in the musical comedy *Once Upon a Mattress* at the Drury Lane Theatre. She then went on to win the 2008 Joseph Jefferson Award for best actress in a supporting role in a musical for her performance as Carrie Pipperidge in *Carousel*. She also performed in the *Fiddler on the Roof, All Shook Up, Merrily We Roll Along, A Christmas Carol, Animal Crackers, Meet Me in St. Louis*, and *Shenandoah*, among others. And finally in 2011, she had her breakout year in Chicago.

In February 2011, she played the role of Miss Adelaide in the old-fashioned musical comedy *Guys and Dolls*, as interpreted by director Matt Raftery. As Chris Jones wrote in a profile for the *Chicago Tribune* (22 Dec. 2011), in which Mueller was dubbed Chicagoan of the year in theater, "The show had its problems—this was, after all, Raftery's directing debut—but Mueller was one of his key solutions. Even though she was known mostly for playing sweet-voiced ingénues, and even though she is younger than ideal for this role, Mueller suddenly unleashed a comic persona with startling force." Mueller played the role of Miss Adelaide, a woman who has been engaged to a "louse" of a man for fourteen years, with "humor, power, charm, vulnerability, and enough spark to set that . . . stage ablaze," as Jones wrote.

In June of that year, Mueller appeared in *Shout*, which Jones called "another mediocre show" but once again praised Mueller for her performance, particularly of the song "How Can I Be Sure?" Her rendition of that song, wrote Jones, was "so technically superb and emotionally rich that it nearly took one's breath away."

BROADWAY BACKSTORY

Mueller being cast in the Broadway revival of the musical *On a Clear Day You Can See Forever* began in 2010, even before her breakout year in Chicago. That year the Tony Award–winning director Michael Mayer was looking for a female lead for *On a Clear Day*. Speaking about Mueller's audition to Patrick Healy years later for the *New York Times* (9 June 2014), Mayer recalled, "I got very excited about her ability to conjure a kind of old-school performance style fueled by a contemporary sensibility." Mayer commended Mueller not only for her "extraordinary voice" but also her ability to be "seriously funny yet vulnerable" and for having a "surprising strength dressed in her unguarded humanity." Mueller was in fact concerned about moving to New York, where she knew she would, for all practical purposes, have to start over. But after she was cast, move she did.

BROADWAY DEBUT

A remake of the musical comedy *On a Clear Day You Can See Forever* premiered on Broadway in New York City in December 2011 with Mueller as the female lead, Melinda Wells. Although she was well known in the Chicago theater world, she was without any Broadway or Off-Broadway experience and thus virtually unknown in New York. And on top of that, she appeared on the Broadway stage opposite Harry Connick Jr., an established star well known for his acting, singing, and charm.

The musical itself was somewhat different from the 1965 original. In the original, a male psychoanalyst hypnotizes his not-so-bright female patient Daisy and she seemingly goes to some sort of past life from centuries ago in which she is a bright, interesting young woman named Melinda. The psychoanalyst falls for "Melinda," but Daisy thinks he has actually fallen for her. The 2011 Broadway revival version puts a new twist on this plot, which is set in 1974, by having the Daisy character be a gay man named David Gamble (David Turner). The therapist (Connick), who is a heterosexual widower, falls for the Melinda character, who this time is a 1940s classy jazz dame. David, of course, thinks the therapist has fallen for him, and comedy ensues.

But the critics were not laughing—at least not enough for the show to have a long run. *On a Clear Day* closed about six weeks after opening, but no one had anything other than praise for Mueller. In his review of the musical for *Vulture* (12 Dec. 2011), Scott Brown observed, "Mueller combines period vocal technique with natural, uninflected charisma and an onstage relaxation not often seen outside of Chi-town. Her voice contains notes of [Judy] Garland, but she's no diva—this is a star of supreme self-possession, one who doesn't need to blind us to impress us." Her performance earned Mueller her first Tony Award nomination in the category of best performance by an actress in a featured role in a musical.

IN DEMAND IN NEW YORK

After *On a Clear Day* closed on January 29, 2012, Mueller was suddenly in demand. She played Cinderella in the 2012 revival of the musical *Into the Woods*, by Stephen Sondheim and James Lapine, which was performed at the famed Delacorte Theatre in Central Park as part of the annual Shakespeare in the Park performance series. She then went on to appear in yet another Broadway revival, this time *The Mystery of Edwin Drood*, in which she played the twin Helena Landless. For that role, which she performed from November 2012 through March 2013, Mueller received a Drama Desk Award nomination for outstanding featured actress in a musical.

Her next role was her first leading role on Broadway: Billie Bendix in a revival of the musical *Nice Work If You Can Get It*, directed and choreographed by three-time Tony Award winner Kathleen Marshall. In March 2013, Mueller replaced the beloved and acclaimed Broadway actor Kelli O'Hara, who had the role of Billie since the show's opening the previous April. The show also starred Matthew Broderick, known both for his film and theater acting. At thirty Mueller was acting in her third Broadway show, often in the professional company of veteran actors, directors, and producers.

BEAUTIFUL

When Mueller auditioned for her next role, *Beautiful: The Carole King Musical*, about the life and career of singer-songwriter Carole King, one of the people whom Mueller had to impress was King herself. King recalled to Patrick Healy how that audition went: "Jessie just came across to me as very devoted to the material, respectful about the music and the story, and had a wonderful energy to her." Mueller got the part and went on to perform the lead role, that of Carole King, from November 2013 to March 2015. *Beautiful* is a jukebox musical, like the very popular *Jersey Boys*, which essentially means there is a thread of a life story woven though the show but its main focus is on the staging and performance of songs—in this case, the songs of Carole King, such as "You've Lost That Lovin' Feelin'," "It's Too Late," and "(You Make Me Feel Like) A Natural Woman."

Mueller's performance, which earned Mueller her first Tony Award and her first Drama Desk Award, received much critical praise. Ben

Brantley, writing for the *New York Times* (12 Jan. 2014), called the show a "friendly, formulaic bio-musical" but went on to praise Mueller's performance in a multitude of ways. Brantley wrote, "What makes Ms. Mueller's performance so touching is its projection of a lack of confidence." Later he observed that Mueller "evokes Ms. King's distinctively throaty, ever-yearning voice without mimicry. Most important, you never doubt the intrinsic connection between the singer—a woman we feel we have come to know intimately—and her songs."

WAITRESS

After almost two years with *Beautiful*, it was time to move on. Mueller joined the cast of the original Broadway musical *Waitress* as the star of the show. The musical, directed by veteran Broadway director Diane Paulus, opened in April 2016, and it once again showed how versatile Mueller can be. She played Jenna, a down-on-her-luck waitress who is miserable in her marriage and works hard at a diner, where she not only bakes but serves a variety of pies. This was Mueller's fifth Broadway show, for which she received another Tony Award nomination, and she had critical praise coming her way from every direction. Writing for *Variety* (24 Apr. 2016), Marilyn Stasio offered what by that point had become a nearly unanimous opinion: "Mueller can really act as well as sing her heart out."

PERSONAL LIFE

Mueller lives in the New York City borough of Queens. She has been romantically involved with actor and writer Andy Truschinski since 2009.

SUGGESTED READING

Healy, Patrick. "Taking Her Tony Home: Jessie Mueller, as Herself, after Her Tony Win as 'Carole King.'" *The New York Times*, 9 June 2014, www.nytimes.com/2014/06/10/theater/theaterspecial/jessie-mueller-as-herself-after-a-starry-night.html. Accessed 14 Nov. 2016.

Isherwood, Charles. "Jessie Mueller Serves a Slice of Life (With Pie) in Sara Bareilles's 'Waitress.'" Review of *Waitress*, directed by Diane Paulus. *The New York Times*, 24 Apr. 2016, www.nytimes.com/2016/04/25/theater/review-jessie-mueller-serves-a-slice-of-life-with-pie-in-sara-bareilless-waitress.html. Accessed 14 Nov. 2016.

Mueller, Jessie. Interview by Victoria Myers. *The Interval*, 11 Oct. 2016, theintervalny.com/interviews/2016/10/an-interview-with-jessie-mueller. Accessed 14 Nov. 2016.

SELECTED WORKS

On a Clear Day You Can See Forever, 2011; *Nice Work If You Can Get It*, 2012; *The Mystery of Edwin Drood*, 2012; *Beautiful: The Carole King Story*, 2014; *Waitress*, 2016

—*Dmitry Kiper*

Garbiñe Muguruza

Date of Birth: October 8, 1993
Occupation: Tennis player

The Venezuelan-born Spanish tennis player Garbiñe Muguruza has drawn comparisons to all-time greats Serena Williams and Maria Sharapova for her powerful serve, blistering returns, and fearless style of play. Standing at six feet tall, Muguruza has emerged as a force on the Women's Tennis Association (WTA) Tour since enjoying a breakout 2014 season, during which she captured her first singles title and defeated several top-ranked players, among them Williams, one of her childhood heroes.

In 2015, Muguruza reached her first Grand Slam final at the Wimbledon Championships, which she lost to Williams. She finished second to Williams that year in prize money and achieved a then-career-high singles ranking of number three. Building on that success, Muguruza solidified her status as the "next big thing" in tennis during the 2016 season, upsetting Williams in the French Open final to claim her first Grand Slam title. Her victory led many observers to tout her as the most likely heir to Williams, although the sentiment was not a new one; in

Jean Catuffe/Getty Images

advance of the 2015 Wimbledon final, Christopher Clarey wrote for the *New York Times* (9 July 2015), "Muguruza is that rare player with the tool kit to match up with Williams's strengths."

EARLY LIFE

Garbiñe Muguruza Blanco was born on October 8, 1993, in Caracas, Venezuela, to a Basque father, José Antonio Muguruza, and a Venezuelan mother, Scarlet Blanco. She began playing tennis at the age of three and has said that her first memory of the game is of playing tennis with her two older brothers, Asier and Igor. Muguruza is known for her on-court fearlessness, a trait she attributes to her parents. "I always had that," she told Reem Abulleil for the United Arab Emirates–based sports newspaper *Sport360*. "I think my parents always told me, 'You have to be brave and don't be scared of anything.'"

When Muguruza was around six years old, she moved to Spain with her family. At age seven she began training at the Bruguera Tennis Academy, near Barcelona, which was founded by the legendary Spanish coach Lluís Bruguera and his son, Sergi, who won back-to-back French Open titles in 1993 and 1994. It was there where Muguruza's tennis talent began to blossom. "You could see her talent from the beginning," Sergi Bruguera said, as quoted by Clarey.

One of Muguruza's favorite tennis players growing up was Swiss star Martina Hingis, a five-time Grand Slam singles champion who used a combination of skills and smarts to compensate for her relatively small stature. Inspired by Hingis and by Spanish players Conchita Martínez and Arantxa Sánchez Vicario, Muguruza initially adopted a style of play that relied more on stamina and baseline defensive tactics and trained almost exclusively on Spain's ubiquitous red clay courts. However, as she grew older and taller, she transitioned to a power game modeled after players such as Serena Williams and Pete Sampras and switched her focus to hard courts, which better suit players with powerful serves and returns. She started playing in national tournaments at around the age of twelve but mostly skipped the junior circuit, save for competing at the French Open Junior Championships and a handful of European tournaments.

By age fourteen Muguruza had already won two Spanish national championships. This was enough for Lluís Bruguera, who oversaw much of Muguruza's early tennis career, to predict that she would one day become a top-five player. Bruguera began entering her in the qualifying draws of WTA and International Tennis Federation (ITF) tournaments. She played in her first WTA tournament in Barcelona in 2008, and over the next four years she collected seven singles titles on the ITF circuit.

RISE UP THE WTA RANKINGS

Muguruza turned professional in March 2012, at age eighteen. After winning her seventh ITF singles title earlier that month, she made her WTA main draw debut at the Miami Open, entering as a wild card ranked at number 208, and reached the fourth round. In the second round of that tournament, only her second WTA-level match, Muguruza defeated then-ninth-ranked Vera Zvonareva of Russia, matching the record for fastest defeat of a top-ten player (a distinction shared by American player Andrea Leand and French player Julie Coin). She subsequently reached her first WTA quarterfinal at a tournament in Fes, Morocco, and finished the 2012 season ranked at 104.

Muguruza continued to progress in 2013, notching fourth-round finishes at both the Indian Wells Masters and the Miami Open. She also reached the second round in three of the four WTA Grand Slam tournaments: the Australian Open, the French Open, and Wimbledon. Following Wimbledon, however, Muguruza was forced to undergo surgery on her right ankle, which sidelined her for the entire second half of the season.

Over the ensuing six months, Muguruza practiced tennis drills while sitting in a chair to expedite her return to the court. It was during that "very significant time" that she realized that she "really wanted to play tennis," as she recalled to Abulleil. Her drive and tenacity paved the way for what would become a breakout 2014 season.

Muguruza started the season in auspicious fashion, earning her first WTA singles title at the Hobart International in Australia, where she won eight matches as a qualifier without dropping a set and defeated Czech player Klára Koukalová in the final. One week later, Muguruza reached the fourth round of the Australian Open. She then advanced to her second WTA final at the 2014 Brasil Tennis Cup in Florianópolis, Brazil, before losing to Koukalová in three sets.

Muguruza's most notable performance of 2014 came during the second round of the French Open, when she defeated defending champion Serena Williams in straight sets. In total, Muguruza dropped only four games to Williams, who suffered her worst loss to date in a Grand Slam tournament. She went on to reach the quarterfinals, where she lost to eventual champion Maria Sharapova in three sets. Muguruza finished the season at number twenty-one in the WTA singles rankings, marking the first time her year-end ranking cracked the top twenty-five.

FIRST GRAND SLAM FINAL

Prior to the 2015 season, tennis legend Martina Navratilova, an eighteen-time Grand Slam winner, pegged Muguruza as one of only two legitimate rivals for Williams. Despite again being slowed by an ankle injury at the start of the season, Muguruza advanced to the fourth round of the Australian Open for the second consecutive year. She lost to Williams in the fourth round, 2–6, 6–3, 6–2, in a match that was described by Christopher Clarey as "big-bang, first-strike tennis."

Muguruza next showcased her punishing power game at the 2015 French Open, where she reached the quarterfinals for the second straight year, losing to eventual runner-up Lucie Šafářová. She struggled, however, to start the grass-court season, suffering a pair of early-round defeats at tournaments in Birmingham and Eastbourne, England. Muguruza nonetheless bounced back at Wimbledon, successively defeating top-seeded veteran players Angelique Kerber, Caroline Wozniacki, Timea Bacsinszky, and Agnieszka Radwańska to advance to her first Grand Slam final.

In the run-up to the championship match, in which Muguruza would again square off against Williams, Williams's coach, Patrick Mouratoglou, described Muguruza as "a super-dangerous opponent," according to Clarey, citing her first-rate serve, her "aggressive returns," her "flat strokes," and "the way she takes the ball early" as causes for concern. Despite losing to Williams in straight sets, Muguruza moved up to number nine in the world singles rankings following the tournament.

However, Muguruza failed to build on her success during the US Open Series, losing to qualifiers in the opening rounds of tournaments in Toronto, Canada, and Cincinnati, Ohio, and then losing in the second round of the US Open. Following that defeat, Muguruza parted ways with her Spanish coach, Alejo Mancisidor, with whom she had been working since 2010. In September 2015 she began working with French coach Sam Sumyk, who had previously guided the Belarusian player Victória Azárenka to number one in the world.

Muguruza's partnership with Sumyk paid immediate dividends, as she reached the final of the 2015 Wuhan Open in China the following month. She then followed up that performance by winning her second career WTA singles title at the 2015 China Open in Beijing. She subsequently reached the semifinals of the year-end WTA Finals, helping her secure a career-high year-end singles ranking of number three. She finished the year with $4.5 million in prize money, second only to Williams's earnings on the WTA tour.

FIRST GRAND SLAM TITLE

Muguruza entered the 2016 season with the expectation that she would compete again for a Grand Slam title. However, she was dogged by plantar fasciitis and inconsistent play during the first half of the season, which resulted in a number of early-round losses. Still, Muguruza remained undaunted. During the run-up to the 2016 French Open, she told Paul Newman for the *Independent* (19 Apr. 2016), "I always think that I can win a tournament. I've never felt a situation where I don't see myself as a possible champion. Some people question that, but you have to believe that you can do it."

That confident mindset served Muguruza well at the French Open, where she dropped only one set en route to advancing to her second Grand Slam final in as many years. In the championship match, she again faced Williams, whom she convincingly defeated in straight sets, 7–5, 6–4, to win her first Grand Slam title. Demonstrating unflappable poise and composure, Muguruza "held her ground just inside the baseline, head down, firing bullets back at the most ferocious ball-striker in WTA history," Peter Bodo wrote for *ESPN.com* (4 June 2016). "She showed that she can stand in there and go blow for blow with anyone."

With her victory, Muguruza, then twenty-two, became the youngest singles champion since Azárenka won the Australian Open in 2012, as well as the first Spanish woman to win a Grand Slam title since Arantxa Sánchez Vicario in 1998. Muguruza's win prevented Williams from equaling Steffi Graf's modern-era record of twenty-two Grand Slam singles titles. It marked Williams's third consecutive loss in a Grand Slam final, lending credence to those touting Muguruza as the future of women's tennis.

Following the French Open, Muguruza ascended to number two in the WTA rankings. She failed to build on her convincing Grand Slam win, however, and struggled with inconsistency for the remainder of the 2016 season, which saw her suffer a second-round exit at Wimbledon and third-round defeat at the 2016 Olympic Games in Rio de Janeiro, Brazil. As Nick McCarvel wrote of Muguruza for *USA Today* (30 Aug. 2016), "Her game, one of bludgeoning power off of both wings that cascades from her strong six-foot frame, is one that can turn ugly when it goes awry."

Muguruza and her coach nonetheless remain optimistic about her future. "If she's not as consistent as other people want, well, it doesn't matter what they want," Sumyk told McCarvel. "We are trying to evolve and move forward; that's all that matters." Muguruza, meanwhile, said to the same writer, "You go out and you try to win. That's all I do. It's always the same."

In addition to singles tournaments, Muguruza has regularly played in women's doubles competitions. She has won five WTA doubles titles—one in 2013 with partner María Teresa Torró Flor; two in 2014, one with Romina Oprandi and one with Carla Suárez Navarro; and two in 2015, both with Suárez Navarro—and she and Suárez Navarro finished as runners-up at the 2015 WTA Finals in Singapore. Muguruza has also represented Spain in the Fed Cup, the ITF's annual international team competition in women's tennis.

PERSONAL LIFE

One of Spain's most marketable athletes, Muguruza, who is known for her charismatic personality and striking looks, holds endorsement deals with Adidas, Babolat, and Rolex, among others. In her spare time, she enjoys cooking, dancing, and listening to music.

SUGGESTED READING

Abulleil, Reem. "Interview: Garbine Muguruza—Sizzling Spaniard on Fast Track to Stardom." *Sport360*, 16 Feb. 2015, sport360.com/article/international/32812/interview-garbine-muguruza-sizzling-spaniard-fast-track-stardom. Accessed 21 Nov. 2016.

Bodo, Peter. "Why Garbine Muguruza Is Here for the Long Haul." *ESPN*, 4 June 2016, www.espn.com/tennis/french16/story/_/id/15949933/french-open-why-garbine-muguruza-here-long-haul. Accessed 21 Nov. 2016.

Clarey, Christopher. "Wimbledon 2015: Garbiñe Muguruza Realizes a Dream, but Faces Nightmarish Odds." *The New York Times*, 9 July 2015, www.nytimes.com/2015/07/10/sports/tennis/garbine-muguruza-realizes-a-dream-but-faces-nightmarish-odds.html. Accessed 21 Nov. 2016.

McCarvel, Nick. "Garbine Muguruza Isn't Worried about Others' Expectations." *USA Today*. USA Today, 30 Aug. 2016, www.usatoday.com/story/sports/tennis/open/2016/08/29/garbine-muguruza-us-open/89561628/. Accessed 21 Nov. 2016.

Newman, Paul. "French Open 2016: Garbine Muguruza Warns Rivals They'll Be Stepping into 'My Territory' at Roland Garros." *The Independent*, 19 Apr. 2016, www.independent.co.uk/sport/tennis/french-open-2016-garbine-muguruza-warns-rivals-theyll-be-stepping-into-my-territory-at-roland-garros-a6991461.html. Accessed 21 Nov. 2016.

—*Chris Cullen*

Jeffrey Mayer/WireImage/Getty Images

Ibtihaj Muhammad

Date of Birth: December 4, 1985
Occupation: Olympic fencer

Ibtihaj Muhammad is an Olympic saber fencer and bronze-medal winner. She was ranked second in the United States and seventh in the world as of November 2016; earlier that year, she was named to *Time* magazine's "100 Most Influential People" list. At the 2016 Olympic Games in Rio de Janeiro, Brazil, Muhammad, an African American Muslim woman, became the first American athlete to wear hijab in an Olympic competition. Swimmer Michael Phelps, the most decorated Olympian in history, was chosen to carry the United States flag at the opening ceremonies in Rio, and Muhammad, who reportedly garnered the second-highest number of votes for the honor, walked beside him.

Muhammad's prominent place in the festivities was particularly meaningful in light of the divisive rhetoric of president-elect Donald Trump, who, during his 2016 presidential campaign, said that the United States should ban Muslims from entering the country and later insulted the parents of a Muslim American army captain who died in Iraq. *Time* magazine endorsed her to perform the ceremonial role in early August for these reasons, and Muhammad herself has spoken out against Trump, who takes office this month. "When you incite hateful speech and rhetoric like that, the people who say it never think about the repercussions and how that affects Muslims. Specifically Muslim women who wear their religion every single day," she told Sean Gregory for *Time* (2 Aug. 2016). "So then you start to think, 'Am I going to be safe?'"

EARLY LIFE AND EDUCATION

Ibtihaj Muhammad, whose first name means "Joy" and whom family and friends call Ibti, was born in Maplewood, New Jersey, on December 4, 1985. She and her four siblings—three sisters and one brother—were raised in the Muslim faith. Her mother, Denise, worked as a special education teacher, and her father, Eugene, is a retired narcotics detective. Muhammad displayed her athletic gifts at an early age, swimming, running track, and playing volleyball, tennis, and softball. As she got older, her participation became trickier, though her parents initially saw sports as a way to integrate into their community. "We're African American and we're Muslim," Muhammad's mother told Robin Wright for the *New Yorker* (4 Mar. 2016). "I'm an educator. I know how important it is for kids to be a part of the community. Sports helps them integrate. Families and fans always unite around teams." Many Muslim women cover their legs, head, and arms as a sign of their faith, but Muhammad's attempts to reconcile her athletic gifts and her religion invited harassment from her teammates. As Muhammad tells it, one day she and her mother were driving past the local high school. Through the large windows, they saw several girls in full fencing gear—uniforms include pants, a long-sleeved shirt, and a full mask—practicing in the cafeteria. "I don't know what that is, but when you get to high school, you're doing it," Muhammad recalled her mother saying, as quoted by Sarah Kaplan for the *Washington Post* (14 Mar. 2016). Muhammad began competing at thirteen and, as a student at Columbia High School, joined the fencing team in 1999.

Muhammad did not fall in love with fencing right away, but she displayed a natural aptitude for the sport. As captain of the fencing team for two years, she helped her team win two state championships. She also played volleyball. Outside of her sporting success, Muhammad's high school career was complicated by the terrorist attacks on September 11, 2001. She was in advanced placement English class when the World Trade Center towers, located just across the Hudson River, fell. After the attack, Muhammad and her family felt a visceral shift in the way they were treated as American Muslims. Muhammad and her siblings were shunned, and people yelled at her mother when she drove down the street. Even in fencing, Muhammad told Wright, things were difficult. Fencing was a predominantly white sport, she said. "Not many people looked like me. There were no role models. When I competed in local tournaments, there were often comments about me—being black, or being Muslim. It hurt."

EARLY CAREER

In high school, Muhammad met Peter Westbrook, a bronze medal–winning Olympic fencer-turned-coach in New York City. Westbrook, who is African American, runs the Peter Westbrook Foundation, an organization that aims to attract young people of color to the predominantly white sport. When Muhammad began training with Westbrook, she switched from épée

to saber. There are three disciplines in fencing, based on weapon: épée, saber, and foil. Saber is all about strategy and speed; Muhammad told Chaya Babu for *Duke Magazine* (2 June 2016) that she thinks of it as "physical chess," whereas Maggie Hendricks, writing for *the Win* (29 July 2016), compared it to the 100-meter dash in track. Unlike épée or foil, saber fencers can score with the edge of their blade as well as the tip. "It's the closest representation of who I am," Muhammad told Victor Mather for the *New York Times* (9 Feb. 2016). "I'm very aggressive, that's who I am."

Muhammad looked at ten universities, but ended up attending Duke University on a partial academic scholarship in 2003. She was named All-American three times. In 2005 she was the Junior Olympic National Champion and finished the season ranked fifteenth nationally among Senior Women's Saber. In 2006 Muhammad went to the School for International Training in Rabat, Morocco, where she studied Moroccan culture and completed courses in intensive Arabic. She graduated in 2007 with bachelor's degrees in African and African American studies and international relations.

In 2009 she began training with Akhi Spencer-El, a different coach with the Westbrook Foundation. Muhammad had always viewed fencing as a means to an end—a college scholarship or a championship—but Spencer-El was the first to convince her to pursue the sport with the aim of becoming one of the best in the world. She poured all of her energy into making the Olympic team—an expensive dream, as fencers must spend tens of thousands of dollars on training camps and international competitions. Muhammad lived with her parents, became a substitute teacher, and coached her old high school team to make ends meet.

Muhammad became a member of the US National Fencing Team in 2010 but tore a hand ligament in 2012. The injury prevented her from qualifying for the Olympics in London, although a complication in the Olympic fencing rules was also a contributing factor. Including both men's and women's events, there are twelve potential medal events in fencing, but the International Olympic Committee allots the sport only ten. To comply with this rule, men and women skip one team event every Olympics, and in individual competitions of that discipline, countries are allotted only two fencers instead of three. In 2012 there were no team saber events, and Muhammad, who was ranked third in the United States in saber, missed individual qualification by one slot. In 2013 she won a team silver medal in the World Cup, and in 2014 she won a team gold medal at the World Fencing Championship in Russia.

RIO OLYMPICS

Muhammad made the United States Olympic fencing team in January 2016, at the age of thirty—uncommonly old for a first-time Olympic fencer. The only woman on the team who was older than Muhammad was Mariel Zagunis, a thirty-year-old, gold medal–winning saber fencer competing in her fourth Olympics. Of the fourteen starters on the Team USA fencing team, Muhammad was the only one who had not fenced internationally at the junior level. Excitement built around Muhammad's Olympic quest, and in February, President Barack Obama, in a meeting at the Islamic Society of Baltimore, mentioned Muhammad by name, urging her to win gold. In April, she met Michelle Obama, and gave the first lady a fencing lesson—with foam swords—in New York City's Times Square. Muhammad is an envoy for the US State Department's Empowering Women and Girls through Sports Initiative, founded in 2012. Fencing has been an Olympic sport since the first modern Olympic Games in 1896—but women have only been allowed to compete in épée since 1996. Women's saber, Muhammad's discipline, was first included in 2004, when Muhammad herself was a college student.

By the Rio Olympic Games in August 2016, Muhammad was ranked as the number two fencer in the United States and eighth in the world. On August 8, Muhammad competed in the individual saber event. She lost in round sixteen to Cécilia Berder from France. A few days later, Muhammad, alongside teammates Dagmara Wozniak, Monica Aksamit, and Mariel Zagunis, beat the Italians to win a bronze medal in the team saber event.

LOUELLA

In 2014 Muhammad and her siblings started Louella, an online clothing company named after their grandmother. After lamenting the lack of contemporary, inexpensive clothing for Muslim women, the Muhammads were inspired to begin making their own clothes. "We felt we needed [Louella] because there was clothing that was either not very fashionable or too expensive and we wanted something we'd wear," Muhammad said, as quoted by Porochista Khakpour for Rolling Stone (8 Aug. 2016). At Louella, Muhammad designs the clothes—long flowing tunics, empire-waist maxi-dresses, and loose-fitting jumpsuits—and her brother manufactures them in Los Angeles. Muhammad is the public face of the company and handles all of its marketing and publicity. Louella is in keeping with Muhammad's larger aim, as she told talk show host Stephen Colbert for The Late Show with Stephen Colbert on August 6, 2016, to "challenge misconceptions" about Muslims and Muslim Americans.

Muhammad is an internationally known athlete, yet she still regularly encounters ignorance and harassment. When she travels, Transportation Security Administration (TSA) agents often assume she does not speak English, and when she walks into a room, she told Wright, people "avoid eye contact." When she was invited to speak on a panel at the 2016 South by Southwest festival in Austin, Texas, a volunteer demanded that she take off her head covering to be issued an identification badge, and in New York City, she has said in a number of interviews, she is routinely harassed on the street. Such incidents are the "norm," she told Wright. "Do I hope it changes soon?" she asked Kaplan. "Yes, every day."

SUGGESTED READING

Babu, Chaya. "This Alumna Is Ready for Olympian Combat." Duke Magazine, 2 June 2016, dukemagazine.duke.edu/article/this-alumna-is-ready-for-olympian-combat. Accessed 11 Nov. 2016.

Hendricks, Maggie. "A Muslim Fencer Broke Stereotypes, but Now She Wants Olympic Gold." For the Win, 29 July 2016, ftw.usatoday.com/2016/07/ibtihaj-muhammad-muslim-us-olympian. Accessed 10 Nov. 2016.

Kaplan, Sarah. "Meet Ibtihaj Muhammad, the History-Making Olympian Who Called Out SXSW for Telling Her to Remove Her Hijab." Washington Post, 14 Mar. 2016, www.washingtonpost.com/news/morning-mix/wp/2016/03/14/meet-ibtihaj-muhammad-the-history-making-olympian-who-called-out-sxsw-for-telling-her-to-remove-her-hijab/. Accessed 7 Nov. 2016.

Khakpour, Porochista. "Rio Olympics: Ibtihaj Muhammad Is America's Olympic Game Changer." Rolling Stone, 8 Aug. 2016, www.rollingstone.com/sports/ibtihaj-muhammad-first-american-olympian-in-hijab-w432942. Accessed 14 Nov. 2016.

Mather, Victor. "Olympic Fencer, a Muslim, Settled on a 'Sport without Alteration.'" The New York Times, 9 Feb. 2016, www.nytimes.com/2016/02/10/sports/olympics/olympic-fencer-a-muslim-settled-on-a-sport-without-alteration.html. Accessed 10 Nov. 2016.

Wright, Robin. "Will America's Olympic Flag Bearer Be Wearing a Hijab?" The New Yorker 4 Mar. 2016. Web. 7 Nov. 2016.

—Molly Hagan

Alaa Murabit

Date of birth: October 26, 1989
Occupation: Activist, physician

Dr. Alaa Murabit founded the Voice of Libyan Women to promote and safeguard women's rights in Libya, the birthplace of her parents and the country she considers home, despite not having lived there before age fifteen. A pediatrician, she has also been a member of or adviser to several advocacy groups, including the international nonprofit organization Ashoka and the Council on Foreign Relations. In 2013 the Thomson Reuters Foundation awarded her the Trust Women Hero Award, which "celebrates an innovator whose bold thinking and high-impact work has helped women defend and advance their rights," according to the foundation's website.

Murabit encourages young leadership. "I have a duty to every child to recognize and cultivate their own sense of leadership, because had it not been for my mother, I would not have recognized or claimed my own space to lead," she wrote for the United Nations Foundation's Global Moms Challenge website (9 May 2016). In 2017 *Forbes* named her one of its "30 under 30" innovators and entrepreneurs in the field of health care, citing her work on health security issues for the United Nations (UN), and Harvard Law School named her its youngest ever "Women Inspiring Change" honoree. Former *Daily Show* host Jon Stewart described Murabit, who began medical school when she was fifteen, as "the Libyan Doogie Howser," alluding to the television show *Doogie Howser, MD* (1989–93), about a precocious young man who completed medical school at age fourteen.

EDUCATION AND EARLY CAREER

Murabit was born in Saskatoon, Saskatchewan, Canada, where she spent the first fifteen years of her life. She was the sixth of eleven children, with five sisters and five brothers. "My parents, both devout Muslims, always created an environment that promoted and supported their eleven children . . . equally," she recalled in an interview for the Al-Madina Institute's online publication *ImamWire* (7 Apr. 2017). "Both in and out of the home we shared responsibilities, and priority was always given to education." One of her older sisters, Amera, became an inspiration to her, finishing medical school and becoming a pediatric plastic surgeon; another sister chose to become a stay-at-home wife and mother. Their mother supported each of her daughters' ideas and decisions. As Murabit wrote of her for the Global Moms Challenge, "She would feed the ideas in my brain with her experience, and with her belief in me. And when it got difficult? When I wanted to quit? She was my courage, my

By Creampuff3201 (Own work) [CC BY-SA 4.0], via Wikimedia Commons

backbone, and even 6,000 miles away, the greatest online enthusiast on my behalf."

For Murabit, culture shock ensued when her family moved back to her parents' native Libya. Having already completed high school in Saskatoon, she began medical school at the University of Zawia at the age of fifteen. There, she found herself frustrated by the way her professors dismissed and passed over the women students. "I started realizing that regardless of how much I studied, or how much smarter I was than my male classmate, his opinion always trumped mine," she said, as reported by the Canadian Press (CP) for CBC News (29 Nov. 2014). "I felt very much robbed of my own opportunity and my own rights." She petitioned the school to allow women to sit on the medical college's student council, which had previously not been permitted, and later that year became the first woman elected to the council.

THE VOICE OF LIBYAN WOMEN

During her fifth year of medical school, in the wake of the 2011 Libyan revolution that led to the deposition of Muammar el-Qaddafi, Murabit founded the Voice of Libyan Women (VLW), hoping to effect real change in the lives of women. During the revolution, she also worked in makeshift clinics and the Zawia Teaching Hospital.

For her activism in the Libyan uprisings of 2011, Murabit became one of eleven women on Qaddafi's most-wanted list. "The idea behind [the list] was that these women should be, if found, arrested," she explained, according to CBC News. "We had seen what had happened to the men on the previous lists that had been released by the government at the time." The families of the women on the list were able to hide them.

Then just twenty-one years old, Murabit had seen women active in the revolution and had been dismayed when they returned to their traditional domestic roles afterward, abandoning public life. To identify the biggest problems facing Libyan women, she initially invited women to her home for tea to zdiscuss the issues and determine how best to approach them. After trying—and failing—to distribute fliers and other informational materials to the public, the VLW tried a new strategy: using Islamic teachings about women, which Murabit is familiar with from her upbringing, to promote women's rights and condemn violence against women. "Islam is the constant scapegoat for the state of women's rights in Libya and in the region—but rather than Islam, it is our own man-made culture and traditions, as well as recently imported ideals, which hinder our growth not only as women, but Libyans," she said to *ImamWire*. In contrast, she said, "My own upbringing has always been affirmation to me of the rights and the elevation of women in Islam. . . . I have always looked to women in Islam, the mothers of our faith, who were pioneers in education, economy, politics, and even security, for inspiration."

VLW CAMPAIGNS
The VLW's first national-level campaign was International Purple Hijab Day, which debuted on February 12, 2012. "Purple has no real significance in Islam," Murabit wrote for the *Christian Science Monitor* (14 Mar. 2013). "It is not the pitch black of despair, and it has universal meaning as a color of hopeful grief. Here it expresses hope for a solution that simply needs to be discovered." In this case, the problem in need of a solution is domestic violence. "Mistakenly, many [Libyans] . . . believe myths about Islam condoning violence against women," Murabit wrote. In fact, Islam takes "a strict stance against domestic violence." At a seminar at a high school in Zaiwa, the VLW distributed anonymous surveys asking attendees what domestic violence meant to them, whether they had been personally affected by it, and what the government could do to help end it. The surveys from this and other schools were presented to then prime minister Abdurrahim El-Keib, who subsequently declared his support for the campaign, wearing a purple scarf in solidarity and speaking out against domestic violence and in favor of legislative reform.

The next year, inspired by the success of International Purple Hijab Day, the VLW launched the Noor Campaign, which Murabit described to *ImamWire* as "a national campaign utilizing media and seminars to shed light on the proper treatment of women in Islam through ayas

[verses] from the Quran and hadiths [accounts of the prophet Muhammad]." The Arabic word *noor*, meaning "light," has long been used in Islam to refer to "the enlightenment of an individual from a position of darkness and ignorance to a position of understanding and wisdom," she explained. Murabit recruited support from thirty-five municipal councils, the Libyan business council, and five government ministries for the campaign. Using radio, television, billboards, and social media, the campaign disseminates positive messages about women and the rights they have under Islam. By doing so, they are attempting to dismantle the taboos against speaking about the role and rights of Muslim women. To combat accusations that the group was twisting religion for its own ends, Murabit and other campaign leaders had the Fatwa House, Libya's official fatwa (authoritative interpretation of Islamic law) organization, authenticate the hadiths they planned to use. The Noor Campaign has since been replicated internationally.

WORKING WITH THE UNITED NATIONS
In March 2016, the secretary-general of the United Nations (UN) appointed Murabit to the UN High-Level Commission on Health Employment and Economic Growth. She was the youngest person to be named to that level and the only one under the age of forty-five. She also has been appointed to a high-level advisory board for the Global Study on the Implementation of United Nations Security Council Resolution 1325, a resolution regarding women, peace, and security that was originally adopted in 2000, and was named a UN sustainable development goal (SDG) advocate. Seventeen SDG advocates were chosen to assist the secretary-general in achieving the sustainable development goals adopted by UN member states in 2015.

Also in 2016, Murabit founded a global mentorship program for young people interested in taking a leading role in issues of international peace and security, policy, and human rights. Interns are given the opportunity to work with Murabit in her activism and to attend various UN meetings. Additionally, she cofounded the Omnis Institute, a nonprofit organization dedicated to empowering women and young people as local leaders. In January 2017, she became the executive director of Phase Minus 1, a company that "provides thought leadership in peacebuilding, conflict resolution, sustainable development, national security, security cooperation and defense technology," according to its website.

PERSONAL LIFE
Murabit lives in the city of Zawia (also spelled Zawiya or Zawiyah) in northwest Libya, not far from the capital city of Tripoli. She earned a master's degree with distinction in international strategy and diplomacy from the London School

of Economics in 2016, and as of 2017 she was a PhD candidate in leadership and security at King's College London.

Murabit is a friend of Nobel Peace Prize laureate Malala Yousafzai, who was shot by a Taliban member in 2012 for seeking an education and has since become an advocate for women's education worldwide. "Her message is the kind of message we need to be delivering everywhere," Murabit said of Yousafzai, according to CBC News. She added, "If you can empower women economically, politically, if you can empower them socially, it completely changes the international dynamic."

SUGGESTED READING

Murabit, Alaa. "How My Mother Raised Me to Be a Global Advocate for Girls and Women." *Global Moms Challenge*, United Nations Foundation, 9 May 2016, www.globalmomschallenge.org/2016/05/mother-created-space-lead/. Accessed 6 Sept. 2017.

Murabit, Alaa. "In Libya, Islam—and a Purple Hijab—Help Spurn Domestic Violence against Women." *The Christian Science Monitor*, 14 Mar. 2013, www.csmonitor.com/Commentary/Opinion/2013/0314/In-Libya-Islam-and-a-purple-hijab-help-spurn-domestic-violence-against-women. Accessed 6 Sept. 2017.

Murabit, Alaa. "Interview with Alaa Murabit, Founder, Voice of Libyan Women." Interview by José Vericat. *IPI Global Observatory*, 28 Sept. 2012, theglobalobservatory.org/2012/09/interview-with-alaa-murabit-founder-voice-of-libyan-women/. Accessed 6 Sept. 2017.

Murabit, Alaa. "A Voice for Libyan Women: Alaa Murabit." *ImamWire*, Al-Madina Institute, 29 May 2014, almadinainstitute.org/blog/a-voice-for-libyan-women-alaa-murabit/. Accessed 6 Sept. 2017.

Murabit, Alaa. "The Voice of Libyan Women: A Progressive Voice amid Violence and Insecurity." Interview by Isabel Marler. *AWID*, 12 Jan. 2016, www.awid.org/news-and-analysis/voice-libyan-women-progressive-voice-amid-violence-and-insecurity. Accessed 6 Sept. 2017.

"Saskatchewan Woman, Alaa Murabit, Was One of Gadhafi's Most Wanted." *CBC News*, CBC/Radio-Canada, 29 Nov. 2014, www.cbc.ca/news/canada/saskatchewan/saskatchewan-woman-alaa-murabit-was-one-of-gadhafi-s-most-wanted-1.2854924. Accessed 6 Sept. 2017.

—*Judy Johnson*

Ruth Negga

Date of birth: January 7, 1982
Occupation: Actor

"Ruth Negga's eyes and frown, as she plays Mildred Loving in *Loving*—Jeff Nichols's film about the landmark interracial marriage case—offer deep reserves of sadness. If [Amedeo] Modigliani ever painted the Delta blues, it would look something like Negga's expression in this movie," Wesley Morris opined in a discussion of the most captivating performances of 2016 with A. O. Scott for the *New York Times* (8 Dec. 2016). Negga appeared in what was widely described as her breakthrough role back in 2005 when she portrayed the best friend of the transgender main character in Neil Jordan's *Breakfast on Pluto*. But she came to much wider mainstream attention when she was nominated for a Golden Globe Award for best actress for her work in the 2016 film *Loving*, which tells the true story of an interracial couple arrested in Virginia on charges of miscegenation who successfully took their case to the US Supreme Court.

She also earned an Academy Award nomination for the quiet but powerful role, becoming one of six black actors—a record number—on that year's ballot for the Oscar. "Diversity needs to operate on every level," Negga asserted to Ryan Gilbey for *The Guardian* (17 Mar. 2016), amid early buzz that she would be tapped during awards season for her sensitive portrayal of Mildred Loving. "It's great that the Oscars have highlighted it, but black actors getting

By Georges Biard [CC BY-SA 3.0], via Wikimedia Commons

nominated shouldn't be the only result. There's so much more that needs to be done."

Of Ethiopian and Irish descent, Negga frequently discusses how her race and nationality have affected her career. "People have always made assumptions about me," she explained to Gaby Wood for *Vogue* (7 Dec. 2016). "I become very territorial about my identity because it's been hijacked by so many people, with their own projections." In a feature article for *Time* (30 Nov. 2016), she recalled to Joe McGovern, "I did an interview a few years back [with the *Irish Sun*] and the headline was something like, 'Ruth Negga Believes Her Heritage Is Holding Her Back.' That was quite a funny phrasing, because I didn't mean my heritage at all. I was talking about other people's preconceptions of what actors who look like me are able to play. It's not the color of my skin that's limiting, it's people's perceptions."

Film, she believes, can help its audience bridge seemingly insurmountable cultural divides and encourage empathy for others. "It's what drew me to acting in the first place," she explained to Gilbey. "It can crystallize one story but speak for many. I've always thought that art can be a balm."

EARLY LIFE

An only child, Ruth Negga was born in Addis Ababa, Ethiopia, on January 7, 1982. Her father, a doctor, was Ethiopian, and her mother, a nurse, was Irish. The couple had met while both were working at Tikur Anbessa (Black Lion), a large public hospital affiliated with Addis Ababa University.

The family lived in Ethiopia until Negga was four, when political and economic upheaval forced many to flee the country. Negga moved with her mother, Nora, to County Limerick in Ireland, waiting for her father to join them there. He was prevented from doing so by the turmoil then rocking Ethiopia, and when Negga was seven, he died in a car accident. Her distraught mother never remarried.

While in Limerick, Negga attended Scoil an Spioraid Naoimh, a small primary school in the town of Ballysheedy, and ran with a large group of male cousins from her mother's side of the family. "We weren't allowed in the house from about 9:00 till about 7:00," she told Wood. "I was an attention seeker, always in trouble."

When Negga was about eleven years old, she moved to London to attend school there. For the first time, she became aware that she was different. "I remember thinking, I'm just *me*," she recalled to Wood. "When you're a kid, you're just you, aren't you? It was when I moved to England that I felt it, because I was Irish *and* black." She found some consolation in the work of black American authors such as Toni Morrison and Maya Angelou. "I didn't have that many black people in my life, so I had to sort of search them out," she explained to Wood. "And I didn't grow up in America, but I identified as much with their writing about the black experience as I did with their writing about the human experience." She felt a deep sense of dislocation when she returned to Africa as a young adult to see her father's grave, realizing that Ethiopia is home to dozens of languages and dialects, yet she spoke none of them.

EDUCATION

Negga knew that she wanted to become an actor from an early age. "You know when you're a kid and you get to pick a movie every Friday? I watched everything," she told Lesley Goldberg for the *Hollywood Reporter* (10 May 2016). "There's no particular genre that was appealing. I just loved the idea that you could dress up and play." That ambition deepened after she saw the 1986 film *Labyrinth*, starring David Bowie, whom she has described as her first girlhood crush, and intensified even further after she watched the 1995 French film *La haine* (*Hatred*), which explored themes of poverty and racial violence, and the 1996 British dark comedy *Trainspotting*, with its look at urban squalor and heroin addiction. She thought, as she told Wood, "OK, I'm going to be eighteen soon, so I'll just go away and figure out how to do that."

Negga studied drama at Trinity College Dublin's Samuel Beckett Centre, becoming enamored of the works of George Fitzmaurice and Seamus Heaney and impressing the theater industry figures who saw her acting in student productions. She graduated with a bachelor's degree in 2002, with a sense that her somewhat peripatetic upbringing had prepared her well for her chosen profession. "Maybe it's informed why I'm an actor," she explained to Matthew Amer for the Official London Theatre website (20 Oct. 2010). "You do become a chameleon when you have to continually make new friends. You go to a new school and you observe first and you try and make yourself fit in, which is what acting is."

EARLY ACTING CAREER

Not long after she graduated, Negga made her professional stage debut as the title character in a Dublin production of *Lolita*. In a review for the Irish *Independent* (8 Sept. 2002), Emer O'Kelly described her work as "breathtaking" and wrote that "the performance howls with sincerity." The following year Negga took on a main role in *Duck* at London's Royal Court Theatre. The play, by the Irish writer Stella Feehily, follows the life of a young bar hostess in love with an aging alcoholic, and Negga's performance won her a prestigious Olivier Award nomination for best newcomer of 2003.

In 2004 Negga made her screen debut in the Irish drama *Capital Letters*, in which she starred as a victim of human trafficking who makes her escape. Her character, like many of those she later portrayed, lived on the margins of society. "History is written by the winners. My job as an artist is to speak up for those who might be perceived as the losers," she asserted to Goldberg. "Or those who can't shout. . . . There are a lot of heroes who don't have loud voices."

When the acclaimed director Neil Jordan set out to make *Breakfast on Pluto*, a film about a transgender character living in Northern Ireland during the era of nationalist conflict known as the Troubles, he hired such widely recognized Irish actors as Liam Neeson and Stephen Rea. He has told interviewers that as soon as Negga, then unknown to him, appeared at an audition, he decided to write a character as biracial so that he could cast her. The role—that of the pregnant girlfriend of a terrorist for the Irish Republican Army—earned Negga an Irish Film and Television Award (IFTA) nomination. Later, when *Breakfast on Pluto* was screened at the Berlinale Film Festival, she was named a "shooting star of 2006."

ACHIEVING GREATER PROMINENCE
Although suddenly in great demand, Negga chose her subsequent roles with care. "I'm not in any rush to get anywhere," she told Tom Lamont for *The Guardian* (3 Nov. 2012). "There's a pressure on actors to get somewhere before it's over. But everyone wants longevity, don't they? . . .Why be that flash-in-the-pan, taking every job out of worry it'll soon be over?" Among her next credits were the television miniseries *Criminal Justice* (2008); the series *Personal Affairs* (2009); a turn on the stage as Ophelia in *Hamlet* (2010), which was broadcast to cinema audiences by National Theatre Live; the superhero series *Misfits* (2010); the biblical miniseries *The Nativity* (2010); and the title role in the 2011 biopic *Shirley*, which told the story of the music legend Shirley Bassey and for which Negga won an IFTA Award for best actress.

In 2013 Negga had a small part in the big-budget Brad Pitt film *World War Z*, and that year she became a series regular on the ABC series *Marvel's Agents of S.H.I.E.L.D.*, playing the mutant antihero Raina. She portrayed Raina until 2015, when the character died. Later that year, she appeared in the big-screen drama *Iona*, about a woman who flees with her son to the small Scottish island where she was raised after leaving an abusive relationship.

The year 2016 was a particularly notable one for Negga. In May the AMC network premiered the series *Preacher*, based on a comic book about a man of the cloth from a small town in Texas who is possessed by a supernatural creature and embarks on a quest to (literally) find God.

In the series, Negga portrays the preacher's romantic interest, Tulip O'Hare, an assassin-for-hire. Her casting was something of a surprise to fans of the comic book, who noted that Tulip had been drawn by the artists as a buxom Caucasian blonde.

That same month *Loving*, directed by Jeff Nichols and costarring Joel Edgerton, premiered at the Cannes Film Festival; the film went into wide release in November. Negga has told journalists that in the course of filming the picture, Mildred Loving became a personal hero to her. "Mildred shied away from the spotlight completely, but she changed the course of American legal history," the actor told Gilbey.

Critics praised Negga's performance, calling her "luminous" and "transcendent," among other such descriptors. Peter Debruge wrote in a review for *Variety* (16 May 2016) that Negga "embodies [her character] with a quiet dignity and deep inner strength."

PERSONAL LIFE
Describing Negga, an enthusiastic practitioner of the martial art Krav Maga, Wood wrote: "Her gift for self-mockery and her appetite for the *craic*—an Irish expression for fun or gossip or high jinks—are matched only by her levels of propulsion: Her neat, tiny frame always seems to move forward at great speed."

Since 2010 Negga has been romantically involved with English actor Dominic Cooper, who now costars with her in *Preacher*. The two originally met while appearing together in a 2009 National Theatre production of Jean Racine's *Phèdre*, starring Helen Mirren. The couple lives in London.

SUGGESTED READING
Gilbey, Ryan. "Ruth Negga: 'I Never Fitted Anywhere—in Life or in Hollywood.'" *The Guardian*, 17 Mar. 2016, www.theguardian.com/film/2016/mar/17/ruth-negga-hollywood-12-years-a-slave-misfits-preacher-iona-loving. Accessed 20 Jan. 2017.

Goldberg, Lesley. "Hollywood's Next Big Thing: *Preacher* Breakout Ruth Negga Heads to Cannes with New Jeff Nichols Film." *The Hollywood Reporter*, 10 May 2016, www.hollywoodreporter.com/news/hollywoods-next-big-thing-preacher-889430. Accessed 20 Jan. 2017.

Lamont, Tom. "Ruth Negga: 'I'm Not in Any Rush to Get Anywhere.'" *The Guardian*, 3 Nov. 2012, www.theguardian.com/tv-and-radio/2012/nov/04/ruth-negga-secret-state-interview. Accessed 20 Jan. 2017.

McGovern, Joe. "Labor of Loving." *Time*, 30 Nov. 2016, time.com/collection-post/4573644/american-voices-ruth-negga. Accessed 20 Jan. 2017.

Morris, Wesley, and A. O. Scott. "The Year's Most Captivating Film Performances." *The New York Times*, 8 Dec. 2016, www.nytimes.com/2016/12/08/magazine/great-performers-la-noir-the-years-most-captivating-film-per-formances.html. Accessed 20 Jan. 2017.

Sands, Nicole. "Who Is Ruth Negga? All About the Oscar-Nominated Star of *Loving*." *People*, 24 Jan. 2017, people.com/movies/who-is-ruth-negga-the-loving-star-earns-oscar-buzz. Accessed 20 Jan. 2017.

Wood, Gaby. "*Loving* Star Ruth Negga on Bira-cial Politics: 'I Get Very Territorial About My Identity.'" *Vogue*, 7 Dec. 2016, www.vogue.com/article/ruth-negga-january-cover-loving-movie-interview. Accessed 20 Jan. 2017.

SELECTED WORKS

Breakfast on Pluto, 2005; *Personal Affairs*, 2009; *Misfits*, 2010; *Shirley*, 2011; *Secret State*, 2012; *World War Z*, 2013; *Marvel's Agents of S.H.I.E.L.D.*, 2013–15; *Loving*, 2016; *Preacher*, 2016–

—*Mari Rich*

Maggie Nelson

Date of birth: 1973
Occupation: Writer

Maggie Nelson is a writer who is hard to classify. And that is no accident. She is the author of many books, including *Jane: A Murder* (2005), *Bluets* (2009), and *The Argonauts* (2015), all of which defy genre. Nelson's writing combines the lyricism of poetry, the narrative of memoir, and the insights of philosophical aphorisms to create a new kind of literature. In her best-known work, *The Argonauts*, for which she won the 2015 National Book Critics Circle Award for criticism, Nelson mines her private life—specifically her pregnancy and her transgender partner's hormone therapy—for insights about love, family, gender, parenthood, and the examination of dichotomies, categories, and language in general. In 2016 she was one of twenty-three individuals to receive the prestigious MacArthur Fellowship, commonly known as the "genius grant," in recognition of her achievements in nonfiction writing. The MacArthur Foundation website (21 Sept. 2016) cited her "empathetic and open-ended way of thinking" as "offer[ing] a powerful example for how very different people can think and live together" and noted, "Through the dynamic interplay between personal experience and critical theory, Nelson is broadening the scope of nonfiction writing while also offering compelling meditations on social and cultural questions."

John D. & Catherine T. MacArthur Foundation

TROUBLE AT HOME

Maggie Nelson was born in 1973 to parents Bruce and Barbara Nelson. She and her older sister, Emily, were raised in Marin County, California, in the San Francisco Bay Area. According to a profile by Hilton Als for the *New Yorker* (18 Apr. 2016), Nelson's father, a lawyer, traveled a lot for his job, which would often leave Nelson's mother as the sole caretaker of her two daughters. Both of Nelson's parents encouraged intellectual exploration and a love of literature; her mother had written her dissertation on the works of Virginia Woolf at San Francisco State University, and her father—who was "a great talker," Nelson told Als—cut out articles on topics she was interested in, such as theater and dance, for her to read.

When Nelson was seven years old, her mother found another romantic interest, and her parents subsequently divorced. Nelson and her sister split their time between their parents' homes until Nelson was ten years old, when her father died of a heart attack at age forty. For some time after, the closeness between Nelson, her sister, and their mother suffered as a result of their shared grief and misplaced blame. Emily spent time with a "rough crowd," according to Als, while Maggie tried to be a model child: staying out of trouble, providing emotional support to her mother, and mostly doing well in school.

One way that Nelson expressed herself from a young age was by writing. She won a poetry contest at the age of twelve and was thrilled, although, as she told Paul Laity for *The Guardian* (2 Apr. 2016), her winning entry was a "terrible poem" that drew heavily on the lyrics of an album by the Cure, at the time her favorite band. The idea that someone had actually selected her poem from all the others was, she said to Laity, "an incredible thought."

FOLLOWING HEROES, FINDING HER VOICE

When Nelson was 17 years old, she left the West Coast to attend Wesleyan University in Middletown, Connecticut, where she majored in English. She chose Wesleyan in part because of its proximity to New York City, having visited the city several times during her teens, as a result of which, she told Laity, her "needle pointed that way." While at Wesleyan, she attended writing classes taught by the writer Annie Dillard, who won the Pulitzer Prize for general nonfiction in 1975. She also met Eileen Myles, a poet and performance artist who conducted a write-in campaign as the first "openly female" presidential candidate for the 1992 US general election, during one of her campaign stops at the Wesleyan campus. After completing her undergraduate studies, Nelson moved to New York in large part to be close to Myles, whom she greatly admired. Much later, in a speech about Myles delivered at the Pasadena Central Library as part of the Poetry Society of America's Voice of Women in American Poetry series (18 Sept. 2014), Nelson said that she was deeply affected by the poem Myles had read at the campaign event and that she went to New York "to find [Myles's] body, her voice, to be near whatever it was that I saw and heard that night."

While supporting herself with various bartending and restaurant jobs, Nelson attended poetry workshops that Myles held at her East Village apartment, and eventually the two became friends. Nelson became part of what Laity described as "an avant garde, DIY, punk poetry scene involving the small indie Soft Skull Press." "I wasn't the kind of writer who was saying, oh if only the *New Yorker* would publish me," she told Laity. "Self-publishing wasn't what you did because you were rejected by HarperCollins; it was what you did because it was fun to make zines and run around with them."

Nelson started graduate school at the City University of New York (CUNY), the city's public higher-learning institution, in 1998. One of her teachers there was the poet and cultural critic Wayne Koestenbaum, who said to Als of Nelson, "The language of criticism fit her like a glove. She already had the whole personality and she was much more fluent than I am, or anyone I know—with just putting together a paragraph so that it flows and pursues an argument in a nonpedestrian way. A quality of being on fire with questions." Koestenbaum's writing and mentorship was crucial to Nelson's development as a writer and thinker, and she still holds dear one of the most important pieces of advice he ever gave her. "I remember when I first met Wayne

he told me, 'Don't get bogged down by the heavyweights,'" she recalled to Als. "It sounds so simple, but it was very freeing advice. A sense of permission."

Nelson graduated from CUNY with a PhD in English literature in 2004. In her dissertation, which was later published as *Women, the New York School, and Other True Abstractions* (2007), she explored how machismo played into the New York School painting and poetry movement of the 1950s and 1960s and how gay poets such as Frank O'Hara and James Schuyler and women abstract artists such as Joan Mitchell defied various concepts of hypermasculinity. The book also analyzes the work of Barbara Guest, Bernadette Mayer, Alice Notley, and Eileen Myles. In what would become a theme in her work, Nelson asks readers, by analyzing art and the language people use to describe and categorize art, to reexamine and reevaluate their preconceptions of artistic schools and the notion of the avant-garde.

BEYOND CATEGORY

By the time *Women, the New York School, and Other True Abstractions* was published in 2007, Nelson already had published four books of poetry: *Shiner* (2001), *The Latest Winter* (2003), *Jane: A Murder*, and *Something Bright, Then Holes* (2007). The most critically acclaimed of these, and the one that had brought her most attention, was *Jane: A Murder*, which tells the true story of her aunt Jane Louise Mixer, her mother's younger sister, who, in the spring of 1969, was brutally murdered at the age of twenty-three, a crime that went unsolved for decades. *Jane* is no ordinary book of poetry, not only because of its evocative language and underlying narrative but also because it incorporates documents such as newspaper clippings, crime reports, and letters and diary entries. "Nelson's identification with Jane's intellectualism and political interests are all rendered in the book with a watchful intensity that takes the reader into Jane's lost and reimagined body and Maggie's living and inventing mind," Als wrote of *Jane*, which was a finalist for a PEN/Martha Albrand Award for the Art of the Memoir.

Two years after *Jane: A Murder*, Nelson published a work of nonfiction prose that served as a sort of follow-up to the story of her aunt's murder: *The Red Parts: A Memoir* (2007, republished in 2016 with the subtitle *Autobiography of a Trial*). The inspiration for the book was the reopening of her aunt's murder investigation in late 2004 and the subsequent trial in 2005. Nelson attended the trial, which sparked in her a number of questions about the nature of violence, entertainment, and the combination of the two, as well as much self-examination. In the preface to the 2016 new edition, Nelson wrote, "After attending the suspect's trial in July 2005, I felt an intense rush to record all the details before being swallowed up, be it by anxiety, grief, amnesia, or horror; to transform myself or my material into an aesthetic object, one which might stand next to, or in for, or as the last impediment to, the dull speechlessness that makes remembering and formulating impossible." Later, in *The Art of Cruelty: A Reckoning* (2011), Nelson continued to explore the use of violence and cruelty in the media—particularly in "higher" arts, such as literature, theater, fine arts, and poetry. In a review for the *New York Times* (14 July 2011), Laura Kipnis praised the book, writing, "This is an important and frequently surprising book. By reframing the history of the avant-garde in terms of cruelty, and contesting the smugness and didacticism of artist-clinicians . . . Nelson is taking on modernism's (and postmodernism's) most cherished tenets." The book was included in the *New York Times'* list of notable books of the year.

Before *The Art of Cruelty*, Nelson published *Bluets*, another work of nonfiction prose that earned her more critical praise and a new following. The book is a collection of more than two hundred philosophical aphorisms—pithy, insightful reflections—that are interwoven together. It has poetic qualities, in that it uses brief, lyrical descriptions; and it has essayistic qualities, in that it offers analysis and insights. *Bluets* is a kind of collage about art, love, religion, the human condition, and the color blue. But, true to Nelson's defiance of categories and genre, it is neither poetry nor an essay; it is both and neither. The book opens with the sentences, "Suppose I were to begin by saying that I had fallen in love with a color. Suppose I were to speak this as though it were a confession; suppose I shredded my napkin as we spoke." In a representative review for the literary journal *Brick* (26 Nov. 2015), Jocelyn Parr wrote, "A critical examination of Nelson's irreverence reveals how her writing heralds a new kind of order. Just as we've not heard enough about the female gaze, we've heard too much about the male gaze and all the ways that it disciplines the female body. Nelson establishes the new order by taking down the old one." In 2015, *Bookforum* magazine named *Bluets* as one of the best ten books of the past twenty years.

THE ARGONAUTS

The Argonauts (2015) is Nelson's most personal and critically acclaimed work to date. Like her previous works, it is neither an essay nor a memoir, yet it is somehow both, providing a detailed, intimate exploration of her relationship with artist Harry Dodge. Nelson met Dodge, who is fluidly gendered and uses male pronouns, in 2007, when she was teaching at the California Institute of the Arts. The two quickly developed an intimate, intellectual relationship. Although they did not initially plan to marry, they did so early in November 2008, fearing—correctly, as it

turned out—that California would pass Proposition 8, which would abolish legal recognition of any marriage not between a man and a woman, in the upcoming general election.

Nelson wrote the book mainly in the second person, addressing Dodge as "you"—a conceit she has long maintained in her poetry as well. "I barely ever had third-person pronouns in poetry," she said to Als. "It was always such a pleasure that it could all just be a 'you.' Pronouns are, you know, so bossy and noisy." Indeed, one of the issues Nelson rigorously examines and questions in *The Argonauts* is such dichotomies as "he" or "she." She also examines the notion of family, including in her discussion the theorists who, to her, are a type of literary family: Gilles Deleuze, Judith Butler, and Eve Kosofsky Sedgwick.

The Argonauts received overwhelmingly positive reviews. Writing for the *Los Angeles Times* (30 Apr. 2015), Sara Marcus observed, "Although Nelson's discussions are grounded in real life, they're amply fed by—though never roped off inside—abstract thought. She points out how misogynistic it is to equate the maternal with the humdrum, but rather than simply flashing the red card of sexism she drives the point home through narrative." In a May 2015 review for National Public Radio (NPR) website, Tomas Hachard wrote, "Nelson's writing dances to avoid the cage. There are more questions broached here than conclusions offered. . . . The instability gives the book life because it reflects a way of life." *The Argonauts* received a multitude of acknowledgements, notably as one of the best books of the year, from publications including the *Chicago Tribune*, the *Village Voice*, and NPR. It also earned Nelson the 2015 National Book Critics Circle Award for criticism.

PERSONAL LIFE

Nelson married artist Harry Dodge in November 2008. They have a son, Iggy, born in 2012. Nelson is also the stepmother of Dodge's son from a previous relationship.

SUGGESTED READING

Als, Hilton. "Immediate Family." *The New Yorker*, 18 Apr. 2016, www.newyorker.com/magazine/2016/04/18/maggie-nelsons-many-selves. Accessed 17 Mar. 2017.

Laity, Paul. "Maggie Nelson Interview: 'People Write to Me to Let Me Know That, in Case I Missed It, There Are Only Two Genders.'" *The Guardian*, 2 Apr. 2016, www.theguardian.com/books/2016/apr/02/books-interview-maggie-nelson-genders. Accessed 17 Mar. 2017.

"Maggie Nelson." *MacArthur Foundation*, 21 Sept. 2016, www.macfound.org/fellows/962/. Accessed 17 Mar. 2017.

Nelson, Maggie. "Maggie Nelson: Inflections Forever New." Interview by Ariel Lewiton.

Guernica, 16 Mar. 2015, www.guernicamag. com/inflections-forever-new/. Accessed 17 Mar. 2017.

Nelson, Maggie. "Maggie Nelson on Eileen Myles." The Voice of Women in American Poetry. Poetry Society of America, 18 Sept. 2014, Pasadena Central Library, Pasadena, CA. Transcript. *Poetry Society of America,* www.poetrysociety.org/psa/poetry/crossroads/tributes/ maggie_nelson_on_eileen_myles/. Accessed 17 Mar. 2017.

SELECTED WORKS

Shiner, 2001; *The Latest Winter,* 2003; *Jane: A Murder,* 2005; *The Red Parts: A Memoir,* 2007; *Something Bright, Then Holes,* 2007; *Women, the New York School, and Other True Abstractions,* 2007; *Bluets,* 2009; *The Art of Cruelty: A Reckoning,* 2011; *The Argonauts,* 2015

—*Dmitry Kiper*

Manuel Neuer

Date of birth: March 27, 1986
Occupation: Professional soccer player

Manuel Neuer, a professional soccer player for Bayern Munich and the German national team, is widely regarded as the best goalkeeper in the world. Tending goal can be a lonesome business. "Even as a child, a goalie realizes that there's a madness inherent in what he does and who he is: He can never succeed, only not fail," Andrew Corsello wrote for *ESPN Magazine* (25 May 2016). Neuer's style of play flips this tradition on its head. He is known as the ultimate "sweeper-keeper," meaning that he covers an enormous amount of ground outside of his goalie box. Neuer makes the most of this sweeping because his skills range far beyond defending the goal. "Neuer's unwillingness to be bound by the lines of his penalty area has changed the way Germany plays," Gregor Aisch, Andrew Das, and Joe Ward wrote for the *New York Times* (12 July 2014) during the 2014 World Cup. "Confident that Neuer has the instincts and the foot skills to deal with defensive problems before they emerge, Germany's field players have been free to press opponents deep into their own half and keep them there." The International Federation of Football History and Statistics (IFFHS) has named Neuer the world's best goalkeeper four years running, and in 2014, he was the first goalkeeper to be shortlisted for FIFA's Ballon d'Or, an award that recognizes the world's best male soccer player. That same year, Neuer led the German national team to a World Cup victory over Argentina, winning the Golden Glove Award for best goalkeeper in the process.

By Steindy [CC BY-SA 3.0], via Wikimedia Commons

EARLY LIFE AND *NERVENSTÄRKE*

Neuer was born on March 27, 1986, and raised in Gelsenkirchen, Germany, which used to be a thriving coal-mining city in the Ruhr valley. His older brother Marcel is a referee in the Verbandsliga, a German football league. Neuer started playing soccer hometown club Schalke 04 when he was five years old, and says he was assigned to play goal because no one else wanted to do it. Early on, his coaches introduced him to the word *Nervenstärke,* which translates to "strong nerves," but has become a philosophy of play for Neuer. Neuer told Corsello, "It is a mental thing, where at every moment, no matter what, you are starting at zero. You stay calm. You don't dwell on mistakes." This concept of Nervenstärke, Corsello contends, has defined Neuer's success as a player. Neuer explained to Corsello that he projects calm confidence to his teammates, and a different kind of confidence to his opponents. He explained using a penalty kick as an example. "Normally, before [the kicker] is going to the ball, it's in his eyes—and that's where I look," he told Corsello. "But the more important thing is I have to be confident and show him that I am confident. I have to show him, even before he begins to make his move, that I will take the ball, that I already have it."

SCHALKE 04

Neuer attended the Gesamtschule Berger Feld school. Like Neuer, most athletes in Europe join their hometown club at a young age and depending on their talent and desire, continue to play for that team into adulthood. (The controversy surrounding Neuer's decision to leave the club at twenty-five is a testament to that honored tradition.) As a teenager, Neuer ascended the ranks at Schalke 04 (the "04" represents 1904, the year the club was founded), and when he was fourteen began working with veteran goalkeeping coach Lothar Matuschak, who was shocked at how small the young Neuer was. Soon after, Schalke 04 considered dropping Neuer, but Matuschak, who had only worked with his charge for a short time, was certain the team would come to regret if they dropped a talent like Neuer.

Neuer, who grew to be six feet, four inches, signed a contract with the club's professional team, nicknamed die Knappen ("the miners"), when he was nineteen. He made his Bundesliga (the German professional league) debut at the beginning of the 2006–07 season. Neuer substituted for goalie Frank Rost in his first game, but quickly replaced Rost as the team's starter, starting twenty-seven games during his first season, including fourteen shutouts. In 2008 Neuer enjoyed a breakout moment, and what is still considered one of the best performances of his career. In a Champions League game against Portuguese team FC Porto, Neuer made a series of unbelievable saves, single-handedly forcing a penalty shootout. The win took Schalke 04 to their first Champion League quarterfinals in club history. "We only had the chance because of Manuel Neuer's performance," Schalke 04 coach, Mirko Slomka told the Agence France-Presse, as published in the *Daily Star* (7 Mar. 2008).

In 2009 Neuer helped Germany win the title, beating England 4–0, at the UEFA European Under-21 Championship in Sweden. His performance brought him to the attention of Karl-Heinz Rummenigge, the head of FC Bayern Munich. That season, Neuer was one of the top three goalkeepers in Germany. In November, the first-ranked Robert Enke committed suicide, and Rene Adler, the other top-ranked goalkeeper, suffered an injury. Thus, Neuer was unexpectedly promoted to the German national team as a starter for the 2010 World Cup in Johannesburg, South Africa. Germany lost to Spain in the semifinals, but Neuer impressed coach Joachim Low enough to be kept on as the team's starting goalkeeper, even after Adler had returned to full health. Neuer's stunning performance in an ultimately losing game against Manchester United in April 2011 made him a household name in Germany. Sir Alex Ferguson, then-manager of United, said of Neuer after the game, as quoted by Alima Hotakie for the soccer magazine *FourFourTwo* (11 Mar. 2014), "In my time at United it's the finest display of goalkeeping against us." Neuer was named Footballer of the Year in Germany in 2011.

BAYERN MUNICH

The young goalie announced that he would not be renewing his contract with Schalke 04, forcing the club to sell him to Bayern Munich in 2011. Negotiations between the two clubs were fraught. Ultras (the nickname for hardcore fans) on both sides hated Neuer: Schalke fans because they saw their hometown hero as a traitor, and Bayern fans, perversely, because they refused to accept a star that was once beloved by another team. During preseason games with Bayern, Neuer was subject to banners that read, as reported by Hotakie: "You can save as many balls as you like, we will never accept you in our shirt."

Bayern fans eventually warmed to their new star as Neuer proved his worth. He went on nine-match run without allowing a single goal. In a Champions League semifinal against Real Madrid, Neuer brilliantly demonstrated his nervenstärke by dramatically saving two penalty shots, one of them from four-time Ballon d'Or winner Cristiano Ronaldo. Bayern made it to the final, where they bested the United Kingdom's Chelsea team to win the title. During the 2012–13 season, Neuer set records in Germany for most shutouts with twenty-one, and fewest goals against, with eighteen. In 2013 Neuer was named the IFFHS World's Best Goalkeeper for the first time.

Neuer shutout Portugal and the United States in the group stages of the 2014 World Cup in Brazil. When Germany faced Algeria in the first knockout round, Neuer's aggressive "sweeper" performance provoked criticism and awe. News outlets like the *New York Times* published heat maps depicting where Neuer was during that game, as well as in Germany's game against France, and Neuer appeared to cover an astonishing amount of defensive ground outside the box. Pundits heralded the multifaceted Neuer as a goalkeeper for a new era of soccer. Germany defeated Brazil, the home team, in the semifinals, and faced Argentina in the World Cup final. The game went into extra-time before the German's scored a goal, winning 1-0.

The World Cup win was technically Germany's fourth, but it was a first win for unified Germany. (The last time the team won was 1990.) At the end of the tournament, Neuer claimed the Golden Gloves Award, for best goalkeeper of the World Cup. In 420 minutes of knockout play, Neuer conceded only two goals. Neuer was again named the world's best goalkeeper (and again in 2015 and 2016). In 2016 Neuer extended his contract with Bayern until 2021, though his previous contract was not set to expire until 2019. He succeeded Bastian Schweinsteiger, who retired from international play, as the new captain of the German national team in September 2016.

In July 2016, seasoned Italian coach Carlo Ancelotti took the helm of Bayern. In the first half of the 2016–17 season, Bayern experienced some growing pains as the team adjusted to the new leadership. Neuer's role, in particular, changed as Ancelotti introduced new strategy into play and Neuer did not play as much as a sweeper keeper, but instead played closer to the goal. Ancelotti came under fire for his tactics and relaxed coaching style, but Neuer came to the defense of his coach and, as he told Grant Wahl for *Sports Illustrated* (7 Mar. 2017), he enjoys the change, "I can speak much more to my players in front of me because of this, and it's closer. I can reach the midfielders. It was impossible before to reach a midfielder when you shout and try to help them with something. And that's different and again a new job for me."

PERSONAL LIFE

Neuer, a devout Catholic, founded a charity called the Manuel Neuer Kids Foundation in 2010; the charity provides aid to disadvantaged youth in the Ruhr valley. Gelsenkirchen, the city where Neuer grew up, has a particularly high poverty rate. He was inspired to create the foundation remembering children that he went to school with who could not afford to eat lunch or go on field trips. The foundation pays for school meals, and offers tutoring, music programs, and summer camps for kids who would normally would not be able to afford those things.

SUGGESTED READING

Agence France-Presse. "Slomka Thanks Neuer." *Daily Star*, 7 Mar. 2008, www.thedailystar.net/news-detail-26464. Accessed 15 Mar. 2017.

Aisch, Gregor, Andrew Das, and Joe Ward. "Manuel Neuer's Wanderlust." *The New York Times*, 12 July 2014, www.nytimes.com/interactive/2014/07/12/sports/worldcup/manuel-neuer-goalkeeper.html. Accessed 15 Mar. 2017.

Corsello, Andrew. "The Stunning, Strange, Beautiful Game of Manuel Neuer." *ESPN Magazine*, 25 May 2016, www.espn.com/espn/feature/story/_/page/enterprise-neuer160525/bayern-munich-manuel-neuer-changing-means-goalie. Accessed 15 Mar. 2017.

Hotakie, Alima. "How Neuer Finally Found Love at Bayern Munich." *FourFourTwo*, 11 Mar. 2014, www.fourfourtwo.com/us/features/how-neuer-finally-found-love-bayern-munich. Accessed 15 Mar. 2017.

Wahl, Grant. "No Longer a Sweeper-Keeper? Neuer's Newer Role at Bayern under Ancelotti." *Sports Illustrated*, 7 Mar. 2017, www.si.com/planet-futbol/2017/03/07/manuel-neuer-carlo-ancelotti-bayern-munich. Accessed 17 Mar. 2017.

—*Molly Hagan*

Dianne Newman

Occupation: Microbiologist

For researcher Dianne Newman, a professor of biology at the California Institute of Technology (Caltech), some of the smallest organisms on Earth are also some of the most important. An award-winning scientist whose work spans the fields of microbiology, geobiology, and genetics, Newman studies microbes—or microscopic organisms—such as bacteria that have a vast range of capabilities and have affected the larger world in myriad ways. Although her devotion to such tiny lifeforms may seem surprising to some, she and her colleagues would not have it any other way. "Every microbiologist in the field has affection for the organisms they study, and this moral obligation to speak up for the little guys—literally—because they are tiny but they have such an outsize influence on the world and have had that for billions of years of history," she explained to Dina Fine Maron for *Scientific American* (22 Sept. 2016).

As a researcher, Newman has devoted much of her time to studying microbes capable of surviving in anaerobic environments, or environments with little to no oxygen, which range from the ancient Earth to the layers of mucus that build up within the lungs of a person with cystic fibrosis. By learning more about the characteristics and capabilities of such microbes, she sheds light not only on the history of life on Earth but also on the causes of certain chronic infections. In light of such research and her potential to

John D. & Catherine T. MacArthur Foundation

make further breakthroughs, she was awarded the prestigious MacArthur Fellowship in 2016. However, although she has received significant attention for her work, particularly following the MacArthur announcement, she prefers to divert that attention toward the microbes themselves. "They are so much more interesting than we are," she told Deborah Netburn for the *Los Angeles Times* (21 Sept. 2016). "We basically have two ways of making energy. These guys have evolved ways to grow under every conceivable habitable condition."

EARLY LIFE

Dianne K. Newman was born in Argentina to Yale and Jo Ann Newman. She has three older siblings from her father's first marriage. Her father, a former television news correspondent, was working for the US Foreign Service at the time of her birth, and she spent much of her childhood in Argentina, Venezuela, and Panama. The family later returned to the United States, where they lived in Virginia and California.

As a child and teen, Newman had a variety of hobbies and interests, participating in her school debate team and carrying out science experiments that she showcased at science fairs. She has attributed much of her early enthusiasm for such differing areas to her parents' influence. "I have to credit them as people who always appreciated new things and encouraged my wide-ranging interests," she told Sarah C. P. Williams for the *HHMI (Howard Hughed Medical Institute) Bulletin* (Feb. 2009). When she was a sophomore in high school, she traveled to Puerto Rico to participate in the Intel International Science and Engineering Fair, which proved to be a formative experience for her.

EDUCATION

After graduating from high school, Newman enrolled in Stanford University, where she majored in German studies and became a member of the Phi Beta Kappa honor society. Although primarily studying German, she remained fascinated by a number of scientific fields, particularly materials science and environmental science. "I loved everything, that was my problem," she told Williams. "I was an advising nightmare." After several years of mingling major requirements and science courses, she earned her bachelor's degree from Stanford in 1993.

Following her graduation from Stanford, Newman enrolled in the Massachusetts Institute of Technology (MIT) to pursue graduate studies in environmental engineering. Although she initially planned to leave after earning her master's degree, inspired by an environmental engineering course she had taken back in her first semester, she ultimately decided to work toward a career in scientific research. She began pursuing doctoral studies under the supervision of Professor François Morel, a scientist specializing in the interactions between microbes and metals.

While working in Morel's lab, Newman first developed a strong interest in the interactions between microbes and metals when another student gave her a sample of bacteria capable of metabolizing arsenic. "It was this really bright yellow color, and the only thing I knew how to do—from my materials science background—was to figure out what compound was making it yellow," she recalled to Williams. Her early research into the bright yellow sample sparked a new fascination with metal-metabolizing microbes, and her newfound interest would shape the course of her career. She likewise developed an interest in the field of genetics as a graduate student, taking courses in the subject at institutions such as the Cold Spring Harbor Laboratory (CSHL), a nonprofit research center on Long Island. Morel moved to Princeton University partway through her studies, and she spent some time in his lab at Princeton prior to earning her doctorate from MIT in 1997.

ACADEMIC CAREER

After earning her PhD, Newman began a postdoctoral fellowship in 1998 at Harvard Medical School (HMS), where she worked under microbiologist Roberto Kolter. Her research during that period combined her background in microbiology with her interest in genetics. Looking back on that time, Kolter still recognizes the revolutionary nature of Newman's studies and the extent of her talent: "Nobody else at the time was thinking of combining environmental microbiology and genetics. She paved the way for a new field," he told Williams. After two years, Newman obtained her first faculty position, joining Caltech as the Clare Boothe Luce Assistant Professor of Geobiology and Environmental Science.

Since 2000, Newman has spent much of her career at Caltech, becoming an associate professor in 2005 and a full professor in 2006. In 2007, she returned to Massachusetts to take a position at MIT, where she served for a time as the John and Dorothy Wilson Professor of Biology and Geobiology. She later returned to her professorship at Caltech. Over the course of her career, she had also served as a HHMI investigator as well as a visiting senior research fellow at St. John's College in Oxford, England. Named the Gordon M. Binder/Amgen Professor of Biology and Geobiology at Caltech in 2016, the following year she was appointed the school's executive officer for molecular biology.

RESEARCH

As a researcher, Newman is primarily interested in microbes, which she considers to be of key importance to the planet and everything on it.

"Microbes dominate the biosphere on earth," she told Netburn. "They have impacted—and continue to impact—not only the physical environment, but the chemical and biological environment in really profound ways. For example, we owe all the oxygen in the atmosphere today to the biochemical invention of ancient microorganisms."

Newman initially focused in large part on the interactions between microbes and various minerals, particularly metals. Microbes examined during that period included *Pseudomonas aeruginosa*, a bacterium capable of metabolizing iron. Such an ability is of great interest to Newman and her fellow researchers, as it makes the bacterium far less reliant on the presence of oxygen than some of its counterparts. As an oxygen-rich atmosphere is a relatively recent development in the history of Earth, microbes that existed prior to its development must have been capable of using other elements to maintain their critical functions. Further areas of interest included the ability of microbes to serve as catalysts for the formation of minerals. She and her colleagues later studied the genetic factors that control various processes in bacteria and the ways in which the observations gleaned from studying microbe-mineral interactions apply to other scientific fields.

MEDICAL IMPLICATIONS

Among Newman's many areas of research, it is her work on *Pseudomonas aeruginosa* that has perhaps attracted the most attention outside of the field of microbiology. That bacterium, which she began studying early in her career due to its ability to metabolize iron, is at times found in the lungs of individuals with the genetic disease cystic fibrosis, where it can cause chronic infections. Among other effects, cystic fibrosis causes thick mucus to build up in the lungs. The layers of mucus create an environment in which there is very little oxygen, where bacteria capable of surviving in oxygen-deprived environments—such as *Pseudomonas aeruginosa*—can thrive.

For Newman, who has worked alongside researchers from the Children's Hospital Los Angeles and the University of Southern California's Keck Hospital to study bacteria found in the lungs of cystic fibrosis patients, the subject as a whole is quite reminiscent of her studies of microbes in other low-oxygen environments. "It's the same problem at a very basic level," she explained to Maron. "How do bacteria survive when they are limited for oxygen or an iron oxide mineral or anything else that could be an oxidant—something that can be used by cells at the end of the electron transport chain in respiration to pick up electrons and make the whole process go—to power metabolism? How do they cope? It's a neat problem." By studying *Pseudomonas aeruginosa* further, Newman and her colleagues hope to uncover a means of preventing the bacterium, which has proven highly resistant to antibiotics, from surviving in the lungs.

MACARTHUR FELLOWSHIP

In the fall of 2016, the John D. and Catherine T. MacArthur Foundation announced that Newman was one of twenty-three individuals selected as members of the prestigious MacArthur Fellows Program. Often known colloquially as the genius grant, the MacArthur Fellowship is granted to individuals who have made significant accomplishments in their respective fields and show great potential for further achievement. In addition to drawing significant public attention to the recipients, the fellowship includes a grant of $625,000 for each recipient.

Although Newman herself objects to the media and public's tendency to refer to MacArthur fellows as "geniuses," as she does not think of herself in that way, she was stunned and pleased to have been selected as a fellow, an experience she described to Maron as "pretty surreal." In addition to using the fellowship funds to promote scientific projects she cares deeply about, she hopes to dedicate a portion of the money to promoting careers in science. "I'd also like to use it in the local community to help people recognize what a science career is like and how accessible it can be," she explained to Maron. "Most people don't realize if you go to grad school in science to get a PhD, it's often covered by grants your advisor gets. I think that's pretty great. I think it's a fantastic thing about the sciences, and it makes it more accessible to people regardless of their background."

PERSONAL LIFE

Newman is married to Jonas Peters, an inorganic chemist who has taught at MIT and Caltech. They have a son named Ronen. Although receiving the MacArthur Fellowship was a major milestone for Newman professionally, she has noted in interviews that the prestigious fellowship has had little bearing on her life outside of the lab. "This is a great honor, but it doesn't change who I am," she told Netburn. "My family is proud and happy, but they know what an idiot I am in real life."

SUGGESTED READING

"Dianne Newman." *MacArthur Foundation*, 21 Sept. 2016, www.macfound.org/fellows/963. Accessed 10 Apr. 2017.

Lemonick, Sam. "Microbiologist Dianne Newman Wins MacArthur 'Genius' Grant." *Forbes*, 28 Sept. 2016, www.forbes.com/sites/samlemonick/2016/09/28/microbiologist-dianne-newman-wins-genius-grant. Accessed 10 Apr. 2017.

Maron, Dina Fine. "MacArthur 'Genius' Grant Winner Battles Drug-Resistant Infections."

Scientific American, 22 Sept. 2016, www.scientificamerican.com/article/macarthur-genius-grant-winner-battles-drug-resistant-infections. Accessed 10 Apr. 2017.

Netburn, Deborah. "Bacteria Have Sculpted the World We Live In, and That's Why MacArthur Winner Dianne Newman Studies Them." *The Los Angeles Times*, 21 Sept. 2016, www.latimes.com/science/sciencenow/la-sci-sn-dianne-newman-macarthur-award-20160921-snap-story.html. Accessed 10 Apr. 2017.

Newman, Dianne. "Dianne Newman." *American Academy of Microbiology*, www.asm.org/index.php/aam-fellows/news-views/interviews-with-fellows/item/5131-dianne-newman. Accessed 10 Apr. 2017.

Williams, Sarah C. P. "Between a Rock and a New Place." *HHMI Bulletin*, vol. 22, no. 1, 2009, pp. 26–31.

—*Joy Crelin*

Photo by Joe Robbins/Getty Images

Gift Ngoepe

Date of birth: January 18, 1990
Occupation: Baseball player

Many avid baseball players could be said to have grown up in the ballpark, but for Gift Ngoepe, that statement is literal. The son of the clubhouse attendant for a South African amateur team, Ngoepe lived with his family in a small storage room in the team's clubhouse and grew up watching the team play right outside of his home. A talented player, he captured the attention of the Pittsburgh Pirates while attending a European training camp in 2008 and was quickly signed to the organization, becoming the first baseball player born in Africa to sign with a professional team. "This just shows it doesn't matter where you come from," Ngoepe told Stephen J. Nesbitt for the *Pittsburgh Post-Gazette* (26 Apr. 2017). "No matter where you are, who you are, you can still make it."

Joining the Pirates organization in 2009, Ngoepe began his professional baseball career with the Gulf Coast League Pirates, the team's rookie-level affiliate. He went on to play more than seven hundred games with a variety of developmental teams, working to improve his offensive skills while excelling as a defensive player. In April 2017, after more than eight years in the minors, Ngoepe was called up to the major-league Pittsburgh Pirates, appearing in his first game with the team on April 26. Although happy to have made his major-league debut, Ngoepe nevertheless remained aware that staying on the team would take a great deal of effort. "It's hard," he told Bob Nightengale for *USA Today* (23 May 2017). "You've got to do everything you can to the best of your abilities to stay in this league." Ngoepe joined the minor-league Indianapolis Indians in June 2017, with the goal of returning to the Pirates after developing his offensive abilities further.

EARLY LIFE AND EDUCATION

Mpho' Gift Ngoepe was born on January 18, 1990, in Pietersburg, now Polokwane, South Africa. When he was a toddler, his mother, Maureen, traveled to look for work while Ngoepe and his older brother, Christopher, remained with their grandparents. Ngoepe's mother found work in Randburg, a suburb of Johannesburg, where she managed the clubhouse of the amateur Randburg Mets baseball team in exchange for room and board. Ngoepe later joined her at the clubhouse, where he and his mother—and later his older and younger brothers as well—lived in a storage room that measured less than eighty square feet. Despite their unusual living circumstances, Ngoepe remembers his family being happy during that time. "We didn't have a whole lot of things, but everything that we had, we just made it work," he told Tyler Kepner for the *New York Times* (8 May 2017).

Growing up at the ballpark, Ngoepe learned to play baseball at a very young age, observing the Randburg Mets players and learning from them directly. As a child, he practiced his throwing and catching skills by throwing a ball against the wall of the clubhouse. "The wall, that was my best friend," he recalled to Nightengale. "The wall just kept throwing the ball back to me. I didn't need anybody else. Really, it was my perfect playground." In addition to priming Ngoepe to become a baseball player, the family's ballpark home had a similar effect on his younger brother, Victor, who would begin playing for the Pittsburgh Pirates' minor-league affiliate teams in 2016.

As a teenager, Ngoepe began to play baseball on national youth teams, representing South Africa at competitions in locales such as Brazil, Mexico, and Cuba. His trips abroad were funded in part by the members of the Randburg Mets, who helmed fundraising efforts in his honor. In addition to playing baseball, Ngoepe enjoyed watching American major-league teams play on television and was a fan of the Boston Red Sox in particular. He likewise spent time playing sports such as soccer and cricket, which were far more popular in South Africa than the somewhat niche sport of baseball.

SIGNING WITH THE PIRATES

To improve his skills, Ngoepe attended the Major League Baseball (MLB) European Academy in Italy, a training camp for promising teenage players, in 2007 and 2008. During his second session, he caught the attention of Pittsburgh Pirates scout Tom Randolph, who had previously seen Ngoepe play on the South African youth team in 2005. The Pirates offered to sign Ngoepe to a professional contract, prompting him to make a difficult decision. "They said they liked the way I worked and my talent. They said they wanted to sign me. So I had to make a decision between soccer, which I still played, and baseball," he recalled to David Manel for *SBNation* (24 May 2015). "With soccer I could stay at home with my family and be comfortable. Or, go to a different country. I love traveling and get to experience so much." Although unhappy about the idea of leaving his mother, with whom he was very close, Ngoepe ultimately chose to sign with the Pirates organization, which agreed to pay for annual flights to South Africa so that he could visit his family. Signing the contract in September 2008, Ngoepe became the first black South African to sign with an MLB team, a particularly significant achievement for a player born under apartheid.

Upon arriving in the United States, Ngoepe began to adjust to his new living circumstances, facing a few challenges along the way. "It was a little bit harder, I guess, living in America. The people are a little bit different," he told Hannah Keyser for *Deadspin* (27 Apr. 2017). "They didn't quite understand me because I spoke with slang that I had from South Africa. And my English was very fast, when it came out of my mouth. Like I had to break it down." Beginning

his professional baseball career during the 2009 season, Ngoepe joined the Gulf Coast League Pirates, a rookie-level team in the Pirates organization. He played in forty-seven games with the team and ended the season with a batting average of .238. Particularly talented as a defensive player, Ngoepe played as second baseman and shortstop during his debut season and achieved fielding percentages of .978 and .961, respectively, in those positions. Also in 2009, Ngoepe once again represented South Africa in international competition, this time in the World Baseball Classic.

MINOR-LEAGUE CAREER

Over the years following his first season in professional baseball, Ngoepe played with six different minor-league teams, including the Bradenton Marauders, the West Virginia Power, and the Altoona Curve. He continued to perform well as a defensive player and worked to improve his batting as he progressed from rookie-level to Double-A teams. Despite his passion for the sport and continual improvement, Ngoepe considered quitting baseball in 2013, following the death of his mother, who succumbed to pneumonia at the age of forty-five. "It was so hard, because my mom meant everything to me," he told Nightengale. "She was always there for me." However, Ngoepe ultimately chose to return to his sport, inspired by his mother's belief in his potential. "I know she would have wanted me to go on. She never wanted me to quit," he explained to Nightengale. "So I kept pushing and pushing. I had to stay strong. I had to overcome my failures. Now, I believe I can be an inspiration."

Ngoepe played with the Double-A Altoona Curve in the 2014 season, appearing in 131 games with the team and splitting his time between the positions of second baseman and shortstop. He remained with the team for much of the 2015 season before advancing to the Indianapolis Indians—a Triple-A team, the highest level of the minor leagues—in June 2015. He remained with the Indians in 2016, primarily playing shortstop.

MAJOR-LEAGUE DEBUT

In April 2017, the Pittsburgh Pirates announced that they were calling Ngoepe up to the major leagues. He made his major-league debut on April 26, in a game against the Chicago Cubs. For Ngoepe, the opportunity to play for the Pirates after spending the better part of a decade on the team's minor-league affiliates was both exciting and nerve-wracking. "I was nervous. I was just thinking, 'It's okay. Just go out there and play,'" he recalled to Keyser. "I was basically sort of talking to myself about how I'd be and being as positive as I can and stay as calm as I can be so I can have a chance to put up a quality [at-bat] against [Cubs pitcher] Jon Lester." His strategy proved successful: Ngoepe hit a single during his first at bat, and he later displayed his defensive capabilities by participating in the double play that resulted in the final out of the game. The Pirates defeated the Cubs 6–5, rendering Ngoepe's debut appearance an unqualified success.

Including his first game, Ngoepe played in twenty-eight games with the Pirates. Primarily playing second baseman but also at times taking the positions of third baseman and shortstop, he continued to demonstrate his skills as a defensive specialist and ultimately achieved a fielding percentage of 1.000 for all three positions, having made no fielding errors during his appearances. He was less effective as an offensive player, batting .222 on average over twenty-eight games, or twelve hits in fifty-four at-bats. On June 2, the Pirates announced that Ngoepe would be returning to the minor leagues, where he would rejoin the Indianapolis Indians and work on his offensive play for a time. Although the demotion represented a setback for Ngoepe, team management informed him that if he demonstrated improvement upon his eventual return to the major leagues, such a setback would not occur again.

PERSONAL LIFE

Although Ngoepe primarily lives in the United States, he regularly returns to South Africa in the off-season to spend time with family. He particularly enjoys visiting the ballpark in Randburg, where his older brother, Christopher, still lives. "I grew up there and all my memories are there," he told Kepner. "I do love being there, knowing that I can practice and work on my baseball stuff on that same field I grew up on."

SUGGESTED READING

Associated Press. "Pirates Demote Gift Ngoepe, First African-Born Major Leaguer." *ESPN*, 2 June 2017, www.espn.com/mlb/story/_/id/19523297/pittsburgh-pirates-demote-gift-ngoepe-first-african-born-major-leaguer. Accessed 11 Aug. 2017.

Kepner, Tyler. "First African to Play in the Major Leagues Is a 'Pinnacle' for Baseball." *The New York Times*, 8 May 2017, nytimes.com/2017/05/08/sports/baseball/gift-ngoepe-south-africa-pittsburgh-pirates.html. Accessed 11 Aug. 2017.

Manel, David. "Pirates Prospect Gift Ngoepe on Hitting, Adjusting to Life in the US, and Helping His Teammates." *SBNation*, 24 May 2015, www.bucsdugout.com/platform/amp/2015/5/24/8651935/pirates-prospect-gift-ngoepe. Accessed 11 Aug. 2017.

Nesbitt, Stephen J. "Gift Ngoepe: 'No Matter Where You Are . . . You Can Still Make It.'" *Pittsburgh Post-Gazette*, 26 Apr. 2017, www.post-gazette.com/sports/pirates/2017/04/26/gift-ngoepe-pirates-african-born-mlb-debut-south-africa/stories/201704260180. Accessed 11 Aug. 2017.

Ngoepe, Gift. "A Conversation with Gift Ngoepe, Your New Favorite Baseball Player." Interview by Hannah Keyser. *Deadspin*, 27 Apr. 2017, deadspin.com/a-conversation-with-gift-ngoepe-your-new-favorite-base-1794721065/amp. Accessed 11 Aug. 2017.

Nightengale, Bob. "Pirates' Gift Ngoepe, First MLB Player from Africa, Wants 'To Be an Inspiration.'" *USA Today*, 23 May 2017, www.usatoday.com/story/sports/mlb/columnist/bob-nightengale/2017/05/23/gift-ngoepe-pirates-first-african-mlb-player-south-africa/102058280. Accessed 11 Aug. 2017.

Smith, Gary. "A Gift from Africa." *Sports Illustrated*, 10 Aug. 2009, www.si.com/vault/2009/08/10/105844802/a-gift-from-africa. Accessed 11 Aug. 2017.

—*Joy Crelin*

Viet Thanh Nguyen

Date of birth: March 13, 1971
Occupation: Author

Few authors have won the Pulitzer Prize, and fewer still have won it for their debut novel. Viet Thanh Nguyen did just that. His debut novel, *The Sympathizer* (2015), won the 2016 Pulitzer Prize for fiction. The story is written as a confession of a spy, a Vietnamese man who served as a double agent during the Vietnam War. Although the book has elements of both genres, it is neither a thriller nor a suspense novel. It is a serious work of literary fiction, and it explores such themes as memory and identity. Nguyen followed the success of his debut novel with a collection of short stories, simply titled *The Refugees* (2017). Though subtler in tone than *The Sympathizer*, the collection explored similar themes. "*The Refugees* comes at a time when Americans are being forced to reckon with what our country is becoming, what values we truly hold dear," wrote Michael Schaub for *NPR* (9 Feb. 2017). "It's hard not to feel for Nguyen's characters, many of whom have been dealt an unfathomably bad hand. But Nguyen never asks the reader to pity them; he wants us only to see them as human beings."

FLEEING VIETNAM

Viet Thanh Nguyen (pronounced "win") was born in Ban Me Thuot (now Buon Me Thout), Vietnam, on March 13, 1971. In the mid-1950s Vietnam was divided into North and South Vietnam. The North was under communist control,

By Fourandsixty (Own work) [CC BY-SA 4.0], via Wikimedia Commons

so Nguyen's parents, who were religious Catholics, moved to South Vietnam to avoid possible persecution. His mother's family also moved south, while his father's parents stayed in the north. In March 1975, when Nguyen was about four years old, the North Vietnamese army invaded his village. As Nguyen recalled to Terry Gross in an interview on NPR's *Fresh Air* (17 May 2016), at the time of the invasion, his father was on a business trip in Saigon (now Ho Chi Minh City), and because the North Vietnamese army cut off communication, his mother could not get a hold of him. So she fled by foot, taking her four-year-old son and his ten-year-old brother, and leaving behind—thinking that she would return—her sixteen-year-old adopted daughter. Nguyen's mother and her sons fled to a nearby port, where they boarded a barge, not knowing for certain whether Nguyen's father would be on that boat. Fortunately, however, he was.

ARRIVING IN AMERICA

The Nguyen family arrived in the United States as refugees in March 1975. They were first sent to Fort Indiantown Gap, Pennsylvania. For a few months the family had to split up, because no sponsor would take a family of four. He was taken in by a "white family" at the age of four, Nguyen told Gross, and "that's when my memory begins." He first stayed with a young couple. Then he was sent to a couple that had kids, and had a better idea of how to deal with children; there he was treated well. Even though Nguyen was separated from his parents for only a few months, he told Gross, "It was really traumatic for me." Not

having his older sister by his side, knowing she was left behind in Vietnam to an unknown future was also traumatizing. While growing up, he told Gross, he was "always haunted by that face . . . thinking, why is she there and not here?" He added "that sense of loss and of haunting had always stayed with me."

A few years later, in 1978, the family moved from Pennsylvania to San Jose, California, a city about an hour south of San Francisco. The family moved to downtown San Jose, which in his official website biography Nguyen called a "rough place to live." By this point, various Vietnamese communities had sprung up in California, especially in San Diego and the Bay Area. A friend of his mother was a businesswoman who had opened one of the first—Vietnamese grocery stores in the area. After working for that woman, his parents opened their own Vietnamese grocery store. They worked hard, putting in fourteen-hour days, seven days a week, and taking only three vacation days a year.

On Christmas Eve when Nguyen was about nine years old, he and his older brother were at home and got a phone call saying that his parents had been shot in their store. He was watching cartoons and did not know what to say. They were released from the hospital the next day and slowly but surely moved on with their lives. While speaking of the shooting during his interview with Gross, Nguyen offered historical and sociological insight about the shooting and Vietnamese Americans' relationship to violence at the time. "A lot of Vietnamese refugees to the United States brought violence with them," Nguyen said. "There was a lot of domestic violence, a lot of domestic abuse. People were traumatized. They were hurt. They were scared. The men faced downward mobility and alienation. And of course, they took it out on their families—their wives and their children. And these children, a lot of them joined gangs." By the time he was in high school he knew Vietnamese American teens in "real gangs" who carried guns and robbed houses. Nguyen and his family also faced racial discrimination.

WHO IS TELLING THE STORY?

One of the first profoundly life-changing moments happened when, around the age of ten, Nguyen watched the Francis Ford Coppola film *Apocalypse Now*. The film, a cinematic classic, takes place in 1970 in Vietnam during the war, though when it came out in 1979, the war had been over for a few years. Nguyen remembers rooting for the American soldiers—until the moment they started killing the Vietnamese characters who looked like him. The film left him confused about whose side he should be on. In a larger sense, it left him confused about identity. But it also sparked a realization that in the

United States, the Vietnam War was being told only from the American perspective. According to a profile by David Streitfeld for the *New York Times* (21 June 2016), Nguyen would go on "wrestling" with the film for the rest of his life, from boyhood to college and academia to his debut as a novelist. The film, in fact, inspired scenes in *The Sympathizer* and philosophical reflections about point of view. In an interview with Streitfeld, Nguyen said that although *Apocalypse Now* is an "important work of art," he will not "bow down before it. I'm going to fight with it because it fought with me."

Nguyen attended high school at Bellarmine College Preparatory High School. He attended both the University of California, Riverside (UC Riverside) and the University of California, Los Angeles (UCLA) before deciding on UC Berkeley. He received undergraduate degrees in English and ethnic studies in 1992. He earned his doctorate in English from UC Berkeley in 1997.

THE SYMPATHIZER
Although he had been writing short stories for journals and magazines for years—publishing in *Narrative*, *TriQuarterly*, and others—Nguyen did not publish a novel until 2015. His debut novel, *The Sympathizer*, attracted a great deal of critical attention and praise, especially after winning the Pulitzer Prize for fiction in 2016. In the novel the story is told by an unnamed narrator in the form of a forced confession written to a "commandant," who also does not have a name, as the Vietnam War comes to an end. The book opens with these words: "I am a spy, a sleeper, a spook, a man of two faces. Perhaps not surprisingly, I am also a man of two minds . . . able to see any issue from both sides." This thing he thought was a talent, in fact, he calls a "hazard." The tone of the book's opening was inspired by Ralph Ellison's 1952 novel *Invisible Man*, which tells the story of a young black man, from his perspective, who feels "invisible" to many people in both the black and white communities. Like Ellison's novel, Nguyen's is also about identity and point of view.

What Nguyen is exploring through the viewpoint of his narrator is a split identity. In a book review for the *New York Times* (2 Apr. 2015), Philip Caputo observed that such an identity is "literally in the protagonist's blood." He is the son of an unmarried couple, a French Catholic priest and a Vietnamese teen. The narrator loves his mother, while he despises his father. The duality of the protagonist is not only internal, however. His two good friends, Bon and Man, are on the opposite sides of the conflict. The narrator's mission eventually takes him to the United States, where he is brought on the set of a film, which seems to resemble *Apocalypse Now*, by a director who needs him to be an authenticity consultant.

The director is concerned with "authentic" details, such as wardrobe, but the point of view of the film, as a whole, is that of the American soldiers. The experience leaves the narrator disillusioned. At this point the mood of the book "darkens," according to Caputo.

The Sympathizer received generally excellent reviews and ended up on many best books of the year lists. Caputo called the book "remarkable," noting that it "fills a void in the literature, giving voice to the previously voiceless while it compels the rest of us to look at the events of forty years ago in a new light." For the *Guardian* (12 Mar. 2016), Randy Boyagoda observed, "*The Sympathizer* is an excellent literary novel, and one that ends, with unsettling present-day resonance, in a refugee boat where opposing ideas about intentions, actions and their consequences take stark and resilient human form." Aside from the Pulitzer Prize, the book also earned Nguyen other notable honors, including the Andrew Carnegie Medal for Excellence in Fiction from the American Library Association (ALA), the First Novel Prize from the Center for Fiction, a Gold Medal in First Fiction from the California Book Awards, and the Asian/Pacific American Literature Award from the Asian/Pacific American Librarian Association.

NOTHING EVER DIES
A year after the publication of *The Sympathizer*, Nguyen published the critical work *Nothing Ever Dies: Vietnam and the Memory of War* (2016), which many saw as the nonfiction addition to his debut novel. It also deals with themes of identity, both national and personal. The book explores how the Vietnam War has been remembered by people within a given culture, in monuments, and in books, films, and other works of art. The book looks at perceptions of the war not only in the United States and Vietnam, but also other Asian countries, such as South Korea, the Philippines, Laos, and Cambodia. "All wars are fought twice," writes Nguyen in the book. "The first time on the battlefield, the second time in memory." This philosophical book of essays, even though heavily about memory, both cultural and personal, is also about compassion. In a review for the *San Francisco Chronicle* (9 May 2016), Elizabeth Rosner concluded, "Those who risk searching among the borderless embers and ashes of war will find much to learn in Nguyen's pages." This book was a finalist for the National Book Award.

THE REFUGEES
Nguyen's next work of fiction, *The Refugees* (2017), was a collection of eight short stories. This much-anticipated work did not disappoint. The first short story, "Black-Eyed Women," is about a highly traumatized woman who lives

with her mother and works as a ghostwriter. After her mother is visited by her son's "ghost," she suspects her mother is losing her mind. But the narrator is later visited by the same "ghost," at which point she realizes that no matter how much she has tried to forget her brother—who was killed on a boat to America—she simply cannot let go of that painful memory. In the short story "The Other Man," an eighteen-year-old young man named Liem comes to the United States from Vietnam as a refugee. He ends up living with two men, one from England, the other from Hong Kong. He is later surprised to learn that they are a gay couple. Mia Alvar, in a review for the *New York Times* (13 Feb. 2017) called the book "superb." Later in the review she noted that the book's "subtle, attentive prose and straightforward narrative style perfectly suit the low-profile civilian lives it explores."

PERSONAL LIFE

Nguyen lives in Los Angeles with his wife, Lan Duong, and son, Ellison. He teaches English and American studies at the University of Southern California, where he has been a professor since 1997.

SUGGESTED READING

"Bio." *Viet Thanh Nguyen*, 2017, vietnguyen. info/author-viet-thanh-nguyen. Accessed 12 Apr. 2017.

Boyagoda, Randy. "*The Sympathizer* by Viet Thanh Nguyen Review—A Bold, Artful Debut." Review of *The Sympathizer*, by Viet Thanh Nguyen. *The Guardian*, 12 Mar. 2016, www.theguardian.com/books/2016/mar/12/the-sympathizer-viet-thanh-nguyen-review-debut. Accessed 12 Apr. 2017.

Caputo, Philip. Review of *The Sympathizer*, by Viet Thanh Nguyen. *New York Times*, 2 Apr. 2015, www.nytimes.com/2015/04/05/books/review/the-sympathizer-by-viet-thanh-nguyen.html. Accessed 12 Apr. 2017.

Nguyen, Viet Thanh. "Author Viet Thanh Nguyen Discusses *The Sympathizer* and His Escape from Vietnam." Interview by Terry Gross. *NPR*, 17 May 2016, www.npr.org/2016/05/17/478384200/author-viet-thanh-nguyen-discusses-the-sympathizer-and-his-escape-from-vietnam. Accessed 12 Apr. 2017.

Nguyen, Viet Thanh. "The Vietnam War, The American War." Interview by Ricardo Herrera. *Los Angeles Review of Books*, 9 Apr. 2016, lareviewofbooks.org/article/the-vietnam-war-the-american-war. Accessed 12 Apr. 2017.

Streitfield, David. "For Viet Thanh Nguyen, Author of *The Sympathizer*, a Pulitzer but No Peace." *New York Times*, 21 June 2016, www.nytimes.com/2016/06/22/books/

viet-thanh-nguyen-prizewinning-author-of-the-sympathizer-still-wrestles-with-apocalypse-now.html. Accessed 12 Apr. 2017.

SELECTED WORKS

The Sympathizer, 2015; *Nothing Ever Dies*, 2016; *The Refugees*, 2017

—*Dmitry Kiper*

Jay Nixon

Date of birth: February 13, 1956
Occupation: Governor of Missouri

The fifty-fifth governor of Missouri, Jay Nixon is a Democratic politician who also served as a state senator and was the state's longest-serving attorney general.

EARLY LIFE AND EDUCATION

Jay Nixon was born on February 13, 1956, in De Soto, Missouri, into a family with long roots in public service. One of his ancestors was a sheriff in Philadelphia who reportedly first read the Declaration of Independence to the public in 1776. His father, Jeremiah "Jerry" Nixon, served as the mayor of De Soto and a municipal judge. His mother, Betty, was a teacher and school board president.

Nixon attended De Soto High School, graduating in 1974, and then enrolled at the University of Missouri–Columbia, from which he graduated with a bachelor's degree in political science in 1978. He then entered the University of Missouri School of Law, earning a juris doctor degree in 1981. Upon completing his studies, Nixon worked in private practice in De Soto until 1986.

POLITICAL CAREER

Nixon entered politics in 1986 when he was elected to the Missouri Senate. He began his political career by working across party lines to pass legislation, including an expansion of prenatal care for pregnant women. He served three terms in the state senate, holding office from 1987 to 1993. In 1988, Nixon unsuccessfully ran for US Senate against incumbent Missouri senator John Danforth. After winning less than one-third of the vote, he put his ambitions for national office on hold and remained in the state senate.

In 1992, Nixon announced his plan to run for attorney general of Missouri. He successfully faced three candidates in a close election to win the Democratic primary. In his campaign for the state's top prosecutor position, he focused on several issues, including cleaning up corruption in the state and ending the desegregation busing program. His claim that the busing program was ineffective and cost the state more than $400 million annually, which he argued could better be spent in local school districts, pleased some voters but created a deep rift with African Americans, who represented a large share of the state's Democratic voters. Despite the loss of this support, Nixon won the general election against Republican David Steelman by a narrow margin and was sworn in on January 11, 1993, becoming Missouri's first Democratic attorney general in twenty-four years.

One of Nixon's first priorities was to restore the integrity of the attorney general's office and the public's confidence following a scandal in which his predecessor, William L. Webster, was investigated for embezzlement and conspiracy. Webster was later found guilty of a corruption charge and served time in a federal prison.

Nixon was reelected attorney general by a wide margin in 1996. In 1998, he made another bid for the US Senate. Despite having the public support of President Bill Clinton, Vice President Al Gore, and House Majority Leader Dick Gephardt, Nixon failed to gain the support of many African American Democrats, who remembered Nixon's plan to end state busing for desegregation, and he lost the election to incumbent candidate Kit Bond.

Nixon was reelected attorney general in 2000 and 2004, ultimately serving a record four terms. His achievements as attorney general include helping clean up government corruption, reducing crime, protecting the environment, and protecting consumer rights. He also helped reinstate campaign contribution limits, arguing before the US Supreme Court in *Nixon v. Shrink Missouri Government PAC* in 1999. He filed a lawsuit against tobacco companies that resulted in multibillion-dollar settlements. He also created a no-call telemarketing program that served as a model for other states.

In 2008, Nixon ran for governor of Missouri against Republican Kenny Hulshof. Echoing then–presidential candidate Barack Obama's call for change, Nixon also ran a change-based campaign, promising to increase access to health care and lower health-care costs, create jobs, provide tax relief for seniors, create a free college scholarship program, and improve government efficiency, accountability, and transparency. By this time, he had improved his relationship with many African American voters and found common ground with voters concerned about the rising costs of food, consumer goods, health insurance, medical care, and higher education. Nixon won the race by 19 percentage points and was sworn in on January 12, 2009, as the fifty-fifth governor of Missouri.

Nixon's achievements as governor include investments in education, job creation, and the passage of the Missouri Manufacturing Jobs Act, which gave auto manufacturers incentives to stay in the state. He also showed leadership in his handling of natural disasters, such as a catastrophic tornado that struck the city of Joplin on May 22, 2011.

On November 6, 2012, Nixon was reelected to a second term, defeating Republican challenger Dave Spence with 54.7 percent of the vote.

IMPACT

Having gained recognition as a politician who united people and breached partisan divides, Nixon stated that if Hillary Clinton did not run for president in 2016, he might consider doing so. However, his chances of positioning himself as a candidate for the Democratic nomination for the presidential election were shot down in 2014 following his handling of the violent protests that followed a police shooting of Michael Brown, an unarmed African American teenager, in Ferguson, Missouri, in August 2014. Many people were critical of Nixon's lack of decisiveness during the crisis and felt he had demonstrated a lack of leadership needed for higher office.

PERSONAL LIFE

Nixon and his wife, Georganne Wheeler Nixon, have two adult sons, Jeremiah and Willson.

SUGGESTED READING

"About the Governor." *Office of Missouri Governor Jay Nixon*. Office of Missouri Governor, n.d. Web. 4 Nov. 2015.

Glueck, Katie. "Jay Nixon Won't Rule Out 2016 Run." *Politico*. Politico, 21 Feb. 2014. Web. 4 Nov. 2015.

Lieb, David A. "Mo. Gov. Candidate Stresses Political Background." *USA Today*. Gannett, 23 Sept. 2008. Web. 3 Nov. 2015.

Lieb, David A. "Mo. Gov. Nixon Sworn In, Calls for Cooperation." *Southeast Missourian*. Southeast Missourian, 14 Jan. 2013. Web. 4 Nov. 2015.

Smith, Mitch. "Missouri Governor Jay Nixon's Legacy Firmly Linked to Ferguson." *New York Times*. New York Times, 23 Sept. 2015. Web. 4 Nov. 2015.

Yokley, Eli. "Why Jay Nixon Missed His Moment." *Politico*. Politico, 21 Aug. 2014. Web. 4 Nov. 2015.

—*Barb Lightner*

Issey Ogata

Date of birth: February 22, 1952
Occupation: Actor, comedian

Issey Ogata, a veteran Japanese actor and comedian, has gained attention in the United States for his role in the 2016 Martin Scorsese picture *Silence*. The film, based on a 1969 novel by Shūsaku Endō about Portuguese Jesuit missionaries in seventeenth-century Japan, was years in the making. Ogata, for instance, was cast in 2009, but Scorsese's vision began during a trip to Japan in 1989. The film, which is about Christian persecution and the nature of faith, was a passion project for the famous director. Ogata was praised for his detailed portrayal of Inoue Masashige, known as the Inquisitor, a government official who tortures Christian missionaries in an effort to understand but ultimately rid them of their faith. Among his other notable film performances are *Yi Yi* (2000), *Tony Takitani* (2004), and *The Sun* (2005).

Ogata began his career as a comic monologist in the 1980s. To date, he has created more than six hundred characters, like a beleaguered white-collar worker, a bored housewife, or a musician who can't get a date, for his long-running series of one-man shows presented under the title *A Catalogue of City Life*. "I describe people who are trying to fill the gap between themselves and reality," he explained to James Sterngold for the *New York Times* (26 Sept. 1993). "I'm not making fun of them. What they're doing is natural behavior, under the circumstances." His subtle parody of Japanese city life, paired with appearances on television, made him one of the most famous comedians in Japan in the 1990s. Though his sketches incorporate dialogue, Ogata, who performs on a bare stage with only a handful of props, is best known for his mime and impression work. He has been compared to physical comedy greats Charlie Chaplin and Buster Keaton.

EARLY COMEDY

Ogata was born in Fukuoka Prefecture, on the north shore of Japan's island of Kyushu, in 1952. When Ogata was a child, his father's job reportedly required the family to move frequently, and he used humor to make friends with each new uprooting. After failing his university exam, he joined an acting school and, later, an acting troupe. He began performing his own work in the 1970s while also holding a job as a construction worker. In 1980, he performed his first one-man show, *Twelve Rough Sketches of a Bartender*, and in 1981, he won a television competition for comedians called *Owarai Star Tanjo!*. He began performing his best-known series, *Toshi seikatsu katarogu* (or *A Catalogue of City Life*), in Tokyo

Photo by Todd Williamson/Getty Images

in 1982. His first audience members, his manager, Morita Kiyoko, told Simon Fanshawe for the London *Sunday Times* (15 Feb. 1998), were "students, people who liked the music of [experimental composer] John Cage and a bunch of math professors from the university." Ogata was an important part of Japan's burgeoning underground theater scene. Most theater in Japan, and most comedy, was at that time defined by strict tradition. Ogata, has proudly noted that he did not come up through the traditional master-student system of *manzai*, a stylized Japanese stand-up comedy that involves one straight man and one funny man.

"From the beginning," Ogata told Yoko Hani for the *Japan Times* (6 Mar. 2005), "I have regarded myself as a performer who cannot fit into the existing system." Ogata drew inspiration from his days as a construction worker, during which he quietly observed people as they moved through the city. The white-collar corporate workers (or *sarariman*, as they are called in Japan) all dressed the same, but Ogata also saw their individual characters and wondered what they thought about and what they did with their days. One his favorite characters, a blundering sarariman named Yama-chan, verges on the absurd. In one sketch, Yama-chan suffers from a sudden bout of amnesia before a client meeting; in another, he finds a nearly dead crow on the street. He carries the crow around all day, surprised that no one cares about it.

STARDOM

With his longtime collaborators, a husband-and-wife team of stage director Morita Yuzo and producer-manager Morita Kiyoko, Ogata continued to develop sketches and perform across Japan through the 1980s. His fame as a theater artist grew after he began appearing on Japanese television shows, and by 1998, his official fan club numbered over 56,000 members. He first brought his show, *A Catalogue of City Life*, to New York in 1993. It was his first international engagement. Ogata was initially worried that his humor would confuse a foreign audience, but a team of translators—non-Japanese speaking audience members are given a headset and receive simultaneous translation—facilitate his performance. The result is, for the most part, very successful, though in one performance, Ogata's translator skipped ahead six pages in the script. "He noticed it pretty quickly, though," Ogata recalled to Ed Harris for the London *Evening Standard* (19 Oct. 2001). Ogata offers subtle social commentary of Japanese mores in his work. "He tries to look at the gap between how people view themselves and how other people view them," Duncan Hamilton, an Irish translator of Ogata's, told James Rampton for the UK *Independent* (21 Feb. 1998). "One of his main concerns is to burst that bubble. All his characters are hopeless. Issey concentrates on people who are unintentionally dislocated from society."

FILM CAREER

Ogata has appeared in a number of films over the course of his career, in addition to directing and writing. One of his best known is *Yi Yi* (2000; also known in English as *A One and a Two*), a celebrated film by the late Taiwanese American filmmaker Edward Yang, a leading figure of the New Taiwan film movement in the 1980s. *New York Times* critic A. O. Scott described *Yi Yi* as an "intimate epic of a middle-class Taipei's [*sic*] family's everyday struggles" in his October 4, 2000, review. It follows the tribulations of software engineer and patriarch NJ, his family members, and his long-lost high school sweetheart. A lot happens in the film, but as Scott noted, the plot never descends into melodrama. Ogata plays NJ's work friend, Mr. Ota. The film premiered at the 2000 Cannes Film Festival—where Yang won an award for best director—and opened in New York in October 2000, the first of Yang's films to receive US distribution.

Ogata went on to star in the 2004 film *Tony Takitani*, based on a 2002 Haruki Murakami short story of the same name and directed by Jun Ichikawa. It won a special jury prize at the Locarno Film Festival that year. Ogata plays Tony, a lonely man who draws technical illustrations of machines, and his wife, Eiko (played by Rie Miyazawa). In nearly every respect, the couple enjoys an idyllic marriage, but Tony is irked by his wife's obsession with buying expensive clothes. Tony has enough money to afford his wife's habit, but his request that she spend less leads to their undoing. As Manohla Dargis wrote in a positive review for the *New York Times* (29 July 2005), the film can be interpreted as an oblique allegory about consumerism and postwar Japan. *Tony Takitani*, she wrote, is a "delicate wisp of a film with a surprisingly sharp sting."

Ogata next starred in Russian director Alexander Sokurov's 2005 film *Solnze*, or *The Sun*, about Japanese emperor Hirohito. Ogata played Hirohito as he made the decision to offer an unconditional surrender to the Allies to end World War II. In an interview for the *Japan Times*, Ogata said that for the difficult role, he had to draw on his twenty-five years of acting experience. Dargis, in her *Times* review (7 Oct. 2005), dubbed his performance "mesmerizing." Hirohito may have been revered as a deity, but Ogata successfully found moments that emphasized his humanity. Director Martin Scorsese, when he cast Ogata in his film *Silence*, told the actor that he was impressed by one scene in particular. "It's a scene where the Emperor met with [General Douglas] MacArthur, and he's about to leave, and nobody's there to open his door—and he's never opened his own door, so he's very carefully opening his door," Ogata explained to Nick Newman for the blog the *Film Stage* (21 Dec. 2016). "Marty liked that scene very much."

SILENCE

In 2009, Ogata sent Scorsese an audition tape, hoping to secure a role in the director's long-anticipated film *Silence*. Ogata met Scorsese the same year when the latter visited Japan. He was cast, but the movie was postponed for six years. In the interim, Ogata read Shūsaku Endō's novel and developed his character based on the scene he had from his audition. In an interview with Jazz Tangcay for the blog *Awards Daily* (9 Jan. 2017), Ogata said that he employed a similar process for discovering Inoue's character to that which he used to flesh out characters in his own comedic work. "I went from external"—facial expressions, body language, and tone of voice—"to internal," he said. The film also stars Andrew Garfield, Liam Neeson, and Adam Driver. Ogata's performance was widely praised. Cara Buckley, writing for the *New York Times* (13 Jan. 2017), expressed incredulity that Ogata had not received an Academy Award nomination because he "brought such depth, twinkling humor and curiosity to the part." Nevertheless, the film was poorly received. Critics praised its actors and stunning visuals but lamented its lack of cohesion. Ogata felt differently, telling Tangcay, "It's a film that will stay with me for life."

SUGGESTED READING

Dargis, Manohla. "He's an Isolated Fellow; She's Addicted to Shopping." *The New York Times*, 29 July 2005, www.nytimes.com/2005/07/29/movies/hes-an-isolated-fellow-shes-addicted-to-shopping.html. Accessed 13 June 2017.

Dargis, Manohla. "New York Film Festival Reviews; The Sun." *The New York Times*, 7 Oct. 2005, query.nytimes.com/gst/fullpage.html?res=9C00E2D91E30F934A35753C1A9639C8B63. Accessed 13 June 2017.

Newman, Nick. "'Silence' Star Issey Ogata on Martin Scorsese Cinephilia and the Kindness of Edward Yang." *Film Stage*, 21 Dec. 2016, thefilmstage.com/features/silence-star-issey-ogata-on-martin-scorseses-cinephilia-and-the-kindness-of-edward-yang. Accessed 13 June 2017.

Ogata, Issey. "Interview: Issey Ogata on How Martin Scorsese's Silence Made Him Question His Own Beliefs." Interview by Jazz Tangcay. *AwardsDaily*, 9 Jan. 2017, www.awardsdaily.com/2017/01/09/interview-issey-ogata-martin-scorseses-silence-made-question-beliefs. Accessed 13 June 2017.

Rampton, James. "Issey for Real?" *Independent* [UK], 21 Feb. 1998, www.independent.co.uk/life-style/issey-for-real-1146147.html. Accessed 13 June 2017.

Scott, A. O. "Film Festival Review; Of Taiwan's Bourgeoisie and Its Affecting Cinema." *The New York Times*, 4 Oct. 2000, www.nytimes.com/2000/10/04/movies/film-festival-review-of-taiwan-s-bourgeoisie-and-its-affecting-charms.html. Accessed 13 June 2017.

Yoko Hani. "Issey Ogata: Comic Chameleon." *Japan Times*, 6 Mar. 2005, www.japantimes.co.jp/life/2005/03/06/to-be-sorted/issey-ogata-comic-chameleon. Accessed 13 June 2017.

SELECTED WORKS

Yi Yi, 2000; *Tony Takitani*, 2004; *The Sun*, 2005; *Silence*, 2016

—*Molly Hagan*

Nneka Ogwumike

Date of birth: July 2, 1990
Occupation: Basketball player

Despite being a relative latecomer to the sport of basketball, Nneka Ogwumike has managed to rack up an impressive list of accomplishments. After helping Cy-Fair Shock's youth club advance to the 2004 Amateur Athletic Union (AAU) National Championships, the six-foot-two Ogwumike and the Lady Bobcats of Cy-Fair High School reached the 2006–7 University

By SusanLesch (Own work) [CC BY 4.0], via Wikimedia Commons

Interscholastic League (UIL) Girls Basketball State Finals before capturing their first 5A state title in 2008. She subsequently found success at the college level, guiding the Stanford Cardinal to four straight Final Fours and a National Collegiate Athletic Association (NCAA) championship game appearance.

Ogwumike has also made her mark on the Women's National Basketball Association (WNBA). In 2012, the Los Angeles Sparks forward was voted rookie of the year. Since then, Ogwumike has made three consecutive All-Star Game appearances under her belt. Her greatest achievement came in 2016, when she won her first WNBA title and was also named the regular-season most valuable player (MVP). Penny Toler, the Sparks' general manager, attributes the rising star's success to her work ethic and poise. "She's so good, but with room to grow," Toler told Michelle Smith for *espnW* (14 July 2012). "Anybody who has ever met Nneka can see she has a maturity about her. . . . With her high basketball IQ and her athleticism, she is going to be a huge star."

RAW TALENT

Nnemkadi "Nneka" Chinwe Victoria Ogwumike was born to Nigerian immigrants on July 2, 1990, in Tomball, Texas. She grew up with three younger sisters—Chinenye "Chiney," Chisom "Olivia," and Ernima "Erica"—in the Houston suburb of Cypress, where her mother, Ify Ogwumike, serves as assistant superintendent of student services for the Cypress-Fairbanks (Cy-Fair) Independent School District. Her father, Peter Ogwumike, is an engineer in the tech sector. Growing up, Ogwumike and her siblings were encouraged to take up sports by their mother, an avid runner who told Adam Coleman for the *Houston Chronicle* (12 Nov. 2013), "It was about . . . helping them become strong women and giving them an outlet." Ogwumike was enrolled in gymnastics for a while.

At the suggestion of her mother's coworker, Ogwumike tried out for the Cy-Fair Shock, a local AAU girls' basketball club, at the age of eleven. Despite never having played previously, the sixth-grader was recruited by the team's coach, Albert Coleman, who was impressed by her stature and sheer athleticism. "I told her mom she was going to be phenomenal," he confided to Tom FitzGerald for the *San Francisco Chronicle* (30 Dec. 2010). He added, "She couldn't make a layup, but she was the most athletic kid on the court." Ogwumike quickly dedicated herself to learning how to play the game. "I wasn't real coordinated. I didn't have much knowledge of the game," she shared with Todd Hveem for the *Houston Chronicle* (26 Jan. 2006). She continued, "It took me about a year or maybe two years. At the 13-under nationals, I started to play hard and have a full understanding of the game." Ogwumike and her Cy-Fair Shock teammates tied for ninth at the 2004 AAU 13-Under Division I National Championship.

MULTISPORT EXCELLENCE

Ogwumike also had success as a member of Cy-Fair High School's girls' varsity basketball team, which went undefeated (36–0) in 2005–6 before losing to the Westside Wolves in the UIL's Class 5A Region III semifinal. Following the addition of Ogwumike's sister Chiney, the Lady Bobcats remained unbeaten (38–0) in 2006–7, narrowly losing the 5A Girls Basketball State Championship in overtime to Rockwall's Lady Jackets. Ogwumike capped off her final season at Cy-Fair (2007–8) by averaging 18.2 points and 9.3 rebounds per game for the Bobcats, who finished with a 39–2 record and claimed their first-ever Class 5A state title in March 2008. Along with being named state tournament MVP and homecoming queen, Ogwumike was the Gatorade State Player of the Year and *MaxPrep.com*'s Girls National Athlete of the Year.

Basketball was not the only sport in which Ogwumike excelled. In 2005 she was named District 17-5A Newcomer of the Year after leading the Bobcats volleyball squad to the first round of the state playoffs. As a senior Ogwumike—joined by Chiney—helped the Bobcats reach the 2007–8 Class 5A state volleyball state tournament qualifier, where they lost to the Amarillo Sandies. In addition to basketball and volleyball, Ogwumike also joined varsity track and

field for a year. During that time, she captained the team.

STANFORD CARDINAL

In the fall of 2008, after being recruited by Duke and Baylor Universities, among others, Ogwumike enrolled at Stanford University in Palo Alto, California, where she majored in psychology. "Ever since I can remember, [my parents have] told me, 'Your education will take you a long way. That always comes first,'" she recalled to Mechelle Voepel for *espnW* (10 Nov. 2009). "I saw in Stanford my best opportunity for having a career in basketball and a wonderful life after basketball." Ogwumike made fourteen starts and averaged 10.6 points and 6.1 rebounds in thirty-eight appearances for the Stanford Cardinal, which finished the 2008–9 year with the Pacific-10 Conference's regular-season and tournament titles as well as a 2009 NCAA Final Four berth. Ogwumike, who led the league in shooting percentage (62.9 percent), also placed into the Pac-10 All-Freshman and All-Tournament teams.

By her sophomore season, Ogwumike had improved her vertical jump, shooting stroke, and footwork. This was evident in the 18.5 points and 9.9 rebounds she averaged in thirty-eight games, which included 23 rebounds—a school record—against Oregon. The Cardinal women went on to repeat their performance as Pac-10 regular-season and tournament champions before reaching the 2010 NCAA women's final. Not only was Ogwumike named Pac-10 Player of the Year and Pac-10 Tournament Most Outstanding Player, she was also a finalist for the Wade Trophy and John R. Wooden Award.

Over the next two years, the Cardinal squad, which then included Chiney as well, kept a stranglehold on the conference's regular-season and tournament titles. During her junior season, Ogwumike's team-leading 17.5 points per game and 58.6 shooting percentage helped guide her team to a 33–3 overall record, including a third consecutive NCAA Final Four appearance, which they narrowly lost to Texas A & M, 62–63. Ogwumike, an All Pac-10 first-team selection, was voted to the State Farm Coaches' All-American team while also earning All-America honors from the Associated Press (AP) and US Basketball Writers Association (USBWA). She was also a candidate for the Wade and Naismith trophies as well as the Wooden Award.

During this period, Ogwumike also began playing at the international level. A year after winning the FIBA Americas U18 Championship, Ogwumike claimed her second consecutive gold medal at the 2009 U19 World Championship, scoring (13.6 points per game) and rebounds (9.9 per game). Her third gold medal came courtesy of Team USA's first-place finish at the 2011 Summer Universiade in Shenzhen, China.

WNBA CAREER

In her final college season (2011–12), Ogwumike posted career-high averages in points (22.5), rebounds (10.2), and free-throw percentage (.830). She reached her fourth straight Final Four, scoring a game-leading 22 points in the Cardinal loss against Baylor and ending her career as the second all-time leading scorer. In mid-April the Los Angeles Sparks selected Ogwumike as the WNBA's top draft pick; by late April, the team had signed her to its roster.

With her athleticism, maturity, and mid-range jump shot, Ogwumike made what she herself termed a "seamless transition" to the WNBA. Under Coach Carol Ross, the Sparks' starting power forward led all rookies in several categories: points (14 ppg), rebounds (7.5 rpg), blocked shots (0.8 bpg), and double-doubles (9). For her effort Ogwumike was the top vote-getter for 2012 WNBA Rookie of the Year. Her team finished second (24–10) in the Western Conference, defeating San Antonio to reach the conference finals, where they lost to the Minnesota Lynx. During the offseason, Ogwumike played in Poland, averaging 17.5 points for CCC Polkowice, which reached the EuroLeague Women Final Eight in 2013. She won the Tom Hansen Medal for leadership and athletic excellence as well.

Ogwumike put up nearly identical numbers during the 2013 season, averaging 14.6 points and 7.6 rebounds per game. She made her All-Star debut as a reserve and was among the league leaders in field-goal percentage (.566) and offensive rebounds (95). For the second straight year, the Sparks were division runners-up, with a 24–10 record, before falling to the Phoenix Mercury in the Western Conference Semifinals.

By the start of the 2014 season, a new collective bargaining agreement had been reached, and an investment group led by NBA legend Magic Johnson and former player Lisa Leslie acquired the financially struggling Sparks. The team underwent another change when general manager Penny Toler replaced Ross as head coach. Despite this, Ogwumike averaged 15.8 points and 7.1 rebounds per game for the Sparks, who were fourth-place finishers in the Western Conference. At the 2014 WBNA All-Star Game—Ogwumike's second consecutive appearance—she and Chiney, the Connecticut Sun's top pick, made history by becoming the first pair of sisters to take part in the event.

CHALLENGES AND VICTORIES

Ogwumike missed the first four games of the 2015 season, following an ankle injury. When she returned to the Sparks, the roster was missing a key player: All-Star forward Candace Parker, who announced she would sit out the first half following a grueling offseason playing professionally overseas. Under a new coach, Brian Agler, the Sparks, who opened the season with a record seven-game winless streak, relied on Ogwumike, Jantel Lavender, and Kristi Toliver for scoring. Despite the slow start, after Parker's return, they finished the season with an overall 14–20 record, fourth place in the Western Conference, and a berth in the playoffs, where they suffered a first-round elimination to Minnesota. With her average of 15.8 points and 7 rebounds per game, Ogwumike was the team's second-leading scorer, behind Parker. Accolades included a third All-Star appearance and an All-Defensive First Team selection.

Ogwumike went on to have her best season to date in 2016. She averaged 19.7 points, 9.1 rebounds, 3.1 assists, and 1.1 blocks per game— all professional career-highs—while also leading the league in field-goal percentage (.665) and free-throw percentage (.869). Her team was equally impressive, opening the 2016 season with eleven straight victories. They followed that up by winning nine of the next ten games, for a 20–1 record. By season's end, the Sparks had the league's second-best record (26–8), clinching the second seed in the WNBA Playoffs. Ogwumike was overwhelmingly the 2016 MVP pick, earning thirty-one of the thirty-nine first-place votes.

WNBA TITLE

Ogwumike put on a show in the Western Conference Semifinals. She shot 60 percent while averaging 21 points, 8.5 rebounds, 3.5 assists, 1.7 blocks, and 2 steals to help the Sparks reach the WNBA Finals. The series against Western Conference rival Minnesota Lynx was among the league's most memorable. Ogwumike had nineteen points and nine rebounds in her team's nail-biting 78–76 Game 1 victory. She followed that up with a double-double (14 points and 12 rebounds) in the series-tying 60–79 loss. Although Ogwumike's 21 points and 9 rebounds helped the Sparks clinch Game 3 (92–75) and regain the series lead, her 11 points and 8 rebounds were not enough in their Game 4 loss (79–85).

Ogwumike was a critical factor in the Sparks' final possession of the deciding game. Her offensive rebound and put-back propelled the franchise to a 77–76 victory and a championship title. However, the Game 5 victory was marred when league officials admitted that they had missed calling a violation on another fourth-quarter shot made by Ogwumike—after the clock had expired, with 1:14 to go. In October 2016 Ogwumike added another title to her

WNBA résumé: president of the Women's National Basketball Players Association (WNBPA).

After spending her third postseason playing for the Russian team Dynamo Kursk, Ogwumike returned to the Sparks ready to defend their title. She had signed a contract extension for an undisclosed amount in February 2017.

PERSONAL LIFE

Off the court, Ogwumike, whose two other sisters play basketball for Rice University, serves as an advocate for fellow Nigerian women. In the spring of 2014, she and Chiney promoted the social media campaign #BringBackOurGirls to raise awareness regarding the kidnappings of hundreds of Nigerian schoolgirls by extremist group Boko Haram. They also raised money for UNICEF programs aimed at providing Nigerian girls with access to a quality education.

SUGGESTED READING

Coleman, Adam. "Ogwumikes Thriving with Basketball as Family Business." *Chron*, Houston Chronicle (TX), 12 Nov. 2013, www.chron.com/neighborhood/champions-klein/sports/article/Ogwumikes-thriving-with-basketball-as-family-9519175.php. Accessed 8 June 2017.

FitzGerald, Tom. "Stanford's Ogwumike Sisters a Powerful Combination." *SFGate.com*, San Francisco Chronicle, 30 Dec. 2010, www.sfgate.com/sports/article/Stanford-s-Ogwumike-sisters-a-powerful-combination-2451863.php. Accessed 8 June 2017.

Hveem, Todd. "Girls Basketball: Cy-Fair's Ogwumike Is Truly Amazing." *Chron*, Houston Chronicle (TX), 26 Jan. 2006, www.chron.com/neighborhood/cyfair-sports/article/Girls-basketball-Cy-Fair-s-Ogwumike-is-truly-1897652.php. Accessed 8 June 2017.

Smith, Michelle. "Nneka Ogwumike Fits Right In." *espnW*, 14 July 2012, www.espn.com/wnba/story/_/id/8164160/transition-pros-seamless-los-angeles-sparks-rookie-nneka-ogwumike. Accessed 8 June 2017.

Voepel, Mechelle. "It's School First for Ogwumike." *espnW*, 10 Nov. 2009, www.espn.com/ncw/preview2009/columns/story?id=4640058&columnist=voepel_mechelle. Accessed 8 June 2017.

—*Bertha Muteba*

Johannes Öhman

Date of Birth: July 1967
Occupation: Artistic director of the Royal Swedish Ballet

Johannes Öhman is the Swedish artistic director at the Royal Swedish Ballet (RSB). In 2016, he and Sasha Waltz, a German contemporary dance choreographer, were named the new artistic directors of the Staatsballet Berlin. The two are slated to assume their posts in 2019, but the announcement of their appointment shocked and angered dancers involved with the theater. A petition protesting Öhman and Waltz, circulated by the dancers, garnered five thousand signatures in a week. The reasons for this reaction are complicated. According to the official petition, dancers were first and foremost opposed to Waltz, a well-known choreographer whom they feel will challenge the theater's long-standing commitment to classical ballet. Hiring her, the petition said, as quoted by Roslyn Sulcas for the *New York Times* (16 Sept. 2016), "has to be compared to an appointment of a tennis trainer as a football coach."

This sentiment may be exacerbated by the fact that the two will follow Nacho Duato, a Spanish choreographer with a taste for modern dance, when Duato's tenure ends in 2019. A classically trained dancer himself, Öhman, the petitioners feel, is more appropriate to the theater's mission, but they reject the idea of hiring two artistic directors. They would prefer, as quoted by Sulcas, one director "with a clear artistic vision and relevant experience."

But artistic differences are only part of the story—politics and cultural identity play an important part, too. In their petition, the dancers note the unusual timing of the announcement to appoint Waltz and Öhman. Duato was only two years into his five-year contract when the announcement of his departure was made, but Berlin's mayor, Michael Müller, made the announcement on September 7, several days before an important state election. The dancers believe he engineered the good news—replacing a deeply unpopular artistic director with a well-known modern choreographer—to win votes.

The Staatsballett Berlin was officially founded in 2004, but was the result of a merger of the ballet companies at the Staatsoper Berlin, the Deutsche Oper Berlin, and Komische Oper Berlin. Historically, Berlin has allotted generous public funds for opera and dance, but after the fall of the Berlin Wall in 1990, a unified city was left with too many houses and too few funds to support them all. The Staatsballett Berlin sought to address this problem through consolidation and became Germany's largest ballet company in the process. With this distinction came the heavy mantle of German artistic tradition in a city eager to reclaim its cultural dominance. "Who should embody [the] tradition if not us?" Elinor Jagodnik, a dancer and a representative of the petitioners, asked Sulcas. "There are twenty times more contemporary dance companies here, specially in Berlin. Why would you mix that up? We cannot leave the classical heritage to Moscow and Paris."

EARLY LIFE AND DANCE CAREER

Öhman was born in Stockholm, Sweden, in July 1967. At fourteen, he enrolled at the Royal Swedish Ballet School, where he studied with the late Raymond Franchetti, the former director of the Paris Ballet de l'Opéra; Russian teacher Konstantin Damianov; and the Swedish ballerina and film star Ellen Rasch, who died in 2015. In 1986 he became a soloist with the Basler Ballet in Basel, Switzerland. It was a big year for Öhman, as he also won the Prix de l'AROP (Association pour le Rayonnement de l'Opéra National de Paris) at the Paris International Dance Competition and first prize at the Swedish Eurovision competition for young dancers. He was also a finalist at the prestigious Varna International Ballet Competition in Varna, Bulgaria. Öhman was invited to return to Stockholm and dance for the Royal Swedish Ballet (RSB) in 1987; he was appointed soloist in 1991. During his career, Öhman danced soloist parts from a number of artistically disparate choreographers, including the neoclassical New York City Ballet founder George Balanchine and the more cerebral and experimental American dancer William Forsythe. He also danced pieces choreographed by Mats Ek, a fellow Swede with whom Öhman would work closely as the director of the RSB.

STOCKHOLM 59° NORTH AND GÖTEBORG DANCE COMPANY

In 2001, Öhman became the artistic director of a neoclassical-contemporary dance company called Stockholm 59° North. (The name refers to Stockholm's latitude.) Madeleine Onne, a soloist with the Royal Swedish Ballet, founded the company, made up of fellow RSB dancers, in 1997. The ensemble made their debut at the Jacobs Pillow Dance Festival in Becket, Massachusetts, the same year. In her review for the New York Times (16 Aug. 1997), Jennifer Dunning wrote that the Royal Swedish Ballet had not performed in the United States in twenty-one years. "One wonders why these exhilarating performers have been absent for so long," she wrote. The troupe focuses on contemporary Swedish choreographers and the avant-garde. A performance at Jacobs Pillow in 2005, during Öhman's tenure as artistic director, was more eclectic; it featured short pieces from Virpi Pahkinen, a

Finnish choreographer; Örjan Andersson from Sweden; and Ek. Öhman left the company and retired from dance in 2007. He was appointed artistic director at the contemporary Göteborg Dance Company (formerly the Gothenburg Ballet) in Gothenburg, Sweden, the same year. Under his leadership, the company collaborated with artists like Ek, his future co–artistic director Waltz, the Belgian choreographer Wim Vandekeybus, and Swedish choreographer Johan Inger.

ROYAL SWEDISH BALLET

Öhman became the artistic director of the Royal Swedish Ballet, where he had trained as a teenager and danced as a soloist as a young man, in 2011. Founded in 1773, the Royal Swedish Ballet is one of the oldest professional ballet companies in the world. The company performs classical work, but under Öhman's direction, it also made an effort to include more contemporary pieces in its repertoire. In 2013 Öhman and the RSB commissioned Ek—who is the son of the late experimental choreographer, Birgit Cullberg—to choreograph a retelling of William Shakespeare's Romeo and Juliet for the company's 240th anniversary. It was Ek's first full-length ballet in seventeen years, and he was enthusiastic about his partnership with Öhman. "I think the direction taken by Johannes is thrilling and I am happy to be part of that initiative," he told Maggie Foyer for Dance Europe (1 July 2013). Ek's version of the tragic romance places young Juliet at its center, focusing on the young woman's anguish, choosing between her lover, Romeo, and the will of her family. "She's sweet, but she's also very, very strong," Öhman told Christina Campodonico for the Los Angeles Times (8 June 2016) of Ek's Juliet.

The ballet, titled Juliet and Romeo, was also inspired by the Arab Spring, a spate of protests, demonstrations, and revolution that swept through the Arab world beginning in Tunisia in 2010. Campodonico wrote that Ek saw parallels "between the lovers' fervor for each other and the fearlessness of Arab youth." That inspiration was reflected in the show's design. Ek also saw fit to trade Sergei Prokofiev's iconic score for the music of Pyotr Ilyich Tchaikovsky—a decision Foyer praised in her review. The reworked orchestral music liberates the work, she wrote, allowing "Ek to fashion a new drama: simple, lucid [with] amazing levels of intensity."

In a review for CriticalDance (1 Oct. 2013), Foyer called the ballet a "tremendous coup" for Öhman. "We can be grateful to Johannes Öhman's persistence in persuading Ek to make this new creation for the company as it stands among his best," she wrote.

In 2015, Öhman commissioned Alexander Ekman to choreograph a full-length adaptation of Shakespeare's *A Midsummer Night's Dream*. The production was one of the most successful of Öhman's tenure thus far. A reviewer for the blog *Totally Stockholm* (1 Sept. 2016) called the production, featuring music from Mikael Karlsson and vocals by Anna von Hausswolff, a "visual feast."

STAATSBALLETT BERLIN

When Öhman joined the Göteborg Dance Company, he was criticized for being too classical for such a contemporary company; when he returned to RSB, his years of working in contemporary dance miffed critics, and he suffered the opposite criticism. In 2016, when it was announced that he would join Sasha Waltz as artistic director of the Staatsballett Berlin, a vocal chorus objected on similar grounds. Ballet tends to be a traditional art form; for much of its history, the correct way to dance a role was taught by one generation of performers to the next. At the same time, revered twentieth-century choreographers like Balanchine made a career of modernizing the classics. Dance has always maintained a healthy tension between these two values.

Duato, the Staatsballett director preceding Öhman and Waltz, is unpopular among dancers and critics alike. He was appointed in 2014, and in 2015, performances were cancelled when dancers went on strike over a payment dispute. Still, Duato's style (however poorly received) is more classical than that of Waltz. The head of her own Berlin-based company, Sasha Waltz & Guests, Waltz is considered a big name in Germany. Jennifer Stahl, for *Dance Magazine* (7 Sept. 2016), described her aesthetic this way: "Although she is already a darling of the Berlin dance scene, the dance theater choreographer is known for wildly avant garde collaborations, sometimes literally setting stages on fire." (The phrase "dance theater" in this description is important; for the dancers at the Staatsballett Berlin, there is a big difference between classical ballet and the less prestigious "dance theater.") Perhaps most troubling for the dancers is that Waltz will be largely responsible for creating new works, whereas Öhman will focus on administrative and executive director duties. Waltz also plans to keep her job with her own company. Still, Waltz and Öhman have said that fears about their impending appointment are unfounded.

Öhman worked with Waltz while he was the artistic director of the Göteborg Dance Company, and according to the Berlin press, their partnership was her idea. In early September, both Öhman and Waltz were scheduled to meet the company for the first time. (Öhman admits that, prior to his appointment, he had never seen the Staatsballett Berlin perform.) Waltz opted not to attend the meeting, leaving Öhman to soothe the dancers himself, though he was unsuccessful. After the meeting Öhman and Waltz released a joint statement: "We find it very unfortunate that the representative's current tone, aggressive discourse and spread of disinformation harms the institution of the Staatsballett."

SUGGESTED READING

Campodonico, Christina. "'Juliet and Romeo'? Royal Swedish Ballet Gives Shakespeare a Twist at Segerstrom." *Los Angeles Times*, 8 June 2016, www.latimes.com/entertainment/arts/la-et-cm-royal-swedish-ballet-juliet-20160607-snap-story.html. Accessed 15 Nov. 2016.

Dunning, Jennifer. "An Odd Romantic Duet: The Grass Gets the Man." *The New York Times*, 16 Aug. 1997, www.nytimes.com/1997/08/16/arts/an-odd-romantic-duet-the-grass-gets-the-man.html. Accessed 15 Nov. 2016.

Ek, Mats. Interview by Maggie Foyer. *Dance Europe*, 1 July 2013, pp. 13+.

Foyer, Maggie. "Royal Swedish Ballet: Julia & Romeo." Review of *Julia and Romeo*, choreographed by Mats Ek. *CriticalDance*, 1 Oct. 2013, criticaldance.org/royal-swedish-ballet-julia-romeo. Accessed 16 Nov. 2016.

"A Midsummer Night's Dream." Review of *A Midsummer Night's Dream*, choreographed by Alexander Ekman. *Totally Stockholm*, 1 Sept. 2016, totallystockholm.se/arts-culture/midsummer-nights-dream. Accessed 16 Nov. 2016.

Stahl, Jennifer. "Nacho Duato Out, Sasha Waltz In at Staatsballett Berlin." *Dance Magazine*, 7 Sept. 2016, dancemagazine.com/news/nacho-duato-sasha-waltz-staatsballett-berlin. Accessed 16 Nov. 2016.

Sulcas, Roslyn. "Dancers Protest New Leadership Plans at Staatsballett Berlin." *The New York Times*, 16 Sept. 2016, www.nytimes.com/2016/09/17/arts/dance/dancers-protest-new-leadership-plans-at-staatsballett-berlin.html. Accessed 15 Nov. 2016.

—*Molly Hagan*

Yoshinori Ohsumi

Date of birth: February 9, 1945
Occupation: Cell biologist

Although Yoshinori Ohsumi dreamed of one day winning the Nobel Prize when he was a child, as an adult he never expected that the prestigious award would be within reach. For decades Ohsumi, a prize-winning Japanese cell biologist, has dedicated his career to researching the

process of autophagy—in which a cell transports a portion of its contents to a specialized organelle for degradation—in yeast. Such a focus is decidedly unglamorous and has historically been relatively unpopular among researchers, but for Ohsumi, the low profile of his field has been a feature rather than a downside to his work. "I don't feel comfortable competing with many people, and instead I find it more enjoyable doing something nobody else is doing," he told Hannah Devlin and Ian Sample for the *Guardian* (3 Oct. 2016). "In a way, that's what science is all about, and the joy of finding something inspires me." Yet despite Ohsumi's under-the-radar approach, his work on autophagy gained widespread attention within the international scientific community, particularly in light of autophagy's potential relevance to major medical conditions such as cancer and Parkinson's disease. For his research into autophagy, Ohsumi was awarded the Nobel Prize in physiology or medicine for 2016.

Although widely lauded for his groundbreaking research, Ohsumi is quick to point out that the work of scientists researching autophagy is far from over. "Even when you have figured one problem out a new problem presents itself. I think that is the nature of science," he explained to fellow scientist Akihiko Nakano in an interview for *Japan Academy* (7 Dec. 2015). "I do not even really feel like I understand all that much about autophagy. When something is broken down by autophagy, for instance, we do not yet really know how much of an effect that has on cell metabolism. I would like to try to answer these kinds of questions with experiments

on yeast. Ten years from now, I would like Japan to have a lab about which it can be said, 'Their work with yeast is prescient and makes a real contribution.'"

EARLY LIFE AND EDUCATION

Ohsumi was born on February 9, 1945, in Fukuoka, a city in southern Japan. The youngest of four siblings, he was born into an academic family: his father was an engineering professor at Kyushu University, and his grandfather had worked for a university as well. As a young boy, Ohsumi enjoyed exploring the natural world, collecting insects, and stargazing. Over the years, he developed an interest in chemistry, and he initially decided to study chemistry while attending the University of Tokyo. After a time, however, Ohsumi began to rethink his choice of field. "I quickly discovered chemistry wasn't so attractive to me, because the field was already quite established," he explained to Caitlin Sedwick for *JCB* (16 Apr. 2012). "But I was lucky, I think, because the early 1960s was the golden age of molecular biology. I decided I wanted to work on that instead."

As an undergraduate, Ohsumi joined the University of Tokyo's Department of Basic Science, where he met Kazutomo Imahori, who would later serve as one of his graduate advisers. After earning his bachelor's degree in 1967, Ohsumi continued on as a graduate student at the University of Tokyo, studying within the Department of Biochemistry. Ohsumi studied a variety of topics related to molecular biology during that period, including protein synthesis within the bacterium *Escherichia coli*, or *E. coli*. He conducted a portion of his graduate research at Kyoto University in southern Japan, working under the supervision of researcher Akio Maeda, but later returned to the University of Tokyo, from which he earned his doctorate in 1972.

EARLY CAREER

After completing his studies at the University of Tokyo, Ohsumi remained at the university as a research fellow in the Department of Agricultural Chemistry. Beginning in 1974, Ohsumi spent three years in the United States, where he completed a postdoctoral fellowship at New York's Rockefeller University, working under Nobel Prize–winning professor Gerald Edelman. Working in Edelman's lab, Ohsumi began to research mammalian biology and embryology, work that he found frustrating. "That was the hardest time in my life," he told Sedwick. Midway through his fellowship, however, Ohsumi joined one of his fellow researchers in studying yeast. Although yeast are single-celled organisms, they share many characteristics with human cells and thus enable biologists to study complex mechanisms at work in both.

In 1977, Ohsumi joined the University of Tokyo's biology department as a research associate, working under Professor Yasuhiro Anraku. As a member of Anraku's laboratory, Ohsumi decided to continue his work with yeast, setting out to study yeast vacuoles, which are organelles—or specialized structures within the cell—enclosed by membranes. "At that time, many people were studying the transport of ions and small molecules at the plasma membrane, but few people had started looking at transport across other organelle membranes," he recalled to Sedwick. "The vacuole was thought to be just a garbage can in the cell, and not very many people were interested in its physiology, so I thought it would be good to study transport in the vacuole because I would not have much competition." Over the following years, Ohsumi determined that vacuoles carry out a number of important functions within cells, including transporting compounds such as amino acids. He remained with Anraku's laboratory until 1986, when he joined the biology department as a lecturer.

OHSUMI LABORATORY

In 1988, Ohsumi took the position of associate professor with the University of Tokyo's biology department, establishing his own laboratory. He would later hold positions at such institutions as the National Institute for Basic Biology (NIBB) and the Graduate University for Advanced Studies, and in 2009 he joined the Tokyo Institute of Technology as a professor. He was named a professor of the Institute of Innovative Research at the Tokyo Institute of Technology in 2016. Having established his own laboratory, Ohsumi set out to perform further research into the functions of vacuoles in yeast. Although focused on a particular area of research, Ohsumi was less interested in developing and testing hypotheses than in observing natural processes and drawing conclusions from there. "My style is basically to just examine some phenomenon and then through the process of observation build an understanding of things," he told Nakano. "That's the way I like to work."

Ohsumi focused primarily on the role played by vacuoles in the degradation of proteins. "All of life is made possible by the wide range of roles that proteins carry out in our bodies," he explained to Nakano. "As scientists have come to understand the importance of proteins, a great deal of research has been conducted on the synthesis of proteins, which is in fact the product of gene expression. However, proteins are not simply created one after another in the body ad infinitum; rather, I believe we have come to understand that life is a balance of protein synthesis and protein degradation. Degradation

necessarily means that something is broken down, making this area of research difficult." Nevertheless, Ohsumi developed a means of studying protein degradation within yeast vacuoles and over time determined the mechanisms of the process taking place, which was known as autophagy.

AUTOPHAGY

The term *autophagy* was coined in the 1960s by Belgian researcher Christian de Duve, who had previously discovered the lysosome, a vacuole-like organelle found within animal cells. Deriving from *auto*, or "self," and *phagy*, or "eating," *autophagy* refers specifically to the process in which cells destroy, or eat, parts of themselves by isolating specific contents and sending them to the vacuole or lysosome, where they are broken down and recycled. In their studies of yeast, Ohsumi and his colleagues determined not only how that process functions, but also some of the specific genes involved in triggering and controlling autophagy. Ohsumi went on to publish numerous papers on his findings, and he was recognized for his work with awards such as the Japan Academy Prize, the Kyoto Prize, and the Paul Janssen Award for Biomedical Research.

According to Ohsumi, his discoveries related to autophagy were in many ways happy accidents. "I did not start this research with any grandiose idea of leading the way in autophagy research," he told Nakano. Nevertheless, his findings proved groundbreaking not only because of their significance to the study of single-celled organisms such as yeast but also because of their broader application to other forms of life, specifically humans. Although human cells and yeast cells differ in various ways, autophagy is carried out in a similar manner in both, and Ohsumi's findings have aided scientists in coming to a better understanding of how the process works in humans. Furthermore, as medical conditions such as Parkinson's disease and some cancers have been linked to faulty autophagy processes, Ohsumi's team's discovery of genes linked to autophagy could contribute significantly to the development of gene-based treatments for such conditions.

NOBEL PRIZE

In October 2016, the Nobel Assembly, the body responsible for awarding the prestigious Nobel Prizes, announced that Ohsumi had been selected as the recipient of that year's Nobel Prize in physiology or medicine. Notably, Ohsumi was the sole scientist chosen to receive that year's award, which is often given to multiple researchers who worked in groups or studied similar topics; in fact, he was the first single scientist to receive the award since British physiologist Robert G. Edwards in 2010. In addition to a gold medal and a diploma, Ohsumi was granted an award of 8 million Swedish krona, or about 882,000 US dollars.

Although surprised by the honor, Ohsumi has noted a broader increase in interest in the area of autophagy since his early days researching the topic. "When I started my work, probably every year twenty or less papers appeared on autophagy," he told Adam Smith for Nobelprize. org (Oct. 2016). "Now more than five thousand or something like that. It's a huge change within probably these fifteen years or so." In a speech delivered at the Nobel Banquet on December 10, 2016, he explained that although his own contributions and those of his colleagues have been essential to the understanding of autophagy, further research will enable scientists to learn more about the role autophagy plays in disease. "There is no greater satisfaction as a scientist than seeing your ideas and efforts transform a field of research," he said, "and I am as happy as I could be."

PERSONAL LIFE

Ohsumi met his wife, Mariko Ohsumi, while pursuing his doctorate. A fellow graduate student, she would go on to hold a professorship in the department of bioscience at Japan's Teikyo University. The couple have collaborated on a number of papers dealing with autophagy and related subjects. They have two sons and live in Oiso, a coastal town within the Tokyo metropolitan area.

SUGGESTED READING

Devlin, Hannah, and Ian Sample. "Yoshinori Ohsumi Wins Nobel Prize in Medicine for Work on Autophagy." *The Guardian*, 3 Oct. 2016, www.theguardian.com/science/2016/oct/03/yoshinori-ohsumi-wins-nobel-prize-in-medicine. Accessed 7 Apr. 2017.

Ohsumi, Yoshinori. "An Interview with the Recipient of the 31st International Prize for Biology." Interview by Akihiko Nakano. *Japan Academy*, 7 Dec. 2015, www.jsps.go.jp/english/e-biol/data/2016/31th_intavew_e.pdf. Accessed 7 Apr. 2017.

Ohsumi, Yoshinori. "Yoshinori Ohsumi: Autophagy from Beginning to End." Interview by Caitlin Sedwick. *JCB*, 16 Apr. 2012, jcb.rupress.org/content/197/2/164. Accessed 7 Apr. 2017.

Ohsumi, Yoshinori. "Yoshinori Ohsumi—Banquet Speech." *Nobelprize.org*, 10 Dec. 2016, www.nobelprize.org/nobel_prizes/medicine/laureates/2016/ohsumi-speech_en.html. Accessed 7 Apr. 2017.

Ohsumi, Yoshinori. Interview By Adam Smith. *Nobelprize.org*, Oct. 2016, www.nobelprize.org/nobel_prizes/medicine/laureates/2016/ohsumi-interview.html. Accessed 7 Apr. 2017.

Wanklyn, Alastair. "Japanese Microbiologist Yoshinori Ohsumi Wins Nobel in Medicine for Autophagy Research." *The Japan Times*, 3 Oct. 2016, www.japantimes.co.jp/news/2016/10/03/world/japanese-microbiologist-yoshinori-ohsumi-wins-nobel-prize-in-medicine-for-autophagy-research. Accessed 7 Apr. 2017.

Woollaston, Victoria. "How Autophagy Could Lead to a Cure for Cancer and Spell the End for Diabetes." *Wired*, 5 Oct. 2016, www.wired.co.uk/article/autophagy-cells-explained. Accessed 7 Apr. 2017.

—*Joy Crelin*

Angel Olsen

Date of birth: January 22, 1987
Occupation: Musician

Angel Olsen launched her solo career in 2011 with the studio EP *Strange Cacti*, and she soon made a name for herself in the world of folk- and country-tinged indie rock. By 2014, with the release of her well-received full-length album *Burn Your Fire for No Witness*, her audience had grown and her reputation as a brooding singer-songwriter was well established. As Bella Todd wrote in a profile for the *Guardian* (29 Aug. 2016), "The indie world had itself a new dark lady."

Yet despite her rapid success, Olsen chafed at the media's attempts at characterizing her and her music. "I think people are like, 'Where do we put Angel Olsen? Oh, let's put her in a venue and get some folding chairs up, because this is gonna be a quiet show,'" Olsen explained to Hazel Cills for *MTV News* (24 Aug. 2016). "It angers me, because I'll always have those albums that represent that character and that part of my music, and I can't really get away from it. Even if I were to make all electronic music from here on out—which I won't—but if I did, I'd still come up in some article as folk rock or country."

In that light, Olsen's 2016 album *My Woman* aimed in some part to distance her from the gloomy folk-rock pigeonhole. The more pop-oriented release and accompanying performances showcased the artist's versatility, including a more upbeat side. "Her set is full of sharp contrasts—from winding psych-rock furor to country balladry to . . . synthy lilt," Suzy Exposito noted for *Rolling Stone* (29 Sept. 2016). "*My Woman* is all about self-possession—Olsen's declaration of ownership over her work, her image, her experience." Though some fans may have been surprised by the transformation, Olsen had in fact been rejecting simple labels

By Abby Gillardi [CC BY 2.0], via Wikimedia Commons

for years. "Here's the deal," she asserted in 2003, as quoted by Mike Applestein for the *Riverfront Times* (23 Apr. 2014). "I'm not prep, I'm not punk, I'm not grunge, I'm not emo. The only label I go by is my name."

EARLY LIFE AND EDUCATION

Angel Olsen was born on January 22, 1987. Shortly after birth she was taken in by a foster family who officially adopted her when she was three years old. Her new family, which already included seven children (some old enough to have children themselves), lived in the Richmond Heights section of St. Louis, Missouri. Her parents continued to regularly foster children after her arrival, although Olsen was the last they adopted. She would later credit the fact that her parents were already middle-aged by the time she joined the family with her interest in older forms of music.

"Because there are so many decades of difference between us, I became more interested in what their childhood was like," Olsen recalled to David Bevan for *Spin* (24 Mar. 2014). "I fantasized about what it was like to be young in the '30s and '50s." She became enamored of songs by artists like Skeeter Davis, Patsy Cline, Roy Orbison, and the Everly Brothers. She often sang herself to sleep, not always a totally acceptable practice in a large household filled with others trying to fall asleep themselves.

Given a small Yamaha keyboard as a gift by a biological uncle, Olsen often holed up in the bathroom and recorded herself singing and playing on an old cassette recorder, pretending to

be in an R&B group. "I was always waiting for my voice to change," she told Todd. "I wanted to be able to sing like it was the last thing that was going to happen before I died—to sing with all of my body, like the soul singers in the Baptist churches."

Olsen attended Tower Grove Christian High School, and during her teen years she taught herself to play the guitar and began writing her own songs. She performed out on the street in front of a local store called Vintage Vinyl and at local coffee shops. With her musical taste evolving, she made friends on a now-defunct Saint Louis–centered social network called STL Punk and attended frequent concerts—some punk, others Christian rock. She also played in a jam-rock band known as Goodfight, playing local shows and developing songs.

COLLABORATIONS AND SOLO DEBUT

Two years after graduating from high school, Olsen decided to move to Chicago, Illinois, to try forging a music career. To appease her conservative parents, she also studied sports massage therapy at Chicago's Soma Institute while performing at whatever small club or venue would have her. She lasted two years in the program before being required to take a pathology class, at which point she realized that she was not suited for the profession and dropped out.

While in Chicago, Olsen began collaborating with local musician Emmett Kelly, who fronted a group called the Cairo Gang. He introduced her to fellow musician Will Oldham, who performed as Bonnie "Prince" Billy, among other stage names, and had already established a popular, if enigmatic, profile. The three sometimes appeared together as the Babblers, taking the stage in pajamas and sunglasses for lively sets comprised of cover tunes and original material. Olsen and Oldham harmonized so well together that he asked her to join his tour, marking her first time on the road. She also participated in his albums *The Wonder Show of the World* (2010) and *Wolfroy Comes to Town* (2011), further introducing her to a national audience well outside the confines of Chicago.

Despite the demands of touring and recording with an established artist, Olsen did not neglect her own music. In 2010 Jon Hency, the owner of a small record label, Bathetic Records, had come across recordings of her singing and playing the guitar online. He became particularly intrigued by one track, "Creator, Destroyer," which she had written about a former boyfriend. After coming to Chicago to see her perform live, he released her debut EP, *Strange Cacti* (2011), which contained six tracks. According to Bevan, "her voice—ululating, warbling, yodeling, obliterating—often felt transcendent: at once impossibly close and painfully distant, new and antique, feminine and masculine, immediate yet uncompromising."

HALF WAY HOME AND BURN YOUR FIRE FOR NO WITNESS

Olsen next worked with Bathetic to release a full-length debut album, *Half Way Home* (2012). It included a mixture of old songs and newer ones she had written while on the road with Oldham. The album was a revelation to many in the music press, opening eyes to Olsen's true talent. Much of the praise focused on her vocals, remarkable for both technical ability and depth of emotion. "Olsen's voice is possessed of an intensely dramatic range; one minute she's barely singing . . . but the next, she's a tragic heroine of the Weimar cabaret, tremendously poised but letting emotion rag her throat as if a freight train were passing through," Laura Snapes wrote in a review for *Pitchfork* (12 Sept. 2012). "Hers is not a voice made for modern laptop speakers."

It soon became apparent that Olsen was poised for great success as a solo artist. In mid-2012 she made the difficult decision to move on from working with Oldham, who had become something of a mentor. "I ended up feeling like I was cheating myself by not following my own course," she told Bevan. "By not taking my own chance, by not doing what he was doing, but for myself." Although the split was not on bad terms, Olsen suggested that Oldham's notoriously inscrutable personality made it relatively awkward.

Olsen hired musicians to work on her next solo album, which she ended up recording in Asheville, North Carolina. *Burn Your Fire for No Witness* was released on the indie label Jagjaguwar in early 2014 and soon earned a spot on the Billboard 200. This "feverish set of high-wire torch songs," as Bevan described the album, attracted new fans and further impressed critics. "There is a lot of heartbreak on *Burn Your Fire for No Witness*, as well as a lot of pleasing anachronism; a lot of hard-won resignation and what you might call stern vulnerability," Kitty Empire opined in a review for the *Guardian* (16 Feb. 2014). The widespread accolades and the album's more mainstream label release catapulted Olsen to a new level of popularity. Her breakthrough also changed her perspectives somewhat—"I lost some friends, and I also realized some people were really valuable to me," she told Cills.

MY WOMAN

Olsen's success came with an increasing feeling that she was being stereotyped in various ways, and she often expressed skepticism of the mainstream music press. Uncomfortable with being cast as an eternally gloomy folk singer, she consciously sought out new territory for her next project. Her complex identity emerged more fully on the album *My Woman* (2016), which included more upbeat and optimistic songs than her previous work. "It still has its share of echoey seven-minute meditations on love and isolation," Todd wrote of the record. "But they increasingly coexist with simple, throwback grunge-pop. . . . The resulting tone is appealingly untidy."

Though *My Woman* was successful and received strong reviews, it did confuse some fans who interpreted the shifting sound as a sellout. Olsen herself often commented to interviewers about such a backlash, including people's reactions to a glittery silver wig she wore in several music videos. "It's always funny to hear what people think, because they're like, 'She's just trying to be Sia,' or, like, 'Are you Grimes now? Who are you?'" she told Cills. "I'm still me. I'm still writing my music. I just want to have fun just like everyone else." Regarding the wig in particular, she variously told interviewers that it was simply chosen due to the lack of a stylist for her videos or that she deliberately chose the look to confound people's expectations.

Olsen was also frequently asked about her take on feminism and gender roles due to the album's lyrical themes and the title's suggestion of possessiveness. "Of course I am a feminist, but I would also say I'm a humanitarian and I believe that we should all be equal," she told April Clare Welsh for the British arts magazine *Fact* (3 Sept. 2014). She noted that while artists like herself increasingly had opportunities, the music business as a whole, as well as other industries, continued to struggle to find gender equality.

PERSONAL LIFE

Olsen moved to Asheville, North Carolina, after recording *Burn Your Fire for No Witness* there, finding its arts scene supportive. She has expressed surprise that fans sometimes approach her to ask about her emotional health, concerned by the persona she projects on stage. "Little do they know," she quipped to Bevan. "When I'm home, I'm usually watching *Twin Peaks* and flatulating under the covers." Though her songs can be deeply personal, she counters suggestions that she is gloomy or depressed.

Olsen acknowledged that for years she consciously rejected the idea of having a family of her own, perhaps in reaction to her mother's role in caring for so many children. She also said she would only consider allowing her music to be used commercially if she had children to support.

SUGGESTED READING

Applestein, Mike. "Angel among Us: An Oral History of Angel Olsen's Time in St. Louis." *Riverfront Times*, 23 Apr. 2014, www.riverfronttimes.com/musicblog/2014/04/23/

angel-among-us-an-oral-history-of-angel-ol-sens-time-in-st-louis. Accessed 3 Apr. 2017.

Bevan, David. "Angel Olsen Will Be Heard." *Spin*, 24 Mar. 2014, www.spin.com/featured/angel-olsen-march-2014-cover-story-interview. Accessed 3 Apr. 2017.

Cills, Hazel. "Angel Olsen Isn't Who You Think She Is." *MTV News*, 24 Aug. 2016, www.mtv.com/news/2922790/angel-olsen-my-woman-feature. Accessed 3 Apr. 2017.

Exposito, Suzy. "Angel Olsen on Finding Inner 'Boss Lady,' Audacious New LP." *Rolling Stone*, 29 Sept. 2016, www.rollingstone.com/music/features/angel-olsen-on-finding-inner-boss-lady-audacious-new-lp-w442590. Accessed 3 Apr. 2017.

Mapes, Jillian. "This Woman's Work: The Many Lives of Angel Olsen." *Pitchfork*, 11 Aug. 2016, pitchfork.com/features/profile/9933-this-womans-work-the-many-lives-of-angel-olsen. Accessed 3 Apr. 2017.

Tang, Estelle. "Angel Olsen Is Nobody's Woman." *Elle*. Hearst Corp., 29 Aug. 2016. Accessed 18 Feb. 2017.

Todd, Bella. "Angel Olsen: Indie's Dark Star Tackles 'the Complicated Mess of Being a Woman.'" *The Guardian*, 29 Aug. 2016, www.theguardian.com/music/2016/aug/29/angel-olsen-my-woman. Accessed 3 Apr. 2017.

Welsh, April Clare. "My Woman, Not Your Woman." *Fact*, 3 Sept. 2016, www.factmag.com/2016/09/03/angel-olsen-my-woman-interview. Accessed 3 Apr. 2017.

SELECTED WORKS

Strange Cacti, 2011; *Half Way Home*, 2012; *Burn Your Fire for No Witness*, 2014; *My Woman*, 2016

—Mari Rich

Victoria Orphan

Date of birth: March 10, 1972
Occupation: Geobiologist

Microbes, geobiologist Victoria Orphan told Marcus Y. Woo for *Engineering and Science* (2010), "are an integral part of almost every facet of our planet. While many researchers would agree with that statement, Orphan is perhaps especially capable of demonstrating just how integral microbes truly are. A professor of environmental science and geobiology at the California Institute of Technology, also known as Caltech, Orphan has devoted much of her career to studying the ways in which marine microbes process a variety of gases. Through her research, she has shown that while substantial

John D. & Catherine T. MacArthur Foundation

amounts of methane gas naturally emerge from deposits located near the seafloor, microbes dwelling in that environment use the methane as a fuel source, preventing as much as 80 percent of it from entering the atmosphere. As methane is a greenhouse gas, the marine microbes thus play a substantial role in preventing potential global warming.

As a working researcher and the head of the Caltech's Orphan Lab, Orphan seeks to explore the depths of the sea, an area still full of surprising discoveries for scientists. "Very little of the deep sea has been studied by scientists—probably less than 1 or 2 percent of all the seafloor," she told Amelia Urry for *Grist* (29 Sept. 2016). In recognition of her completed work and ongoing attempts to understand more about the functions of marine microbes, Orphan was awarded the prestigious MacArthur Fellowship, commonly known as the "genius grant," in 2016. With the financial support of the MacArthur Foundation, she hopes to pursue further research that will allow her to learn more about microbial ocean life before that life is threatened by industry, climate change, and more. "There are critical knowledge gaps that we need to fill before we start decimating the seafloor for industrial purposes," Orphan told Urry. "It's very hard to come up with predictive models without understanding this fundamental information."

EARLY LIFE AND EDUCATION

Victoria Jeanne Orphan was born in California's San Diego County on March 10, 1972, to Victor and Jeanne Orphan. Long fascinated by the ocean, Orphan decorated her room in an ocean theme as a child and dreamed of becoming a marine biologist. She attended San Dieguito High School Academy in Encinitas, where her mother worked as a teacher. Orphan graduated from the school in 1990.

After high school, Orphan attended the University of California (UC), Santa Barbara. Although not initially interested in the field of microbiology, which would become the focus of much of her professional career, she quickly developed a fascination with the subject while taking a marine microbiology course taught by Professor Edward DeLong. "It just totally changed my whole worldview of the importance of microorganisms," she recalled to Jim Logan for the *UC Santa Barbara Current* (7 Oct. 2016). "It not only brought me to the fields of global science and marine ecosystems, but it also was a perfect merger of environmental science and the issues involved in this field." She continued, "Working on this topic, when it was in its infancy and with lots of discovery potential—that was the beginning for me. I was just so hooked on microbes at that point. I switched almost exclusively to marine microbiology." Orphan's devotion to marine microbiology deepened when a graduate student showed her a sample of seawater under a microscope. "It was like looking at the Milky Way," she told Amina Khan for the *Los Angeles Times* (21 Sept. 2016). "It was just an incredible amount of microscopic life. I've never looked at a glass of seawater the same way since."

Orphan earned her bachelor's degree in 1994 and went on to pursue her PhD, studying microbes in marine sediment. She performed some of her graduate research at the Monterey Bay Aquarium Research Institute, a nonprofit research facility in Moss Landing, California. Orphan completed her doctorate in 2002.

TEACHING CAREER
After earning her PhD, Orphan first took a position as a national research council associate at the National Aeronautics and Space Administration (NASA) Ames Research Center in northern California, a role she held into 2004. That year, Orphan joined the faculty of the California Institute of Technology, or Caltech, as an assistant professor. She remained in that position until 2010, when she was promoted to associate professor. She advanced to full professorship later that year. In 2016, Orphan was named the James Irvine Professor of Environmental Science and Geobiology at the university. In addition to her work at Caltech, she has served as an adjunct scientist at the Monterey Bay Aquarium Research Institute.

During her time at Caltech, Orphan has taught courses in a number of subjects, including evolution and microbial ecology. Her molecular geobiology seminar focuses on the latest research in a specific topic, which changes each term the seminar is offered. Overall, Orphan's courses, much like her research, blend different disciplines to allow for a fuller understanding of the topic at hand. Indeed, for Orphan, the interplay between different scientific fields is essential to the study of geobiology. "The study of anaerobic methane oxidation started with geology and geochemistry," she explained to Woo. "The whole field of geobiology has blossomed because of those close interactions between geologists, geochemists, and microbiologists."

RESEARCH
As a researcher, Orphan focuses primarily on marine microbes that are involved in cycling certain gases—that is, they take in certain compounds as a source of fuel and release different ones. Although she has performed work dealing with elements such as carbon and sulfur, she is best known for her work concerning the gas methane, a compound composed of four hydrogen atoms and one carbon atom. Methane is one of a number of "greenhouses gases," which trap heat in the atmosphere. When more greenhouse gases enter the atmosphere and more heat becomes trapped, global warming occurs. Although humans are able to limit the output of greenhouse gases from industrial processes and everyday actions, gases such as methane are also released naturally. Large amounts of methane are found in undersea deposits of a substance known as methane hydrate, and when the ice-like substance melts due to changes in water temperature or pressure, it releases the gas into the water and, eventually, the atmosphere. In studying deep-sea microbes, Orphan learned that certain microbes have the ability to process methane released under the water and prevent a significant portion of it from entering the atmosphere. "It turns out that these microorganisms are very effective—as much as 80 percent of the methane that could potentially be released from the seafloor is consumed before it gets into the overlying waters and up into the atmosphere," she explained to Urry about her findings. "It's a globally important process."

In keeping with the nature of her work, Orphan spends much of her research time at sea. She frequently sails on the naval research ship *Atlantis*, operated by the Woods Hole Oceanographic Institution (WHOI),Woods Hole, MA, and travels deep into the ocean aboard the three-person submersible *Alvin*. Many of the microbes Orphan studies can live only in the deep ocean, so taking samples to the lab for further study is a difficult process. "We've learned over time to at least keep them going in the lab," she told Erin Blakemore for the *Washington Post* (29

Sept. 2016). "We create our own sort of artificial methane sea world. It's not glamorous."

Over the course of her career, Orphan has collaborated extensively with her fellow geobiologists and researchers from a variety of fields, a process she considers essential. "It's important to diversify your life in terms of the scientists you interact with across different fields," she told Khan. "This leads to discoveries in unexpected ways." The prolific author and coauthor of numerous papers, Orphan has shared her insights into the functions of microbes such as bacteria and archaea in publications including the journals *Geobiology*, *Environmental Microbiology*, and *Frontiers in Microbiology*. In October 2016, she delivered a talk on some of her findings, titled "Ocean Microbes: Small Size, Global Impact," at the TEDxOlympicBlvdWomen conference, held in Culver City, California.

MACARTHUR GENIUS

In September 2016, the John D. and Catherine T. MacArthur Foundation announced that Orphan was one of twenty-three individuals chosen as that year's MacArthur Fellows. Often referred to as the "genius grant," the MacArthur Fellowship is a prestigious honor that recognizes individuals who are making significant contributions to their respective fields and have the potential to carry out further groundbreaking work. In addition to the prestige of the fellowship, the MacArthur Foundation provides each fellow with a grant of $625,000, distributed over five years. For Orphan, being named a MacArthur Fellow was nearly unbelievable. "It's not totally sunk in yet," she told Logan not long after the announcement. "I am hearing from a lot of people I haven't talked to for a long time. It is a nice opportunity to touch base with old friends and reminisce about the trajectory of your career—even if being the center of attention can be uncomfortable for me."

With its $625,000 grant, the MacArthur Fellowship presents numerous possibilities for Orphan, who told Blakemore that she hopes to put much of the money toward what she termed "risky science endeavors." Further research into the ability of microbes to prevent gases such as methane from entering the atmosphere remains of great importance, as concerns about climate change increase worldwide. By revealing how such microbes function, Orphan may stimulate research that could be used to lessen the detrimental effects of greenhouse gases. Her research likewise has further implications beyond microbiology, as deep-sea explorations of any type tend to reveal more of the deep ocean's secrets. "Every time we go to one of these environments, we discover totally new forms of life," Orphan told Blakemore.

PERSONAL LIFE

Orphan's life partner, Shana Goffredi, is an associate professor of biology at Occidental College. Goffredi previously worked as a senior research associate at Caltech, and the couple have collaborated on numerous papers. They live in Pasadena, California.

SUGGESTED READING

Blakemore, Erin. "Ask a MacArthur 'Genius': Could Elusive Deep-Sea Microbes Help Fight Climate Change?" *Washington Post*, 29 Sept. 2016, www.washingtonpost.com/news/speaking-of-science/wp/2016/09/29/ask-a-macarthur-genius-could-elusive-deep-sea-microbes-help-fight-climate-change/. Accessed 10 Feb. 2017.

Jacobson, Stuart. "Victoria J. Orphan: Deep Partnerships." *The Scientist*, 1 Dec. 2006, www.the-scientist.com/?articles.view/articleNo/24541/title/Victoria-J--Orphan--Deep-Partnerships/. Accessed 10 Feb. 2017.

Khan, Amina. "MacArthur Winner Victoria Orphan Showed How Deep-Sea Microbes Keep Greenhouse Gas out of the Atmosphere." *Los Angeles Times*, 21 Sept. 2016, www.latimes.com/science/sciencenow/la-sci-sn-victoria-orphan-macarthur-award-20160921-snap-story.html. Accessed 10 Feb. 2017.

Logan, Jim. "A Gaucho Genius." *UC Santa Barbara Current*, 7 Oct. 2016, www.news.ucsb.edu/2016/017265/gaucho-genius. Accessed 10 Feb. 2017.

Nadin, Elisabeth. "Partnerships of Deep-Sea Methane Scavengers Revealed." *Caltech*, 9 May 2008, www.caltech.edu/news/partnerships-deep-sea-methane-scavengers-revealed-1424. Accessed 10 Feb. 2017.

Urry, Amelia. "She Studies Underwater Methane-Eating Microbes that Keep Our Planet in Balance. Genius!" *Grist*, 29 Sept. 2016, grist.org/climate-energy/she-studies-underwater-methane-eating-microbes-that-keep-our-planet-in-balance-genius. Accessed 10 Feb. 2017.

Woo, Marcus Y. "Diving for Microbes." *Engineering and Science*, vol. 71, 2010, pp. 12–19. *Caltech Engineering and Science*, calteches.library.caltech.edu/705/2/Microbes.pdf. Accessed 10 Feb. 2017.

—Joy Crelin

Anderson .Paak

Date of birth: February 8, 1986
Occupation: Musician

Anderson .Paak is a singer-songwriter, rapper, and drummer from Southern California. In 2017, .Paak was nominated for a Grammy Award for best new artist, and his 2016 sophomore album, *Malibu*, was nominated for best urban contemporary album. Although these Grammy nominations recognized his musical talent and style, .Paak's road to success was not an easy one. As a child and teenager, .Paak saw the arrests of both of his parents. Later, struggling to make ends meet for a small family of his own, .Paak was briefly homeless. The kindness of a few musicians, however, helped him get back on his feet and make music, which would eventually catch the ear of hip-hop mogul Dr. Dre. In 2015, .Paak was heavily featured on *Compton*, Dr. Dre's comeback album. Buoyed by that success, he was able to launch his own successful music career.

By The Come Up Show [CC BY 2.0], via Wikimedia Commons

Although .Paak had released his first album, *Venice*, in 2014, his career did not take off until 2016, when he released the Grammy-nominated *Malibu*. "The last year has been the best of my life," .Paak told Jon Pareles for the *New York Times* (8 Feb. 2017), marveling at his own success. "I've traveled the world, and I've actually gotten to make some money from my music and help be a provider for my family. But simultaneously, I feel like the world is kind of crumbling around me, and people are going through hell." As a "groove-based artist," .Paak added, "I want [my music] to help people get through these times."

EARLY LIFE AND EDUCATION

Anderson .Paak was born Brandon Paak Anderson in Oxnard, California, on February 8, 1986. He was estranged from his late father, a former air force mechanic, who served time in prison for assaulting .Paak's mother when the singer was seven. His father died before .Paak ever saw him again. .Paak's mother, who is from Seoul, South Korea, remarried and started a roadside produce stand. Soon her business blossomed into a large company, selling strawberries to restaurant chains and grocery stores. The family, which also included .Paak's younger sister, moved from a small apartment to a mansion.

.Paak began his music career drumming in church when he was eleven. "My godsister invited me to church when I was about eleven years old after I had learned to play a couple beats," he told Scott Simon for NPR's *Weekend Edition* (30 Jan. 2016). "She was like, 'You should come to the church. You gotta see the choir and you gotta see the church band.' I went, and I saw the choir

and the church band and I was hooked." A few years later, he started rapping under the name Breezy, after a childhood nickname.

In 2003, when .Paak was seventeen, he made a demo and began meeting with producers. Those producers, however, were looking for rappers similar to the Ying Yang Twins, a crunk rap duo. .Paak, a singer and drummer who preferred the music of Jay Z and Kanye West, thought the style was too much of a stretch. "I didn't want to be that guy that was just chasing sounds," he told Andy Hermann for *LA Weekly* (25 July 2016).

Meanwhile, back home, .Paak's mother was having major problems. Due to the tremendous growth of her business, she had purchased strawberry fields. The timing, however, was unfortunate because the climatic event El Niño had arrived, destroying the fields. Later, his mother and stepfather ended up in prison for tax evasion. The mansion was foreclosed and .Paak, a senior in high school, and his sister found themselves on their own.

Anguished, .Paak quit making music and sold all of his equipment. He stayed with family and friends until he graduated from high school, and then devoted all of his energy to finding a job. He began working for an assisted-living facility and lived in his friend's garage. During that time, .Paak played drums for a few punk bands, but music was not a priority.

After briefly attending culinary school, he moved to Los Angeles, California, where he took drumming classes at the Musicians Institute of Hollywood. Furthermore, .Paak began rapping again—this time under the name Breezy Lovejoy—and formed a short-lived group called Block Cheddar. They recorded a demo of covers of Coldplay songs called *The Cold Tapes*.

EARLY CAREER AND THE FREE NATIONALS

In 2009, Block Cheddar briefly toured with Mandi Perkins, the lead singer of the band Verona, but quit the group in 2010. Afterward, he began playing shows with guitarist Jose Rios and keyboardist Ron Avant. Their band, called the Free Nationals, made little money, and .Paak had a pregnant partner to care for. With the help of Rios, he got a job working in the fields at a legal marijuana farm in Santa Barbara, California, and the two men sold pot on the side. The enterprise was going well until .Paak was unexpectedly fired in 2011.

Homeless, the family moved to Los Angeles, sleeping on friends' couches while .Paak performed around town as Breezy Lovejoy. He also continued performing with the Free Nationals, who became something of a house band for a club called Little Temple in East Hollywood. Moreover, .Paak and his family moved in with Shafiq Husayn, a member of the hip-hop group Sa-Ra Creative Partners. "At one point, I was his videographer and chauffeur, his assistant, his weed roller, his chef," .Paak told music experimentalist Flying Lotus for *Interview Magazine* (7 Mar. 2017). "In the short time that I was living with him, I picked up a lot of knowledge from that dude aside from just production and writing, a lot of historical stuff." Husayn kept .Paak housed and employed long enough for him to finish two albums. In 2012, he released *O.B.E. Vol. 1* and *Lovejoy*.

That same year, .Paak got a job touring as a drummer for Haley Reinhart from *American Idol*, a reality television show, and then for rapper Dumbfoundead. He also decided to trade the name Breezy Lovejoy for Anderson .Paak, a variation of his birth name. "It just [had] a little more class and timelessness to it," he admitted to Hermann. The period before .Paak, he has said, signifies attention to detail.

VENICE

In 2014, .Paak released a full-length album called *Venice*. His timing was strategic; he had already recorded a good amount of what would be his next album, *Malibu* (2016), but he wanted to introduce himself with a bang. "I thought before I do *Malibu*, let's do *Venice*," he told Gerrick D. Kennedy for the *Los Angeles Times* (4 Mar. 2016). "It'll be all fun, excess, modern, house, and trap. I wanted to go where *Malibu* is eventually—the soul music—but I wanted to have fun first. I wanted more people paying attention before I showed them a matured sound, and hopefully they still cared." *Venice*,

particularly the popular single "Drugs," earned him an underground following, as did NxWorries, his collaboration with the prolific producer Knxwledge, also known as Glen Boothe. The duo's song "Suede," the lead single of their debut EP, became a viral hit.

Around the same time, his manager arranged an introduction between .Paak and rap legend Dr. Dre. .Paak played "Suede" for Dre, and after he had listened to it three times, the rapper invited .Paak to appear on his album *Compton* (2015)—Dre's first record in sixteen years. .Paak appeared on six tracks, including "All Days Work," "Deep Water," and the political song "Animals." "Anderson .Paak, a young multitalent from Los Angeles who's all over *Compton*, finds his star turn here," Jay Balfour wrote in his review for *Pitchfork* (11 Aug. 2015), referring to the song "Animals." With the help of *Compton*, .Paak's career started to take off.

MALIBU AND YES LAWD!

In 2016, .Paak released *Malibu* independently, but signed with Dre's Aftermath label soon after. The album garnered positive reviews from music critics. "*Malibu*—his second album under this moniker, following a stretch under the name Breezy Lovejoy—is multilayered," Jon Caramanica wrote for the *New York Times* (20 Jan. 2016). "It's also incisive, languorous and deeply felt, a warm bath of studiously relaxed hip-hop and soul." Moreover, many reviewers of the album compared .Paak to his friend and fellow rapper Kendrick Lamar. "Much like Kendrick Lamar, .Paak skillfully depicts his surroundings while remaining in the foreground," Marcus J. Moore wrote for *Pitchfork* (11 Jan. 2016). In 2017, *Malibu* was nominated for a Grammy Award for best urban contemporary album, and .Paak was nominated for best new artist.

Also in 2016, NxWorries released their first full-length album, *Yes Lawd!* The album collects the duo's songs, such as "Suede," from the years 2015 and 2016. "*Yes Lawd!* is another accomplishment in Anderson .Paak's continued rise, a beautiful beat tape made with the producer Knxwledge that nods to classic Stones Throw duos," Jonah Bromwich wrote for *Pitchfork* (18 Oct. 2016). The album was influenced by the late J Dilla—a record producer who worked with A Tribe Called Quest, The Roots, and Erykah Badu—and church music.

In April of that same year, .Paak performed at the Coachella festival, earning a reputation as a master showman. In concert, he moves seamlessly from the front man microphone to the drum kit. "Vividly reimaging the songs from *Malibu*, .Paak entered full beast mode: scatting, gyrating, prowling around the stage, ripping off his jacket, sweating, and unleashing and flipping between raw odes to over-consumption to take me to church falsetto's," Jeff Weiss wrote for *Noisey* (18 Apr. 2016).

In 2017, .Paak started touring with pop star Bruno Mars. He also started working on a new album with his band the Free Nationals.

PERSONAL LIFE

.Paak married after high school but soon divorced. In 2011, he married Hey Oun, a Korean vocal student whom he met at the Musicians Institute of Hollywood. They live in Los Angeles, California, with their son, Soul.

SUGGESTED READING

Caramanica, Jon. "Review: On *Malibu* Anderson .Paak Takes In All That His Surroundings Offer." Review of *Malibu*, by Anderson .Paak. *The New York Times*, 20 Jan. 2016, www.nytimes.com/2016/01/21/arts/music/review-on-malibu-anderson-.Paak-takes-in-all-that-his-surroundings-offer.html. Accessed 5 Apr. 2017.

.Paak, Anderson. "Anderson .Paak." Interview by Flying Lotus. *Interview*, 7 Mar. 2017, www.interviewmagazine.com/music/anderson-.Paak. Accessed 5 Apr. 2017.

.Paak, Anderson. "Anderson .Paak Hits Big Time in LA after Struggling Up the Road but a World Away in Oxnard." Interview by Gerrick D. Kennedy. *The Los Angeles Times*, 4 Mar. 2016, www.latimes.com/entertainment/music/la-ca-ms-anderson-.Paak-20160306-story.html. Accessed 5 Apr. 2017.

.Paak, Anderson. "Anderson .Paak's Long, Hard Road to Fame Was Worth the Wait." Interview by Andy Hermann. *LA Weekly*, 25 July 2016, www.laweekly.com/music/anderson-.Paaks-long-hard-road-to-fame-was-worth-the-wait-7169706. Accessed 3 Apr. 2017.

.Paak, Anderson. "Anderson .Paak, a Singing, Rapping, Drumming Grammy Nominee, Doesn't Fit into Any Box." Interview by Jon Pareles. *The New York Times*, 8 Feb. 2017, www.nytimes.com/2017/02/08/arts/music/grammys-anderson-.Paak.html. Accessed 5 Apr. 2017.

SELECTED WORKS

Venice, 2014; *Malibu*, 2016; *Yes Lawd!* (with Nx-Worries), 2016

—Molly Hagan

Zach Parise

Date of birth: July 28, 1984
Occupation: Hockey player

For Minnesota Wild left-winger Zach Parise, ice hockey is more than a sport—it is a family tradition. The son of professional hockey star and coach Jean-Paul Parise and the younger brother of player Jordan Parise, he grew up in a family with deep ties to the game. "I think it was in my blood," he told Oliver Janz for *Hockey's Future* (9 Mar. 2003).

After a successful high school career playing hockey for the Shattuck–St. Mary's Sabres, Parise spent two seasons playing for the University of North Dakota before being drafted by the New Jersey Devils National Hockey League (NHL) team, which he would go on to lead to the Stanley Cup Final in 2012. He later returned to his home state of Minnesota to join the Wild. A frequent member of US national teams, Parise has also competed in the Olympic Games on two occasions. "I remember growing up watching the Olympics and then getting the chance to play in two of them," he told Sean Leahy for the *Yahoo Sports!* blog *Puck Daddy* (7 May 2017). "There's nothing like it."

EARLY LIFE AND EDUCATION

Zachary Parise was born on July 28, 1984, in Minneapolis, Minnesota, to Jean-Paul and Donna Parise. His father, known as J. P., was a Canadian hockey coach who played left wing

By Resolute (Own work) [CC BY-SA 3.0], via Wikimedia Commons

for NHL teams such as the Boston Bruins and the Minnesota North Stars in the 1960s and 1970s. Following his retirement, he found work as a coach in the NHL before taking charge of the highly competitive hockey program at the Shattuck–Saint Mary's School in Faribault, Minnesota.

Hockey was a constant presence during Parise's childhood. He and his older brother Jordan began playing as children—a pastime their father encouraged. "It was always a benefit to have him supporting my brother and me," Parise told Janz. "He brings a huge amount of knowledge to me and helps me with whatever I need to work on. He helps every aspect of my game." Both brothers would go on to pursue careers in professional hockey. As an adult, Jordan played as a goaltender for several teams, including the Chicago Steel and the Waterloo Black Hawks. He also played competitively in Europe before his retirement in 2013. "We were born with it in our genes, and we excelled in it," Parise explained to Janz. "Both my brother and I loved to play it all the time."

Parise attended Shattuck–St. Mary's, where his father served as director of the hockey program. After making his freshman debut on the school's bantam team, he went on to play for the prep team for the remainder of his high school career. Parise graduated from Shattuck–St. Mary's in 2002.

COLLEGE HOCKEY

After graduating from high school, Parise attended the University of North Dakota, where he played for the Fighting Sioux hockey team. The team was led by head coach Dean Blais, whose expertise was one of the deciding factors in Parise's decision to enroll in the university. "Coach Blais is an incredible motivator," he told Janz. "He makes you want to play your best, and he makes you excited to come to the rink and go to practice. Our relationship has been great. We can always joke around with him, and he is a players' coach."

Coming from a relatively small high school, attending the much larger University of North Dakota was a major adjustment for Parise. Nevertheless, he soon acclimated to the school, which his brother also attended. Although he expected to remain at the university for three or four years, he ultimately spent only two years there, having been drafted into the NHL after his freshman year. He returned to the university for his sophomore year but left after the end of the year to pursue his professional hockey career. During his two seasons with the Fighting Sioux, Parise distinguished himself as a talented player and was nominated for the Hobey Baker Award for best National Collegiate Athletics

Association (NCAA) ice men's hockey player on two occasions.

NEW JERSEY DEVILS

In June 2003, the teams of the NHL held their annual draft to select new players. Although not yet in his twenties, Parise was chosen as the seventeenth pick of the first round by the New Jersey Devils. Following his second year at the University of North Dakota, he planned to join the Devils for the 2004–5 season. A labor dispute, however, prompted the cancellation of the entire NHL season, and Parise was instead sent to play for the Albany River Rats, the Devils' American Hockey League affiliate.

Parise joined the Devils in 2005, playing in eighty-one games over the course of the season. Over the following years, he established himself as a valuable member of the team. In 2008, he was named alternate captain, and at the start of the 2011–12 season, Parise became team captain. During that postseason, his last with the Devils, Parise led the team to the Stanley Cup Final for the first time. The Devils defeated teams such as the Florida Panthers and the New York Rangers to face off against the Los Angeles Kings in the championship in the summer of 2012. They, however, were ultimately defeated 4–2.

Although disappointed by the loss to the Kings, Parise was proud of what the Devils had accomplished. "We played against our bitter rival in the conference final and beat them in overtime to make it to the Stanley Cup Finals, but to be a part of one of the last two teams remaining was surreal," he told Mike Mazzarone for *Alternative Nation* (9 Oct. 2014). "Once it's over, you pray and hope that you get back to that stage again and get another chance. It goes by quick, and you never know if you'll ever get there again."

MINNESOTA WILD

Following the end of his contract with the Devils, Parise became a free agent. Returning to his home state, he signed a thirteen-year contract with the Minnesota Wild. Although his first season with the Wild (2012–13) was shortened by a lockout, Parise and his teammates were able to play for about half of the originally scheduled season and demonstrate their skills as a team. At the end of the season, the team entered the Stanley Cup playoffs but was eliminated in the first round by the Chicago Blackhawks. The Wild were regular contenders in the playoffs over the following years, although they seldom proceeded past the tournament's first round. They were eliminated by the Blackhawks in early rounds in 2014 and 2015, and the team was knocked out in the first round by the Dallas Stars in 2016. In

2017, the Minnesota Wild lost to the St. Louis Blues in the first round of the playoffs.

During his time with the Wild, Parise sustained many injuries, including multiple knee injuries and a broken foot. "It's frustrating because you trained really hard in the summer, want to have a good season, expect to have a good season, and then the last two years get injured early in the year," he told Leahy. "It just kind of derailed a little bit."

In January 2015, Parise's tenure with the Wild was briefly interrupted by family tragedy when his father died after a battle with lung cancer. He would later honor his father on the rink, wearing J. P. Parise's old gloves and helmet during warm-ups at the end of the 2016–17 season. "I was sitting at my house the night before and I had seen the pictures of the jerseys in the locker room the day before," he told Leahy of his decision. "I was thinking I wonder if my mom can find that stuff, so I asked her and I asked my brother. My mom dug it up and she still had it in one of his bags in the garage."

INTERNATIONAL CAREER

Parise has also represented the United States internationally since he was a teenager. In 2002, he accompanied the US Men's National Under-18 Team to the International Ice Hockey Federation (IIHF) Men's Under-18 World Championship in Slovakia—where the team claimed a gold medal.

Perhaps most exciting for Parise was the opportunity to play in the Winter Olympic Games. He made his first Olympic appearance in 2010, when he joined the US team at the games in Vancouver, Canada. The team ultimately claimed a silver medal after an intense game against the Canadian national team, during which Parise played a pivotal role. With less than twenty-five seconds left in the game, Canada led the United States 2–1. Parise managed to score a goal, which tied the score and gave the United States another chance to challenge the hosts. "I was really excited," he recalled to Manish Mehta for *NJ.com* (28 Feb. 2010). "We got another crack at it to win. I was happy. We were happy. We just couldn't finish the job." The United States was unable to score an additional goal, and a goal scored by Canada in overtime brought the game's final score to 3–2.

In 2014, Parise returned to the Winter Olympics as US team captain, leading the team to Sochi, Russia. The team made it through the early stages of the tournament as well as through the quarterfinals. In the semifinals, however, they lost to Canada. Facing off against Finland in the bronze medal game, the United States was unable to score a single goal, and Finland ultimately claimed the medal.

In April 2017, the NHL announced that players from the league will not be allowed to play at the 2018 Winter Olympics in Pyeongchang, South Korea, as the games would interrupt the NHL season. Disagreeing with this decision, Parise told interviewers that he hoped league leadership would reconsider. "It's the one time you get best on best in hockey," he told Leahy of the Olympics.

PERSONAL LIFE

Parise met his wife, Alisha Woods, in college. The couple married in 2012, and their twins Emelia and Jaxson were born in 2014. The family lives in Minnesota.

SUGGESTED READING

Allen, Kevin. "Parise Has a Family Connection." *USA Today*, 19 June 2003, usatoday30.usatoday.com/sports/hockey/draft/2003-06-19-us-draft-prospects_x.htm. Accessed 12 May 2017.

Brehm, Mike. "Grieving Zach Parise Due Back in Minnesota Wild Lineup." *USA Today*, 10 Jan. 2015, ftw.usatoday.com/2015/01/grieving-zach-parise-returns-nhl-preview. Accessed 12 May 2017.

Mehta, Manish. "Zach Parise's Game-Tying Goal against Canada Made Olympic Gold Medal Game One to Remember." *NJ.com*, New Jersey On-line, 28 Feb. 2010, www.nj.com/olympics/index.ssf/2010/02/zach_parises_game-tying_goal_a.html. Accessed 12 May 2017.

Parise, Zach. "*HF*'s Interview with Zach Parise." Interview with Oliver Janz. *Hockey's Future*, Crave Online Media, 9 Mar. 2003, www.hockeysfuture.com/articles/5765/hfs_interview_with_zach_parise/. Accessed 12 May 2017.

Parise, Zach. "Interview: Zach Parise Bashes NHL Expansion, Talks Upcoming Season and Marty Brodeur." Interview by Mike Mazzarone. *Alternative Nation*, 9 Oct. 2014, archive.alternativenation.net/zach-parise-bashes-expansion-talks-upcoming-season/. Accessed 12 May 2017.

Parise, Zach. "Zach Parise on Wild's Season, Olympic Decision (Puck Daddy Q&A)." Interview by Sean Leahy. *Puck Daddy*, Yahoo Sports, 7 May 2017, sports.yahoo.com/news/zach-parise-wilds-season-olympic-decision-puck-daddy-qa-142401517.html. Accessed 12 May 2017.

"Zach Parise." *Minnesota Wild*, NHL.com, 2017, www.nhl.com/player/zach-parise-8470610. Accessed 12 May 2017.

—*Joy Crelin*

Inbee Park

Date of birth: July 12, 1988
Occupation: Golfer

Despite being one of the most difficult of her decade-long career, 2016 was a year of firsts for the South Korean professional golfer Inbee Park. In June and at the age of twenty-seven, she qualified for the LPGA (Ladies Professional Golf Association) Hall of Fame, becoming the youngest player to achieve that honor. Two months later she won a gold medal in the Summer Olympic Games in Rio de Janeiro, Brazil, the first Olympics in over a century to feature golf events. These historic accomplishments came despite a thumb injury that plagued her all season and forced her to withdraw for the year's opening tournament in January.

Park began her career with a record when she won her first major title: the US Women's Open in 2008 at the age of nineteen. For the next four years, she struggled to live up to the promise of that first win. She considered quitting the sport but then in 2012 won her second LPGA title, the Evian Championship. "I always try to look back to the hard times I had," she told Bill Fields for ESPN (9 Sept. 2015). "I never try to forget that. It still feels like yesterday that I went through them. I totally remember how I felt. I am feeling good and having good results, but I try not to get too cocky and to stay humble. When I think about those low moments, I can appreciate what is happening right now."

EARLY LIFE AND JUNIOR CAREER

Inbee Park was born in Seoul, South Korea, on July 12, 1988. Her father, Gun Gyu Park, introduced her to golf when she was ten years old, just days after Se Ri Pak, known to many as the godmother of Korean golf, won the US Women's Open. Park's father taught her to "read the greens," Park told Fields, and encouraged her to develop her putting, which is now considered one of her greatest strengths. Park quickly became the top junior golfer in Korea. She and her mother, Sung, moved to a suburb of Orlando, Florida, in 2002, and Park and her younger sister Inah attended Mount Dora Bible. (Park's father stayed in Korea to run his business.) The girls began learning English and slowly adjusted to their new school—their old school in Korea had been far stricter.

At the 2002 US Girls' Championship, fourteen-year-old Park won both the stroke and match play portions of the competition, the first person to do so since 1997. She also became the youngest golfer to win the Polo Golf Junior Player of the Year. In 2003 she led her middle school team to its first state tournament, and in 2004 she played in her first LPGA event, the Takefuji

Classic, as an amateur. She finished in a tie for eighth place.

Park's family moved to Las Vegas, Nevada, in 2004, and she continued to hone her golf game with Shawn Callahan at the Butch Harmon School of Golf. At Bishop Gorman High School, she won individual state championships in 2004 and 2005. Still an amateur, Park played the Takefuji Classic again, placing fifth. Park turned professional after graduating from high school in 2006, and then embarked on the Futures Tour (now Symetra Tour). She finished the season ranking third among the tour's money winners and qualified for the LPGA.

2008 US WOMEN'S OPEN AND A COMEBACK

Park, who changed the spelling of her first name from In-Bee to Inbee to make it easier for fans to remember, struggled her first year on the LPGA tour but finished tied for fourth place at the US Women's Open and just missed finishing in the top ten at the British Open. The 2008 season was better for Park when she made the top ten in three consecutive events, including a major tournament: playing in the US Women's Open at the Interlachen Country Club in Edina, Minnesota, in June 2008 and at the age of nineteen, Park beat every player and became the youngest player to win that tournament. The trophy marked her first victory since turning professional.

This career-launching win, however, was followed by a four-year drought. Park performed poorly throughout 2009, despite finishing the season with two top-ten placements. In 2010, she played both the LPGA and the JLPGA

(LPGA of Japan) tours, and the following year she won the first event on that tour, the Daikin Orchid Ladies Open. Park also began training with a new swing coach, former professional golfer Gi Hyeob Nam. The two had been dating since 2008, and Park attributes some of her comeback to his calming presence on tour. "I really started playing well since I started traveling with him, and he has been a big help on my swing and mentally and everything," Park told Ron Sirak for *Golf Digest* (19 June 2013).

In July 2012, Park won the first Evian Masters, her first LPGA title since 2008. Joe Versage for *Bleacher Report* (29 July 2012) reported Park as exclaiming, "It feels great," when asked to describe the win. "It's been four years. It felt more than four years." The win was attributed by many to Park's putting skills. She finished second in three of the four LPGA Majors that year, and Evian became the fifth Major in 2013. She completed the season ranking fourth in the world.

WINNING STREAK IN 2013

In April 2013, Park won her second major tournament of her career at the Kraft Nabisco Championship (now known as the ANA Inspiration Championship) at the Mission Hills Country Club in Rancho Mirage, California. She won handily, clinching the lead by a comfortable margin in the third round. Two months later at the KPMG Women's PGA Championship (then Wegmans LPGA Championship) at Locust Hill Country Club in Pittsford, New York, Park was ranked number one in the world. Although Park played well, she struggled through the last few holes and ended the tournament tied for first place with veteran golfer Catriona Matthew of Scotland, which forced a three-hole playoff. Park won the playoff after sinking an 18-foot putt to birdie the third hole. This second consecutive major win of the season prompted talk of a Grand Slam, which would be even more challenging since 2013 was the first season that the LPGA boasted five major tournaments instead of four. (Ironically, Park had won the fifth major, Evian, the year before when it was still considered a regular tournament.)

Despite the added pressure of a Grand Slam, Park continued her winning streak and was undefeated through June. At the end of the month, she played in her third major of the season: the US Women's Open at the Sebonack Golf Club in Southampton, New York. Steve DiMeglio for *USA Today* (30 June 2013) wrote that Park maintained an "authoritative" lead in the home stretch, winning the tournament with four strokes. Her victory was hard-earned and historic. Park became the second woman in LPGA history since the legendary Babe Zaharias in 1950 to win a season's first three major tournaments.

Park maintained her characteristic cool even after her victory as her teammates doused her in champagne, but she later told DiMeglio that she was ecstatic over her win. "I just hope this is not a dream," she said.

Unfortunately, Park was unable to secure wins in the final two major tournaments, but she rallied at the end of the season to become the first Korean to win the LPGA Player of the Year trophy. In an unexpectedly candid acceptance speech in November, Park revealed how she struggled with the media attention that came with her new fame. She referenced her nickname, the "Silent Assassin," which was inspired by her effortless calm on the green, and explained to award ceremony attendees, as reported by *Golfweek* in its online reprint of Park's acceptance speech, that "just because I don't show my feelings, doesn't mean that I don't feel anything."

CAREER GRAND SLAM AND 2016 SUMMER OLYMPIC GAMES

Park's 2014 season was solid, if subdued, compared to her previous golden season. She angled to complete her career Grand Slam at the British Open in July, but she stumbled in the final round and finished fourth. In August, however, she came from behind to best Brittany Lincicome in a play-off at the KPMG Women's PGA Championship to win her second consecutive title. Park's fifth major victory tied her with Se Ri Pak as the winningest Korean golfer in history. She surpassed Pak in 2015 when she won the KPMG Women's PGA Championship for a third time by five strokes. In August 2015, Park finally clinched her career Grand Slam when she won the RICOH Women's British Open in Scotland. Kevin Garside for the *Independent* (2 Aug. 2015) wrote of Park's achievement that day: "The world No. 1 could thread a needle from twenty paces. She gives nothing away behind her inscrutable demeanor, which gives her unerring putting stroke an even more lethal aura."

A sore back and a thumb injury forced Park to withdraw from the first tournament in the 2016 season, but by June, Park had officially filled all of the requirements to earn a slot in the LPGA Hall of Fame. Although she was the twenty-fourth inductee, she was also the youngest. Still, her nagging injuries led many to speculate that the wunderkind might sit out the Olympic Games in Rio in August. It was the first time since 1904 that golf was included in the Games, and Park was determined to play. After failing to make the cut at the KPMG Women's PGA Championship in June, a major she had won three times in the past, Park decided to sit out both the US Women's Open and the Women's British Open in order to prepare for Rio. As a member of South Korea's four-member team,

Park deemed her thumb only "80 percent fit," she told Lisa D. Mickey for the *New York Times* (14 Sept. 2016), but played admirably through the pain. In the end, she beat Lydia Ko, with whom she had vied for number-one ranking, by five strokes to win the gold. Exhausted after Rio, Park opted to take some more time off. "I used my body a lot for the last ten years," she told Mickey. "It's a little bit worn out, and I just have to take some rest."

PERSONAL LIFE

Park's sister, Inah, is also a golfer and played throughout her four years at the University of Southern California (USC). Park married her swing coach, Gi Hyeob Nam, in 2014. She lives in Las Vegas.

SUGGESTED READING

Fields, Bill. "How Inbee Park Could Climb the Ladder in Golf History." *ESPN*, 9 Sept. 2015, www.espn.com/espnw/news-commentary/article/13616636/how-inbee-park-climb-ladder-golf-history. Accessed 21 Dec. 2016.

Garside, Kevin. "Women's British Open 2015: 'Golfing Gods' Help Inbee Park Win Seventh Major." *Independent*, 2 Aug. 2015, www.independent.co.uk/sport/golf/womens-british-open-2015-golfing-gods-help-inbee-park-win-seventh-major-10434103.html. Accessed 21 Dec. 2016.

"Inbee Park's POY Speech Proves to be Inspirational." *Golfweek*, 24 Nov. 2013, golfweek.com/2013/11/24/lpga-inbee-park-speech-player-of-year. Accessed 21 Dec. 2016.

Mickey, Lisa D. "Inbee Park's Up-and-Down Year." *New York Times*, 14 Sept. 2016, www.nytimes.com/2016/09/15/sports/golf/inbee-park-evian-championship.html. Accessed 21 Dec. 2016.

Sirak, Ron. "She's Back in the Picture." *Golf Digest*, 19 June 2013, www.golfdigest.com/story/gwar-inbee-park-0624. Accessed 21 Dec. 2016.

Versage, Joe. "Evian Masters 2012: South Korea's Inbee Park Wins First Evian Masters Title." *Bleacher Report*, 29 July 2012, bleacherreport.com/articles/1276888-evian-masters-2012-south-koreas-inbee-park-wins-first-evian-masters-title. Accessed 21 Dec. 2016.

—*Molly Hagan*

Daniel Pemberton

Date of birth: November 3, 1977
Occupation: Composer

Daniel Pemberton is an award-winning British composer best known for his work on films such as *The Man from U.N.C.L.E.* (2015) and *Steve Jobs* (2015), for which he was nominated for a Golden Globe Award for best original score in 2016. After spending over twenty years composing music for television and video games, he scored his first feature film, *The Awakening*, in 2011. His big break however, came after working on Ridley Scott's *The Counselor* in 2013. Although the film itself divided critics, Pemberton, who had spent years plying his trade in the relative obscurity of British public television, became a Hollywood commodity. The theme song that he worked on alongside director Stephen Gaghan, Iggy Pop, and Danger Mouse for the film *Gold* (2016) was also nominated for a 2017 Golden Globe Award.

Praised for his versatility and originality, Pemberton typically enters the filmmaking process early on, an unusual strategy for a score composer that, as he explained to Melinda Newman for *Billboard* magazine (6 July 2016), he felt helps him achieve the most effective results: "There's a period of working out what is the tone of this movie, so you kind of have to help them explore that. That's a long, long process, and it means you have to bin tons of work you do, but I always think that's the way you're going to get the best new work done."

George Pimentel/WireImage/Getty Images

EARLY LIFE

Daniel Pemberton was born on November 3, 1977, and raised in England. Although he was not especially musical when he was a young child, when he was about ten years old, he recalls his father taking him to a laser show at the planetarium in London. The soundtrack, he told Daniel Schweiger for *Film Music Magazine* (5 Aug. 2015), featured a lot of synthesizer music. "It was like a switch was pressed in my head. Suddenly I became obsessed by it." He began collecting records, particularly electronic and instrumental records, and saved up enough money to buy his own synthesizer and tape recorder.

Pemberton began writing and recording his own music. Plugged into the local underground scene, the enterprising youth soon made contact with a record company, and he released an album titled *Bedroom* in 1994. He described his debut to Schweiger as "quite a mad record of Avant-garde ambient electronic music." Somehow, British television director Paul Wilmshurst heard it and offered Pemberton a job scoring a documentary for Britain's public-service Channel 4. At the time, he told Jessica Pace for *Music Connection* magazine (22 Jan. 2016), composing music for television was seen as an "unclean" way to make money, but he enjoyed the freedom of the work. Scoring was, at first, a pleasant after-school hobby for him, but it soon became much more.

TELEVISION AND JOURNALISM CAREERS

Pemberton continued to work with Wilmshurst before eventually branching out to collaborate with other television directors. "I started out during a golden age for certain types of music and worked on a lot of small scale [documentaries] at a time when Channel 4 had a really innovative and experimental culture," he told a reporter for *M* magazine (23 Sept. 2013). "TV shows were being made because directors wanted to make great TV shows." In the 1990s, he also worked as a music and video game journalist, writing tip columns for various publications.

According to Pemberton, he has scored hundreds of television episodes over the course of his career. Some of those songs are collected on the compilation album *TVPOPMUZIK* (2007). Highlights from Pemberton's television career include his theme song for the cult classic Channel 4 sitcom *Peep Show* (2003–15), the score for the Wilmshurst-directed television documentary *Hiroshima* (2005), and the popular theme "From Fiji with Love" for the British dating reality show *Love Island* (2005). He also composed music for Gordon Ramsay's cooking show *Hell's Kitchen*, the BBC Two's *The Great British Menu*, and the six-part drama series *Desperate Romantics*, for which he won an Ivor Novello Award in 2009. At the same time, he even composed music for a few video games, including the soundtracks for *The Movies* computer game and *LittleBigPlanet* for PlayStation 3, which were nominated for British Academy of Film and Television Arts (BAFTA) Awards in 2006 and 2008, respectively.

BREAKING INTO FILM

Pemberton had previously collaborated with BAFTA Award–winning television director Nick Murphy on the BBC drama series *Occupation*. When Murphy began working on his first film, a World War I–era horror about a haunted boarding school called *The Awakening*, starring Rebecca Hall and Dominic West, he brought Pemberton on board to compose the score. It was Pemberton's first film as well, and he approached his task with gusto; he has told interviewers that it remains one of his favorite scores.

Working on *The Awakening*, Pemberton found, was an illuminating experience that served him well going forward. He employed an orchestra and a choir but ultimately found that the "spookiest sounds," he wrote for *The Guardian* (15 Nov. 2011), were the ones he recorded alone with a slide whistle and time-stretching software on his computer. These humble tools allowed him to "create 'foggy' textures that made certain scenes extra creepy." He added, "Sometimes the most effective musical moments in films aren't always the biggest and most expensive—they can often be the simplest and cheapest."

The Awakening, which was released in theaters in 2011, did not perform as well as its team had hoped, but it introduced Pemberton to the film world and Hollywood. Ridley Scott, a prolific director best known for science-fiction classics such as *Alien* (1979) and *Blade Runner* (1982), was deeply impressed by Pemberton's unique score. His years of working in television also appealed to Scott. "When Ridley and I met, he told me, 'You've done your 10,000 hours in the garage,'" he recalled to Newman.

Scott asked Pemberton to score his 2013 thriller *The Counselor*. With a screenplay written by Pulitzer Prize–winning novelist Cormac McCarthy, *The Counselor* features a star-studded cast including Michael Fassbender, Penélope Cruz, Cameron Diaz, Javier Bardem, and Brad Pitt. The film is about a drug cartel, but, with McCarthy at the helm, could more accurately be described as a dense and bleak meditation on greed. Pemberton's score is percussive, and in his interview with Newman, he suggested that he was inspired by moments of tension, such as one involving a dead body in an oil barrel. "I like to try and find an unusual palette and work from there outwards," he said. Although *The Counselor* also had a disappointing performance at the box office, he has emphasized that he remains proud of the film and his contribution, which he finds more important than attracting record numbers of viewers.

THE MAN FROM U.N.C.L.E.

With word of his talent spreading, Pemberton continued to find work. Over the next few years, he contributed scores to British films in a range of genres, including *In Fear* (2013) and *Cuban Fury* (2014). As further proof of his growing reputation, he was named as the discovery of the year at the World Soundtrack Awards in 2014.

In 2015, Pemberton teamed up with director Guy Ritchie on a film based on the 1960s NBC show *The Man from U.N.C.L.E.* Pemberton's work on the film, an action comedy about international spies, provided a stark contrast to his work on *The Counselor*. Ritchie, he told Newman, wanted music to drive the action of the movie. Working closely with Ritchie's editor, James Herbert, he created a score that was both integral to the film yet sounded like a piece of music unto itself—as per Ritchie's instructions. "He didn't want it to feel like score," Pemberton told Matt Patches for *Esquire* (15 Aug. 2015) of the director. "He wanted it to feel like a great piece of music that was just being dropped on the scene." To achieve an appropriately retro-cool score, he employed a dizzying array of instruments that included a jazz and a bass flute, harpsichords, synthesizers, and bongos. For the movie's final music cue, he even found a vocalist to wail underneath an echoing, 1960s-era wall of sound. According to Schweiger's assessment of the score, Pemberton drew from the swinging scores of classic spy thrillers of the past to create a score that was bold and distinctive without succumbing to satire.

STEVE JOBS

Pemberton's score for Danny Boyle's 2015 film *Steve Jobs*, about the late Apple founder, was bold in a very different way. Written by the famously verbose Academy Award–winning Aaron Sorkin, Pemberton had the formidable task of creating music for a film that appeared on the page as solid dialogue. Whereas Ritchie wanted the music in *The Man from U.N.C.L.E.* to be a member of the cast, Boyle needed the score of *Steve Jobs* to be an important part of the scenery. Sorkin wrote the film in the manner of a stage play, with three separate acts, each set in one location and telling the story of a separate moment in Jobs's career. The first act is set in 1984, moments before Jobs unveils the first Macintosh personal computer; the second act is set in 1989, before Jobs launches a computer called NeXT for his short-lived company of the same name; and the third act is set in 1998, after Jobs has been reinstated at Apple, just before he introduces the first iMac. Pemberton embraced each act in itself, creating three separate scores

to complement the tone and even the technology of the time in each. In an interview with Cory Woodroof for *PopMatters* (13 Nov. 2015), Pemberton summarized how he and Boyle approached this innovative structural strategy: "He explained the film to me in this really great way. He said, 'The first act is vision, the second act is revenge, and the third act is wisdom,' and I really liked that clarity of what the underlying principles behind each act were."

Explaining the score, which he wanted to match the complexity of Jobs's personality, Pemberton told Woodroof that he chose one of his favorite instruments, the synthesizer, for the first act to not only elicit a period sound, but also to capture a sense of optimism, the "belief that computers were going to change our lives." He even sourced vintage synthesizers, using only ones that would have been available in 1984. In the second act, Jobs confronts his old partner, Steve Wozniak, in an opera theater, and Pemberton sought to emulate the drama of the scene in his operatic score. This was especially challenging given Sorkin's dense dialogue. Fittingly, for the film's third act, Pemberton stepped out of the studio and used his own Apple computer to compose a digital-sounding score. "There was something quite special . . . watching it and thinking 'Wow, I did that in my flat, and now it's on this massive screen in Hollywood being played to thousands of people," he told Woodroof.

In 2016, Pemberton was tapped once again, this time to work on Stephen Gaghan's adventure drama *Gold*, which stars Matthew McConaughey and Bryce Dallas Howard. Based on a true story, the film focuses on a contemporary prospector's attempt to find gold in the jungles of Indonesia. He also composed the score for the 2016 French film *Mal de pierres* (From the land of the moon), which is set in the World War II era and stars Marion Cotillard. Despite being in growing demand, he has remained committed to maintaining a smaller workload to ensure quality: "I don't want to be the guy who takes on twenty films, has twenty assistants who write everything, and ends up with scores that all sort of sound the same," he explained to Paul Weedon for *Clash* (11 Nov. 2015). "I kind of want to take a couple of projects on a year, if that, and just do them really well."

SUGGESTED READING

Pemberton, Daniel. "Daniel Pemberton Talks Working with Ridley Scott, Danny Boyle & More on Film Scores That Make You Go 'Wow.'" Interview by Melinda Newman. *Billboard*, 6 July 2016, www.billboard.com/articles/news/7430910/daniel-pemberton-composer-interview. Accessed 15 Dec. 2016.

Pemberton, Daniel. Interview by Daniel Schweiger. *Film Music Magazine*, 5 Aug. 2015, www.filmmusicmag.com/?p=14948. Accessed 15 Dec. 2016.

Pemberton, Daniel. "Sometimes the Best Film Soundtracks Are the Most Simple." *The Guardian*, 15 Nov. 2011, www.theguardian.com/music/musicblog/2011/nov/15/best-film-sountracks-simple. Accessed 15 Dec. 2016.

Pemberton, Daniel. "Sounds of Spycraft: The Secrets behind *Man from U.N.C.L.E.*'s Gnarly, Retro-Rock Soundtrack." Interview by Matt Patches. *Esquire*, 15 Aug. 2015, www.esquire.com/entertainment/music/a37195/the-man-from-uncle-soundtrack-music-secrets/. Accessed 15 Dec. 2016.

Woodroof, Cory. "A Symphony in Three Parts: Breaking Down the *Steve Jobs* Score with Composer Daniel Pemberton." *PopMatters*, 13 Nov. 2015, www.popmatters.com/feature/a-symphony-in-three-parts-breaking-down-the-steve-jobs-score-with-composer-/. Accessed 15 Dec. 2016.

SELECTED WORKS
The Awakening, 2011; *The Counselor*, 2013; *The Man from U.N.C.L.E.*, 2015; *Steve Jobs*, 2015; *Gold*, 2016

—*Molly Hagan*

Adam Pendleton

Date of birth: 1984
Occupation: Artist

Adam Pendleton is a New York–based conceptual artist, best known for an avant-garde practice he calls Black Dada. When Kevin McGarry asked him to describe Black Dada for the *New York Times*'s *T Magazine* (27 May 2010), Pendleton quoted his 2008 manifesto on the subject: "Black Dada is a way to talk about the future while talking about the past. It is our present moment." Pendleton, a Virginian by birth, takes the term Black Dada from a 1964 poem by Amiri Baraka called "Black Dada Nihilismus." Loosely speaking, Black Dada is an exploration of blackness in the manner of Dada, the influential anti-art movement of the early twentieth century. Dada grew out of the horror and disillusionment of World War I. Dadaists rejected the modern capitalist society that had created the war, and their work, illogical and strange, willfully resisted interpretation according to any known set of artistic values. Pendleton's Black Dada presents large black-and-white photographic images, typically with a few letters or words printed over top of them; initially the letters were drawn from the

words "Black Dada," but later series incorporated other phrases from African American life and history, most recently the phrase and movement "Black Lives Matter." Pendleton has been compiling writing (his own and the work of others) for a book called the *Black Dada Reader* for over a decade, and it is due to be published in the fall of 2017. Since a presentation of his breakthrough performance work, *The Revival*, at the Performa biennial performance art exhibition in New York City in 2007, Pendleton's star has been on the rise. His work has been presented at the Venice Biennale, and is included in the collections at New York's Museum of Modern Art (MoMA), the Guggenheim, and London's Tate Modern.

EARLY LIFE AND FIRST COLLECTOR
Pendleton was born in 1984 and grew up in Richmond, Virginia. His father ran a construction company and was a musician. His mother, who worked as a teacher, was a voracious reader. Pendleton spent his early years perusing his mother's book collection—in particular the work of poet Adrienne Rich and writer and activist Audre Lorde. He made a studio in the family basement, and studied the art of Jasper Johns and Robert Rauschenberg, in books culled from the local bookstore. Pendleton attended the private Collegiate School in Richmond. As a student, his father would take him on trips to New York City to visit galleries and museums. "It was an encounter with something extraordinary," he told Ellen Gamerman for the *Wall Street Journal* (16 Apr. 2015) of his first taste of the art world. In

2000, Pendleton participated in an independent art study program in Pietresanta, Italy.

Pendleton graduated from Collegiate in 2002, when the ambitious artist was eighteen years old. He and his father loaded the family van with a few of his paintings and made the trip to New York City. He sent slides of his work to galleries throughout the city, and followed up in person, asking if the proprietors had seen the slides. One day, Pendleton and his father visited Gallery Onetwentyeight on Manhattan's Lower East Side with one of Pendleton's paintings in tow. Owner Kazuko Miyamoto was then an assistant to the late minimalist artist Sol LeWitt. Miyamoto liked the painting, and decided to include it in the gallery's summer group show. Later, LeWitt, visiting Miyamoto, saw the painting and offered to buy it, trading one of his own works. The famous artist became Pendleton's first collector.

EARLY CAREER AND *THE REVIVAL* (2007)
Pendleton continued to develop his voice, living and working in the Fort Greene neighborhood of Brooklyn. "I always say to people that I went to art school in public," he told Steven Kurutz for the *New York Times* (18 Apr. 2017). He presented his first solo show at the now closed Yvon Lambert Gallery in Chelsea in 2005. The show, titled "Deeper Down There," showcased Pendleton's works that incorporate found text from literature and poetry. Pendleton continues to be interested in making language visual in his work, in an effort to explore the relationship between text and meaning. Also included in the show were paintings bearing titles like *American Negro History Volume Two*. *New York Times* critic Ken Johnson (20 May 2005) compared Pendleton to Glenn Ligon, a conceptual artist who incorporates block text in his work, 1960s artist Lawrence Weiner, and artist Ed Ruscha, but added: "Mr. Pendleton has his own smooth graphic style and enigmatic sense of purpose. Is he satirizing cliché black culture, collecting them like a sociologist, or trying to prompt more subtle thinking about language and identity? The provocative reticence is itself a strength of his work."

In 2007, Pendleton moved to Germantown, New York, in the Hudson Valley. In the solitude of his rural studio, Pendleton first began to articulate Black Dada with a series of abstract, monochromatic paintings featuring text. Pendleton spent the same year developing a performance piece for Performa 07, called *The Revival*. In it, Pendleton, accompanied by a thirty-person gospel choir in a room filled with black cube sculptures, delivers a roving monologue—incorporating scraps of language from poets and writers—that Holland Cotter described in his rapturous review for the *New York Times* (9 Nov. 2007) as "a soliloquy, part sermon, part aria, of spliced-together quotations about family, marriage, AIDS and racism." The piece launched Pendleton's star, and marked the beginning of his Black Dada practice. He wrote his Black Dada manifesto a year later, in 2008.

BLACK DADA
Pendleton began his Black Dada series in 2008 with a collection of silkscreen images. Some of the paintings make reference to LeWitt's famous incomplete open cube sculptures; the scrambled letters of the words "Black Dada" are often imposed over the image. (MoMA acquired one piece in the series, *Black Dada (LK/LC/AA)*, in 2011.) In 2009, Pendleton made a series called *System of Display*. For it, Pendleton mounted black boxes framing text imposed over found images—some from art publications, others film stills—that had been photocopied and silkscreened on mirrors. The mirrors, Pendleton told Thom Donovan for *Bomb* magazine (Winter 2011), allow "for a deconstruction of the image that exists inside the frame, because it literally brings things that are outside of the frame into the frame, into the space." Pendleton also made a video work called *BAND* in 2009. The three-channel, twelve-minute film is inspired by Jean Luc-Godard's 1968 documentary featuring the Rolling Stones, *Sympathy for the Devil*. It shows the indie rock band Deerhoof making their song, "I Did Crimes for You," a song the band wrote after watching *Sympathy for the Devil*. Like Godard's film, Pendleton intersperses footage of the band with footage and audio from another source, in this case the 1971 documentary *Teddy*, about radical politics and a black teenager's experience of the late 1960s and early 1970s. "The resulting video follows the formal logic of Godard's film, but the scenario it presents is strikingly more ambiguous," Tom Williams wrote for *Art in America* (9 Feb. 2011). "As Deerhoof rehearses the confrontational rhetoric of the late 1960s, the voiceovers from *Teddy* reflect, quite thoughtfully, on both the prospects for change and the efficacy of violence."

BLACK LIVES MATTER (2015)
In 2010, Pendleton participated in *Greater New York*, an exhibition at the art gallery MoMA PS1 in Queens, showcasing the work of New York artists. For it, he made an installation called *The Abolition of Alienated Labor*. The title of the piece was taken from a 1963 work by artist Guy Debord, which in turn superimposes text onto work by another artist, Giuseppe Pinot-Gallizio. Pendleton described the installation as a coming together of Black Dada works and *System of Display*. The installation incorporated audio based on a jazz composition called "Triptych: Prayer/Protest/Peace," by Max Roach and Abbey Lincoln.

In 2012, Pendleton became the youngest artist represented by the prestigious Pace Gallery in over forty years. He made his Venice Biennale debut in 2015, with *Black Lives Matter*, a piece named for the movement Black Lives Matter. "Black Lives Matter, and the political situation that it has raised awareness of, has been around for a long time," Pendleton told Antwaun Sargent for *Vice* (9 Sept. 2015). "The political dynamic isn't new. What's new is the language that is at once a public mourning, a rallying cry, and a poetic plea." The piece sought to connect the contemporary movement to its historical predecessors, like the Black Power movement of the 1970s, Pendleton told Sargent. The mixed-media installation features black and white paintings and vinyl. It incorporates text—it explodes the words "Black Lives Matter" much as Pendleton's earlier works had exploded and scrambled "Black Dada"—mirrors and photocopied images. (In 2017, he told Kurutz that his trusty old photocopier was the "queen" of his studio.)

In December 2016, Pendleton opened the exhibit *Midnight in America* at the Galerie Eva Presenhuber in Zürich, Switzerland. As Sophie Gilbert, who interviewed Pendleton about the exhibit for the Atlantic (5 Dec. 2016), pointed out, the work, about American history, past and future, took on a new resonance when it was presented after the election of President Donald Trump. The exhibit includes six new paintings and features text from W. E. B. Dubois and Che Baraka. Despite the foreboding title, Pendleton insisted there was "exuberance" in the juxtaposition of objects in the show. "I think that it articulates that arriving at one place or political situation or dynamic that isn't desirable just means there's somewhere else to go," he told Gilbert.

PERSONAL LIFE
Pendleton lives in Brooklyn with his husband, entrepreneur Karsten Ch'ien. He works at a studio in the Sunset Park neighborhood of Brooklyn.

SUGGESTED READING
Cotter, Holland. "Art Is Brief. You Just Have to Be There." *The New York Times*, 9 Nov. 2007, www.nytimes.com/2007/11/09/arts/design/09perf.html. Accessed 13 July 2017.

Gamerman, Ellen. "Adam Pendleton: The Making of an Art-World Star." *The Wall Street Journal*, 16 Apr. 2015.

Gilbert, Sophie. "Adam Pendleton on Art's Turbulent Moment." *The Atlantic*, 5 Dec. 2016, www.theatlantic.com/entertainment/archive/2016/12/adam-pendleton/509459/. Accessed 14 July 2017.

Kurutz, Steven. "The Rising Art World Star behind 'Black Dada.'" *The New York Times*, 18 Apr. 2017, www.nytimes.com/2017/04/18/
style/adam-pendleton-black-dada-moma-guggenheim-tate-modern.html. Accessed 13 July 2017.

Pendleton, Adam. "Greater New Yorkers." Interview by Kevin McGarry. *T Magazine*, 27 May 2010, tmagazine.blogs.nytimes.com/2010/05/27/greater-new-yorkers-adam-pendleton/. Accessed 13 July 2017.

Pendleton, Adam. Interview by Thom Donovan. *Bomb*, Winter 2011, bombmagazine.org/article/4718/adam-pendleton. Accessed 14 July 2017.

Sargent, Antwaun. "'Black Lives Matter' Makes It to the Venice Biennale." *Vice: Creators*, 9 Sept. 2015, creators.vice.com/en_us/article/mgp5yn/black-lives-matter-makes-it-to-the-venice-biennale. Accessed 14 July 2017.

SELECTED WORKS
The Revival, 2007; *BAND*, 2009; *System of Display*, 2009; *Black Lives Matter*, 2015

—*Molly Hagan*

Perfume Genius

Date of birth: September 25, 1981
Occupation: Musician

Perfume Genius is the stage name of the openly gay, gender-bending, and emotionally expansive singer-songwriter Mike Hadreas. He came onto the music scene in 2010, seemingly out of nowhere. His MySpace page was noticed by a studio executive, which led to a record deal, even though he had never performed at a club. He was signed on the strength of his singing and keyboard playing, and has since released such songs as "Mr. Peterson," about a suicidal teacher who has an inappropriate relationship with a student, and "Dark Parts," about his mother's experience of childhood sexual abuse, as well as lighter fare, such as "Queen," which boldly expands upon gay stereotypes and pokes fun at those who stereotype. There is also the love song "Alan," about his longtime romantic and musical partner, Alan Wyffels. "The honesty in Perfume Genius's music has attracted him a devoted audience," wrote Alex Frank for the *Fader* (21 Feb. 2017), "and he receives a lot of messages on Twitter from young kids going through the process of coming out, or dealing with their own addictions."

EARLY LIFE
Mike Hadreas was born on September 25, 1981. He grew up in Everett, Washington, a city near Seattle. He has a younger brother, Matt. When Hadreas was a boy, he took piano lessons, but they did not go very well. "I was a bad student,"

[CC BY 2.0], via Wikimedia Commons

Hadreas recalled, speaking to William Van Meter for the *New York Times* (12 Sept. 2014). "My teachers gave up trying to teach me how to read music." Around the beginning of high school, his parents were in the process of divorcing, so life at home was difficult and unstable. Hadreas also faced enormous challenges at school, where he was harassed and beaten up regularly for being openly gay. "I'd get death threats," he told Van Meter. "I would print them out and say: 'This is what people are doing to me. What are you going to do about it?' They didn't do a damn thing. . . . I wish I toughed it out, instead of standing outside smoking and weeping, which is what I did." Hadreas would also partake in painting and writing for himself. He also listened to music, and was particularly fond of powerful singers such as Liz Phair, Nina Simone, and PJ Harvey.

Hadreas's mother, Carmen Boggs, a special-education teacher, told Van Meter that in high school the football players would beat her son up and spit on him. "Also during this," she told Van Meter, "I was drinking, and there were times when he needed support, and I wasn't there." (Boggs would eventually, along with her new romantic partner, get sober.) During his senior year Hadreas dropped out of high school, unable to take any more harassment and abuse. A few years later, as he was walking down the street in his neighborhood, he was viciously attacked by a group of young men. His injuries were so bad that he had to be hospitalized. After he recovered, he left Everett, moving to New York City.

DRUG ADDICTION, RECOVERY, AND CREATIVITY

Hadreas wanted to move to New York City to become a thriving artist, a successful painter, but instead he spent his time doing odd jobs and staying up late partying. During this time, he developed a drug addiction. "I don't like to get specific," he told Van Meter, "but I'd have one drink and be on the phone with my dealer." His mother and stepfather began to worry. Even though Hadreas was thousands of miles away, they could tell that he was having a hard time and in really bad shape. Hadreas returned home to Washington in 2005 to stay at a live-in drug rehabilitation facility, after which he moved in with his mother and stepfather, both of whom at the time were recovering addicts. Such a living situation was difficult for Hadreas. His mother, speaking to Van Meter, described it as a "house of two recovering people who were not going to allow him to kill himself with drugs, and we did mini A.A. [Alcoholics Anonymous] meetings as a family. I wanted him to not just be sober but to love himself."

About three years after his return home, Hadreas finally moved out of his parents' house and moved in with his brother, Matt. The year was 2008 and the social media website MySpace was still very popular; Hadreas made a MySpace page and began posting his music there. One day a music executive at Turnstile, a record company based in London, England, discovered Hadreas's home-made videos of himself playing the piano and singing. He was so impressed that he got in touch with Hadreas and then helped the young singer-songwriter reach out to Matador Records.

LEARNING

Perfume Genius's first album, *Learning* (2010), is noteworthy for several reasons, not the least of which is the fact that Hadreas was signed to Matador Records based solely on the strength of the musical talent and abilities evident in his self-made videos. He had not yet performed his music at an actual music venue. The first single off his debut album was called "Mr. Peterson," a story of a relationship, implied to be sexual, between a student and his teacher, who goes on to commit suicide. In a review for AllMusic, Heather Phares wrote, "At times Hadreas's songs suggest personal notes or diary entries set to music—not because they're too literal, but because of the emotional weight implied in them. He reveals only the smallest but most telling parts of his stories, playing cat and mouse with details . . . . But what makes Hadreas's songwriting remarkable is the empathy he holds for his characters."

The songs feel personal, intimate, and non-judgmental. In a review for the music website *Pitchfork* (16 July 2010), Larry Fitzmaurice called the songs "eviscerating and naked, with heartbreaking sentiments and bruised characterizations delivered in a voice that ranges from an ethereal croon to a slightly cracked warble." In the song "Write to Your Brother," Perfume Genius sings of a girl taking special care to hide mouthwash from her mother, presumably because mouthwash contains alcohol. Many of his songs swing pendulum-like between hope and optimism on the one hand and gloom and anguish on the other. Yet despite all this, slivers of light manage to break through the cracks. The song "Perry," for example, ends with the following lines: "Whatever good is left / Put your trust in it / You know we already have." For the tour, Perfume Genius was accompanied by Alan Wyffels, whom Hadreas met in rehab.

PUT YOUR BACK N 2 IT

On his second album, *Put Your Back N 2 It* (2012), just as he did on his first, Perfume Genius continued to explore themes such as drug addiction, physical and emotional abuse, despair, and anxiety—and just as he did on the first album, he let some light shine through these dark themes and feelings. There were again comparisons to such sensitive storytelling singers as Sufjan Stevens, and the album overall received high praise. In a profile of Hadreas for the *New Yorker* (22 Sept. 2014), Sasha Frere-Jones not only praised the second album, but also states that Perfume Genius "comes clearly into focus" on the album, on which he fully realizes his style. Writing about the song "Dirge"—which features such lyrics as "All you loved of him lies here / Do your weeping now"—Frere-Jones calls it a "secular kind of hymn." In a review for AllMusic, Phares observed, "The unabashedly lush sound of songs such as 'AWOL Marine,' which, with its sweeping synth strings and piano, feels like a missing piece of Angelo Badalamenti's melodramatic and knowing score for *Twin Peaks*, only highlights how tremulous Hadreas's voice still is, but he finds strength in his fragility." Even more than before, on *Put Your Back N 2 It* Perfume Genius goes boldly into territory rarely dealt with in pop music. For example, in the song "Dark Parts" he speaks to someone who has been the victim of molestation—presumably Hadreas's mother at the hands of her father—singing, "I will take the dark part of your heart into my heart."

TOO BRIGHT

Noticeably different from his first two albums, *Too Bright* (2014), his third, featured a greater range of instrumentation and sounds, as well as some notable collaborators: Adrian Utley of Portishead and PJ Harvey collaborator John Parish. Perfume Genius is also more comfortable being funny and clever on this record. On the glam-rock track "Queen," for example, he throws out one homophobic stereotype after another, and

sings, "No family is safe when I sashay," referring to the unfounded stereotype that gay people are out to destroy the nuclear family or "convert" children to the "gay lifestyle." He also has some fun on the song "Fool," which explores the way that some straight women like to have a gay man as a best friend as a kind of accessory. On this album, wrote Frere-Jones, with its "battery of synthesizers and unusual instruments, Hadreas sings more confidently than before; he also increases the level and range of creepy things in his lyrics." For example, on the song "My Body," in what Frere-Jones called a "strangled falsetto," Perfume Genius sang, "I wear my body like a rotted peach. You can have it if you handle the stink. I'm as open as a gutted pig."

"A lot of these songs are me trying to claim some power in situations that would typically depress or alienate or victimize me," Hadreas said, as quoted by Brandon Stosuy for *Pitchfork* (23 Sept. 2014). "I've seen faces of blank terror when I walk by. Sometimes from seemingly strong, macho dudes—somehow my presence confuses and ultimately scares them. There is a strange power to it that I've only recently begun to understand and embrace." And though the sexuality of Hadreas—and therefore Perfume Genius—is an important and undeniable part of his aesthetic and persona, he is, Stosuy writes, "above all a human—one who's spoken about battling addiction and sickness and sadness, and one who possesses the ability to write about it in a way that feels universal." This is a unique album, wrote Frere-Jones, because unlike most pop musicians, Perfume Genius offers "emotional heaviness" by being, more than anything else, himself.

NO SHAPE

On his fourth album, *No Shape* (2017), Perfume Genius continues down the road of growing up and self-discovery and moves into a sort of acceptance. Sonically it is also different. Phares writes, "Producer Blake Mills' Technicolor arrangements and sonic tricks help Perfume Genius make good on the subversive lavishness *Too Bright* promised." Phares pointed to the "glittering choruses" on the song "Otherside," which opens the album, and called "Just Like Love" a kind of "orchestral synth-pop" and "Go Ahead" "daring electro." There is also the trip-hop-inspired "Die 4 You," somewhat reminiscent of Portishead, and the love song, "Alan," that he wrote for his real-life partner.

The album, like Perfume Genius's previous ones, was very well received, and at times music writers had to employ seemingly distant analogies, images, and phrases to properly describe the atypical music. "These songs swoop and chatter like flocks of mad starlings, light up like religious paintings, flounce like all the pink frills in Sofia Coppola's *Marie Antoinette*, make the cosmos explode inside your ribs," wrote Laura Snapes for *Pitchfork* (5 May 2017). "*No Shape* rebukes tasteful minimalism and embraces beauty at its most transgressive, harking back to the aestheticism and decadence movements of the nineteenth century, as well as Kate Bush and Prince's most lurid extroversions." In a review for the *New Yorker* (8 May 2017), Jia Tolentino summed up how this album is different from Perfume Genius's other work: "This time, though, the songs aren't reaching across horror toward grace—they are simply, and boldly, graceful."

PERSONAL LIFE

Hadreas has been in a relationship with Wyffels since about 2009. The couple live together in Tacoma, Washington. Their house is painted the color of a lemon on the outside; inside it is the color of a lime.

SUGGESTED READING

Frank, Alex. "How Perfume Genius Grew Up and Started Thriving." *The Fader*, 21 Feb. 2017, www.thefader.com/2017/02/21/perfume-genius-cover-story-interview-sobriety. Accessed 6 July 2017.

Frere-Jones, Sasha. "Growth Spurt." Review of *Too Bright*, by Perfume Genius. *The New Yorker*, 22 Sept. 2014, www.newyorker.com/magazine/2014/09/22/growth-spurt. Accessed 6 July 2017.

Phares, Heather. "Perfume Genius: Artist Biography." *AllMusic*, 2017, www.allmusic.com/artist/perfume-genius-mn0002455573/biography. Accessed 6 July 2017.

Snapes, Laura. Review of *No Shape*, by Perfume Genius. *Pitchfork*, 5 May 2017, pitchfork.com/reviews/albums/23137-no-shape. Accessed 6 July 2017.

Stosuy, Brandon. Review of *Too Bright*, by Perfume Genius. *Pitchfork*, 23 Sept. 2014, pitchfork.com/reviews/albums/19798-perfume-genius-too-bright. Accessed 6 July 2017.

Van Meter, William. "Lashing Out at His Tormentors, at Last." *The New York Times*, 17 Sept. 2014, www.nytimes.com/2014/09/21/arts/music/an-aggressive-new-album-from-perfume-genius.html. Accessed 6 July 2017.

SELECTED WORKS

Learning, 2010; *Put Your Back N 2 It*, 2012; *Too Bright*, 2014; *No Shape*, 2017

—*Michael Tillman*

Rick Perlstein

Date of Birth: 1969
Occupation: Journalist, author

Rick Perlstein, whose career as a journalist has had an unabashedly liberal slant, has come to be acclaimed as one of the preeminent historians of the modern conservative movement. With three popular and highly acclaimed histories—*Before the Storm: Barry Goldwater and the Unmaking of the American Consensus* (2001), *Nixonland: The Rise of a President and the Fracturing of America* (2008), and *The Invisible Bridge: The Fall of Nixon and the Rise of Reagan* (2014)—Perlstein has garnered considerable praise from critics on the right, the left, and all points in between. This is due in part to the exhaustive research he puts into his work as well as to the balanced way in which he discusses his conservative subjects and their liberal critics. His fascination with mid- and late twentieth-century politics dates back to his teenage years, but it truly coalesced when he was in graduate school. In an interview with Jason Saltoun-Ebin for the *Huffington Post* (5 Aug. 2014), he said, "When I was in graduate school I . . . became fascinated with the different tribes in America. I was fascinated by the fact that there were just millions of Americans who saw the world in radically different ways than I did. So I began this exploration of the internal anthropology of America."

EARLY LIFE AND EDUCATION

Eric S. Perlstein was born in 1969 to a Reform Jewish American family in Milwaukee, Wisconsin. His fascination with the 1960s, and the so-called culture wars between liberals and conservatives that sprang from them, came while he was still a teenager. He recalled to Saltoun-Ebin, "When I was a teenager in Milwaukee in the 1980s life was pretty boring and I found myself riveted by the sheer melodrama of everyday life of the 1960s. I'd go to this crazy bookstore in Milwaukee called Renaissance Books. . . . They had crazy old books: ones with America spelled with three *K*s, books on the John Birch Society. I ended up getting my own archive on the 1960s culture wars. That's where it started."

Perlstein entered the University of Chicago in 1988 and earned his bachelor's degree in history in 1992. After graduating, he wrote several pieces of his cultural criticism for the left-leaning *Baffler*. He then attended the University of Michigan, where he spent two years working toward a doctorate in American cultural studies but left before completing his PhD.

EARLY CAREER AND *BEFORE THE STORM*

After moving to New York City in 1994, Perlstein began working at *Lingua Franca* magazine, first

Martin Lengemann/ullstein bild via Getty Images

Before the Storm earned the 2001 *Los Angeles Times* Book Prize for history and was cited by the *Chicago Tribune*, the *New York Times*, and the *Washington Post* as one of the best books of the year. A critic for *Kirkus Reviews* (15 Jan. 2001) praised Perlstein's evenhanded approach, writing, "Perlstein, who writes for the *Nation*, clearly delights at relating Johnson's landslide defeat of the Arizona senator, yet he conveys the mindset of a Goldwater supporter with respect, asking readers to put themselves in the shoes of small businessmen bogged down by unions and the New York financial establishment."

Perlstein subsequently served as chief national political correspondent for the *Village Voice* from 2003 to 2005, during which time he covered the 2004 presidential election, and an online columnist for the *New Republic* and *Rolling Stone*. In 2005 he published *The Stock Ticker and the Superjumbo: How the Democrats Can Once Again Become America's Dominant Political Party* (2005), which contained Perlstein's essay on the titular topic along with a collection of responses from such notable contributors as Robert Reich, Elaine Kamarck, and Ruy Teixeira.

NIXONLAND

Perlstein's next book was *Nixonland: The Rise of a President and the Fracturing of America* (2008), a chronicle of the political career of President Richard M. Nixon. After narrowly losing the presidency to John F. Kennedy in 1960, Nixon triumphantly returned to the political stage in 1968 to defeat incumbent vice president and presidential candidate Hubert Humphrey. The election was held against the backdrop of a United States fractured by divisions over the Vietnam War, race riots, and a general uptick in crime. Nixon took advantage of the situation by appealing to the so-called silent majority of Americans—primarily white, middle-class voters who were distressed by what they viewed as the unraveling of the country's moral fabric. Nixon went on to win a second term in 1972 in a rout over his Democratic rival, Senator George McGovern, but he resigned in disgrace two years later following his involvement in the cover-up of the Watergate scandal.

Like its predecessor, *Nixonland* earned considerable praise for its exhaustive research and attention to detail, and it was named one of the best books of 2008 by more than a dozen major publications. It also received plaudits from all points on the political spectrum and became a *New York Times* Best Seller. In a review for the *Atlantic* (May 2008), Ross Douthat wrote, "*Nixonland* reads marvelously. Perlstein has the rare gift of being able to weave social, political, and cultural history into a single seamless narrative, linking backroom political negotiations to suburban protests over sex education in schools to the premiere of *Bonnie and Clyde*. And he has the

as an intern and eventually as an associate editor. At the same time, he began publishing freelance journalism, book reviews, and essays in such notable magazines and newspapers as the *Village Voice*, the *Nation*, the Long Island–based *Newsday*, and the then–newly formed online magazine *Slate*.

Perlstein's reputation as a gifted historian and chronicler of the modern conservative movement began in 2001 with the publication of *Before the Storm: Barry Goldwater and the Unmaking of the American Consensus*, which received widespread acclaim on both sides of the political aisle. It describes the life and career of Senator Barry Goldwater, a conservative Republican from Arizona who believed unflinchingly in American exceptionalism and decried a number of happenings during his political career: the rise of unions, which he believed oppressed working people; the creation of civil rights laws, which he believed would start the United States down the road to becoming a police state; and what he believed to be the ineffectual response of American leaders to Soviet aggression and expansionism. Although nominated for the presidency by Republicans during the 1964 election, he lost in a landslide to the sitting president, Lyndon B. Johnson, who would leave office in disgrace in 1969 due to his mishandling of the Vietnam War. Goldwater, however, would later prove to have been ahead of his time: Ronald Reagan became one of the most popular presidents of the second half of the twentieth century based on a similarly conservative ideology.

eye of a great documentarian, fastening not only on the obvious historical set pieces (Kent State, Watts, Attica), but on the not-so-obvious ones as well."

THE INVISIBLE BRIDGE

For his next book, Perlstein did not jump directly to the presidency of Ronald Reagan, the two-term conservative icon who served as president from 1981 to 1989. Instead, as evidenced by the subtitle, he decided to chronicle the period between Nixon and Reagan in *The Invisible Bridge: The Fall of Nixon and the Rise of Reagan*, which was published in 2014 to rave reviews. While the main focus of the work is Reagan, who was serving as governor of California during Nixon's time in the Oval Office, another central character of the book is the United States during the 1970s, a period of unrest and transition that is often described as the "hangover" of the 1960s. As belief in American institutions was waning—the Vietnam War was lost, a president had left office in disgrace, crime was on the rise, and the economy was in the doldrums—Reagan came to prominence, declaring that the country's best days were still ahead. Although Reagan ultimately failed to seize the 1976 Republican nomination for president from incumbent Gerald Ford, who had succeeded to the presidency following Nixon's resignation, he left the Republican National Convention (RNC) more highly regarded than when he arrived, effectively setting up his successful run for the presidency in 1980.

Like Perlstein's previous works, *The Invisible Bridge* topped numerous year-end best-of lists and received a considerable amount of critical acclaim. In the *Wall Street Journal* (1 Aug. 2014), Max Boot wrote, "Rick Perlstein has established himself as one of our foremost chroniclers of the rise of the modern conservative movement. It's an unexpected niche for a card-carrying liberal. But if he's occasionally tart in his comments about conservatives, he is not entirely unsympathetic either. In fact, he reserves some of his most cutting barbs . . . for clueless establishment liberals who all too readily dismissed the significance of conservative champions such as Barry Goldwater, Richard Nixon, and Ronald Reagan." A critic for *Kirkus Reviews* (1 Sept. 2014) wrote, "Perlstein once again delivers a terrific hybrid biography of a Republican leader and the culture he shaped," adding that he "deftly . . . taps into the consciousness of bicentennial America."

In recent years, Perlstein's journalism and essays have appeared in such prestigious periodicals as the *New York Times*, the *Washington Post*, the *Chicago Tribune*, the *San Francisco Chronicle*, the *Los Angeles Times*, the *London Review of Books*, the *Columbia Journalism Review*, and the *New Yorker*.

PERSONAL LIFE

Rick Perlstein married Kathy Geier, a fellow writer and public-policy researcher, in April 2001. The couple met in 1998 when Perlstein responded to Geier's personal ad in the *Nation*. They moved from New York to Chicago, Illinois, in 2002.

In his interview with Saltoun-Ebin, Perlstein said he was working on a fourth book about American conservatism that would cover Reagan's 1980 reelection campaign, then added, "After that I'm not sure. I've been working on this since 1997. Twenty years will probably be enough." When not working, Perlstein enjoys yoga and playing jazz piano.

SUGGESTED READING

Alter, Alexandra. "Reagan Book Sets Off Debate." *The New York Times*, 4 Aug. 2014, www.nytimes.com/2014/08/05/business/media/rick-perlsteins-the-invisible-bridge-draws-criticism.html. Accessed 11 Nov. 2016.

Boot, Max. Review of *The Invisible Bridge: The Fall of Nixon and the Rise of Reagan*, by Rick Perlstein. *The Wall Street Journal*, 1 Aug. 2014, www.wsj.com/articles/book-review-the-invisible-bridge-by-rick-perlstein-1406927765. Accessed 11 Nov. 2016.

Douthat, Ross. "E Pluribus Nixon." Review of *Nixonland: The Rise of a President and the Fracturing of America*, by Rick Perlstein. *The Atlantic*, May 2008, www.theatlantic.com/magazine/archive/2008/05/e-pluribus-nixon/306765/. Accessed 11 Nov. 2016.

Perlstein, Rick. *Before the Storm: Barry Goldwater and the Unmaking of the American Consensus.* 15 Jan. 2001. *Kirkus Reviews*, 24 June 2010, www.kirkusreviews.com/book-reviews/rick-perlstein/before-the-storm-2/. Accessed 11 Nov. 2016.

Perlstein, Rick. "*The Invisible Bridge*: 10 or So Questions with Rick Perlstein." Interview by Jason Saltoun-Ebin. *The Huffington Post*, 5 Aug. 2014, www.huffingtonpost.com/jason-saltounebin/the-invisible-bridge-10-o_b_5648712.html. Accessed 11 Nov. 2016.

Perlstein, Rick. "*The Invisible Bridge: The Fall of Nixon and the Rise of Reagan*", *Kirkus Reviews*, 1 Sept. 2014, p. 67.

Prager, Emily. "Vows: Kathy Geier and Rick Perlstein." *The New York Times*, 6 May 2001, www.nytimes.com/2001/05/06/living/vows-kathy-geier-and-rick-perlstein.html. Accessed 11 Nov. 2016.

SELECTED WORKS

Before the Storm: Barry Goldwater and the Unmaking of the American Consensus, 2001; *The Stock Ticker and the Superjumbo: How the Democrats Can Once Again Become America's*

Dominant Political Party, 2005; *Nixonland: The Rise of a President and the Fracturing of America*, 2008; *The Invisible Bridge: The Fall of Nixon and the Rise of Reagan*, 2014

—*Christopher Mari*

Kelsey Plum

Date of birth: August 24, 1994
Occupation: Basketball player

Professional basketball player Kelsey Plum was the first overall pick—the first of all eligible players to be chosen—in the 2017 Women's National Basketball Association (WNBA) draft. The left-handed, five-feet-eight point guard for the San Antonio Stars became a national sensation while she was still in college at the University of Washington, leading the Washington Huskies to three consecutive National Collegiate Athletic Association (NCAA) tournaments, including an appearance in the Final Four of the 2016 NCAA Division I Women's Basketball Tournament. In her senior year at Washington, Plum scored a total of 1,109 points, breaking the NCAA women's basketball record for points scored in a single season, and ended the season with a career total of 3,527 points scored—another record in NCAA women's basketball and the second-highest career total in NCAA basketball overall, just 140 points behind the male record holder, former Louisiana State University player Pete Maravich.

Despite a rough start to her professional career thanks to an ankle injury in May 2017, Plum's future in the WNBA is full of promise. Her style of play has been compared to that of National Basketball Association (NBA) star James Harden of the Houston Rockets, and a video intercutting clips of the two players went viral in early 2017. The Harden comparison was good publicity, but Plum was not shy about challenging the underlying assumption that, as Seth Berkman wrote for the *New York Times* (13 Apr. 2017), "female players can be validated only through association with their male counterparts." "It started off as really flattering, but hopefully we can move past that because I think comparing men to women is kind of . . . disheartening," Plum said to Natalie Weiner for *Bleacher Report* (12 May 2017). "Fans come in expecting something specific, and then they leave disappointed. I don't even really want to play like other women—I want to play like me, the best version of me."

EARLY LIFE

Kelsey Plum was born on August 24, 1994, in Poway, California, in San Diego County. She

By Jennifer Buchanan [CC BY-SA 4.0] via Wikimedia Commons

comes from a family of athletes: her maternal great-grandfather was Arthur "Mickey" McBride, the founder of the Cleveland Browns football team; her father, Jim Plum, was a star football player at San Diego State University in the early 1980s; and her mother, Katie McBride, played Division I volleyball for the University of California, Davis (UC Davis), as did, years later, her oldest sister, Kaitlyn. Another sister, Lauren, played volleyball for the University of Oregon before graduating and going on to play professionally overseas. Her little brother Dan played football for UC Davis.

Like her mother and sisters, Plum played volleyball as a child, both indoor and beach, but she was captivated by the pickup basketball games she watched her father play. While still in elementary school, she began practicing her free throws, keeping track of how many she made each day. "I learned from an early age, if you want something, go make it happen," she explained to Daniel Uthman for *USA Today* (22 Feb. 2017). "It's not anyone else's job." She cited as an example a time in fourth grade when, feeling that she was too old for fourth grade and too young for fifth, she asked her parents to tell the principal that she wanted to switch into a class made up of both fourth- and fifth-graders. Her father urged her to talk to the principal herself and make her own case. Plum did so, and successfully switched classes; more importantly, she learned the power of her own agency.

LA JOLLA COUNTRY DAY SCHOOL

When Plum was in seventh grade, she began joining in her father's pickup games with his friends. As an adolescent playing with grown men, she was determined to improve and to justify her place in their games. "I think the first thing I learned was, I gotta be able to shoot if I'm going to stay on the court," she said to Uthman. "And then also I gotta make shots, because if you lose at pickup, you're off and you have to wait like two hours to get back on." When she entered high school, she broke precedent with her older sisters, who had attended Poway High School; instead, Plum went to La Jolla Country Day School, the alma mater of WNBA star Candace Wiggins, and played for coach Terri Bamford, who was named Cal-Hi Sports Girls State Coach of the Year in 2012. Bamford and Plum took to each other immediately. "She's one tremendous leader, as competitive as they come," Bamford said to Lee Michaelson for the women's basketball website *Full Court* (1 May 2012). "Her work ethic is off the charts—and not just on the court, but also in the weight room, in individual skill work."

Bamford also called Plum "one tough kid," but even that description seems an understatement. At the 2011 Nike Tournament of Champions in Chandler, Arizona, Plum dove for a ball in a game against Northern California's Dougherty Valley High School and caught an elbow to the face, knocking out four of her front teeth. She was determined to keep playing, and Bamford and her mother had to force her to come out of the game. That year, she was named Cal-Hi Sports Sophomore of the Year, having averaged 19.6 points and 4.8 assists per game.

In 2012, Plum truly came into her own as a player, averaging 22 points, 4.5 rebounds, and 4.5 assists per game and earning the title of California Interscholastic Federation (CIF) Division IV Player of the Year. At state finals, she scored a game-high 32 points, including five three-point shots, leading La Jolla to their first championship victory since 2002. During her senior year, she averaged 27.1 points, 8.5 rebounds, and 3.3 assists per game. She was named Ms. Basketball 2013 by Cal-Hi Sports—the second player in the school's history to earn the honor, Wiggins having won in 2004. That summer, Plum was selected for the US women's national under-nineteen basketball team, which went on to win the gold medal at the 2013 Fédération Internationale de Basketball (FIBA) Under-19 World Championship for Women in Lithuania.

Through it all, Plum visited countless colleges and spoke with hordes of recruiters. Finally, inspired by her older sister Lauren, who attended a university with a low-ranked volleyball team and helped lead that team to the NCAA championships for the first time ever, Plum decided that she wanted to play for a school that, as her mother put it to Jayda Evans for the *Seattle Times* (14 Sept. 2014), "hadn't gotten 'there' yet. . . . Kelsey was like, 'I want to do that, I want to go in and help build a program and help get a program to the next level.' It gave her that vision."

Plum committed to the University of Washington, which had not reached an NCAA tournament since 2007, but she nearly ended up not going. In April 2013, Huskies head coach Kevin McGruff left the school for Ohio State University. Plum was blindsided. Recruiters began calling again as she was granted a release from her letter of intent, but Plum turned off her phone. "I felt like I got broken up with," she said to Adam Jude for the *Seattle Times* (24 Mar. 2016). Still, she kept in contact with the assistant coach, Mike Neighbors, promising to attend the school if he stayed there. When he was promoted to head coach, she kept her word.

WASHINGTON HUSKIES

Plum showed up to her first Huskies practice still jet-lagged from her gold-medal-winning trip to Lithuania. In her first season (2013–14), she was second in the nation among freshman scorers and broke the school's freshman scoring record with 38 points in a game against the University of Oregon in February 2014. She also set a freshman record of 37.3 minutes played per game. Plum fulfilled the promise of her stellar high school career by effectively putting the Huskies on the national map of tournament contenders, but that success came at a cost. Before the season began, Neighbors named her team captain; the decision rankled her elder teammates and made Plum enormously unpopular. According to one anecdote, the star player was forced to walk almost three miles home from a game in the rain because none of her teammates offered her a ride. The experience informed Plum's rookie season with the Stars, and she has said repeatedly that her primary goal is to serve her teammates and her team.

In her sophomore season (2014–15), Plum led the Huskies to the first round of the NCAA tournament; in her junior year (2015–16), she led the team to the Final Four for the first time in its history. During her senior year (2016–17), Plum made a national name for herself as a fearless and aggressive player with a killer shot, averaging 31.7 points per game, breaking the NCAA women's single-season scoring record with 1,109 points, and setting the NCAA women's career scoring record with 3,527 points. She led the Huskies to the NCAA tournament for a third consecutive year, although the team's bid for the championship ended in the regional semifinals (also known as the Sweet Sixteen). At the end of the season, Plum was named the Associated Press Women's College Basketball Player of the

Year and the Naismith College Player of the Year, and was awarded the John R. Wooden Award for women's player of the year. She also won the Dawn Staley Award for best guard in women's Division I basketball, the Nancy Lieberman Award for best point guard in women's Division I, and the Ann Meyers Drysdale Award for women's national player of the year.

2017 DRAFT AND THE SAN ANTONIO STARS
As the WNBA draft rolled around, Plum found a friend in Markelle Fultz, the University of Washington's star male basketball player. "We became friends because there were a lot of expectations of both of us, so we connected on certain things that we'd both go through," she said to Weiner. Plum was the first pick of the WNBA draft, going to the San Antonio Stars in April; Fultz was selected first in the NBA draft, going to the Philadelphia 76ers in June. It was the first time that both the male and the female first overall draft picks came from the same school in the same year.

The Stars' 2017–18 season got off to a rocky start, as the players learned to work as a unit and to balance the talents of its three star guards: Plum, Moriah Jefferson (the number-two draft pick in 2016), and Kayla McBride (number-three pick in 2014). Learning a new system built for three powerful guards was made all the harder for Plum after she sprained her ankle in May. "It's been difficult to try and get back, and not even to get back but play at the level I'm capable at," she said to Tim Booth for the Associated Press (16 June 2017). "It's a tough shift regardless for rookies, so it's been an experience for me that is going to help me in the long run. For now, it's not easy." But as the summer wore on, Plum relaxed into her new role. In early August, she scored a career-high 23 points in a game against the Seattle Storm, boding well for the team's future prospects.

SUGGESTED READING
Berkman, Seth. "Kelsey Plum Is a Lot Like James Harden. But Is It a Left-Handed Compliment?" *The New York Times*, 13 Apr. 2017, www.nytimes.com/2017/04/13/sports/basketball/kelsey-plum-wnba-draft-james-harden-comparisons.html. Accessed 17 Aug. 2017.

Booth, Tim. "Kelsey Plum Returns to Seattle after Rough Start as a Pro." *AP News*, Associated Press, 16 June. 2017, www.apnews.com/a273accd26074da4baf520bb1513565c/Kelsey-Plum-returns-to-Seattle-after-rough-start-as-a-pro. Accessed 13 Aug. 2017.

Evans, Jayda. "Husky Basketball Star Kelsey Plum Finds Inspiration at Home." *The Seattle Times*, 14 Sept. 2014, www.seattletimes.com/sports/uw-huskies/husky-basketball-star-kelsey-plum-finds-inspiration-at-home/. Accessed 13 Aug. 2017.

Jude, Adam. "How Kelsey Plum and Mike Neighbors Formed the Perfect Player-Coach Pairing." *The Seattle Times*, 24 Mar. 2016, www.seattletimes.com/sports/uw-husky-basketball/how-kelsey-plum-and-mike-neighbors-formed-the-perfect-player-coach-pairing/. Accessed 13 Aug. 2017.

Michaelson, Lee. "Passion, Toughness Define La Jolla Country Day's Kelsey Plum." *Full Court*, 1 May 2012, www.fullcourt.com/lee-michaelson/5896/passion-toughness-define-la-jolla-country-days-kelsey-plum. Accessed 13 Aug. 2017.

Plum, Kelsey. "No. 1 Pick Kelsey Plum Talks Sexism, Launching T-Shirts & Beating Markelle Fultz." Interview by Natalie Weiner. *Bleacher Report*, 12 May 2017, bleacherreport.com/articles/2709295-no-1-pick-kelsey-plum-talks-sexism-launching-t-shirts-beating-markelle-fultz. Accessed 13 Aug. 2017.

Uthman, Daniel. "Most Likely to Succeed: Washington's Kelsey Plum Nears NCAA Scoring Record." *USA Today*, 22 Feb. 2017, www.usatoday.com/story/sports/ncaaw/2017/02/22/washington-kelsey-plum-jackie-stiles-ncaa-womens-basketball-scoring-record/98264130/. Accessed 13 Aug. 2017.

—Molly Hagan

Victor Ponta
Date of birth: September 20, 1972
Occupation: Prime Minister of Romania

Victor Ponta is a Social Democratic Party politician and was the prime minister of Romania until his resignation in November 2015.

EARLY LIFE AND EDUCATION
Victor Ponta was born in Bucharest, Romania, on September 20, 1972, to Ninel Ponta and Cornelia Naum. His family is of Albanian and Italian descent. As a child, Ponta distinguished himself as both a dedicated student of history and a basketball star. In interviews his mother has stated that although the young Ponta expressed an interest in becoming a priest like his grandfather, he secretly nurtured a dream to become a politician. His participation in politics began at the age of seventeen when he took to the streets to protest Romania's communist government.

After graduating from Ion Neculce High School in 1991, Ponta attended the University of Bucharest to study law. From 1995 to 1998, he worked as a prosecutor at a courthouse in the wealthy sector 1 neighborhood. During this time he also taught criminal law at the

Romanian-American University. He went on to work as an anticorruption prosecutor at the Supreme Court of Justice, with a focus on financial crimes. He served in this position from 1998 to 2001, and in 2003, Ponta received his doctorate in criminal law from the University of Bucharest. The degree would later prove problematic when allegations that large parts of his thesis were plagiarized came to a head. He relinquished his PhD title in 2014, stating that once his political career concluded he would pursue a new doctorate and better adhere to the University of Bucharest's ethical standards.

POLITICAL CAREER

Ponta entered the political arena in 2001 when he was appointed chief of the prime minister's control department. He rose quickly through the ranks of the Social Democratic Party under the guidance of former prime minister, Adrian Năstase. After winning the Gorj constituency seat in the 2004 parliamentary elections, Ponta became one of the youngest members of parliament in Romanian history. In 2006, he was elected vice president of the Social Democratic Party.

Upon his reelection to the Romania's parliament in 2008, Ponta was appointed to the prime minister's cabinet. His term was cut short, however, when he and several other Social Democrats resigned in 2009 in an act of protest against the dismissal Dan Nica, fellow party member and vice prime minister. In 2010, Ponta became the president of the Social Democratic Party, replacing the incumbent leader, Mircea Geoană. As the party's president, Ponta spearheaded the formation of the Social Liberal Union, a coalition with the National Liberal Party, the Centre Right Alliance, and the Conservative Party. Together, the coalition was able to dilute the power of the governing Democratic Liberal Party and eventually earn a majority in the parliament.

Following the resignation of Emil Boc and the dismissal of his successor, Mihai-Răzvan Ungureanu, Ponta was appointed prime minister of Romania in May 2012. At only thirty-nine, Ponta had become the youngest leader in Europe. As prime minister, he promised to facilitate economic growth by creating more jobs in the private sector. However, in reality his first few months in office were spent trying to impeach President Traian Băsescu. Widely unpopular among the public, Băsescu was a former Communist Party member known for championing austerity measures and abusing his constitutional powers. Despite Ponta's extensive efforts to remove Băsescu from office, the president remained in office until 2014. Meanwhile, the conflict between the two men crippled the already weakened Romanian economy and furthered tensions with the European Union (EU), which had helped the country secure a €5 billion loan from the International Monetary Fund (IMF).

Ponta began to significantly lose favor with the Romanian public in 2014. In addition to the plagiarism allegations surrounding his PhD thesis, Ponta refused to nominate National Liberal Party leader Klaus Iohannis as his deputy prime minister. Ponta's conflict with Iohannis escalated when the two ran against one another during the 2014 presidential elections. Iohannis defeated Ponta, who then remained prime minister.

Ponta's reputation suffered further when Romania's National Anti-Corruption Directorate (DNA) announced on June 5, 2015, that it was investigating the prime minister for multiple counts of forgery, money laundering, and tax evasion. Led by director Laura Codruţa Kövesi, who was delegated by the European Union to crack down on the eastern member's corruption, the DNA put Ponta on trial in September 2015. Although President Iohannis called for him to step down, Ponta refused stating that only the parliament could dismiss him.

When a fire at a Bucharest nightclub killed thirty-two people and injured hundreds more in late October 2015, the public outcry for Ponta's resignation became impossible to ignore. The nightclub was permitted to have only one exit, a fact that Romanians viewed as an extension of the government's apathy and corruption. On November 4, 2015, in the face of an estimated twenty-thousand protestors gathered in Bucharest, Ponta resigned as prime minister citing the need for high-ranking political accountability. Two weeks later, the independent Dacian Cioloş was appointed prime minister.

IMPACT

As prime minister, Victor Ponta led Romania into some of its most tumultuous political years since the fall of communism in 1989. The Romanian public's long-standing frustration with the government boiled over as a result of his corrupt actions and conflicts with other high-ranking officials. Investigations of Ponta by the national anti-corruption group marked a new chapter in Romania's history when the government would insist on accountability.

PERSONAL LIFE

Ponta lives in Bucharest, Romania, with his wife Daciana Sârbu and their daughter Irina Ponta. Ponta has a son, Andrei, with his first wife Roxana Ponta.

SUGGESTED READING

Beauchamp, Zachary. "The Romanian Protests That Forced Out the Prime Minister, Explained." *Vox*. Vox Media, 5 Nov. 2015. Web. 11 Mar. 2016.

Chandler, Adam. "How a Nightclub Fire Brought Down a Prime Minister." *Atlantic*. Atlantic Media, 4 Nov. 2016. Web. 11 Mar. 2016.

"Clear Victory, Uncertain Future." *Economist*. Economist Group, 15 Dec. 2012. Web. 11 Mar. 2016.

"EU Warns Romania PM Victor Ponta over Political Crisis." *BBC*. BBC, 12 July 2012. Web. 11 Mar. 2016.

Gillet, Kit, and Palko Karasz. "Victor Ponta, Romania's Premier, Steps Down after Outcry over Corruption." *New York Times*. New York Times, 4 Nov. 2015. Web. 11 Mar. 2016.

—*Emily Turner*

Charlie Puth

Date of Birth: December 2, 1991
Occupation: Singer-songwriter

JB Lacroix/WireImage/Getty Images

Rising pop singer Charlie Puth was destined for greatness—a bold declaration made in 2012 by his close friend Vail Cerullo, a former Berklee College of Music classmate who died in a tragic motorcycle accident months later. "He said 'you're going to have a No. 1 single someday,'" Puth shared with Bobby Olivier for *NJ.com* (23 Apr. 2015). This prediction became reality three years later, when "See You Again," a song he cowrote with Cerullo in mind, topped Billboard's Hot 100, eventually becoming one of the chart's longest-running number-one rap singles following twelve weeks at the top position overall. Overwhelmed by his almost overnight success, he explained the experience to Jen Yamato in an interview for the *Daily Beast* (7 Apr. 2015): "I use the word 'insane' a lot and I'm going to say it again. This whole thing has been *insane*."

Puth emerged from relative obscurity after his YouTube version of an Adele hit garnered the attention of comedian Ellen DeGeneres, who invited him to perform on her talk show. He has since earned cowriting credit for several songs performed by other major artists, including the rapper Pitbull and singer Jason Derulo. In addition to his behind-the-scenes role, the little-known Puth was able to sing lead, launching him as a solo artist. His full-length debut album, *Nine Track Mind*, spawned the multiplatinum hits "Marvin Gaye" and "One Call Away," as well as the gold-certified single "We Don't Talk Anymore."

EARLY LIFE

The oldest of three children, Charlie Puth was born to Debra and Charles Puth on December 2, 1991, in the beach town of Rumson, New Jersey. His earliest musical exposure came from his mother, a piano instructor; while pregnant with her firstborn, she introduced him to the songs of folk icon James Taylor by placing headphones over her belly. He credits his father with exposing him to several R & B greats, including Motown legend Marvin Gaye, Barry White, and The Isley Brothers.

When Puth was four, his mother started teaching him to play the piano and realized that he possessed perfect pitch, or the rare ability to distinguish musical notes. "He'd tell me the sound of the wind, or the sound of a dime dropping on the floor, and say 'Mommy, that's an A flat, or a D sharp,'" she told Olivier for *NJ.com* (28 Jan. 2016). Only a few years later, Puth was taking jazz and improv classes at the Academy of Music and Drama in Little Silver, New Jersey, where he also learned to record music on a computer, under the watchful eye of the school's director, Jim Josselyn. The musical prodigy also honed his improvisational skills in the youth jazz arts program at the Count Basie Theatre's Performing Arts Academy.

PRODUCING HIS OWN MUSIC

However, jazz was not the only genre that Puth embraced. He also became enthralled with pop music and the actual process of making a song, closely admiring the work of Max Martin, the Grammy Award–winning songwriter/producer responsible for several hits by Britney Spears and the Backstreet Boys during the late 1990s. Inspired to buy his first production keyboard, Puth began making his own CDs, eventually creating a holiday album for which he handled every aspect of production. In addition to creating the artwork and assembling the jewel cases for each

CD, he successfully peddled the discs door-to-door, eventually contributing his earnings to the local church. He also served as a piano accompanist for local school plays and productions. It was around this time that he remembers realizing his gift for recognizing and memorizing music and pitch himself, telling Clay Skipper in an interview for *GQ* (1 Feb. 2016), "From just going to church, I had already memorized all the music. So when the organist didn't show up on Ash Wednesday, my twelve-year-old self went up to the organ—I didn't even know how to play it—and just played the whole Mass from memory. But again, I thought it was just a normal thing. . . . But apparently it is a little bit more rare."

Though Puth has confided to interviewers that he suffered verbal abuse and bullying while attending Rumson-Fair Haven Regional High School, which generally made him shy away from public performances and eventually pushed him toward the YouTube format, he did not give up on his talent. Saturdays were spent commuting to the Manhattan School of Music, where he studied jazz and classical music as a member of the pre-college program. In 2009, he launched his very own YouTube channel, on which he posted cover tunes and parody videos.

Upon graduating from high school in 2010, Puth accepted a full scholarship to attend the Berklee College of Music in Boston, Massachusetts. As a freshman, he recorded the independent EP *The Otto Tunes* (2010) in his dorm room—the same one once occupied by Berklee alumnus and Grammy Award–winning singer-songwriter John Mayer. In September 2011, his cover of Adele's "Someone Like You"—a duet with classmate Emily Luther—won an online contest sponsored by gossip blogger Perez Hilton.

EMERGING FROM OBSCURITY

Puth subsequently uploaded the video to YouTube—a decision that would prove to be life changing. Within a week, the duo's rendition of "Someone Like You" had amassed one million views, catching the attention of actor Portia de Rossi, the wife of comedian and talk show host Ellen DeGeneres, who immediately tracked him down and contacted him. In October 2011, he and Luther performed the song on *The Ellen Show* before being jointly signed to DeGeneres's record label, eleveneleven. They closed out the year by collaborating on another cover—Lady Antebellum's "Need You Now"—and "Break Again," a self-released tune cowritten by Puth.

The duo started 2012 on a high note, winning the award for best cover song at the inaugural PopCrush Music Awards and performing "Need You Now" and "Break Again" on the January 25 episode of *The Ellen Show*. Puth credited DeGeneres with giving his budding career a boost. "Those two appearances got me my international base and shot my YouTube subscribers up," he told Trevor Anderson for *Billboard* (17 Mar. 2015). "One of the best things from it is that it actually inspired me to write more music for myself."

After earning a degree in music production and engineering in 2013, Puth returned to his parents' New Jersey home, where he stayed for the next six months. In October, he independently released *Ego* (2013), subsequently filming and uploading YouTube videos for many of the album's tracks. He performed at New York City's The Bitter End the following March to promote his sophomore EP.

In the summer of 2014, the independent Artist Publishing Group (APG) courted the budding performer, signing Puth to a publishing deal. "I also secretly wanted to be an artist, but I thought the best way to go about that was to write songs first," he admitted to Rob LeDonne for *American Songwriter* (23 Apr. 2015). Immediately upon re-settling on his own in Los Angeles, he penned a new song—an ode to Gaye.

BREAKING OUT WITH "SEE YOU AGAIN"

On his second day in Los Angeles, Puth entered the studio with fellow APG recruit and producer Justin "DJ Frank E" Franks to compose a melody and chorus for the closing song of the highly anticipated new installment of the Fast and the Furious franchise *Furious 7*, which would pay tribute to star Paul Walker, who had died tragically in a car crash the previous November. The first-time collaboration, which was inspired by the similar motorcycle death of Puth's close friend and fellow Berklee alumnus, proved seamless. "We didn't know each other, [but] we wrote the hook in, like, ten minutes," he told Madison Vain for *Entertainment Weekly* (24 Apr. 2015). "What was interesting was that we were writing the song for Paul, but we didn't tell each other that we had both lost somebody recently. It was pretty powerful. The moment we finished it, we hugged."

The filmmakers, as well as executives from Universal Pictures and Atlantic Records (who had also seen Puth's performances on *The Ellen Show*), responded equally well to the song, which was ultimately approved. Rapper Wiz Khalifa was then enlisted to add the finishing touches. When Puth was shown a rough cut of the film, he made a pleasant discovery: they had decided to keep his vocals from the demo recording rather than using an established artist such as Sam Smith. He experienced more good news in December 2014, when he signed an artist deal with Atlantic Records. "Marvin Gaye," his debut single under the new label and duet with fellow young rising star Meghan Trainor, was released in February 2015.

By the end of the following month, before *Furious 7* had even premiered in theaters, "See You Again" had entered Billboard's Hot 100 at number one hundred. The single's music video, which premiered in early April, was followed by Puth's mid-April return appearance on *The Ellen Show*. After the release of the film helped to boost "See You Again" into the top ten by April 18, he scored his first-ever number one hit a week later, when the song dethroned Mark Ronson and Bruno Mars's "Uptown Funk" after fourteen consecutive weeks at the top of the Hot 100.

Some Type of Love, Puth's third EP and his first release under Atlantic Records, hit the shelves in May 2015 and included "Marvin Gaye" as one of the four tracks. That same month, he performed alongside Khalifa on *Saturday Night Live*.

NINE TRACK MIND

In July 2015, Puth served as the opening act on Trainor's North American summer tour while starting to work on his full-length debut for a major label. By late August 2015, he had released "One Call Away," the first single from his upcoming album, and attended the 2015 MTV Video Music Awards, where "See You Again" was nominated twice. While performing in the Philippines in October 2015, he penned "We Don't Talk Anymore," a breakup song and duet with Selena Gomez. For his upcoming disc, he decided to shun recording studios and continue to produce his songs on his laptop from locations such as his bedroom. "No vocal booth, no studio treatment. Nothing fancy. It's more personal that way," he explained to Skipper.

In January 2016, about a month after completing the iHeartRadio Jingle Ball tour and receiving nominations for both Grammy Awards and a Golden Globe Award, Puth and Khalifa claimed the best song prize at the Critics' Choice Awards for "See You Again." Later that same month, he released his long-awaited debut CD, *Nine Track Mind*, to lukewarm reviews. In his review for *Newsday* (28 Jan. 2016), Glenn Gamboa wrote, "Puth shows promise, but he can't quite pull off everything he wants on *Nine Track Mind*." Despite the mixed critical reactions, the album reached number six on the Billboard 200 and has since been certified gold.

To promote *Nine Track Mind*, Puth embarked on a headlining tour of the United States and Canada in March 2016. Two months later, he released "We Don't Talk Anymore," which became his second top-ten hit after reaching number nine on Billboard's Hot 100. He debuted the duet live during the last US date of Gomez's Revival tour in July. The fall leg of Puth's tour kicked off in September but he canceled his October 7 appearance in Raleigh, North Carolina after being hospitalized with the flu. Later that month he canceled the rest of the tour, stating his need to fully recover.

PERSONAL LIFE

In 2016, Puth purchased a Mediterranean-style home in the Hollywood Hills. Although he has been romantically linked to Trainor and Gomez and eventually addressed these rumors, he has remained focused on his music and has generally opted to keep the details of his personal life private.

SUGGESTED READING

Anderson, Trevor. "Charlie Puth Talks Meghan Trainor Duet 'Marvin Gaye' & His Plea to James Taylor." *Billboard,* 17 Mar. 2015, www.billboard.com/articles/columns/popshop/6502317/charlie-puth-tonight-show-interview. Accessed 15 Nov. 2016.

LeDonne, Rob. "Q&A: Singer-Songwriter Charlie Puth on Current Number One Hit 'See You Again.'" *American Songwriter,* 23 Apr. 2015, americansongwriter.com/2015/04/qa-singer-songwriter-charlie-puth-current-number-one-hit-see/. Accessed 15 Nov. 2016.

Olivier, Bobby. "How Blossoming N.J. Star Charlie Puth Became Pop's Ascendant Hit-Maker." *NJ.com,* New Jersey On-Line, 28 Jan. 2016, www.nj.com/entertainment/music/index.ssf/2016/01/charlie_puth_blossoms_into_njs_hottest_pop_star_th.html. Accessed 15 Nov. 2016.

Olivier, Bobby. "How an N.J. Singer's Simple Hook Became the No. 1 Song in the World." *NJ.com,* New Jersey On-Line, 23 Apr. 2015, www.nj.com/entertainment/music/index.ssf/2015/04/how_an_nj_singers_simple_hook_became_the_no_1_song.html. Accessed 15 Nov. 2016.

Skipper, Clay. "We Confronted Charlie Puth, the Guy Who Made You Cry Like a Baby at *Furious 7.*" *GQ,* 1 Feb. 2016, www.gq.com/story/charlie-puth-interview. Accessed 15 Nov. 2016.

Vain, Madison. "Breaking Big: Charlie Puth." *Entertainment Weekly,* 24 Apr. 2015, www.ew.com/article/2015/04/24/breaking-big-charlie-puth. Accessed 15 Nov. 2016.

Yamato, Jen. "Charlie Puth on His Geeky YouTube Beginnings and Chart-Topping Paul Walker Tribute Anthem." *Daily Beast,* 7 Apr. 2015, www.thedailybeast.com/articles/2016/11/16/48-hours-in-facebook-s-unreality.html. Accessed 15 Nov. 2016.

SELECTED WORKS

The Otto Tunes, 2010; *Ego,* 2013; *Some Type of Love,* 2015; *Nine Track Mind,* 2016

—*Bertha Muteba*

Dorit Rabinyan

Date of birth: 1972
Occupation: Author

An acclaimed Israeli writer, Dorit Rabinyan is the recipient of numerous Israeli literary awards, including the Itzhak Vinner Prize, the ACUM (Association of Composers, Authors and Publishers of Music) Award, and the Prime Minister's Prize. She is also the winner of the prestigious Bernstein Prize for her third novel, *All the Rivers*, which was met with critical acclaim upon its publication in Israel in 2014. The novel, which has been translated into seventeen languages, including English, explores the intense romantic relationship between an Israeli woman and a Palestinian man—a subject that remains taboo in some quarters of her native country. In 2015 a group of teachers requested that the novel be added to the recommended high school curriculum in Israel, but the Israeli Ministry of Education found the book to be inappropriate and declined its inclusion. Naftali Bennett, the education minister, defended the novel's removal from the approved reading list, asserting "intimate relations between Jews and non-Jews threaten to subvert our distinct identity." The book's removal sparked a firestorm in Israel and abroad, and sales of the novel surged in response, as literary figures and ordinary citizens rallied to the author's defense.

Although taken aback by the official condemnation of her work, Rabinyan continues to believe that the only way to promote peace between Israelis and Palestinians is through open dialogue and understanding. As an artist, she hopes to promote peace through her writing. "Art and literature are about a magical appeal to identity and empathy. How an identity in literature is transferred into your own identity so that you care for a fictional stranger so that you get into his skin and wear his gaze," Rabinyan told Peter Beaumont in an interview for the *Guardian* (8 Apr. 2017). "This is what is so powerful. It is an antidote to the armoury we are requested to put on. This shield of ignorance and indifference and apathy. Because if you really sense everything, if you don't wear this shield, it is painful."

EARLY WRITING CAREER

Little has been published in English about Rabinyan's formative years. She was born in 1972 in Kfar Saba, a city in the Central District of Israel, to a family of Iranian Jewish ancestry. When she was eighteen years old, she served two years in the Israel Defense Forces. During that time she worked as a reporter for the Israeli army's magazine. She became a published writer at a young age, when her collection of poetry, *Yes, Yes, Yes,* was published in Israel in 1990. She followed this success with a pair of novels, which were

By רשנ סיריא :תמלצ [CC BY 3.0], via Wikimedia Commons

first published in Hebrew and then released under the English titles *Persian Brides* (1995) and *Strand of a Thousand Pearls* (1999). Both became international best sellers and were translated into more than a dozen languages. *Persian Brides* earned the Jewish Quarterly Wingate Prize in 1999.

In *Persian Brides*, which was translated into English by Yael Lotan and published in the United States in 1998, Rabinyan describes the relationship and lives of two young cousins born into a Jewish community in Persia in the early twentieth century. Flora is fifteen, recently married, and now pregnant with the child of her husband, a cloth merchant who has deserted her. Her cousin, Nazie, is just eleven but is longing to marry Flora's brother. Life for the two cousins proves difficult, especially in a time and place where husbands often physically and emotionally abuse their wives. Michael Lowenthal, reviewing the book for the *New York Times* (15 Mar. 1998), called the novel "lush, lyrical, and disturbing." Lowenthal praised Rabinyan's "unwaveringly authentic period detail" and her "marvelously digressive style and rich prose." He added, "Rabinyan grounds her themes of sexual politics in scenes mingling exotic beauty and gritty horror. Only twenty-three when her book was published in Hebrew, she writes with the wise and leisurely assurance of a town bard recounting communal myths. . . . *Persian Brides* is an auspicious debut."

STRAND OF A THOUSAND PEARLS

Rabinyan's follow-up novel was published in the United Kingdom under the title *Our Weddings* and in the United States as *Strand of a Thousand Pearls*. The British edition was published in 2001 and met with considerable acclaim there. The novel, unlike its predecessor, moves into the modern world and describes a family collapsing under the weight of broken dreams. Solly and Iran Azizyan watch as their once successful and happy family falls apart: their son, Maurice, is spoiled; their grown daughters, Sofia, Marcelle, and Lizzie, grieve over personal losses; and Iran, once a controlling matriarch, now does little to care for her family. The youngest daughter, Matti, who is just eleven, spends much of her time talking with her deceased twin. Throughout the novel, the narrative moves from the past to the present, as Solly and Iran's early life and marriage is contrasted with their middle-aged struggles. In a review for the *Guardian* (5 Aug. 2001), Stephanie Merritt declared: "Aside from her descriptive powers, Rabinyan's great strength is her perceptive portrayal of the thousand frustrations, conflicts and misunderstandings that make up family life, particularly for the women in a culture that hasn't yet learnt to acknowledge their freedom." *Strand of a Thousand Pearls* earned the Eshkol Award in Israel.

Following the publication of her second novel, Rabinyan attended the International Writing Program at the University of Iowa in 2002.

ALL THE RIVERS

Rabinyan's next novel was published in Israel in 2014. The novel was later published in English under the title *All the Rivers*, although its working title in English was *Borderlife* for a period of time. This third novel took many years to complete, in part because it was based on her friendship and romance with the Palestinian artist Hassan Hourani, who drowned near the Port of Jaffa in Israel, in August 2003. Hourani was born in 1974 in Hebron and attended the Academy of Fine Arts in Baghdad, Iraq. His art was shown in exhibits in Egypt, Jordan, Qatar, the United Arab Emirates, and South Korea. After arriving in New York, his work was displayed in the United Nations building. At the time he was introduced to Rabinyan, he was at work on a children's book, *Hassan Everywhere*.

The pair met while both were living in New York City. Much of their relationship revolved around their shared homeland, despite their differing visions for its future. Hourani was an optimist and believed that Israel would someday be a state shared by Israelis and Palestinians equally; Rabinyan believed the only way to peace would be a two-state solution, with a sovereign Palestine existing alongside but separate from Israel. She felt it was impossible for Israel to exist as anything other than a Jewish homeland. Rabinyan recalled their friendship in a poignant article she wrote for the *Guardian* (2 Apr. 2004): "During the interminable games of backgammon that we played, I heard myself talking to you about Israel without a single drop of cynicism souring the words. Suddenly, and how ironic that it should happen with you of all people, I found in my voice a true love of homeland." Despite their different backgrounds, Rabinyan and Hourani both longed for their homeland and missed the Mediterranean Sea. She recalled, "The expression on our faces was the same expression, the vista was of the same homeland, only the passports in our coat pockets were different; the passports of enemies."

All the Rivers is somewhat autobiographical in nature, in that it describes an intense relationship between a Palestinian painter named Hilmi and an Israeli Fulbright scholar named Liat, who are both studying in New York City in the period following the terrorist attacks of September 11, 2001, in which nearly three thousand people were killed. Hilmi and Liat, having different religions and ethnic backgrounds but sharing a common country, find themselves becoming more and more committed to one another, even as it seems unlikely that their relationship could long endure once they return to their homeland.

The novel became an immediate best seller in Israel, was named one of the ten best books of the year by the Israeli newspaper *Haaretz*, and was awarded the prestigious Bernstein Award for Literature. It was quickly translated into more than a dozen languages and met with serious critical acclaim when it was published in English. "It is a realistic relationship that sparks with vitality and vitriol, jumping through blissful rendezvous, heated arguments, and shameful secrets that build upon each other," a critic declared in a review for *Publishers Weekly* (27 Feb. 2017). "While their political, cultural, and religious differences should be of little importance in multicultural New York City, there remains an obscure, impenetrable wall between them. Rabinyan beautifully loops the story from season to season, depicting Liat and Hilmi's lives and love vividly and memorably."

CONTROVERSY AND BACKLASH

Despite the book's critical and commercial success, *All the Rivers* became the center of a political scandal in Israel in late 2015: the Ministry of Education announced it would remove the book from the country's approved high school curriculum. The removal spun out of the book's popularity with educators, who in 2015 requested it be added to high school literature classes. When the Ministry of Education reviewed the book, it came to the conclusion that it was not appropriate for Israeli schools, as it promoted assimilation and intermarriage between Israelis and Palestinians.

Rabinyan recalled how she learned of the ban to Beaumont: "I received a call from the reporter on the Israeli newspaper *Haaretz* who would expose the whole affair. To be honest, we were laughing at first because the reasons given for rejecting the book seemed so absurd. That this book of mine was a threat to the Jewish separate identity. Because it might encourage young readers to get intimately involved with non-Jewish residents of the country."

But the ban proved no laughing matter. As the news of the ban spread, some conservative Israelis began to see Rabinyan as having betrayed them by having a Jewish woman fall in love with a Palestinian man in her novel. In an article published in *Time* (27 Apr. 2017), Rabinyan recalled how she was confronted by a shopkeeper and a female customer. They berated her for writing terrible things about Israeli soldiers in her novel, despite neither of them having read it. She wrote: "As I went out into the street, into the downpour, I put down my bags to open my umbrella. As though mocking me, a gust of wind blew it inside out. Just then, the woman from the shop hissed at me in disgust: 'You worthless piece of trash.' She spat at me. 'You're not worth the sole of a soldier's boot.'"

Support for Rabinyan soon followed. A number of Israeli literary luminaries, among them A. B. Yehoshua, David Grossman, Amos Oz, Sami Michael, and Meir Shalev, expressed their support and condemned the government's actions. Sales of the book surged. Rabinyan even received a fan letter from Angela Merkel, the German chancellor, who read the German translation.

Although the controversy surrounding the book and its subsequent ban continues to swirl, Rabinyan remains defiant, believing that the only way to achieve true peace in her homeland is through fostering understanding and dialogue between Israelis and Palestinians. She told Ian Fisher for the *New York Times* (3 May 2017): "I refuse to let go of my instinct of being in contact with others' pain. This is turning your back. I refuse."

SUGGESTED READING

Review of *All the Rivers*, by Dorit Rabinyan. *Publishers Weekly*, 27 Feb. 2017, www.publishersweekly.com/978-0-375-50829-5. Accessed 7 July 2017.

Beaumont, Peter. "Censored in Israel, Praised by Merkel: The Novelist Who Is a 'Threat to Jewish Identity.'" *The Guardian*, 8 Apr. 2017, www.theguardian.com/world/2017/apr/08/dorit-rabinyan-novel-censorship-israel. Accessed 7 July 2017.

Fisher, Ian. "It's Complicated: The Path of an Israeli-Palestinian Love Story." *The New York Times*, 3 May 2017, www.nytimes.com/2017/05/03/books/its-complicated-the-path-of-an-israeli-palestinian-love-story.html. Accessed 7 July 2017.

Lowenthal, Michael. "The Family Honor." Review of *Persian Brides*, by Dorit Rabinyan. *The New York Times*, 15 Mar. 1998, www.nytimes.com/books/98/03/15/bib/980315.rv132127.html. Accessed 7 July 2017.

Merritt, Stephanie. "Iran's Children Grow Bitter with the Death of Their Dreams." Review of *Our Weddings*, by Dorit Rabinyan. *The Guardian*, 5 Aug. 2001, www.theguardian.com/books/2001/aug/05/fiction.features2. Accessed 7 July 2017.

Rabinyan, Dorit. "The Day Israel Banned My Book from Schools." *Time*, 25 Apr. 2017, time.com/4754208/all-the-rivers-dorit-rabinyan-book-ban. Accessed 7 July 2017.

Rabinyan, Dorit. "The Exile's Return." *The Guardian*, 2 Apr. 2004. www.theguardian.com/books/2004/apr/03/fiction.israelandthepalestinians. Accessed 7 July 2017.

SELECTED WORKS

Yes, Yes, Yes, 1990; *Persian Brides*, 1995; *Strand of a Thousand Pearls*, 1999; *All the Rivers*, 2014

—Christopher Mari

Issa Rae

Date of birth: January 12, 1985
Occupation: Entertainer

Since her days as a student at Stanford University, multitalented entertainer Issa Rae has created filmed content that accurately represents herself and the people and places around her, often with a comedic twist. From her early web mockumentary *Dorm Diaries* to her acclaimed viral web series *The Misadventures of Awkward Black Girl* to her HBO series *Insecure*, Rae has highlighted a diverse array of perspectives—primarily African American and female—that are rarely seen onscreen. "How hard is it to portray a three-dimensional woman of color on television or in film?" she wrote in her 2015 memoir, also titled *The Misadventures of Awkward Black Girl*, about her frustrations with existing media representation. "I'm surrounded by them. They're my friends. I talk to them every day. How come Hollywood won't acknowledge us?"

In her web and television series, Rae seeks to depict the kinds of situations she and her friends encounter in their everyday lives—situations that are often characterized by awkward humor and simmering insecurities, as the titles of her two best-known series suggest. "Everybody has awkward moments. I know everybody has insecurities," she told Julia Felsenthal for *Vogue* (7 Oct. 2016). "Your insecurities can inhibit you in a way that awkwardness can't. It feels more real,

She began acting while in fifth grade when she was cast as Demetrius in *A Midsummer Night's Dream*, and she was active in the drama program while attending King/Drew Magnet High School of Medicine and Science in South Los Angeles. She also began writing screenplays. "I didn't necessarily think I could make a career out of my creative interests until I saw *Love & Basketball* when I was in high school," she recalled to Jessica Grose for *Elle* (25 Feb. 2015). "That movie—written, directed, and coproduced by a black woman, and shot in my neighborhood—really made me feel like I could do it, too."

EDUCATION AND EARLY CAREER

After graduating from high school, Rae enrolled in Stanford University, where she majored in African and African American studies and minored in political science. Disappointed by many of the plays being produced within the school's drama program and inspired by friends who were creating their own work, Rae struck out on her own, putting on a theatrical adaptation of the Spike Lee film *School Daze*. She also began to experiment with making short videos that she posted to the newly created video-sharing site YouTube.

Perhaps the most popular of Rae's creations then was the web series *Dorm Diaries*. A mockumentary about African American student life at Stanford, the series became popular among Stanford students as well as students at other colleges, and it demonstrated the potential of the web series medium in an era of increasing Internet-based media consumption. In a profile of Rae for the *New York Times Magazine* (4 Aug. 2015), Jenna Wortham wrote, "Rae learned that she had a knack for portraying everyday black life—not made special by its otherness or defined in contrast to whiteness, but treated as a subject worthy of exploration all of its own." Rae remarked to Wortham that creating *Dorms Days* was her "epiphany moment."

After graduating from college in 2007, Rae moved to New York City, where she landed a fellowship at the Public Theater and also took on freelance videography work. Her own creative endeavors suffered a major setback when thieves broke into her apartment and stole her film equipment and works in progress. She eventually moved back to Los Angeles to live with her mother and seriously considered enrolling in law school or business school. However, she returned to creating web series in 2009 with *Fly Guys Present "The 'F' Word"*—a mockumentary series about her brother's music group.

THE MISADVENTURES OF AWKWARD BLACK GIRL

In early 2011, Rae launched a new web series that would be her most popular creation yet. Titled *The Misadventures of Awkward Black Girl,*

Earl Gibson III/WireImage/Getty Images

more kind of dire to me. And it encompasses so much more: the instability of it, the identity issues, the gender issues, the feeling of angst, like you're doing things wrong. That's what I wanted to tap into." Indeed, Rae has accomplished just that, creating series that have earned her a dedicated fan base as well as critical acclaim.

EARLY LIFE

Issa Rae was born Jo-Issa Rae Diop in Los Angeles, California, on January 12, 1985. She was the third of five children born to Abdoulaye Diop, a doctor, and Delyna Hayward Diop, a teacher. The Diop family moved frequently when Rae was young and spent two years living in Dakar, Senegal, where her father grew up. Back in the United States, the family spent some time in Potomac, Maryland, and also lived for many years in the Windsor Hills neighborhood of South Los Angeles. The area left a lasting impression on Rae, who later sought to depict it onscreen in projects such as *Insecure*. Speaking of South Los Angeles and neighboring Inglewood, she told Felsenthal, "You have so many different types of people, so many different classes, so many different backgrounds. That's what I know it to be. That's where I grew up. There's poverty and affluence, and communities mesh. That's just the culture."

During her childhood and teen years, Rae developed an interest in television comedies, particularly enjoying shows such as *The Fresh Prince of Bel-Air* and *Living Single*, whose styles of comedy and predominantly African American casts helped to shape much of her later work.

the show stars Rae as J, a young woman who frequently finds herself in uncomfortable—but often humorous—social situations. After the first few episodes of the series, produced on a shoestring budget, gained an enthusiastic fan base, Rae and coproducer Tracy Oliver turned to the crowdfunding website Kickstarter, where they raised more than fifty thousand dollars to fund additional episodes.

Drawing from comedy influences such as the television shows *Seinfeld* and *Curb Your Enthusiasm* as well as elements from Rae's life, *Misadventures* points out the humor that can be found in the most awkward moments. "I just think embarrassment is funny," Rae explained to Kayla Kumari Upadhyaya for *Complex* (7 Oct. 2016). "There's nothing more funny and relatable than people's discomfort. Being like, 'Oh my god, you'll *never* believe what happened to me.' 'Oh my god, that happened to you, too? Let me tell you *my* story!' There's just something funny about the simple to me."

Misadventures proved popular with viewers, gaining significant media attention as the episodes went viral. Rae and her team ultimately created twenty-four episodes of the series, divided into two seasons. Thanks to the nature of the web series medium, they were able to adjust their approach as needed, which gave the creative process a flexibility not found in traditional television. "We were creating in real time and with audience feedback, so you could automatically know if something worked or if it didn't," she explained to Estelle Tang for *Elle* (11 Oct. 2016). Although the series concluded after two seasons, the spirit of the titular awkward black girl continued to resonate with the show's audience, and in 2015 Rae published a memoir, also titled *The Misadventures of Awkward Black Girl*, that shared some of her own awkward life experiences.

In addition to *Misadventures*, Rae has worked on a number of unrelated web series as an actor, writer, and producer, including *The Number*, *Roomieloverfriends*, *The Choir*, and *Ratchetpiece Theatre*. In 2012, she came close to launching her first television series after successfully pitching her show *I Hate L.A. Dudes* to television powerhouse Shonda Rhimes's production company. Although the pilot sold to ABC, the network ultimately passed on the series. For Rae, this was ultimately a good thing. "I compromised my vision, and it didn't end up the show that I wanted," she explained to Wortham. "It wasn't funny anymore."

INSECURE

Rae's next major project, the show *Insecure*, premiered on HBO in October 2016. Starring and cowritten by Rae, the show follows a Los Angeles woman named Issa who deals with a variety of challenges related to her personal relationships. *Insecure* is in many ways a spiritual successor to *Misadventures*, but it is undoubtedly its own series. "I just wanted a completely different show," Rae explained to Felsenthal. "By the time I got the HBO opportunity, we had twenty-four episodes [of *Misadventures*] online. We had the merch, the book. I felt like I had done enough. But I'm always going to be awkward. That's still how I identify. . . . Now, being thirty, thirty-one, I wanted to tell a new story that was closer to me, felt more grounded."

Although Rae's earlier projects had been small-budget affairs initially created by a small team of friends and colleagues, *Insecure* was a significantly larger project from the beginning, gaining a far greater budget and featuring contributions from entertainment veterans such as comedian Larry Wilmore, who cocreated the show, and singer Solange Knowles, who served as the music consultant. For Rae, one of the most important contributors to the show was director Melina Matsoukas, who offered a valuable new perspective. "She has such a good eye, and she pays attention to *everything* . . . like the pattern on the table that's in the background that nobody sees, or handpicking extras to be in every scene," Rae told Caroline Framke for *Vox* (9 Oct. 2016). "It all matters to this larger aesthetic, and I'm so impressed by that."

Following its premiere in 2016, *Insecure* gained critical acclaim, and its characters' struggles with feelings of insecurity resonated with the show's viewers. "It's one of those universal elements—feeling like you're not doing things right, that you don't have it all together," Rae told Tang. "I was tapping into a time when I was teetering: whether my relationship would work, whether my career would work, and what it was about me that was messing things up along the way." In recognition of her work in *Insecure's* eight-episode first season, Rae was nominated for the Golden Globe Award for best performance by an actress in a television comedy or musical. HBO announced it had renewed *Insecure* for a second season in November 2016.

PERSONAL LIFE

Although Rae draws somewhat from her own life when creating her shows, she frequently notes in interviews that there are significant differences between her and her characters, particularly *Insecure's* Issa. "She's basically me if I didn't know what I wanted to do, and if I made different decisions in life," she told Quinn Keaney for *PopSugar* (13 Oct. 2016). "I say 75 to 80 percent. I think I'm a bit more empathetic than she is, and I'd like to say that I wouldn't put my friends on blast in the way that she did in the pilot, but I probably have. I've probably done that to a degree. She's generally my essence, for sure."

Rae lives in Los Angeles.

SUGGESTED READING

Felsenthal, Julia. "*Insecure* Is the Candid, Funny, Sharp Issa Rae Show We've Been Waiting For." *Vogue*, 7 Oct. 2016, www.vogue.com/article/insecure-issa-rae-interview. Accessed 10 Feb. 2017.

Framke, Caroline. "'I Just Wanted It to Be a Regular Story about Black People': Issa Rae on Creating and Starring in HBO's *Insecure*." *Vox*, 9 Oct. 2016, www.vox.com/culture/2016/10/7/13176104/issa-rae-insecure-hbo-interview. Accessed 10 Feb. 2017.

Rae, Issa. "Issa Rae Takes Aim at the 'Old Boys' Club' of Television." Interview by Estelle Tang. *Elle*, 11 Oct. 2016, www.elle.com/culture/movies-tv/interviews/a39920/issa-rae-insecure-interview. Accessed 10 Feb. 2017.

Rae, Issa. "Issa Rae on Why *Insecure* Is the Show TV Needs Right Now: 'We're Touching a Nerve.'" Interview by Quinn Keaney. *PopSugar*, 13 Oct. 2016, www.popsugar.com/entertainment/Interview-Issa-Rae-October-2016-42535883. Accessed 10 Feb. 2017.

Upadhyaya, Kayla Kumari. "Issa Rae's 'Insecure' Isn't Niche—It's Just Never Been Done Before." *Complex*, 7 Oct. 2016, www.complex.com/pop-culture/2016/10/issa-rae-insecure-hbo-interview. Accessed 10 Feb. 2017.

Wortham, Jenna. "The Misadventures of Issa Rae." *New York Times Magazine*, 4 Aug. 2015 www.nytimes.com/2015/08/09/magazine/the-misadventures-of-issa-rae.html. Accessed 10 Feb. 2017.

SELECTED WORKS

The Misadventures of Awkward Black Girl, 2011–13; *The Number*, 2012–13; *The Choir*, 2013–15; *Insecure*, 2016–

—*Joy Crelin*

Natacha Ramsay-Levi

Date of birth: January 17, 1980
Occupation: Creative director of Chloé

When Natacha Ramsay-Levi was named the new creative director of the fashion brand Chloé in March 2017, her appointment to the position came as a surprise to some within the fashion industry. The Chloé brand, founded in 1952 by French designer Gaby Aghion, is often described as having a particularly distinctive feminine and romantic style, and Ramsay-Levi, with her more androgynous and edgy fashion sense, seemed a somewhat unusual choice for the brand. Even more unusual was the fact that

Photo by Jacopo Raule/Getty Images for Chloe

unlike many previous Chloé creative directors, including her immediate predecessor Clare Waight Keller, she had not yet served as director of a fashion house. For Ramsay-Levi, however, her leadership position at Chloé was less a surprise and more the culmination of over a decade of work in the fashion industry. "Chloé for me feels super natural," she told Ellie Pithers for *Vogue UK* (15 July 2017). "I was very ready for the position."

Although initially a student of history, Ramsay-Levi found herself drawn to the world of fashion and particularly to the style promoted by designer Nicolas Ghesquière, who at the time led the fashion house Balenciaga. After completing her studies in fashion at the prestigious Studio Berçot in 2002, she made working with Ghesquière her goal, moving from a low-level position at Balenciaga to the role of design director over the course of a decade. When Ghesquière left the company in 2012, Ramsay-Levi followed, joining her mentor at Louis Vuitton the following year. Having established herself not only as Ghesquière's second in command but also as a fashion leader in her own right through her work as director of Louis Vuitton's women's ready-to-wear line, Ramsay-Levi views her new position at Chloé not as a challenge to be overcome but as an opportunity. "The idea of 'challenge,'" it's the idea of climbing a mountain," she explained to Pithers. "I don't feel I am climbing a mountain. I feel I am just walking strongly on a path that I love."

EARLY LIFE AND EDUCATION

Ramsay-Levi was born in Paris on January 17, 1980. Her father, Jean-Pierre Ramsay-Levi, worked in the film industry, primarily as a producer. As a young woman, Ramsay-Levi wanted to become a historian and began studying history at Université Paris 8 in 1997. She was also interested in fashion and spent some of her spare time designing her own clothing.

A major shift in Ramsay-Levi's career outlook came when she first became aware of the fashion house Balenciaga, which since 1997 had been headed by creative director Nicolas Ghesquière. The brand captivated and inspired Ramsay-Levi, changing her career and lifestyle aspirations forever. "The silhouette! The girl that Nicolas Ghesquière had in mind! I really wanted to be a Balenciaga girl: young, cool, androgynous," she recalled in an interview with the German edition of *Interview* magazine, as quoted by Kyle Munzenrieder for *W* (4 Jan. 2017).

Ramsay-Levi's newfound devotion to Balenciaga fueled her existing interest in fashion, and she ultimately "threw everything aside," as quoted by Munzenrieder, to pursue a new career in the field. To gain the necessary skills and knowledge, she enrolled in Studio Berçot, a prestigious fashion design institute in Paris, in 2000. Founded in 1954, the institution was known for producing numerous working designers and emphasized not only classroom learning but also internships and apprenticeships with successful fashion houses.

ENTERING THE WORLD OF FASHION

Throughout her time at Studio Berçot, Ramsay-Levi remained a devotee of Balenciaga and continued to aspire to work for the company, which was a major force in the Parisian fashion industry and beyond. Founded in 1919 by Spanish designer Cristóbal Balenciaga, the company had moved to Paris in 1937, during the Spanish Civil War, and established itself as one of the most influential couture brands of the mid-twentieth century. Although Cristóbal Balenciaga closed the company in 1968, it was revived in 1986, fourteen years after his death. Ghesquière became the third creative director to head the fashion house following its revival. The brand thrived under his leadership and came to encompass lines of clothing for women and men as well as handbag and shoe lines.

In 2002, after completing her fashion studies, Ramsay-Levi applied for and secured an internship with Balenciaga. Like interns with many major companies, she was initially expected to perform relatively mundane tasks that had little to do with fashion design. "They told me that I would do nothing else but to cook coffee and sort documents," she told the German edition of *Interview*, as quoted by Munzenrieder.

"But I did not care." Ramsay-Levi was later hired on permanently as a stylist, a position she held until 2007.

BALENCIAGA AND LOUIS VUITTON

Over the course of her years at Balenciaga, Ramsay-Levi rose within the fashion house's ranks, gaining further responsibilities as she demonstrated her affinity for design and developed a strong working relationship with Ghesquière. In 2007, she was named head designer of the brand's women's precollections, collections of new clothing that are released in between the biannual collections traditionally released by couture houses. Ramsay-Levi continued to work on the women's precollections until 2011, when she transitioned into the role of design director.

As design director for Balenciaga, Ramsay-Levi effectively became Ghesquière's second in command and worked closely with the designer, whom she considered a mentor. "He taught me everything," she told Pithers. "When I arrived [at Balenciaga] I was obsessed already with what he was doing. I felt it was so strong, I really wanted to be that woman. I thought it was the coolest thing ever." Ramsay-Levi's high-ranking position at the company made her a rumored choice to succeed Ghesquière upon his departure from the fashion house in November 2012, an abrupt separation that was all the more surprising to industry insiders because of Ghesquière's fifteen years of service with the company. Although some in the fashion media suggested that Ramsay-Levi, as Ghesquière's protégé and longtime employee, was a natural choice to succeed him, the role of creative director ultimately went to American designer Alexander Wang.

In the fall of 2013, the fashion and accessories brand Louis Vuitton announced that Ghesquière would be joining the company as artistic director of its women's lines, succeeding American designer Marc Jacobs. Ramsay-Levi likewise moved to Louis Vuitton, taking on the title of director of women's ready-to-wear clothing. Building upon her decade of work with Ghesquière, she served as a crucial link between the designer and the company's design staff, helping facilitate the creation of clothing based on Ghesquière's designs. Ramsay-Levi soon established a strong working relationship with her team at Louis Vuitton, with whom she would work to produce a variety of clothing items for the well-known luxury brand. "The team is like a family to me," she told the German edition of *Interview*, as quoted by Steff Yotka for *Vogue* (20 Mar. 2017). Ramsay-Levi remained with Louis Vuitton into early 2017.

CHLOÉ

In January 2017, the fashion media reported that British designer Clare Waight

Keller would be leaving her position at the French fashion house Chloé, where she had served as creative director since 2011. Ramsay-Levi quickly became the rumored front-runner for the position with the company, which had been founded in 1952 by designer Gaby Aghion. Since its founding, the company had been led by eight different creative directors, which included not only Aghion and Keller but also prominent designers such as Karl Lagerfeld and Stella McCartney.

Despite the rumors surrounding her potential appointment to the position, Ramsay-Levi was a somewhat unlikely choice for the role, as she had not yet served as creative director of a fashion house. Indeed, she was not on the initial list of candidates considered by Geoffroy de la Bourdonnaye, the chief executive officer of Chloé, and came to his attention only after being recommended by a recruiter. De la Bourdonnaye soon recognized Ramsay-Levi as the right candidate for the position, and in March 2017, the company officially announced that she would succeed Keller as creative director. "Natacha was trained in the couture ateliers, and she perfectly embodies the spirit of Chloé," de la Bourdonnaye told Vanessa Friedman for the *New York Times* (10 Mar. 2017). "She is daring, charismatic, joyful, confident, and knows where she's going."

CREATIVE DIRECTOR

Officially joining Chloé in April, Ramsay-Levi worked not only to get her bearings at a new company but also to make a statement about what her leadership would mean for the brand. Accustomed to working collaboratively, she emphasized the importance of transparency and teamwork to the fashion house's success. "At Chloé, everybody is luminous, joyful, people get along very well together," she told Pithers. "I need to be in a position where I feel we are all working in the same team, building the same thing. I like to be super open about what I do."

Ramsay-Levi likewise sought to find a productive balance between her own sense of style—which tends toward somewhat androgynous, edgy, and structured pieces—and the long-established look of the so-called Chloé girl, which is characterized by flowing fabrics, bohemian styles, and a distinct take on femininity and romanticism. Although Ramsay-Levi may leave a mark on Chloé's overall sensibility in the long run, she has reassured fans of the company that she intends to remain true to Chloé's long-standing aesthetic. "I am not doing Natacha's brand, I am doing Chloé's brand," she explained to Pithers. "The bags have to stay Chloé, the clothes have to stay Chloé." The first opportunity to show Ramsay-Levi's take on Chloé would come in September of 2017, when the brand was scheduled to show its Spring 2018 collection at Paris Fashion Week.

PERSONAL LIFE

Ramsay-Levi lives in Paris. She has a son, Balthus, with Olivier Zahm, a French fashion photographer and journalist who serves as editor in chief of the fashion and culture magazine *Purple*. Ramsay-Levi has made numerous appearances in *Purple* in addition to a variety of other fashion publications.

SUGGESTED READING

Friedman, Vanessa. "Chloé Names Natacha Ramsay-Levi as Creative Director." *The New York Times*, 10 Mar. 2017, www.nytimes.com/2017/03/10/fashion/chloe-natacha-ramsay-levi.html. Accessed 11 Aug. 2017.

Moss, Hilary. "Is Natacha Ramsay in the Running for the Balenciaga Job?" *The Cut*, 8 Nov. 2012, www.thecut.com/2012/11/natacha-ramsay-balenciaga.html. Accessed 11 Aug. 2017.

Munzenrieder, Kyle. "Everything You Need to Know about Natacha Ramsay-Levi, Chloé's Rumored New Creative Director." *W*, 4 Jan. 2017, www.wmagazine.com/story/natacha-ramsay-levi-chloe-creative-director/amp. Accessed 11 Aug. 2017.

Pithers, Ellie. "Natacha Ramsay-Levi on What We Can Expect from Her Chloé." *Vogue UK*, 15 July 2017, www.vogue.co.uk/article/natacha-ramsay-levi-chloe-vogue-interview. Accessed 11 Aug. 2017.

Wendlandt, Astrid, Reuters. "Report: Louis Vuitton's Natacha Ramsay-Levi to Take Lead at Chloé." *Business of Fashion*, 4 Jan. 2017, www.businessoffashion.com/articles/news-analysis/report-louis-vuittons-natacha-ramsay-levi-to-take-lead-at-chloe. Accessed 11 Aug. 2017.

Yotka, Steff. "Who Is Natacha Ramsay-Levi? Meet Chloé's New Creative Director." *Vogue*, 20 Mar. 2017, www.vogue.com/article/natacha-ramsay-levi-chloe-biography/amp. Accessed 11 Aug. 2017.

—*Joy Crelin*

Dee Rees

Date of birth: November 30, 1976
Occupation: Director and screenwriter

Many independent films are screened at the prestigious Sundance Film Festival, but only a select few attract widespread attention and critical praise, elevating their creators to new heights and opening doors to countless opportunities.

Photo by Gabriel Olsen/FilmMagic

At the 2017 Sundance Film Festival, one such film was *Mudbound*, a historical drama based on the 2008 novel of the same name that explores issues such as race relations and family relationships in the aftermath of World War II. The second feature film written and directed by filmmaker Dee Rees, *Mudbound* earned immediate acclaim and, by the end of the festival, was acquired by the streaming service Netflix for $12.5 million. For Rees, the success of the film is tied in part to her overall approach to her artistic medium. "Art breaks down otherness," she explained to Marlow Stern for the *Daily Beast* (24 Jan. 2017). "Art makes you see people as individual, unique human beings. Art, in that way, allows us to see each other in particulate, as opposed to in aggregate."

Although Rees has experienced widespread success as an independent filmmaker, she did not initially pursue that career path, instead spending several years working in marketing for large corporations. After completing graduate studies in film at New York University (NYU), where she was mentored by veteran filmmaker Spike Lee, she launched her career in cinema with the short film *Pariah*, which brought Rees her first wave of critical acclaim following its screenings at film festivals. Her feature film of the same name, an expanded version of the short, likewise earned critical praise and won a cinematography award following its premiere at Sundance in 2011. Later projects such as the television biopic *Bessie* were similarly well received. Although appreciative of her positive critical reception, Rees focuses primarily on

creating compelling works that highlight strong, three-dimensional characters. "I just want to tell stories that are meaningful and have inspiration to them; people can watch it and take away something or maybe they'll just think about themselves differently, or think about the world differently," she told Deenah Vollmer for *Interview* magazine (21 Dec. 2011). "I just want to create characters that live on."

EARLY LIFE

Rees was born Diandra Rees in Tennessee on November 30, 1976. She grew up in Antioch, a suburb of Nashville. Her father was a police officer, and her mother a university scientist. Both of her grandfathers were veterans of foreign wars, which she has referenced as an inspiration in her filming of *Mudbound*. After graduating from high school, Rees enrolled in Florida A&M University in Tallahassee. There she earned a master's degree in business administration.

After completing her degree, Rees took a marketing job with the corporation Procter & Gamble in Cincinnati, Ohio, but was laid off. Continuing her career in marketing, she next worked for New York–based Schering-Plough (now part of Merck), a pharmaceutical company that owned the foot care brand Dr. Scholl's. She also went on to work for Colgate-Palmolive.

FILM EDUCATION

After several years in corporate marketing, Rees found herself dissatisfied with her career and seeking a new direction. A turning point came when she worked on the set of a commercial for a Dr. Scholl's shoe insole. "I liked being on set. I asked one of the ad guys how to get into something like this, and he said, 'You have to go to film school,'" she recalled to Vollmer. "And I was like, 'Okay. So what film schools do I go to?' 'Oh, NYU, but you won't get in there.'" Inspired by her experience on set, Rees disregarded the idea that she would not get into NYU and applied anyway. She was ultimately accepted into the university's graduate-level film program and enrolled in the university in 2003.

While attending NYU's Tisch School of the Arts, Rees learned not only about the craft of filmmaking but also about the business side of the process, which is particularly critical for independent filmmakers such as Rees, who make films without the backing of major studios. "Filmmaking is the intersection of art and commerce," she told Vollmer. "All that training helped us get investors, business plans, and people to help finance the film." Throughout her graduate studies, Rees learned a great deal from veteran filmmaker Spike Lee, who had taught at Tisch since 1993. In addition to attending Lee's office hours, during which he gave notes on her work in progress, she interned for his 2006 film *Inside Man* and the television documentary *When the Levees Broke*. She also completed her first short film, *Orange Bow* (2005), as a graduate student.

EARLY CAREER

Near the end of Rees's time at NYU, she set out to create a short film that would serve as her thesis project. The eventual short, *Pariah*, was completed in 2006. Based on an excerpt from the feature-length screenplay that Rees was working on, the film tells the story of teenager Alike (Adepero Oduye), a lesbian who struggles with her sexual orientation being hidden in plain sight from those around her. Screened at dozens of international film festivals in 2007, *Pariah* won more than two dozen awards for best short or student film.

After earning her master of fine arts degree from NYU, Rees participated in the Sundance Institute's 2007 June Screenwriters Lab. This annual writers' workshop enables developing screenwriters to workshop their scripts with more experienced filmmakers. Rees's experience at the Screenwriters Lab proved valuable, helping her to cut more than forty pages from her original draft screenplay for the feature-length version of *Pariah*. The following year, she participated in the Sundance Directors Lab, which gave her the opportunity to workshop scenes from her screenplay with actors and hone her skill as a director. In addition to continuing to develop *Pariah*, Rees created the 2007 documentary *Eventual Salvation*, about her grandmother's return to her former home in Liberia, and the 2009 short film *Colonial Gods*.

PARIAH

Having refined her script for *Pariah*, Rees set out to create the full-length incarnation of the film, which would again feature Oduye in the lead role of Alike but would expand upon the characters and world presented in the short film. Lee served as an executive producer for the film, and Rees sought out funding for the work with the help of producer Nekisa Cooper. A portion of the funds for the film were raised through the crowdfunding website *Kickstarter* between December 2010 and January 2011.

For Rees, the experience of making *Pariah* was highly personal. Although the film is not strictly autobiographical, it shares some elements with its creator's own life. "Like Alike, when I came out, I had a struggle with my parents accepting who I was, and I also had the internal struggle of realizing that my spirituality and my sexuality were not mutually exclusive," Rees explained to Amita Swadhin for *GLAAD* (29 Dec. 2011). "That's what Alike comes to realize on top of her journey—discovering that even within the gay world she doesn't have to

check a box, she doesn't have to be hard, she doesn't have to be soft, she can just be herself." Imbued with authentic emotion as well as strong writing, acting, and directing, *Pariah* met with significant acclaim upon its premiere at the Sundance Film Festival in January of 2011. The film won the festival's Excellence in Cinematography Award. It also went on to win the NAACP Image Award for outstanding motion picture.

TELEVISION PROJECTS

Following *Pariah*'s warm reception at Sundance, Rees became widely cited as an up-and-coming filmmaker to watch, and she took on a variety of new opportunities. In addition to developing different potential films, she began to take on television projects, most notably the 2015 biopic *Bessie*. The television film, which premiered on HBO in May of that year, tells of the rise of early-twentieth-century blues singer Bessie Smith, played by actor and recording artist Queen Latifah.

For Rees, who directed the film and cowrote the screenplay with Christopher Cleveland and Bettina Gilois, the process of creating a film for HBO differed in many ways from the process of creating her earlier independent work, in large part due to the increased budget. At the same time, she remained focused on the film's key characters and moments, seeking to shed light on who Smith was as a person. "The extra money gets you lights, it gets you bigger equipment, but it doesn't get you better performances," she explained to Anna Lisa Raya for *Deadline* (Aug. 2015). The work of *Bessie*'s cast and crew paid off: the film won four Emmy Awards, including the awards for outstanding made-for-television movie and outstanding cinematography for a miniseries or movie. Rees herself was nominated for the Emmy Awards for outstanding writing in a miniseries or special and directing for a miniseries movie or special. She also won several additional awards, including the NAACP Image Award for outstanding directing in a motion picture (television) and the Directors Guild of America Award for the category of movies for television and miniseries.

In addition to her long-form work on *Bessie*, Rees directed several shorter televised works, including a 2015 episode of the music industry drama *Empire*. She likewise directed one part of the 2017 four-part miniseries *When We Rise*, about the history of the gay rights movement. The year 2017 also brought Rees's first foray into science fiction with her writing and directing contributions to the sci-fi anthology series *Philip K. Dick's Electric Dreams*.

MUDBOUND

Rees's second feature film, *Mudbound*, premiered at the Sundance Film Festival on January

21, 2017. A historical drama, *Mudbound* was Virgil Williams's adaptation of Hillary Jordan's 2008 novel of the same name; Rees edited his script to tell the story from different viewpoints and directed the final version. *Mudbound* focuses on the lives of two families—one African American and one Caucasian—living on a southern farm and the experiences of young men from both families as they return to the United States following World War II.

Mudbound performed well at Sundance, earning a standing ovation, and became one of the most talked-about films from the 2017 festival. Near the end of the festival, the streaming service Netflix announced that it had purchased the distribution rights to the film for $12.5 million. In addition to making the film available to stream toward the end of 2017, Netflix planned a limited release in theaters to ensure the film's eligibility for awards such as the Academy Awards. While undoubtedly happy with the film's critical success, Rees was also particularly proud of the feats that the film's cast and crew managed to pull off, even with the limited budget and capabilities common among independent films. "Shooting a tank battle before lunch, to me, was the biggest triumph of the making of the film," she told Stern. "We should get T-shirts made that say, 'We shot a tank battle before lunch!'"

Following the premiere of *Mudbound*, Rees worked on developing a few different products, including an adaptation of a book by English writer Zadie Smith. She is reportedly also developing a horror film about a lesbian couple living in a rural town. Rees has likewise noted that she wants to explore the Western genre. "I like the extreme angles and the standoffs and the showdowns," she told Raya. "This is actually just Western language. Maybe I should do one because that's the stuff I'm responding to."

SUGGESTED READING

Rainey, James. "Dee Rees Brings 'Mudbound' and Thoughts beyond Race to Sundance." *Variety*, 21 Jan. 2017, variety.com/2017/film/news/dee-rees-brings-mudbound-thoughts-beyond-race-to-sundance-1201966116. Accessed 11 Aug. 2017.

Rees, Dee. "'Bessie' Director Dee Rees Follows Up with 'Empire,' a Zadie Smith Project and, Possibly, a Western—Emmys." Interview by Anna Lisa Raya. *Deadline*, Aug. 2015, deadline.com/2015/08/bessie-dee-rees-interview-queen-latifah-empire-1201508251/amp. Accessed 11 Aug. 2017.

Rees, Dee. "GLAAD Interviews 'Pariah' Director Dee Rees." Interview by Amita Swadhin. *GLAAD*, 29 Dec. 2011, www.glaad.org/blog/glaad-interviews-pariah-director-dee-rees. Accessed 11 Aug. 2017.

Rees, Dee. "How Dee Rees Built a Cocoon." Interview by Deenah Vollmer. *Interview*, 21 Dec. 2011. www.interviewmagazine.com/film/dee-rees-pariah. Accessed 11 Aug. 2017.

Rees, Dee. "Sundance Interview: 'Pariah' Director Dee Rees Discusses Her Powerful Debut." Interview by Matt Patches. *CinemaBlend*, 2011, www.cinemablend.com/new/Sundance-Interview-Pariah-Director-Dee-Rees-Discusses-Her-Powerful-Debut-22888.html. Accessed 11 Aug. 2017.

Stern, Marlow. "'Mudbound': How Dee Rees Made One of the Most Gripping Films in Sundance History." *The Daily Beast*, 24 Jan. 2017, www.thedailybeast.com/mudbound-how-dee-rees-made-one-of-the-most-gripping-films-in-sundance-history. Accessed 11 Aug. 2017.

Winfrey, Graham. "'Mudbound' Is a Major Step for Dee Rees, but Underrepresented Storytellers Remain—Sundance 2017." *IndieWire*, Jan. 2017, www.indiewire.com/2017/01/mudbound-dee-rees-underrepresented-artists-sundance-2017-1201771644/amp. Accessed 11 Aug. 2017.

SELECTED WORKS

Eventual Salvation, 2008; *Pariah*, 2011; *Bessie*, 2015; *Mudbound*, 2017

—*Joy Crelin*

Thomas Rhett

Date of birth: March 30, 1990
Occupation: Singer-songwriter

Thomas Rhett is regarded as one of country music's rapidly rising stars, following the release of his country-pop debut, *It Goes Like This* (2013), which has spawned three consecutive number-one singles, including the platinum title track. Rhett has proven himself adept at songwriting, having cowritten most of his album's twelve tracks as well as major hits for some of country's biggest acts—Jason Aldean, Florida Georgia Line, and Lee Brice, among others.

Rhett's follow-up, *Tangled Up* (2015), featured a more progressive sound, incorporating elements of soul, funk, R & B, and hip-hop. "I didn't grow up listening to just one style of music," he recalled on his personal website. "So I don't know how to write just one style of music. Whether these songs have more of a pop influence or more of a hip-hop influence or a completely country influence, they all—in some crazy way—cohesively sound like a me song." Country audiences embraced this new direction. *Tangled Up* achieved platinum status and

Noam Galai/FilmMagic/Getty Images

also amassed three straight number-one singles, like its predecessor.

A PASSION FOR MUSIC

Thomas Rhett was born Thomas Rhett Akins Jr. on March 30, 1990, in Valdosta, Georgia. At the age of two, he relocated with his parents to Nashville, Tennessee, where his father pursued a music career and became an accomplished Nashville hit maker. Despite growing up in the epicenter of country music, Rhett and his sister, Kasey, were also exposed to other genres. "I listened to Led Zeppelin, Aretha Franklin, Frank Sinatra, Hank Williams, and Merle Haggard," he shared with Hugh McIntyre for *Forbes* (11 Oct. 2015). "I grew up listening to so many different things, and having a dad that also sang, music was innately born into me." Rhett, who often accompanied his father on tour, made his onstage debut at about age nine, singing "Gettin' Jiggy Wit It" by actor-rapper Will Smith during his father's weekend gig.

The two also bonded during Rhett's early teens, when his father helped him develop guitar-playing basics. "When I was 12 or 13, my dad taught me a couple of different chords," he told Alison Richter for *Guitar World* (16 Mar. 2015). "I never learned to read music, but . . . I learned songs that had the chords I knew." Rhett honed his guitar skills at Goodpasture Christian School, in Madison, Tennessee, and served as the drummer for the High Heel Flip Flops, a punk rock quartet he formed with three of his classmates.

Besides music, Rhett was actively involved in several sports, including baseball and football.

However, he excelled mostly at soccer until his junior year of high school, when he was sidelined by a torn ligament in the first game of the season, ending any hopes of playing college soccer but also sparking an interest in sports medicine. "I wanted to be a physical therapist because I had torn up my knee and thought it was interesting with the rehab," Rhett shared with Alanna Conaway for *Taste of Country* (21 July 2011).

LANDING A PUBLISHING DEAL

After graduating from high school in 2008, Rhett enrolled in Nashville's Lipscomb University, where he briefly considered studying kinesiology and then business before eventually deciding on communications. While attending college, he fronted the cover band Brassfish and performed at frat parties and local college bars. Rhett's life took a pivotal turn when his father booked Brassfish as an opening act for rising country singer Frankie Ballard. "I'd been writing a lot of songs with Frankie Ballard, and Carol Ann Mobley, who was A&R [artists and repertoire] at Warner Bros. at the time, asked me how I could get college kids to Frankie's show [at Nashville's 2nd Avenue Live club]," father Rhett Akins recalled to Abby White for BMI (27 July 2015). "So Thomas Rhett opened for Frankie. A bunch of industry people were there. . . . He blew everybody away."

Among the attendees was EMI Music Publishing's vice president of A & R Ben Vaughn, who was so impressed by Rhett's performance that he offered him a contract—despite a lack of songwriting experience. After signing his publishing deal in February 2010, Rhett juggled school and songwriting sessions, including a first-time collaboration with Jaron Boyer and Ben Stennis that resulted in the song "I Ain't Ready to Quit."

SIGNING WITH VALORY MUSIC

Just days after submitting the demo to EMI, Vaughn informed Rhett that a well-known country artist was considering the song for his upcoming record. The singer in question, Jason Aldean, eventually included "I Ain't Ready to Quit" on his fourth studio album, *My Kinda Party*, which was released in November 2010. Not content to rest on his laurels, Rhett began seriously pursuing a recording contract, with Vaughn's help. "Ben started taking me to labels, just to get my name out there by playing an acoustic set for the A&R people at the labels," he recalled to Conaway. "I played at Sony, Warner Bros., Universal, Big Machine, Capitol [. . .] after I played every one of those places, everyone offered me a record deal."

In 2011 Rhett not only signed with the Valory Music Co., an imprint of the Big Machine Label Group, but also decided to leave Lipscomb University, with one year remaining. Over the next couple of years, he worked on his debut album while still continuing to amass songwriting credits, including "Write My Number on Your Hand" from Scotty McCreery's 2011 debut CD, *Clear as Day*, and "She's Just Like That" from *It's All Good* (2011), Joe Nichols's seventh studio album.

EP RELEASE

Rhett officially embarked on a solo career in January 2012, with the release of the country-rock single "Something to Do with My Hands" and an accompanying live music video. Following his Grand Ole Opry debut in May, Rhett served as one of the opening acts on Toby Keith's Live in Overdrive summer tour. While Rhett was on the road, his tune was enjoying a steady climb up the Billboard Hot Country Songs chart, peaking at number fifteen in early August. Later that month Rhett dropped his self-titled EP—a five-track preview of his upcoming full-length album. Within a few hours, it topped iTunes' Country Albums chart and eventually reached number three on Billboard's Top Heatseekers chart. His second single from the disc, the soul-searching mid-tempo ballad "Beer with Jesus," made the top 30, but also stirred up controversy among some country music fans who objected to the idea of mixing religion and alcohol. Rhett later had to defend the song in several radio interviews. That fall, Rhett supported Chris Young during his headlining Liquid Neon tour.

TOPPING THE CHARTS

The year 2013 was a memorable one for Rhett. As a songwriter he cowrote several tunes that were recorded by some of Nashville's biggest stars: "Parking Lot Party," a country-style party anthem for Lee Brice; "Round Here," a chart-topper for Florida Georgia Line; and "1994," a country hip-hop ballad for Aldean, who featured Rhett in the companion video and on his Night Train tour. In May Rhett unveiled "It Goes Like This," the first-ever single from his upcoming disc, and performed several album tracks at the CMA Music Fest 2013. He achieved a milestone on September 9, when three of the songs that he had written, cowritten, or sung ("Parking Lot Party," "Round Here," and "It Goes Like This") occupied the top 15 of Billboard's Country Airplay chart.

A month later Rhett released his debut studio album, *It Goes Like This* (2013), featuring the previously released tracks "Something to Do with My Hands" and "Beer with Jesus." He scored his first-ever number-one in late October, when his title track held the top position of the Country Airplay chart, eventually earning him a new artist of the year nod from the 2013 American Country Awards. In mid-November Rhett, whose album had entered the Billboard 200, released "Get Me Some of That"; the following May, it became Rhett's second consecutive number-one song on Country Airplay. (He also cowrote and sang on Brantley Gilbert's Country Airplay top-10 hit "Small Town Throwdown.") Rhett's next single, "Make Me Wanna," spent thirty weeks on the Country Airplay chart before claiming the number-one spot at the end of February 2015. With three consecutive chart toppers on Billboard's Country Airplay chart, Rhett became the first male solo act since 1994 to accomplish this feat from a full-length debut album.

MIXING GENRES

In early April Rhett, who was working on his follow-up, released the lead single: the funky, R & B–inspired "Crash and Burn," which was a clear departure from his previous material. "I wanted to explore a different side of my voice, a more soul-filled side of my songwriting," he shared with Kurt Wolff for *Radio.com* (9 Apr. 2015). The risk paid off; country fans responded well to the song, which hit number two on the Country Airplay chart in September 2015, giving Rhett his fourth number-one hit—and the fastest-rising song of his career. Both milestones were eclipsed by the emotional country-pop ballad "Die a Happy Man." Rhett's ode to his wife and childhood sweetheart ruled Billboard's Country Airplay chart for six weeks. It went on to earn single of the year honors at the 2016 Academy of Country Music (ACM) and Country Music Association (CMA) Awards and be named the top country song at the 2016 Billboard Music Awards.

Both singles helped Rhett's sophomore album, *Tangled Up*, reach the top 10 of the Billboard 200 and Top Country Albums charts. Bruno Mars's throwback sound deeply influenced Rhett's second album. In the first half of 2016, Rhett released two new tracks: "T-Shirt," the album's third number-one song; and the feel-good tune "Vacation," a top-30 hit on Country Airplay.

Rhett also cohosted the *CMA Music Festival: Country Music's Night to Rock* (2016) with Brett Eldredge; the duo had headlined the CMT On Tour's Suits & Boots together the fall before. To promote his platinum album, Rhett performed at Country to Country (C2C), the UK and Ireland's biggest country music festival, and embarked on his first-ever headlining European tour in November 2016. Rhett ended the year on a high note, earning his first-ever Grammy Award nod in the best country song category for "Die a Happy Man."

PERSONAL LIFE

In October 2012, Rhett married Lauren Gregory Akins. She has starred in several of his music videos, including "Get Me Some of That," "Die a Happy Man," and "Star of the Show."

SUGGESTED READING

"About." *ThomasRhett.com*, www.thomasrhett. com/about. Accessed 15 Dec. 2015.

Akins, Rhett, and Thomas Rhett. "A Conversation with Rhett Akins and Thomas Rhett." Interview by Abby White. *BMI*, 27 July 2015, www.bmi.com/news/entry a_conversation_ with_rhett_akins_and_thomas_rhett. Accessed 15 Dec. 2015.

Rhett, Thomas. "Country Star Thomas Rhett Explains Why He's Got Pop and Hip-Hop on His Album." Interview by Hugh McIntyre. *Forbes*, 11 Oct. 2015, www.forbes.com/sites/ hughmcintyre/2015/10/11/country-star-thomas-rhett-explains-why-hes-got-pop-and-hip-hop-on-his-album/#67fbfbdd5c90. Accessed 15 Dec. 2015.

Rhett, Thomas. "Thomas Rhett Gets His Turn in the Spotlight." Interview by Alanna Conaway. *Taste of Country*, 21 July 2011, tasteofcountry.com/thomas-rhett-interview. Accessed 15 Dec. 2015.

Rhett, Thomas. "Thomas Rhett on His Next Album, Picking Style and Being a Well-Rounded Musician." Interview by Alison Richter. *Guitar World*, 16 Mar. 2015, www.guitarworld. com/features-news-interviews/thomas-rhett-his-next-album-picking-style-and-being-well-rounded-musician. Accessed 15 Dec. 2015.

Rhett, Thomas. "Thomas Rhett Talks New Single 'Crash and Burn' and His Upcoming 'Soul-Filled' Album." Interview by Kurt Wolff. *Radio.com*, 9 Apr. 2015, radio.com/2015/04/09/ thomas-rhett-crash-and-burn-new-album-interview. Accessed 15 Dec. 2016.

SELECTED WORKS

Thomas Rhett, 2012; *It Goes Like This*, 2013; *Tangled Up*, 2015

—*Bertha Muteba*

Margot Robbie

Date of Birth: July 2, 1990
Occupation: Actor

The Australian actor Margot Robbie first achieved Hollywood fame for her role in Martin Scorsese's 2013 film *The Wolf of Wall Street*. "One doesn't have to be a professional casting director to recognize that Robbie is as perfect a specimen of young womanhood as a film-maker could hope to find," Alex Bilmes wrote for *Bazaar* (4 Aug. 2016). "With her honeyed skin, her mega-watt eyes, and her widescreen smile, it's

Gage Skidmore/CC BY-SA 3.0/Wikimedia Commons

almost as if she'd arrived pre-CGI'd, a Disney princess sprung to life." Journalists are frequently moved to describe Robbie in similarly rapturous terms. In addition to her physical beauty, however, Robbie is often cited for her easygoing but driven nature, her down-to-earth charm, and her natural acting ability. As Bilmes noted, "She's sunny, lively, unpretentious. . . . But she's no pushover."

These qualities helped make Robbie a major star after only a handful of film and television roles. Her breakthrough success was followed by high-profile roles in several big-budget Hollywood films, including *The Legend of Tarzan* and *Suicide Squad*, both released in the summer of 2016. These roles further transformed Robbie from a virtual unknown into a box-office draw, and her name was quickly attached to a variety of projects as one of Hollywood's hottest names.

EARLY YEARS AND EDUCATION

Margot Robbie was born on July 2, 1990, and grew up in Gold Coast, a city in Queensland, Australia. Her parents divorced when she was young. Robbie, who was nicknamed "Maggot" as a child, grew up with three siblings—a sister and two brothers. The four were raised by their mother, Sarie, a physiotherapist. After she became famous, Robbie would describe Sarie to interviewers in glowing terms and claim that one of her proudest moments was when she earned enough money to pay off her mother's mortgage. She had little contact with her father, a farmer.

Robbie often spent time with extended family that lived in Dalby, a small, rural town where it was not unusual to spot kangaroos, dingoes, and other quintessentially Australian sights. "I don't like to talk about it [because it] encourages stereotypes," she told Rich Cohen for *Vanity Fair* (Aug. 2016). "People always want to know, 'Did you have kangaroos outside your bedroom window?' I'm like, 'Yes, but none of my other friends did.' Or 'Did you have snakes running around?' And again, 'Yes, in our house, but this isn't an Australian thing.'"

Robbie was an active child who took trapeze lessons and dreamed of becoming a magician. Although money was always tight, her mother managed to send her to an academically rigorous private school. "It was weird because a lot of my friends were very wealthy," she recalled to Aaron Gell for *Marie Claire* (Mar. 2015). "It was interesting to see what you can have in life and know what it was like not to have it. It makes you very ambitious. It seemed horrible at the time, but I'm grateful I had it that way, because I knew what I wanted to achieve." To earn cash, Robbie worked at a series of odd jobs, including making sandwiches at an Australian Subway franchise. (Later, as a professional actor, she filmed a commercial for the popular chain.)

BUDDING ACTING CAREER

As a child, Robbie naively believed that acting was a profession only for those born in Hollywood. Once, however, while watching television, the thought came to her that she could deliver lines better than the actor on the screen. She began watching videos over and over, and she acted in every play that was staged at her school. At age sixteen, she was asked to appear in a low-budget independent picture that a local film student was shooting nearby.

Although she has described the finished product as embarrassing, the experience gave Robbie the push she needed to head to Melbourne, where most Australian television shows are made. In short order, she had found an agent, gone on a round of auditions, and had been hired to appear in a children's program called *The Elephant Princess*. In Melbourne, she stayed with a succession of friends, sleeping on their sofas until she sensed she was wearing out her welcome. It was far from an easy way of life, but her determination paid off, and she gradually began to be cast in small parts.

She subsequently set her sights on appearing in the popular daily Australian soap opera *Neighbours*. Several Hollywood stars, including Russell Crowe, Naomi Watts, and Heath Ledger, had gotten their start on Australian soaps, and Robbie hoped to follow in their footsteps. "Robbie's beauty and speed of ascent mask her ambition, the part hustle and savvy have played," Cohen asserted, explaining that the aspiring actor hunted down the name of the soap's production company and began to doggedly call again and again in hope of securing an audition.

When she finally got a producer on the phone, *Neighbours* was fortuitously casting teenage actors. Robbie was hired to play the role of Donna Freedman, a garrulous groupie who matures into a warm, sensitive young woman over the course of her run on the show, which lasted from 2008 to 2011. Because her character was so talkative, and the show aired an episode every weekday evening, Robbie sometimes had sixty pages of script to memorize at a time and worked long hours for five days a week.

Once Robbie's *Neighbours* contract ended she declined to renew, instead opting to try launching a Hollywood career. "I remember watching American movies and TV shows growing up and thinking, 'Oh, God, these crazy characters doing these outlandish things, how do the writers come up with it?'" she recalled to Cohen. "Then I moved to America and met so many people just like the people in the movies, and I realized, 'Oh, so this is just real life in America.'"

Robbie was soon hired to play a flight attendant on the ABC series *Pan Am*. Despite playing upon nostalgia for mid-twentieth-century New York, the show ran for only one season, from 2011 to 2012. It was notable, however, for showcasing Robbie's facility with accents—a talent that would serve her breakthrough role.

THE WOLF OF WALL STREET

While working on *Pan Am*, Robbie continued to audition for films. In 2012 she landed a supporting role in *About Time*, a romantic comedy starring Rachel McAdams that was released in 2013 to generally positive reviews. However, it was another 2012 audition that would lay out Robbie's path to stardom—one for Martin Scorsese's 2013 film *The Wolf of Wall Street*. Along with seemingly every other young, blonde actor in the business, she sent a tape to the iconic director, hoping to be considered for the role of Naomi, the Brooklyn-born girlfriend (and later, wife) of Leonardo DiCaprio's lead character, a hotshot financial trader. Also known as "the Duchess of Bay Ridge," Naomi is described in the script as "the hottest blonde ever."

Called to New York to audition, Robbie initially showed up in jeans and flat shoes. The casting director sent her out to buy "a really tight, short dress and the highest pair of heels you can find," as the actor recalled to Bilmes. Once clothed in her hastily purchased outfit, Robbie began performing scenes with DiCaprio. After the first, she felt she was failing to keep up with the experienced actor, who improvised some lines. The next scene called for the pair to have a raging argument, after which DiCaprio's character, Jordan Belfort, was to demand a kiss. Instead of complying, Robbie improvised herself, cursing and slapping DiCaprio hard across the cheek. "The room just went dead silent and I froze," she told Bilmes. "I'm thinking, 'You just hit Leonardo DiCaprio in the face. They're going to arrest you because that's assault. You're definitely never going to work again, that's for sure. They'll probably sue you as well.'" Instead, both DiCaprio and Scorsese laughed, and a week later Robbie was offered the part.

While the film got mixed reviews, Robbie's portrayal of Naomi received fascinated attention, particularly in the sexually charged scenes. "Whether she's tempting Jordan with her legs spread open in their baby's nursery or throwing a glass of water in his face and screaming at the top of her lungs, she commands the screen," Marlow Stern wrote for the *Daily Beast* (8 Jan. 2014). Robbie, now being compared to other breakout sex-symbol stars such as Michelle Pfeiffer, Sharon Stone, and Cathy Moriarty, worried that her overnight success had set the bar too high. "I was worried that people would be expecting too much of me now, like, 'If Scorsese cast her in a film, she must be brilliant!'" she told Eliza Berman for *Time* (4 Aug. 2016). "Instead of having the chance to surprise people, I was worried that I'd disappoint them."

AN ESTABLISHED STAR

Although far from disappointing, Robbie's next few roles did not garner the attention of *The Wolf of Wall Street*. In 2014's *Suite Française* she played a defiant farm girl in Nazi-occupied France, and the following year she played a thief being mentored by a veteran con man (played by Will Smith) in *Focus*. In early 2016 she portrayed a war reporter in the Tina Fey vehicle *Whiskey Tango Foxtrot*. It was a pair of notable roles in big-budget films released in the summer of 2016, however, that truly continued Robbie's rise to the top of Hollywood, getting her on the cover of major magazines and interviewed on talk shows.

The first of these films was *The Legend of Tarzan* (2016), a new version of the classic Tarzan story. Robbie became involved with the film in part because she was deeply attracted to the prospect of working with director David Yates, who had helmed the last four films in the Harry Potter franchise. Robbie was such an enormous fan of Harry Potter that as a child she once faked poor vision so that she could get glasses like those worn by the hero, and when Yates approached her to play Jane opposite Alexander Skarsgård's Tarzan, she agreed. Though the resulting CGI-heavy film got middling reviews, the acting was generally commended.

Robbie's next project was even more hotly anticipated: the DC Comics film *Suicide Squad* (2016), about a group of imprisoned supervillains coerced into taking on risky missions. She played Harley Quinn, a deranged sidekick of the famous Batman villain the Joker who had become a fan-favorite character in animated works and comics. Calling *Suicide Squad* "the most tweeted about movie of the summer," Berman wrote that "Harley Quinn's pig-tailed insanity is one of its biggest draws. . . . She's a candy-coated madwoman." Robbie reached out to fans to get their take on playing the character, and she read up extensively on codependence—a trait she felt might explain Quinn's attachment to an evil character like the Joker. "All the roles I've played are very strong and very flawed," she told Berman. "I look for a really strong point of view. They know who they are or they know what they want—not necessarily both."

Though *Suicide Squad* was a major commercial success, becoming one of the highest-grossing films of the year, it received negative reviews from critics. However, Robbie's acting was seen as one of the movie's bright spots. Plans were quickly laid for a Harley Quinn solo film, which Robbie signed on to produce as well.

PERSONAL LIFE

Robbie entered a long-term relationship with Tom Ackerley, an assistant director she met while shooting *Suite Française*. She maintains as normal a life as possible and calls herself an optimistic, trusting person. Robbie is an amateur tattoo artist who has worked on many of her friends and costars, and she also plays in an amateur hockey league.

SUGGESTED READING

Berman, Eliza. "Why Margot Robbie Thought Her Career Was Over After Making *The Wolf of Wall Street*." *Time*, 4 Aug. 2016, time.com/4368577/margot-robbie-suicide-squad-harley-quinn/. Accessed 7 Nov. 2016.

Bilmes, Alex. "From Australia's Gold Coast to *The Wolf of Wall Street*, Margot Robbie Is the Latest Girl from Nowhere to Become a Hollywood Star." *Harper's Bazaar*, 4 Aug. 2016, www.harpersbazaar.co.uk/fashion/fashion-news/news/a33706/margot-robbie-is-bazaars-april-cover-star. Accessed 7 Nov. 2016.

Cohen, Rich. "Welcome to the Summer of Margot Robbie." *Vanity Fair*, Aug. 2016, www.vanityfair.com/hollywood/2016/07/margot-robbie-cover-story. Accessed 7 Nov. 2016.

Gell, Aaron. "Exclusive Sneak Peek: Marie Claire March Cover Star Margot Robbie." *Marie Claire*, 5 Feb. 2015, www.marieclaire.com/celebrity/news/a13235/exclusive-sneak-peek-margot-robbie/. Accessed 7 Nov. 2016.

Heigl, Alex. "9 Things You Didn't Know About Margot Robbie as We Gear Up for *Suicide Squad*." *People*, 25 July 2016, people.com/celebrity/margot-robbie-suicide-squad-actress-trivia/. Accessed 7 Nov. 2016.

Van Meter, Jonathan. "*Tarzan*'s Margot Robbie on Why She's No Damsel in Distress." *Vogue*, 13 May 2016, www.vogue.com/13435036/margot-robbie-june-cover-wolf-of-wall-street-jane-legend-of-tarzan/. Accessed 7 Nov. 2016.

SELECTED WORKS
Neighbours, 2008–11; *Pan Am*, 2011–12; *About Time*, 2013; *The Wolf of Wall Street*, 2013; *Suite Française*, 2014; *Focus*, 2015; *Z for Zachariah*, 2015; *Whiskey Tango Foxtrot*, 2016; *The Legend of Tarzan*, 2016; *Suicide Squad*, 2016

—*Mari Rich*

Maggie Rogers

Date of birth: April 25, 1994
Occupation: Musician

Maggie Rogers has enjoyed a remarkably rapid ascent to popularity thanks to the viral power of the Internet, transforming from a young, unknown singer-songwriter to an up-and-coming star in a matter of months. She first drew significant attention in 2016, when a video of her singing her song "Alaska" during a university master class with musician and producer Pharrell Williams was shared by users of the content-rating site Reddit. That video quickly racked up more than two million views, and a version of the song later uploaded to the music-streaming service Spotify soon had more than twenty-six million plays. By early 2017, Rogers had thousands of followers on social media and released her major-label debut, the EP *Now That the Light Is Fading* (2017).

Yet in some ways, Rogers was an unlikely candidate for pop success. For one thing, she was no social-media savvy self-promoter. "I went viral on Reddit, and I didn't know what Reddit was," Rogers told Claire Landsbaum for *New York Magazine* (10 Feb. 2017). "I'm a strange person to be a person of the Internet, but I'm indebted to it because this is the only thing I've ever wanted to do." She was also previously known as mainly a folksy banjo player, with a few self-released albums that had attracted only minor attention. But even those works were eagerly sought out by fans as she earned critical attention.

Rogers always had faith in the creative process: "I've always really thought that if you make good music, then people will find it," the singer told Audrey White for the music magazine *Pitchfork* (26 June 2016). "I know that's a really naïve statement and that isn't always the case, there is so much good music that doesn't get heard, but it's been really wild watching people find my old

music. It kind of reaffirms my belief that if you make what you want to make, maybe somebody will find it, even if it takes four years."

EARLY LIFE AND EDUCATION
Maggie Rogers grew up in a rural town on the eastern shore of Maryland. Her first musical love was classical—Gustav Holst and Antonio Vivaldi were particular favorites—and at the age of seven she began playing the harp. Meanwhile, her mother played neo-soul artists such as Lauryn Hill and Erykah Badu, which she subconsciously absorbed. She connected deeply to music from a very young age, associating it strongly with other senses, especially color, a phenomenon known as synesthesia.

By middle school, Rogers had started expanding her horizons, listening to a wide variety of artists, including 311, Incubus, Vampire Weekend (the first record she ever played on repeat, she has said), Phish, the Grateful Dead, and Jack Johnson. She learned to play several other instruments, including piano and guitar, and began dreaming of making music a career. In sixth grade, Rogers would act as a DJ during recess, playing tracks by the likes of Usher, Alicia Keys, and Missy Elliott, who were then topping the charts. A few years later, nursing a broken heart after she and her boyfriend broke up, she wrote her first song.

In 2008 Rogers graduated from her small private middle school and entered St. Andrews, an Episcopal boarding school in Middleton, Delaware, where she hoped to find a larger community of fellow musicians than in her tiny hometown. There, one of her dorm mates was a girl from North Carolina who often asked Rogers to help her tune her banjo. Rogers discovered a love for the instrument and began borrowing it regularly.

At St. Andrews, much of the technology beloved by teenagers was prohibited: there was no television, cell phone usage, or Internet access. Through an art teacher who loved such artists as Bob Dylan, the Beatles, and Carol King she became influenced by vintage folk and folk-rock. This eventually led her to modern indie-folk artists such as Bon Iver and Fleet Foxes. Folk music became her primary obsession, and she began writing and playing music frequently.

DEVELOPING AS A SONGWRITER

During her junior year of high school, Rogers found out about a five-week summer program being held at the Berklee School of Music, in Boston, Massachusetts. She applied, thinking it would be a good opportunity to see if she wanted to pursue music in college, and was accepted based on the strength of one of her compositions. "I learned so much from that program, especially when it comes to vocal and music theory," she told Gerard Marcus for the independent music website *ThrdCoast* (7 Mar. 2016). "And it was the first time I felt creatively on fire. I was just making stuff all the time, and it was so crazy to feel that and be in a community of people who wanted to just sit around and talk about music all day."

While at Berklee, Rogers won a student songwriting contest, and during a performance singing with a band she realized she wanted to dedicate herself to music. Feeling encouraged, she turned a small broom closet into a recording booth upon her return to St. Andrews for her senior year. It was there that she made her first album, *The Echo* (2012), recording everything herself and doing all the mixing and mastering. "I didn't even know what production was at that point. I was just like, 'I'm going to make this,'" she told Marcus. She sent some of the songs as part of her college application to Clive Davis Institute of Recorded Music at New York University (NYU) and was accepted.

NEW YORK UNIVERSITY

As a college freshman, Rogers sang, played banjo, and wrote songs with the band Del Water Gap. By the end of her sophomore year she had recorded and self-released a second album, *Blood Ballet* (2014). However, she soon went through a period of self-doubt and stopped writing her own songs. She left NYU to study in Paris, France, for a semester, and while in Europe she went, under some protest, to a nightclub in Berlin, Germany. "When someone said, 'Let's go to a club' in New York, it often meant heels and tight dresses and money," Rogers explained to Katherine Cusumano for *W* (13 Feb. 2017). In Berlin, however, everyone wore sneakers so that they could dance all night, and Rogers discovered she loved the rhythms of electronic dance music and the feelings it could inspire in listeners. "Watching a group of people move in the same way so instinctually was so connective," she recalled to Landsbaum. "I realized how instinctive human rhythm is."

Rogers went back to NYU revitalized, and she focused on merging her folk roots with her new love of dance and pop music. Still learning and evolving, in her senior year she took a course taught by Questlove, a multi-instrumentalist and producer best known as the drummer for the band the Roots. However, it was a master class featuring a surprise appearance by musician and producer Pharrell Williams that would have the greatest impact—though not right away. Rogers graduated in May 2016 and returned home to figure out her future. She assumed that she would work at a coffee shop or do freelance writing (she had once interned at the magazine *Elle*) and make music whenever possible.

VIRAL BREAKTHROUGH

Rogers's expectation to join the ranks of artists struggling to make their mark was quickly upturned. The master class she had participated in with Pharrell had been filmed, and in June 2016 the video began to go viral. It shows the famed producer (perhaps best known for his blockbuster single "Happy") providing critiques on the students' musical compositions. The students had been told only to prepare a song as a homework assignment and were unaware that Pharrell would be in attendance, so they appear understandably star struck. However, it was Pharrell's reaction to Rogers's song that spurred the video's popularity.

In the clip, each student discusses and plays their track, and Pharrell provides suggestions. At Rogers' turn, she plays a song she wrote called "Alaska," inspired by her experience hiking on a pristine glacier. She had written it in fifteen minutes and quickly created a demo mix, which was the only track she had ready to submit to the class. It features a pulsing beat, partly made up of simple samples such as a hand slapping a knee, with a background of natural sounds for the ethereal vocals. The video shows Rogers introduce the song by describing her synthesis of traditional folk with electronic dance music.

As the track plays, Pharrell's face memorably expresses a mixture of surprise and appreciation, with his eyes even appearing to tear up. When the song is over he is almost speechless: "I have zero, zero, zero notes for that," he says. "I've never heard anyone like you before." Eventually he recommends that the rest of the class aspire to finding a similar blend of influences that combine to create something new and unique.

Viewers across the Internet shared Pharrell's stunned reaction, racking up millions of plays of the video, which was widely shared on social media sites such as Reddit. Rogers was immediately seen as an up-and-coming talent, attracting a sizable social media following. Plays of her old albums, available online, skyrocketed. She scrambled to release a fully mixed and mastered version of "Alaska" on the streaming services Spotify and SoundCloud, and it soon was heard by millions of eager fans.

MAJOR LABEL DEBUT
The tumult surrounding the master class video as it went viral overwhelmed Rogers. The same day she released the official version of "Alaska" she left for a previously planned hiking trip to the Alps. Upon her return, record companies began heavily courting her—including one that sent a pristine first edition of Virginia Woolf's *To the Lighthouse* as a gift. Rogers ultimately signed with Capitol and began work on her major-label debut.

Her first EP, *Now That the Light Is Fading*, was released in February 2017. In addition to "Alaska," the five-song set included the singles "Dog Years," which prominently features the pan flute, and "On + Off." Music videos for the singles were shot, mostly featuring natural settings Rogers was drawn to and with her family and friends as actors. She also appeared on major television programs such as *The Tonight Show Starring Jimmy Fallon* to promote the work, further boosting her profile.

The EP was received enthusiastically by fans and critics alike. Many reviewers referred to Rogers as an artist to watch and praised her use of original sampling, such as the sounds of a mourning dove and conversations recorded from a Moroccan marketplace included on "Alaska." However, some critics also cautioned that Pharrell's suggestion that Rogers's sound was wholly unique might be a bit overblown; while her songs are strong, they follow in the tradition of so-called folktronica artists such as Beth Orton and Ellie Goulding and viral pop stars such as Lorde. In a mixed review for *Pitchfork* (16 Feb. 2017), for example, Katherine St. Asaph opined that the EP was simply the beginning for a very young and less than fully formed artist: "She has a platform. She's got ideas. But like all discovery stories, the real reward lies in what comes next."

SUGGESTED READING
Cusumano, Katherine. "First, Maggie Rogers's Music Enchanted Pharrell—Now, the Rest of the World." *W*, 13 Feb. 2017, www.wmagazine.com/story/maggie-rogers-musician-pharrell-alaska-profile. Accessed 2 May 2017.

Guiducci, Mark. "How Maggie Rogers Is Harnessing Viral Fame to Go Her Own Way." *Vogue*, 29 Sept. 2016, www.vogue.com/article/maggie-rogers-musician-producer-alaska-pharrell-williams. Accessed 2 May 2017.

Landsbaum, Claire. "Maggie Rogers Is More Than the Musician Who Made Pharrell Freak." *New York Magazine*, 10 Feb. 2017, nymag.com/thecut/2017/02/maggie-rogers-is-more-than-the-musician-who-floored-pharrell.html. Accessed 2 May 2017.

Petrusich, Amanda. "Maggie Rogers: An Artist of Her Time." *The New Yorker*, 13 Mar. 2017, www.newyorker.com/magazine/2017/03/13/maggie-rogers-an-artist-of-her-time. Accessed 2 May 2017.

Pollard, Alexandra. "Maggie Rogers on the Song that Left Pharrell Speechless: 'It Tumbled Out in 15 Minutes.'" *The Guardian*, 16 Mar. 2017, www.theguardian.com/music/2017/mar/16/maggie-rogers-pharrell-williams-speechless-tumbled-15-minutes-alaska. Accessed 2 May 2017.

Rogers, Maggie. Interview by Gerard Marcus. *ThrdCoast*, 7 Mar. 2016, www.thrdcoast.com/read/2016/3/6/interview-maggie-rogers. Accessed 2 May 2017.

White, Audrey. "Pharrell's Stunned Face Launched Maggie Rogers' Career. Now What?" *Pitchfork*, 26 June 2016, pitchfork.com/thepitch/1206-pharrells-stunned-face-launched-maggie-rogers-career-now-what/. Accessed 2 May 2017.

SELECTED WORKS
The Echo, 2012; *Blood Ballet*, 2014; *Now That the Light Is Fading*, 2017

—Mari Rich

Tracee Ellis Ross
Date of Birth: October 29, 1972
Occupation: Actor

An award-winning actor known for her positivity and dedication to female empowerment, Tracee Ellis Ross has taken a somewhat unusual path in her journey to fame. The daughter of famed singer Diana Ross and music executive Robert Ellis Silberstein, she acknowledges that her famous parentage could have opened doors for her in Hollywood. However, Ross was reluctant to pursue acting work because of such connections, which brought her additional scrutiny and pressure to live up to her famous mother's example. Beginning her career instead in the fashion industry, Ross ultimately decided to pursue an acting career on her own terms, taking on a variety of

Mingle Media TV/Flickr/CC BY-SA 2.0/ Wikimedia Commons

small roles before breaking through to a new level with her starring role in the sitcom *Girlfriends*, which aired on United Paramount Network (UPN) and then the CW Television Network for eight seasons.

Ross returned to the spotlight in 2014, joining the cast of the sitcom *Black-ish* as doctor and mother Rainbow Johnson. Created by Kenya Barris and costarring actor Anthony Anderson, *Black-ish* follows the lives of a wealthy African American family and mixes family comedy with insightful and thoughtfully handled musings on race and class. "To be on a show that is willing to keep telling the truth through the lens of this family means a lot to me," she told Ashley Weatherford for the *New York* magazine blog the *Cut* (18 Mar. 2016) about *Black-ish*. "The fact that the writers are willing to keep addressing what American families are dealing with right now—and sometimes, like the police-brutality episode, what black families are dealing with right now—is really exciting and makes me feel really proud." Having begun its third season in September 2016, *Black-ish* remains a popular and critically acclaimed addition to ABC's lineup, providing Ross further opportunities to explore and develop her well-regarded character.

EARLY LIFE AND EDUCATION
Ross was born Tracee Joy Silberstein on October 29, 1972, in Los Angeles, California. Her mother is the singer Diana Ross, while her father, Robert Ellis Silberstein, is a music executive who served for a time as his wife's manager. Ross's parents later divorced, and she has several siblings from their multiple marriages. When Ross joined the Screen Actors Guild (SAG) later in life, she changed her name to Tracee Ellis Ross to honor both of her parents. Ross lived in numerous places during her early life, including California, Switzerland, and France, and she attended schools such as New York's prestigious Dalton School.

As a child, Ross was inspired by the work of comedian and actor Lucille Ball, whose influence shaped her own comedic sensibilities. "I didn't have a lot of examples of silly women around me," she told Jenna Wortham for the *New York Times Magazine* (22 Jan. 2015). "Lucy made me feel not crazy, not too much, not too big. She taught me that I could be both glamorous and elegant and sophisticated and beautiful—and still really stupid, silly, and funny."

Growing up, Ross was highly aware of her mother's career as a singer and success in the field. However, she was unsure whether she wanted to pursue a career in show business, particularly acting, herself. While being the child of a celebrity such as Diana Ross could potentially benefit an aspiring actor, Ross found that her famous parentage actually placed her under more scrutiny. "It's not that it opened doors, it was like people unlocked the door, sat on the other side of it with their arms crossed, and were, like, 'How's she going to walk in?'" she recalled to Stacy Lambe for *Backstage* (13 Jan. 2016).

EARLY CAREER
Rather than pursuing acting work, Ross initially entered the fashion industry as a model. She made her runway debut in 1991, appearing alongside her mother as well as supermodels such as Naomi Campbell in designer Thierry Mugler's Paris Fashion Week show. Although she found the experience terrifying, Ross has since described it as the best birthday ever, as the runway show happened to fall on her eighteenth birthday. She again walked in a Mugler show in the spring of 1992 and also found various smaller modeling jobs while represented by the modeling agency Wilhelmina Models. Despite her initial success as a model, Ross has noted in interviews that her personality was not suited to the career and recalled that a photographer once asked her to "stop talking and try to look sexy," as quoted by Carl Swanson for the *New York* magazine blog *Vulture* (14 June 2006).

Ross attended Brown University, where she studied theater arts. She earned her bachelor's degree from the university in 1994. Ross remained interested in the fashion industry while at Brown and worked as an intern for the women's magazine *Mirabella*. After graduating from college, she returned to *Mirabella* as a contributing editor and also worked for a time in the fashion department of *New York* magazine.

FILM AND TELEVISION ROLES

Although still unsure whether she wanted to pursue work as an actor, Ross began to move in that direction in the early 1990s. While at Brown, she auditioned for director Spike Lee's 1992 film *Malcolm X*. Although she did not get the part, she received positive feedback from casting director Robi Reed that inspired her to keep looking for acting work. Although Ross acknowledges that her connection to her mother could potentially have benefited her search, she takes pride in the fact that she instead went through countless auditions, embarking on the career trajectory of a working actor rather than simply the child of a celebrity. Indeed, she initially struggled to find work and at one point was told that she did not "pop," she recalled to Lambe. However, Ross persevered and soon began to find work, making her film debut in 1996's *Far Harbor*. "I figured out how to enjoy the process," Ross told Lambe about her experience competing for work. "And to me, auditioning is an opportunity for me to play the role that I want."

Over the following years, Ross appeared in several films, including the 1997 drama *Sue* and the 2000 comedy *Hanging Up*. In 2000 she moved in a new direction with her appearance in *The Lyricist Lounge Show*, a short-lived comedy and hip-hop show that aired on MTV. Her true breakthrough, however, came in the fall of 2000, when the comedy series *Girlfriends* began to air on UPN. Airing for eight seasons between 2000 and 2008, *Girlfriends* followed the lives of lawyer Joan Carol Clayton, played by Ross, and several of her female friends. The show moved to the CW following the merger of UPN and the WB Television Network in 2006. *Girlfriends* proved popular with viewers, and Ross won several awards, including a NAACP Image Award and a BET Comedy Award, for her performance.

Ross appeared in a variety of film roles while *Girlfriends* was on the air, and following its conclusion in 2008, she began to take on additional television work. In 2011 she appeared in several episodes of *CSI: Crime Scene Investigation* and also began starring in the sitcom *Reed between the Lines*. Ross left *Reed between the Lines* after the first season.

BLACK-ISH

In 2014 Ross returned to television as one of the stars of the sitcom *Black-ish*, which premiered on ABC in September of that year. Following the lives of the members of the Johnson family, the show deals with topics such as race and class while at the same time presenting a humorous take on everyday family life. For Ross, *Black-ish* represents an important step forward in the media representation of African Americans. "I think that for years, people have been watching white families and identifying with them [and seeing] how we're all the same," she told Shantell E. Jamison for *Ebony* (24 June 2016). "But this is an opportunity for other people to see a Black family and identify with us and connect to that place where families are families. Funny is funny and some of the situations might be handled in different ways, or have a more specific historical context because of the specificity of your race or religion or whatever those things may be, but in essence, a family is a family."

The critical response to *Black-ish* was overwhelmingly positive, and it was renewed for second and third seasons by the network. Ross's character, Rainbow Johnson, was particularly well received, and she was nominated for the Emmy Award for outstanding lead actress in a comedy series in 2016 for her performance. In addition to facilitating Ross's return to television, her role in *Black-ish* has dramatically increased her public profile, and she has steadily gained a reputation as a positive person dedicated to female empowerment, particularly in regard to African American women and girls. "I really feel like there's a paradigm shift that has occurred in the last ten years for how black women in this country are seen, the voice that we have, how we see ourselves, how we our images are portrayed," she told Ashley Weatherford. "I want to see images that remind me that I am beautiful and I am enough, so that I don't have to waste any energy feeling ashamed of myself or any of that, so I can actually go out and do extraordinary things. Using my voice to recognize and celebrate other women is a joy for me."

PERSONAL LIFE

Ross lives in California. In addition to her television work, she has a substantial social media presence and frequently posts videos in which she takes on different personas, including that of rapper T-Murda. Ross was awarded an honorary doctorate of fine arts from Brown University in 2015.

SUGGESTED READING

Jamison, Shantell E. "5 Things with Tracee Ellis Ross." *Ebony*, 24 June 2016, www.ebony. com/entertainment-culture/tracee-ellis-ross. Accessed 10 Nov. 2016.

Lambe, Stacy. "Why Tracee Ellis Ross Loves Auditioning." *Backstage*, 13 Jan. 2016, www. backstage.com/interview/why-tracee-ellis-ross-loves-auditioning. Accessed 10 Nov. 2016.

Merritt, Jennifer. "8 Things You Didn't Know about Tracee Ellis Ross." *InStyle*, 15 July 2016, www.instyle.com/videos/tracee-ellis-ross-interview-video-facts-about. Accessed 10 Nov. 2016.

Ross, Tracee Ellis. "Tracee Ellis Ross Is 'A Woman Who Speaks Up for Herself': BUST

Interview." Interview by Jenni Miller. *BUST*, Dec. 2015–Jan. 2016, bust.com/tv/15422-tracee-ellis-ross-bust-interview.html.   Accessed 10 Nov. 2016.

Ross, Tracee Ellis. "Tracee Ellis Ross: 'That Hurt Like the Bejesus.'" Interview by Jenna Wortham. *The New York Times Magazine*, 22 Jan. 2015, mobile.nytimes.com/2015/01/25/magazine/tracee-ellis-ross-that-hurt-like-the-bejesus.html. Accessed 10 Nov. 2016.

Swanson, Carl. "*Black-ish*'s Tracee Ellis Ross on Being a Sitcom Mom, Her Own Mother, and Her Alter Egos." *Vulture*, 14 June 2016, www.vulture.com/2016/06/black-ish-tracee-ellis-ross.html. Accessed 10 Nov. 2016.

Weatherford, Ashley. "Tracee Ellis Ross Wants to Make TV That Reflects Black People's Real Lives." *The Cut*, 18 Mar. 2016, nymag.com/thecut/2016/03/tracee-ellis-ross-race-black-ish-black-girls-rock.html. Accessed 10 Nov. 2016.

SELECTED WORKS

Far Harbor, 1996; *Hanging Up*, 2000; *The Lyricist Lounge Show*, 2000; *Girlfriends*, 2000–8; *Reed between the Lines*, 2011; *Black-ish*, 2014–

—*Joy Crelin*

Bozoma Saint John

Date of birth: January 21, 1977
Occupation: Chief brand officer at Uber

Bozoma "Boz" Saint John is the chief brand officer (CBO) at the ride-sharing company Uber. She originally intended to become a doctor, but her interests and talents led her to work in marketing for Pepsi, Apple Music, and director Spike Lee's advertising agency Spike DDB. At Apple, she was the brains behind popular ads featuring stars such as Kerry Washington, Taylor Swift, and Drake.

Saint John began her job as CBO at Uber—she is the first person to ever serve in the role—during a dark period in the company's brief history. In January 2017, the car service appeared to capitalize on the crowds protesting President Donald Trump's travel ban that targeted Muslim-majority countries. Uber's decisions during the upheaval, whatever their intention, led about 200,000 people to delete their Uber accounts. In June, after an extensive investigation by a third party, Uber fired twenty employees for sexual harassment; around the same time, controversial chief executive Travis Kalanick resigned at the behest of shareholders. Meanwhile, the company is under investigation by the Department of Justice for using secret software to

Photo by D Dipasupil/FilmMagic

evade authorities in areas where ride hailing is restricted. With all of this in mind, Saint John is charged with making the brand appear more humane. Saint John claims to be undaunted by this task and is excited about the idea of engineering a "turnaround" for the company, as she told Amy Dubois Barnett for *Glamour* (24 July 2017). "It's really about assessing what the brand is today and then figuring out a way to connect what is emotional and human about the brand—the drivers and riders and the cities that we're in—to our customer," she said. Saint John was inducted into the American Advertising Federation's Advertising Hall of Achievement in 2014, and she was named executive of the year at the Billboard Women in Music Awards in 2016.

EARLY LIFE AND EDUCATION

Saint John was born Bozoma Arthur on January 21, 1977 in Middletown, Connecticut, where her father, Appianda Arthur, was earning his PhD in ethnomusicology at Wesleyan University. When she was six months old, her family returned to her parents' native Ghana, where her father was a member of Parliament from 1979 until a coup d'état in 1981. Her mother, Aba Enim, designed and sold clothes. Saint John's family, which includes her parents and three younger sisters, sought political asylum in the United States and eventually settled in Colorado Springs when Saint John was twelve years old. Her mother worked hard to instill a love for African culture in her daughters, but Saint John, one of only a few black children in her town, just wanted to fit in. She became well versed in popular culture and developed a deep and abiding love for hip-hop. Eventually, she grew more comfortable in her own skin. "Being the authentic me always got me attention," Saint John told Barnett. "Sometimes too much attention makes you a target, but you take the hits and push forward." As a student at Liberty High School, Saint John was captain of both the cheerleading squad and the track team. She ran for student council with the slogan "Ain't Nothin' but a Boz Thing," a play on her nickname and Dr. Dre's then-hit song "Nuthin' but a G Thang."

Like her father, Saint John attended Wesleyan University, where she majored in English and African American studies. She was still a student when rapper Tupac Shakur was murdered in 1996. Saint John approached a professor, suggesting he teach a class on Shakur. Instead, the professor helped Saint John develop her own noncredit course, for which she used her cassette tape player to painstakingly transcribe every single one of the rapper's songs. "We had thirty students for this noncredit course—a course just to learn something," she said later in a speech at Wesleyan, as quoted by Cynthia Rockwell for the Wesleyan website (25 Apr. 2016). "The next semester, we had thirty people in the class and a sixty-person wait list, and the semester after that, [the professor] took it on himself."

EARLY CAREER

Saint John graduated in 1999 with plans to attend medical school, but she decided, with the blessing of her parents, to take a gap year instead. She moved to New York City, where she took a number of odd jobs through a temp agency. After working for a caterer and a dog salon, she took a job with director Spike Lee's advertising firm, Spike DDB. Saint John was supposed to answer the phones while Lee looked for a permanent assistant, but according to Lee, in an interview with Sheila Marikar for the *New York Times* (22 July 2017), "She walked in, she got the job. It was evident that she was going to go places." There, Saint John helped Lee develop a successful advertisement for Pepsi in 2002. The ad featured Beyoncé, who had just embarked on a solo career, singing new lyrics to the familiar aria from the opera *Carmen*. "That became the turning point where, O.K., I can actually use my knowledge of pop culture, running around these streets with my friends, knowing the inside track on things, to help inform business decisions," Saint John told Marikar.

Saint John went on to work for the ad agency Arnold Worldwide and to serve as the vice president of Ashley Stewart, a women's fashion brand. She joined Pepsi as the head of music and entertainment marketing and created a sponsorship program called the Pepsi DJ Division, which included such performers as DJ Khaled.

During her tenure, she negotiated endorsement deals with such artists as Nicki Minaj, Kanye West, and Eminem. She also continued to work with Beyoncé, and in 2012, negotiated a $50 million deal for Pepsi to sponsor the singer's tour. In 2013, Saint John orchestrated Beyoncé's Super Bowl halftime performance (featuring the former members of Destiny's Child) in New Orleans. Saint John described the halftime show to Barnett as a "career highlight."

BEATS AND APPLE MUSIC

In February 2014, Saint John met with Jimmy Iovine of Interscope Records. Iovine had just founded a streaming service called Beats Music, with Dr. Dre. In her interview with Marikar, Saint John admitted that, at the time, she knew nothing of streaming—she did not even know who Iovine was—but the meeting offered her a change in perspective. "I needed something to give me some hope for the future," she told Marikar. "I needed something that could help me see further. When he was talking about all this newfangled stuff, I said: 'That sounds like the future! I'm going to the future!'" Saint John resigned her job at Pepsi and moved to Los Angeles to become the head of global marketing for Beats.

Fortuitously, Apple bought Beats for $3 billion in May 2014, just a few months after Saint John joined the company. She rose through the ranks at the company to become the global head of marketing for iTunes and, as the service was launched in June 2015, Apple Music. In September, orchestrated by Saint John, the company premiered a series of commercials featuring actors Taraji P. Henson and Kerry Washington, as well as Grammy Award–winning hip-hop artist Mary J. Blige. (Ava DuVernay directed the commercials.) Though the ads were wildly popular, Apple Music suffered a rocky start as it struggled to assert itself against competitors and appease artists and subscribers. "The question we ask is: In the normal course of your day, how are you actually interacting with music?" Saint John told Reggie Ugwu for *Buzzfeed News* (26 Sept. 2016). "What are you going to it for? And how can we better serve that up?" Apple Music relaunched in June 2016.

With the relaunch came what is widely considered Saint John's breakout moment, when she appeared onstage at the annual Apple Worldwide Developers Conference (WWDC). She played "Rapper's Delight," the classic 1979 hip-hop record from the Sugarhill Gang, and encouraged an auditorium full of middle-aged white men to rap along. Around the same time, she appeared in a commercial for Apple Music featuring late-night television host James Corden. She went on to work on advertisements featuring Taylor Swift and Drake working out to each other's music. In

December 2016, she was named executive of the year at the Billboard Women in Music Awards.

JOINING UBER

In June 2017, Saint John resigned her job at Apple to join Uber as the company's first chief brand officer, though she first caught the attention of media maven and Uber board member Arianna Huffington in 2016. According to a post on Instagram, Saint John called an Uber to attend a business dinner in Austin, Texas. The car was in shambles when it arrived. Saint John made a joke about the sorry state of the vehicle, but the driver told her that the car had been vandalized and that he did not have the money to fix it. He also lamented that he had been saving money to see Iggy Pop perform as part of the festival Saint John was in town to attend. Saint John who, as it happened, was on her way to a dinner with Iggy Pop, invited the beleaguered driver along. "We're all rushing in our lives, and I was so concerned with getting from here to there, and if not for the moment of humanity where we just started talking, that connection would not have happened," she told Marikar. Huffington was impressed by Saint John's good deed, and later, spearheaded the effort to hire her at Uber.

PERSONAL LIFE

Saint John was married to advertising executive Peter Saint John, whom she met while they were both working at Spike DDB. Peter Saint John died in December 2013 of Burkitt's lymphoma, with which he had been diagnosed only months before. Saint John and her daughter, Lael, live in Los Angeles.

SUGGESTED READING

Marikar, Sheila. "Is This the Woman Who Will Save Uber?" *The New York Times*, 22 July 2017, www.nytimes.com/2017/07/22/style/uber-bozoma-saint-john.html. Accessed 10 Aug. 2017.

Rockwell, Cynthia. "Apple Music's Saint John '99 Recalls Formative Wes Moments in WesFest Keynote." *Wesleyan University*, 25 Apr. 2016, newsletter.blogs.wesleyan.edu/2016/04/25/bozoma. Accessed 10 Aug. 2017.

Saint John, Bozoma. "Uber's New Exec Bozoma Saint John on Sexism, Embracing Fear, and Bringing Her 'Whole Self' to Work." Interview by Amy Dubois Barnett. *Glamour*, 24 July 2017, www.glamour.com/story/bozoma-saint-john-uber-chief-brand-officer. Accessed 10 Aug. 2017.

Ugwu, Reggie. "Inside Apple Music's Second Act." *Buzzfeed News*, 26 Sept. 2016, www.buzzfeed.com/reggieugwu/inside-apple-musics-second-act. Accessed 10 Aug. 2017.

—*Molly Hagan*

Gary Sánchez

Date of birth: December 2, 1992
Occupation: Baseball player

New York Yankees catcher and designated hitter Gary Sánchez began his major league career in early August 2016, and by the end of his first month with one of baseball's most storied franchises, he had logged more home runs than any other Yankees player in history. Sánchez was born in the Dominican Republic, and moved to the United States after signing a contract with the Yankees when he was fifteen years old. One of the team's best prospects in recent memory, he grew up, often painfully, while rising through the ranks of the minor leagues. He was called up to the majors twice before his history-making debut in 2016, and as he headed into the 2017 season, he was already one of the team's most popular players. With the 2016 retirement of Alex Rodriguez, the team's most famous player at the time, the franchise hopes to capitalize on Sánchez's blockbuster potential. Filip Bondy for the *New York Times* (16 Jan. 2017) dubbed him the "face of the rebuilding Yankees." Sánchez, a strong defensive player, was noted as being notoriously inconsistent in the minor leagues. However, he is also one of only a handful of Yankees to have 11 RBIs in his first fifteen career major league games. Another player on that list is Joe DiMaggio. As a regular member of the team in 2017, Sánchez is focused more on winning than on achieving records. When asked what success looked like in the new season, Sánchez told Tyler

By Bryan from Florida [CC BY 2.0], via Wikimedia Commons

Kepner for the *New York Times* (1 Mar. 2017), "I would say winning the World Series—getting to the World Series and winning it. That would be a successful season."

EARLY LIFE

Sánchez was born on December 2, 1992, and raised in the small community of La Victoria in Santo Domingo in the Dominican Republic. His parents separated when he was young, and Sánchez, his three brothers and one sister, were raised primarily by their mother, Orquidia Herrera, a nurse, and their grandmother, Agustina Pena. Sánchez often saw his father who lived nearby. Growing up, he and his older brother Miguel, who went on to play briefly in the minor leagues for the Seattle Mariners, would spend their days looking for doll heads to use as baseballs that they would then hit with their broomstick bats. Baseball is enormously popular in the Dominican Republic, and with major league scouts working with *buscones*, or street agents, to scour the country for the next big talent, the sport is also potentially an enormously lucrative endeavor. Even amongst the competition, Sánchez stood out at an early age.

Sánchez was fourteen years old when he was first brought to the attention of major league scouts. He was fifteen when he first met Mark Newman, the former Yankees vice president of player development, at a training camp in Boca Chica. He had already won the admiration of people like Donny Rowland, the Yankee's director of international scouting, and area scouts Victor Mata and Ray Sánchez. They pushed Newman to consider signing the teen, so Newman offered Sánchez a challenge: hit home runs to right field, centerfield, and then left field. Sánchez completed the challenge in four swings. "We didn't have many other kids do that," Newman recalled to Brendan Kuty for *NJ.com* (29 Aug. 2016).

In February 2009, Yankees general manager Brian Cashman flew to the Dominican to see Sánchez for himself. Sánchez worked out for the Yankees that morning, and then he worked out for the New York Mets the same afternoon, which underscored for everyone that his talents were in demand. With Cashman on board, the Yankees offered fifteen-year-old Sánchez a contract and a $3 million bonus, which was reportedly the largest signing bonus the franchise had given an international amateur player. The team was investing in Sánchez's multifaceted potential. "He had such a good arm for a fifteen-year-old," Newman told Kuty. "He could catch the ball. He wasn't a technically solid catcher back then, but his hands were fine. His arm was a plus. The power was a plus. His bat—he had solid hitting ability."

MINOR LEAGUE CAREER

During the summer of 2010, Sánchez played in the minor leagues for the Gulf Coast Yankees and the Staten Island Yankees, a short-season minor league team in the franchise. Sánchez, who was only seventeen years old at the time, struggled to adjust to his new life. He was lonely, and despite attending the team's mandatory English classes, he had difficulty learning the language. The game of baseball was different for him too. The pitchers threw more precise pitches, and there were games almost every day. "I only have one thing on my mind," Sánchez told Kevin Flood for SILive (25 Aug. 2010) through teammate and interpreter, Luis Parache. "I want to play my best no matter what level I'm at, help my team win games, and get to the big leagues as quick as I can. From what I've seen so far, New York is a nice place to play baseball."

Sánchez impressed baseball insiders with his stellar first season in the minor leagues, hitting a combined .329 with 8 home runs and 43 RBIs in forty-seven games. *Baseball America* ranked him the number two Yankees prospect, and number thirty in the minor leagues. During his second season, however, Sánchez's troubles off the field began to spill into his performance on the field. During the summer of 2011, he was sent to the Charleston RiverDogs, a Class-A minor league team in the South Atlantic League, but he struck out more than sixty times in his first thirty-two games. His batting average was a meager .238, and he was developing a reputation for coasting on his talent without trying to work on improving, which Andrew Marchand for ESPN (7 Sept. 2016) contended, "would stick with him for years." The franchise benched him hoping to motivate him to work harder. When that proved unsuccessful, the Yankees sent him to a Tampa, Florida, training camp for two weeks.

When Sánchez returned to Charleston to finish out the season, Andrew Miller of the Charleston *Post and Courier* (17 June 2012) reported that Sánchez was a new man. "You could see the difference in him right away," RiverDogs hitting coach Greg Colbrunn explained to Miller. "Gary was much more relaxed at the plate, he was patient, and he was so much better defensively. He was a completely different guy off the field, too." Sánchez finished the season's final fifty games with 13 home runs and 31 RBIs, and he was twice named the South Atlantic League's player of the week. Sánchez returned to Charleston for the start of the 2012 season, but midseason he was promoted to the Tampa Yankees, a Class-A Advanced minor league team in the Florida League. By September, the MLB Prospect Watch ranked Sánchez the number one New York Yankees prospect and number three overall among catchers.

Sánchez began the 2013 season at Tampa where he hit .254 with 16 home runs and 61 RBIs. In August, the franchise promoted the now twenty-year-old again, this time to the Trenton Thunder, a Double-A minor league team in the Eastern League. Despite the promotion, Sánchez began to struggle once again, and he dropped in the prospect rankings but finished out the season strong with 2 home runs and 10 RBIs. He was officially added to the New York Yankee's forty-man roster at the end of the 2013 season, a move that had more to do with the complexities of MLB rules than it did Sánchez's timetable for joining the major leagues, but it emphasized the franchise's commitment to Sánchez, who began the 2014 season with the Trenton Thunder.

In June 2014, Sánchez was suspended for five games for a rule violation. Although the nature of the violation was not disclosed, the suspension appeared to be the same kind of wrist slapping that the franchise employed when Sánchez regressed. That year was a milestone in Sánchez's personal life, however, in that his wife, Sahaira, gave birth to a baby girl named Sarah. The event also served to push Sánchez to want to reach his full potential in baseball. "It is a beautiful experience to become a dad," Sánchez told Marchand. "It was very important because, when she was born, it was kind of like a new life began for me because it is a lot of responsibility, so you want to make sure that you can give it your all so you can get to the big leagues and you can stay in the big leagues and, definitely, it is a changing experience."

MAJOR LEAGUE DEBUT

Sánchez began the 2015 season with the Thunder, and in June the Yankees selected him to play in the All-Star Futures Game. The following month he was promoted to play for the Triple-A Scranton/Wilkes-Barre RailRiders in Pennsylvania. He memorably hit a home run at his first at-bat, ending the season with a .274 average, with 18 home runs in 374 at-bats. In October, he was called up to the major league as a pinch hitter, and then he was assigned to the off-season Arizona Fall League where he led the league in home runs. Although he had hoped to start the 2016 season with the Yankees, he played poorly at spring training in 2016 and was sent back to Scranton/Wilkes-Barre. He was called up to play a Yankees home game in May.

On August 3, Sánchez was called up for a third time and turned in a solid, if unimpressive, performance. He continued to play with the Yankees, and within four weeks, he had "transformed from talented prospect into a phenom," Mike Vorkunov wrote for the *New York Times* (26 Aug. 2016). Sánchez, with an astonishing .400 batting average, became the first rookie in franchise history to log 10 home runs in his first

month and the third player in major league history to hit 10 home runs in his first twenty-two games. In a September game against the Tampa Bay Rays, Sánchez hit his eighteenth and nineteenth home runs of the season, setting a major league record for the most home runs recorded in a player's first forty-five career games.

In addition to his skill as a slugger, Sánchez proved to be one of the most productive catchers in the league. He suffered a brief slump at the end of his first, record-breaking season, but in fifty-three games with the Yankees in 2016, Sánchez finished with a .299 batting average, 20 home runs and 42 RBIs. He narrowly missed being named Rookie of the Year.

SUGGESTED READING

Bondy, Filip. "Hello, Fans. We're the New Yankees. Sandwich?" *The New York Times*, 16 Jan. 2017, www.nytimes.com/2017/01/16/sports/baseball/new-york-yankees.html?_r=0. Accessed 16 Mar. 2017.

Flood, Kevin. "Staten Island Yankees' Sánchez Already Thinking Big." *SILive.com*, 25 Aug. 2010, archive.is/20130111104300/www.silive.com/siyankees/index.ssf/2010/08/staten_island_yankees_sanchez.html. Accessed 15 Mar. 2017.

Kepner, Tyler. "Gary Sánchez, Yankees' Young Slugger, Faces a Bar He Set High." *The New York Times*, 1 Mar. 2017, www.nytimes.com/2017/03/01/sports/baseball/gary-sanchez-new-york-yankees.html. Accessed 16 Mar. 2017.

Kuty, Brendan. "How a 15-Year-Old Gary Sánchez Convinced the Yankees." *NJ.com*, 29 Aug. 2016, www.nj.com/yankees/index.ssf/2016/08/how_a_15-year-old_gary_sanchez_convinced_the_yanke.html. Accessed 15 Mar. 2017.

Marchand, Andrew. "Oh, Baby! Gary Sánchez Owes August for the Ages to Hard Work, Maturity—and His Daughter, Sarah." *ESPN*, 7 Sept. 2016, www.espn.com/mlb/story/_/id/17476422/new-york-yankees-gary-sanchez-owes-august-ages-daughter-sarah. Accessed 16 Mar. 2017.

Miller, Andrew. "Charleston RiverDogs Catcher Gary Sánchez Having Breakout Season." *The Post and Courier*, 17 June 2012, www.postandcourier.com/sports/charleston-riverdogs-catcher-gary-sanchez-having-breakout-season/article_efa8e553-0bfd-559c-bf87-6060379d6285.html. Accessed 16 Mar. 2017.

Vorkunov, Mike. "As Gary Sánchez Ascends, Yankees See Their Fortunes Beginning to Rise." *The New York Times*, 26 Aug. 2016, www.nytimes.com/2016/08/27/sports/baseball/buoyed-by-youth-ny-yankees-beat-baltimore-orioles.html. Accessed 16 Mar. 2017.

—*Molly Hagan*

Kathryn Schulz

Occupation: Journalist

Kathryn Schulz has been a staff writer at the *New Yorker* since 2015. In the pages of that magazine she has written on topics as varied as death certificates, the psychology and technology of being "unseen," a philosophical analysis of "No" phrases that are used to signal agreement (such as "No, totally" and "No, definitely"), an examination of the Lewis Carroll–inspired expression "rabbit hole" and its figurative uses, the mind-expanding act of running long distances, the way novelists have used weather symbolically in their fiction, and the complex history of the Underground Railroad, which was used in the mid-nineteenth century by slaves escaping to free states.

The long-form article that got her the most public recognition and critical acclaim appeared in the July 20, 2015, issue of the *New Yorker*, titled "The Really Big One," about the real and frightening possibility of a powerful earthquake hitting the northwest coast of the United States within the next fifty years. The article went viral and received a Pulitzer Prize for feature writing and a National Magazine Award. Schulz is also the author of the book *Being Wrong: Adventures in the Margin of Error* (2010).

HOUSE OF EDUCATORS

Kathryn Schulz grew up in the small town of Shaker Heights, Ohio. Her father was a lawyer and the head of the Cleveland Bar Association; he also served on the school board. Her mother was a French teacher. Schulz has a sister, Laura Schulz, who went on to become a professor of cognitive science at the Department of Brain and Cognitive Sciences at the Massachusetts Institute of Technology (MIT) in Cambridge, Massachusetts. As Kathryn Schulz wrote in a reflective, autobiographical essay for the *New Yorker* (13 Feb. 2017), her family members are "fairly similar," but they do differ with regard to how "scatterbrained" they are. Whereas she and her mother are very organized, her sister and father are "sublimely unconcerned with the everyday physical world." Her sister loses things all the time. Her father, for example, "once spent an entire vacation wearing mismatched shoes." He only realized this when airport security asked him to take his shoes off. Schulz's mother, on the other hand, once adjusted a crooked picture at the Cleveland Museum of Art.

In the essay, which was about losing things and people, Schulz reminisced about her father, who was born in Tel Aviv, Israel, and then moved with his parents to Germany after World War II, in 1948. When her father was twelve years old, he arrived in the United States with his family as a refugee. In the United States he learned English—his sixth language, after Yiddish, Hebrew, Polish, French, and German. Her father spoke English "with Nabokovian fluency and panache," Schulz wrote, referring to Vladimir Nabokov, the Russian-born writer who is generally considered to have had a facility with the English language unusual even among native speakers. Schulz added that her father "loved to talk—I mean that he found just putting sentences together tremendously fun, although he also cherished conversation."

Schulz has said she got an "incredible education" from her parents, as well as from the schools in Shaker Heights. She specifically mentioned her writing and history teachers. The most valuable lessons, it seemed, had to do not with specific facts but an overall view of the world: her teachers taught her, she said, that the world is a "big and interesting" place, and they taught her to "ask questions about it."

While attending Shaker Heights High School, Schulz did graphic design and layouts for the high school newspaper, the *Shakerite*. However, she told Emily Bamforth for *Cleveland.com* (19 Apr. 2016), she was eventually lured in by the writing. She had been writing since elementary school, she told Bamforth, but she did not initially think journalism was going to be her actual career.

HIGHER EDUCATION AND EARLY CAREER

Schulz graduated from Shaker Heights High School in 1992 and went on to attend Brown University in Providence, Rhode Island. Though she did not study journalism at Brown or join the writing staff at the school newspaper or magazine, she did learn a lot. Speaking to Julianne Center for the *Brown Daily Herald* (26 Apr. 2016), Schulz said she got "an incredible education in critical thinking. I learned to be curious." She was open-minded and embraced new ideas and perspectives. She explained, "I had a sense that it was fine to be ignorant and go tromp into some new field, ask a lot of questions to try to teach yourself about it, and ask other people to share their knowledge with you—all of that is really core to journalism."

After graduating from Brown University in 1996, Schulz moved to Portland, Oregon, for a few years. She went on to report for the Chilean English-language newspaper *Santiago Times*. Starting in 2001 she served as the editor at the environment-focused magazine *Grist*, for which she covered such issues as the overlap of environmental conditions and the economy, as well as environmental justice issues, such as pollution, lead paint in housing, asthma rates, and contaminated water. In 2004 she received the Pew Fellowship in International Journalism.

Later she wrote for *New York* magazine, primarily reviewing books.

BEING WRONG

In 2010 Schulz saw the publication of her first book, *Being Wrong: Adventures in the Margin of Error.* The book, though hard to categorize, is a work of nonfiction that combines philosophy, psychology, sociology, neuroscience, thoughtful introspection, and fearless examination of the most basic human tendencies regarding being right—the need to be right and to avoid the feeling of being wrong. Most people would say being wrong feels bad, embarrassing, or uncomfortable. However, Schulz wrote, this feeling actually accompanies not "being wrong" itself but the realization of that fact. Being wrong without being aware of it, she said in a TED Talk (Mar. 2011), feels like "being right." Her book has many such paradoxes. For most of the book, Schulz is interested in being wrong, in human error, "as an idea and as an experience." Regarding the former, the idea, she calls that a "meta-mistake"—in other words, a mistake about the idea of erring. "We are wrong about what it means to be wrong," Schulz writes in the book. "Far from being a sign of intellectual inferiority, the capacity to err is crucial to human cognition. Far from being a moral flaw, it is inextricable from some of our most humane and honorable qualities: empathy, optimism, imagination, conviction, and courage."

Being Wrong was very well received. Schulz, a first-time book author—although by that point a respected journalist and critic—was commended for her thoughtful, interdisciplinary approach. Dwight Garner, in a review for the *New York Times* (10 June 2010), called her book a "funny and philosophical meditation on why error is mostly a humane, courageous, and extremely desirable human trait. She flies high in the intellectual skies, leaving beautiful sunlit contrails." In a review for the *Guardian* (27 Aug. 2010), Stuart Jeffries called Schulz a "forbiddingly clever and vexingly wise American journalist."

"THE REALLY BIG ONE"

Schulz became a staff writer at the *New Yorker*, one of the most prestigious and respected English-language literary magazines, in 2015. She had begun writing for the magazine as a freelancer in 2014. In the pages of the magazine, Schulz has published many engaging, thoughtful pieces, but the story that got Schulz the most public attention and critical acclaim—as well as the Pulitzer Prize for feature writing and the National Magazine Award—was about the potential for a powerful earthquake to devastate the northwest coast of the United States. This earthquake had not yet happened, but promised to be, as the name of the article suggests, "The Really Big One."

As Schulz wrote, although most Americans know of the San Andreas Fault in California, few know of the fault line called the Cascadia subduction zone, which is north of the San Andreas Fault. "The 'subduction zone' part," she wrote, "refers to a region of the planet where one tectonic plate is sliding underneath (subducting) another. Tectonic plates are those slabs of mantle and crust that, in their epochs-long drift, rearrange the earth's continents and oceans." Generally these plates move slowly and are "harmless." However, where the borders of those plates meet, the movement can cause a major earthquake. In the article, Schulz did something that is at times quite challenging for science writers: conveying complex scientific information and data in a language that is both easy for average readers to understand and also engaging enough for them to keep reading. One device she used was asking her readers to use their hands to simulate how the plates would interact. "Take your hands and hold them palms down, middle fingertips touching," Schulz wrote. "Your right hand represents the North American tectonic plate, which bears on its back, among other things, our entire continent, from One World Trade Center to the Space Needle, in Seattle. Your left hand represents an oceanic plate called Juan de Fuca, ninety thousand square miles in size. The place where they meet is the Cascadia subduction zone. Now slide your left hand under your right one. That is what the Juan de Fuca plate is doing: slipping steadily beneath North America." The potential earthquake that could result, she wrote, would have a magnitude of at least 8.0 and as much as 9.2, which she calls a "very big one."

The affected area in the Pacific Northwest would be approximately 140,000 square miles, including Portland and Seattle as well as Olympia, the capital of Washington, and Salem, the capital of Oregon. The projected human toll is grim: thirteen thousand dead, twenty-seven thousand injured, and more than two million that would need food and water. The odds of a big earthquake happening in the next fifty years, she wrote, are "roughly one in three." The odds of the "very big one" are about "one in ten." But, as Schulz immediately points out, the numbers, though indeed frightening, do not convey how unprepared the region is for even a big—let alone a very big—earthquake.

Soon after the story appeared on the *New Yorker* website (28 July 2015), it went viral. A week later Schulz wrote a short article for the website answering the most frequently asked questions from readers, such as who would be at risk from the tsunami that would result from the earthquake. One line in the story that especially aroused fear and concern was a quote from Kenneth Murphy, the regional director of the Federal Emergency Management Agency (FEMA) responsible for Cascadia. Murphy said, "Our operating assumption is that everything west of Interstate 5 will be toast." One of the questions Schulz answered in her follow-up article was whether everything west of freeway Interstate 5 really would be "toast." Schulz acknowledged that "toast" is not a "precise description." Not everyone in that area would be killed or even injured, she wrote, but the situation would be seriously chaotic: most of the ports, potable water sources, fire stations, waste-water treatment plants, airports, hospitals, railways, and schools would be destroyed. So a better analogy than "toast," she wrote, is the following: "The Cascadia earthquake is going to hit the Pacific Northwest like a rock hitting safety glass, shattering the region into thousands of tiny areas, each isolated from one another and all extremely difficult to reach."

SUGGESTED READING

Garner, Dwight. "To Err Is Human. And How! And Why." Review of *Being Wrong: Adventures in the Margin of Error*, by Kathryn Schulz, and *Wrong: Why Experts Keep Failing Us—And How to Know When Not to Trust Them*, by David H. Freedman. *The New York Times*, 10 June 2010, www.nytimes.com/2010/06/11/books/11book.html. Accessed 5 Apr. 2017.

Schulz, Kathryn. "How to Stay Safe When the Big One Comes." *The New Yorker*, 28 July 2015, www.newyorker.com/tech/elements/how-to-stay-safe-when-the-big-one-comes. Accessed 5 Apr. 2017.

Schulz, Kathryn. "In Conversation: Kathryn Schulz '96." Interview by Julianne Center. *The Brown Daily Herald*, 26 Apr. 2016, www.browndailyherald.com/2016/04/26/in-conversation-kathryn-schulz-96. Accessed 5 Apr. 2017.

Schulz, Kathryn. "When Things Go Missing." *The New Yorker*, 13 Feb. 2017, www.newyorker.com/magazine/2017/02/13/when-things-go-missing. Accessed 5 Apr. 2017.

—*Dmitry Kiper*

Michael Schur

Date of birth: October 29, 1975
Occupation: Writer; producer

"Someone once asked Joe DiMaggio why he played so hard every day," television creator Michael Schur told Anthony D'Alessandro for *Deadline* (2 June 2014). "His answer was,

Photo by Alberto E. Rodriguez/WireImage

'Because you never know when there's someone in the crowd who hasn't seen me play.' That's how I feel about TV: You don't know when one person will see your show for the first time." For viewers of American television comedies in the first decades of the twenty-first century, there have been numerous opportunities to see one of Schur's shows for the first time. Since 2009, shows created or cocreated by Schur have aired on networks such as NBC and Fox as well as in syndication, introducing audiences to the comedic sides of areas as disparate as town government, policing, and the afterlife.

A writer, producer, and showrunner, Schur began his career in the *Saturday Night Live* writers' room before joining the American remake of *The Office* as a writer, producer, and occasional reluctant actor. In 2009, he joined veteran showrunner Greg Daniels to create the sitcom *Parks and Recreation*, a critically acclaimed series following the titular department of the government of a fictional Indiana town. Schur went on to partner with writer and producer Daniel Goor to create the police comedy *Brooklyn Nine-Nine* before embarking on his first solo project, the series *The Good Place*, in 2016. Although often challenging, the process of running his own shows appeals to Schur like nothing else. "It's a very rare thing that you get to do, especially running a show that actually sticks around," he told Greg Rosenstein for the *Hartford Courant* (31 July 2014). "I really wouldn't want any other job."

EARLY LIFE AND EDUCATION

Michael Herbert Schur was born on October 29, 1975, in Ann Arbor, Michigan. His parents, Anne and Warren, moved the family to Connecticut when Schur was still a young child and later spent a year in Wellesley, Massachusetts. Schur grew up primarily in West Hartford, Connecticut, where he attended William H. Hall High School. Schur participated in the school's drama program and later became president of the drama club, and he also played junior varsity baseball. He graduated from Hall High School in 1993.

Schur was drawn to comedy at a young age and as a teenager enjoyed creating comedy shorts that were broadcast on the local community television station. Although he gained acting experience at school and through his independent projects, he soon found that he preferred writing for actors over being one. "I felt like I knew exactly how the words should sound coming out of my mouth, and I just couldn't make it sound that way. It used to really frustrate me," he recalled to Rosenstein. "Then one day, I was like, 'Oh, I don't have to say them. I can be the person who writes them and have better people say them. Then everybody wins.'"

After graduating from high school, Schur enrolled in Harvard University. As a freshman, he joined the staff of the *Harvard Lampoon*, a humor magazine published by undergraduates since the nineteenth century. Many of the publication's alumni have gone on to succeed as comedians and comedy writers, and Schur described the *Lampoon* to Rosenstein as "a natural sort of feeder into TV comedy writing." Schur later became president of the *Lampoon*. He earned his bachelor's degree from Harvard in 1997.

EARLY CAREER

After graduating from Harvard, Schur moved to New York, where he attempted to settle on a career path. "I didn't know what I wanted to do when I grew up," he told Rosenstein. "I gave myself about a year to see if I could make it as a TV comedy writer." Shortly after entering the workforce, he briefly worked for comedian Jon Stewart, pitching ideas for the book Stewart was writing at the time. When friends who worked for the television sketch comedy institution *Saturday Night Live* encouraged Schur to apply for a job in the show's writers' room, he took their advice and applied. Although he was not initially offered a job, he was hired on not long afterward and joined the writing staff at the weekly live sketch show.

Over the next several years, Schur moved up in the ranks at *Saturday Night Live*, eventually becoming a producer for the show's Weekend Update segment, then hosted by Tina Fey and Jimmy Fallon. A notoriously high-pressure comedy environment, *Saturday Night Live* proved to be an educational—if challenging—workplace for Schur. "It's a very special place. It's very difficult, it's very Darwinian, it's very trial-by-fire," he explained to Rosenstein. "If you can survive the initial wave of crushing anxiety and misery that awaits you there, it can be super, super fun."

In 2004, Schur decided to leave *Saturday Night Live* and pursue new opportunities in Los Angeles, California. He first found work as a writer and producer for the short-lived comedy *The Comeback*, an HBO series about a has-been actor, played by Lisa Kudrow, as she attempts to regain her relevance. The show was cancelled after one season in 2005, although it would later return for a second season in 2014, without Schur's involvement. While working on *The Comeback*, Schur also gained the attention of established television creator Greg Daniels, who was working with British comedians Ricky Gervais and Stephen Merchant to develop *The Office*, the American remake of Gervais and Merchant's mockumentary series of the same name. Daniels hired Schur as a writer and producer on the show, roles he filled for the next several years. Schur also played the character of Mose—the beet-farming cousin of character Dwight Schrute (Rainn Wilson)—in thirteen episodes over the series' nine-season run.

PARKS AND RECREATION

In 2009, Schur and Daniels partnered to create a new series, the comedy *Parks and Recreation*. Although initially planned to be a spin-off of *The Office*, the show, which featured a similar mockumentary style, ultimately developed its own universe and distinctive viewpoint. Set in the fictional town of Pawnee, Indiana, the show follows town employee Leslie Knope (former *Saturday Night Live* cast member Amy Poehler) as she attempts to improve her town and the lives of those in it. The show premiered on NBC in April 2009.

Following the release of its six-episode first season, *Parks and Recreation* met with largely negative reviews, with many critics characterizing it as a lackluster knockoff of *The Office*. The following season, however, fared much better with critics, an improvement that Schur has credited in part to the show's writers' increasing understanding of the characters. "We got some feedback that Leslie came across as 'ditzy' sometimes," he told Alan Sepinwall for the *Star-Ledger* (17 Sept. 2009) prior to start of the second season. "That surprised us, because we didn't intend that at all. I think what the writers intended as 'takes her job too seriously' read to some people as 'oblivious.' So we corrected a little for that this year in the scripts." Over the course of seven seasons, *Parks and Recreation* gained an enthusiastic fan base of viewers who appreciated the show's characters, humor, and optimism. *Parks and Recreation* was nominated for numerous awards during its run, including an Emmy Award for outstanding comedy series.

BROOKLYN NINE-NINE

Schur's next series was created in collaboration with Daniel Goor, a friend from Harvard who had previously worked with Schur on *Parks and Recreation*. The pair set out to create a comedy set in a police station, building on a longstanding trend of television shows centered on law enforcement. "The last fifteen years of American television have been strewn with hour-long cop dramas—there have been, like, twelve *Law & Order*s and fourteen *CSI*s, all the way back to *NYPD Blue*," Schur told Stephanie Palumbo for the *Believer* (Fall 2015). "But the way a police precinct functions hasn't really been used recently for comedy instead of drama. Setting that tone is hard—those shows are dramas because the stories tend to be horrifying." With *Brooklyn Nine-Nine*, Schur and Goor sought to present a show that incorporated aspects of realistic police work while falling solidly within the comedy genre.

Set in the New York borough of Brooklyn's ninety-ninth precinct, *Brooklyn Nine-Nine* stars former *Saturday Night Live* cast member Andy Samberg as detective Jake Peralta, Andre Braugher as precinct captain Ray Holt, and a host of other talented comedic actors as their law enforcement colleagues. Following its premiere on Fox in September 2013, *Brooklyn Nine-Nine* was received well by critics and viewers, and it won the 2014 Golden Globe Award for best comedy series for its first season. *Brooklyn Nine-Nine*'s fifth season began airing in September 2017.

THE GOOD PLACE

For his next project, Schur sought to explore a new direction, creating a comedy that dealt with more philosophical ideas. "I've wanted to write about what it means to be either a good person or a bad person. And I think I wanted to do that because I didn't think I knew. And I still don't know," he told P. Claire Dodson for *Esquire* (19 Sept. 2016). "I wanted to poke around and see what it means to be good or bad."

The resulting television show, *The Good Place*, premiered on NBC in September 2016 and follows a woman named Eleanor Shellstrop who, after dying in an accident, finds herself in the titular afterlife realm. Upon realizing that she was sent to the Good Place by mistake, she attempts to conceal her previous questionable behavior so that she can remain in that realm, which she eventually learns may not be what it seems. The first season of *The Good Place* received overwhelmingly positive reviews, and a second season began to air in late 2017.

OTHER WORK

In addition to his work on shows such as *Parks and Recreation*, *Brooklyn Nine-Nine*, and *The Good Place*, Schur has contributed to a variety of additional projects as a writer or producer, including the science-fiction anthology series *Black Mirror*, the 2009 film *Brief Interviews with Hideous Men*, and the Netflix television series *Master of None*. A longtime fan of the 1996 David Foster Wallace novel *Infinite Jest*, Schur holds the film rights to the novel and hopes to adapt it eventually, although he has noted that such an undertaking will be a monumental one. "The challenges of adapting it are numerous, and although much of the book is very filmic, certain aspects, like the footnotes—and, more specifically, the effect the footnotes have on the reader as part of the experience of reading the book—are not, really," he explained to Palumbo. Also a lover of baseball, Schur at times writes about sports under the name Ken Tremendous and previously ran the sports blog *Fire Joe Morgan* with fellow television writers Alan Yang and Dave King.

PERSONAL LIFE

Schur met his wife, Jennifer "J. J." Philbin, while they were both working at *Saturday Night Live*. Philbin is a television writer and producer and is also the daughter of well-known television host Regis Philbin. Schur and Philbin have two children, William and Ivy. They live in Los Angeles.

SUGGESTED READING

Martin, Denise. "Making Bureaucracy Work: How NBC's 'Parks and Recreation' Overcame Bad Buzz." *Los Angeles Times*, 18 Nov. 2009, latimesblogs.latimes.com/showtracker/2009/11/parks-and-recreation.html. Accessed 8 Sept. 2017.

Schur, Michael. "Emmy's Q&A: 'Brooklyn Nine-Nine' Co-Creator Michael Schur on Comedic Cops." Interview by Anthony D'Alessandro. *Deadline*, 2 June 2014, deadline.com/2014/06/brooklyn-nine-nine-michael-schur-creator-interview-739199/. Accessed 8 Sept. 2017.

Schur, Michael. "*The Good Place* Creator Michael Schur Has an Idea of Who's Going to Make It to Heaven." Interview by P. Claire Dodson. *Esquire*, 19 Sept. 2016, www.esquire.com/entertainment/tv/q-and-a/a48706/the-good-place-michael-schur-interview/. Accessed 8 Sept. 2017.

Schur, Michael. "'Good Place' Creator Michael Schur Talks Trump, Ron Swanson, and Comedy vs. Politics." Interview by Maureen Ryan. *Variety*, 3 Aug. 2016, variety.com/2016/tv/

features/michael-schur-the-good-place-parks-and-recreation-trump-comedy-ron-swanson-1201829738/. Accessed 8 Sept. 2017.

Schur, Michael. Interview. By Stephanie Palumbo. *Believer*, Fall 2015, www.believermag.com/issues/201511/?read=interview_schur. Accessed 8 Sept. 2017.

Schur, Michael. "*Parks and Rec* Creator Remembers Childhood in West Hartford." Interview by Greg Rosenstein. *Hartford Courant*, 31 July 2014, www.courant.com/hartford-magazine/people/hc-hm-interview-august-20140731-story.html. Accessed 8 Sept. 2017.

Schur, Michael. "*Parks and Recreation*: Interviewing Co-Creator Mike Schur." Interview by Alan Sepinwall. *The Star-Ledger*, 17 Sept. 2009, www.nj.com/entertainment/tv/index.ssf/2009/09/parks_and_recreation_interview.html. Accessed 8 Sept. 2017.

SELECTED WORKS

Saturday Night Live, 1997–2004; *The Comeback*, 2005; *The Office*, 2005–8; *Parks and Recreation*, 2009–15; *Brooklyn Nine-Nine*, 2013– ; *The Good Place*, 2016–

—*Joy Crelin*

Walter McBride/WireImage/Getty Images

Alex Sharp

Date of birth: February 2, 1989
Occupation: Actor

To say that Alex Sharp's story is unlikely may be an understatement. After being homeschooled and on the road with his parents in England until the age of seven, he started acting and fell in love with the art, only to have his dreams crushed after secondary school, when every great British drama school he applied to rejected him. He then came to the United States; did some traveling and manual labor; got into Juilliard, one of the top drama schools in the country; and then auditioned for a Broadway play. Even though it was his first ever audition for the New York stage, Sharp got the role: the lead in the play *The Curious Incident of the Dog in the Night-Time*, for which he received a great deal of critical praise and won several awards, most notably the 2015 Tony Award for best actor in a leading role in a play. After leaving the show, Sharp landed roles in two movies scheduled for release in 2017.

ON THE ROAD

Alex Sharp was born on February 2, 1989, in London, England. Until he was about seven years old, Sharp and his family traveled around a lot. His mother was a teacher and his father, after having done well in real estate, retired at the age of thirty-five. During this time of frequent travel, he was homeschooled by his mother, who had a rather unorthodox approach to education. As Rebecca Keegan wrote in a profile for the *Los Angeles Times* (4 Oct. 2014), Sharp's mother would come up with multidimensional approaches to learning: for example, not only would she have her son read about a castle, he would also go to the castle itself to explore it and then write a story about the castle. Recalling that time, Sharp told Ronni Reich for *NJ.com* (14 Sept. 2014), "It was such a wild and free experience." When the family stopped moving and Sharp began attending a regular school, he found it very challenging to sit still and relate to the lessons; it was hard for him to pay attention to material he had no interest in. "I don't think I ever adjusted to sitting behind a desk and being told hour by hour what you have to learn," he told Reich.

In retrospect, however, there was at least one positive—and life-changing—side effect to attending a regular school: Sharp began acting, and he quickly realized how much he loved the experience. His first stage role, when he was seven years old, was as Piglet in a stage version of *Winnie the Pooh* at a school in Devon, England. And that was it: he was bitten by the acting bug, in part because it suited his personality, even as a young boy. "I was really interested in observing people," Sharp told Tim Teeman for the *Daily Beast* (7 Dec. 2014). "From a young age, I wouldn't listen to what an adult was saying—I was obsessed with other people's body language. I took in their gestures, facial expressions, I'd listen to the rhythm, intonations, and melody of their voice." Sharp went on to perform in regional theater in the area, such as the Octagon Theatre in Yeovil and the Northcott Theater in Exeter. At the Northcott Theater, according to Teeman, Sharp was encouraged by the head of youth theater, Rachel Vowles, "to be free on stage, to never play it safe." Vowles elaborated, adding that a truly "transcendent" performance can only happen when an actor puts everything on the line and risks "looking like an absolute fool."

As a teenager, Sharp applied to all the major drama schools in the United Kingdom. To his great disappointment, he received only rejections. So after finishing secondary school, Sharp stayed in Devon, with no career prospects or life plan, working at a deli. "I was so incredibly depressed but had this unbelievable high amount of energy," he told Keegan. "I was very frustrated and kind of trapped."

Sharp then decided to leave England and travel. He came to the United States and, with a friend, began buying cheap homes and renovating them and then selling them right after for a quick profit, a practice known as "flipping houses." In addition to that he did handyman work, everything from painting to repairs. During this time, he also traveled in South America, where he climbed mountains and hitchhiked, among other adventurous activities. Much like his parents, he enjoyed being on the move. But Sharp still had not given up on his dream of studying acting. When he asked around about the top acting schools in the United States, he was told the best schools were the Yale School of Drama in New Haven, Connecticut, and Juilliard in New York City. Sharp wanted to be in New York, so the decision to apply to Juilliard was an easy one. In his audition for Juilliard he did a scene from Hamlet and another from a play he wrote himself, which he claimed was written by an unknown English playwright, as Juilliard does not allow prospective students to write their own material for auditions. He got in.

JUILLIARD DRAMA
Sharp studied at Juilliard in the drama division (the school also has dance and music divisions), where he encountered stricter discipline and structure than he ever had before. The Juilliard approach to teaching drama, according to its official website, "combines vocal and physical training, extensive work on the written word, and appreciation of style with a fierce commitment to emotional honesty, immense physical energy, and imaginative daring." On several occasions Sharp wanted to quit, but he stayed in the program because he knew it was essential for his development as an actor. In fact, the list of respected actors who graduated from the drama division is very diverse and extensive, including Jessica Chastain, Ving Rhames, Oscar Isaac, Kelsey Grammer, Kevin Spacey, Viola Davis, Robin Williams, and many more. During his time at Juilliard, Sharp not only acted but also directed; for example, he directed a stage adaptation of the Anthony Burgess novel *A Clockwork Orange* (1962).

Around this time Sharp, on the advice of a staff member at Juilliard, auditioned for a Broadway play, *The Curious Incident of the Dog in the Night-Time.* Sharp knew it would be a challenge, not only because it was his first audition for a play in New York, but also because the play is about an autistic boy who, for all his intelligence, has trouble communicating and understanding various emotions. Yet Sharp, as he told Teeman, had never wanted a role as badly as this one in his life. When he was younger, he had read the Mark Haddon novel of the same name, on which the play is based. He was intrigued by the question of how the director would create on the stage the intricate world that exists in the novel. The director, Marianne Elliott, had reservations of her own—but was still won over by Sharp's audition. "Yes, I had trepidations about casting a newcomer," Elliott told Keegan. "He's never off the stage and drives every scene. However, I was seduced by his youth and vulnerability. He has a lovely clarity about him—you can read what he's thinking and feeling." Sharp got the part. After graduating from Juilliard, in the spring of 2014, he would go on, only a few months later, to play the lead role in a major and highly anticipated Broadway production.

THE CURIOUS INCIDENT OF THE DOG IN THE NIGHT-TIME
The Curious Incident of the Dog in the Night-Time opened on Broadway in October 2014, with Sharp playing the central character, Christopher Boone. Christopher is a fifteen-year-old boy who attends a special school and lives with his father near London. On the one hand, he can be especially sensitive to noise or being touched, and he has trouble communicating—at one point he says, "I find people confusing"—but on the other hand, he is exceptionally gifted when it comes to math. His whole way of seeing and understanding the world is filtered through mathematics: numbers are his language. Christopher is very comfortable in this highly abstract world, though he has trouble living in this world, which is full of people. The show's plot turns when Christopher finds out that Wellington, his neighbor's dog, has been killed—though Christopher insists the dog was "murdered." For him the logic is clear: whoever murdered the dog must be punished, but he first needs to solve the mystery of who did it. In the play's second act, Christopher goes to London and continues his investigation.

The city, understandably, is overwhelming—the sounds and lights and massive amount of people incessantly moving from place to place. He travels with a pet rat, which he brought with him to London to keep him company.

"The boy is never more endearing than when he's applying his mathematically logical mind to a problem, like analyzing the kind of person who might kill a dog, or explaining to the vicar why there is no heaven and no God," wrote Marilyn Stasio in a review of the play for *Variety* (5 Oct. 2014). "Young Sharp is quite wonderful at such moments, his face so open and receptive to thought." Stasio was only one of many critics to praise Sharp's performance as engaging, emotionally open, and sensitive. In a review for *The Guardian* (6 Oct. 2014), Alexis Soloski called Sharp's performance "marvelous," adding that the way he played Christopher is "studied—the blinking, the shifting, the chin held too low or too high so as to avoid eye contact—but also emotionally resonant." For his performance Sharp received a great deal of recognition and several awards in 2015, including the Theatre World Award, the Drama Desk Award for outstanding actor in a play, and most notably, the Tony Award for best performance by an actor in a leading role in a play.

Sharp left the cast of *The Curious Incident of the Dog in the Night-Time* in September 2015. Shortly afterward, he was cast in a leading role opposite Elle Fanning in the science-fiction romantic comedy film *How to Talk to Girls at Parties*, adapted from a short story by award-winning speculative fiction author Neil Gaiman and directed by John Cameron Mitchell. The movie began filming in November 2015 and was scheduled to be released in 2017. In April 2016 Sharp was cast in *To the Bone* (2017), a dark comedy film about a girl struggling with anorexia, directed by Marti Noxon.

PERSONAL LIFE

Sharp lives in New York when not filming. As of 2015, he was dating Wallis Currie-Wood, whom he met at Juilliard. Currie-Wood is also an actor, best known for her role as the protagonist's daughter in the television show *Madam Secretary*.

SUGGESTED READING

Clark, Nick. "Tony Awards 2015: Best Actor Winner Alex Sharp Was Rejected by the UK's 'Good Drama Schools.'" *Independent*, 8 June 2015, www.independent.co.uk/arts-entertainment/theatre-dance/news/tony-awards-2015-best-actor-winner-alex-sharp-was-rejected-by-the-uks-good-drama-schools-10306244.html. Accessed 20 Dec. 2016.

Keegan, Rebecca. "Actor Alexander Sharp's Curious Beginning to a Promising Career." *Los Angeles Times*, 4 Oct. 2014, www.latimes.com/entertainment/arts/theater/la-et-cm-ca-curious-incident-20141005-story.html. Accessed 20 Dec. 2016.

Reich, Ronni. "Alexander Sharp Makes His Broadway Debut in 'Curious Incident.'" *NJ.com*, 14 Sept. 2014, www.nj.com/entertainment/index.ssf/2014/09/alexander_sharp_makes_his_broadway_debut_in_curious_incident.html. Accessed 20 Dec. 2016.

Soloski, Alexis. Review of *The Curious Incident of the Dog in the Night-Time*, dir. Marianne Elliott. *The Guardian*, 6 Oct. 2014, www.theguardian.com/stage/2014/oct/06/the-curious-incident-of-the-dog-in-the-night-time-review-broadway.

Stasio, Marilyn. Review of *The Curious Incident of the Dog in the Night-Time*, dir. Marianne Elliott. *Variety*, 5 Oct. 2014, variety.com/2014/legit/reviews/broadway-review-curious-incident-dog-night-time-1201321871. Accessed 20 Dec. 2016.

Teeman, Tim. "The Brit Who Stormed Broadway." *The Daily Beast*, 7 Dec. 2014, www.thedailybeast.com/articles/2014/12/07/the-brit-who-stormed-broadway.html. Accessed 20 Dec. 2016.

—*Dmitry Kiper*

Blake Shelton

Date of birth: June 18, 1976
Occupation: Singer

Blake Shelton is perhaps best known as one of the celebrity judges on *The Voice*, the hit reality game show in which novice singers compete against one another for a shot at a recording contract and superstardom. But his longtime fans know him as something far more than that: a megastar who racked up more than twenty number-one country hits after his debut single in 2001. He is one of the most popular country artists on the planet, having sold more than 10 million albums and 30 million singles and generated 1.7 billion streams worldwide. Moreover, owing to his widespread appeal and high profile as a judge on *The Voice*, he is widely credited with helping to bring country music to a wider audience.

In the *New York Times* (7 July 2011), Jon Caramanica noted Shelton's appeal: "He's one of the most affable celebrities in Nashville and one of the most unpredictable, cheekier than all his male counterparts put together. Handsome and 6-foot-5, he's one of the highest-profile

By Department of Defense Warrior Games via Wikimedia Commons

country stars to appear regularly in prime time since the days Buck Owens hosted 'Hee Haw.'" Indeed, his fame has at times outstripped his music, as his personal life, including high-profile relationships with fellow musicians Miranda Lambert and Gwen Stefani, often drew heavy media attention.

EARLY LIFE

Blake Tollison Shelton was born in Ada, Oklahoma, on June 18, 1976. His father, Richard, was a used-car salesman; his mother, Dorothy, was the owner of a beauty salon. The youngest of three children, he had an older brother and a sister. His brother, Richie, died in a car accident when Blake was just fourteen.

Shelton came to love country music at a very early age and quickly learned to play guitar. As a teenager, he began performing in local bars, often performing his own songs. Success came early, too: he won the Denbo Diamond Award, which is given to up-and-coming Oklahoma entertainers.

Just two weeks after graduating from high school in 1994, Shelton traveled to Nashville, Tennessee, hoping to make a name for himself at the epicenter of country music. He got by the next few years in Nashville by doing odd jobs as a mover or a painter while attempting to break into the music scene. He was also able to earn some money as a staff songwriter at a music production company and by occasionally singing a demo for established recording artists.

CAREER IN COUNTRY

Shelton's big break came through a songwriter he knew, who put him in contact with the famed songwriter and producer Bobby Braddock. Braddock had written a great number of country hits, including George Jones's "He Stopped Loving Her Today" and Tammy Wynette's "D-I-V-O-R-C-E," and he saw great potential in Shelton. Braddock's latest piece, "Same Old Song," was looked on as another potential hit by many country stars, but the writer refused to let anyone record it until a label agreed to pick up the new young recording artist he had discovered. In 1998, Giant Records agreed to take Shelton on, and he and Braddock worked together on material.

Despite giving Shelton a contract, Giant did not immediately release his work. It was not until 2001 that the company finally released his first single, "Austin"; the label went bankrupt soon after. Warner Bros. brought Shelton aboard after buying Giant, and the move buoyed his debut single, boosting it to the top of the country charts for five weeks. He followed it with his first album, the self-titled *Blake Shelton* (2001), which went on to reach number three on the country charts and be certified platinum. His second record, *The Dreamer* (2003), did not do as well, achieving only gold status, but did have a number one single, "The Baby."

Shelton followed these albums with *Blake Shelton's Barn & Grill* (2004) and *Pure BS* (2007), both of which generated a number of hit singles and were certified gold, but neither of which proved to be blockbusters. In 2008, his fifth album, *Startin' Fires*, proved to be something of a flop despite two hit singles. At this point, fearing that his career might be over, Shelton began to transition out of his emotive style of singing and into a more rhythmic style, prompted by new producer Scott Hendricks. He also began to style himself differently: the mullet he had defiantly sported was cut, and his cowboy attire was toned down in favor of dark suits with vests.

Yet the diversity of Shelton's music remained. In his songs he often took on a variety of personas: lover, son, wisecracking drunk, prisoner, scoundrel. His first greatest hits collection, *Loaded: The Best of Blake Shelton* (2010), highlighted his multifaceted image and went platinum. "If there's anything that I hope that I have contributed to country music, it's probably not going to be song of the year, or to sing some amazing note people will talk about forever," Shelton told Caramanica. "I hope that people learn from me, it's O.K. to be yourself. It's O.K. to offend somebody, and as a matter of fact, please be polarizing. If you're not polarizing, you failed in my opinion. If you don't stand for something, how can anyone respect what you do?"

CROSSING OVER WITH *THE VOICE*

Despite consistent success on the country music charts, Shelton arguably was not a true superstar until 2011. And ultimately, his breakthrough to real mainstream success was due less to his musicianship than to his personality. Though a strong singer and a talented, if sometimes controversial, songwriter, most critics agreed his charm was his best celebrity asset. "I tell him he's the Dean Martin of our generation—a handsome devil who comes across as lackadaisical even though he's extremely driven," Warner executive John Esposito told Rob Tannenbaum for *Billboard* (28 July 2016). "His wit and charm translate to the music—you can see the twinkle in his eye, and you get sucked in."

In 2011, Shelton put out *Red River Blue*, which was his first album to top both the Billboard 200 and the country charts. It also spawned four platinum hit singles: "Honey Bee," "God Gave Me You," "Drink on It," and "Over." But what made Shelton a household name across the United States was taking a role as one of the four celebrity judges for *The Voice*, a reality television game show in which unknown singers compete against each other to win a cash prize and a record deal. The celebrity judges, all musicians, also act as mentors to teams of competitors, vying against the other coaches to produce the winning contestant. The show was an instant success and catapulted Shelton to new fame as its representative of country music. Though he had previously appeared as a judge on the reality series *Nashville Star* and *Clash of the Choirs* in 2007, never before had he had such broad national exposure.

On the initial season of *The Voice*, Shelton competed for emerging talent against fellow judges Christina Aguilera, Cee Lo Green, and Adam Levine. Stars of pop, hip-hop, and rock, respectively, all three entered the show with arguably higher profiles than Shelton, who was virtually unknown outside the country scene despite his longstanding success. Despite this imbalance, Shelton quickly became one of the most popular parts of the show, with fans enjoying his often-witty banter with Levine and his general demeanor. Caramanica noted that the country singer "emerged as the spiritual conscience of 'The Voice,' an earnest and warm coach with a naughty streak. That the breakout star of the show wouldn't be one of the contestants but instead one of the coaches, and the country one at that, was an unanticipated outcome." Although the show's coaches would vary over future seasons, Shelton remained a stable and popular presence.

COUNTRY SUPERSTAR

While not working on *The Voice*, Shelton continued to record and promote his albums, which included *Cheers, It's Christmas* (2012), a collection of holiday songs; *Based on a True Story . . .* (2013); and *Bringing Back the Sunshine* (2014). Between his established fan base and the new attention from his national television presence, his records were consistently successful, making him one of country's bona fide superstars. For example, *Based on a True Story . . .* sold more than 1.4 million copies and included the smash hits, "Sure Be Cool If You Did," "Boys Round Here," "Mine Would Be You," "Doin' What She Likes," and "My Eyes." *Bringing Back the Sunshine* shot to the top of the Billboard Top 200 charts the week it was released and produced hits like "Neon Light," "Lonely Tonight," and "Sangria." In 2015 he released his second greatest hits album, *Reloaded: 20 #1 Hits*, which also included a new single, "Gonna."

Shelton's next studio album was *If I'm Honest*, released in 2016. The record, deemed by critics more personal than any of his earlier efforts, tracked the decline of his marriage to fellow country artist Miranda Lambert and the beginning of a new relationship with singer Gwen Stefani. Shelton recalled in an interview with Patrick Doyle for *Rolling Stone* (1 June 2016), "When I started going through what I went through last year, the last thing on my mind was making a record. I was trying to figure out how I was going to piece my life back together. And I figured out making this record helped me get that out of my system." The album debuted at the top of the country charts and at number three on the Top 200. It produced several hit singles, including "Came Here to Forget," "Savior's Shadow," "She's Got a Way with Words," "A Guy with a Girl," and "Every Time I Hear That Song."

PERSONAL LIFE

Shelton was married to Kaynette Gern from 2003 to 2006. He then married Lambert, whom he had dated for several years, in 2011. They were widely seen as darlings of the country world, a powerhouse couple who often made the covers of national magazines. In July 2015, the couple announced they were divorcing, shocking many of their fans and drawing intense tabloid coverage. Several months later, Shelton announced that he was dating Stefani, who had been a fellow coach on *The Voice* for several seasons and had recently gone through a divorce of her own. Shelton remarked to Cindy Watts for the *Tennessean* (18 May 2016), "The fact that we were able to be there for each other and relate to each other in that way like nobody else on earth . . . There's so much out there that is crazy, to have a shoulder and somebody that can be there for you and relate and understand, it literally saved my life."

Shelton lives in his native Oklahoma when not touring or filming *The Voice*. He is known for a lifestyle that lives up to his country lyrics, as he told Doyle: "Unless it's raining, I'm hunting or fishing or farming."

SUGGESTED READING

Caramanica, Jon. "Country Boy for the Whole Country." *The New York Times*, 7 July 2011, www.nytimes.com/2011/07/10/arts/music/blake-shelton-the-voice-coach-makes-good-countrywide.html. Accessed 1 Aug. 2017.

Erlewine, Stephen Thomas. "Blake Shelton: Artist Biography." *AllMusic*, www.allmusic.com/artist/blake-shelton-mn0000046814/biography. Accessed 1 Aug. 2017.

Shelton, Blake. "Blake Shelton on Gwen, Twitter, Mistakes and Tabloid Trouble." Interview by Patrick Doyle. *Rolling Stone*, 1 June 2016, www.rollingstone.com/music/features/blake-shelton-on-gwen-twitter-mistakes-and-tabloid-trouble-20160601. Accessed 1 Aug. 2017.

Tannenbaum, Rob. "Blake Shelton on Heartache, Falling in Love Again and Starting Over after Being in the 'Middle of Hell.'" *Billboard*, 28 July 2016, www.billboard.com/articles/news/7453469/blake-shelton-billboard-cover-divorce-miranda-lambert-gwen-stefani-relationship-the-voice-if-im-honest-album. Accessed 1 Aug. 2017.

Watts, Cindy. "Blake Shelton Finds Grace in God, Gwen Stefani." *Tennessean*, 18 May 2016, www.tennessean.com/story/entertainment/music/2016/05/18/blake-shelton-finds-grace-god-gwen-stefani/84508738/. Accessed 1 Aug. 2017.

SELECTED WORKS

Blake Shelton, 2001; *The Dreamer*, 2003; *Blake Shelton's Barn & Grill*, 2004; *Pure BS*, 2007; *Startin' Fires*, 2008; *Red River Blue*, 2011; *Cheers, It's Christmas*, 2012; *Based on a True Story . . .*, 2013; *Bringing Back the Sunshine*, 2014; *If I'm Honest*, 2016

—Christopher Mari

Taylor Sheridan

Date of birth: May 21, 1970
Occupation: Actor, screenwriter, director

Taylor Sheridan was getting by as an actor. He was not famous by any means, but by 2008, he had landed a steady role on the popular and acclaimed FX series *Sons of Anarchy*. When it came to renegotiating his contract for his part, however, it was made clear to him that he was not quite as valuable as he had hoped he would be. So, in 2011, he put acting behind him—permanently.

Photo by Amanda Edwards/WireImage

At the same time, he wanted to take one more shot at making a name for himself in the film industry by penning the kinds of screenplays he had always wished had come his way. The result: three critically acclaimed suspense-thrillers— *Sicario* (2015), *Hell or High Water* (2016), and *Wind River* (2017)—that made him one of the most highly sought-after screenwriters in Hollywood as of late 2017. With a 2017 Academy Award nomination for best original screenplay for *Hell or High Water* under his belt, he even took a shot at doing double duty as director of *Wind River*, about the murder of a young girl on an American Indian reservation.

Sheridan explained to David Marchese for *Vulture* (26 July 2017) how his three screenplays form a sort of trilogy: "They're a thematic trilogy. Each is exploring the modern American frontier and how it's changed since being settled—how much do the consequences of actions taken 130 years ago reverberate today? So that's the landscape of the films, but you can't make a movie about a landscape. The true theme of the trilogy is failed fathers—how they failed and how they overcame that failure. Then I wrap that into a suspense-thriller package."

That said, Sheridan is not much of a fan of overtly didactic films and would never put any of his films in that category. "I don't like being lectured to when I go to the movies, and I don't imagine other people do either. I'm here to entertain. I like playing against expectations. And if you can tell my political affiliations by watching one of my movies, then I've failed," he told David Fear in an interview for *Rolling Stone* (11 Aug.

2017). "But . . . I want people leaving the theater with something to think—and think hard—about. My job is not to give you all the answers. My job is to ask the questions."

EARLY LIFE AND ACTING CAREER

Taylor Sheridan was born on May 21, 1970 and was raised near the small town of Cranfills Gap, Texas. He and his family lived on a ranch, but following his parents' divorce, the property was lost during the economic recession of the early 1990s. Growing up, he was also exposed to the types of films that would inspire him in his later years as a writer as he watched select Westerns several times on the few channels available on the family television. After attending Paschal High School, he enrolled at what is now Texas State University for a time but dropped out after failing a number of classes. He then found himself living in Austin, and it was there that he met a talent agent who set him up with an audition in Chicago. "I figured I might as well take the free trip," he recalled to Brooks Barnes in an interview for the *New York Times* (9 Feb. 2017).

After this opportunity secured him his first acting gigs and he moved to New York to continue appearing in several commercials, Sheridan relocated to Los Angeles and soon found himself getting small roles on television, including shows such as *Walker, Texas Ranger* (1995) and the made-for-television film *Her Costly Affair* (1996). He would continue to get bit parts through the 1990s and early 2000s, primarily on television series such as *VIP* (2001), *Strong Medicine* (2002), *The Guardian* (2003), *Star Trek: Enterprise* (2004), *NYPD Blue* (2004), *CSI: NY* (2005), *CSI: Crime Scene Investigation* (2005), and *Veronica Mars* (2005–7). The work was steady but not entirely fulfilling and gave him little expectation of ever becoming a star. He recalled in an interview with Michael O'Sullivan for the *Washington Post* (11 Aug. 2016), "You only have to look at my résumé to know that I wasn't doing groundbreaking work as an actor. I paid the bills. I worked on largely procedural network shows, and then I did some really small, really bad movies, and auditioned for thousands more."

Sheridan's highest-profile role as an actor came as Deputy Chief David Hale on FX's drama *Sons of Anarchy* (2008–10), about an outlaw motorcycle club in the fictional town of Charming, California. When it came time to renegotiate his contract, however, it became clear to him that it might be time to make a career change. He told O'Sullivan, "I made a very conscious decision to quit acting. I was on a series and we were in the process of renegotiating. They had an idea of what they thought I was worth, and I had an idea that was quite different. My wife was pregnant. I wasn't a movie star. People have a misconception

of what a journeyman actor makes—not a lot of money. . . . You can't get rich."

BECOMING A SCREENWRITER

Although Sheridan thought about returning to his ranching roots and relocating his family to Wyoming, he also wanted to take a stab at writing the kind of script he always wanted to receive. He had read untold numbers of screenplays in his acting career, all rigidly structured in three acts, none particularly daring or inventive. So, he sat down—in his forties and with no experience as a screenwriter—and began to work on his first script, as he told Barnes that he had "read enough scripts to know what not to do." As he wrote, he abandoned all the rules the business expected scripts to follow, composing simple plots about complex people living in tough parts of rural America. He went wherever his imagination took him: "I don't outline," he said to Barnes. "I sit down to write and I take the ride. If something starts to not feel right, I go back to the last place that felt like jazz to me."

Sheridan's first screenplay would become the 2015 drug-war thriller *Sicario*, which stars Emily Blunt, Benicio Del Toro, Josh Brolin, and Victor Garber. Initially, however, no producer seemed to be interested in it, and Sheridan, not optimistic, moved on to writing his second and, he felt, more marketable script, *Hell or High Water*. Although *Hell or High Water* did find a buyer first, after the script for *Sicario* fell into the hands of respected French Canadian director Denis Villeneuve, who wanted to make it as his next film, the top-name actors also came on board, making it his first effort to reach theaters. *Sicario* met with widespread critical acclaim upon its release and several critics, including Richard Roeper, called it one of the best films of the year. Buoyed by this achievement, Sheridan continued to emphasize his dedication to writing scripts conscious of those responsible for making it come to life on the screen: "I would love nothing more than to be considered an actor's writer," he told Matt Grobar for *Deadline Hollywood* (7 Dec. 2015).

Sicario's success was quickly followed by *Hell or High Water*, which debuted in theaters in 2016. It is a tale of two bank-robbing brothers, played by Chris Pine and Ben Foster, who steal from financial institutions across West Texas during the Great Recession and mortgage crisis, which began in late 2007. The brothers then use the money to pay back predatory loans their family had taken out in an effort to save their family's ranch. Following them are two Texas Rangers, played by Jeff Bridges and Gil Birmingham, who, although friends, have a relationship imbued with racial overtones. (Bridges's character is white; Birmingham's is half Comanche and half Mexican.) Like its predecessor,

Hell or High Water met with rave reviews, many of which pointed out Sheridan's tight and powerful script as a highlight. This recognition was further solidified by his nominations for a Golden Globe Award for best screenplay for a motion picture and an Academy Award for best original screenplay.

WIND RIVER

The first two screenplays Sheridan had written with a mind to sell them to well-known directors. *Wind River*, on the other hand, which was released in 2017 and stars Jeremy Renner and Elizabeth Olsen, was crafted with the idea of directing it himself. The plot of the film involves a wildlife tracker, played by Renner, and a Federal Bureau of Investigation (FBI) agent, played by Olsen, investigating the murder of a teenage girl who lived on the American Indian reservation nearby. Sheridan felt personally connected to the story, having grown up with people who lived on reservations, and he wanted to shine a light on this subject. Sheridan explained to Colin Covert for the *Star Tribune* (10 Aug. 2017), "It's a really deeply personal story. It's about some subject matter that I was scared another director might have a different vision for. I felt responsible to the people I know in Indian country to shepherd the vision my way, success or fail. At least I'd know it would be presented in a manner which they'd respect."

Wind River was shot in the snowy mountains of Utah and Wyoming over about thirty days. Equipment and actors endured very cold and inconsistent conditions, but Sheridan felt that the effort showed in the final product. At the same time, he admits he was not entirely sure if he could pull the directing off, having only ever directed one previous film, the low-budget horror film *Vile*, in 2011. "I didn't know if I could make a *good* movie," he told Fear. "But I knew I could make a respectful one."

In the end, *Wind River*, which was screened at the prestigious Cannes Film Festival and earned Sheridan the event's award for best director, met with high praise similar to his two previous screenwriting efforts. Writing for the *New York Times* (3 Aug. 2017), Glenn Kenny proclaimed, "Taylor Sheridan, the screenwriter of last year's socially conscious crime drama *Hell or High Water*, proves an undeniably strong director with his second effort in that job, *Wind River*."

UPCOMING PROJECTS

With these three films behind him, Sheridan has continued to find his skills in demand. His next project, *Soldado*, the sequel to *Sicario* featuring Del Toro's character, is directed by Stefano Sollima and is due out in 2018. Additionally, he has been working on writing and directing

Yellowstone, a ten-episode television series about the Dutton family, who own the largest contiguous ranch in the country but must also contend with issues around its borders, including Yellowstone National Park, an American Indian reservation, and greedy land developers. The show will star veteran actor Kevin Costner and will air on the Paramount Network, which will be the rebranded version of Spike TV. Sheridan remarked to Lesley Goldberg for the *Hollywood Reporter* (3 May 2017), "The show is both timely and timeless. As much as it explores themes painfully relevant to the world today, it explores the very essence of family, and how the actions of one member can alter the course of generations."

PERSONAL LIFE

Sheridan lives with his wife and son in Wyoming.

SUGGESTED READING

Barnes, Brooks. "Taylor Sheridan on His Oscar-Nominated Screenplay for *Hell or High Water*." *The New York Times*, 9 Feb. 2017, www.nytimes.com/2017/02/09/arts/a-respected-film-a-vivid-script-an-oscar-chance.html. Accessed 6 Sept. 2017.

Fear, David. "*Wind River*: Taylor Sheridan on Why He Needed to Make This Modern Western." *Rolling Stone*, 11 Aug. 2017, www.rollingstone.com/movies/features/wind-river-taylor-sheridan-on-why-he-needed-to-make-this-modern-western-w497058. Accessed 6 Sept. 2017.

Grobar, Matt. "*Sicario* Scribe Taylor Sheridan on Next Projects and Brutality in Drug War Film: 'I Didn't Make That Up.'" *Deadline Hollywood*, 7 Dec. 2015, deadline.com/2015/12/sicario-screenplay-taylor-sheridan-interview-oscars-2015-1201653398/. Accessed 6 Sept. 2017.

Sheridan, Taylor. "Actor-Turned-Screenwriter Taylor Sheridan, on His Love Letter to Texas." Interview by Michael O'Sullivan. *The Washington Post*, 11 Aug. 2016, www.washingtonpost.com/entertainment/actor-turned-screenwriter-taylor-sheridan-on-his-love-letter-to-texas/2016/08/11/1ac2e68e-5e80-11e6-9d2f-b1a3564181a1_story.html. Accessed 6 Sept. 2017.

Sheridan, Taylor. "Taylor Sheridan Has Two Tips for Becoming an Oscar-Nominated Screenwriter." Interview by David Marchese. *Vulture*, 26 July 2017, www.vulture.com/2017/07/taylor-sheridans-tips-for-oscar-nominated-screenwriting.html. Accessed 6 Sept. 2017.

SELECTED WORKS

Sons of Anarchy, 2008–10; *Sicario*, 2015; *Hell or High Water*, 2016; *Wind River*, 2017

—*Christopher Mari*

Margot Lee Shetterly

Date of birth: 1969
Occupation: Writer

Before she published her first book, Margot Lee Shetterly had a successful career in finance. However, she wanted to shine light on the stories of the African American women who worked at the National Aeronautics and Space Administration (NASA) Langley Research Center beginning in the 1930s. Her debut book, *Hidden Figures* (2016), not only won awards but was adapted into an award-winning film of the same name (2016). Shetterly feels that telling the story of ordinary people who do extraordinary work is key. As she told Asha French for *espnW* (6 Sept. 2016): "For too long, history has imposed a binary condition on its black citizens: either nameless or renowned, menial or exceptional, passive recipients of the forces of history or superheroes who acquire mythic status not just because of their deeds but because of their scarcity."

By NASA/Aubrey Gemignani via Wikimedia Commons

EARLY LIFE AND EDUCATION

Shetterly was born and raised in Hampton, Virginia, where she grew up with two younger sisters, Lauren and Jocelyn. Shetterly's mother was an English professor at Hampton University. Her father was a climate scientist at NASA's Langley Research Center, and five of his seven siblings were engineers or technologists. As a young child, Shetterly met his coworkers, the women who were the "human computers"—excellent mathematicians—for NASA. She told Jonathan Black for Virginia's *Daily Press* (3 Sept. 2016), "I would go to my dad's office and see them. They were people that I knew that were my parents' friends and colleagues. I never thought about what they did."

After graduating from Phoebus High School in 1987, Shetterly studied finance at the University of Virginia's McIntire School of Commerce, earning a bachelor's degree in 1991. She began her career in New York City working as a junior trader at J. P. Morgan and later became a senior associate at Merrill Lynch. In the mid-1990s, she left Wall Street to work as a consultant for several digital media startups. There she met writer and historian Aran Shetterly, whom she later married.

EXPATRIATE

In 2005, Shetterly and her husband relocated to Oaxaca, Mexico, and launched *Inside Mexico*, an English-language publication targeting the expatriate community from the United States and Canada as well as tourists and business travelers. Although there were approximately one million Canadians and Americans living in Mexico

by 2007, there was at that time no English-language journal regularly in print.

Shetterly acted as both president of the company and the journal's managing editor, although neither she nor her husband, who was editor in chief and chief executive officer, had any previous newspaper experience. They worked with a staff of eight, evenly divided between expats and Mexicans, to produce a publication they modeled on New York City's *Village Voice*, an alternative news weekly. The print run of the magazine reached twenty thousand. As Shetterly told Reed Johnson for the *Los Angeles Times* (14 Feb. 2007), "We were frankly surprised at the numbers, for the sheer size of the market. This is the kind of opportunity that comes along only once in a lifetime." They also had a weekly newsletter, *The Tip*, which had a circulation of ten thousand.

The monthly magazine, which focused on arts and culture rather than business or politics, ran until 2009, after which the couple remained in Mexico, working as consultants and translators. Shetterly's husband expressed interest in the stories she told him about the women in her hometown who worked at NASA. As Shetterly told Black, "I began to hear the names of these other women and dug into the details of the work that had been done. The more I scratched the surface, the more I became hooked on this story."

FINDING THE HIDDEN FIGURES

Shetterly continued to visit Virginia while living in Mexico. In December 2010, she interviewed one of her former Sunday school teachers, Kathleen Land, who was a retired NASA "human computer." Her next interview was with Katherine Johnson, the last surviving human computer who had worked at the Langley Research Center in the 1960s, who helped Shetterly make further connections with the women who did such important work. Shetterly told Black, "It really did start with Katherine Johnson and understanding her story. From there it was any number of different sources, tracking down stories and oral histories from people that worked with those women." Johnson, who was born in 1918, worked at NASA for more than three decades and helped to calculate the flight trajectory for Alan Shepard, the first American in space.

Shetterly spent the next six years pursuing original research at both Langley Research Center and the National Archives. She told Black, "I spent tons of time in the National Archives, digging through boxes that I knew I was the first person to open the box. It was like water-logged, dried-up yellow paper." To support her research efforts while she was writing the book, the Alfred P. Sloan Foundation gave Shetterly a $50,000 grant in 2014.

THE WORK IN PRINT

To make the project manageable and interesting to others, Shetterly limited herself to four women's stories. "It wasn't enough to be a talented mathematician, but it really was the women who were willing to occupy all the space they could get and then some. A lot of it had to do, and still has to do, with being in people's blind spots." The idea of a blind spot gave the book its title, Hidden Figures, itself a play on words.

Shetterly saw the research as a way to combine areas of information that were usually separated by academic discipline. Her research focused on intersection of race, gender, the space race, the civil rights movement, and the Cold War. She submitted her completed manuscript to sixteen publishers; all but two said they were not interested.

Shetterly then applied to a doctoral program at the University of Virginia, expecting her book to become her thesis project. After being accepted for the program in 2014, she heard from William Morrow and Company; they wanted to publish her work. As she told Black, "There are times when you have to do things and push and push and push, taking all of your effort. Then there are times when you do something and it feels like even before you get to the door, people are opening it."

THE WORK ON FILM

Doors continued to open for Shetterly's research when Levantine Films optioned the book. Academy Award–winning producer Donna Gigliotti,

who saw Shetterly's fifty-five-page book proposal, was determined to see the story come alive on the big screen. With producing credits such as Shakespeare in Love (1998) and Silver Linings Playbook (2012), Gigliotti was a good fit for the project. When she called Shetterly from New York to make an offer, the author was heading home after visiting Johnson at her retirement home.

Pharrell Williams, who had grown up near Hampton, Virginia, heard about the project from his producing partner Mimi Valdes after she met with Gigliotti. He was tapped to compose songs and score the film with Hans Zimmer and Ben Wallfisch; he also became one of the producers. As he told Cara Buckley for the New York Times (20 May 2016), "[Gigliotti] knew I was going to lose my mind upon hearing about it. And when I did, we got on the phone with everybody, and we begged."

Gigliotti began shooting the movie, which was filmed in Atlanta, Georgia, before the book was published, citing its strong characters and untold, true story as powerful motivators for taking on the film. Allison Schroeder, who grew up near Cape Canaveral and completed an internship at NASA during high school, completed the screenplay in May 2015. The entire process of adapting Hidden Figures for film moved at warp speed, filming in forty-six days and opening in limited release in December 2016 with high-profile stars Octavia Spencer and Kevin Costner in the major roles. Hidden Figures has grossed $230 million on a production budget of $25 million; the film was also nominated for three Academy Awards, including best picture and best adapted screenplay, and two Golden Globes Awards.

THE HUMAN COMPUTER PROJECT

As an outgrowth of her research, Shetterly founded the Human Computer Project in 2014. Her colleague on the project is Duchess Harris, who is a professor of American studies at Macalester College, in St. Paul, Minnesota. One of the goals of the project is to record the names of women who worked at NASA in the mid-twentieth century and to document their achievements. As Shetterly told Black of her research, "It was like being a detective. I have this one bit of information, but what more can I find? It was addicting." One of the interesting connections Shetterly made was that Dorothy Vaughan had taught at Robert Russa Moton High School in Farmville, Virginia, which became part of the 1954 landmark Supreme Court case Brown v. Board of Education that led to the desegregation of public schools.

A secondary goal of the Human Computer Project is to increase interest in science, technology, engineering, and math (STEM), especially among young women and people of color, who are particularly underrepresented and needed in these areas. As Tara Jefferson reported for the website of the Anisfield-Wolf Book Award (8 Feb. 2017), Shetterly rhetorically asked an audience at Case Western Reserve University, "A thousand women working as professional mathematicians, getting up and going to work at NASA, every day for decades. Why didn't we turn them into professional role models and use them to pull generations of young people, particularly young women, into science careers?" The story of Katherine Johnson, one of the central figures of the book and the film, is featured as one of the "Inspiring STEM stories from history" on the Human Computer Project's website. Johnson was honored for her achievements with the Presidential Medal of Freedom, the highest civilian honor in the United States, which she received from President Barack Obama in November 2015, and by having a new Langley Research Center building named for her in May 2016.

PERSONAL LIFE

Shetterly is working on the second book of a three-book deal she regards as a trilogy. She told Danielle Young for the *Root* (6 Jan. 2017), "The new story [I'm working on] is also unseen but not quite untold. It deals with midcentury. Anything I will ever do in life will not be as consuming and overwhelming as *Hidden Figures*."

Shetterly's hobbies include knitting, as she told Chris Kornelis for the *Wall Street Journal* (13 Jan. 2017), "I'm a knitter and I cannot live without knitting needles. I used addi Turbo needles to knit my wedding dress—and, no, it didn't look like a big sweater! When the feet wear out of my socks, I will darn them to fix them up. I just replace the feet; the legs never wear out."

SUGGESTED READING

Black, Jonathan. "Hampton Native Releases 'Hidden Figures' After 6-Year Journey." *The Daily Press*, 4 Sept. 2016, www.dailypress.com/entertainment/books/dp-fea-hidden-figures-book-0904-20160903-story.html. Accessed 3 Aug. 2017.

Cox, Ana Marie. "Margot Lee Shetterly Wants to Tell More Black Stories." *The New York Times Magazine*, 13 Sept. 2016, www.nytimes.com/2016/09/18/magazine/margot-lee-shetterly-wants-to-tell-more-black-stories.html. Accessed 3 Aug. 2017.

French, Asha. "'Hidden Figures' Author Tells the Story of the Black Women Who Helped Win the Space Race." *espnW*, 6 Sept. 2016, www.espn.com/espnw/culture/feature/article/17476115/hidden-figures-author-margot-lee-shetterly-tells-story-black-women-helped-win-space-race. Accessed 3 Aug. 2017.

Hammond, Jane. "Phoebus High Throws Surprise Pep Rally for Alumna Margot Lee Shetterly." *The Daily Press*, 10 Mar. 2017, www.dailypress.com/news/education/dp-nws-shetterly-phoebus-appearance-20170309-story.html. Accessed 3 Aug. 2017.

Jefferson, Tara. "Author Margot Lee Shetterly Shares 'Hidden Figures' Origin Story at Case Western Reserve University." *Anisfield-Wolf Book Awards*, 8 Feb. 2017, www.anisfield-wolf.org/2017/02/author-margot-lee-shetterly-shares-hidden-figures-origin-story-at-case-western-reserve-university. Accessed 3 Aug. 2017.

Johnson, Reed. "Speaking the Same Language." *The Los Angeles Times*, 14 Feb. 2007, articles.latimes.com/2007/feb/14/entertainment/et-mexpaper14. Accessed 3 Aug. 2017.

Young, Danielle. "Hidden Figures is Margot Lee Shetterly's 1st Book, Which Proves #BlackGirlMagic Knows No Limits." *The Root*, 6 Jan. 2017, www.theroot.com/hidden-figures-is-margot-lee-shetterly-s-1st-book-whic-1791134217. Accessed 3 Aug. 2017.

—*Judy Johnson*

Iliza Shlesinger

Date of birth: February 22, 1983
Occupation: Comedian

Comedian Iliza Shlesinger has been described as an "absolute monster on stage." Stephie Grob Plante for the *Times of Israel* (21 Jan. 2015) added that "Shlesinger dominates the stage with an intensity that at times borders on manic, manipulating her voice with the ease and range of a classically trained actor, unafraid to let physical comedy render her unsexy. (It doesn't.) She is a comedy beast." In fact, Shlesinger is well-known for one particularly beastly character that she often describes in her act and that she believes will be familiar to most young women: the "party goblin."

"Your party goblin sleeps in the back of your brain, and she waits on piles of regrets and rags and old *Tiger Beat* magazines," Shlesinger jokes in her act. "She will awaken when she hears you say, 'I guess I'll just come out for one drink.'" So popular is Shlesinger's party goblin character, which the comedian voices in a deep growl, that fans have been known to attend her shows with their faces painted green in homage.

The party goblin growl is not the only voice in Shlesinger's arsenal. She regularly employs a wide variety of sounds, which are usually high-pitched, to satirize the foibles of her fellow young women. "At first blush, it's easy to mistake

Heather Kennedy/Getty Images for SXSW

Shlesinger's raptor shrieks and alien bleats as mockery," Plante wrote. "But Schlesinger . . . [is] along for the ride, breaking down the behavioral peccadilloes and complicated thought patterns universal to all women, Shlesinger included."

The comedian affirms that she has no intention of being simply mean-spirited. "I think what differentiates my act from other female acts is that I'm not there to vilify anyone," she explained to Plante. "[When I began my career] I'd make fun of the girls, and every girl was like, 'Oh my God, I know a girl who does that.' And I'd say, 'No, you don't know a girl who does that. You are that girl. Because I am that girl. We all do the same stuff.'"

EARLY YEARS AND EDUCATION

Iliza Vie Shlesinger was born on February 22, 1983. She grew up in Dallas, Texas. Her father, Fred, left the family when Shlesinger was young, and growing up, she rarely saw him. (The two did not rekindle their relationship until Shlesinger was an adult and had launched her career.) "I always wished my dad was there to intimidate my boyfriends or something," she recalled to Jordan Smith for *Esquire* (14 Apr. 2011). "It's supposed to be your dad giving your guy friends the stink-eye for sneaking beer through your house, not your mom."

The family is Jewish, and Shlesinger attended synagogue services and Sunday school; had Bat Mitzvah and confirmation ceremonies; and was active for a time in B'nai B'rith Youth Organization (BBYO), a social and leadership-training organization for Jewish teens. "I had the chemical outline of a Jewish upbringing," she told Plante. "We did all the holidays, but it was Reform," a less tradition-bound branch of the religion, "so I could wear what I wanted, and I ate a lot of bacon," which is forbidden to those who consume only kosher foods.

Despite her less-than-rigorous adherence to religious ritual, Shlesinger—who often incorporates references to literature, sociology, and other such scholarly topics into her act—feels her Jewish background helped shape her career path. "I think part of being Jewish is that innate desire to question things," she explained to Plante. "Rabbis sit around all day and question the Torah. Giving yourself the room to question things in a religion just breeds thinking." Shlesinger also credits her time at the Greenhill School, a progressive, private institution where she was a member of the swim team and the only girl in the improvisational comedy troupe. "I wasn't a great student, but I loved learning, and I loved facts," she recalled to Joel Keller for *TV Insider* (11 Oct. 2016). "I will sit in front of a dictionary and just read. . . . I like accumulating knowledge. There's just an oddly academic approach I've taken with stand-up, and those facts, they're seamlessly woven in. . . . I think that you write what you know."

Shlesinger was a fan of comedy from an early age, avidly watching cartoons such as *The Ren & Stimpy Show* and *Rugrats*, which she has told interviewers sparked her interest in doing different voices. Later, she watched sketch shows like *In Living Color* and *Kids in the Hall*, even as her friends were developing crushes on the actors in nighttime dramas like *ER*.

After graduating from Greenhill in 2001, Shlesinger attended Emerson College, which is located in Boston and is a liberal arts college with a primary focus on communication and performing arts studies, where she majored in visual and media arts. Shlesinger has said in interviews that she was the only woman in her sketch-comedy group who wanted to write her own material. She once mounted a one-woman show using characters she had developed in her sketch group and subsequently discovered that she had an affinity for monologues.

Shlesinger, who earned her undergraduate degree in 2004, considers one of the defining experiences of her college years to be her participation in Semester at Sea, a ship-based study-abroad program. It was during this time that she initially performed her stand-up comedy at open-mic nights, and although she did not have any real entertainment-industry connections, the positive response she received fueled her decision to move to Los Angeles after graduation.

COMEDY CAREER

Once in California, Shlesinger, who was then in her early twenties, joined Whiteboy Comedy, a group that organizes stand-up shows. Under their auspices, she became a popular act at the Improv, a renowned comedy club in Hollywood, and in 2007 she won "So You Think You're Funny," a contest launched by the then-popular social media outlet Myspace. The following year her career received an enormous boost when she became the first woman and youngest performer to win the sixth season of NBC's *Last Comic Standing*.

Shlesinger was surprised when her victory was met with some vitriol in the highly charged and competitive world of stand-up comedy. "I was there with all my heart and soul, thought everyone was my friend, and then I won the competition and found out, oh, these grown men you just beat are definitely *not* your friends," she recalled to Marlow Stern for the *Daily Beast* (28 Oct. 2016). "They got really catty and bitchy. . . . It was weird to see grown men acting like *Mean Girls*. . . . Nothing in my show-business career will be as hard as doing competitive stand-up and then being hated by people you thought were your friends."

Still, Shlesinger was determined to use her win to her advantage, and a variety of other offers and jobs began to pour in. After winning *Last Comic Standing*, Shlesinger hosted a segment called "The Weakly News" on the website TheStream.tv and appeared as herself in the 2009 comedy *Surviving the Holidays with Lewis Black*. In 2010 she released an on-demand comedy video, *Man Up and Act Like a Lady*, and an on-demand comedy album, *iliza LIVE*. She also hosted *Excused*, a syndicated dating show that aired for two seasons starting in 2011, and in 2014 she launched a semiweekly podcast, *Truth and Iliza*, that features a mix of celebrity guests and friends. On July 13, 2016, ABC-digital (the network's digital platform) released Shlesinger's short-form comedy series *Forever 31*, which follows a group of single friends in their thirties who struggle with the demands of adulthood. Also in 2016, Shlesinger co-hosted the TBS game show *Separation Anxiety*, was a contestant on the game show *Celebrity Name Game*, and judged the children's cooking show *Chopped Junior*.

Perhaps her most high-profile partnership thus far, however, has been with Netflix, which has released three of Shlesinger's comedy specials: *War Paint* (2012), *Freezing Hot* (2015), and *Confirmed Kills* (2016). "I feel like for the first time in my life, 'Oh, I got to the cool kids' table,'" Shlesinger told Plante of her work with Netflix.

In their reviews of Shlesinger's specials, critics often comment on the physicality of her performances. "It's very hard to get an attractive picture of me doing stand-up," she explained to Keller, "because I'm always hunched over or making some sort of whimsical creature face. Part of it comes from my desire to get a message across, and it pours out of me so intensely that it manifests itself in a voice or in the physicality of it. . . . I want to crawl into the audience's brain and into their heart and make a nest."

PERSONAL LIFE

Shlesinger has reportedly dated fellow comic Bret Ernst. One of her most popular tales, however, concerns a man she refers to as "Brian," who, she explains, told her such an increasingly implausible string of lies that she was forced to finally break up with him. Her dog, Blanche, she says now constitutes the bulk of her social life.

Her nonfiction book, *Girl Logic*, is scheduled for release in mid-2017, and she is currently developing an as-yet-unnamed comedy pilot for ABC; it will follow the adventures of a recently divorced New York caterer who moves to Dallas with her two small children.

"It's a lot of good stuff happening at once," Shlesinger told Stern. "It seems like it's all a tsunami, but I've been at this for a really long time. People don't see the failed pilots, blind script deals, network deals, auditions, screen tests, screenplays that get some attention . . . and then nothing."

SUGGESTED READING

Plante, Stephie Grob. "Sexy 'Comedy Beast' Makes It to the Netflix Cool Kids' Table." *The Times of Israel*, 21 Jan. 2015, www.timesofisrael.com/sexy-comedy-beast-makes-it-to-the-netflix-cool-kids-table. Accessed 15 Jan. 2017.

Shlesinger, Iliza. "Iliza Shlesinger Talks Women in Comedy: 'I Don't Think the Bar is Set Very High.'" Interview by Emily Krauser. *ET Online*, 27 Aug. 2015, www.etonline.com/news/170745_iliza_shlesinger_talks_women_comedy_i_dont_think_the_bar_is_set_very_high. Accessed 15 Jan. 2017.

Shlesinger, Iliza. "Iliza Shlesinger on Her Netflix Special, *Forever 31*, and How Women Need to Treat Each Other." Interview by Joel Keller. *TV Insider*, 11 Oct. 2016, www.tvinsider.com/100295/iliza-shlesinger-interview. Accessed 15 Jan. 2017.

Shlesinger, Iliza. "The Evolution of Iliza Shlesinger." Interview by Isaac Kozell. *Splitsider*, The Awl, 10 Oct. 2016, splitsider.com/2016/10/the-evolution-of-iliza-shlesinger. Accessed 15 Jan. 2017.

Shlesinger, Iliza. "Killer Instincts." Interview by Jonathan Soroff. *The Improper Bostonian*, 19 Aug. 2016, www.improper.com/life-style/killer-instincts. Accessed 15 Jan. 2017.

Smith, Jordan. "Iliza Shlesinger Is the Woman of Your Dreams." *Esquire*, 14 Apr. 2011, www.esquire.com/entertainment/a9765/iliza-shlesinger-bio-5560896. Accessed 15 Jan. 2017.

Stern, Marlow. "Iliza Shlesinger Is about to Be a Pretty Big Deal—and It's about Damn Time." *Daily Beast*, 28 Oct. 2016, www.thedailybeast.com/articles/2016/10/28/iliza-shlesinger-is-about-to-be-a-pretty-big-deal-and-it-s-about-damn-time.html. Accessed 15 Jan. 2017.

—*Mari Rich*

Sturgill Simpson

Date of birth: June 8, 1978
Occupation: Singer-songwriter

With the arrival of his second album, *Metamodern Sounds in Country Music* (2014), Sturgill Simpson gained a passionate following and critical acclaim from fans of country and rock music alike. Though deeply indebted to traditional country music and those who put their own spins on the genre, Simpson also finds inspiration in rock singers such as Van Morrison, Joe Cocker, and Kurt Cobain as well as the legendary soul singer Marvin Gaye. But it is not just Simpson's music that is unique in country—his lyrics talk about soul searching and exploring metaphysical questions in a way that is entirely his own. *Rolling Stone* magazine placed the album on its best albums of 2014 list. Simpson's third album, *A Sailor's Guide to Earth* (2016), is a concept album inspired by his young son. In it Simpson branches out even further musically, incorporating jazz and soul, weaving in various sounds and genres to create something of his own.

EARLY LIFE

Born John Sturgill Simpson in 1978, Simpson grew up in the small coal-mining town of Jackson in southeast Kentucky. Simpson is an only child. His mother worked as a secretary, and his father as a state police officer who mainly served in the undercover narcotics division. Simpson would grow up to be the first man in his mother's family to not become a coal miner. His great-grandfather worked in deep mines, and his grandfather and uncle worked in strip mines. Simpson has recalled in interviews that Jackson was a small town with a Main Street and mom-and-pop stores and people knowing one another.

Simpson got his first guitar around the age of nine. At that place and time, it was not unusual for anyone to play guitar or sing, but it was not something people considered for their livelihood. Playing music was, as Simpson told

Duncan Cooper for *Fader* magazine (15 July 2014), "what you do when you're done with your real job."

MUSIC LESSONS

During Simpson's early teen years, the family moved to Versailles, a town in central Kentucky. Before moving, Simpson's mother had had enough of his father's dangerous job and had given him an ultimatum: choose between her and working in undercover narcotics. His father asked for a transfer, and the family moved to Versailles. (Despite the job change, Simpson's parents did eventually divorce.) During the summers, Simpson visited his grandparents in Jackson. His mother's brother played organ and harmonica, and he would take young Simpson, once he had shown some proficiency on guitar, to a friend's house where they would all jam. During these jam sessions, Simpson learned to play in a band and the importance of listening to bandmates, instead of playing over them.

Simpson's maternal grandfather also had a profound musical influence on him from childhood. Together they watched the country-music variety television program *Hee Haw* (1969–92), and his grandfather told him which artists he liked and who was really playing guitar and who was just holding it as a prop. Meanwhile, Simpson's paternal grandfather was a mandolin player, who exposed young Sturgill to bluegrass music.

It was while attending high school in Versailles, however, that Simpson discovered hard rock and blues from the 1960s and 1970s. Simpson, who has readily admitted that he was not the greatest student in high school, told Marc Maron during an interview on the *WTF* podcast (13 May 2016) that he drove a 1998 Toyota Corolla, worked at McDonald's, and was a "stringy, greasy pot head." His cousin exposed him to a great variety of music, namely Led Zeppelin, Jimi Hendrix, Eric Clapton and Cream, and Peter Green of early Fleetwood Mac, as well as the Texas blues player Stevie Ray Vaughan. His neighbor exposed him to the first Guns N' Roses record, *Appetite for Destruction* (1987), a gritty hard-rock album. Simpson's mother did not like her son listening to such hard-core rock, so when she found the album she threw it out.

During high school, Simpson also became more serious about playing music, practicing, and singing. He equipped himself with an amplifier and electric guitar. He later went on to listen to—and be influenced by—great, revolutionary singers such as Marvin Gaye, David Bowie, Joe Cocker, Van Morrison, and Kurt Cobain.

FITS AND STARTS
Simpson "barely graduated" from high school, he told Cooper, and then "made some bad decisions which limited my options." Within weeks of graduating high school, Simpson enlisted in the US Navy and served from 1996 to 1999. He worked a series of odd jobs after leaving the navy.

In 2004 Simpson formed the bluegrass rock band Sunday Valley, along with bassist Gerald Evans and drummer Edgar Purdom III, with whom he would perform off and on until 2012. He moved to Nashville, Tennessee, for about nine months in 2005 and tried to break through but found the music scene divided between the old guard and a glut of pop-country stars, with little room for anyone of his mindset. Broke, drunk, and no more known than when he arrived, Simpson left Nashville for Utah to work on the railroad.

Before long, Simpson's grandfather became very sick, and he moved back to Kentucky to help his mother care for his grandfather. While at home, he met his future wife, Sarah, who encouraged him to seriously consider music as a career. They had moved back to Utah, and he had taken a management position for the railroad company he worked for. That period in his life, he told Rachel Martin for National Public Radio (25 May 2014), was "the most depressed state I've ever been in my life. I think I put on like thirty-five pounds and as a result, starting pulling the guitar out of the closet for the first time in about three years and really, really writing a lot."

HIGH TOP MOUNTAIN
Simpson's wife encouraged him to keep writing and playing and to try to make a career of

his passion before it was too late. So they sold a lot of their possessions and moved to Nashville, where Simpson began to perform live. He decided he would not try to court a major label or try to "make it" by becoming popular at the expense of his personal art. He decided to seek success on his own terms, without a publicist, instead using Twitter and word of mouth. He did send out four hundred emails to managers and other music insiders to get his name out there, however, and the one person who responded became his manager. Simpson spent about two weeks in the studio with session musicians and recorded his first album, *High Top Mountain* (2013). Veteran session musicians, such as pianist Hargus "Pig" Robbins and steel-guitar player Robby Turner, contributed significantly to its sound.

The resulting album is one that Simpson has labelled both serious and classic country. Although Simpson's music draws from many musical influences, many critics picked out the influence of hard-country musician Waylon Jennings; Simpson's voice is even reminiscent of Jennings. The irony is, however, that Simpson was not drawing from Jennings; in fact, he is very aware of his influences and knows that to make the album stand out, it has to be personal. In the song "Life Ain't Fair and the World Is Mean," he draws from his personal life with the line: "the most outlaw thing I've ever done is to give a good woman a ring." He also mined his early childhood and his family history for song material, in such songs as "Old King Coal" and "Hero," the latter about his grandfather. "He's got a powerful, slurry singing voice that really puts the moan in his material," wrote Stuart Munro in a review for the *Boston Globe* (2 July 2013), "and he's a fine songwriter with a penchant for making art out of his own life." Initially, the album did not get much attention in the press, but that changed with the release of his second album.

METAMODERN SOUNDS IN COUNTRY MUSIC
Metamodern Sounds in Country Music (2014), recorded in only four days at a Nashville studio, went on to give Simpson a bigger fan base, more critical praise, and greater recognition for his unique combination of traditional country and modern sensibilities. The title is a direct reference to the revolutionary, genre-crossing Ray Charles album *Modern Sounds in Country and Western Music* (1962). On the opening track, "Turtles (All the Way Down)," he is a spiritual seeker, interested in everything from cosmology to Buddhism to hallucinogenic drugs. Simpson has noted that reviewers and listeners alike honed in on the drug references, which became his calling card, although Simpson has explained that the album is really about ruminations on love and human experience.

In a review for the influential indie-music web magazine *Pitchfork* (16 May 2014), Stephen M. Deusner wrote, "With a sharp mind to match that Hag burr of a voice, Simpson not only owns the best name in current country music but comprehends the genre as a vehicle for big, unwieldy ideas about human consciousness and the nature of life." Deusner added that the "heady" material on the album, all the metaphysical searching, could potentially be too much, but it somehow works, primarily because Simpson "favors clear melodies, careful structures, and riffs that draw on Nashville and Bakersfield traditions without sounding revivalist." John Caramanica for the *New York Times* (14 May 2014) called *Metamodern Sounds in Country Music* a "triumph of exhaustion, one of the most jolting country albums in recent memory, and one that achieves majesty with just the barest of parts."

A SAILOR'S GUIDE TO EARTH

If Simpson's second album pushed new musical elements onto traditional country—such as psychedelic rock and modern ideas and problems having nothing to do with country music clichés—then his third album, *A Sailor's Guide to Earth* (2016) went a step further. Aside from the music itself—there are elements of jazz and soul, and strings aplenty—it is also a concept album, one that tells a story from beginning to the end, or focuses on a single theme or experimentation. Also, unlike what many expect from a country singer, Simpson is openly against war, against consumerism, and for experimentation.

A Sailor's Guide to Earth, observed Jeremy D. Larson in a review for *SPIN* (13 April 2016), is indeed a guide: "an epistolary album lovingly addressed to his two-year-old son. It's designed to serve as the boy's own pocket atlas for navigating the world, written by someone who's seen its many angels and demons." The album was also inspired by a letter his grandfather wrote to his wife and child while fighting in World War II, in case he did not come home. In a review for *Pitchfork* (19 Apr. 2016), Corban Goble noted the differences between this album and Simpson's previous one: "The premise—a concept album addressed to his own son and wife—might sound corny, but the result is a beautiful and earnest record that flips the defeatist subtext of *Metamodern* on its head." Goble added that the "instrumentation on songs like 'Keep It Between the Lines'—much of it provided by Sharon Jones's backing band, the Dap-Kings—is denser, bolder, and more rhythmic than anything Simpson has steered previously." Simpson earned a Grammy for best country album for *A Sailor's Guide to Earth* at the 2017 Grammy Awards in February 2017 and performed live with the Dap-Kings.

PERSONAL LIFE

Simpson lives with his wife, Sarah, and son in Nashville. After having battled alcoholism, Simpson became sober at the age of twenty-eight while working in Utah.

SUGGESTED READING

Caramanica, Jon. "A Country Lament Sinks into Despair; Sturgill Simpson's *Metamodern Sounds in Country Music*." Review of *Metamodern Sounds in Country Music*, by Sturgill Simpson. *The New York Times*, 14 May 2014, www.nytimes.com/2014/05/15/arts/music/sturgill-simpsons-metamodern-sounds-in-country-music.html. Accessed 14 Feb. 2017.

Deusner, Stephen M. "Sturgill Simpson *Metamodern Sounds in Country Music*." Review of *Metamodern Sound in Country Music*, by Sturgill Simpson. *Pitchfork*, 16 May 2014, pitchfork.com/reviews/albums/19386-sturgill-simpson-metamodern-sounds-in-country-music. Accessed 14 Feb. 2017.

Goble, Corban. Review of *A Sailor's Guide to Earth*, by Sturgill Simpson. *Pitchfork*, 19 Apr. 2016, pitchfork.com/reviews/albums/21758-a-sailors-guide-to-earth/. Accessed 14 Feb. 2017.

Larson, Jeremy D. "Review: Sturgill Simpson Preps a Son of a Sailor on *A Sailor's Guide to Earth*." *SPIN*, 15 Apr. 2016, www.spin.com/2016/04/review-sturgill-simpson-a-sailors-guide-to-earth. Accessed 14 Feb. 2017.

Munro, Stuart. "Album Review: Sturgill Simpson, *High Top Mountain*." Review of *High Top Mountain*, by Sturgill Simpson. *The Boston Globe*, 1 July 2013, archive.boston.com/ae/music/2013/07/01/album-review-sturgill-simpson-high-top-mountain/kAoxN7i1hwfVlzGPBuirCM/story.html. Accessed 14 Feb. 2017.

Simpson, Sturgill. "Another Country; A Freewheeling Hour with Sturgill Simpson." Interview by Duncan Cooper. *Fader*, 15 July 2014, www.thefader.com/2014/07/15/another-country-a-freewheeling-hour-with-sturgill-simpson. Accessed 14 Feb. 2017.

Simpson, Sturgill. "Sturgill Simpson / John C. Reilly." Interview by Marc Maron. *WTF with Marc Maron*, 12 May 2016, www.wtfpod.com/podcast/episode-706-sturgill-simpson-john-c-reilly. Accessed 14 Feb. 2017.

SELECTED WORKS

High Top Mountain, 2013; *Metamodern Sounds in Country Music*, 2014; *A Sailor's Guide to Earth*, 2015

—*Dmitry Kiper*

Alexander Skarsgård

Date of birth: August 25, 1976
Occupation: Actor

Alexander Skarsgård is a Swedish actor best known for the HBO series *True Blood*.

EARLY LIFE AND EDUCATION

Alexander Johan Hjalmar Skarsgård was born in Stockholm, Sweden, on August 25, 1976. He is the oldest of the six children of physician My Skarsgård and actor Stellan Skarsgård, who is one of Sweden's most famous actors. (Alexander Skarsgård has an additional two siblings from his father's second marriage.)

Skarsgård was raised in the SoFo (south of Folkungagatan) neighborhood on Södermalm, an island district in Stockholm. Skarsgård's upbringing in Sweden included vacationing at his family's compound on the island of Öland on the Baltic Sea. Skarsgård's family was constantly in the public eye when he was a child, due to his father's celebrity status. Skarsgård grew up watching his father perform at Stockholm's Royal Theatre from backstage and occasionally traveling with him to movie sets.

Skarsgård acted in his first film, *Ake and His World*, in 1984. He landed his first starring role at age thirteen in *The Dog That Smiled* (1989). Skarsgård became an object of young, female attention; many visited his home hoping to meet him. He felt nervous being written about in the press when he was still in a formative period of his youth, and he disliked the experience of being a public figure. The public attention he received after the release of *The Dog That Smiled* led to his decision to give up acting.

Instead of pursuing a career in acting, Skarsgård joined the Swedish Royal Navy at age eighteen, serving in its antiterrorist SäkJakt division. He later recalled that he wanted to serve in the military as a way of distinguishing himself from merely being the son of a celebrity. He served in the navy for fifteen months.

In 1996 he attended Metropolitan University in Leeds, United Kingdom, for six months and rediscovered his interest in acting. He left Leeds to attend Marymount Manhattan College's drama program and begin acting again. He returned to Sweden after a year at Marymount.

ACTING CAREER

After his return, Skarsgård appeared in several Swedish films. His first Hollywood film appearance was in the comedy *Zoolander* (2001), in which he played a goofy male model. He wrote and directed a short film, *To Kill a Child* (2003), in Sweden. It received critical praise and was screened at the Cannes and Tribeca Film Festivals.

Over the next several years, Skarsgård appeared in a mix of Swedish and Hollywood films, including the independent dramas *The Last Drop* (2005), *Om Sara* (2005), and *Kill Your Darlings* (2006). To facilitate auditioning and performing in some of those roles, Skarsgård moved to Hollywood in 2004.

Skarsgård gave many auditions during this period and was eventually cast in the HBO miniseries *Generation Kill* (2008), in which he plays Sergeant Brad "Iceman" Colbert, a soldier in the US Marine Corps during the 2003 invasion of Iraq. His role in the critically acclaimed miniseries was a breakthrough for his career and paved the way for larger opportunities in American film and television.

He soon landed his second HBO series, *True Blood* (2008–14). The horror fiction program centered on a group of vampires was a major hit that elevated Skarsgård to greater fame in the United States. Skarsgård plays Eric Northman, a millennium-old vampire who is the sheriff of Bon Temps, the fictional setting in Louisiana where vampires and other mythological creatures live. Skarsgård's part was relatively small in the first season, but he became a fan favorite in the second season when a love triangle developed between Eric, Sookie Stackhouse (Anna Paquin), and Bill Compton (Stephen Moyer). Amid his rise to fame through *True Blood*, Skarsgård appeared in a 2009 Lady Gaga music video for her song "Paparazzi."

The popularity of *True Blood* touched off a string of Hollywood film opportunities for Skarsgård. In 2011, he starred in a remake of the 1971 suspense drama *Straw Dogs*. In the 2011 remake, Skarsgård plays the film's antagonist alongside actress Kate Bosworth.

Skarsgård had his first opportunity to act opposite his father in *Melancholia* (2011), a Lars von Trier film about the apocalypse. His character is a mild-mannered groom who picks his wife's boss to be his best man, played by Stellan Skarsgård. Skarsgård considered the role a welcome departure from the alpha-male typecasting that had come to characterize many of the roles offered to Skarsgård as a result of his success on *True Blood*.

In 2012, Skarsgård's dramatic film roles continued with a critically acclaimed film adaptation of Henry James's novel *What Maisie Knew*. He then starred in *Battleship* (2012), a widely panned action film loosely based on the strategy board game of the same name. The film was nominated for six Golden Raspberry Awards (better known as the Razzies), which recognize failure in filmmaking. Seemingly unaffected by the critical ire for *Battleship*, Skarsgård's dramatic film career continued through the concluding years of *True Blood*, during which he also appeared in an episode of the HBO comedy series *Eastbound & Down* (2013).

Skarsgård starred in a string of independent dramas including *Disconnect* (2013), *The East* (2013), and *The Giver* (2014). In 2015 he starred in *The Diary of a Teenage Girl*, a film adaptation of the popular Phoebe Gloeckner graphic novel of the same name. His third HBO series, *Big Little Lies*, began filming in 2016. He also starred in the title role of the action epic *The Legend of Tarzan*, which was released in July 2016.

IMPACT

Though his family is famous throughout Sweden, Skarsgård became more widely popular in the United States with the success of *True Blood*. For his portrayal of Eric Northman on *True Blood*, Skarsgård won two Scream Awards for best horror actor in 2010 and 2011.

PERSONAL LIFE

Skarsgård's brothers Gustaf, Bill, and Valter are actors in Sweden. Skarsgård lives in Hollywood Hills, California, but he spends much of his free time in Sweden with his family.

SUGGESTED READING

"Alexander Skarsgård." *Bio*. A&E Television Networks, n.d. Web. 1 May 2016.

Hicklin, Aaron. "Alexander Skarsgård: Interview with a Vampire." *Guardian*. Guardian News and Media, 10 Sept. 2011. Web. 30 Apr. 2016.

Martin, Brett. "Here Comes the Viking." *GQ*. Condé Nast, 17 May 2011. Web. 30 Apr. 2016.

Ramsdale, Suzannah. "Alexander Skarsgård: 9 Things You Need To Know." *Marie Claire*. Time, 30 Mar. 2016. Web. 30 Apr. 2016.

Skarsgård, Alexander. "Alexander Skarsgård." Interview by Win Butler. *Interview*. Interview, 31 May 2011. Web. 30 Apr. 2016.

SELECTED WORKS

Zoolander, 2001; *Kill Your Darlings*, 2006; *Straw Dogs*, 2011; *Generation Kill*, 2008; *True Blood*, 2008–14; *Melancholia*, 2011; *Battleship*, 2012; *What Maisie Knew*, 2012; *Disconnect*, 2013; *The Giver*, 2014; *The Diary of a Teenage Girl*, 2015; *The Legend of Tarzan*, 2016; *Big Little Lies*, 2016

—*Richard Means*

Shaka Smart

Date of birth: April 8, 1977
Occupation: College basketball coach

Shaka Smart is the head coach of Longhorns, the men's basketball team at the University of Texas (UT) at Austin, although he is best known for his tenure at the Virginia Commonwealth University (VCU). In his second year as head coach at VCU, Smart shepherded the Rams to the Final Four in the 2011 NCAA tournament. The team, which many pundits argued did not deserve to be included in the tournament at all, was seeded eleventh in the Southwest regional semifinals. The Rams ultimately lost to Butler, but their shocking rise made Smart, the brain behind the devastatingly effective defensive strategy known as Havoc, a celebrity in college sports. John Branch for the *New York Times* (26 Mar. 2011) dubbed him the "tournament's breakout star." But Smart's success was by no means overnight; by March 2011, the thirty-three-year-old former Kenyon College point guard had already coached at five universities. He took up his post at UT Austin in 2015.

EARLY LIFE

Smart was born on April 8, 1977, and raised by his mother, Monica King, in a town called Oregon, Wisconsin. His name, given by his Trinidadian father, Winston Smart, is in honor of the legendary Zulu warrior Shaka Zulu. When Smart was a child, his father left for a short vacation

in Trinidad; he did not return until Smart was in high school. According to Gary Parrish for *CBS Sports* (3 Dec. 2014), Smart's father was highly educated, with four college degrees, but abusive. He discouraged Smart and his brother from playing sports. Smart's father left again, at King's request, on December 12, 1994, during Smart's senior year in high school. Smart's maternal grandfather, Walter King, was a stronger presence in Smart's life during his childhood.

Smart also has an older half-brother, film critic and writer, J. M. Tyree. When the boys were young—Smart was eight—their mother sent them to spend several weeks living with a financially strapped family in Greenville, Mississippi. Monica King, who worked at a community center, arranged the trip in an effort to have her sons experience and understand the frustration of financial hardship and to counter what she saw as her sons' growing sense of entitlement. Smart recalls the experience to this day. King, who is white, also made a point of introducing Smart to nearby black communities, to better understand his own background. "As difficult as that was to go through," King told Jonathan Abrams for the *Bleacher Report* (10 Nov. 2016), "it really solidified Shaka's concept of who he is and what he stands for and what his family is about, even though his family has a lot of white people in it." In middle school, Smart joined two different basketball teams as a point guard: the mostly white one at his school and a traveling team called the Madison Spartans that was mostly black.

People in Smart's life say that he is known for his kindness and his acute perception of how other people feel and what they need. In high school, he convinced his mother to adopt another biracial student, Alfie Olson, who estimates that there were only ten students of color out of about two thousand in the school district (Mike Finger, writing for the *Houston Chronicle* on April 11, 2015, reported an estimate of about 1,200 students in the district). The two boys found comfort and friendship in one another after enduring racist harassment from their classmates. "Dealing with those little indignities, you've got to tell yourself you're a person and stick to that," Smart told Abrams. "And that helps define you versus *I'm black, I'm white,* or *I'm a jock, I'm a nerd.*"

EDUCATION AND COLLEGE CAREER

At Oregon High School, Smart and Olson became the basketball team's stars, and coach Kevin Bavery became a father figure, one of several such men in Smart's life. Smart was a three-year starter and a second-team All-Badger Conference pick as a senior. He also set the school record for assists in three categories: career, with 458; season, 201; and in a single game, 20. In

addition to his skills on the court, Smart excelled in school, and he earned an almost perfect score on his SAT. He graduated in 1995 and was accepted to three Ivy League universities, including Harvard, Yale, and Brown. But a visit to Yale, a wealthy university located in the economically depressed city of New Haven, Connecticut, left a bad taste in his mouth. "He said, 'Get me out of here,'" King recalled to Finger (11 Apr. 2015). "That elitism was not for him." Smart chose instead to attend Kenyon College, a small liberal arts school in Gambier, Ohio. He played point guard for the Lords, the school's Division III basketball team. The Lords' coach, Bill Brown, was a major factor in Smart's decision to attend the school. The two men became very close; Smart even lived with Brown's family during his freshman year.

When Brown took a job at California University of Pennsylvania that summer, Smart was crushed by Brown's departure and debated transferring schools. He ultimately chose to stay at Kenyon and play for the Lords, becoming a three-year captain and the school's all-time leader in assists. A history professor, Peter Rutkoff, first noticed Smart's natural teaching abilities when the student held forth in a class about the Great Migration, the mass migration of African Americans from the South to the Midwest during the early twentieth century and the subject of Smart's honors thesis. "I realized right away that he was in fact first a teacher, and it happened that he was going to teach the thing he liked most in the world, which was basketball," Rutkoff told Abrams. Smart graduated magna cum laude with a degree in history in 1999. After graduation he joined his mentor, Brown, at California University, where he served as assistant coach and earned master's degree in social science.

EARLY COACHING CAREER AND BREAKOUT SEASON

Two years after joining the staff at California University, coach Oliver Purnell offered Smart a job as the director of basketball operations at the University of Dayton in 2001. From there, he went to the University of Akron, where head coach Keith Dambrot made his coaches spend at least ten minutes with players after each practice. The custom taught Smart the importance of developing relationships with his players. Three years later, Smart rejoined Purnell at Clemson University in South Carolina, and two years after that, in 2008, he began working for coach Billy Donovan at the University of Florida. Just a year later, Donovan encouraged Smart to take an unexpected offer from Virginia Commonwealth University (VCU) in Richmond, Virginia. Smart accepted the position of Rams' head coach in 2009.

During Smart's first season at VCU, in 2010, the team won twenty-seven games as well as the College Basketball Invitational (CBI). This success could be attributed to Smart's signature style, an aggressive defensive strategy that he called Havoc. "We are going to wreak havoc on our opponents' psyche and their plan of attack," he told the team, as quoted by Shane Ryan for the now-defunct online magazine *Grantland* (5 Mar. 2013). Havoc involves a full-court press focused on keeping the ball from the opponent's guards. It's a fast-paced, "man-to-man style," Ryan wrote, "but with constant adjustments and double-teams."

For Smart's second season at VCU, in 2011, the Rams suffered a losing stretch in February, leading pundits to protest the team's inclusion in the NCAA bracket a month later. College basketball analyst and ESPN commentator Jay Bilas called the selection committee's decision "indefensible" and wondered on air whether the committee "knows if the ball is round," as quoted by Dan Fogarty for the blog *Sports Grid* (13 Mar. 2011). Bilas's outrage was no longer merited, however, after eleventh-seed VCU blew through its first two games, beating the University of Southern California (USC) by 13 points and Georgetown by 18 in the 64-team bracket. The Rams wreaked havoc on Purdue, beating them by 18 points to advance to the Sweet Sixteen for the first time in the school's history. There, they beat Florida State in overtime, 72–71. The team's historic run continued into the Elite Eight, where they managed to upset top-seeded Kansas, 71–61. "Once again we felt like nobody really thought we could win going into the game," Smart told Branch (27 Mar. 2011). "But these guys believed we could win. They knew we could win. And we talked before the game about how nobody else really matters." The Rams lost to Butler in the Final Four.

UNIVERSITY OF TEXAS AT AUSTIN
The Rams' stunning success made Smart one of the most sought-after coaches in college basketball. Though he ultimately chose to stay at VCU, he was offered lucrative posts at North Carolina State, Illinois, Tennessee, Minnesota, and the University of California, Los Angeles (UCLA), which offered to double his salary. When people asked why he chose to stay at VCU, Smart cited his commitment to his players and his own experience with his college coach, Brown. "I know what it's like for a coach who is your father figure to leave, and I understand, maybe better than most, how me leaving will affect more than just me and my family," he told Parrish. Under Smart, VCU returned to the NCAA tournament in 2012 and narrowly missed advancing to the Sweet Sixteen. After three more seasons and the graduation of a generation of players, Smart accepted the head coaching position at the University of Texas (UT) at Austin in the spring of 2015.

The Longhorns reportedly offered Smart $22 million over seven years, but Smart's brother, Olson, told Abrams that money was not the only appeal for Smart. "He wants to be in a place where it's in need of some change where he feels like he is needed, when he's really needed by his players," he said. After firing their previous coach, Rick Barnes, UT was ready for such a change, but two seasons in, Smart continues to struggle to build the team and unite it under a winning strategy. Although Smart has appeared particularly frustrated by his players' attitudes, which oscillate between fearful and entitled, he remains optimistic about the team's prospects. "I feel really good about that group of guys turning into a good team," he told Finger for the *Chronicle* (28 Dec. 2016). "The question is when." The Longhorns ended the 2016–17 season with an overall record of 11–22 in March after losing to West Virginia in the Big 12 quarterfinal.

PERSONAL LIFE
Smart is married to community advocate, journalist, and Harvard graduate Maya Payne Smart. The couple has a daughter named Zora Sanae, who was born in 2011. They live in Austin.

SUGGESTED READING
Abrams, Jonathan. "Shaka Smart Is Wreaking Havoc on College Basketball." *Bleacher Report*, 10 Nov. 2016, thelab.bleacherreport.com/shaka-smart-wreaking-havoc-college-basketball. Accessed 1 May 2017.

Branch, John. "First Four to Final Four: V.C.U. Stuns Kansas." *The New York Times*, 27 Mar. 2011, www.nytimes.com/2011/03/28/sports/ncaabasketball/28southwest.html. Accessed 1 May 2017.

Branch, John. "V.C.U.'s Brightest Star May Be the Head Coach." *The New York Times*, 26 Mar. 2011, mobile.nytimes.com/2011/03/27/sports/ncaabasketball/27vcu.html. Accessed 1 May 2017.

Finger, Mike. "Shaka Smart Facing Familiar UT Challenge." *Houston Chronicle*, 28 Dec. 2016, www.chron.com/sports/longhorns/article/Shaka-Smart-facing-familiar-UT-challenge-10823569.php. Accessed 1 May 2017.

Finger, Mike. "Smart's Vision Was a Lifetime in the Making." *Houston Chronicle*, 11 Apr. 2015, www.houstonchronicle.com/sports/article/Smart-s-vision-was-a-lifetime-in-the-making-6194139.php. Accessed 1 May 2017.

Parrish, Gary. "The Shaping of Shaka." *CBS Sports*, 3 Dec. 2014, www.cbssports.com/collegebasketball/feature/24862342/the-shaping-of-shaka. Accessed 1 May 2017.

Ryan, Shane. "Whiz Kids." *Grantland*, 5 Mar. 2013, grantland.com/features/shaka-smart-brad-stevens-butler-vcu. Accessed 1 May 2017.

—*Molly Hagan*

Jordan Spieth

Date of birth: July 27, 1993
Occupation: Golfer

Since turning professional in 2012, Jordan Spieth has built up an impressive résumé. The relative unknown first made a name for himself by capturing the 2013 John Deere Classic, becoming the youngest PGA Tour winner in eighty-two years and earning Rookie of the Year honors. Spieth is regarded among golf's elite, following a runner-up finish at the 2014 Masters and an impressive breakout 2015 season during which he clinched back-to-back majors, the world's number-one ranking, and the FedEx Cup.

Much of Spieth's early success is attributed to a talent and poise that belie his age and that have also earned him comparisons to one of the game's best players. "Spieth is a natural-born finisher," Johnny Miller told Jaime Diaz for *Golf Digest* (30 Mar. 2016). "So many guys today seem to win by accident, but Spieth doesn't. His game is ruled by that most important word: intent. Like Tiger . . . he truly plays every tournament intending to win."

EARLY LIFE AND EDUCATION

Jordan Alexander Spieth was born in Dallas, Texas on July 27, 1993, to Shawn and Mary Christine (Julius) Spieth. Athleticism runs in Spieth's family. His mother played basketball at Moravian College, in Bethlehem, Pennsylvania; his father was a member of neighboring Lehigh University's baseball team. Spieth's love of golf began at eighteen months, when his parents bought him a set of plastic golf clubs. He became so enamored that he transformed his front yard into a makeshift putting green. Spieth was eight when his parents joined Dallas's Brookhaven Country Club, where he first caught the eye of instructor Joey Anders. "It wasn't so much that he could hit the ball [well]. Lots of kids can do that. It was that he never hit the ball bad," Anders shared with John McAlley for *Golf* (16 Dec. 2015).

With his parents' encouragement, Spieth took up team sports (basketball, baseball, and football) at St. Monica Catholic School, to develop social skills while spending summer vacations on the golf course. In June 2006 Spieth, a competitor on the Northern Texas PGA Junior Tour, entered—and won—the boys' twelve-year-old division title at the Starburst Junior Golf Classic in Waco, Texas.

By early July, Spieth had switched coaches from Anders to Cameron McCormick, the director of instruction at Brook Hollow Golf Club in Dallas. Despite his raw talent, Spieth was not without his idiosyncrasies. "I had a big loop in my swing, a very weak grip, misaligned, shoulders open," he told Jim Moriarty for *Golf Digest* (3 Dec. 2013). McCormick honed Spieth's mechanics by having him swing with a rubber ball between his arms and also engaged him in putting contests to improve his short game. Within six months, Spieth had also adopted a cross-handed grip.

ON THE JUNIOR CIRCUIT

Spieth's coaching change paid off. In April 2007 he was victorious at the Junior All-Star at Walnut Creek—his American Junior Golf Association (AJGA) tournament debut. Two months later, he claimed the Championship Boys title at the Starburst Classic. After graduating from St. Monica in 2007, Spieth attended the all-boys Jesuit College Preparatory School of Dallas, where he played under former LGPA golfer Cathy Marino. As a member of the Rangers team (2007–11), Spieth won three consecutive Texas University Interscholastic League (UIL) 5A state boys championship titles in 2009, 2010, and 2011—the only golfer ever to accomplish this feat.

Spieth also had success on the junior-golf circuit. Three months after his March 2008 victory at the AJGA Championship at Traditions, Spieth became the youngest-ever winner of the

HP Byron Nelson Junior Championship. In early July he and other US juniors competed at the 2008 Wyndham Cup, a match-play event held at the Stanwich Club in Greenwich, Connecticut. Spieth represented a West squad that dominated the East, 30–20. Later that month he was runner-up at the R&A Junior Open and reached the semifinals of the sixty-first US Junior Amateur Championship.

Despite falling short in a sudden-death playoff at the 2008 Junior PGA Championships in August, Spieth's second-place finish earned him an appearance at September's Junior Ryder Cup, where his 3–0 record helped lead the US squad to its first-ever win in the prestigious international match-play competition. Spieth rallied from a four-stroke deficit to cap off an exciting come-from-behind victory at the PING Invitational in October 2008. "That one proved to me I could close the deal," he confided to Jon Mahoney for ESPN (18 May 2010).

The following June, Spieth successfully defended his title at the 2009 Byron Nelson Junior Championship while also setting the course record (62) at Dallas's Lakewood Country Club. A month later, Spieth, now the country's top-ranked junior golfer, made history at the 2009 US Junior Amateur, earning medalist honors during the thirty-six-hole stroke-play qualifying rounds and defeating San Diego's Jay Hwang in the thirty-six-hole match-play finals to win his first Junior Amateur crown. After achieving runner-up status for a second consecutive year at the Junior PGA Championship in August, he was honored by the AJGA as the 2009 Rolex Player of the Year.

PGA TOUR DEBUT AND NCAA TITLE

In January 2010 the sixteen-year-old Spieth received a golf sponsor exemption from the PGA Tour's HP Byron Nelson Championship—the tournament's first amateur exemption in fifteen years. To prepare for the four-day event in May, Spieth added strength training to his workout routine. He had a respectable debut, becoming the sixth-youngest player to make a PGA Tour cut and finishing tied for sixteenth.

Spieth's first 2010 victory came in June, at the Byron Nelson Junior Championship, where he clinched a record third consecutive title. He earned another PGA Tour exemption to the FedEx St. Jude Classic, where he missed the cut by one shot. A month later Spieth was part of the Junior Ryder Cup team that gave the United States its first-ever victory on European soil. After missing the Junior PLAYERS Championship in September 2008 and 2009 due to illness, Spieth came within one stroke of winning the tournament in 2010. He followed that up with his second consecutive PING Invitational title,

which Spieth handily won by nine strokes—an AJGA record.

Spieth's next history-making achievement came in July 2011, when he claimed the US Junior Amateur, joining Tiger Woods as the event's only other multiple winner. Other 2011 amateur achievements included a second-place finish at the Jones Cup Invitational, a fifth-place showing at the Azalea Invitational, quarterfinal appearances at the Western Amateur and US Amateur championships, and a record (2–0–1) at the Walker Cup.

In the fall of 2011, after graduating from Dallas Jesuit, Spieth, a three-time AJGA First Team All-American (2008–10), enrolled at the University of Texas (UT) with one objective in mind. "When I committed I told [head] coach [John Fields], 'I have . . . one main goal here. That's to accomplish a team national championship,'" he shared with Scott Michaux for the *Augusta Chronicle* (2 Apr. 2016). Spieth made good on his promise. As a freshman, he was the stroke average leader (70.92) for the Longhorns, who closed out the 2011–12 regular season with seven tournament crowns, the number-one ranking, a second-place finish at 2012 Big 12 Men's Championship, and a berth in the 2012 NCAA Men's Golf Championship, where his team bested Alabama for their first national crown since 1972.

In addition to earning Big 12 Conference Player of the Year and Freshman of the Year honors, Spieth was named a Ben Hogan Award finalist (2012), as well as a First Team All-American and All-Big 12 Team. On the PGA Tour, he competed in the 2012 US Open as an alternate and finished as the low amateur, tied for twenty-first with Tiger Woods, among others. Spieth's performance moved him to the top of the World Amateur Golf Rankings and earned him an exemption into the second stage of Qualifying School. Despite failing to earn PGA Tour status, Spieth left UT in December 2012 to turn professional, initially competing in *Web.com* and PGA tournaments.

JOINING THE PGA TOUR

By March 2013, Spieth had been granted temporary PGA Tour membership, following top-ten results at two pairs of *Web.com* and PGA events. Over the next four months, he finished in the top ten at three more events. The nineteen-year-old finally earned full membership in July, when he captured his first PGA title, the John Deere Classic—a victory that gave him automatic entry to the 2013 Open Championship. After top-five finishes at the Wyndham, Deutsche Bank, and TOUR Championships, along with top-twenty results at the Barclays and the BMW Championship, Spieth was tapped as PGA Rookie of the Year and represented the United States at the 2013 Presidents Cup. He ended the season ranked number ten among the PGA Tour's money leaders and twenty-two in the world.

Spieth started off 2014 with a successful first appearance at the Hyundai Tournament of Champions, finishing second to Zach Johnson. Spieth's next-best results came in February, when he placed fourth at the AT&T Pebble Beach National Pro-Am and reached the quarterfinals of WGC-Accenture Match Play Championship. Spieth had an impressive debut at the first major of the season, the 2014 Masters Tournament in April, where he shared a third-round lead with past champion Bubba Watson before finishing in second place. He was the second-youngest runner-up in Masters history.

The next month Spieth was also in contention to win the 2014 Players Championship before finishing in a fourth-place tie. In July he unsuccessfully defended his John Deere Classic title, dropping into a tie for seventh. His only other top-ten result was at the BMW Championship in September—the same month he became the youngest member of the US Ryder Cup team. Spieth followed that up with his first international win at the Emirates Australian Open on the PGA Tour of Australasia, before closing out the year with an overwhelming ten-stroke margin at the Tiger Woods Hero World Challenge in Orlando, Florida.

COMPETING IN MAJORS

Spieth's second PGA Tour title came in March 2015, with a three-way playoff win at the Valspar Championship, followed by runner-up results at the Valero Texas Open and the Shell Houston Open. Spieth continued his strong play into his next event, the Masters, where he was among the favorites to win. The twenty-one-year-old took a first-round lead with nine birdies—the youngest player to accomplish this feat. Spieth maintained a comfortable lead in the final round, clinching his first major title—and his first green jacket. The win, Spieth's third overall victory, propelled him to number two in the world golf rankings.

In June 2015 Spieth, a runner-up at the Crowne Plaza Invitational and third-place finisher at the Memorial Tournament, competed at his second major, the US Open, in which he secured his second major title, and the fourth victory of his career.

The next month Spieth reclaimed the John Deere Classic title—his second in three years—after winning a two-hole playoff against Tom Willis. However, his Grand Slam quest ended in a fourth-place tie at the Open Championship in late July, where he fell one stroke shy of the playoff. Spieth came close to a third major title, with his second-place finish at the 2015 PGA Championship. He closed out an impressive

season with a victory at the Tour Championship—a sixth career win that also earned him a $10 million bonus and the world's number-one ranking.

Spieth's first title of the 2016 season came at the Hyundai Tournament of Championships. He joined Tiger Woods and Horton Smith as one of three players to amass seven PGA Tour victories by the age of twenty-two. In April the reigning champion defended his Masters title at Augusta. Spieth maintained a close lead going into the final round, but after a spectacular failure on the twelfth hole, he finished tied for second.

Spieth tried to move on from his heartbreaking Masters loss with his eighth PGA Tour win at the 2016 Dean & Deluca Invitational in May. He played for the Ryder Cup team that gave the United States its first victory since 2008 and secured him a spot at the WGC Bridgestone Invitational, where he finished in a four-way tie for third. Spieth qualified for the FedEx Cup Playoffs, a series of four tournaments that determine the season's champion. His top-ten showings at the Barclays and BMW, twenty-first-place tie at the Deutsche Bank Championship, and top-twenty finish at the Tour Championship placed him ninth on the final leaderboard. In November 2016 Spieth captured his second Emirates Australian Open in three years.

Spieth had a solid start to 2017, with third-place results at the Tournament of Champions and the Sony Open. He claimed his first victory at Pebble Beach, making him only the second player (behind Woods) to have nine PGA Tour wins before age twenty-four.

Asked what made Spieth stand out among other golfers, NBC Sports analyst Jimmy Rogers, who had a front-row seat for Spieth's performance in the 2015 FedEx Cup, told McAlley, "He doesn't appear to be overwhelmed by the moment—he seizes it. . . . The moment seems to fuel him. It doesn't intimidate him in any way. Plenty of athletes say, 'Yeah, I live for these moments.' But for how many of them is that truly the case?"

PERSONAL LIFE

Spieth lives with his partner Annie Verret in a $2.3 million home in Preston Hollow he purchased in April 2015. Inspired by his younger sister, Ellie, Spieth founded an eponymous family foundation devoted to fundraising for special needs children. In January 2017 Spieth, currently in the second year of a ten-year endorsement contract with Under Armour, debuted Spieth One, his first signature shoe.

SUGGESTED READING

Diaz, Jaime. "Quick Learner: Jordan Spieth." *Golf Digest*, 30 Mar. 2016, www.golfdigest.

com/story/quick-learner-jordan-spieth.   Accessed 11 Mar. 2017.

Mahoney, Jon. "Jesuit's Spieth Cool under Pressure." *ESPN*, 18 May 2010, www.espn.com/dallas/news/story?id=5197742. Accessed 11 Mar. 2017.

McAlley, John. "The Hunger Game: Why Does Spieth Play as If His Soul Is on Fire?" *Golf.com*, 16 Dec. 2015, www.golf.com/tour-and-news/jordan-spieth-plays-soul-on-fire.   Accessed 11 Mar. 2017.

Michaux, Scott. "Spieth's Career Forged with Magic Moments." *The Augusta Chronicle*, 2 Apr. 2016, www.augusta.com/masters/story/news/spieth's-career-forged-magic-moments. Accessed 11 Mar. 2017.

Moriarty, Jim. "Newsmakers of the Year: Jordan Spieth." *Golf Digest*, 3 Dec. 2013, www.golfdigest.com/story/jordan-spieth-1-newsmakers. Accessed 11 Mar. 2017.

—*Bertha Muteba*

Photo by Jim Spellman/WireImage

Keith Stanfield

Date of birth: August 12, 1991
Occupation: Actor

After playing a lonely, troubled teen in the film *Short Term 12* (2013), the actor LaKeith "Keith" Stanfield has received one opportunity after another. Stanfield has played a variety of different characters. Among them are a civil rights activist in the Martin Luther King Jr. biopic *Selma* (2014); a gang member in the coming-of-age dramedy *Dope* (2015); and a heroin-addicted jazz musician in *Miles Ahead* (2015). In *Straight Outta Compton* (2015) he portrays the rapper Snoop Dogg; and in the Jordan Peele horror comedy *Get Out* (2017), he portrays Andrew Logan King, a role that is impossible to explain without giving away the suspenseful plot. He is also one of three main characters on the television series *Atlanta* (2016–), in which he plays Darius, a strange young man who many critics agree has stolen the show from series creator and costar Donald Glover, who is best known as the rapper Childish Gambino. Stanfield himself is also a rapper, and he performs as a member of the duo Moors.

EARLY LIFE

LaKeith Lee Stanfield was born on August 12, 1991, in San Bernardino, California. He is one of five children. In San Bernardino he encountered poverty and gang violence. In an interview with Ian Servantes for *Complex* (6 Sept. 2016), Stanfield said that as a boy in San Bernardino he was often "codeswitching," meaning using different lingo and slang and taking on different attitudes and mannerisms depending on the group he was hanging out with. He could just as easily hang out with "white guys," whom the gangbangers considered "corny dudes," as he would with the gangbangers themselves. "That was something I realized early on," Stanfield told Servantes. "Like, 'What is my identity?' And I realized my identity is in all of those. I learned how to survive that way, and it's been valuable for my career." In a way, Stanfield was neither, and he was both. Even as a boy he refused to be pigeonholed. Many of his friends played gangsta rap while he gravitated more toward Disney soundtracks and the emotional hard rock of Slipknot and Marilyn Manson.

Life in San Bernardino was also tough for Stanfield for various reasons. He often went hungry, which he has said he eventually got used to, as he told Servantes. "Baloney sandwiches with no mayo and no cheese," he recalled. "And that was it, but it was cool. I learned to be strong. I learned to be a hustler, a fighter. I learned to never give up." He also encountered serious violence at home. On several occasions he witnessed his mother being beaten by her boyfriend at the time. One time he called 911 and the man was arrested; on another occasion, the police handcuffed both his mother and her boyfriend. During these episodes, Stanfield, though young, became aware that telling the police or protective services could mean that he and his four siblings, two of whom have autism, could be taken away to foster care. As a boy Stanfield was sometimes beaten by his mother's boyfriend as well, he told Servantes. He recalled one incident in which he was hit with the "buckle end of a belt."

When Stanfield was about eleven, he and his mother and siblings moved to Victorville, California, where he spent the rest of his formative years. The town, still being built, was essentially a desert. The family lived in a two-story house and generally had a more peaceful existence there than in San Bernardino. But there was not much to do, so Stanfield and his friends had to make their own fun. Stanfield and some friends started a record company, called Stay Intelligent Records, and used a karaoke microphone to record their music. In high school he fell in love with acting. He did not do very well in most subjects, but in drama he was a star. And he took the prospect of being a professional actor very seriously. He got headshots, took classes at a modeling and acting school, and searched online for acting opportunities around Los Angeles.

BREAKOUT ROLE

While still in high school, Stanfield auditioned and got the lead role in an independent short film, *Short Term 12* (2008). The character, Mark, is a lonely, musically gifted teenager living in a group home for troubled teens. Stanfield was himself transitioning during this time from being a teenager to being a young adult, which is part of the reason he related so strongly to the character. The film was directed by Destin Daniel Cretton, who at the time was working on his master's degree at San Diego State University.

After high school, Stanfield set himself on a path to pursue acting as a career. He was determined to make it work, but he also needed to support himself. He moved to Sacramento, California, to pursue a relationship with his biological father. In Sacramento he held various jobs, including selling cable television subscriptions door to door. It was there that he found he had a chance to audition for a role that would open one door after another.

Cretton had decided to direct a full feature-length version of *Short Term 12*, and he asked Stanfield to audition for the role of Mark, now Marcus. Halfway through the audition Stanfield noticed that Cretton was crying because he was so moved by Stanfield's performance. The film, which also stars Brie Larson, went on to premiere at the South by Southwest (SXSW) Festival in March 2013. At the festival and later in general release, Stanfield received a great deal of praise for his portrayal of Marcus, a boy who is about to turn eighteen. In the film, Marcus lives in a group home for troubled kids, where he feels lonely and scared. Grace (Larson) plays one of the workers. Larson, in an interview with Servantes, said that Stanfield was so committed to his role as an isolated teen that he would not interact with her, not even to eat lunch,

during breaks between shooting. It was only after the end of filming that Larson and Stanfield became friends.

For his performance, Stanfield received nominations for two 2014 Black Reel Awards, as well as a nomination for best supporting male actor at the Independent Spirit Awards. At the Independent Spirit Awards show he met director Ava DuVernay, who would go on to direct him in *Selma* (2014). DuVernay, who saw something in the young actor, explained why she thought Stanfield stood out: "He feels like a real guy who has some weight on his shoulders, and yet you look in his eyes and see this vulnerability and this sweetness," DuVernay told Servantes. "For me that really encapsulates the vibe of so many African American men that I know and love. But in film and television we either see the alpha or the emasculated. He represents this beautiful hybrid of all that complexity."

STRAIGHT OUTTA COMPTON, SELMA, MILES AHEAD

After the festival premiere of *Short Term 12*, Stanfield was offered roles in other projects. He played Young Ghoul Face in the sci-fi action-horror movie *The Purge: Anarchy* (2014). Stanfield also portrayed civil rights activist Jimmy Lee Jackson in the film *Selma* (2014), which was about Dr. Martin Luther King, Jr. and other civil rights activists and their nonviolent campaign to gain voter rights with a march from Selma to Montgomery, Alabama. Though the role of Jackson was not a big one, it gave viewers a deeper understanding of Stanfield's range. The role also made Stanfield more reflective and thankful for the sacrifices made by Dr. King and other civil rights activists.

After playing a gang member named Bug in the coming-of-age drama-comedy *Dope* (2015) and a young drug-addicted trumpet player named Junior in the Miles Davis biopic *Miles Ahead* (2015), starring and directed by Don Cheadle, Stanfield appeared in yet another music-themed film, *Straight Outta Compton* (2015), about the gangster-rap group NWA, which included many rappers who went on to have successful solo careers, namely Dr. Dre and Ice Cube. In the film, Stanfield takes the part of Snoop Dogg, Dr. Dre's protégé. Though Stanfield is a rapper in his own right, when it came time to rap as Snoop in the film, he had to do so in a higher register than he was used to. Stanfield studied Snoop's mannerisms, body language, manner of speaking, and rap delivery style. Stanfield again stayed in character during shooting, as he did for *Short Term 12* and *Miles Ahead*—for the latter he did not go anywhere without his trumpet. In an interview with Andrew Barker for *Variety* (13 Aug. 2015), he described his method for playing Snoop: "I tried to constantly be in his sort of energy, be real cool on the set. [My costars] helped me out a bit—everyone referred to me as Snoop. Now, I didn't leave set still doing Snoop or anything. But a big inspiration for that was just trying to be in a high mind-state a lot of the time, just having that disposition of always being high."

ATLANTA

In the TV series *Atlanta*, Stanfield plays a strange guy named Darius—one of three central characters. The FX show is the creation of actor, writer, and rapper Donald Glover, also known as Childish Gambino. The show received major critical acclaim and gave Stanfield yet another platform to show his range and depth as an actor. In the series, Earn (Glover), a Princeton University dropout, decides to try to manage the career of his cousin Alfred (Brian Tyree Henry), a rapper known as Paper Boi. Stanfield's Darius is Alfred's friend and roommate.

Writing for the *New York Times* (19 Oct. 2016), Wesley Morris elaborated on exactly how Darius, "whom Keith Stanfield plays as a nincompoop visionary," is weird. "He's wonderful, too, a snoopy, Snoopy-looking guy, who can't be upstaged by high-on-drugs costumes (a Bedouin turban and a T-shirt, say). He, Alfred, and Earn are weirdos to one another and to other black people, too. On any other show, they'd be played by fitter, hotter actors. But *Atlanta* isn't going for sexy. It's going for a warped kind of real— and sometimes winds up at sexy anyway." In another review for the *New York Times*, James Poniewozik (5 Sept. 2016) noted that because Glover plays an observant, laid-back character, other characters have room to shine: "The show's breakout character may be Alfred's stoner-philosopher roommate, Darius."

PERSONAL LIFE

Stanfield lives in Los Angeles, California. He and his partner, actor Xosha Roquemore, announced in March 2017 that they are expecting their first child.

SUGGESTED READING

Cabe, Matthew. "Straight Outta Victorville." *Daily Press*, 8 Sept. 2015, www.vvdailypress.com/article/20150908/NEWS/150909737. Accessed 14 June 2017.

Morris, Wesley. "'Atlanta' Walks a Line between Magical Realism and Keeping It Real." Review of *Atlanta*, created by Donald Glover. *The New York Times*, 19 Oct. 2016, www.nytimes.com/2016/10/23/arts/television/atlanta-has-brilliant-characters-and-some-of-the-best-acting-on-tv.html. Accessed 14 June 2017.

Nicholson, Amy. "Keith Stanfield Is Stepping into Big Shoes—Snoop Dogg's." *LA Weekly*, 6 May 2015, www.laweekly.com/arts/keith-stanfield-is-stepping-into-big-shoes-snoop-doggs-5534239. Accessed 14 June 2017.

Poniewozik, James. "Review: In FX's 'Atlanta,' a Princeton Dropout Works the Angles Back Home." Review of *Atlanta*, created by Donald Glover. *The New York Times*, 5 Sept. 2016, www.nytimes.com/2016/09/06/arts/television/atlanta-fx-donald-glover.html. Accessed 14 June 2017.

Servantes, Ian. "How Lakeith Stanfield Went from Stealing Subs to Stealing Donald Glover's 'Atlanta.'" *Complex*, 6 Sept. 2016, www.complex.com/pop-culture/2016/09/keith-stanfield-atlanta. Accessed 14 June 2017.

Stanfield, LaKeith. "'Straight Outta Compton's' Lakeith Stanfield on Playing Snoop Dogg." Interview by Andrew Barker. *Variety*, 13 Aug. 2015, variety.com/2015/film/features/lakeith-straight-outta-compton-snoop-dogg-1201567858. Accessed 14 June 2017.

Staple, Justin. "Straight Out of Compton Actor Keith Stanfield Is Breaking into Music with Moors." *Noisey*, Vice, 28 Apr. 2015, noisey.vice.com/en_us/article/moors-keith-stanfield-gas-video-premiere-interview. Accessed 14 June 2017.

SELECTED WORKS

Short Term 12, 2013; *Selma*, 2014; *Dope*, 2015; *Miles Ahead*, 2015; *Straight Outta Compton*, 2015; *Atlanta*, 2016–; *Get Out*, 2017

—*Dmitry Kiper*

Jill Stein

Date of birth: May 14, 1950
Occupation: Politician

Jill Stein is an American physician and politician who, as a Green Party candidate, ran for governor of Massachusetts and president of the United States. In 2012, she received the largest percentage of the popular vote for a female presidential candidate in a general election.

EARLY LIFE AND EDUCATION

Jill Stein was born in Chicago on May 14, 1950 and was raised in Highland Park, Illinois, a suburb north of Chicago. Her mother was a homemaker and her father was a small business attorney. She has two older sisters and one brother. Stein has described her family as largely apolitical, but she became interested in politics following a trip to Sweden in the summer of 1967 with the Experiment in International Living while she was in high school. Stein later permanently relocated to Massachusetts after graduating magna cum laude from Harvard College in 1973 and attending Harvard Medical School, where she earned a medical degree in 1979. She began practicing internal medicine, which became her primary career. She worked as an internist at Harvard Community Health Plan and the Simmons College Health Center.

She became concerned about the epidemic levels of asthma, autism, obesity, diabetes, and other conditions that she was seeing in her clinical practice, so she began working as an activist with the public-health organization Physicians for Social Responsibility. Unsatisfied with political response to emerging research about environmental toxins affecting children, Stein became active in politics in 1998, testifying before legislative panels about the negative health impacts of pollution. Stein influenced the Massachusetts legislature to update the state's fish advisories regarding mercury contamination. She also helped to lead a campaign to clean up the state's coal plants, leading to the passage of legislation that imposed the most protective coal regulations in effect at the time. She also advocated for campaign finance reform and promoted the state's Clean Elections Law, which was approved by voters with a two-to-one margin in 1998 but repealed by the state legislature in an unrecorded voice vote in 2003. From 1982 to 2006, she was an instructor of medicine at Harvard Medical School.

POLITICAL CAREER

Stein first ran for public office in 2002, as the Green-Rainbow Party's candidate for governor of Massachusetts. She earned 3.5 percent of the vote in her first gubernatorial campaign. This was seen as a successful effort for a minor third-party candidate. Her campaign for governor saw her debate the eventual winner, Mitt Romney, whom she later faced in the 2012 presidential race.

The Green Party, the fourth-largest political party in the United States, was closely associated with Ralph Nader during his 1996 and 2000 presidential campaigns. Stein effectively assumed leadership of the party with her 2012 campaign, which foregrounded many of the party's long-held concerns regarding environmental protection, military spending, health care access, and civil rights.

Following unsuccessful campaigns for election to the Massachusetts House of Representatives in 2004 and the office of the Massachusetts Secretary of the Commonwealth in 2006, Stein was elected to the town meeting in Lexington, Massachusetts, in 2005 and was reelected in 2008. Following another run for the office of governor of Massachusetts in 2010, Stein announced she would run as the Green Party's candidate for president of the United States.

Stein's 2012 campaign was built on a "Green New Deal," a platform that sought to deliver meaningful legislation to address the effects of climate change while creating jobs and providing stimulus funds for environmentally positive initiatives. Modeled on Franklin D. Roosevelt's New Deal policies of the 1930s, the proposed program was touted as an economic solution as much as an environmental one. In addition to environmental and social issues, Stein's presidential platform centered on campaign finance reform. Known for employing bold rhetoric, Stein has used the phrase "business-as-usual politics" to criticize politicians in the United States whose campaigns are funded by large private businesses. In 2015, she described the field of presidential contenders as "corrupt and sold out."

Stein and her running mate, Cheri Honkala, were arrested for blocking traffic in October 2012 while protesting outside a presidential debate hosted at Hofstra University, which no third-party candidates were invited to attend. Stein told the reporters the debate was "fake and contrived," and that, as a candidate on 85 percent of general election ballots, she should be allowed to debate the Republican and Democratic candidates.

While she openly acknowledges the unlikelihood of winning the presidency, Stein has often said her campaigning is intended to highlight social and political issues she feels are not addressed in the traditional two-party electoral process.

Stein's 2012 campaign raised roughly $1 million, following the Green Party's policy of denying any donations from private corporations. In 2015, Stein pointed to this figure in comparison to the $900 million Koch Industries allocated to funding candidates for the 2016 election. On June 22, 2015, Stein announced her intention to seek the Green Party's nomination in the 2016 presidential campaign.

IMPACT

Stein received 0.36 percent of the vote in the 2012 general election, making her the most successful female presidential candidate in any general election in United States history. Her popularity during the 2012 race led to her being the second-ever Green Party candidate, after Nader in 2000, to receive federal matching funds.

PERSONAL LIFE

Stein enjoys playing and writing music. Stein has two sons, Ben and Noah, with her husband, fellow physician Richard Rohrer. Stein lives in Lexington, Massachusetts.

SUGGESTED READING

"About Jill Stein." *Jill2016.com*. Jill2016 Exploratory Committee, n.d. Web. 13 Oct. 2015.

Bachko, Katia. "The Occupy Candidate." *New Yorker*. Condé Nast, 19 Sept. 2012. Web. 12 Oct. 2015.

Henneberger, Melinda. "Is Jill Stein Crazy, or Are We?" *Washington Post*. Washington Post, 20 Oct. 2012. Web. 12 Oct. 2015.

Nader, Ralph. "Why Run for President If You Don't Have a Real Chance?" *Los Angeles Times*. Los Angeles Times, 15 May 2015. Web. 12 Oct. 2015.

Nichols, John. "A Presidential Candidate Willing to Get Arrested to Fight Foreclosure Abuse." *Nation*. Nation, 2 Aug. 2012. Web. 12 Oct. 2015.

Oremus, Will. "Finally, a Presidential Debate Tackles Climate Change." *Slate*. Slate Group, 24 Oct. 2012. Web. 12 Oct. 2015.

Saulny, Susan. "Party Strains to Be Heard Now That Its Voice Isn't Nader's." *New York Times*. New York Times, 12 July 2012. Web. 12 Oct. 2015.

Stein, Jill. Interview by Paul Jay. *TheRealNews.com*. Real News Network, 15 Feb. 2015. Web. 4 Nov. 2015.

—*Richard Means*

Photo by Gregg DeGuire/WireImage

Amandla Stenberg

Date of birth: October 23, 1998
Occupation: Actor

A year after Amandla Stenberg debuted in the 2011 action thriller *Colombiana*, she costarred opposite Jennifer Lawrence in the film adaptation of Suzanne Collins's 2008 young-adult (YA) novel *The Hunger Games*. Stenberg spent the next three years racking up small-screen credits in the Fox supernatural drama *Sleepy Hollow* and the NBC comedy *Mr. Robinson*. She then made the leap from supporting actor to lead actor with *As You Are* (2016), a teen-angst drama that won a Special Jury Award at the Sundance Film Festival.

The following year Stenberg took center stage in another YA book adaptation: Nicola Yoon's best-selling *Everything, Everything*, a teen romance between a black girl with a rare immune disorder and her white neighbor. For Stenberg, *Everything, Everything* represented more than just her first leading role. "Diversity is something that people desperately want. I'm lucky enough to be here and see what's happening and take those roles when they do appear," she confided to Anthony Breznican for *Entertainment Weekly* (27 Apr. 2017). "I'm very aware of how special it

is that I get to have this experience of creating representation while talking about representation at a time where people really, really want to see black girls as leads in movies."

Stenberg continues to tackle hot-button issues in *Where Hands Touch*, an interracial World War II romance between German teens, and *The Hate U Give*, inspired by the Black Lives Matter movement. "There's a lack of representation for different kinds of people, and so I want to provide that. Especially focusing on stories that feature and star women of colour—that's very important to me," she told Sirin Kale for *Dazed* (24 Mar. 2016).

THE ACTING BUG BITES
Los Angeles, California, native Amandla Stenberg was born to Karen Brailsford and Tom Stenberg on October 23, 1998. Stenberg's African American mother was an entertainment reporter, while her Danish-born father worked in the music business. She has two older half-sisters.

Acting captivated Stenberg at age three. "The daughter of one of my mom's friends was doing commercials, and when I heard about it, I said, 'You'll see me on TV,'" she recalled to Iain Blair for *Variety* (20 Oct. 2011). Stenberg's prediction quickly came true. Following a brief stint as a model for Disney print catalogs, the four-year-old appeared in commercials for Walmart and McDonald's, as well as a public service announcement for the Martin Luther King Jr. National Memorial.

Stenberg also took an early interest in music. She learned to play the guitar from her father and took violin lessons in elementary school. Drums became part of Stenberg's repertoire when she enrolled in the RockSTAR Music Education program. Stenberg went on to be an instrumentalist for the back-to-back winners of RockSTAR's annual Battle of the Bands competition (2007–8). She received the 2008 Los Angeles City Elementary Schools Music Association violin scholarship and in 2009 performed with the LA Unified School District Honors Orchestra.

BREAKTHROUGH

A year later Stenberg was cast in her first feature film, *Colombiana* (2011), portraying the younger version of the lead character, Cataleya Restrepo, an assassin seeking to avenge her parents' murder by a ruthless Colombian drug lord. During the film's opening sequence, the kingpin's henchmen pursue Cataleya through the favelas, or slums; for that scene, Stenberg tackled several stunts with the help of David Belle, the pioneer of Parkour, a training discipline of running and athletics to enable efficient movement through all environments. Stenberg's big-screen debut caught the eye of critics, including Mike Hale, who, in his *New York Times* review (25 Aug. 2011), hailed "her portrayal of the future deadly-but-sensitive killer [as] such a perfect combination of trembling emotion, action chops and deadpan humor."

Around this time, Stenberg also landed uncredited roles in the Tyler Perry sequel *Why Did I Get Married Too?* (2010) and the crime thriller *The Texas Killing Fields* (2011). She played a part in the pilot of the TNT summer sci-fi drama *Falling Skies* as well.

By May 2011, the newcomer was already filming the much-anticipated movie adaptation of *The Hunger Games*, Suzanne Collins's popular YA trilogy. To play Rue, the youngest participant in the titular death-defying contest and surrogate sister to series' heroine Katniss Everdeen (Jennifer Lawrence), Stenberg read the first book five times. However, the role, which required tree climbing, involved little physical training. "I didn't have to do any of the hard-core stuff, but I got strapped in my custom harness. I flew around the room and jumped from tree to tree," she shared with Web Behrens for *TimeOut Chicago* (30 Jan. 2012).

When *The Hunger Games* premiered in March 2012, critics hailed Stenberg's performance. Richard Corliss lauded her "underage winsomeness" for *Time* (21 Mar. 2012). Ty Burr remarked in his *Boston.com* review (22 Mar. 2012), "The youngest and most vulnerable of the 24 contestants, Rue bonds with Katniss in a relationship that, on the page, packs a wallop. Stenberg plays the role with sensitivity and fire but without the otherworldly spookiness that made

the character so memorable." Stenberg shared the 2012 Teen Choice Award for choice movie chemistry with Lawrence, and was nominated for the 2013 NAACP Image Award for supporting actress in a motion picture.

SMALL-SCREEN CREDITS

Next came Stenberg's costarring turn in the dramatic short film *Mercy* (2013) as a violinist and the daughter of a limousine driver, played by singer Robin Thicke. *Mercy* represented Thicke's directorial debut.

In October 2013 Stenberg played herself in an online Funny or Die spoof centering on a former child actor-turned-psychologist, Kiernan Shipka, who now counsels fellow child stars. Stenberg followed that up with a four-episode guest stint during the 2013–14 season of the Fox drama *Sleepy Hollow*. Next, she voiced the character Bia in the hit animated sequel *Rio 2*, released in April 2014.

Soon after *The Hunger Games*, Stenberg had been cast alongside comedian Craig Robinson in an unnamed NBC pilot, which the network did not pick up until 2014. By then, the show had undergone several changes: filming shifted from single camera to multicamera, actresses Meagan Good and Peri Gilpin were added, and Stenberg's character, Irene, was renamed Halle. When *Mr. Robinson* finally premiered in August 2015, critics and audiences alike panned the show and it was cancelled after only six episodes.

GRADUATING TO LEAD ACTOR

Stenberg achieved lead-actor status in *As You Are*, Miles Joris-Peyrafitte's directorial debut. In the 1990s coming-of-age drama, Stenberg plays Sarah, a straight-laced student who bonds with two misfit classmates and accompanies them on a road trip of self-discovery. *As You Are* debuted at the 2016 Sundance Film Festival, where it won the US Dramatic Special Jury Award and was picked up by Amazon. After making the rounds on the festival circuit, *As You Are* had its New York premiere in February 2017.

That same year, Stenberg also starred in the adaptation of *Everything, Everything*, Nicola Yoon's 2015 novel of the same name. Stenberg was immediately drawn to the script. "This project was really special because not only was the director a black woman, it was written by a black woman, featuring a main character who is biracial, who is in an interracial relationship," she shared with Mehera Bonner for *Marie Claire* (8 May 2017). "There are so many different layers—it's just a more accurate reflection of our world today." *Everything, Everything* also struck a chord with audiences; following its May release, the teen romance earned over $56.4 million worldwide on a $10 million budget.

OTHER PROJECTS

In late 2016 Stenberg performed in another interracial love story: the landmark *Where Hands Touch*, in which Stenberg plays Leyna, a biracial German teen who falls for a Hitler Youth soldier—a role for which she shaved her head. Sony Pictures picked up the film rights at the 2017 Cannes Film Festival, but a release date was not announced. Stenberg next landed a role as a teen fugitive with telekinetic powers in the forthcoming adaptation of Alexandra Bracken's 2012 dystopian thriller *The Darkest Minds*. Filming began in the spring of 2017, and its release is scheduled for September 2018. She also headlines in the screen adaptation of Angie Thomas's *The Hate U Give*, playing a teenager whose best friend is killed by a police officer. The production on the film was set to begin in September 2017.

The rising actor is also a budding filmmaker. In 2014 Stenberg wrote, filmed, and directed her first short, *The Yellow Wallpaper*, inspired by the Charlotte Perkins Gilman tale about an obsessive, mentally ill woman whose physician husband confines her to a room covered with the titular wallpaper. *Blue Girls Burn Fast* (2016), Stenberg's nineteen-minute short about a friendship between a foster teen and her intrusive neighbor, earned her admission to New York University to study directing and cinematography.

Stenberg has also collaborated on print and musical projects. She and Sebastian A. Jones cowrote two related comic book series about a mixed-race female warrior, *NIOBE: She Is Life* and *NIOBE: She Is Death*. She released two EPs with Honeywater, her folk-rock duo with Zander Hawley, 2015 and 2016; collaborated with Dev Hynes, "Blood Orange," on three music videos for his 2015 album *Freetown Sound*; and appeared in the music video for Beyoncé's 2016 visual album, *Lemonade*, and the companion HBO special.

SOCIAL ACTIVIST AND TRENDSETTER

Stenberg has been outspoken regarding issues facing the black community and women. In April 2015, she posted "Don't Cash Crop My Cornrows," a four and a half minute YouTube video—and history class assignment—discussing how mainstream white culture appropriates black culture. Two months later Stenberg became embroiled in a social media feud when she criticized Kylie Jenner's Instagram self-portrait featuring cornrows. Stenberg, who promotes the No Kid Hungry campaign and supports the Ubuntu Education Fund, also advocates for girls becoming involved in science, technology, engineering, and math. The Ms. Foundation for Women named Stenberg its Feminist Celebrity of 2015, *Time* magazine listed her among its 30 Most Influential Teens of 2015, and the 2016 Black Girls Rock! Young, Gifted and Black Award.

Also in 2016, Stenberg was tapped to advertise POP, Stella McCartney's new fragrance. The budding fashion icon—and front-row attendee at Chanel's Fall 2017 Couture show in Paris—has graced the covers of *Teen Vogue*, *Elle UK*, and *Nylon*, among others.

PERSONAL LIFE

Stenberg made headlines when she revealed her bisexuality during her January 8, 2016, appearance on the *Teen Vogue* Snapchat. That April she openly identified as gender nonbinary (not exclusively male or female). Stenberg prefers the pronouns "they" and "them" personally but "she" and "her" for business.

Stenberg began dating director Tucker Tripp in the spring of 2016; they met while filming a Blood Orange music video. The couple share a West Los Angeles bungalow.

SUGGESTED READING

Bonner, Mehera. "Amandla Stenberg's New Movie Is Bringing Diversity to the White-Washed World of Teen Romance." *Marie Claire*, 8 May 2017, www.marieclaire.com/celebrity/news/a27000/amandla-stenberg-everything-everything-interview. Accessed 7 Sept. 2017.

Breznican, Anthony. "Amandla Stenberg: 'People Really, Really Want to See Black Girls as Leads in Movies.'" *Entertainment Weekly*, 27 Apr. 2017, ew.com/movies/2017/04/27/everything-everything-amandla-stenberg-interview. Accessed 7 Sept. 2017.

Burr, Ty. Review of *The Hunger Games*, directed by Gary Ross. *Boston.com*, Boston Globe Media Partners, 22 Mar. 2012, archive.boston.com/ae/movies/articles/2012/03/22/hunger_games_movie_aims_for_solid_entertainment_and_hits_the_mark. Accessed 7 Sept. 2017.

Corliss, Richard. "*The Hunger Games*: The Odds Are Not in Your Favor." Review of *The Hunger Games*, directed by Gary Ross. *Time*, 21 Mar. 2012, entertainment.time.com/2012/03/21/the-hunger-games-the-odds-are-not-in-your-favor/?iid=ent-main-lede. Accessed 7 Sept. 2017.

Hale, Mike. "She Walks in Beauty, and Brings Along a Bazooka." Review of *Colombiana*, directed by Olivier Megaton. *The New York Times*, 25 Aug. 2011, www.nytimes.com/2011/08/26/movies/zoe-saldana-in-colombiana-review.html. Accessed 7 Sept. 2017.

Kale, Sirin. "Amandla Stenberg to Star in a Black Lives Matter Film." *Dazed*, 24 Mar. 2016, www.dazeddigital.com/artsandculture/article/30512/1/

amandla-stenberg-to-star-in-a-black-lives-matter-film. Accessed 7 Sept. 2017.

Stenberg, Amandla. "Amandla Stenberg of *The Hunger Games*." Interview by Web Behrens. *TimeOut Chicago*, 30 Jan. 2012, www.timeout.com/chicago/kids/activities/amandla-stenberg-of-the-hunger-games-interview. Accessed 7 Sept. 2017.

SELECTED WORKS

Colombiana, 2011; *The Hunger Games*, 2012; *As You Are*, 2016; *Everything, Everything*, 2017

—*Bertha Muteba*

Javaka Steptoe

Date of birth: April 19, 1971
Occupation: Author and illustrator

A prolific and nationally renowned illustrator of children's books, Javaka Steptoe is also the 2017 winner of the Randolph Caldecott Medal, which, according to the prize's website, has recognized the "most distinguished American picture book for children." Steptoe was honored for his distinctive collage work for *Radiant Child: The Story of Young Artist Jean-Michel Basquiat*, a 2016 book that celebrated the life of the acclaimed abstract painter, who died in 1988. (One of Basquiat's paintings sold at auction for more than $110 million in 2017.) The award was a capstone on Steptoe's already distinguished career: he has received several honors for his books, including the Coretta Scott King Award for illustration, and earned numerous positive reviews for his work from both critics and readers.

Steptoe is the son of artists; his father, John Steptoe, was also a celebrated children's book illustrator. Throughout his life, Steptoe has studied and worked with a wide variety of materials, including, as he did with *Radiant Child*, canvases of scavenged wood that he painted and collaged with photos. His collage work is informed by the black experience in the United States but, like all great art, expands beyond it, making the art accessible to people from all walks of life. In addition to his work as a children's book artist, Steptoe is also a lecturer and has spoken often throughout the country on the importance of children's education.

EARLY LIFE

Steptoe was born on April 19, 1971, in New York City. He is the son of the artists Stephanie Douglas and John Steptoe. His father, whose parents hailed from Virginia, was born in Brooklyn, New York, in 1950. He published his first picture book, *Stevie*, at age eighteen. He went on to illustrate sixteen books before his early death at the age of thirty-eight in 1989, writing ten of those himself. A pioneering African American children's book illustrator, John Steptoe earned two Caldecott Honors, one in 1985 for *The Story of Jumping Mouse: A Native American Legend* and one in 1988 for *Mufaro's Beautiful Daughters: An African Tale*. He also won the Coretta Scott King Book Award for illustration twice: in 1982 for *Mother Crocodile* and in 1988 for *Mufaro's Beautiful Daughters*.

Much of Javaka's artistic education came through serving as a model and inspiration for his father, as well as watching his parents at work. In an interview with *Mosaic Magazine* (12 Apr. 2017), Steptoe recalled to Mariahadessa Ekere Tallie: "I was a consistent witness to their creativity. I was learning from them either in their studio or in the next room. I'd be drawing and if I had any questions I'd ask them how do you do this or that. They'd take a couple of seconds and show me and then I'd keep on doing what it is that I was doing."

Later on, he would engage with art through the myriad of art museums in New York City, although his first trip to a museum was not one devoted entirely to art. Steptoe recalled for Peter Stamelman for the *Brooklyn Daily Eagle* (11 Nov. 2016): "Like most New York City kids, the first museum I visited wasn't an art museum, it was the Museum of Natural History. Those dinosaurs . . . they were iconic and really resonated for me. Later on, when I was a bit older, my parents would take me to art museums."

EDUCATION AND EARLY CAREER

By the time he finished high school, Steptoe was certain he would follow in his parents' footsteps and become an artist. He studied at the Cooper Union for the Advancement of Science and Art, where he took foundation classes in drawing, photography, printmaking, and sculpture. Upon his graduation, he soon found work as an illustrator of children's books, beginning with *In Daddy's Arms I Am Tall: African Americans Celebrating Fathers*, which was published in 1997. His debut work earned him a number of notable awards, include the Coretta Scott King Book Award for illustration and a nomination for outstanding children's literature work at the 1998 NAACP Image Awards. The book was also named a finalist for the Bluebonnet Award for Excellence in Children's Books. His early success made him quickly realize that he had found his true vocation, for a variety of reasons. As Steptoe told Tallie, "Creating books for children is therapeutic. It's an opportunity to go back and really dig around and explore that stuff you need to figure out so that you can go forward. When I worked on *In Daddy's Arms I Am Tall*, my father had recently passed away and the book was a way for me [to] deal with that."

Steptoe followed his initial success with *In Praise of Our Fathers and Mothers: A Black Family Treasury by Outstanding Authors and Artists* (1997), a collection of stories by famous artists and writers compiled by Cheryl Hudson and Wade Hudson; *Do You Know What I'll Do?* (2000), by Charlotte Zolotow; and *A Pocketful of Poems* (2001), by Nikki Grimes. *The Jones Family Express*, published in 2003, was the first book that Steptoe both wrote and illustrated. The book, about a young African American boy who awaits his world-traveling aunt's postcards by using a discarded model train to create his own tales of travel, received excellent reviews from such magazines as *Booklist* and *School Library Journal*. Like its predecessors, it employed a wide variety of materials to create Steptoe's eye-catching collages.

Steptoe followed this success with a collaboration with writer Karen English, *Hot Day on Abbott Avenue* (2004), about two young girls who refuse to play together anymore—until something brings them back together again. The book was named a 2005 honor book by Jane Addams Children's Book Award. "*Hot Day on Abbott Avenue* was a really fun book for me to do," Steptoe said to Stamelman. "The language is very musical. I created these two characters going through their day, playing 'Double Dutch' and hopscotch, other games. So, the reader hears the rhythm of these games."

MAKING A NAME FOR HIMSELF

By the mid-2000s, Steptoe was a well-regarded illustrator, noted for his inventive use of collage. Work came quickly and included *Sweet, Sweet Baby!* (2005), a cloth book for infants and toddlers; *All of the Above* (2008), a middle-grade novel by Shelley Pearsall; and *Rain Play* (2008), a children's book written by Cynthia Cotten. In 2009 he got the opportunity to illustrate *Amiri and Odette: A Love Story*, a poem written by the noted children's author Walter Dean Myers. "*Amiri and Odette: A Love Story* is a haunting story," Steptoe recalled, as quoted on the Scholastic website. "I was struck by this poem that reminds readers that love does survive among the drug deals and gang violence of the inner city. In preparing the artwork, I wanted the reader to feel the grit, noise, and urgency of the streets." To achieve this effect, he used acrylic paint on slabs of asphalt and incorporated everyday items such as candy wrappers, plastic bags, and jewelry.

He followed these works with *Jimi: Sounds Like a Rainbow: A Story of the Young Jimi Hendrix*, a children's book about the rock pioneer, written by Gary Golio and published in 2010, and *What's Special about Me, Mama?* (2011), a children's book written by Kristina Evans that discusses how children need to understand they are important, as seen through the eyes of an African American family. In interviews Steptoe has often noted that he is highly conscious of his audience while he works on his children's book illustrations. Steptoe told Tallie, "Children are dealing with their lives and whatever they were given. . . . It's really all about the journey that person is going to take. I just see myself as someone who is going to put out an option. My work says 'There is also this in the world if you're interested.'"

THE CALDECOTT MEDAL

Steptoe's greatest success to date has come through his children's book *Radiant Child: The Story of Young Artist Jean-Michel Basquiat*, which was published in 2016. Basquiat was an abstract artist who died tragically young, at the age of twenty-seven, in 1988. During his short career, he was considered one of the leading lights of the New York City art scene. Steptoe, in developing his book, did not use any of Basquiat's works but instead created his own original artwork that drew its inspiration from Basquiat. "I think one of the things that drew me to Basquiat is that he was celebrating things that were happening in my life; my experiences," Steptoe noted to Shannon Maughan for *Publishers Weekly* (23 Jan. 2017). "He uses skelzie boards in his art and I played skelzies growing up. . . . It's like marbles, but instead of marbles, you use weighted bottle caps and crash them into each other while trying to slide the caps into the boxes on the board."

Steptoe's *Radiant Child* earned widespread critical acclaim and, most notably, the 2017 Caldecott Medal. The award has been one of the highlights of his career thus far and what he considers to be a very humbling experience. "The most important thing it does is bring my voice to more people," he told Maughan. "Whatever I'm interested in saying—and people don't necessarily have to agree with me—if I have something to say, I have a voice that's going to be heard. It's kind of like Spider-Man: with great power comes great responsibility. I appreciate that. I hope to be seen as someone who thinks deeply and cares about the world and cares about what's going on."

SUGGESTED READING

"About Javaka Steptoe." *Javaka Steptoe*, www.javaka.com/bio.html. Accessed 24 May 2017.

"Javaka Steptoe." *Scholastic*, www.scholastic.com/teachers/authors/javaka-steptoe. Accessed 1 June 2017.

Maughan, Shannon. "'A Very Incredible Day': Javaka Steptoe on His 2017 Caldecott Medal." *Publishers Weekly*, 23 Jan. 2017, www.publishersweekly.com/pw/by-topic/childrens/childrens-authors/article/72585-a-very-incredible-day-javaka-steptoe-on-his-2017-caldecott-medal.html. Accessed 24 May 2017.

Steptoe, Javaka. "Interview with Javaka Steptoe: 'Art Outside the Lines.'" Interview by Peter Stamelman. *Brooklyn Daily Eagle*, 11 Nov. 2016, www.brooklyneagle.com/articles/2016/11/30/interview-javaka-steptoe-'art-outside-lines'. Accessed 24 May 2017.

Steptoe, Javaka. Interview by Mariahadessa Ekere Tallie. *Mosaic Magazine*, 12 Apr. 2017, mosaicmagazine.org/javaka-steptoe-interview. Accessed 24 May 2017.

SELECTED WORKS

In Praise of Our Fathers and Mothers: A Black Family Treasury by Outstanding Authors and Artists, 1997; *Do You Know What I'll Do?*, 2000; *The Jones Family Express*, 2003; *Hot Day on Abbott Avenue*, 2004; *Sweet, Sweet Baby!*, 2005; *All of the Above*, 2008; *Amiri and Odette: A Love Story*, 2009; *Jimi: Sounds like a Rainbow: A Story of the Young Jimi Hendrix*, 2010; *What's Special About Me, Mama?*, 2011; *Radiant Child: The Story of Young Artist Jean-Michel Basquiat*, 2015

—Christopher Mari

Lindsey Stirling

Date of birth: September 21, 1986
Occupation: Violinist, dancer, and performance artist

Performance artist Lindsey Stirling's compositions combine classical, electronic, and dance music. Stirling made it to the quarterfinals on the reality television show *America's Got Talent* in 2010. She capitalized on the exposure to beat her own path to stardom, posting covers of popular theme music from the video game *The Legend of Zelda* and a medley of themes from the Lord of the Rings film series on her YouTube channel, LindseyStomp. Her elaborate costumes and exuberant choreography underscored the swelling energy of her music. In 2012, Stirling posted one of her original compositions, something she had done before, but she was nervous. "I was worried my subscribers wouldn't like it," Stirling told Aly Comingore for the Santa Barbara *Independent* (7 Nov. 2012). But the video for the dubstep song, "Crystallize," garnered more than one million views in less than two days. "That was the moment when I decided I was going to really go for it," Stirling recalled to Comingore.

Since then, Stirling has released three albums, all of which have topped the Billboard Top Dance/Electronic Albums chart. The title track to her second album, the independently produced *Shatter Me* (2014), debuted in the number-two slot on the Billboard 200 chart, and the album itself won a Billboard Music Award for best dance/electronic album in 2015. Her 2016 album, *Brave Enough*, claimed the same prize in 2017.

EARLY LIFE AND EDUCATION

Stirling was born to a Mormon family in Santa Ana, California, on September 21, 1986. Her father, Stephen J. Stirling, worked first as a freelance writer and a teacher while Stirling was growing up. Stirling's mother, Diane Leigh, taught her to make do without much money. Growing up in Mesa, Arizona, Stirling and her four siblings were poor, but the experience taught her to use her imagination.

Despite a happy childhood, Stirling struggled in school, unable to learn to read until partway through the first grade. A doctor told her that she had a complex learning disability called "cross dominance." Basically Stirling's eyes were seeing words on a page, but that information, what the words actually said, was getting scrambled on the way to her brain. To correct what is essentially a vision problem, young Stirling had to wear an eye patch for an hour each day. She hated wearing the patch until she discovered a costume pirate hat in a closet. In a decision that would prove emblematic of Stirling's lemons-to-lemonade personality, she became a full-fledged pirate for that daily hour. (The experience gives Stirling's 2016 autobiography, written with her sister Brooke Passey, its title *The Only Pirate at the Party*.)

Stirling's parents, classical music lovers if not musicians themselves, inspired her to pick up the violin. Her father often took her to see free community concerts. She first asked her parents for lessons when she was just six years old. She began to learn to play but recalls her hands shaking with nerves at recitals. It was not until she became a backup instrumentalist for the rock band Stomp on Melvin as a teen that she began to actually enjoy performing onstage. "There were these rocking audiences that just wanted to have a good time, which was so different from the classical scene," Stirling told Comingore. "That was kind of what sparked my interest."

Stirling soon got her start filming and editing music videos, using basic software her father gave her for her sixteenth birthday. She made videos for Stomp on Melvin but also choreographed and directed her friends in videos for popular songs such as Avril Lavigne's "Sk8er Boi." She even learned how to rig her own green screen and create special effects. Stirling also began writing her own music.

After graduating from Mesquite High School, Stirling enrolled at Brigham Young University in Provo, Utah. She took eighteen months off after her sophomore year to serve as a missionary—a mandatory activity for young Mormons—in New York City. Stirling eventually finished her bachelor's degree in recreation management and therapeutic recreation in 2015.

IN COMPETITION

In 2005, Stirling competed in the Arizona Junior Miss Pageant and performed one of her own compositions while dancing. It was the first time Stirling had danced while playing the instrument. When George Varga for the *San Diego Union-Tribune* (13 May 2014) asked her how she got the idea for the performance, she said, simply, "So many girls in the pageant were doing entertaining stuff, and I didn't want to be the boring one." Stirling went on to win the Arizona Junior Miss Pageant and won the Spirit Award at the America's Junior Miss finals.

In 2007, she was desperate to perform on *The Ellen DeGeneres Show.* Eventually, she got in contact with one of the show's producers, who advised her to upload a video of herself playing the violin and dancing on YouTube, a relatively new site at the time. Stirling did—she posted a video of herself playing along to "Pump It" by the Black Eyed Peas. The video did not land her a spot on the show, but it did go viral, capturing the attention of some producers with the reality television show *America's Got Talent.* The producers encouraged Stirling to audition for the show, and she did. She billed herself as a hip-hop violinist. She first appeared on the show during its fifth season in 2010, performing a song of her own composition. All three judges—actor Howie Mandel and media personalities Sharon Osbourne and Piers Morgan—gave her a "yes" vote, ushering her into the second round of the competition. She passed that round as well, moving into the show's quarterfinals in Hollywood. For that performance, Stirling played along to "Break Your Heart," by Taio Cruz featuring Ludacris, and Kesha's "Tik Tok." The act went over poorly with judges, particularly Morgan, who hit his buzzer of disapproval while Stirling was still performing. In an effort to incorporate more dancing, the judges agreed, Stirling's violin playing suffered. Their criticism stung; Morgan even told her that there were moments in the song "where it sounded, to me, like a bunch of rats being strangled," as quoted by Varga. Stirling, who did not garner enough audience votes to stay in the competition, was eliminated from the show.

YOUTUBE CELEBRITY

The experience took its toll on the young performer, but it taught her a valuable lesson, she told Comingore. While the show was taping, the crew kept her in high spirits, telling her how talented she was. "It puts you up on this crazy plane, but then it only took one word from the judges

to send me right back down to one of the lowest points of self-esteem I've ever experienced," she said. "When I looked back on that roller-coaster ride, I realized that I didn't want to go through that . . . . I learned to be myself and to not let other people's opinions bring me up and down." This attitude would prove useful to Stirling, who seems to draw particularly cruel criticism for her work and persona. In 2014, two music critics for the *New York Times*, one specializing in pop and the other in classical music, ridiculed her popularity and discussed how poorly acquitted she was to perform in either genre. They described her millions of fans derisively as a bunch of "nerdy teenage girls" (2 May 2014).

In the wake of her ouster from *America's Got Talent*, Stirling made a promotional video and résumé. She drove to Las Vegas and tried to book a gig. Not a single talent agency called her back. But there were other opportunities on the horizon. She poured her energy into her YouTube channel, LindseyStomp (a nod to Stomp on Melvin), and teamed up with cinematographer Devin Graham to make more elaborate music videos. About eight months after her appearance on *America's Got Talent*, Stirling's career began to take off. In February 2012, she published a video for an original violin dubstep song called "Crystallize." It was viewed one million times in less than two days. Stirling quickly became one of the most popular channels on the website. Today, her videos, posted to both LindseyStomp and LindseyTime, have garnered more than 1.8 billion views in total.

ALBUMS

Stirling self-released a debut album, *Lindsey Stirling*, in 2012. The album included her hit song, "Crystallize," which, by the end of 2012, was the eighth most-viewed video on YouTube with 42 million views. (By mid-2017, the song boasted over 175 million views.) The album fared particularly well in Europe, but it was really thanks to her YouTube channels that Stirling began performing sold-out shows for thousands of fans. In April 2013, she signed with Lady Gaga's manager, Troy Carter, but no recording companies.

Shatter Me, Stirling's sophomore effort, self-released in April 2014, marked her first collaborations with vocalists. Her lead single, "Shatter Me," featuring singer-songwriter Lzzy Hale, debuted in the number-two slot on the Billboard 200 chart. The lyrics explore Stirling's struggle with anorexia as a college student. Moving from Arizona to Utah for school, Stirling became obsessed with counting calories. She did not realize she had a problem until she began working at mental health treatment center for teen girls. The song combines elements of pop, electronica, and dubstep. The album, which also features a collaboration with singer-songwriter Dia Frampton (who appeared on the first season of the reality television show *The Voice*), "digs a lot deeper, musically and emotionally," than her first album, Stirling told Gary Graff for *Billboard* magazine (1 May 2014). "I feel like I pushed the limits in every way. The violin is, like, much more classical but at the same time the electronic side is much more in-your-face, up-front, hard-hitting. I took both styles of music to a little more extreme rather than testing the waters like I did on the first one." Within months of *Shatter Me* coming out, Stirling and Hale were given the opportunity to perform on an episode of *America's Got Talent*, to great applause.

Stirling's third album, *Brave Enough*, was released just before the musician's thirtieth birthday, in August 2016. It explores the death of a close friend and bandmate as well as the final illness of her father (who died of skin cancer in January 2017). The album features guest vocalists Rivers Cuomo (formerly of the band Weezer), hip-hop artist Lecrae, singer-songwriter Christina Perri, country duo Dan + Shay, and singer-songwriter Andrew McMahon, among others.

SUGGESTED READING

Caramanica, Jon, and Zachary Woolfe. "Defining an Online Phenomenon: Virtuoso or a Wedding Band Star?" *The New York Times*, 2 May 2014, nytimes.com/2014/05/03/arts/music/lindsey-stirlings-music-combines-classical-and-dance.html. Accessed 14 July 2017.

Comingore, Aly. "Lindsey Stirling: From Small Screens to Big Stages." (Santa Barbara) *Independent*, 7 Nov. 2012, www.independent.com/news/2012/nov/07/lindsey-stirling-small-screens-big-stages. Accessed 14 July 2017.

Graff, Gary. "Lindsey Stirling Talks 'Powerful' Single with Lzzy Hale, Tour Choreography." *Billboard*, 1 May 2014, www.billboard.com/articles/news/6077156/lindsey-stirling-shatter-me-lzzy-hale-new-album-tour. Accessed 15 July 2017.

Stirling, Lindsey, and Brooke S. Passey. *The Only Pirate at the Party*. Simon & Schuster, 2016.

Varga, George. "Lindsey Stirling Bows Way to the Top." *The San Diego Union-Tribune*, 13 May 2014, www.sandiegouniontribune.com/entertainment/music/sdut-lindsey-stirling-interview-2014may13-htmlstory.html. Accessed 14 July 2017.

SELECTED WORKS

Lindsey Stirling, 2012; *Shatter Me*, 2014; *Brave Enough*, 2016

—*Molly Hagan*

A. G. Sulzberger

Date of birth: 1980
Occupation: Deputy publisher of the *New York Times*

Arthur Gregg Sulzberger was named the deputy publisher of the *New York Times* in October 2016 and editor of the paper's opinion page in 2017. He is a fifth-generation heir of the Ochs-Sulzberger clan, the family that bought the prestigious newspaper in 1896. The promotion put him in the position to succeed his father, Arthur Ochs Sulzberger Jr., as the paper's publisher and chair of the New York Times Company, continuing the family-run tradition of what it widely viewed as the United States' most influential newspaper. However, the appointment was not without controversy, as some observers critiqued the perceived nepotism involved.

While Sulzberger's rise at the *New York Times* was certainly helped by his family background, it was made possible by years of journalism experience and tough competition against other family members with eyes for the publisher's seat. Sulzberger wrote for Rhode Island's *Providence Journal* and the *Oregonian* in Portland, Oregon, before joining the *Times* as a Metro reporter in 2009. He later headed a Midwest bureau of the *Times* in Kansas City, Missouri, and was named editor of the Metro section in 2012. In 2014, he published an explosive internal critique that outlined controversial measures

Bowers/Getty Images

for upping the paper's readership and embracing digital technology. The report was leaked by other news outlets, forcing Sulzberger to defend his proposals to a sometimes skeptical staff. His success in this regard bolstered his standing as a key voice of the next generation for his family's company.

EARLY LIFE AND CAREER

Arthur Gregg Sulzberger, known as A. G., was born in 1980 to Arthur Ochs Sulzberger Jr. and Gail Gregg. His great-great-grandfather, Adolph Simon Ochs, the son of wealthy Bavarian immigrants, bought the New York Times, which had been founded in 1851, in 1896 when he was only thirty-eight years old. Under Ochs's leadership as owner and publisher, the paper blossomed. When Ochs died in 1935, control of the newspaper was passed down to his son-in-law, Arthur Hays Sulzberger, beginning a tradition of succession within the family for the role of publisher. Arthur Hays Sulzberger's son Arthur Ochs "Punch" Sulzberger became publisher of the Times in 1963 (following a brief stint in which his brother-in-law held the job), and Punch named his own son, Arthur Ochs Sulzberger Jr., publisher in 1992. Sulzberger's mother, Gail Gregg, was a journalist turned artist.

Sulzberger grew up in Manhattan, New York City, with his parents and sister, and he attended the prestigious Ethical Culture Fieldston School in the Riverdale area of the Bronx. Author and journalist Gabriel Sherman, in a piece about succession within the Sulzberger-Ochs clan for New York Magazine (23 Aug. 2015), described an upbringing steeped in "Times mythology." Copies of the family's newspaper were placed on each garden bench at the family's old estate in Connecticut. Sulzberger's parents, like other members of the family, taught their children that they were "stewards of the public trust."

However, Sulzberger was not always keen on following in his family's footsteps. He studied political science at Brown University and graduated in 2003. It was only when one of his professors, an investigative reporter at the local Providence Journal named Tracy Breton, recommended him for a two-year internship at the Journal that he turned toward a career in news. "I hadn't always wanted to go into journalism," Sulzberger told James Barron for the New York Times (19 Oct. 2016), "but she really pushed me to give it a shot." According to his coworkers, Sulzberger worked hard to make his own name, refusing to rely on his powerful and well-known family.

Soon after becoming a reporter, Sulzberger discovered a love for political writing, and in August 2006 he took a staff position at the Oregonian in Portland, Oregon. Stephen Engelberg,

then that paper's managing editor and a former New York Times employee who knew Sulzberger's father, oversaw the young writer's training. Engelberg paired him with veteran reporter Les Zaitz on a high-profile investigation that led to the resignation of Multnomah County Sheriff Bernie Giusto two years later.

JOINING THE FAMILY BUSINESS

While Sulzberger was at the Oregonian, senior editors at the New York Times monitored his development. In 2008, the Times's managing editor Jill Abramson deemed Sulzberger mature enough to join the paper, and his father was reportedly excited to bring him into the family business. As the elder Sulzberger told Sherman, "Our promise to members of the Ochs-Sulzberger family who want to work at the New York Times and have the skill set to do so is to give them careers." Sulzberger himself, however, was unsure about accepting the offer. "He didn't think he was talented enough," a source told Sherman. It was Abramson who finally convinced him to make the shift back to New York, where he joined the paper's Metro division in 2009.

Meanwhile, Sulzberger's cousins—Samuel Dolnick, a reporter who cut his teeth at the New York Village Voice and the Associated Press, and David Sulzberger Perpich, a tech investor and financial consultant—were also joining the company. Both were also widely seen as potential heirs to the publisher's desk. As a past succession had caused a traumatic family rift, an internal board called the "Family Career Development Committee" was created to ensure a level playing field among the three men. According to Sherman, this was orchestrated by family members who were wary of Sulzberger being groomed to become publisher without competition. Dolnick soon joined the Metro desk with Sulzberger.

In 2010, Sulzberger was transferred to Kansas City, where he opened a Midwest bureau of the Times. There, he wrote several well-received human interest stories, including a piece about a man who built a replica of San Francisco's Golden Gate Bridge on his property and a feature about the last machine in the world capable of processing Kodachrome film. The latter article even inspired the development of a movie. Sulzberger also got experience with breaking news and was on the scene to cover the deadly tornado that tore through Joplin, Missouri, in May 2011.

Sulzberger returned to New York in 2012 and became an editor on the Metro desk in March of that year. This promotion led to increased attention to the training of the fifth generation of the Ochs-Sulzberger family (Dolnick was given a parallel promotion soon after). As the cousins rose through the ranks of the Times—Sulzberger and Dolnick in the newsroom and Perpich in the business department—editors Abramson and Dean Baquet began inviting them to monthly meetings to discuss major editorial decisions. The family also hired a consulting psychologist and family-business specialist to monitor the progress of Sulzberger and the other heirs.

INNOVATION REPORT

In 2013, Abramson gave Sulzberger leadership of a committee aimed at looking into ways to improve the *Times*'s financial prospects. At the time, the paper was struggling to navigate plummeting print ad sales and an audience thirsty for unique digital content. The committee was supposed to be an exploratory effort, while providing a chance for Sulzberger to acquaint himself with another aspect of the day-to-day life of the paper. However, as the committee continued to dig, Sulzberger realized that the paper's failure to capitalize on digital journalism and other modern innovations was a threat to the entire company.

Sulzberger and his team went on to author a controversial report, later dubbed the "innovation report," in May 2014. In it, Sulzberger described an outdated newsroom culture and outlined a radical path for the newspaper. The report struck a chord with many *Times* employees, as it identified not only issues regarding print versus digital content, but serious ideological issues embedded in the very fabric of the company. The *Times*'s editorial leadership released a condensed version of the report and a statement supporting it, though Baquet characterized the document to Sherman as "a slap in the head." Then a series of unusual events occurred: the elder Sulzberger fired Abramson and promoted Baquet to editor-in-chief. Soon after, Sulzberger's full report was leaked to the online news outlet *BuzzFeed*.

The leak forced Sulzberger to defend the full report to the public and his colleagues far sooner than he had anticipated. Central to his findings was a failure to deliver the news to readers. In other words, whereas the *New York Times* focused on making good work, it was not very successful in making sure people read it. To this end, Sulzberger proposed an audience development team. The report's most internally controversial proposal called for ending the division between newsroom and business departments. This in particular rankled writers. "News people were in a state of shock," a veteran *Times* reporter recalled to Sherman. But Sulzberger won staff over a few people at a time in a spate of meetings, in which he was reportedly humble about the limitations of his findings but effective at making the case for implementing his ideas.

DEPUTY PUBLISHER

Many of the recommendations in Sulzberger's innovation report soon began to be enacted at the *Times*, and it became an influential guiding document even for other news organizations and media companies. This attention raised Sulzberger's profile, and speculation increased that he was the leading candidate to eventually succeed his father as publisher of the *Times*. He was named senior editor for strategy in July 2014 and an associate editor in August 2015. However, the internal competition with his cousins remained fierce, with Dolnick receiving similar appointments around the same time and Perpich increasing his newsroom presence.

In October 2016, Sulzberger's mix of experience on both the business and newsroom ends of the company paid off when he was named deputy publisher. This appointment effectively put him next in line for his father's job, putting to rest longstanding rumors over which of the cousins would take over as publisher. At age thirty-six, he was dedicated to continuing the effort to bridge the gap between traditional newspaper journalism and the type of digital media that was increasingly shaping the twenty-first century. As he told Benjamin Mullin for *Poynter* (25 Oct. 2016), "We've got a pretty different business model from most other publishers, which is built more on loyalty than scale. The vast majority of our revenue comes directly from our most dedicated readers. That's a good thing, since it aligns our business model with our journalistic mission. We need to make journalism that is so original, useful, and engaging that it's worth paying for."

Sulzberger took on increased responsibilities as deputy publisher, many of which built on the findings of the 2014 innovation report and the successful changes made in the ensuing years. The *Times* was in the midst of finalizing a similar, updated report for 2020, meant to guide organizational initiatives for years to come. In early 2017, Sulzberger also took over for his father as the editor of the paper's opinion page, another position seen as a clear indication of his favored status. In all his roles, he continued to keep an eye toward satisfying current readership as well as building new generations of readers through a commitment to quality journalism and up-to-date digital platforms.

SUGGESTED READING

Barron, James. "A.G. Sulzberger: Leading Change at the *New York Times* as Journalism Evolves." *The New York Times*, 19 Oct. 2016, www.nytimes.com/2016/10/20/business/media/ag-sulzberger-leading-change-at-the-new-york-times-as-journalism-evolves.html. Accessed 12 July 2017.

Benton, Joshua. "The Leaked New York Times Innovation Report Is One of the Key Documents of This Media Age." *Nieman Lab*, 15

May 2014, www.niemanlab.org/2014/05/the-leaked-new-york-times-innovation-report-is-one-of-the-key-documents-of-this-media-age. Accessed 12 July 2017.

Sherman, Gabriel. "The Heirs." *New York*, 23 Aug. 2015, nymag.com/daily/intelligencer/2015/08/new-york-times-heirs.html. Accessed 12 July 2017.

Sulzberger, A. G. "A.G. Sulzberger on His New Job, Transforming the New York Times and the Thing that Keeps Him Up at Night." Interview by Benjamin Mullin. *Poynter*, 25 Oct. 2016, www.poynter.org/2016/a-g-sulzberger-on-his-new-job-transforming-the-new-york-times-and-the-things-that-keep-him-up-at-night/435977. Accessed 12 July 2017.

—*Molly Hagan*

By Arturo Pardavila III [CC BY 2.0], via Wikimedia Commons

Noah Syndergaard

Date of birth: August 29, 1992
Occupation: Baseball player

Although he made his Major League Baseball (MLB) debut with the New York Mets in 2015 at the young age of twenty-two, Noah Syndergaard quickly established himself as one of the best pitchers in baseball. With a fastball speed that often exceeds 100 miles per hour and averages higher than any other starting pitcher, he makes for an intimidating presence and a formidable opponent on the pitcher's mound. "I want the hitter to know it's not going to be a comfortable at bat," he told Clay Skipper for *GQ* (30 June 2016) of his approach.

Despite his rapid rise to MLB stardom, however, Syndergaard's skills on the field were many years in the making. The athlete—known to friends and teammates as Thor—began playing baseball as a child but was insecure about his body as a young teen, struggling with his weight and a series of growth spurts that left him towering above his classmates. After developing a passion for weightlifting and spending nearly five years honing his skills in the minor leagues, Syndergaard made a triumphant entrance into the majors as part of a resurgent Mets team that reached the World Series in his first season. For Syndergaard, the experience was a dream come true. "I've been wanting to get to this level since I could pick up a baseball," he told Steve Serby for the *New York Post* (30 May 2015).

EARLY LIFE AND EDUCATION

Noah Seth Syndergaard was born on August 29, 1992, in Mansfield, Texas, a suburb in the Dallas–Fort Worth area. He grew up in the area as it was undergoing significant growth. "When my

parents moved there, there was one road that went through the entire city. Now there's six or seven high schools in the whole city, it's got close to a population about 100,000," Syndergaard told Serby. "Not a whole lot to do there, but it's home." Syndergaard's mother, Heidi Syndergaard, worked for a medical device manufacturer, while his father, Brad Syndergaard, raised and trained horses. Although he was the only child born to the couple, he had two older half-sisters from his father's previous relationship.

Syndergaard developed an interest in baseball early in life. He began playing on local teams and practicing with his father at an early age, persevering despite a lack of self-confidence caused by his clumsiness (his childhood nickname was Bumpy, after the many accidental bumps he endured). While still a youth, he impressed onlookers by hitting a home run over the park fence. "My grandfather was at my game, and he decided since he was at that game that he wanted to sign my baseball for me—his name," he recalled to Serby. "I was like seven years old at the time. I wasn't gonna like tell him, 'No, I don't want you to do that.' He did it anyways and I spent the whole night I think trying to get the signature off my ball, and just in tears." In addition to showing skill as a hitter, Syndergaard played as a pitcher from early on, and over time he became capable of throwing baseballs at speeds that stunned onlookers.

Syndergaard began his high school career at Mansfield High School, before switching to Mansfield Legacy High School for his sophomore year. Quiet, awkward, and insecure about his weight, he decided to work to change his appearance. In addition to playing for the Broncos baseball team, he began to focus on weightlifting, following workouts from magazines while at the local YMCA. "I'd always been self-conscious of my weight, how I appeared to other people," he explained to Ben Reiter for *Sports Illustrated* (8 Feb. 2017). "I wanted to change that. Then I got hooked." While working to burn fat and build muscle, Syndergaard also experienced a growth spurt that left him far taller than many of his classmates. He ultimately reached an adult height of six feet six inches. His height and added muscle improved his pitching; before his senior year his fastball velocity was in the low 80s, but that increased steadily into the mid and even upper 90s by the time Syndergaard graduated from Mansfield Legacy in 2010.

MINOR LEAGUE CAREER

Syndergaard had received little attention from scouts through most of his high school career, and he initially planned to attend Texas Baptist University, which had offered him a baseball scholarship, rather than immediately attempt to play professionally. However, the uptick in velocity during his senior year drew considerable attention, as few starters even in the majors threw so hard so consistently. Syndergaard began to be listed as one of Texas's top prospects, though his late emergence and the fickle nature of pitcher development meant many teams were still skeptical. A Toronto Blue Jays scout who had been closely following Syndergaard advocated strongly in favor of drafting him, and in June 2010, the Blue Jays selected Syndergaard as the thirty-eighth overall pick in that year's MLB Draft. Still only seventeen years old, Syndergaard was excited to pursue a professional career, which gave him the opportunity to explore the world beyond Texas. "I had been kind of growing up in this bubble," he told Reiter. "Once I got drafted, I finally figured out what was outside of it."

Like most players, Syndergaard still faced a long road to the majors. He was first assigned to the Gulf Coast League Blue Jays, one of Toronto's minor league developmental affiliates. Syndergaard spent several years in the minors, refining his pitching and batting skills and playing for a variety of teams at different levels. He joined the Bluefield Blue Jays in June 2011 and over the next several months moved to the Vancouver Canadians, the Lansing Lugnuts, and again to Vancouver. He returned to Lansing in March 2012. In Vancouver and Lansing, Syndergaard came to be considered one of three talented young pitchers, known as the Vancouver Trio and the Lansing Trio, who played together and were considered high-level prospects with the potential to be top starters. In addition to Syndergaard, the trio included Aaron Sanchez and

Justin Nicolino, who would go on to play for the Blue Jays and the Miami Marlins, respectively.

In December 2012, the Blue Jays traded Syndergaard, then ranked by most evaluators as one of Toronto's top three prospects, to the New York Mets as a key piece in a deal for R. A. Dickey, then the reigning winner of the Cy Young Award for the league's best pitcher. Syndergaard was initially assigned to the St. Lucie Mets affiliate team, and in June 2013 moved to the Binghamton Mets at the AA level. He joined the AAA Las Vegas 51s in March 2014. Syndergaard struggled in Las Vegas, and he later noted in interviews that the experience made him doubt whether he would ever pitch in the major leagues. However, the team's pitching coach, retired major league pitcher Frank Viola, helped him overcome such doubts. "He really got me to understand that baseball's a game and I need to go out there and have fun with it," Syndergaard told Skipper.

MAJOR LEAGUE DEBUT

After nearly five years in the minor leagues, Syndergaard was called up to the Mets' big-league club from Las Vegas in May 2015. He made his debut with the team on May 12 in a game against the Chicago Cubs. Although the Mets lost that game 6–1, Syndergaard proved to be a valuable addition to the team over the course of the season. He pitched in a total of twenty-four games during the regular season, serving as starting pitcher in each, and managed a solid earned run average (ERA) of 3.24 over 150 innings. Playing in the National League (NL), Syndergaard also hit, posting a .209 batting average but recording a home run. His imposing height and ferocious fastball speed, along with his long hair, earned him the nickname Thor, after the Norse god of thunder. Syndergaard joined fellow young starters Matt Harvey and Jacob DeGrom in helping lead the Mets to a NL East division championship with a 90–72 record.

The team beat the Los Angeles Dodgers in the first round of the 2015 play-offs, though Syndergaard lost his only start in that series. The Mets then swept the Chicago Cubs in the National League Championship Series, with Syndergaard winning the second game, to claim a spot in the World Series. Facing off against the American League champions, the Kansas City Royals, the Mets lost the first two games in the series. Syndergaard started Game 3 against the Royals' Yordano Ventura, and he sparked controversy with his first pitch, a 98-miles-per-hour fastball that came very close to Royals batter Alcides Escobar's head. Although some on the Royals thought that Syndergaard had been trying to hit Escobar, the pitcher asserted otherwise. "My intent was to make them uncomfortable, and I feel like I did that," Syndergaard said after the game, as quoted by Joel Sherman for the *New York Post* (31 Oct. 2015). "I didn't think he would want to swing at that one."

Controversy aside, Syndergaard struggled at first, giving up three early runs before settling in. He ultimately earned the win in a 9–3 Mets victory. It proved to be the team's high point, as they dropped the next two games to lose the series. Still, Syndergaard was happy to have had the opportunity to go to the World Series during his first season in the majors. He was also ranked fourth for the NL Rookie of the Year Award.

NEW YORK METS

Having established himself as a valuable team player during his first season with the Mets, Syndergaard had developed a strong relationship with his teammates going into the 2016 season. "We're all pretty competitive with one another, we're all close friends, which makes it even better," he told Steve Kettmann for the *New Yorker* (24 Feb. 2016). "That gives us a camaraderie, a little brotherhood. We all push each other and try to learn from each other."

During the 2016 regular season, Syndergaard built upon his impressive debut. He posted an impressive 2.60 earned run average for the season to go with a 14–9 record and 218 strikeouts. He even hit three home runs, proof of his raw strength. In July of that year, he was selected to join the National League roster for the MLB All-Star Game for the first time. Though a contender for the honor of starting that game, he ended up not playing due to an injury.

Syndergaard earned votes for both the NL Cy Young and NL MVP awards in 2016, though he did not win either. He was a major reason the Mets finished the regular season with an 87–75 record, good enough to earn a spot in the postseason NL Wildcard Game. There the Mets faced the San Francisco Giants, with Syndergaard chosen to start opposite the Giants' ace Madison Bumgarner in a must-win situation. The game was a classic pitchers' duel, with both starters pitching shutouts and Syndergaard maintaining a no-hitter into the sixth inning. However, Syndergaard was removed after the seventh inning in favor of relievers. The Mets ultimately lost 3–0 and were eliminated from the play-offs.

Syndergaard started off the 2017 season strong, serving as the opening day starter. However, during an April 30 game against the Washington Nationals, he was forced to leave the game during the second inning due to what at first seemed to be a muscle strain. He was later determined to have torn the latissimus dorsi muscle, which affected his throwing arm. Initially placed on the ten-day disabled list, Syndergaard was later moved to the sixty-day disabled list as he recovered from the injury, missing a significant amount of the season. The Mets struggled without him, posting a losing record around the All-Star break.

PERSONAL LIFE

After joining the Mets, Syndergaard enjoyed living in New York City, which he contrasted with suburban Texas. "I love how you can go out and do basically whatever you want and have the most unbelievable food you've ever eaten at anywhere around the corner," he told Serby. He often returns to Texas to visit family and friends during the off-season. He is an avid fan of golf, as well as of the television show *Game of Thrones*. In the spring of 2017, it was announced that Syndergaard would make a cameo appearance in the seventh season of the show.

SUGGESTED READING

Elliott, Bob. "How Former Blue Jays Prospect Noah Syndergaard Was Discovered." *Toronto Sun*, 19 May 2015, www.torontosun.com/2015/05/19/how-former-blue-jays-prospect-noah-syndergaard-was-discovered. Accessed 14 July 2017.

Kettmann, Steve. "Noah Syndergaard and the Very Confident New York Mets." *The New Yorker*, 24 Feb 2016, www.newyorker.com/news/sporting-scene/noah-syndergaard-and-the-very-confident-new-york-mets. Accessed 14 July 2017.

Reiter, Ben. "Synderella: How Noah Syndergaard Went from Awkward Kid to Mets Ace." *Sports Illustrated*, 8 Feb. 2017, www.si.com/mlb/2017/02/08/noah-syndergaard-mets-synderella-yearbook-photo. Accessed 14 July 2017.

Sherman, Joel. "Noah Syndergaard's 98-MPH Bullet Flipped World Series on Its Head." *New York Post*, 31 Oct. 2015, nypost.com/2015/10/31/brash-syndergaards-98-mph-bullet-flipped-world-series-on-its-head/. Accessed 14 July 2017.

Syndergaard, Noah. "Mets Ace Noah Syndergaard Shares the Secret to His Norse God Hair." Interview by Clay Skipper. *GQ*, 30 June 2016, www.gq.com/story/noah-syndergaard-mets-hair-baseball-interview. Accessed 14 July 2017.

Syndergaard, Noah. "Noah Syndergaard on '6 Aces,' Onesies, and 'Game of Thrones.'" Interview by Steve Serby. *New York Post*, 30 May 2015, nypost.com/2015/05/30/noah-syndergaard-on-6-aces-onesies-and-game-of-thrones/. Accessed 14 July 2017.

Syndergaard, Noah. "Noah Syndergaard Wants Jay Z to Write a Rhyme about Him, Watched 'Game of Thrones' with His Mom." Interview by Aaron Mansfield. *Complex*, 13 Apr. 2017, www.complex.com/sports/2017/04/

—*Joy Crelin*

David Szalay

Date of birth: 1974
Occupation: Author

Few modern authors depict the struggles of contemporary men as honestly or as intimately as David Szalay. In 2016, Szalay's fourth novel, *All That Man Is*, was placed on the short list for the Man Booker Prize—one of the most prestigious literature awards in the world—adding to his ever-growing list of literary accomplishments. Since the appearance of his debut novel, *London and the South East*, in 2008, Szalay has cemented his reputation as one of the most distinctive British authors working today, despite the fact that he was born in Canada and now resides in Budapest, Hungary.

Yet, despite the widespread critical acclaim he has received for his novels, Szalay does not feel any great sense of satisfaction from his work. As Szalay noted to Ari Shapiro in an interview for the National Public Radio program (NPR) *All Things Considered* (10 Oct. 2016), "I think no matter how much success you pile up, I do feel that set against mortality, there will always be times when it looks pretty flimsy, pretty minor, pretty vanishing almost."

EARLY LIFE AND EDUCATION

David Szalay was born in 1974 in Montreal, Quebec, Canada. His father was Hungarian, and his mother was Canadian. Shortly after he was born, his family moved from Canada to Beirut, the capital city of Lebanon, but they left the country after the Lebanese civil war broke out in 1975. His family then settled in London, England, where they intended to live for only a few months, but they ended up remaining in England for nearly three decades.

Szalay has said that he first decided he wanted to become a writer when he was twelve years old. He studied English at the University of Oxford. After graduating from Oxford, he tried and failed to find a publisher for a novel he had written. Before embarking on a successful career as a novelist, he worked in a variety of jobs, including media sales. He later wrote a number of radio dramas for the BBC.

Although his writing style has been described as strongly representative of modern Britain, he, like many Europeans of his generation, also has a continental aspect to his identity.

Kaveh Kazemi/Getty Images

As he told Shapiro: "I have this personal experience of traveling around the continent. But I don't think I mean I'm far from unique or even unusual in that. I mean the nature of contemporary Europe is very much one in which people are making themselves new lives in other places or simply traveling on shorter trips but on a regular basis. So they're constantly decontextualizing themselves." He continued to describe the influence of this cross-cultural exchange, adding, "There is an opportunity for reinvention. There are also the possible downsides of that kind of movement. I mean it can be lonely. It can be isolating. You can feel deracinated and confused."

LONDON AND THE SOUTH EAST

Szalay's debut novel, *London and the South East* (2008), took a scathing look at modern working life through the experiences of a salesman named Paul Rainey. Paul is a good salesperson but is working in a field that is rapidly shrinking due to changes in technology: he attempts to sell print ad space in trade magazines that have few readers other than advertisers themselves. When Paul attempts to better his life by joining a rival company, he is tricked and suddenly finds himself unemployed. As the novel progresses, he finds himself in ever more dismal and menial jobs. He eventually is even excited by the prospect of working in a cemetery before he realizes he must return to the drudgery and relative safety of sales and the London commute.

London and the South East earned considerable critical acclaim. In a review for the *Independent* (12 Apr. 2008), Brandon Robshaw declared,

"The novel is brilliant on the day-to-day texture of the workplace—the rhythms, routines and procedures, the spite, envy, resentment and camaraderie, the all-embracing familiarity of the environment, the lunch-hours in the pub, the chorus of 'How was your weekend?' on Monday morning, the shadowy sense one has of the lives of one's coworkers outside the office." Robshaw praised *London and the South East* as "a funny, painful, graphic demonstration that our job is a crucial part of our identity." Reviewing the book for the *Guardian* (1 May 2009), Alfred Hickling remarked, referring to a Pulitzer Prize–winning play by David Mamet, "Szalay's debut is a Connex South Eastern *Glengarry Glen Ross* suffused with a sense of the salesman's sleepless despair. . . . Szalay's satire is sharp, though his depictions of rush-hour raise the blood pressure to levels that may not be advisable."

In 2009, *London and the South East* won the Betty Trask Award and the Geoffrey Faber Memorial Prize. These two awards are given to the debut novel of young authors who are citizens of current or former British Commonwealth countries.

THE INNOCENT

Szalay switched gears for his second novel, *The Innocent*, which was published in 2009. Instead of depicting modern life in London, he moved back in time to describe the experiences of a former officer for the Soviet Ministry of State Security—the predecessor of the Soviet State Security Committee (KGB)—named Aleksandr, who, in 1972, is haunted by a case he took on in 1948. In that year he was sent by his superiors to see Anatoly Yudin, who had been shot in the head and suffered serious mental impairment as a result. Aleksandr wanted Yudin's doctors to release him into his care to see if he was actually faking his condition to avoid confrontation with his paranoid superiors, who were working under the autocratic Soviet leader Joseph Stalin. Like its predecessor, Szalay's second novel provides an intensely intimate character study of a man caught up in the cogs of a societal system that operates beyond his control.

The Innocent found widespread praise upon its publication in the United Kingdom. Writing for the *Guardian* (18 Sept. 2009), Chris Petit observed: "*The Innocent* is muted and sparse in detail, written in trimmed prose, marked by private regret and a controlled laconicism that is shown to be in keeping with how personal emotion becomes a victim to self-censorship in states of repression." Similarly, Lesley McDowell remarked in a review for the *Independent* (14 Aug. 2010): "Szalay's multi-layered narrative does not make for an easy read, and his knowledge of the period is formidable, but he twists both the politics and the human drama into an intelligent, commanding shape that draws us irresistibly on."

SPRING

For his third novel, *Spring* (2011), which was published both in the United Kingdom and the United States, Szalay produced an intimate look at a romantic relationship between a thirtysomething former dot-com millionaire named James and a hotel manager named Katherine, who is now separated from her husband, Fraser. The pair's affair begins after Katherine discovers that her husband had a fling with an underwear model, but her relationship with James is complicated by the fact that her estranged husband is doing all he can to win her back. James, for his part, is a somewhat shady character; since his fall from the dot-com world, he has pursued a number of get-rich-quick schemes, including one that involves working as a tipster for horse races.

Despite their flaws, the characters have a certain degree of likability that makes them compelling, according to reviewers. "Szalay provides a sharp and occasionally humorous portrait not only of these two people but of the mores of twenty-first-century romance among those for whom romance has had its old glamour grubbed up a bit by age, world-weariness and the demands of everyday life," a critic wrote for *Kirkus Reviews* (29 Dec. 2011). "Subtle in its psychology, elegantly written, with lively and amusing minor characters—an impressive novel, but one with a slight morguelike chill."

In 2013, just two years after publishing his third novel, Szalay was named one of the best of young British novelists by the prestigious literary magazine *Granta*.

ALL THAT MAN IS

Szalay may have cemented his reputation as one of the best up-and-coming novelists with the publication of his fourth work of fiction, *All That Man Is* (2016), which is not so much a novel but rather a novel-length collection of nine interconnected stories. The book examines nine stages of a man's life, with each story focusing on a different male character at various ages. The youngest character is a seventeen-year-old boy who is traveling across Europe with a friend; the eldest is a seventy-three-year-old retired government official reflecting on his increasing frailties. Other characters include a journalist, an academic, and a billionaire. Each, while no means unsympathetic, is suffering from an ennui that Szalay believes troubles many modern men, but particularly ones who live in Europe, where there is a sense that the continent's best years are behind it and that Europe itself faces its own mortality, just as many of Szalay's characters do in this unique work of fiction.

In an interview for the *Paris Review* (Summer 2016), Szalay described his own concerns prior to writing his most recent work: "I sat down to think about writing a new book and just didn't see the point of it. What's a novel? You make up a story and then you tell that story. I didn't understand why or how that could be meaningful."

Despite its less-than-celebratory depiction of modern manhood, *All That Man Is* was widely hailed by critics, in large part because of the deft way its author depicted its central characters. William Skidelsky wrote in a review for the *Guardian* (3 Apr. 2016): "As the title (taken from [W. B.] Yeats's Byzantium) implies, this book aims to be a reckoning with 'all that man is.' And here, it has to be said, Szalay's verdict is depressing. Far from celebrating's man's infinite variety, the book reveals his endless repetitiveness." Skidelsky elaborated, explaining, "The characters we encounter, no matter how ostensibly different, are all caught up in the same narrow set of concerns, chief among which are love and money (or variations thereof). They're all fundamentally lonely, and have a tendency to drift, in mild befuddlement, through life." In a review for the *Spectator* (16 Apr. 2016), Jude Cook declared: "Though it doesn't present itself as a novel, the book hangs together: The predicaments of the various tormented men come together to produce a rich exploration of male vulnerability. . . . With *All That Man Is*, he emerges as a writer with a voice unlike any other."

In September 2016, *All That Man Is* was named to the short list for the prestigious Man Booker Prize, the leading literary prize for English-language novels.

SUGGESTED READING

Cook, Jude. "All That Man Is: A Novel View of Masculinity." Review of *All That Man Is*, by David Szalay. *The Spectator*, 16 Apr. 2016, www.spectator.co.uk/2016/04/all-that-man-is-a-novel-view-of-masculinity. Accessed 14 Nov. 2016.

McDowell, Lesley. Review of *The Innocent*, by David Szalay. *The Independent*, 14 Aug. 2010, www.independent.co.uk/arts-entertainment/books/reviews/the-innocent-by-david-szalay-2049876.html. Accessed 14 Nov. 2016.

Petit, Chris. Review of *The Innocent*, by David Szalay. *The Guardian*, 18 Sept. 2009, www.theguardian.com/books/2009/sep/19/innocent-david-szalay-review. Accessed 14 Nov. 2016.

Robshaw, Brandon. Review of *London and the South-East*, by David Szalay. *The Independent*, 12 Apr. 2008, www.independent.co.uk/arts-entertainment/books/reviews/london-and-the-south-east-by-david-szalay-5340499.html. Accessed 14 Nov. 2016.

Shapiro, Ari. "David Szalay's 'All That Man Is' Charts Life of Man in 9 Stories." *All Things Considered*, 10 Oct. 2016, www.npr.org/2016/10/10/497423550/david-szalays-all-that-man-is-charts-life-of-man-in-9-stories. Accessed 14 Nov. 2016.

Skidelsky, William. "Tales of Love and Money." Review of *All That Man Is*, by David Szalay. *The Guardian*, 3 Apr. 2016, www.theguardian.com/books/2016/apr/03/all-that-man-is-review-david-szalay-short-story-collection. Accessed 14 Nov. 2016.

Szalay, David. "Writing *All That Man Is*: An Exchange." Interview by Lorin Stein. *The Paris Review*, 2016, www.theparisreview.org/miscellaneous/6478/writing-iall-that-man-is-i-an-exchange-david-szalay. Accessed 14 Nov. 2016.

SELECTED WORKS

London and the South East, 2008; *The Innocent*, 2009; *Spring*, 2011; *All That Man Is*, 2016

—*Christopher Mari*

Ruby Tandoh

Date of birth: 1992
Occupation: Baker, writer

For baker and food writer Ruby Tandoh, cooking is about far more than just food. "Cooking is a really creative, tactile thing, and I love that way of working," she told Beth Maiden for *Autostraddle* (27 Feb. 2017). "I think that pushes me towards visual approaches to my work—drawing sketches of foods, making recipe mind maps, color coding literally everything. I like my work to feel colorful and woven through with my personality." Indeed, Tandoh's personality has been deeply connected to her culinary creations since she first entered the public eye in the fourth season of the wildly popular televised baking competition *The Great British Bake Off*. Only twenty years old at the time of the competition, which she ultimately finished as a runner up, Tandoh was a favorite of many of the show's viewers and went on to establish herself as a food writer and cookbook author.

Perhaps most compelling for socially conscious gourmands, however, has been Tandoh's writings on and strong opposition to the "clean eating" movement, which she has linked not only to eating disorders but also to deeply ingrained class divisions in both British and global society. "There's still so much snobbery about food," she told Anna Pointer for *Grazia Daily* (1 Aug. 2016). "I hate how people on already limited budgets are told to buy things like buckwheat flour and coconut oil, for no good reason. The assumption is that these things are healthier, but they're just expensive fads. It's misinformation which reinforces class division."

EARLY LIFE AND EDUCATION

Ruby Alice Tandoh was born in England in 1992. The oldest of four children, she was raised in Southend-on-Sea, a coastal community in the county of Essex. During her childhood, her father worked for the Royal Mail, and her mother was an administrator at a school. Tandoh's parents enjoyed cooking, and Tandoh began to learn about food and recipes at a young age. She was an avid reader of cookbooks and particularly enjoyed books that featured pictures of the completed dishes. To make the most of their limited grocery budget, the family often ate meat-free meals and filling helpings of pasta, and her early understanding of the importance of such foods would shape her later opposition to diets necessitating the purchase of expensive foods in the name of wellness.

After graduating from Southend High School for Girls, Tandoh attended University College London, where she studied art history and philosophy. While in high school and university, she struggled with mental health challenges that included disordered eating, a topic about which she would later speak out extensively. "It's something that comes to me worst when I'm feeling insecure and anxious, and when my depression is bad, though what I've noticed over the years is that even when I'm reasonably well and happy, there's always an undercurrent of that disordered thinking around food," she said in an interview with Eve Simmons for the eating-disorder-focused website *Not Plant Based* (19 Sept. 2016). "I think that's really important for me and for anyone: recognizing, even on good days, that you could slip back in disordered eating. It sounds pessimistic, but actually it's so freeing to be able to say: 'That's my past, and I carry it with me even now—I'm not scared to acknowledge that it's there, and I want to fight it.'"

In her late teens, Tandoh briefly worked as a model and was represented by the agency Models 1. After having a breakthrough in regard to her relationship with food, however, she decided to give up the profession. "My own epiphany came when I calculated that the number of minutes I'd spent counting calories that day was greater than the number of calories eaten," she wrote for *Elle UK* (11 Feb. 2015). "I stopped returning my agency's calls and enjoyed a valedictory ice cream, though not without making a mental note to run off those fifteen grams of fat later at the gym." Tandoh went on to work various jobs related to food and cooking, including a stint in a cake shop and a summer working in the kitchen of a hostel in Lisbon, Portugal.

THE GREAT BRITISH BAKE OFF

In 2013, Tandoh went from an unknown college student to a well-known television figure following her debut appearance in the beloved competitive cooking show *The Great British Bake Off*. The show, which aired on BBC Two before moving to BBC One and later Channel 4, first premiered in 2010 and quickly earned a devoted audience who enjoyed the low-key drama resulting from high-stakes baking and the amusing and sometimes bawdy commentary of the show's hosts. Also aired on PBS in the United States under the title *The Great British Baking Show*, the series has gained an avid international viewership as well.

Having begun regularly practicing her baking skills while in university, Tandoh decided to audition for a spot in the competition, but she did not believe she would make the cut. "I hadn't been baking very long when I went on. I had just started university and had a kitchen to myself for the first time," she recalled to David Tamarkin for *Epicurious* (28 Apr. 2015). "I applied to the show, thinking that if I had the pressure of applying it would be good practice. I never thought it would lead to anything."

To Tandoh's surprise, she was accepted as a contestant for the fourth season of *The Great British Bake Off*. At the age of twenty, she was the youngest contestant to appear in the series at that point, and she faced intense competition from talented bakers who had far more experience. Nevertheless, Tandoh traveled to the show's filming location every weekend for ten weeks, distinguishing herself as a skilled baker in her own right. After a difficult start in the first episode, during which she narrowly escaped elimination, she was named star baker in three episodes and ultimately proceeded to the finale, where she faced off against eventual winner Frances Quinn and fellow runner-up Kimberley Wilson.

FOOD WRITING

Following her strong performance on *The Great British Bake Off*, Tandoh briefly returned to University College London to continue her studies. However, her newfound professional commitments proved too time consuming, and she eventually left university to focus on her work. Having established herself as a talented baker and engaging personality, Tandoh found a niche as a food writer whose topics of interest encompassed not only baking but also broader forms of cooking. In addition to publishing one-off pieces in a variety of publications, she regularly wrote a baking column, Ruby Bakes, for the *Guardian*.

The life of a freelancer took some getting used to for Tandoh, who initially struggled to manage her time and assignments. "I used to be a real chancer, just taking commissions as and when, and working all night to meet deadlines that I'd forgotten I had," she told Maiden. "As time goes on, though, I've got much better at keeping on top of work, logging my assignments as they come in and taking control of my work-life balance."

A longtime lover of cookbooks, Tandoh relished the opportunity to write cookbooks of her own, developing recipes for the types of food she would most like to eat. Her first cookbook, *Crumb: The Baking Book*, was published in the United Kingdom in 2014 and features recipes for a variety of sweet and savory baked goods. The book was published in the United States as *Crumb: A Baking Book* the following year. Her next cookbook, *Flavour: Eat What You Love*, debuted in the United Kingdom in 2016. In addition to baked goods, the book features recipes for soups, appetizers, and other flavorful dishes.

ACTIVISM

In conjunction with her work as a food writer, Tandoh is an outspoken advocate for eating a variety of delicious foods and not cutting out certain ingredients or food groups in the name of wellness. Her views on the subject became common knowledge when, in May 2016, her article "The Unhealthy Truth behind 'Wellness' and 'Clean Eating'" was published on *Vice* magazine's website. In the article, Tandoh denounced the trend of eliminating supposedly "unclean" foods such as gluten, sugar, and meat from one's diet based on little to no scientific evidence. For Tandoh, the tendency to brand foods as "clean" or "unclean" ties into disordered eating—particularly an eating disorder known as orthorexia, in which one develops an unhealthy obsession with defining different foods as good or bad and constricts one's diet accordingly. "Subscribing to the idea of wellness as a mask for my eating disorder is something that I had done in the past, so there was that really personal motivation to shine a light on it," she told Simmons. "But also, as someone who works in the food press, I was just so pissed off that people were making a lot of money, using their influence, making a mark, selling these stupid fad diets. I was so furious to see these people not only peddling crappy, elitist diet regimes, but also then having the nerve to market those diets as 'morally superior' . . . . That's what really broke my heart: seeing really restrictive diets wrapped up in the language of self-care and (for many) of eating disorder recovery."

Although Tandoh did not expect that the public would be receptive to her article, it ultimately sparked numerous conversations within the food-writing community and brought Tandoh a new audience beyond the one she had amassed from *The Great British Bake Off*. "The response was amazing," she said to Pointer. "People were

so supportive, which is rare for me. I'm more used to upsetting everyone." Since the publication of her *Vice* piece, Tandoh has continued to speak out about the dangers of the clean-eating movement and has at times feuded with its advocates on social media. "They're not going out of business any time soon," she told Pointer in an earlier article for the *Telegraph* (16 July 2016). "And I'm sure they don't feel threatened by me. But I hope the current is changing, and that the public see there's an alternative, moderate way to do things."

PERSONAL LIFE

Tandoh lives in Sheffield, England, with her partner, Leah Pritchard. In early 2017, the couple collaborated on a one-off zine dealing with mental health, using the crowdfunding platform Kickstarter to raise funds for the publication. The zine, titled *Do What You Want*, was published in April 2017. Proceeds from *Do What You Want*'s sales were donated to a variety of relevant charities.

SUGGESTED READING

Pointer, Anna. "'Half a Courgette instead of a Plate of Pasta—Where's the Energy in That?' Ruby Tandoh on Self-Doubt, Misogyny and Carbs." *The Telegraph*, 16 July 2016, www. telegraph.co.uk/women/life/half-a-courgette-instead-of-a-plate-of-pasta--wheres-the-energy/. Accessed 15 May 2017.

Pointer, Anna. "Ruby Tandoh: 'I Feel Sorry for People Who Document Every Meal in Pictures.'" *Grazia Daily*, 1 Aug. 2016, lifestyle. one/grazia/news-real-life/real-life/ruby-tandoh-bake-interview/. Accessed 15 May 2017.

Tandoh, Ruby. "Follow Your Arrow: *Great British Bake Off* Star Ruby Tandoh Shares Her Love of Food." Interview by Beth Maiden. *Autostraddle*, Excitant Group, 27 Feb. 2017, www.autostraddle.com/follow-your-arrow-food-writer-ruby-tandoh-shares-her-love-of-food-367726/. Accessed 15 May 2017.

Tandoh, Ruby. "Ruby Tandoh Likes Buns, Doesn't Get Excited about Cupcakes." Interview by David Tamarkin. *Epicurious*, Condé Nast, 28 Apr. 2015, www.epicurious.com/expert-advice/interview-ruby-tandoh-crumb-cookbook-article. Accessed 15 May 2017.

Tandoh, Ruby. "Ruby Tandoh: My Life in Food." *Elle UK*, 11 Feb. 2015, www.elleuk.com/life-and-culture/news/a24668/ruby-tandoh-my-life-in-food-article-november-2014-issue/. Accessed 15 May 2017.

Tandoh, Ruby. "Ruby Tandoh on Recovery, Depression & Coffee Ice Cream Cravings." Interview by Eve Simmons. *Not Plant Based*, 19 Sept. 2016, www.notplantbased. com/2016/09/19/ruby-tandoh-interview/. Accessed 15 May 2017.

Tandoh, Ruby. "The Unhealthy Truth behind 'Wellness' and 'Clean Eating.'" *Vice*, 13 May 2016, www.vice.com/en_uk/article/ruby-tandoh-eat-clean-wellness. Accessed 15 May 2017.

—Joy Crelin

Madeleine Thien

Date of birth: May 25, 1974
Occupation: Author

Madeleine Thien is a Canadian-born author who has written a collection of short stories, *Simple Recipes* (2001), and three novels, *Certainty* (2006), *Dogs at the Perimeter* (2011), and *Do Not Say We Have Nothing* (2016), the most recent of which was short-listed in 2016 for the prestigious Man Booker Prize.

Although Thien was born in Canada, her parents are of Chinese ancestry, and her older brother and sister were born in Malaysia. Thien's writing explores the people and landscape of her ancestry as well as many of the political, historical, and cultural events and trends throughout the region and their effects on the people living there. For example, *Do Not Say We Have Nothing* explores everyday life in China during the mid-1900s through the early 1990s amid extreme cultural and political suppression and the ramifications such repression had for many Chinese people. In her 2003 essay "But, I Dream in Canadian," Thien reflects on her Canadian upbringing and on being the child of immigrants. She also provides insight into why so many of her works are set in Asia, explaining that "children of immigrants often seek to return to the country that our parents have left behind. . . . We want to open what our parents have closed."

Thien examines difficult and wide-reaching themes, and her writing has been described as beautiful and universally appealing. Many of her stories and novels have been translated into over twenty languages.

EARLY LIFE

Madeleine Thien was born in Vancouver, British Columbia, in 1974, several months after her parents and two older siblings emigrated from Malaysia. Thien is the only member of her immediate family who was born in North America and whose first language is English. "When I was young, my world was Vancouver. I was proud . . . of the way I needed no map, no instruction, no guide," Thien wrote in her 2008 essay "My Mother's Dresses."

Thien's mother was raised in Kowloon, Hong Kong, and attended school in Australia, where

she met Thien's father, who is ethnically Chinese but was raised in Malaysia. After marrying, Thien's parents lived in East Malaysia and had two children before immigrating to Canada in the mid-1970s in order to escape the increasing violence and political disruptions in Malaysia.

Thien grew up speaking English because, as she explained in "My Mother's Dresses," it was important to her parents that she and her siblings "speak and think in the language of the new home." The children were also enrolled in Chinese language and calligraphy classes, and because their mother "believed that all the opportunities of the world" were in Canada, the children took lessons in dance, painting, swimming, acrobatics, ballet, and piano. Thien's mother, who was the primary wage earner in the family, worked as a purchasing manager for a paper company and taught business courses in the evening at a local community college. She also helped found a Vancouver support group for recent immigrants.

As a child, Thien spent a lot of time on her own. Her parents struggled financially, which meant the family moved often and friendships were difficult to establish and maintain. Recalling her childhood in "My Mother's Dresses," Thien remembers feelings of optimism and anticipation because "in each new neighborhood, no matter our circumstances, we arrived hopeful. The unfamiliar kitchen sink, the empty cupboards, the windows with their different vistas, each was romantic and mysterious."

Despite the constant opportunities to explore and reinvent, the atmosphere in Thien's home was often difficult and isolating for her, and, as she described in "My Mother's Dresses," her parents offered very little solace: "My parents—always complex, always unfathomable—were harried and melancholy and distant. We shared so few confidences." Her older siblings took little interest in being with or speaking to her. Thien soon learned that books and stories would "ease the loneliness," however, and would allow her to "move forward," she explained to Claire Armitstead for *The Guardian* (8 Oct. 2016). Despite spending "long hours on her own, walking to and from school through 'quite rough neighborhoods,'" Thien explained to Armitstead that she drew strength and purpose from "these magical things, books, that made an imaginative space other people could inhabit."

Thien's siblings left home when they were young, and Thien's father left the family permanently when she was sixteen.

EARLY WRITING AND EDUCATION
Thien's childhood and adolescence were lonely, confusing years to be sure, but it was during this time that she discovered books and that words and imagination could help fill in the missing pieces of her family life and home. Thien writes in "My Mother's Dresses" that as a young girl, she read story after story and often resisted returning books to the library, and came to believe that writers were "the bearers of secrets: imaginary ones, real ones." She explained that her relationship with books became "a kind of love affair."

The sudden departure of Thien's father was a confusing and painful time for her because he "simply disappeared" without warning or explanation. As an adult and with the benefit of time, hindsight, and maturity, she views the event differently, as she explained in an interview with *Mason Fiction* (23 June 2009). Thien felt that she was put in a "strange position" because although she was "at that age when adolescents are usually the ones leaving the family," the reverse had happened when her father left.

Although understandably a confusing and painful time for then-teenaged Thien, she also described it to Scott Douglas Jacobsen for *InSight* as a "pivotal moment" for her as a writer. Her siblings had moved out of the home, and she was living alone with her mother, with whom she felt disconnected emotionally. Thien described to Jacobsen that she was unable to voice what she thought or how she felt because her thoughts and feelings were too private and personal and she believed they would be too hurtful for others to hear. "Writing," she explained, "became a way to express things that were unsayable. . . . Writing was a space to lay things down."

Thien had a talent for dance and won a scholarship to study ballet and contemporary dance at Simon Fraser University, a public research university in British Columbia. Excited by the new intellectual environment, she took advanced fourth-year literature and philosophy courses, which, as she explained to Armitstead, "was a leap too great," and she ultimately lost her scholarship. Deciding then to pursue a literature degree instead of dance, Thien worked at a clerical job at an academic press while she wrote short stories in her spare time. She was eventually offered a scholarship to the University of British Columbia, where she completed her MFA in creative writing in 2001.

SIMPLE RECIPES
The same year that Thien received her MFA, she published her first work, *Simple Recipes*, a collection of short stories that were based on her master's thesis. The collection gained immediate critical acclaim, in part because Thien was only in her mid-twenties when the book was published. She was awarded the 2001 Canadian Authors Association Air Canada Award for the most promising writing under thirty, the 2001 City of Vancouver Book Award, and the 2002 Ethel Wilson Fiction Prize, and was a regional finalist for the Commonwealth Writers Prize for Best First Book. Janice P. Nimura wrote in a review of *Simple Recipes* for the *New York Times* (29 Sept. 2002) that Thien's young age "makes the austere grace and polished assurance of her prose remarkable." She noted that two stories—the title story, which opens the collection, and "A Map of the City," which closes it—"explore the intimate interiors of immigrant families . . . and that it's very difficult, finally, to understand any family but your own." Both stories are narrated by a Canadian-born daughter of immigrants, and Vancouver features prominently throughout the collection, yet all of the stories are universal in their treatment of the forces and subtleties of family dynamics across generations.

NOVELS
Thien's first novel, *Certainty* (2006), became a 2007 finalist for the Kiriyama Book Prize and won the Ovid Festival Prize. Like many of the stories in *Simple Recipes*, there are underlying themes of a confused and disjointed father-daughter relationship, a need to reconcile the past with the present, and the feelings of displacement and fragmentation felt by many immigrants. Ian McGillis for the *Montreal Review of Books* (Spring 2006) described the book as "a moving, richly textured, and immaculately nuanced study of war, grief, displacement, love, renewal, photography, and much more." Thien explained to Armitstead that she felt "dissatisfied" with the book, however, because she had "tried to tell the

story of her father's Malaysian background" but had not known as much as she thought she did. She did admit that *Certainty* was "a daughter's book" and was something she "had to write so [she] could move on."

Thien's next novel, *Dogs at the Perimeter* (2011), is about the aftermath of the Cambodian genocide by the Khmer Rouge in the 1970s and the individuals who survived. Thien told Jacobsen that she wanted to explore "how people begin again, how they remember, and how they forget." *Dogs at the Perimeter* garnered Thien even more attention than her previous novel and won the Frankfurt Book Fair's Literaturpreis award in 2015 and was short-listed for the International Literature Prize in Berlin. In his review for *The Guardian* (15 Feb. 2013), Alfred Hickling wrote, "Thien's observations of the ravaged country maintain a fine balance between lyricism and horror."

Thien's third novel, *Do Not Say We Have Nothing* (2016), also explores the aftermath of an actual event. In the spring of 1989, student activists in China demonstrated against the Communist government in Beijing's Tiananmen Square. On June 4, 1989, the demonstrations turned violent in what came to be known as the Tiananmen Square Massacre when government troops killed several hundred pro-democracy protesters. Thien's novel explores the aftermath of the protests and tells the story of revolution, idealism, and suppression of cultural endeavors. *Do Not Say We Have Nothing* won the Scotiabank Giller Prize and the Governor General's Award for English-Language Fiction. It was also short-listed for the prestigious Man Booker Prize. Jennifer Senior, writing for the *New York Times* (23 Oct. 2016), called the novel "a beautiful, sorrowful work" and noted how well Thien "captures painfully well the depersonalization and numbness of living through the Cultural Revolution, particularly the 'day-to-day insincerity' of casual conversation, larded with perfunctory praise for the party and [Chinese dictator] Chairman Mao." Isabel Hilton, critic for *The Guardian* (14 July 2016), wrote that *Do Not Say We Have Nothing* "deserves to cement Thien's reputation as an important and compelling writer."

PERSONAL LIFE

Thien married a Dutch citizen in 2004 and lived for a short time in the Netherlands. They later divorced, and she returned to Vancouver before relocating to Montreal, Quebec. She lives with her partner, Lebanese novelist Rawi Hage.

SUGGESTED READING

Armitstead, Claire. "Madeleine Thien: 'In China, You Learn a Lot from What People Don't Tell You." *The Guardian*, 8 Oct. 2016, www. theguardian.com/books/2016/oct/08/madeleine-thien-interview-do-not-say-we-have-nothing. Accessed 10 Jan. 2017.

Hickling, Alfred. Review of *Dogs at the Perimeter*, by Madeleine Thien. *The Guardian*, 15 Feb. 2013, www.theguardian.com/books/2013/feb/15/dogs-perimeter-madeleine-thien-review. Accessed 12 Jan. 2017.

Jacobsen, Scott Douglas. "Madeleine Thien: Writer-in-Residence, Simon Fraser University." *In-Sight*, 22 Feb. 2014, in-sightjournal.com/2014/02/22/madeleine-thien-writer-in-residence-simon-fraser-university. Accessed 11 Jan. 2017.

Senior, Jennifer. "In 'Do Not Say We Have Nothing,' a Portrait of Souls Snuffed Out." Review of *Do Not Say We Have Nothing*, by Madeleine Thien. *New York Times*, 23 Oct. 2016, www.nytimes.com/2016/10/24/books/review-in-do-not-say-we-have-nothing-a-portrait-of-souls-snuffed-out.html. Accessed 11 Jan. 2017.

Thien, Madeleine. "But, I Dream in Canadian." *The Globe and Mail*, 27 Dec. 2003, www.theglobeandmail.com/opinion/but-i-dream-in-canadian/article774677/?page=all. Accessed 11 Jan. 2017.

Thien, Madeleine. Interview. *Mason Fiction*, 23 June 2009, gmufictionmfa.blogspot.com/2009/06/interview-with-madeleine-thien.html. Accessed 11 Jan. 2017.

SELECTED WORKS

Simple Recipes, 2001; *Certainty*, 2006; *Dogs at the Perimeter*, 2011; *Do Not Say We Have Nothing*, 2016

—*Dmitry Kiper*

Isaiah Thomas

Date of birth: February 7, 1989
Occupation: Professional basketball player

Isaiah Thomas is the five-foot-nine, powerhouse point guard for the Boston Celtics. Thomas's rise may seem surprising to some basketball fans—he was selected sixtieth, the last pick of the 2011 National Basketball Association (NBA) draft by the Sacramento Kings, and languished on the Phoenix Suns before being traded to the Celtics in early 2015—but for the player himself, superstardom was the only option. "Some people's opportunity comes and they waste it, because they're not ready for that moment," Thomas told Kevin O'Connor for the sports website *The Ringer* (23 Jan. 2017). "I remember [veteran NBA shooting guard] Jason Terry always telling me, 'Opportunity doesn't go away, it goes to

By Keith Allison from Hanover, MD, USA[CC BY-SA 2.0], via
Wikimedia Commons

somebody else.' You just gotta be ready for that moment. To this day, I've always been ready for the moment that came my way." The 2017 season was a landmark one for Thomas; he led the Celtics to the best regular season record in the Eastern Conference, and enjoyed, as sportswriter Bill Simmons put it mildly for *The Ringer* (12 May 2017), a "prolonged hot streak" that began in December. Thomas developed a reputation as the King of the Fourth, famous for delivering in the clutch in the fourth quarter. His hot streak culminated in May, in an Eastern Conference Semifinals game against the Washington Wizards in which Thomas scored a whopping 53 points. But Thomas's legendary season ended in personal tragedy, as his career-defining game came just two weeks after the sudden death of his younger sister.

EARLY LIFE

Isaiah Jamar Thomas was born on February 7, 1989. He was named after the Detroit Pistons point guard and 1980s All-Star, Isiah Thomas. Before Thomas was born, his father, James, a Los Angeles Lakers fan, made a bet with a friend: if the Pistons beat the Lakers in the 1989 NBA Finals, he would name his son after the team's star. Tina Baldtrip, Thomas's mother, gave birth several months before the Pistons won their first championship, but the couple honored the bet, changing only the spelling of the name to the biblical Isaiah. It is ironic that Thomas would not only grow up to become an All-Star point guard himself, but also that he would play for the Celtics. The Pistons-Celtics rivalry is one

of the most storied in the NBA, and during his heyday, Thomas's namesake was one of the most hated men in Boston.

Thomas grew up in Tacoma, Washington. He learned to play ball at gyms across the city, including the Al Davies Boys and Girls Club. Thomas was tough; as the smallest player on the court, he played as though he had something to prove. Two NBA players from Seattle, Jason Terry and Jamal Crawford, became his mentors. At Curtis High School, he was a local celebrity, averaging 31 points a game by his third year. Thomas was a star on the court but fared poorly in the classroom. If he did not have the grades to play in college, he would never make it to the NBA. With this in mind, Thomas made the difficult decision to leave Tacoma for the all-boys' South Kent School in rural Connecticut in 2006. "Back then I hated it," he told Alan Siegel for *Boston Magazine* (Nov. 2016). "But it was the best thing that's happened for me. It made me grow up."

COLLEGE CAREER AND NBA DRAFT

Thomas graduated from South Kent in 2008 and enrolled at the University of Washington. He was a galvanizing, if polarizing, figure for the Huskies; in a November 2008 interview, Percy Allen reported for the *Seattle Times* (12 May 2011), Thomas, then an incoming freshman, accused the team, which had not played in a National Collegiate Athletic Association (NCAA) tournament in two years, of having lost its "swagger." Over the course of his three-year tenure, Thomas worked to bring that swagger back. He was named the Pacific-10 Freshman of the Year in 2009, led the team to back-to-back Pac-10 Conference Tournament Championships in 2010 and 2011, and was named most outstanding player for both games. In the March 2011 game, after playing the full forty-five minutes, Thomas sunk a fadeaway jumper at the buzzer to break a tie with the University of Arizona and win the championship 77–75. "I knew I had a smaller guy on me, so I could get a shot off and I just made a little step back and God made the ball go in the hoop," Thomas told a reporter for the Associated Press (13 Mar. 2011). Thomas also took the Huskies to three NCAA tournaments, making it to the Sweet Sixteen in 2010. He was also named to the All-Pac-10 First-Team in his junior year. When he left the school in 2011, Thomas ranked sixth on the University of Washington's scoring list, with an average of 16.4 points a game.

Not long after his game-winning shot in 2011, Thomas announced that he would opt out of his senior year with the Huskies and enter the NBA draft. Thomas had previously announced that he would stay with the team but changed his mind. "I feel like with the guards coming out this year I have a really good chance of going high in this draft," he told Percy Allen for the *Seattle Times* (31 Mar. 2011). That scenario, of course, did not come to pass. Some predicted that Thomas might go late in the second round, but Thomas waited so long that he eventually left a celebration party at his apartment and headed to the gym. He came home, and stepping onto the elevator, he received a phone call from his agent: he been selected sixtieth, the last pick of the 2011 NBA draft by the struggling Sacramento Kings. It was not an ideal match, but Thomas was energized. "All I wanted," he told Siegel, "was a chance."

EARLY NBA CAREER

Thomas made All-Rookie second team in 2012 and, in 2014, was averaging 20.3 points a game. In January, he scored 38 points in a losing game against the Oklahoma City Thunder. That season, he signed his first endorsement deal with a Northern California–based chain restaurant called Pizza Guys. As Siegel points out, the ads did not make Thomas huge sums of money, but they did make him a "cult favorite" among fans and players. But the Kings were not quite sure what to do with their young talent. The team traded him to the Phoenix Suns in the summer of 2014. Thomas played only half a season with the Suns before he was traded to the Celtics in February 2015. In his very first game, a matchup against the Los Angeles Lakers, Thomas scored 21 points in the first three quarters but was ejected in the fourth for disputing a foul call. The Celtics lost the game in overtime. Coach Brad Stevens was frustrated with Thomas's ejection but said later that he admired his new player's ferocity. "That's a powerful, powerful thing if that energy is funneled correctly," Stevens told Siegel. "Here was a guy dying to win." Stevens' respect put Thomas at ease.

As a reserve player during his first season with the Celtics, Thomas averaged 19.0 points and 5.4 assists a game. During his second season, 2016, he was a starter. In January, he was named an Eastern Conference All-Star reserve, becoming the lowest-picked player to be so chosen in twenty-seven years. He also tied Calvin Murphy, San Diego Rockets player from 1970 to 1983, as the shortest player ever selected for an All-Star team. The Celtics finished the season ranked second in the Atlantic Division of the Eastern Conference and made it to the first round of the playoffs where they faced the Atlanta Hawks. Though Thomas managed to score 42 points to win Game 3, the Celtics ultimately lost the series, 4–2.

BREAKOUT SEASON

During the 2016–17 season, Thomas led the Celtics to a number-one ranking in the Eastern Conference; the team boasted a better season record than the defending 2016 champions, the Cleveland Cavaliers. Thomas's hot streak began in late December, when he scored a then career high 44 points in a victory against the Memphis Grizzlies. Ten days later, he obliterated that personal record, scoring 52 points in a win against the Miami Heat. Thomas scored 29 of those points in a single quarter, becoming the only player in franchise history to achieve that feat. The team record, 24 points, was set by Hall of Famer Larry Bird in 1983 and tied by Todd Day in 1995. The game solidified Thomas's reputation as the King of the Fourth.

In January 2017, Thomas averaged 32.5 points a game and was named an All-Star player for the second year and an Eastern Conference Player of the Month. In February, Thomas broke a team record from 1971, recording forty-three straight games with at least 20 points. In March, he recorded his two hundredth three-point shot, one of only three Celtics players in franchise history to do so. The same month, he became the sixth Celtic ever to score 2,000 points in a single season.

Just before the Celtics faced the Chicago Bulls in the first round of the conference playoffs, Thomas's twenty-two-year-old sister, Chyna, was killed in a car accident. After leading the Celtics to a 4–2 victory in the series, he returned home for her funeral. During Game 1 of the second round against the Washington Wizards, Thomas lost a front tooth when he was elbowed in the mouth by Otto Porter. Thomas played the rest of the game, which the Celtics won, but spent the next day undergoing dental surgery to reinsert his tooth. Thomas returned for Game 2—on what would have been Chyna's twenty-third birthday—and turned in the most stunning performance of his career to date, scoring 53 points, including 29 in the final quarter. O'Connor, who was at the game, described the evening for *The Ringer* (3 May 2017) as particularly "special." "There are nights when a player enters the zone, and then there are nights when an entire arena reaches those heights collectively. They're part of something bigger than one game, or one series, or one season. The player and the crowd are connected in a moment, feeding off each other in a virtuous cycle. Isaiah Thomas seemed to understand the moment he was in," O'Connor wrote. The Celtics won the series in seven games to make it to the Eastern Conference Finals, where they lost to the Cleveland Cavaliers in five games. Though Thomas and his team did not make it to the NBA Finals, his 53-point performance against the Wizards could be a harbinger of a career yet to come. "I always dream of moments like this," Thomas told O'Connor later. "Those are where legends are born. One day I want to be one of those guys."

PERSONAL LIFE

Thomas married longtime girlfriend Kayla Wallace in August 2016. He has two sons, James and Jaiden.

SUGGESTED READING

Allen, Percy. "Huskies' Isaiah Thomas Says He Will Enter the NBA Draft." *The Seattle Times*, 31 Mar. 2011, www.seattletimes.com/sports/uw-huskies/huskies-isaiah-thomas-says-he-will-enter-nba-draft. Accessed 12 June 2017.

Associated Press. "Isaiah Thomas' Fadeaway Beats Buzzer, Crowns Washington as Pac-10 Champions." *ESPN*, 13 Mar. 2011, www.espn.com/mens-college-basketball/recap?gameId=310710012. Accessed 12 June 2017.

Keh, Andrew. "Diminutive All-Star Isaiah Thomas Finds Shoulders to Stand On." *The New York Times*, 2 Feb. 2016, www.nytimes.com/2016/02/03/sports/basketball/diminutive-all-star-isaiah-thomas-finds-shoulders-to-stand-on.html. Accessed 12 June 2017.

O'Connor, Kevin. "Isaiah Thomas's 53-Point Night Deserves to Be in Boston's Postseason Pantheon." *The Ringer*, 3 May 2017, theringer.com/2017-nba-playoffs-isaiah-thomas-boston-celtics-washington-wizards-game-2-53-points-582b0d6d9c7c. Accessed 12 June 2017.

O'Connor, Kevin. "The King of the Fourth." *The Ringer*, 23 Jan. 2017, theringer.com/isaiah-thomas-celtics-fourth-quarter-4404c2f7ae93. Accessed 11 June 2017.

Siegel, Alan. "Isaiah Thomas: The Biggest Little Man in Boston." *Boston Magazine*, 1 Nov. 2016, www.bostonmagazine.com/news/article/2016/11/06/isaiah-thomas/. Accessed 12 June 2017.

Simmons, Bill. "Isaiah and LeBron." *The Ringer*, 12 May 2017, theringer.com/2017-nba-playoffs-lebron-james-isaiah-thomas-cleveland-cavaliers-boston-celtics-2fd60f3d5434. Accessed 12 June 2017.

—*Molly Hagan*

Heather Ann Thompson

Date of birth: August 17, 1963
Occupation: Historian

"My obligation as a historian is to recount history no matter what it is," professor and award-winning historian Heather Ann Thompson told Courtney Harrell for the *National Book Foundation*'s website (2016). "That means that if I find stuff that shocks even me, that can't change my story." Indeed, much of Thompson's historical

Photo by Sylvain Gaboury/Patrick McMullan via Getty Images

research has dealt with topics that not only shock but also prompt readers to consider the ways in which the systemic injustices at the heart of past events continue to manifest in the twenty-first century. A professor of history who has taught at Temple University and the University of Michigan, Thompson is particularly interested in the criminal justice system and mass incarceration, labor history, and activist movements of the mid-twentieth century. Her published works have considered how such topics intersected in places such as 1960s Detroit, which became the focus of her first book, *Whose Detroit?: Politics, Labor, and Race in a Modern American City* (2001).

In 2016, Thompson gained significant media attention for her second book, *Blood in the Water: The Attica Prison Uprising of 1971 and Its Legacy*. Documenting the bloody Attica prison rebellion and the subsequent cover-up carried out by law enforcement and the state government of New York, the book proved difficult to write due in large part to the government's suppression of records dealing with the incident, which made the process of researching and writing the book a monumental and at times frustrating undertaking. "It was supposed to take a couple of years, and it ended up being a thirteen-year journey," Thompson told Harrell of the book. Despite such difficulties, her dogged pursuit of the facts paid off: following its publication, *Blood in the Water* revealed long-hidden truths about Attica to the public, and it went on to claim the 2017 Pulitzer Prize in history.

EARLY LIFE AND EDUCATION

Thompson was born on August 17, 1963, in Lawrence, Kansas. She was the first of two daughters born to Ann Curry Thompson and Frank Wilson Thompson, who were students at the University of Kansas at the time of her birth. Her mother went on to become an attorney specializing in labor and employment law, while her father later became a professor of economics at the University of Michigan. The family moved on several occasions during Thompson's childhood, and she spent a portion of the early 1970s in Oxford, England, while her father was studying at Oxford University.

When Thompson was a teenager, her family moved to Detroit, Michigan, where they settled in northwest Detroit's Rosedale Park neighborhood. The city of Detroit was in the midst of political, social, and racial turmoil at the time, as fallout from economic instability, white flight, and mass incarceration related to the federal government's war against crime took their toll on the city. "Everything was happening at once," she told Ana Marie Cox for the *New York Times Magazine* (10 May 2017). "I was growing up in the epicenter of America, a white girl in a mostly black city trying to understand all of that politically." While attending Cass Technical High School, a magnet school in downtown Detroit, she began to gain a personal understanding of such issues as people she knew were arrested for minor crimes and received disproportionately harsh sentences. At the same time, she did not yet fully understand the complex political and social mechanisms at work. "Back in that time we would say, 'So-and-so, what an idiot! Why didn't he get his act together and instead go to college?'" she told Bill McGraw for *Bridge* (2016). "We didn't understand we were in the middle of one of the biggest buildups of criminal justice resources in human history. We didn't understand that we were in the middle of mass incarceration." Thompson's later research into the criminal justice system would deepen her understanding of the Detroit of the 1970s and 1980s, granting her a new perspective on the events of her teen years.

After graduating from Cass Technical in 1981, Thompson enrolled at the University of Michigan to study history. She remained at the university until 1987, earning her bachelor's degree as well as a master's degree. Continuing her study of history, she went on to attend Princeton University, where she worked toward a PhD. She received a number of awards and fellowships during her time as a doctoral student, including the Shelby Collum Davis Merit Prize and the Princeton University Fellowship Award. She completed her doctorate in 1995.

BEGINNING AN ACADEMIC CAREER AND WRITING HER FIRST BOOK

Following her graduation from Princeton, Thompson returned to Michigan to take a position as a visiting assistant professor at the University of Michigan. In addition to working within the Department of History, she had a joint appointment with the Residential College, an interdisciplinary program within the university's College of Literature, Science, and the Arts. Thompson served as a visiting assistant professor for nearly two years, leaving in the summer of 1997 to take an assistant professorship in the history department of the University of North Carolina at Charlotte. She spent more than a decade at the university and was promoted to associate professor in 2002.

Shaped in large part by her time living in Detroit, Thompson's research interests have reflected many issues relevant to that city's development in the twentieth century, including political and racial conflict, mass incarceration, activist movements and particularly African American activism, and labor history. In her first book, *Whose Detroit?: Politics, Labor, and Race in a Modern American City*, she addresses many of those issues specifically in regard to Detroit, detailing the civil rights and labor rights movements active in the city during the 1960s and 1970s as well as discussing the 1967 Detroit riot and its implications. Although the book touched upon numerous issues related to the criminal justice system, which would go on to become a major focus of her research, she did not yet fully draw the connection between justice issues and mid-twentieth-century Detroit. "It's chock full of stories about policing, arrests, about criminalizing urban space, but I didn't quite see it that way until years later," she told McGraw of *Whose Detroit?*. "One of the reasons that is the case is that I lived in Detroit, and when you're in it, when you're experiencing historical moments and you're in the center of them, you don't have depth perception, you don't quite know what's happening." Originally published by Cornell University Press in 2001, *Whose Detroit?* was reissued by the publisher in 2017.

CONTINUING TO TEACH AND WRITE HISTORY

In August 2009, Thompson moved to Philadelphia, Pennsylvania, where she joined the faculty at Temple University. Working as an associate professor within the Department of History and the Department of African American Studies, she remained at the university into the summer of 2015. In addition to teaching, she served as associate director of Temple's Center for the Humanities beginning in 2010. At the same time, she served as a visiting scholar at the University of Wisconsin–Madison's A. E. Havens Center for Social Justice in 2012 and 2013. In July

2015, she returned to the University of Michigan, where she became a full professor within the Department of History, the Department of Afroamerican and African Studies, and the Residential College.

Further complementing her primary academic positions, Thompson has appeared as a guest speaker at institutions such as Duke University, Oxford University, Yale University, and Germany's University of Tübingen. By this point, in addition to *Whose Detroit?*, she had also published numerous shorter works during her career, including book chapters on topics such as Detroit history and prison reform. Her papers have been published in journals such as the *Journal of Urban History*, *Socialism and Democracy*, and the *Journal of Law and Society*. Beginning around 2011, she became a frequent contributor to newspapers and popular magazines, writing largely about the criminal justice system, mass incarceration, and protest movements. She has also served as an editor or series editor for a variety of works, including the 2010 book *Speaking Out: Activism and Protest in the 1960s and 1970s*.

BLOOD IN THE WATER

The most significant work of Thompson's career to date was published in 2016, thirteen years after she began work on the project. *Blood in the Water: The Attica Prison Uprising of 1971 and Its Legacy* tells the story of the titular rebellion, which began on September 9, 1971, at New York's Attica Correctional Facility. During that event, more than one thousand of the facility's prisoners—the majority of whom were African American—took over the facility and held prison workers hostage while attempting to negotiate with the state for better treatment, including improved medical care. After four days of negotiations, the state of New York sent armed state troopers and prison officers to end the rebellion. Thirty-nine individuals were killed in the process, including both prisoners and hostages. After the event, many of Attica's prisoners were prosecuted, but the troopers and corrections officers known to have killed inmates and hostages in the fighting or tortured prisoners were not. Instead, the state sought to cover up the events that took place and prevented researchers—including Thompson—from accessing many key records.

Over more than a decade, Thompson researched the rebellion extensively and embarked on a lengthy search for the relevant historical documents, which she was largely unable to obtain from the state of New York. "I had to think about who had the original copy of anything that the state of New York had, which took me to all kinds of peripheral state institutions, archives, and local collections," she recalled to Harrell. "But it also brought me to the survivors to see what they had saved and to hear their stories." Thompson's interviews with survivors of the uprising, who included both former prisoners and former prison employees who had been held hostage, provided her with a deeper understanding of the event and its aftermath and enabled her to demonstrate how both the event itself and the state's response to it affected those involved.

CRITICAL RECEPTION

In addition to discussing Attica specifically, *Blood in the Water* has prompted an ongoing discussion regarding prison conditions, which were a key issue behind the rebellion and remain a major concern in the twenty-first century. "Things are much worse today than they were in 1971," Thompson told Cox. "We have people serving decades in solitary confinement. We have more life sentences than we've ever had. We have more children in solitary confinement. And the overcrowding is worse than it was during Attica." Although the events of the Attica prison rebellion are decades in the past, Thompson asserts that the lessons of the incident remain more relevant than ever.

Following its publication, *Blood in the Water* met with widespread critical acclaim. The book was a finalist for the 2016 National Book Award and was named one of the most notable books of the year by publications such as the *New York Times*, *Publishers Weekly*, and *Newsweek*. The production company TriStar Pictures purchased the film rights to the book in 2016. Perhaps the most significant recognition came in 2017, when the Pulitzer Prize Board awarded the book the Pulitzer Prize in history. Honored to receive the award, Thompson was particularly pleased that the survivors' experiences were at last being recognized. "I am so incredibly and deeply grateful that their story is being honored in this way," she said in a press release issued by the University of Michigan (10 Apr. 2017).

PERSONAL LIFE

Thompson has two sons, Dillon and Wilder, from her first marriage. She later married historian Jonathan Daniel Wells, a professor at the University of Michigan and the author of numerous works on nineteenth-century Southern history. She and Wells have a daughter, Ava. They live in Michigan.

SUGGESTED READING

Craig, Gary. "New Book on Attica Uprising Will Reopen Old Wounds." *Democrat & Chronicle*, 13 Aug. 2016, www.democratandchronicle.com/story/news/2016/08/13/new-book-attica-uprising-reopen-old-wounds/88496714. Accessed 17 July 2017.

Thompson, Heather Ann. "Heather Ann Thompson." Interview by Courtney Harrell. *National*

Book Foundation, 2016, www.nationalbook. org/nba2016finalist_nf_thompson_blood-in-the-water.html. Accessed 17 July 2017.

Thompson, Heather Ann. "Heather Ann Thompson Thinks the Justice System Is Unfair." Interview by Ana Marie Cox. *The New York Times Magazine*, 10 May 2017, www.nytimes. com/2017/05/10/magazine/heather-ann-thompson-thinks-the-justice-system-is-unfair.html. Accessed 17 July 2017.

Thompson, Heather Ann. "The War on Crime, Not Crime Itself, Fueled Detroit's Post-1967 Decline." Interview by Bill McGraw. *Bridge*, 2016, www.bridgemi.com/detroit-bankruptcy-and-beyond/war-crime-not-crime-itself-fueled-detroits-post-1967-decline. Accessed 17 July 2017.

"U-Michigan Historian Wins Pulitzer for Attica Book." *Michigan News*, University of Michigan, 10 Apr. 2017, ns.umich.edu/new/releases/24746-u-michigan-historian-wins-pulitzer-for-attica-book. Accessed 17 July 2017.

SELECTED WORKS

Whose Detroit?: Politics, Labor, and Race in a Modern American City, 2001; *Speaking Out: Activism and Protest in the 1960s and 1970s*, 2010; *Blood in the Water: The Attica Prison Uprising of 1971 and Its Legacy*, 2016

—Joy Crelin

Jeff Kravitz/Getty Images for The Meadows

Bryson Tiller

Date of birth: January 2, 1993
Occupation: Singer

Singer Bryson Tiller first came to public attention on October 9, 2014, when he uploaded his track "Don't" to SoundCloud, an online platform that allows users to create their own music, share it privately or publicly, promote their work, and engage directly with listeners. Recorded using just six hundred dollars' worth of studio equipment, "Don't" quickly went viral, attracting millions of listeners. Just a few months later, he signed with a major label, RCA Records, and his first full-length studio album, *T R A P S O U L*, was released on October 2, 2015. Debuting at number eleven on the Billboard 200 album chart, it ultimately went platinum.

Erika Ramirez, writing for *Fuse* (29 Feb. 2016), attributes Tiller's breakout success to his mastery of "the art of seduction by taking a note from 90s R & B greats like Boyz II Men and 112, but instead of catering to nostalgia junkies and recreating a sound from an ended era, the singer engages a listener by making you feel like it's only you in the room."

Tiller explained to Ramirez why he was inspired by those artists and what qualities he hopes to emulate, "If you listen to the lyrics, they're honest—they're not afraid to be," he told her. "It's the way they say certain things, the way they talk to a woman on a song—that's what I try to do with my music. Some people talk *at* women, and they talk *to* women."

EARLY LIFE AND EDUCATION

Bryson Djuan Tiller was born on January 2, 1993, in Louisville, Kentucky. He has four siblings, but when he was four years old, his mother died, and the family was separated. Tiller and his younger brother were sent to live with their grandmother.

His musical talent was evident early on. "I used to sing in church," he recalled to Brittany Lewis for the online pop culture magazine *Global Grind* (2015). "Not like in the choir or anything, but for people around the church . . . on the church bus going home and Christmas plays." He was initially moved by the music his grandmother played; among her favorites were such artists as Gladys Knight and Earth, Wind & Fire. Later, his uncle introduced him to the works of the rap and soul group Dru Hill, the R & B quartet known as 112, and the rapper Omarion. The latter and singer Chris Brown inspired him to pursue a career in the music industry.

Tiller was shy by nature and could most often be found in his house playing video games or watching television. "You would think because I stayed to myself and I was shy that I'd be a good student, but actually I was a bad student," Tiller admitted to Lewis. "I was in detention a lot, mainly for cutting, being late to class. I was in tardy hall a lot. I hate the idea of homework. I don't get it." His grandmother, whom he has described as "old-fashioned," resorted to yelling a lot and frequently calling his teachers. In March of 2016, however, he gave a different impression during a visit to Stephen Foster Elementary School in his hometown where he told an enthusiastic audience of fifth graders that English had been his favorite subject because it had helped him in his songwriting.

When Tiller was about fifteen years old, he found that performing was an effective way to impress girls at Iroquois High School. A fellow student heard him singing in the hallway to a group of girls one day and offered the use of a home recording studio he had set up. Not everyone encouraged his musical aspirations however. Tiller said that a teacher had told him that he had a greater chance of getting hit by a meteorite than of finding success as a professional musician.

In 2011, Tiller graduated from Iroquois High School and that same year he released a homemade mixtape, *Killer Instinct*, but it received little attention. "I was just trying way too much back then," he told Dan Hyman in an interview for *GQ* (18 Jan. 2016). "Doing too many harmonies and too many runs and all the crazy stuff. Rapping all funny and animated."

Tiller found work at Papa John's pizza restaurant and the UPS delivery company. Although some sources claim that during this period he was virtually homeless, sleeping in his car, he continued to work on his music.

MUSIC CAREER

In 2014 Tiller's luck took a turn for the better. A friend lent him $600 to purchase studio equipment of his own. Because he didn't own a drum machine—an electronic instrument designed to imitate the sound of drums and other percussion instruments, as well as bass lines—he downloaded a free beat from a website called SoundClick and used it to compose and record "Don't." "That was the last beat that I ever had to download," he told Elias Leight for *Rolling Stone* (30 Oct. 2015).

The song's explicit lyrics take the form of a man's plea to a woman to make their relationship work: "I wanna give you better / Baby it's whatever / Somebody gotta step up / Girl, I'm that somebody / So I'm next up." Its style, a mixture of hip-hop, R & B, and rap, has been called trap music. Trap musicians make liberal use of the Roland TR-808 drum machine along with resampled hip-hop and rap vocals.

After Tiller uploaded the song to SoundCloud, the track quickly garnered more than 20 million listens, and music producer Timbaland, a distant acquaintance, suggested that he quit his day jobs and fly to Miami, where the music scene was more dynamic. Tiller also caught the attention of fellow rapper and singer-songwriter Drake, who offered Tiller a contract at OVO Sound, a record label he had cofounded. Tiller found the offer exceptionally flattering. "I just feel like [Drake] makes the best music, quality-wise and everything-wise, basically," he told Brittany Spanos for *Rolling Stone* (1 Feb. 2016). "For him to reach out early in my career and say that he likes my music was crazy for me. I was shocked."

After careful consideration, Tiller chose to sign with RCA Records instead, and *T R A P S O U L*, his first studio album, was released on October 2, 2015.

T R A P S O U L

T R A P S O U L includes "Don't" as its lead single. Among the other tracks on the album are "Exchange," an appeal for an ex-lover to grant the singer a second chance, and "Sorry Not Sorry," a scathing indictment of gold diggers coproduced by Timbaland.

In addition to RCA Records, Apple Music was instrumental in Tiller's success. "Don't" was dubbed a "heatseeker" on iTunes Radio, and when the company launched the more genre-specific Beats 1 Radio, his tracks were featured prominently. The week that *T R A P S O U L* became available for preorder, Tiller was featured in the iTunes "New Artist Spotlight."

The album attracted a wide variety of opinions. "This is somber, lyrically candid music, in which getting what you want doesn't sound much different from coming up short," Leight wrote. "The tracks are simultaneously sludgy but precise; the vocalists' delivery is frictionless." Others, however, were less impressed. "[The tracks] vary little in pace, ranging from leaden to liquid, rooted in sparse constructions that consist of deeply booming bass, rattling percussion, and synthesizer accents that stir and swarm," Andy Kellman wrote in a review for *AllMusic*. "As monochromatic as the tracks are, they're the right settings, ideal backdrops for Tiller's limited vocal and lyrical range. . . . Tiller has his sound and image nailed down, but not much of the content here has lasting value."

Mixed reviews did little to dissuade Tiller's fans, however. Within seven months of its release, they had purchased a million albums—enough to certify *T R A P S O U L* as platinum—and just a year after the official music video for "Don't" had been posted on YouTube, it had been viewed more than 150 million times. At MTV's 2016 Video Music Awards, "Don't" was nominated as best male video of the year and best hip-hop video, while Tiller was nominated as best new artist. At the 2016 BET Awards, he took home statuettes for best male R & B/pop artist and best new artist. In December of 2016, it was announced that Tiller' song "Exchange" had been nominated for a 2017 Grammy for best R & B song.

PERSONAL LIFE

Tiller has a daughter named Harley, with whom he is often pictured on social media. The artist credits his daughter for his success. "Having a kid made me care more about the things that I love—I started taking music more serious," he explained to Ramirez.

Tiller is said to be working on a second album. "I feel like I'm still defining who I am as an artist," he told Hyman. "I've got a lot of showing up to do. People try to change up my method but I'm gonna keep doing it the same way I've been doing it: going in the room by myself and making a song."

SUGGESTED READING

Hyman, Dan. "Meet Bryson Tiller, the New Surprise Hero of R&B." *GQ*, 18 Jan. 2016, www.gq.com/story/bryson-tiller-the-new-surprise-hero-of-r-b. Accessed 6 Jan. 2017.

Leight, Elias. "Bryson Tiller: Drake, Apple Music and the Making of a Trap-Soul Star." *Rolling Stone*, 30 Oct. 2015, www.rollingstone.com/music/news/bryson-tiller-drake-apple-music-and-the-making-of-a-trap-soul-star-20151030. Accessed 6 Jan. 2017.

Tiller, Bryson. "Bryson Tiller: A Conversation in the Key of '*T R A P S O U L*.'" Interview by Ashley Monaé. *Vibe*, 6 Oct. 2015, www.vibe.com/2015/10/bryson-tiller-trapsoul-interview. Accessed 6 Jan. 2017.

Tiller, Bryson. "Bryson Tiller's Music Saved Him. Now He Wants to Save Your Relationship." Interview by Erika Ramirez. *Fuse*, 29 Feb. 2016, www.fuse.tv/2016/02/bryson-tiller-interview-dont-trapsoul. Accessed 6 Jan. 2017.

Tiller, Bryson. "Bryson Tiller Talks 'Trapsoul' Breakthrough, Drake Co-Sign." Interview by Brittany Spanos. *Rolling Stone*, 1 Feb. 2016, www.rollingstone.com/music/features/bryson-tiller-talks-trapsoul-breakthrough-drake-co-sign-20160201. Accessed 6 Jan. 2017.

Tiller, Bryson. "From Nothing to Something: The Life & Times of Bryson Tiller." Interview by Brittany Lewis. *Global Grind*, 2015, globalgrind.com/4117715/bryson-tiller-interview. Accessed 6 Jan. 2017.

Tiller, Bryson. "Interview: Bryson Tiller." By Asia Burris. *Saint Heron*, 27 Oct. 2015, saintheron.com/featured/interview-bryson-tiller. Accessed 6 Jan. 2017.

—*Mari Rich*

Allison Tolman

Date of birth: November 18, 1981
Occupation: Actor

Although Allison Tolman had wanted to act all her life, she had little expectation that she would find her breakthrough moment after age thirty. Like many struggling actors before her, Tolman worked a variety of odd jobs while toiling away in the theater, earning some recognition for her skills at improvisation but little in the way of steadily paying gigs. The occasional bit role on television or in a commercial would crop up, but after years of work with few breaks, she began to assume that her life-changing moment would never come. Yet that moment did come, in the form of her award-winning performance as the brilliant Deputy Molly Solverson in the television series *Fargo*, which was based on a 1996 film of the same name and premiered to critical acclaim in 2014. Tolman was seen as the breakout performer of the series' first season, which also featured such heavyweight actors as Billy Bob Thornton, Keith Carradine, Colin Hanks, and Martin Freeman.

Since that success, Tolman has sought to take on roles that appeal to her—guest spots on television shows, supporting roles in horror and comedy films, and work on a television pilot—all in an effort to make herself as experienced an actor as possible. She also hopes to hone her comedic writing skills, with an eye toward writing for television. "I want to vary my résumé and my experiences as much as I can," Tolman told Mark

Dominick D/CC BY-SA 2.0/Wikimedia Commons

Lieberman in an interview for the news magazine the *Week* (8 Oct. 2015). "And I don't want to ever be pigeonholed. I don't want to pigeonhole *myself*. I'm difficult in that way, I guess."

EARLY LIFE AND EDUCATION

Allison Cara Tolman was born in Houston, Texas, on November 18, 1981, to Davis Nichols Tolman and Valerie Clohecy. She was raised in England until age four, when her parents returned to the United States, eventually settling in Sugar Land, Texas, near Houston. She took to acting very early, according to her mother. "Seriously, she was 2 or 2 1/2, playing in the bathtub and there was a mirror on the back wall: She would say, 'This is me happy,' 'This is me surprised,'" Valerie Tolman told Don Maines for the *Houston Chronicle* (11 Apr. 2014).

Encouraged and supported by both of her parents, Tolman began taking acting classes at the Ford Bend Theatre in Stafford at age eight. She continued to perform in junior high school and high school; while a student at Clements High School, she told Maines, she was "an officer in Thespian Troupe No. 3689." Her favorite high school show was *The Kentucky Cycle* (1991), a series of nine one-act plays by Robert Schenkkan that won the 1992 Pulitzer Prize for Drama.

After graduating in 2000, Tolman went on to study theatrical performance at Baylor University, earning her bachelor's degree in 2004. In interviews she has described her experiences at Baylor's Department of Theatre Arts as being instrumental to her development as an actor, but initially she was not sure if the school was right for her. "I went to Baylor kind of by accident," she said to Randy Fiedler in an interview for *Baylor Arts & Sciences* magazine (12 May 2015). "At first I didn't think it was going to end up being the school for me. . . . I was just going to be there for a year, but I fell in love with the theatre department. I thought, 'I don't want to leave—this is where I'm supposed to be. This is where I want to study. I want to have a degree from this institution.'"

COMEDY THEATER AND EARLY TELEVISION

Upon her graduation, Tolman and a few fellow Baylor alums moved to Dallas, where they helped establish Second Thought Theatre. In 2009, after five years in Dallas, she moved to Chicago, Illinois, having been accepted into the conservatory program at the Second City improvisational comedy theater. While there, she developed her skills at writing sketch comedy; she would later perform sketch comedy in a number of venues in Chicago, in addition to working on the *City Life Supplement*, a monthly comedy podcast.

During this period, Tolman had only landed the occasional small role in television programs, appearing as a nurse in a 2006 episode of *Prison Break* (2005–9), as a mother on *Barney & Friends* (1992–2009) in 2007, and as a recurring character Tink on *Sordid Lives: The Series* (2008). When not working in the theater, she supported herself with a wide variety of odd jobs, including veterinarian receptionist, personal assistant, children's theater teacher, vocal coach, phone sales associate, client services representative, and dog walker, to name a few. She then heard about a part in a television adaptation of brothers Joel and Ethan Coen's Academy Award–winning black comedy *Fargo* (1996), about a pregnant police chief in Fargo, North Dakota. The television series would feature an entirely new cast of characters and center on a new crime. The first season, set in 2006, starred Billy Bob Thornton, Colin Hanks, and Martin Freeman.

FARGO

Describing her selection for *Fargo* as a "total fluke," Tolman recalled how she got her life-changing role to Christina Radish for *Collider* (9 Feb. 2015): "I just put myself on tape at my agency in Chicago, with a bunch of other girls, and I magically kept rising through the ranks." She continued, "In the end, they were like, 'We don't know who this girl is, but we've obviously liked her for this long. We probably should bring her in with all of these other legitimate actresses and give her a screen test.' . . . I guess I was able to deliver on what they thought they saw in my original tape, so they took a chance and cast me, which was awesome."

In the series, Tolman portrayed Deputy Molly Solverson, who teams with Duluth police officer Gus Grimly (Hanks) to solve a series of murders that may be linked to characters Lorne Malvo (Thornton) and Lester Nygaard (Freeman). Describing Molly to Radish, Tolman explained, "She's the heart and the little engine that could of this show. I love the fact that she's this determined, dogged policewoman who's really just putting her head down and plowing through things, for the entire series, against all odds. . . . She knows how to play a long game and be patient, which is nice."

Although most series have a regular cast of characters who remain from one season to the next, series creator Noah Hawley decided to move in a different direction with *Fargo*, instead setting season 2 in 1979 and focusing on a new murder with an entirely different set of characters. (A third season, set in 2010, will premier in 2017.) The change in direction was met with a considerable outcry by fans of the series, who were particularly disappointed that Tolman's character would not be returning. Tolman's performance was seen as a standout by both critics and viewers alike, earning her the 2014 Critics' Choice Television Award for best supporting actress in a movie or miniseries and a nomination for the 2013–14 Emmy Award for outstanding supporting actress in a limited series or movie (ultimately won by Kathy Bates for her performance in *American Horror Story*). Although disappointed that she would not be returning for another season of *Fargo*, Tolman has said in interviews that she is comfortable with where her character ended up at the end of the ten-episode first season.

LOOKING AHEAD

After leaving *Fargo*, Tolman began searching for the right jobs to fit her interests, being selective about the projects she chose to be involved with. She made several guest appearances on television shows, including a two-episode run on *The Mindy Project* (2012–) as Abby Berman, a historical romance novelist who becomes romantically involved with the character of Dr. Peter Prentice (Adam Pally), in 2014. The following year she appeared in the Christmas horror comedy film *Krampus* (2015), which was filmed in New Zealand through the production company of noted director Peter Jackson, and *The Gift* (2015), a psychological thriller directed by actor Joel Edgerton and starring Jason Bateman and Rebecca Hall. Both of the films appealed to Tolman's love of horror movies, a genre that she had asked her agent to look into after she left *Fargo*.

Tolman has also appeared in a number of films scheduled to be released in 2017, including the musical drama *La Barracuda* and the Will Ferrell–Amy Poehler comedy *The House*, and filmed a comedy pilot for a television series titled *Downward Dog*. In addition to acting, she plans to continue to work on her own comedic writing skills. "I need to find some good software, I need to lock myself for a few hours in my office every day, and I need to learn to write television shows," she told Lieberman.

BODY IMAGE

In an industry that puts a premium on picture-perfect beauty, Tolman has been outspoken against body-shaming—the practice of criticizing a person's looks or weight for not conforming to a narrowly defined standard of beauty. Tolman, who as a size 12 is in the normal range of weight, has been the target of such attacks, which do not bother her specifically. She is much more angered by what such attacks might mean to impressionable young girls such as her niece. She also thinks that another problem that "average-looking" women actors face is typecasting, particularly if they are more than thirty years old. "Average-looking women tend to play more wholesome characters who tend to have their s—— together. Which . . . is a misrepresentation," Tolman said to Lieberman. "All sorts of people make bad choices and questionable

decisions in the real world. And those are the characters that are really fun to play."

SUGGESTED READING

Hinkley, David. "Fargo Creator Noah Hawley Calls His Firing of Allison Tolman a 'Crime and a Tragedy.'" *NY Daily News*, 22 July 2014, www.nydailynews.com/entertainment/tv/fargo-creator-noah-hawley-hated-firing-allison-tolman-article-1.1876141. Accessed 4 Jan. 2017.

Lieberman, Mark. "How *Fargo* Star Allison Tolman Is Taking Her Newfound Celebrity in Stride." *The Week*, 8 Oct. 2015, theweek.com/articles/572992/how-fargo-star-allison-tolman-taking-newfound-celebrity-stride. Accessed 4 Jan. 2017.

Maines, Don. "Clements Grad Stars in *Fargo*." *The Houston Chronicle*, 11 Apr. 2014, www.chron.com/neighborhood/fortbend/news/article/Clements-grad-stars-in-Fargo-5396294.php. Accessed 4 Jan. 2017.

Tolman, Allison. "Allison Tolman Talks *Fargo*, How She Got the Role, Taking to the Accent, Working with the Talented Cast Including Keith Carradine, and the Tone of the Ending." Interview by Christina Radish. *Collider*, 9 Feb. 2015, collider.com/allison-tolman-fargo-interview. Accessed 4 Jan. 2017.

Tolman, Allison. "Q&A with Allison Tolman." Interview by Randy Fiedler. *Baylor Arts & Sciences*, Baylor University College of Arts & Sciences, 12 May 2015, blogs.baylor.edu/artsandsciences/2015/05/12/allison-tolman. Accessed 4 Jan. 2017.

SELECTED WORKS

Fargo, 2014; *The Gift*, 2015; *Krampus*, 2015

—*Christopher Mari*

Paul F. Tompkins

Date of birth: September 12, 1968
Occupation: Comedian

Accumulated over more than three decades, the body of work of comedian Paul F. Tompkins can be quite difficult to categorize—and for good reason. "My career is made up of many different things," he said to Arian Brumby for *Austinist* (23 May 2012). "I have standup and television stuff and there's auditions and there's all sorts of things that make up the career of someone like me who does not have a regular steady gig." A fixture in the Los Angeles comedy scene since the mid-1990s and a working stand-up and sketch comic for a decade before that, Tompkins has split his time between a variety of pursuits,

By RangerRick (Benjamin Reed) [CC BY-SA 2.0], via Wikimedia Commons

including live performances, television guest appearances, and extended hosting stints on multiple podcasts and web series.

The Pennsylvania-born Tompkins, whose work has often been categorized as alternative comedy, began performing stand-up comedy at Philadelphia's Comedy Works club as a teenager. He took his career in a new direction in the 1990s, when he moved to California and joined the writing staff and cast of the HBO sketch comedy series *Mr. Show with Bob and David* (1995–98). Numerous television appearances followed, including a regular gig on VH1's *Best Week Ever* (2004–9), and Tompkins likewise gained attention for his live performances and recorded specials, particularly his DVD releases *Paul F. Tompkins: You Should Have Told Me* (2010) and *Paul F. Tompkins: Laboring under Delusions* (2012). With such projects as the Netflix animated series *BoJack Horseman* (2014–), in which he voices an anthropomorphic dog named Mr. Peanutbutter, and podcast projects such as the improv-focused *SPONTANEANATION with Paul F. Tompkins*, Tompkins has since explored new avenues of comedy to critical acclaim. Above all, he values a comedic approach that is more joyful than cynical. "Increasingly, I enjoy less the comedy of uncomfortable things and sad things being funny. I enjoy silliness," he said to fellow comedian and actor Ben Schwartz for *Vulture* (4 Feb. 2016). "I feel like, man, life is hard enough."

EARLY LIFE AND EDUCATION

Paul Francis Tompkins was born in Philadelphia, Pennsylvania, on September 12, 1968. The fifth of six children, he grew up in the Mount Airy neighborhood of Philadelphia. His father worked for a train company, while his mother was a receptionist. Tompkins had a distant relationship with his parents, who did not support his career aspirations, and that aspect of his early life would later inform some of his stand-up and podcast appearances.

As a child and teenager, Tompkins found himself drawn to comedy, particularly to the performance aspect of it. "I always wanted to be a performer," he recalled to Mark Rozeman for *Paste* (2 Sept. 2014). "When I first started doing stand-up back in Philadelphia, the idea of being a professional writer was completely beyond me. It didn't even occur to me that that was something you could do." Although some of Tompkins's later projects, including *SPONTANEANATION*, would focus heavily on improvisational comedy, he never pursued formal training in that area, instead focusing primarily on stand-up. After graduating from Bishop McDevitt High School in Wyncote, Pennsylvania, he moved to downtown Philadelphia and enrolled in Temple University. However, he dropped out after less than a year to pursue a career in comedy.

EARLY CAREER

Tomkins began performing stand-up at Philadelphia's Comedy Works in 1986, while still a teenager. He soon formed a sketch comedy duo with fellow comedian Rick Roman, and they performed together for more than a year. Roman would later move to Chicago, where he would cofound the influential Upright Citizens Brigade comedy group.

In 1994, Tompkins left Philadelphia and moved to California, settling in the Los Angeles area. Not long afterward, he and comedian Jay Johnston formed a comedy group called the Skates, which performed live sketch comedy in the area. Their work captured the attention of more established performers in the Los Angeles comedy scene, and both Tompkins and Johnston were soon hired as writers and cast members for the sketch comedy series *Mr. Show with Bob and David*. Starring established comedians Bob Odenkirk and David Cross, *Mr. Show* has since become a cult favorite, although it had a limited audience at the time of its original release. Tompkins rejoined many of the show's stars and writers for a limited revival series, *W/ Bob & David*, which was released on Netflix in 2015.

LIVE COMEDY

During his tenure on *Mr. Show with Bob and David*, Tompkins came to realize that he enjoyed performing much more than writing, and over the next decade-plus he primarily sought out performing opportunities. In 2002 he began hosting a live variety show, featuring Tompkins himself in addition to an array of comedians and musicians, at the Largo nightclub in Los Angeles. *The Paul F. Tompkins Show* was a regular feature at Largo through 2012.

As a comedian who began his career in stand-up, Tompkins has devoted much of his career to that medium, performing widely in comedy clubs throughout the United States. Over time, however, he came to tire of the usual method of scheduling performances, which involved booking gigs and then hoping that audiences would attend and appreciate Tompkins's particular strain of humor. "I would go do a show and part of doing the show was the preparation. Like, 'Well, I have to win these people over. I have to prove to them that I'm funny,'" he explained to John Wenzel for the *Denver Post* blog the *Know* (25 May 2011). "Whereas going into an audience of people who are fans of mine, they're already assuming I'm going to be funny. They know who I am and my sensibility." In light of that realization, Tompkins began booking performances based on Facebook groups known as Tompkins 300s: if a group had at least three hundred members who would commit to attending a performance in a given city, he would schedule a show in that city. This strategy enabled Tompkins to limit his touring schedule while also ensuring that his performances would be seen by his core audience of dedicated fans.

In addition to his live shows, Tompkins has recorded stand-up comedy albums, beginning with 2007's *Impersonal*. His live comedy specials include the 1998 HBO special *Paul F. Tompkins: Driven to Drink* and two installments of *Comedy Central Presents*, in 2003 and 2007, as well as *You Should Have Told Me* and *Laboring under Delusions*. His special *Paul F. Tompkins: Crying and Driving*, which aired on Comedy Central in 2015, tackles his experience of learning to drive in his forties, among other topics.

TELEVISION AND FILM

Since 1995, Tompkins has appeared in numerous film and television projects, both as an actor and as himself. He appeared in multiple episodes of shows such as *Tenacious D* (1997–2000) and *The Sarah Silverman Program* (2007–10) and was a supporting cast member on the short-lived sitcom *DAG*, which aired for one season on NBC in 2000–2001. Tompkins also made single-episode guest appearances in shows such as *NewsRadio* (in 1999), *Frasier* (in 2003), *Pushing Daisies* (in 2008), *Community* (in 2010), and *Curb Your Enthusiasm* (in 2011) and has played small roles in a variety of films, including—in a perhaps unexpected move away

from comedy—the Academy Award–winning 2007 drama *There Will Be Blood*.

As himself, Tompkins has contributed and often hosted a variety of comedy projects. He was a frequent contributor to the weekly VH1 clip show *Best Week Ever* following its premiere in 2004, and in 2008 he took over as host of the show, which was renamed *Best Week Ever with Paul F. Tompkins*. "That whole experience from start to finish was unlike anything I had ever been through before," he told Kyle Ryan for the *AV Club* (20 Apr. 2012) of his time on *Best Week Ever*. Tompkins returned to the project for *Best Week Ever*'s short-lived revival in 2013–14. He went on to host several additional projects, including the television show *No, You Shut Up!* (2013–16), which featured debating puppets, and the web series *Speakeasy* (2012–15), in which Tompkins interviewed various celebrities over drinks.

Tompkins has also found work as a voice actor, contributing voices to animated projects such as the Disney film *Tangled* (2010) and the television shows *King of the Hill* (in 2005), *Regular Show* (in 2010–12), and *Bob's Burgers* (in 2011–14). Perhaps his best-known vocal role is that of Mr. Peanutbutter, the former sitcom actor and anthropomorphic dog in the Netflix series *BoJack Horseman*. The optimistic counterpart to the titular cynical and depressed horse, Mr. Peanutbutter became a fan-favorite character following the show's debut in 2014. For Tompkins, the character provides an important perspective in a show that can at times become quite dark in tone. "Mr. Peanutbutter is saying to the audience: All of these flawed characters, as flawed as these people are, these creatures are—they're doing reprehensible things sometimes—they're human beings. And we all do deserve love," he said to Miranda Popkey for *GQ* (8 Sept. 2017). He continued, "I think that a lot of times Mr. Peanutbutter is absolutely speaking directly to the audience and saying basic, human truths that we need to hear."

PODCASTS

In addition to his work in more traditional forms of media, Tompkins has been an active contributor to the world of podcasts, series of recorded shows available for download or online streaming that somewhat resemble radio programs but often concern more niche topics and perspectives. "A big difference between podcasts and radio is the intimacy," Tompkins explained to Schwartz. "Radio oftentimes feels big and loud. To me, podcasting is closest to that weird late-night stuff, whether it's late-night love-song request lines, or it's some talk radio show where you feel like you're the only person listening to it. I always like things that shrink the world for me, that make me feel a strange connection, not just to the person that I'm listening to but to the world."

Tompkins launched his personal podcast, *The Pod F. Tompkast*, in 2010 and released regular episodes through 2012. From 2011 to 2015 he hosted *The Dead Authors Podcast*, a semi-improvisational show in which Tompkins, in character as writer H. G. Wells, interviewed deceased writers played by other comedians. He launched the improvisational comedy podcast *SPONTANEANATION with Paul F. Tompkins* in 2015. Tompkins has also frequently contributed to additional podcasts, including *Comedy Bang! Bang!*, *Superego*, and *The Thrilling Adventure Hour*.

PERSONAL LIFE

Tompkins married actor Janie Haddad Tompkins in 2010. They live in Los Angeles. Although Tompkins has been very prolific since his early days in comedy, he has become "more discerning as time goes on," as he told Brumby. He added, "I am trying to take time more to myself, have more of a life, have a social life and get to enjoy the things that I like to enjoy. I love my job and I love the things that I get to do and I really do have a lot of fun, but at the end of the day there's more to life than just show business, and I want to get to enjoy those things."

SUGGESTED READING

Tompkins, Paul F. "Ben Schwartz Talks to Paul F. Tompkins about *Comedy Bang! Bang!* and an Idea for a *Hamilton* Podcast." Interview by Ben Schwartz. *Vulture*, New York Media, 4 Feb. 2016, www.vulture.com/2016/02/ben-schwartz-talks-to-paul-f-tompkins.html. Accessed 12 Sept. 2017.

Tompkins, Paul F. "*Bojack Horseman*'s Paul F. Tompkins Is the Happiest Part of the Saddest Show." Interview by Miranda Popkey. *GQ*, 8 Sept. 2017, www.gq.com/story/bojack-horseman-paul-f-thompkins-interview. Accessed 12 Sept. 2017.

Tompkins, Paul F. "Bringing 'Dead Authors' to Life for Book-Smart Comedy." Interview by Arun Rath. *NPR*, 11 Jan. 2014, www.npr.org/2014/01/11/255575642/bringing-dead-authors-to-life-for-book-smart-comedy. Accessed 12 Sept. 2017.

Tompkins, Paul F. "Catching Up with Paul F. Tompkins." Interview by Mark Rozeman. *Paste*, 2 Sept. 2014, www.pastemagazine.com/articles/2014/09/catching-up-with-paul-f-thompkins.html. Accessed 12 Sept. 2017.

Tompkins, Paul F. "An Interview with Paul F. Tompkins: A Very Fancy Man." Interview by Arian Brumby. *Austinist*, Gothamist, 23 May 2012, austinist.com/2012/05/23/paul_f_tompkins_a_fancy_man.php. Accessed 12 Sept. 2017.

Tompkins, Paul F. "Paul F. Tompkins on Why He's More Storyteller Than Comedian These Days." Interview by Kyle Ryan. *The AV Club*, Gizmodo Media Group, 20 Apr. 2012, tv.avclub.com/paul-f-tompkins-on-why-he-s-more-storyteller-than-come-1798230912. Accessed 12 Sept. 2017.

Tompkins, Paul F. "Why So Serious, Paul F. Tompkins?" Interview by John Wenzel. *The Know*, Denver Post, 25 May 2011, theknow.denverpost.com/2011/05/25/paul-f-tompkins-interview/. Accessed 12 Sept. 2017.

SELECTED WORKS

Mr. Show with Bob and David, 1995–98; *Comedy Central Presents: Paul F. Tompkins*, 2003, 2007; *Best Week Ever*, 2004–13; *You Should Have Told Me*, 2010; *Paul F. Tompkins: Laboring Under Delusions*, 2012; *Comedy Bang! Bang!*, 2012–16; *BoJack Horseman*, 2014– ; *W/ Bob and David*, 2015; *Paul F. Tompkins: Crying and Driving*, 2015; *Bajillion Dollar Propertie$*, 2016–

—*Joy Crelin*

Karl-Anthony Towns

Date of birth: November 15, 1995
Occupation: Basketball player

Minnesota Timberwolves center Karl-Anthony Towns was named National Basketball Association (NBA) Rookie of the Year for the 2015–16 season. The New Jersey–born athlete was a local celebrity by the time he was in middle school. He was a standout at St. Joseph High School, a Catholic prep school in Metuchen, New Jersey, and became a member of the Dominican Republic national team when he was just fifteen. In college, Towns played for the University of Kentucky, and was selected by the Timberwolves as the first pick of the NBA draft in 2015. Towering seven feet tall and wearing a size 20 shoe, Towns in many ways fits the classic "big man" mold of an NBA player. But he is also something entirely new. Today's game is much faster, and big men, Kevin Arnovitz wrote for *ESPN Magazine* (17 Nov. 2016), are expected to do more—shoot threes, pick and roll, guard, run the floor—than just stand as "an immovable force, dominating as a defensive presence in the paint." Towns can do it all, often better than anyone else. As Arnovitz argues, similar players like Draymond Green and Serge Ibaka developed the necessary new big-man skills over the course of their NBA career. Towns, who turned twenty-one in 2016, has been training for the new game his whole life, and his versatility is the result of conscious effort. "I don't limit myself," he told Arnovtiz. "If

Dennis Adair/CC BY-SA 2.0/Flickr/Wikimedia Commons

my coach needs me to guard 1 through 5, I have worked tremendously hard to have the ability to do that. If I need to shoot, I can shoot. If I need to post up and be a bruiser, I can be a bruiser. I try to be great at all skills."

EARLY LIFE

Karl-Anthony Towns was born in Edison, New Jersey, on November 15, 1995, to Jacqueline Cruz-Towns and Karl Towns. He and his older sister, Lachelle, were raised in Piscataway, New Jersey. Karl Towns, a former basketball player for Monmouth University in New Jersey in the 1980s, worked as a coach at Piscataway Technical High School. (He stepped down to follow his son's basketball career after the 2014 season.) Towns's father, at six feet five inches, was once one of the leading college rebounders in the nation, but it was clear from an early age that Towns would surpass his father in height—and perhaps even in talent. When Towns was eight, the family decided to raise the ceiling in their dining room and had a special bed built for their son. He ate so much that he perfected the art of collecting coupons, just to help his parents pay for all the food he consumed. By the time he was in the fifth grade, he was over six feet tall. But it was not merely his height that suggested his gift for basketball. As his mother recalled to Zach Schonbrun for the *New York Times* (3 Apr. 2015), "He was so graceful, even though he was so big. That's when I knew he was going to do something with basketball."

Towns attended Our Lady of Fatima School, and transferred to Theodore Schor Middle School, repeating the seventh grade in the shuffle. Already a standout in the eighth grade, Towns accepted a $40,000 scholarship to the Pennington School, a boarding school outside of Princeton. But before the school year began, Towns got a phone call from Pennington rejecting his admission because of his growing celebrity. With the encouragement of Dave Turco, head coach at St. Joseph High School, Towns eventually chose to attend St. Joseph, a Catholic prep school in Metuchen. He excelled as a student there, enjoyed studying finance and religion, and was elected president of his freshman class. He played ultimate Frisbee, golf, and flag football; he learned to play piano, joined the social justice club, and worked for local charities. He also maintained a nearly 4.0 grade point average in high school and graduated in three years.

HIGH SCHOOL CAREER

Towns began practicing with his father's junior varsity team after school when he was in fifth grade. Karl Towns drilled his son on the fundamentals; Towns was big but he was agile, and he could dribble, pass, and defend like a player twice his age. By the time he was a high school freshman, he had scholarship offers from Michigan State, Syracuse University, and the University of Connecticut. That same year, 2011, Towns played for the Dominican Republic's under-seventeen national team, for which he was eligible because his mother is Dominican. There, he was coached by Oliver Antigua, brother of Orlando Antigua, the former assistant coach at the University of Kentucky. Antiqua told Keith Pompey for the *Philadelphia Inquirer* (29 May 2011), "He has a great feel for the game. Once his body catches up and fills out, he will be able to do anything."

When Towns, a high school sophomore, turned seventeen the next year, he was invited to play on the Dominican national team, where he met Kentucky coach John Calipari and played alongside NBA players Al Horford, Charlie Villanueva, and Francisco Garcia. He played against Team USA—he was guarded by Anthony Davis—in an Olympic qualifying game in 2012. Turco, Towns's high school coach, employed a very specific and unusual strategy with his star player. "Karl was on the perimeter, because if the [opposing team's] big man stayed inside, we'd get Karl the ball and he'd knock down threes, and if he went outside then [another player] would get to the rim pretty easily," he told Adam Figman for *Slam* magazine (1 Sept. 2016). Towns led the team in three-pointers.

As a senior during the 2013–14 season, Towns was selected to play in the McDonald's All-American game in Chicago, and named a Gatorade Player of the Year, a national award for high school student-athletes. By the end of his high school career, he had scored 1,670 career points and 1,160 rebounds, and made 484 blocks and 127 three-pointers. Towns became a proto-celebrity, signing autographs and taking pictures with fans after games. He told one reporter in 2014 that he began shopping online because he could not go the mall without being recognized.

COLLEGE CAREER

Unsurprisingly—but controversially in the eyes of some other recruiters—Towns chose to attend the University of Kentucky, and play for the Wildcats and coach Calipari. Arnovitz called Calipari's program a "veritable finishing school for NBA big men." Past Kentucky players include John Wall and Anthony Davis, both of whom went first in their NBA draft years, in 2010 and 2012, respectively. Calipari had very different but also more traditional ideas for using Towns, reversing Turco's approach with the young athlete. "I did not let him shoot three-point shots," Calipari told Figman. Towns, he said, "was gonna get next to that basket and every day he was gonna get better." Towns, who was already well known as a hard worker and perfectionist, worked to accommodate his coach's taste.

As a freshman forward during the 2014–15 season, Towns had already developed his reputation as a renaissance man, with guard skills, a three-point jump shot, and a point guard's passing ability. But Calipari pushed him to develop his weaker skills, to "play low" and get down and dirty in scuffles under the basket. The coach wanted him to get tough, to drop his usually friendly demeanor on the court and learn quickly—the latter being something, Calipari later wrote for *Sports Illustrated* (16 Nov. 2016), that Towns struggled mightily to do. "It wasn't just post play he had to learn," Calipari wrote. "On defense, I was teaching him to guard pick and rolls, the most difficult skill—and increasingly, one of the most important skills—for any big man. With the professional game more wide open, and shooters spread all over the court, a big player has to be able to compete around the hoop and jump out on smaller players to either prevent open three-point shots or impede them if they try to drive to the hoop. Our team needed Karl to learn that and Karl needed it for his future."

Thanks to Towns and other standout players, the season was one of the best in Kentucky Wildcats history. The team was undefeated in the regular season, and made it to the Final Four, a personal goal for Towns, with a 38–0 record. But there, they were upset by the Wisconsin Badgers who went on to face Duke in the National Championship. Towns continues to work on two degrees from Kentucky, one in kinesiology, the study of body movement, and one in business. After his NBA career—or "after the basketball goes flat," as he put it to Calipari—he hopes to become a doctor.

2016 ROOKIE OF THE YEAR

By the end of the 2015 season, Towns was the presumed number-one draft pick, but when draft night came, the player was still incredibly nervous waiting at a table for his name to be called. "I was trying to drink the water and I was shaking uncontrollably," Towns told Jerry Zgoda for the Minneapolis *Star Tribune* (30 June 2015). As expected, however, he was selected first by the Minnesota Timberwolves. His selection was in large part thanks to the late Timberwolves president Flip Saunders, who told Zgoda at the time of the draft, "[Towns] plays with a great passion. He plays hard. He's multiskilled. When you see him warming up, you're going to think we drafted a point guard." Saunders, who encouraged a mentoring relationship between Towns and veteran Kevin Garnett, died just before the season 2016 season began; Towns has said that he plays in honor of the man's memory, as it is clear Saunders had hoped to build the franchise around the rookie's talents.

According to Figman, Towns had one of the best rookie seasons ever, averaging 18.3 points, 10.5 rebounds and 1.7 blocks per game. He was unanimously named Rookie of the Year, only the fifth player in NBA history to win every first-place vote. Kevin Pelton even argued for *ABC News* (16 May 2016) that Towns's might be the best NBA prospect since four-time MVP LeBron James. As he has such talent at only twenty-one years old, the sky could very well be the limit for Towns, Pelton wrote. "His rookie season suggested the potential to become a talent unlike any we've seen before."

SUGGESTED READING
Arnovitz, Kevin. "Real Big Deal." *ESPN*, 17 Nov. 2016, www.espn.com/espn/feature/story/_/id/18063065/minnesota-timberwolves-karl-anthony-towns-face-nba-big-man-revolution. Accessed 14 Feb. 2017.

Calipari, John. "How John Calipari Helped Karl-Anthony Towns Ditch 'Nice Guy' Persona on Court." *Sports Illustrated*, 16 Nov. 2016, www.si.com/college-basketball/john-calipari-book-excerpt-kentucky-karl-anthony-towns. Accessed 15 Feb. 2017.

Figman, Adam. "The Perfect Storm." *Slam*, 1 Sept. 2016, www.slamonline.com/the-perfect-storm/. Accessed 14 Feb. 2017.

Pelton, Kevin. "Karl-Anthony Towns Is the NBA's Best Prospect since LeBron James." *ABC News*, 16 May 2016, abcnews.go.com/Sports/karl-anthony-towns-nbas-best-prospect-lebron-james/story?id=39143283.   Accessed 15 Feb. 2017.

Pompey, Keith. "A Towering Hoops Talent—and Only in Eighth Grade." *Philly.com*, 29 May 2011, www.philly.com/philly/blogs/sports/sixers/Karl-Anthony-Towns-ways-back-when-.html. Accessed 14 Feb. 2017.

Schonbrun, Zach. "Two Parts to His Name, but Karl-Anthony Towns Is One Complete Player." *New York Times*, 3 Apr. 2015, www.nytimes.com/2015/04/04/sports/ncaabasketball/two-parts-to-his-name-but-karl-anthony-towns-is-one-complete-player.html. Accessed 13 Feb. 2017.

Zgoda, Jerry. "Karl-Anthony Towns Taken No. 1 by the Wolves; Tyus Jones Acquired in Trade with Cavaliers." *Star Tribune* [Minneapolis], 30 June 2015, www.startribune.com/karl-anthony-towns-drafted-no-1-overall-by-timberwolves-as-expected/309936841. Accessed 15 Feb. 2017.

—*Molly Hagan*

John Cordes/Icon Sportswire via Getty Images

Julio Urías

Date of birth: August 12, 1996
Occupation: Baseball player

During game 4 of the National League Division Series in October 2016, Julio Urías, a twenty-year-old, left-handed pitcher for the Los Angeles Dodgers, became the youngest player to start in a postseason game. Urías's rise from Mexican Baseball League (LMB) star to Dodgers minor league standout, could only be described as meteoric. As journalists like to point out, Urías accomplished his lifelong dream of playing for a major league team before he was old enough to buy a beer. The young pitcher, who was first discovered at age fourteen by legendary Dodgers scout Mike Brito, is known for his 97-mph fastball, among other pitches in his arsenal. In 2016, Zachary D. Rymer for *Bleacher Report* (10 Feb. 2016) called Urías "the best left-handed pitching prospect in the game, as well as a consensus top-10 overall prospect." Rymer also praised Urías's control when he quoted Ben Badler of *Baseball America* who said, "[Urías] manipulates the shape and speed of his curve, giving it top-to-bottom depth at times, then getting wide and slurvy [a slurve is a slider thrown like a curveball] at others. He also mixes in a short slider at times. He deliberately throws from multiple arm angles, adding and subtracting from his pitches." For all his potential, however, the Dodgers management is not in any hurry to push Urías for fear of injury. In February, the franchise said that Urías would not be a full-time starter for the Dodgers in the 2017 season, though it is likely that toward the end of the season he will be called up again from the minor leagues.

EARLY LIFE

Urías was born on August 12, 1996, in Culiácan, Sinaloa, in northeastern Mexico. His father, Carlos, is a former pitcher who played in a local municipal league in Sinaloa and introduced his son to baseball when Urías was a toddler. In addition to his father and his mother, Juana Isabell, Urías's family includes two younger siblings, Carlitos and Alexia.

Growing up in the tiny town of La Higuerita just outside of Culiácan, Urías idolized Óliver Pérez, another left-handed pitcher from Culiácan, who went on to play for the Washington Nationals. "As we like to say, he's 'un caballo,'" slang that roughly means "the man," Urías told Dylan Hernandez for the *Los Angeles Times* (22 June 2016). As a ten-year-old, Urías met Pérez, and nine years later, Pérez was in the visiting bullpen watching Urías pitch one of his first major league games.

As a child, Urías practiced the game on a dirt field that his grandfather and relative had built in the middle of farmland, and from an early age, baseball was his singular ambition. Urías's father recalled the many birthday parties and family gatherings his son did not attend because he was at practice. "He missed out on some childhood activities, but he enjoyed being out on the field and had a dream, and thank God he accomplished it," Carlos Urías told Jorge L. Ortiz for *USA Today* (13 June 2016).

SIGNING WITH THE LOS ANGELES DODGERS

By the time Urías was fourteen years old, he was traveling with the Mexican professional baseball team the Diablos Rojos del México (the Mexico City Reds). Dodgers scout Mike Brito saw Urías play that year and made him and his family a promise. "I told his father . . . 'You're going to be with the Dodgers,'" Brito recalled to Doug Padilla for ESPN (7 June 2016), but he was unable to sign Urías at the time because Urías was too young. Nearly two years later in 2012, former Dodgers scouting director Logan White was in Mexico City and decided to make the two-hour trip by plane to Oaxaca to see a showcase of young Mexican League players. There he watched a fifteen-year-old Urías throw a 92-mph fastball. "When I saw this kid, I said, 'My goodness, he has really got a chance to be something special,'" White recalled to Mark Saxon for ESPN (18 June 2013).

Urías was still too young to officially sign with the Dodgers, but there was another problem: As a small child, Urías had a tumor removed from his left eyelid, which left that eye permanently and noticeably droopy. Urías's eyelid spawned all kinds of rumors among scouts, including that he was blind in that eye, that he had cancer, that he needed chemotherapy, and that he was dying. The Dodgers were unable to substantiate any of the claims, and in August 2012, just a few days after Urías turned sixteen, the team signed him for $450,000, though most of that money went to the Mexican League. Urías was thrilled to see his major league dreams begin to take shape. "That's how God works," Urías told Hernandez (23 Feb. 2015). "He gave me a bad left eye but a good left arm."

MINOR LEAGUE CAREER

After signing with the Dodgers, sixteen-year-old Urías moved from his home in Mexico to Midland, Michigan, in order to play with a Dodgers-affiliated minor league team, the Great Lakes Loons. Although he had been playing on the road since he was ten, the move still took its toll. Away from his family's cooking, Urías ate a lot of fast food, and Victor J. Corona of the *Sporting Nation* (30 Apr. 2014) joked that the weight Urías gained was the inevitable "freshman 15."

Urías made his US debut in May 2014 when the Loons played the Dayton Dragons, pitching three shutout innings and striking out six hitters. Fans took to social media to express their disbelief at the pitcher's age. During the 2014 season, Urías also played for California's Rancho Cucamonga Quakes and was a standout in that league as well, pitching a perfect inning in an exhibition game against the San Diego Padres and striking out 109 batters in 87 2/3 innings.

At the end of the 2014 season, the seventeen-year-old was selected to play in the all-star showcase Futures Game at Target Field in Minneapolis. He did not disappoint, throwing a perfect fifth inning, which included one strikeout and eleven strikes in fourteen pitches. The week preceding the game, Urías was named the Dodgers top prospect.

Fans gleefully predicted Urías's rise to the majors, but the pitcher began the 2015 season with the minor league Tulsa Drillers, a Dodgers affiliate in the Texas League. Urías also missed over a month of play following Dodger-requested cosmetic surgery to correct the appearance of his droopy eyelid, which Kevin Henry for *Tulsa World* (30 July 2015) observed seemed to bother others more than it bothered Urías. "Growing up, people made fun of me," Urías told Henry. "I've always stood out, but I think I've stood out because I was always the best one on the team." In late August, Urías made his debut with the Oklahoma City Dodgers, a Triple-A Dodgers affiliate in the Pacific Coast League. He also began the 2016 season with that team, but in May he received a long-awaited but unexpected phone call.

MAJOR LEAGUE DEBUT

Urías made his major league debut with the Dodgers on May 27, 2016, against the New York Mets at Citi Field. The young pitcher received the call on May 26, and he immediately phoned his family in Mexico. The family stopped off at Iglesia de La Lomita Virgen de Guadalupe, a local Catholic Church, to give thanks before getting on a plane to attend the game, arriving in New York City at 5:30 in the morning on game day.

Urías struggled in his major-league debut and gave up three runs in the first inning. He was then replaced by veteran pitcher Chris Hatcher in the third inning. Urías was nervous, he told reporters after the game. Ken Gurnick for *MLB.com* (28 May 2016) reported Urías explaining that when he walked out on to the field, "I started thinking of everything I've had to go through to get here. But when I was on the mound, I was able to settle down, be a little more comfortable. Unfortunately, we weren't able to get the results we wanted." At nineteen years old, Urías was the youngest Dodgers pitcher to start a game in fifty-three years.

Urías was called back to the minor leagues in July. The decision was based on an innings limit more than it was on his performance. "As an experiment, Urías in the bigs was a mixed bag," Craig Calcaterra wrote for NBC Sports (5 July 2016). "He was below average to be sure, but he's painfully young and pitched in some bad luck at times as well. . . . Ultimately, however, his not being dominant in the bigs was probably a blessing for his long-term development." But the injury-plagued team recalled Urías only a few weeks later. By this time, the young pitcher had found his groove, and in August he led the team to break a three-game losing streak after throwing six scoreless innings in a game against the Cincinnati Reds. By September, he led the majors in pickoffs. The following month and at age twenty Urías started for the Dodgers and became the youngest starting pitcher in major league playoff history.

All in all, 2016 was a huge leap for Urías's career, not only in his move from the minor league to the major league, but also thanks to his career-high 127 2/3 innings, up from his previous high of 87 2/3 in 2014. Concerned that pushing Urías to pitch a similar load might injure him, the Dodgers will likely send him to extended spring training in 2017 and recall him to the majors toward the end of the season.

SUGGESTED READING

Gurnick, Ken. "Urías's MLB Debut Doesn't Go as Planned." *MLB.com*, 28 May 2016, m.mlb.com/news/article/180675066/julio-urias-struggles-in-mlb-debut-for-dodgers/. Accessed 17 Feb. 2017.

Hernandez, Dylan. "Despite Eye Condition, Prospect Julio Urías Dazzles on the Mound." *Los Angeles Times*, 23 Feb. 2015, www.latimes.com/sports/dodgers/la-sp-dodgers-urias-20150224-story.html. Accessed 16 Feb. 2017.

Hernandez, Dylan. "It's a Memorable Night for Dodgers' Julio Urías, Pitching with His Hero, Washington's Oliver Perez, in the House." *Los Angeles Times*, 22 June 2016, www.latimes.com/sports/dodgers/la-sp-urias-perez-hernandez-20160622-snap-story.html. Accessed 16 Feb. 2017.

Ortiz, Jorge L. "Dodgers' 19-Year-Old Rookie Julio Urías Holding Up under Bright Spotlight." *USA Today*, 13 June 2016, www.usatoday.com/story/sports/mlb/dodgers/2016/06/13/julio-urias-los-angeles-dodgers-san-francisco-giants-nl-west/85816850/. Accessed 16 Feb. 2017.

Padilla, Doug. "How Teenage Phenom Julio Urías Became a Dodger." *ESPN*, 7 June 2016, www.espn.com/blog/los-angeles/dodger-report/post/_/id/19970/how-teenage-phenom-julio-urias-became-a-dodger. Accessed 17 Feb. 2017.

Rymer, Zachary D. "Breaking Down MLB's Next Golden Era of Pitching Prospects." *Bleacher Report*, Turner Broadcasting System, 10 Feb. 2016, bleacherreport.com/articles/2615064-breaking-down-mlbs-next-golden-era-of-pitching-prospects. Accessed 17 Feb. 2017.

Saxon, Mark. "How the Dodgers Found the Youngest Prospect in MLB." *ESPN*, 18 June 2013, www.espn.com/blog/los-angeles/dodger-report/post/_/id/5781/how-the-dodgers-found-the-youngest-prospect-in-mlb. Accessed 17 Feb. 2017.

—*Molly Hagan*

Meg Urry
Occupation: Astrophysicist

For astrophysicist Meg Urry, some of the most exciting discoveries in space are the ones that cannot be perceived by the human eye. The Israel Munson Professor of Physics and Astronomy at Yale University, Urry conducts research focusing on the qualities and behavior of supermassive black holes at the centers of active galaxies. "For the past fifteen years, I've been discovering where and when black holes grew," she explained to Claudia Dreifus for the *New York Times* (28 Nov. 2016). "My tools have been ground and space telescopes such as Keck and Hubble." Urry and her fellow researchers have identified and analyzed emissions such as x-rays to study phenomena that occurred light-years from Earth. Prior to joining Yale in 2001, Urry worked for more than a decade as an astronomer at the Space Telescope Science Institute. She also served as the president of the American Astronomical Society (AAS) from 2014 to 2016.

Alongside her career in astronomy and astrophysics, Urry has been an outspoken advocate for increasing diversity in the sciences. She has worked for decades to combat the implicit biases and sexist treatment that women scientists at times encounter within the scientific community. At the same time, she seeks to encourage more young women to pursue studies and careers in the sciences, which she argues will ultimately have a far-reaching positive effect on scientific fields as a whole. "It's been demonstrated that diversity of thought leads to innovation," Urry told Richard Panek for the *Yale Alumni Magazine* (Mar./Apr. 2014). "If diversity of faculty means diversity of thought . . . then science will benefit enormously from this change."

EARLY LIFE

Claudia Megan Urry was the second of four children born to Grant and Lillian Urry. Her parents met while working as docents at the Museum of Science and Industry in Chicago and had both studied science at the University of Chicago: Her mother had trained in zoology, while her father earned his PhD in chemistry. Urry spent her early years in Indiana before moving

to Massachusetts with her family after her father joined the faculty of Tufts University in 1968.

As a teenager, Urry enjoyed researching and writing papers that were not for school assignments, demonstrating the curiosity that would serve her well as a scientist. Although Urry did not yet know what career path she wanted to pursue, she was strongly influenced by her chemistry teacher, who encouraged her to consider a career in science. "She said I thought like a scientist because I was always comparing things to one another," Urry recalled to Dreifus.

EDUCATION

After graduating from Winchester High School in 1973, Urry enrolled at Tufts. She began her college experience as a "thoroughly undecided undergraduate," as she told Karen Masters for the *Galaxy Zoo* blog (2 May 2010). When she took a freshman physics class, she found herself drawn to the subject and soon began to pursue further studies in physics and mathematics. "I chose physics because it was clean and elegant," she told Dreifus. "I didn't go through that thing that often happens to teenage girls where they fall off of the cliff of self-confidence and get discouraged about science. The discouraging things happened later on."

It was during the summer before Urry's senior year, however, that her academic path found even further focus. That summer, she completed a research internship at the National Radio Astronomy Observatory (NRAO) in Charlottesville, Virginia. There, she worked under the supervision of astronomer Richard Porcas,

assisting with the astronomical research carried out at the facility. "One of my main jobs was to use the Palomar Sky Survey prints to find optical counterparts to radio sources from the Jodrell Bank high declination survey," Urry recalled to Masters. "I kept a notebook carefully describing the fields around each radio source." She found the work fascinating and enjoyed her time at the observatory, which introduced her to career paths that had not yet come to her attention. "It was amazing to realize people earned a living doing something so interesting," she told Masters. "After that experience, I was going to do astronomy and astrophysics if at all possible."

After earning her bachelor's degree from Tufts in 1977, Urry went on to enroll at Johns Hopkins University in Baltimore, Maryland, where she pursued graduate studies in physics. She worked as a scientific data aide for the x-ray group of the Smithsonian Astrophysical Observatory in 1977. While at Johns Hopkins, she also conducted research at the Goddard Space Flight Center, a facility operated by the National Aeronautics and Space Administration (NASA) in Goddard, Maryland. Urry's research at the facility focused on blazars, which are a type of active galactic nuclei (AGN), galaxies that have extraordinarily luminous cores due to the presence of supermassive black holes at their centers. Blazars are distinct from other types of AGN in that they emit a highly variable stream of electromagnetic radiation directly toward Earth, which makes it appear as if the emitted material is moving faster than the speed of light. Studying blazars enables astrophysicists to observe the effects of energies that are orders of magnitude greater than can be achieved in accelerators on Earth.

In addition to her research efforts, Urry also gained teaching experience while at Johns Hopkins, serving as a teaching assistant throughout her time at the school and teaching a six-week physics course to Air Force personnel overseas. She completed her master's degree in physics from Johns Hopkins in 1979 and earned her doctorate in 1984 with a thesis titled "X-Ray and Ultraviolet Observations of BL Lacertae Objects."

ASTRONOMY CAREER

After earning her PhD, Urry returned to Massachusetts to take a postdoctoral fellowship at the Center for Space Research at the Massachusetts Institute of Technology (MIT), where she worked under physics professor Claude Canizares. She remained at MIT until 1987, when she returned to Baltimore to join the Space Telescope Science Institute. Located on the Johns Hopkins campus, the institute was founded in 1981 and, following the Hubble Space Telescope's launch into orbit in 1990, came to manage the telescope's operations on behalf of NASA.

Urry spent more than a decade at the Space Telescope Science Institute, serving first as a postdoctoral fellow before taking on the role of assistant astronomer and chief of the institute's research support branch in 1990. She gained tenure at the institute in 1995 and became head of the institute's science program selection office in 1996. She remained in that role until 2001, when she left to take a professorship at Yale University.

YALE

Since 2001, Urry has served as the Israel Munson Professor of Physics and Astronomy at Yale University in New Haven, Connecticut. She has likewise served as the director of the Yale Center for Astronomy and Astrophysics, which Urry has been credited with growing from a fledgling department into an active center of research and study and establishing a prestigious postdoctoral fellowship program. From 2007 to 2013, she also served as the chair of the university's physics department.

Urry's research has continued to focus on black holes, blazars, and related concepts such as active galaxies, which she described to Masters as "galaxies whose central supermassive black hole is actively accreting and thus producing lots of non-stellar light." Researchers in her lab seek to determine how supermassive black holes grow over time and understand their coevolution with galaxies. Urry is excited by the potential for further research represented by new tools, such as the James Webb Space Telescope, scheduled to be launched into orbit in 2018. Space telescopes like the Webb and its predecessors have the ability to detect emissions put out by black holes, which in turn allow researchers to learn about distant phenomena. "It appears that every black hole emits x-rays," Urry explained to Dreifus. "The newest space telescopes spot them instantly."

A prolific researcher and writer, Urry has written or contributed to more than 270 papers and is the coeditor of several books. In addition to her research and teaching work, she served as president of the American Astronomical Society from 2014 to 2016. She is a member of numerous scientific organizations, including the American Physical Society (APS), the American Academy of Arts and Sciences, and the National Academy of Sciences (NAS).

ADVOCACY FOR WOMEN IN SCIENCE

In addition to her work as an astronomer, researcher, and professor, Urry has long been a dedicated advocate for the rights and representation of women in science. She has worked to call attention to the forms of discrimination that women studying or working in scientific fields sometimes face, which include both outright forms of discrimination and subtler forms rooted in deep-seated institutional and personal biases. "Discrimination isn't a thunderbolt, it isn't an abrupt slap in the face. It's the slow drumbeat of being underappreciated, feeling uncomfortable, and encountering roadblocks along the path to success," she wrote in a piece for the *Washington Post* (6 Feb. 2005). "These subtle distinctions help make women feel out of place."

In 1992, Urry organized a meeting for women in astronomy in Baltimore. The conference resulted in the writing of a document known as the Baltimore Charter for Women in Astronomy, which asserted that "women should not have to be clones of male astronomers in order to participate in the mainstream of astronomical research" and made recommendations with the goal of eliminating inequality in the field. Among other recommendations, the charter recommended that astronomy institutions work to avoid gender biases or other biases in documents or discussions and to implement sexual harassment awareness programs. However, despite the efforts of Urry and her fellow signatories, the charter did not attain widespread support. "We thought it was the Magna Carta of astronomy," she told Panek. "And then we tried to get places to endorse it. They just thought it was a totally radical document."

Over the course of her career, Urry has continued to write and speak extensively on the experiences of women in science, both identifying ongoing issues within the scientific community and encouraging young women to pursue careers in scientific fields. She took further action while serving as head of the American Astronomical Society, speaking out against harassment occurring at scientific conferences and arguing that individuals with a history of harassing others be banned from attending the organization's meetings. "We had a situation where we had young female astronomers reporting conference experiences that were very different from those of their male counterparts," she explained to Dreifus. "The men came and used the event to network. The women came and sometimes found themselves worried about people propositioning them. I wanted to make clear what our values are. I said straight out, 'Look, our meetings are not *The Dating Game*. This is a professional environment. Act professionally.'"

PERSONAL LIFE

Urry met her husband, Andrew Szymkowiak, on her first day at the Goddard Space Flight Center. A fellow physicist, Szymkowiak is a research scientist at Yale. They have two daughters, Amelia and Sophia, and live in Guilford, Connecticut.

SUGGESTED READING

Masters, Karen. "She's an Astronomer: Meg Urry." *Galaxy Zoo*, 2 May 2010, blog.galaxy-zoo.org/2010/05/02/shes-an-astronomer-meg-urry. Accessed 10 Mar. 2017.

"Meg Urry." *The Women of Hopkins*, women.jhu.edu/urry. Accessed 10 Mar. 2017.

Panek, Richard. "Astronomy and Gender Politics." *Yale Alumni Magazine*, Mar./Apr. 2014, yalealumnimagazine.com/articles/3843-astronomy-and-gender-politics. Accessed 10 Mar. 2017.

Pollack, Eileen. "Why Are There Still So Few Women in Science?" *The New York Times Magazine*, 3 Oct. 2013, www.nytimes.com/2013/10/06/magazine/why-are-there-still-so-few-women-in-science.html. Accessed 10 Mar. 2017.

Urry, Meg. "C. Megan Urry, Peering into the Universe, Spots Bias on the Ground." *The New York Times*, 28 Nov. 2016, www.nytimes.com/2016/11/28/science/c-megan-urry-peering-into-universe-spots-bias-on-the-ground.html. Accessed 10 Mar. 2017.

Urry, Meg. "Diminished by Discrimination We Scarcely See." *The Washington Post*, 6 Feb. 2005, www.washingtonpost.com/wp-dyn/articles/A360-2005Feb5.html. Accessed 10 Mar. 2017.

—*Joy Crelin*

Max Verstappen

Date of birth: September 30, 1997
Occupation: Racing driver

Formula One racer Max Verstappen's driving style has at times been characterized as aggressive, but the driver could not disagree more. "I'm pretty relaxed but maybe sometimes on the track it looks like I'm quite aggressive," he told Amanda Davies and Eoghan Macguire for *CNN* (17 May 2017). "As a person, I'm pretty relaxed in the car, I think." Indeed, considering Verstappen's background, it is unsurprising that he would be relaxed or even comfortable in a car hurtling around a racetrack at more than two hundred miles per hour. The son of two former racers, Formula One driver Jos Verstappen and kart driver Sophie Kumpen, Verstappen grew up surrounded by racing vehicles and their drivers and began racing karts himself at the age of four. Since joining the competitive circuit, Verstappen has progressed through the various levels of vehicles and teams, moving from karts to racing cars as a teenager.

In 2014 Verstappen began competing in Formula One, the fastest form of organized car

By Morio (Own work) [CC BY-SA 4.0], via Wikimedia Commons

racing in the world, joining the Red Bull racing organization. After developing his skills further as a member of Red Bull's junior team, Scuderia Toro Rosso, he moved to the senior Red Bull team, Red Bull Racing, in mid-2016. Making his debut with the team at the Spanish Grand Prix, he ultimately claimed first place in the competition, becoming the youngest driver ever to do so. Although clearly proud of his achievement, Verstappen credits much of his success to those around him. "It's a great feeling and achievement for the whole team," he said in an interview for *Sport360* (23 May 2016).

EARLY LIFE AND EDUCATION

Max Emilian Verstappen was born on September 30, 1997, in Hasselt, Belgium. Racing was undoubtedly in his blood: his father, Dutch-born racer Jos Verstappen, competed in Formula One, while his mother, Belgian racer Sophie Kumpen, was a kart racer. His younger sister, Victoria-Jane Verstappen, also races karts, and their father operated his own kart team when the children were young. As his parents' careers might suggest, Verstappen was exposed to the world of racing at a young age and soon developed an interest in trying it out himself. When he was four years old, his parents gave him his first kart as a Christmas present, and he began to learn to race the vehicle, albeit not competitively. "You're allowed to race from seven years onwards, so I just started having fun driving laps," he recalled to Josh Kruse for *Crash.net* (2 June 2017). "When you're seven years old it starts to get a bit more serious."

In addition to the hands-on racing experience he received throughout his childhood, Verstappen was the recipient of ongoing guidance from his father, who stopped racing himself to focus on his son's racing career. Providing technical guidance and mechanical support, Jos Verstappen likewise advised Verstappen on the business- and team-related aspects of the sport throughout his developing career. "Because he did F1 he also knows the bad sides of it and what can happen to you if you go too quickly into a very good team," Verstappen explained to Brad Spurgeon for the *New York Times* (28 Nov. 2014). "And that is always where he tries to prevent me from making a mistake."

Although Verstappen initially worked to balance his schoolwork with his racing obligations, he eventually found the two to be incompatible and left school at the age of fifteen. "It was just difficult to combine," he explained to Kruse. "I was two weeks away, one week at school, so it was very hard to catch up." Although confident in his decision, Verstappen has acknowledged that it presented the risk that if his racing career progressed poorly, he might have to return to school at a later date. "That was my motivation to try to do well, so I didn't have to go back to school afterwards," he told Kruse.

EARLY CAREER

As a young child, Verstappen made his first competitive racing appearance in a karting competition in Emmen, in the northern Netherlands. "It was actually a very good weekend," he recalled to Kruse. "I qualified on pole and won both races. I could see my dad because he was my mechanic, and he was so nervous because it was my first race and the procedures and everything was new to me." Over the course of his first three seasons of competition, Verstappen won nearly all of his races, establishing himself as an up-and-coming racer to watch.

After several years as a kart racer, Verstappen sought to move on to more advanced levels of racing, transitioning from karts to race cars. That transition is a significant step for any racer, for while race cars differ from each other in design and capabilities, "in general a racing car is a racing car," Verstappen explained to Spurgeon. Karts and race cars, however, were fundamentally different vehicles, and the young racer had a great deal to learn. He began testing Formula Three cars in 2013 and in 2014 officially launched his international career as a Formula Three racer, competing in events such as the Florida Winter Series and the International Automobile Federation (Fédération Internationale de l'Automobile, or FIA) Formula Three European Championship and drawing further attention from major racing teams for his strong competitive performances. Due to his success on that circuit, Verstappen's

Formula Three career proved short; in 2014, he began training with the Red Bull racing organization, a major force in Formula One racing.

FORMULA ONE

Overseen by FIA and featuring the use of lightweight and incredibly fast racing cars, Formula One competitions occupy a much higher level of competition than their Formula Three counterparts, and Verstappen's transition into Formula One represented a significant turning point in his career. In August 2014, the Red Bull racing organization announced that Verstappen would join the Scuderia Toro Rosso Formula One racing team beginning in the 2015 season. Owned by the energy drink company Red Bull, which sponsors a variety of extreme and speed-focused athletes and sporting events, Toro Rosso serves as a junior team that allows talented drivers to develop their skills while competing in high-level Formula One events. The team is the counterpart of the senior-level Red Bull Racing, a successful team on the international racing circuit.

Raised in a racing household, Verstappen was well aware of the continual need for self-improvement among racers and recognized the opportunity he was being granted to compete and hone his skills. "All the people in Formula One are very talented but talent alone is not enough, you have to work hard also to achieve the best result possible," he later told *Sport360*. "It's not just doing a great lap but also spending time with your engineers to improve the car, to improve yourself every time."

As a member of Toro Rosso, Verstappen competed in a variety of races in 2015, beginning with the Australian Grand Prix in March of that year. By competing in that race, his first at that level, Verstappen became the youngest Formula One driver of all time, at only seventeen years old. He went on to compete in grand prix races throughout Europe, Asia, and North America. The following season, Verstappen raced in several grand prix competitions, earning respectable finishes that cemented his reputation as a talented racer with significant potential. The Red Bull racing organization took notice of Verstappen's performance, and on May 5, 2016, Red Bull Racing announced that Verstappen would be leaving Toro Rosso and joining their main Formula One team, switching places with Russian driver Daniil Kvyat. Although surprised by this sudden change, particularly because it was taking place mid-season, Verstappen was thrilled by the opportunity to race with the senior-level team. "When you get that chance you take it," he told *Sport360*, "and we have started off in a very positive way."

RED BULL RACING

Verstappen's move to Red Bull Racing came less than two weeks before the 2016 Spanish Grand Prix, an event held on May 15 of that year. The grand prix became his competitive debut with the team, which consisted of Verstappen and Daniel Ricciardo, an Australian driver nearly a decade Verstappen's senior. His former team, Toro Rosso, likewise competed in the race, along with teams sponsored by car manufacturers such as Ferrari, McLaren, and Mercedes. Held at the Circuit de Barcelona-Catalunya in northeastern Spain, the Spanish Grand Prix consisted of sixty-six laps around the circuit, for a total distance of nearly two hundred miles. Verstappen completed the race with a time of one hour, forty-one minutes, and just over forty seconds, claiming first place. The victory was a major one for Verstappen, who began his tenure with Red Bull Racing on a triumphant note. In addition to proving conclusively that he was a good fit for the team, the eighteen-year-old Verstappen likewise claimed the title of youngest racer to win or even qualify for a podium position at a grand prix.

Following his impressive performance in Spain, Verstappen continued to race as a member of Red Bull Racing, competing in more than fifteen events and earning podium positions in several of them. He ended the 2016 Formula One season ranked fifth among all drivers at his level, two places below Red Bull teammate Ricciardo. Pleased with his performance, Verstappen noted in interviews that he felt at home with his new team and credited the Red Bull racing organization with providing the support necessary for him to excel as a racer. "I am massively enjoying myself and I am super happy with the team," he said in an interview for the official *Formula One* website (2 July 2016). "They give me a lot of confidence—and that in return gives me the results that I am getting. I am always trying to do my best."

The 2017 Formula One season began in March with the Australian Grand Prix, in which Verstappen placed fifth. He went on to compete in the first several races of the season and by June 2017 was ranked sixth in the season's championship standings.

PERSONAL LIFE

Although Verstappen grew up in Belgium and in 2015 moved to Monaco, he generally considers himself to be Dutch and represents the Netherlands in international competitions. He is particularly interested in promoting racing within the Netherlands and providing new and younger drivers with opportunities to develop their skills. "My dream is to build a go-kart track . . . in [the Netherlands] to give something back because at the moment we don't really have go-kart tracks," he told Davies and Macguire.

SUGGESTED READING

Davies, Amanda, and Eoghan Macguire. "Pushing to the Max: Verstappen a Rookie No More." *CNN*, 17 May 2017, www.cnn.com/2017/05/17/motorsport/max-verstappen-spanish-grand-prix-monaco/index.html. Accessed 9 June 2017.

Johnson, Daniel. "How Max Verstappen Learnt from His Father Jos's Silent Treatment in His Progression to F1." *The Telegraph*, 2 Nov. 2014, www.telegraph.co.uk/sport/motorsport/formulaone/11204319/How-Max-Verstappen-learnt-from-his-father-Joss-silent-treatment-in-his-progression-to-F1.html. Accessed 9 June 2017.

Keith, Paul. "Max Verstappen to Red Bull Racing." *Red Bull*, 5 May 2016, www.redbull.com/us-en/verstappen-to-red-bull-racing-fomula-1. Accessed 9 June 2017.

Spurgeon, Brad. "Max Verstappen, a Young Man in a Hurry to the Top of World Racing." *The New York Times*, 28 Nov. 2014, nytimes.com/2014/11/29/sports/autoracing/max-verstappen-interview-becoming-the-youngest-driver-in-formula-one-history.html. Accessed 9 June 2017.

Verstappen, Max. "'I Am Still Surprising Myself'—Exclusive Max Verstappen Q&A." *Formula 1*, 21 July 2016, www.formula1.com/en/latest/interviews/2016/7/_i-am-still-surprising-myself---exclusive-max-verstappen-q-a.html. Accessed 9 June 2017.

Verstappen, Max. "Interview: Max Verstappen—Red Bull's New Star." *Sport360*, 23 May 2016, sport360.com/article/motorsport/formula-one/179427/interview-max-verstappen-red-bulls-new-star-is-taking-life-as-it-comes/. Accessed 9 June 2017.

Verstappen, Max. "10 Minutes with . . . Max Verstappen." Interview with Josh Kruse. *Crash.net*, 2 June 2017, crash.net/f1/interview/251044/1/10-minutes-with-max-verstappen.html. Accessed 9 June 2017.

—Joy Crelin

Melissa Villaseñor

Date of birth: October 9, 1987
Occupation: Comedian

Before the fall of 2016, Melissa Villaseñor had been best known to television viewers as a finalist on the sixth season of *America's Got Talent*, which aired in 2011. That changed when the producers of *Saturday Night Live* (SNL) announced

Kyle Mizono/CC BY 2.0/Wikimedia Commons

that Villaseñor would be joining the cast on October 1, 2016, when the iconic sketch-comedy show began its forty-second season.

Villaseñor's hiring came after a period of harsh public criticism about the lack of diversity among the show's cast and staff of writers. The criticism reached a particularly feverish pitch when producers invited then–presidential candidate Donald Trump to host, despite the fact that during his campaign he had made pointed attacks on Mexicans and immigrants.

There was therefore widespread approval when it was announced that Villaseñor, who is Mexican American, would be the first Latina cast member ever to appear on *SNL*. (The show had featured two men of Latin heritage, Horatio Sanz and Fred Armisen.) "The hiring of Villaseñor is cause for celebration for the Hispanic community, because it opens a door that was once presumed locked," Luis Miguel Echegaray wrote for *The Guardian* (13 Sept. 2016).

Villaseñor debuted, as promised, and has gradually made a name for herself on the show. Since starting on the show, she has distinguished herself with a number of impressions and sketches as she continues to establish her place among her cast mates.

EARLY YEARS AND EDUCATION

Melissa Villaseñor was born on October 9, 1987, and raised in Whittier, California, a city within Los Angeles County. She was an enormous fan of 1990s-era comedy acts and particularly loved watching Jim Carrey movies and Dana Carvey sketches on *SNL*. At about the age of twelve she

discovered that she had a talent for impressions and entertained her friends by mimicking Britney Spears and other popular artists' songs.

As a student at Ramona Convent, an all-girls' Catholic high school in Alhambra, California, she participated avidly in choir and performed in the occasional play. She also took part in a talent show during her sophomore year, an experience that solidified her determination to become a comedian. "That talent show was my first time realizing, 'Oh my goodness, I love comedy!'" she recalled to Gordon Downs for *SanDiego.com* (4 Jan. 2012). "I did like six singing impressions. I did little parodies and rewrote their songs. It was only three or five minutes. It was pretty great."

When Villaseñor was fifteen, she attended the Laugh Factory Comedy Camp. "It turned out that was for kids who need help in life and stuff," she told Downs. "I ended up doing it because I was like, 'I just want to perform!' Then I was just looking online wondering, 'Where am I going to do stand-up?' According to the camp's website, the camp is actually intended to be a "safe haven for at risk or underprivileged children."

During her junior and senior years, she took an improvisation class in Orange County, which was closer to her home than Hollywood and did not necessitate asking her parents to drive a long distance. So eager was Villaseñor to perform that she asked everyone she knew whether she could entertain at their birthday parties or other celebrations.

After graduating from Ramona Convent, Villaseñor attended a community college in order to please her parents, although she had little interest, by then, in academia.

BUILDING A COMEDY CAREER

Villaseñor tried her hand at various open-mic nights around Los Angeles, including a regular Sunday show at the Ice House Annex in Pasadena, and she served as an intern on the set of the NBC soap opera *Days of Our Lives*. From time to time, she performed comedy sketches or interviewed the soap's stars when there was no show taping in progress, and NBC would often post those clips on the official website.

When she was nineteen years old, a friend passed along a few videos of Villaseñor performing stand-up to Frank Caliendo, a comedian and impressionist who had appeared on the Fox sketch-comedy show *MADtv*. In 2007 he launched his own short-lived program, *Frank TV*, on TBS and he invited Villaseñor to appear on it. She did an impersonation of fellow comic Sarah Silverman and was well received enough that she was approached by an agent, who wanted to represent her.

In about 2009, Villaseñor began uploading original videos to the video-sharing site YouTube, and she gradually gained a large following. One video, simply titled "Melissa Villaseñor's Impressions," garnered almost 2 million views. Among her most popular impressions were Owen Wilson, Jennifer Lopez, Kathy Griffin, Miley Cyrus, and Christina Aguilera.

Since those early days of watching Dana Carvey perform on *SNL*, Villaseñor had dreamed of one day appearing on the show herself. In 2009 she got the chance to audition for Lorne Michaels, *SNL*'s producer. Her first audition impressed Michaels enough to call her in for a second audition. She performed a range of impressions, including Barbara Walters, but she did not make the cut. Reflecting on the experience with an interviewer from *Bird* magazine, she said, "I'm starting to understand that when I visualize something happening and believe in it, I start seeing results. So I put myself out there. . . . I feel like the universe will give back what's best for me."

In 2011 Villaseñor appeared on *America's Got Talent*, a popular reality show competition that featured Nick Cannon as host and Piers Morgan, Sharon Osbourne, and Howie Mandel as judges. Villaseñor performed a remarkable roster of impressions during her appearances on the show, and while she was eliminated during the semifinals, she garnered positive reviews from the judges.

The name recognition Villaseñor attained during the show helped propel her stand-up career. One video of her performing on *America's Got Talent* was viewed almost 9 million times. She embarked on a national tour of clubs and colleges with a set comprised partially of impressions and partially of comic stories about herself. During this period of touring, she really honed her comedy set. She commented to an interviewer for *Bird* magazine, "My set is a balance of telling stories about me and using impressions to tell my point of view. I think I started strengthening my set on the road and after I was on *America's Got Talent*. . . That stage time really forced me to get to that place, and that's when I started to piece it together."

She performed two different one-woman shows, directed by Ron Lynch, at the Steve Allen Theater in Hollywood. She was also hired to provide voices for popular animated shows. She voiced Nora Ephron in an episode of *Family Guy* and a number of characters on *Adventure Time*, and also did voice work for *TripTank*.

SNL

SNL has long been under fire for its lack of diversity. Before Villaseñor joined the cast at the end of 2016, the show boasted only six African American female cast members in its four-decade history and no Latina cast members.

Tensions with the Latino community reached a head when the show invited Republican

presidential candidate Donald Trump to host. Trump had characterized Mexicans as rapists and criminals and had called for building a new border wall to keep them out of the country.

The activists pointed out that Armisen and Sanz, the only two Latino cast members in the show's history, were not Mexican American, the most predominant ethnicity of the nation's largest minority. Furthermore, they noted, there had been no more than a handful of Latino guest hosts. The writers, as well, were mostly white, thanks to a system whereby current staffers recommended friends (likely to also be white) for positions.

SNL producer Lindsay Shookus and co–head writer Rob Klein assured the gathering that the show would make every effort to rectify the situation. A few months earlier, Lorne Michaels had launched Más Mejor, a digital platform meant to promote Latino comedians and engage Latino millennials. Villaseñor was recruited for the initiative and appeared in a number of videos in a series titled "Daily Itineraries" doing impressions, the most notable of which are videos where she plays Jennifer Lopez and Owen Wilson. Shortly after, she was tapped to join the *SNL* cast for the forty-second season.

Soon after her hiring was announced, however, a Twitter user and writer for *Grist*, Aura Bogado, noticed that Villaseñor had locked her Twitter account to followers and deleted some 2,000 tweets. Suspicious, Bogado tracked down other tweets Villaseñor had written and discovered many of them to be xenophobic and racist. The offensive tweets denigrated black people and other groups in blunt terms; SNL made no official comment, and Villaseñor did not make any response.

Villaseñor has appeared in a good number of sketches since the 2016 season opened. One week she played Elaine Quijano, a CBSN anchorwoman who moderated the vice-presidential debate between Tim Kaine and Mike Pence; Villaseñor broke the fourth wall to explain in the sketch that although she is Latina she is playing a figure of Filipino descent, "because baby steps." She has also played or impersonated Sacagawea, Sarah Silverman, and Sue Perkins in sketches, among other characters.

Aside from *SNL*, in 2016 Villaseñor also appeared in the low-budget comedy *Laid in America* and was featured on an episode of the sketch comedy show *Nuclear Family*.

PERSONAL LIFE

Little has been published about Villaseñor's social life; she jokes on occasion about using the dating app Tinder, having boyfriend woes, and being attached to her cat. She is also very close with her family and sees them weekly when in Los Angeles.

In an interview with the online publication *Bird*, which is devoted to profiles of interesting women, she was asked if she found performing comedy therapeutic. "Yeah, it is," she replied. "There are some nights where I'm not in the mood. I'm like, 'I don't want to go onstage. I'm not feeling happy now.' And then my bits really make me happy. When I walk out there I think, 'Oh man, that voice just makes me feel good.' Even if it's not a voice bit, if it's just me complaining about something, it feels great."

SUGGESTED READING

Andrews, Travis M. "Melissa Villaseñor, of *America's Got Talent* Fame, Becomes SNL's First Latina Cast Member." *Washington Post*, 13 Sept. 2016, www.washingtonpost.com/news/morning-mix/wp/2016/09/13/melissa-villasenor-becomes-snls-first-latina-cast-member/?utm_term=.a677acc0437f. Accessed 25 Oct. 2016.

Downs, Gordon. "Melissa Villasenor Has Got Talent." *SanDiego.com*, 4 Jan. 2012, www.sandiego.com/articles/2012-01-04/melissa-villasenor-has-got-talent. Accessed 25 Oct. 2016.

Echegaray, Luis Miguel. "Melissa Villaseñor Will Blaze a Trail for Latinas on SNL." *The Guardian*, 13 Sept. 2016, www.theguardian.com/tv-and-radio/2016/sep/13/melissa-villasenor-snl-cast-first-latina. Accessed 25 Oct. 2016.

Schroeder, Audra. "New 'SNL' Cast Member Melissa Villaseñor Criticized for Old Tweets." *Daily Dot*, 23 Sept. 2016, www.dailydot.com/upstream/melissa-villasenor-snl-tweets. Accessed 25 Oct. 2016.

Slead, Evan. "Who Is Melissa Villaseñor?" *Entertainment Weekly*, 12 Sept. 2016, ew.com/article/2016/09/12/snl-melissa-villasenor. Accessed on 25 Oct. 2016.

Villaseñor, Melissa. Interview. *Bird*, www.wearebird.co/melissa-villasenor. Accessed 20 Dec. 2016.

SELECTED WORKS

Family Guy, 2012; *Adventure Time*, 2012–16; *Saturday Night Live*, 2016–

—*Mari Rich*

Denis Villeneuve

Date of birth: October 3, 1967
Occupation: Film director, screenwriter

In 2017, Award-winning French Canadian film director Denis Villeneuve was nominated for an Academy Award for best director for his science-fiction thriller *Arrival* (2016). Based on a short

Kevin Winter/Getty Images

story called "The Story of Your Life" by Ted Chiang, *Arrival* was nominated for eight Oscars, including best picture. Although the film is not Villeneuve's first, it represents the fulfillment of a childhood dream. Villeneuve's love of science fiction, in particular the film *Close Encounters of the Third Kind* (1977), led him to consider a career making films as a child. He expressed his desire to direct a science-fiction film several years ago, just after his film *Incendies* (2010), which was nominated for an Academy Award for best foreign language film, brought him into the Hollywood fold. In Los Angeles, he met screenwriter Eric Heisserer who was working on an adaptation of Chiang's structurally tricky, but powerful story about a female linguist charged with interpreting an alien language. The two men worked on the script for several years; *Arrival* was eventually released to critical acclaim in 2016. Villeneuve's two upcoming projects—the *Blade Runner* sequel, *Blade Runner 2049* (2017), and the long-awaited adaptation of the science-fiction epic, *Dune*—are sending Villeneuve's career down the path of his childhood imaginings.

EARLY LIFE

Villeneuve was born on October 3, 1967, and raised in the small village of Gentilly, located northeast of Montreal in Quebec on the St. Lawrence River. He was the oldest of four children. In addition to his father, a notary, and his mother, a homemaker, his grandmothers were important figures in his young life. "I'm the first generation of men that was in contact with those new ideas of feminism," he told Cara Buckley for the *New York Times* (10 Nov. 2016). "I was raised in a way that I didn't feel threatened by those ideas. I felt that it was a beautiful thing."

As for his love of film, Villeneuve jokes that he became a filmmaker because he was a terrible hockey player. As a boy growing up in Canada, he told Shannon M. Houston for *Paste Magazine* (20 Mar. 2014), "your identity is built on hockey." Relegated to the bench, Villeneuve took pleasure in daydreams, and science-fiction stories, eventually falling in love with films like Steven Spielberg's *Close Encounters of the Third Kind*. Villeneuve began writing his own stories inspired by Spielberg and the way the famous director was able, as he told Houston, "deal with *le merveilleux*—the wonders" in his work. Spielberg led him to the French director François Truffaut and the French New Wave. By then, Villeneuve knew he wanted to be a film director, specifically a sci-fi director. "It wasn't logical at all," he told Jennifer Vineyard for *Vulture* (25 Jan. 2017). "But it was a calling."

Villeneuve attended the University of Quebec in Montreal. He was a student there when he signed up for a Canadian television competition called *La course destination monde* ("Destination world race"). Participants were given a camera and every week, were expected to shoot a five-minute piece in a different country. The competition lasted for seven months. The show, Villeneuve told Vineyard, "was the best school I ever had." Villeneuve won first place in the contest in 1991, and then took a job with the National Film Board of Canada. He made a couple of short films, including *REW FFWd* (1994), a documentary about Jamaica, and "Le Technetium," a segment of a larger film called *Cosmos* (1996).

EARLY FILMMAKING CAREER

Villeneuve made his first feature film, a drama called *August 32nd on Earth* (originally released as *Un 32 août sur terre*) in 1998. The film is about a woman who decides she wants to have a baby after surviving a terrible car crash. *August 32nd on Earth* premiered at the Cannes Film Festival, where it was nominated for best film. It was Canada's official submission to the Academy Awards in the best foreign language film category, though it was not ultimately nominated. "The most striking thing about *August 32nd on Earth* is the visuals, and there's no question Villeneuve has real talent in that department," Brendan Kelly wrote for *Variety* (21 May 1998). "But the scripting is a lot less assured. Commercial prospects do not look especially bright."

The director's second feature, *Maelstrom* (2000), which he wrote and directed, won a slew of Genie Awards (the Canadian equivalent of the Academy Awards) including best motion picture, best achievement in direction, and best screenplay. The film is narrated by a dead fish, and, like its predecessor, takes as its subject the spiritual crisis of a young woman. Its pivotal scene also involves a car accident. In a largely positive review for the *New York Times* (25 Jan. 2002), Stephen Holden praised the film for its unusual imagery and stylistic flourishes. He wrote, "*Maelstrom* is a meditation on the disconnection between the glossy surfaces of high-end urban existence and the life-and-death realities they camouflage."

Despite their modest success, Villeneuve was unhappy with his first two films. "They were not strong enough," he told Vineyard. "There was a weakness in the way they were written." He did not make another film for nine years, during which time he helped raise his children, and honed his writing. His next film, a crime drama called *Polytechnique* (2009), was based on a 1989 school shooting at Montreal's École Polytechnique in which fourteen female engineering students were killed by a man who claimed to be "fighting feminism." Villeneuve was criticized for his decision to make the film, but after it was released, *Polytechnique* was widely praised. The film won nine Genie Awards, including best motion picture.

In 2010 Villeneuve made a film called *Incendies*, based on the 2003 play of the same name by Lebanese Canadian playwright Wajdi Mouawad. In it, adult twins venture from Canada to an unnamed country in the Middle East to fulfill their mother's last wishes—one is to seek a father they never knew, the other to seek a long-lost brother. The film is a mystery as well as a social commentary; though it never explicitly identifies Lebanon as its location, it is a sharp commentary on that country's politics and tumult. Villeneuve intertwines the stories of mother and children to powerful effect, critics noted. In addition to a slew of glowing reviews, *Incendies* was nominated for an Academy Award for best foreign language film.

HOLLYWOOD DEBUT

"It was clear to us that the filmmaker behind *Incendies* was for real," producer Shawn Levy told Buckley. "The command of tone, and visuals in service of tone, was so confident." Indeed, the success of the film brought Villeneuve to Hollywood, where he signed on to direct his first English language film, *Prisoners* (2013), about two young girls who go missing. The drama featured a star-studded cast including Hugh Jackman (who played a father-turned-vigilante), Jake Gyllenhaal, Paul Dano, Viola Davis, Terrence Howard, and Melissa Leo. The film received moderately positive reviews; critics tended to focus more on Villeneuve's directing and the cinematography of Roger Deakins (who was nominated for an Academy Award for his work) than on the movie's script.

Villeneuve's next film, a thriller called *Enemy*, was also released in 2013. (Both *Prisoners* and *Enemy* premiered the same year at the Toronto Film Festival.) *Enemy* is based on a 2002 novel by Nobel Prize–winning Portuguese author Jose Saramago called *The Double*. In the film, Jake Gyllenhaal plays a man who discovers his doppelganger in a movie. He becomes obsessed with the man, also played by Gyllenhaal. Critics were divided on the film; some found it confusing and self-indulgent, while Peter Bradshaw of *The Guardian* (1 Jan. 2015) called it Villeneuve's "most accomplished film so far."

SICARIO (2015)

Villeneuve directed stars Emily Blunt, Josh Brolin, and Benicio Del Toro in a 2015 thriller about Mexican drug cartels called *Sicario*. In it, Blunt plays an FBI agent who is drawn into an operation involving the Sonora cartel on the US–Mexico border. The film scrambles the lines between good guys and bad guys, with Blunt's character caught in the middle. In his review of the film, A. O. Scott of the *New York Times* (17 Sept. 2015) noted that Villeneuve's films have the inclination to explore violence and evil on a philosophical level rather than merely portray them for effect. On this note, *Sicario* is less successful than his previous work, Scott wrote. "Mr. Villeneuve conjures an atmosphere of menace and pervasive cruelty, but after a while *Sicario* starts to feel too easy, less an exploration than an exploitation of the moral ambiguities of the drug war," Scott wrote. "We glimpse mutilated bodies hanging from bridges, hear stabbings and shootings just out of sight and study the face of a man whose family is being killed in front of him. But after a while these sounds and images start to feel like expressions of technique, and they become at once numbing and sensational, and instead of a movie about violence we're watching another violent movie, after all." Nonetheless, *Sicario* was nominated for three Academy Awards, in cinematography, original score, and sound editing.

ARRIVAL (2016)

Relative to the films he made directly preceding it, Villeneuve's *Arrival* (2016), was the most hopeful in Villeneuve's body of work up to that point. In it, Amy Adams plays a linguist named Louise who is called upon to translate the whale-like language of an alien species after space ships arrive on Earth. The aliens, when viewers see them, look like octopuses and speak using symbols drawn from their ink. Over the course of the film, Louise learns to understand them. Louise's interior, emotional world is plagued by the painful memories of the death of her young daughter. Her work is also complicated by the petty gamesmanship of national leaders. Critics celebrated the emotional core of the film, though Anthony Lane, writing for the *New Yorker* (14 Nov. 2016), complained that the political aspect of the film hijacks the more interesting interactions between Louise and her alien charges. The meditative movie about an alien visitation struck a deep resonance—about how nations interact with one another and the remarkable smallness of human life. "The movie is a model of faithful, transformative film adaptation," Jia Tolentino of the *New Yorker* (16 Nov. 2016) wrote, citing Chiang's classic story. "It's also an exploration of a humble and brave ontological position that, in the aftershock of the Presidential election, feels as sublime, unfamiliar, and vaguely oracular as the iron-gray spaceships that hover in the film."

PERSONAL LIFE

Villeneuve was married to Canadian actor Macha Grenon, with whom he has three children. The director is currently married to Tanya Lapointe, a Canadian journalist, and lives in Montreal.

SUGGESTED READING

Bradshaw, Peter. "*Enemy* Review—A Thrilling Take on the Doppelganger Theme." Review of *Enemy*, directed by Denis Villeneuve. *The Guardian*, 1 Jan. 2015, www.theguardian.com/film/2015/jan/01/enemy-review-jake-gyllenhaal-denis-villeneuve. Accessed 15 Feb. 2017.

Buckley, Cara. "Denis Villeneuve of *Arrival* Leans in to Strong Heroines." *New York Times*, 10 Nov. 2016, www.nytimes.com/2016/11/13/movies/denis-villeneuve-interview-arrival.html. Accessed 15 Feb. 2017.

Kelly, Brendan. "Review: *August 32nd on Earth*." Review of *August 32nd on Earth*, directed by Denis Villeneuve. *Variety*, 21 May 1998, variety.com/1998/film/reviews/august-32nd-on-earth-1117477558/. Accessed 15 Feb. 2017.

Lane, Anthony. "The Consuming Fervor of *Arrival*." Review of *Arrival*, directed by Denis Villeneuve. *New Yorker*, 14 Nov. 2016, www.newyorker.com/magazine/2016/11/14/the-consuming-fervor-of-arrival. Accessed 15 Feb. 2017.

Villeneuve, Denis. "Catching Up with *Enemy* Director, Denis Villeneuve." Interview by Shannon M. Houston. *Paste*, 20 Mar. 2014, www.pastemagazine.com/articles/2014/03/catching-up-with-enemy-director-denis-villeneuve.html. Accessed 15 Feb. 2017.

Vineyard, Jennifer. "Denis Villeneuve Has Arrived. Now He's about to Take the Next Step." *Vulture*, 25 Jan. 2017, http://www.vulture.com/2017/01/

denis-villeneuve-intervew-blade-runner-dune-arrival.html. Accessed 15 Feb. 2017.

SELECTED WORKS
Incendies, 2010; *Prisoners*, 2013; *Sicario*, 2015; *Arrival*, 2016

—*Molly Hagan*

John Wall

Date of birth: September 6, 1990
Occupation: Basketball player

By Keith Allison from Hanover, MD, USA (John Wall) [CC BY-SA 2.0], via Wikimedia Commons

John Wall is an All-Star point guard for the Washington Wizards. After playing one year with the University of Kentucky Wildcats, Wall was the first pick of the 2010 National Basketball Association (NBA) draft. In seven seasons with the Wizards, Wall has established himself as a singularly agile player, known for his incredible speed. To paraphrase Juliet Litman for the *Ringer* (22 July 2017), Wall might not be the best-known player in the NBA, but he is "undoubtedly one of the best." In July 2017, he signed a four-year $170 million contract extension with the Wizards, after he led the team to the Eastern Conference semifinals, nearly felling the Boston Celtics. During a troubled childhood, basketball became his lifeline. He was discovered at an elite basketball camp in 2007. Wall's NBA career has been tied to the Wizards' arduous path to relevancy. Washington, DC, welcomed the rookie as a savior—the mayor declared the day after he was drafted "John Wall Day"—but Wall's greatness, and his synergy with the shifting team, would take time to develop. The team slowly built itself up around Wall, and in 2014, he took them to the playoffs for the first time in six years. By 2017, Wall was a rising league superstar—an improbable but exhilarating position given the hard road that got him there. "Hell of a lot of experts said John Wall might not have it," John Thompson, former basketball coach at Georgetown and sports commentator, told Mike Wise for *ESPN* (13 Feb. 2015). "Now look. John is that guy coming out of the dust."

EARLY LIFE
Johnathan Hildred Wall was born in Raleigh, North Carolina, on September 6, 1990. His mother, Frances Pulley, worked a series of odd jobs—she drove a bus for children and worked at a hotel—to support Wall and his younger sister, Cierra. Wall's father, John Carroll Wall, was a maintenance man. The elder Wall had been incarcerated for second-degree murder before he met Pulley. The two dated for eight years before Wall was born. In September 1991, the elder Wall robbed a convenience store at gunpoint, and found himself in prison once more. Wall's mother took the children to visit their father almost every weekend. Wall idolized his father. "He was good to us," Wall recalled to Wise. "You never thought, 'Oh, my father's in prison.' That was just his home in our eyes." His parents were married while his father was incarcerated. In 1998, the elder Wall was diagnosed with liver cancer, and was released the following year, a month early. Wall, who was nine, and his family took a vacation to White Lake, North Carolina, that summer. Wall considers the trip one of his fondest memories, but on the last day, his father's liver burst. He hemorrhaged in the hotel bathroom and died the next day.

Wall was traumatized by his father's death. He lashed out at his family, including his older stepsister, Tonya, who often served as his babysitter, and his classmates. (Wall also has an older half-brother named John Carroll Wall Jr.) For a period of time, Wall's mother would drop him off at elementary school, but then wait in the parking lot for him to be released. He was often sent home in less than two hours for bad behavior. She was worried about her son, but Wall was determined to push everyone away. When he was eleven, he met LeVelle Moton, who ran a basketball camp for young people. Moton recognized Wall's pain and brought him into the camp for free. Wall was kicked out of the camp his first year, but the sport gave him purpose. "Once I figured it out, I just said, basketball is my escape. This is the best way for me to do it," he told Eric Prisbell for the *Washington Post* (20 June 2010).

"I just build it into me and basically play every game for [my dad]. I feel like I have to step on the court every night and be dominant. He's down there watching me, so if he can't be in the stands, he'll be at the top." Wall returned to the camp a year later, ready to play.

HIGH SCHOOL CAREER

Wall excelled at Moton's camp, and kept his cool when Moton made bad calls against him as a test. When the camp was over, Wall was named MVP. He continued to play summer leagues, and later, played two years for Garner High School. When his family moved, Wall transferred to Broughton High School in Raleigh. For reasons that remain unclear—though some friends point to Wall's poor attitude—Wall was cut from the team. His summer league coaches, Tony Edwards and Brian and Dwon Clifton, and his mother helped him transfer again, this time to Word of God Christian Academy, where he repeated his sophomore year. Wall continued to struggle with his anger, but coach Levi Beckwith worked with Wall's mentors to overcome it. Beckwith often visited Wall at his house to talk through his issues. Despite the emotional rollercoaster, Wall was quickly becoming one of the best young players in North Carolina. In 2007, he was invited to the Reebok All-American Camp in Philadelphia. His outstanding performance there established him as a national phenomenon. As Moton put it to Prisbell, Wall's talent suddenly "clicked." Brian Lee, the head of Reebok Global Basketball, told Joseph Santoliquito for *Max Preps* (23 July 2011) that Wall exemplified the mission of the camp. The camp, he said, is "about giving kids like John Wall, those kids that fly under the radar, a chance to show what they can do. John had to drive eighteen hours round-trip to even get an invitation to this camp. He took his week at this camp very seriously, and he was discovered here."

UNIVERSITY OF KENTUCKY

Wall, who finished his high school career ranked number one among high school point guards and fifth overall, was actively recruited by colleges. He graduated from Word of God in 2009, the same year he was arrested for breaking and entering and sentenced to community service. Wall overcame the setback and enrolled at the University of Kentucky to play for Coach John Calipari and the Wildcats. Wall knew when he moved to Lexington that he would stay for only one year; still he developed a deep love for the community and a familial relationship with Calipari. Wall began his college career with a two-game suspension—he was barred from an exhibition game and the season opener—for violating National Collegiate Athletic Association (NCAA) rules about college visits, but once

he was allowed on the court, he became one of the team's star players. He averaged 16.6 points, 6.5 assists, and 1.8 steals per game, won the 2009–10 Adolph Rupp National Player of the Year and Southeastern Conference Player of the Year awards, and was named first team All-American. At the NCAA tournament—with the public encouragement of then President Barack Obama—he led the Wildcats to the Elite Eight. As the NBA draft approached, Wall was considered the obvious candidate for first pick. As Jonathan Abrams for the *New York Times* (23 June 2010) wrote, "In a draft of few guarantees, Wall is one." Sure enough, on June 24, 2010, Wall was selected, first overall, by the Washington Wizards.

WASHINGTON WIZARDS

The struggling Wizards embraced Wall like a long-lost son. At a press conference the day after the draft, fans swarmed the Verizon Center (now the Capital One Arena) to catch a glimpse of the new star and watch then Washington, DC, Mayor Adrian Fenty declare June 25, 2010, "John Wall Day." Despite the pressure, Wall performed well early. In his third NBA game, and first home game, he scored 29 points, and made 13 assists and 9 steals. He scored his first triple-double (double-digit points in three statistical categories)—19 points, 13 assists, and 10 rebounds—in a game against the Houston Rockets a week later. At the Rookie Challenge during All-Star weekend in 2011, Wall won the MVP award, with a record 22 assists. At the end of the season, Wall came in second in the voting for Rookie of the Year. (The title went to Blake Griffin of the Los Angeles Clippers.) His sophomore season, Wall returned to the NBA All-Star Weekend to play in the Rising Stars Challenge. A knee injury sidelined him for several months during the 2012–13 season. When he returned to the court during a game against the Atlanta Hawks in January, he received a standing ovation from fans. In March, he scored a career-high 47 points in a game against the Memphis Grizzlies. Wall signed a five-year contract extension with the Wizards in 2013. "He is the cornerstone of our team," Wizards owner Ted Leonsis told the Associated Press (31 July 2013) at the time. "And we have clearly expressed our desire to build around him."

In January 2014, Wall made his first NBA All-Star team, and won the competitive slam dunk contest. At season's end, Wall led the team to its first postseason game in six years. The Wizards ultimately lost to the Indiana Pacers in the Eastern Conference semifinals. In December, Wall played one of the best games of his career—scoring 26 points and a career-high 17 assists—against the Boston Celtics. He dedicated his performance to the memory of a young girl he had met who died of cancer earlier in the day. At the end of the 2015 season, Wall led the Wizards to the playoffs once more, sweeping the Toronto Raptors but losing, again, in the second round, this time to the Atlanta Hawks. Wall began to hit his individual stride in 2016, though the Wizards did not make it to the playoffs that year. During the off-season, Wall underwent two surgeries on his knees, making the start of the 2016 season a rocky one, but Wall went on to have the best season of his career, averaging 23.1 points, 10.7 assists, and 2.0 steals. In April 2017, he broke a franchise record for most assists in a single season with 802; he racked up 831 assists by season's end. Behind the scenes, he assumed the mantle of team leader. He led the Wizards to a victorious first round of the playoffs, beating the Hawks in six games. In the second round, the Wizards forced the Celtics to Game 7, but ultimately lost their shot at the finals 115–105.

SUGGESTED READING

Abrams, Jonathan. "Wall Leaves His Troubled Past for the Top of the Draft List." *The New York Times*, 23 June 2010, www.nytimes.com/2010/06/24/sports/basketball/24wall.html. Accessed 7 Sept. 2017.

Associated Press. "Wizards, Wall Agree to Contract Extension." *NBA*, NBA Media Ventures, 31 July 2013, www.nba.com/2013/news/07/31/report-wizards-extend-wall.ap/. Accessed 7 Sept. 2017.

"John Wall." *NBA*, NBA Media Ventures, 2017, www.nba.com/players/john/wall/202322. Accessed 11 Sept. 2017.

Litman, Juliet. "John Wall Finally Has a Contract Worthy of His Talent." *The Ringer*, 22 July 2017, www.theringer.com/2017/7/22/16078322/john-wall-finally-has-a-contract-worthy-of-his-talent-bfc088560371. Accessed 7 Sept. 2017.

Prisbell, Eric. "Despite the Angst That His Father's Jail Stint and Death Created, John Wall Reveres Him." *The Washington Post*, 20 June 2010, www.washingtonpost.com/wp-dyn/content/article/2010/06/19/AR2010061902948.html. Accessed 6 Sept. 2017.

Santoliquito, Joseph. "John Wall Shares His Road to Discovery." *Max Preps*, 23 July 2011, www.maxpreps.com/news/gwwYALFtEeCk-hgAcxJSkrA/john-wall-shares-his-road-to-discovery.htm. Accessed 6 Sept. 2017.

Wise, Mike. "Little John Wall's Unvarnished Climb." *ESPN*, 13 Feb. 2015, www.espn.com/nba/story/_/id/12300588/wizards-guard-john-wall-long-uphill-road-raleigh. Accessed 6 Sept. 2017.

—*Molly Hagan*

Lori Wallach

Date of birth: 1964
Occupation: Director of Global Trade Watch

As director of the consumer advocacy group Global Trade Watch, Lori Wallach is one of the best-known experts on global trade deals and bodies such as the World Trade Organization (WTO)—and one of their fiercest opponents. Since the mid-1990s, Wallach has spoken out against trade policies that she believes unfairly benefit corporations at the expense of the working and middle classes. "Our secretive trade negotiating process gives a privileged role to hundreds of official US trade advisors representing corporate interests," she wrote in an opinion piece for the *Huffington Post* (24 Mar. 2016). "They have turned our 'trade' agreements into delivery mechanisms for an array of retrograde policies, many unrelated to trade, that have hurt most Americans."

Wallach began her career in trade advocacy after spending several years fighting for food safety protections as part of the consumer-rights organization Public Citizen. Upon realizing that trade deals such as the North American Free Trade Agreement (NAFTA) often prevented countries from making their own decisions about important issues such as health and safety, she devoted herself to fighting such deals full time, founding Global Trade Watch as a division of Public Citizen in 1995. Although proponents of free trade deals such as NAFTA argue that such agreements benefit the member countries

Michael Nagle/Bloomberg/Getty Images

significantly, Wallach is adamant that they ultimately hurt far more than they help. "The data show that not only has this model failed to deliver its promised benefits, but that conditions are worse economically, environmentally and socially for a majority of people in a majority of the countries involved," she told Margie Kelley for the *Harvard Law Bulletin* (1 Sept. 2006).

EARLY LIFE AND EDUCATION

Lori Wallach was born in Wisconsin in 1964. She and her two brothers grew up in Wausau, a city in central Wisconsin. Her parents, Peter and Toby, owned and operated the Wausau Steel Corporation, a steel and recycling company founded in the 1950s by Wallach's paternal grandfather.

Growing up in Wausau, Wallach learned a great deal about the importance of fighting for one's beliefs and livelihood from her entrepreneur parents as well as from the example set by her grandparents, who had fled Nazi Germany in 1938. As one of the few Jewish children in town, and in the surrounding region, she faced bullying and has recalled in interviews that she at times had to fight to defend herself, an experience that shaped her later outlook. "I think my upbringing gave me a combination of what [activist] Ralph Nader calls an early learned scrappiness from just defending myself, and the notion of being able to accomplish almost anything you really feel is worth fighting for," she told Moisés Naím for *Foreign Policy* (Spring 2000).

After graduating from Wausau East High School in 1982, Wallach enrolled in Wellesley College to study political science. She earned her bachelor's degree from the college in 1986. After leaving Wellesley, Wallach pursued a law degree at Harvard Law School. Her enrollment overlapped that of future president Barack Obama, whose trade policies she would later strenuously oppose. Indeed, at Harvard Wallach had the opportunity to debate with her professors and fellow students about key issues, which in turn helped shape her own political and economic viewpoint. "One influence there was the impact of some knock-down-drag-out fights with our classic Chicago School-line-economics dean, Bob Clark," she recalled to Naím. "If I wasn't already heading in a progressive direction—and I was—that really did it." Wallach graduated from Harvard Law in 1990.

EARLY CAREER

Although Wallach had earned her law degree, she quickly realized that she was not interested in pursuing many of the traditional lines of work for a lawyer, instead feeling drawn to activism. "I'm a trade lawyer by training, but an activist by necessity," she explained in an interview for the 2002 public television program *Commanding*

Heights. Not long after graduating from Harvard, Wallach took a position with Public Citizen, a consumer advocacy group based in Washington, DC. Founded by activist (and fellow Harvard Law alumnus) Ralph Nader in 1971, Public Citizen advocates for consumer rights and safety through lobbying, litigation, and public awareness campaigns, among other strategies. Joining the organization in the early 1990s, Wallach focused on Public Citizen's food safety efforts, working to find regulatory solutions to concerns about pesticide use and meat inspection.

While lobbying for Public Citizen, Wallach soon noticed that food industry lobbyists who opposed food safety regulations often claimed that trade deals such as NAFTA and the General Agreement on Tariffs and Trade (GATT) would not allow Public Citizen's proposed regulatory changes to be made. "I heard this over and over enough times, and it didn't seem like the corporations who should be fighting us on the food-safety bills were fighting us face to face," Wallach recalled in her interview for *Commanding Heights*. "I started to get this feeling . . . that there was another door; I was guarding only one door to the bank, and someone was ripping off the loot through another door."

After researching the trade agreements in question, Wallach realized that many such agreements, although ostensibly focused on financial policies such as tariffs, effectively prevented the member countries from making their own decisions regarding environmental and health and safety issues. Wallach soon shifted her focus to global trade and in 1995 founded the Global Trade Watch division of Public Citizen.

GLOBAL TRADE WATCH

Since its early years, Global Trade Watch has researched the effects of trade deals and globalization on the economy, public health and safety, the environment, and other key areas and sought to educate the public and policymakers about the detrimental aspects of existing or proposed trade agreements. Wallach, as director of the organization, has served as the public face of Global Trade Watch, making media appearances and testifying before lawmakers on numerous occasions over more than two decades in the role.

Although Global Trade Watch has actively opposed a number of different agreements and bodies, the World Trade Organization (WTO) became one of the group's perennial opponents. Since early 1995, the WTO has sought to regulate global trade and oversee the operations of ongoing trade agreements. Wallach, however, argues that the WTO ultimately promotes commerce in a manner that harms the member countries and their residents, by taking away their ability to act independently on issues of national and local concern. "The basic idea was to fence in the range of government action so as to establish a single global market with uniform rules," she explained in an interview for the *Multinational Monitor* (Oct.–Nov. 1999). "Human beings are either labor or consumers. Water, trees, animals—basically all of nature—is a resource to be exploited. To exploit these human and natural resources most efficiently, all barriers breaking up this single world market must be eliminated—so as to maximize efficiency of scale." This way of perceiving the world, she argues, is inherently flawed. "What the corporate interests saw as market 'fragmentation' is the diversity of policies, values, cultures and laws that one would consider the blessing of democracy," she told the *Multinational Monitor*. "The WTO was to be a body that would continuously promulgate international standards that would be biased towards promoting commerce over other values and with powerful enforcement to knock down any divergent national standards."

Working to draw attention to the negative aspects of the WTO, Wallach and others organized the large-scale protests that broke out against the WTO Ministerial Conference held in Seattle, Washington, in 1999. She is also the coauthor with Patrick Woodall of the 2004 book *Whose Trade Organization? A Comprehensive Guide to the WTO*, which documents many of the objections to the WTO as well as some proposed solutions.

OPPOSING THE TPP

International trade deals gained substantial media and public attention in 2015 and 2016, as a proposed deal known as the Trans-Pacific Partnership (TPP) became a key point of debate in the US presidential primaries and general election. Signed in early 2016 but not yet ratified and put into effect by the end of that year, the TPP was an agreement among a dozen countries, including the United States, Canada, Australia, Japan, Vietnam, and Chile. The stated purpose of the agreement was to improve economic growth and create jobs within the member countries, as well as remove barriers to trade, such as tariffs, between them. As the countries involved represented 40 percent of world trade, the ratification of such an agreement would likely have a significant effect on the global economy. Among the proponents of the trade deal were President Barack Obama and many key members of his administration. However, the TPP proved politically controversial, and opposition to the deal became a key talking point during the 2016 campaign. Republican candidate Donald Trump opposed the deal, as did Democratic candidate Hillary Clinton—who had supported the deal during its initial stages of development but later spoke out against it—and her principal primary challenger, Bernie Sanders. Following his election in November 2016, Trump claimed that he would withdraw the United States from the TPP upon taking office.

Strongly opposed to TPP, which she referred to as "NAFTA on steroids" in the *Huffington Post*, Wallach was pleased by the public attention given to the deal, particularly in light of the secretive development of many such deals. "Americans have become aware that our trade agreements have been hijacked by corporate interests that use the free-trade brand to Trojan-horse into place special protections," she told *Politico* (2016). "The TPP is a pivot point because it comes at a time of rising anger about the influence corporations have over governments."

Wallach, who has written about the TPP for numerous publications, argues that the deal would, like its predecessors, have a detrimental effect on the people of the member countries while benefiting only corporate interests and politicians. She attributes the loss of US manufacturing jobs and the prevalence of international outsourcing to global free-trade agreements and argues that passing further agreements will do little to improve the employment outlook within the country. In addition to her economic reasons for opposing the TPP, Wallach has noted that entering into a trade agreement with nations such as Brunei and Malaysia will effectively make the United States complicit in human-rights abuses taking place in those countries. In light of objections made by the TPP's proponents, Wallach seeks to remind policymakers and the public that opposing free-trade deals such as the TPP does not mean that one opposes all trade. Rather, she hopes to work toward the development of trade agreements that improve the lives of each member country's people rather than merely increasing the profits of corporations.

PERSONAL LIFE

Wallach lives in the Washington, DC, area.

SUGGESTED READING

Kelley, Margie. "Dangerous Liaisons?" *Harvard Law Bulletin*, 1 Sept. 2006, today.law.harvard.edu/dangerous-liaisons. Accessed 6 Jan. 2017.

"Michael Froman, Lori Wallach." *Politico*, 2016, www.politico.com/magazine/politico50/2016/michael-froman-lori-wallach. Accessed 6 Jan. 2017.

Wallach, Lori. "The Choice Is Not between TPP or No Trade." *The Huffington Post*, 24 Mar. 2016, www.huffingtonpost.com/lori-wallach/the-choice-is-not-between_b_9541300.html. Accessed 6 Jan. 2017.

Wallach, Lori. "Lori's War." Interview by Moisés Naím. *Foreign Policy*, vol. 118, Spring 2000, pp. 29–54.

Wallach, Lori. Interview. *Commanding Heights.* WGBH, 2002, www.pbs.org/wgbh/commandingheights/shared/minitext/int_loriwallach.html. Accessed 6 Jan. 2017.

Wallach, Lori. "The WTO's Slow Motion Coup against Democracy." *Multinational Monitor,* Oct.–Nov. 1999, www.multinationalmonitor.org/mm1999/101999/interview-wallach.html. Accessed 6 Jan. 2017.

—*Joy Crelin*

Yuja Wang

Date of birth: February 10, 1987
Occupation: Musician

Classical pianist Yuja Wang maintains an active Twitter feed on which she has quoted everyone from composer Gustav Mahler ("Tradition is tending the flame, it's not worshiping the ashes") to fashion icon Coco Chanel ("A girl should always be two things: classy and fabulous"). Vivian Schweitzer wrote for the *New York Times* (6 Apr. 2012): "Mahler and Coco Chanel are unusual bedfellows, but . . . Wang, who at 25 is one of the most gifted pianists of her generation, would make Mahler and Chanel equally proud."

Schweitzer explained that duality, writing, "She has attracted attention both for her prodigious talents and for her attire, which has raised eyebrows in the tradition-bound world of classical music. A passionate performer, Ms. Wang meshes an impeccable technique and insightful artistry, evident both on disc and in live concerts."

Wang has, indeed, garnered ecstatic notices for her playing. In a review of a Carnegie Hall performance of Ludwig von Beethoven's *Hammerklavier* Sonata, Anthony Tomassini wrote for the *New York Times* (15 May 2016): "Wang's virtuosity goes well beyond uncanny facility. Right through this Beethoven performance she wondrously brought out intricate details, inner voices and harmonic colorings. The first movement had élan and daring. The scherzo skipped along with mischievousness and rhythmic bite. In the grave, great slow movement, she played with restraint and poignancy."

On the other hand, there are those who find her propensity to dress in tight, flashy clothing while on stage an affront to tradition. "Her dress [at a Hollywood Bowl performance] was so short and tight that had there been any less of it, the Bowl might have been forced to restrict admission to any music lover under 18 not accompanied by an adult," Mark Swed wrote in an oft-quoted review for the *Los Angeles Times* (3 Aug. 2011).

For her part, Wang takes the opinions of all reviewers—fans and detractors alike—in stride. She remarked to Ivan Hewett of the *Telegraph* (5 Feb. 2014), "Anyway I have many different styles, I don't only wear short. I don't understand why I have to explain this, I just do what is natural for me." In another Twitter post, she asserted, "Music criticism should be to musicians what ornithology is to birds."

EARLY YEARS AND EDUCATION

Wang was born on February 10, 1987, in Beijing, China. Her father, Wang Jianguo, was a percussionist, and her mother, Zhai Jieming, was a dancer. She has described them as conventional people who were never allowed to develop to their full potential because of China's repressive cultural and political environment.

A quiet and shy child, Wang began taking piano lessons at the age of six. Her mother had taken her to a performance of *Swan Lake.* "I absolutely loved the music, but I didn't want to dance. I was too lazy," she related to Schweitzer. "That's why I liked the piano—you get to sit down!" While Wang is best known on the video-sharing site YouTube for a rapid-fire rendition of "Flight of the Bumblebee" that went viral, other videos show her as a young girl confidently playing the music of Frederic Chopin. "My dad is really good with rhythm and was always correcting me and telling me, 'You're rushing,'" she admitted to Schweitzer. "That's my weakness. Even back then I was rushing."

Wang studied with respected instructors at Beijing's Central Conservatory of Music, and she was soon giving recitals in Australia and Germany. At age fourteen, she attended the Mount Royal Conservatory in Calgary, Alberta, Canada. That year she also won the Special Jury Award at the first Japan Sendai International Music Competition, where she was the youngest competitor. She lived with a volunteer family while in Canada but chafed when they corrected her English (her English is now exceptionally fluent).

CURTIS INSTITUTE OF MUSIC
At age fifteen, Wang traveled alone to Philadelphia, Pennsylvania, to study at the Curtis Institute of Music. Her mother had planned to chaperone, but visa problems prevented her from doing so. Wang, who as a teenager was far from shy, rented her own apartment rather than staying with a host family and reveled in the freedom of being independent. At the school, she studied with noted pianist Gary Graffman, with whom she continues to maintain a warm and close friendship. During her first year under his tutelage, she won the concerto competition at the Aspen Music Festival, and she was also a featured performer in the Canadian Broadcasting Corporation's Up and Coming series.

She was happy, she asserted, to be away from her native land. "Being a classical musician is almost like being a pop star in China, and it's more about power and fame and money," she explained to Schweitzer. "That's why so many kids are playing. It's like sports in America. It's for being more famous, and I don't really like that."

While still a student, Wang undertook a series of high-profile appearances with major orchestras. In 2005, for example, she performed Beethoven's *Fourth Piano Concerto* with the National Arts Centre Orchestra in Ottawa. She had been called to replace renowned Romanian pianist Radu Lupu, who was ill, with just a single day's notice, and she received a spate of media attention, with many of the reviews announcing, "A star is born!"

In 2006 she debuted with the New York Philharmonic, as well as the symphony orchestras of Chicago, San Francisco, and Houston. She also took home the hotly contested Gilmore Young Artist Award. In 2007 she had other "star is born" turns when she stepped in for an ailing Martha Argerich with the Boston Symphony Orchestra and for Yefim Bronfman (again at a day's notice) with the Swedish Radio Symphony Orchestra.

RECORDINGS AND REVIEWS
By the time Wang graduated from the Curtis Institute of Music in 2008, her career was already well underway. In 2009 she signed a recording deal with Deutsche Grammophon, through which she has since released a series of albums. Her first, *Sonatas & Etudes by Chopin, Scriabin, Liszt & Ligeti* (2009), led Grammophon to name her its Young Artist of the Year, and she was nominated for a Grammy Award in the category of best classical instrumental solo for her 2011 effort, *Rachmaninov with the Mahler Chamber Orchestra and Claudio Abbado*. She released two additional albums through Grammophon in the next few years: *Fantasia* (2012) and *Masterpieces in Miniature* (2014). In April 2016 she released her album *Ravel: Complete Orchestral Work*.

In addition to her recording career, Wang has performed live on numerous occasions. In the summer of 2014, Wang completed a four-night residency with the London Symphony Orchestra. In May 2016, she gave a Beethoven recital at the Walt Disney Concert Hall alongside veteran pianist Murray Perahia. Wang performed the *Hammerklavier* at this performance as well, and the *Los Angeles Times* critic Mark Swed commented that she made the notoriously difficult piece "look easy" (3 May 2016). In the fall of 2016, Wang was named the Musical America 2017 Artist of the Year.

Her recordings and performances sometimes attract mixed reviews, with some critics lauding her technical virtuosity while bemoaning her lack of emotional depth. Despite the occasional detractors, she still has many who sing her praises. Graffman told Schweitzer that it was her "intelligence and good taste" in her interpretations that made her stand out. Clive Gillison, in conversation with Barbara Jepson for the *Wall Street Journal* (18 Oct. 2011), noted, "She's not only a remarkable player, but she also has a remarkable ability to connect with audiences."

BREAKING THE RULES
Even as Wang, an Avery Fisher Career Grant recipient, blazed a trail through the great concert halls of the world, her live performances have similarly been subject to divided scrutiny, with some critics enthralled by her playing and others dismissive of her presentation. Ever since Wang came to international attention, Jepson asserted, "Her handlers have rightfully endeavored to show that she's a serious young artist with more to her formidable talent than jaw-dropping technique." Wang's disregard for accepted dress and the attention it has garnered, however, have gotten in the way of those efforts, according to Jepson. "The thigh-baring orange dress Ms. Wang wore for an August performance with the Los Angeles Philharmonic at the Hollywood Bowl sparked bicoastal debate, pitting those who deemed *Los Angeles Times* critic Mark Swed's honest, if overheated, reaction 'sexist' against those who thought the outfit showed poor professional judgment," Jepson wrote. "Her cancellations during the past two years have raised hackles in some quarters. And the pianist hasn't yet shed the 'flying fingers' image generated by YouTube videos of her performing

an arrangement of Nikolai Rimsky-Korsakov's 'Flight of the Bumblebee' at warp speed."

Of that infamous Hollywood Bowl dress, Wang has expressed some confusion. She had already worn the garment, a figure-hugging mini dress with strategic cut-outs, at a recital in Switzerland, where it had attracted little notice. "[In Los Angeles] they were paying attention to this rather than the music," she lamented to Schweitzer. "Which makes sense, as LA is kind of superficial and more visual. But they have rules about what classical musicians should be wearing, which I think is stupid." Still, she added mischievously, the publicity had no doubt helped sell tickets to her Carnegie Hall debut, which she made just a few months later. Anthony Tomassini later summed up the debate, writing, "In any event, [Wang] is a lovely young woman. If you've got it, flaunt it. What matters is that Ms. Wang has got it as a pianist."

PERSONAL LIFE

Although Wang once enjoyed the excitement of traveling to concert gigs during her student days, she now considers it a sometimes exhausting part of her job rather than a glamorous perk. She maintains a home on the Upper West Side of Manhattan, not far from Lincoln Center, but she has told interviewers that she is so seldom there that the doorman does not recognize her. She spends her rare downtime in New York, however, and prefers reading on her Kindle to going out on the town. (Her taste in books ranges from genre fiction to Virginia Woolf and Immanuel Kant.)

Wang, a fan of such disparate musical artists as Rihanna, the Black Eyed Peas, Keith Jarrett, and Ella Fitzgerald, has said that if she had not become a professional pianist, she might have considered a career as a fashion designer, given her deep love of fashion.

SUGGESTED READING

Jepson, Barbara. "The Fast and the Serious." *Wall Street Journal*, 18 Oct. 2011, www.wsj.com/articles/SB10001424052970203914304576628961037766644. Accessed 21 Oct. 2016.

Malcolm, Janet. "Yuja Wang and the Art of Performance." *New Yorker*, 5 Sept. 2016, www.newyorker.com/magazine/2016/09/05/yuja-wang-and-the-art-of-performance. Accessed 21 Oct. 2016.

Midgette, Anne. "Which Offends? Her Short Dress or Critic's Narrow View?" *Washington Post*, 12 Aug. 2011, www.washingtonpost.com/lifestyle/style/2011/08/10/gIQAMvtO-BJ_story.html. Accessed 21 Oct. 2016.

Schweitzer, Vivian. "Talented, Eye-Catching, Unapologetic." *New York Times*, 6 Apr. 2012, www.nytimes.com/2012/04/08/arts/music/yuja-wang-pianist-and-fashion-plate.html. Accessed 21 Oct. 2016.

Swed, Mark. "Review: Yuja Wang Slays Beethoven's Monster Piano Piece—and Makes It Look Easy." Review of the *Hammerklavier* Sonata, performed by Yuja Wang. *Los Angeles Times*, 3 May 2016, www.latimes.com/entertainment/arts/la-et-cm-yuja-wang-review-20160503-snap-story.html. Accessed 10 Nov. 2016.

Tomassini, Anthony. "Flaunting Virtuosity (and More)." Review of the *Hammerklavier* Sonata, performed by Yuja Wang. *New York Times*, 21 Oct. 2011, www.nytimes.com/2011/10/22/arts/music/yuja-wang-at-carnegie-hall-review.html. Accessed 21 Oct. 2016.

Wang, Yuja. "Yuja Wang Interview: 'I Can Wear Long Skirts When I'm 40.'" Interview by Ivan Hewett. *Telegraph* [London], 5 Feb. 2014, www.telegraph.co.uk/culture/music/classical-music/10617975/Yuja-Wang-interview-I-can-wear-long-skirts-when-Im-40.html. Accessed 21 Oct. 2016.

SELECTED WORKS

Sonatas & Etudes by Chopin, Scriabin, Liszt & Ligeti, 2009; *Transformation: Stravinsky, Scarlatti, Brahms*, 2010; *Fantasia*, 2012; *Masterpieces in Miniature*, 2014; *Ravel: Complete Orchestral Works*, 2016

—*Mari Rich*

Junya Watanabe

Date of birth: 1961
Occupation: Fashion designer

One of the most internationally famous Japanese fashion designers, Junya Watanabe may initially seem to present a mass of contradictions. An intensely private person who rarely speaks about his personal life and gives few interviews about his professional work, he nevertheless makes his design work available for widespread public scrutiny multiple times a year, just as he has for decades. His clothing often features innovative shapes and unusual textiles, yet at the same time, his collections experiment with classic forms and styles and at times can even be characterized as Americana. Yet such juxtapositions are business as usual for Watanabe, who has experienced significant success in fashion since joining the Japanese fashion label Comme des Garçons as a pattern cutter in the mid-1980s. Having quickly risen through the ranks at the groundbreaking fashion house, he launched his own label under the Comme des Garçons umbrella, Junya Watanabe Comme des Garçons, in 1992. Since then, he has gained widespread praise for his work, which has diverged from the avant-garde creations of Comme des Garçons' founder, Rei Kawakubo, and veered toward styles that are artistically innovative yet distinctly more practical in form and function. For Watanabe, such practicality informs his overall approach to fashion. "I think that fashion is a way to express myself, and in that sense it is close to art," he explained to Olivier Zahm for *Purple Magazine* (2014). "But the very reality of fashion is business. And I work on that basis.'"

EARLY LIFE AND EDUCATION

Junya Watanabe was born in Fukushima, Japan, in 1961. He was drawn to the field of fashion design at a young age, an interest that he has hinted was fueled by his family background. "There's nothing in particular that made me want to start fashion and create clothes. But if I were to mention something, it would be the fact that my mother used to have a little made-to-order shop," he told Alexander Fury for the *New York Times* (17 Oct. 2016). "That may have been an influence."

During his early years, he was inspired by the work of figures such as French fashion designer Pierre Cardin and Japanese designer Issey Miyake. He was particularly intrigued by fashion that had innovated shapes and unusual structures. "I was drawn to the fact that designers before Miyake, like Dior and big names, would create clothes that were formfitting," he explained to Fury. "Issey totally changed the idea, completely different, and that impact was profound on me. Of making me want to create something, the idea of clothing much different from previous designers."

Watanabe attended Bunka Fashion College, a well-regarded institution based in Tokyo. The college focuses on fashion design as well as associated fields such as marketing and textile production. He graduated from the college in 1984.

COMME DES GARÇONS

Shortly after completing his education, Watanabe found a job as a pattern cutter for Comme des Garçons. Founded by designer Rei Kawakubo in the 1960s, the company was based in the Aoyama district of Tokyo, where it had opened its first store in 1975. Although first gaining notice in Japan, Comme des Garçons' clothing found a far greater international audience beginning in 1981, when Kawakubo debuted a collection in Paris for the first time. Although initially focused on women's clothing, the company later came to encompass a menswear line as well as lines of perfumes and accessories.

Although Watanabe started his fashion career in a relatively low position at Comme des Garçons, he soon rose through the ranks at the company and was named the design director of the Tricot line in 1987. Specializing in knitwear, the Tricot line featured more casual clothing than the pieces typically included in Comme des Garçons' main collections. Watanabe also played a role in the company's menswear lines and by the beginning of the 1990s was a major figure in the design house.

Although Watanabe appreciated Kawakubo's design aesthetic, he eventually came to understand that his own varied significantly from hers. "My idea of something being beautiful or aesthetically pleasing is completely different from what Rei Kawakubo's vision of beauty is," he explained to Fury. "To this day, seeing Rei Kawakubo's work, I feel the same. I understand certain points and I can relate to certain areas. . . . That doesn't mean that I completely agree. As a person-to-person relationship, I feel that I have a different idea, and I'll always have a different vision of what is beautiful. Another reason, perhaps, I didn't end up working right alongside Kawakubo is perhaps she felt that I had a different vision of my own. Maybe that's why we parted, in terms of creating something that was different." Where many of Kawakubo's designs could be described as avant-garde or sculptural, Watanabe favored more functional designs that riffed on classic styles. He would soon be able to explore his preferred aesthetic as head of his own fashion label under the Comme des Garçons banner, Junya Watanabe Comme des Garçons.

JUNYA WATANABE COMME DES GARÇONS

In 1992, Watanabe founded his own label, Junya Watanabe Comme des Garçons. Although the label is sometimes referred to as Watanabe's own company, he is quick to correct that misconception. "It is not my company," he explained to Zahm. "It is Rei Kawakubo's company and I work in it." Although the label is technically part of Comme des Garçons, Watanabe had creative control from the start, which allowed him to explore clothing styles that would not necessarily have fit in with the rest of Comme des Garçons' offerings.

Watanabe launched Junya Watanabe Comme des Garçons in 1992 with a line of women's clothing, holding his first fashion show at Ryogoku Station, a train and subway station in Tokyo, that year. Unlike Kawakubo, who made her Paris debut more than a decade after founding her company, Watanabe presented his first collection at Fashion Week the following year, showing a collection of women's clothing in Paris for the first time in 1993 for the Spring/Summer 1994 season. He would go on to design the Comme des Garçons Homme line in 2001. Both lines would be met with acclaim from many fashion critics, boosting Watanabe's popularity as a designer worldwide.

AESTHETIC

As an innovative designer, Watanabe frequently plays with shape and form, yet at the same time, he also has a somewhat utilitarian perspective. "I'm not very interested in various design philosophies or ideas," he told Zahm. "What matters to me more is the content and reality of design. The everyday work." Often drawn to styles of clothing that are frequently described as wardrobe essentials, such as jeans and classically shaped jackets, Watanabe is particularly known for his experiments with Americana-influenced menswear. Even as the clothing's style is the most visible point, however, he remains devoted to presenting clothing that serves a particular purpose. "When I design menswear, it's important for me to consider where you wear the clothes and what purpose they serve," he told *Interview* magazine (27 Feb. 2009). "This season, I started off with the idea of 'wear it two ways,' or, reversible clothes. Then as I thought about what scenes you would wear them in, I came up with travel."

Despite his emphasis on practicality, Watanabe nevertheless produces many experimental creations, from sculptural pieces to collections influenced by styles such as punk and grunge. One of Watanabe's major areas of experimentation has been that of textiles, as he has frequently experimented with fabrics that have been rarely or never used in fashion contexts. In 1999, for instance, he debuted a collection that featured waterproof textiles. Notably, he demonstrated the capabilities of the clothing by simulating rain above the runway during the fashion show.

DESIGN PROCESS

Working out of his Aoyama office, Watanabe collaborates with a team of employees to develop the designs that have made him famous. Business and logistical concerns are of key importance to his design process. "My ideas come out squeezed and pressured, on deadlines," he explained to Zahm. "So I could say that the starting point of my creation would be a calendar and a schedule."

Moving beyond that starting point, Watanabe works to bring his ideas to life, step-by-step. "It all begins inside my head," he told Fury. "I start to look for strings of ideas that interest me. From then, I put my ideas to words. I work alongside my pattern makers, trying to put my words into creating and actually seeing it come to life. Photographs, artist's work, anything that may seem relatable to what I am speaking about." Next, Watanabe told Fury, "they start to craft." Just as Watanabe himself began his career working with

patterns for Comme des Garçons, so too has he employed a number of people who would go on to have their own lines under the Comme des Garçons umbrella or on their own; the designer Tao Kurihara, for instance, worked under Watanabe before launching her own signature line for Comme des Garçons.

The next stage in the design process includes piecing together the crafted elements to form complete garment designs, and in turn a cohesive collection. "After creating pieces and little constructed elements, then I start to think about the relationship of these pieces with the body and how it could be formed onto the body," Watanabe told Fury. "All these ideas, little by little, they form garments, clothing. Then I create the collection."

COLLABORATIONS

In addition to his original designs for Junya Watanabe Comme des Garçons, Watanabe is well known for his collaborations with other design brands, which have resulted in the creation of clothing and accessories that mesh with his interests and preferred aesthetics while expanding the reach of his brand. Among other companies, he has worked with the German shoe manufacturer Heinrich Dinkelacker, creating a line of men's shoes that play on classic styles, and the Spanish designer Loewe, designing a small collection of handbags. Other brands with which he has collaborated include the denim-focused Levi's and Mackintosh, a designer and manufacturer of raincoats made from rubberized fabric. In January 2017, Watanabe further emphasized his spirit of collaboration through his fall-winter runway show at Paris Fashion Week. Focusing largely on outerwear, the show introduced a variety of clothing items that featured reworked designs from brands such as Levi's, Carhartt, and the North Face.

PERSONAL LIFE

Watanabe is reticent about his personal life and rarely grants interviews. He is divorced, and lives and works in Tokyo.

SUGGESTED READING

"Beyond the Brand: Junya Watanabe." *Journal*, 11 Oct. 2011, www.mrporter.com/journal/journal_issue34/7. Accessed 10 Mar. 2017.

Fury, Alexander. "Junya Watanabe, One of Fashion's Foremost Thinkers." *The New York Times*, 17 Oct. 2016, nytimes.com/2016/10/17/t-magazine/junya-watanabe-interview.html. Accessed 10 Mar. 2017.

"Junya Watanabe." *Business of Fashion*, 2016, www.businessoffashion.com/community/people/junya-watanabe. Accessed 10 Mar. 2017.

"Junya Watanabe." *The Cut*, 2017, nymag.com/thecut/fashion/designers/junya-watanabe. Accessed 10 Mar. 2017.

Kennedy, Alicia, Emily Banis Stoehrer, and Jay Calderin. "Junya Watanabe." *Fashion Design, Referenced: A Visual Guide to the History, Language, and Practice of Fashion*. Rockport Publishers, 2013, pp. 400–401. *eBook Collection (EBSCOhost)*, search.ebscohost.com/login.aspx?direct=true&db=nlebk&AN=576544&site=ehost-live. Accessed 13 Mar. 2017.

Watanabe, Junya. Interview by Olivier Zahm. *Purple Magazine*, 2014, purple.fr/magazine/ss-2014-issue-21/junya-watanabe. Accessed 10 Mar. 2017.

Watanabe, Junya. "Sentimental Journey." *Interview*, 27 Feb. 2009, www.interviewmagazine.com/fashion/junya-watanabe. Accessed 10 Mar. 2017.

—*Joy Crelin*

Photo by Vincent Sandoval/FilmMagic

Carole Boston Weatherford

Date of birth: February 13, 1956
Occupation: Author

"I aim to mine the past for family stories, forgotten struggles, and fading traditions," Carole Boston Weatherford said in an interview for the blog *The Brown Bookshelf* (20 Feb. 2008), which is devoted to African American children's literature. "I feel that I have succeeded when a child asks for more information about the trials and triumphs I have chronicled. I want kids to read my books and then dig deeper." Many of her books include an introduction, an author's note, and a glossary to provide further resources and context for her readers who are looking to learn more about a topic.

Weatherford is best known for such award-winning volumes as *The Sound That Jazz Makes* (2000), *Moses: When Harriet Tubman Led Her People to Freedom* (2006), *Birmingham, 1963* (2007), *Voice of Freedom: Fannie Lou Hamer* (2015), *You Can Fly: The Tuskegee Airmen* (2016), and *Freedom in Congo Square* (2016). Much of what Weatherford writes is based on real-life events. "I want kids to know, because they can't fathom that these kinds of injustices existed in the USA," she explained to Linda M. Castellitto for *BookPage* (Feb. 2016). "We have to continually tell them this happened in the past. It wasn't a video game, a TV series, a movie with a prequel or sequel. It happened."

Although there has been a gradual increase in the number of major publishers willing to promote books with characters of color, Weatherford remembers when that was not always the case. As she recalled in her interview for *The Brown Bookshelf*: "The biggest mountain was getting editors to read my work and to regard my subjects as more than so-called 'footnotes to history.' Before black authors can enlighten and inspire young readers, we must educate those editors who assume that if they themselves are not aware, then the topic is not important or not universal."

EARLY LIFE

Carole Boston Weatherford was born on February 13, 1956, in Baltimore, Maryland. Her parents, Joseph Alexander Boston and Carolyn Virginia Boston, were both educators. She has told interviewers that books were a central feature of her life from a young age; family lore has it that once, when she was a few months old, someone unthinkingly handed her a book upside down, and she promptly turned it in the proper direction.

She recalls having a picture she drew featured in *Highlights*, a venerable children's magazine that accepts reader submissions, and she began writing poetry while in first grade. Her father taught printing at a local high school, and he printed her early efforts on his classroom's letterpress. Seeing her own words in print—a rarity in the days before home computers and laser printers—gave her a thrill that she still fondly remembers.

Besides her parents' love of literature, she was influenced by their musical tastes. Her father kept an impressive collection of jazz records, and as a child, Weatherford often devised dance numbers to perform as he played them. "Here is a snapshot of my formative years in the 1960s," she recalled in her interview for *The Brown Bookshelf*. "My father's jazz collection was the soundtrack."

Weatherford loved going to the library and has made special mention of Gloria Johnston, the school librarian at Baltimore's Edgewood Elementary School. Although she harbored some dreams of becoming a fashion designer, she also wanted to become a librarian, thanks to Johnston's influence. "I must have been a bit odd as a child," she recalled to Toni Buzzeo for *LibrarySparks* (Aug. 2013). "Who catalogs their own books? Well, I cut #10 envelopes in half and glued those pockets in the backs of my books. For each book, I wrote the title and author on a file card that I slid into the pocket. I may have even had a rubber stamp that I used to check out books."

EDUCATION

Although Edgewood's all-black faculty members made sure to introduce their students to African American history and stressed the accomplishments of black scientists, athletes, authors, and artists, Weatherford was disappointed to realize that few books featured people of color. "When I was growing up, there was no multicultural literature. There probably wasn't even the term 'multicultural,'" she told an interviewer for *Reading Rockets* (23 Apr. 2014). "I was an avid reader but I probably only read maybe two books that included girls who looked like me, and one of them was a book that was published in the 1940s that my mother recommended that I read . . . . So that was a void in my life."

Still, at that stage she did not consider becoming a professional author herself. "It never dawned on me that the people who were writing the books I was reading were making money, or even alive," she admitted to Castellitto. "I never saw any of them, and authors weren't celebrities then like they are now."

Weatherford attended American University, in Washington, DC, where she took part in an independent study program that allowed her to design her own course of study. Combining her love of music and literature, she devised a course called "The Poetry of the Blues." After graduating with a bachelor's degree in 1977, she embarked on a varied career that included stints as a public-school teacher, field representative for the American Red Cross, host and producer of the *Black Arts Review* radio talk show, and director of communications for the National Bar Association.

Although she published an occasional poem during this time, it was not until she had married and started a family that she decided to pursue a master's degree in fine arts and try her hand at writing for children. "I was taking my own kids to the library, and there were so many more multicultural books for them than there had been for me as a child," she told Castellitto. "I was still writing adult poetry, plus things on the side to entertain my kids. I thought, maybe I can try to write for children."

In 1982 Weatherford received a master of arts in publications design from the University of Baltimore, and she later earned an MFA in creative writing from the University of Carolina at Greensboro, in 1992.

BOOKS

In 1995 Lee & Low Books, a well-known publisher of multicultural children's books, released *Juneteenth Jamboree*, Weatherford's tale of a girl who has recently moved to Texas and is introduced to the joyful holiday commemorating the events of June 19, 1865, when slaves in that state finally learned about their emancipation. Aimed at readers from first to fourth grade, the brightly illustrated book earned laudatory reviews.

Since then, she has written more than forty other books for children and young adults. Among the best known is *Moses: When Harriet Tubman Led Her People to Freedom*, which won both a prestigious Caldecott Honor and a Coretta Scott King Award for illustrations and garnered critical acclaim for its verse. A reviewer for *Publishers Weekly* (Sept. 2006) called it a "gorgeous, poetic picture book." In a review for the *New York Times* (11 Feb. 2007), Rebecca Zerkin asked, "How do you add to the already impressive body of children's literature about Harriet Tubman? Write a fictional account, in three voices, of Tubman's heart-rending escape from slavery and get Kadir Nelson to illustrate it."

In her interview for *The Brown Bookshelf*, Weatherford recalled writing *Moses*, explaining that it "began as a story to be read aloud and lay dormant for five or more years until being performed by my [pastor] husband's church. That performance showed me the work's potential as a children's book. . . . *Moses* propelled my career to another level."

Birmingham, 1963 (2007), Weatherford's book about the horrific 1963 bombing of a black church—an act of terrorism that killed four young girls—also garnered multiple laurels for the author, including the 2008 Jane Addams Children's Book Honors Award, the Lee Bennett Hopkins Poetry Award, and the Jefferson Cup Award.

Her more recent works include volumes about the Tuskegee Airmen, a celebrated group of African American pilots who fought in World War II; a devastating flood that ravaged the town of Princeville, North Carolina, which had been founded by freed slaves; and the historic Harlem neighborhood known as Sugar Hill that has been home to such notable figures as W. E. B. Du Bois, Thurgood Marshall, Duke Ellington, and Miles Davis; and the nonviolent sit-ins that took place at the height of the civil rights movement in Greensboro, North Carolina.

She has also written well-received biographies of such figures as Barack and Michelle Obama; arctic explorer Matthew Henson; singers Billie Holiday, Leontyne Price, and Lena Horne; photographers Dorothea Lange and Gordon Parks; activist Fannie Lou Hamer; and media personality Oprah Winfrey. Her 2016 book *Freedom in Congo Square* earned Weatherford the Charlotte Zolotow Award, which is given annually for outstanding writing in a picture book.

ACADEMIC CAREER
In addition to writing, Weatherford also teaches creative writing, children's literature, and adolescent literature. In 2002 Weatherford joined the faculty of Fayetteville State University's Department of English, where she is now a full professor. She is widely recognized there as a pioneer in online course development and has created several new courses, including Hip Hop: Poetry, Politics, and Pop Culture.

PERSONAL LIFE
Carole Boston Weatherford lives in High Point, North Carolina. She married Ronald Jeffrey Weatherford in February 1985. Together, they authored the 1998 treatise *Somebody's Knocking at Your Door: AIDS and the African-American Church*, and had a daughter, Caresse Michele, and a son, Jeffery Boston. Weatherford's son is an artist who illustrated her 2016 book *You Can Fly: The Tuskegee Airmen.* (She has told interviewers that she used to have to chastise him for doodling at school instead of focusing on his teachers.) Though the Weatherfords are now divorced, they talk frequently.

SUGGESTED READING
Buzzeo, Toni. "Meet the Author: Carole Boston Weatherford." *LibrarySparks*, Aug. 2013, librarysparks.com/wp-content/uploads/2016/06/lsp_mta_caroleweatherford_aug13.pdf. Accessed 1 Sept. 2017.

Vander Linde, Rebecca. "Inspired by Lady Day, Carole Boston Weatherford, KSB/BA '77, Writes Jazzy Poetry and Prose." *American University Alumni News*, www.american.edu/alumni/success/Carole-Boston-Weatherford.cfm. Accessed 1 Sept. 2017.

Weatherford, Carole Boston. Interview. *The Brown Bookshelf*, 20 Feb. 2008, thebrownbookshelf.com/2008/02/20/carole-boston-weatherford. Accessed 1 Sept. 2017.

Weatherford, Carole Boston. Interview. *Reading Rockets*, 23 Apr. 2014, www.readingrockets.org/books/interviews/weatherford. Accessed 1 Sept. 2017.

Weatherford, Carole Boston. Interview by Linda M. Castellitto. *BookPage*, Feb. 2016, bookpage.com/interviews/19365-carole-boston-weatherford. Accessed 1 Sept. 2017.

Weatherford, Carole Boston. Interview by Daryl Grabarek. *School Library Journal*, 2 Feb. 2016, www.slj.com/2016/02/interviews/freedom-in-congo-square-an-interview-with-carole-boston-weatherford. Accessed 1 Sept. 2017.

Zerkin, Rebecca. Review of *Moses: When Harriet Tubman Led Her People to Freedom*, by Carole Boston Weatherford. *The New York Times*, 11 Feb. 2007, www.nytimes.com/2007/02/11/books/review/Zerkin.t.html. Accessed 1 Sept. 2017.

SELECTED WORKS
Juneteenth Jamboree, 1995; *The Sound That Jazz Makes*, 2000; *Remember the Bridge: Poems of a People*, 2002; *Freedom on the Menu: The Greensboro Sit-Ins*, 2005; *Moses: When Harriet Tubman Led Her People to Freedom*, 2006; *Birmingham, 1963*, 2007; *I, Matthew Henson*, 2007; *Voice of Freedom: Fannie Lou Hamer, Spirit of the Civil Rights Movement*, 2015; *You Can Fly: The Tuskegee Airmen*, 2016; *Freedom in Congo Square*, 2016

—Mari Rich

Pete Wells
Date of birth: ca. 1964
Occupation: Restaurant critic

Pete Wells cares deeply about food, but his approach to dining is perhaps not what one might expect from the restaurant critic for the *New York Times*. Since beginning his tenure with the *New York Times* in 2011, Wells has often challenged prevailing notions of what makes a restaurant good, including the long-established tenets of fine dining. "I don't like pretension in any form, but I do like old-fashioned things when they're done really well," he told Isaac Chotiner for *Slate* (21 Jan. 2016). "I just think that restaurants that are trying to follow the very traditional and formal modes of service really have to know what they're doing, and they have to do it with conviction, or it seems fake, and when it seems fake, it's not pleasurable."

Wells has attracted attention from both within and beyond the culinary industry with a number of reviews that went viral. In 2012, he visited celebrity chef Guy Fieri's Times Square restaurant, Guy's American Kitchen & Bar, and subsequently composed a scathing yet humorous review that was widely read and discussed. He has not shied away from criticizing popular fine-dining establishments as well: in early 2016, he demoted chef Thomas Keller's acclaimed Per Se from four stars to two, noting that the restaurant no longer met the high standards it had previously set for itself. For the most part, however, Wells's reviews are intended to educate prospective diners rather than make waves. "Above the simple recommendation, I generally try to put a place into context. If it's a less familiar cuisine I try to put in some background about what this kind of food is," he explained to W. Blake Gray for the *Gray Report* (19 Jan. 2016). "The restaurant column goes beyond the simple consumer service approach. I try to make sense of what the place is up to. Separately, I look at how well they deliver on what they try to do."

EARLY LIFE AND EDUCATION

Peter Andrew Wells grew up in the suburbs of Providence, Rhode Island. His father, Raymond, was an electrical engineer who worked for the New England Electrical System, while his mother, Shirley, was a nurse who later served as executive director of an assisted living community. Wells was adopted when he was a baby, and he began to research his biological parents later in life; however, they did not play a role in his upbringing.

Wells attended Cumberland High School in northeastern Rhode Island. As a teenager, he was active in the school's theater program. After graduating, he went on to enroll in the University of Pennsylvania, where he studied history. He earned his bachelor's degree from the university in 1985.

By the time he was in college, Wells was already demonstrating the strong interest in food that would shape the development of his career. For a time, he reportedly lived off campus in a house known as Beulah's Supper Club, which he shared with fellow food aficionados Betsy Andrews, who later served as executive editor of the cooking magazine *Saveur*, and Lisa Futterman, a future food writer and cheese monger. During that period, Wells is said to have learned to cook and enjoyed many of Philadelphia's signature foods.

EARLY CAREER

After graduating from the University of Pennsylvania, Wells began a career in journalism, beginning as a fact checker for publications such as the *New Yorker*. He later moved to the *New Yorker*'s public relations department. In 1999, he became an editor for *Food & Wine* magazine, for which he wrote the column Always Hungry. He remained at *Food & Wine* until 2001, when he left to become an articles editor for *Details*, a

men's fashion and lifestyle magazine. Wells spent five years with the publication, leaving *Details* in 2006. During his time at *Details*, Wells won five James Beard Foundation Awards for his writing, including articles published in *Food & Wine*, for which he remained a contributing editor.

In 2006, Wells moved to the publication that would bring him the greatest recognition yet. As dining editor for the *New York Times*, he proved himself again to be a dedicated food writer, and he demonstrated his strengths as a critic as well when he briefly filled a vacancy in the restaurant critic position. In addition to overseeing the dining section, Wells at times answered reader questions as part of the newspaper's Talk to the Newsroom column.

RESTAURANT CRITIC

In September 2011, *New York Times* restaurant critic Sam Sifton left the position to become a national editor for the newspaper. Seeking a replacement, the *Times* promoted Wells to the role, hiring editor Susan Edgerley to replace him as the editor of the dining section. Wells officially began his tenure as restaurant critic in January 2012.

The position of *Times* restaurant critic originated in 1962, when food editor Craig Claiborne began to print regular restaurant recommendations based on the merits of the restaurants. The following year, he introduced a four-star system that has remained in place for decades. Unlike many star rating systems, in which one star indicates a poor rating, the *Times* system considers one star to be good. All restaurants considered poor to satisfactory receive no stars, and a rating of two stars, though considered mediocre in many ratings systems, can have a dramatically beneficial effect on a new restaurant when awarded by the *Times*.

Over the years, the position of *Times* restaurant reviewer has been held by a number of luminaries in the field, including critics Gael Greene and Ruth Reichl. Wells became the twelfth critic to hold the position, which brought with it a significant platform but also substantial scrutiny. In his new role, Wells sought to continue the longstanding tradition of which he was now a part while also reflecting the realities of dining in twenty-first-century New York.

REVIEW PROCESS

Throughout his years as critic, Wells developed a review process that built upon the traditional procedures established by previous *Times* critics. Traditionally, a reviewer visits a restaurant at least three times to get a full idea of its offerings and quality. Wells frequently visits restaurants with groups of friends so that they can order multiple items, with the goal of evaluating more menu options than a lone reviewer could.

At times, if Wells is unable to visit three times or chooses not to, he writes a less detailed piece that is not considered a full review.

Choosing which restaurants to visit is of particular importance, as Wells seeks to highlight lesser-known restaurants while also meeting the expectations of his readers. "Some [restaurants] get so much buzz they become more or less mandatory," he explained to Susan Lehman for the *New York Times* (16 Feb. 2015). "You hear about them so often that you want to know what they're like." However, he tries to balance such reviews with less expected ones. "I'll look for something a little unusual, like a neighborhood that isn't really on the foodie radar, or a cuisine that hasn't reached market saturation yet, or an idea that just sounds novel," he told Lehman.

For Wells, the work of a restaurant critic varies significantly from that of other varieties of critics, in large part because of the wide range of prices and quality inherent to the restaurant industry. "All movies cost the same, and all books are in the same range, and that's not true for restaurants," he told Chotiner. "Movie critics in particular generally review everything that's in wide release. So, they review the schlock, even if the critics would rather not spend their time in that theater. If I do schlock, it's because I think it's interesting schlock."

VIRAL REVIEWS

Although Wells's restaurant reviews were regularly read by devoted fans of the *Times* and its dining section as well as many seeking restaurant recommendations in New York, he gained widespread attention as a reviewer when several of his reviews went viral. Perhaps the most significant of those was his 2012 review of Guy's American Kitchen & Bar, a restaurant in Times Square that was owned by celebrity chef and Food Network star Guy Fieri, who was best known as the host of shows such as *Diners, Drive-Ins, and Dives*. In accordance with his typical process, Wells visited the restaurant several times prior to writing his review. As the published review suggested, he did not enjoy his meals there. In his scathing review of the restaurant, published in November 2012, As Not Seen on TV, Wells asks Fieri a series of questions, from "Is the entire restaurant a very expensive piece of conceptual art?" to "Why did the toasted marshmallow taste like fish?" Quickly reaching far beyond Wells's usual readership, that review of Guy's American Kitchen & Bar soon became the fifth most e-mailed *Times* article of 2012.

After Wells's review went viral, some commentators questioned why Wells had visited the restaurant in the first place. Wells, however, noted that his visits to the restaurant were, in fact, warranted. "The *New York Times* is published right off Times Square. Hence the name. Do you think we sit at our desks at lunchtime every day, holding our noses in the air because we're too good to go outside in search of a meal? We do not," he wrote for the *New York Times* (3 Dec. 2012) in response to a reader question. "We eat in the neighborhood pretty often. So do the editors at Condé Nast and the lawyers at Proskauer Rose and a lot of other people. A few tourists get hungry in that neighborhood, too. Those people deserve better than most of the food I was served at Guy's American Kitchen & Bar."

Wells again sparked significant discussion in early 2016, when he reviewed Per Se, a fine-dining restaurant opened by acclaimed chef Thomas Keller in 2004. Although the restaurant, one of the most expensive in the world, had previously received four stars from the *Times*, Wells found that it no longer measured up to its previous quality. He rated the restaurant only two stars, a rating that could dramatically improve the outlook of a new restaurant but, when given to a restaurant as established and expensive as Per Se, came as a shock to much of New York's culinary community. The review became the topic of much debate among New York's restaurateurs, critics, and diners, tying into ongoing discussions about the future of fine dining.

PERSONAL LIFE

Wells met his wife, novelist Susan Choi, while working for the *New Yorker*. They have two sons and live in Brooklyn, New York. Although Wells eats many of his meals at the restaurants he is reviewing, he enjoys snacking on Oreo cookies at home. "I find the Oreo and all of its imitators pretty hard to stay away from," he confessed to Chotiner. "I just think it's an amazing cookie."

SUGGESTED READING

Alexander, Kevin. "Finding Pete Wells: A Search for America's Most Dangerous Restaurant Critic." *Thrillist*, 6 Apr. 2016, www.thrillist.com/eat/nation/finding-pete-wells-a-search-for-americas-most-dangerous-restaurant-critic. Accessed 10 Nov. 2016.

Parker, Ian. "Pete Wells Has His Knives Out." *The New Yorker*, 12 Sept. 2016, www.newyorker.com/magazine/2016/09/12/pete-wells-the-new-york-times-restaurant-critic. Accessed 10 Nov. 2016.

Wells, Pete. "As Not Seen on TV." *The New York Times*, 13 Nov. 2012, www.nytimes.com/2012/11/14/dining/reviews/restaurant-review-guys-american-kitchen-bar-in-times-square.html. Accessed 10 Nov. 2016.

Wells, Pete. "A Conversation with Pete Wells." Interview by Isaac Chotiner. *Slate*, 21 Jan. 2016, www.slate.com/articles/arts/culturebox/2016/01/a_conversation_with_new_york_times_food_critic_pete_wells.html. Accessed 10 Nov. 2016.

Wells, Pete. "Pete Wells, Restaurant Critic, Answers Readers' Questions." *The New York Times*, 3 Dec. 2012, www.nytimes.com/2012/12/03/dining/questions-for-pete-wells-restaurant-critic.html. Accessed 10 Nov. 2016.

Wells, Pete. "Restaurant Critic Pete Wells on How He Does His Job." Interview by Susan Lehman. *The New York Times*, 16 Feb. 2015, hwww.nytimes.com/times-insider/2015/02/16/restaurant-critic-pete-wells-on-how-he-does-his-job. Accessed 10 Nov. 2016.

—*Joy Crelin*

Andrew Toth/Getty Images

Elaine Welteroth

Date of birth: December 10, 1986
Occupation: Editor in chief, *Teen Vogue*

Elaine Welteroth made history in the spring of 2016 when she was named editor in chief of the magazine *Teen Vogue*. The second editor to head the magazine since its debut in 2004, Welteroth was likewise only the second African American to serve as editor in chief of a Condé Nast publication and, at twenty-nine years old, the youngest person to do so. Although as editor in chief, Welteroth would be responsible for overseeing all areas of the magazine's editorial operations, the role was in many ways a continuation of her previous work as the magazine's beauty and health director. "I was hired to bring a fresh perspective on beauty for teens who love fashion," she told Kerry Folan for *Racked* (22 May 2013) of her earlier role. "It's a very specific reader, not just because she's young, but because of her sensibilities. Our reader has upscale taste, she's in the know, and her obsession with beauty really ties back to this budding love affair with fashion."

As an editor who brought both significant experience working for magazines such as *Ebony* and *Glamour* and her own millennial perspective to the table, Welteroth was perhaps the ideal person to lead *Teen Vogue* further in its ongoing transition from a publication focusing primarily on fashion and oriented toward readers from a limited range of demographics to a more socially conscious magazine that values diversity both on and off its pages. Under her leadership, *Teen Vogue* has expanded its coverage of politics and current events while also highlighting a broad range of fashion insiders, trends, and viewpoints. Ultimately, the magazine seeks to reach a readership that is far more politically and socially aware than ever before and for whom fashion and beauty play a valuable role in self-expression—a mission for which Welteroth is particularly well suited. "I think you've got to be able to relate to what teens are going through," Welteroth explained to Folan. "I joke that I've always had this sort of insatiable 'big sis' complex—which is odd given that I am the baby of the family with no sisters! It's the reason I have such a powerful desire to connect with girls and encourage them. So, it's a natural fit for me to have a job that's like the editorial version of an older sister to a million girls."

EARLY LIFE AND EDUCATION

Welteroth was born on December 10, 1986. She grew up in Newark, California, a city in the southernmost region of northern California's Bay Area. Welteroth attended Newark Memorial High School, where she participated in track and field. She graduated from Newark Memorial High in 2004.

After high school, Welteroth enrolled in California State University, Sacramento, where she studied communication studies and minored in journalism. While in college, she completed internships in marketing and communications, serving as an account management intern for the New York–based advertising agency Ogilvy and Mather. In addition to those positions, Welteroth began to establish herself as a journalist during her college years, contributing articles to publications such as *Figure* magazine and the *State Hornet* student newspaper. Welteroth earned her bachelor's degree from California State University in the winter of 2007.

EARLY CAREER

After graduating from college, Welteroth first found work as a content producer for the entertainment company SomaGirls.TV, based in the Bay Area. In that role, she discovered that she both enjoyed and excelled at writing about fashion and beauty. She remained with SomaGirls. TV into 2008. In the summer of that year, she relocated to New York to join the staff of *Ebony* magazine. Welteroth first joined the influential magazine as an unpaid intern, having previously worked in a restaurant for several months in order to save the money necessary to pay for her living expenses. She was soon hired on as *Ebony*'s beauty and style editor.

Welteroth spent several years at *Ebony* before her departure in the fall of 2011. At that time, she joined *Glamour* magazine, published by the media powerhouse Condé Nast, as a beauty writer and editor. Welteroth was successful in that role, and she was later promoted to senior beauty editor.

TEEN VOGUE

In October 2012, Welteroth switched publications yet again, this time remaining under the Condé Nast banner as she joined the magazine *Teen Vogue*. A spin-off of the long-running fashion magazine *Vogue*, *Teen Vogue* was founded in 2004 to provide a youth-oriented take on the fashion and lifestyle topics typically featured in *Vogue*. At the time of Welteroth's hiring, the magazine's editorial operations remained under the direction of Amy Astley, who had served as the magazine's editor in chief since its first publication. *Teen Vogue*'s various departments were the responsibility of a number of different editors, and Welteroth assumed the role of beauty and health director for the publication.

While serving as beauty and health director, Welteroth was responsible not only for overseeing content production in those topic areas but also for keeping up with industry trends and key influencers. Among the many industry events relevant to her work was New York Fashion Week, a high-profile extravaganza of fashion shows, parties, and other events of interest to any fashion publication. For Welteroth, Fashion Week presented the opportunity to identify new products of interest as well as models whose personalities and looks would resonate with *Teen Vogue*'s readers. "When I'm backstage, I'm looking for that extra sort of 'It' factor—someone who's really comfortable in her skin and who has something to say [or] offer even if it's a cool element of their look," she explained to Gemma Kim for *Fashionista* (16 Feb. 2016). "They're not just clones of each other, which is sometimes how they appear on the runway." While Welteroth enjoyed her work, which allowed her to express her long-standing interest in health- and

beauty-related topics, she likewise remained aware of her ultimate responsibility to *Teen Vogue*'s young readership. "It's fun to sniff and slather on beauty products, but the end goal is finding what appeals most to *Teen Vogue* readers and reporting on it in the most compelling way," she wrote for a *Teen Vogue* article documenting a day in her life.

EDITOR IN CHIEF

In May 2016, Condé Nast announced that Astley, *Teen Vogue*'s editor in chief, was leaving the magazine to become editor of *Architectural Digest*. Welteroth was named as Astley's replacement and was tasked with running the magazine's editorial operations in conjunction with digital editorial director Phillip Picardi and creative director Marie Suter. The decision to promote Welteroth, who was twenty-nine years old at the time, reaffirmed *Teen Vogue*'s youth-oriented focus, and many observers in the fashion industry saw Welteroth's ascension to the role as a step forward for diversity in magazine publishing, as she became only the second African American to hold the position of editor in chief for a Condé Nast publication.

Under Welteroth's leadership, *Teen Vogue* continued to document trends in fashion and beauty as well as to highlight the designers, cosmetics creators, models, and fashion and beauty influences who play key roles in the industry. At the same time, the magazine has sought to explore other topics of interest to its teenage readers, including politics, current events, and social justice issues. This shift in editorial focus is in keeping with the shifting attitudes and priorities among *Teen Vogue*'s readers. "We're not speaking to [the reader] in the way we were speaking to her thirteen years ago, [because] the world has changed a ton," Welteroth explained to Lauren Sherman for the *Business of Fashion* (4 Aug. 2016). "Our whole goal is to evolve with her . . . . Certainly, we're a fashion magazine still, but we're also so much more than that."

PRINT VS. DIGITAL

In addition to its evolving audience and editorial mission, one of the primary challenges facing *Teen Vogue*, both prior to and during Welteroth's tenure as editor in chief, was the decline in print magazine sales. The popularity of print media declined significantly in the first decades of the twenty-first century, a trend that manifested in dramatic decreases in magazine subscriptions. In light of such trends, *Teen Vogue*, like many other magazines, sought to explore options for digital publishing. In addition to publishing articles on its website, *Teen Vogue* maintains an active presence on social media and has likewise explored digital avenues that are popular with teens, such as Instagram and Snapchat.

Although Welteroth, herself an avid user of social media, is a supporter of such new-media efforts, she remains confident that the print edition of *Teen Vogue* still has an important role to play in an increasingly digital world, in part because of its ability to present more fleshed-out, complex articles than the content available online, which is often shorter and based more on current events or celebrities. "Our readers are in high school and college [and] fashion week doesn't have a lot to do with their real lives. There has to be a real world connection for them, [so] a lot of the [online] content will be inspired by a familiar face like [models] Kendall Jenner or Gigi Hadid," she explained to Kim. "Whereas in [print], you have the time to reflect and think about what could come together as a really special piece in book." In November 2016, *Teen Vogue* announced that it would shift to a quarterly publication schedule for the print edition, which would be printed in a larger size and take on more collectible qualities.

PERSONAL LIFE

As Welteroth's career trajectory might suggest, she has a deep interest in fashion and believes that fashion and beauty are key to personal expression. "I truly believe that getting dressed in the morning is about deciding who you want to be, what you're saying in the world, and how you want people to see you," she told *BET* (14 July 2016). "It's so much more than superficial. I feel like people in fashion get a bad rep sometimes, but fashion is truly an art form and a means of self-expression. It's a way of commanding respect and constructing an image that you're proud of."

Welteroth lives in the West Village neighborhood of New York City.

SUGGESTED READING

Sherman, Lauren. "Inside the New *Teen Vogue*." *Business of Fashion*, 4 Aug. 2016, www.businessoffashion.com/articles/intelligence/new-teen-vogue-millenials-generation-z-anna-wintour. Accessed 15 Dec. 2016.

Welteroth, Elaine. "24 Hours with: *Teen Vogue's* Beauty and Health Director Elaine Welteroth." *Teen Vogue*, www.teenvogue.com/gallery/day-in-the-life-of-a-beauty-editor. Accessed 15 Dec. 2016.

Welteroth, Elaine. "Interview: 'Teen Vogue' Editor Elaine Welteroth Talks Favorite Denim Looks and Style Alter-Egos." Interview by Shiona Turini. *BET*, 14 July 2016, www.bet.com/shows/how-to-rock/denim/interviews/teen-vogue-elaine-welteroth.html. Accessed 15 Dec. 2016.

Welteroth, Elaine. "*Teen Vogue's* First African American Beauty Director Elaine Welteroth on Diversity." Interview by Kerry Folan. *Racked*, 22 May 2013, www.racked.com/2013/5/22/7669359/teen-vogues-first-african-american-beauty-director-elaine-welteroth. Accessed 15 Dec. 2016.

Welteroth, Elaine. "What Fashion Week Is Like for Elaine Welteroth, Beauty and Health Director of 'Teen Vogue.'" Interview by Gemma Kim. *Fashionista*, 16 Feb. 2016, fashionista.com/2016/02/elaine-welteroth. Accessed 15 Dec. 2016.

—*Joy Crelin*

Danny Willett

Date of birth: October 3, 1987
Occupation: Golfer

Although the title of "overnight success" might seem to fit professional golfer Danny Willett, it does not tell the full story. The English golfer's 2016 win at the Masters Tournament, one of the four major tournaments in professional golf, surprised onlookers, many of whom favored defending champion Jordan Spieth, and brought Willett real international attention for the first time in his career. However, as he would be quick to point out, his win was in fact the culmination of many years of effort. "People see a good result and say 'this could be the making of him' but they don't realize the work you've put in over the last fourteen years," he explained to *Today's Golfer* (18 Mar. 2015). "People call you an overnight success because you've won, but actually it's taken over a decade and a hell of a lot of hard work."

Having learned to play golf as a child, Willett quickly demonstrated a gift for the sport and worked to improve his skills throughout his teen years. He spent two years playing college golf in the United States before moving first into amateur golf and then into professional competition in 2009. It was only after seven years in the field, during which time he won minor tournaments but none of the sport's most notable ones, that he secured his Masters win at Georgia's Augusta National Golf Club. Although pleased to have won his first major tournament, Willett remained focused on continual self-improvement. "Winning the Masters was unbelievable," he told Nick Westby for the *Yorkshire Post* (10 Dec. 2016). "But then a few weeks later, you're back out there trying to get better."

EARLY LIFE AND EDUCATION

Daniel John Willett was born on October 3, 1987, in Sheffield, England. His father, Steve, was a vicar, and his mother, Elisabet, worked as a math teacher. As a child, Willett attended City

such as the Yorkshire Amateur Championship and the South of England Amateur Championship. In 2007, he claimed first place at the English Amateur championships, held at the prestigious Royal St. George's Gold Club in southeastern England. He would later return to that course in 2011 for that year's Open Championship. By 2008 he ranked as the number-one amateur in all of Europe.

Although Willett proved successful as an amateur golfer, the idea of going pro was a daunting one. "England's got a fantastic amateur golfing body, but we don't integrate it into professional ranks as well as other countries do which is why you get the gaps," he told *Today's Golfer*. "It takes a few years to adjust, regardless of how good your game is or how mature you are mentally." To demonstrate his readiness for professional competition, Willett competed in the European Tour Qualifying School, or q-school, a three-stage competition that grants the top twenty-five players the right to play on the professional-level European Tour. Willett placed fourth in the 2008 q-school, earning the right to begin playing on the European Tour in 2009.

PROFESSIONAL GOLF

Entering the European professional golf circuit, Willett had a relatively slow start in 2009, ranking fifty-eighth by the end of the season. Over the following years, however, he began to find success on the European Tour, earning his first second-place finish in a tour event in 2010. He reached a particularly exciting milestone in 2012, when he secured his first victory on the European Tour with a win at the BMW International Open. He went on to win additional tournaments such as the Nedbank Golf Challenge and the Omega European Masters in 2014 and 2015, respectively. Although Willett's victories were relatively infrequent, he noted that the mere experience of competing alongside more successful players contributed greatly to his own improvement as a golfer. "The more you play with great players, the more you realize that a) you're a great player yourself and b) that you can take things from what they do and how they cope under pressure," he explained to Westby.

Among the highest-pressure events on Willett's annual tour schedule were the competitions known as the majors, the four most important events in golf. Key events in both the European Tour and the US–focused PGA Tour, the majors include the Masters Tournament, the US Open, the Open Championship (also known as the British Open), and the PGA Championship. Willet made his first appearance in the PGA Championship in 2010 but did not make it past the cutoff point that determines which players may compete in the final rounds of the

School in Sheffield and enjoyed playing sports such as soccer. He developed an interest in golf early in life, in part due to the competitive nature of his relationship with his three brothers. "I had to find some sport that I could beat them in," he told Derek Lawrenson for the *Daily Mail* (24 Jan. 2015). "It's funny when golf gets its hooks into you. I would practice for hours on my own. It takes over your childhood." In addition to playing golf on a sheep field while vacationing with his family in Wales, Willett began to practice his sport frequently at his local course, soon distinguishing himself as a talented young player.

When Willett was sixteen, he left school to focus on playing golf full time. He competed in a variety of amateur competitions in his late teens and went on to travel to the United States, where he enrolled in Alabama's Jacksonville State University to play college golf in 2005. The experience required some adjustments from Willett, who was unaccustomed to the intensely competitive nature of college sports in the United States. "Every single college sport, not just golf, is so competitive over there," he told the *Star* (7 Aug. 2007). "I'm learning how to win. It's teaching me how to come down that final stretch and win, whatever the opposition." Willet ultimately left Jacksonville State University after two years.

EARLY CAREER

As a teenager and young adult, Willett made numerous strong showings on the amateur golf circuit. He was named the Ohio Valley Conference freshman of the year in 2006, and over the following years he performed well in competitions competition. His appearance in the 2011 Open Championship had a similar outcome.

In 2013, however, Willett made it past the cutoff point at both the PGA Championship and the Open Championship, tying for fortieth and fifteenth places, respectively. He competed in all four majors in 2015 and performed even better, tying for sixth place in the Open Championship. For Willett, the 2015 Open Championship proved that a majors victory could one day be achievable. "Playing with [American golfer] Zach Johnson in the final round, who went on to win it, was massive," he told Westby, adding that the experience helped him realize "you've not got to be super-human to win a major."

SUCCESS AT THE MASTERS

Although Willett made frequent appearances in all four majors during his professional career, his real breakthrough success came at the Masters Tournament. Held in April each year at the Augusta National Golf Club in Augusta, Georgia, the Masters consists of four rounds of play, each with eighteen holes. Willett was first invited to the 2015 Masters, having performed well enough in competition in 2014 to rank among the top fifty players worldwide and thus gain eligibility. Upon receiving his invitation to the prestigious tournament, Willett was thrilled by the opportunity ahead of him. "I knew I'd made it to Augusta by what I'd done at the end of last year but there's still nothing like holding the official invitation," he told Lawrenson. "It just feels awesome to be setting out on a new season knowing you can plan your early year schedule around a trip to Augusta." Willett ultimately tied for thirty-eighth place at the tournament, which was won by American golfer Jordan Spieth.

At the end of 2015, Willett was invited to compete in the Masters a second time. Returning to Augusta in 2016, he joined a competitive tournament that featured numerous talented players, including defending champion Spieth. Despite early indications that Spieth might claim a second consecutive victory, Willett unexpectedly overcame the previous champion in the final round to claim first place. "It is unbelievable. There is nothing that can compare to that feeling down the stretch in a major and, in my case, shooting 67 to get it done," he told Ewan Murray for the *Guardian* (32 Mar. 2017). "It is a great source of inspiration."

In addition to being Willett's first major win, his victory at the Masters marked the first time in twenty years that an English player had won the competition. In recognition of his win, Willett was awarded $1.8 million in prize money as well as a lifetime invitation to compete in the tournament and a five-year guaranteed invitation to the other three majors. In addition, he was catapulted to a new level of international recognition and media attention. He rose to an official ranking of ninth in the world and accepted a spot on the PGA Tour.

CONTROVERSY AND SETBACKS

Although Willett's victory at the Masters started his 2016 season off on a high note, the golfer struggled to remain on that level during the remainder of the year. He achieved a second-place finish at the Italian Open and a third-place finish at the BMW PGA Championship, but otherwise he did not place in the top ten during any other European Tour competitions. In addition, Willett became the center of controversy after his brother Pete wrote an article for the *National Club Golfer* (27 Sept. 2016), in which he insulted American golf fans during the lead-up to the 2016 Ryder Cup, a competition between American and European teams of golfers. Willett faced heckling during his matches and ultimately performed poorly, losing the three matches in which he played.

The 2017 season was similarly difficult for Willett, who achieved a fifth-place finish in February's Maybank Championship but did not place higher than thirty-ninth in the subsequent nine matches on the European Tour. During his return to the Masters, he played in the first rounds of the competition but did not meet the cutoff to advance to the final rounds. He similarly missed the cut at the PGA Championship and in June 2017 withdrew from the US Open before the start of the second round due to a back injury.

In August of that year, Willett announced that he would be taking some time off from competition to work on his skills, address his recurring back pain, and reevaluate his overall approach to his sport. "It might need a drastic change," he told Lawrenson for the *Daily Mail* (7 Aug. 2017). 'Swing-wise, everything—I'm going to have a proper think. I don't want to make rash decisions but quite clearly it can't go on any longer like this." Although he lost his PGA Tour eligibility for the 2018 season, Willett noted in interviews that he considered the break from competition necessary for his career and also looked forward to spending more time with his family. In addition to the time off, Willett ended his relationship with coach Pete Cowen and began working with Sean Foley, who had previously coached golf legend Tiger Woods.

PERSONAL LIFE

Willett and his wife, Nicole, married in 2013. Their first child, Zachariah, was born only days before Willett's 2016 win at the Masters, nearly causing him to miss the tournament. Willett's other interests include soccer, pool, and snooker, and he is an avid reader. "I always read books about people who are fantastically amazing at what they do, but drive themselves mental with trying to perfect in every way in their sport," he told Adam Shergold for the *Daily Mail* (11 Apr. 2016).

SUGGESTED READING

Lawrenson, Derek. "Danny Willett Plans Time Out to Search for His Lost Mojo after Dismal Run for Masters Champion." *The Daily Mail*, 7 Aug. 2017, www.dailymail.co.uk/sport/golf/article-4769476/amp/Danny-Willett-plans-time-search-lost-mojo.html. Accessed 11 Aug. 2017.

Lawrenson, Derek. "Rising Star Danny Willett Looks to Lead England's New Wave after Masters Invite." *The Daily Mail*, 24 Jan. 2015, www.dailymail.co.uk/sport/golf/article-2924888/Rising-star-Danny-Willett-looks-lead-Englands-new-wave-Masters-invite.html. Accessed 11 Aug. 2017.

Murray, Ewan. "Danny Willett: 'There Have Been Massive Highs but Some Pretty Low Lows." *The Guardian*, 31 Mar. 2017, amp.theguardian.com/sport/2017/mar/31/danny-willett-masters-golf-augusta-interview. Accessed 11 Aug. 2017.

"The Rookie: Danny Willett." *Today's Golfer*, 18 Mar. 2015, www.todaysgolfer.co.uk/news-and-events/tour-features/the-masters-2015/interviews/the-rookie-danny-willett. Accessed 11 Aug. 2017.

Shergold, Adam. "Masters Champion Danny Willett Is the Son of a Vicar from Sheffield Who Honed Skills in a Sheep Field, Is Inspired by Rocky and Nearly Missed Augusta Due to Son's Birth." *The Daily Mail*, 11 Apr. 2016, www.dailymail.co.uk/sport/sportsnews/article-3533582/Masters-champion-Danny-Willett-son-vicar-Sheffield-honed-skills-sheep-field-inspired-Rocky-missed-Augusta-baby-son-due.html. Accessed 11 Aug. 2017.

Westby, Nick. "Saturday Interview: Masters Champion Danny Willett Now Coping with His Major Shift." *Yorkshire Post*, 10 Dec. 2016, www.yorkshirepost.co.uk/sport/golf/saturday-interview-masters-champion-danny-willett-now-coping-with-his-major-shift-1-8283365. Accessed 11 Aug. 2017.

"Willett Learning How to Acquire Winning Habit." *The Star*, 8 Aug. 2007, www.thestar.co.uk/sport/willett-learning-how-to-aquire-winning-habit-1-359748. Accessed 11 Aug. 2017.

—*Joy Crelin*

Maisie Williams

Date of birth: April 15, 1997
Occupation: Actor

Few actors' first roles bring them worldwide fame, but British actor Maisie Williams is undoubtedly one of those few. Then an unknown performer who had never acted on camera, she impressed the casting team for the HBO series *Game of Thrones* during her auditions in 2009, ultimately winning the role of young Arya Stark. Portraying a fan favorite character from the *A Song of Ice and Fire* novels on which *Game of Thrones* is based, Williams had a built-in fan base from the moment the series premiered in 2011, as well as an exciting journey ahead of her character. "I'm so grateful that the first job I ever landed taught me to never take a role that was 'less,'" she told Leila Brillson for *Nylon* (15 Apr. 2016) of her work on the series. "I've had the opportunity to play a lot of actors' dream role—I don't want to ever settle."

Over the course of *Game of Thrones*' run, Williams has established herself as a talented actor and impressed critics with her performance, earning an Emmy Award nomination in 2016 for her work. In addition to the series, she has appeared in a number of television shows and films, including the British science-fiction series *Doctor Who* and the 2016 drama *The Book of Love*. Although she once worried that her career as an actor could not possibly last, the critical acclaim she has received for *Game of Thrones* and the many other opportunities that have

Gage Skidmore from Peoria, AZ, United States of America /CC BY-SA 2.0/Wikimedia Commons

presented themselves suggest otherwise. "Now all of a sudden I feel like I've got a bit of a hold of my career," she told Alex Clark for the *Evening Standard* (20 Aug. 2015). "Now I'm like, actually I don't have to worry about that any more, I should actually look to the future, and look at what I'm going to do next. Rather than thinking that I'll make the most of this because it's gonna end, I've realized, no, I'm going to make sure this continues . . . *forever.*"

EARLY LIFE AND EDUCATION

Margaret Constance Williams was born in Bristol, England, on April 15, 1997. Known as Maisie since early childhood, she is the youngest of four siblings. Following her parents' divorce, Williams lived with her mother, Hilary, a university administrator who eventually left her job to serve as Williams's assistant. Williams's mother later remarried.

Williams developed an interest in performing at a young age. "I always wanted to make people laugh," she told Clark. "I was so much more confident making a dick out of myself, basically. When I was little I didn't care about that, I had no reservations. I loved to do funny accents and make my mum, my stepdad and brothers and sisters laugh." Despite her apparent talent, Williams had no interest in acting or taking drama classes and instead focused on dance lessons. While performing at a showcase, Williams was spotted by an agent, who signed the young performer and convinced her to begin acting.

As a child, Williams attended Clutton Primary School and Norton Hill School. She later enrolled in Bath Dance College, a performing arts school in southern England. She left school when she was fourteen to pursue acting full time and studied with tutors until two years later.

GAME OF THRONES

In 2009, the production team of the in-development HBO show *Game of Thrones* was seeking to cast many of the series' principal cast members. Although many of the adult roles went to established actors, the casting team was prepared to cast lesser-known or even unknown actors in the show's child roles. Based on award-winning fantasy writer George R. R. Martin's popular series *A Song of Ice and Fire, Game of Thrones* is set on the continent of Westeros, a region characterized by decade-long seasons, hidden magic, and frequent political upheaval. Although very much an ensemble show, the series focuses significantly on the members of the Stark family, who are thrown into various forms of political, military, and magical conflict over the course of the show's run. As the younger Stark children were among the most popular characters from the novels, the casting team knew that they had their work

cut out for them when it came time to fill those roles on-screen.

After a series of auditions, Williams landed the part of Arya Stark, one of the family's middle children and a particularly popular character in the novels. Although excited about the role, she was unaware of how popular *Game of Thrones* would truly become and was more focused on how it might affect her day-to-day life. She was "really obsessed" about buying her own laptop computer, she recalled to Sarah Hughes for *The Guardian* (22 Apr. 2016). "My stepdad, Gary, just looked at me and said: 'I think there'll be enough for a couple of laptops, Maisie.'" She added, "Suddenly I could pay for my own dancing lessons and school trips, all those things my mum had always paid for. I was able to help out."

After filming for a substantial period of time in locales such as Malta and Northern Ireland, *Game of Thrones* premiered on HBO in April of 2011. Viewers responded positively to the show and to Williams's portrayal of Arya, who quickly became a fan favorite even among viewers who had not read the original novels. "Arya is really popular with a lot of people because she's just a broadly funny character—witty, dry, ballsy, feminist," Williams explained to Brillson. The series was renewed for a second season only two days after its premiere, and it would continue for the next several years, with the sixth season starting in April 2016.

GROWING UP AS ARYA

Like many of *Game of Thrones*' central characters, Arya evolves greatly over the course of the series as the challenging circumstances in which she finds herself force her to hide her noble heritage, to learn to fight, to kill when necessary, to travel across her homeland and beyond, to train as an assassin, and more. Fans responded well to her growth as a character, often expressing their approval of Arya at surprising times. At the 2014 premiere of the fourth season's first episode, held at New York City's Lincoln Center, audience members broke into applause during a scene in which Arya kills a man who had previously murdered one of her friends. "It was crazy. And really embarrassing!" Williams recalled to Jennifer Vineyard for *Vulture* (6 Apr. 2014). "I just lit up so much, I buried my head. I'm glad people liked it, because something is finally starting to go right for Arya. She's finding what she's good at."

As is often the case for young celebrities, Williams sometimes struggled with growing up in the public eye, particularly when fans and the media were seemingly unable to distinguish her from the character she plays. She has noted in interviews that she was sometimes criticized for wearing skirts or makeup by people who failed to realize that she is several years older than Arya is in-show, and she was angered when a number of British newspapers criticized her family for allowing her to drop out of school. Nevertheless, Williams's experience playing Arya was largely positive, earning her significant praise on the part of critics as well as a nomination for the 2016 Emmy Award for outstanding supporting actor in a drama series.

In the summer of 2016, HBO confirmed that *Game of Thrones* would continue for at least two more abbreviated seasons. As the series had already moved past most of the events depicted in *A Song of Ice and Fire* novels published to that point, fans were left to await the next seasons anxiously, hoping to learn the fates of characters such as Arya.

NEW ROLES

Although Williams's primary commitment is to *Game of Thrones*, she has had the opportunity to take on a number of additional roles during breaks in filming. Having begun her career in television, she went on to appear in several additional programs, including the BBC One miniseries *The Secret of Crickley Hall*. In 2015, Williams guest-starred in four episodes of the long-running British science-fiction series *Doctor Who*, playing an immortal Viking who encounters the time-traveling protagonists at various points in history. Williams made her feature film debut with a part in the 2014 action movie *Heatstroke*. She followed that role with appearances in films such as 2014's *The Falling*, the 2015 television movie *Cyberbully*, and the 2016 drama *The Book of Love*.

Although Williams has found work in a variety of film and television projects, she has expressed frustration with the limited roles available for young women. "There are a lot of roles that come in that are 'the girlfriend' or 'the hot piece' in a movie or TV series," she told Clark. She continued, "That's the way your character is described, so going into an audition you are channeling 'hot,' which isn't like a person, that's not who a person is. That's what I see and that's what needs to change. I've been lucky enough to play a very great female character from a young age, who is a fantastic role model for girls."

PERSONAL LIFE

When not filming, Williams lives in Bath, England. Like many actors of her generation, she is an avid user of social media, and she has worked to present an authentic view of her personality and life both online and off. "Being perfect is a bit disheartening," she told Brillson. "Life's too short and I want to inspire people to have fun and not take life too seriously. And if that means I make mistakes and say the wrong thing, then so be it. That's kind of what being young and growing up is about. I'm learning like everyone else."

SUGGESTED READING

Brillson, Leila. "Maisie Williams Is Not Having Hollywood Nonsense." *Nylon*, 15 Apr. 2016, www.nylon.com/articles/maisie-williams-nylon-may-cover-star. Accessed 6 Jan. 2017.

Clark, Alex. "Maisie Williams Talks Resisting Stereotypical Roles as She Prepares to Take Hollywood by Storm." *EveningStandard*, 20 Aug. 2015, www.standard.co.uk/showbiz/celebrity-news/whats-driving-miss-maisie-a2917456.html. Accessed 6 Jan. 2017.

Hughes, Sarah. "*Game of Thrones*' Maisie Williams: It's Not All Fun and Games." *The Guardian*, 22 Apr. 2016, www.theguardian.com/tv-and-radio/2016/apr/22/game-of-thrones-maisie-williams-its-not-all-fun-and-games. Accessed 6 Jan. 2017.

Williams, Maisie. "'*Game of Thrones*' Maisie Williams on Arya's Hard Road, Dreamy Brad Pitt, and Why She'll Never Get Married." Interview by Jennifer Vineyard. *Vulture*, 6 Apr. 2014, www.vulture.com/2014/04/maisie-williams-arya-game-of-thrones-season-4-interview.html. Accessed 6 Jan. 2017.

Williams, Maisie. "'*Game of Thrones*': Maisie Williams: 'You Are Either a Normal Person or a Sexist.'" Interview by James Hibberd. *Entertainment Weekly*, 4 Apr. 2016, ew.com/article/2016/04/04/game-thrones-maisie-williams-interview-2. Accessed 6 Jan. 2017.

Williams, Maisie. "Maisie Williams on '*Game of Thrones*,' Blind Arya and Impatient Fans." Interview by Jeremy Egner. *New York Times*, 24 Apr. 2016, www.nytimes.com/2016/04/24/arts/television/hbo-game-of-thrones-arya-interview.html. Accessed 6 Jan. 2017.

Williams, Maisie. "Maisie Williams Knows Arya Stark Is a Force to Reckon With." Interview by Eleanor Laurence. *Making Game of Thrones*. HBO, 30 May 2016, www.makinggameofthrones.com/production-diary/606-interview-with-maisie-williams. Accessed 6 Jan. 2017.

SELECTED WORKS

Game of Thrones, 2011–; *The Secret of Crickley Hall*, 2012; *The Falling*, 2014; *Cyberbully*, 2015; *Doctor Who*, 2015; *The Book of Love*, 2016

—Joy Crelin

Martin Wolf

Date of birth: 1946
Occupation: Journalist

Martin Wolf is a British journalist, author, and the associate editor of the London *Financial Times*. One of the most influential economic reporters in the world, Wolf became an outspoken critic of the response to the financial meltdown in 2008.

EARLY LIFE AND EDUCATION

Martin Wolf was born in London in 1946. His father, Austrian playwright Edmund Wolf, saw most of his extended family die in the Holocaust, as did his mother, a Jewish refugee from Holland. The horror of the war made Wolf skeptical of political extremism and continues to inform his largely centrist views. In 1965 he enrolled at Corpus Christi College at Oxford University to study classics; he switched to politics, philosophy, and economics two years later. In 1966 he was involved in the formation of the school's Democratic Labour Club, and in 1967, he became its chairman.

In 1969 Wolf enrolled at Nuffield College, Oxford, where he received a master's degree in economics. In 1971 he got a job at the World Bank, which was then led by former defense secretary—and architect of the Vietnam War—Robert McNamara. McNamara advocated for lending large amounts of money to developing countries, but his antipoverty strategy resulted only in a massive debt crisis in the 1980s. Wolf worked in East Africa from 1972 to 1974, and in India between 1974 and 1977. In 1978 he was a team member on the first World Development Report. During his time with the World Bank, Wolf developed a more conservative, pro-trade view, and by the end of the 1970s, had grown disillusioned with the organization. Wolf believed that the bank relied too heavily on lending and that McNamara, while a man of great personal conviction, was woefully lacking in common sense. In the preface to his 2004 book *Why Globalization Works*, Wolf criticized the bank for its indiscriminate lending practices, lending to both governments that needed the help and those that were corrupt. He left in 1981, and joined the Trade Policy Research Centre, a think tank in London. He served as director of studies for six years, primarily focusing on the role of developing countries in global trade.

WRITING FOR THE *FINANCIAL TIMES*

By 1986 the Trade Policy Research Centre was nearing the end of its funds. Wolf began looking for a new job, and was offered a position as an editorial writer for the *Financial Times*. He had contributed to the newspaper a handful of times in the past, and in 1987 he joined the writing staff. He began writing his own weekly column on international economics in 1996. The *Financial Times* is an influential newspaper, and over the course of his long career, Wolf has established himself as one of its leading contributors. He is a notoriously didactic and dense writer, but he has been candid about his political evolution. Among the many reasons that Wolf

has garnered such tremendous respect among economists and policy makers is his intellectual honesty: he is willing to admit his own mistakes and, if need be, criticize the policies of his high-powered friends.

Throughout the late 1980s and 1990s, Wolf was a vocal proponent of financial liberalization, or the deregulation of markets, as espoused by politicians like British prime minister Margaret Thatcher. He believed, as he wrote in *Why Globalization Works*, that such policies would raise the standard of living across the globe. In his 2014 book *The Shifts and Shocks*, however, Wolf blames financial liberalization—and the related belief that rapid growth makes for a more stable system—for the financial crisis of 2008. The book, which provides an exhaustive analysis of the crisis itself, goes on to indict measures taken in its wake, and call for radical reforms. Six years after the recession, he writes, the global economy remains sluggish because policy makers have not taken bold enough action to repair—or overhaul—that which has been broken. Policy makers mistakenly pushed for austerity when they should have accepted larger fiscal deficits, Wolf writes. His proposals seek to reverse this blunder, though they remain largely theoretical.

IMPACT

Wolf has been described as the ultimate economic insider. His influence is so great that some of the most powerful people in the world vie for his approval. When US treasury secretary Timothy Geithner announced the details of the Public-Private Investment Program, a part of the financial bailout in 2009, he called Wolf to defend the reasoning behind it. Wolf heard Geithner's case, but brutally attacked the program the next day in his column. In recognition for his achievements as a financial journalist, Wolf was made a Commander of the British Empire (CBE) in 2000.

PERSONAL LIFE

Wolf is married to Alison Wolf, an influential author and professor at King's College London. They have three children.

SUGGESTED READING

"How to Fix a Broken System." Rev. of *The Shifts and Shocks*, by Martin Wolf. *Economist*. Economist Newspaper, 6 Sept. 2014. Web. 9 Sept. 2015.

Ioffe, Julia. "Call of the Wolf." *New Republic*. New Republic, 16 Sept. 2009. Web. 9 Sept. 2015.

Krugman, Paul. "Why Weren't Alarm Bells Ringing?" Rev. of *The Shifts and Shocks*, by Martin Wolf. *New York Review of Books*. NYREV, 23 Oct. 2014. Web. 9 Sept. 2015.

Salmon, Felix. "A Radical Response." Rev. of *The Shifts and Shocks*, by Martin Wolf. *New York Times*. New York Times, 25 Sept. 2014. Web. 9 Sept. 2015.

Toye, Richard. "What We've Learned from the Crash." Rev. of *The Shifts and Shocks*, by Martin Wolf. *Guardian*. Guardian News and Media, 2 Oct. 2014. Web. 9 Sept. 2015.

SELECTED WORKS

Why Globalization Works, 2004; *The Shifts and Shocks: What We've Learned—and Have Still to Learn—from the Financial Crisis*, 2014

—*Molly Hagan*

Kao Kalia Yang

Date of birth: December 17, 1980
Occupation: Writer

Kao Kalia Yang has mixed memoir, family history, and the history of the Hmong people of Southeast Asia to remarkable effect in her two books, *The Latehomecomer: A Hmong Family Memoir* (2008) and *The Song Poet: A Memoir of My Father* (2016). For the latter, she received the 2017 Minnesota Book Award in Creative Nonfiction/Memoir, and she was also a finalist for the highly prestigious PEN USA Literary Award in Nonfiction. Margaret Flanagan for *Booklist Online* (15 Mar. 2016) called *The Song Poet* a "hauntingly lyrical tribute to her beloved father," as well as a "memorable and moving immigrant story." Yang has managed to not only write engaging stories, both personal and historic, but also to inform her readers of the little-known history of the Hmong people.

NEW HOME IN MINNESOTA

Kao Kalia Yang's parents fled the ethnic cleansing of the Hmong people in Laos by crossing the border to the Ban Vinai refugee camp in Thailand, where Yang was born in December 1980. In 1987 her parents found out that they would have the opportunity to leave the camp for the United States. They learned basic English phrases and received some simple clothes to take with them, such as shoes, socks, sweaters, and collared shirts. The family moved to St. Paul, Minnesota, where they sought to begin a new life for themselves.

When she arrived in St. Paul, Yang had a very hard time with the English language, and with her family's immigrant status. In a 2011 interview with *Minnesota Public Radio*, she told the story of going to K-Mart with her mother as a child. Her mother wanted to buy some light bulbs, but didn't know the word for them in English. So, as Yang recounted, she asked for "the thing that made the world shiny." The clerk ignored her and walked away. In that moment, Yang recalled, "I decided if the world didn't need to hear my mom and dad, then surely it didn't need to hear me. So I stopped talking the next day." Not speaking, of course, did not help her spoken language skills. Her words became "rusty," she said. "When I tried to speak, kids laughed. So I stopped completely." Eventually, Yang turned to writing as an outlet, noting, "The words had to go somewhere. So they went onto the page. . . . On the page, I got more tries, so my voice grew strong, and it grew natural."

BECOMING A WRITER

Though Yang received some encouragement from teachers in high school, she really came into her own as a writer at Carleton College, in Northfield, Minnesota. Although she entered college expecting to one-day study medicine, a couple of events pointed her toward the less financially secure career path of a writer. During her junior year at Carleton she studied abroad in Thailand, in a program called "Global Development and the Rural Poor." Though she had grown up poor herself, in Thailand Yang experienced poverty of another scale, and then realized that if she could survive poverty—which she became sure she could—then she could become a writer. She told interviewer Annie Choi for Coffee House Press, "I became involved with writing like it is a love affair the moment I chose to leave safety behind (the promise of medical school and a career in 'helping' people)."

Yang's change of career path was also influenced by the death of her grandmother. "I did not want to forget my grandmother," Yang told Kerry Xiong for the *Hmong Times* (June 16, 2015). "[So] I wrote about her in one of my college classes." The professor assigned a five-page paper, but Yang turned in thirty pages. She said the professor told her, "I think we have something very special here." The roots of her first book were in that paper.

Yang graduated from Carleton College with a bachelor's degree in American studies, women's and gender studies, and cross-cultural studies. She then moved to New York City and completed a master of fine arts degree focused on creative nonfiction at Columbia University. She went on to cofound Words Wanted, a company offering writing and translating services to immigrants, before her own writing career launched.

THE LATEHOMECOMER

Yang's first book, *The Latehomecomer: A Hmong Family Memoir*, was published in 2008. It is the true story of the Yang family, but also of the Hmong people of the mountains of Laos, where they were recruited by the US Central

Intelligence Agency to fight in the Vietnam War. When the United States left Vietnam, however, in 1975, it did not offer any real help to most Hmong people, who were now the targets of an extermination campaign by the victorious Communists in both Vietnam and Laos. Some, like the Yang family, made it to Thailand, where they lived for years in refugee camps before coming to the United States in the late 1980s.

A major theme of *The Latehomecomer* is that of the search for a home—both her family's and her people's search. The Hmong had come to settle in Vietnam and Laos only in the eighteenth century, having been driven out of China, and they were in many ways, historically, a people without a country—just as, after the conflict in Southeast Asia, Yang's family was driven from country to country before settling in the United States. In the prologue to her book, Yang explains that growing up in the United States, she learned to answer the questions, "What is Hmong? Where is your country? What are you doing here, in America?" with, "Hmong is an ethnic minority. We don't have a country. We are here looking for a home." She told Choi that the title of the book comes from a German word that "was used to described the Jews who had returned late from the internment camps, back to homes that were no longer so. I saw the relevance of it to my work immediately." She said she regards people like her grandmother, as well as the Hmong people, as "latehomecomers."

The Latehomecomer did not make a big impact right away, but slowly the press coverage increased and the list of awards began to grow. A reviewer for *Publishers Weekly* wrote, "Yang tells her family's story with grace; she narrates their struggles, beautifully weaving in Hmong folklore and culture. By the end of this moving, unforgettable book, when Yang describes the death of her beloved grandmother, readers will delight at how intimately they have become part of this formerly strange culture." A reviewer for *Kirkus Reviews* (20 May 2008) had some reservations, calling the book an "uneven but inspiring memoir." The reviewer emphasized that Yang told a story of a people that really needed to be told, but that "the prose needs serious tightening and burnishing."

Accolades for *The Latehomecomer* continued for years after its publication: it received the 2008 Outstanding Book Award from the Gustavus Myers Center for the Study of Bigotry and Human Rights; the 2009 Skipping Stones Honor Award; the 2009 Minnesota Book Awards in Creative Nonfiction/Memoir and Readers' Choice; and the 2012 Jeannette Fair Memorial Award for Distinguished Writing. It was also a finalist for the 2010 PEN USA Award for Creative Nonfiction/Memoir.

THE SONG POET

In Yang's next book, *The Song Poet: A Memoir of My Father* (2016), published a full eight years after her first, she continued to explore her family history, specifically that of her father, Bee Yang, and his unique talent for Hmong poetry and song. In 1989, about two years after arriving in the United States, the Yang family was celebrating the Hmong New Year at an event in St. Paul. Yang was about eight years old at the time. There, for the first time, she saw her father take the stage, microphone in hand, and sing his song poems, addressing topics such as life, love, family, history, politics, and so on. Yang notes in *The Song Poet* that her father began composing these poems when he was twelve years old. He later wrote songs about the Hmong people's role in the Vietnam War, and how after the war the North Vietnamese soldiers searched for Hmong to capture and kill. A few years after his impromptu New Year's performance, in 1992, Yang's father released a six-song recording of his song poems, which circulated among the Hmong community in St. Paul.

In a review for the *Minneapolis Star Tribune* (8 May 2016), Kevin Canfield described *The Song Poet* as being about "art, resilience and the opportunities and indignities that come with life in a new country." Canfield praised Yang's "perfectly paced" chapters about her father's boyhood, and how he coped with his father's death by climbing trees. Other tales include how her father was forced to deliver opium to gun-carrying drug dealers while in the refugee camp in Thailand, and how, throughout the years, he lovingly cared for his wife. A reviewer for *Kirkus Reviews* (15 Feb. 2016) wrote, "Yang's evocative, often moving memoir, told from Bee's perspective, reveals a life of struggle, hardship, deep love, and strong family ties." The reviewer concluded by noting, "Yang's gentle prose captures her father's sufferings and joys and serves as a loving celebration of his spirit."

Yang received some very notable awards for *The Song Poet*, including the 2017 Minnesota Book Award in creative nonfiction/memoir, and she was again a finalist for the prestigious PEN USA Literary Award in nonfiction. The book was also a finalist for the 2017 National Book Critics Circle in biography and the Chautauqua Prize.

Yang has held teaching positions at American colleges and universities, including a visiting professorship at her alma mater, Carleton College, in 2016–17.

PERSONAL LIFE

She lives with her husband, Aaron Hokanson, and their three children, in St. Paul, Minnesota.

SUGGESTED READING

Canfield, Kevin. Review of *The Song Poet*, by Kao Kalia Yang. *Star Tribune*, 8 May 2016, www.startribune.com/review-the-song-poet-by-kao-kalia-yang/378330461/. Accessed 13 Sept. 2017.

"Kao Kalia Yang: 'I Grew on the Page.'" *Minnesota Public Radio*, 2011, minnesota.publicradio.org/projects/2011/writing-minnesota/kao-kalia-yang/. Accessed 13 Sept. 2017

Review of *The Song Poet*, by Kao Kalia Yang. *Kirkus Reviews*, 15 Feb. 2016, www.kirkusreviews.com/book-reviews/kao-kalia-yang/the-song-poet/. Accessed 13 Sept. 2017.

Xiong, Kerry. "How a Writer Became—An Interview with Hmong Writer Kao Kalia Yang." *Hmong Times Online*, 16 June 2015, www.hmongtimes.com/main.asp?SectionID=49&SubSectionID=218&ArticleID=5495&TM=50941. Accessed 13 Sept. 2017.

Yang, Kao Kalia. Interview. By Annie Choi. *Coffee House Press*, coffeehousepress.org/authors/kao-kalia-yang/. Accessed 13 Sept. 2017.

—*Michael Tillman*

Tu Youyou

Date of birth: December 30, 1930
Occupation: Chemist

Tu Youyou discovered the revolutionary antimalarial drug artemisinin using traditional Chinese medicine as inspiration. She shared the 2015 Nobel Prize in Physiology or Medicine for the global impact of her work.

EARLY LIFE AND EDUCATION

Tu Youyou was born on December 30, 1930, in the city of Ningbo, in Zhejiang province on the east coast. She was the only daughter among five children. Growing up, Tu attended two prestigious schools, Xiaoshi Middle School and Ningbo Middle School, to complete her secondary education. She entered Peking University School of Medicine (later renamed Beijing Medical College) in 1951 to pursue a graduate degree in pharmaceutical sciences, which she obtained four years later.

Still interested in medicine, Tu joined the Institute of Materia Medica to study traditional Chinese medicine. She has said that her decision to study traditional medicine was spurred mostly by one of her professors from Peking University, phytochemist Lin Qi Shou.

Tu never obtained a postgraduate degree because they simply were not available in China at the time. She also never studied or worked in any labs abroad, and she never joined any national academic societies. As a result, she has earned the nickname "The Professor with Three Nos," though this nontraditional academic path did not prevent her from making significant scientific and medical discoveries.

LIFE'S WORK

With her graduate studies in traditional Chinese medicine complete, Tu traveled to Beijing to begin work at the China Academy of Traditional Chinese Medicine. Her time there coincided with China's involvement in the Vietnam War and the Chinese Cultural Revolution. During these tumultuous times, North Vietnamese officials asked for help from their Chinese allies in finding ways to combat malaria, which plagued much of the globe except the far northern and southern regions. Malaria is a parasitic disease that is transmitted by mosquitoes and can result in death. The only preventative treatment at the time, chloroquine, was quickly becoming obsolete as the parasite responsible for the disease was becoming resistant to the medication.

As Malaria ravaged the North Vietnamese and Chinese troops, China's leader Mao Zedong created a top-secret project in response: Project 523, which began on May 23, 1967. The project's goal was to develop a new treatment for malaria, and Tu was put in charge of the effort. Meanwhile, similar efforts in the United States were unsuccessful. Tu used her training in traditional Chinese medicine to guide her research team and spent two years delving into ancient texts and compiling a list of some 380 solutions made from some 200 different herbs that appeared to have been used to treat malaria in the past. The herb known as sweet wormwood (*Artemisia annua*) in the West and *qīnghāo* in Chinese, seemed a particularly promising candidate.

Tu and her team tested various extractions from the plant, but none worked until Tu found a recipe dating back to the fourth century, titled "Emergency Prescriptions Kept Up One's Sleeve," that described an extraction process she had not yet tried: steeping the herb in cold water and not boiling it. This technique worked, and the extract proved effective at combating malaria in animals. Eventually, Tu tested the drug on herself first, and then proceeded to confirm with volunteers that it worked in humans as well.

It took until the 1970s for the full benefit of Tu's research to be realized, and her work was published in 1977 after the cultural tumult in China had abated. Tu was forced to submit the paper anonymously in order to adhere to the egalitarian ethos of Chinese society at the time. The specific compound that was effective in destroying the parasite responsible for infecting humans with malaria was identified as artemisinin. Its chemical structure was described, and labs around the world were able to produce it synthetically. Meanwhile, Tu had accidentally discovered a stronger form of artemisinin, dihydroartemisinin, which was ten times as effective as its progenitor and has remained a standard in malaria treatments for decades since.

Tu eventually became the chief scientist at the China Academy of Traditional Medicine and remained there for the rest of her career.

IMPACT

Despite the impact her discovery had on health worldwide, Tu remained largely unknown until around 2011 when malaria researchers began to ask who had discovered the wonder drug artemisinin. As her role spearheading the discovery of artemisinin became more widely known, Tu began to receive international recognition.

In 2015 Tu was awarded the United States' top prize in medical science, the Lasker Award, which recognizes individuals "who have made major advances in the understanding, diagnosis, treatment, and prevention of human disease." The award is often considered an indicator of future Nobel Prize winners. In October 2015, Tu was awarded a half-share of the Nobel Prize in Physiology or Medicine for her revolutionary work in developing novel treatments for malaria. At the time, she was eighty years old.

PERSONAL LIFE

Tu's husband, Li Tingzhao, is a metallurgical engineer. She met him as a classmate at Xiaoshi Middle School. The two live in Beijing and have two daughters.

SUGGESTED READING

"Artemisinin Therapy for Malaria." *Lasker Foundation.* Albert and Mary Lasker Foundation, 2011. Web. 28 June 2016.

McKenna, Phil. "Nobel Prize Goes to Modest Woman Who Beat Malaria for China." *New Scientist.* Reed Business Information, 5 Oct. 2015. Web. 1 June 2016.

Padmanaban, G. "Nobel Shot in the Arm for Neglected Infectious Disease Research." *Current Science* 109.9 (10 Nov. 2015): 1537. Print.

Perlez, Jane. "Answering an Appeal by Mao Led Tu Youyou, a Chinese Scientist, to a Nobel Prize." *New York Times.* New York Times, 7 Oct. 2015. Web. 1 June 2016.

"Tu Youyou on Being Awarded the Nobel Prize." *Chinese American Forum* 31.2 (Oct. 2015): 19. Print.

Wenzong, Li. "Tu Youyou: Bringer of Traditional Chinese Medicine to the World." *China Today.* China Internet Information Center, 2 Dec. 2015. Web. 1 June 2016.

—*Kenrick Vezina*

Zhang Zanbo

Date of birth: 1973
Occupation: Filmmaker

Zhang Zanbo is a documentary filmmaker who grew up in a peasant family in a poor, rural village in China's Hunan Province. His films, shot in the cinéma vérité style, explore poverty, greed, and power in the rapidly growing country. For his most recent project, *The Road* (2015), Zhang spent over three years filming the construction of a highway through Hunan. In a statement for the film's website (www.TheRoad2015.com), Zhang writes that the "road" in the title is both literal and metaphorical; marked by violence and corruption, the construction of the road is a "fable" of the path China has chosen for itself.

Zhang's first film, *Falling from the Sky* (2009), about a village plagued by falling satellite debris, was banned in China, where the filmmaker's work is often censored. The pushback makes him "feel powerless" at times, he admitted to Stephen Heyman for the *New York Times* (9 Sept. 2016), but he remains committed to speaking out against the Chinese government and criticizing the country's commercial film industry for failing to hold Communist Party of China (CPC) officials accountable. He told Heyman, "If a country only likes to make a show of its 'glory' and refuses to face its dark side and do something real to change it, its power and greatness are fragile and even hallucinatory."

EARLY LIFE AND EDUCATION

Zhang Zanbo was born in Hunan Province in southern China in 1973. His parents were subsistence farmers in the mountainous region. Growing up, Zhang worked with them in the fields. "When I tell my experience as a peasant boy to others now, many of them think that I am joking," he told Heyman. "There are about 800 million peasants in China, who are at the very bottom of the society. Through my personal experience I know just too well the difficulties in their lives. . . . They suffer from not only poverty, but also various forms of social injustice and discrimination. Their dignity and rights are not respected and well maintained."

Zhang attended secondary school in Hunan and received his master's degree from the Beijing Film Academy in 2005. He began teaching at the school but quit after his first film, *Falling from the Sky*, was banned in 2009. Working as an independent filmmaker, Zhang first relied on savings to support himself. He is also a writer—he wrote a companion book to his 2015 film, *The Road*—and makes some money as a cameraman for his friends' projects. Still, in his 2016 interview with Heyman, Zhang described himself as "nearly penniless."

FALLING FROM THE SKY

Zhang traveled to Suining County in Hunan Province in July 2008, the same year that China was hosting the Summer Olympic Games in Beijing and was touting its burgeoning space program. But for the 160,000 people of Suining, national pride in these events was tempered by fear. In preparation for the games, the Chinese government scrambled to launch satellites for television broadcasts. The poor villages in Suining County are in the path of Xichang Satellite Launch Center, and since the 1990s they have suffered under the constant threat of falling debris from rocket launches. The summer of 2008 was no exception.

Zhang's 2009 film *Falling from the Sky* tells the story of the people of Suining. In an interview with Kyle Mullin for the *Beijinger* (25 Apr. 2012), Zhang recalled how villagers bought television sets to watch the Olympic Games. In one scene, a child watches the opening ceremonies, his eyes "shining with excited light." In another scene, the most challenging for Zhang to film, villagers are running through the rain, away from a field where another satellite has crashed. The juxtaposition of the scenes, like the film as a whole, Zhang told Mullin, shows that the villagers "loved their country and their homes. But that feeling was complicated by the fact that they're victims of the national will."

THE INTERCEPTOR FROM MY HOMETOWN

Zhang shot his next film, *The Interceptor from My Hometown* (2012), which was also released under the alternative title *Solemn Tranquility*, in 2010. In it, he trails an old high school classmate, the vice mayor of a rural town whom Zhang gives the pseudonymous name He Xiaozhou. In the film, He is visiting Beijing to "intercept" petitioners, his constituents, before they air their grievances at a special central government agency that exists for that purpose. For Americans, an appropriate analogy might be traveling to Washington, DC, to meet with the Department of Veterans Affairs, only to be intercepted, bribed, and sent home by their local congressperson. The petitioners in the film include Korean War veterans, farmers whose land has been sold to developers, victims of the Cultural Revolution, and laid-off workers. Though the complaints are varied, local officials fear, quite rightly, that any complaint from a constituent will hurt their own chances of promotion. Thus an entire cottage industry—referred to in the film as "buying stability"—arose to keep people from complaining at all.

Louisa Lim, in a piece for *All Things Considered* (30 Oct. 2012), talked about one scene that features special-forces veterans who worked on a secret nuclear program in the 1970s and are now suffering from health problems. After arriving by train in Beijing, the veterans are detained in their local representative's office, located in "an unmarked apartment in a secret location." The veterans plead with the official for help, but he turns them away, telling them, "As veterans, you should share the country's difficulties, not make trouble for your motherland."

As the star of the film, He is candid about the nature of his job. In his role as an interceptor, he oversees a vast system of bribes—bribes to keep petitioners from voicing their complaints, bribes to erase complaints already lodged, even bribes for the train conductors who tip off officials when petitioners are on their way to Beijing. He insists that he does not agree with the system, but he makes clear that he is expected to participate in it. Zhang draws a powerful metaphor for the silencing of petitioners from one of He's anecdotes about visiting Zhongnanhai, a Beijing community where top party leaders live. He observes that "the place is filled with a solemn tranquility"; such silence can only be achieved, Zhang told Lim, "by sacrificing the voices of those outside."

"LIKE FIGHTING A WAR"

Zhang's third film, *The Road* (2015), was also inspired by an old school friend. Zhou Binhe is a construction worker; intrigued by his stories, Zhang decided to make a film about the construction of the massive Xu-Huai highway in Hunan Province, part of a $586 billion infrastructure plan meant to stimulate the Chinese economy after the global recession in 2008 and 2009. He began shooting in 2010, focusing on one rural village bisected by the roadway and following the construction workers, local villagers, and project managers for nearly four years.

A central figure in *The Road* is a construction manager called Mr. Meng. "The highway is like a golden apple: Everyone wants a bite," Mr. Meng says, as quoted by a reporter for the *Economist*'s literary and cultural blog *Prospero* (8 July 2016). For Mr. Meng, however, certain players seem to deserve those bites more than others. While he fights with locals who demand compensation for the seizure and destruction of their homes and migrant workers who endure what the *Economist* blogger described as "medieval" and dangerous conditions for paychecks that never seem to arrive, government officials overseeing the project are freely plied with envelopes of cash and cigarettes.

Zhang captures a number of harrowing scenes in his film. In one, an old woman yells at a construction crew as their blasts rain rocks down on her house. Later in the project, road authorities employ gangsters to attack workers with knives. According to the *Economist*, Zhang captures one of their injuries on film: A worker offers his hand to show skin growing up around metal fragments from the weapon. The workers, who were forced to lug away mud-filled buckets in wheelbarrows, demand medical treatment and compensation for their injuries. That compensation is so difficult to procure that in another scene, captured in the film's trailer, a worker and his wife lie behind the back wheels of a work truck to get the manager's attention. The man's wife has tears streaming down her face. "Did you treat us as humans?" he demands. The violence of the film surprised many viewers, but of course, not its participants. "Building a highway is like fighting a war," Mr. Meng says at one point.

Zhang told interviewers that access was not a problem. He trailed participants in the project for so long that the men and women in the film eventually forgot he was even there. As for the construction company, which conceivably stands to lose the most from the film, the *Economist* blogger reported that Zhang was upfront about his intentions: "I just told them that I wanted to make a film about how difficult a highway was constructed in China." The company officials were so used to the propaganda films of Chinese television, he said, that they never bothered to modify their behavior, expecting that the unsavory details would be edited out.

One of the most striking scenes in the film, the *Economist* blogger wrote, is one of its least dramatic. Zhang captures highway workers lounging in their underwear watching a solemn ceremony commemorating the anniversary of the CPC on television. They laugh at the pomp of their government and speak derisively of the party, wondering how long it will take for it to finally be overthrown. Outsiders might be surprised that the workers would say such things so casually in a nation so intent on suppressing them, but Zhang insists that social dissent is common. "The people's words and wishes are like water, which can't be blocked," he said, according to the *Economist*.

SUGGESTED READING

"The Chinese Documentaries Exposing the Communist Party's Flaws." *Prospero*, The Economist, 8 July 2016, www.economist.com/blogs/prospero/2016/07/politics-and-film. Accessed 14 Dec. 2016.

Lim, Louisa. "In China, a Ceaseless Quest to Silence Dissent." *China: Change or Crisis*, NPR, 30 Oct. 2012, www.npr.org/2012/10/30/163658996/in-china-a-ceaseless-quest-to-silence-dissent. Accessed 14 Dec. 2016.

Zhang Zanbo. "The Road Taken: Controversial Filmmaker Zhang Zanbo Knows the True Meaning of Independence." Interview by Sidney Leng. *South China Morning Post* [Hong Kong], 13 Aug. 2016, www.scmp.com/news/china/society/article/2002982/road-taken-controversial-filmmaker-zhang-zanbo-knows-true-meaning. Accessed 14 Dec. 2016.

Zhang Zanbo. "Unidentified Falling Objects in Rural China." Interview by Kyle Mullin. *The Beijinger*, 25 Apr. 2012, www.thebeijinger.com/blog/2012/04/25/unidentified-falling-objects-rural-china. Accessed 14 Dec. 2016.

Zhang Zanbo. "Zhang Zanbo: A Chinese Documentary Filmmaker Returns to His Roots." Interview by Stephen Heyman. Translated by Ning Xin, *New York Times*, 9 Sept. 2016, www.nytimes.com/2016/09/09/arts/international/zhang-zanbo-a-chinese-documentary-filmmaker-returns-to-his-roots.html. Accessed 14 Dec. 2016.

SELECTED WORKS

Falling from the Sky, 2009; *The Interceptor from My Hometown*, 2012; *The Road*, 2015

—Molly Hagan

Zendaya

Date of birth: September 1, 1996
Occupation: Actor, singer

"Zendaya has been on a trajectory of fame that shows no signs of peaking," Cori Murray wrote for *Essence* (Aug. 2016). Beginning with her first role on the Disney Channel's *Shake It Up* in 2010, the multitalented performer went on to release a studio album, star in another Disney Channel series that she also helps to produce, and earn a place in the ensemble of a major feature film, all before turning twenty. In summing up her additional impact as a public figure, Murray added, "For millennials, Zendaya is a clear voice, unafraid of challenging stereotypes and calling out racial and gender bias."

Even those who do not follow social media, watch the Disney Channel, or enjoy television dance competitions (she was a finalist on *Dancing with the Stars* in 2013) likely became familiar with Zendaya in the summer of 2017, when the big-budget, highly anticipated superhero film *Spider-Man: Homecoming*, in which she appears in a pivotal role, was released. "What I've been doing is slowly transitioning and allowing my fans to grow with me," she told Nolan Feeney for *Time* (2 Nov. 2015). "I have no shame in the fact that I'm still on the Disney Channel. I'm able to have two careers going at different times. I'm able to grow up and do awesome things with an older audience, and all the kids who were watching when they were fourteen, they all grow up with me."

Mingle MediaTV [CC BY-SA 2.0], via Wikimedia Commons

Despite frequently being referred to as a role model for her young fans, Zendaya quibbles with that terminology. "I like the word real model a little bit better. . . . I'm just completely being myself. And in being myself and being true to myself, that in turn inspires and helps other people," she explained to Julia Lee for *Tiger Beat* (21 Aug. 2016).

EARLY YEARS AND EDUCATION

Zendaya Maree Stoermer Coleman was born on September 1, 1996, in Oakland, California, to Claire Stoermer and Kazembe Ajamu Coleman (born Samuel David Coleman, he took his African name later in life). In interviews and appearances, Zendaya has explained how her full name is a representation of her rich heritage: "I have my African first name, I have a middle name that is [my mom's] middle name, which is French, but we did it African spelling, so it's literally me in a name," the performer explained in a video honoring Immigrant Heritage Month, as quoted by Allison Takeda in *Us Weekly* (9 June 2015). "And then you have Stoermer, and then you have Coleman. I literally have, like, a timeline in history in my name." Zendaya means "to give thanks" in Shona, a Bantu language spoken in Zimbabwe. Discussing her mixed heritage, she told Kristen Yoonsoo Kim for *Complex* (Dec. 2015/Jan. 2016), "You get the best and the worst of both worlds. . . . I had to learn about both sides of myself and be really proud of and educated in both."

Zendaya is the only child her parents, both former teachers, have together, although she has several half siblings. According to Zendaya, her parents became estranged, eventually divorcing in 2016 while reportedly maintaining an amicable connection. She initially attended the predominately white private school where her father taught physical education and later moved on to the Oakland School for the Arts.

Though exceptionally shy as a small child, early on Zendaya harbored dreams of performing. "I just watched Disney Channel a lot. I really liked it and had an attraction to it and I couldn't see myself doing anything else," she told Kim. "It wasn't like I was that kid that was like, 'I want to be an astronaut.' I wanted to do this. I wanted to be an entertainer." Besides teaching fifth grade at a public school, her mother worked as a house manager at the California Shakespeare Theater in Orinda, and Zendaya often pitched in to collect raffle tickets and seat patrons. She also began to train at the company's student conservatory program, and she was soon dancing in a kids' hip-hop group called Future Shock, modeling for such brands as Macy's and Old Navy, and appearing in shows at local venues that included the Berkeley Playhouse and Palo Alto's Theatre-Works. (One of her higher-profile gigs was as a backup dancer in a Sears commercial featuring Selena Gomez.)

When she was about thirteen, she was approached by an agent, and she subsequently moved with her father to Los Angeles to pursue a professional career while her mother remained in Oakland to work. Within months, she had been hired by Disney.

SMALL SCREEN AND MUSIC CAREER

In 2010, *Shake It Up* premiered on the Disney Channel, with Zendaya starring as Rocky Blue, who—along with her friend CeCe Jones (played by Bella Thorne)—tries to make it as a professional dancer while dealing with school, siblings, and rivals. Although the show attracted few rave critical reviews, it was largely well received by viewers, particularly between the ages of nine and fourteen, bringing in significant ratings for the channel. Many of the songs Zendaya performed as Rocky Blue in *Shake It Up* were released as singles; one, "Watch Me," a duet with Thorne, landed on Billboard's Hot 100 chart in 2011.

Quickly gaining a positive reputation, Zendaya won a lead role in the 2012 Disney Channel film *Frenemies*. In 2013, the year she made it to the finals of *Dancing with the Stars*, she released an eponymous debut album through the Hollywood Records label whose lead single, "Replay," became a viral hit, with the video viewed online some twenty million times within just a few weeks of its debut. At the same time, she became a published author when the Disney-Hyperion imprint released her paperback book

Between U and Me: How to Rock Your Tween Years with Style and Confidence (2013), which offers advice for young people about friendship, fashion, crushes, and more.

Shake It Up, which aired until 2013, was popular enough with viewers to earn Zendaya a role in the Disney Channel film *Zapped* (2014) and lend her further influence with studio executives. When they approached her to star in a second series, tentatively titled *Super Awesome Katy*, she, having gained confidence from her experience, countered with a list of demands. She insisted that the show's title and main character's name be changed, on the grounds that she did not look like a Katy; that a family of color be featured; and that she be listed as a producer. Additionally, she had particular views about how her character should be portrayed: "I wanted to make sure that she wasn't good at singing or acting or dancing. That she wasn't artistically inclined. . . . There are other things that a girl can be," she told Abby Aguirre for *Vogue* (15 June 2017). "I want her to be martial arts–trained. I want her to be able to do everything that a guy can do. I want her to be just as smart as everybody else. I want her to be a brainiac. I want her to be able to think on her feet. But I also want her to be socially awkward, not a cool kid. I want her to be normal with an extraordinary life." The first episode of *K. C. Undercover*, as the show was ultimately titled, aired in early 2015 and, as per Zendaya's directives, it follows the adventures of a savvy young spy equally adept at martial arts and computer technology.

BREAKING THROUGH TO THE BIG SCREEN

While making *K. C. Undercover*, Zendaya continued to participate in the music world, including a high-profile appearance in Taylor Swift's music video for the hit single "Bad Blood," in addition to earning a guest role on the ABC sitcom *Black-ish* in 2015. After several years of balancing school and her increasingly flourishing career, she also graduated that year from Oak Park High School, which she had attended through an independent study program. In early 2016, she released another well-received single, "Something New," characterized by a more R&B style and featuring guest vocals by Chris Brown.

Zendaya also learned in 2016 that she would be making her debut in a major feature film when she was tapped to appear in *Spider-Man: Homecoming*, which focuses on the popular Marvel Comics superhero's high school years in his true identity as Peter Parker. As this new film would be the first opportunity for Marvel Studios to bring Spider-Man into its cinematic universe after reaching a deal with Sony, its release was highly anticipated. However, Zendaya has explained in interviews that although she had been waiting for the right role to serve as her

introduction to feature films, she initially did not know what film she was submitting an audition tape for due to the secrecy surrounding the project. Once she found out, however, she knew that she wanted to have a part, large or small, in the venture. "I would much rather have one line in a great movie than be the lead of a s—— one," she told Ramin Setoodeh for *Variety* (8 Aug. 2017). Though director Jon Watts was immediately impressed by her despite being unfamiliar with her work, she was unsure of whether she would get a role: "I didn't know they were going to switch up the characters and really cast the best people for the roles, instead of what's most like the comic book. I think that was the coolest part for me, knowing they embraced the diversity," she explained to Setoodeh.

Given that Zendaya figured prominently in the studio's publicity push for the summer 2017 blockbuster, appearing alongside star Tom Holland on numerous talk shows and in the pages of entertainment magazines, unsuspecting viewers were surprised that her role as Peter's classmate Michelle seemed to be a small one: she has only a short amount of actual screen time, and the titular main character evinces little romantic interest in her. There was, however, an important twist to her casting, as the film's ending implies that her character will likely play a much larger role in future installments. Regardless, the film was a great success upon its release, faring well at the box office and receiving positive critical reviews. Yohana Desta, writing for *Vanity Fair* (7 July 2017), called Zendaya "a comic delight" in the film, opining, "Zendaya manages to pack the character with abundant personality in the few scenes she has, strongly piquing our interest to see what she can do with a bigger role in the next installment."

Zendaya's next big-screen role will be in the P. T. Barnum biopic *The Greatest Showman*, starring Hugh Jackman and Zac Efron. The picture, in which she plays a trapeze artist, is slated to open on Christmas Day 2017.

PERSONAL LIFE

Zendaya, who purchased her first home in California in 2016, has long had an interest in fashion design, and she now oversees a line called Daya by Zendaya, which has been celebrated for being neither overtly feminine nor masculine as well as for its extended size range, from zero to twenty-two. Her own red-carpet style is often lavishly praised by the fashion press for its originality and verve.

Tabloids often speculate about who Zendaya is dating, linking her to figures such as National Football League (NFL) player Odell Beckham Jr. "Any male that I've ever been around in my life, if they follow me on Twitter, if they look at me, if they breathe the same air as me, we've dated," she explained to Kim.

SUGGESTED READING

Aguirre, Abby. "Zendaya Talks *Spider-Man*, Her First Love, and Reinventing Disney Stardom." *Vogue*, 15 June 2017, www.vogue.com/article/zendaya-interview-july-vogue-cover-spider-man-homecoming. Accessed 7 Sept. 2017.

Lee, Julia. "Why Zendaya Says She's Not a Role Model." *Tiger Beat*, 21 Aug. 2016, tigerbeat.com/2016/08/zendaya-role-model-inspiration/. Accessed 7 Sept. 2017.

Murray, Cori. "Flying Down to Rio." *Essence*, Aug. 2016, pp. 76–81.

Setoodeh, Ramin. "How Zendaya Fell in Love with Spider-Man and Launched a Movie Career." *Variety*, 8 Aug. 2017, variety.com/2017/film/features/zendaya-spider-man-homecoming-kc-undercover-1202516631/. Accessed 7 Sept. 2017.

Takeda, Allison. "Zendaya Gets to the Heart of Her Family Tree for Immigrant Heritage Month." *Us Weekly*, 9 June 2015, www.usmagazine.com/celebrity-news/news/zendaya-digs-deep-into-her-past-for-immigrant-heritage-month-video-201596. Accessed 7 Sept. 2017.

Zendaya. "Real Good." Interview by Kristen Yoonsoo Kim. *Complex*, Dec. 2015/Jan. 2016, www.complex.com/pop-culture/zendaya-interview-2015-cover-story. Accessed 7 Sept. 2017.

Zendaya. "Zendaya on Body Image, Being an Influential Teen and How *Scandal* Got Her into Politics." Interview by Nolan Feeney. *Time*, 2 Nov. 2015, time.com/4093271/zendaya-interview-influential-teen/. Accessed 7 Sept. 2017.

SELECTED WORKS

Shake It Up, 2010–13; *Frenemies*, 2012; *Zapped*, 2014; *K. C. Undercover*, 2015–; *Spider-Man: Homecoming*, 2017

—*Mari Rich*

Ben Zobrist

Date of birth: May 26, 1981
Occupation: Baseball player

In more than a decade as a professional baseball player, Ben "Zorilla" Zobrist has established himself as a dependable presence both on and off the field. "He's a metronome," manager Joe Maddon, who oversaw Zobrist's tenure with both the Tampa Bay Rays and the Chicago Cubs, told Susan Slusser for *SFGate* (11 Oct. 2016). "He

By Arturo Pardavila III from Hoboken, NJ, USA [CC BY 2.0], via Wikimedia Commons

comes out there every day. And if you watch his work, it's meticulous." Drafted by the Houston Astros in 2004, Zobrist began his major-league career with Tampa Bay, spending nine seasons with the team and accompanying the Rays to the franchise's first World Series in 2008.

The most exciting moments to date, however, came in close succession following his departure from Tampa. Moving to the Kansas City Royals for the 2015 season, Zobrist joined the team in its successful push through the postseason, claiming his first World Series win. After a move to the Chicago Cubs, he assisted that franchise in winning the 2016 World Series, the franchise's first championship in more than one hundred years. While contributing to two back-to-back World Series victories was undoubtedly a major achievement, Zobrist focuses less on winning and more on the happiness of his teammates and the fans. "Being put in arenas that you're not used to being put in—just because you were able to do something as an athlete—is pretty special," he explained to Patrick Mooney for *CSN Chicago* (19 Feb. 2017). "It's special to know that you were able to do something that made a lot of people happy."

EARLY LIFE AND EDUCATION

Benjamin Thomas Zobrist was born on May 26, 1981, in Eureka, Illinois. He was the second of five children born to Cindi and Tom Zobrist. His father served as the pastor of Liberty Bible Church, and Zobrist grew up planning to follow in his father's footsteps despite demonstrating talent in sports such as baseball, basketball, and football at an early age. "I never even thought about playing professionally," he told Tyler Kepner for the *New York Times* (3 Nov. 2016). "I didn't think that was a possibility for a little kid from Illinois. I just wanted to play the game and win."

After graduating from Eureka High School in 2001, Zobrist planned to attend Calvary University (formerly Calvary Bible College) in Kansas City, Missouri, which his father had previously attended. However, after attending a baseball tryout camp, he attracted the attention of college representatives who sought to recruit him to join their teams. The most compelling offer came from Olivet Nazarene University in Bourbonnais, Illinois, which competed in the National Association of Intercollegiate Athletics' Division II. Zobrist told his parents that he felt he was "not done with baseball yet," as his father recalled to Vahe Gregorian for the *Kansas City Star* (22 Oct. 2015), and he ultimately decided to change his plans and accept Olivet Nazarene's offer. He later transferred to Dallas Baptist University, a member of the National Collegiate Athletic Association's Division I, and played for the university's Patriots baseball team for the 2004 season.

PROFESSIONAL BASEBALL

In June 2004, Zobrist was drafted by the Houston Astros in the sixth round of the 2004 Major-League Baseball (MLB) draft. He spent his first years as a professional baseball player gaining experience while playing for a number of the Houston Astros' minor-league affiliate teams, including the Tri-City ValleyCats and the Lexington Legends. Although he spent two years in with Astros affiliates, he did not play any games for the major-league team and was instead traded to the Tampa Bay Devil Rays, later known simply as the Tampa Bay Rays, in July 2016. Zobrist made his major-league debut with the Rays on August 1, 2006, in a game against the Detroit Tigers. Over the course of the season, he appeared in fifty-two games with Tampa Bay and scored a total of ten runs.

Following his debut with the Rays, Zobrist spent nearly a decade with the team and its minor-league affiliates, with which he played on several occasions. In 2008, he joined the team as they defeated the Boston Red Sox to win the American League Championship Series in the postseason and proceeded on to the World Series, the franchise's first. The Rays faced off against the Philadelphia Phillies in the World Series but fared poorly, winning only one of the five games played. Despite the team's defeat by the Phillies, Zobrist and his teammates were pleased to have had the opportunity to compete in the World Series, which represented a significant milestone for the relatively young franchise.

The Tampa Bay Rays competed in the postseason again in 2010, 2011, and 2013 but were unable to claim a second American League pennant during Zobrist's tenure with the team.

In the years after Tampa Bay's World Series effort, Zobrist established himself as a reliable contributor to the team, playing full or nearly full seasons in 2009 through 2014. A versatile athlete, he played in a variety positions for the Rays, including the positions of shortstop and second baseman. Zobrist's time with the Rays came to an end in January 2015, when the team's management traded Zobrist to the Oakland Athletics. Injuring his knee in April of that year, Zobrist was placed on the disabled list and sent on rehabilitation assignments with affiliate teams such as the Stockton Ports. He rejoined the Athletics in late May 2015 but ultimately played a total of only sixty-seven games for Oakland before being traded to the Kansas City Royals in July of that year.

KANSAS CITY ROYALS

Making his debut with the Royals on July 30, 2015, in a game against the Toronto Blue Jays, Zobrist joined the roster at an exciting time for the Royals franchise. The team had played in the previous year's World Series but had ultimately lost to the San Francisco Giants. Energized by that close call with the championship, the Royals had their eyes on the goal of winning in 2015, which would mark the franchise's first series win in thirty years. "This club has got a little bit more of a mix of guys that are experienced, they're ready to be here and want to win it," Zobrist told Steve Garner for *USA Today* (28 Oct. 2015) of his new team's World Series aspirations. "In Tampa Bay, we were just happy to be there and couldn't believe we had made it there."

Over the course of the regular season, in which Zobrist played in fifty-nine games, the Royals amassed a strong win record to place first in the division. Zobrist remained with the Royals into the postseason, helping the team defeat the Blue Jays to win the American League championship and proceed on to the 2015 World Series, held between October 27 and November 1 of that year. In the series, the Royals faced off against the New York Mets, playing a total of five games and defeating the Mets 4–1. Over the course of the series, Zobrist scored five runs with twenty-three at bats and hit a batting average of .261, and he made a substantial contribution to the team with his work as a second-baseman.

CHICAGO CUBS

On November 2, 2015, only a day after claiming his first World Series victory, Zobrist was granted free agency, a status that meant that he was no longer under contract with a team and could therefore join any team that made him an offer. After assessing several offers, including one from the Giants, on December 8, he signed with the Chicago Cubs in a four-year, $56 million deal. Although the Cubs' lucrative offer could not have hurt, Zobrist was also interested in joining the Cubs so that he could return to Illinois, where he would be closer to his parents.

Zobrist's first game with the Cubs, on April 4, 2016, set the tone for an extraordinary year as the Cubs beat the Los Angeles Angels of Anaheim 9–0. Over the course of the regular season, he played in 147 games, scored a total of ninety-four runs, and played second base for the National League in the All-Star Game that July. The most exciting achievement, however, came in the postseason, as the Cubs beat the Los Angeles Dodgers to win the National League Championship Series. Their win marked the first time that the Cubs had made it into the World Series since 1945. Even more significant was the fact that the Cubs had not won a World Series since 1908; Zobrist and his teammates had the opportunity to claim the first victory in more than one hundred years.

2016 WORLD SERIES

The 2016 World Series began on October 25 of that year, with the Cubs facing off against the Cleveland Indians. The first game was a disappointment for Chicago, as Cleveland claimed a 6–0 victory. Game 2 was a marked improvement and a Cubs victory, but the Indians won the following two games, pitching a shutout during Game 3. Rallying, the Cubs won Games 5 and 6, tying the series and rendering Game 7 a tie-breaker with immense implications for their team. Thanks in part to Zobrist, whose batting enabled a fellow player to score a pivotal run, the Cubs overcame Cleveland, winning the game 8–7. Zobrist was named most valuable player of the series for his contributions to the Cubs' historic victory.

Although the 2016 series marked Zobrist's third World Series appearance and second win, the intensity of the competition and the monumental nature of the Cubs' win was nevertheless striking to him. "It was like a heavyweight fight, man, just blow for blow, everybody playing their hearts out," he told Kepner. "The Indians never gave up, either, and I can't believe we're finally standing, after 108 years, finally able to hoist the trophy." Following the historic win, the Cubs were determined not to wait another century for their next victory, pushing hard to replicate their success in 2017. "Everybody was super-hungry to make it happen last year. We have to push each other to realize it's going to be even harder this year," he told Mooney. "For us to be able to do something like repeating a championship in Chicago would be even greater than what we were able to do last year."

PERSONAL LIFE

Zobrist and his wife, Christian pop singer Julianna Zobrist, married in 2005. They have three children. Their youngest daughter, Blaise Royal Zobrist, was born days after the 2015 World Series and named in part after Zobrist's championship-winning team. The family lives in Chicago and also owns a home in Tennessee.

SUGGESTED READING

"Cubs, Ben Zobrist Agree to Terms on Four-Year Deal Worth $56M." *ESPN*, 9 Dec. 2015, www.espn.com/mlb/story/_/id/14324454/ben-zobrist-chicago-cubs-agree-terms-4-year-56-million-deal. Accessed 9 June 2017.

Gardner, Steve. "Ben Zobrist Doing It All for the Royals: 'Thank God We Got Him.'" *USA Today*, 28 Oct. 2015, www.usatoday.com/story/sports/mlb/2015/10/28/ben-zobrist-royals-world-series/74742222. Accessed 9 June 2017.

Gregorian, Vahe. "Before He Was a Royal, Ben Zobrist's Baseball Career Hinged on a $50 Tryout Camp." *Kansas City Star*, 22 Oct. 2015, www.kansascity.com/sports/spt-columns-blogs/vahe-gregorian/article41120313.html. Accessed 9 June 2017.

Kepner, Tyler. "With a Curse-Breaking Hit, Ben Zobrist Lives a Dream He Never Expected." *The New York Times*, 3 Nov. 2016, www.nytimes.com/2016/11/03/sports/baseball/world-series-game-7-ben-zobrist-chicago-cubs.html. Accessed 9 June 2017.

Mooney, Patrick. "After Surreal Offseason, Ben Zobrist Comes to Cubs Camp in Style as World Series MVP." *CSN Chicago*, 19 Feb. 2017, www.csnchicago.com/chicago-cubs/after-surreal-offseason-ben-zobrist-comes-cubs-camp-style-world-series-mvp. Accessed 9 June 2017.

Schwarz, Alan. "For Rays' Zobrist, Versatility Meets Opportunity." *The New York Times*, 18 July 2009, www.nytimes.com/2009/07/19/sports/baseball/19zobrist.html. Accessed 9 June 2017.

Slusser, Susan. "Cubs' Ben Zobrist Trying for 2nd Ring in a Row." *SFGate*, 11 Oct. 2016, www.sfgate.com/giants/article/Cubs-Ben-Zobrist-trying-for-second-ring-in-a-9965676.php. Accessed 9 June 2017.

—*Joy Crelin*

OBITUARIES

Magdalena (Marta) Abakanowicz

Born: Falenty, Poland; June 20, 1930
Died: Warsaw, Poland; April 20, 2017
Occupation: Sculptor

With art being highly regulated by Poland's Communist government, Magdalena Abakanowicz, a world-renowned sculptor, defied the government's oversight by creating abstract figures out of fiber. Her early work in tapestry design informed her art for the rest of her life.

Magdalena Abakanowicz's birth name was Marta. She was born into an aristocratic family who were direct descendants of Genghis Khan. The family lived in a country estate east of Warsaw. Her childhood was peopled with servants and tutors, and she was always drawn to the grandeur and mystery of the forest surrounding her home. When German tanks rolled through in 1939, her life was irrevocably altered. She would spend much of her life living in a one-room apartment. Following the Nazi occupation and 1944 Warsaw uprising, former aristocrats were considered "enemies of the people." By hiding her family background, Abakanowicz won acceptance into the Academy of Fine Arts in Warsaw. In 1950s Poland, the only officially sanctioned art was that favored, by the dictator, Joseph Stalin. Though admitted as a painting student, Abakanowicz's reaction was to work on tapestry design, which eventually led to her crafting abstract sculptures from old fiber ropes. By the 1970s her work was widely recognized and dubbed "Abakans." The large, eerie figures she constructed were reminiscent of World War II images of prisoners lined up in concentration camps. She even characterized her creations as reminiscent of the mangled victims she helped nurse during the Soviet invasion of Nazi-occupied Warsaw. Later in her career, Abakanowicz used more traditional sculpting materials like wood and steel. One of her most powerful works was titled "War Games," in which she used discarded tree trunks and steel blades to depict the horror and mystery of war.

Magdalena Abakanowicz worked as a professor of art at the Academy of Fine Arts in Poznan, Poland. She was named both an officer and chevalier of France's Order of Arts and Letters. In 1965 she married a civil engineer, Jan Kosmowski. The couple had no children. Mr. Kosmowski is her sole survivor.

See Current Biography 2001

Peter Abrahams

Born: Johannesburg, South Africa; March 3, 1919
Died: Kingston, Jamaica; January 18, 2017
Occupation: Author

Peter Abrahams is often considered to be the first African author to achieve worldwide acclaim. Though he spent most of his life abroad, the majority of his novels take place in South Africa, Abraham's spiritual home.

Peter Abraham's father was Ethiopian and his mother was "colored," the daughter of a white French mother and black father. His father died when Abrahams was quite young, and the boy had to work, selling firewood to help support himself and his mother as they managed to survive in a spirit-crushing atmosphere of racism in pre-apartheid South Africa. He was eleven years old before he could enter school at the colored school in Vrededorp where he first experienced a passion for literature. He won a scholarship to the Diocesan Training College in Grace Dieu, outside of Pietersburg. After graduation Abrahams taught for a year in Cape Town, and began writing and publishing poetry in *Bantu World*. In 1939 he got a job as a ship's stoker and began traveling around the world, eventually landing in London, England, where he worked in a Marxist bookstore. His first collection of short stories and essays, *Dark Testament,* was published in 1942 and, his first novel, *Song of the City,* was published in 1945. Many of his stories were about the tragic misunderstandings among his own people and the "complex interplay between British imperialism and African nationalism and tribalism." In 1957 the British colonial office hired him to write a history of Jamaica called *Jamaica: An Island Mosaic.* Abrahams became involved with London's African community and he befriended Jomo Kenyatta of Kenya and Kwame Nkrumah of Ghana, who were each destined to lead their post-colonial, free nations.

Abrahams was awarded the Musgrave Gold Medal from the Institute of Jamaica. He married Dorothy Pennington in 1942, but the marriage was dissolved in 1948. In 1956 Abrahams made Jamaica his permanent home with his second wife, the former Daphne Miller, and their three children. His survivors include his wife of sixty-eight years and his three children.

See Current Biography 1957

Alexei Abrikosov

Born: Moscow, Russia, USSR; June 25, 1928
Died: Sunnyvale, California; March 29, 2017
Occupation: Russian-born physicist

Nobel laureate, Alexei Abrikosov, is credited with pioneering contributions to the theory of superconductivity. He recognized a flaw in the equation that his predecessors, Vitaly L. Ginzburg and Lev Landau, had overlooked in their examination of superconductivity. Abrikosov's breakthrough explained how superconductors allow magnetism and super conductivity to co-exist.

Alexei Abrikosov was born to two Russian physicians. His father apparently supervised the autopsy of Vladimir Lenin, in 1924, and his mother once attended to Joseph Stalin. Abrikosov graduated from Moscow State University in 1948 and earned two doctorate degrees in physics from the Kapitsa Institute for Physical Problems. After examining the Landau-Ginzburg equations, Abrikosov was able to posit that magnetic fields formed, like ropes through holes in alloys, while still allowing the material to remain superconducting. "With his theory of vortices, Abrikosov invented a whole new discipline," according to Brian Schwartz, the vice president for research at the Graduate Center of the City University of New York (CUNY) in his interview with the *Washington Post* (8 Oct. 2003). Abrikosov's work led to numerous technological advances such as magnetic resonance imagining (MRI), used by medical doctors in diagnosing disease, and particle-beam accelerators like those used in the Large Hadron Collider in Switzerland. In 1965 Abrikosov became the head of the L. D. Landau Institute of Theoretical Physics of the USSR Academy of Sciences in Moscow. He also taught at Moscow State University, Gorky University, and the Moscow Physical English Institute. In 1988 he became the head of the Institute of High Pressure Physics in Moscow. Disillusioned with life in Communist Russia, Abrikosov moved his family to the United States in 1991, just months shy of the collapse of the USSR. In the United States he joined the Argonne National Laboratory, in Illinois, in 1991.

In addition to his Nobel Prize, Alexei Abrikosov also received the Lenin Prize, the Fritz London Award, the USSR Academy of Sciences' Landau Award, and the International John Bardeen Award. His survivors include his wife, Svetlana, his three children, and four grandchildren.

See Current Biography 2007

Richard Adams

Born: Newbury, England; May 9, 1920
Died: Oxford, England; December 24, 2016
Occupation: Writer

Richard Adams is most remembered as the author of the now classic novel, *Watership Down,* which was published in 1972.

Richard Adams was born and raised in the rolling Berkshire countryside, which would one day provide the setting for his first novel, *Watership Down.* His parents lived in a spacious house with three acres of garden. Adams was the last of three children in the family, and with his siblings being nine and seven years older, he had a lot of time on his own. His father was a surgeon who loved to read Hugh Lofting's *Dr. Doolittle* stories to his children. Adams attended Bradfield College, a boarding school where he was a classmate of Christopher Milne, the son of A. A. Milne, the author of *Winnie the Pooh.* He attended Oxford University, graduating in 1938. He fought with the British Airborne Forces during World War II, after which he returned to Oxford where he received an MA in modern history. He joined the British home civil service shortly thereafter, and remained there well into his fifties. At the time he left his civil service career, Adams was an assistant secretary in what would become the Department of the Environment.

Adams' anthropomorphic animal fantasy was conceived on a car ride with his wife and children. The children were bored so he made up a story about a society of rabbits, one of whom knows their warren is about to be destroyed and tries to warn the others who won't believe him. He and a small band venture out to find a new home and become embroiled in a bloody war before they can fully settle into their new home, Watership Down. Four publishers and three literary agents rejected the novel before Rex Collings picked it up. Since its publication in 1972, the book has been ranked beside George Orwell's *Animal Farm* and the fantasy fiction of C. S. Lewis, J.R.R. Tolkien, and A. A. Milne. With the publication of his second novel, *Shardik,* in 1974, Adams resigned his civil service position and became a visiting professor of poetry appreciation at the University of Florida, and then the writer-in-residence at Hollins College in Virginia. Other novels include *The Plague Dogs, Maia,* and *The Girl in the Swing. Watership Down* was adapted for an animated film in 1978. Adams was inducted into the Royal Society of Literature in 1975.

Richard Adams married his wife, Barbara Elizabeth Acland, in 1949. They had two daughters. Information about his survivors is not available. *See Current Biography 1978*

Roger Ailes

Born: Warren, Ohio; May 15, 1940
Died: Palm Beach, Florida; May 18, 2017
Occupation: Television executive, media consultant

As the chairman and chief executive of the Fox television network, Roger Ailes knew how to put on a good show. At one time he was the most sought-after media consultant for Republican political candidates, and was credited with the successful campaigns of Richard Nixon and George Bush, among numerous others.

Roger Ailes was born in Warren, Ohio, the son of a maintenance foreman at the Packard Electric Plant. He worked his way through Ohio University where he was a disc jockey on the college radio station. After graduation he worked as a prop boy for KYW, the NBC–affiliated television station in Cleveland. Within three years he was the producer of the *Mike Douglas Show*. In 1967 and 1968 Ailes won two Emmy Awards for the show. His career took an unexpected turn when he met Richard Nixon who appeared as a guest on the show. Nixon persuaded Ailes to become his media advisor. Ailes' approach was to restrict Nixon's major media appearances to a carefully controlled series of media events. He essentially orchestrated Nixon's every move with attention to creating an image. For Ailes, image took precedent over substance. His credo was "You are the message." After his success with the Nixon campaign, in 1969 Ailes created his own communications consulting company, providing media advice to Republican candidates. In 1996 Ailes partnered with the wealthy media mogul, Rupert Murdoch to create the conservative, Republican cable news program *Fox News*, which made common household names of Bill O'Reilly and Sean Hannity. It was said that Ailes had two speeds: attack and destroy, and his news network reflected that same energy where hosts have often attacked political opponents. In fact, the phenomenon of the "attack ad" was Ailes' greatest weapon in creating the myths voters responded to.

In 2016 numerous female employees accused Roger Ailes of sexual harassment and revealed a culture of misogyny at Fox. Murdoch was forced to fire Ailes. Roger Ailes was married three times. His survivors include his wife, Elizabeth Gilson, and their son.

See Current Biography 1989

Sulaiman Bin Abdul Al Rajhi

Born: Saudi Arabia; 1920
Died: June 27, 2017
Occupation: Saudi Arabian financier

As the founder of Al Rajhi Bank, the world's largest Islamic bank, Sulaiman Bin Abdul Al Rajhi, was one of the wealthiest men in the world, and the wealthiest non-royal in the kingdom of Saudi Arabia. *Forbes* estimated his wealth to be $7.7 billion in 2011. His net worth changed dramatically when he donated most of his wealth, half to his children and the other half to charitable endowments. At his death he was worth roughly $590 million.

Sulaiman Bin Abdul Al Rajhi was born into poverty and began his career as an entrepreneur when he was just nine years old, working as a porter at a local hotel. At one time he also worked as a chef. As a teenager Al Rajhi sold imported kerosene for the wholesale market, and he worked for his brother Saleh, at his currency exchange. In 1970 he separated from his brother to create his own exchange, which quickly blossomed to more than thirty branches throughout Saudi Arabia. At the same time Al Rajhi is said to have earned a bachelor's degree from King Abdul Aziz University. He also studied at the Wharton School of Business and Cranford School of Management in the UK. As his money exchange enterprises grew, Al Rajhi established the Al Rajhi Bank, the oldest financial institution in Saudi Arabia. The bank adhered to Islamic law meaning it could not charge interest on loans or invest in anti-Islamic businesses. The bank earned income through buying and reselling or leasing properties, and exchanging stock or other commodities. In the 1990s Al Rajhi expanded into the poultry business, naming his farm Al-Watania, which produced as much as half a million chickens a day by 2006.

Al Rajhi came under considerable international scrutiny as he was suspected of aiding Islamic terrorists such as Hamas and al-Qaeda through his charitable SAAR organization. (The name was an acronym formed by Al Rajhi's initials.) He also established the non-profit Sulaiman Al Rajhi University. Late in his life Al Rajhi dispersed his wealth to his children and to his charitable foundation.

Sulaiman Bin Abdul Al Rajhi had multiple wives, according to Islamic law, and had at least twenty-three children.

See Current Biography 2006

Dwayne O. Andreas

Born: Worthington, Minnesota; March 4, 1918
Died: Decatur, Illinois; November 16, 2016
Occupation: Business executive

From humble beginnings as the son of a Mennonite Iowa farmer, Dwayne Andreas became one of the most powerful business executives in the world. He was the chairman and chief executive of Archer Daniels Midland (ADM), the "supermarket to the world," manufacturing everything from animal feed and ethanol, to high-fructose corn syrup and veggie burgers. He was just as comfortable in the boardroom, among the world's most powerful statesmen, as he was on a farm in America's heartland.

Dwayne Andreas was the fourth of five sons born to Lydia (Stoltz) Andreas and Reuben Peter Andreas, a Mennonite farmer near Worthington, Minnesota. Andreas reportedly started working on the farm's grain elevator when he was nine years old. In 1936 the family moved to Cedar Rapids, Iowa, where they built a soybean meal processing plant, which would become one of the largest in the country. Andreas briefly attended Wheaton College in Illinois. In 1947 Andreas married Dorothy Inez who was the single mother of a little girl.

In the mid-1960s the farm products manufacturers, the Archer and Daniels families, invited the Andreas family to purchase shares and work as executives for their company (ADM). Dwayne Andreas would remain the chief executive from 1970 to 1997. The company came under federal investigation for price-fixing in the 1990s and ADM paid a record $100 million fine.

Though he never ran for political office, Dwayne Andreas wielded behind the scenes political influence, making frequent donations to political campaigns, both Republican and Democratic. He was close to President Nixon and, according to Keith Schneider of *The New York Times* (16 Nov. 2016) Andreas "helped arrange the first meeting between Reagan and Mr. Gorbachev." Included among his closest friends were Senator Bob Dole, House Speaker "Tip" O'Neill, Howard Baker, and broadcast newsman David Brinkley.

Dwayne Andreas is survived by a son, two daughters, nine grandchildren, and twenty-three great grandchildren.

See Current Biography 1992

Cecil D. Andrus

Born: Hood River, Oregon; August 25, 1931
Died: Boise, Idaho; August 24, 2017
Occupation: US Secretary of the Interior, governor of Idaho

In January of 1977, Cecil Andrus headed the US Interior Department at a time when energy needs and conservation programs were often in conflict. He was best known for his ability to balance environmental conservation with economic development. He was also a three-term governor of Idaho.

Born and raised in Hood River, Oregon, Cecil Andrus grew up on a farm in logging country, where his father was a sawmill operator. Early in his career he worked the forests and lumber mills of northern Oregon, where he acquired his conservationist views. He attended Oregon State College for two years, and served in the US Navy from 1951 to 1956. He later went back to work as a lumberjack for Tru-Cut Lumber Corporation in Orofino, Idaho. He entered politics and was elected to the Idaho State Senate in 1961. At the time he was the youngest state senator in Idaho history. Elected for a second term, he served until 1966. He made a bid for the 1966 Idaho Democratic gubernatorial nomination, but was narrowly defeated by John Charles Herndon. Two weeks later Herndon was killed in an accident and Andrus became the Democratic nominee, though he lost in the general election. Andrus was elected four years later with a campaign promise to preserve Castle Peak in the White Cloud Mountains, and became Idaho's first Democratic governor in twenty-four years. In 1974 he successfully opposed the Pentagon's plan to launch Minuteman missiles from Montana over portions of Idaho and Oregon.

Andrus met Jimmy Carter in 1970 and helped him with his 1974 campaign. Carter rewarded his efforts by making Andrus his nominee as the Secretary of the Interior. At the time, the interior agency's control covered the National Parks Service, the Fish and Wildlife Service, the Bureau of Mines, the Geological Survey, the Bureau of Land Management, and the Bureau of Indian Affairs. Andrus was instrumental in preserving Alaska's wilderness areas from mining operations. Following his service on Carter's cabinet, Andrus ran for governor of Idaho once more, serving one more term.

Cecil Andrus married Carol Mae May in 1949. They had three daughters. His wife, three daughters, three grandchildren, and one great-grandchild survive him.

See Current Biography 1977

Antony Armstrong-Jones

Born: London, England; March 7, 1930
Died: London, England; January 13, 2017
Occupation: Husband of Princess Margaret of Great Britain and photographer

Princess Margaret and Antony Armstrong-Jones surprised the world when they announced their engagement in January of 1960. They had carried on a clandestine courtship for several years. Armstrong-Jones was the first commoner to marry British royalty in over four hundred years.

Antony Armstrong-Jones was born a commoner, the only son of Sir Ronald Owen Lloyd Armstrong-Jones and the former Anne Messel. His parents divorced when he was small and his mother married Sir Laurence Michael Harvey Parsons, the Sixth Earl of Rosse. Antony preferred being called Tony. He first attended the Sandroyd School and then went on to attend Upcott's house at Eton in 1943. While there he contracted polio, which left him with a permanent, though slight, limp. While recovering from polio, his mother bought him a camera, which led to his lifelong love affair with photography. In 1948 he entered Jesus College at Cambridge University. He studied architecture but failed his exams and was expelled. He worked as a court photographer and set up his own basement studio, living a rather bohemian lifestyle. He won great popularity for his photography among fashionable circles. Armstrong-Jones's photography appeared in fashion magazines like *Vogue* as well as in common advertisements. He was appointed an official court photographer in 1958, taking pictures of the royal family. In addition to royalty, he photographed such notable personalities as T. S. Eliot, Charlie Chaplin, and Sir Laurence Olivier. He first met Princess Margaret at a London party in early 1958, and they continued a secret courtship until they agreed to marry in 1960. When the princess became pregnant, Queen Elizabeth named her brother-in-law the Earl of Snowdon and Viscount Linley of Nymans in the County of Sussex. The couple had two children. By the late 1960s their marriage was crumbling as the two were linked with others romantically. They formally separated in 1976 after Princess Margaret was photographed with a young male companion. They divorced in 1978. Within months, Lord Snowdon married Lucy Mary Lindsay-Hogg who gave birth to their daughter seven months later. The two divorced in 2000. Lord Snowden also had several children out of wedlock. His five children survive him.

See Current Biography 1960

John Ashbery

Born: Rochester, New York; July 28, 1927
Died: Hudson, New York; September 3, 2017
Occupation: American poet

Arguably, John Ashbery's greatest work of poetry, and his greatest poem, was *Self-Portrait in a Convex Mirror*. Published in 1975, the book won Ashbery the National Book Critics Circle Prize, the National Book Award for poetry, and the 1976 Pulitzer Prize for poetry. He was reportedly considered for a Nobel Prize in literature. In 2011 he was recognized with a National Book Award for lifetime achievement, and a National Humanities Medal.

John Ashbery was born in Rochester, New York, to a fruit farmer. Ashbery's mother had been a biology teacher before her marriage. The death of his only brother at the age of nine left John Ashbery a solitary child. He spent his summers working on the family orchard in Sodus, New York, and was close with his grandfather, Henry Lawrence, who was the chairman of the University of Rochester's physics department. Ashbery was recognized early for his intellect, winning a contest that made him one of "The Quiz Kids," a popular radio program in the 1940s that starred gifted children. He earned a scholarship to attend the prestigious Deerfield Academy for the last two years of high school. He earned his degree in English literature from Harvard in 1949, and then continued to study contemporary literature at Columbia University, earning a master's degree in 1951. For the next five years Ashbery worked as a copywriter for Oxford University Press and McGraw-Hill. In 1955 W. H. Auden selected Ashbery's chapbook *Some Trees*, as the winner of the Yale Younger Poets competition. The same year he won a Fulbright fellowship to France to translate and edit an anthology of contemporary French poetry. The fellowship was renewed for a second year, and Ashbery remained in France for ten years. He also began contributing to *Art News* Magazine. In 1965 he would become the executive editor. He also began publishing volumes of poetry. In 1960 and 1964 he earned the Poet's Foundation grant, and he earned two Guggenheim fellowships in 1967 and 1973. In 1966 his *Rivers and Mountains* was nominated for the National Book Award, and Ashbery was recognized as one of the "New York Poets," which included such poets as Donald Hall, Robert Bly, Barbara Guest, and Kenneth Koch.

John Ashbery was married to David Kermani who survives him.

See Current Biography 1976

Brenda Barnes

Born: Chicago, Illinois; November 11, 1953
Died: Naperville, Illinois; January 17, 2017
Occupation: Business executive

Brenda Barnes held a number of high-ranking executive positions, primarily at PepsiCo and Sara Lee Corp. She shocked the business world in 1997 when she announced that, after twenty-two years at PepsiCo and heir apparent to the CEO, she was resigning to spend more time with her family.

Brenda Czajka was the third of seven daughters born to her mother, a homemaker, and her father, a factory worker. She grew up in Franklin Park, Illinois, and attended Augustana College in Rock Island, Illinois, graduating in 1975 with a degree in business and economics. She worked sorting mail on the night shift at the Chicago post office before her job as a business manager for Wilson Sporting Goods, then a subsidiary of PepsiCo. While working, she took night classes at Loyola University in Chicago, and earned her master's degree in business administration. She then proceeded to rise through the executive ranks until 1996 when she became the president and chief executive officer (CEO) of Pepsi-Cola. Under her tenure, she oversaw the acquiring of bottling operations that resulted in a tripling of sales, with record operating profits of $1.43 billion. In 1997 she shocked the business world by resigning from her $2 million-per-year position, citing a desire to devote more time to her husband, Randall C. Barnes, a retired PepsiCo executive, and their three young children. For a short time she filled in as president and CEO of the Starwood Hotels and Resorts in White Plains, New York. In 2004, as her children grew and began leaving home, Barnes accepted a position as the president and CEO of the Chicago-based Sara Lee Corp. At that time, *Forbes* magazine ranked her eighth on its list of the world's most powerful women, a step ahead of Oprah Winfrey. The *Wall Street Journal* named her one of its "50 Women to Watch."

In 2010 Barnes suffered a debilitating stroke. She then served on the board of the Rehabilitation Institute of Chicago where she was also a patient. Her three children survive her.

See Current Biography 2006

Chuck Barris

Born: Philadelphia, Pennsylvania; June 3, 1929
Died: Palisades, New York; March 21, 2017
Occupation: Television producer, writer

Chuck Barris is most remembered as the creator of the wildly popular television game shows *The Dating Game, The Newlywed Game,* and *The Gong Show.* He was alternately called the "godfather of TV," and the "king of schlock."

Chuck Barris's father died when Barris was quite young, leaving his mother to raise her two children with little money. Barris drifted from college to college, attending six in all, before graduating from Drexel University in 1953. He lacked a sense of direction, working at various jobs, including a stint at US Steel. He worked as a page at NBC Studios in New York City and conned his way into a management trainee program. In the late 1950s, during the payola scandals, he was paid to keep an eye on Dick Clark for any signs of corruption. The two became fast friends. Barris worked for awhile as the director of ABC's daytime programming. At this time he penned the song "Palisades Park," which shot to the number three position on the pop charts. Barris left ABC after he was reprimanded for participating in a civil rights march in Selma, Alabama. Barris set out on his own as an independent producer. With a $20,000 loan from his mother's second husband, Barris created *The Dating Game,* which became a huge success, occupying prime spots on both the daytime lineup and an evening prime time spot—the first television show to do so. He had similar success with *The Newlywed Game,* which premiered in 1966. Barris then penned his best-selling novel, *You and Me, Babe.* In 1976 he created *The Gong Show,* a spoof of old-time amateur shows. The daytime version of the show captured seventy-eight percent of young viewers.

In 1980 Barris sold off his various business enterprises, baffling the entertainment industry, and penned his own autobiography, *Confessions of a Dangerous Mind,* in which he confessed to having been an assassin for the Central Intelligence Agency (CIA). The CIA has never corroborated the claim. A movie adaptation, directed by George Clooney, was released in 2002. In 1998 Barris lost his only child to a drug overdose, and in 2010, he published *Della: A Memoir of My Daughter.* His third wife, the former Mary Clagett, survives him.

See Current Biography 2005

Walter Becker
(Steely Dan)

Born: New York, New York; February 20, 1950
Died: Maui, Hawaii; September 3, 2017
Occupation: Rock/jazz musician, songwriter

Walter Becker was the co-founder of the popular band, Steely Dan whose music is a smooth fusion of rock and jazz. He and his partner, Donald Fagen, were one of the most popular bands of the 1970s.

Walter Becker met Donald Fagen when the two were both students at Bard College. Upon Fagen's graduation, Becker dropped out and the two moved to New York City where they met Kenny Vance of Jay and the Americans, a pop group from the 1960s. Vance helped them record some demo tapes and sold one song, "I Mean to Shine," to Barbara Streisand. Vance also arranged for the duo to perform as backup musicians for Jay and the Americans on their 1970 live tour. At the same time, Becker and Fagen met the young producer Gary Katz who persuaded them to move to Los Angeles and work as staff songwriters for ABC Records. With Katz's guidance, they put together a group of musicians proficient enough to do their complicated arrangements justice. The vocalist David Palmer briefly worked with Becker and Fagen. They then decided to record a record under the name "Steely Dan," a slang term for a sexual device from the William Burroughs novel *Naked Lunch*. Two songs from their first album, *Can't Buy a Thrill*, hit the charts: the Latin-tinged "Do it Again," and "Reelin' in the Years." Being perfectionists, both Becker and Fagen shunned improvisation and for most of their careers, only performed in the studio. They put together three albums in the early 1970s. The album *Pretzel Logic*, which included the hit "Rikki Don't Lose That Number," reached number eight on the charts and went gold. The duo began picking individual musicians for specific album tracks, leading producer Gary Katz to characterize Steely Dan as a floating workshop rather than a band. In 1980 Becker was hit by a taxi and his girlfriend died from an overdose in his apartment. He himself became addicted to heroin. Steely Dan announced their dissolution in 1981, though Becker and Fagen remained friends. Becker moved to Maui, becoming an avocado farmer, and beating his addiction. Becker and Fagen renewed their partnership in the early 1990s and began touring, putting out several new albums. Their album *Two Against Nature* sold over a million copies and won Steely Dan a Grammy Award. Becker released a solo album in 2008.

Information about the cause of death and survivors is not available.

See Current Biography 2000

Chester Bennington (Linkin Park)

Born: Phoenix, Arizona; March 20, 1976
Died: Palos Verdes Estates, California; July 20, 2017
Occupation: American singer, songwriter

Chester Bennington was the front man for the popular, trans-genre, nu-metal band called Linkin Park. Over the course of Bennington's career, Linkin Park was nominated for nine American Music Awards, winning five; six Grammy nominations with two wins; and fourteen Billboard Music Award nominations, with one win. Linkin Park was also awarded a Global Leadership Award by the United Nations Foundation.

Chester Bennington was born the youngest of four children to Lee and Susan Bennington who divorced when their youngest child was eleven years old. It had a profound effect on their youngest son, who moved in with his father, having felt abandoned by his mother. He endured bullying in school and took solace in drugs and alcohol, addictions that he fought for the rest of his life. He devoted himself to song writing in the 1990s, drawing on the pain of his addictions and the trauma of sexual child abuse. He co-created the band Grey Daze, which produced three albums in the early 1990s. He then joined the band Xero, which changed its name to Linkin Park, and in 2000 they produced their first album, *Hybrid Theory*. It was an immediate success, rising to the number two spot on Billboard's charts, winning the band several Grammy Awards, and selling over thirty million copies. Bennington co-founded and produced a new album with the group Dead by Sunrise in 2005.

In 2013 he fulfilled a life-long dream and made an album with his childhood idols, Stone Temple Pilots.

Bennington married his first wife, Samantha Olit, in 1996 and they had one son. The couple divorced in 2005. In 2006 he married a school-teacher, Talinda Bentley and they had three children. He also had two sons from a relationship with Elka Brand. His wife and six children survive him.

See Current Biography 2002

Leo Leroy Beranek

Born: Solon, Iowa; September 15, 1914
Died: Westwood, Massachusetts; October 10, 2016
Occupation: Acoustic engineer, educator, author

Leo Beranek was a pioneer in sound technology who designed acoustics for numerous high-profile venues such as the United Nations General Assembly Hall, the music hall at the Tanglewood Music Center in Lennox, Massachusetts, and the Philharmonic Hall at Lincoln Center in New York. He was responsible for setting worldwide noise standards for public buildings and airports. He also co-founded the firm Bolt, Beranek & Newman, which won a US Department of Defense research grant to design the first computer-based network known as Arpanet, a precursor to the modern Internet.

Leo Beranek earned his undergraduate degree in physics and mathematics from Cornell College in Mount Vernon, Illinois, and then attended Harvard University where he earned his graduate degree in physics and communications engineering. From 1940 to 1946 he taught at Harvard as an assistant professor and became the director of Harvard's Electroacoustic Lab, charged with improving communications systems for the US military during World War II. Beginning in 1947, with a John Guggenheim Fellowship, Beranek conducted joint research at Harvard and Massachusetts Institute of Technology (MIT), in acoustic materials and auditorium design. He was chairman of a panel on acoustics with the Department of Defense, and a member of a joint committee on hearing and bioacoustics of the National Research Council. In 1948 Beranek partnered with Richard Bolt and Robert Newman to found Bolt, Beranek & Newman (BBN), which delved into the brand-new field of computer networking. According to Glenn Rifkin, writing for *The New York Times* (17 Oct. 2016), "the company developed one of the best software research groups in the country."

Leo Beranek was married twice. His first wife, Phyllis Knight, died in 1982. He later married Gabriella Sohn who survives him along with his two sons, two stepsons, and a granddaughter.

See Current Biography 1963

Rosamond Bernier

Born: Philadelphia, Pennsylvania; October 1, 1916
Died: New York, New York; November 9, 2016
Occupation: Art lecturer, writer, editor

A friend to such legendary artists as Henri Matisse and Pablo Picasso, Rosamond Bernier drew upon her experiences with artists to write and lecture on their art. She was *Vogue* magazine's first European features editor, and co-founded the magazine *L'ŒIL* a high-end, lavish, bi-lingual publication that became required reading for the international art world in Paris, London, and New York. She also published sixteen influential art books. She became a much sought-after lecturer at universities and museums around the world.

Rosamond (Rosenbaum) Bernier was born into a home of high-culture. Her father was vice president of the Philadelphia Orchestra, and guests to her home included the likes of Sergei Rachmaninoff. Her mother died when Bernier was eight. For three years she attended the Sherborne School for Girls in Dorset, but was sent home after she contracted tuberculosis. She attended Sarah Lawrence College in New York, leaving early to marry her first husband, Lewis Riley. They settled in Acapulco, Mexico, where Rosamond became fluent in Spanish. (Her fluency eventually earned her a close friendship of Pablo Picasso.) After her first divorce, Bernier was offered a job at *Vogue* magazine as assistant to the fashion editor. She later became *Vogue's* first European features editor. While establishing herself in Paris, Bernier met and married Georges Bernier, a former journalist. They partnered with the art dealer Eugene V. Thaw, selling a Cezanne watercolor to David Rockefeller. They soon co-founded their magazine *L'ŒIL*, which quickly earned the respect of the art world. Bernier was the first journalist to be invited by Henri Matisse to see his designs for the chapel in Venice. The Berniers also published sixteen art books.

After an unexpected divorce, Rosamond Bernier returned to the United States where a friend and art historian, Michael Mahoney, suggested she give a series of lectures on modern art to his students at Trinity College. (He was the head of the fine arts department.) She was asked to lecture at the New York Metropolitan Museum of art in 1971, thus launching a successful career as an art lecturer.

Rosamond Bernier was awarded the French Order of Arts and Letters, and won a Peabody award for her work on a PBS program about modern art. A stepson and stepdaughter survive her.   *See Current Biography 1988*

Chuck Berry

Born: St. Louis, Missouri; October 18, 1926
Died: Ladue, Missouri; March 18, 2017
Occupation: Rock and roll icon, musician

Some critics consider Chuck Berry, rather than Elvis Presley, the father of rock and roll music. Many of his songs are considered classics, such as "Johnny B. Good," "Roll Over Beethoven," and "Rock n' Roll Music." He had a major influence on other rock legends, including the Beatles and the Rolling Stones.

Chuck Berry grew up in a middle-class home with his two parents and his five siblings. His earliest musical training was with the Antioch Baptist Church choir in St. Louis. Later he sang bass in the Sumner High School glee club. He taught himself to play the six-string Spanish guitar. Berry worked in a factory assembly line and took night classes in cosmetology, hoping to become a hairdresser. In the early 1950s he supplemented his income with money he earned from gigs playing guitar. He also formed a trio with pianist Johnny Johnson and drummer Ebby Harding and they began doing regular weekend gigs at the Cosmopolitan Club in East St. Louis. While vacationing in Chicago, Berry met the legendary Muddy Waters who introduced him to Leonard Chess, president of Chess Records. Berry and Johnny Johnson auditioned with an original song titled "Maybelline," which soon became his first hit, and would become the first song ever to simultaneously occupy three number one slots on Billboard's charts: rhythm-and-blues, country-and-western, and pop. For the following five years, Berry continued a steady parade of hits on the Chess label.

With his newfound wealth, Berry moved his wife and children into a mansion and he opened Chuck Berry's Club Bandstand. When he fired a hatcheck girl at the club, she claimed to have been under age when she met Berry, and that he transported her from New Mexico to St. Louis for immoral purposes. Though it was eventually proven that the girl lied, Berry spent two years in prison. He was released in 1964, a changed man. His records continued to sell, but he had lost his momentum with writing and performing new music. He released a number of albums in the early 1970s. His Risqué "My Ding-A-Ling" had more than a million sales. In 1973 he took part in a touring rock and roll festival that included vintage rock stars like Chubby Checker, Bo Diddley, and Bill Hale and the Comets. Though he didn't write new music in the 1980s and 1990s, he kept a vigorous concert schedule. He continued to perform well into his eighties.

In 1985, Berry received the Lifetime Achievement Award at the 27th Annual Grammy Awards, and he was inducted into the Rock and Roll Hall of Fame in 1986. In 2000, he received a Kennedy Center honor, and in 2003, *Rolling Stone* magazine named him number six on its list of Greatest Guitarists of All Time.

His survivors include his wife of sixty-eight years, Themetta Berry (Suggs), and their four children.

See Current Biography 1977

William Peter Blatty

Born: New York, New York; January 7, 1928
Died: Bethesda, Maryland; January 12, 2017
Occupation: Novelist, filmmaker

Although William Peter Blatty wrote a dozen novels and the same number of screenplays, he will always be remembered as the author of *The Exorcist,* a horror novel that was made into a movie that, at the time, was the biggest money-maker in cinema history.

William Peter Blatty was the fifth child born to his Lebanese immigrant parents who separated when he was six, leaving him to be raised by his eccentric mother, who earned a meager living by selling homemade quince jelly on the street. Blatty won a scholarship to Brooklyn Prep, a Jesuit school for the wealthy, and later, he attended Georgetown University in Washington, DC on a scholarship. After graduation he sold Electrolux vacuum cleaners door-to-door and drove a beer truck before enlisting in the US Navy, working in aerial resupply and the communications wing, where he directed psychological warfare policy. He then returned to Georgetown to earn his master's degree in English literature. (He later earned a doctorate from Georgetown.) From 1955 to 1957 he lived in Beirut, Lebanon, working for the US information agency and edited the *News Review*, a weekly magazine. In collaboration with James Cullen, Blatty wrote his first novel, *Ulysses and the Cyclops: A Tale from Homer's Odyssey.* His second book, *Which Way to Mecca, Jack?* came out in 1960. Early film credits include *A Shot in the Dark*, starring Peter Sellers as the bumbling inspector Clouseau, *Gunn, Darling Lili,* and *What Did You Do in the War, Daddy?*

Shortly after his mother's death in 1967, Blatty retired to a cabin near Lake Tahoe, California, where he completed his new novel, *The Exorcist.* While critics judged it little more than a skillfully wrought horror story, the sales belied their assessment. It sat on the *New York Times'* bestseller list for fifty-five weeks and was translated into a dozen languages. In 1971 Blatty sold the film rights and acted as both screenwriter and producer, hiring Academy Award-winning director William Friedkin to direct the film version of the novel. The movie was released in 1973 to record-breaking crowds. The film was nominated for ten Oscars, but won only two.

Blatty was married four times and had seven children. His wife of thirty-three years, and his children survive him.

See Current Biography 1974

William Bowen

Born: Cincinnati, Ohio; October 6, 1933
Died: Princeton, New Jersey; October 20, 2016
Occupation: University president; educator, economist

William Bowen served as the president of Princeton University from 1972 to 1988, transforming the university from a preserve of the wealthy, white male academic to a diverse and inclusive institution that championed women and minorities in higher education. Bowen was elected president when he was just thirty-eight making him one of the youngest university presidents in the country. He also served as president of the Andrew W. Mellon Foundation for nearly two decades.

Born in Cincinnati, Ohio, to a salesman of calculating machines, William Bowen's early life was humble. He attended Denison University in Ohio on scholarships, playing varsity tennis in the Ohio Conference. He was the first university graduate in his family. He entered Princeton University as a Woodrow Wilson, Danforth, and Ford Foundation fellow, earning his PhD in economics, and he was immediately appointed to the Princeton faculty as an assistant professor. He served for five years as the university provost before being elected Princeton University president in 1972. Under his leadership, Bowen tripled Princeton's endowments. He ushered in the residential college system with a sixty-three percent growth in the faculty. Following his tenure as Princeton University president, Bowen served for nearly two decades, from 1988 to 2006, as the president of the Andrew W. Mellon Foundation, where he helped establish global electronic academic archives such as JSTOR, ARTstor and ITHAKA.

William Bowen wrote or co-wrote numerous books, including *The Shape of the River: Long-Term Consequences of Considering Race in College and University Admissions*, a groundbreaking book on the value of affirmative action in higher education, written with Derek Bok, the former president of Harvard University. In 1993, a new science and engineering research building was named Bowen's Hall in Bowen's honor. In 2012 President Barack Obama awarded Bowen the National Humanities Medal.

William Bowen married the former Mary Ellen Maxwell (whom he met in the fourth grade) in 1956. She, their two children, and five grandchildren survive him.

See Current Biography 1973

Jimmy Breslin

Born: New York, New York; October 17, 1930
Died: New York, New York; March 19, 2017
Occupation: Writer

Jimmy Breslin was a columnist for several New York newspapers. He was a key contributor in the development of "new Journalism," bringing narrative nonfiction to newspaper columns. He was unique in that he wrote stories from the perspective of those present: the gravedigger who dug President Kennedy's grave, a child witnessing the civil rights march in Selma, Alabama. In 1986 he won a Pulitzer Prize for his story about the AIDS epidemic from the perspective of David Camacho, an early AIDS victim.

James Earle Breslin was born and raised in Jamaica, Queens in New York City where he learned the brash "Queens English" that became an integral part of his style. It is questionable whether he graduated from high school, which he attended for five years. Shortly thereafter he began working at the *Long Island Press* newspaper. At the time, his only real interest was sports writing. Throughout the 1950s Breslin moved from newspaper to newspaper, but was never able to settle with one. He turned to writing books, and his first novel, *Sunny Jim: The Life of America's Most Beloved Horseman, James Fitzsimmons*, was published. The following year he published his second book, *Can't Anybody Here Play This Game?: The Improbable Saga of the New York Mets, First Year*. Mets fans loved it, including the brother of Mets owner Mrs. Charles Shipman Payson who was also the publisher of the *New York Herald Tribune*. Breslin became a regular columnist at the paper. In 1967 he began writing pieces for *New York*, a magazine that he helped launch.

Breslin's stories were primarily short nonfiction narratives—something called "mood pieces." He wrote about the Vietnam War, the Selma civil-rights march, from the perspective of a child, and the assassinations of the Kennedys, written from the perspective of an attending surgeon. Breslin was with Robert Kennedy when Kennedy was assassinated. The gravedigger piece won Breslin the Columbia School of

Journalism's Meyer Berger Award and the Newspaper General Reporting Award of the Sigma Delta Chi journalism fraternity.

Breslin's first wife, Rosemary Dattolico, died in 1981. His survivors include his second wife, Ronnie Eldridge, four sons, three stepchildren, a sister and twelve grandchildren.

See Current Biography 1973

Trisha Brown

Born: Aberdeen, Washington; November 25, 1936
Died: San Antonio, Texas; March 18, 2017
Occupation: Choreographer, dancer

Trisha Brown was a unique, avant-garde presence in the dance community. She founded the Judson Dance Theater group and the dance collective, Grand Union, and created her own troupe, the Trisha Brown Dance Company. She won some of the dance world's most prestigious awards, including several National Endowment for the Arts (NEA) fellowships, a MacArthur foundation "genius" grant," and a Samuel H. Scripps American Dance Festival Award. In 1988 France named her a chevalier of the Order of Arts and Letters, the equivalent of a British knighthood.

Trisha Brown was born in Washington State where she spent her childhood hunting, fishing, and climbing trees. She claimed her father "forgot his third child was a girl." She also took dance classes, learning tap, jazz, and acrobatics. As she matured she realized she needed to do something with her natural athleticism. She was a dance major at Mills College in Oakland, California, where she learned techniques developed by Martha Graham. Reed College hired Brown to start a dance program. In 1959 she attended a workshop led by the guru of improvisational movement and founder of post-modern dance, Anna Halprin, who rejected traditional dance techniques in favor of more natural movements. Brown moved to New York City where she joined like-minded dancers, choreographers, and artists that became known as the Judson Dance Theater. By 1970 Brown had gained enough confidence to form her own dance company.

Trisha Brown began to create using new tools such as pulleys, ropes, climbing gear, tracks, and cables—a time referred to as her "equipment" phase. Around the same time, Brown joined her colleague, Yvonne Rainer, in a collective company known as Grand Union, which became a hotbed of creativity. The dancers in both endeavors performed in non-stage settings such as in a museums and parks. She even performed in a dark parking lot in Ann Arbor, Michigan, where a parked car's headlights provided her stage

lighting. The 1980s brought international prestige with Brown's piece titled "Set and Reset." Mikhail Baryshnikov sought Brown as a collaborator in modern dance. Late in her career, she began choreographing and performing to classical music.

Trisha Brown's survivors include two siblings, her son, and four grandchildren. Her husband, Burt Barr, predeceased her only months earlier, in November of 2016.

See Current Biography 1997

Zbigniew Brzezinski

Born: Warsaw, Poland; March 28, 1928
Died: Falls Church, Virginia; May 26, 2017
Occupation: Former US national security advisor, social scientist, educator

Zbigniew Brzezinski was a foreign affairs advisor to successive US presidents for more than four decades, and was the national security advisor to President Jimmy Carter.

Zbigniew Brzezinski was born into a family of diplomats; his father, Tadeus Brzezinski was a Polish diplomat, and Brzezinski spent most of his childhood in France and Germany. In 1938 the family moved to Canada where Brzezinski's father served as the Polish consul general in Montreal throughout World War II. Brzezinski entered McGill University in 1945 earning degrees in economics and political science. He earned his PhD degree from Harvard University in 1953, after which he worked as a research fellow and instructor in government. He taught at Harvard from 1953 until 1960 when he was appointed an associate professor in public law and government at Columbia University. In 1961 he served as a foreign policy advisor to President-elect John F. Kennedy. He earned a seat on the State Department's Policy Planning Council in 1966, where he defended the US involvement in Vietnam. In 1973 Brzezinski sat on the Trilateral Commission, a group of business leaders founded by David Rockefeller to examine the challenges faced by the industrialized countries of North America, Europe, and Japan. He invited the new star of the Democrats, Jimmy Carter, to join the commission, and two years later he became an advisor on foreign affairs to president-elect Jimmy Carter. He soon became Carter's national security advisor. He was a chief instigator of the botched attempt to rescue nine American hostages held by the Ayatollah Khomeini's revolutionary forces in Iran. He had an ongoing feud with Secretary of State Cyrus Vance that eventually ended with Vance's resignation. Brzezinski made it his personal mission to thwart the Soviet Union, no matter the cost.

When the Soviets invaded Afghanistan, Brzezinski supported arming Islamic militants—a move that would haunt the United States a decade later. Over the course of his career, he published over a dozen books including a memoir. In 2003 Brzezinski was one of the few foreign policy experts to warn against the invasion of Iraq.

Zbigniew Brzezinski was married to Czech-American sculptor Emilie Benes. She survives him in addition to their two children and five grandchildren.

See Current Biography 1970

Glen Campbell

Born: Delight, Arkansas; April 22, 1936
Died: Nashville, Tennessee; August 8, 2017
Occupation: Country and western performer, singer, musician, songwriter

At the height of his career, Glen Campbell was one of the most popular performers in the country. Although ostensibly a country and western singer, he also had songs on the pop charts. Campbell won ten Grammy Awards, including a lifetime achievement award, eleven Academy of Country Music Awards, and three American Music Awards. He appeared with John Wayne in the classic movie, *True Grit*, and his song for the movie's soundtrack was nominated for an Academy Award.

Glen Travis Campbell was born the last of twelve children, to a poor sharecropper at the height of the Depression. As a boy he helped supplement the family's income by picking cotton. He started to learn to play the guitar by the age of four, and by the time he was six, Campbell was playing for local radio stations. At fourteen he made appearances at the Houston Nightclub in nearby Galveston. He quit high school after the tenth grade and performed across the western states after joining his uncle Dick Bill's country band. By 1958 he had his own band known as the Western Wranglers. In 1960 Campbell moved to Hollywood. He eventually found steady work as a background artist, playing with such great performers as Frank Sinatra, Nat King Cole, Dean Martin, and Elvis Presley. In one year, he filled 586 recording dates. He toured with the Beach Boys in the mid-1960s. His first hit, *Turn Around—Look at Me*, led to his signing a long-term contract with Capitol Records. In 1967 he performed "Gentle on My Mind," which became a runaway hit and Campbell was awarded four Grammy Awards. In 1968 Campbell signed a six-picture contract with Hollywood film producer Hal Wallis. His first film was a Western called *True Grit*, starring John Wayne. Campbell's song was nominated

for an Academy Award and he received a Golden Globe nomination for his role. In 1969 Campbell hosted his own television variety show, *The Glen Campbell Good Time Hour.*

In the 1980s Campbell fell into alcoholism and drug abuse, which he fought for the rest of his life. He performed well into his seventies, covering such popular groups as U2 and Green Day. Though diagnosed with Alzheimer's disease, Campbell launched "The Glen Campbell Goodbye Tour," playing 151 sold-out shows. A film crew recorded his performances, and the documentary film, *Glen Campbell: I'll Still Be Me*, was highly acclaimed. Campbell also won himself another Grammy and an Academy Award nomination for the song "I'm Not Gonna Miss You."

Campbell was married four times and had eight children. Besides his children, Campbell's survivors include his wife and numerous grandchildren, great-grandchildren, and great-great-grandchildren.

See Current Biography 1969

Robert Campeau

Born: Chelmsford, Ontario, Canada; August 3, 1923
Died: Ottawa, Canada; June 12, 2017
Occupation: Canadian entrepreneur

Robert Campeau was a Canadian real-estate developer and retail magnate who, at one time, owned such retail chains as Brooks Brothers, Ann Taylor, I Magnin, Filenes, and Bloomingdales.

Robert Campeau was raised in abject poverty after his family lost nearly everything during the Depression. Of the fourteen children in his family, only seven survived past infancy. Campeau was forced to leave school at fourteen so he could work. As he had an aptitude for mechanical things, he completed a four-year training program in two years and, at the age of sixteen, joined Canadian International Paper as the manager of a pulp and paper mill in Ottawa. He became involved in construction after selling an unfinished house he had been building at a $3,000 profit. In the booming postwar economy, he invested in farmland and converted it into a fifty-house subdivision. The Campeau Construction Company incorporated in 1953. During the 1960s the company shifted its operations to include commercial developments. In 1968 one of Campeau's best friends, Pierre Trudeau was elected prime minister of Canada. Any time the government needed office space for an expanding bureaucracy, they called Campeau. Campeau's tight relationship with the government brought criticism from his opposition in the business community. During the 1970s, Campeau's marriage fell apart when it was discovered he had a long-time mistress who had two of his children. The two eventually married. In 1983 Campeau decided to leave the residential housing business and go into commercial real-estate development. He moved to New York where he attempted to take over Allied Stores, the third largest retail chain in the United States, stunning the Wall Street business community. He withdrew his bid, and when share prices tumbled, Campeau purchased a large percentage of Allied shares through a Los Angeles broker who had arranged the deal on Campeau's behalf. It was the largest single block of shares ever traded in American corporate history at that time. Campeau's unorthodox entrepreneurial style was his audacity in risk-taking, which eventually caught up with him when Allied and Federated declared bankruptcy in 1990.

Robert Campeau lived the rest of his life as something of a recluse in Switzerland. He was married three times. His wife, Cristal Dettman, his son, Daniel, and eight grandchildren survive him.

See Current Biography 1989

Fidel Castro

Born: Oriente, Cuba; August 13, 1926
Died: Havana, Cuba; November 25, 2016
Occupation: President of Cuba

Fidel Castro was the young Cuban revolutionary who, with a small force of rebels, overthrew the forces of the military dictator Fulgencio Batista. He became Cuba's prime minister and, at first, declared his alignment with Western Democracies. However, relations with the United States quickly deteriorated as Castro drew closer to the Soviet Union. Tense relations came perilously close to war with the US invasion of the Bay of Pigs and, a year later, its blockade of ships carrying Soviet missiles to Cuba. Castro declared Cuba a "Socialist country." Castro's regime became repressive and violent. He aligned his country with guerrilla revolutionaries in Central and South America, a direct affront to the United States. He remained in power until 2008 when he resigned, and his brother, Raul, took over leadership.

Fidel Castro's parents were immigrant laborers from Galacia, Spain who eventually acquired an estate of more than twenty-three thousand acres. Castro was born on their sugar plantation. Though he worked in his father's fields as a boy, Castro was determined to get an education. He was educated in several Jesuit schools and in 1945, he enrolled in the Faculty of Law at the University of Havana where he studied law, diplomacy, public administration, and social sciences. After earning his doctoral degree, Castro started his own practice. In 1952, General Fulgencio Batista overthrew the Cuban government and established a military dictatorship. Castro brought a legal suit to the Court of Constitutional Guarantees, charging the dictator with violating the Constitution of 1940. The suit was rejected and Castro led a small force of men in an attack on the Moncada Barracks in Santiago de Cuba. Castro was caught and sentenced to fifteen years imprisonment at the Isle of Pines. After two years he was released under general amnesty and continued his campaign against Batista. He traveled to Mexico City where he met Ernesto "Che" Guevara who would become a key figure in the Cuban revolutionary movement. After another failed attempt on the government, the two waged continuous guerrilla warfare against the Batista troops until 1959 when, after realizing his defeat, Batista went into exile. The early days of Castro's provisional government saw wholesale arrests, trials, and the executions of Batista supporters.

As relations with the United States quickly soured, Castro sought trade with the Soviet Union and declared Cuba a Socialist country. Cuban industry was nationalized and its agriculture collectivized. Public speech was tightly monitored, with dissidents jailed or executed. Relations with the United States hovered on the brink of war after a US–backed force of Cuban dissidents invaded Cuba at the Bay of Pigs. The effort failed. US intelligence learned that the Soviet Union was building bases in Cuba for long-range ballistic missiles and set up a blockade. The maneuver, known as the Cuban missile crisis, brought the two super-powers to the brink of nuclear warfare. The crisis was averted after Russia's Khrushchev agreed to remove the missiles and President Kennedy lifted the blockade.

Relations between the United States and Cuba remained chilly for decades as disaffected Cubans sought asylum in the United States. In 2008 Castro resigned as President of Cuba and, with failing health, retired in seclusion.

Fidel Castro was married twice and had nine children. He is reported to have had a daughter out of wedlock.

See Current Biography 2001

Eugene Cernan

Born: Chicago, Illinois; March 14, 1934
Died: Houston, Texas; January 16, 2017
Occupation: Astronaut

Eugene Cernan was the commander of the Apollo 17 lunar mission and the last man to walk on the moon, as of this writing, in December of 1972. He was the second man to walk outside of an orbiting spacecraft, tethered to his ship. He piloted Apollo 10, coming within eight nautical miles of the moon's surface, the final rehearsal for the first manned landing on the moon with Apollo 11.

Eugene Cernan was born to first-generation Czechoslovak-American parents in Chicago, Illinois. He shared an especially close relationship with his father who worked as a supervisor at a naval installation near Chicago. He was quite a successful athlete but rejected a number of college football scholarships to study electrical engineering at Purdue University. He had not been particularly interested in flying until he spent several summer vacations as a construction worker at Chicago's O'Hare Airport. His experience there and his exposure to the Naval Reserve Officer Training Program (ROTC) at Purdue led him to seek a career as a pilot. He completed flight training with his commission in the US Navy. He began graduate study in aeronautical engineering, at the Naval Postgraduate School (NPS) in Monterey, California, while also serving as a test pilot. He applied and was accepted to train as a National Aeronautics and Space Administration (NASA) astronaut. His first flight in space was on the Gemini 9 mission, a three-day orbit around the Earth in 1966, making him the youngest astronaut to fly in space at age thirty-two. Of importance in his mission was a two-hour and ten-minute tethered "walk" outside the space capsule. He served as backup pilot for Gemini 12 and lunar module pilot for Apollo 7 and Apollo 10. He was the commander of Apollo 17, the last manned mission to the moon. He retired from the navy and from NASA in 1976 and became an executive for Coral Petroleum in Houston. He also founded his own aerospace consulting company, Cernan Corporation in 1981. From 1994 to 2000, he was the chairman of Johnson Engineering.

Captain Cernan was awarded the NASA Distinguished Service Medal, the NASA Exceptional Service Medal, the Manned Spacecraft Center Superior Achievement Award, and the Navy Distinguished Service Medal. Cernan married Barbara Jean Atchley, and they had a daughter. They divorced, and Cernan married Jan Nanna, who survives him along with his daughter, two stepdaughters, and nine grandchildren.

See Current Biography 1973

Leonard Cohen

Born: Montreal, Quebec, Canada; September 21, 1934
Died: Los Angeles, California; November 7, 2016
Occupation: Canadian author, songwriter, poet, singer

Leonard Cohen was one of the most highly regarded singers and songwriters of the late twentieth and early twenty-first centuries. He published thirteen volumes of poetry and two novels in addition to numerous short stories.

Leonard Cohen was born into a prosperous Jewish family in Montreal, Canada. He majored in English at McGill University, winning a Mac-Naughton Prize in creative writing. He started primarily as a poet, publishing five volumes in quick succession from 1961 to 1964, and he was regarded as one of Canada's most promising young poets. (In 1960 and 1961 Cohen received a Canadian Council grant, and in 1964 he was awarded the Quebec Prize for Literature.) He studied law at Columbia University in New York. His first novel, *Beautiful Losers*, was published in 1966. In the late 1960s Cohen emerged as a folk-rock singer and composer, meeting his mentor, Judy Collins, in 1966 and appearing with her in concerts. In 1967 he performed at the Newport Folk Festival, and in 1968 he released his first album, *The Songs of Leonard Cohen*. Cohen was ranked with the likes of Bob Dylan and John Lennon.

Cohen took a break from writing and recording in the early 1990s, spending five years in a Zen Buddhist retreat and becoming ordained as a Buddhist monk. He officially returned to recording in 2001. In 2004 his album *Dear Heather* topped 131 in Billboard's 200. He contributed tracks to tribute albums for such artists as Paul Simon, Joni Mitchell, and his former mentor, Judy Collins. His final album, *You Want It Darker*, was released just before his death, and debuted at number ten on the Billboard 200 (the second of Cohen's albums to reach the top ten in the United States).

Leonard Cohen had a long-standing friendship with Marianne Ihlen who inspired a number of Cohen's best-known songs. He had two children with the artist Suzanne Elrod. His two children and three grandchildren survive him.

See Current Biography 1969

William T. Coleman, Jr.

Born: Philadelphia, Pennsylvania; July 7, 1920
Died: Alexandria, Virginia; March 31, 2017
Occupation: Former US Secretary of Transportation, civil rights attorney

William Coleman led a long and distinguished career as a lawyer and civil rights activist. As the secretary of transportation in President Gerald Ford's cabinet, Coleman was the second African American to serve in a cabinet position. In 1995 President Bill Clinton presented him with the Presidential Medal of Freedom.

William Coleman was born the second of three children to a solidly middle–class family that claimed six generations of teachers and Episcopal ministers. His father, William T. Coleman, Sr., served for forty years as the director of the Germantown Boys Club. As such, he met some of America's most distinguished black leaders, including W.E.B. DuBois, co-founder of the National Association for the Advancement of Colored People (NAACP), and Supreme Court Justice, Thurgood Marshall. The young Coleman was one of seven token black students admitted to the prestigious Germantown High School. There the swim team disbanded rather than integrate and allow Coleman to join. He graduated from the University of Pennsylvania in 1941, cum laude, and he entered Harvard University Law School, but he dropped out in 1943 to enlist in the US Army Air Corp where he served as defense counsel in eighteen courts-martial cases. Back at Harvard, Coleman was a member of the board of editors of the *Harvard Law Review*, winning the Joseph E. Beale Prize, graduating first in his class in 1946. He was admitted to the Pennsylvania bar in 1947. He occupied a long list of distinguished positions, including law clerk to Associate Justice Felix Frankfurter of the US Supreme Court.

Coleman specialized in transportation law and represented several cities in mass-transit and labor matters. He became a director of Pan American World Airways and eventually became a member of the board of governors of the American Stock Exchange. He co-authored the brief presented to the Supreme Court in *Brown vs. Board of Education*, which desegregated schools across the country. He was co-counsel in the historic *McLaughlin vs. Florida*, which established the constitutionality of racially mixed marriages. In 1966 he was co-chair of the White House Conference on Civil Rights. In 1971 he was elected president of the NAACP Legal Defense and Education Fund. In 1973 Coleman declined an invitation to become the Watergate special prosecutor. In 1975, however, President Gerald Ford offered the life-long Republican the post of Secretary of Transportation, the fourth largest federal agency, which he accepted. In all, Coleman argued nineteen cases before the US Supreme Court.

Coleman met Lovida Hardin when they both attended college in Boston. They had three children. He leaves behind his wife of seventy years, three children, and four grandchildren.

See Current Biography 1976

Barbara Cook

Born: Atlanta, Georgia; October 25, 1927
Died: New York, New York; August 8, 2017
Occupation: American actress, singer

At the height of her career, Barbara Cook was one of the brightest singing stars, and is most remembered for her role of librarian, Marian, in Meredith Willson's *The Music Man*, when it opened in 1957. Cook won a Tony Award for her performance. Later in her life, Cook launched a second career, singing in music halls and cabarets in New York and London.

When Barbara Cook was a small child, her eighteen-month-old sister died from contracting whooping cough and pneumonia from her older sister. It's something that haunted Barbara Cook for most of her life. At the age of seven, she began taking tap dancing, and several years later she began performing at amateur night performances in movie theaters. At fifteen she earned herself a job as a chorus girl in Atlanta's Roxy Theatre and sang over local radio stations. After graduating from Girl's High School in Atlanta in 1945, Cook headed to New York. She worked as a typist, a file clerk, and at the Flushing, New York post office, as she tried to make a career as a performer. After working as a resort entertainer for the summer in 1950, Cook opened in her first Broadway musical, Flahooley. In 1953 she was cast in the role of Ado Annkie in a revival of *Oklahoma!* and later in the revival of another Rodgers and Hammerstein classic, *Carousel*. On December 19, 1957, Cook premiered in Majestic Theatre's *The Music Man* in which she played the plain librarian who reforms the fast-talking, heart-of-gold con man, played by Robert Preston. It was an enormous hit and Cook won a Tony Award for her performance. Several years later she played Anna in the City Center revival of *The King and I*.

Cook married drama coach, David LeGrant, in 1952 and they had one son. After the marriage fell apart, Cook fell into alcoholism and deep depression. That might have been her end, except she met pianist and composer Wally Harper who recognized her talent. The two began performing in cabarets and music halls, and garnering critical acclaim. In 1975 Cook performed at

Carnegie Hall and revitalized her singing career. For her eighty-fifth birthday, she gave another Carnegie Hall performance.

Barbara Cook's son survives her.

See Current Biography 1963

Denton Cooley

Born: Houston, Texas; August 22, 1920
Died: Houston, Texas; November 18, 2016
Occupation: Surgeon

Dr. Denton Cooley was a noted heart surgeon who pioneered surgeries in the removal of aneurysms, the replacement of damaged heart valves, and the development of the heart-lung bypass. He was the first surgeon to implant an artificial heart into a patient. His work sparked some controversy surrounding the question of how and when the medical community determines death. He was the founder of the renowned Texas Heart Institute.

Doctor Cooley was born to a prosperous Houston dentist. He studied zoology at the University of Texas where he was also a varsity basketball star. He earned his MD degree at Johns Hopkins University School of Medicine where he shared first place with another student in his graduating class. He was a protégé of the noted heart surgeon, Alfred Blalock. He served in the Army Medical Corps where he was the chief of surgical service in Linz, Austria. In 1951 Cooley was an associate professor of surgery at Baylor University College of Medicine, working with noted vascular surgeon, E. DeBakey with whom he would eventually have a notorious and heated rivalry. In the 1960s Cooley became famous for his work with congenital heart disease, especially in infants. He pioneered surgery in the replacement of diseased aortic or mitral heart valves with artificial ones. Cooley came under attack from his old mentor, Dr. DeBakey, who charged Cooley with violating federal guidelines on human experimentation, after he implanted a man-made heart into a patient. He was censured by the board of governors of the American College of Surgeons, though Cooley claimed Dr. DeBakey was trying to limit his research. Cooley left his professorship and affiliation with Baylor University and became chief surgeon of the Texas Heart Institute, which he had founded.

Dr. Cooley was honored with the International Surgical Society's highest honor, the Rene Leriche Prize in 1967. He was awarded the Presidential Medal of Freedom in 1984, and in 1999 President Bill Clinton honored him with the National Medal of Technology.

In 1949 Denton Cooley married Louise Goldsborough Thomas. They had five daughters. His wife and one daughter predeceased Dr. Cooley who is survived by his four daughters, sixteen grandchildren, and seventeen great-grandchildren.

See Current Biography 1976

Liam Cosgrave

Born: Castleknock, Ireland; April 30, 1920
Died: Dublin, Ireland; October 4, 2017
Occupation: Former prime minister of Ireland

Though his tenure as taoiseach was relatively short (he only served one four-year term), Irish Prime Minister Liam Cosgrave is most remembered for his role in brokering the Sunningdale Agreement, a short-lived power-sharing agreement with Northern Ireland that helped break the decades-long cycle of violence between the Republic of Ireland and Northern Ireland.

Liam Cosgrave was born into a family of Irish politicians. His father was president of the executive council of the Irish Free State (the equivalent of prime minister) from 1922 until 1932. Cosgrave attended Christian Brothers' School in Dublin, Castleknock College, and he studied law at King's Inns. He was called to the bar in 1943, and then served in the National Army from 1943 to 1948. From 1948 to 1951 he was parliamentary secretary to the minister of Industry and Commerce, and from 1954 to 1957 he was Minister for External Affairs. In 1956 he led the first delegation to the General Assembly to the United Nations (UN). In 1958 he was called to the inner bar, becoming a senior counselor to the government. He became the leader of his party, Fine Gael, in 1965 and remained there until 1977. In 1973 he was elected taoiseach. Cosgrave, a devout Catholic, surprised his own cabinet when he voted against his own government's bill to legalize contraception. He retired from politics in 1981.

Liam Cosgrave married Vera Osborne in 1952. She predeceased her husband in 2016. Their three children survive him.

See Current Biography 1977

José Luis Cuevas

Born: Mexico City, Mexico; February 26, 1934
Died: Mexico City, Mexico; July 3, 2017
Occupation: Mexican artist

An artist of unusual vision, José Luis Cuevas had his first one-man show at the age of thirteen. He was always a controversial figure for his perceived self-conceit and challenges to popular art. In 1992 Cuevas opened the José Luis Cuevas Museum in Mexico City. In 2008 a retrospective of Cuevas' work was held at the Museum of the Palace of Fine Arts in Mexico City.

José Luis Cuevas grew up with his extended family that lived over a paper and pencil factory, which may have stimulated his early interest in art and drawing. When he was ten years old, he suffered from a bout of rheumatic fever, which had him bed-ridden for two years, leaving him plenty of time to explore his artistic talents. Except for one semester at the National School of Painting and Sculpture, Cuevas was self-taught. His subjects were largely the grotesque or profane, beggars covered with sores, hunchbacks, prostitutes, or impoverished and filthy children. One of his favorite subjects was the Marquis de Sade. One famous oil painting was titled "The Marquis de Sade as a Child." He explained that he realized drawing was "the best vehicle for expressing [his] daily struggle with death." Cuevas gained widespread attention in the early 1950s after Pan American Union artistic director, José Gómez-Sicre, showed his work. More shows followed in New York and Paris. It was reported that Pablo Picasso bought two of Cuevas's drawings. As he aged Cuevas turned to sculpting.

In 1961 Cuevas married Bertha Lilian Riestra, a psychologist he met at La Castaneda psychiatric hospital where Cuevas used patients as models. She and their three children survive him.

See Current Biography 1968

Edward E. David, Jr.

Born: Wilmington, North Carolina; January 25, 1925
Died: Bedminster, New Jersey; February 13, 2017
Occupation: Former science advisor to President Nixon, corporate executive

For twenty-eight months, Edward David served as the director of the office of Science and Technology, and as chairman of the President's Science Advisory Committee to President Richard Nixon. In 2012 David co-authored an article for the *Wall Street Journal* that claimed there was no scientific evidence to compel drastic action due to climate change.

Edward David was raised in Atlanta, Georgia, and received his BS degree in electrical engineering from the Georgia Institute of Technology in 1945. He earned a master's and doctorate degree from the Massachusetts Institute of Technology (MIT) where he specialized in microwaves and noise theory. In 1950 he joined Bell Telephone Laboratories as a specialist in underwater sound, concentrating on developing undersea warfare techniques. He was named the director of visual and acoustic research in 1958. In the early 1960s he conducted research in acoustical psychophysics and in the interpretation of neural information by the brain. He helped develop a low-cost artificial larynx to help correct speech disorders after surgery. Though he worked primarily in the corporate world, he maintained close contact with the academic world, attending symposiums and publishing scientific papers. He co-authored a textbook in technical concepts applied to actual community problems such as traffic control, road flooding, and air and water pollution.

In 1970 President Richard Nixon selected David to serve as the director of the Office of Science and Technology and as science advisor to the president. Acting on David's recommendation, Nixon allotted additional funds for academic research, increased the budget for the National Science Foundation (NSF), and increased spending in environmental and medical research. He was the principal architect of Nixon's "clean energy" plan, submitted to Congress on June 4, 1971. He was also an advocate of international scientific cooperation, visiting Poland and the Soviet Union to sanction joint research in medical science, agriculture, ecology, and urban planning. Despite his many accomplishments, David often clashed with Nixon over policy matters, and he resigned after two years. He subsequently worked at Gould, Inc., a technology company and was the president of Exxon Research from 1977 to 1986. He also served on NATO's Science Committee.

David married Ann Hirshberg in 1950, and they had one daughter. His wife and daughter survive him.

See Current Biography 1974

Frank Deford

Born: Baltimore, Maryland; December 16, 1938
Died: Key West, Florida; May 28, 2017
Occupation: Sportswriter, novelist, television and radio commentator

Frank Deford was a sportswriter and commentator of unusual talent. In the span of his career he wrote for *Sports Illustrated* for more than thirty years. He appeared on numerous broadcast networks including NBC, CNN, and ESPN, and on NPR's *Morning Edition*, offering 1,656 weekly commentaries by the time he retired. He was named the Sportswriter of the Year no less than six times, and was a member of the National Sportscasters and Sportswriters Hall of Fame. In 2013 President Barack Obama awarded him the National Humanities Medal. He was the first sportswriter to receive the honor.

Frank Deford was born in Baltimore, Maryland, and attended Princeton University where he worked on the school paper, the *Daily Princetonian*. From the time he was a young boy, Deford had wanted to be a writer. Following graduation he joined the staff of *Sports Illustrated*, in New York City, where he would remain, off and on, for over thirty years. For more than twenty years, he appeared with Bryant Gumbel on HBO's *Real Sports with Bryant Gumbel*. In 1990 Deford was recruited, along with several of sports journalism's top talent, to be co-founder and editor in chief for *National Sports Daily* (also known as *The National*). The venture lasted just under two years.

Deford wrote more than a dozen books, both fiction and nonfiction, most notably *Alex: The Life of a Child* (1983) about his daughter, Alex, who died at eight years old from cystic fibrosis. The book was made into a television movie in 1986. He served as the national chairman of the Cystic Fibrosis Foundation for sixteen years. In 2012 he published a memoir, *Over Time: My Life as a Sportswriter*.

Frank Deford's survivors include Carol, his wife of over fifty years, his son, Christian, an adopted daughter, Scarlet, and two grandchildren.

See Current Biography 1996

Frank Delaney

Born: County Tipperary, Ireland; October 24, 1942
Died: Danbury, Connecticut; February 21, 2017
Occupation: Irish writer

Frank Delaney was a popular broadcaster and author who is most recognized for his insight into Irish literature, history, and culture. National Public Radio (NPR) named him "the most eloquent man in the world" and he was frequently sought as a judge for literary panels, including the Man Booker Prize.

Born the youngest of eight children, Frank Delaney was raised in a busy household. His parents were both teachers who helped found the Irish teacher's union, and who filled their home with books. Delaney always assumed he would one day be a writer, though he got off to a rocky start. He attended an abbey school where corporal punishment was the rule. He failed to do well enough on his exit exams to attend a university so he took an exam for a job at the Bank of Ireland where his older brothers already worked. He stayed there for eleven years, while also writing and publishing book reviews and short stories in the *Irish Times*. When he was twenty-eight, Delaney became a newsreader for Raidió Teilifís Éireann (RTE), Ireland's national broadcasting company. In 1978 he moved to London to host the radio program, *Bookshelf*, a show he pitched to the British Broadcasting Corporation (BBC). He interviewed over 1,000 authors, including John Updike and Margaret Atwood. He published his first book, *James Joyce's Odyssey: A Guide to the Dublin of Ulysses*, an attempt to make Joyce's novel more accessible to the masses. In 1986, still working for BBC, he hosted a six-part series about the Celts. Delaney published his first work of fiction, *My Dark Rosaleen*, in 1989. In the early 1990s he wrote a series of books set in Deanstown, a village in Tipperary, between 1925 and 1927. The first book in the series was short-listed for the Sunday Express Book of the Year award. In 2004 he released his first novel in the United States, a fictionalized account of Irish history, simply titled *Ireland*. In 2010 Delaney released daily, popular five-minute podcasts about *Ulysses*.

Frank Delaney nearly died from septicemia, blood poisoning, in 1995 after sustaining a small cut at his gym. Delaney suffered a stroke the day before his death. His survivors include his second wife, Diane Meier, three sons from his first marriage, and three grandchildren.

See Current Biography 2005

Jonathan Demme

Born: Baldwin, New York; February 22, 1944
Died: New York, New York; April 26, 2017
Occupation: American filmmaker

The most widely recognized films that Jonathan Demme directed are *Silence of the Lambs* (1991), which garnered five Academy Awards, including

Best Director for Demme, *Philadelphia* (1993) starring Tom Hanks and Denzel Washington, and *The Manchurian Candidate* (2004).

Jonathan Demme was born in Long Island, New York. His father was an airline publicist and an editor who would one day help his son enter the world of filmmaking. The young Demme attended high school in Miami, Florida. He worked part time at an animal hospital and had every intention of becoming a veterinarian when he entered the University of Miami. A failed chemistry test persuaded him otherwise. While there, he realized the school newspaper needed a movie critic. Demme became a filmmaker by happenstance when producer and Embassy Pictures founder, Joseph Levine met Jonathan Demme's father while vacationing in Miami. Demme's review of the movie, *Zulu* so impressed Levine (who was the film's executive producer) that he offered the young Demme a job. He moved to New York to work in the publicity department at Embassy. After a few years he moved to London and earned his first movie credit as the music coordinator for the movie *Sudden Terror*. Demme's passion for music would become central to his work for the rest of his career. His big break happened when Thom Mount of Universal Pictures called on Demme to direct the movie *Melvin and Howard*, a true story about Howard Hughes. The movie received rave reviews at the New York Film Festival and won two Academy Awards. It was named the best picture of the year by the National Society of Film Critics. Demme also produced a number of documentary films. He worked frequently with David Byrne of Talking Heads, most remarkably on the 1984 concert film *Stop Making Sense*.

Jonathan Demme was married twice. His wife, Joanne Howard, survives him as well as his three children.

See Current Biography 1985

Lou Duva

Born: New York, New York; May 28, 1922
Died: Paterson, New Jersey; March 8, 2017
Occupation: Boxing trainer and promoter

Lou Duva's boxing business, Main Events, became one of the most powerful outfits in the boxing world, comparable to the operations of Don King and Bob Arum. He trained and represented such great boxers as Evander Holyfield, Pernell Whitaker, Mark Breland, and Meldrick Taylor. All would go on to win world titles. He was inducted into the International Boxing Hall of Fame in 1998.

Lou Duva's parents were Italian immigrants who came to the United States in 1920. He was one of seven children. The family lived in utter poverty during the Depression, and Duva worked odd jobs delivering newspapers, shining shoes, and setting up bowling pins to help the family get by. He joined the Civilian Conservation Corps (CCC) in 1938 where he learned to drive a truck. In 1942 he enlisted in the army, working as a boxing instructor in Camp Hood, Texas. In 1947 he started a trucking company. During this time he was also a professional welterweight, accumulating a 15-7 record, but he realized he would never be a great contender. Still, his experienced factored heavily into his success as a boxing trainer, promoter, and manager. He eventually sold his trucking company to become a bail bondsman and Teamsters Union organizer. He also partnered with Rocky Marciano, world heavyweight champion from 1952 to 1956, in promoting fights and managing boxers.

Duva's son, Dan, opened Main Events in Totowa, New Jersey, in 1978. Duva suffered a heart attack in 1979. The incident spurred him to give up his work as a bail bondsman and president of Teamster Local 286. Main Events' big break came in 1981 when the company won promotional rights to the Sugar Ray Leonard-Thomas Hearns welterweight title fight. Main Events would go on to represent such young talent as Tony Ayala, Mitch Green, and Johnny Bumphus. Duva's success helped persuade members of the 1984 Olympic boxing team to sign on with Main Events. After Duva's son Dan died from a brain tumor in 1996, the family split up, with Dan's widow running Main Events, and the rest of the family forming Duva Boxing.

Lou Duva's wife of thirty-seven years, the former Enes Rubio, died in 1986. His survivors include four children, eleven grandchildren, and four great-grandchildren.

See Current Biography 1999

Helen T. Edwards

Born: Detroit, Michigan; May 27, 1936
Died: June 21, 2016
Occupation: American particle physicist

Physicist Helen Edwards was one of the most successful and best-known physicists of the Twentieth Century, who led the effort to build the Tevatron, the world's most powerful particle accelerator.

Helen Edwards grew up in the suburbs of Detroit and attended an all-girls school near Washington, DC. She attended Cornell University, receiving her bachelor's degree in physics in

1957. She continued at Cornell for her graduate degrees, earning her PhD in 1966. She continued there as a research associate for four years at Cornell's Laboratory for Nuclear Studies. In 1970, the director of Fermilab, Robert Wilson, invited Edwards to join him as Associate Head of the Booster Group. She remained there until 1989 when she left Fermilab to help construct the Superconducting Supercollider, a particle accelerator, housed in a fifty-four–mile tunnel outside Dallas, Texas. She returned to Fermilab in 1992 and remained there until 2010.

Edwards numerous professional honors included a 1989 National Medal of Technology, a 1988 MacArthur Foundation "genius" award, the US Department of Energy's Ernest O. Lawrence Award, and a 1985 Prize for Achievement in Accelerator Physics and Technology.

Edwards married fellow physicist Donald Edwards while the two were at Cornell University. Information about her survivors is not available.

See Current Biography 2001

Vernon Ehlers

Born: Pipestone, Minnesota; February 6, 1934
Died: Grand Rapids, Michigan; August 15, 2017
Occupation: US congressman from Michigan, research physicist

Vernon Ehlers was a research physicist who served in the US House of Representatives from 1994 to 2011. He was the first nuclear physicist to be elected to Congress, and he considered it his personal mission to educate lawmakers about scientific matters that pertained to legislation.

Vernon Ehlers was the son of a Christian Reform minister. He spent several years at Calvin College, a Christian liberal arts school in Michigan, before transferring to the University of California (UC) at Berkeley. He earned his undergraduate degree in physics in 1956. He continued as a research assistant at the university while earning his PhD, which was awarded to him in 1960. In 1961 he won a two-year North Atlantic Treaty Organization (NATO) research fellowship, with which he devoted himself to research at the University of Heidelberg in West Germany. He returned to Calvin College in 1966 as a professor of physics. He remained there until 1983. He concurrently served on the Board of Commissioners of Kent County, and as the county commissioner, from 1975 to 1982. In 1983 he was elected to the Michigan House of Representatives and was promptly appointed assistant to the Republican floor leader. From 1986 to 1993, he served as a state senator

and was a member of the Senate Appropriations subcommittee overseeing aspects of higher education. After US Congressman Paul Henry of Michigan died, Ehlers successfully ran to succeed him. He was sworn in to the 103rd Congress on January 25, 1994. Ehlers sat on the House Science Committee and the Transportation and Infrastructure Committee, and he built a reputation as the foremost congressional authority on scientific and technological matters. He was a relentless advocate for scientific causes, from elementary-school education to research and development. He also held positions on the Education and the Workforce Committee, the House Administration Committee, and the Joint Committee on the Library of Congress. He was a staunch environmentalist and sat on the environment committee as well and the Federal Clean Air Act Advisory Committee. Ehlers co-wrote three books on Christian perspectives on world hunger and environmental management.

Vernon Ehlers married the former Johanna Meulink in 1958 and they had four children. She, their children, five grandchildren, and three great-grandchildren survive him.

See Current Biography 2005

Arthur Finkelstein

Born: New York, New York; May 18, 1945
Died: Ipswich, Massachusetts; August 18, 2017
Occupation: Political consultant

Political consultant Arthur Finkelstein is credited with making the word "liberal" a dirty epithet, and he was instrumental in generating the phenomena of negative political campaigns. His work helped elect or re-elect such high-profile politicians as Alfonse M. D'Amato, Jesse Helms, Orrin Hatch, Ronald Reagan, and Israel's Benjamin Netanyahu.

Arthur Finkelstein was one of three sons born to Jewish immigrants from Eastern Europe. He grew up in Brooklyn, New York, and attended Queens College where he earned a bachelor's degree in economics and political science. While in college, Finkelstein worked as a radio interviewer for the Libertarian ideologue and novelist, Ayn Rand, whose ideas reinforced his own political philosophy. Finkelstein got involved in the 1970 New York senatorial campaign of the Conservative party candidate James Buckley, who won the race. Word of Finkelstein's work reached North Carolina's Jesse Helms who hired him as a pollster and political consultant. Word of his success spread and four years later, Finkelstein worked with Ronald Reagan who was challenging President Gerald Ford.

Reagan was about to drop out of the race when he brought in Finkelstein who recommended he take a more hawkish stance on national defense and strongly criticize Ford's foreign policy. Though Reagan lost, many pundits consider 1976 a turning point in American politics as it marked a turn in Reagan's career, and helped insure his winning presidential campaign in 1980. In the late 1970s Finkelstein advised New York's aggressive Alfonse D'Amato in one of the most brutal Senate campaigns ever, launching a campaign focused on attacking D'Amato's opponent, Jacob Javits. Finkelstein demonstrated he could manipulate voters, politicians, and the electoral process itself toward his own ends. Later, in the 1990s, Finkelstein worked as a consultant for Israel's right-wing Likud Party, advising Benjamin Netanyahu's campaign for prime minister.

Finkelstein guarded his privacy assiduously. Ironically, he helped elect the very politicians who formed the core opposition to gay rights. Arthur Finkelstein married Donald Curiale, his partner of more than fifty years, in 2004. They had two daughters. Finkelstein's two brothers, Mr. Curiale, their two daughters, and a granddaughter survive him.

See Current Biography 1999

Carrie Fisher

Born: Beverly Hills, California; October 21, 1956
Died: Los Angeles, California; December 27, 2016
Occupation: Actress, author

As the daughter of Hollywood icons Debbie Reynolds and Eddie Fisher, Carrie Fisher was born for show business. Though she starred in a number of movies, her most recognized role was as Princess Leia in the George Lucas blockbuster film *Star Wars* and its two sequels, *The Empire Strikes Back,* and *Return of the Jedi.* Fisher also wrote the best-selling novel, *Postcards from the Edge,* a semi-autobiographical novel about a young actress who enters a drug rehabilitation center after nearly overdosing on Percodan.

Carrie Fisher was the first-born child of the actress Debbie Reynolds and Eddie Fisher, one of the most recognized couples in Hollywood in the 1950s, who divorced when their daughter was eighteen months old. Her father then married Elizabeth Taylor. Fisher's mother, Debbie Reynolds, married a wealthy shoe executive, Harry Karl. Carrie Fisher entered show business at a very young age, performing with her mother in Las Vegas. At fifteen Fisher dropped out of Beverly Hills High School to join the chorus of *Irene,* the Broadway revival that also starred her mother. Her movie debut was for *Shampoo,* in 1975 and she earned a photoplay nomination as the best newcomer of 1975. Fisher then went to London for two years to study at the Central School of Speech and Drama. She left after she earned the role of Princess Leia in the *Star Wars* movie franchise, which became the highest grossing film venture in Hollywood history. Her role made Fisher a household name. In 1980 she worked with John Belushi and Dan Aykroyd in the musical comedy *The Blues Brothers.* Fisher's first stage appearance was in John Pielmeier's Broadway production of *Agnes of God,* though she was forced to give up the role due to tracheal bronchitis. In 1985 Fisher took a trip to India, Nepal, and Sri Lanka, returning as a heavy user of LSD and Percodan. She nearly died of a drug overdose then spent thirty days in a drug rehabilitation facility. She later learned that she suffered from bi-polar disorder and attributed much of her drug use to her attempts to self-medicate.

Fisher's first novel, *Postcards From the Edge,* was a successful, semi-autobiographical novel about a young actress who enters a drug rehabilitation clinic after nearly overdosing on Percodan. She wrote the screenplay version of her novel, which was made into a movie released in 1990, starring Meryl Streep and Shirley MacLaine. Fisher continued to act in movies, though usually in supporting roles, and on television. She earned an Emmy nomination in 2008 for her guest appearance in the television series, *30 Rock.* In 2006 Fisher began developing a one-woman play titled *Wishful Drinking,* which met with high praise and received a Grammy Award nomination for best spoken word album in 2010. She returned to her role as Princess Leia in *Rogue One: A Star Wars Story.* Shortly thereafter, she suffered a heart attack during a flight and was hospitalized. She died two days later. Her mother, Debbie Reynolds, died the following day from a stroke.

Carrie Fisher's daughter, Billie Lourde, her brother, Todd Fisher, and two stepsisters survive her.

See Current Biography 1991

Zsa Zsa Gabor

Born: Budapest, Austria-Hungary; February 6, 1917
Died: Bel Air, California; December 18, 2016
Occupation: Actress, socialite

Zsa Zsa Gabor was best known as a glamorous socialite, but she starred in quite a few movies and was a common guest on television talk and game shows. She also published four books. She was married nine times, and divorced seven. (One marriage was annulled.)

Zsa Zsa Gabor's real name was Sari Gabor, but she acquired the nickname Zsa Zsa when she was quite young. Gabor and her sisters, Eva and Magda, were groomed to be socialites. Her parents, Vilmos and Jolie (Tillman) Gabor were of Jewish ancestry and heirs to a jewelry fortune. In Jolie's own words, she trained her girls to be "rich, famous, and married to kings." Gabor attended Madame Subilia's School for Young Ladies in Lausanne, Switzerland. She then became a student at the Academy of Music and Dramatic Arts in Vienna. In 1936 she was crowned Miss Hungary. Her first marriage was to Burhan Belge, a Western-educated Turk who was the press director of the Turkish foreign ministry. Gabor became a close confidante of Turkey's President Kemal Ataturk. She left Belge and traveled to Hollywood where her sister, Eva, had settled. She met and married the hotel tycoon, Conrad Hilton in 1942. They divorced in 1947, setting up a pattern of short-lived marriages that ended in divorce. She soon took up with Magda's ex-husband, actor George Sanders. He was her entrée into show business when Sanders' brother recommended her for a spot on the CBS television show *Bachelor Haven*. Gabor gained national attention for her humor, and she soon developed a nightclub act. Some of her humor was published in the compendium *How to Catch a Man, How to Keep a Man, How to Get Rid of a Man*. Gabor had a busy acting career in both television and on the big screen. In the late 1950s, she became a semi-regular guest on talk shows, especially the *Jack Parr Tonight Show*. She made her theater debut with her sister, Eva, in a revival of *Arsenic and Old Lace* in Chicago in 1975.

Her numerous marriages aside, Gabor was embroiled in a number of controversies. She apparently became involved with Rafael Trujillo Jr., the son of the Dominican Republic dictator, and the married father of six. In 1989 she slapped a police officer who had pulled her over. An open bottle of alcohol was found in her car. A 2002 car crash left her confined to a wheelchair. Then, in 2009, Gabor was listed as a victim of the Bernard Madoff Ponzi scheme in which she reportedly lost $7-10 million. Gabor was plagued with significant health issues in the last decade of her life. She died just weeks shy of her one-hundredth birthday. Gabor had one daughter, Francesca Hilton, who predeceased her in 2015. Gabor's ninth husband, Frederic Prinz von Anhalt, survives her.

See Current Biography 1988

James Galanos

Born: Philadelphia, Pennsylvania; September 20, 1924
Died: West Hollywood, California; October 30, 2016
Occupation: Fashion designer

James Galanos was a fashion designer who clothed the moneyed elite of America. Having never transformed his success to a mass market, his name was not recognized by the general public, but he was well known to the stars.

James Galanos was born to a working-class immigrant family from Greek Macedonia who ran a restaurant in southern New Jersey. He graduated from the Traphagen School of Fashion in New York City in 1943, and spent the first few years of his career selling sketches. He was eventually hired as an assistant to Jean Louis, the head designer for Columbia Studios, a job that lasted only six months, but was enough time to make a few important connections. He obtained an apprenticeship in the Piquet house of couture. His former mentor, Jean Louis, encouraged Galanos to strike out on his own by lending him enough capital to get started, and introducing him to a dressmaker. His success was unlike that of most fashion designers in that he never transformed his designed for the mass market, neither did he stage fashion shows.

Galanos designs were always a sign of privilege. He made costly luxury clothing for the wealthy elite that included celebrities like Marlene Dietrich, Diana Ross, Grace Kelly, and Nancy Reagan who wore a Galanos design to four of her husband's inaugural balls. He once famously quipped that his clothes were "too chic for most women," and he exhorted his customers to "live up to" his designs.

James Galanos won numerous industry awards and accolades including several Coty Awards. (He was the youngest designer ever to win one.) The Council of Fashion Designers of America awarded Galanos with a lifetime achievement award, and he was honored with a bronze plaque on the Fashion Walk of Fame in New York City.

Galanos's survivors include his sister, Dorothy Chrambanis, and numerous nieces and nephews.

See Current Biography 1976

Nicolai Gedda

Born: Stockholm, Sweden; July 11, 1925
Died: Tolochenaz, Switzerland; January 8, 2017
Occupation: Singer

An accomplished lyric tenor, the Swedish native, Nicolai Gedda, recorded more complete operas than any other tenor of his day. He performed in such great venues as Italy's La Scala in Milan, London's Covent Garden, the Paris Opera, and New York's Metropolitan Opera House. He was also one of opera's most long-lived performers, appearing on stage well into his seventies.

Nicolai Gedda was born into humble circumstances. His teenaged, unwed parents intended to consign him to an orphanage at birth. However, an aunt, Olga Gädda, his father's sister, decided to raise him as her own. She later married Michail Ustinoff, a Russian-born singer who became the choirmaster at the Russian Orthodox Church in Leipzig, Germany. He was a cruel father, but he recognized his son's gift of perfect pitch. By age five, the boy was playing the piano and singing with the church choir. Having spent his early childhood in Germany with a Swedish mother and a Russian father, Gedda was fluent in Swedish, German, Russian and, eventually, English. With the rise of Adolph Hitler, the family returned to Olga's Sweden. After graduating from high school, Gedda worked as a bank clerk in Stockholm and studied at the Royal College of Music. At twenty-six, Gedda debuted at the Royal Swedish Opera. His performance gained the attention of Walter Legge, a record producer with Electric and Musical Industries (EMI). Legge introduced Gedda to the notable conductor, Herbert von Karajan. Gedda would later debut at La Scala as Don Ottavio in Mozart's Don Giovanni. He received high praise for his American debut in 1957 at the Pittsburgh Opera. He would go on to perform in three hundred and sixty-seven music productions at the Metropolitan Opera House.

Nicolai Gedda married three times. His first two marriages ended in divorce. He had one daughter, Tatiana, with his first wife, the Russian pianist, Nadja Nova. Gedda's third wife, Aino Sellermark Gedda, who also co-authored Gedda's 1999 memoir, *Nocolai Gedda: My Life & Art*, survives him.

See Current Biography 1965

John Glenn, Jr.

Born: Cambridge, Ohio; July 18, 1921
Died: Columbus, Ohio; December 8, 2016
Occupation: Astronaut, US senator

John Glenn was the first American to orbit the Earth in 1962. He later became the US senator from Ohio, serving in the senate for twenty-four years.

John Glenn was the only son of John Herschel Glenn, a railroad conductor and proprietor of a heating and plumbing business. Glenn grew up in New Concord, Ohio. The high school he attended has been renamed in his honor. He attended Muskingum College in New Concord, graduating with a degree in engineering. He also began taking flying lessons. In 1942 he volunteered for the Naval Aviation Cadet program and, a year later, he joined the Marine Corps. He earned two Distinguished Flying Crosses and ten Air Medals.

At the end of the Korean conflict, Glenn trained to become a military test pilot. In the meantime, the USSR had succeeded in sending a man into space, leaving the US government to initiate an ambitious space program. In 1959 Glenn and six others were selected to undergo rigorous training with National Aeronautics and Space Administration (NASA). On February 20, 1962 Glenn was propelled into space, completing three orbits of the Earth. Though he was anxious to return to space, President Kennedy blocked his efforts, likely due to politics. Frustrated at not being allowed to return to space, Glenn resigned in 1964 to pursue a career in politics.

He had a rough start, losing in several election cycles, but in 1974 he succeeded in becoming a senator for Ohio. He sat on the Foreign Relations Committee, the Government Affairs Committee, and the Special Committee on Aging. His nuclear weapons anti-proliferation stance put him at odds with President Ronald Reagan. In the late 1980s Glenn was embroiled in a scandal due to his association with the savings and loan operator, Charles Keating, who was later convicted of fraud. Though Glenn was found innocent of influence peddling, his name and reputation suffered as he became one of the "Keating Five," along with four other senators. Glenn announced his retirement from the senate in 1998. In January 1998 NASA announced that Glenn would return to space, becoming the oldest person ever to be sent into space, as part of a study on aging, and on the biological effects of space flight on the human body. In his retirement Glenn chaired the National Commission on Mathematics and Science Education for the 21st Century, with the goal of recruiting and retaining high-quality math and science teachers. He also worked at the new John H. Glenn Institute for Public Service and Public Policy that he founded at Ohio State University.

In 2012 President Barack Obama awarded Glenn the prestigious Presidential Medal of Freedom, the country's highest civilian honor. John Glenn married his high school sweetheart, Anna Margaret Castor, in 1943 and they had two children. His wife, two children, and two grandsons survive him.

See Current Biography 1999

C. Jackson Grayson, Jr.

Born: Fort Necessity, Louisiana; October 8, 1923
Died: Houston, Texas; May 4, 2017
Occupation: US government official, educator

In 1971 President Richard Nixon appointed C. Jackson Grayson to chair his Price Commission charged with curbing runaway inflation and stabilizing the nation's economy. At the time Grayson was the dean of the business school at Southern Methodist University. After his tenure on the Price Commission was over, Grayson created the American Productivity and Quality Center (APQC), an economic research and training group.

C. Jackson Grayson was born into a farming family in Louisiana. He spent the first fifteen years of his life milking cows and tending soybean and cotton crops. In 1944 he earned his BBA degree at Tulane University. He then served as a naval gunnery officer during World War II. Upon his return, he obtained an MBA degree from the University of Pennsylvania's Wharton School of Finance and Commerce in 1947. He served in the Federal Bureau of Investigation (FBI) for two years and was nearly killed in an armed robbery. He ran the family farm for several years before earning his DBA (professional doctorate degree) degree from Harvard University's School of Business Administration. He then returned to Tulane, this time as an associate professor, and eventually as dean of the school of business administration. In 1968 he left Tulane to serve as dean of Southern Methodist University's School of Business Administration.

President Nixon wanted the Price Commission to be comprised of individuals not involved in government or public service. George Shultz, the director of the Office of Management and Budget, recommended Grayson to the president after working with him at the Ford Foundation. Grayson left in 1973 when inflation seemed to be holding at under four percent. He subsequently founded an economic research group, the American Productivity and Quality Center, to help private companies measure productivity and improve worker performance.

Grayson's first three marriages ended in divorce. His fourth wife, Carla O'Dell, served as the chairwoman and chief executive of APQC. In addition to his wife, Grayson's survivors include three sons and four grandchildren.

See Current Biography 1972

Dick Gregory

Born: St. Louis, Missouri; October 12, 1932
Died: Washington, DC; August 19, 2017
Occupation: Comedian, social activist

Dick Gregory was an African American comedian who created a new take on "negro humor," quite apart from the humor of Amos n' Andy, Moms Mabley, and Nipsey Russell who catered to African American audiences. He paved the way for other great African American comedians who catered to a white audience, like Richard Pryor and Bill Cosby.

Richard (Dick) Claxton Gregory was born into utter poverty. His father abandoned his wife and six children, leaving the family to scrape out an existence. Gregory began working at the age of seven, shining shoes in a pool parlor, or carrying packages and lugging groceries. He attended the Summer High School of St. Louis where he became a track star, winning the Missouri State mile championship. After receiving a number of track scholarship offers, he attended Southern Illinois University where he ranked third, nationally, for the half-mile. However, he was no student and left college in 1956. From there he drifted from one odd job to another. Wherever he worked, he kept his co-workers entertained. He spent two years in the US Army, practicing comedy routines in GI shows. Following his stint in the army, Gregory began performing at small clubs in Chicago. In 1961 he was asked to audition at Chicago's Playboy Club, filling in for an ailing Irwin Corey. However, there was some concern because the audience was filled with southern white business executives. Gregory began, "I understand there are a good many Southerners in the room tonight. I know the South very well. I spent twenty years there one night." He was a huge success. In 1961 *Time* published a profile of Gregory, and Jack Paar of *The Tonight Show* had him appear several times. In April of 1962 Gregory appeared at Carnegie Hall.

In 1962 Gregory became active in the civil rights movement. In 1965 he was shot in the leg, trying to be a peacemaker during the Watts riots in Los Angeles. He began fasting for certain causes, from South African apartheid to the Vietnam War and police brutality. His protest activity did not help his comedy career.

In the late 1950s, Gregory married Lillian Smith, a secretary at the University of Chicago. They had eleven children. Besides his wife, Lillian, Gregory's ten children, sixteen grandchildren, and five great grandchildren survive him.

See Current Biography 1962

Tammy Grimes

Born: Lynn, Massachusetts; January 30, 1934
Died: Englewood, New Jersey; October 30, 2016
Occupation: Actress, comedienne

Tammy Grimes is most remembered for her title role in the Broadway production of *The Unsinkable Molly Brown*, for which she won a Tony Award. She was just twenty-six years old at the time. She won a second Tony Award for her role in Noel Coward's *Private Lives* in 1969.

Tammy Grimes was born to Luther Nichols Grimes who managed the Country Club in Brookline, Massachusetts. She attended the Beaver Country Day School in Chestnut Hill outside of Boston. She attended Stephens College in Columbia, Missouri, majoring in English though she claimed to have chosen the school for its flourishing theater department. Through the mid-1950s Grimes acted in various small playhouses throughout New England and New York, including the Falmouth Playhouse and the Neighborhood Playhouse in New York. Her big break came when playwright Noel Coward saw her perform at the New York supper club, Downstairs at the Upstairs. He had her audition for the lead role in his play *Look after Lulu*. The play did not last long, but Grimes won recognition nevertheless. She was elevated to star status for her performance in *The Unsinkable Molly Brown* at the Winter Garden Theater. Grimes also appeared on film in *Play It as It Lays, The Last Unicorn,* and *Slaves of New York*. She also appeared in numerous television roles.

In 1956 Grimes married actor Christopher Plummer, but the marriage ended in 1960. She was also briefly married to television actor, Jeremy Slate. Her third husband was musician and composer Richard Bell. The two were married from 1971 until his death in 2005. Her survivors include her daughter, Amanda Plummer, and a brother.

See Current Biography 1962

Ruth Gruber

Born: New York, New York; September 30, 1911
Died: New York, New York; November 17, 2016
Occupation: Journalist, humanitarian

As a young Jewish woman in her early twenties, Ruth Gruber managed to slip inside countries under Communist rule, documenting the lives of ordinary citizens, just as Hitler's regime was rising to power. During World War II she risked her life to escort nearly one thousand refugees to the United States. She documented the Israeli War of Independence, and attended the trials of Nazi war criminals. She counted Eleanor Roosevelt and Israeli Prime Minister, Golda Meir among her closest friends.

Ruth Gruber was born the fourth of five children, to Polish Jewish immigrants. Her father, David Gruber owned and ran a liquor store in Brooklyn. Gruber was a precocious child, graduating from high school when she was fifteen. She studied German and journalism at New York University, and earned her master's degree from the University of Wisconsin. She earned a fellowship at the University of Cologne, in Germany, just as extreme nationalism and anti-Semitism were on the rise, earning her doctorate in one year's record time, and becoming the youngest person in the world to earn a PhD at that time.

Gruber was the first Western journalist to travel to Siberian Russia, and even gained entry into the Soviet Gulag forced-labor camps. Her aim was to document the lives of ordinary women across Europe, under various forms of government, from Communism to capitalism. She became the special assistant to the US secretary of the interior, Harold Ickes, traveling to Alaska to scout possible homesteads for war veterans. In 1944 when President Roosevelt granted permission for a thousand Holocaust refugees to enter the United States, Gruber insisted on acting as an interpreter—she spoke Russian, German, Yiddish, Polish, and French—during the voyage, at great personal risk. Following the war, she documented conditions of the Displaced Persons camps for Jews who could not return to their homes, followed the activities of the UN Special Committee on Palestine, and witnessed the birth of the state of Israel.

Ruth Gruber continued to travel widely throughout her career and wrote sixteen books. She was married twice. She had two children with her first husband, attorney Philip Michaels. He died in 1968 and Ruth married Henry Rosner in 1974. Her book, *Raquela: A Woman of Israel*, won the National Jewish Book Award in 1979 for the best book on Israel. Other awards include the Na'amat Golda Meir Human Rights

Award and awards from the Simon Wiesenthal Center's Museum of Tolerance. Ruth Gruber passed away at the age of one hundred and five. Her children and grandchildren survive her.

See Current Biography 2001

Ferreira Gullar

Born: São Luís, Maranhão, Brazil; September 10, 1930
Died: Rio de Janeiro, Brazil; December 4, 2016
Occupation: Brazilian poet, art critic

One of Brazil's pre-eminent poets, artists, and art critics, Ferreira Gullar, helped found the Neo-Concretist movement in art in 1959. His greatest work was a long, book-length, autobiographical poem titled "Poema Suo" ("Dirty Poem"). His work demonstrated the subversive nature of art, which he believed distinguished human beings from other animals. In 2002 Gullar was nominated for a Nobel Prize in Literature.

Ferreira Gullar was one of eleven children born to Newton Gullar, a merchant. He began writing poetry during his teens, and with the encouragement of a teacher, Gullar published his first poem. He published his first book of poetry, *Un Pouco Acima Do Chao* (*A Little above the Ground*), when he was still a teenager. He moved to Rio de Janeiro in 1951 where he became acquainted with other young artists and the art critic, Mario Pedrosa. He began writing about art for *O Cruzeiro* (*The Cruise*), one of Brazil's most influential magazines. In 1954 he became the editor of the popular magazine, *Manchete* (*Headline*), and published his second poetry collection, *a luta corporal* (*The Body Fight*), which became a benchmark in modern Brazilian lyric, establishing Gullar as a promising new poet. He participated in the first National Exposition of Concrete Art in São Paulo, and published his first book of art criticism, *Teoria do nao-objeto* (*The Theory of the Non-Object*), and penned his Neo-Concrete manifesto. In 1961 Gullar was appointed the director of the Fundação Cultural de Brasilia, a cultural foundation, though he soon resigned, having become disillusioned with avant-garde and experimental poetry. In 1963 he was elected president of the Centro Popular de Cultura (CPC, the Popular Culture Center), a left-wing organization, which was shut down a year later after a military dictator seized power.

Gullar ran afoul of the ruling power with his "subversive" art and writings, and he was imprisoned and denounced as a Communist. He fled the country and spent several years living in Moscow, Russia; Santiago, Chile; Lima, Peru;

and Buenos Aires, Argentina, and wrote under the pseudonym Frederica Marques. His exile from his wife and children inspired his greatest work, *Poema Sujo* (*Dirty Poem*). In 2002 he was nominated for a Nobel Prize in Literature. That same year he was awarded the Prince Claus Prize from the Netherlands Academy of Arts and Sciences. He was considered one of the most influential Brazilians of the twentieth century, writing more than fifty books.

Information about his survivors is not available.

See Current Biography 2004

Albert Ramsdell (A. R.) Gurney, Jr.

Born: Buffalo, New York; November 1, 1930
Died: New York, New York; June 13, 2017
Occupation: American playwright, novelist

Most of AR Gurney's plays explored the quickly fading culture of American white Anglo-Saxon Protestant (WASP) society from which he had emerged. He was a recipient of the Everett Baker teaching award of Massachusetts Institute of Technology (MIT), a Rockefeller playwright's award, and a playwriting award from the National Endowment of the Arts (NEA).

Albert Ramsdell Gurney, who went by his initials "AR," was born to a prosperous real estate and insurance executive, enjoying a relatively privileged childhood in Buffalo, New York. He began making up plays as early as kindergarten. Gurney's grandmother who loved theater had a strong influence on him, as did his father's tales about F. Scott Fitzgerald, a fellow Buffalo resident. He attended private school at St. Paul's prep in New Hampshire, where he won a prize for his first play, *Buffalo Meat*, a story about his family background. He attended Williams College, along with his contemporary, Stephen Sondheim who was already writing musicals. After graduating in 1952, Gurney joined the navy where he wrote shows to entertain military personnel. He enrolled at Yale University's school of drama under the GI Bill, and wrote his first musical, *Love in Buffalo*, which starred two Yale students, Dick Cavett and Carrie Nye. He received his MFA from Yale in 1958. In the beginning of 1960 Gurney began teaching American literature and the humanities at MIT. He would remain there for twenty-five years, while also establishing his reputation as a playwright. He originally wrote under the pseudonym, Pete Gurney. His first off-Broadway play, *The David Show*, a satire about politics in the 1960s, closed after just one night. Though his work did not set the theater world ablaze, his work was included in the 1969 and 1970 volumes of *Best Short Plays*. Gurney's first major theatrical successes came in the 1982 season with New York productions of three of his plays: *The Middle Ages*, *What I Did Last Summer*, and *The Dining Room*. Gurney's most widely applauded play, *The Cocktail Hour*, was produced in 1988. Gurney also authored three novels: *The Gospel According to Joe*, *Entertaining Strangers*, and *The Snow Ball*.

He married the former Mary Forman Goodyear in 1957. She, the couple's four children, and eight grandchildren survive him.

See Current Biography 1986

Louis Harris

Born: New Haven, Connecticut; January 6, 1921
Died: Key West, Florida; December 17, 2016
Occupation: Public opinion analyst, journalist

One of the best-known, highly regarded public opinion pollsters of the twentieth century, Louis Harris was the president of his own firm that became widely recognized for its accuracy in determining public opinion and forecasting public trends from political ideology to brand recognition.

One of three children, Louis Harris was born in New Haven, Connecticut. His father was a real-estate developer. He became interested in journalism and politics while working on the school newspaper. He attended the University of North Carolina at Chapel Hill, graduating with a degree in economics in 1942, just in time to join the US Navy as a captain of a patrol boat. His first experience in polling occurred when he was assigned to Boston's Naval Receiving Station after World War II. His first poll was to determine whether sailors awaiting demobilization felt they were being treated properly. He became the national research director for the American Veterans Committee in 1946. In 1947 Harris met Elmo Roper, a pioneer in market research and opinion polling, joining Roper's firm to write newspaper columns and radio scripts. In 1951 he began working in political research. He left in 1956 to create his own organization, Louis Harris and Associates, Inc., refining interviewing techniques to discover the whys and wherefores behind the answers he uncovered. In 1958 Senator John F. Kennedy hired Harris in his bid for re-election to the Senate. Harris's expertise in public opinion and his political insight made him a political campaign strategist. In 1962 Harris replaced Roper as the public opinion analyst for the CBS network where he conducted polls and appeared on TV to present

his findings. According to Harris, the purpose of political pollsters was not to predict the outcome of an election but to give directions to candidates by informing them of changing trends. In 1963 he began writing columns for the *Washington Post*, which were then syndicated to other newspapers.

Louis Harris married Florence Hickox Yard in 1943 and they had three children. His wife predeceased him in 2004. His three children and four grandchildren survive him.

See Current Biography 1966

Tom Hayden

Born: Royal Oak, Michigan; December 11, 1939
Died: Santa Monica, California; October 23, 2016
Occupation: Social activist, politician, author

Tom Hayden was an anti-war and pro-civil rights activist in the 1960s and 1970s. He worked with the Student Nonviolent Coordinating Committee and co-founded the Students for a Democratic Society. He was one of the "Chicago seven" prosecuted for his anti-war activities. He was instrumental in bringing US prisoners of war home from North Vietnam in the early 1970s. He was a California state assemblyman from 1982 to 1992 when he was elected to the California State Senate.

Thomas Emmet Hayden was born in Royal Oak, Michigan, an only child of a conservative working-class couple. His father left shortly after his birth and Hayden was raised by his single mother and attended a conservative, private Catholic school. He attended the University of Michigan at Ann Arbor where he was inspired by the demonstrations against the House Un-American Activities Committee by the students at the University of California at Berkeley, and by the lunch counter sit-ins by black students in Greensboro, North Carolina. He was the editor of the *Michigan Daily*, the university's campus newspaper. After graduation Hayden worked full time with the Student Nonviolent Coordinating Committee (SNCC), which published his pamphlet *Revolution in Mississippi* in 1961. He helped found the Students for a Democratic Society (SDS) and wrote the famous "Port Huron Statement," which became the organization's manifesto, attacking "complacency" in American politics, the arms race, racial discrimination, and apathy in the face of poverty. In 1964 he co-wrote the Economic Research and Action Project to help the poor organize themselves. He hit a turning point in his life when he traveled to North Vietnam and later, to Bratislava, Czechoslovakia to meet with North Vietnamese leaders.

His work led to the release of three American prisoners of war. He was a pallbearer at the funeral of assassinated Senator Robert F. Kennedy whom he came to know through his civil rights and anti-war activities. He was a major planner of anti-war demonstrations in Chicago, coinciding with the Democratic National Convention, which grew into riots. Hayden and six others were indicted for inciting a riot, and they became known as the "Chicago seven." Though he was found guilty and sentenced to five years in prison, the conviction was overturned in appeals court.

Hayden was elected to the California State Assembly in 1982 where he remained until 1992 when he was elected to the state senate. Over the course of his lifetime, Hayden authored more than twenty books. He was married three times. His second wife was the actress, Jane Fonda, with whom he had a son, actor Troy Garity. His third wife, Barbara Williams, and his two sons survive him.

See Current Biography 1976

Hazzard became a staunch opponent of the UN, and much of her non-fiction dealt with the corruption and secrecy inherent in the bureaucracy. Her polemical *Defeat of an Ideal: A Study of the Self-Destruction of the United Nations,* revealed the "sacred-cow treatment" she felt the UN received from the press. In *Countenance of Truth: The United Nations and the Waldheim Case,* Hazzard revealed that national interests of the powerful UN members made it possible for a man with a Nazi record to serve as secretary general from 1972 to 1982.

Hazzard received numerous accolades and awards including a National Book Award, a first-place O. Henry Award, and the PEN/Faulkner Award. She was awarded a guest lectureship at Princeton University in 1982. Hazzard never attended college herself. She married Francis Steegmuller, a fellow writer and Flaubert scholar, in 1963. He predeceased her in 1994. They had no children. Information about her survivors is not available.

See Current Biography 1991

Shirley Hazzard

Born: Sydney, Australia; January 30, 1931
Died: New York, New York; December 12, 2016
Occupation: Author

Shirley Hazzard was an award-winning novelist, short story writer, and the author of six books of non-fiction. She won the 1980 National Book Critics Circle Award for her first novel, *The Transit of Venus,* and the 2003 National Book Award for fiction for *The Great Fire.*

Shirley Hazzard was born in Australia to Reginald Hazzard, a Welshman, and Catherine (Stein) Hazzard from Scotland. She graduated from the Queenwood School in Sydney and accompanied her parents to Hong Kong where her father was sent as a government official on a diplomatic mission. At just sixteen years old, Hazzard worked for the British Combined Intelligence in Hong Kong. She worked from 1949 to 1951 at the United Kingdom Commissioner's Office in Wellington. When her father was sent to New York, Hazzard joined the staff of the United Nations (UN) Secretariat where she worked on economic and social problems of underdeveloped countries. In 1967, while working at the UN, Hazzard published her first collection of short stories, *People in Glass Houses,* which satirized life in a bureaucracy. Her first novel, *The Evening of the Holiday,* was published in 1966. Much of her work appeared in *The New Yorker* prior to its publication in book form. After leaving the UN to work full time as a writer,

Hugh Hefner

Born: Chicago, Illinois; 9 April 1926
Died: Los Angeles, California; September 27, 2017
Occupation: Publisher, entrepreneur

Hugh Hefner created a publishing empire when he released his first issue of *Playboy* magazine, the most successful magazine in the mid-twentieth century. In addition to his magazine, Hefner's empire comprised Playboy Clubs, a series of nightclub/restaurant key clubs, and eventually, vacation resorts, and casinos.

Hugh Hefner was born in Chicago, Illinois, to a devout, Methodist couple who raised their children under rigid Protestant fundamentalist ethics. Hefner reported that he never felt free of their moral code until he published the first issue of *Playboy.* In his adolescence, Hefner was something of an introvert, a far cry from the individual who had continual parties at his Playboy Mansion. Hefner earned a bachelor's degree at the University of Illinois in 1949, and later he did one semester's graduate work in psychology at Northwestern University. He married his high school sweetheart, Millie Williams and dabbled in writing comic strips, supported his growing family by working at *Esquire* as a writer of subscription promotion copy. He left *Esquire* in 1952, convinced that the time was ripe for a daring mens' magazine. He put together the first issue of *Playboy* using his entire savings of six hundred dollars, and by selling ten thousand dollars worth of stocks. The first issue featured a celebrated nude calendar shot of Marilyn Monroe. It immediately sold out its press run of 53,991 copies. In an interview with Oriana Fallaci for *Look* magazine (10 January 1967), Hefner explained that *Playboy* came at the right time, when the United States was experiencing a sexual revolution. By including the stories of such classic writers as James Baldwin, PG Wodehouse, Irwin Shaw, and Isaac Singer, Hefner added class and literary sophistication to his magazine of female nudes. By 1960 Hefner's magazine had a circulation that exceeded one million copies, bringing in revenues of $1,058,000 from newsstands sales alone, and Hefner decided to branch out into other fields of entertainment. He created a series of international Playboy Clubs where scantily clad waitresses and hosts catered to club members. This was the birth of the Playboy Bunnies. With the rise of the Internet *Playboy's* subscriptions plummeted to fewer than one million copies, though the magazine produced an online version. In 2015 *Playboy* made the bold, but short-lived decision to stop including nudes in its copy.

Hefner divorced his first wife, Millie, in 1959. In 1989 he married the Playmate of the Year, Kimberley Conrad. They had two children. They divorced in 2010. On New Year's Eve, 2012, Hefner married his third wife, twenty-five-year-old, Crystal Harris. She survives along with Hefner's four children.

See Current Biography 1968

Henry Heimlich

Born: Wilmington, Delaware; February 3, 1920
Died: Cincinnati, Ohio; December 17, 2016
Occupation: Surgeon, medical inventor/researcher

The name "Heimlich" has become a household name since Henry Heimlich invented a procedure, called the "Heimlich maneuver," that has saved countless lives. The maneuver involves a sudden upper thrust that expels air from a choking victim's lungs to dislodge the object that blocks his or her airway. Heimlich also invented a surgical method for constructing a new esophagus, and a method for enabling stroke victims to learn to swallow again.

Doctor Henry Heimlich grew up in Wilmington, Delaware. His father was a social worker who focused his attention on prison reform. When Heimlich was ten years old, his father sent him to a camp for delinquent boys to expose him to a broader environment. Heimlich attended Cornell University, graduating in 1941.

He obtained his medical degree from Cornell in 1943. His career was put on hold when World War II broke out. Heimlich volunteered for especially hazardous duty, serving as a surgeon with Chinese guerrillas behind Japanese lines. (He was honored in 1984 by the Chinese ministry of health for his service to the Chinese people.) He completed his residency in thoracic surgery in several New York City hospitals.

Heimlich's first medical innovation was a procedure for constructing a new esophagus using stomach tissue, thus allowing affected patients to eat normally. The technique has become standard practice. He invented the "Heimlich valve" used to drain fluids from the chest cavity due to chest surgery or emergency injury. Heimlich moved to Cincinnati in 1977 where he was the director of surgery at the Jewish Hospital. It was here that he developed the maneuver for dislodging a blockage in a victim's airway. Many restaurants post Heimlich maneuver instructions for saving the lives of choking victims. (At the time of the Heimlich maneuver's invention it was estimated that four thousand people died from choking each year, many of them children.) Heimlich left the Jewish Hospital in 1977 and was appointed a professor of advanced clinical sciences at Xavier University, where he established the Heimlich Institute to work on further inventions.

Henry Heimlich wrote two books and created a cartoon series for children. Presented on ABC, the series won an Emmy award in 1980. He received the Albert Lasker Public Service Award, the Golden Plate Award and was inducted into the Engineering and Science Hall of Fame.

In 1951 Henry Heimlich married Jane Murray—the daughter of Arthur Murray of dance studio fame. She co-authored a book on holistic medicine. They had two sons and twin daughters. Jane Murray Heimlich passed away in 2012. Henry Heimlich's children survive him.

See Current Biography 1986

Florence Henderson

Born: Dale, Indiana; February 14, 1934
Died: Los Angeles, California; November 24, 2016
Occupation: Actress, singer

Though she had an illustrious Broadway career and even had her own television cooking show for nine years, Florence Henderson is most remembered for her role as Carol Brady on the popular television series *The Brady Bunch*, which aired from September 1969 to March 1974. She was the first female to receive the

CARTA Award given by the Catholic Apostolate of Radio, Television and Advertising.

Florence Henderson was born, the last of ten children, to a tobacco sharecropper, Joseph Henderson and his wife, Elizabeth (Elder) Henderson. Hers was a poor family of Roman Catholic, Irish descent, harvesting tobacco on rented land in Owensboro, Kentucky. She attended a Catholic school, St. Francis Academy, in Owensboro. She learned to sing from the Benedictine sisters. During her senior year, relatives of a friend offered financial help so she could attend a two-year course of study at the American Academy of Dramatic Arts. Her first big role was as Laurey in Rodgers and Hammerstein's *Oklahoma!* in 1952. In 1954 she played the title role in the musical *Fanny.* In a *Variety* poll early in the year, Henderson was chosen as the most promising young actor of the season. She continued studying voice with Dolf Swing, and took acting lessons with Mary Tarcai from 1955 to 1959. Henderson studied dance and took lessons in French and Italian, and learned the operatic role of Mimi in *La Boehme.* Her role as Maria Rainer in *The Sound of Music* won Henderson the Sarah Siddons Award in 1962. In 1964 she played Nellie Forbush in the Lincoln Center revival of *South Pacific.* Her film debut was an ABC production of *Song of Norway* in which Henderson played the wife of composer Edvard Grieg. She also made appearances on a number of television variety shows, including the *Dean Martin Show, Jackie Gleason Show,* and the *Jonathan Winters Show.* Henderson later became the first female to stand in for Johnny Carson on *The Tonight Show.* In 1969 Henderson earned her iconic role as the effervescent, cheerful Carol Brady on the television series, *The Brady Bunch,* which aired from 1969 to 1974.

Florence Henderson married Ira Bernstein in 1956, and they had four children. They divorced in 1985, and she later married John Kappas who predeceased her in 2002. Survivors include her four children and five grandchildren.

See Current Biography 1971

Nat Hentoff

Born: Boston, Massachusetts; June 10, 1925
Died: New York, New York; January 7, 2017
Occupation: Journalist, novelist

Nat Hentoff was a remarkably prolific writer whose freelance career made him one of the most visible writers in the country. He wrote more than thirty-five books, fiction and nonfiction, on such broad topics as Jazz music, education reform, censorship, civil liberties, and abortion.

Nathan Irving Hentoff was born in Boston, the first child of his parents, Simon Hentoff, a haberdasher, and Lena (Katzenberg) Hentoff, who were Russian Jewish immigrants. Hentoff grew up in the Jewish ghetto in the Roxbury section of Boston. At that time and place were broad political debates among socialists, anarchists, and Communist ideologues, thus exposing the young Hentoff to social criticism. He attended the Boston Latin School, the oldest public school in the country, and one of the most rigorous. He became addicted to books, which he bought with the money he earned working three jobs. His other passion was jazz music. Classified 4-F during World War II, Hentoff went straight to college from high school. He attended Northeastern University where he was editor of the school newspaper, and he began working at the radio station WMEX where he remained for nine years, except for the year he spent in graduate school at Harvard University on scholarship. He also spent a year in Paris on a Fulbright fellowship.

In 1953 Hentoff moved to New York and began a career as a freelance writer. He would become one of the most recognized writers in the United States with articles published in the *New Yorker, Esquire, Harper's, Hi Fi/Stereo, The Reporter, Playboy,* the *Washington Post,* and the *Commonweal* (to name only a few). His career with the *Village Voice* lasted for fifty years. His work was widely distributed through syndication. Hentoff was particularly enamored with jazz music and wrote liner notes for countless jazz record albums. His book *The Jazz Life,* a collection of essays, explored numerous social, economic, and psychological elements that create the context of modern jazz, including the effects of racial prejudice and discrimination. He became an activist for racial equality and wrote novels for young adults. He was a mystery writer as well as a scholar on the Constitution.

Hentoff's first two marriages ended in divorce. At the time of his death he had been married to Margot Goodman since 1959. She survives him along with his three children, a stepdaughter, a sister, and ten grandchildren.

See Current Biography 1986

Aileen Hernandez

Born: Brooklyn, New York; May 23, 1926
Died: Irvine, California; February 13, 2017
Occupation: Former NOW president, EEOC member

Aileen Hernandez was the second president of the National Organization for Women (NOW) following the group's founder and first president, Betty Friedan. She was the only female appointed to President Lyndon B. Johnson's Equal Employment Opportunity Commission (EEOC).

Aileen Hernandez was born in Brooklyn, New York, to Jamaican immigrants. She graduated as class salutatorian in 1943 from Bay Ridge High School, with a scholarship to Howard University in Washington, DC, which was still a "Southern" city. She was shocked to discover that the nation's capital had not a single restaurant, theater, or hotel open to black people. She became an active member of the National Association for the Advancement of Colored People (NAACP) and edited the campus newspaper. She graduated magna cum laude in sociology and political science in 1947 and enrolled as a graduate student in public administration at New York University (NYU). There she became active in politics, volunteering on the Congressional campaign of Franklin D. Roosevelt, Jr. In 1950 she trained as a labor leader with the International Ladies Garment Workers Union (ILGWU). In 1951 she was assigned to the ILGWU's Pacific Coast Regional Office, working as an organizer and assistant educational director from 1951 to 1959. She was the director of public relations and education from 1959 to 1961. Simultaneously, she earned a master's degree in government from Los Angeles State College. In 1961 Hernandez left the ILGWU to become campaign coordinator for Democrat Alan Cranston, who was elected California State Comptroller. He appointed Hernandez assistant chief of the California Fair Employment Practices Commission. In 1965 President Lyndon B. Johnson appointed her to the EEOC where she was the only female on the commission. She resigned a year later due to the EEOC's lack of progress. In 1970 she was elected the second president of NOW, a civil rights organization modeled closely on the NAACP. Her goal was to change NOW's elitist, middle-class image to include black and low-income women.

In 1957 Hernandez married a Mexican-American garment cutter. They were divorced two years later. She has no immediate survivors.

See Current Biography 1971

Howard Hodgkin

Born: London, England; August 6, 1932
Died: London, England; March 9, 2017
Occupation: British artist

Howard Hodgkin was an artist of world-renown whose broad-brush style was often painted on rough wood, and often incorporated a frame as integral to the artwork itself. He was appointed Commander of the Most Excellent Order of the British Empire (CBE) and was knighted in 1992. He was made a Companion of Honour in 2003.

Howard Hodgkin was born into an upper-middle-class Quaker family that had earned distinction for its pioneering accomplishments in meteorology, antiquarianism, engineering, and other fields of intellectual endeavor. An ancestor, Thomas Hodgkin, was the first to describe the fatal lymphoma that bears his name. Other relatives include several Nobel Prize winners in science. By the age of five he resolved to become a painter. During World War II, he was evacuated from England to a household on Long Island, New York. (The house had been the setting for F. Scott Fitzgerald's *The Great Gatsby*.) He could visit museums in nearby Manhattan where he studied the paintings of French artists including Vuillard, Matisse, Degas, and Bonnard, who would greatly influence his artwork. He was also greatly influenced by paintings from India. From 1949 to 1950 Hodgkin studied at the Camberell School of Art in London. He then spent four years at the Bath Academy of Art in Corsham. He began teaching art at Charterhouse School in London in 1954. In 1956 he moved to the Bath Academy of Art where he remained for a decade. Hodgkin had his first one-man show in 1962 at Arthur Tooth and Sons in London.

Hodgkin used wooden forms as his canvas, embracing the enclosed-playpen approach, something American painting had outright rejected, by underlining the containing frame in different ways, either by thick painted borders or by using actual three-dimensional wooden strips. His paintings were more representational than abstract, featuring "pictures" of emotional situations and feelings that arise in social interactions. He would spend two or three years on a single picture, but remarkably, his paintings looked almost spontaneous—vivacious, brisk, and exuberant.

In 1955 Hodgkin married a fellow art student, Julia Lane. They had two sons. In 1978 he separated from Lane and came out as a gay man, partnering with Antony Peattie, a music critic. Survivors include his two sons and Peattie.

See Current Biography 1991

Ivor Noël Hume

Born: London, England; November 4, 1927
Died: Williamsburg, Virginia; February 4, 2017
Occupation: British archaeologist, antiquary

Ivor Noël Hume, a largely self-taught archaeologist, was responsible for unearthing the remains of an early, long-lost British settlement known as Wolstenholme Towne and Martin's Hundred in present-day Virginia. His was among the most important archaeological finds ever made in the United States. Noël Hume essentially transformed the discipline in the United States from "little more than a treasure hunt" to a rigorous scientific discipline.

Ivor Noël Hume was born into an aristocratic home, and was largely brought up by servants. He attended a series of boarding schools and became interested in theatre while attending St. Lawrence College where he wrote and directed two plays. His theatre experience would become a major factor in his later approach to archaeology. Upon graduating from St. Lawrence, Noël Hume began working as an assistant stage manager at the J. Arthur Rank school at the Connaught Theatre in Worthing, Sussex. He enjoyed walking along the banks of the Thames, scavenging for old Roman coins or pieces of pottery—traces of London's ancient past. He sold some of his treasures to the Guildhall Museum and became its sole volunteer. He eventually joined the staff as the curator's assistant, but within days, he would replace his boss who had fallen ill. He became curator and the City of London's sole staff archaeologist. When the museum was in danger of closing, Noël Hume drew upon his theatre experience to generate public interest in history.

While at the Guildhall, Noël Hume met and married Audrey Baines, another volunteer and graduate with a degree in archaeology. She would play pivotal role in his education and remarkable success as an archaeologist. In 1956, Noël Hume served as a consultant in historical archaeology in Colonial Williamsburg Virginia, where, remarkably, he and his wife joined the staff, she as a curator, and Noël Hume as the chief archaeologist. In 1964 he became the director of archaeology at Colonial Williamsburg. He was an honorary research associate with the Smithsonian Institution from 1959 onward.

Noël Hume published more than two dozen books on archaeology. He was made a member of the Order of the British Empire (OBE) in 1992. Noël Hume's wife, Audrey, predeceased him. Survivors include his second wife, Carol Glazier, three children, and nine grandchildren.

See Current Biography 1997

John Hurt

Born: Chesterfield, England; January 22, 1940
Died: Norfolk, England; January 25, 2017
Occupation: British actor

As an actor, John Hurt's skills ranked among some of the best of his time. Though a great stage actor, he is remembered for his lead roles in such highly acclaimed films as *The Elephant Man* and *Midnight Express*, each earning Hurt Academy Award nominations. He earned the British Academy of Film and Television Arts (BAFTA) award for his supporting role in *Midnight Express*, which also won Hurt a Golden Globe Award.

John Hurt was the youngest of three children born to the Anglican minister, Reverend Arnould Herbert Hurt, and his engineer wife, Phyllis (Massey) Hurt. He wanted to become an actor from an early age and starred in a number of school productions while attending Lincoln School in Cleethorpes, Lincolnshire. His parents insisted that he train for a second career so he attended art school. He received a full scholarship from the prestigious Royal Academy of Dramatic Art (RADA) in London. Hurt won acclaim as the "most promising newcomer of the year" from the London critics for his portrayal as Len in Harold Pinter's comedy *The Dwarfs*. During the mid-1960s Hurt joined the Royal Shakespeare Company and he appeared in a variety of films. He first gained attention from American audiences for his 1976 role in the PBS Classic Theatre series, *The Playboy of the Western World*. With that role, Hurt earned a 1975 best actor award from the British Academy of Film and Television Arts (BAFTA) and an Emmy award. Hurt's film career took off in the late 1970s when he appeared in several high-profile films, including *Midnight Express* and *Alien*. He received the British Academy Award, the Golden Globe award, and an Academy Award nomination as best supporting actor. Arguably his greatest role was as John Merrick, the victim of neurofibromatosis, who was exploited as a carnival freak in David Lynch and Mel Brooks' production of *The Elephant Man*. Hurt earned another Oscar nomination for the role. Hurt won an Emmy award and another BAFTA Award for best children's program for his work in Jim Henson's television series, *The Storyteller*.

John Hurt was made a Commander of the Order of the British Empire (CBE) in 2004 and was knighted in 2015 for his services to drama. He married four times and had two sons with his third wife, Joan Dalton. His survivors include his wife, Anwen Rees-Myers and two children.

See Current Biography 1982

Gwen Ifill

Born: New York, New York; September 29, 1955
Died: Washington, DC; November 14, 2016
Occupation: Broadcast journalist

Gwen Ifill was the first woman and the first African American to host the show *Washington Week in Review* on the Public Broadcasting Service (PBS). She later became the anchor and managing editor for PBS *NewsHour*, the network's nightly news show. Ifill moderated the vice-presidential debates in the 2004 and 2008 elections, and the Democratic presidential candidate debate in the 2016 primary. She was a correspondent for several national newspapers including the *New York Times* and the *Washington Post*.

Gwen Ifill was one of six children born to the African Methodist minister, O. Urcille Ifill, a Panamanian immigrant, and his wife, Eleanor Ifill who emigrated from Barbados. Gwen Ifill explained that it was a family ritual to sit and watch the national news broadcasts on television, which inspired her to seek a career as a journalist. The family was poor and moved frequently, and Ifill spent her high school years living in public housing in Buffalo, New York. She would later remark, while working on a story about public housing, that she was likely the only correspondent there who had lived in public housing. Ifill attended Simmons College, a women's school in Boston, earning her degree in communications studies in 1977. A professor, Alden Poole, helped Ifill get an internship at the *Boston Herald American,* which later hired her to cover politics.

After a decade of working for print news, with occasional television appearances, at the urging of Tim Russert, moderator of NBC's program *Meet the Press,* Ifill entertained the idea of working in broadcast news. She accepted a position as the senior political correspondent for the popular PBS show *NewsHour* with Jim Lehrer, as well as her own slot on the political show *Washington Week,* carried by ninety percent of PBS stations around the United States. Ifill went on to moderate several vice-presidential and primary debates.

Gwen Ifill wrote the book *The Breakthrough: Politics and Race in the Age of Obama,* which became a best seller. She was a presenter at the News and Documentary Emmy Awards, and was the master of ceremonies at the 2015 LBJ Liberty & Justice for All Award ceremony. She received a Peabody Award in 2008, was inducted into the National Association of Black Journalists Hall of Fame, was nominated for an NAACP Image Award, and received a lifetime achievement award from Women's Media Center, and

the Fourth Estate Award from the National Press Club.

Gwen Ifill died on November 14, 2016 of breast and endometrial cancer. Her survivors include her brother and a sister.

See Current Biography 2005

Michael Ilitch

Born: Detroit, Michigan; July 20, 1929
Died: Detroit, Michigan; February 10, 2017
Occupation: Founder of Little Caesars Pizza, baseball and hockey team owner

Michael Ilitch founded the Little Caesars Pizza franchise in 1959 and was ranked 389th on the 2004 Forbes list of the 400 richest Americans. He purchased the Detroit Red Wings hockey team in 1982, and the Detroit Tigers baseball team in 1992.

Michael Ilitch grew up in Detroit, Michigan, the son of Macedonian immigrant parents. His father, Sotir, was a tool-and-die worker at Chrysler. Ilitch was a talented baseball shortstop with a .340 batting average, who dreamed of playing in the major league. He was sidelined by injuries and spent his youth at various jobs, including a successful metal awning business. Ilitch married in 1954 and the two pooled their savings to open a pizzeria in a strip mall in Garden City, Michigan. Little Caesars would grow to become the fourth largest pizza chain in the United States, and ranked 36th in US food-service sales in 2002. Known as "Mr. I," Ilitch was a humble man and his restaurant chain mirrored his personality. Half of the company's vice presidents started as hourly employees.

In 1982 Ilitch bought the Detroit Red Wings hockey team, which has won four Stanley Cups. Its worth increased from $184 million in 1998 to $245 million in 2003. Ten years later Ilitch purchased the foundering Detroit Tigers. He contributed $245 million to help build a new, 40,000-seat baseball stadium, Comerica Park, which opened in 2000. Ilitch also founded the Little Caesars Love Kitchen Foundation, feeding more than 1.5 million needy people through a mobile pizza kitchen. President Bill Clinton awarded the organization the Volunteer Action Award in 1994. His Ilitch Charities for Children (ICC) is dedicated to improving the lives of children in health, education, and recreation. Ilitch also created the Little Caesars AAA Hockey Scholarship program for outstanding high school athletes to attend the colleges of their choice. He received the Ellis Island Medal of Honor from the National Ethnic Coalition of Organizations (NECO).

Michael and Marian Ilitch were married in 1954 and had seven children. Michael Ilitch is survived by his wife, seven children, twenty-two grandchildren, and three great-grandchildren.

See Current Biography 2005

Albert Innaurato

Born: Philadelphia, Pennsylvania; June 2, 1947
Died: Philadelphia, Pennsylvania; September 24, 2017
Occupation: Playwright, opera critic

Albert Innaurato is most remembered for his hit Broadway play, *Gemini*, which had a four-year run, and was an early exploration of gay rights and the gay lifestyle. He was honored with two Obies, a Guggenheim fellowship, and grants from the Rockefeller Foundation and the National Endowment for the Arts (NEA).

Albert Innaurato was born and raised in the Italian section of South Philadelphia. He was gifted as a child. By the age of twelve, he was reading Nietzsche and Freud, and began writing plays before graduating from Central high school. He attended Temple University, then transferred to the California Institute of the Arts where he earned his bachelor's degree in fine arts. He earned his master's degree in fine arts from Yale University where he became friends with such notables as fellow playwright, Christopher Durang, Sigourney Weaver, and Meryl Streep. While still in graduate school, Durang and Innaurato collaborated on the play, *The Idiots Karamazov*, which featured Meryl Streep in its cast. Innaurato's greatest work was his play *Gemini*, about a gay boy growing up in the mean streets of a tough Italian neighborhood in South Philadelphia. The show opened on May 21, 1977 at the Little Theatre on Broadway, and ran for more than four years, until September 5, 1981. Innaurato became a well-known aficionado of opera, writing frequent critiques for *Opera News*. He also wrote for the PBS television show, *The Days and Nights of Mollie Dodd*.

Albert Innaurato apparently died in his sleep and was found by a cousin. No immediate relatives survive.

See Current Biography 1988

Roy Innis

Born: St. Croix, US Virgin Islands; June 6, 1934
Died: New York, New York; January 8, 2017
Occupation: Civil rights activist

Roy Innis was a black nationalist who rose through the ranks of the Congress of Racial Equality (CORE) to become its autocratic national leader.

Roy Innis was born in St. Croix, in the US Virgin Islands. His father was a police officer who was killed when Innis was six years old. He moved to Harlem with his mother in 1946 and attended Stuyvesant High School in Manhattan, graduating in 1952. He studied chemistry at the City College of New York (CCNY) but left before earning his degree to work as a research chemist at Vicks Chemical Company, and at Montefiore Hospital where he was the union representative for Local 1199 of the Hospital Workers Union. He joined CORE in 1963 and was considered an extremist for his neo-nationalist views. In 1965 he was elected chairman of the Harlem chapter. Two years later he was elected second national vice-chairman, and in 1968 Innis was named CORE's permanent national director. In 1982 he became the CORE's national chairman. In later years, members would try to depose him for his autocratic leadership style.

Roy Innis was always a controversial figure in politics and in the civil rights movement where his views resembled a Republican political platform. He did not espouse the ideals of nonviolent civil disobedience and fought desegregation. He did not envision equality in white society, but strength in an independent black society. He felt integration would rob African Americans of their distinct, unique identity, which he sought to strengthen. Innis supported the candidacy of Richard Nixon and later, that of Ronald Reagan, urging African Americans to join the Republican Party. In the 1980s Innis was embroiled in several suits alleging he participated in illegal fundraising and misused CORE money. Though he lost two sons to gun violence he was a life member and a director of the National Rifle Association. In the 1980s he ran for congress twice, and in 1990 he ran in the Democratic mayoral primary but lost to David Dinkins. Innis was involved in two on-air talk show scuffles, in one case pushing the Reverend Al Sharpton to the ground.

Roy Innis married several times and was said to have nine children who survive him.

See Current Biography 1969

Arthur Janov

Born: Los Angeles, California; August 21, 1924
Died: Malibu, California; October 1, 2017
Occupation: American psychologist

Arthur Janov was the first psychotherapist to develop "primal scream therapy." He wrote well over a dozen books about this new form of therapy, and established the Janov Primal Center in Malibu, California.

Arthur Janov was born and raised in Los Angeles, California, and he attended Los Angeles High School, graduating in 1943. Shortly thereafter, Janov joined the US Navy and fought in both the Pacific and European theatres. Upon returning home, Janov went to the University of California at Los Angeles (UCLA), graduating with a bachelor's degree in social sciences. He conducted research for his thesis at the Los Angeles Veterans Hospital. He earned his master's degree in social work in 1951 and set up his own practice while also working on the staff of the Los Angeles Children's Hospital. He earned his PhD in clinical psychology from Claremont Graduate School, specializing in neurophysiology. He happened upon the idea of the primal scream while leading a group therapy session that included a young, withdrawn college student. He suggested the student cry out for his parents. Though resistant at first, the patient began crying with a piercing, deathlike scream, and writhing on the floor in agony. Janov succeeded in repeating the experiment with his other patients. He wrote of the basic tenets of his method in the book, *The Primal Scream,* published in 1970. Soon he was overwhelmed with prospects for this new therapy. His most famous patients included John Lennon, Yoko Ono, and James Earl Jones, who certainly helped popularize Janov's methods. Although some critics felt Janov's theories lacked sufficient evidence to be a bona-fide new methodology, his techniques have persisted and have brought some healing for neuroses.

Dr. Janov's first marriage to Vivian Glickstein ended in divorce in 1980. Within the following year he married France Daunic, who survives along with Dr. Janov's two sons, two grandchildren, and a great-grandchild.

See Current Biography 1980

Al Jarreau

Born: Milwaukee, Wisconsin; March 12, 1940
Died: Los Angeles, California; February 12, 2017
Occupation: Singer, songwriter

Though he didn't begin his singing career until his thirties, Al Jarreau won seven Grammy Awards, combining elements of jazz, soul, Latin, and pop singing styles.

Al Jarreau was born into a musical family. His mother, Pearl, was a piano teacher, and his father, Emile, played the musical saw. Jarreau, along with his parents and five siblings, performed at church benefits and other local venues. Though his father had been trained as a minister, he earned his living as a welder in a Milwaukee foundry. In high school Jarreau performed Broadway show tunes in school productions. He was also a talented athlete, winning a basketball scholarship to Ripon College where he graduated with a degree in psychology. He earned his master's degree in psychology, specializing in rehabilitation and counseling, from the University of Iowa in 1964. After a brief stint in the US Army Reserve, Jarreau worked as a counselor at the California Division of Rehabilitation in San Francisco. He quit in 1968 to follow his passion for music. He partnered with a Brazilian guitarist, Julio Martinez, and the two began performing for overflow crowds at Gatsby's club in Sausalito, California. Jarreau would continue to perform in clubs even after achieving some fame.

Al Jarreau's first album, *We Got By*, was released in 1975 and he embarked on a successful European tour. In 1976 *Record World* named him the number one jazz vocalist of the year. He won his first Grammy Award for his double album, *Look to the Rainbow.* In all, Jarreau earned seven Grammy Awards, with well over a dozen additional nominations. He also performed the theme song for the popular television series, *Moonlighting.*

Al Jarreau married his wife, Susan in 1976 and they had one son. His wife and son survive him.

See Current Biography 1992

F. Ross Johnson

Born: Winnipeg, Manitoba, Canada; December 13, 1931
Died: Jupiter, Florida; December 29, 2016
Occupation: Business executive

F. Ross Johnson was the chief executive officer of RJR Nabisco Company. He helped define an era of corporate greed and deal making when he attempted a leveraged buyout (LBO) of the nineteenth-largest corporation in the United States. The book *Barbarians at the Gate: The Fall of RJR Nabisco*, documented the ordeal. A movie version of the book was produced in 1990 with James Garner playing F. Ross Johnson.

Johnson was born in Winnipeg, Canada, the only child of Frederick and Caroline (Green) Johnson. His father was a businessman who became the head of the Canadian division of the Schlage lock company. Johnson seemed to have been born for business. As a child he rented out his comic books to friends and won a bicycle for selling *Liberty* magazine subscriptions. He was always highly competitive and aggressive. He attended the University of Manitoba, graduating in 1952 with a bachelor's degree in commerce. His first job was as an accountant with Canadian General Electric in Toronto. He took night classes at the University of Toronto to earn his MBA. In 1971 he became the president and Chief Executive Officer (CEO) of the Canadian division of Standard Brands Limited, a multinational food products company. He moved up the ladder of command quickly and by 1976 he was the CEO and chairman of the board of the entire company. He was forty-four years old. In 1981 Johnson successfully guided the company into a merger with Nabisco, and by 1985 the company employed over 70,000 people in fifty-five countries, with annual sales topping $6 billion. Johnson oversaw the friendly takeover of RJ Reynolds Industries, creating the firm RJR Nabisco, with Johnson as the CEO of the new venture. In 1988 Johnson and a team of seven other managers proposed a leveraged buyout of $17.6 billion. Within days the powerful Wall Street investment firm Kohlberg, Kravis, Roberts and Company tendered a higher bid, initiating a hostile bidding war, which Johnson eventually lost. He retired with a $50 million severance package. He

Johnson was married twice. His wife Susan, his two sons and two grand daughters survive him.

See Current Biography 1989

George Keyworth

Born: Boston, Massachusetts; November 30, 1939
Died: Monterey, California; August 23, 2017
Occupation: Physicist, Director of US Office of Science and Technology Policy

George Keyworth was a proponent of the weapons defense system commonly referred to as "Star Wars," that gained traction during the Reagan administration. Using space technology, the defense system would intercept missiles fired at the United States. Some historians have argued that just the possibility of such a defense system eventually led to the end of the Cold War, and even the disintegration of the Soviet Union.

George Keyworth was raised outside of Boston, Massachusetts, attending the elite private boys school, Deerfield Academy. He attended Yale University where he earned his BS degree in physics in 1963. He immediately moved to Duke University where he earned his graduate degree in nuclear physics. Upon graduation Keyworth joined the staff of physicists at Los Alamos Scientific Laboratory in New Mexico, where he eventually became the director of experimental physics, supervising several hundred scientists and technicians. In May of 1981, President Ronald Reagan announced that Keyworth would be the new director of the Office of Science and Technology Policy, charged with implementing Reagan's Strategic Defense Initiative, commonly known as "Star Wars" because of its potential use of space-based particle beams or lasers to shoot down incoming missiles. The system was controversial and not universally backed by the scientific community, which feared it was, at best, impossible to implement. Keyworth countered that the program's goal was not perfection but effective deterrence. After Reagan's first term, Keyworth resigned in 1985 and served on the board of General Atomics Corp. and as director at Hewlett-Packard. He was a senior fellow and co-founder of the Progress & Freedom Foundation, a technology policy think tank.

Dr. Keyworth's first wife, Polly Lauterbach Keyworth, died in 2004. His survivors include his second wife, Marion Schwartz Keyworth, his two children and four grandchildren from his first marriage, three stepchildren, and ten step-grandchildren.

See Current Biography 1986

Adnan Khashoggi

Born: Mecca, Saudi Arabia; July 25, 1935
Died: London, England; June 6, 2017
Occupation: Saudi Arabian corporation executive, arms dealer

Adnan Khashoggi, one of the world's wealthiest men, was a Saudi Arabian commission agent who made his fortune by brokering financial transactions between Western corporations and Middle-Eastern governments.

Adnan Khashoggi was born to a devout Muslim family. His father, Mohamed Khashoggi was a personal physician to the late king ibn Saud, and was the first Western-trained physician in Saudi Arabia. He was instrumental in importing the country's first x-ray machine, and also setting up Mecca's first power plant. His son Adnan was ambitious. He attended an elite British-style boarding school, Victoria College, in Alexandria, Egypt. The future King Hussein of Jordan was a classmate. While in school Khashoggi earned his first business fee by introducing two of his classmates' fathers to each other for a business deal. Upon returning from school, the boy helped his family establish the Alnasr Trading and Industrial Corporation, which was guaranteed a fifty-year monopoly on developing gypsum deposits. He attended college in the United States, at California State University at Chico, and at Stanford University. With his family ties to the royal Saudi family, he was able to broker deals for many things, from Kenworth trucks and Rolls Royce, to F-104 Starfighter combat aircraft. During the 1970s Khashoggi was a conduit for about eighty percent of all Saudi foreign defense systems. During the mid-1970s the US Justice Department and the Securities and Exchange Commission investigated the legality of Khashoggi's American connections. In the mid-1980s Khashoggi facilitated the Iran-Contra Affair in which the United States traded weapons through Israel to Iran in exchange for a hostage release. It was Khashoggi who connected Iranian and Israeli arms dealers. It was Khashoggi who worked with the US Central Intelligence Agency (CIA), which eventually revealed that the United States had exchanged 508 TOW anti-tank missiles to Iran for the release of one hostage, and diverted millions of dollars from the proceeds to the Contra guerrillas in Nicaragua. In 1988 Khashoggi was convicted of concealing funds in the bankruptcy of the Bank of Credit and Commerce International. He spent three months in a Swiss jail before being extradited to the United States to stand trial for fraud and racketeering. He was acquitted of the charges but lost many of his clients and creditors.

In 1961 Khashoggi married an English woman, Sandra Daly. They had four children and divorced in 1974. His second wife was a seventeen-year-old Italian woman named Laura Biancolini. They had one child. He took a third wife, as allowed under Islamic law, an Iranian woman named Shahpari Azam Zanganeh. Adnan Khashoggi's six children survive him.

See Current Biography 1986

Helmut Kohl

Born: Ludwigshafen, Germany; April 3, 1930
Died: Ludwigshafen, Germany; June 16, 2017
Occupation: German chancellor

Helmut Kohl served as the chancellor of West Germany, and later the unified Germany, from 1982 to 1998, staying in office for an unprecedented sixteen years, overseeing the fall of the Berlin Wall and Germany's reunification.

Helmut Kohl was born into a conservative, Roman Catholic home. His father was an officer in the German Army during World War II, who later became a finance official in the civil service. Kohl worked as a farming apprentice, and completed his secondary education at the Oerrealschule in Ludwigshafen. He studied law, political science, history, and sociology at the universities of Frankfurt and Heidelberg, while working as a research assistant in political science at Heidelberg's Alfred-Weber Institut. He earned his doctorate in 1958. From 1958 to 1969 Kohl was the department head in an industrial association, the Industrieverband Chemie. His first political sympathies were with the left, and he joined the conservative Christian Democratic Union (CDU) where he helped found the Ludwigshafen branch of the Junge Union (Young Union) of the CDU. He then rose through party ranks. Kohl was then hand picked by Peter Altmeier, the aging chief executive of the CDU, to succeed him as the Minister-President, which made Kohl a member of the Bundesrat, the upper house of the federal parliament. In 1969 he was elected vice-chairman of the federal CDU. In 1975 the CDU unanimously nominated Kohl to be the federal candidate for the chancellorship. In 1982 the Free Democratic Party (FDP), which had supported Chancellor Schmidt in 1976, removed their support and joined the CDU-CSU (Christian Social Union) coalition, effectively passing a vote of no confidence against Chancellor Schmidt. He resigned and Kohl was placed as chancellor of West Germany. In 1989 the Berlin Wall came down and Kohl started focusing his attention on promoting a unified Germany. In 1990 he signed a treaty with

East Germany, unifying German economic and social-welfare systems, and granting an equal currency exchange with East Germany's now-defunct currency, a highly controversial move. Later that year, East Germany was dissolved and a unified Germany was created. In 1990 Kohl won the first free, all-German parliamentary elections since 1931. He was reelected in 1994, making him the longest serving chancellor in modern German history. In 1999 Kohl became embroiled in a corruption scandal after he accepted at least $1 million in illegal donations.

Helmut Kohl's wife, Hannelore, took her own life in 2001 after suffering for several years from a rare allergy to light. In 2008 Kohl suffered a head injury that left him in a wheelchair, with difficulties speaking. He died in 2017 at his home in Ludwigshafen, Germany. His two sons survive him.

See Current Biography 1977

Mauno Koivisto

Born: Turku, Finland; November 25, 1923
Died: Helsinki, Finland; May 12, 2017
Occupation: President of Finland, banker

Mauno Koivisto served two six-year terms as president of Finland, from 1982 to 1994. His foreign policy skills helped Finland remain stable and balanced in its relationships with the Soviet Union and the United States during the height of the Cold War.

Mauno Koivisto came from a working-class family. His father was a carpenter who died when his son was ten, and the family's meager circumstances meant Koivisto would have to work to support himself throughout his college career. At the age of sixteen, Koivisto volunteered to fight for Finland against the Soviet Union in the Winter War from 1939 to 1940, and the Continuation War from 1941 to 1944. Following the war he joined the Social Democrat Party, and worked his way through college, earning a doctorate in sociology from Turku University. During that time he wrote two books: *Social Relations in Turku Harbor* and *Laajempaan Kansanvaltaan* (*More Power to the People*). In 1958 Koivisto joined the Helsinki Workers Savings Bank, and within a year he became the managing director. He entered government banking in 1966, and by 1968 he became governor of the Bank of Finland, a powerful institution, largely independent of Parliament. His lengthy tenure there made Koivisto one of the most enduring presences on the national economic scene, and he earned the respect of those in the Social Democratic Party. Koivisto sat in several cabinet posts before being elected to the presidency in 1982. He would remain there until 1994. Before the collapse of the Soviet Union, Koivisto steered Finland out of his predecessor's isolationist policies, and in 1990 he hosted a summit in Helsinki between George Bush of the United States and Mikhail Gorbachev of the Soviet Union. In 1992 Koivisto forwarded Finland's application to join the European Community, precursor of the European Union (EU). In 1994 Finland was admitted.

Koivisto's wife of sixty-five years, Tellervo Koivisto, and their daughter survive him.

See Current Biography 1982

Peter-Hans Kolvenbach

Born: Druten, Netherlands; November 30, 1928
Died: Beirut, Lebanon; November 26, 2016
Occupation: Superior General of the Society of Jesus, Roman Catholic priest

Father Peter-Hans Kolvenbach was the superior general of the Jesuit order of priests, the largest and most influential Roman Catholic religious order of men.

Peter-Hans Kolvenbach was born in the village of Druten, Holland, near Nijmegen. His father was of Dutch and German descent, and his mother was of Italian descent. Raised in the Armenian rite, Kolvenbach claimed to feel at home in the liturgies of both the east and the west. (He eventually learned many languages. In addition to Dutch and Armenian, Kolvenbach spoke fluent English, German, French, Russian, Italian, and Spanish.) At nineteen, Kolvenbach entered the Society of Jesus at Mariendaal, in the Netherlands. Following two years of spiritual training at the Jesuit novitiate, he took his vows of poverty, chastity, and obedience. He studied philosophy at the University of Nijmegan for three years, followed by four years of theology at St. Joseph University in Beirut, Lebanon, a place that would become his spiritual home. He was ordained in 1961. Following his ordination, Kolvenbach earned his doctorate and returned to Beirut as a professor of general linguistics. In 1981 he was appointed to the faculty of the Gregorian University in Rome. During this time tension arose between Pope Paul VI and Kolvenbach's predecessor, the Superior General Pedro Arrupe, as Arrupe seemed to advocate more radical activism. In August of 1981, Arrupe suffered a stroke and could no longer function as the superior general. In the fall of 1983, the Jesuits held their General Congregation 33, and elected Father Peter-Hans Kolvenbach as their superior general. According to Jesuit Father Joseph McShane, president of Fordham University who was interviewed by Daniel Cosacchi, writer for *Americanmagazine.org* (26 Nov. 2016), Father Kolvenbach was known for "his humility, holiness, integrity and savvy diplomacy… [which] stabilized the society after one of the roughest periods of [its] history… [he was] the quintessential peacemaker between the papacy and the society."

After twenty-five years, Father Kolvenbach resigned as superior general in 2008, a rare occurrence as superior generals are elected for life. He spent his final years as assistant librarian for the Jesuits in Beirut.

See Current Biography 1984

Melvin Laird

Born: Omaha, Nebraska; September 1, 1922
Died: Fort Myers, Florida; November 16, 2016
Occupation: US Secretary of Defense, senator

Melvin Laird served as Richard Nixon's first secretary of defense. He also served nine terms in the US House of Representatives.

Melvin Laird was born, the third of four sons, into a political family. His father was a minister who served in the Wisconsin state senate from 1939 until his death in 1946. His grandfather on his mother's side was a chairman of the Wisconsin Republican party and served as the Wisconsin Lieutenant Governor.

Laird's mother was a former member of the University of Wisconsin board of regents and was a delegate to the 1948 Republican National Convention. Laird attended Carleton College in Northfield, Minnesota, where he majored in political science. Upon his graduation he enlisted in the United States Navy where he served aboard the destroyer USS Maddox. He was wounded twice and was awarded the Purple Heart.

Upon his father's death, Laird won his father's senate seat making him the youngest state senator in the United States at that time. Six years later he was elected to the US House of Representatives serving on the powerful Appropriations Committee, where he sponsored legislation to expand the National Institutes of Health (NIH), including the creation of cancer research centers across the country. In the 1960s he was the chair of the House Republican Conference and worked closely with future president, Gerald Ford. President Richard Nixon appointed him defense secretary in 1969, but the two rarely agreed on strategy for ending the Vietnam War. Laird felt that the war could only end through diplomacy, whereas Nixon and Secretary of State, Henry Kissinger, favored more

bombing. Under Laird's command the draft was suspended and he helped institute an all-volunteer military in the 1970s. At one point his relationship was so adversarial with Nixon, that Nixon had Laird's chief aid's phone tapped. He was often at loggerheads with the Secretary of State, Henry Kissinger, and once had an aid obtain copies of secret documents from Kissinger's office. Laird was instrumental in getting Nixon to reach a strategic arms limitation agreement with the Soviet Union. When the Vice President, Spiro Agnew resigned, Melvin Laird helped convince Nixon to replace him with Gerald Ford. Upon retiring from government service, Laird worked for the Reader's Digest Association as a senior advisor on national and international affairs.

Melvin Laird married his college sweetheart, Barbara Masters. They had two children. After Barbara's death in 1991, Laird married Carole Howard. Melvin Laird is survived by his wife, his three children, a stepdaughter, four grandsons, and a step-granddaughter.

See Current Biography 1964

Martin Landau

Born: New York, New York; June 20, 1928
Died: Los Angeles, California; July 15, 2017
Occupation: Actor, teacher

Although many people will remember Martin Landau as Rollin Hand on the television series *Mission: Impossible* from the late 1960s, he was a highly decorated film star with three Academy Award nominations and one win for his role in the 1995 movie *Ed Wood*, starring Johnny Depp. He also won three Golden Globe Awards and was nominated for six television Emmy Awards.

Martin Landau grew up in Brooklyn, New York, and attended Brooklyn's Pratt Institute, though he left before earning his degree. He also studied at the famous Art Student's League. At seventeen he began working as an artist and cartoonist for the *New York Daily News*. In his early twenties he auditioned and gained admittance to the renowned New York City Actors Studio. (According to some sources, he and Steve McQueen were the only students, out of several thousand, who were accepted that year.) During that time he began picking up television roles in popular shows such as *Gunsmoke, Maverick, The Twilight Zone,* and *The Outer Limits.* He also landed his first feature film, *Pork Chop Hill,* a Korean War drama starring Gregory Peck. In 1966 he was selected to play Rollin Hand in the wildly popular series *Mission: Impossible.* He left the show after its third season, but found he had become so closely identified with his character that he had trouble finding new roles for several decades. In 1974 he moved with his family to London where he and his wife, actress Barbara Bain, landed roles in the television series *Space: 1999*. Finally, after a long dry spell in Landau's career, Francis Ford Coppola cast him as Abe Karatz in *Tucker: The Man and His Dream*. He earned his first Academy Award nomination for the role. In 1988 Woody Allen selected Landau to play the principle male lead in *Crimes and Misdemeanors*. Perhaps Landau's greatest achievement was his depiction of Bela Lugosi in Tim Burton's *Ed Wood*. For his role he received a Golden Globe Award and awards from the New York Film Critics Circle (NYFCC), the National Society of Film Critics (NSFC), and the Screen Actors Guild (SAG). He also won an Academy Award for best supporting actor. In addition to his acting, Landau taught at the Lee Strasberg's Actors Studio. Among his students were Jack Nicholson, Anjelica Huston, and Oliver Stone.

Martin Landau acted in well over fifty feature films, and he accumulated more than five hundred television credits. In 2001 he received his star on Hollywood's Walk of Fame. He and Barbara Bain married in 1957 and divorced in 1993. They had two daughters who survive him.

See Current Biography 1997

Frédérick Leboyer

Born: Paris, France; November 1, 1918
Died: Vens, Switzerland; May 25, 2017
Occupation: French physician, author, photographer

Frédérick Leboyer is most well known for the birthing method that bears his name, the "Leboyer method," which he described at length in his seminal book *Birth Without Violence*. Leboyer advocated a calm atmosphere in the birthing room, including dimmed lighting, soft voices, gentle massage, and a warm bath for the newborn.

Frédérick Leboyer was not forthcoming about his early life. He was born in Paris and attended the Faculty of Medicine at the University of Paris, graduating as an advanced scholar in 1937. Following his military service in World War II, he practiced in Germany, serving displaced persons. During the war, Leboyer and his brother changed their names from Levi to Leboyer to hide the fact they were Jews. (Leboyer was born Alfred Lazare Levy.) After 1955 Leboyer devoted himself exclusively to obstetrics. In 1958 he traveled to India, and it was there that he came to realize that modern childbirth

focused on the mother's suffering while ignoring that of the baby. He felt that the trauma of birth was a source of anxiety and stress later in life. He was convinced the newborn is highly sensitive to light and sound and that the trauma of birth was exacerbated by the ambiance of most delivery rooms. In 1974 Leboyer published his *Pour Une Naissance Sans Violence* in Paris. The following year, Alfred A. Knopf published the book under the title *Birth Without Violence*. Strangely, the book was written as a long prose poem, which may have contributed to its mixed reviews. The book and Leboyer's methods brought a wide range of reactions, from broad outright dismissal to tempered enthusiasm. Leboyer stopped practicing medicine in large measure, to eliminate the appearance of a conflict of interest on his part.

Frédérick Leboyer married late in life and had no children. His survivors include his wife, Mieko Yoshimura, a niece and a nephew.

See Current Biography 1982

Jerry Lewis

Born: Newark, New Jersey; March 16, 1926
Died: Las Vegas, Nevada; August 20, 2017
Occupation: Comedian, producer, director, philanthropist

Jerry Lewis was a comedian whose zany, slapstick act served as a perfect counter to his fellow actor, the smooth, suave, night-club crooner, Dean Martin. Their partnership was remarkably short, about six years from 1946 to 1953, given the impact they had on show business. They each went on to have successful solo careers. Jerry Lewis is also remembered as the spokesman who led telethons for Muscular Dystrophy research. He was chairman of the Muscular Dystrophy Association for fifty-five years. His work earned him a Nobel Peace Prize nomination.

Jerry Lewis shot to fame shortly after World War II, when he was only twenty years old. His parents were both performers and often had to leave their young son with relatives, engendering a deep insecurity and need for attention in their son. By the time he was sixteen, he had dropped out of high school, developed a comedy routine, and gave himself the stage name Jerry Lewis. (He was born Joseph Levitch.)

He performed in vaudeville and burlesque stages across the region, going as far as Detroit where he met Patti Palmer. The two were married several months later. In 1946 he met lounge singer, Dean Martin and the two began working on an act. Representatives from Broadway and *Billboard* magazine began taking notice. The duo's rise was meteoric. Copacabana producer Hal Wallis signed them to a five-year contract with Paramount Pictures. They ended up making six movies in short order, from 1951 to 1956. However, the relationship between Lewis and Martin became strained when Lewis wanted more artistic control with an eye towards producing and directing. Martin decided to renew his solo career. Shortly thereafter, Jerry Lewis launched a singing career and his first album, *Jerry Lewis Just Sings*, shot to number three on Billboard's top hits. In the early 1960s, Lewis tried his hand at directing, and found great success, especially with his 1963 hit, *The Nutty Professor*. By the early 1970s, Lewis's act was going out of style and his career hit a dry spell. Throughout the 1980s and 1990s, Lewis appeared in a number of television roles.

Jerry Lewis served as the spokesman and national chairman of the Muscular Dystrophy Association, and in 1966 he began hosting telethons, which would become an annual affair. Lewis raised over $2 billion over the fifty-five years he served.

Jerry Lewis and his wife, Patti, divorced in 1980. They had four children. In 1983 he married SanDee Pitnick, and they had one daughter. Lewis's survivors include his wife, SanDee, his five children, and several grandchildren.

See Current Biography 1970

Harvey Lichtenstein

Born: New York, New York; April 9, 1929
Died: New York, New York; February 11, 2017
Occupation: President of the Brooklyn Academy of Music

Harvey Lichtenstein is credited with transforming the Brooklyn Academy of Music (BAM), revitalizing it to become the leading avant-garde performing arts center in the country.

Harvey Lichtenstein was born to eastern European immigrants. His father, Samuel, was from Poland and his mother, Jennie (Walodarsky), was from Russia. He grew up in the Bushwick section of Brooklyn and attended Brooklyn Technical High School. He studied history and English literature at Brooklyn College, winning a scholarship to study dance at the Connecticut College of School and Dance. He won another dance scholarship to Bennington College in Vermont. For one summer, he studied under Merce Cunningham at the experimental Black Mountain arts school in North Carolina, and in the early 1950s Lichtenstein became a professional dancer with the Sophie Maslow Dance Company, based at Connecticut College. In 1964

the Ford Foundation Entertainment Fellowship awarded Lichtenstein an internship in cultural administration with the New York City Ballet where he eventually joined the staff to manage ticket subscriptions. In 1967 Lichtenstein was selected to be the president of the Brooklyn Academy of Music where he would remain for the rest of his life.

Lichtenstein has been credited with transforming BAM from a staid, tradition-bound academy to the undisputed leading avant-garde performing arts center in the United States, recognized internationally as a showcase for innovative music, dance, and opera. He led an aggressive corporate campaign, which resulted in generous contributions from such industrial giants as AT&T and Philip Morris, and he earned substantial ongoing support from the Ford and Rockefeller foundations and the National Endowment for the Arts (NEA). Late in his life, Lichtenstein devoted his energy into revitalizing downtown Brooklyn.

Harvey Lichtenstein was awarded the National Medal of the Arts in 1999, and in 2013 he earned New York City's highest award for artistic achievement, the Handel Medallion. He was married twice and had two sons who survive him.

See Current Biography 1987

Peter Mansfield

Born: London, England; October 9, 1933
Died: London, England; February 8, 2017
Occupation: Physicist

Peter Mansfield was the primary architect and inventor of Magnetic Resonance Imaging (MRI), creating a revolution in diagnostic medicine. In 2003 he received the Nobel Prize for physiology or medicine.

Peter Mansfield was born the youngest of three boys to his working-class parents. World War II interrupted his education, but the experience sparked his interest in the V1 and V2 German rockets that terrorized London. A school guidance counselor recommended he not pursue an ambitious career in physics, so he worked in a print shop, while also exploring his interests in rocketry in his spare time. He was conscripted in the army where he spent any spare time studying for his A-levels in preparation to attend college. He was accepted into Queen Mary College, at the University of London. As an undergraduate he began studying nuclear magnetic resonance (NMR). His aim was to create a portable NMR detector to be used in architectural research, detecting objects underground. After earning his

PhD in physics in 1962, Mansfield worked as a research associate in physics at the University of Illinois. In 1964 he became a lecturer in physics at the University of Nottingham where he would eventually become a full professor and remain until his retirement in 1994. On 6 October 2003 the Karolinska Institute awarded the Nobel Prize in Physiology or Medicine to Mansfield and Paul Lauterbur, a professor at the University of Illinois, "for their discoveries concerning magnetic resonance imaging," widely regarded as one of the most transformational innovations in medicine of the preceding fifty years.

In addition to his Nobel Prize, which had been awarded decades late, Mansfield was elected fellow of the Royal Society in 1987 as well as its Wellcome and Mullard medals. He was knighted in 1993. He is survived by his wife of more than fifty years, Jean, their two daughters, and four grandchildren.

See Current Biography 2007

Alec McCowen

Born: Tunbridge Wells, England; May 26, 1925
Died: London, England; February 6, 2017
Occupation: British actor

Alec McCowen, whose full name was Alexander Duncan McCowen, was born to a working-class family. His father ran a pram store. His mother had been a professional dancer before her marriage. McGowan attended the Skinners' School in Tunbridge Wells until he was sixteen, when he entered the Royal Academy of Dramatic Arts in London. He never finished his course of study, and instead, made an education for himself in repertory theatre. In 1948 he spent two weeks in New York City, watching performers like Marlon Brando, Jessica Tandy, and Karl Malden. The experience transformed his understanding of acting, and he left determined to infuse his own performances with the depth he had observed. He made his London debut in 1950 and a year later, he appeared on Broadway beside Sir Laurence Olivier and Vivien Leigh in Olivier's production of *Caesar and Cleopatra* and *Antony and Cleopatra*. In 1959 he joined London's Old Vic, performing Shakespeare for the first time. In 1962 he joined the Royal Shakespeare Company.

McCowen came to international fame when he played the lead in *Hadrian VII*, a role previously turned down by Alec Guinness and John Gielgud. It was an instant success, earning McCowen a clean sweep of best actor awards in London. A New York production of the play followed at the Helen Hayes Theatre in 1969,

earning McCowen his first Tony nomination. By the end of his career he had earned three Tony nominations. His most significant stage performance was in his own composition, a one-man play called *St. Mark's Gospel*. For his performance, he memorized the entire New Testament book of Mark. He performed the play at the White House for an audience that included President Jimmy Carter.

McCowen is also remembered for several remarkable movie roles including *Travels with My Aunt*, opposite Maggie Smith, and the character Q in the James Bond film, *Never Say Never Again*, starring Sean Connery.

In 1972 McCowen was made an Officer of the Order of the British Empire (OBE), and Commander of the Order of the British Empire (CBE) in 1986. His survivors include his sister, Jean, two nieces and two nephews.

See Current Biography 1969

George Michael

Born: London, England; June 25, 1963
Died: Goring-on-Thames, England; December 25, 2016
Occupation: Pop musician

Originally part of the highly successful pop duo known as Wham!, with hit songs like "Enjoy What You Do," "Young Guns," and "Wake Me Up Before You Go-Go," George Michael also had a successful career as a solo artist.

George Michael was born Georgios Kyriakos Panayiotou, the youngest child of a Greek Cypriot immigrant restaurant owner. The young George Michael's biggest dream was to become a recording star. On his seventh birthday he was given a tape recorder and he spent much of his free time singing and recording pop tunes. When he was twelve the family moved to Bushey, a prosperous London suburb where Michael met fellow Wham! co-creator Andrew Ridgeley. The two would become inseparable, spending their spare time recording their creations on Michael's old tape recorder. Michael's parents did not approve of the friendship, considering Ridgeley a bad influence on their boy. Their fears were not unfounded. Ridgeley convinced Michael to drop out of school and form a band. Their first band, The Executive, was short-lived but Michael and Ridgeley soon created Wham!, an upbeat pop duo. They came to the attention of talent scout Mark Dean who signed them with Innervision. Their first album, *Fantastic*, had four hit singles. "Young Guns" made it to number four on the British pop charts, and "Bad Boys" rose to number two. The duo's next album became a number one hit in the United States, England, Australia, Belgium, The Netherlands, Norway, Austria, and Denmark. They were nominated for a Grammy and won a prize from the American Video Awards. Michael was honored with the Ivor Novello Award for best songwriter in 1985. They became the first major Western pop band to perform in the People's Republic of China. In 1986 Michael left Wham! and reinvented himself as a less "pop," more rugged and sexual performer. He earned a Grammy Award for his worldwide number one single "I Knew You Were Waiting for Me," which he recorded with Aretha Franklin. In 1987 Michael's new album *Faith* hit the charts, becoming the first album to feature four number-one singles. The album also became the first by a white soloist to reach Billboard's black album chart.

Personally, Michael's life was plagued with drug addiction. In 1998 he was arrested in Los Angeles for engaging in "lewd conduct" in a public restroom. The incident led him to come out as a gay man. In 2010 he was convicted of driving under the influence after crashing his car in London. He spent four weeks in prison.

George Michael died suddenly from heart failure on Christmas day, 2016. He was fifty-three years old.

See Current Biography 1988

Robert Michel

Born: Peoria, Illinois; March 2, 1923
Died: Arlington, Virginia; February 17, 2017
Occupation: United States congressman

Robert Michel was the Minority Leader in the US House of Representatives for fourteen years, the longest term of anyone in US history. He served in Congress from 1957 to 1995.

Robert Michel was born to working-class parents in Peoria, Illinois. After graduation from Peoria public high school, he enlisted in the US Army in 1942. He served in England, France, Belgium, and Germany. He was severely wounded and given a disability discharge. For his service Michel earned two Bronze Stars, the Purple Heart, and four battle stars. Upon returning home he attended Bradley University where he earned a degree in business administration. The following year he became an administrative assistant to the rabid anti-Communist representative, Harold H. Velde from Illinois' Eighteenth Congressional District. When Velde retired, Michel sought his House seat. Michel was a conservative lawmaker who sought bipartisan cooperation. Recognizing his peacemaking abilities, President Nixon asked him to head the White House Congressional liaison office. Michel's

refusal may have saved him from being inadvertently embroiled in the Watergate scandal that led to Nixon's resignation. Michel was elected minority whip in 1974.

Congressman Michel was a fiscal conservative, leading the call to cut costly social programs, which he considered largely responsible for the runaway inflation of the 1970s. He became a close advisor to the president during Ronald Reagan's term. Michel announced his retirement in 1994 and did not seek reelection for the following term.

In 1948 Michel married the former Corinne Woodruff and they had four children. She predeceased him in 2003. His survivors include a sister, his four children, five grandchildren, and two great grandchildren.

See Current Biography 1981

Kate Millett

Born: St. Paul, Minnesota; September 14, 1934
Died: Paris, France; September 6, 2017
Occupation: American feminist writer

Kate Millett has been credited with launching the "second-wave" feminism with the publication of her thesis *Sexual Politics* in 1970. The book explained how gender is a function of social construction rather than biological difference.

Kate Millett's father, James Millett, abandoned his family when Kate was fourteen. Even though her mother, Helen, was a college graduate she could only find work in menial jobs following World War II, especially with the influx of returning service men. In addition, she found that men were often paid much more than women. Kate Millett, the oldest of three daughters, contributed to the family income by working at a department store and by babysitting. In 1952 she entered the University of Minnesota, graduating with a bachelor's degree, magna cum laude and Phi Beta Kappa, in 1956. With the help of a wealthy aunt, Millett continued her education at St. Hilda's College at Oxford University in England. After a brief return to the United States, she moved to Tokyo where she studied sculpting with the Japanese sculptor, Fumio Yoshimura, who she married in 1965. Millett began teaching English at several universities around the United States including at Barnard, Bryn Mawr, and the University of California at Berkeley. She joined the Congress of Racial Equality (CORE) and the National Organization for Women (NOW), where she served as the chairperson of the education committee from 1965 to 1968. While teaching at Barnard she completed her PhD at Columbia University. Six months later, Doubleday published her doctoral thesis titled

Sexual Politics. Intense scrutiny by the media and by some feminists soon followed. Millett was depicted on the cover of *Time* magazine in the August 1970 women's issue. Throughout the 1970s she wrote and filmed several documentaries about her interviews with prostitutes and a female legal aid worker. She continued to detail her travels, love affairs, and her state of mind in several autobiographical books. Millett later revealed that she had tried to kill herself as she suffered from bi-polar disorder, an illness that required her to take lithium. She later wrote several books about her experience with mental illness. In her later years she established an art colony in upstate New York.

She divorced Fumio Yoshimura in 1985. She later married Sophie Keir who survives her.

See Current Biography 1995

Maryam Mirzakhani

Born: Tehran, Iran; May 3, 1977
Died: Palo Alto, California; July 14, 2017
Occupation: Mathematician, educator

Maryam Mirzakhani was the first and only woman to win the prestigious, highly coveted "Fields Medal," the equivalent of a Nobel Prize for mathematics.

Maryam Mirzakhani was born in Tehran, Iran, shortly before the Iranian Revolution that saw the overthrow of the shah and the implementation of an Islamic Republic under Ayatollah Khomeini. She originally dreamed of becoming a writer, but by the time she reached high school at the Farzanegan high school for girls, she had developed an interest in mathematics. She secured a position on Iran's historically male International Mathematical Olympiad team, winning a gold medal in 1994, and achieving a perfect score in 1995. She attended Sharif University of Technology in Tehran, graduating with a bachelor's degree in 1999. She attended graduate school at Harvard University. Mirzakhani specialized in an area of mathematics known as Riemann surfaces. Her doctoral thesis advisor was Curtis McMullen, another noted mathematician who had received the Fields Medal in 1998. She completed her doctoral thesis in 2004, and served as both an assistant professor of mathematics at Princeton University, and as a Clay Mathematics research fellow from 2004 to 2008. In 2008 she became a full professor of mathematics at Stanford University.

Maryam Mirzakhani received a number of prestigious awards, including her merit fellowship from Harvard University, the Clay Research Award, and the Ruth Lyttle Satter Prize from the American Mathematical Society (AMS). She received the Fields Medal in 2014. Mirzakhani married Jan Vondrak, a fellow mathematics professor at Stanford. They had one daughter, Anahita. Mirzakhani died from metastatic breast cancer at the age of forty. Her husband and daughter survive her.

See Current Biography 2015

Constantine Mitsotakis

Born: Halepa, Crete, Greece; October 18, 1918
Died: Athens, Greece, May 29, 2017
Occupation: Prime minister of Greece

Constantine Mitsotakis was a life-long politician who served as the prime minister of Greece from 1990 to 1993.

Constantine Mitsotakis was essentially born into politics. His father, grandfathers, and uncles were all members of parliament. One of his grandfathers founded the liberal party, Komma Xipoliton, "the barefooted Ones." His most prominent forebear was Eleutherios Venizelos who served as prime minister several times, and founded the Liberal party that Mitsotakis would eventually join. He earned a degree in law and economics from the University of Athens and started a law practice, but World War II interrupted his plans. He fought against the Germans on the Greek-Bulgarian border, then retreated to Crete where he became involved in the Greek Resistance. He narrowly escaped execution twice. Both Britain and Greece decorated him for his military service.

Mitsotakis ran for the Greek parliament in 1946, as a liberal anti-monarchist, won re-election in 1951, and served in a cabinet post under the secretary of finance in Prime Minister George Papandreou's cabinet. The 1950s saw a lot of political strife over the ruling party's failure to dismantle repressive measures that had been implemented by the anti-Communist, right-wing government of the late 1940s. When Papandreou became embroiled in a bitter feud with King Constantine II, who essentially unseated Papandreou, Mitsotakis joined in the pro-monarchist forces. Several years later, when a pro-Papandreou military coup failed, Papandreou was arrested and died under house arrest. The Papandreou family blamed Mitsotakis, and their animus would plague him for years thereafter. He would also have to overcome a reputation of right-wing militancy and opportunism. A seven-year dictatorship ensued and Mitsotakis was forced into exile in France. By the 1970s, the populace was discontent with the deteriorating economy and strife with Turkey. Mitsotakis was allowed to return to parliament when the military junta collapsed; he established the New Liberation party, and set about reviving the economy. He was appointed the foreign minister and sought to strengthen Greece's ties with the North Atlantic alliance. However, Andreas Papandreou had become wildly popular and worked to undo Mitsotakis' accomplishments. Several years later he would become embroiled in scandal, and in 1989 he, along with five of his ministers, had to stand trial for financial misconduct. On April 22, 1990 Mitsotakis was sworn in as prime minister.

Constantine Mitsotakis married Marika Giannoukou in 1953. She predeceased him in 2012. Their four children, grandchildren and great-grandchildren survive him.

See Current Biography 1990

Mary Tyler Moore

Born: New York, New York; December 29, 1936
Died: Greenwich, Connecticut; January 25, 2017
Occupation: Actress, comedian

Mary Tyler Moore played the role of Laura Petrie on the popular program *The Dick Van Dyke Show* in the early 1960s. In the 1970s she played the role of the independent young woman, Mary Richards, in *The Mary Tyler Moore Show.* She won seven Emmy Awards, a Tony Award, a Lifetime Achievement Award from the Screen Actors Guild (SAG), and she was nominated for an Oscar Award.

Mary Tyler Moore was born in Brooklyn, New York, to George Tyler Moore, a utility clerk, and Marjorie Hackett Moore. The family moved to Los Angeles when Moore was nine. The day after graduating from Immaculate Heart High School in 1955, she did her first commercial as the "Happy Hotpoint" pixie. Hotpoint Appliances was the sponsor for the popular television show *The Adventures of Ozzie and Harriet.* Shortly thereafter, Moore married Dick Meeker. Her son Richie was born in 1956. She had caught the eye of Danny Thomas who suggested she try for the role of Laura Petrie on *The Dick Van Dyke Show.* She ended up broadening the role significantly with her comedic talents. Shortly after the show's debut, Moore divorced her first husband and married Grant Tinker, an NBC programming executive. In 1969 Moore and Tinker formed MTM Enterprises, an independent production company. CBS bought their first offering, which became *The Mary Tyler Moore Show*, a groundbreaking hit. For the first time a young woman, Mary Richards, was portrayed as independent and career-minded. Moore won five of her seven Emmy Awards for her role in the show.

Following her television success, Moore starred in the Broadway play *Whose Life Is It Anyway?* earning herself a Tony Award. In 1976, Moore starred in Robert Redford's *Ordinary People.* In this serious role she was a cold, uptight mother whose eldest son had drowned, and her second son had attempted suicide. She earned an Oscar nomination for her performance.

The following decade was rough for Moore. Her sister, Elizabeth, died of an overdose and, two years later, Moore's son, Richie accidently shot himself in the head. Moore divorced Grant Tinker in 1981. She remarried in 1983, and in 1984 Moore checked herself into the Betty Ford Clinic for alcoholism. Information about her survivors is not available.

See Current Biography 1997

Roger Moore

Born: London, England; October 14, 1927
Died: Montana, Switzerland; May 23, 2017
Occupation: British actor

Roger Moore became the longest-running actor to play the title role of Ian Fleming's James Bond. Moore starred in six James Bond films from *Live and Let Die* in 1973 to *A View to a Kill* in 1985. He also starred in several television series.

Roger Moore grew up in South London, the son of a policeman. He was overweight as a boy and endured enormous teasing and bullying, but in adolescence, Moore lost the weight and began to acquire his "male starlet" good looks. He dropped out of school at fifteen, intending to become a painter. However, he took a temporary job as an apprentice at Publicity Picture Productions, an animated cartoon studio. In 1945 he became an extra in the film *Perfect Strangers*, which was released as *Vacation from Marriage* in the United States. The co-director, Brian Desmond Hurst, took an interest in Moore and helped him enroll in the Royal Academy of Dramatic Arts. In 1953 Moore went to the United States to appear in a live television drama, and ended up being cast in a flurry of television roles. Columbia's Screen Gems division signed Moore to play the title role in its series based on *Ivanhoe,* in a loose adaptation of Sir Walter Scott's novel. He appeared in a number of short-lived television series that won him recognition to an American audience. In 1960 to 1961, he took on the lead role in the series *Maverick* once James Garner departed. Throughout the sixties, Moore played Simon Templar, the lead character in *The Saint,* which was wildly popular in Britain and, worldwide, became the most widely viewed British series ever produced at that time. Several years later, Moore starred with Tony Curtis in

The Persuaders!, another British-made television series. At the same time, Harry Saltzman and Albert Broccoli pegged Moore for their eighth James Bond film, *Live and Let Die*. Moore would appear in five more James Bond films before he was through.

Later in his life, Moore became a UNICEF good-will ambassador. He was made a Commander of the British Empire (CBE) in 1999, and he was knighted in 2003. He was married four times and had three children. His fourth wife, the Swedish-born Kristina Tholstrup, and Moore's three children survive him.

See Current Biography 1975

Jeanne Moreau

Born: Paris, France; January 23, 1928
Died: Paris, France; July 31, 2017
Occupation: French actress

Jeanne Moreau was an unusual actress for her time. Although she was beautiful, it was her intensity and unique seductiveness that had her creating a new perspective on modern womanhood. She helped usher in the "French new wave." She won the Cannes Best Actress Award for her role in the film *Moderato Cantabile* in 1960, and she won two British Academy Film Awards (BAFTA), and was honored with a BAFTA fellowship.

Jeanne Moreau was born to a French restaurateur and his wife, an Irish dancer. Moreau's father lost his business at the end of the 1930s, and was drafted into the army in 1939. He remained in southern France during the occupation. His wife and two daughters were forced to stay in Paris, living over a brothel in a shabby hotel. She attended the Lycée Edgar Quinet where she discovered theater. When she told her father she wanted to be an actress, he reportedly slapped her and called her a whore. (The two reconciled several years before his death in 1975.) Her parents divorced and her mother returned to Britain. When Moreau was eighteen, she attended the Conservatoire National d'Art Dramatique. At twenty Moreau became the youngest member of the Comedie Francaise where she performed twenty-two roles before leaving in 1952. Moreau was cast in *The Dazzling Hour* with Suzanne Flon. However, two days before the premier, Ms. Flon became ill and Moreau covered both of their roles, proving herself to be a tour de force as she portrayed both the wife and mistress to one man. She became a Paris theater phenomenon, starring in numerous roles over the next few years. Her attempts to achieve some acclaim in movies took longer. She made twenty-two films

before meeting the fledgling director, Louis Malle. In their first picture, *Frantic*, Malle put aside the flattering lights and cosmetics, allowing the camera to concentrate on the drama in Moreau's face. A new image, a new way of photographing women, was the result. The two released some controversy with their film *The Lovers*, in which Moreau appeared in partially nude love scenes.

Jeanne Moreau was married twice and had a number of affairs. She had a five-year relationship with the fashion designer Pierre Cardin. Her son, Jérôme Richard survives her.

See Current Biography 1966

Bharati Mukherjee

Born: Calcutta, India; July 27, 1940
Died: New York, New York; January 28, 2017
Occupation: Writer

Originally from India, Bharati Mukherjee became an American writer who chronicled the transformation of culture often experienced by Asian émigrés to the West.

Born in Calcutta, India, Bharati Mukherjee's upbringing was relatively circumscribed when compared to her later life in North America. Her household comprised a large family, which extended to nearly thirty people, and included many servants and bodyguards. Her father was a chemist with his own pharmaceutical company. Mukherjee grew up with wealth, privilege, and the centuries-old social and religious traditions of the Brahmin. She explained that in such a world, one's primary identity is as a community. A desire for privacy was considered selfish.

Mukherjee attended the University of Calcutta and the University of Baroda where she earned two master's degrees in English and ancient Indian culture. After expressing her desire to be a writer, Mukherjee attended the Iowa Writers' Workshop at the University of Iowa where she studied under Philip Roth and Vance Bourjaily. She married her husband, Clark Blaise, a fellow student, after a two-week courtship, and they had two sons. Mukherjee earned her PhD from the University of Iowa in 1969, and she and Blaise taught at several universities before settling at McGill in Montreal, Canada. She became a full professor in 1978, however, after experiencing rabid racial discrimination, they relocated to the United States. Mukherjee published her first novel, *Tiger's Daughter*, in 1972, followed by her second novel, *Wife*, published in 1975. She and Blaise collaborated on a book of non-fiction, *Days and Nights in Calcutta*, which was made into a movie in 1990. For most of her career, Mukherjee lived apart from her husband and children. Blaise spent most of his teaching career at the University of Iowa, while his wife taught across the country in relatively short-term assignments, mostly in the Northeast. From 1989 onward, Mukherjee taught at the University of California at Berkeley.

Mukherjee's short story collection, *The Middleman and Other Stories*, won her a National Book Critics Circle Award for fiction in 1988. She is survived by her husband, two sisters, a son, and two granddaughters.

See Current Biography 1992

Gardnar Mulloy

Born: Washington, DC; November 22, 1913
Died: Miami, Florida; November 14, 2016
Occupation: Amateur athlete, coach, lawyer

Gardnar Mulloy, commonly referred to as "Gar," was an amateur tennis player who won more than one hundred and twenty-five national tournaments. He championed senior tennis tournaments, and became the oldest player to win a men's doubles tournament at Wimbledon when he was forty-three. At one hundred and two, he had been the oldest living honoree in the International Tennis Hall of Fame.

Though he was born in Washington, DC, Gardnar Mulloy spent most of his life in Miami, Florida, where his father was in the lumber business. At his father's behest, Mulloy began playing tennis when he was nine years old. He was a natural athlete and went to the University of Miami on a football scholarship. His father urged him to quit football, however, fearing injuries might affect his tennis game. Mulloy approached the college president who gave him permission to start the Miami Hurricanes tennis team, and he went on to win the eastern intercollegiate singles title. He graduated with a law degree from the University of Miami. After setting up his own law practice, he continued to coach the Hurricanes without pay. He was responsible for recruiting Pancho Segura who went on to win three National Collegiate Athletic Association (NCAA) singles championships for the school. Mulloy and his father paired to win the US Father and Son doubles title in 1939, 1941, and 1942. At that time he was ranked seventh among national players. In 1942 Mulloy was commissioned to the US Naval Reserve to fight in World War II where he saw action in Anzio and Salerno, Italy. His greatest achievement on the court was in the Wimbledon doubles championship in 1957 when he paired with Budge Patty to upset the reigning champions, Australia's Lew Hoad and Neale Fraser, in four sets. He teamed with

Bill Talbert to win the US National men's title in 1942, '45, '46, and '48.

Mulloy wrote two memoirs, *The Will to Win: An Inside View of the World of Tennis* in 1960s and *As It Was*, in 2009. His first wife, Madeleine Cheney died in 1993. His second wife, Jacqueline Mayer, survives him along with two daughters, a sister, four grandchildren, and eight great-grandchildren.

See Current Biography 1957

Manuel Antonio Noriega

Born: Panama City, Panama; February 11, 1934
Died: Panama City, Panama; May 29, 2017
Occupation: Panamanian dictator

Manuel Noriega took command of the Panamanian army in 1983 and ruled the country until his ouster in 1989. He was a vicious leader who sold US secrets to its enemies, supported a robust drug trade, and murdered anyone who crossed him. Eventually the United States invaded Panama and seized Noriega to stand trial in the United States, France, and Panama.

Manuel Noriega was born in a poor barrio in Panama City. After graduating from Instituto Naciona, Panama's premier high school, he hoped to study medicine but his family could not afford it. He accepted a scholarship to attend the Military School de Chorrillos in Lima, Peru. Upon his return home, he joined the national guard and became a favorite of Captain Omar Torrijos. Noriega rose quickly in the ranks and joined rebel "Combo" forces that staged a successful coup against Panamanian President Arnulfo Arias. Noriega was appointed chief of military intelligence, and interacted with the American intelligence community, seemingly as an ally. He became involved in drug trafficking in 1972 and his relationship with the United States quickly soured. Upon the death of then President Torrijos in a plane accident, strongman General Dario Paredes took control and appointed Noriega his chief of staff. Noriega would succeed him and promoted himself to general. In 1984 Noriega's candidate for president, Nicolas Ardito Barletta, won the election, but Noriega became disappointed in his handling of the economy. It was later learned that Noriega had him removed because he had been pressing an investigation into the grisly murder of Dr. Hugo Spadafora, who had charged Noriega with drug trafficking. A *New York Times* exposé revealed that Noriega had been a double agent and had released highly classified manuals to Cuba. The United States called upon the Panamanian government to remove Noriega and investigate his alleged crimes. Rioters attacked the American embassy and the United States cut off all military and economic aid to Panama. José Isabel Blandón Castillo, consul general of Panama in New York, was placed under United States protection and was subpoenaed to testify before a Miami grand jury that had been investigating charges of racketeering and international drug trafficking against Noriega. In 1989, it was declared that the US and Panama were in a state of war as US troops invaded Panama City. He was tried in a federal court in Florida, found guilty of drug trafficking, racketeering, and money laundering, and sentenced to forty years. In 2010 he was extradited to stand trial in France. A year later he was extradited to Panama where he was tried for the disappearance and murder of his political opponents. Found guilty, he would remain in custody for the rest of his life.

Noriega's wife, Felicidad Sierio, and three daughters survive him.

See Current Biography 1988

Michael Novak

Born: Johnstown, Pennsylvania; September 9, 1933
Died: Washington, DC; February 17, 2017
Occupation: Social critic, philosopher, writer

Michael Novak was a scholar, theologian, and a prolific writer, whose ideology conflated religion, economics, politics, and morality, swinging broadly from a decidedly liberal slant as a young man, to a staunch conservative in the latter half of his life.

Michael Novak was born to a working-class, Catholic family of Slavic descent. At the age of fourteen he became a junior seminarian in the Congregation of the Holy Cross. (A younger brother followed him into the religious community and became a missionary priest who was killed in riots in Dacca in 1964.) Novak received a degree in philosophy from Stonehill College in Massachusetts, and a degree in theology from the Gregorian University in Rome, Italy. He earned a master's degree from Harvard University in 1966.

Novak began his career while still a seminarian, writing for the liberal Catholic journal *Commonweal*, and the Jesuit weekly, *America*. His first novel, *The Tiber Was Silver,* was published in 1961. A recurrent theme in his early writing was the "renewal and reform" of the church following the second Vatican Council in the early 1960s. He argued the case for Christian theism in a "post-religious" age, engendered by a philosophy of self-knowledge. He became an assistant professor of humanities at Stanford University from 1965 to 1968 at the height of student antiwar activism. His social criticism argued that ethnic diversity is a myth imposed by a dominant WASP culture. He founded the Ethnic Millions Political Action Committee (EMPAC), to shape a new white ethnic consciousness into a "progressive force." He wrote speeches for Senator Edward Muskie and was a member of George McGovern's campaign staff. He was the director of humanities at the Rockefeller Foundation in the early 1970s and, from 1977 to 1979, he taught at Syracuse University as a resident scholar. His philosophy took a turn to the right during the presidential candidacy and eventual success of President Ronald Reagan, going so far as to excoriate the liberal theologians who, he felt, subverted Catholic doctrine. With former Secretary of the Treasury, William Simon, Novak headed the Lay Commission on Catholic Social Teaching and the US Economy, praising the capacity of US capitalism to create jobs and lower the poverty level.

In 1994 Novak was awarded the Templeton Prize for Progress in Religion, which came with a million-dollar award. He married artist Karen Laub in 1963. She predeceased him in 2009. Novak's survivors include his three children and four grandchildren.

See Current Biography 1985

Russell Oberlin

Born: Akron, Ohio; October 11, 1928
Died: New York, New York; November 25, 2016
Occupation: Countertenor singer

Russell Oberlin was naturally gifted with a rare voice, with a countertenor scale that ranged well over two octaves, between tenor and soprano ranges, without using a falsetto voice.

Russell Oberlin was raised in Akron, Ohio, a descendant of Jean Frederic Oberlin, an eighteenth-century clergyman and educator for whom Oberlin, Ohio, and Oberlin College are named. His music career began when Oberlin was still a small boy, performing in boy choirs from the age of six. When he was sixteen his voice changed to baritone tenor, but gradually rose to a light tenor range. He was a soloist for a church in Cleveland. After his high school graduation in 1946, Oberlin attended the Julliard School of Music in New York City, graduating with a diploma in voice in 1951. In 1953 he became a leading soloist with New York's Pro Musica Antiqua, a group of singers and instrumentalists dedicated to performing the forgotten music of the Middle Ages and the Renaissance.

He appeared with a number of important music organizations, including the New York Philharmonic Orchestra, the Chicago Symphony, the American Opera Society, and the Washington Opera and Choral Societies. Oberlin also performed in Broadway theater, including Lillian Hellman's 1955 adaptation of *The Lark,* starring Julie Harris. Leonard Bernstein composed songs especially for Oberlin's voice. Oberlin also appeared with the American Shakespeare Festival Theatre in Stratford, Connecticut. In the summer of 1959, he performed in the Cambridge Drama Festival production of *Twelfth Night.* Oberlin retired early, at the height of his career, when he was just thirty-eight. He taught voice and the history of the countertenor at Hunter College of the City University of New York (CUNY).

His sister, Jean Lundin, survives him.

See Current Biography 1960

Ara Parseghian

Born: Akron, Ohio; May 21, 1923
Died: Granger, Indiana; August 2, 2017
Occupation: Football coach

At the time that football coach Ara Parseghian arrived at Notre Dame University, its football team never won more than five games in a season from 1956 to 1963. Ara Parseghian is credited with turning around the school's long decline, guiding his fabled "Fighting Irish" to five consecutive winning seasons, one national championship, and a consistent rating at or near the top in collegiate football.

Ara Parseghian was born the second of three children, to Michael Parseghian, an Armenian immigrant and Amelie (Bonneau) Parseghian, a French woman the senior Parseghian had met during World War I. Parseghian's mother had forbid him to play on his high school football team, so he did so secretly until he came home injured. After graduating from South Akron High School, he enrolled at the University of Akron but left soon after to join the navy. Upon his discharge, Parseghian entered Miami University at Oxford, Ohio. He led the team to an undefeated season during his senior year and earned the Little All-American honors. Just six credits shy of graduation, Parseghian left the university for the Cleveland Browns in 1947. In the second game of his second season, Parseghian sustained a career-ending hip injury and turned to coaching. He returned to his alma mater, becoming the head coach at Miami University, and a year later, moved to Ohio State. He also coached at Northwestern for four years before moving on to Notre

Dame in 1964. That year the Fighting Irish won nine games, and lost only one game in the final minutes of the final game. Parseghian's quarterback, John Huarte, won the Heisman Trophy. Notre Dame was ranked number three in the nation, and was awarded the MacArthur Bowl by the Football Hall of Fame. Parseghian shared Coach-of-the-Year honors with Frank Broyles of Arkansas University. Parseghian retired in 1974 and became a commentator for *ABC Sports* from 1975 to 1981. In 1988 he worked for *CBS Sports.*

Ara Parseghian married his wife Kathleen in 1948 and they had three children. One daughter died in 2012. In 1994 Parseghian founded the Ara Parseghian Medical Research Foundation to support research in Niemann-Pick Type C disease, a genetic disorder that killed three of his grandchildren. His survivors include his wife and remaining two children.

See Current Biography 1968

Roberta Peters

Born: New York, New York; May 4, 1930
Died: Rye, New York; January 18, 2017
Occupation: Opera singer

Roberta Peters quickly rose to stardom the night she debuted at the Metropolitan Opera. With just five hours to prepare for her role as Zerlina in Mozart's opera *Don Giovanni,* she had to substitute for Nadine Conner. Peters became the Metropolitan's "most-celebrated pinch-hitter," with a career that lasted decades longer than most opera divas.

Roberta Peters was born Roberta Peterman, the daughter of Ruth (Hirsch) Peterman and Solomon Peterman, of Jewish Austrian decent. Her grandfather was a maître d' at Grossinger's summer resort in the Catskills. When Peters was thirteen, her grandfather asked renowned tenor, Jan Peerce, to hear her sing. He recognized her potential and suggested she leave school to study music full time. She began a rigorous course of singing, dancing, and drama lessons. With special permission from the New York Board of Education, she finished school with a special tutor and never attended high school. She studied with William Herman who taught numerous opera stars. He demanded rigorous physical training. She was once pictured in *Life* magazine, with the 175-pound trainer standing on her diaphragm to demonstrate her muscle strength. As part of her rigorous training, the young singer mastered twenty roles. Peters signed with the Metropolitan in January of 1950 where she received advanced training in acting, stage deportment, foreign languages, and vocal interpretation with Kathryn Turney Long. In November of 1950, opera management called her to substitute for Nadine Conner. Critics were overwhelmed and Peters became the Met's brightest coloratura prima donna.

Roberta Peters performed around the world in such respected institutions as the Vienna State Opera and the Berlin Opera. She performed at the Salzburg Festival and became the first American singer to perform in the People's Republic of China. She performed on Broadway, on television, and even in a television commercial. By her twenty-fifth anniversary at the Met, Peters had sung in more than three hundred performances of her twenty roles in nineteen operas. At age fifty she was still going strong and continued with the Met until 1985.

In 1952 Peters married baritone, Robert Merrill. The marriage lasted mere months. She married hotel executive, Bertram Fields in 1955 and they had two sons. In 1998 Peters was honored with the National Medal of Arts. Two sons and four grandchildren survive her.

See Current Biography 1954

Tom Petty

Born: Gainesville, Florida; October 20, 1950
Died: Santa Monica, California; October 2, 2017
Occupation: Rock icon, singer, songwriter, musician

Tom Petty and the Heartbreakers were one of the most widely respected rock-n-roll bands of all time. They received a star on the Hollywood Walk of Fame in 1999, and were inducted into the Rock-n-Roll Hall of Fame in 2002. They performed in the 2008 Super Bowl halftime show. In 1996 Tom Petty received the George and Ira Gershwin Award for Lifetime Musical Achievement. In 2016 he was inducted into the Songwriters Hall of Fame.

As a child, Tom Petty was a huge fan of rock-n-roll and, more specifically, Elvis Presley, whom Petty met when Presley was in Gainesville for a video shoot. Petty's mother bought him a guitar from a Sears' catalogue, and he began to school himself in guitar playing by listening and copying riffs by the Beatles and the Rolling Stones. By the time he was fourteen, Petty was playing with local bands in the Gainesville area. He dropped out of school and began performing with Mudcrutch, one of the area's best bands. Several members would make up the core of Petty's Heartbreakers band. Petty was also writing his own songs. Concerned that he might be stuck in Gainesville forever, Petty went to Los Angeles

with a Mudcrutch demo recording and landed a contract with Shelter Records. In 1975 Petty and several Mudcrutch members formed a new band called the Heartbreakers. They quickly became one of the most popular bands in Los Angeles, and released their first album, *Tom Petty and the Heartbreakers* in 1976. In 1979 Petty declared bankruptcy over a contract dispute with MCA and Shelter Records, which allowed him to contract with the newly minted Backstreet Records. In 1985 Petty participated in the Live Aid benefit concert, the No Nukes show, and appeared in another benefit event to help farmers. In 1986 Petty and the band embarked on a world tour with Bob Dylan. Petty fell into a deep depression following his divorce from Jane Benyo in 1996, and he began using drugs. He eventually went into rehabilitation and chronicled his experiences in a 2015 biography titled *Petty: The Biography*, in an effort to dissuade young fans from following in his footsteps. In 2014 Tom Petty and the Heartbreakers produced a new album, *Hypnotic Eye*, which was their first album to rise to the top of the charts. In 2017 they launched a fortieth anniversary tour, capped off by a performance on September 22 at the Hollywood Bowl. Petty died suddenly on October 2.

Petty's survivors include his second wife, Dana, a stepson, his former wife, Jane, their two daughters, and one grandchild.

See Current Biography 1991

Oleg Popov

Born: Vyrubovo, Russia; July 3, 1930
Died: Rostov-on-Don, Russia; November 2, 2016
Occupation: Soviet circus clown

Oleg Popov was a world-renowned circus clown from the Soviet Union. He won the admiration of the French mime, Marcel Marceau, and he was a big hit at the July 1958 World's Fair in Brussels, Belgium.

Oleg Popov was born and raised in the Kuntsevo district of Russia's Moscow region. His father was a watch mechanic and his mother was a photograph retoucher. Popov started school when he was eight, but quit five years later, in 1943, to work as an apprentice fitter in the print shop of the Russian newspaper, *Pravda*. He spent a great deal of time at the gymnasium where he met students from the nearby State School of Circus Art. He so impressed the faculty with his agility and self-taught acrobatics that he was accepted into the school in 1944. In the Soviet Union, the circus was highly esteemed, and circus clowns were as admired and highly paid as ballerinas and opera singers. He embarked on a six-year curriculum that included his finishing secondary school, and graduated in 1950 as a tightrope-walking performer. When the circus's clown, Bobovrikev, broke an arm, Popov took his place and was a big success. By 1955 he was well enough established as a clown to join the Moscow State Circus. He was just twenty-five years old at the time, a considerable achievement. In 1956 the circus visited France, Belgium, and England where Popov became known as "the sunny clown" for all his good cheer. Belgian journalists described him as contributing to the circus in the same manner that Charlie Chaplin had contributed to moving pictures. Popov appeared on the 1957 Bob Hope broadcast from Moscow, and first visited the United States in 1963 when the Moscow Circus toured seven cities. In 1969 he was given the title of "The People's Artist of the Soviet Union."

Oleg Popov was on tour when he died of a heart attack. His second wife, Gabriela Lehmann, a German circus performer, and his daughter from his first marriage survive him.

See Current Biography 1964

Rene Préval

Born: Port-au-Prince, Haiti; January 17, 1943
Died: Port-au-Prince, Haiti; March 3, 2017
Occupation: Two-term president of Haiti

Rene Préval was elected twice to serve as the president of Haiti, the only president who also served a term as prime minister, and the first to oversee the peaceful transfer of power to an opposition president-elect.

Rene Préval was born into a politically active family. His father was Haiti's minister of agriculture. After a 1957 coup, the family was exiled to Belgium where Préval studied agronomy at the University of Jembloux. He moved to New York in the early 1970s, working as a messenger and janitor. He returned to Haiti in 1975, working at the ministry of mines. In the 1980s he owned and operated a bakery in Port-au-Prince where he befriended Jean Bertrand Aristide, who would become Haiti's president.

Préval became involved in grass-roots politics while serving in a children's shelter—LaFanmi Selavi ("The Family Is Life")—founded by Aristide, who became the first democratically elected president of Haiti in 1990. Aristide appointed Préval as Haiti's prime minister. He was unpopular with the Haitian Parliament and, following a coup by General Raoul Cedras, both Aristide and Préval were exiled. However, Aristide's popularity only flourished during his absence and, assisted by the US military, he returned to the

presidency in 1994. This time Aristide appointed Préval the director of the Fund for Economic and Social Assistance. In 1996 Préval won the presidency with many voters assuming he would be an Aristide puppet. He surprised many with his bold action, mapping out his own plan to bring peace and economic stability with recommendations from the International Monetary Fund (IMF). Unfortunately, violent crime increased and the popular former President Aristide broke with Préval, forming his own party known as the Fanmi Lavalas (FL). Their primary bone of contention was the privatization of industry. Préval's prime minister, Rosny Smarth, was unpopular as he advocated for cuts in government spending, and soon strikes and anti-Smarth protests developed. Smarth resigned and Haiti's parliament refused to vote a new one into office until potential election fraud by Jean Bertrand Aristide was investigated. The ensuing government stalemate led to huge unemployment and inflation. Préval was put under extreme pressure after a 7.0 magnitude earthquake felled buildings and over 300,000 people were killed. Following his term as president, Préval created an agricultural cooperative, a juice factory, and an education center.

In addition to his wife, Préval is survived by his sister and chief confidant, Marie-Claude Préval Calvin, two daughters, two sons, and two grandchildren.

See Current Biography 2006

Om Puri

Born: Ambala, Punjab, India; October 18, 1950
Died: Mumbai, India; January 6, 2017
Occupation: Indian actor

Om Puri was one of India's most highly acclaimed actors, as at home in Hollywood as he was in Bollywood.

Om Puri was born in a rural area in Punjab. Originally Puri had planned to follow in his father's footsteps in the Indian military. However, while in college he acted in plays and realized his passion for theater. He enrolled in the National School of Drama in Delhi, and also studied at the film institute in Poona. After his graduation, Puri moved to Bombay, India's film capital. His performance in Satyajit Ray's *Sadgati* (1981) won him the admiration of Western filmmakers. He was cast in Richard Attenborough's movie, *Gandhi*, a film that earned eight Academy Awards out of eleven nominations. He was known in Britain for his roles in *My Son the Fanatic* and *East Is East*. The popular Bollywood actor appeared in well over one hundred twenty-five movies. His honors include his honorary Officer of the Order of the British Empire (OBE) in 2004, and a Filmfare Lifetime Achievement award in 2009.

Puri was married twice. His first marriage to Seema Kapoor ended after eight months. His second wife, Nandita Puri, wrote a biography of Puri's life titled *Unlikely Hero: The Story of Om Puri* that angered the actor because of the intimate details she revealed. In 2013 she charged Puri with domestic abuse and the marriage ended shortly thereafter. They had one son together.

See Current Biography 2000

Ali Akbar Hashemi Rafsanjani

Born: Bahereman, Kerman, Iran; August 25, 1934
Died: Tehran, Iran; January 8, 2017
Occupation: President of Iran

Ayatollah Ali Akbar Hashemi Rafsanjani was an enigmatic and unpredictable president of Iran from 1989 to 1997. A longtime disciple of the late Ayatollah Ruhollah Khomeini, Rafsanjani was a founding member of the Islamic Republican party that gained control of the government after the ouster of the Shah Mohammed Riza Pahlevi in 1979.

Hashemi Rafsanjani was born to a prosperous pistachio farmer. He left home at age fourteen for his religious training. In the 1950s he studied under Ruhollah Khomeini at the Qom theological seminary. The shah's arrest of Ayatollah Khomeini in 1962 had a radicalizing effect on Rafsanjani. When Khomeini was exiled in 1964, he relied on Rafsanjani to organize an underground movement. Rafsanjani was arrested in 1975 and served three years of a six-year sentence. In 1979 he helped found the Islamic Republican party and served on the Revolutionary Council, overseeing the transition from a monarchy to a theocracy in Iran. He was elected to the Majlis, the Iranian parliament, which made him speaker, the second most powerful official after Khomeini. Beginning in 1980 he also served as the Imam Jomeh, the leader of Friday prayer services in Iran. His pulpit was monitored nationally and abroad as he used his role to make policy pronouncements and communicate with foreign leaders.

Beginning in 1979 Iran had held fifty-two hostages, taken when Iranian militants stormed the American embassy. Rafsanjani agreed to free the hostages in exchange for American arms needed for the war with Iraq. Rafsanjani's enemies leaked the negotiations to reveal his association with one of Islam's most reviled enemies, the United States. The revelation, which was referred to as the Iran-Contra scandal, also created havoc for US President Ronald Reagan's administration. Rafsanjani was a major architect of the eight-year war with Iraq and was named the commander in chief of Iranian armed forces. It was at Rafsanjani's urging that Khomeini accepted the UN cease-fire resolution in 1988, thus ending the war. Rafsanjani then sought to normalize relations with the West.

After the death of the Ayatollah Khomeini, Rafsanjani was elected president and took office in August of 1989. He soon set about purging hard-liners from the government. Sometimes referred to as a pragmatist, his adversaries called him an opportunist, as he changed his views based on political expedience.

Hashemi Rafsanjani amassed quite a fortune over his lifetime. He owned Iran's second largest airline, had control of Azad, Iran's largest private university, and ran a robust pistachio trade. He married Effat Marashi in 1962, and they had five children. One daughter, Faezeh, became an activist for women's rights. No information on survivors is available.

See Current Biography 1989

Irina Ratushinskaya

Born: Odessa, Ukraine; March 4, 1954
Died: Moscow, Russia; July 5, 2017
Occupation: Soviet dissident writer

Irina Ratushinskaya is most remembered for her poetry, which she committed to memory while in a Soviet prison. She had been sentenced to seven years of hard labor and five years of internal exile, the harshest punishment meted out to a woman since the days of Joseph Stalin. She spent most of 1985 and 1986 in solitary confinement.

Irina came from a family of rebels. Her paternal great grandfather spent time in a prison in Siberia for protesting forced conscription in the Russian Army. Her maternal grandparents took part in the 1863 Polish uprising, and her father fought against the Bolsheviks. Ratushinskaya was a precocious child who began reading and writing at a very young age. She attended the University of Odessa where she majored in physics, and in 1976 she began teaching physics and mathematics. She was fired in 1978 for protesting anti-Semitism in her school's admission policy. In 1979 she married her childhood friend, Igor Gerashchenko, and the two settled in Kiev where Gerashchenko was an engineer specializing in thermo physics at the scientific institute. In 1981 Ratushinskaya and her husband signed an open letter to the Supreme Soviet protesting the exile of the nuclear physicist, Andrei Sakharov. They became more active in human rights endeavors, and continued to distribute banned literature through a clandestine operation called "Zamizdat." In December of 1982, Ratushinskaya was arrested for writing poetry that slandered the state. While in prison, Ratushinskaya wrote more than 300 poems, committing her work, originally written on bars of soap, to her memory. Her poems were smuggled out to her husband, by word of mouth, and he saw that they were published in the West. On October 9, 1986, the day before the Reykjavik summit between Gorbachev and Reagan, the KGB released her. She and her husband moved to the UK to seek medical treatment. Ratushinskaya was later appointed a poet in residence at Northwestern University in Chicago. In 1998 the couple returned to Moscow.

Irina Ratushinskaya wrote eleven books including an autobiography and a novel, in addition to her poetry. She was awarded the Religious Freedom Award. Her survivors include her husband and their two sons.

See Current Biography 1988

Janet Reno

Born: Miami, Florida; July 21, 1938
Died: Miami, Florida; November 7, 2016
Occupation: US attorney general

Janet Reno was the US attorney general for eight years during President Bill Clinton's two terms. She was the first woman to hold the post. She is most remembered for the FBI assault on the Branch Davidian cult compound in Waco, Texas, in which eighty-six people died, and for the decision to return the six-year-old Cuban refugee, Elián González, to his father in Cuba.

Janet Reno was born and raised in the area outside of Miami, Florida. Her parents were somewhat eccentric and that had a profound impact on their daughter. Her mother, an investigative reporter, literally built their home with her own hands. Reno attended Cornell University, earning a degree in chemistry in 1960. She then enrolled in Harvard Law School, one of sixteen women in a class of more than five hundred. In 1971 she was named staff director of the Judiciary Committee of the Florida House of Representatives, and in 1973 she worked in the state attorney's office. She became the Dade county state's attorney in 1978, the first woman to hold the position, with over nine hundred employees and more than one hundred twenty thousand cases a year under her watch.

President Bill Clinton heard about Reno's work through his brother-in-law, Hugh Rodham, a public defender. He nominated her and the US Senate confirmed her unanimously on March 12, 1993. Her most difficult decision was the call to have federal authorities flush out cult members of the Branch Davidian compound using teargas after evidence suggested the children there were being abused. Rather than surrender, the cult members set the compound on fire, killing eighty-six people including seventeen children. Ironically, Reno's candor and quick admission of her culpability in the case won her the admiration of the American people. She was tangentially involved in the Whitewater investigation, which sought to determine whether Bill and Hillary Clinton had improperly benefited from real-estate deals in Arkansas. What's more, the investigation uncovered Bill Clinton's relationship with the young White House intern, Monica Lewinsky. Clinton was impeached for lying to investigators. Her Justice Department also sued the tobacco industry for health violations and filed the landmark anti-trust case against Microsoft. Her last major case was that of Elián González, a young Cuban boy who washed ashore in Florida following his mother's death after their boat, full of Cuban refugees, wrecked. The boy's father wanted him returned to Cuba, and there followed an intense custody battle between Cuban relatives in the United States and Elián's father. Reno sided with the father, significantly damaging her relationship with the Cuban community.

While she was still in office, Reno was diagnosed with Parkinson's disease, which eventually took her life. Her sister and seven nieces and nephews survive her.

See Current Biography 1993

Debbie Reynolds

Born: El Paso, Texas; April 1, 1932
Died: Los Angeles, California; December 28, 2016
Occupation: Actress

Debbie Reynolds was a highly successful actress who became an icon in the 1950s through the 1970s, characterized as a perky "pretty little package" by Bosley Crowther, film reviewer for the *New York Times*. Her film credits include *The Daughter of Rosie O'Grady*, *The Unsinkable Molly Brown*, and *Singing in the Rain*.

Until she was eight years old, Debbie Reynolds was born and raised in El Paso, Texas at which time her father, a carpenter for the Southern Pacific Railroad, was transferred to southern California. The family settled in Burbank, California. On a whim in 1948, Reynolds entered the Miss Burbank contest and won the title. As a result, she caught the attention of a Warner Brothers talent scout who invited her for a screen test. They gave her a minor role in *The Daughter of Rosie O'Grady*. When not acting, she stuffed envelopes and conducted studio tours. After leaving Warner Brothers, Reynolds was picked up by MGM to act in *Three Little Words*, along with Fred Astaire and Red Skelton. Reynolds ended up singing the smash hit song "Abba Dabba Honeymoon," which sold more than a million copies when released as a single. Her dancing skills were featured in the now classic film, *Singing In the Rain*, which also starred Gene Kelly and Donald O'Connor. Reynolds' was generally cast in the role of a bright, young ingénue, though one of her most famous roles was as Molly Brown in the movie *The Unsinkable Molly Brown*, a rags-to-riches chronicle of a high-spirited Colorado woman. Reynolds received an Academy Award nomination for her efforts.

Her famous marriage with the singer and actor Eddie Fisher came under intense public scrutiny after it was revealed that Fisher was having an affair with Reynold's friend Elizabeth Taylor. The two divorced and Fisher eventually married Ms. Taylor. Reynold's second husband, businessman Harry Karl, had a serious gambling problem, leaving Reynolds deeply in debt. The couple divorced in 1972 and Reynolds performed in a number of one-woman song-and-dance revues in nightclubs to try to recoup her losses. During the 1970s Reynolds starred in the Broadway musical *Irene,* which became a major hit. Reynold's sixteen-year-old daughter, Carrie Fisher, also performed in the chorus alongside her mother. Reynolds continued acting well into her seventies.

Debbie Reynolds had two children with Eddie Fisher. She married a third time to Richard Hamlett, but that marriage also ended in divorce in 1996. On December 23, 2016, Reynolds was shocked to learn that her daughter, Carrie Fisher, suffered a heart attack on a flight from London to Los Angeles. She died several days later. While making funeral arrangements, Debbie Reynolds suffered a major stroke and passed away on December 28, 2016. Her survivors include her son, Todd Fisher, and her granddaughter, Billie Lourd.

See Current Biography 1997

Don Rickles

Born: New York, New York; May 8, 1926
Died: Los Angeles, California; April 6, 2017
Occupation: Comedian

For most of his life, Don Rickles was a standup comedian who made his living, not so much because of great jokes, but by spewing caustic barbs at his audiences.

Don Rickles was born in Queens, New York, the son of a gregarious insurance salesman. He reportedly kept his family in stitches from the time he was five, and he developed a passion for acting in high school. He graduated from high school in 1944 and immediately joined the navy where he spent the remainder of World War II in the Philippines. Following the war he enrolled in the American Academy of Dramatic Arts where he studied alongside Anne Bancroft, Grace Kelly, and Jason Robards. He graduated in 1948 but failed to land acting roles and became a salesman. He moonlighted in nightclubs and at Catskill resorts. During the 1950s he performed in Las Vegas where he gradually realized he was better at insulting the audience than in delivering standard comedic monologues. His big break came in 1957 while he filled in at the Slate Brother's Club, a favorite hotspot for famous Hollywood actors. One night Frank Sinatra came in and, without missing a beat, Rickles barked, "Hey Frank, make yourself at home. Hit somebody!" Evidently, Sinatra roared with laughter and began bringing his friends to catch Rickles performances. He came to widespread acclaim after appearing on Johnny Carson's *Tonight Show* on October 7, 1965. He became a regular on Carson. Rickles' forays into television and movies were not successful. However, in 1995 he appeared in Marin Scorsese's ode to mob-run Las Vegas, *Casino,* with Robert DeNiro and Joe Pesci. He played the voice of Mr. Potato Head in the computer-animated blockbuster *Toy Story* (and later, *Toy Story 2*).

Don Rickles was forty when he married Barbara Sklar in 1965. They had two children. His son, Lawrence, died in 2011. His survivors include his wife, daughter, and two grandchildren.

See Current Biography 2000

David Rockefeller

Born: New York, New York; June 12, 1915
Died: Pocantico Hills, New York; March 20, 2017
Occupation: Banker, philanthropist

David Rockefeller was the son of John D. Rockefeller, Jr., and the grandson of John D. Rockefeller, Sr., one of the wealthiest men in the world. David Rockefeller made his own fortune in banking, working as the chairman and chief executive of Chase Manhattan Bank, the largest bank in New York City, and the second largest bank in the country at that time. He was the last surviving Rockefeller son.

David Rockefeller was born into one of the wealthiest families in the world. His grandfather, John D. Rockefeller, Sr., made his fortune through investments, largely in oil. The Rockefeller children were taught that their enormous wealth came with a public responsibility, and should be used as much to benefit others as for themselves. Rockefeller attended the Lincoln School of Columbia University's Teachers College for twelve years, and earned his bachelors degree from Harvard University in 1936. He continued graduate studies in economics at Harvard and the London School of Economics, and earned his PhD from the University of Chicago in 1940. Rockefeller enlisted as a private in the army in 1942, serving in North Africa and France. He had achieved the rank of captain before his discharge, and was awarded the Legion of Merit, the Commendation Ribbon, and the French Legion of Honor. In 1946 he joined the staff of the Chase National Bank of New York where his uncle, Winthrop W. Aldrich, was chairman of the board. He was appointed senior vice president in 1952. He was made executive vice president in 1955, and was chairman of the board of directors in 1957. As a banker, Rockefeller had enormous influence in the United States and abroad, often receiving honors customarily accorded to foreign state dignitaries. He came under scrutiny for his business ties to foreign leaders hostile to the United States. In 1979 he helped persuade President Jimmy Carter to allow the deposed Shah of Iran into the US for medical treatment. Enraged revolutionaries in Iran seized the United States Embassy there, holding American diplomats hostage.

In 1940, Rockefeller married Margaret McGrath, who died in 1996, and they had six children. A daughter, Eileen Margaret predeceased her father in 1996. His son Richard died in a plane crash in 2014. David Rockefeller was 101 years old when he passed away. Survivors include four daughters, ten grandchildren, and ten great-grandchildren.

See Current Biography 1959

Harold Rosen

Born: New Orleans, Louisiana; March 20, 1926
Died: Pacific Palisades, California; January 30, 2017
Occupation: Electrical engineer

Sometimes referred to as the "father" of the synchronous satellite, Harold Rosen, along with his brother, Benjamin Rosen, created the first commercially viable electrically powered automobile engine.

Harold Rosen studied electrical engineering at Tulane University in New Orleans, graduating in 1947, following a stint in the US Navy as an electronics technician. He received a doctoral degree in the same discipline from the California Institute of Technology (Caltech), and immediately went to work as an engineer with the Raytheon Corporation. At Raytheon's military test site in Point Mugu, California, he developed antiaircraft guided missiles. Rosen's younger brother, Benjamin, also attended Caltech, and then received his master's degree in electrical engineering from Stanford University. The two brothers' careers ran parallel and, years later, with Benjamin's sizeable wealth, the two would form the innovative technology company, Rosen Motors. By 1956 Harold Rosen had commenced a thirty-seven-year career with the Hughes Aircraft Company, where he helped establish Hughes as the premier satellite and communications systems developer. Harold Rosen helped develop more than one hundred and fifty satellites. He was awarded more than fifty patents and numerous engineering prizes.

President Ronald Reagan honored Rosen with the National Medal of Technology and Innovation in 1985. In 1993, Harold and Benjamin Rosen founded Rosen Motors with the aim of developing a hybrid-electric power train for automobiles. Theirs would be the first such hybrid-electric automobile technology.

Harold Rosen's first wife, Rosetta Hirschfeld Rosen predeceased him in 1969. His survivors include his brother Benjamin, his second wife, Deborah Castleman, their two children, and three grandchildren.

See Current Biography 1997

James Rosenquist

Born: Grand Forks, North Dakota; November 29, 1933
Died: New York, New York; March 31, 2017
Occupation: Artist

In the style of his contemporaries Andy Warhol and Roy Lichtenstein, James Rosenquist was an artist who used his expertise in painting billboards and enormous advertising murals, to add a unique perspective that helped launch the Pop Art movement.

James Rosenquist was raised in North Dakota and Minnesota, the only son of Louis Andrew and Ruth Clara Hendrickson who worked in the aviation industry. His father serviced B-17 and B-24 bombers in World War II. Rosenquist's aptitude for art earned him a School Scholastics Scholarship to study at the Minneapolis School of Art in 1948. He graduated from high school in 1952 and took a summer job painting signs on huge gasoline tanks. He attended the University of Minnesota for three years, graduating with an Associate of Arts degree. He won a competitive, one-year scholarship with the Arts Student's League in New York City in 1955. While there he continued to earn money painting large advertisements and joined the Amalgamated Sign and Pictorial Painters Union of America, Local 230. As a billboard artist, Rosenquist earned enough money to free himself from a routine job, devoting at least a year to thinking and painting without interruption. His idiom grew out of his billboard work. His first one-man show in 1962 at the Green Gallery in New York, sold out. His most controversial painting "F-111," was made up of fifty-one interlocking canvas panels that measured eighty-six by ten feet when placed together. It filled four entire walls of a room at the gallery. The collection was Rosenquist's protest of the ever-growing American military complex. He had intended to sell the panels as separate pieces, but the art collector, Robert Scull, bought the entire collection and kept it whole.

In 1978 President Jimmy Carter appointed Rosenquist to a six-year term on the National Council of the Arts (NEA), which advises the National Endowment for the Arts. He published an autobiography, *Painting Below Zero: Notes on a Life in Art,* in 2009, in which he discussed his role in the Pop Art movement. Rosenquist's first marriage ended in divorce. His survivors include his second wife, Mimi Thompson, a son from his first marriage, a daughter from his second, and one grandson.

See Current Biography 1970

Hans Rosling

Born: Uppsala, Sweden; July 27, 1948
Died: Uppsala, Sweden: February 7, 2017
Occupation: Global health expert, statistician

A highly regarded expert on global health, Hans Rosling created the nonprofit think tank, the Gapminder Foundation, which Rosling referred to as a "fact tank that promotes a fact-based world view," with the aim of presenting statistics in a new, dynamic format that challenged the assumptions of "first world" and "third world" categorization.

Hans Rosling was born to a Swedish, working-class family. He was the first in the family to receive a higher education, graduating from Uppsala University with a degree in statistics in 1967. A trip to Bangalor, India, in 1972, to attend a course in public health, changed the

trajectory of Rosling's life. He discovered that the Indian students were much better educated than their Western counterparts, and Rosling realized the Western world would not continue to dominate the world forever. He completed his medical degree from Uppsala University in 1974, and he studied international aid and disaster relief in Sandö, Sweden. His other degrees included a diploma in nutrition, public health, and tropical medicine, with a PhD in medical sciences from Uppsala University.

As part of his training, Rosling worked as a district medical officer in Nacala, Mozambique, and was shocked by the dearth of doctors available to such a large population. He claimed to have suffered an attack of "numerical trauma"—there were two doctors for 300,000 people, whereas in Sweden there were 800 doctors for such a population. While in Africa he identified a mysterious ailment that caused paralysis as "konzo," caused by the ingestion of high concentrations of cyanide in cassava root, the only food source available during famine.

In 2005, with his son, Ola, and his daughter-in-law, Rosling founded the Gapminder Foundation with the aim of informing the Western world about built-in misconceptions and assumptions regarding the quality of life in so called third-world countries. In 2006 he was invited to speak at an annual Technology, Entertainment, and Design (TED) conference where he presented "The Best Stats You've Ever Seen," in which he discussed recent global changes in fertility, life expectancy, child survival, and poverty, debunking preconceived myths about the third world. He has been referred to as a "popstar" statistician.

Hans Rosling married child and adolescent psychiatrist, Agneta Thordeman. She, their three children, and a brother survive him.

See Current Biography 2014

Alain Senderens

Born: Hyères, Var, France; December 2, 1939
Died: Saint-Setiers, France; June 25, 2017
Occupation: French chef

Alain Senderens was a French chef whose Parisian restaurant L'Archestrate helped establish nouvelle cuisine. He received numerous accolades including the title of officer in the French Legion of Honor on 2004. He was also named a knight of the Order of Agriculture, and a knight in the Legion of Honor.

Alain Senderens was born into a family that believed good food was an essential part of life. He claimed food in his grandmother's house was considered sacred. He began his apprenticeship as a chef at the Ambassador Hotel in Lourdes, France, when he was eighteen. (This was considered a late start as most gourmands begin apprenticeships by the age of ten.) At twenty-one Senderens moved to Paris to work at La Tour d'Argent. In 1968 Senderens opened his own restaurant, l'Archestrate, a tiny restaurant with just seven tables, where he began experimenting with new combinations of flavor while also studying ancient cuisine, adapting recipes from as early as the Roman Empire. He was committed to making French cuisine simpler, and focused on acquiring exceptional ingredients, becoming one of the first proponents of organic produce. In 1978 L'Archestrate was awarded a third star, the highest rating possible, by the *Michelin Red Guide*, the premier guide to European cuisine. At the time only seventeen restaurants in France received the honor. That same year Senderens spent several months in China, returning to include unusual food pairings such as Chinese spice powder with fruit salad. He was also a pioneer in the art of pairing the best wines with food. He moved to New York City in the 1980s, working as a consultant chef at the new Parker Meridien Hotel, and published his first cookbook for English audiences. In 1989 Senderens helped form the Conseil National des Arts Culinaire (National Council of Culinary Arts) with the culture minister of France, Jack Lang. He remained president of the organization until 1998. In 2002 he fought the introduction of genetically modified crops and livestock in France. He published four books in the United States: *The Three-Star Recipes of Alain Senderens*, *Dining with Proust*, *The Table Beckons*, and *Alain Senderens and Jérôme Bancel in Your Kitchen*.

Alain Senderens's wife, Eventhia Pappadinas Senderens, co-wrote his books with him. Information about his survivors is unavailable.

See Current Biography 2005

Sam Shepard

Born: Fort Sheridan, Illinois; November 5, 1943
Died: Midway, Kentucky; July 27, 2017
Occupation: American playwright, actor, musician

Sam Shepard was an artist of remarkable versatility. He won a Pulitzer Prize for his play *Buried Child* in 1978, and was nominated for an Oscar Award for his role as Chuck Yeager in *The Right Stuff*, a movie based on Thomas Wolfe's novel. He wrote songs with John Cale and Bob Dylan, most notably, his song "Brownsville Girl" that was featured on Dylan's album, *Knocked Out*

Loaded. Shepard played drums with the group called Holy Modal Rounders that once opened for the group Pink Floyd.

Sam Shepard was born into a military family. His father was a career army man, which meant the family moved from South Dakota to Guam. They finally settled in Duarte, California, where Shepard graduated from high school. He briefly attended San Antonio Junior College before moving to New York where he began a writing career. To support himself, Shepard bussed tables at the Village Gate, a Greenwich Village cabaret, where he met Ralph Cook who encouraged Shepard to write for Off Off Broadway theatre. (Cook would make a name for himself as an Off Off Broadway pioneer.) Shepard began turning out one-act plays at a furious pace. He reached an important milestone when Richard Barr, Clinton Wilder, and Edward Albee decided to include one of his plays in their New Playwright series at the Off Broadway Cherry Lane Theatre. Three of Shepard's plays received Off Broadway theatre Obie Awards in the 1965–66 season. Shepard received a Rockefeller Foundation grant in 1967 and a Guggenheim grant in 1968, giving him the resources to write full time. Shepard's plays have been noted for their surrealist qualities, impressionistic and moody. He often wrote about the American West. At the Lincoln Center production of his play *Operation Sidewinder*, Shepard's musical band, the Holy Modal Rounders, performed musical interludes. Though he had acted in his early twenties, his first recognized role was in Terrence Malick's *Days of Heaven* in 1978. Over the course of his career, Shepard wrote fifty-five plays and appeared in more than fifty films.

He married the actress, O-Lan Jones Dark in the late 1960s. They had one son. He met Jessica Lange when the two performed in the movie *Frances* in 1982. Their relationship lasted for thirty years and they had two children together. Shepard's three children and two sisters survive him.

See Current Biography 1979

Stanislaw Skrowaczewski

Born: Lwów, Poland; October 3, 1923
Died: Minneapolis, Minnesota; February 21, 2017
Occupation: Conductor, composer

Stanislaw Skrowaczewski was the youngest man to ever hold the position of permanent conductor with a major American symphony. He was appointed conductor of the Cleveland Symphony in 1960 out of a pool of one hundred candidates.

Skrowaczewski's father was a brain surgeon and his mother was a concert pianist. As a child he learned to play the piano, flute, and violin, and he composed his first symphony when he was just eight years old. The Lwów Philharmonic performed his first overture that same year. After his musical training at the Conservatory of the Lwów Music Society, and graduating from secondary school, Skrowaczewski studied composition and conducting at the State Conservatory in Lwów. Upon graduating in 1945, Skrowaczewski studied composition with Roman Palester and conducting with Walerian Bierdiajew at the Krakow State Higher School of Music. He received a fellowship from the French government to study in Paris with Nadia Boulanger and Paul Kletzki. By his mid-twenties, Skrowaczewski was achieving international recognition as a composer. According to Richard Sandomir, writer for the *New York Times* (26 February 2017), Skrowaczewski "composed at least three dozen orchestral and chamber works and, between 1954 and 1960, eight scores for Polish films." During World War II, a wall collapsed on his hands, leaving him permanently disabled. In 1956 he won the international conducting competition at the Academia di Santa Cecilia in Rome, and the music director for the Cleveland Orchestra asked him to perform as a guest conductor. He later traveled with the New York Philharmonic and the Philadelphia Orchestra.

Stanislaw Skrowaczewski married Krystyna Jarosz and the two escaped the oppressive atmosphere of Communist Poland with a convenient performance in Amsterdam. The two left all of their belongings except for two suitcases and made their way to Minneapolis. Skrowaczewski's wife died in 2011. Their three children and two grandchildren survive him.

See Current Biography 1964

Mario Soares

Born: Lisbon, Portugal; December 7, 1924
Died: Lisbon, Portugal; January 7, 2017
Occupation: President and prime minister of Portugal

Mario Soares was a life-long politician who oversaw Portugal's transition from a fascist dictatorship to a parliamentary democracy. He served as Portugal's prime minister twice, from 1976 to 1978, and from 1983 to 1985. He was Portugal's president from 1986 to 1996.

Mario Soares' father, João Lopes Soares, was an educator and a government minister prior to the dictatorship of Antonio de Oliveira Salazar. In 1942 the young Soares studied literature at

the University of Lisbon and helped found the United Democratic Youth Movement until it was outlawed in 1948. He obtained his degree in 1951 and attended law school at the Sorbonne in Paris. Upon returning home, he rallied in opposition to the Salazar dictatorship, joining the Democratic-Social Directive. The 1960s saw the wars of independence for the Portuguese African colonies in Angola, Mozambique, and Portuguese Guinea, creating a rally-point of resistance to the Salazar regime. Soares became a leading figure in the anti-Salazar movement. He provided legal counsel to political prisoners and to the family of the mysteriously murdered opposition leader, General Humberto Delgado, earning Soares international recognition. Soares' opposition to Salazar's regime earned him additional jail time. In all, Soares was arrested twelve times, and spent three years in prison. He was banished in 1968 to the remote island of São Tomé. Months later a stroke incapacitated Salazar and his successor, Marcello Caetano, began to loosen the reigns of the dictatorship. In 1974 the dictatorship fell in a bloodless coup known as the "Carnation Revolution." Soares was the foreign minister for the transitional government, and was elected prime minister in 1976. Under his leadership, through a series of difficult negotiations, Portugal's African colonies of Guinea-Bissau, Mozambique, and Angola became independent. In 1986 Soares became the first democratically elected president of Portugal since 1926.

Mario Soares married Maria Barroso, a prominent Portuguese actress, in 1968, while he was imprisoned by the Salazar government. (The Salazar regime promptly banned her from the stage in Portugal.) She was later elected to the National Assembly. Maria Barroso died in 2015. They had two children who survive her.

See Current Biography 1975

Harry Dean Stanton

Born: West Irvine, Kentucky; July 14, 1926
Died: Los Angeles, California; September 15, 2017
Occupation: Actor, singer

While Harry Dean Stanton played mostly supporting roles in his early career, often as a rugged outlaw, it wasn't until he was in his late fifties, that he was cast as the lead in Wim Wenders' *Paris, Texas*, which won the Grand Prize at the 1984 Cannes Film Festival.

Harry Dean Stanton was born to a strict Southern Baptist tobacco farmer. His parents fought constantly, and eventually divorced when

Stanton was in his late teens. He served in the navy during World War II and then attended the University of Kentucky, though he dropped out before earning his degree. He moved to Los Angeles and began performing at the Pasadena Playhouse. His first television roles were in Westerns like *Gunsmoke, Bonanza, The Big Valley,* and *Rawhide*. His first movie role was in *Tomahawk Trail* in 1957, followed by *The Proud Rebel* in 1958. Stanton narrowly escaped being typecast as the perpetual rugged villain. Over time Stanton achieved cult status for his appearances in many genre films. In Ridley Scott's *Alien* (1979), Stanton and Yaphet Kotto provided comic relief as two exasperated crew members of a doomed space ship. In 1983 producer Sam Shepard met with Stanton and decided to cast Stanton as the lead in his movie *Paris, Texas*. He was the quintessential Shepard male lead. Thereafter, Stanton refused to play a violent character, even turning down a role in Beth Henley's *Crimes of the Heart*. Over the course of his career, Stanton worked with some of the greatest film directors in America, including John Houston, Francis Ford Coppola, and Martin Scorsese. He counted among his close friends, the actors Jack Nicholson and Marlon Brando.

Information about Stanton's nearest survivors is not available.

See Current Biography 2000

Thomas Starzl

Born: LeMars, Iowa; March 11, 1926
Died: Pittsburgh, Pennsylvania; March 4, 2017
Occupation: Surgeon, medical researcher

Dr. Thomas Starzl was a pioneer in organ transplantation, performing the first liver replacement surgery in 1963. His research in the use of drugs to suppress the body's rejection of transplanted organs made liver transplantation a standard surgical procedure. He also masterminded the first xenograft, or cross species transplant, when he replaced a human patient's liver with that of a baboon.

Thomas Starzl was born to Anna Laura (Fitzgerald) Starzl and Roman F. Starzl who was the editor and publisher of the local paper, the *Globe Post*. He was also a science fiction writer. His mother, who Starzl considered his "guiding light," worked as a surgical nurse until she married. Following World War II when Starzl fought in the navy, he entered the premedical program at Westminster College in Fulton, Missouri. In 1947 he entered Northwestern University's medical school while working as a news writer for the *Chicago Tribune* and working as a

paramedic in the office of an industrial surgeon. He also worked as an assistant to Horace W. Magoun, a professor of neuroanatomy, whom Starzl credited with teaching him "the true meaning of research." Starzl's work with Magoun helped earn him a PhD degree in neurophysiology from Northwestern in 1952, and an MD degree in the same year. Upon graduation, Starzl entered the prestigious surgical training program at Johns Hopkins University Hospital, and he spent a year as a resident at the University of Miami School of Medicine. In 1958 he accepted a one-year fellowship in thoracic surgery at Northwestern. By the time he passed the thoracic surgery boards in 1959, he received two awards: a five-year grant from the National Institutes of Health (NIH) to study insulin metabolism and transplantation, and a five-year Markle Scholarship. His experience led him to commit to staying in university research for the rest of his life. His decision to specialize in transplantation grew out of his desire for a "lifetime challenge."

Starzl performed his first kidney transplant in 1962 at the University of Colorado School of Medicine where he was soon named professor of surgery. (In 1972 he became chairman of the department of surgery.) He attempted the world's first liver transplant in 1963. In early 1980 Starzl became convinced the University of Colorado was no longer interested in transplantation and he transferred to Presbyterian University Hospital, which is affiliated with the University of Pittsburgh, where he would remain for the rest of his life. He made Pittsburgh a hub of a nationwide organ procurement network. The University of Pittsburgh's Transplantation Institute is the largest, most active transplant facility in the world. Starzl came under scrutiny from animal rights groups who felt he was using animals as "spare parts" for humans. His research in cyclosporine and other anti-rejection drugs led Starzl to attempt simultaneous, multiple-organ transplants.

Thomas Starzl's first marriage ended in divorce after twenty-two years. They had three children. In 1981 he married Joy Conger. She, a son and a grandson survive him.

See Current Biography 1993

David Storey

Born: Wakefield, England; July 13, 1933
Died: London, England; March 27, 2017
Occupation: British playwright, novelist

The writer, David Storey, was unusual in that he achieved substantial success as both a novelist and as a playwright. He won the Man Booker

Prize in 1976 for his novel *Saville,* while two other novels were shortlisted for the prize. The New York Drama Critics Circle designated three of his works "best plays" for four years running. His work also earned him two Tony nominations.

Much of Storey's writing could be considered autobiographical, depicting life in a poor mining community. He was born to a poor coal miner in Wakefield Yorkshire, one of four sons. One of Storey's brothers died of "privation" in childhood. Storey's parents encouraged their children to get an education to rise above the poverty of their early years. David Storey was interested in becoming an artist and attended school at the Slade School of Art in London, while playing rugby under contract with the Leeds team. The juxtaposition of this arrangement would flavor much of Storey's work. He published his first novel, *This Sporting Life,* in 1960, winning the Somerset Maugham Fiction Award and the John Llewellyn Rhys Memorial Prize. The film version of the novel, scripted by Storey, was awarded the International Film Critics prize at the 1963 Cannes Film Festival. He earned a Tony Nomination in 1970 for his play *Home,* which also brought nominations for the actors John Gielgud, Ralph Richardson, and Mona Washbourne, and a nomination for the director, Lindsay Anderson. He reportedly wrote the play in three days. His play, *The Changing Room,* likewise won Storey a Tony nomination.

In 1956 David Storey married Barbara Hamilton. They had four children. Barbara predeceased Storey in 2015. His survivors include his four children, a brother and six grandchildren.

See Current Biography 1973

Seijun Suzuki

Born: Tokyo, Japan; May 24, 1923
Died: Tokyo, Japan; February 13, 2017
Occupation: Japanese filmmaker

Towards the end of his life, Seijun Suzuki, who reached the height of his fame when he was in his seventies and eighties, lamented that either his films were made too early, or his audience came too late. But a large part of his success has been his legacy and the impact of his genius on contemporary artists like David Lynch, John Woo, and Quentin Tarantino.

Upon finishing high school, Seijun Suzuki was drafted into the Japanese military and served in the navy during World War II. He survived two shipwrecks. Upon returning home, he failed the entrance exam at the ministry of agriculture's university. He found a job as an assistant filmmaker at the Shochiku film company where he

worked with well-established directors like Minora Shibuya and Noboru Nakamura. There he learned how to make films quickly on a small budget. For the first half of his career, he was a relatively dispassionate filmmaker, cranking out the work expected of a "B" filmmaker. For the young Suzuki, it was a way to make a living. Of the fifty films he directed in his fifty-year career, forty were produced in the first twelve years.

In 1954 Suzuki moved to Nikkatsu studios, a company notorious for its massive output of violent, sexually explicit pictures. While there he adopted the pseudonym Seitaro Suzuki. From 1956 to 1967 Suzuki cranked out forty-two low-budget movies. But he grew restless with virtually the same scripts and low budgets time after time. He came into his own as a filmmaker, with the film, *Youth of the Beast.* He subverted convention by shifting points of view. He gained some recognition with the gangster movie, *Tokyo Drifter* and *The Fighting Elegy.* In 1967 he filmed *Branded to Kill,* which established his enduring reputation. The film was so shocking to Nikkatsu that they immediately fired Suzuki. He was embroiled in a breach of contract suit with the company for over ten years, effectively blacklisting him, and he made a sparse living working on television productions. He won the suit and a monetary award, but a huge part of his career was over. In 1980 he made a successful comeback with a supernatural love story, *Ziguenerweisen,* which won Suzuki the equivalent of a Japanese Academy Award. By the time of his death, Suzuki had gained a cult following among young moviegoers.

Suzuki's wife, Takako, and a brother, Kenji, survive him.

See Current Biography 2005

Jalal Talabani

Born: Kelkan, Kurdistan, Iraq; November 12, 1933
Died: Berlin, Germany; 3 October 2017
Occupation: Iraqi politician, first president of Iraq after Saddam Hussein's ouster

Jalal Talabani was Iraq's first post-war president following the US–led ouster of the dictator Saddam Hussein.

Jalal Talabani was born into a powerful Kurdish family. By the time he was eighteen, he became a ranking member of the Kurdistan Democratic Party (KDP). He attended law school at Baghdad University where he helped found the Kurdistan Student Union. He had to flee briefly because of his role in founding the union, traveling to China where he met the Premier Zhou Enlai. He returned to Baghdad and graduated from law school in 1959. He became an overseas envoy for the KDP. In 1975 he founded the Patriotic Union of Kurdistan (PUK), a rival group to the KDP. In 1987 Saddam Hussein killed thousands of Kurds in a gas attack. Talabani snuck out of the country, landing in the United States, serving as a messenger to the West regarding Hussein's atrocities. He spoke at the United Nations (UN), with the US government, and to the press. Western allies imposed a "no-fly zone," allowing some sense of security for the Kurds. In 2003 the United States launched a war with Iraq to depose Iraq's dictator, Saddam Hussein. After Hussein's fall, Iraq wrote a new constitution that called for free and open elections. Out of more than 5,000 candidates, Jalal Talabani was elected president. He was re-elected in 2006 and in 2010; however, poor health led to his resignation in 2014.

Jalal Talabani's wife, Hero, whom he married in 1970, their two sons, and three grandchildren survive him.

See Current Biography 2005

David Tang

Born: Hong Kong, China; August 2, 1954
Died: London, England; August 29, 2017
Occupation: Chinese entrepreneur

David Tang was a well-known Chinese entrepreneur and socialite who founded numerous well-known business ventures including the Pacific Cigar Company, the sole distributor of Cuban cigars in the Asia Pacific region. In 2008 he was knighted for his charitable work.

David Tang Wing-Cheung was born to a wealthy family in Hong Kong. He attended the exclusive Perse School in Cambridge, though he didn't speak English and was the only Asian boy at the school. He later graduated from King's College, part of the University of London, earning a law degree several years later. After briefly teaching English in Beijing, Tang returned to Hong Kong and began casting about for entrepreneur opportunities and ended up founding the Pacific Cigar Company in the late 1980s. His first store, called Cigar Divan, was in the lobby of the Mandarin Oriental Hotel in Hong Kong. Within a short while, he had opened numerous stores in places like Bangkok, Jakarta, Singapore, and Macau. His clubs attracted not only businessmen but also celebrities like Richard Gere, Kevin Costner, Sarah Ferguson, and the late Diana, Princess of Wales. In 1994 Tang opened his first department store, the Shanghai Tang, in Hong Kong, and designed many of the items the store carried. He soon had stores

around the world. Tang was an avid art collector and helped create Hong Kong's Hanart TZ Gallery. He also managed several investment funds and became part owner of the restaurant Cipriani, in London. He also wrote an advice column for Hong Kong's newspaper, the *Apple Daily*.

Tang was well known in celebrity circles for his lavish parties. He died from cancer just a week before his scheduled "farewell party." Tang's first marriage to Susanna Cheung ended in divorce. They had two children. His survivors include his two children and his second wife, Lucy (Wastnage) Tang.

See Current Biography 2006

Alan Thicke

Born: Kirkland Lake, Ontario, Canada; March 1, 1947
Died: Burbank, California; December 13, 2016
Occupation: Actor, songwriter, television performer, producer

Although Alan Thicke had a long and varied career, and played many roles, he is most remembered as one of the best television dads in the medium. He played Dr. Jason Seaver, a psychiatrist who practices from home and cares for his three children, on the hit situation comedy, *Growing Pains*, from 1985 to 1992.

Alan Thicke was born in the small mining town of Kirkland Lake in Ontario, Canada, to William Jeffery and his wife. His parents divorced when he was six years old, and his mother married a physician who had a strong influence on him as a boy, and whose surname Thicke adopted. In deference to his stepfather, Thicke chose to major in pre-medicine at the University of Western Ontario, but was more interested in communications and sports writing. He auditioned with the Canadian Broadcasting Corporation (CBC) in Toronto and began his career as a "gofer." While there he began writing material for television shows. He moved to Los Angeles in 1970. Having been an avid hockey player in Canada, he had a number of friends who played for the Los Angeles Kings, and who introduced him to show-business people they knew. His first major American credits were for a Flip Wilson comedy special. He joined the writing team for Richard Pryor and *Saturday Night Live*. In 1977 he was a member of a team that won an Emmy award for a Barry Manilow special, and an Emmy for *Saturday Night Live* the following year. Thicke also wrote and sang theme music for more that thirty television shows. Impressed with Thicke's ability to ad lib, casting director John Crosby recommended Thicke as the lead for the situation comedy *Growing Pains.* Following *Growing Pains,* Thicke appeared on a number of comedy and variety shows. He also acted in three *Growing Pains* follow-up movies.

Alan Thicke had two children with his first wife, Gloria Loring. His son Robin became a successful pop singer. He had another son with his second wife, Gina Tolleson. He married for a third time in 2005, to actor and model Tanya Callau. Thicke died suddenly while playing hockey with his youngest son, Carter. His wife and three children survive him.

See Current Biography 1987

Grant Tinker

Born: Stamford, Connecticut; January 11, 1926
Died: Los Angeles, California; November 28, 2016
Occupation: Broadcasting executive

Grant Tinker was a broadcast and television executive responsible for some of the most successful television shows in the 1970s and 1980s.

After graduating from Dartmouth College in 1949, Grant Tinker was a management trainee in the NBC radio network. He was appointed operations manager until 1954 when he became the deputy director of Radio Free Europe. From 1958 through 1961, he worked with Benton & Bowles, a top advertising agency. Shortly thereafter, he returned to NBC as a general program executive in the television division. In 1966 he was promoted to vice-president of programming, but he resigned a year later, moved to Los Angeles and created his own independent television production company, MTM, founded with his second wife, the actress Mary Tyler Moore. The *Mary Tyler Moore Show* was the first to feature an independent career woman in the lead role. Successful spin-off programs included *Lou Grant* and *Rhoda.* Tinker returned to NBC ten years later, as the chairman and chief executive. His winning, "hands-off" management style gave free reign to his creative people. The network's profits increased ten-fold, and a number of television's most successful shows, including *Cheers, The Cosby Show, Family Ties, St. Elsewhere,* and *Hill Street Blues,* came out of that time period.

Grant Tinker was married three times. He had four children with his first wife, the former Ruth Byerly. He was married to Mary Tyler Moore from 1963 to 1981, and they had no children. Tinker's third wife, Brooke Knapp, survives along with a sister, his four children, ten grandchildren, and numerous great-grandchildren.

See Current Biography 1982

Y. A. Tittle

Born: Marshall, Texas; October 24, 1926
Died: Stanford, California; October 8, 2017
Occupation: American professional football player

Y. A. Tittle was the star quarterback for the New York Giants and at the time, was the most productive passer in the history of the team. He led the Giants to three Eastern Division championships. The United Press International (UPI) named him Player of the Year in 1957, and in 1962, UPI named him Most Valuable Player (MVP) in the National Football League (NFL). He is also remembered for the iconic picture of an aging warrior quarterback, after he was brutally taken down, kneeling and injured, suffering a concussion, a bloodied face, and cracked ribs. The photo of Tittle became an icon, winning the National Headline Award for best sports photograph of 1964. It sits in the Pro Football Hall of Fame.

YA Tittle's given name was Yelberton Abraham, a family name. He was the middle child in a family with three boys. He attended Marshall High School where he was named all-star halfback in 1943. He was picked up by Louisiana State University (LSU), which he attended on an athletic scholarship. While there, Tittle was named MVP for three years running, and was named twice to the Southeast Conference Squad. In 1948 he was picked up by the Cleveland Browns who immediately traded him to the Baltimore Colts, where he was the starting quarterback in the 1948 and 1949 seasons. When the All-America league folded, Tittle went to the San Francisco Forty-niners. In 1961 he was traded to the New York Giants. At the end of 1961, Tittle was voted the most popular New York Giant. He led the Giants to Eastern Conference titles in 1961, 1962, and 1963.

Tittle's daughter, two sons, seven grandchildren, and nine great grandchildren survive him. His wife of sixty-four years, Minnette, died in 2012.

See Current Biography 1964

William Trevor

Born: Mitchelstown, Ireland; May 24, 1928
Died: County Cork, Ireland; November 20, 2016
Occupation: Irish writer

William Trevor was arguably one of the best short-story-writers of the last century and he was widely anthologized. He also wrote more than fifteen novels.

William Trevor's father worked for the Bank of Ireland, which meant the family moved often, from one provincial town to another. He attended Trinity College in Dublin, earning a degree in history in 1950. He taught history in Armagh, Northern Ireland, from 1950 to 1952. Trevor's passion was art however, and he obtained a position as an art teacher in Rugby, England, thus allowing himself more time for sculpture. He did relief carvings for All Saints Church in Braunston, near Rugby. In 1956 he moved to Somerset where he continued working as a church sculptor and had one-man exhibitions in Dublin and Bath. For economic reasons he took a position as an advertising copywriter in London, and launched his career as a writer. As a sculptor Trevor was known by his full name, William Trevor Cox, so he adopted the pseudonym, William Trevor, to use for his writing. His short stories were widely anthologized. He was known especially for his ability to shape his characters through dialogue, and many of his stories have been adapted into short plays for British radio and television, and several of his titles were adapted for the stage. He continued writing prolifically well in the 2000s. His final novel, *Love and Summer*, was published in 2009.

Trevor received numerous awards for his writing. He won the Whitebread prize three times. His second novel, *The Old Boys,* won the Hawthornden Prize. His late novel, *The Story of Lucy Gault*, was short-listed for the Man Booker Prize. He was a member of the Irish Academy of Letters and was named a Commander of the Order of the British Empire (OBE) in 1977.

Trevor married his wife, Jane Ryan, in 1952 and they had two sons. His wife, sons, and one granddaughter survive him.

See Current Biography 1984

administration strikes were resolved with railway workers, postal workers, and coal miners.

W. J. Usery liked to be called Bill. His father was a postal worker at the Central State Hospital in Milledgeville, Georgia, and his mother worked in the laundry facilities and as a nurse's aid. He had planned to study law and enrolled at the Georgia Military College in Milledgeville. However, his plans were interrupted when World War II broke out and Usery worked as a welder in the naval shipyards. He then joined the navy where he served aboard a repair ship in the Pacific. Upon his return home he began working for the Armstrong Cork Company where he was a founding member of the local chapter of the International Association of Machinists (IAM). He attended night school but never graduated with a degree. Recognized for his gregarious personality, the IAM sent Usery to coordinate union activities at the aerospace installations at Cape Canaveral, Florida, where the union membership roster rose from seventeen to four thousand, six hundred. President Kennedy appointed Usery to the President's Missile Sites Labor Committee in Florida. While in Florida, Usery became involved in the civil rights movement. In 1969 the secretary of labor George Shultz offered Usery the job of assistant secretary of labor. In 1973 Usery was appointed director of the Federal Mediation and Conciliation Service (FMCS) where he initiated a series of experimental programs designed to help unions establish more amicable relationships. Most unions praised Usery's skills as a mediator. In 1976 President Ford nominated Usery to fill the unexpected vacancy as the secretary of labor.

Bill Usery married Gussie Mae Smith in 1942. She died in 2005. The couple had one son who survives, along with Usery's second wife, the former Frances Pardee, and one granddaughter.

See Current Biography 1976

W. J. (Bill) Usery

Born: Midway-Hardwick, Georgia; December 21, 1923
Died: Eatonton, Georgia; December 10, 2016
Occupation: US secretary of labor

Willie Julian Usery, Jr., a Democrat, had the unusual distinction of working in the administrations of two Republican presidents. He was the US assistant secretary of labor in the Nixon administration, and the secretary of labor in the Ford administration. Under Usery's watch the federal government conceded to give organizing and collective bargaining rights to federal employees. With his leadership in the Nixon

Ely Ould Mohamed Vall

Born: Nouakchott, Mauritania; 1953
Died: Zouerat, Tiris Zemmour, Mauritania; May 5, 2017
Occupation: Mauritanian head of state

Ely Ould Mohamed Vall led a bloodless coup on August 3, 2005, seizing control of the country and helping to establish a new constitution to help ensure a democratic future for the small nation of Mauritania.

Ely Ould Mohamed Vall was born in the capital of Mauritania, Nouakchott, in 1952 or 1953. He was sent to France for his schooling and received his baccalaureate in 1973. He then joined the prestigious military academy of Meknes in Morocco. Some sources claim he also studied for a law degree. Upon returning home, he was given command of several troops near the border of the Western Sahara. In 1982 Vall was given a military command in Rosso, and later, he earned a military command in Nouakchott, placing him near the center of Mauritanian power. In 1984 Vall helped the army chief of staff and prime minister, Maaoya Sid'Ahmed Ould Taya, overthrow the president who had come into power through a coup four years earlier. (Mauritania had experienced ten coups or coup attempts since it gained independence from France in 1960.) Taya would remain in power for two decades, winning elections in 1997 and 2003, though fraud and intimidation were likely factors in his wins. Political unrest leading to the 2005 coup stemmed largely from tribal conflicts between African ethnic groups. When Taya left to attend the funeral of King Fahd of Saudi Arabia, Vall and other military commanders took control in a bloodless coup, which was widely supported by the Mauritanian citizens. In June of 2006 a referendum was held in which about 96 percent of voters approved constitutional changes limiting future presidents to two five-year terms. Vall assumed leadership and stated that neither he nor anyone in his seventeen-member junta would run for office. The coup was largely condemned and the fifty-three-member African Union announced it was suspending Mauritania's membership until constitutional order was achieved. Vall assured the UN that Mauritania would honor all its international treaties and agreements.

In October Vall assembled seven hundred delegates to find a consensus on a democratic system. Vall also worked to strengthen his country's international ties, and in May, the European Union (EU) agreed to resume aid to Mauritania.

Little information is available about Vall's survivors. He was married and had several children.

See Current Biography 2006

Robert Vaughn was born into a show business family, though his parents divorced shortly after his birth. His father, Gerald Walter Vaughn, was a radio actor, and his mother was the Broadway actress, Frances Gaudel. Vaughn's grandparents raised him in Minneapolis, Minnesota. He claimed to have had a miserable childhood that seemed to improve as he entered high school and discovered his own athletic abilities. Vaughn studied at the University of Minnesota on an athletic scholarship. During summers in his teen years, Vaughn lived with his mother in New York where he acted for various network radio shows. Following the death of his grandparents, Vaughn moved to Los Angeles to live with his mother. He earned a degree in theater arts from Los Angeles State College. He was inducted into the army, serving as a private from 1956 to 1957. He returned to school and received an MA in theater from the University of Southern California (USC). (He would earn his PhD from USC in 1970.) During that time, he made his first film, *No Time to Be Young*, in which he co-starred with Roger Smith. In 1959 Vaughn was nominated for an Academy Award for best supporting actor for his role in *The Young Philadelphians* (Warner Brothers, 1959). In 1960 he co-starred with Yul Brynner in *The Magnificent Seven* (United Artists, 1960). The role that would make Vaughn a household name came to him in 1964 when he signed to play Napoleon Solo in *The Man from U.N.C.L.E.* (U.N.C.L.E. was an acronym for the United Network Command for Law and Enforcement.) Vaughn was also politically active and became friends with the late Senator Robert F. Kennedy. He served as the chairman of the speakers' bureau of the Southern California Democratic Central Committee. In 1967 he became the chairman of Dissenting Democrats, an organization that promoted the end of the war in Vietnam.

Robert Vaughn married Linda Staab in 1974 and they had two children. She, their two children, and two grandchildren survive him.

See Current Biography 1967

Robert Vaughn

Born: New York, New York; November 22, 1932
Died: Ridgefield, Connecticut; November 11, 2016
Occupation: Actor

The actor Robert Vaughn is most remembered for his role as Napoleon Solo in the television series *The Man from U.N.C.L.E.*, which aired from 1964 to 1968. Vaughn earned an Emmy Award in 1978 for his role in the miniseries *Washington Behind Closed Doors*.

Simone Veil

Born: Nice, France; July 13, 1927
Died: Paris, France; June 30, 2017
Occupation: French politician, president of the European parliament

One of the most highly regarded public figures in France, Simone Veil served as the minister of health under President Giscard d'Estaing, from 1974 to 1979. She was the second woman to hold a cabinet post. Under her tenure, France legalized birth control devices and legalized abortion, enacting a law that still bears her name, the Veil Law. She was the first woman to be elected president of the European Parliament, the legislative arm of the European Community.

Simone Veil, née Jacob was born the youngest of four children, to a French Jewish architect. The day after she graduated from the Lycée de Nice, the equivalent of an American high school, she, her sister, and mother were deported to Auschwitz, and later, to Bergen-Belsen concentration camp. While there, her mother died of typhus. Veil would never see her father and brother again. Following the war Veil studied law and political science at the Institute for Political Studies in Paris, where she met her future husband, Antoine Veil. (His sister had been a fellow inmate at Auschwitz.) They married in 1946. Veil became a magistrate in 1956 and accepted a position as attaché with the Ministry of Justice. In 1969 she served as the technical advisor to the Minister of Justice, René Pleven, and from 1970 to 1974, Veil was secretary-general of the High Council of the Magistrature. In 1974, newly elected President Valéry Giscard d'Estaing appointed her minister of health. Veil was an unwavering supporter of women's rights and under her watch, Giscard's government legalized birth control devices and abortion, no small feat in a Roman Catholic country. In 1979 Veil was elected to the European Parliament and resigned as France's minister of health. She was the so-called "President of Europe," a great irony given that thirty-five years after Hitler's failed "final solution," a Jewish woman presided over the European Parliament.

Simone Veil was honored with several doctorates from Princeton, Yale, Edinburgh, and Cambridge universities. She was decorated a Chevalier de l'Ordre national du Mérite in France, a Grand Croix du Senegal, and a Grand-Croix de l'ordre du Phénix (from Greece). The Veil's had three sons. The middle son and Veil's husband predeceased her. Her survivors include her two sons and twelve grandchildren.

See Current Biography 1980

Derek Walcott

Born: Castries, St. Lucia; January 23, 1930
Died: Gros Islet Quarter, St. Lucia; March 17, 2017
Occupation: Poet, playwright

West Indian poet, Derek Walcott was a master of Caribbean patois, crafting a body of work that reflects his history and identity as a "perpetual outsider." Walcott won the Nobel Prize for literature in 1992.

Derek Walcott was of African, Dutch, and English descent. Mixed descent was not uncommon in his native West Indies. His parents were both schoolteachers. His father died when Walcott was an infant. He graduated from St. Mary's College in St Lucia and accepted a scholarship to the University of the West Indies in Jamaica, where he majored in French, Latin, and Spanish. When he was eighteen, Walcott published three slim volumes of poetry. Walcott returned to teach at St. Mary's College, at Boys Secondary School in Grenada, and at Kingston College. He wrote art and literary criticism for the *Trinidad Guardian*. Two of his plays were produced in 1954. He received a Rockefeller Foundation grant in 1957 and 1958, and he attended José Quintero's directing classes and rehearsals at the Phoenix Theatre's repertory company. He founded his own repertory company, the Little Carib Theater Workshop, which would later become the Trinidad Theater Workshop. Walcott's most widely recognized play was *Dream on Monkey Mountains,* which was produced in Waterford, Connecticut in 1969, and off Broadway in 1971. His first collection of poetry, *In a Green Light,* was published in 1962 and was hailed by critics as a landmark in Caribbean literature. Walcott explained it was a way for him to come to terms with "the immutable historic wrongs [done] to his people." He wrote a book-length, autobiographical poem, *Another Life,* in which he looks back on his childhood and his magical rites of poetic passage as part of a Caribbean way of life. Walcott's themes include life as a wanderer, home, "the ancient war between obsession and responsibility," and the elusiveness of peace. Arguably, Walcott's greatest achievement was his Homeric, book-length poem, *Omeros.* Walcott received numerous literary awards, including an Obie Award for his play, *Dream on Monkey Mountain,* a MacArthur Foundation "genius award," a Royal Society of Literature Award, and a Nobel Prize.

Walcott was married three times and had three children. His survivors include his longtime companion, Sigrid Nama, his three children, and several grandchildren.

See Current Biography 1984

Robert James Waller

Born: Charles City, Iowa; August 1, 1939
Died: Fredericksburg, Texas; March 10, 2017
Occupation: Novelist, educator

Robert Waller was an economist and professor of management at the University of Northern Iowa, when he began his writing career. In 1991, over the course of two weeks, Waller wrote the break-out bestseller, *The Bridges of Madison County.* He would continue to write several additional best sellers, *Slow Waltz in Cedar Bend* and *Border Music.*

Robert Waller was the only son of Robert Waller, Sr., a chicken wholesaler, and his wife, Ruth Waller. The boy's earliest ambition was to become a musician. He entered the University of Iowa on a basketball scholarship. After his first year there, he transferred to the University of Northern Iowa to study math and economics. He earned his PhD in business management from Indiana University. When not studying, Waller played guitar, banjo, and ukulele at the local Holiday Inn; Charles Kuralt found him and filmed one of his performances for a segment of *CBS Evening News*'s series, "On the Road." Robert F. Kennedy became something of a fan, and invited Waller to sing on his campaign train in Indiana before the State's Democratic presidential primary.

Waller became a professor of management at the University of Northern Iowa, earning the position of dean of the university's business school. He also served as a management consultant to corporations and government agencies. During this time, he began writing essays for the *Des Moines Register* newspaper, and eventually published some of his pieces in a single volume, *Just Beyond the Firelight: Stories and Essays by Robert James Waller.* Waller continued to publish several more volumes of his essays. While on a leave of absence from the university, he visited Iowa's Madison County, taking pictures of old covered bridges. Soon thereafter, Waller began writing *The Bridges of Madison County.* The novel was completed within two weeks. Though the book did not fair well among literary intellectuals, it became a runaway best seller, remaining on *The New York Times* bestseller list for three years. In 1993 Waller recorded the album, *The Ballads of Madison County.* Four of the songs were Waller's own creations. He would continue his writing career with two additional bestsellers, *Slow Waltz in Cedar Bend* and *Border Music.*

Waller was married to Georgia Ann Wiedemeier, a potter, for thirty-six years. The marriage ended in divorce. They had one daughter. Waller's survivors include his second wife, Linda Bow, his daughter, and a granddaughter.

See Current Biography 1994

Joseph Wapner

Born: Los Angeles, California; November 15, 1919
Died: Los Angeles, California; February 26, 2017
Occupation: Television personality, retired judge

The honorable judge, Joseph Wapner, became a household name in the 1990s when he presided over a real courtroom known as *The People's Court,* a wildly popular television show where real plaintiffs and defendants brought their small claims for adjudication.

Joseph Wapner was born to a relatively well-to-do Jewish family in Los Angeles, California. He attended Hollywood High School where he briefly entertained the idea of a career in show business, and dated a girl named Judy Turner, who eventually dyed her hair blond and became the famous actress, Lana Turner. Joseph Wapner's film career seemed forever doomed when he was dismissed from the cast of the school play because he was told he had no talent. He attended the University of Southern California (USC), graduating in 1941 with a degree in philosophy. He enlisted in the US Army and fought in the Pacific theater during World War II. He was shot by sniper fire and received a Purple Heart and the Bronze Star for heroism. He returned to USC where he attained his law degree and was admitted to the California bar in 1949.

Wapner practiced law with his father for several years before setting out on his own. In 1958 Wapner worked in Edmund G. Brown's successful gubernatorial campaign, and was rewarded a year later with an appointment as judge of the Los Angeles Municipal Court. In 1961 he was promoted to the Los Angeles Superior Court. After eight years, he was elected presiding judge to supervise more than two hundred judges and eight hundred employees. There he remained until his retirement in 1979. Several years later, a friend, Christian Markey, recommended him to the television producer, Ralph Edwards, and his partner, Stu Billett, who had worked on numerous successful shows and were looking to produce a daytime show about real court cases. Wapner was a natural and *The People's Court* was an instant ratings hit. As with real court cases, there were no rehearsals or scripts. Joseph Wapner became a household name and was invited to speak to law students across the country. His name was more widely recognized than those of the Supreme Court justices.

Joseph Wapner married Mickey Nebenzahl in 1945 and they had three children. She and two of their sons survive. A daughter, Sarah, died in 2015.

See Current Biography 1989

Fritz Weaver

Born: Pittsburgh, Pennsylvania; January 19, 1926
Died: New York, New York; November 26, 2016
Occupation: Actor

Fritz Weaver was a versatile character actor who performed on the stage as well as on television and movie screens. He received a Tony nomination for his Broadway debut where he played a fussy butler in Enid Bagnold's play *The Chalk Garden* in 1955. He won a Tony Award in 1970 for his role in the drama *Child's Play*. He won an Emmy Award for his role as a German Jewish doctor, Joseph Weiss, slain by the Nazis in the television mini-series, *Holocaust* in 1978.

Fritz Weaver's father was an economist who conducted radio and television discussion programs in the Pittsburgh area. After graduating from high school, Weaver registered as a conscientious objector when he was called for military service during World War II, and worked at various camps under the Civilian Public Service program. He entered the University of Chicago, graduating with a degree in physics in 1950. He discovered his love of theater while at the university, and he performed in many campus productions. He decided to make acting his career and joined different acting troupes in the early 1950s. His New York stage review was in 1954 in the Proscenium Productions revival of *Congreve's Way of the World*. He won the Clarence Derwent Award as the season's best supporting actor for his role as a secretary in George Bernard Shaw's remake of a seventeenth century tragedy called *The White Devil*. (Shaw's remake was called *The Doctor's Dilemma*.) He was then invited to join the original company of the American Shakespeare Festival in Stratford, Connecticut. Beginning in the 1950s, Weaver also performed on television in popular shows such as *Mission Impossible* and *The Twilight Zone*. Weaver's movie credits include *The Day of the Dolphin, Marathon Man,* and *The Thomas Crown Affair*. Later in his career, Weaver did a number of voice-over performances, narrating many shows on the History Channel.

Fritz Weaver was married twice. His second wife was the actress Rochelle Oliver who survives him along with his two children and a grandson.

See Current Biography 1966

Mark White

Born: Henderson, Texas; March 17, 1940
Died: Houston, Texas; August 5, 2017
Occupation: Governor of Texas

Mark White's term as governor of Texas, from 1983 to 1987, is most remembered for his education reform measures, including the infamous "no pass, no play" rule. Students who failed to pass their classes were barred from participating in extra curricular activities, including sports. Though unpopular, White's reforms remain largely in place over thirty years later.

Mark White was born in Henderson, Texas, near the Louisiana border. His father was a ship fitter and his mother was a schoolteacher. He attended Lamar High School in Houston, and earned his degrees in business administration and law from Baylor University in Waco, Texas. He passed the Texas bar in 1965 and went to work for the state attorney general's office. He began his political career in 1973 when the Democratic governor, Dolph Briscoe, appointed him Texas secretary of state where he learned valuable lessons in running campaigns. He was the Democratic nominee for state attorney general in 1978. His was a rough term however, as he clashed with the Republican Governor William Clements. During this time the Texas economy took a big downturn as the price of oil, so vital to the state economy, plummeted. In addition, Mexico experienced an economic crisis that influenced the border economy. The political animosity between the two came to a head when White challenged Clements in the following gubernatorial elections. After winning the election, White set about improving Texas education, which in White's view was key to attracting new businesses to Texas, especially in the computer, aerospace, and other high-tech industries. Texas passed the Education Reform Act in 1984. The "no pass, no play" portion of the reform was hugely unpopular given the role high school football played in the state's social fabric. The act also included competency testing for teachers and a passing grade on student competency exams before a student could advance to the next grade. White lost his re-election bid to his old rival, William Clements. According to White one of his greatest honors was having a school named after him.

Mark White's wife, three children, and nine grandchildren survive him.

See Current Biography 1986

Roger Wilkins

Born: Kansas City, Missouri; January 29, 1932
Died: Kensington, Maryland; March 26, 2017
Occupation: Lawyer, activist, journalist, educator

Roger Wilkins was an assistant US attorney general in the Johnson administration. He was an officer of the Ford Foundation and worked on the editorial staff of the *Washington Post* and the *New York Times*. He coordinated Nelson Mandela's visit to the United States in 1990, sat on the board of the Pulitzer Prize, and served as a trustee on the board of the University of the District of Columbia. He was a professor at George Mason University, and served ten years as a fellow at the Institute for Policy Studies, a Washington think tank.

Roger Wilkins was the only child of Earl Wilkins, an advertising executive, and Helen Jackson Wilkins, the first black woman to serve on the national board of the Young Women's Christian Association (YWCA). His uncle, Roy Wilkins, was an assistant executive secretary of the National Association for the Advancement of Colored People (NAACP). Wilkin's father died in 1941 and the family moved to the Sugar Hill section of Harlem. In 1943 Wilkin's mother remarried and the family moved to an all-white neighborhood in Grand Rapids, Michigan. His two years in Harlem near his uncle, Roy Wilkins, had a major influence on his identity, as did his childhood years in a white neighborhood in Grand Rapids. Wilkins attended the University of Michigan in Ann Arbor where he was the president of his graduating class. He graduated with a law degree in 1956 and moved to New York City to practice law. In 1962 Wilkins was recruited to work as a special assistant to the administrator of the Agency for International Development in Washington, DC. A few years later the Community Relations Service (CRS) tapped him to oversee a program to defuse and prevent riots. Before he was thirty-four, President Johnson promoted him to direct the CRS. Shortly thereafter, he received the rank of assistant US attorney general. When Richard Nixon became president, Wilkins joined the Ford Foundation where he oversaw funding for job training, drug rehabilitation, and education for the poor. In 1972 he began writing for the *Washington Post*, and later, he joined the staff at *The New York Times*.

Wilkin's received the Roger Baldwin Civil Liberties Award. He was one of the first African Americans to sit on the Pulitzer Prize board. Wilkins was married three times and had three children. His survivors include his third wife, Patricia King, his three children, and two grandsons.

See Current Biography 1994

Daniel Yankelovich

Born: Boston, Massachusetts; December 29, 1924
Died: La Jolla, California; September 22, 2017
Occupation: Social scientist

Daniel Yankelovich was a social scientist and pollster who became an advisor to presidents, and conducted research for such large corporations as IBM, AT&T, General Electric, and the *New York Times*. He was more interested in social movements and conduct than he was in political polling.

Daniel Yankelovich was born to Russian immigrants, one of two children. His mother died when he was a small boy, and his father painted houses to support his family during the Great Depression. Yankelovich studied philosophy and social relations at Harvard University. He took a break from college during World War II to serve in the US Army. He returned to graduate magna cum laude and Phi Beta Kappa in 1948. He remained at Harvard for two more years, studying clinical psychology on a Rantoul fellowship. He received his master's degree in 1950 and studied for his PhD at the Sorbonne in Paris, France. Upon returning to the United States in 1952 Yankelovich rose quickly through the ranks of the market research firm Nowland & Company, becoming president and director of research within six years. He left in 1958 to establish his own research firm, Daniel Yankelovich, Inc. His early research was on the direction of foreign trade, and unlike his peers, George Gallup and Louis Harris, Yankelovich was not interested in election polls, preferring to study social movements like the 1970s "generation gap," and the women's movement. He was the first to adopt the term "baby boomers" when referring to the first post-war generation. Though he did not focus on election polls, Yankelovich did work with several presidents including Jimmy Carter, Gerald Ford, and Bill Clinton. Yankelovich authored more than a dozen books and published numerous articles for professional journals.

Daniel Yankelovich married Hasmieg Kaboolian in 1959 and they had one daughter. After they divorced he married Mary Komarnicki who was killed in an auto accident four years later. He and his third wife, Barbara Lee were separated at the time of his death. His survivors include his long-time companion, Laura Nathanson, his daughter, Nicole, and a granddaughter.

See Current Biography 1982

Clayton Yeutter

Born: Eustis, Nebraska; December 10, 1930
Died: Potomac, Maryland; March 4, 2017
Occupation: Former US Secretary of Agriculture, international trade negotiator

Clayton Yeutter was a trade negotiator under President Ronald Reagan, and the secretary of agriculture under President George Bush. He was integral to the creation of the World Trade Organization (WTO). Probably his greatest legacy was the creation of the Canada–US Free Trade Agreement, which eventually served as the foundation for the North Atlantic Free Trade Agreement (NAFTA). He later became the chairman of the Republican National Committee (RNC).

Clayton Yeutter was born into a farming family with a 2,500-acre "corn and cow farm" that barely survived the Great Depression. Though his family wanted him to help run the farm, Yeutter wanted a college education. He graduated from the University of Nebraska in 1952, designated the nation's most outstanding graduate in animal husbandry. He served in the US Air Force from 1952 to 1957, and attended law school on the Korean GI Bill. Yeutter simultaneously earned his PhD in agriculture economics at his alma mater while also managing the family farm. He earned his law degree in 1963 and his PhD in 1966. He entered state politics when he served from 1966 to 1968 as the Nebraska governor, Norbert Tiemann's executive assistant. He also held positions in the Department of Agriculture and the Office of the Special Trade Representative. In 1970 Yeutter was tapped to administer the Consumer and Marketing Service of President Nixon's Department of Agriculture, after which he served as secretary for marketing and consumer services under Secretary of Agriculture, Earl Butz. In 1978 Yeutter became the chief executive of the Chicago Mercantile Exchange, fostering a period of tremendous growth. Subsequently, he was a trade negotiator for President Ronald Reagan's administration and the secretary of agriculture in President George Bush's cabinet beginning in 1989 through 1991, and in 1992 he was made Bush's counselor for domestic policy.

Clayton Yeutter married the former Jeanne Vierk in 1957, and they had four children. She died in 1993, and Yeutter married Cristena Bach in 1995, who survives him. Other survivors include his four children from his first marriage, three daughters from his second, nine grandchildren, and one great-grandchild.

See Current Biography 1988

Yevgeny Yevtushenko

Born: Zima, Irkutsk, Russia; July 18, 1932
Died: Tulsa, Oklahoma; April 1, 2017
Occupation: Russian poet, writer, filmmaker

Yevgeny Yevtushenko was a poet of great stature in post-Stalin Russia. Although he was hailed as a poet for the masses and the oppressed, one of a small group of rebel poets and writers who brought hope to a new generation, he was criticized for his artistic compromises, made to maintain favor with the Russian government.

Yevgeny Yevtushenko was born in a small lumber station in Siberia. His father was a geologist and an intellectual who exposed his son to the world of classic western literature. His parents divorced when he was quite young, and he lived in Moscow with his mother and assumed her surname. During World War II he was evacuated to Siberia for his own safety. There he became interested in the folk songs and ballads, the speech patterns and rhythms of peasant life. After the war Yevtushenko nearly became a professional athlete, but the broad acceptance and publication of some of his early poems led him to pursue a literary life.

Like many of his generation he was deeply affected by Stalin's death in 1953. His first book of poetry was published in 1952, and he was admitted to the Soviet Writer's Union and the Literary Institute. His reading of his long, autobiographical poem "Zima Junction" touched many people and marked the rebirth of the Russian tradition of the "public poet," where poets read verse to enthusiastic crowds. In the year 1961 alone, he gave 250 poetry readings. He was granted official permission to read his poetry abroad, traveling to Eastern Europe, the United States, Great Britain, Cuba, East Africa, and Australia. His most popular poem, "Babiy Yar" was an indictment of Russian and German anti-Semitism. The Russian composer Dmitri Shostakovich developed his Thirteenth Symphony around it and several other Yevtushenko poems. Though he came to the defense of fellow writers, including Aleksandr Solzhenitsyn, whom Yevtushenko felt was being mistreated by Soviet officials, Yevtushenko was criticized by many in literary circles for compromising his art to maintain favor with the government.

Yevtushenko was married four times and had five children. His survivors include his wife, Maria, four sons, and one granddaughter.

See Current Biography 1994

CLASSIFICATION BY PROFESSION

ACTIVISM
Amal Clooney
Alaa Murabit
Lori Wallach

ARCHITECTURE
David Adjaye

ART
Olivia Bee
Vera Brosgol
Marion Coutts
Carson Ellis
Kellie Jones
Chen Man
Helen Marten
Adam Pendleton
Javaka Steptoe
Lindsey Stirling

BUSINESS
Sam Altman
Patrick Awuah
Kayvon Beykpour
Bozoma Saint John

COMEDY
Iliza Shlesinger
Paul F. Tompkins

DANCE
Jérôme Bel
Michaela DePrince
Sara Mearns
Johannes Ohman

EDUCATION
Carol Anderson
Patrick Awuah
Andrew Bacevich
Anne Case
Mike Duncan
Sara Goldrick-Rab
Adam Grant

ENTERTAINMENT
Mike Duncan

FASHION
Roksanda Ilincic
Azede Jean-Pierre
Natacha Ramsay-Levi
Junya Watanabe

FILM
Riz Ahmed
Mahershala Ali
Melissa Benoist
Sofia Boutella
Sônia Braga
Janicza Bravo
Damien Chazelle
Derek Cianfrance
Lily Collins
Mike Colter
Kelly Fremon Craig
Adam Curtis
Loretta Devine
Mark Duplass
Luke Evans
Elle Fanning
Claire Foy
Julia Garner
Tyrese Gibson
Luca Guadagnino
Rebecca Hall
Corey Hawkins
Simon Helberg
Tom Holland
Barry Jenkins
Daniel Kaluuya
Pom Klementieff
Sasha Lane
Joe Manganiello
Melina Matsoukas
Gugu Mbatha-Raw
Ben Mendelsohn
Ruth Negga
Issey Ogata
Daniel Pemberton
Dee Rees
Margot Robbie
Tracee Ellis Ross
Taylor Sheridan
Keith Stanfield
Amandla Stenberg
Allison Tolman
Denis Villeneuve
Zhang Zanbo
Zendaya

GASTRONOMY
Massimo Bottura
Vivian Howard
Christopher Kimball
Ruby Tandoh
Pete Wells

GOVERNMENT & POLITICS, FOREIGN
Elio di Rupo
Joachim Gauck
Ameenah Gurib
Ollanta Humala
Klaus Iohannis
Emmanuel Macron
Victor Ponta

GOVERNMENT & POLITICS, U.S.
Denis Daugaard
Neil Gorsuch
Vanita Gupta
Carla Hayden
Jay Nixon
Jill Stein

JOURNALISM
Daniel Berehulak
Rukmini Callimachi
David Fahrenthold
Jeffrey Goldberg
Andrew Kaczynski
Rick Perlstein
Kathryn Schulz
A. G. Sulzberger
Martin Wolf

LAW
Amal Clooney

LITERATURE
Kwame Alexander
Chris Bachelder
Kelly Barnhill
Ali Benjamin
Emma Cline
Matt de la Peña
Adam Gidwitz
Garth Greenwell
Yaa Gyasi
Elena Ferrante
Angela Flournoy
John Green
Tyehimba Jess
Deborah Levy
Lisa Lucas
Karan Mahajan
Hisham Matar
Tarell Alvin McCraney
Ottessa Moshfegh
Maggie Nelson
Viet Thanh Nguyen
Dorit Rabinyan
Javaka Steptoe
David Szalay
Madeleine Thien
Carole Boston Weatherford
Kao Kalia Yang

MUSIC
Riz Ahmed
Mahershala Ali
Avery Amereau
Piotr Anderszewski
Kelsea Ballerini
Camila Cabello
Cam
Chance the Rapper
Tasha Cobbs
Daveed Diggs
Imagine Dragons
Perfume Genius
Tyrese Gibson
Clio Gould
Mirga Gražinytė-Tyla
David Guetta
Halsey
Justin Hurwitz
Nicky Jam
Solange Knowles
Zara Larsson
Little Big Town
Susanna Mälkki
Shawn Mendes
MØ
Angel Olsen
Anderson Paak
Daniel Pemberton
Charlie Puth
Thomas Rhett
Maggie Rogers
Blake Shelton
Sturgill Simpson
Keith Stanfield
Lindsey Stirling
Bryson Tiller
Yuja Wang
Zendaya

NONFICTION
Carol Anderson
Rick Perlstein
Kathryn Schulz
Margot Lee Shetterly
Heather Ann Thompson

PUBLISHING
Elaine Welteroth

SCIENCE
Jacob Hooker
Thomas Lindahl
Arthur B. McDonald
Dianne Newman
Yoshinori Ohsumi
Victoria Orphan
Meg Urry

SPORTS

Giannis Antetokounmpo
Tina Charles
Jason Day
Michael Fulmer
A. J. Green
Brooke Henderson
Laurie Hernandez
Marcel Hirscher
Braden Holtby
Al Horford
Eric Hosmer
Dustin Johnson
Ariya Jutanugarn
Mary Jepkosgei Keitany
Angelique Kerber
Chloe Kim
Si Woo Kim
Carli Lloyd
Tyronn Lue
Simone Manuel
Angel McCoughtry
Connor McDavid
Tatyana McFadden
Conor McGregor
Von Miller
Garbiñe Muguruza
Ibtihaj Muhammad
Manuel Neuer
Gift Ngoepe
Nneka Ogwumike
Zach Parise
Inbee Park
Kelsey Plum
Gary Sánchez
Shaka Smart

Jordan Spieth
Noah Syndergaard
Isaiah Thomas
Karl-Anthony Towns
Julio Urías
Max Verstappen
John Wall
Danny Willett
Ben Zobrist

TELEVISION

Pamela Adlon
Melissa Benoist
Tituss Burgess
Mike Colter
James Corden
Loretta Devine
Claire Foy
Simon Helberg
Daniel Kaluuya
Chrissy Metz
Issa Rae
Tracee Ellis Ross
Michael Schur
Alexander Skarsgård
Keith Stanfield
Melissa Villaseñor
Maisie Williams
Zendaya

THEATER

Tituss Burgess
Daveed Diggs
Marin Ireland
Jessie Mueller
Alex Sharp

LIST OF PROFILES

List of Profiles